October 15–18, 2012
São Paulo/SP, Brazil

AF765110

Association for
Computing Machinery

Advancing Computing as a Science & Profession

WebMedia'12

Proceedings of the 2012 Brazilian Symposium on
Multimedia and the Web

Sponsored by:

Brazilian Computer Society (SBC)

In cooperation with:

ACM SIGMM & ACM SIGOPS

Association for Computing Machinery

Advancing Computing as a Science & Profession

The Association for Computing Machinery
2 Penn Plaza, Suite 701
New York, New York 10121-0701

Copyright © 2012 by the Association for Computing Machinery, Inc. (ACM). Permission to make digital or hard copies of portions of this work for personal or classroom use is granted without fee provided that copies are not made or distributed for profit or commercial advantage and that copies bear this notice and the full citation on the first page. Copyright for components of this work owned by others than ACM must be honored. Abstracting with credit is permitted. To copy otherwise, to republish, to post on servers or to redistribute to lists, requires prior specific permission and/or a fee. Request permission to republish from: permissions@acm.org or Fax +1 (212) 869-0481.

For other copying of articles that carry a code at the bottom of the first or last page, copying is permitted provided that the per-copy fee indicated in the code is paid through www.copyright.com.

Notice to Past Authors of ACM-Published Articles
ACM intends to create a complete electronic archive of all articles and/or other material previously published by ACM. If you have written a work that has been previously published by ACM in any journal or conference proceedings prior to 1978, or any SIG Newsletter at any time, and you do NOT want this work to appear in the ACM Digital Library, please inform permissions@acm.org, stating the title of the work, the author(s), and where and when published.

ISBN: 978-1-4503-1706-1

Additional copies may be ordered prepaid from:

ACM Order Department
PO Box 30777
New York, NY 10087-0777, USA

Phone: 1-800-342-6626 (USA and Canada)
+1-212-626-0500 (Global)
Fax: +1-212-944-1318
E-mail: acmhelp@acm.org
Hours of Operation: 8:30 am – 4:30 pm ET

Printed in the USA

Preface and Chairs' Welcome

It is our great pleasure to welcome you to the *18th Brazilian Symposium on Multimedia and the Web – WebMedia 2012*. WebMedia is an annual symposium sponsored by the Brazilian Computer Society (SBC) and is the most important forum for researchers and professionals in the Multimedia, Hypermedia and Web areas in Brazil. This is WebMedia's 18th edition and it seeks to bring together researchers, students and practitioners, both from Brazil and from abroad, to present and discuss research problems related to any and all of the Symposium's topics.

WebMedia 2012 is being held in São Paulo, capital of the state of the same name, from October 15 to 18. This edition of WebMedia is being organized together with two other relevant events: the 27th Brazilian Symposium on Databases (SBBD), and the 9th Brazilian Symposium on Collaborative Systems (SBSC). The co-location of these symposia provides intellectual synergies for the researchers, practitioners and students in all three fields as well as providing organizational synergies.

WebMedia 2012 is principally organized by the University of São Paulo (USP) and has many other sponsors and supporters including academic institutions, industry, government and learned societies. The sponsors and supporters are listed elsewhere in these proceedings.

The Symposium's program is composed of technical sessions, mini-courses, panels, 3 inner workshops (Thesis and Dissertation Workshop, Tools and Applications Workshop and Undergraduate Research Workshop), as well as international and invited talks.

The papers accepted for publication in the WebMedia 2012 proceedings include 33 full papers and 30 short papers. These papers were selected from 108 full paper submissions and 62 short paper submissions, for acceptance rates of 31% and 48%, respectively. The Symposium's Program Committee worked very hard to perform the selection of papers that will be presented and published from among many submissions of excellent quality. We thank all the submitting authors for their research efforts and for their submissions and congratulate those who had their work accepted.

Finally, we would like to thank the members of the Program and Organization committees, as well as the reviewers. Their volunteer work was essential to the success of WebMedia 2012. We hope you enjoy the Symposium.

WebMedia 2012 General Co-Chairs

Graça Bressan
University of São Paulo

Regina Melo Silveira
University of São Paulo

WebMedia 2012 Program Co-Chairs

Maria da Graça C. Pimentel
University of São Paulo

André Santanchè
State University of Campinas

Ethan V Munson
University of Wisconsin-Milwaukee

Table of Contents

Session 3: Digital TV I

Session 4: Multimedia and Graphics Performance

Session 5: Ubiquitous Computing I

Session 6: Social Networks I

Session 7: Web: Semantics and Services

Session 8: Digital TV II

Session 9: Multimedia: Annotation, Tagging, and Human Issues

Session 10: Web: Detection and Recommendation

Session 11: Ubiquitous Computing II

Session 12: Social Networks II

Session 13: Web: Selecting and Analyzing

Session 14: Digital TV III

WebMedia 2012 Organization

General Chairs:	Graça Bressan *(University of São Paulo, Brazil)* Regina de Melo Silveira *(University of São Paulo, Brazil)*
Program Chairs:	Ethan V. Munson *(University of Wisconsin-Milwaukee, USA)* Andre Santanchè *(State University of Campinas, Brazil)* Maria da Graça Campos Pimentel *(University of São Paulo, Brazil)*
Workshop of Undergraduate Research Chairs:	Leônidas Brandão *(University of São Paulo, Brazil)* Luciana Zaina *(Federal University of São Carlos, Brazil)*
Workshop on Tools and Applications Chairs:	Anarosa Alves Franco Brandão *(University of São Paulo, Brazil)* Seiji Isotani *(University of São Paulo, Brazil)*
Workshop on Ongoing Thesis and Dissertations Chairs:	Rudinei Goularte *(University of São Paulo, Brazil)* José Maria Parente Oliveira *(Aeronautical Institute of Technology, Brazil)*
Tutorial Chairs:	Alessandra Alaniz Macedo *(University of São Paulo, Brazil)* Itana Stiubiener *(Federal University of ABC, Brazil)*
Steering Committee Chairs:	Celso Alberto Saibel Santos *(Federal University of Espírito Santo, Brazil)* Fernando Antônio Mota Trinta *(Federal University of Ceará, Brazil)*
Steering Committee:	Jussara Almeida *(Federal University of Minas Gerais, Brazil)* Eduardo Barrére *(Federal University of Juíz de Fora, Brazil)* Fábio Gomes *(Federal Institute of Piauí, Brazil)* José Valdeni de Lima *(Federal University of Rio Grande do Sul, Brazil)* Maria da Graça Campos Pimentel *(University of São Paulo, Brazil)* Valter Roesler *(Federal University of Rio Grande do Sul, Brazil)* Luiz Fernando Gomes Soares *(Pontifical Catholic University, Brazil)* Guido Lemos de Souza Filho *(Federal University of Paraíba, Brazil)* Mário Meireles Teixeira *(Federal University of Maranhão, Brazil)* Roberto Willrich *(Federal University of Santa Catarina, Brazil)*

Program Committee: Eduardo Albuquerque *(Federal University of Goiás, Brazil)*
Jussara Almeida *(Federal University of Minas Gerais, Brazil)*
Junia Anacleto *(Federal University of São Carlos, Brazil)*
Rossana Andrade *(Federal University of Ceará, Brazil)*
Regina Araujo *(Federal University of São Carlos, Brazil)*
Rodrigo Assad *(Federal University of Pernambuco, Brazil)*
Laercio Baldochi *(Federal University of Itajubá, Brazil)*
Jorge Barbosa *(University of the Sinos Valley, Brazil)*
Eduardo Barrere *(Federal University of Juíz de Fora, Brazil)*
Thais Batista *(Federal University of Rio Grande do Norte, Brazil)*
Daniela Barreiro Claro *(Federal University of Bahia, Brazil)*
Renato de Freitas Bulcão-Neto *(Federal University of Goiás, Brazil)*
Jorge Campos *(Salvador University, Brazil)*
Renan G. Cattelan *(Federal University of Uberlândia, Brazil)*
Silvio Cazella *(University of the Sinos Valley, Brazil)*
Marco Pinheiro Cristo *(Federal University of Amazonas, Brazil)*
José Maria Nazar David *(Federal University of Juíz de Fora, Brazil)*
Kelvin Dias *(Federal University of Pernambuco, Brazil)*
Jean-Marie Farines *(Federal University of Santa Catarina, Brazil)*
Carlos Ferraz *(Federal University of Pernambuco, Brazil)*
Renato Fileto *(Federal University of Santa Catarina, Brazil)*
Renata Pontin M. Fortes *(University of São Paulo, Brazil)*
Vinicius Cardoso Garcia *(Federal University of Pernambuco, Brazil)*
Jerome Gensel *(Grenoble Informatics Laboratory, France)*
Fabio Gomes *(Federal Institute of Piauí, Brazil)*
Rudinei Goularte *(University of São Paulo, Brazil)*
Ronaldo Husemann *(Federal University of Rio Grande do Sul, Brazil)*
Jose Valdeni de Lima *(Federal University of Rio Grande do Sul, Brazil)*
Bernadette Farias Lóscio *(Federal University of Ceará, Brazil)*
Daniel Lucredio *(Federal University of São Carlos, Brazil)*
Lau Cheuk Lung *(Federal University of Santa Catarina, Brazil)*
Alessandra A. Macedo *(University of São Paulo, Brazil)*
Marcelo Manzato *(University of São Paulo, Brazil)*
Joberto Martins *(Salvador University, Brazil)*
Marcelo Moreno *(Federal University of Juíz de Fora, Brazil)*
Anselmo Paiva *(Federal University of Maranhão, Brazil)*
José Gonçalves Pereira Filho *(Federal University of Espírito Santo, Brazil)*
Maria da Graça Campos Pimentel *(University of São Paulo, Brazil)*
Carlos Eduardo Pires *(Federal University of Campina Grande, Brazil)*
Cassio Prazeres *(Federal University of Bahia, Brazil)*
José Fernando Rodrigues Júnior *(University of São Paulo, Brazil)*
Valter Roesler *(Federal University of Rio Grande do Sul, Brazil)*
Luciana A. S. Romani *(University of São Paulo, Brazil)*
Gustavo Rossi *(National University of La Plata, Argentina)*
Débora Christina Muchaluat Saade *(Federal Fluminense University, Brazil)*
Ana Carolina Salgado *(Federal University of Pernambuco, Brazil)*
Celso A. S. Santos *(Federal University of Espírito Santo, Brazil)*

Program Committee (continued):

João Benedito dos Santos Junior *(Pontifical Catholic University, Brazil)*
Daniel Schwabe *(Pontifical Catholic University, Brazil)*
Frank Siqueira *(Federal University of Santa Catarina, Brazil)*
Carlos Soares Neto *(Federal University of Maranhão, Brazil)*
Damires Souza *(Federal Institute of Paraíba, Brazil)*
Guido Souza Filho *(Federal University of Paraíba, Brazil)*
Luiz Fernando Gomes Soares *(Pontifical Catholic University, Brazil)*
Tatiana Tavares *(Federal University of Paraíba, Brazil)*
Cesar Teixeira *(Federal University of São Carlos, Brazil)*
Mario M. Teixeira *(Federal University of Maranhão, Brazil)*
Luis C. Trevelin *(Federal University of São Carlos, Brazil)*
Fernando Trinta *(Federal University of Ceará, Brazil)*
Samyr Vale *(Federal University of Maranhão, Brazil)*
Windson Viana *(Federal University of Ceará, Brazil)*
Vaninha Vieira *(Federal University of Bahia, Brazil)*
Patrícia Vilain *(Federal University of Santa Catarina, Brazil)*
Roberto Willrich *(Federal University of Santa Catarina, Brazil)*
Leandro Krug Wives *(Federal University of Rio Grande do Sul, Brazil)*
Zeyun Yu *(University of Wisconsin-Milwaukee, USA)*
Luciana Zaina *(Federal University of São Carlos, Brazil)*

Additional reviewers:

Marcelo Amorim
Roberto Azevedo
Rodolfo Barriviera
Carlos Eduardo Batista
Maria da Conceição Batista
Rodrigo E. Botelho-Francisco
Jose Camacho-Guerrero
Alberto Bastos do Canto Filho
Reinaldo Castro
Everton Cavalcante
Carlos Eduardo Cirilo
Eduardo Cruz
Diego Dias
David Fernandes
Raoni Simões Ferreira
José Gilvan
Arthur Godoy
Rodrigo Laiola Guimaraes
Guilherme Coan Hobold
Anelise Jantsch
Bruno Y. L. Kimura
Alessandro Kraemer
Jim Lau
Guilherme Lima
Marcia Lima
Rodrigues Maia
Fabiana Marinho
Diogo S. Martins
Hamilton F. de Moraes Junior
Vivian Genaro Motti
Leandro Nascimento
Fabia Nishida
Lucas Bueno Ruas de Oliveira
Diogo C. Pedrosa
Ivan Ricarte
Ricardo Rios
Kamila Rodrigues
Joel dos Santos
Matheus Santos
Núbia S. Rosa Santana dos Santos
Flavio Seixas
Anderson Silva
Julia Silva
Paulo Silveira
Caio Viel

WebMedia 2012 Sponsors & Supporters

Sponsors:

Sociedade Brasileira de Computação

In cooperation with:

Supporters:

The Other Side of the Social Web: A Taxonomy for Social Information Access

Peter Brusilovsky
School of Information Sciences
University of Pittsburgh
Pittsburgh, PA 15217, USA
+1 412 6249404
peterb@pitt.edu

ABSTRACT
The power of the modern Web, which is frequently called the Social Web or Web 2.0, is frequently traced to the power of users as contributors of various kinds of contents through Wikis, blogs, and resource sharing sites. However, the community power impacts not only the production of Web content, but also the access to all kinds of Web content. A number of research groups worldwide explore what we call *social information access* techniques that help users get to the right information using "collective wisdom" distilled from actions of those who worked with this information earlier. This invited talk offers a brief introduction into this important research stream and reviews recent works on social information access performed at the University of Pittsburgh's PAWS Lab lead by the author.

Categories and Subject Descriptors
H.3.3 [Information Systems]: Information Search and Retrieval – *search process, information filtering, relevance feedback;* **H.5.3 [Information Interfaces and Presentation]**: Group and Organization Interfaces – *collaborative computing;* **H.5.4 [Information Interfaces and Presentation]**: Hypertext and Hypermedia – *navigation;*

General Terms
Algorithms, Human Factors

Keywords
Social information access, social navigation, social search, social tagging, social visualization.

1. INTRODUCTION
The power of the modern Web, which is frequently called the Social Web or Web 2.0, is frequently traced to the power of users as contributors of various kinds of contents through Wikis, blogs, and resource sharing sites. However, the community power impacts not only the production of Web content, but also the access to all kinds of Web content. A number of research groups worldwide explore what we call *social information access* techniques that help users get to the right information using "collective wisdom" distilled from actions of those who worked with this information earlier. Social information access technologies capitalize on the natural tendency of people to follow direct and indirect cues of others' activities, e.g. going to a restaurant that seems to attract many customers, or asking others what movies to watch.

Social information access can be formally defined as a stream of research that explores methods for organizing users' past interaction with an information system (known as explicit and implicit feedback), in order to provide better access to information to the future users of the system. It covers a range of rather different systems and technologies operating on a different scale - from a small closed corpus site to the whole Web. While the technologies located on the different sides of this stream may not even recognize each other as being a part of the same whole, the whole stream is driven by the same goals: to use the power of a user community for improving information access.

An important feature of all social information access systems is self-organization. Social information access systems are able to work with little or no involvement of human indexers, organizers, or other kinds of experts. They are truly powered by a community of users. Due to this feature, social information access technologies are frequently considered as an alternative to the traditional (content-oriented) information access technologies. In most of the cases, social information access can run in parallel with the traditional one, helping users to find resources that would be hard to find in a traditional way. In other cases where traditional information access is hard to organize (for example, in a collection of non-indexed images), social mechanisms (such as tagging) can provide a handy replacement. However, it has been more and more frequently demonstrated that most benefits could be obtained by integrating social and traditional technologies, for example, building hybrid recommender systems, which integrate collaborative and content-based recommender mechanisms [1].

The goal of this invited talk is to provide a brief overview of the emerging social information access research stream and to promote integrative and hybrid social information access technologies. To achieve this goal we offer two approaches. First, we introduce a brief taxonomy that defines the space of social information access and shows both, place of traditional technologies within this space and the opportunities for integrative work. Second we provide a review of recent works on social information access performed at the University of Pittsburgh's PAWS Lab lead by the author. These works provide various examples of bringing together different social information access technologies.

Permission to make digital or hard copies of all or part of this work for personal or classroom use is granted without fee provided that copies are not made or distributed for profit or commercial advantage and that copies bear this notice and the full citation on the first page. To copy otherwise, or republish, to post on servers or to redistribute to lists, requires prior specific permission and/or a fee.
WebMedia'12, October 15–18, 2012, São Paulo/SP, Brazil.
Copyright 2012 ACM 978-1-4503-1706-1/12/10...$15.00.

2. A TAXONOMY FOR SOCIAL INFORMATION ACCESS

Two aspects have to be considered to understand differences between modern social information access systems and technologies. Most important is the type of information access they are attempting to support. In earlier papers on the topic we distinguished four major information access paradigms to classify adaptive information access systems: ad-hoc information retrieval, information filtering (recommendation), hypertext browsing, and information visualization [2; 3]. In ad-hoc information retrieval (IR), users get access to relevant information by issuing a query to an IR system or search engine and analyzing/accessing a ranked list of documents (for example, book records), which are returned as a result. In information filtering (IF) an information system attempts to recommend documents, which match the user's long-term interests. Traditional IF systems match a user-provided profile against a flow of incoming documents (for example, news articles) to select the most relevant items for the user. Modern recommender systems (often considered as an extension of IF) construct dynamic user profiles by observing user interactions, and as a result can produce new recommendations even in stable document collections. In hypertext browsing, a user attempts to find relevant documents by browsing links that connect documents in a collection. In information visualization, a set of documents is presented to the user using some visualization metaphor in 2 or 3 dimensions; the user observes or, in the case of interactive visualization, interacts with the visualized set to find the most relevant documents.

The type of supported information access is, however, only a part of the picture. From the "social" prospect it is also important to consider what kinds of actions of past users a specific system or technology uses to enhance traditional information access. In the field of personalized and social systems these actions are frequently called as *user feedback*. The reason for this name is that in the oldest adaptive filtering and retrieval system user feedback (typically provided as a yes/no or a multi-point scale rating) was the only kind of user actions that these systems were able to trace. User ratings are an example of so-called explicit feedback - actions that the users explicitly provide to express some opinion about an information item. While users ratings are still very popular source of information in some social information access systems (for example, collaborative recommendation systems), it has long been recognized that user ratings form a very small fraction of user interaction with information. As a result, more recent work focused on various *implicit feedback* indicators [4] that assess user attitude to an information items provided *implicitly* i.e., through various users actions that were not specifically performed to express this attitude. Most popular source of implicit feedback is user clicks and dwell time (known together as *clickstream*). Both clicks and time provide a good evidence of user interest to an item or item usefulness for a given user. While this evidence is less reliable, it is more readily available in many contexts. A more reliable evidence could be extracted by tracing various kinds of user manipulations with a document – from mousing over document to saving, bookmarking, or printing a document [5].

Explicit ratings and clickstream are the extreme points of implicit-explicit continuum of feedback. Nowadays, social information access system employ a whole range of user actions that bridge the gap between these two extremes such as user queries, comments, and tags. These new kinds of actions are harder to classify into explicit/implicit bins. For example, tagging is certainly an explicit action and to some extent it expresses user attitude to an item. Yet, tagging is typically done not to express feedback or attitude, but to organize personal or social information space. As for comments, while in some systems (like e-commerce) comments are done to express attitude (i.e., clearly explicit feedback), in other systems (like online reading) comments are mostly notes to oneself.

The kind of supported information access and the kind of considered user actions form two dimension of the taxonomy that defines the space of social information access technologies (Table 1). Presenting this space in two dimensions shows that this space is not really well explored. The table shows some well-explored pockets on the crossroads of information access types and trackable actions surrounded by larger *terra incognita*. The reason for this is that classic social information access technologies were developed in tight conjunction with corresponding information access paradigms and with little interest to what *other* paradigms can offer. As a result, the type of information access supported by a specific technology to a large extent determined the kind of social enhancement provided by the technology and the kind of user actions that the "social" version of this paradigm harvested to provide social access.

For example, classic *social navigation* technologies (history-enriched environments) were developed to support browsing-based access. This context requires navigation support systems, which can help the users to decide, which of many links on the current page to follow. The natural approach to using the community wisdom is to show "where did the people go" [6] by augmenting links with digital "wear" indicators. The natural approach to collect this wisdom is to track user page visits [7] or link traversals [8].

Collaborative filtering technologies were designed as an extension of traditional information filtering that has been long based on user explicit feedback [9]. As a result, the majority of collaborative filtering systems still use ratings as the only kind of feedback. Ratings are tightly integrated into the very algorithms of traditional collaborative filtering.

Social search technologies were developed to support traditional IR information access. In this context, users expect to see a ranked list of relevant resources. The natural approach to using the community wisdom is to insert community-relevant links into the list or results [10; 11] or stress, which of the returned documents are not only relevant, but also appreciated by the community [12; 13]. A reliable approach to collecting this wisdom is to track connections between queries and items selected [11] or rated [10; 13] by the community members in the context of these queries.

While the social search technology shows an example of horizontal integration (using several kind of feedback to support one kind of information access), *social bookmarking* technology presents a different integration case in social information access. In this case, a single kind of user feedback is used (tagging), yet this feedback is engineered to enhance at least two different kinds of information access. Not only social tags are used to improve search by bridging the well-known author-user mismatch, they also provide an alternative mechanism to browse information through tag indexes and tag clouds.

The simple integration examples provided by social search and social tagging shows that the kind of supported information access and the kind of tracked user actions should not be necessary connected into tight couples. I.e., within one system, one kind of information access can be supported by social wisdom extracted from several different kinds of feedback. Excellent examples of horizontal integration are provided by modern recommender systems that explored how almost every possible kind of feedback can be used for recommendations. Yet, even in this area a single system uses one, rarely two kinds of feedback. The cases of vertical integration where a specific kind of tracked actions could be used to support more than one kind of access are even more rare.

One of the goals of our recent work at PAWS Lab was exploring the space of integrated social information access technologies. Next sections attempt to provide a few examples of social systems that integrate several technologies and spans several "cells" on the social information access map (Table 2).

Table 1. The space of social information access

Past User Behavior	Explicit Actions			Implicit Actions		
Supported Access Types	**Tags**	**Comments**	**Ratings**	**Queries**	**Clicks/Time**	**Manipulations**
Search	Social tagging systems		Social search			
Browsing					Social Navigation	
Recommendation			Collaborative Filtering			
Visualization						

Table 2. Examples of integrative social information access systems

Past User Behavior	Explicit Actions			Implicit Actions		
Supported Access Types	**Tags**	**Comments**	**Ratings**	**Queries**	**Clicks/Time**	**Manipulations**
Search		KS, ASSIST		ASSIST	KS, ASSIST	
Browsing	CoMeT	KS, ASSIST	CourseAgent	ASSIST	CoMeT, KS, ASSIST	CoMeT
Recommendation			CourseAgent			
Visualization		KS			KS	

3. TOWARDS INTEGRATED SOCIAL INFORMATION ACCESS SYSTEMS

3.1 CourseAgent

One of the simplest kinds of integration is using a specific kind of user feedback to support two types of social information access: one that is traditionally based on this feedback and one that usually exploits another kind of feedback. An example of this integration is CourseAgent [14]. CourseAgent is a system that helps graduate students at our School to select courses that are most relevant to their career goals. The kind of feedback exploited by CourseAgent is user ratings. A student is expected to rate the relevance of each taken course to one or more career goals using explicit 5-point scale. This kind of feedback typically drives social recommendation mechanism. CourseAgent does offer course recommendations. However, more visible form of social information access offered by this system is social navigation support. Relevant courses are annotated with different adaptive visual cues in every context where the courses are shown to students like course schedules or course catalogs. This allows the system to provide in-context guidance beyond the usual rating list. Title and Authors

3.2 CoMeT

Another simple kind of integrated information access is using a range of observable user actions to offer an extended version of a specific kind of social information access. A good example of this is CoMeT, a system that guides its users to most interesting research talks offered by several universities in Pittsburgh [15]. CoMeT recognizes that users are rarely interested to rate research talks so it attempts to use several implicit evidences of interest: accessing a talk, adding a talk to one's schedule or calendar, sending information about a talk to friends, tagging a talk. This feedback is used to offer integrated social navigation: i.e., it guides users to interesting talks right in the context where these talk are shown – day, week, and month calendars.

3.3 Knowledge Sea (KS)

An extensive exploration of social information access was performed in the Knowledge See (KS) project. Knowledge See is an educational system that was designed to guide students in a class to most useful and relevant reading fragments. KS started as a traditional social navigation system [7]: it tracked class document access and offered visual cues that indicated cumulative student traffic. Thus the system guided the users to the pages that were most visited by a class as a whole. Traffic, however, appeared to be a relatively noisy indicator of interest. Subsequent versions explored more reliable indicators – time spent reading [16] and annotations created by the users while reading [17]. The system was also extended with a social search [12] and a social visualization [18] components that used both the clickstream and the annotations to support search and visualization-based access to class readings.

3.4 ASSIST

Our most advanced attempt to create an integrated system for social information access was performed collaboratively with a research team from Dublin lead by Barry Smith. When we started this collaboration, our team accumulated a lot of experience in various kinds of social navigation while Barry's team with its work on several versions of I-Spy [11] had a great experience in social search. Yet, at that time both teams followed traditional approaches. Our team delivered browsing support using clickstream left by the users when browsing and Barry's team focused on queries and page access combinations left by the users in the search process. Both teams recognized, however, that a typical Web information access session includes a combination of search and browsing where users most typically start from search, but then follow a sequence of link to the destination. What we attempted to do is to design an integrated system that can support both kinds of information access using both kinds of implicit feedback. The result was the ASSIST architecture. It was implemented and explored in several contexts such as social access to ACM Digital Library and social exploration of YouTube videos [19; 20].

4. ACKNOWLEDGMENTS

A number of students working in PAWS Lab provided critical contributions to the work presented in this talk. The author wants to specifically acknowledge Rosta Farzan, Jaewook Ahn, Chirayu Wongchokprasitti, Sherry Sahebi, and Denis Parra. This work was partially supported by NSF grants IIS 0447083 and DUE 0840597 to the author.

5. REFERENCES

[1] Burke, R. Hybrid Web recommender systems. In: Brusilovsky, P., Kobsa, A. and Neidl, W. (eds.): The Adaptive Web: Methods and Strategies of Web Personalization. Lecture Notes in Computer Science, Vol. 4321. Springer-Verlag, Berlin Heidelberg New York, 2007, 377-408.

[2] Brusilovsky, P. and Tasso, C. Preface to special issue on user modeling for Web information retrieval. User Modeling and User Adapted Interaction, 14, 2-3 (2004), 147-157.

[3] Brusilovsky, P. Social Information Access: The Other Side of the Social Web. In: Geffert, V., et al. (eds.) Proc. of SOFSEM 2008, 34th International Conference on Current Trends in Theory and Practice of Computer Science, Springer Verlag, 5-22.

[4] Claypool, M., Le, P., Wased, M., and Brown, D. Implicit interest indicators. In: Proc. of 6th International Conference on Intelligent User Interfaces, ACM Press, 33-40.

[5] Goecks, J. and Shavlik, J. Learning user's interests by unobtrusively observing their normal behavior. In: Lieberman, H. (ed.) Proc. of 2000 International Conference on Intelligent User Interfaces, ACM Press, 129-132.

[6] Dieberger, A., Dourish, P., Höök, K., Resnick, P., and Wexelblat, A. Social navigation: Techniques for building more usable systems. interactions, 7, 6 (2000), 36-45.

[7] Brusilovsky, P., Chavan, G., and Farzan, R. Social adaptive navigation support for open corpus electronic textbooks. In: De Bra, P. and Nejdl, W. (eds.) Proc. of Third International Conference on Adaptive Hypermedia and Adaptive Web-Based Systems (AH'2004), Springer-Verlag, 24-33.

[8] Wexelblat, A. and Mayes, P. Footprints: History-rich tools for information foraging. In: Proc. of ACM Conference on Human-Computer Interaction (CHI'99), 270-277.

[9] Konstan, A., Bradley, N.M., Maltz, D., Herlocker, J.L., Gordon, L.R., and Riedl, J. GroupLens: Applying collaborative filtering to usenet news. Communications of the ACM, 40, 3 (1997), 77-87.

[10] Jung, S., Harris, K., Webster, J., and Herlocker, J.L. SERF: Iintegrating human recommendations with search. In: Proc. of ACM 13th Conference on Information and Knowledge Management, CIKM 2004, 571-580.

[11] Smyth, B., Balfe, E., Freyne, J., Briggs, P., Coyle, M., and Boydell, O. Exploiting Query Repetition and Regularity in an Adaptive Community-Based Web Search Engine. User Modeling and User-Adapted Interaction, 14, 5 (2004), 383-423.

[12] Ahn, J.-w., Farzan, R., and Brusilovsky, P. Social search in the context of social navigation. Journal of the Korean Society for Information Management, 23, 2 (2006), 147-165.

[13] Kantor, P.B., Boros, E., Melamed, B., Meñkov, V., Shapira, B., and Neu, D.J. Capturing human intelligence in the net. Communications of the ACM, 43, 8 (2000), 112-116.

[14] Farzan, R. and Brusilovsky, P. Encouraging User Participation in a Course Recommender System: An Impact on User Behavior. Computers in Human Behavior, 27, 1 (2011), 276-284.

[15] Sahebi, S., Wongchokprasitti, C., and Brusilovsky, P. Recommending research colloquia: a study of several sources for user profiling. In: Proc. of the 1st International Workshop on Information Heterogeneity and Fusion in Recommender Systems (HetRec 2010) at the 2010 ACM conference on Recommender systems, RecSys '10, ACM, 32-38

[16] Farzan, R. and Brusilovsky, P. Social navigation support in E-Learning: What are real footprints. In: Anand, S.S. and Mobasher, B. (eds.) Proc. of IJCAI'05 Workshop on Intelligent Techniques for Web Personalization, 49-56.

[17] Farzan, R. and Brusilovsky, P. AnnotatEd: A social navigation and annotation service for web-based educational resources. New Review in Hypermedia and Multimedia, 14, 1 (2008), 3-32.

[18] Ahn, J.-w., Farzan, R., and Brusilovsky, P. A two-level adaptive visualization for information access to open-corpus educational resources. In: Brusilovsky, P., Dron, J. and Kurhila, J. (eds.) Proc. of Workshop on the Social Navigation and Community-Based Adaptation Technologies at the 4th International Conference on Adaptive Hypermedia and Adaptive Web-Based Systems, 497-505.

[19] Farzan, R., Coyle, M., Freyne, J., Brusilovsky, P., and Smyth, B. ASSIST: adaptive social support for information space traversal. In: Proc. of 18th conference on Hypertext and hypermedia, HT '07, ACM Press, 199-208.

[20] Coyle, M., Freyne, J., Brusilovsky, P., and Smyth, B. Social Information Access for the Rest of Us: An Exploration of Social YouTube. In: Nejdl, W., Kay, J., Pu, P. and Herder, E. (eds.) Proc. of 5th International Conference on Adaptive Hypermedia and Adaptive Web-Based Systems (AH'2008), Springer Verlag, 93-102.

Socially-Aware Multimedia: Adding Personal and Temporal Contexts to Media

Dick C.A. Bulterman

CWI: Centrum Wiskunde & Informatica, and
VU University Amsterdam

dick.bulterman@cwi.nl

ABSTRACT

Multimedia data has two general characteristics that separate it from other types of ICT data: it is inherently intended for human consumption and it is inherently temporal. In this context, it is interesting to note that most multimedia research has held neither the user nor the notion of time as central themes. In this keynote presentation, I argue that a fresh look at multimedia is required. This 'fresh look,' which I call *socially-aware multimedia*, is centered on supporting end-user interaction with media in the long-term social context of the user's social environment. This context is inherently personal and temporal: it changes as a person matures and assumes new roles during a lifetime. Notions of media search, media storage and media presentation will need to be modified to reflect a new central role of the user as not only a consumer but also a determining element in defining, selecting and sharing content.

Categories and Subject Descriptors

H.1.2 [**Models and Principles**]: User/Machine Systems – *Human factors*. H.5.1 [**Information Interfaces and Presentation**]: Multimedia Information Systems – *Audio, Video*.

General Terms

Design, Experimentation, Human Factors.

Keywords

Community-based authoring, Community Video Mash-Ups, Hybrid Media Authoring.

1. INTRODUCTION

Multimedia research has typically covered the following list of topics:

- Efficient coding of media content
- Efficient systems for capture and storage of coded content
- Efficient systems for the distribution of coded content
- Efficient systems for delivering and rendering coded content

During the past two decades, the application context of multimedia has shifted from isolated desktops (modelled nicely by a PC with a CD-ROM media disk) through networked desktops (modelled by a set of servers, a highish-speed communication network and a PC), through wide-scale distribution systems (such as is modelled by an interactive television environment), to handheld mobile systems (such as a smartphone or tablet connected to a higher-speed mobile communication system.

The need for efficient systems has influenced the tools, languages and interfaces associated with delivering multimedia content. In many ways, the dominant model for content has been that of a spool of film, as has been used within the motion picture industry for nearly 100 years: content is created, encoded and packaged as an immutable object that needs to be shared in a reliable, cost-effective and predictable manner.

The spool-of-film model has extended beyond the packaging of content to the manner in which the user is provided access to content. The user is allowed to select content, to view content and (sometimes) to temporally fast-forward or rewind content during viewing. The user is also allowed to terminate the viewing experience, either at the end of the object or at some intermediate point in the presentation. All viewers of a particular object see the same content. If there are any dynamic aspects to the presentation, these are in the size or the quality of the encoding.

Although there are many classical problems related to content coding, analysis, storage and transport that still need to be solved, I feel that the time is ripe to move to a more personal media experience paradigm. Here, the user – and the user's context – form a central element of media selection and rendering. Rather than storing and analyzing media for a mass audience, it is time consider tools and technologies for supporting a micro-audience that can be refined to the level of a single person. I argue that doing so requires a fundamental shift in how we view media content and how we support media distribution. It will require adding a temporal and social context to media that is geared to the needs of a socially-evolving user. It will require new content authoring tools that take personalization as a fundamental requirement – rather than as a luxury add-on, as is currently the case. Content storage will need to consider context migration and personal protection (both in terms of content privacy and information integrity). It will also have a host of other fundamental implications for a wide range of media topics.

In this keynote talk, I present a number of personal reflections on a new paradigm for studying user-driven interactions with content in a future generation of multimedia systems. I begin with a short discussion on the nature of personal content. I continue with a (highly selective) historical overview of relevant media research. I then discuss the notion of socially-aware multimedia, viewing end-user interaction with media content as a fundamental authoring activity. I close with a discussion of the impact of socially-aware multimedia systems on a variety of mainstream and emerging media research topics.

2. HIGHLY-PERSONAL MULTIMEDIA

Historically, capturing personal media was a special activity that occurred at major life events. With the ubiquity of media capture

Permission to make digital or hard copies of all or part of this work for personal or classroom use is granted without fee provided that copies are not made or distributed for profit or commercial advantage and that copies bear this notice and the full citation on the first page. To copy otherwise, or republish, to post on servers or to redistribute to lists, requires prior specific permission and/or a fee.
WebMedia'12, October 15–18, 2012, São Paulo/SP, Brazil.
Copyright 2012 ACM 978-1-4503-1706-1/12/10...$15.00.

devices, there is ample evidence that this capture context is shifting: most of the recorded media currently concerns much less structured and more transient daily events: a shared meal, a ride on the bus, a visit with friends. As a result, the complexity of the media management task for user-producers has increased, as has the volume of personal media content.

In addition to media management, we also need to address the issue of *content interaction*: how does an end-user who is not the original content creator interact with content available from personal sources. Note that the qualification "from personal sources" is very important: most commercial content is laden with licensing restrictions that make meaningful interaction (such as incremental selection, linking, copying, extending, enhancing and even redistribution) legally difficult. Personal content is less restricted on potential reuse and intelligent content navigation. This provides unprecedented freedom for end-users to create their own personal media compositions, using multiple sources. In this way, end-user interaction performed during content viewing can flow seamlessly into end-user content authoring of an augmented version of that content. Unfortunately, current content encoding, storage and distribution models effectively prohibit any form of efficient dynamic recombination of user-generated content.

Consider media collection at a high school music concert. Figure 1 shows a redheaded mother who (together with other parents) is capturing part of the event.

This event model is interesting for study because it presents a number of natural content partitioning possibilities: by set, by song, by musician, by solo, by musical role, etc. We can assume that different viewers of this content will have different interests (some will want a three-minute 'taste' of the event, others will want a summary of a single person of interest, others will want a fully-annotated archival version of the concert).

Note that it is difficult to encode these various versions as an *a priori* activity: they flow from the interaction paradigm of a viewer with content. In this context, the way in which people interact with content will ultimately view more useful context information on the viewer than on the media object(s).

Figure 1: Collecting content only a mother could love.

3. SOCIALLY-AWARE MULTIMEDIA

The content types of text, images, video, audio and graphic data have the interesting property that they are primarily intended for human consumption. This imposes a set of temporal and spatial constraints on media processing that have guided much of media research. The majority of this research has, however, focused on properties of the media during production rather than properties of the human ultimately viewing each object.

At its core, the idea that is encompassed by socially-aware multimedia is this: that personal media archives should be constructed in such a way that (future) end users have the ability to dynamically create media objects that are a composite of potentially non-contiguous media fragments stored across a web of content servers, based on the context of the user viewing the object. The resulting video should contain links to associate content that are also generated dynamically based on the context of the end users. By interacting with the media, the end-user should be able to easily create derivative works that can serve as the basis for a next generation of media sharing. Media archives should become living, organic repositories of content, the combination of which should be steered by the demands of the user community.

Consider the media object shown in Figure 2. Here we see a young musician – or, in any case, a young person holding a musical instrument. For nearly all viewers of this media object, this is an anonymous individual who is sitting in a non-descript setting. A content analysis algorithm would probably recognize the lad as a person (even though he has only one hand visible, and his face has only one eye and one-half of a nose in view), but it would almost certainly miss the fact that the instrument being played was a trombone. There is also no indication of the piece being performed, or the location/time of the object capture. There is absolutely no direct information on the phase-of-life context in which the image was taken, other than the main person is young.

For most of us, this context is not particularly interesting information. To be honest, for most of us, this is not even a particularly interesting photograph! There are probably hundreds of similar images that might be found on photo-sharing sites or across web archives. The situation is radically different for the grandmother shown in Figure 3. Here we show a person who is interested in seeing only *this* trombone player. For her, all of the similar pictures of musicians are irrelevant.

It is tempting to think that socially-aware multimedia is simply a meta-data problem that can be solved by adding the kind of highly-personal annotations necessary to support a directed query of the content. I would argue that the problem is not nearly as simple as it seems. Consider, for example, the following query being entered by the grandmother in Figure 3:

Figure 2. A highly-personal media object.

Figure 3. A highly-personal media viewer.

```
Find a picture of my husband making
music before he started playing piano.
```

Now, the young man's context has transformed into his role at the time of the query: as an older gentleman who has (evidently) embarked upon a musical career as a pianist and married the grandmother in question. Tagging the photo as: `name=Frans, date=1939, place=HighSchool instrument=Trombone` no longer is a viable means of providing life-long support for socially aware media. The moment of media capture no longer forms the basis for annotation.

There are other examples. Consider a video mash-up of the performance represented in Figure 1. If this were a large-scale concert event, attended by thousands of adoring fans, it would be relatively straightforward to create a concert mash-up giving an impression of the event. With a thousand fans, 1% of which may contribute their captured media, it is possible to generate multi-view concert summaries. However, only few will concentrate on this trombonist, and fewer yet will be able to tell a concert story that will be compelling during the person's lifetime of development.

4. MEDIA INTERACTION: AN OVERVIEW

Before we peer into the future of increased end-user interaction with media, it is useful to reflect on how we got where we are today. This is a perilous task, since many people have contributed significant bits of technology during the 20-year period we consider. I apologize for excluding important contributions.

In first years of multimedia, two topics dominated the research agenda: the efficient coding of media content and the efficient transfer of that content over public communication networks. We briefly consider each of these in turn. The efficient coding of media content is a difficult challenge, the importance of which is difficult to exaggerate. To understand this challenge, consider the requirements for coding a 60 minute high-definition video of our high school concert. In raw form, this video would require approximately 40 gigabytes of storage space. In 1992, this was more than the total storage available at most university computing centers. Even on current-generation systems, multi-gigabyte files provide a storage and processing burden. Luckily, advances in coding technology can reduce the storage requirements of our video object to fewer than 10% of that space, even in relatively uncompressed form. For viewers willing to sacrifice a bit of quality, the storage size of the video object can be further reduced by one or two orders of magnitude. As we will consider later, this not only allows multiple full-length Hollywood films to be stored on desktop machines, it also allows an entire family video archive to be stored on-line instead of in a box in the attic. This is a significant enabler for supporting socially-aware multimedia.

The second early multimedia research topic that had a significant impact on the interaction of a user with content was the efficient transfer of information across public computer networks. Although media compression and storage has played a fundamental role in enabling the wide-scale representation of media assets, the real catalyst for the multimedia revolution of the past two decades has been the development and deployment of networks that can be used to share this data.

In the early 1990's, using the mega-bit networks only available to universities and research centers, it would have taken more than a week to upload our HD concert video to a remote server. In the past two decades, the speed of national and international backbone networks has grown significantly, but for most European households, it will still require nearly four days at a realistic sustained upload rate of a few kilobytes per second to upload a 40 GB full-HD video to family and friends abroad. In other words, it would take less time to fly from Amsterdam to Atlanta with a video in your pocket, show it to your family over dinner and then fly home, than it does to upload a raw full HD movie to that family member abroad. (If you use a mobile phone for the upload, the round-trip flight probably would be much cheaper as well!)

The increase in aggregate networking capacity in the last two decades has been phenomenal. From a personal end-user perspective, however, the most seminal development in multimedia networking was the ability to incrementally transfer only small portions of a video or audio object from a server to a client using some form of explicit or implicit streaming technology. This has resulted in an interesting paradox: while streaming technology has made personal content broadly accessible, it has largely inhibited any effective interaction with that content by end users. Simple activities such as fast-forwarding through a long video (which is commonplace when interacting with text documents) are nearly impossible because the video presentation becomes non-fluid. Adding hyperlinks to a video, which could enable structured, personalized navigation, has not been used even though the world-wide web provides a compelling existence proof for the power of such links in making interactive content accessible. The baseline technology for such temporal hyperlinking has been available for over a decade in languages such as SMIL, but it has been underutilized by media servers because of the performance implications of rebuffering content.

Effectively interacting with content is a complex problem that extends beyond the existence of communications networks. This is even more so when combined with a notion of integrating end-user content into the distribution process. The following list highlights some of the context related issues:

- There is the inherent complexity and inter-related nature of managing time-sensitive information across fundamentally unreliable computer networks and across an array of diverse presentation devices. In the mid-1990's, this complexity was explicitly addressed by synchronization specification languages, but more recently the complex task of synchronizing media from several sources has all but been abandoned as a priority in media delivery systems.
- Communication across computer networks can be synchronous or asynchronous. In synchronous communication, all parties are active at the same time, as in a video conference. In asynchronous sharing, a message is prepared for later consumption, as in an e-mail message. While synchronous communication has always received the bulk of attention among media researchers, it actually

represents a simplified case of asynchronous transfers among parties. In synchronous communication, issues such as context, state and presentation persistence are often neglected. For asynchronous networking, these are all essential problems that must be solved.

- Media viewing is a highly personalized activity. Each viewer is likely to bring his or her own 'consumption context' that will guide the viewing experience. When give a 48-minute concert view, not all viewers are likely to want to watch the video for the same duration or with the same interest. This is inherently different from professional content, in which sophisticated narrative and production rules are used to maintain view interest. The uncle of a performer at the concert will have different viewing interests than, say, a grandmother or a sibling of the performer. This is captured in the illustration shown in Figure 4. Current media players do not allow the scalable presentation of content based on the semantic properties of the media. This is a lost opportunity for effective sharing.

Figure 4: End-user personalization implies independent paths through source media.

The past two decades of media technology has provided a foundation for a more proactive approach to media consumption by end users. The pro-active approach can be called *socially-aware multimedia*. It goes beyond a personal collection of media to consider the (temporally variant) context in which that media is used.

5. SUPPORT ISSUES

Providing support for socially-aware multimedia will significantly extend the types of research that needs to be performed to support the effective encoding, storage, classification, selection, transmission, protection and sharing of (potentially composite) media objects. The principal reason for this is that the context in which media is used will strongly determine how it is classified and accessed. Annotations and metadata will become multifaceted and dynamic, and will be determined by use rather than by design. The following subsections highlight some of the issues that will need study.

5.1 Measuring Content Engagement

In the early days of radio, listeners starved for news and entertainment were happy to be able to receive a distortion-tainted broadcast signal. In the early days of television, reflection-induced ghosts and intermittent reception were part of the game of watching TV content. As transmitter and receiver technology improved, a focus shifted from quality reception to content engagement.

Of course, measuring content engagement is a difficult social and sociological problem that transcends coding and delivery. Any potential value for engagement is based on understanding not only the content in question, but also the viewing history and personal context of the receiver. This includes not only long-term personal data, but also information on where, when, how and with whom the content experience takes place. This context – or more correctly – these contexts are themselves not static, but they will vary over time. While parts of any context can undoubtedly be shared among users, much of the context definition will depend on a combination of {source, user, access} information tuples.

5.2 Customized Media Selection and Transfer

As hinted earlier, media selection in socially-aware multimedia is not a case of 'find as many essentially equivalent photos as possible', but 'find the relatively few photos that are relevant to me now, based on my context (and that of the people in the photo)'.

To understand the progress that has already been made in managing social media, it is interesting to follow the development through the last 80 years of broadcast media selection. In the period up through the mid-1960's, if we wanted to experience broadcast content, we would need to consult a published program guide, compare its information with a calendar and a clock and then select the content that was available at that moment. This is essentially the same process that had consisted since 1927, when the first widely-available radio broadcasts started in the UK.

The first major innovation to this process came with the wide availability of the video tape recorder. For the first time in history, it was the viewer that determined when content would be watched – on the precondition that it had been broadcast and recorded earlier. A next innovation came with the introduction of the digital set-top box, which included an embedded program guide.

After the introduction of the set-top box, the next logical development is to remove the TV guide altogether and to have the system itself recommend content for the family, which it found based on metadata encoded by the content providers. One drawback of home systems is that a set-top box is typically not aware of who is actually watching TV. There are many potential solutions to this problem, but not many have been deployed yet.

At present, much research is being expended on recommender system technology. These systems depend heavily on producer-generated metadata for determining available candidate content. For socially-aware multimedia, the granularity of the metadata needs to be refocused to personal content. Another change in focus is that content selection will need to move from selecting 'programs' to selecting fragments of content. For a given viewing experience, several fragments typically will need to be dynamically combined to support end-user engagement.

5.3 Media Encoding and Storage

At present, media encoding is based on an agnostic view of content. This has been used to great advantage on sharing websites and physical distribution media. The assumption has been, however, that all of the fragments related to a single story are compressed into a single fixed media object. There are usually no facilities for packaging custom versions of content from a single base encoding. Each personal version of a video (or video fragment) must be re-encoded in a new document.

One important difference required to support the end-user dynamic composition implied by socially-aware multimedia is that small logical groups of media would be stored on several servers, each as individual fragments. These fragments could be mixed/match dynamically at viewing time to support the interests of the viewer. In terms of our concert example, this would mean that all of the individual assets captured by all of the parents could be saved in a cloud over servers. Individual presentations could then be stitched together on demand, as shown in Figure 5.

Figure 5: Each socially-aware media object would be composed of individual fragments, which would be dynamically combined based on end-user interests.

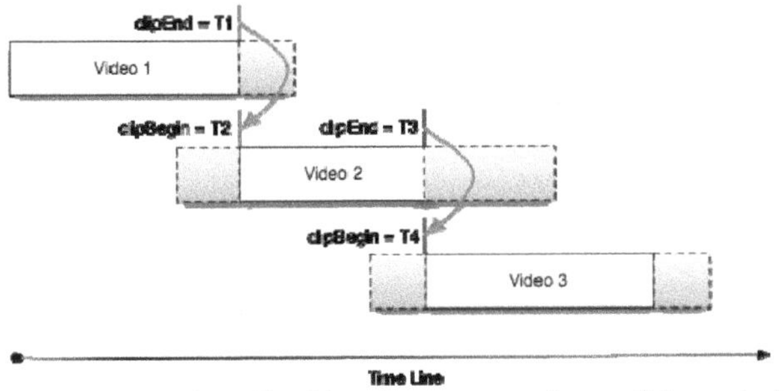

Having a logical media object be constructed out of dynamically combined physical fragments allows customized navigation to be supported. The fact that fragments could be fetched on demand from a wide range of servers has implications for increased efficiency and even increased privacy: access to servers could be monitored more closely if many separate servers were used. It is clear that the current model of content streaming would need to be revised: the seamless integration of individual fragments into a logical whole is a composition concept that most media servers (and certainly media container languages like HTML-5) are ill-equipped to support.

5.4 Media Classification and Annotation

Media classification and labeling (whether informal using a number of personal keywords, or formally using a well-defined ontology) remains one of the biggest challenges for supporting effective sharing that exists in the multimedia research domain. For professional content, the problem is well-structured and the content is often highly segmented along the lines of established commercial distribution models. For personal content, the situation is vastly different.

At present, personal content annotation is driven by device-supplied metadata (clocks, GPS coordinates, file names). For socially-aware multimedia, it is also necessary to encode relative social relationships among interested parties – plus to maintain those relationships over time. As with any large software system, the long-term maintenance costs of media will dominate the short-term development costs. This will require a new generation of iterative, socailly-aware media classification tools. The analysis of content becomes a continuing task, not an import activity.

Figure 6: An overview of media fragments captured at a student concert.

Consider our concert example again. In a recent capture experiment performed in a pan-European project, it would found that parents at a high school concert captured approximately 150 media fragments at a 60-minute, two set student concert. Some of this content overlapped temporally, but much of it was disjoint in terms of its semantic content.

One obvious way to organize the content is to analyze the audio signals on each of the content streams and to align the audio tracks of each object with the audio from one of the always-on main cameras. The result of this alignment, which works surprisingly well, is shown in Figure 6.

Once this alignment has been performed, a composite projection of the available media could be generated at any specific time instance in the concert. (One such instance is shown in Figure 7.) Note that the images are dark and fuzzy and of widely varying quality. Unfortunately, this is the quality of the video that is often taken at these dimly-lit events.

Figure 7: Available fragments at a given point of a concert, based on 8 available cameras.

One of the problems with temporal searching along the timeline in Figure 6 is that it is a highly unstructured activity. The time axis provides no information on the logical structuring of the event, let alone the performers in the concert or their relationships. It will be necessary to replace timeline searching with navigation based on an overlay of structure components. One approach to providing this structure is based on graphs of performers, instruments, songs or solo's. It could also be based on cinemagraphic classifications, such as long shots, pan shots, tight shots.

A screen grammar could be defined to select appropriate shots. If we were filming a soccer game or a wedding instead of a school concert, much of the infrastructure would be the same, but the structuring paradigms might be quite different.

In addition to a content structuring, logical story structuring could also be developed, based on narrative models or other content cues. The main goal of all of this analysis is to delay the moment at which individual content objects are bound to a general narrative structure. The later you bind, the more flexibility you have in creating differentiated, tailored presentations. Of course, the later your bind, the more work you need to do interactively. You can consider this process as recommendation-based content selection at the scene level, rather than at the program level.

5.5 Security and Privacy Concerns

A 'fun' picture shared with friends can become less fun when those friends turn into your enemies. A blown trombone solo can be cute if viewed by your trombone-playing father, but a disaster if it is used to taunt you at school (or in twenty years, at work). Research is required to support content access and content protection that reflects time-variant social and personal relationships. In the same vein, content sharing and content recommendation needs to be sensitive to the context of use: are you watching alone, with your spouse, with your children, with your friends? New management and recommender models are needed to manage this situation.

One aspect of security and privacy of socially-aware multimedia is that personally metadata will likely become too sensitive to simply place on a third-party storage system (like Facebook or Google): all of us will want to take back our identity and maintain our own control of our life-long information. This will require convenient interfaces. It will also probably require users to become accustomed to paying for media access and sharing services!

5.6 Incremental Content Authoring

Most current media authoring is predicated on the notion that content creation is a one-time event. In socially-aware multimedia, content authoring becomes an incremental process of content refinement, sharing and repurposing. "Old" assets remain living entities. This will foster a new generation of create-view-refine-share authoring systems. A key element of this approach is that media gets integrated into some larger narrative story, rather than that the media object is the story itself.

One of the things that makes professional media compelling and engaging is that nearly all media has a well-defined storyline that is packaged for general consumption. Personal media is often fragmented and incident based. Consider, for example, the personal content shown in Figure 8. Here, we can image a short story fragment, but we can see that a coherent long-term message is probably missing.

The lack of a complete 'media message' in personal media content actually presents the viewer of such media with a golden opportunity to superimpose his/her own meaning on top (physically or logically) of the content provided by the media object.

For text media, this is not a new concept. In the Figure 9, you can see how end-user content layering can be applied to a page from a noted technical manuscript. The question is: how can a common base page be transformed into a personal page (from the user's perspective – a page in which own commentary has been added, and thus own value). The answer for conventional books is pretty simple: take a pen and mark up what the base media.

Figure 8: A 'cute trick' media fragment that lacks a larger coherent story.

Changing content brings with it questions of ownership. In printed documents, this is a solved problem: even though the base content is copyright protected, there is a clear distinction between "my" media and that of the original authors. For web pages and on-line content, the relationship is less simple.

If transparent sheets had been placed between all of the pages, we could take all of the user's comments comments and sell them as separate items – all fully within current law. The content added could be further aggregated with the context created across a social network (or across the world), and analyzed. What are the most marked-up pages in the book? Does these represent the most interesting or most unclear sections of text? Do the markup patterns change over time?

A significant authoring challenge is to provide the markup and analysis functionality for all media. When annotating a piece of media – whether it be text, audio, images, or whatever – the implication has been that, as with the book pages shown in Figure 13, the annotations are of a highly personal nature. Of course, if many of these personal notes are collected and analyzed, they could provide valuable insights into the reusability of personal media assets. Even a simple density analysis of multiple media annotations could provide interesting clues for socially-aware recommender systems.

Figure 9: An example of layering (collections of) personal annotations onto existing content.

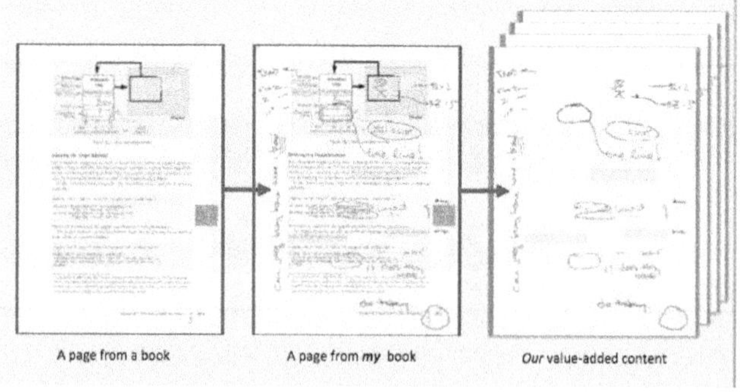

6. ADDITIONAL ISSUES

The entire premise of socially-aware multimedia is that the context of the view becomes more important – or at least equally as important – than that of the content producer. This involves considering context drawn from the experience world of each potential viewer, and realizing that one semantic media size does not fit all users. This brings up many issues of secondary importance that need to be considered and supported. We discuss three of these here.

6.1 Encapsulating Formats for Media

One of the most important technological bases for supporting dynamic composition and content/presentation adaptation is the use of a declarative specification language for encoding composition information. Such a format allows presentations to be generated dynamically, to be verified and to be transformed. One such language is SMIL, which was largely developed by my group at CWI. Other alternatives have also been developed, such as the Brazilian NCL language for use in interactive TV applications. Whatever the language choice, the most important requirement for dynamic control is a unified notion of time *and* that is not based on a scripting metaphor. In this sense, it is disappointing that the highly-hyped HTML-5 is a dramatic technological step backward. By focusing on placing a single media object in a static web page and by concentrating on VCR-only controls, HTML5 has evolved into a useless container format for all but the most simple presentations.

6.2 Encoding Emotional Content

Consider the very formal academic ceremony illustrated in portion of Figure 10(a). Here we see our redheaded Mom, still in her green dress, defending her Ph.D. dissertation. A reasonably-informed content analysis system may be able to capture many important aspects of this situation: it may be able to recognize the mom (as long as she keeps wearing the same dress!) or other prominent people, it may be able to use subtle location cues such as University logos, and it may even be able to identify the degree to which participants are engaged with the presentation. But from a personal perspective, this is kid stuff.

The real power is describing the same scene through the emotional eyes of a 12-year old boy, who is seeing his mother being grilled by a set of self-assured academic fat cats (in his opinion, of course!), smoking virtual cigars and having a grand time at Mom's expense. This is shown in Figure 10(b).

6.3 Dynamically Creating New Content

The media objects we have been studying so far contain content that was captured and (possibly) reordered as part of a viewing process. Here, the focus is on content selection and presentation. This, of course, only scratches the surface of real end-user content manipulation.

Consider the series of three photographs in Figure 11. The first two pictures are 'real' in the sense that they were taken using a real camera. The third is 'real' in the sense that it represents how the event was remembered by the participants. It is an ultimate challenge to have this form of personal synthesis supported automatically.

7. CLOSING THOUGHTS

Much has changed in the world of multimedia. Who would have expected twenty years ago that within two decades, it would be commonplace to not only listen to music via your computer, but it buy it there as well? That books would not only be written on a PC, but that the PC and its technological cousins would become a handy way to read them, or to have them read aloud. That the computer would threaten to replace not only the television, but also the movie theatre as a venue for the shared watching of content. And, perhaps more significantly in the long term, that the computer would not only render a wide range of real and artificial images, but that it would attempt to understand them as well.

In the previous sections, I have outlined what I mean by socially-aware multimedia. Using several examples, I have tried to argue that the impact of support socially-aware multimedia transcends the incremental and provides a number of (fascinating) new challenges that require fundamental research results across a wide range of multimedia disciplines.

This presentation presents the idea of socially-aware multimedia as a next step in the evolution of media processing. By introducing the notional of a temporally-variant social content into media storage, access and sharing, I hope to stimulate a new level of media research in which the multimedia user is given the central role that she deserves.

8. Acknowledgements

The ideas presented in this paper have developed over time based on my work with many talented people at CWI, at the VU University and in over a dozen European projects. They also stem from very fruitful interactions with my research partners in North and South America. I am indebted to the fine interactions that I have had with Pablo Cesar, Jack Jansen, Rodrigo Laiola, Bo Gao. A bit further from home, I acknowledge our long-term partnerships with Luis Fernando Soares Gomes and Maria de Graca Pimentel. Finally, when it comes to interactive interactions, I remain indebted to my dear friend Andy van Dam. The work described here is funded in part by the EU projects Vconect (FP7-ICT-287760) and Reverie (FP7-ICT-287723) .

(a): A formal ceremony, as seen by a camera.

(b): A formal ceremony, as seen by a 12-year old.

Figure 10: Representing Emotional Information

Figure 15: Merging and creating new 'real' content.

Crowdsourcing User Interactions with the Video Player

Konstantinos Chorianopoulos
Ionian University, Corfu, Greece
choko@acm.org

ABSTRACT

Every second millions of users enjoy content streaming on diverse video players (e.g., Web, Apps, social networks) and create billions of interactions within online video, such as *play, pause, seek/scrub*. This collective intelligence of video viewers might be leveraged into useful information for improved video navigation. For example, we can accurately detect and retrieve interesting scenes through the analysis of the aggregated users' *replay* interactions with the video player. Effective crowdsourcing of video interactions is grounded on previous work in multimedia, user modeling, and controlled user experiments. These research issues are described for the case of user-based detection of video thumbnails that stand for the semantics of the video. Moreover, we demonstrate the respective experimental environment with a focus on educational and user generated (e.g., how-to, lecture) videos.

Keywords

User-based, video, key-frame, replay, signal processing.

Catagories and Subject Descriptors

H.5.1 Multimedia Information Systems

INTRODUCTION

There is a growing research interest in user-based video modeling approaches of video interactions on the Web. The research interest has been largely motivated by the popularity of video with Web users, who have become familiar with video content, as an integral part of the Web experience in Web sites, smartphone and tablet Apps, and social networks. Notably, video search results and suggested videos are represented with a video thumbnail. In addition to the title and the short description of the video, the video thumbnail is an important information element that facilitates user navigation [2][3]. Moreover, video thumbnails have been useful as a summary and as a table of contents.

Previous multimedia research has considered content-based systems that have the benefit of analyzing a video without user interactions, but they are monolithic, because the resulting video thumbnails are the same regardless of the user preferences. Nevertheless, most of the existing content-based techniques that extract thumbnails at regular time intervals, or from each shot/scene are inefficient, because there might be too many shots in a video (e.g., how-to video), or rather few (e.g., lecture video).

In addition to the problem of detecting a set of descriptive video thumbnails for a given video, there is also the problem of selecting one of them for representing the video. For example, search results and suggested links in YouTube are represented with a thumbnail that the video authors have manually selected out of the three fixed ones (Figure 1). This approach puts too much trust on the video thumbnails selected by the video author or uploader. Besides the threat of authors tricking the system, the author-based approach does not consider the variability of users' knowledge and preferences. Thus, there is a need for selecting video thumbnails according to the collective wisdom of video viewers.

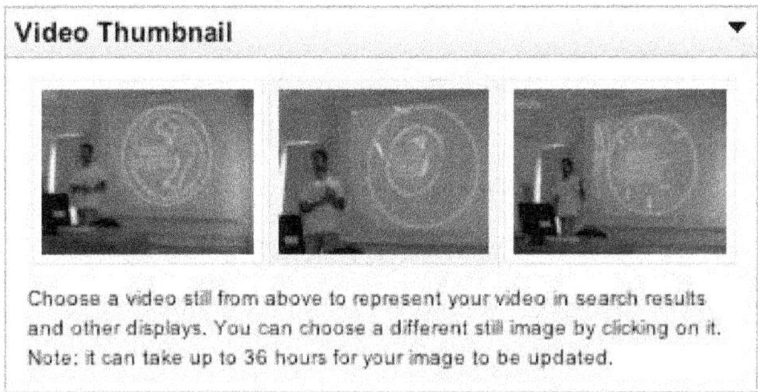

Figure 1 The YouTube upload tool asks the user to manually select a video thumbnail, which has been randomly generated.

Previous user-based research on web video has focused on the meaning of the comments, tags, re-mixes, and micro-blogs, but has not examined simple user interactions with a web-based video player. In the seminal user-based approach to web video, Shaw and Davis [7] proposed that video representation might be better modeled after the actual use made by the users and they analyzed user-comments in order to understand media semantics. Peng et al. [5] have examined the physiological behavior (eye and head movement) of video users, in order to identify interesting key-frames, but this approach is not practical because it assumes that a video camera should be available and turned-on in the privacy-sensitive home environment. Shamma et al. [6] have created summaries of broadcasts (sports and political debate respectively) by analyzing the twitter stream of the respective real-time event. Although comments and tweets are very rich in meaning, they lack the real-time accuracy that is required in the generation of

Permission to make digital or hard copies of all or part of this work for personal or classroom use is granted without fee provided that copies are not made or distributed for profit or commercial advantage and that copies bear this notice and the full citation on the first page. To copy otherwise, or republish, to post on servers or to redistribute to lists, requires prior specific permission and/or a fee.
WebMedia'12, October 15–18, 2012, São Paulo/SP, Brazil.
Copyright 2012 ACM 978-1-4503-1706-1/12/10...$15.00.

user-based video thumbnails, which we describe in the next sections.

USER-BASED VIDEO THUMBNAIL DETECTION

In order to prove that video interactions stand for interesting video segments we have devised an experimental methodology. The evaluation methodology consists of the following parts: 1) customized web video player and cloud-based server that logs user interactions, 2) questions that can be only answered by retrieving information from particular video segments, 3) controlled experiment that produces a clean video interaction data-set, 4) data analysis for automatically generating video thumbnail. For the first couple of parts, the SocialSkip [1] video interaction logging and questionnaire system has been employed.

The experimental web video player (Figure 2, left part) employs few buttons. There is the familiar pause/play button, but instead of the common video seek bar timeline, we used two fixed-seek buttons. The GoBackward goes backward 30 seconds and its main purpose is to replay interesting parts of the video, while the Goforward button jumps forward 30 seconds and its main purpose is to skip insignificant video segments. We did not use a random seek timeline because it would be difficult to analyze users' interactions. Moreover, Li et al. [4] observed that when seek thumb is used heavily, users had to make many attempts to find the desirable section of the video and thus caused significant delays. Next to the buttons, there is the current cue-time and the total time of the video in seconds.

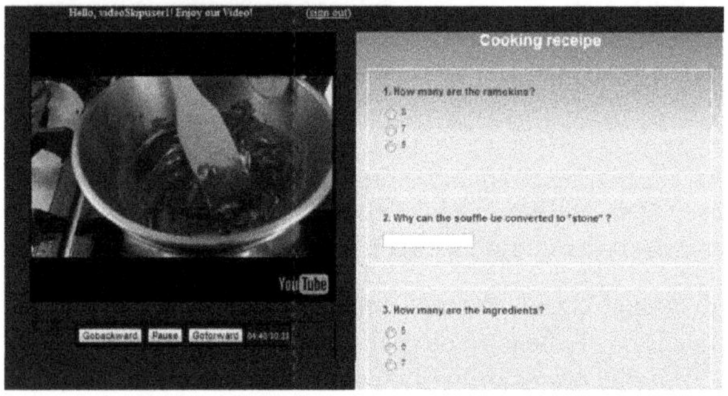

Figure 2 The experimental web video player includes skipping buttons and questionnaire functionality.

A user-centered approach identifies salient signals from human behavior, and not signals present in the video content itself. For the lecture and how-to videos we focus on, the video content tends to be either very static (usually a speaker at a podium), or very dynamic (multiple moving cameras provide alternative views of the same object and/or activity). Thus, signal processing of video content tends to fail, because it produces few or too many key-frames respectively.

In order to experimentally replicate user interest, we created an electronic questionnaire (Figure 2, right part) that corresponds to a few manually selected video segments, which stand for the semantics of the respective video. Indeed, according to Yu et al. [8] there are segments of a video clip that are commonly interesting to most users, and users might browse the respective parts of the video clip in searching for answers to some interesting questions. This assumption might be especially valid in the case of informational videos (e.g., lectures, how-to), when users seek to retrieve important information. The questions were relatively simple to answer, and did not depend on any previous knowledge, besides the information available within the video itself (Table 1). Therefore, the users had to seek/scrub through the video in order to answer those questions.

Video	Indicative questions
Lecture A	• Which are the main research topics? • What the students did not like? • What time does the first part of the talk end?
How-to B	• How many are the ramekins? • How many are the ingredients? • Which is the right order for mixing the ingredients?

Table 1 Example questions from each video. The questions are not supposed to be meaningful, but to direct the users towards a video segment.

The experiment took place in a lab with Internet connection, general-purpose computers, and headphones. Twenty-three university students (18-35 years old, 13 women and 10 men) spent approximately ten minutes to watch each video (buttons were muted). All students had been attending the Human-Computer Interaction courses at a post- or under-graduate level and received course credit in the respective courses. Next, the questionnaire appeared and there was a time restriction of five minutes, in order to motivate the users to actively browse through the video and answer the respective questions. We did not directly encourage the users to actively seek, but we informed the users that the purpose of the study was to measure their performance in finding the answers to the questions within time constraints.

Our goal is to examine whether video interactions are similar to the video semantics. For this purpose, we modeled the user interactions as a time series function and we compared it to the manually selected video semantics. For example, the *replay* function is based on the aggregation (crowdsourcing) of all *replay* interactions along the video cue time. In particular, we modified the value of the time series by one, depending on the type of interaction (e.g., for each GoBackward, we increased the value of the previous 30 cells). Next, we smoothed the signal and we calculated the local maximums. Finally, we constructed the corresponding semantic time series (pulse-like), which models the video semantics. In the next section, we present a comparison between user interactions and video semantics, in order to demonstrate that there is a close match between them.

USER INTERACTIONS STAND FOR VIDEO SEMANTICS

We observed that the interaction counts are similar between the different types of videos, because user behavior was rather motivated by the controlled conditions of the experiment than their own preferences about the content types. Nevertheless, we expect that in a natural setting (e.g., data mining of video logs from a web site) there will be variability depending on the type of the video content. The most popular button was the *skip-forward*, because the users were under time pressure to retrieve the required information in order to answer the questions.

Next, we compared the smooth versions of the *replay* and *skip-forward* time-series to the semantic ones. We observed that the *replay* closely matched the semantics of the videos. Therefore, we computed the local maximums of the *replay* time series for each one of the videos. The video segments with peaks are most likely to attract the viewers' interest. In order to determine the precise position of the peak, a derivative curve is computed. The zero-crossing points from positive to negative on derivative curve are the locations of the peaks. In this way, all key-frames in a video sequence can be identified without the need of any content-based detection. In the following figures, the user time series are plotted with the solid red curve and the experimentally defined ground truths are plotted with the pulse-like solid blue line.

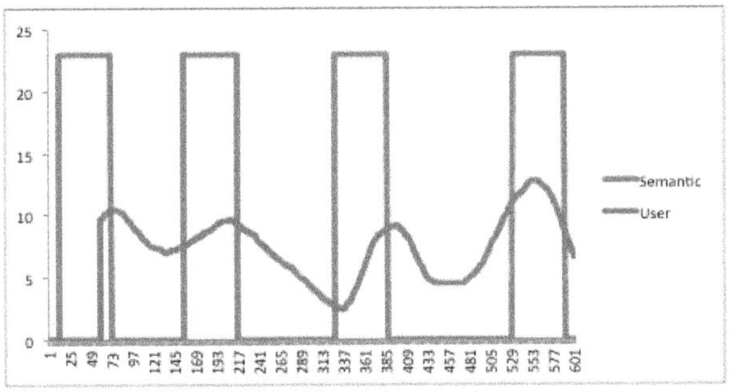

Figure 3 The user interactions function is similar to the semantic one for the lecture video

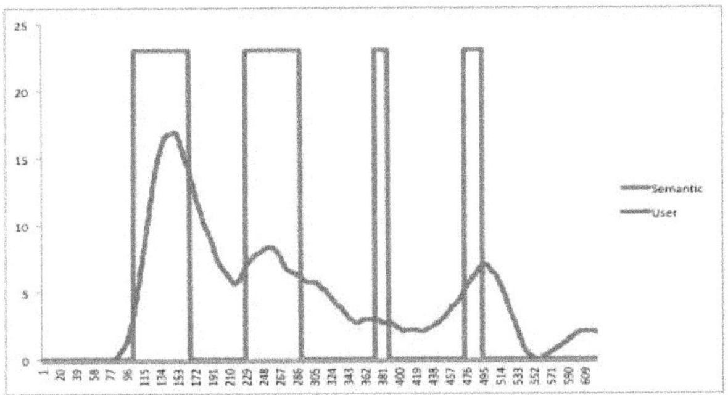

Figure 4 The user interactions function is similar to the semantic one for the how-to video

Although there is an obvious visual matching between the semantics and the user interaction signal, we have also calculated the user interaction signal peaks and the distance from the semantics one. In particular, the local maximum values of the user interaction signal can be used as the rank of the respective key-frame. Based on such a measure, it is convenient to generate a ranking of importance of key-frames. Then, the global maximum of the user interaction value in a video could be used as its representative video thumbnail (Table 2).

Semantics/ Video(secs)	Lecture A (81 interactions)	How-to B (68 interactions)
Semantic 1	33 (40) [10]	45 (105) **[16]**
Semantic 2	13 (145) [10]	21 (230) [8]
Semantic 3	48 (350) [9]	-13 (374) [3]
Semantic 4	1 (554) **[13]**	21 (475) [7]

Table 2 We have calculated the distance of the replay maximum from the semantic start (inside parentheses) and we provide in bold the user activity peak values

Finally, we found that a simple heuristic could automatically generate video thumbnails that are positioned at the start of each interesting video segment. In order to calculate this heuristic we observed that in all cases the distance of the local maximum of the *replay* time series from the start of the respective ground truth is less than 60 seconds. This simple heuristic detects 100% of the interesting video segments (n=8). There is only one case that the local maximum is before the start of the interesting video segment (how-to video, S3). Therefore, we suggest that the position of user-based video thumbnails can be automatically generated for any video by locating the local maximums of the *replay* time series and then selecting the one with the greatest value (Table 2).

In summary, the central contribution of this work is a novel conceptualization of video data-logs that holds the following unique properties: 1) implicit from people's action, 2) video signal/content-free, 3) adaptive based on consumption. The proposed heuristic ("sixty-seconds from local maxima of user activity") explains a methodology to support our core contribution and might hold different values depending on the video and on the distribution of video interactions. Moreover, we present a reproducible method that is verified and explained via qualitative and quantitative sources. Reimplementation of this system would only require a properly instrumented video player.

DISCUSSION AND FURTHER RESEARCH

The concept of crowdsourcing video interactions could be applied to any video, in order to generate user-based and dynamic video thumbnails in web search results, in Apps, and in social networks. In this work, instead of mining real video interaction data, we have devised a controlled experiment, because it provides a clean set of data that might be easier to model and understand. We focused on videos that are as much visually unstructured as possible (e.g., lecture, how-to), because content-based algorithms have already been successful with those videos that have visually structured scene changes (e.g., movies, series).

The majority of previous approaches employed content-based (e.g., detection of object, shot, and scene change) or explicit user-based methods (e.g., comments, tags, re-mix) to improve users' watching and browsing experience. In contrast, we suggest recording users' interactions with video player buttons. In terms of the user activity data, the most relevant work is the Audience Retention tool, which is part of the YouTube Analytics video account. The Audience Retention tool is employing the same set of data as suggested here, but there is no open documentation on the technique employed to map user interactions to a graph and only the video author has access to the data.

Previous work on content-based information retrieval from videos has emphasized the *number of videos* employed in similar experiments, because the respective algorithms treated the content of those videos. In this user-based work, we are not concerned with the content of the videos, but with the user activity *within* a video, thus the granule of analysis is the *number of video interactions*. Nevertheless, it is worthwhile to explore the effect of more videos and interaction types. Therefore, the small number of videos used in the preliminary studies is not an important limitation, but further research has to elaborate on different genres of video (e.g., news, sports, comedy). Notably, video interactions on educational videos might be analyzed in order to understand learning patterns of students.

Our main interest has been with lecture videos for two reasons: 1) they lack any meaningful visual structure that might have been helpful in the case of a content-based system, and 2) they contain lots of audio-visual (verbal and non-verbal) information that a user might actively seek to retrieve. In addition to video lecture, we employed a how-to (cooking) video because it has a rather complicated and active visual structure, which might have created too many false positives for a content-based approach. Moreover, the lecture and how-to video genres represent a growing and useful category of online videos, which facilitate life-long learning in many diverse topics, both theoretical and practical.

Although the *replay* user activity seems suitable for modeling user interest and video semantics, further research should consider the rest of the implicit user activities with the video player. For example, a *pause* might signify an important moment, but a pause that is too long might mean that the user is away. Another direction for further research would be to perform data mining on a large-scale database of video interactions. Nevertheless, we found that the experimental approach is very flexible during the development phase of a system, because it is straightforward to associate user behavior to the respective video interaction logs. Thus, this technique could be applied to novel video players with domain-specific user interfaces.

Finally, we suggest that user-based content analysis has the benefits of continuously adapting to evolving users' preferences, as well as providing additional opportunities for the personalization of content. For example, researchers might be able to apply several personalization techniques, such as collaborative filtering, to the user activity data. Moreover, further research should combine user-based methods in order to link user-comments to finely timed video interactions. In this way, crowdsourcing of video interactions is emerging as a new playing field for improving user experience with online video.

ACKNOWLEDGMENTS

The work reported in this paper has been partly supported by a Marie Curie European Reintegration Grants (CULT (MC-ERG-2008-230894, http://cult.di.ionio.gr) fellowship.

REFERENCES

1. Konstantinos Chorianopoulos, Ioannis Leftheriotis, and Chryssoula Gkonela. 2011. SocialSkip: pragmatic understanding within web video. In Proceddings of EuroITV '11, pages 25-28.
2. Marc Davis. 1995. Media Streams: an iconic visual language for video representation. In Human-computer interaction, Ronald M. Baecker et al. (Eds.). Morgan Kaufmann Publishers Inc., San Francisco, CA, USA
3. Girgensohn, A. Boreczky, J., Wilcox, L, (2001). Keyframe-based user interfaces for digital video, Computer, 34(9):61–67
4. F.C. Li, A. Gupta, E. Sanocki, L.-wei He, and Y. Rui, "Browsing digital video," Proceedings CHI '00, vol. 2, 2000, pp. 169-176.
5. Peng, W.-T., Chu, W.-T., Chang, C.-H., Chou, C.-N., Huang, W.-J., Chang, W.-Y., and Hung, Y.-P. (2011). Editing by viewing: Automatic home video summarization by viewing behavior analysis. Multimedia, IEEE Transactions on, 13(3):539-550.
6. David A. Shamma, Lyndon Kennedy, and Elizabeth F. Churchill. 2009. Tweet the debates: understanding community annotation of uncollected sources. In Proceedings of WSM '09. ACM, 3-10.
7. Ryan Shaw and Marc Davis. 2005. Toward emergent representations for video. In Proceedings of MULTIMEDIA '05, 431-434.
8. Bin Yu, Wei-Ying Ma, Klara Nahrstedt, and Hong-Jiang Zhang. 2003. Video summarization based on user log enhanced link analysis. In Proceedings MULTIMEDIA '03. ACM, 382-391.

An Architecture for Multidimensional Computer Adaptive Test with Educational Purposes

Jean Piton-Gonçalves
University of São Paulo
Federal University of São Carlos
Department of Mathematics
Rod. Washington Luís, Km 235, CP 676,
13565905, São Carlos/Brazil
jpiton@ufscar.br

Sandra Maria Aluísio
University of São Paulo
Institute of Mathematics and Computer Science
Avenida Trabalhador São-Carlense, 400,
13566590, São Carlos/Brazil
sandra@icmc.usp.br

ABSTRACT

Given a set of items, a *Multidimensional Computer Adaptive Test* (MCAT) selects those items from the bank according to the estimated abilities of the student, resulting in an individualized test. MCATs seek to maximize the test's accuracy, based on multiple simultaneous examination abilities (unlike a *Computer Adaptive Test* - CAT - which evaluates a single ability) using the sequence of items previously answered. Although MCATs have been very well studied from a statistical point of view, there is no computational system that covers all the steps needed for its appropriated use such as: the use of a calibrated item bank, proposal of initial and stopping criteria for the test, criteria for estimating the ability of the examinee and criteria to select items. The purpose of this paper is twofold: (i) to present an innovative architecture of an MCAT for real users, as a Web application, and (ii) to discuss the theoretical and methodological development of such MCAT, through a new approach named here *Computer-based Multidimensional Adaptive Testing* (CBMAT). The proof of concept of CBMAT was an implementation called *Multidimensional Adaptive Test System for Educational Purposes* (MADEPT). In simulations, MADEPT proved to be a computer system suitable for applications with real users, secure, accurate and portable.

Categories and Subject Descriptors

K.3 [**Computers and Education**]: Computers and Information Science Education; D.m [**Software**]: Miscellaneous—*Software psychology*

General Terms

Design, Measurement

Permission to make digital or hard copies of all or part of this work for personal or classroom use is granted without fee provided that copies are not made or distributed for profit or commercial advantage and that copies bear this notice and the full citation on the first page. To copy otherwise, to republish, to post on servers or to redistribute to lists, requires prior specific permission and/or a fee.
WebMedia'12, October 15–28, 2012, São Paulo/SP, Brazil.
Copyright 2012 ACM 978-1-4503-1706-1/12/10 ...$15.00.

Keywords

Computer-based Testing, Multidimensional Computer Adaptive Test, Multidimensional Item Response Theory, Web Architeture

1. INTRODUCTION

The first thoughts on Intelligence Quotient tests have been introduced in 1905 by the researches of Alfred Binet (1857-1911), a French psychologist and educator. He realized that it was possible to individualize a test by classifying the items according to their level of difficulty. The adaptive test of Binet (Binet-type Adaptive Test) is an intelligence test based on levels of difficulty that was initially created to gauge the level of intelligence of a child in comparison with his/her chronological age, thus assessing his/her mental age [36].

In the 50ths, more complex psychometric models appeared, giving rise to a discussion on the use of computers in Psychometrics. In the same decade, the Two-Stage Adaptive Testing has been developed, divided into two subtests: one of lower difficulty (Routing Test) and one of higher difficulty (Measurement Test). The items of the Measurement Test are selected according to the correct and wrong answers obtained in the Routing Test. A variation of Binet-type adaptive test is the Stratified Adaptive Test, which is distinguished for electing the next item immediately after each item is answered [36].

Relevant improvements have occurred in the area of psychometric tests, highlighting Lord's work [14] in Item Response Theory (IRT), which has been used in Brazilian large-scale exams, such as the national exam of secondary school, ENEM[1], the basic education evaluation system, SAEB[2] and Prova Brasil[3], among others. Another important advance in psychometric tests is the Computer Adaptive Test (CAT), highlighting Reckase's [24].

In the CAT, the objective is to measure a single ability (unidimensional) or a major construct, in which each examinee receives a different sample of items, resulting in an individualized test. The **Multidimensional Computer**

[1](Exame Nacional do Ensino Médio) tests graduating high school students. Some universities use the scores obtained by the student in the exam as a criterion for admission.
[2](Sistema de Avaliação de Ensino Básico) is a national exam for students of the 4th and 8th grades of basic school, applied in both urban and rural areas, in public and private schools.
[3]Is complementary to SAEB exam and encompasses other aspects of the school system besides students performance.

Adaptive Test (MCAT) considers that the items of the test evaluate the examinee under more than one ability simultaneously. Mathematics, for example, is a knowledge domain that may have a unidimensional interpretation in CAT or receive a multidimensional interpretation, considering the knowledge of the examinee in Algebra, Arithmetic and Geometry. MCAT may be employed in different knowledge domains, as Medicine, Education, Business, Psychology and Industry. Each context has a well-defined goal. For example, an adaptive test in the field of Psychology may determine whether an individual presents traits of anxiety or predisposition for a psychological disorder. In business field, it may help to manage the company's knowledge, administering questionnaires to a group of coordinators.

In the literature, MCAT is often understood as a set of theories, methods and psychometric models, which measures the abilities of an examinee, and not as a computational system. The **Computer-Based Testing (CBT)** performs automatically the assembly of items, the administration, the correction and the report generation, enabling, for example, an MCAT for real examinees. The psychometric properties of MCAT may be determined by the **Multidimensional Item Response Theory (MIRT)**, which proposes a statistical and mathematical interpretation for the examinee's multiple abilities. In our review of the literature, two papers stood out in what concerns a proposal of web architecture for CAT (unidimensional): Marinagi et al. [15] and Phankokkruad and Woraratpanya [20]. We did not find proposals of web architecture for MCAT, which, due to its multidimensional nature, has several particularities and needs that do not exist in CAT.

This paper (i) presents an architecture that enables the administration of MCATs to real users through the Web, an entirely new and innovative proposal, and (ii) discusses theoretical and methodological aspects for the development of the proposed MCAT, which is enabled by a new approach, the **Computer-based Multidimensional Adaptive Testing (CBMAT)**. The CBMAT architecture encompasses six modules: Administrator Module, MCAT Module, Correctness Module, Database Module, Integration Module and Item Module. CBMAT proof of concept was made through the implementation of the Multidimensional Adaptive Test for Educational Purposes (MADEPT), which proved to be safe, correct, portable and suitable for applications with real users.

The Section 2 addresses and classifies the CBTs. The Section 3 discusses the elements required for developing MCATs based in MIRT. A new architecture for CBMAT is proposed in Section 4. The results and discussion related to the development of MCATs and CBMATs is found in Section 5 and the conclusion is presented in Section 6.

2. CBT

A CBT evaluates electronically the knowledge and the abilities of the examinee and may be employed in different knowledge domains, such as, Medicine, Education, Business, Psychology, Industry. A CBT manages and configures the whole process of evaluation of an examinee, administering and correcting items, generating reports of performance and/or results and ensuring the security and accuracy of the test.

In the last decades, there have been innovations both in the CBT conception and in the way reports are generated and analyzed. Bartram [3] reports that some innovations are evident, as for example those that have multimedia items or even virtual objects simulators, enabling a different level of interaction of the examinee with the test.

CBTs may be categorized by the following two criteria: type of score (right/wrong or partial evaluation of the knowledge) and sample of items (same number of items and/or same items and/or variable number of items). The type of score and the sample of items give origin to two process of evaluation [1]: (i) Traditional Computer-based Methods, in which the tests have the same number of items for all the examinees and a dichotomous response (correct/incorrect); and (ii) Alternative Computer-based Methods, which measure the partial knowledge of the examinee (as is the case in the Admissible Probability Measure [5]) or select the items of the test according to the estimated abilities of the examinee (as is the case in the adaptive tests, which are detailed in Section 3).

3. MCAT

In its modern concept, CAT is characterized by selecting the items according to the (one) level of ability (or proficiency of the examinee). Given a set of items, the major characteristic of a CAT is to "individualize" a test, that is, each examinee receives a different sample of items, which may also vary in quantity. CAT aims to maximize the accuracy of the test, based on the knowledge of the examinee given by the previously answered items [37]. In this way, it is possible to administer tests with more flexibility and adaptability, reducing significantly the time required and obtaining immediate results and higher precision in comparison to the tests that present a fixed number of items [18].

Examples of successful systems based in CAT, being used for many years, are the *Adaptive English Proficiency Test for the Web* (ADEPT), administered in the Institute of Mathematics and Computer Sciences, University of São Paulo, Brazil [21, 23] and the computing environment called *Inteligent Evaluation System using Tests for Teleducation* (SIETTE) [9].

The CAT measures only an ability θ (unidimensional) or even a major construct. On the other hand, the tests of psychological assessment are increasingly indicating the assessment of more than one ability simultaneously (multidimensional), due the very nature of the human mind, which is multifaceted. For this, the MCAT assumes that the examinee has more than one mental construct that may be estimated by the MIRT [25].

An example of unidimensional mental construct is the knowledge domain of Mathematics, interpreted unidimensionally in the CAT as the unique ability of the examinee. In what concerns the multidimensional abilities, in the knowledge domain of Mathematics, they may be interpreted, for example, as the ability in Algebra, Arithmetic, and Geometry. In this last case, one may say that the probability space (or parametric space) has dimension three. In the MIRT, the multiple abilities are denoted by a vector of abilities $\boldsymbol{\theta} = (\theta_1, \ldots, \theta_p)$, in which each component represents one ability that may be or not correlated to the others in the p-dimensional probability space.

The development of an MCAT requires a multidimensional model of response (Section 3.1); a calibrated item bank (Section 3.2); a method for estimating the examinees' abilities (Section 3.3); a criterion for item selection (Section

3.44); an initial criterion (Section 3.5), and a stopping criterion (Section 3.6).

3.1 Multidimensional Item Response Model

The *Multidimensional Three Parameter Logistic model* represents the ability of the examinee in the p-dimensional probability space as the vector $\boldsymbol{\theta} = (\theta_1, \theta_2, \ldots, \theta_p) \in \mathbb{R}^p$. The function that models the hit probability of the examinee for an n-th item is

$$P_i(\boldsymbol{\theta}) = P(U_i = \mathbf{1}|\boldsymbol{\theta}, \boldsymbol{a}_i, b_i, c_i) = c_i + \frac{1 - c_i}{1 + e^{-\boldsymbol{a}_i(\boldsymbol{\theta} - b_i \mathbf{1})}}, \quad (1)$$

in which:

U_i: is the random variable that corresponds to the answer to the n-th item. For the dichotomous case (in which only one alternative of response is correct and the others are incorrect), $U_i = 1$ for the correct answer; otherwise, $U_i = 0$.

$\boldsymbol{a}_i = (a_1, \ldots, a_p)$: is the discrimination vector of the n-th item and is related to the slope of the *Item Response Surface* from Equation (1), which is tridimensionally represented in the Figure 1. The *Discrimination Power of the Item* (MDISC) [27], which summarizes the interpretation of the vector $\boldsymbol{a}_i$ is:

$$MDISC_i = ||\boldsymbol{a}_i|| = \sqrt{\sum_{j=1}^{p} a_{i_j}^2}. \quad (2)$$

This value measures the intensity of variation from the low hit probability region to the high hit probability region of the response model. In this way, an item with an ideal discrimination power is the one that all low-ability examinees got wrong and all high-ability examinees got right.

$b_i\mathbf{1}$: is the vector $p \times 1$ of the difficulty parameter b_i of the n-th item and 1 is the vector of 1's.

c_i: represents the probability of a correct answer given an examinee with low-ability estimates. In the educational scenery, this is called "guess".

3.2 Calibrated Item Bank

The item bank is a database that contains items and other related data, as for example (i) the correct answers of the tests that encompasses predetermined answers (objective tests) [16], (ii) statistical data, as the number or examinees that got right/wrong the item, (iii) links related to the item, as texts, videos and audiovisual components, (iv) identifiers and markers of the item (v) psychometric parameters, as the level of difficulty of the item, markers of different contents/issues of the item. As a requirement of the adaptability, in adaptive tests the number of items of the pool must be greater than the number of items administered in the test.

The calibration of the item bank is the determination of the linked parameters. In the case of a test with dichotomous answers, the procedure is performed taking into consideration the number of successes and failures obtained by the examinee in the items previously answered. If the response model is according to Equation (1), the calibration

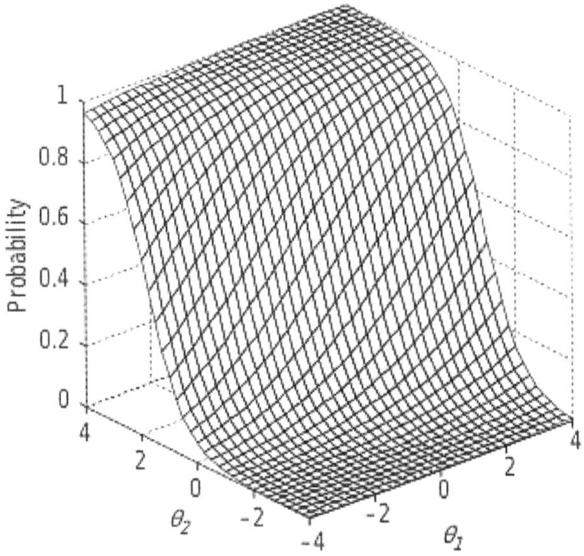

Figure 1: Example of Item Response Surface for $\boldsymbol{\theta} = (\theta_1, \theta_2)$. Extracted from [26].

determines the parameters $\boldsymbol{a}$, b, and c for the items of the bank.

An interesting aspect is the analysis of the dimensionality of the items [12]. Such analysis consists of the analysis of the eigenvalues of tetrachoric correlation matrix and the full information factor analysis [4]. It must be stressed that the calibration of items is a procedure expensive and computationally slow, and must be performed and analyzed previously to the test application. There is a commercial software for multidimensional calibration - the TESTFACT[4].

3.3 Ability Estimation

The ability vector $\boldsymbol{\theta}$ of the examinee is often estimated through the Maximum Likelihood (ML) method or through Bayesian methods, such as (i) Posterior Mode and Posterior Mean [8, 33]. The ML has serious deficiencies, resulting at least in two problems that are aggravated in an adaptive test [31]: (i) the initial adaptation in item selection is hindered by the lack of information to determine the maximum and (ii) the maximum likelihood does not take into consideration the prior knowledge about joint distribution of the ability. Such deficiencies are removed by the Bayesian approach [30] which reveals the value that maximizes the posterior density function

$$f(\boldsymbol{\theta}|\boldsymbol{u}) = L(\boldsymbol{u}|\boldsymbol{\theta}) \frac{f(\boldsymbol{\theta})}{f(\boldsymbol{u})}, \quad (3)$$

in which $\boldsymbol{u}$ is the vector of the observed answers of the examinee and

$$f(\boldsymbol{u}) = \int L(\boldsymbol{u}|\boldsymbol{\theta}) f(\boldsymbol{\theta}) d\boldsymbol{\theta} \quad (4)$$

is the marginal probability of $\boldsymbol{u}$; $f(\boldsymbol{\theta})$ is the prior distribution of $\boldsymbol{\theta}$, and $L(\boldsymbol{u}|\boldsymbol{\theta})$ is the likelihood function of $\boldsymbol{u}$.

[4]http://www.ssicentral.com

The determination of the value that maximizes the Equation (3) falls under the numerical solution of nonlinear equations and $f(\boldsymbol{\theta})$ is often adopted as the Multivariate Normal distribution, $N(\boldsymbol{\mu}, \boldsymbol{\Phi})$. If the adopted estimation is the Posterior Mean, thus the estimated ability $\boldsymbol{\theta}$ for the iteration $j+1$ is:

$$\boldsymbol{\theta}^{(j+1)} = \boldsymbol{\theta}^{(j)} - [\boldsymbol{H}(\boldsymbol{\theta}^{(j)})]^{-1} \times \frac{\partial}{\partial \boldsymbol{\theta}} \log f(\boldsymbol{\theta}^{(j)}|\boldsymbol{u}) \quad (5)$$

for $\boldsymbol{\theta}$ of the iteration $j+1$ and $\boldsymbol{H}(\boldsymbol{\theta}^{(j)})$ is the Hessian matrix $p \times p$ evaluated in the instance j. One advantage of the Bayesian estimators is that, unlike estimators of ML, they always converges [30].

3.4 Item Selection

The MCAT is characterized by selecting the next item of the test according to the model and criterion of selection adopted. Since the last decade, the literature is indicating criteria of item selection that interpret the level of information of the test or of the item which may consider aspects of the Bayesian approach. The aim is to select the item that maximizes the information according to $\boldsymbol{\theta}$; the interpretation of such item may be obtained either by Local [30] or Global Information [6, 35].

Regarding Local Information, the highlights are the criteria based on principles of the Bayesian approach, as for example the Largest Decrement in the Volume of the Bayesian Credibility Ellipsoid, proposed by Segall [30], denoted by V_{i_k} for the n-th item of the pool in the k-th item administered in the test. In such case, we select the k-th item that presents

$$\arg \max_{i_k \in R_k} [V_{i_k}] = \arg \max_{i_k \in R_k} [I(\boldsymbol{\theta}, \hat{\boldsymbol{\theta}}_k) + I(\boldsymbol{\theta}, u_{k+1}) + \boldsymbol{\Phi}^{-1}] \quad (6)$$

In which $I(\cdot,\cdot)$ is the Fisher Information, $\boldsymbol{\Phi}^{-1}$ is the inverse of the covariance matrix of the multivariate normal distribution and R_k is the set of items of the pool that have not yet been administered in the test until the step k. The conditional distribution of $\hat{\boldsymbol{\theta}}_k$ is asymptotically normal, related to the Fisher Information [26].

The Global Information, in what concerns criteria for item selection, may be based on the principles of the Kullback-Leibler Information measure (or Relative Entropy) [11, 10] between two distributions of probability f and g, under a same parametric space. In the continuous case, the Kullback-Leibler Information Measure between two distributions f and g is defined through

$$KL[f||g] = \int f(\boldsymbol{\theta}) \log \frac{f(\boldsymbol{\theta})}{g(\boldsymbol{\theta})} \, d\boldsymbol{\theta}, \quad (7)$$

and that [11]: (i) $KL[f||g] \geq 0$, (ii) if $f = g$ thus $KL[f||g] = 0$ and (iii) $KL[f||g] \neq KL[g||f]$ (they are not symmetric). The works reported in [17, 35, 34, 6] discuss and propose Bayesian criteria for item selection based on Kullback-Leibler Information for unidimensional and multidimensional models, with studies categorized into intentional abilities (known abilities) and nuisance abilities (unpredicted abilities).

In the Global Information, the main criteria for item selection are: (i) Kullback-Leibler Index [6]; (ii) Posterior Expected Kullback-Leibler Information [17]; (iii) Mutual Information [17] and (iv) Kullback-Leibler between Subsequent Posteriors [17].

3.5 Initial Criterion

The first item selected for the examinee is an important point in an MCAT and may be classified in two different ways [19]: with or without prior information on the examinee. In the first way, we use some prior information on the examinee as, for example, the school transcript. In the second way, every examinee has the same initial level of ability and, for this reason, it is possible (i) to fix the initial ability of the examinee and select the item and (ii) to separate a set of items with the same difficulty level and choose randomly the first item for the examinee.

3.6 Stopping Criterion

An adaptive test may finalize when [13]: (i) the item bank runs out of items; (ii) the test reaches a predetermined number of items for the examinee; (iii) the estimated ability reaches a sufficient level of accuracy; (iv) the estimated ability is below a predetermined level; (v) the examinee presents an abnormal behavior such as, for example, to answer an item very quickly or very slowly.

Other criteria may be adopted, such as: the standard error estimate is below a predefined value and/or the item information ceases to exist for an examinee [32]. An MCAT demonstrates integrity if it does not finish until the examinee has performed a minimum number of items, keeping the validity of the test.

4. PROPOSED ARCHITECTURE

This paper proposes an architecture for CBMAT systems, taking as base (i) the gap found in the literature concerning proposals of architectures for MCATs and (ii) the experience of the authors in developing systems based on adaptive tests and CBTs [21, 23, 7, 22].

CBMATs' architecture, represented in Figure 2, is distributed in six modules: *Administrator Module*, *MCAT Module*, *Correctness Module*, *Database Module*, *Integration Module* and *Item Module*. The next sections present details of each module.

4.1 Administrator Module

This is the module in which the system administrators (i) authenticate and authorize the examinees, (ii) configure the setup of MCAT Module and (iii) make operations in the Database Module, such as insertion, alteration and removal of users.

4.2 MCAT Module

The MCAT is the main subsystem and needs to be implemented in a scientific language, suitable for multidimensional statistical and mathematical aspects. Suggestions for free languages and softwares include the language and statistical environment R[5], GNU Octave[6], C++, FORTRAN, among other languages focused on scientific programming which have libraries and packages for this purpose.

This module encompasses, in short, (i) a criterion for initial selection of item; (ii) a model of multidimensional response; (iii) a method for ability estimation and (iv) a stopping criterion. In the model, we added the final ability, computational time, standard errors of the estimators, information measures (when they are available), calculus of

[5]cran.r-project.org

[6]www.gnu.org/software/octave

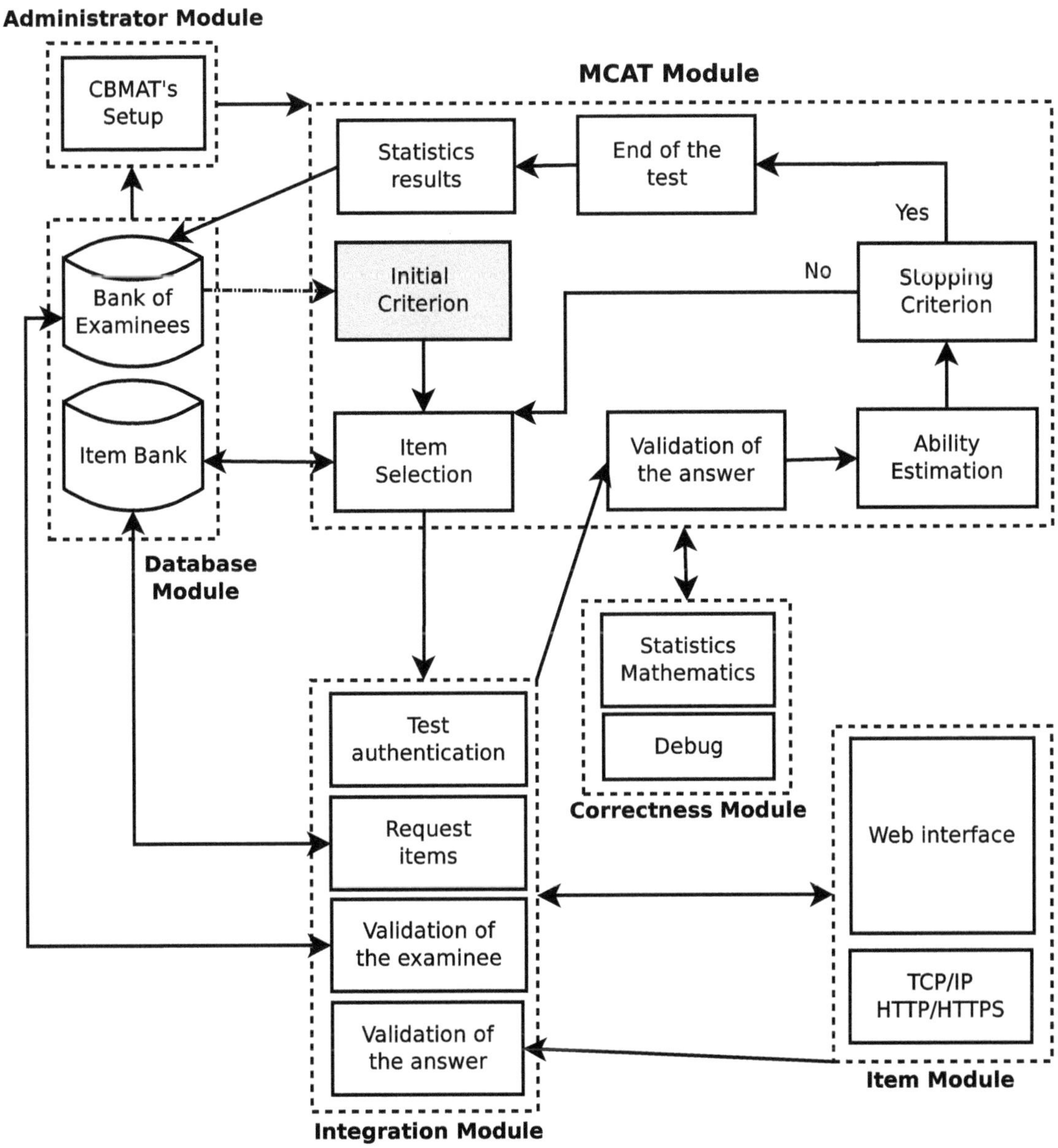

Figure 2: Architecture proposed for the CBMAT.

the *MDISC*, values for future calculation of test accuracy and efficiency, among other statistical measures related to the test (or set of tests) and to the items.

4.3 Correctness Module

The Correctness Module is directly related to the MCAT Module and performs, during the execution time, the following tasks: (i) verify loss of precision with floating points; (ii) validates numerical input and output between the several processes of the MCAT, (iii) corrects the multidimensional method of Newton, which may present problems related to convergence and singularity in the Hessian matrix (in such case we recommend to use Fisher Information matrix); (iv) corrects the multidimensional estimation and integration methods, and (v) log aiming depurating the calculi generated by the MCAT Module.

4.4 Database Module

This module consists of: (i) a calibrated item bank (Section 3.2) with the analysis of dimensionality; (ii) a bank with data from the examinees, such as record of performance in previous tests, personal data, etc.; (iii) a database containing other information on the CBMAT, such as access records, encryption keys, data communication protocols, among others required by a Web system.

4.5 Integration Module

The communication between the Database Module, the Item Module and the MCAT is performed by the Integration Module. This module is composed by (i) test authentications, which validates the data from the MCAT Module; (ii) requests on the item bank; (iii) examinees' validations which check the information from MCAT and (iv) validations of the answers, which check the answers, correct/incorrect, as input data for the MCAT Module. In this way the communication between different languages and softwares becomes more efficient and robust.

4.6 Item Module

In the Item Module the iteration user-computer occurs via Web interface, mediated by TCP/IP, HTTP and HTTPS protocols. The aim is to exhibit the item validated by the integration Module, with the main characteristic of ensuring the security in the exhibition and collection of the examinee's answer.

4.7 Execution of the CBMAT

The execution of the CBMAT starts from the administrator's setup, defining the initial criterion, the criterion for the selection of the next item, the criterion for ability estimation and the stopping criterion. Such definition depends on: (i) the quantity of criteria/methods implemented in the CBMAT and (ii) the purposes of the test.

Accordingly to the architecture represented in Figure 2, as soon as the administrator authorizes the test, an Initial Criterion is adopted and, in the sequence, the Item Selection from the item bank occurs. The Integration Module authenticates the examinee and the item. The Item Module exhibits the item for the examinee in the Web interface, and the answer of the examinee for such item is informed by the Web interface to the Integration Module, which, on its turn, validates the answer for the MCAT Module. The Ability Estimation determines the $\boldsymbol{\theta}$ of the examinee. Next, the Stop Criterion of the test is applied and, if it is not fulfilled, the next item is selected in accordance with the estimated $\boldsymbol{\theta}$ and the adopted criterion. In order to ensure the security of the test, the examinee is periodically authenticated.

The test finishes when the Stop Criterion is satisfied, generating the final result of the test. The Correctness Module acts in every step of the MCAT Module, ensuring the correctness of the calculations. The architecture proposed in this paper was validated by the project and development of the CBMAT addressed in Section 5.

5. RESULTS AND DISCUSSION

In order to validate the proposed architecture, we developed the Web system **Multidimensional Adaptive Test for Educational Purposes (MADEPT)** using: (i) R language for the MCAT and Correctness Module; (ii) PHP, Javascript and JQUERY for the Administrator and Item modules and (iii) MySQL for the Database Module. The Integration Module is hybrid and contains the drivers developed for R, PHP, Javascript, JQUERY and MySQL communication.

The MCAT Module of the MADEPT encompasses: the Bayesian criterion MAP proposed by [30] for estimation of the ability; the Kullback-Leibler information as item selection criterion; the random selection of the first item as initial criterion and a prefixed number of answered items as stop criterion.

In simulations, MADEPT proved to be a computational system suitable for applications with real users, safe, correct and portable, given that it allows the expansion of the MCAT Module with regard to items selection and estimation. In the future, new criteria for estimating and selecting items, as well as for initializing and stopping the test, may be expanded or added.

MADEPT presented the following characteristics: (1) the test time is shorter due to the adaptability of MCAT, reducing substantially the examinees' fatigue, when compared to long tests performed using pencil and paper; (2) it is a system adequate for assessment in Distance Education [28] and in teaching and learning activities held on E-learning environments [38]; (3) once it is guaranteed by the Item Response Theory, the test does no require that all the examinees perform the examination simultaneously [2], (4) the elaboration and multidimensional calibration of the item bank requires an specialized know-how; (5) it may require a server based on distributed applications and parallel processing, due to the high operational cost of multidimensional numerical integration and matrix calculus; (6) the implementation of the MCAT Module is very expensive and labor-intensive because it involves statistical and mathematical theories in a multidimensional field. The algorithms of this nature have to be projected to ensure a correct, secure and fast processing, enabling trustable and reliable results.

The Figure 3 shows a screenshot of an item in MADEPT's interface relating to the Educational Informatics. The item presents: (i) one statement composed by one question and one algorithm and rs(ii) four choices, being one of them correct and the other three incorrect (distractors).

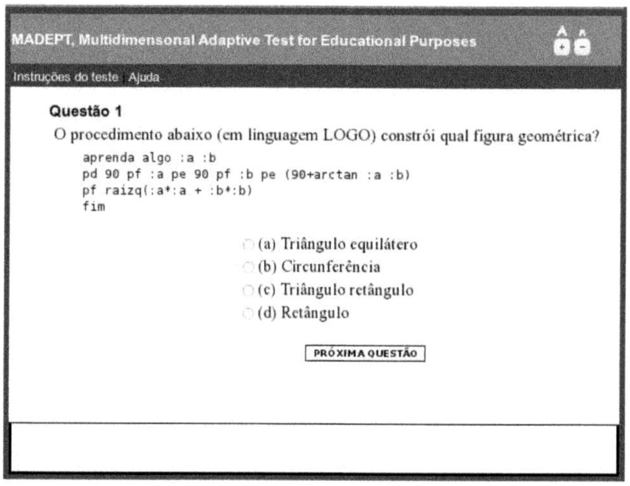

Figure 3: Screenshot of an item in MADEPT's interface.

6. CONCLUSION

If the aim of a test is to measure simultaneously several abilities of the examinee, the MCAT is a solution for educational evaluation. However, to make it applicable to real users, it is necessary an architecture for its development.

In the literature review, we did not find proposals of Web architecture for MCAT. Considering this context, this paper presented an architecture for the CBMAT. CBMAT has an architecture that encompasses six modules: Administrator Module, MCAT Module, Correctness Module, Database Module, Integration Module and Item Module. Every communication between the modules must contain safety controls, such as cryptography and session controls.

For this architecture, the item bank has to be calibrated and the dimensionality analysis must be done. In order to validate such architecture, we developed for the Web the system MADEPT, which in simulations [22] proved to be a computational system suitable for applications with real users, safe, correct and portable.

In what concerns future work, the next steps are: (i) to calibrate multidimensionally, with the TESTFACT, the item bank related to Mathematics of the SARESP[7] Exam [29] and (ii) to test the MADEPT with real students.

7. REFERENCES

[1] S. M. Aluísio, V. T. de Aquino, R. Pizzirani, and O. N. Oliveira. High order skills with partial knowledge evaluation: Lessons learned from using a computer-based proficiency test of english for academic purposes. *Journal of Information Technology Education*, 2(1):185–201, 2003.

[2] D. F. Andrade, H. R. Tavares, and R. da Cunha Valle. *Teoria de Resposta ao Item: Conceitos e Aplicações.* Associação Brasileira de Estatística, São Paulo, 2000.

[3] D. Bartram. *Computer-Based Testing and the Internet: Issues and Advances*, chapter Testing on the Internet: Issues, Challenges and Opportunities in the Field of Occupational Assessment, pages 13–37. John Wiley and Sons, Ltd, 2006.

[4] R. D. Bock, R. Gibbons, and E. Muraki. Full-information item factor analysis. *Applied Psychological Measurement*, 12(3):261–280, 1988.

[5] J. E. Bruno. Admissible probability measures in instructional management. *Journal of Computer-Based Instruction*, 14, 1987.

[6] H.-H. Chang and Z. Ying. A global information approach to computerized adaptive testing. *Applied Psychological Measurement*, 20:213–229, 1996.

[7] M. Curi, J. Piton-Gonçalves, T. A. M. Ricarte, and S. M. Aluísio. Métodos de seleção de itens em teste adaptativo multidimensional. 1o Congresso Brasileiro de Teoria de Resposta ao Item.

[8] Q. Diao and M. D. Reckase. Comparison of ability estimation and item selection mathods in multidimensional computerized adaptive testing. In *Proceedings of the 2009 GMAC Conference on Computerized Adaptive Testing*, 2009.

[9] E. Guzmán, R. Conejo, and E. García-hervás. An authoring environment for adaptive testing. *Educational Technology & Society*, 8:66–76, 2005.

[10] S. Kullback. *Information theory and statistics.* John Wiley and Sons, 1959.

[11] S. Kullback and R. A. Leibler. On information and sufficiency. *The Annals of Mathematical Statitics*, 22(1):79–86, 1951.

[12] Y. H. Li and R. W. Lissitz. An evaluation of the accuracy of multidimensional irt linking. *Applied Psychological Measurement*, 24:115–138, 2000.

[13] J. M. Linacre. Computer-adaptive testing: a methodology whose time has come. Published in Sunhee Chae, Unson Kang, Eunhwa Jeon and J. M. Linacre. Development of computerised middle school achievement test, 2000.

[7] School Performance Assessment System of the State São Paulo/Brasil is a annual exam used to evaluate the performance of state School and High School students of the State of São Paulo.

[14] F. M. Lord. *Application of Item Response Theory to Practical Testing Problems.* Lawrence Erlbaum Associates, Hilsdale, New Jersey, EUA, first edition, 1980.

[15] C. C. Marinagi, V. G. Kaburlasos, and V. T. Tsoukalas. An architecture for an adaptive assessment tool. *Frontiers In Education Conference - Global Engineering: Knowledge Without Borders, Opportunities Without Passports. FIE '07*, (37th Annual):T3D–11 – T3D–16, 2007.

[16] C. McKenna and J. Bull. Design effective objective test questions: an introductory workshop. *Proceedings of the Conference at Loughborough University, Flexible Learning*, (Third):253–257, June 1999.

[17] J. Mulder and W. J. van der Linden. *Elements of Adaptive Testing*, chapter Multidimensional Adaptive Testing with Kullback-Leibler Information Item Selection, pages 77–101. Springer, 2010.

[18] J. Olea, V. Ponsoda, and G. Prieto. *Tests Informatizados Fundamentos y Aplicaciones.* Ediciones Pirámede, 1999.

[19] C. G. Parshall, J. A. Spray, J. C. Kalohn, and T. Davey. *Practical Considerations in Computer-Based Testing.* Springer-Verlag, New York, Inc., 2002.

[20] M. Phankokkruad and K. Woraratpanya. Web service architecture for computer-adaptive testing on e-learning. *Proceedings of World Academy of Science Engineering Technology*, 46:347–351, 2008.

[21] J. Piton-Gonçalves, S. M. Aluísio, L. H. Mendonca, and O. O. Novaes. A learning environment for english for academic purposes based on adaptive tests and task-based systems. In J. Lester, R. Vicari, and F. Paraguaçu, editors, *Intelligent Tutoring Systems*, volume 3220 of *Lecture Notes in Computer Science*, pages 1–11. Springer Berlin Heidelberg, 2004.

[22] J. Piton-Gonçalves, M. Curi, and S. M. Aluísio. Studies in kullback-leibler between subsequent posteriors: defining an information-based stopping critetion. *Psychometrika: New York: Springer (submitted)*, 2012.

[23] J. Piton-Gonçalves, A. J. Monzon, and S. M. Aluísio. Métodos de avaliação informatizada que tratam o conhecimento parcial do aluno e geram provas individualizadas. In *Anais do XX Simpósio Brasileiro de Informática na Educação*, volume 1, Porto Alegre, RS, Novembro 2009. Sociedade Brasileira de Computação.

[24] M. D. Reckase. An interactive computer program for tailored testing based on the oneparameter logistic model. *Behaviour Research Methods and Instrumentation*, 6(2):208–307, 1974.

[25] M. D. Reckase. The difficulty of test items that measure more than one ability. *Applied Psychological Measurement*, 9(4):401–412, 1985.

[26] M. D. Reckase. *Multidimensional Item Response Theory.* Springer: New York - NY, 2009.

[27] M. D. Reckase and R. L. McKinely. The discriminating power of items that measure more than one dimension. *Applied Psychological Measurement*, 15:361–373, 1991.

[28] P. Salcedo, M. Pinninghoff, and R. Contreras. Computerized adaptive tests and item response theory on a distance education platform. In J. Mira and

J. álvarez, editors, *Artificial Intelligence and Knowledge Engineering Applications: A Bioinspired Approach*, volume 3562 of *Lecture Notes in Computer Science*, pages 22–29. Springer Berlin / Heidelberg, 2005.

[29] São-Paulo. *Matrizes de Referência para a Avaliação SARESP 2009*, volume 1. Secretaria da Educação do Governo do Estado de São Paulo, 2009.

[30] D. O. Segall. Multidimensional adaptive testing. *Psychometrika*, 61(2):331–354, June 1996.

[31] D. O. Segall. *Computerized Adaptive Testing: Theory and Practice*, chapter Principles fo Multidimensional Adaptive Testing, pages 53–73. Kluwer Academic Publishers - New York, Boston, Dordrecht, London, Moscow, 2000.

[32] L. J. Simms and L. A. Clark. Validation of a computerized adaptive version for nonadaptive and adaptive personality (snap). *Psychological Assessment*, 17(1):28–43, 2005.

[33] B. P. Veldkamp and W. J. van der Linden. Multidimensional adaptive testing with constraints on the test content. *Psychometrika*, 67(4):575–588, 2002.

[34] C. Wang and H.-H. Chang. Item selection in multidimensional computerized adaptive testing-gaining information from different angles. *Psychometrika*, 76(3):363–384, 2011.

[35] C. Wang, H.-H. Chang, and K. A. Boughton. Kullback-leibler information and its applications in multi-dimensional adaptive testing. *Psychometrika*, 76(1):13–19, 2011.

[36] D. J. Weiss. Adaptive testing by computer. *Journal of Consulting and Clinical Psychology*, 53(6):774–789, 1985.

[37] D. J. Weiss and G. G. Kingsbury. Application of computerized adaptive testing to educational problems. *Journal of Education Measurement*, 21:361–375, 1984.

[38] L. A. M. Zaina, J. F. R. Jr., M. A. C. D. A. Cardieri, and G. Bressan. Adaptive learning in the educational e-lors system: an approach based on preference categories. *IJLT*, 6(4):341–361, 2011.

A Proposal for Managing Multiple Trails in Educational Environments

Wagner L. Cambruzzi, Sandro J. Rigo, Jorge L. V. Barbosa
Universidade do Vale do Rio dos Sinos
Av. Unisinos, 950
São Leopoldo - RS - Brasil
wagner@cambruzzi.com.br, {rigo, jbarbosa}@unisinos.br

ABSTRACT

Mobile computing and localization systems recent diffusion enables the use of contexts and trails in several applications, with the incorporation of resources for content adaptation and distribution. A trail represents a set of user contexts, historically organized. This article presents a proposal for managing multiple trails in mobile computing environments. Its differential is the representation of the data of each entity in several trails. This approach allows the multiple aspects of interest for the entity to be modeled and stored. In addition, facilitates its use in different applications, which may need only part of the elements in this set of trails. In this way, this proposal extends the possibility of context composition for entities, providing greater flexibility to their use. This is demonstrated in two case studies of the application of this model.

Categories and Subject Descriptors

D.2.11 [**Software Engineering**]: Software Architectures—*Domain-specific Architectures.*

General Terms

Management, Design, Experimentation.

Keywords

Mobile Computing, Trails, Context Management.

1. INTRODUÇÃO

Este artigo propõe um modelo para gerenciamento de múltiplas trilhas em ambientes de computação móvel, voltados ao contexto educacional. Nesta proposta o conceito de Múltiplas Trilhas constitui-se em uma ampliação da proposta de trilhas encontrada em UbiTrail [7], a qual é considerada como um conjunto de registros que tem como objetivo armazenar informações de eventos realizados pela entidade em um ambiente computacional. Os registros obedecem a uma estrutura estática e todos os eventos de uma entidade são armazenados em uma mesma trilha.

O modelo proposto possibilita que a interação de cada entidade possa ser armazenada em diferentes trilhas, cada uma delas com um objetivo específico. Desta forma amplia-se a possibilidade de composição do contexto das entidades, pois as características de cada trilha são representadas em ontologia própria, o que proporciona maior flexibilidade e abrangência para sua utilização. Um dos diferenciais desta abordagem é a maior flexibilidade para as aplicações interessadas no tratamento destes dados.

Comprovando os ganhos com a adoção desta abordagem, são descritos e analisados nesse artigo dois estudos de caso aplicando o modelo desenvolvido, em contextos ligados à Educação, sendo um deles desenvolvido no contexto do Ensino Médio e outro no Ensino Superior. Nestes estudos de caso evidenciam-se as vantagens do modelo proposto, pois além de informações de localização, são integrados elementos diversificados, de modo a possibilitar que o modelo seja utilizado no apoio em orientação educacional, na geração de opções de visualização de dados e em conjunto com Mineração de Dados Educacionais.

2. MODELO DE GERENCIAMENTO DE MÚLTIPLAS TRILHAS

O conceito de múltiplas trilhas implica em que, para uma mesma entidade, sejam registradas diversas trilhas nas quais estão organizadas as ações realizadas pela entidade, de acordo com suas características. O termo entidade representa uma pessoa ou um objeto computacional para o qual se deseja registrar as trilhas. Neste cenário, diferentes aplicações estão envolvidas, tanto no registro das trilhas, quanto no uso das informações históricas registradas, o que confere uma ampla flexibilidade ao modelo.

Como exemplo de múltiplas trilhas, podem ser citados os registros de diversos aspectos da vida de uma pessoa, tais como o seu histórico educacional, profissional, o registro das atividades realizadas em ambientes virtuais de aprendizagem ou em comunidades virtuais de relacionamento. Os contextos que fazem parte de cada trilha podem ser consultados ou utilizados a partir de uma dimensão temporal e são aqui denominados de contextos sistêmicos. Na figura 1 estão exemplificadas trilhas para diversos aspectos relacionados a um estudante, com as seguintes denominações e respectivos significados, resumidamente: "Educação formal" (cursos de formação obrigatória, mais ensino superior e pós-graduação) , "Educação complementar" (cursos de extensão), "Profissional" (atividades profissionais realizadas), "Mídias sociais"

Permission to make digital or hard copies of all or part of this work for personal or classroom use is granted without fee provided that copies are not made or distributed for profit or commercial advantage and that copies bear this notice and the full citation on the first page. To copy otherwise, to republish, to post on servers or to redistribute to lists, requires prior specific permission and/or a fee.
WebMedia'12, October 15–18, 2012, São Paulo/SP, Brazil.
Copyright 2012 ACM 978-1-4503-1706-1/12/10 ...$15.00.

(informações veiculadas em mídias sociais) e "Atividades esportivas" (atividades esportivas realizadas).

Porém, ao consultar o contexto sistêmico da entidade, podem ser consideradas relevantes, para uma aplicação específica, apenas algumas das suas trilhas. Por exemplo, na figura 1, pode ser considerado um contexto sistêmico formado pelas trilhas de "Educação Formal" e "Mídias Sociais", em um determinado momento de tempo. Ou então, outro contexto sistêmico pode ser recuperado com o acesso às trilhas de "Atividades Profissionais" e de "Atividades Esportivas", em momento diverso. Assim podem ser avaliadas as informações de contexto de modo flexível e independente, facilitando atender as necessidades de aplicações diversas.

Em especial, destaca-se esta funcionalidade do modelo proposto como importante para atender diversas aplicações de forma eficiente, tal como é demonstrado nos dois estudos de caso detalhados neste trabalho, onde apenas os dados relevantes para cada situação são considerados. Esta flexibilidade deve ser entendida tanto em aspectos de coleta de dados, como no tratamento dos mesmos. Assim, novos dispositivos podem ser agregados ao contexto de aplicações, bem como novas fontes de dados podem ser consideradas para compor o conjunto de dados manipulados quando necessário.

Com base nas possibilidades de ampliação do conjunto de trilhas a cada necessidade ou oportunidade para manutenção do sistema, torna-se importante a integração e interoperabilidade de dados de cada trilha, tendo em vista a sua diversidade e as diversas necessidades de relacionamento. Ontologias vêm sendo utilizadas como forma de organizar conhecimento específico em áreas de conhecimento e também como recurso para promover a interoperabilidade e integração.

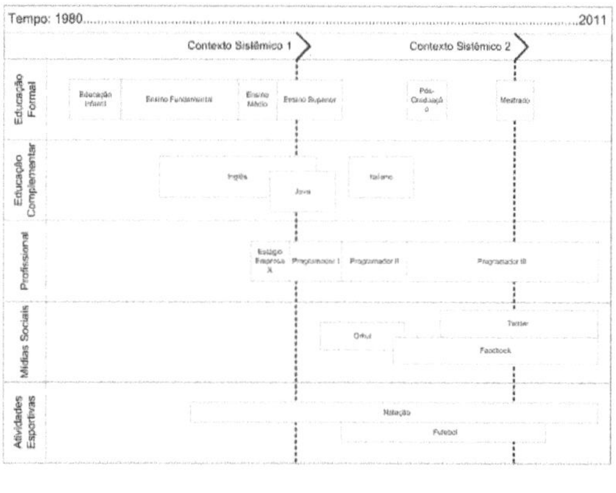

Figura 1. Exemplo de esquema de múltiplas trilhas

A figura 2 ilustra os principais elementos utilizados na ontologia para a integração geral entre dados de trilhas diversas. De acordo com cada componente e com as disponibilidades existentes, é possível a utilização de ontologias já definidas, que descrevem componentes a serem integrados junto do sistema. Por exemplo, especificamente relacionadas com contexto, localização e com perfis, torna-se viável a utilização de ontologias largamente aplicadas na descrição de pessoas, tais como a FOAF (*Friend of a Friend*) [3] ou então ontologias para descrição de elementos de localização, tais como a UbisWorld [8]. Os componentes principais da ontologia proposta são responsáveis por descrever a "trilha", composta por uma "identificação" e por "eventos", conceitos que são especializados de acordo com o contexto tratado. Os elementos da trilha são relacionados de forma independente com "usuários", que podem especializar descrições ou também estar associados com outras representações, como no caso citado, do uso do FOAF (*Friend of a Friend*) [3]. Já os elementos como "componentes"e "origem" identificam elementos da arquitetura responsáveis pela geração e coleta dos dados armazenados e pelo seu processamento. A representação da ontologia é feita com a linguagem OWL (*Ontology Web Language*), visando proporcionar maior expressividade e interoperabilidade.

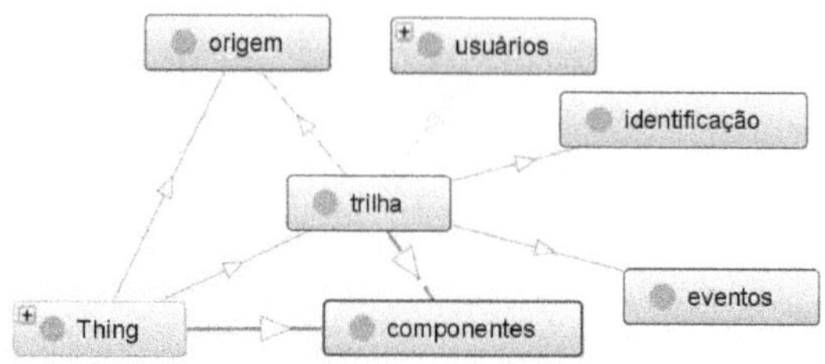

Figura 2. Elementos parciais da ontologia para integração

3. ARQUITETURA PROPOSTA

A arquitetura proposta, representada na Figura 3, está organizada em três camadas: servidor (*MultiTrail Server*), cliente (*MultiTrail Client*) e dispositivos de coleta ou fontes de coleta (*Source Collector/Collector Devices*). O usuário interage com os dispositivos de coleta e com componentes de software que registram suas atividades. De acordo com cada dispositivo, existirá um componente na camada *MultiTrail Client* responsável pela coleta da interação correspondente. Este componente interage através de solicitações de registro com a camada *MultiTrail Server*. O *MultiTrail Server* é responsável por organizar e prover serviços diversos, com base nas trilhas do usuário, atendendo às necessidades de aplicações diversas.

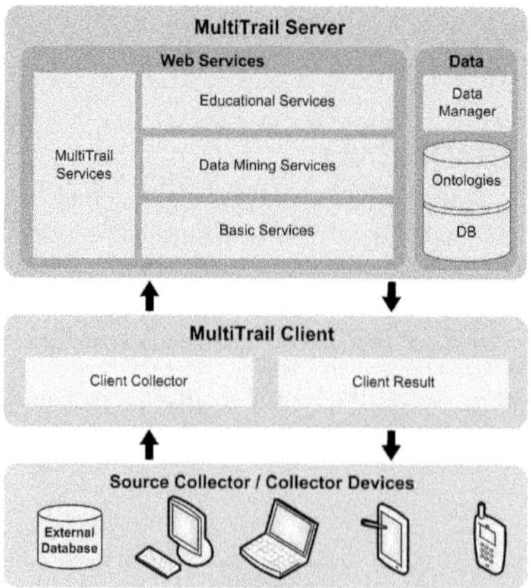

Figura 3. Arquitetura do Modelo MultiTrail

A primeira camada possui como objetivo a implementação do suporte necessário para as atividades de interação e coleta de dados, com o pressuposto de uma ampla flexibilidade para com o tipo de dispositivo e as fontes de dados utilizadas. Assim, está prevista toda a interação do usuário com o sistema através dos dispositivos de coleta ou fontes de dados, sendo estes considerados inicialmente com base nas possibilidades atuais, mas não limitados a esta situação. O modelo proposto prevê flexibilidade para a inclusão e tratamento de novos dispositivos ou novas fontes de dados.

Pode-se considerar que a interação envolvendo os usuários e as aplicações baseadas neste modelo acontece em duas situações distintas, sendo que para ambas ocorre a utilização dos componentes da camada *MultiTrail Client*. A primeira delas no caso em que o dispositivo é utilizado para registrar ocorrência em uma trilha, tratado através da implementação do componente *Client Collector* correspondente. A segunda situação ocorre quando o sistema necessita enviar uma mensagem de alerta para o usuário, sendo que este processo é tratado através da implementação do componente específico do *Client Result*.

A camada *MultiTrail Client* está organizada em dois módulos. O módulo *Client Collector* é responsável pela captura de dados e pelo seu registro nas trilhas correspondentes e no formato adequado. Este módulo pode estar implementado em aplicações localizadas nos dispositivos ou por componentes de software responsáveis pela interação com bases de dados externas. Já o módulo *Client Result* é o responsável pela interação com o usuário e pela adaptação do conteúdo para o dispositivo do usuário. A camada denominada *MultiTrail Server* está organizada em quatro módulos e um repositório de dados. O seu principal objetivo é proporcionar o suporte necessário para o armazenamento dos dados obtidos das diversas fontes e dos múltiplos dispositivos, em conjunto com a integração necessária para o atendimento aos diversos serviços propostos como suporte para as aplicações desenvolvidas.

O módulo *MultiTrail Services* é responsável pelo gerenciamento e manipulação das diferentes trilhas da entidade. Sempre que uma aplicação cliente desejar manipular dados de uma trilha, esse serviço será o responsável pela identificação e manutenção da mesma. O mesmo ocorre com as consulta em trilhas, sejam elas consultas específicas, ou consultas utilizando o contexto sistêmico. O módulo *Basic Services* é responsável pelos serviços de autenticação e gerenciamento da aplicação servidora, responsável pelo gerenciamento dos serviços e pelo atendimento de necessidades de aplicações específicas diversas. O módulo *MultiTrail Data* é responsável por prover uma infraestrutura de manipulação e acesso aos dados para os outros módulos que compõe o *MultiTrail Server*. O módulo *Educational Services* é responsável pelo gerenciamento do suporte de ações educacionais, disponibilizando contextos de visualização e de geração de alertas e análises, com base no uso de classificadores disponíveis no módulo *Data Mining Services*.

4. PROTÓTIPO E ESTUDOS DE CASO

Para avaliação do modelo proposto, foi utilizado o protótipo implementado em um estudo de caso foi desenvolvido em uma escola de Ensino Médio e em outro desenvolvido junto a cursos de graduação de uma universidade.

A implementação do modelo propsto segue a arquitetura descrita na seção anterior e foi realizada com a linguagem ASP.NET para os componentes dedicados à coleta e manipulação dos dados, tendo sido implementados de forma independente dos demais componentes. Para a persistência dos dados foi utilizado o banco de dados SQL Server 2008 R2. Além destes componentes foram implementados módulos de visualização de dados e um componente para mineração de dados utilizado nos estudos de caso para predição de evasão e baixo rendimento escolar, também com a linguagem ASP.NET e com o uso de componentes da ferramenta WEKA [9]. A ontologia utilizada foi descrita em linguagem OWL (*Ontology Web Language*) e editada inicialmente com a ferramenta Protege [6].

O primeiro estudo de caso realizado teve como objetivo analisar dados obtidos no Ensino Médio e a sua utilização no atendimento de diferentes necessidades observadas nesta área. O estudo de caso utilizou o conceito de múltiplas trilhas para organizar informações históricas em três trilhas: "Histórico Escolar", "Atividades Complementares" e "Ocorrências Pedagógicas". O experimento foi realizado em uma instituição de ensino fundamental e médio localizada na cidade de Porto Alegre. As trilhas de 5.921 alunos foram registradas. A figura 4 apresenta trechos parciais da situação histórica de um aluno, onde é possível verificar a idade em que o mesmo cursou cada ano do ensino fundamental e médio, o desempenho do mesmo em cada disciplina, atividades complementares que foram realizadas e ocorrências pedagógicas.

Através desta interface Web é possível a análise de fatores importantes, tais como a influência de atividades complementares no desempenho escolar e no comportamento do aluno. A avaliação empírica e preliminar desta aplicação deu-se através de entrevistas com profissionais da educação, que indicaram a sua expectativa de possibilidades de apoio desta ferramenta para atividades de aconselhamento pedagógico e acompanhamento.

Figura 4. Visualização de trilhas

Como segunda aplicação, ainda neste estudo de caso inicial, foram utilizados dados obtidos com a coleta de trilhas para identificação de perfis possivelmente relacionados à reprovação no 3° ano do ensino médio. O objetivo é destacar a possibilidade de utilização flexível dos dados das múltiplas trilhas em aplicações diversas. Para tal foram realizados experimentos com árvores de decisão, utilizando o algoritmo J48 implementado na ferramenta WEKA [9]. O resultado indicou a idade dos estudantes como característica relevante para reprovação. Em análise estatística complementar, também foi possível validar, para os dados contidos neste estudo de caso, a informação de que estudantes que ingressam no 3° ano com idade entre 16 e 17 anos tem 4% de chance de reprovação, com 18 anos a probabilidade aumenta para 13% e com 19 anos ou mais a probabilidade aumenta para 33%. Essa informação é importante para acompanhamento pedagógico e pode ser usada para desencadear um acompanhamento aos alunos com tais características para minimizar a probabilidade de reprovação.

Já no segundo estudo de caso realizado o objetivo foi utilizar dados obtidos no Ensino Superior, com a seguinte aplicação: Analisar dados de uma turma de alunos na modalidade de Educação a Distância, em um curso de Administração de Empresas, para predição de situações de evasão ou baixo desempenho. O estudo de caso aqui descrito consiste do acompanhamento de dados gerados por 377 alunos de graduação durante uma ocorrência da disciplina, sendo que foram acompanhados e tratados os aspectos de interação e de realização de tarefas de avaliação, bem como troca de mensagens e realização de intervenções em um ambiente virtual de aprendizagem.

Em um dos aspectos evidenciados como importantes para o acompanhamento de possíveis situações demandando atenção, está a interação entre os alunos nas diversas ferramentas de ambientes virtuais de aprendizagem. Para este acompanhamento, foi desenvolvido um componente de visualização que disponibiliza, em forma de um grafo, aspectos relacionados com a interação e desempenho, a partir do qual é possível analisar a relação entre o desempenho dos estudantes e a participação nos fóruns da disciplina. No exemplo da figura 5, o resultado obtido com a análise parcial de uma turma de alunos representa a interação destes alunos de uma disciplina de Matemática para Administração, em um curso de graduação de Administração, realizado na modalidade de Educação a Distância. Os nodos representados em amarelo são os tutores da disciplina, os nodos em verde são os alunos aprovados e os nodos em marrom são os alunos reprovados. As arestas do grafo representam a interação entre os diversos participantes na ferramenta fórum de discussão.

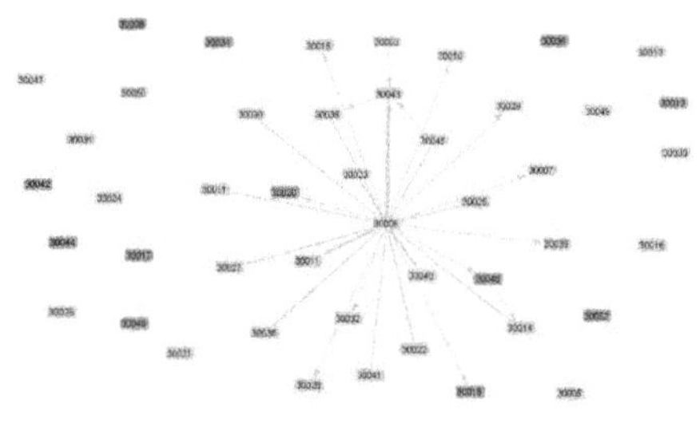

Figura 5. Visualização de interações em fórum

Através de ferramentas de visualização como este grafo é possível prover o suporte para análises relacionando a interação dos alunos no ambiente virtual de aprendizagem e o seu resultado final nas disciplinas. Nos experimentos realizados, em diversos contextos resta evidenciado que a participação ativa nos fóruns desta disciplina está relacionada positivamente com o desempenho, pois alguns dados indicam que enquanto 15% dos alunos que interagiram com maior intensidade reprovaram, o índice de reprovação aumentou para 45% entre os alunos que não interagiram significativamente.

Além das ferramentas para visualização, neste estudo de caso também foram aplicadas técnicas de mineração de dados para a predição do desempenho dos estudantes. Para a análise das informações de interação dos estudantes com finalidade de predição do desempenho foram utilizadas redes neurais artificiais e a topologia adotada foi a Multilayer Perceptron [5].

Com este estudo identificou-se com uma taxa alta de acerto os indivíduos relacionados com o perfil de baixo rendimento, sendo destacados como elementos de análise os dados de interação, atividades e resultados obtidos. Com base nos dados utilizados, foram obtidas taxas de acerto da ordem de 90% para a predição de baixo rendimento, o que foi considerado satisfatório levando-se em conta o volume de dados disponíveis e a quantidade de séries históricas considerada (que foi de apenas uma edição da disciplina).

5. CONCLUSÕES

Este artigo apresentou a proposta de gerenciamento de múltiplas trilhas para uma mesma entidade em ambientes de computação móvel. A partir do estudo de trabalhos relacionados [4, 1, 2], destacou-se que o diferencial desse trabalho é a consideração das entidades interagindo com um conjunto de trilhas ao longo de sua trajetória e com a possibilidade de especificação de diferentes níveis para o tratamento dos dados destas trilhas. Nos trabalhos estudados não foram encontradas abordagens com estas características aqui descritas.

6. AGRADECIMENTOS

Agradecimentos ao CNPQ, a partir do qual foi possível a obtenção de apoio; à Universidade UNISINOS, por ter possibilitado o estudo de caso; e à Unidade de Novos Negócios da GVDASA Informática LTDA por propiciar o desenvolvimento do projeto.

7. REFERÊNCIAS

[1] S. B. H. S. Alf Inge Wang, Carl-Fredrik Sørensen and S. Gimre. The Nidaros Framework for Development of Location-aware Applications. pages 171–186, 2005.

[2] G. Ananthanarayanan, M. Haridasan, I. Mohomed, D. Terry, and C. A. Thekkath. Startrack: a framework for enabling track-based applications. (14):207–220, 2009.

[3] P. FOAF. The Friend of a Friend (FOAF) Project. Disponível em `http://www.foaf-project.org/`, 2012.

[4] E. Gams and S. Reich. The Trailtrecer Framework: Applying Open Hypermedia Concepts to Trails. *Journal of Universal Computer Science*, 8(10):913–923, Outubro 2002.

[5] M. Paliwal and U. A. Kumar. Neural networks and statistical techniques: A review of applications. *Expert Systems with Applications*, 36(1):2–17, 2009.

[6] Protégé. The Protégé Ontology Editor and Knowledge Acquisition System. Disponível em `http://protege.stanford.edu/`, 2012.

[7] J. Silva, J. a. Rosa, J. Barbosa, D. N. F. Barbosa, and L. A. M. Palazzo. Distribuição de Conteúdo em Ambientes Cientes de Trilhas. *WebMedia'09*, 2009.

[8] UbisWorld. UbisWorld - Research on User Modeling and Ubiquitous Computing. Disponível em `http://www.ubisworld.org/`, 2012.

[9] WEKA. Weka 3 - Data Mining with Open Source Machine Learning Software in Java. Disponível em `http://www.cs.waikato.ac.nz/ml/weka/`, 2012.

Engineering Device-spanning, Multimodal Web Applications using a Model-based Design Approach

Sebastian Feuerstack
Universidade Federal de São Carlos
Rodovia Washington Luís, km 235
São Carlos - São Paulo – Brasil
sfeu@dc.ufscar.br

Ednaldo Brigante Pizzolato
Universidade Federal de São Carlos
Rodovia Washington Luís, km 235
São Carlos - São Paulo – Brasil
ednaldo@dc.ufscar.br

ABSTRACT

Nowadays the web is an ubiquitously available source of information that can be accessed through a broad range of devices, such as smart phones, tablets and notebooks. Although web applications can be used through several devices, they are controlled and designed for a one-to-one connection type of interaction, which prevents device-spanning multi-modal interactions.

We propose a model-based run-time framework to design and execute multi-modal interfaces for the web. Different to a model-based design that implements reification, a process to derive concrete models from abstract ones by transformation, we design interactors that keep all design models alive at run-time. Interactors are based on finite state machines that can be inspected and manipulated at run-time and are synchronized over different devices and modalities using mappings. We show the expressiveness of state charts for modeling interactions, interaction resources, and interaction paradigms.

We proof our approach by checking its conformance against common requirements for multimodal frameworks, classify it based on characteristics identified by others, and present initial results of a performance analysis.

Categories and Subject Descriptors

H.5.2 **[Information Interfaces and Presentation]**: User Interfaces - *Input devices and strategies, Interaction styles, Prototyping*; D.2.2 **[Software Engineering]**: Design Tools and Techniques – *User Interfaces.*

General Terms

Design, Human Factors, Languages.

Keywords

Model-based User Interfaces, Multimodal Interfaces, Web Application Development, HCI.

Permission to make digital or hard copies of all or part of this work for personal or classroom use is granted without fee provided that copies are not made or distributed for profit or commercial advantage and that copies bear this notice and the full citation on the first page. To copy otherwise, or republish, to post on servers or to redistribute to lists, requires prior specific permission and/or a fee.
WebMedia'12, October 15–18, 2012, São Paulo/SP, Brazil.
Copyright 2012 ACM 978-1-4503-1706-1/12/10...$15.00.

1. INTRODUCTION

With the ubiquitously available word wide web information can be accessed from any place and any device connected to the internet. Just a web browser is required to search the web or even run web applications in the cloud.

Different to graphical interfaces of web applications that are often adapted to consider different screen sizes, the support for different control modes is often limited to the classic keyboard and mouse based input control. Input controls that go beyond basic touch gestures are not considered or are implemented for specific domains like an in-car control that uses wheels, a touchscreen or voice commands. Multimodal applications that combine several modes into one single application are even more complex to implement. Model-based software development has been successfully performed to support the semi-automated generation of interfaces for different platforms (like HTML [9], XHTML+Voice [9] or even 3D interfaces [9]). But to our knowledge there are still no frameworks available that support the model-based design and execution of multimodal interfaces that can enable a flexible combination of modes and media based on the preferences of the user.

We implement web applications that enable the user to switch devices and modalities or even combine them on demand. The basic idea is to offer a model-based design of custom interactors that are self-executable and that can be distributed and synchronized through several devices and modalities. Different to model-based user interface design (MBUID) that generates isolated interfaces for different platforms by a structured abstract-to-concrete modeling of interaction, we design interactors that are, once they have been designed, assembled by user interface builders to form a multi-modal interface. Therefore, we adapt classical user interface building instead of requiring the developer to learn new languages and processes to create interfaces.

The paper is structured as follows: The next section discusses related work. Thereafter, in section 3 we present our modeling approach that re-uses common MBUID models, such as task, abstract and concrete user interface models for the interactor design. Section 4 explains how the interactors get instantiated at run-time and are executed as part of a web server. Section 5 presents an evaluation of the platform based on practitioners' requirements (5.1), common characteristics for multimodal frameworks (5.2) that have been identified by others and states initial results of a performance evaluation (5.2).

2. RELATED WORK

MBUID has been applied for a long time to reduce the development costs of user interfaces to enable them running on different platforms. Languages, such as USIXML [14] and tools such as [12] have been proposed to form a structured development process. These processes typical start from a very abstract description of the user interface tasks to a more concrete one considering the characteristics of certain modalities (a concrete user interface model) and end up with a final user interface to be executed on a specific platform [3]. This process through several abstractions requires anticipation skills to understand how changes on an abstract level will be reflected in the final user interfaces [14]. Most of the approaches that we are aware of are focusing on design-time support.

Different to these approaches our interactor-based interfaces can be flexibly extended to new modes and media just by adding new interactors and mappings to a running system. Our approach is inspired by the findings of the iCARE platform [13] that supports building multimodal interaction out of components that are connected based on the CARE properties. These properties describe the relations between different modes, such as their complementary, redundant or equivalent combination.

Some frameworks have been already proposed to ease the creation of multimodal interaction controls like the Open Interface Framework [10] that enables a developer to assemble multimodal controls out of components. It focuses on bridging different interaction technologies by enabling the interconnection of device drivers and signal processing algorithms to form new kinds of multimodal interaction setups. But the specification of how an application is controlled with an assembled interaction setup is still done at the source code level.

We are using the same model abstractions as initially summed up by the CAMELEON framework [3], but applying a development process that conforms to classical user interface construction: Using an user interface builder that offers a palette of widgets (that we call interactors) that can be directly assembled to form a multimodal interface. This is an approach that has been followed by Gummy [11] as well, but was focused to create different graphical interface for different sized screens and has to our knowledge no support for extending the existing widget set. User interface builders ease the development of interfaces by offering pre-defined widgets but lack the possibility to add new ones or require the developer to enhance the tool itself on the source code level. Our approach tackles this issue. Therefore, we propose to construct interactors based on State Chart XML (SCXML). SCXML[1] is a general-purpose event-based state machine language that is based on Call Control eXtensible Markup Language and Harel State Tables [7]. It is an easily understandable language composed of only few basic concepts (such as states, actions, transitions and events).

Direct model execution has the advantage that even at run-time the models can be the targets of manipulation to consider context changes that could not be predicted at design-time. The unpredictable context-of-use has been named the effective context-of-use [1] as opposed to the predictive context-of-use that can be considered at design-time. We call MBUID approaches that enable direct model execution Model-driven Run-time-Environments (MRE). The Context Mobile Widget (COMET) architecture style [4] is an early MRE approach that offers self-descriptive interactors that are able to handle a set of different contexts-of-use. At run-time the COMET interactors benefit from

[1] [1] http://www.w3.org/tr/2011/wd-scxml-20110426/, last checked august 25, 2011.

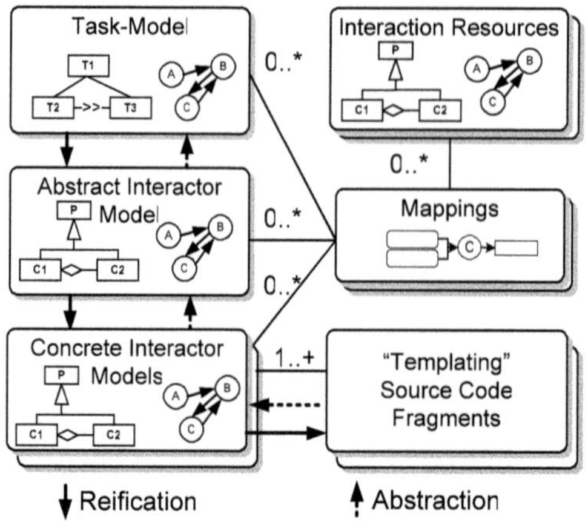

Figure 1. The run-time models of a multimodal application.

querying a semantic network to figure out a transformation path for an adaptation goal. The Multi Access Service Platform (MASP) [2] advances model execution one step further and provides all the logic that defines the behavior of an interface inside the models. Therefore, several meta-models (and a meta-meta-model) are provided that describe the construction of MBUID. Like COMETS, MASP has limited support for considering multimodal interfaces by supporting just equivalent multimodal relations.

3. MINT RUN-TIME MODELS

Figure 1 illustrates the six different types of models that we use to specify a multimodal interface. A task model identifies the tasks that are relevant for the application. An abstract model captures the basic behavior of the interface independent of the mode or media being used. Concrete user interface models complement the abstract model by considering platform specific behavior and data. Interaction resource models describe the characteristics and features of physical (e.g. a mouse, or a smart phone) or virtual devices (e.g. gesture recognition). A final interface model stores interface widget templates (source code fragments) for a specific platform. Finally, a mapping model specifies the way model elements are connected to each other. Mappings link at least interactors of two different models, whereas a source code fragment is directly connected to a corresponding concrete model interactor. If a mapping connects an interaction resource model interactor, we call the mapping "multimodal". Otherwise we refer to the mapping as a "synchronization mapping", as it is used to synchronized interactors between different levels of abstraction.

We call the basic model element an interactor and define it based on the YORK interactor [5] as

"an *executable* component in the description of an interactive system that encapsulates a state, the events that manipulate the state and the means by which the state is made perceivable to the user of the system."

Different to the original definition of the YORK interactor we explicitly require an interactor to be executable. This has the advantage that there is no gap between what is designed and executed and has the result that we instantiate interactors on all model abstraction levels at run-time. Thus, one abstract interactor that represents a choice between several options is instantiated together with its related concrete interactors, for instance a

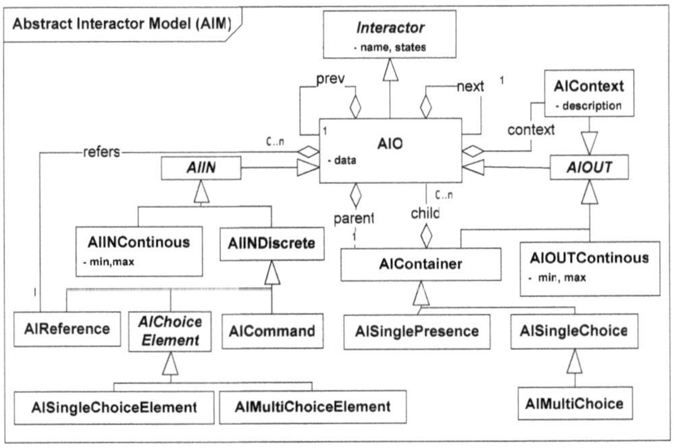

Figure 2. The interactor relations on the abstract level.

graphical pull-down menu or a speech prompt with several corresponding answers to choose from.

We specify interactors by state charts. On the one hand this reduces the entry barrier for developers since no new language has to be learned. On the other hand state charts can be directly transformed to state machines that can then be executed.

In the following subsections we describe the most interesting models in greater detail. A task model and templating mechanisms have been discussed earlier [12][1] and are out of the scope for this work.

3.1 Abstract Interactor Model (AIM)

The abstract interactor model describes the general behavior of all user interface elements that can be used in an interface independently from the control mode or the media being used for presenting the element to the user. Figure 2 depicts the entire interactor class hierarchy of the abstract interactor model. The basic abstract interactor object (AIO) that all other abstract interactors are derived from includes the basic functionality of the core interactor class: a unique name, an observable state, the functionality to instantiate itself as a state machine and to process events. Further on, an AIO interactor implements a basic interface navigation enabling the user to navigate between previous/next and parent/child (through the AIContainer) interactors. An AIO interactor usually is presented in an interface within a certain context (AIContext) that clarifies to the user the relevance of the interactor (e.g. by a textual description, or an interactive help). Additionally, an interactor has one or several related navigation shortcuts (AIReference) like a hotkey or a label that can be used to directly navigate to the interactor.

The two most important classifications of the AIM are the distinction between input and output as well as continuous and discrete types of interaction. The former ones are organizational structures if they are related to output, for instance: lists (AISingleChoice), containments (AIContainer) and commands, or choices like individual list elements if they are input-related. Different to a discrete interactor that defines an identifiable and referable setting, a continuous interactor can only be controlled and observed relatively to its previous settings. Examples are a dimmer to control the light level or a progress bar of a graphical interface.

Figure 3 illustrates the behavior of the AICommand interactor by a state chart. This interactor is used to enable a user initiating single actions. It's general lifecycle has been derived from the abstract AIO interactor that specifies an interactor to be "initialized" upon startup, "organized" if the navigational relationships to its neighbors have been computed, "presenting" while it is part of an active user interface, and finally "suspended" after it disappeared from the active user interface presentation. During the time an interactor is in the "presenting" state the navigation is possible by moving the user focus from one interactor to the next or previous one. Thus, as soon as an interactor receives a "next" event while it is "focused", it figures out its next neighbor and defocuses itself after sending a "focus" event to the next interactor.

What makes the AICommand interactor special is its capability to store an activation state that runs in parallel to the "presenting" super state. If the interactor is in state "presenting" and in the focus of the user it can be "activated". A possible concrete

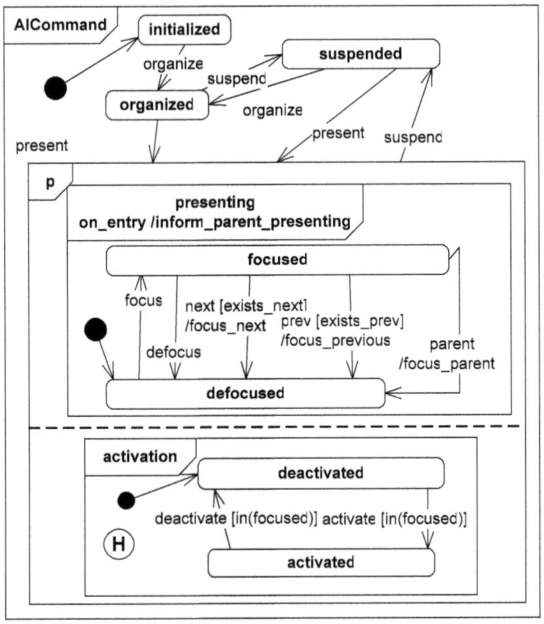

Figure 3. Behavior of the abstract AICommand interactor.

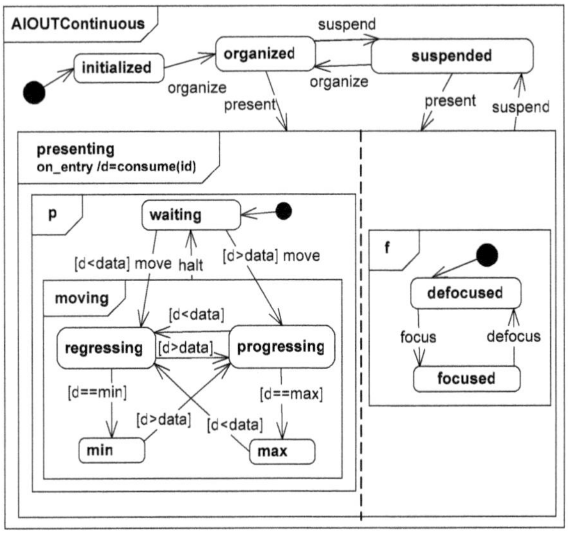

Figure 4. Behavior of the AIOUT Continuous interactor

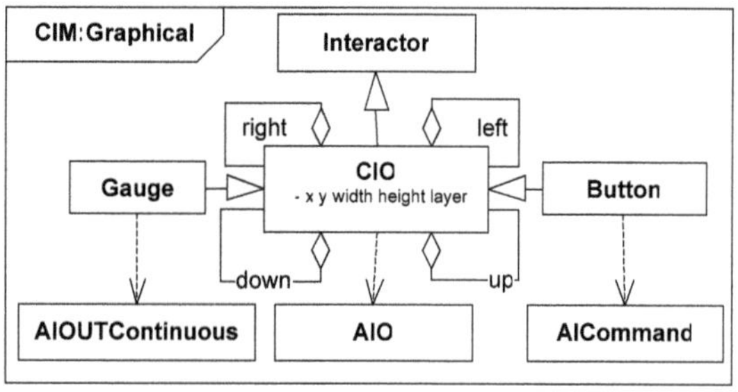

Figure 5. Excerpt from a graphical CIM

interactor that matches this abstract one is a button that we will present later on.

An example of a continuous interactor is shown by figure 4. It implements the same overall lifecycle as the AICommand interactor and represents an output-oriented interactor. Therefore, the interactor listens to data from a streaming source while it is being presented, which we specify by an "on_entry" statement. Depending on the data "d" that it retrieves, the interactor changes its state to be in "regressing" or "progressing". Upon initialization a minimum, maximum as well as a threshold can be defined.

3.2 Concrete Interactor Model (CIM)

The concrete model is in charge of representing an interface on a specific mode and media. Each platform has its own concrete model with two constraints:

1. It can only enhance the data structure and behavior of abstract interactors. Thus, no overlapping definitions between AIM and CIM are allowed.
2. It is required to specify at least one concrete interactor for each AIM interactor. Thus, the AIM is the least common denominator for all mode and media and it is therefore ensured that for an AIM based interface design there is always a complete reification to a CIM one.

Figure 5 illustrates an excerpt of a graphical CIM with the relations to the AIM interactors. Graphical interfaces organize elements in a coordinate system. This is reflected by the Concrete Interactor Object (CIO) that adds the data structure to store positions and sizes. Its lifecycle structure is similar to the AIO, which eases a direct synchronization, but the state semantic is different: It starts by being "initialized", then enters the "positioning" phase during which it is decided e.g. by the task model, what other interactors are presented simultaneously. After the coordinates for each interactor have been calculated based on the layout and screen constraints, it enters "positioned" and

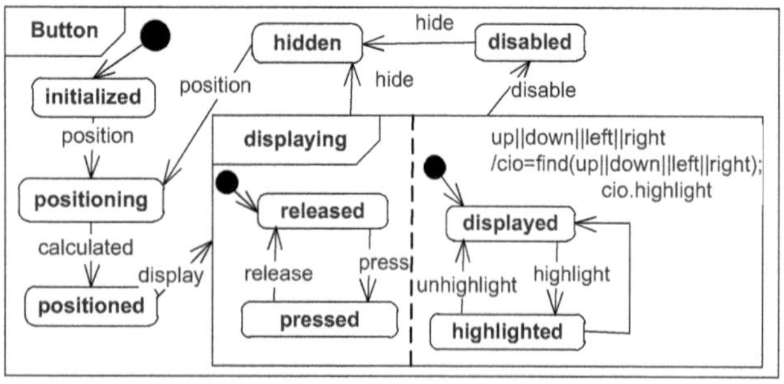

Figure 6. A graphical button interactor

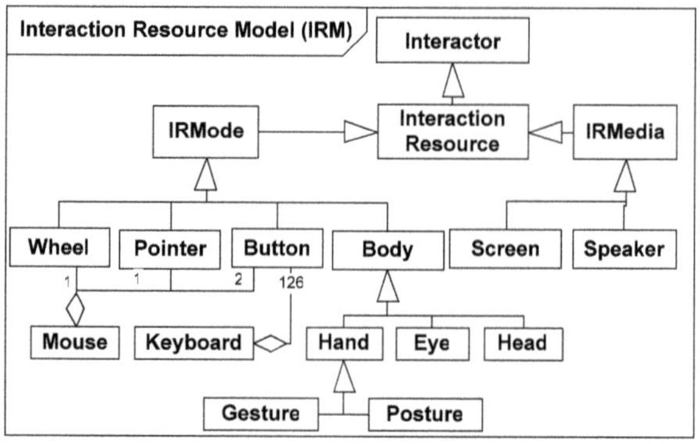

Figure 7. Part of the Interaction Resource Model

"displayed" as soon it is presented to the user. Thereafter it can be "disabled" or "hidden" from the interface.

A coordinate system enables directed navigation options by "up", "down", "left", and "right" events. But usually only little additional behavior needs to be added by the CIM model, since most of the overall behavior is already specified by the AIM. Examples for CIO interactors are a gauge meter that implements a continuous output or a button that represents a command (depicted by figure 6).

3.3 Interaction Resource Model (IRM)

Interactor resource interactors specify characteristics of physical or virtual devices that are used to interact with a system. Physical devices are for instance a mouse, a joystick, or a keyboard. Virtual devices describe software that controls hardware like a gesture or body movement recognition driven by a webcam or a light or a speaker connected to a home automation system.

Figure 7 shows a part of the IRM and depicts the relations between some of the interaction resources (IRs) that we have and will present in this section. Like for the other models, IRs are modeled as interactors. The IRM distinguishes between mode and media IRs. The former represent multimodal control options of the user, the latter specify output-only media.

Figure 8 depicts an aggregated IR representing a mouse. It is composed of a pointer, a button and a wheel. Different to physical devices like the mouse for which the IR specification is fixed and often simple, virtual device IRs are more complex and often are designed with a specific application in mind. Figure 9 depicts an example of a virtual IR that enables basic user interface navigation and selection of elements using the four different hand postures and movements shown on the left of figure 9. Green colored gloves and a webcam are used to capture the different

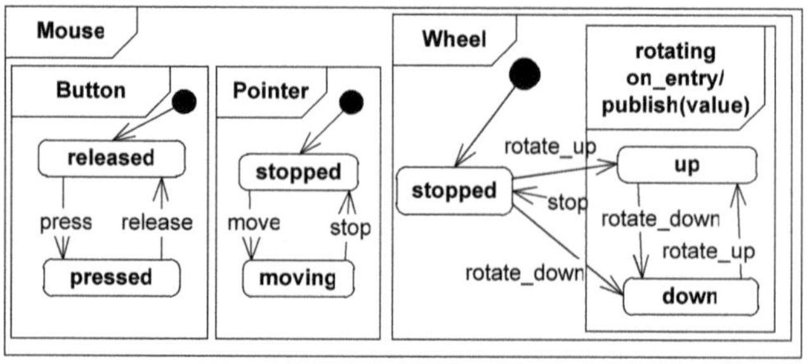

Figure 8. Mouse Interactor

postures and their movements in relation to the cam ("closer" and "farther"). By the state chart-based design specification design decisions can be captured in great detail: First of all, the navigation works with only one hand. Next, there is a fixed default speed of one second per element specified. Therefore, while the previous or next posture is shown, the focus in the interface moves to the previous or next element with each "tick". Then, there is a way to dynamically manipulate the navigation speed (see "movement" super state of figure 8), which replaces the default fixed ticker by considering hand movements (closer to or farther from the cam) to generate "tick" events. Finally, there is an element selection specified, that on the one hand stops the navigation as soon as the select posture is shown and on the other hand requires a second posture to actually confirm the selection (e.g. for security reasons).

Now that the three interface models have been presented they need to be linked together to actually form a dynamic multimodal interaction. Whereas abstract and concrete interactors are synchronized by mappings that are currently defined inside the state charts, the relations between different IRs and the abstract or concrete model are specified by multimodal mappings that we present in the following sub-section.

3.4 Mappings

We use mappings to connect the various models at system run-time and distinguish between two elementary types of mappings: multimodal mappings and synchronization mappings. The former ones a target of a typical application design process, as they are used to describe how an interaction resource (mode) is used to control an interaction. The latter one are used to synchronize the different levels of interactor abstraction and are pre-defined together with most of the interactors.

3.4.1 Multimodal Mappings

Multimodal mappings connect abstract or concrete interactors with interaction resources. They are defined on three different levels of abstraction using a custom, flow-like notation:

- *Application level*: A mapping that connects specific interactor instances; e.g. "If the 'confirm reservation' button is pressed then close the window."

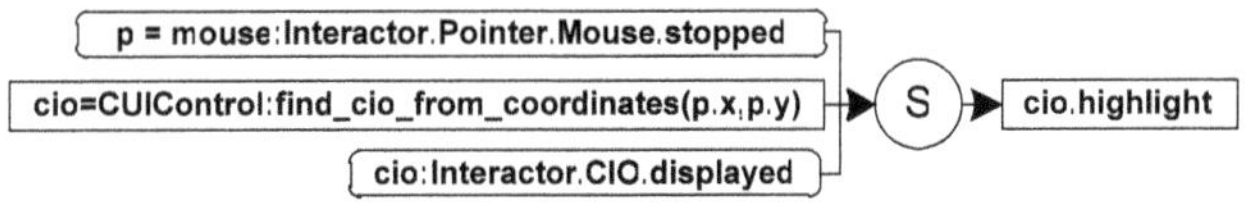

Figure 10. Basic pointer mapping.

- *Interactor level*: A mapping that is pre-defined together with the interactor designs ("the meta level") to be used later on for concrete application development. E.g. "If a button is pressed then play a 'click' sound".
- *Paradigm level*: A mapping that specifies an interaction paradigm, such as e.g. a "drag-and-drop" or a "double-click" that was prepared to work with the designed interactor set.

Figure 10 gives an example for a multimodal mapping that is defined at the interactor level between an IR (a pointer) and interface interactors on the concrete, graphical user interface level: It defines to change the highlighted graphical UI elements based on the current pointing position. It is worth mentioning that some IRs, like the pointer, can only be connected to the CUI model level and not to the abstract one. This is because the pointer is moved in a coordinate system and therefore depends on a graphical interface.

Mappings are specified by a custom flow chart like notation that offers three basic elements: observations, actions and operators. Boxes with rounded edges describe "observations" of state changes. Boxes with sharp edges are used to define actions, which are backend function calls or the triggering of events. The mapping observes the state of the pointer interactor and gets triggered as soon as the pointer enters the state "stopped". There are several operators available that we derived based on the findings of the CARE properties that are used to describe multimodal relations. The sequence operator "S" that is used in figure 10 defines a strict top-down sequence of observations and actions. Thus, the mapping of figure 10 waits for the mouse pointer to stop, then looks up the concrete interactor that is at the current mouse pointer positions and finally checks if this interactor is not already in highlighted and therefore in state "displayed" (compare with the CIO interactor of figure 6).

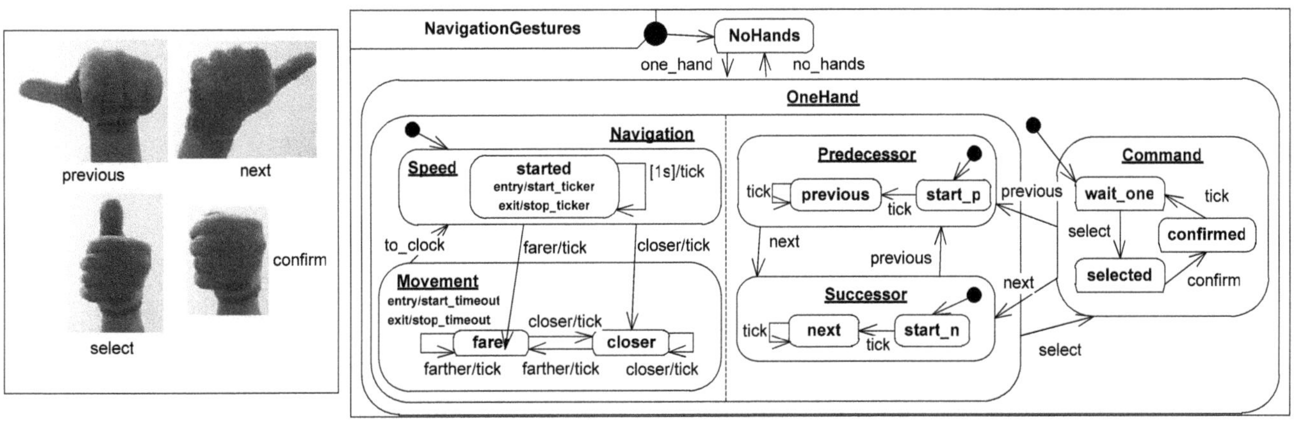

Figure 9. Used postures (left) and a gesture-based user interface navigation IR

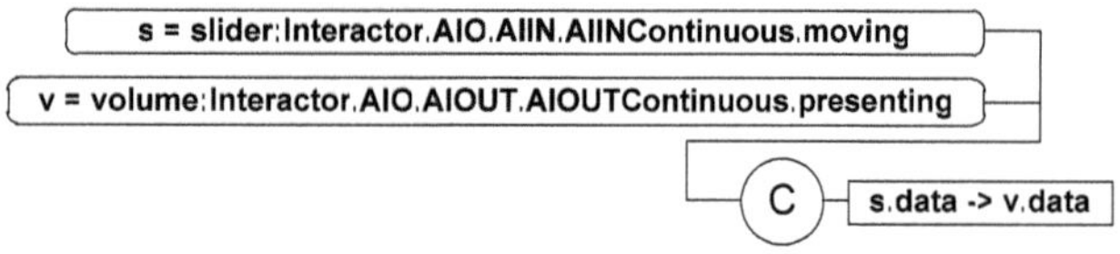

Figure 11. Application level mapping.

Mappings can fail and are then reinitialized automatically. Thus, the pointer mapping of figure 10 can fail for instance if no CIO can be found at the coordinates where the mouse pointer has been "stopped".

Figure 11 gives an example for an application level mapping that has been designed for a specific application in that a slider and a progress bar should be connected so that the slider movements are reflected by the progress bar. Even though the example mapping can be thought to be used for a concrete a slider and a progress bar the mapping itself is defined on the abstract, platform independent level by connecting an AIINContinuous with an AIOUTContinuous interactor (see figure 4). Thus, a "slider" could be as well a dimmer control, and the interactor named "volume" a dimmable light for instance.

The "C" operator that is used in this example defines a "complementary" relation. Therefore, the mapping initiates its action only if both observations are true at the same time: the slider interactor needs to be in state "moving" and the volume interactor in state "presenting". The complementary relation is continuous, which is defined by using lines to connect the operator "C" without arrows indicating a direction. A continuous mapping activates the actions as long as all operations are true and deactivates it otherwise. The mapping of figure 10 forwards all updates of the slider (stored inside the "data" variable") to the "data" variable of the "volume" interactor) as long as the slider is "moving" and the volume is in "presenting" state.

Finally, figure 12 depicts an example for a paradigm level mapping that defines a "drag-and-drop" to be used with an interaction resource that offers a pointer and a button, a mouse for instance. The pointer is implicitly included by using the mapping of figure 10 and a synchronization of "highlighting" to the abstract "focused" state. The Drag-and-Drop mapping utilizes temporary window (Tw) constraints to define the maximum timespan in which all observations are required to be evaluated to true. Further on, a fail statement can be attached to an operator to list the actions to recover from a failed observation. For the Drag-and-Drop such a fail statement is used to recover if the button is released while dragging without a target choice in focus. In this case the fail statement ensures that all dragged elements are re-added to the origin choice list.

3.4.2 Synchronization Mappings

Synchronization mappings are defined to propagate information about state changes between the different abstraction levels of one interactor. Mainly between it's abstract and it's several concrete model representations. Figure 13 depicts such a mapping that is specified in the same notation as a multimodal mapping. It ensures that a "highlighted" interactor of the concrete model (that has been highlighted e.g. by the mouse pointer (see pointer mapping, figure 10) is assumed to be in the user's focus in its abstract model representation.

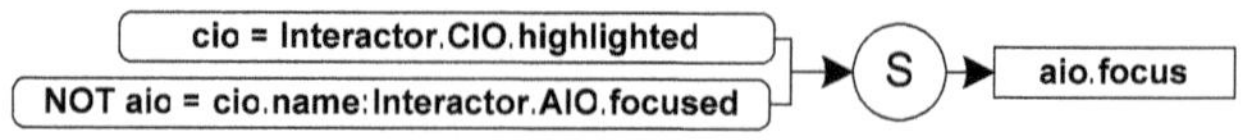

Figure 13. Synchronization Mapping.

In an earlier approach, we used "on_entry" and "on_exit" state actions to synchronize AIM with CIM interactors and did not use separate mappings for model synchronization. This had the advantage that all synchronizations get automatically added if an interactor is used.

The disadvantage was an un-wanted dependency of the AIM to the CIM models, which prevented introducing new concrete model without touching the existing AIM model.

In this section we gave an overview about the models we are using to design and combine multimodal interactors by an abstract, a concrete and a mapping model. Physical or virtual devices are specified by an interaction resource model. The next section introduces the MINT platform, which implements a run-time environment for the models and enables to directly execute them, without a transformation to source code.

4. MINT PLATFORM 2012

Model-driven design of software is performed by designing models and transforming them from platform independent to platform dependent ones. Usually this is a process that is performed during design-time before the application is started the first time and that ends with a final model-to-code transformation.

There are two main reasons, which made us decide to implement a run-time instead of a design-time process: First, different to software backend development, user interface development is a highly interactive and iterative process. Improving the efficiency in including changes in a single iteration would improve the overall development speed since changes can be discussed while giving the targeted audience the opportunity to experience the interface.

Second, modern user interfaces need to consider context changes: different groups of users, devices, environments, cultures, or modalities. Often all these potential context-changes cannot be considered during design-time; therefore problems often first occur during run-time when it is too late to adjust the interface using a traditional model-driven development approach.

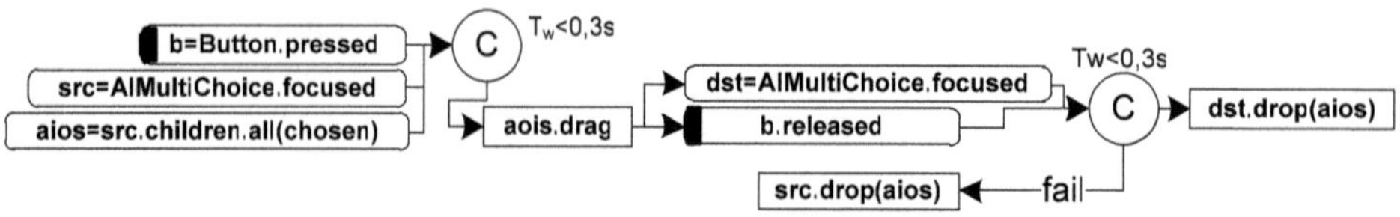

Figure 12. Drag-and-Drop paradigm level mapping.

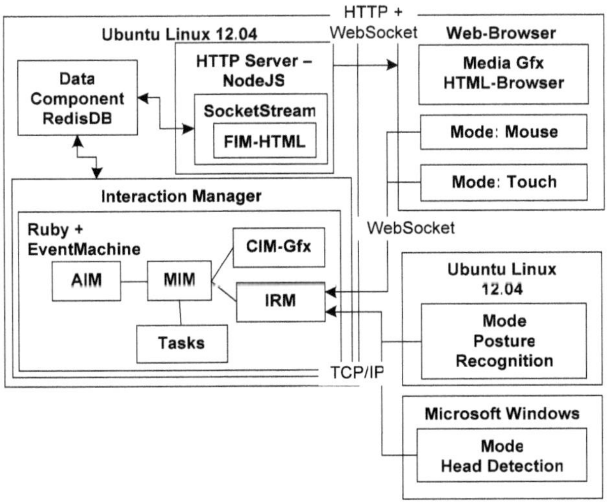

Figure 14. MINT 2012 Basic technical architecture.

Because of that, we implemented a model-based run-time environment (MRE) that is executed as part of a web-server. The main tasks of the MRE are 1) to instantiate the interactors of the Task, AIM, CIM and IRM as state machines, 2) to connect them through the mappings, and 3) to synchronize the modes and media utilized in an interaction by the user. The platform implements the structure of the W3C multimodal framework architecture (W3C-MMI) [17] and its basic component-based architecture is depicted in figure 14. Different to the W3C approach we strictly distinguish between mode and media. Thus, media components such as a web page are pure output components whereas modes implement components that handle user inputs. Therefore, even mouse and keyboard events are synchronized inside the interaction manager on server side instead of by the browser. The left part of the figure shows the server side that consists of a No-SQL data store with publish/subscribe functionality (RedisDB), an asynchronous HTTP Server written in Javascript (NodeJS) and an Interaction Manager that manages all the model instances written in ruby and the Event Machine Framework written in C that enables event-driven I/O based on the reactor pattern with high scalability. Since the main processing and fusion of the different connected modes and media happens on the server-side, all server-side functionality is processed completely asynchronous and event-driven.

Two components of figure 14 have not been discussed so far: The Tasks model in the interaction manager and the final HTML interface model (FIM-HTML) in the HTTP server. The former one is an implementation of a task model interpreter that can process a task tree specified in the ConcurTaskTree notation [12] and is used to define the overall process of an application. It distinguishes between three types of tasks: Interaction In, Interaction Out and Application tasks. Each task type has a behavior specification lifecycle that has been described earlier by the WebTaskModel [1]. The latter one, the final interface model (FIM), represents the graphical CIM model interactors by HTML templates and a widget library (we use jQuery).

The client side consists of the real interaction resources implementing modes and media, like a browser, head movement, posture and gesture recognition, a mouse or a multi-touch surface. User input from the modes is forwarded to the IRM, gets processed there and then is stored and published in the Redis database. The HTTP server subscribes itself to the database to receive relevant interactor updates and forwards them to the connected browsers.

5. Evaluation

Earlier works have suggested several requirements that have to be fulfilled for such a framework to be applicable. We will use these requirements (5.1) and classification criteria (5.2) to discuss the pros and cons of our work and proof the feasibility of a server-sided procession by an inital performance analysis (5.3). Further on, we indent to publish the 2012 version as open source as we did with the previous version [7] as well for others to proof and further evaluate our approach.

5.1 Requirements

As part of the W3C multimodal initiative, [17] has identified several requirements a multimodal toolkit should consider from a practitioner perspective that we discuss and relate in the following to our approach.

5.1.1 Structuration Mechanism

[15] notes that structuration mechanisms are required to "define the overall user interface composition" and mentions that there is currently no fixed overall model and no fixed model to start with as well.

Our approach uses reference integration through mappings that can be defined separately from the other models to link their elements together based on state change observations that can trigger events (actions). A current limitation of our approach is the synchronization mappings that sync between the different abstraction levels (e.g. between the abstract concrete model) of a single interactor. These are currently defined inside the interactor to reduce the amount of mappings that need to be created when designing an interface. This problem is known as the mapping problem [14].

5.1.2 Explicit Control Structures

[15] mentions explicit control structures as a crucial requirement. They are 1) hardly distinguishable from other facets, 2) difficult to track, and 3) difficult to locate if there are several threads of control.

We proposed a three-folded control structure: a macro-level and an inter-interactor as well as an intra-interactor control on the micro-level. The macro-level that specifies the overall control flow, we rely on a task model, where each task consists of a set of active interactor. On the micro-level finite state machines implement the control flow (the behavior) of individual interactors. Between interactors we use mappings to define their control relations.

5.1.3 Extensible Event Definition Mechanisms

[15] requires a multimodal toolkit to use events to connect interaction channels from different modalities and demands a mechanism that "should be extensible so that when a new input or output channel is created it is not necessary to rewrite the event model" [15].

Our approach defines an abstract interactor model (AIM) that specifies the minimal set of interactors that are required to be considered by a new modality (or a certain combination of modes) to allow the user a complete control of all interfaces that have been designed with our approach. Since we rely on SCXML

Table 1. Processing performance of pointer movement (n=250)

Device	Mean Time	Deviation	Variance
Server	9,39 ms	0,72 ms	0,57e-6
iPad Gen. 1 WLAN	14,39 ms	1,9 ms	3,6e-6
NoteBook WLAN	10,21 ms	1,1 ms	1,2e-6

based state charts interactor designs, the basic API is to observe these state changes or trigger them by events. An extension of the event definitions usually has to happen at the concrete model level. Thus, an abstract interactor could be extended to react on new events that are specific to a certain modality.

5.1.4 Data Modeling

[15] requires an explicit data model.

We distinguish between two types of data models. One that is used to capture the data from and present the information to the user and another one that is used by the functional backend of the applications. The former one is designed using class diagrams to express the data and additional functionality that is implemented by each interactor. The latter one depends on the application domain and could be a database, an enterprise server or web services for instance.

5.1.5 Reusable Components

User interfaces are made out of components containing visual parts, interactive behavior and control structures that repeat themselves in different parts of the interface [15].

In our approach interactors encapsulate these functionalities and represent interface elements as re-usable components. Interactors are designed once to specify a concrete way of interaction, like e.g. by a widget on a specific platform, a general way of interacting on the abstract model or by capturing the interaction capabilities of an interaction (as a resource interactor). Once these interactors have been designed they could be part of the palette of a classical user interface builder to enable a designer to assemble interface based on these interactors.

Mappings that glue together the interactors can be re-used as well. As interactor-level mappings they can be automatically established when the interactor is instantiated as part of an application's interface or even can specify overall interaction paradigms that implement a certain way of interacting with the application.

5.2 Programming Framework Characteristics

In a recent publication Dumas et. all. presented a survey of principles, models, and frameworks to create multimodal interfaces [6]. They classified existing frameworks based on their architecture trails, their ease of reusability and four further characteristics: extensibility, pluggability, reusable components, and availability as open source.

From the eight available frameworks to create multimodal interfaces, they state that only three have been made available as open source for others to proof and extend the authors work. During our initial investigations we figured out that the ICARE-Toolkit, differently than mentioned by the study, has not been made available by the authors. From the remaining two frameworks, only one is still being actively developed (Open Interface [10]), whereas the development of the other one (Papier-Mache) has stopped 7 years ago (according to the changes tracked in their open source repository).

Classifying our approach by the suggested criteria, the MINT platform is based on finite-state machine processing and still misses enhanced fusion mechanisms like frame support or symbolical-statistical fusion. It offers a low-level API in ruby, but supports higher-level programming features such as a graphical state-chart design based on the scxmlgui tool and a visual mapping editor to specify the mappings. We have not focus on supporting visual programming so far.

5.3 Processing Performance

Our main concern was the performance loss by processing all user action on the server-side that is required to fuse and distribute information from various connected devices. The most performance critical part of interface is the tracking and processing of user movements. For graphical interfaces this is the mouse pointer. To get an idea about the delay that is caused by the communication overhead, we tracked on the client side how long it takes to capture, send and receive back mouse pointer movements. The results are listed in table 1 for three different devices: (1) Our webserver running on a Intel Core2Duo P8600 notebook using a local browser, a first generation 1 Pad and an Intel Dual Core T2400 Notebook that are connected via WLAN to the server.

The results revealed that server-sided processing is a feasible approach when running the server on a router in a local network. For most applications the cursor tracking does not need to be pixel-precise (different to the pixel precise evaluation test, in our applications even a five pixel movement threshold was not discovered by the users) the delay can be further reduced.

The performance analysis experiment has been performed 500 times based by an automated test, while presenting an interface with 24 parallel running interface interactors, which we consider as medium complexity (like an email client main view for instance). Currently we have only implemented a very small set of interactors, but we intend to evaluate more complex interfaces like the Microsoft Word 2010 main interface view as future work.

6. CONCLUSION

This paper presents the MINT 2012 framework, a run-time platform enabling developers to create multi-modal interactors for the web. Research about model-based user interface design has been previously done to generate interfaces for different platforms. MBUID applies a structured process based on abstract-to-code transformations through several (transient) models. Multimodal interface generation has been considered by MBUI to a very limited extend only. Recent surveys revealed that only a handful of frameworks have been proposed. From those only two were made available for others to use and extend as open source and only one is still being actively developed.

We proposed a new approach based on a model-based design of interactors to represent multimodal interface elements. Interactors are well-known for user interface development and are considered as mature. We decided to use state charts and SCXML, an upcoming W3C standard, to specify the interactors. Different to other approaches all models are kept alive and get synchronized at run-time by mappings. This enables interactor inspection and introducing changes like switching modalities or adding new devices at run-time and closes the often occurring gap between what has been designed and what has been implemented. Interactors run and communicate on the server side and all client-sided devices and modalities are synchronized with the server.

We have focused on a performance evaluation, because we think that it is one basic requirement for user acceptance (how fast a framework is able to process user inputs) and we haven't found performance analyses for other multimodal frameworks that we could proof. The current state of the framework is, that is enables the model-based creation of multimodal interfaces. To proof the efficiency and effectively of the development process we require development tools that we are currently working on.

7. ACKNOWLEDGMENTS

We would like to thank FAPESP for funding the travel grant that enabled Sebastian Feuerstack to attend the WebMedia 2012 conference and present the paper. Further on, Sebastian Feuerstack is grateful to the Deutsche Forschungsgemeinschaft (DFG) for the financial support of his work.

8. REFERENCES

[1] Bomsdorf, B. (2007), The WebTaskModel approach to web process modelling, *in* 'Proceedings of the 6th international conference on Task models and diagrams for user interface design', Springer-Verlag, Berlin, Heidelberg, pp. 240--253.

[2] Blumendorf, M. Lehmann, G. et al.: Executable Models for Human-Computer Interaction; in Interactive Systems. Design, Specification, and Verification: 15th International Workshop, DSV-IS 2008 Kingston, Canada, July 16-18, 2008; S. 238–251; Berlin, Heidelberg; 2008; Springer-Verlag.

[3] Calvary, G., Coutaz J., Thevenin D. ,Limbourg, Q., Bouillon L., and Vanderdonckt J. A unifying reference framework for multi-target user interfaces. Interacting with Computers, 15(3):289–308, 2003.

[4] Demeure, A., Calvary, G., and Coninx, K.: COMET(s), A Software Architecture Style and an Interactors Toolkit for Plastic User Interfaces; S. 225–237; 2008; Design, Specification, and Verification, 15th International Workshop, DSV-IS 2008, Springer Berlin / Heidelberg..

[5] Duke, D. Faconti, G., Harrison, M., and Paternó, F. Unifying views of interactors. In *AVI '94: Proceedings of the Workshop on Advanced Visual Interfaces*, pages 143–152, New York, NY, USA, 1994. ACM, ISBN:0-89791-733-2.

[6] Dumas, B.; Lalanne, D. and Oviatt, S. (2009), 'Multimodal interfaces: A survey of principles, models and frameworks', *Human Machine Interaction*, 3--26.

[7] Feuerstack, S. and Pizzolato, E.B. (2011), Building Multimodal Interfaces out of Executable, Model-based Interactors and Mappings, *in* J.A. Jacko, ed., 'Proceedings of the HCI International 2011; 14th International Conference on Human-Computer Interaction, Part I', Springer, Heidelberg (2011), Hilton Orlando Bonnet Creek, Orlando, Florida, USA., pp. pp. 221—228.

[8] Gonzalez-Calleros, J.; Vanderdonckt, J., and Muoz-Arteaga, J. (2009), A Structured Approach to Support 3D User Interface Development, *in* 'ACHI '09. Second International Conferences on Advances in Computer-Human Interactions, 2009.', pp. 75 -81.

[9] Harel, D. Statecharts: A visual formalism for complex systems. Sci. Comput. Program., 8(3):231–274, 1987.

[10] Lawson,J.-Y.L. , Al-Akkad, A.A., Vanderdonckt, J., and Macq, B. An open source workbench for prototyping multimodal interactions based on off-the-shelf heterogeneous components. In EICS '09: Proceedings of the 1st ACM SIGCHI symposium on Engineering interactive computing systems, pages 245–254, New York, NY, USA, 2009. ACM.

[11] Meskens, J. , Vermeulen, J., Luyten, K., and Coninx, K.. Gummy for multi-platform user interface designs: shape multiply fix use me. In Proceedings of the working conference on Advanced visual interfaces, AVI '08, pages 233–240, New York, NY, USA, 2008. ACM.

[12] Mori, G., Paternò, F., and Santoro, C.. Ctte: Support for developing and analyzing task models for interactive system design. IEEE Trans. Software Eng., 28(8):797–813, 2002.

[13] Nigay, L., and Coutaz, J.: Multifeature Systems: The CARE Properties and Their Impact on Software Design; in Intelligence and Multimodality in Multimedia Interfaces; 1997.

[14] Limbourg Q., and Vanderdonckt, J.(2004), Addressing the mapping problem in user interface design with UsiXML, *in* 'TAMODIA '04: Proceedings of the 3rd annual conference on Task models and diagrams', ACM Press, New York, NY, USA, pp. 155--163.Jean Vanderdonckt and Pierre Berquin. Towards a very large model-based approach for user interface development. In UIDIS, pages 76–85, 1999.

[15] Sire, S., Chatty, C.: The Markup Way to Multimodal Toolkits. In: W3C Multimodal Interaction Workshop (2002)

[16] Stanciulescu,A. (2008), 'A Methodology for Developing Multimodal User Interfaces of Information Systems', PhD thesis, Université Catholique de Louvain.

[17] W3C. Multimodal architecture and interfaces. http://www.w3.org/tr/2011/wd-mmi-arch-20110125/, last checked may 21, 2012, 2012.

Scripts as Source of Information to Contextual Video Advertising

Raoni Ferreira
Univ. de São Paulo
ICMC
São Carlos, SP, Brasil
raonisf@icmc.usp.br

Karla Okada
Intituto Nokia de Tecnologia
Manaus, AM, Brasil
karla.gomes@indt.org.br

Marco Cristo
Univ. Fed. do Amazonas
Instituto de Computação
Manaus, AM, Brasil
marco.cristo@icomp.ufam.edu.br

Klessius Berlt
Univ. Fed. do Amazonas
Instituto de Computação
Manaus, AM, Brasil
klessius@icomp.ufam.edu.br

Edleno S. de Moura
Univ. Fed. do Amazonas
Instituto de Computação
Manaus, AM, Brasil
edleno@icomp.ufam.edu.br

David Fernandes
Univ. Fed. do Amazonas
Instituto de Computação
Manaus, AM, Brasil
david@icomp.ufam.edu.br

ABSTRACT

The wide availability of online video content in the Internet has changed the way users interact with TV. In fact, TV users often watch the news, movies and TV series through the Web. Along with this change, new advertisement of products and services have emerged. The success of contextual advertising in the Web, mainly related to finding advertising keywords on page content, has motivated us to apply them to video. Textual evidence extracted from videos may provide good contextualization source for advertising. In this work, we evaluate the usefulness of movies scripts as a source of information for contextual advertising in video. We adopted a machine learning-based strategy to finding keywords and advertising. We studied not only features proven be useful in earlier studies, as well as novel features proposed and derived from the ad collection. We evaluate the impact of using scripts both in finding keywords and in finding relevant ads. The results indicate that the studies features were more useful for finding keywords than ads. Features derived from the ad collection performed consistently well in finding keywords. We also observed that the best keywords are found in the script section which describes the characters' actions and scenarios than in the one which describes the dialogues.

Categories and Subject Descriptors

H. Information Systems [**H.3 INFORMATION STORAGE AND RETRIEVAL**]: H.3.m Miscellaneous

Keywords

contextual video advertisement, movie scripts, scenes

Permission to make digital or hard copies of all or part of this work for personal or classroom use is granted without fee provided that copies are not made or distributed for profit or commercial advantage and that copies bear this notice and the full citation on the first page. To copy otherwise, to republish, to post on servers or to redistribute to lists, requires prior specific permission and/or a fee.
WebMedia'12, October 15–18, 2012, São Paulo/SP, Brazil.
Copyright 2012 ACM 978-1-4503-1706-1/12/10 ...$15.00.

1. INTRODUCTION

The Internet has changed the way users interact with TV. In fact, it is increasingly common that TV users watch news, movies and even TV series through the Web [11]. Such a transition of users from TV to Internet is accompanied by new investments in product and service advertising which lead to the necessity of new advertising approaches.

In the web, contextual advertising systems (see [1]) operated by companies such as Google and Yahoo! have become the main source of monetization. Its success is mainly due to the advantages they offer to both users and advertisers, such as (a) the display of less intrusive ads, (b) targeted content, that lead users to product and services they are interested in; and (c) performance-based payment, that is, advertisers only pay if their ads are clicked. In such systems, the amount payed by the advertisers is proportional to the clicks provided by the users on ads triggered by a set of keywords. The cost of such keywords is defined in an auction system involving all advertisers. At first, these strategies were focused only on text sources such as search queries and page contents. More recently, they have been applied to other media such as video.

The faster growth of interest in online video [10, 18, 15, 7, 13] makes it important to investigate how specific features of this media should be explored for advertising. The technology used nowadays in contextual video advertising is mainly based on the simple association of the ad text with the video description and surrounding page content [10]. While such general descriptions may be enough for short videos, better scene content analysis can be necessary for long videos, increasingly more common nowadays.

In contextual video advertising, visual elements shown to the user such as the situation and the character actions may be interesting for triggering ads [18]. For instance, consider a movie scene describing a car chase that almost results in an accident. Textual evidence gathered from the general movie description may not provide clues useful enough for finding good ad keywords, such as the ones related to insurance in the given example. In fact, architectures for visual video advertising have already been proposed for TV [3] and, in 2009, some american TV stations started the first mechanisms to display ads on the content of movies and series based on manual labeling of specific scene contents [4]. While this move highlights the importance of targeting specific movie segments, it requires expensive manual labeling, which enforces the necessity of exploring new evidence, available to long video, that support the task of finding ad keywords in video content. One such evidence, which we study in this article, is the video script, largely available in the Web nowadays.

Many previous studies have focused on conbining evidence such as audio, video, images and text description [10, 14, 7, 15]. However, only few authors have reported the use of video scripts [13, 18]. Unlike these studies, (a) we provide a through analysis of the impact of the features derived from the video scripts on the quality of the retrieved ads; (b) we study the scripts sections individually and (c) we study features derived from the ad collection on the task of finding keywords.

In this work, we adopt a machine learning-based strategy to find ad keywords in video scripts. We evaluate the impact of using scripts on finding keywords and relevant ads. Our results indicate that the features were more useful for finding keywords than ads. Features derived from the ad collection performed consistently well on finding keywords. We also observed that better keywords are more common in the metadata section which describes the actions of the characters and the scenarios than in the dialogue section. In fact, the noise introduced by the dialogue section was so high that using the two sections combined was worse than using only the metadata section.

This paper is organized as follows. In Section 2, we provide background information on contextual video advertising. In Section 3, we describe how we modeled the keyword selection for advertising on video scripts. In Section 4, we describe our experiments and datasets, as well as we report our results. In Section 5, we describe the related work. In Section 6, we present our conclusions and future works.

2. BACKGROUND

2.1 Contextual Advertising in Video

Contextual advertising consists in showing an ad or a list of ads related to a content. Existing contextual ad engines, such as Google[1], can deliver text, video and image ads to non-video and video content pages. Theses ads are expected to be relevant to the users, suitable and profitable to the publishers and advertisers. The ads displayed in the list are placed in an order that takes into account, at least: (i) the relatedness and adequacy of ads to the page content and (ii) the amount the advertiser is willing to pay for clicks on their ads [8].

Unlike contextual and sponsored search advertising, many ad formats are available for video advertising, such as static graphic banners, animated banners, and text ads such as those commonly used in sponsored search. These ads appear embedded within the video. They can be placed at several positions, using different sizes and shapes. They also can be interactive, which improves their visibility. For instance, an ad may overlay the video content when the mouse is over it, showing detailed information about the advertised product. Figure 1 illustrates a text ad in an overlay box displayed at the bottom of the video area. In this work, in particular, we use only text ads in videos.

[1]`http://www.google.com`

Figure 1: An overlay ad displayed at the bottom of the video area.

The text ads we used in this article are similar to the ones used in sponsored search. They are composed of three visible structural parts: a title, a description and a hyperlink. The hyperlink points to the page (called *landing page*) where the transaction is started. In the landing page, the user can find more information about the product or service being advertised. Besides these visible parts, a list of keywords is associated with each ad. A keyword is composed of one or more words which are provided by the advertiser to describe the context in which the ad should be placed.

2.2 Video Scripts as Feature Source for Video Advertising

The video script is a written work that is made especially for guiding the production of a movie or a TV serie. Although it is not as widely available as subtitles, it is easily found in web [18]. The script describes actions and dialogues of characters as well as certain technical or dramatic elements. The prose is largely focused on what is audible and what is visible on screen. The format of the text clearly distinguishes the dialogue section from the remaining of the text, which we call here, metadata section.

The dialogue section contains, besides the lines the characters have to speak, information about who are the characters, their voice intonation, and body attitude. In the metadata section, we found descriptions of scenes and character actions. Technical details described in a scene can include camera positions, sound and light effects, time and place in which the scene is performed. Other important elements described in that section are the transitions that define the beginning and the end of a scene.

Note that the metadata section provides a visual perception of the scene and its context, evidence that may be useful for advertising. On the order hand, most of the scripts are composed of dialogues which are normally weakly associated with the scene context, since rarely the characters will verbally describe their surrounding visual context.

Figure 2 shows a fragment of a movie script. The line starts with the label **IN** which stands for "interior" and in-

IN. Monica and Rachel's Kitchen
Scene: Rachel and Ross are eating Chinese.
Ross: Marcel. Bring me the rice, c'mon. Bring me the rice, c'mon. Good boy. Good boy. C'mere, gimme the rice. **[Marcel brings the rice]** Thank you, good boy. Well, I see he's finally mastered the difference between 'bring me the' and 'pee in the'. **[Rachel ignores him]** 'Bring me the' and- Rach?
Rachel: What?
Ross: Hi.
...

Figure 2: Script sample, showing dialogue and action descriptions.

dicates that the scene will be played inside somewhere (in the example, the scene will be played in a kitchen). This label also indicates the beginning of the scene. The second line describes the scene context. Then, the following lines describe the character speeches and comprise which we call the dialogue section. Note that some phrases appear between brackets. They indicate character actions and are considered as part of the meta-data section.

In this paper, we study the text of video scripts to identify useful keywords for contextual advertising. Unlike Web pages or emails where the text content is generally self-contained, the video script textual content is complementary to the audio-visual content, which makes it a very interesting object for study.

3. SYSTEM MODELING

In this section, we model the keyword selection task as a classification problem. We also present the approach we adopted for this task, define keyword relevance, and the set of features we use to represent the keyword candidates.

3.1 Keyword Selection as a Classification Problem

Given a word or a set of words (candidate, for short) extracted from the script, we would like to determine if it is a good keyword for advertising (keyword, for short). That can be viewed as a classification task in which, given a candidate, we want to classify it as a keyword or not. More formally, let $K = \{k_1, k_2, ..., k_n\}$ be a set of candidates. Each candidate k_i is represented by a set of m features $F = \{F_1, F_2, ..., F_n\}$, such that $k_i = \{f_{i1}, f_{i2}, ..., f_{im}\}$ is a vector representing k_i, where each f_{ij} is the value of feature F_j in keyword k_i. Note that the term *feature* describes a characteristic of the candidate that could be useful to identify it as a keyword, such as the fact it appears in the metadata section or it starts with an uppercase letter.

We consider that we have access to some training data of the form $\{(k_1, r_1), (k_2, r2), ..., (k_n, r_n) \subset K \times \{0, 1\}\}$, where each pair $\{k_i, r_i\}$ represents a candidate and its corresponding relevance value, such that if $r_i = 1$, then the candidate k_i is a keyword. Otherwise, it is not a keyword.

The solution to this problem using machine learning approach consists in: (a) determining the set of features used to represent the keyword candidate in K; and (b) applying a classification method to find the best combination of features to predict the relevance value r_i for any given candidate k_i. To accomplish this, we use a logistic regression that, by means of the logistic function (Equation 1), computes the probability of a keyword being relevant for advertising as a function of the values of its describing features.

$$f(z) = \frac{1}{1 + e^{-z}} \tag{1}$$

where, given a candidate k_i, the variable z is defined as $z = \beta_0 + \beta_1 f_{i1} + \beta_2 f_{i2} + ... + \beta_m f_{im}$. The values $\beta_0, \beta_1, ..., \beta_m$ are the regression coefficients which indicate how important are the relevance indicators f_{ij} to estimate the probability of k_i being relevant.

Finally, we perform a regression for each class, setting the output equal to one for training instances that belong to the class and zero for the remaining ones. Then, given a candidate, we calculate the value of the logistic regression expression both for keywords and not keywords and choose the one that is largest. This value is also used to rank the candidates.

Note we chose a logistic regression as our machine learning algorithm because it has been successfully used in very close related works [19, 18]. We also experimented with other algorithms, such as Support Vector Machine[2], but we were not able to reach a better performance when compared to logistic regression, a finding corroborated in a similar work on email context [6].

3.2 Selection of Candidates

To select keyword candidates, we use the same settings of the monolithic combined candidate selector described in [19] since this was found to be the best keyword selector in that work. More specifically, a keyword candidate is any word or phrase (consecutive words up to length 5) that appears in a video script. For example, Portuguese phrases such as "café da manhã" (breakfast), "camera digital" (digital camera) or "dia das mães" (mother's day) are considered as candidates.

Phrases are not selected as candidates if they cross sentence or block boundaries. Further, phrases are taken as individual entities, such that features do not describe statistics about phrase constituent words but the entire phrase. Note that no stemming normalization or stopword filtering was applied. In spite of that, phrases were not selected if they start or finish with stopwords.

3.3 Keyword and Ad Relevance

The training set was built from volunteers judgments of 20 volunteers about the set of the candidates extracted from 100 script scenes. Then, we ask a group of 20 volunteers to watch 15 distinct scenes from five TV series and label as keywords candidates they judged relevant for advertising. Each candidate was evaluated by three different volunteers. Then we assumed as keywords the candidates considered as keywords by, at least, two volunteers. This evaluation approach was adopted so we could have an idea of the relative importance of the candidates by checking the agreement between the judges.

We also intend to evaluate the performance of the selected keywords by verifying how relevant are the ads triggered by them. To accomplish this, we queried the ad collection using each distinct set of previously selected keywords. The top-10 ads retrieved by each query were used to compose the set

[2]In this work, we used a SVMLight library freely available at `http://svmlight.joachims.org`.

of ads for each scene. As done before, we also asked the 20 volunteers to watch the same scenes and select the ads they judged as relevant. Since we got three judgments for each ad, we considered relevant the ad selected by, at least, two volunteers.

3.4 Keyword Representation

This section presents the features used to select advertising keywords on scripts. The system works not only with features proven be useful in earlier studies, as well as novel features proposed and derived from the ad collection.

3.4.1 Earlier Features

- **Information Retrieval Features (IR)**: the TF (term frequency) and DF (document frequency) values of the candidate. The term frequency is the number of times a term appears on the script. The document frequency is the number of scripts in the script collection that contain the candidate. In addition to the original TF and DF, $log(TF + 1)$ and $log(DF + 1)$ are also used as features.
- **Relative location of the candidate (LOC)**: the beginning of the script scene often contains an introduction with important words or phrases. Such part of the text normally include descriptions such as how the characters should act or details of the scene environment (for instance, in a car or in a drugstore). Therefore, the location of the occurrence of the candidate is extracted as a feature. Since the length of a document varies considerably, we use the relative location by considering a normalized document length equal to 1. When the candidate is a phrase, its first word is used as its location. There are three different relative locations used as features: (a) wordRatio: the relative location of the candidate in the sentence; (b) sentRatio: the location of the sentence where the candidate is in divided by the total number of sentences in the document; (c) wordDocRatio: the relative location of the candidate in the document. In addition to these 3 features, we also use their logarithms as features. Specifically, we used $log(1 + wordRatio)$, $log(1 + sentRatio)$, and $log(1 + wordDocRatio)$. Our last location feature was the identification of the script section where the candidate occurred (dialogue or metadata).
- **Sentence and document length (LEN)**: the length (in words) of the sentence (sentLen) where the candidate occurs, and the length of the whole document (docLen) (words in the header are not included) are used as features. Similarly, $log(1 + sentLen)$ and $log(1 + docLen)$ are also included.
- **Length of the candidate phrase (phLEN)**: the length of the candidate phrase (phLen) in words and $log(1 + phLen)$ are included as features.
- **Linguistic Information (LIN)**: although this feature was reported not useful in Web page context by the authors in [19], we included since advertisers often bid on noun keywords associated with their ads. Then, we identify three possibles cases: (1) whether the candidate is a noun, (2) whether the candidate is a proper noun, and (3) whether the candidate is a noun-phrase. We got this information using a Portuguese part-of-speech tagger [5].
- **Query log (QLog)**: The query log of search engine reflects the distribution of the keywords people are most interested in. We use this information to define three features: whether the phrase appears in the query log, the frequency with which it appears and the log value $log(1 + frequency)$.
- **Ad Log (Adword)**: we also considered whether the candidate belongs to the ad collection vocabulary which was extracted from a Brazilian ad collection detailed on the next subsection.
- **Term frequency history (H)**: the frequency values for all occurrences of the candidate in previous scenes (i.e. TF values in earlier scenes). A high **H** value indicates a term commonly used and, thus, probably a good candidate to be a keyword. The term frequency history is expressed as $tf' = tf_{actual} + \pi \dot{t} f_{history}$, where tf_{actual} is the term frequency in the current scene, $tf_{history}$ is the term frequency in earlier scenes and π is the importance of $tf_{history}$. We set $\pi = 0.9$ [9].
- **Situation (Situation)**: this feature represents real world situations in which scenes and candidates are classified. For instance, a scene can be classified as related to "cars" as well as a candidate, such as, for instance, "ferrari". The general intuition behind using situation as a feature is that candidates classified into the same situations as their scenes may have a better chance to be keywords. To classify scenes and candidates we used a pre-defined business taxonomy in which all ads are classified. This taxonomy is detailed later.
  All the scenes were manually classified by the volunteers according to this taxonomy. We use situation to compose three types of features. All theses features were firstly suggested and studied by [18]. The first one is the situation that the scene belongs to. This feature tries to capture the idea that some situations are more suitable for advertising than others. The second feature is the degree of associativity of the candidate in each of the situations considered. This feature captures the idea that the higher the degree of associativity of the candidate, the higher is its chance of being a keyword. The degree of associativity is computed using the pointwise mutual information between the candidate k and the situation s based in co-occurrence information obtained as follows:

$$PMI(k, s) \approx \frac{count(k, s)}{count(k)\dot{c}ount(s)} \quad (2)$$

  where $count(k, s)$ is the total number of keyword candidate k that occur in s, $count(k)$ is the frequency of k in the collection and $count(s)$ is the total number of candidates in the scene mapped to s.
  The last situation-based feature is the difference between candidate's PMI and the average PMI taken over all terms in the targeted scene (except stopwords) for each situation class. The intuition is that the higher the difference, the more the relative chance that the candidate is a keyword among other terms in the scene.

3.4.2 Ad inventory Features (ADCOL)

The ad inventory features are extracted from the ad database. As far as we know, they are used here for the first time in learning methods applied to select keywords to video adver-

Table 1: Script related-statistics extracted from each TV series.

TV serie (IMDB URL)	Genre	#Scenes	#Candidates	#Keywords
Lost (http://www.imdb.com/title/tt0411008)	Sci-fi	25	8.613	423 (4,90%)
The Big Bang Theory (http://www.imdb.com/title/tt0898266)	Comedy	23	10.921	663 (6,00%)
Two and Half Men (http://www.imdb.com/title/tt0369179)	Comedy	15	6.211	329 (5,02%)
Friends (http://www.imdb.com/title/tt0108778)	Comedy	21	6,756	413 (6,11%)
One Tree Hill (http://www.imdb.com/title/tt0368530)	Drama	16	4.776	353 (7,39%)
Total	-	100	37.277	2.181 (5,85%)

tising. As described in Section 2.1, we consider that an ad is composed by a title, a textual description, a hyperlink to the landing page, and a set of keywords. Further, an advertiser can associate several ads with the same product or service. We refer to such group of ads as a *campaign*. Note that only an ad per campaign should be placed in a particular scene in order to ensure a fair use of the scene advertising space and increase the likelihood that the user will find an interesting ad. The proposed features observed and extracted from the ad inventory are:

- **Ad Section TF**: candidate frequency in each of the structural sections of an ad creative. Since an ad has three sections, we use three features to represent them: Ad title TF, Ad description TF, and Ad keyword TF.
- **Ad Section Max-TF**: maximum candidate frequency in each of the structural sections of an ad creative. As for Ad Section TF, we then have: Ad title Max-TF, Ad description Max-TF and Ad keyword Max-TF.
- **Ad Section Avg-TF**: average candidate frequency in the three sections of an ad creative: Ad title Avg-TF, Ad description Max-TF, and Ad keyword Max-TF.
- **Ad Section DF**: number of ads in which candidate occurs in a certain section of an ad creative. The three features are in this case: Ad title DF, Ad description DF, and Ad keyword DF.
- **Campaign Section Max-TF**: maximum candidate frequency in the structural sections of all the ads of a campaign. The three features in this case are: Campaign title Max-TF, Campaign description Max-TF, and Campaign keyword Max-TF.
- **Campaign Section Avg-TF**: average candidate frequency in each of the structural sections of all the ads of a campaign. The three features in this case are: Campaign title Avg-TF, Campaign description Avg-TF, and Campaign keyword Avg-TF.
- **Campaign Section DF**: number of campaigns in which candidate occurs in a certain section of an ad creative. The three features in this case are: Campaign title DF, Campaign description DF and Campaign keyword DF.

These features were chosen given the success of frequency of terms in objects (TF) and of the number of objects where a term occurs (DF) as features in previous work related to information retrieval tasks [8].

4. EXPERIMENTS

In this section we describe the datasets, the experimental methodology we used, the experiments carried out and the results obtained.

4.1 Environment Setup

We train and evaluate our learning methods to select keywords using a test collection built from a set of 100 script scenes from TV series in Portuguese language. These script scenes belong to five TV series and are available on Web. As we have no preference for a specific genre, our collection have scripts from drama, comedy, sci-fi, and adventure series. Table 1 details some statistics extracted from this test collection. Each line refers to a specific TV series. Columns #scene, #candidate and #keywords indicate, respectively, the total number of scenes, the total number of candidates, and the total number of words labeled as keywords in each script. Note that the set of keywords is a subset of candidates.

The ad collection we used in our experiments was sampled from a real case ad collection. In fact, we only use a sample of this collection. This sample is composed of 61,296 ads grouped in 1,059 campaigns provided by 981 advertisers. With these ads, advertisers associated a total of 58,323 keywords. Note that, in spite of these ads having not been designed to be displayed on the video content, they provide a good test collection to our study. In this collection, only one keyword is associated with each ad.

It is important to note this sample is pre-classified according to a situation taxonomy. That taxonomy is composed of 26 general classes (such as music, arts, education etc) derived from category names of businesses/products. These classes suggest general situations. For example, "arts" class, which contains ads related to arts businesses, reminds of art galleries scenes or auctions of arts works scenes. In our taxonomy, the most popular class is "computer" (39% of the ads) and the least one is "arts" (1% of the ads).

The training set was built as follows: first we extracted a set of candidates from each scene. Then, a group of 20 volunteers (each volunteer watched 15 distinct scenes) labeled the candidates they considered as keywords. Thus, for each candidate we had three evaluations from different volunteers. We assumed as keywords the candidates that were considered as keywords by, at least, two volunteers.

The ad relevance assessment was done using the top-10 ads associated with each scene. From this, we obtained a list of judgment pairs (script scene and the ad associated with it). This list was composed of 3,301 distinct pairs, with an average of 33 ads evaluated for each scene.

The features related to query log are statistics obtained from WBR03 query log collection, a database extracted from the Brazilian web which contains queries submitted to TodoBR, a real search engine. The log consists of 12,795,101 queries submitted in 2002, from a total of 2,987,745 distinct queries.

4.2 Methodology

We split the experiments into two phases. The first phase

consisted in evaluating the quality of the keywords labeled by the classifier. In the second phase, we used the labeled keywords to retrieve ads and evaluated their relevance.

In our experiments, we performed ten-fold cross validation, that is, we used a subset of our collection (10%) as test set and the remaining as training set, varying the training and test sets ten times, as described by Witten et al [16]. Thus, the results we reported here were taken as the average of the ten folds. In all comparisons, we applied the Student t-test to determine whether the observed difference in performance among the compared methods was statistically significant. We considered significant p values such that $p <= 0.05$.

In the first phase, we used logistic regression to rank the candidates according to the probability of being keyword. We then considered the top-k ranked items ($k = 1, 3, N$, where N is the maximum number of keywords retrieved by the system) as keywords. To measure performance we used the precision, expressed as the proportion of the correctly classified instances.

In the second phase, we evaluated the quality of the ads obtained using the selected keywords. Note that we used all the sets of keywords returned by each classifier as queries to the ad retriever system. We used the AAK matching function to retrieve the ads [12]. With this evaluation, we intend to determine which set of keywords was the best choice for the task of retrieving relevant ads related to the video content.

4.3 Results

In this section we present the results we obtained by evaluating: (a) the quality of selected keywords and (b) the relevance of the ads retrieved using those keywords. Regarding the first item (a), we are interested in evaluating the performance of set the features used by the keyword classifier. Regarding item (b), we check whether the output of this classifier is able to retrieve relevant ads. In both experiments, we consider two scenarios: (1) the entire script and (2) each section of the script, that is, metadata and dialogue.

4.3.1 *Feature Analysis*

Whereas the ideal evaluation approach would be to study all possible feature combinations, this is prohibitive in practice. Thus, we evaluate each feature by analyzing its impact after removing it or adding it to the set of features.

Table 2 shows the results of removing each one of the features. Each line corresponds to a feature removed from the complete set, with the first one indicating the baseline (none removed). The columns show the gain over the baseline precision obtained for each top-k ranking. Thus, the values in the baseline correspond to precision figures. Statistical significant differences to the baseline are indicated by a † symbol (that is, $p <= 0.05$).

The results indicate that **loc** and **adcol** reached the highest contribution. For instance, if we consider the top-3 ranking, removing **adcol** and **loc** leads to a precision loss of around 14%. We note that features related to statistics of the words within the script (e.g, **ir**, **phlen**, **h**, **len**) do not have much influence on the precision of the classifier. Feature **lin** performed similarly. Feature **qlog**, very useful in the context of Web pages [19], yielded not statistically significant gains in our case. Finally, unlike the observed by [18], removing **situation** improved the classifier performance. This result may be due to the different datasets used in our experiments.

Table 2: Gains/losses obtained by removing each feature used in the baseline

Removed Feature	TOP-1	TOP-3	TOP-N
None	**64.00**	**51.07**	**47.22**
-adcol	−7.81%	−14.65%†	−14.89%†
-loc	−17.19%†	−13.52%†	−15.41%†
-len	−9.38%	−6.20%	−6.46%
-lin	+4.69%	−4.51%	+1.87%
-qlog	0.00%	−3.36%	−2.39%
-h	−1.56%	−1.13%	−1.97%
-ir	−4.69%	−0.56%	+1.59%
-phlen	0.00%	0.00%	+0.53%
-situation	+15.63%†	+15.21%†	+27.26%†

Table 3: Gains/losses obtained by adding each feature to the set used in the baseline.

Added Feature	TOP-1	TOP-3	TOP-N
adcol	**59,00**	**51.83**	**50.59**
+loc	+16,95%†	+22.51%†	+23.71%†
+h	+11,86%	+16.72%†	+11.25%
+lin	+5,08%	+10.93%†	+9.79%†
+len	+8,47%	+8.68%	+8.19%
+ir	+1,69%	+3.54%	−1.25%
+phlen	0.00%	0.00%	−0.19%
+qlog	−6.78%	−3.22%	−4.37%
+situation	−20.34%†	−19.29%†	−28.85%†

Since **adcol** was one of the best features in our previous study, we then used it as our baseline in the next experiments by combining each feature to **adcol**. The results presented in Table 3 show that all the features are useful when combined with **adcol**, except **situation**. The loss in performance with the addition of **situation** enforces the previous finding related to this feature. The linguistic information **lin** contributed significantly, which was expected. During the training, we noted the tendency of the volunteers to consider as keyword noun and noun-phrases candidates. Further, in our ad collection, advertisers often associate noun keywords with their ads.

Among all the combinations we studied, we highlight the **loc** contribution, which indicates that the location of the word in the script is very important. Given that the scripts are comprised of dialogue and metadata sections, we suppose that the location of the word in one of these sections was useful to distinguish the keywords.

4.3.2 *Analysis of the Features in Each Section*

Once the performance of **loc** was satisfactory in the task of selecting keywords, we now study the contribution of each feature when taking into consideration the section it is located. Thus, we also evaluated the impact of removing each one of the features in each section of the script. Table 4 shows the results detailing only the features with statistically significant gains or losses.

Note in Table 4 the large precision figures for the metadata section. For instance, at TOP-N, we observed a gain of about 43% of metadata section over the dialogue section,

Table 4: Gains/losses obtained by removing one feature set to the baseline in each section of scripts.

Removed Feature	Dialogue		Meta-data	
	TOP-1	TOP-N	TOP-1	TOP-N
None	46.00	31,31	72.00	55,66
-adcol	−28.26%	−20.46%	−36.11%	−28.71%
-situation	+17.39%	+35.77%	+11.11%	+23.92%

when considering all the features. This result is due to the high concentration of keywords in the metadata section of the training scripts. More specifically, 11% of the candidates in the metadata section are keywords against only 4% of the dialogue section. This behavior was probably due to the fact that the metadata vocabulary is more concise, restrict and related to the visual content. In contrast, the dialogue vocabulary is generally very noisy and ambiguous.

Thus, keywords are proportionally more common in the metadata than in the dialogue section. We also observed that using both sections combined was not better than using only features extracted from the dialogue section. Such an observation enforces the idea that the dialogue section has much noise. We also observed that removing **adcol** is worse in the metadata section, whereas removing situation was better in the dialogue section.

4.3.3 Impact of the Ads

We now present the results obtained from the ad evaluation carried out by our volunteers. In all results reported, we assume that only one ad per campaign was associated with each scene. Tables 5 and 6 show the top-1 precision (P@1) for each system considering each script section separately. Note that, for the sake of readability, we do not report performance figures using precisions P@3, P@5, and P@10, but they were similar to that obtained using P@1.

In general, the results reported in both tables are very different from those shown in the previous keyword experiments. In the most of the cases we obtained no statistically significant differences to the baseline. Thus, it is hard to claim that any particular feature combination is better than another on the task of placing ads. In general, gains are very low, ranging from 20% to 25%. In spite of that, we observed some coincidences with the keyword evaluation. For instance, we observed, in Table 5, the positive impact of **adcol** in the metadata section. Similarly, Table 6 confirms the poor performance of **situation**. Another important difference is observed on the performance of **ir**. While it was almost irrelevant regarding keyword selection, it is more important when considering the ad evaluation. This change is probably due to the impact of this feature on the matching algorithms.

5. RELATED WORK

In this section we review the research on contextual advertising. In particular, we review studies on tasks such as (a) keyword selection and (b) strategies for matching pages/videos and ads.

The first task, keyword selection, addresses the problem of selecting keywords from textual content to make suggestions for bidders or to trigger ads. In particular, the authors in [2] and in [17] have proposed techniques for suggesting keywords to bidders based on the ones previously selected by the

Table 5: Performance P@1 in relevant ads retrieval by removing one feature set from the baseline.

Removed Feature	Dialogue	Metadata	Dialogue and Metadata
None	0,19	0,23	0,26
-adcol	−15.79%	−30.43%†	−11.54%
-len	−21.05%	−21.74%†	−11.54%
-phlen	−10.53%	0.00%	0.00%
-loc	−21.05%	−8.70%	+3.85%
-qlog	−5.56%	+8.70%	+3.85%
-h	0.00%	0.00%	+3.85%
-ir	−26.32%	−4.35%	+19.23%
-lin	−10.53%	−13.04%	+23.08%
-situation	+5.56%	+26.09%	+19.23%

Table 6: Performance P@1 in relevant ads retrieval by adding one feature set to the baseline.

Added Feature	Dialogue	Metadata	Dialogue and Metadata
adcol	0,10	0.25	0.17
+ir	+90.00%†	+4.00%	+35.29%
+situation	+30.00%	−40.00%†	−23.53%
+len	+30.00%	+24, 00%†	+23.53%
+h	+30.00%	0.00%	+35.29%
+loc	+30.00%	−12.00%	+11.76%
+lin	+20.00%	+12.00%	+11.76%
+phlen	+10.00%	+4.00%	−5.88%
+qlog	+10.00%	+8.00%	+47.06%†

bidders. Whereas these strategies could be used to extract keywords from content, they were not really evaluated in this task. The specific problem of determining which keywords of a text source are more useful for advertising was addressed by Goodman et al [6] and Yih et al [19]. They evaluated several extraction methods based on machine learning using Web page and email contents.

The second task, matching, has to do with matching keywords and ads. Ribeiro-Neto et al[12] proposed several strategies to minimize the mismatch between ad and page vocabularies. From the studied strategies, the best one, not based on keyword expansion, was called AAK. That method consisted in matching the content of the page to the content of the three structural parts of the ad (title, description, and keyword) with the additional requirement that all the words in the keyword should appear in the page. AAK is particularly useful for us, since we chose it as our method to retrieve ads, given its simplicity and good performance. Other alternative methods are based on evidence not publicy available as particular product taxonomies and click-through data.

As in the web contextual advertising, textual content related to video can be exploited for the placement of ads. That is the case of online video services such as Youtube and Yahoo! Video. These services use the textual information found in the page in which the video is embedded which normally includes a video description. Some authors, however, have proposed complex approaches that demand more computer resources. For example, Mei et al [10] proposed a system, called VideoSense which combines image, sound, and text evidence to automatically select ads. It also determines the most appropriate ad insertion point by analyzing the degree of discontinuity and attractiveness of the content. Wang et al [15] proposed an approach based on a model of user attention. The user attention was captured by analyzing the mouse movements over objects and concepts in the video. As long as the users pay attention to these objects and concepts, the higher are the chances they get ads associated with them. In a following work, [14], Wang et al have proposed an interactive format of video advertising.

Other recent work have studied the impact of textual evidence from script and subtitles on the characterization of video content. For instance, the authors in [7] have used subtitles as evidence to support the video classification and summarization tasks. Regarding video advertising, Yi et al [18] have expanded the original set of features proposed by the authors in [19]. In particular, they proposed a novel feature to describe the scene situation. Unlike these studies, we here conducted a systematic analysis of the features in order to find the most important ones for the task of selecting keywords and ads, we proposed new features derived from the ad inventory, and analysed particular sections of the script. Note that we did not use the work in [18] as a baseline because it lacks important implementation details such as how the selected keywords were used to retrieve ads.

6. CONCLUSION AND FUTURE WORK

In this work we evaluated the impact of using scripts both in finding keywords and in finding ads. Our main contributions were not only studying the features proven be useful in earlier works, as well as novel features proposed here and derived from the ad inventory. Further, we evaluated the quality of the ads obtained by using such features.

The results indicate that the features we studied were more useful for finding keywords than ads. Features derived from the ad collection performed consistently well in finding keywords, in particular, feature **adcol**. In contrast, feature **situation** always degraded the results. Regarding the ads evaluation, the best performance was obtained by feature **ir** which, when used earlier for finding keywords, presented a weak performance. Other features were also useful, although less important, such as **lin** and **len**. We also noted that keywords are proportionally more common in the metadata section than in the dialogue section. In fact, the best performance was obtained when using the metadata section, taken in isolation.

As future work, we intent to build a tool to assist human labeling of video content. The reason to invest in this strategy should be the emergence of the first mechanisms adopted by TV companies for displaying ads within the video content according to a manual labeling of specific scene. We also intend to study the impact of movie scripts as a source of evidence to detect the best ad insertion point of the video.

7. ACKNOWLEDGMENTS

The authors would like to thank INdT, UOL (grant 2011-021.521.5200), CNPq (grants 307.861/2010-4, 309.474/2011-6, and 484.816/2011-0), and CAPES for their financial support of this research.

8. REFERENCES

[1] A. Broder, M. Ciaramita, M. Fontoura, E. Gabrilovich, V. Josifovski, D. Metzler, V. Murdock, and V. Plachouras. To swing or not to swing: learning when (not) to advertise. In *Proceeding of the 17th ACM conference on Information and knowledge management*, pages 1003–1012, Napa Valley, California, USA, 2008. ACM.

[2] Y. Chen, G.-R. Xue, and Y. Yu. Advertising keyword suggestion based on concept hierarchy. In *WSDM '08: Proceedings of the conference on Web search and web data mining*, pages 251–260, New York, NY, USA, 2008. ACM.

[3] M. Cristo, A. Bitar, B. Guimaraes, G. Penalber, R. Hanada, C. Teixeira, and E. Melo. Web-like personalized advertising system for interactive digital TV. In *WTVDI/WEBMEDIA 2010*. SBC, 2010.

[4] S. Elliott. *Advertising - TV Advertisers Are Offered Closer Ties With Content*, 2009. Available at http://www.nytimes.com/2009/05/20/business/media/20adco.html?_r\=1\&fta\=y.

[5] E. R. Fernandes, R. L. Milidiú, and C. N. dos Santos. Portuguese language processing service. In *Proceedings of the Web in Ibero-America Alternate Track of the 18th World Wide Web Conference (WWW)*, Madrid, Spain, 2009. ACM.

[6] J. Goodman and V. R. Carvalho. Implicit queries for email. 2005. http://www.ceasc.cc/papers-2005/141.pdf.

[7] P. Katsiouli, V. Tsetsos, and S. Hadjiefthymiades. Semantic video classification based on subtitles and domain terminologies. In *1st Workshop on Knowledge Acquisition from Multimedia Content (KAMC-2007)*, volume 253, Genoa, Italy, July 2007. CEUR-WS.

[8] A. Lacerda, M. Cristo, M. A. Gonçalves, W. Fan, N. Ziviani, and B. Ribeiro-Neto. Learning to advertise. In *Proceedings of the 29th ACM SIGIR conference on Research and development in information retrieval*, pages 549–556, Seattle, Washington, USA, 2006. ACM.

[9] H. Li, D. Zhang, J. Hu, H.-J. Zeng, and Z. Chen. Finding keyword from online broadcasting content for targeted advertising. In *ADKDD '07: Proceedings of the 1st workshop on Data mining and audience intelligence for advertising*, pages 55–62, New York, NY, USA, 2007. ACM.

[10] T. Mei and S. Li. Contextual in-stream video advertising. In X.-S. Hua, T. Mei, and A. Hanjalic, editors, *Online Multimedia Advertising: Techniques and Technologies*, pages 223–233. IGI Global, 2011.

[11] Microsoft. Europe logs on. european internet trends of today and tomorrow. 2009. http://download.microsoft.com/download/9/5/1/951300C9-7F7C-4656-B00F-B19A72363669/EuropeLogsOn.PDF.

[12] B. Ribeiro-Neto, M. Cristo, P. B. Golgher, and E. S. de Moura. Impedance coupling in content-targeted advertising. In *Proceedings of the 28th ACM SIGIR conference on Research and development in information retrieval*, pages 496–503, Salvador, Brazil, 2005. ACM.

[13] T. Tsoneva, M. Barbieri, and H. Weda. Automated summarization of narrative video on a semantic level. In *Conference on Semantic Computing, 2007. ICSC 2007*, pages 169–176, 2007.

[14] B. Wang, J. Wang, L.-Y. Duan, Q. Tian, H. Lu, and W. Gao. Interactive web video advertising with context analysis and search. In *Proceedings of the 20th Conference on Pattern Recognition*, ICPR '10, pages 3252–3255, Washington, DC, USA, 2010. IEEE Computer Society.

[15] J. Wang, Y. Fang, and H. Lu. Online video advertising based on user's attention relavancy computing. In *IEEE Conference on Multimedia and Expo, 2008*, pages 1161–1164, 2008.

[16] I. H. Witten, E. Frank, and M. A. Hall. *Data Mining: Practical Machine Learning Tools and Techniques*. Morgan Kaufmann, Amsterdam, 3. edition, 2011.

[17] X. Wu and A. Bolivar. Keyword extraction for contextual advertisement. In *WWW '08: Proceeding of the 17th conference on World Wide Web*, pages 1195–1196, New York, NY, USA, 2008. ACM.

[18] B.-J. Yi, J.-T. Lee, H.-W. Woo, and H.-C. Rim. Contextual video advertising system using scene information inferred from video scripts. In *Proceedings of the 33rd ACM SIGIR conference on Research and development in information retrieval*, SIGIR '10, pages 771–772, New York, NY, USA, 2010. ACM.

[19] W.-t. Yih, J. Goodman, and V. R. Carvalho. Finding advertising keywords on web pages. In *WWW '06: Proceedings of the 15th conference on World Wide Web*, pages 213–222, New York, NY, USA, 2006. ACM.

A Framework for Processing Business Financial Rules

Fernando Cezar Reis Borges
Salvador University
Postgraduate Program, Master Degree in Systems and Computing, Brasil, Bahia, Salvador
fcssa@yahoo.com.br

Paulo Caetano da Silva
Salvador University
Postgraduate Program, Master Degree in Systems and Computing, Brasil, Bahia, Salvador
paulocaetano.dasilva@gmail.com

ABSTRACT
The processing of business rules usually occurs through its encoding in software applications, causing impacts that hinder their maintenance and reuse. In the financial area, the centralization of business rules represented in technology XBRL Formula promotes reuse by multiple applications and reduces these impacts. However, its use is not widespread and solutions that enable the applications reusing business rules with flexibility are restricted to proprietary solutions. This article proposes a framework for flexible processing of business rules defined with XBRL Formula from the use of services.

Categories and Subject Descriptors
D.3.3 [Language Constructs and Features]: *Frameworks, Web-based services, Domain-specific architectures.*

General Terms
Design, Languages

Keywords
XBRL, *XBRL Formula*, Services, *Web Service*, *Framework*.

1. INTRODUCTION
In the current globalized economic conjuncture of Brazil, the volume of negotiation carried on in the financial market has increased values and the competition, in this market, holds as a success differential the demand of information with more and more quality, transparency, quickness and low cost. Therefore, the pursuit for reduction in enterprise processes complexity using Information Technology (IT) is a challenge sought by software developers. However, the solutions released in the market are not always able to reach the usability expected in the software of a certain domain with business complexity, because, in many cases, the solution aggregates a set of applications with different formats, released to the user, which do not relate with a single solution, creating difficulties in these resources management.

In the past, the exchange of information among financial market entities happened in an inefficient way, using paper-based or electronic-based forms, forwarded by the sender to the receiver, in a scenario of financial information with a great format diversity that mandatorily needed to be converted according to the needs of the information consumer (SILVA, SILVA E AQUINO JUNIOR, 2006). This scenario was changed by using marking languages that, according to Silva (2010), provide a flexibility that favors the creation vocabularies and grammars for specific domains, in which XML distinguishes itself, used as a format for data transmission that facilitates its extension and adaptation for diverse specializations, in different society segments.

One of these specializations is XBRL, a markup language derived from XML aimed at the financial market (HOFFMAN, 2010), which represented an advance for standardization and reduction of different financial report formats in financial information systems. *XBRL Formula* technology, an extension of XBRL, represents the basis for processing business financial rules (ENGEL ET AL, 2009). Some business rules are usually reused in different organizational processes, these rules processing takes place usually through codes rewriting in different systems. This makes the process more expensive and disposed to failures. In this context, this work presents a *framework*, in which, stages business rules processing, represented in *XBRL Formula,* are turned into services with the usage of WS-BPEL language and *web services*, eliminating, thus, the need for codes rewriting in the usage of such stages by other processes.

This paper is organized as follows: in Section 2, issues concerning the technologies used in this project are discussed, in Section 3, correlate works are reviewed, in Section 4, the presentation of the proposed *framework* is carried on, in Section 5, the considerations regarding the proposal and future works are presented.

2. ASSOCIATED TECHNOLOGIES
For comprehending the *framework* some technologies, thereby discussed, distinguish themselves as essential ones: XBRL, *XBRL Formula*, Services, *Web Service* and WS-BPEL.

XBRL: XBRL language was developed from XML to be used in financial data preparation and exchange. These technology functionalities are defined with XLink (DeRose, Maler e Orchard, 2001) and XML Schema (Ezell, Sperberg e Quin, 2001). In order to express financial data with XBRL, in files denominated instances, it is necessary to define a vocabulary, based on XML Schema, and the relation among their terms, defined with XLink.

Figure 1 illustrates XBRL technology set of specifications and its modules with different functions.

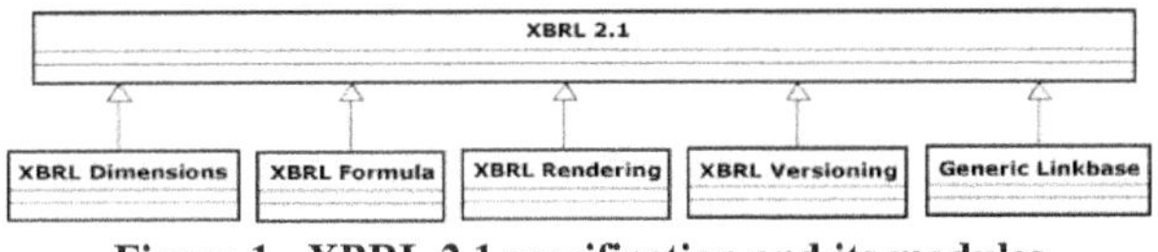

Figure 1 - XBRL 2.1 specification and its modules

Permission to make digital or hard copies of all or part of this work for personal or classroom use is granted without fee provided that copies are not made or distributed for profit or commercial advantage and that copies bear this notice and the full citation on the first page. To copy otherwise, or republish, to post on servers or to redistribute to lists, requires prior specific permission and/or a fee.
WebMedia'12, October 15–18, 2012, São Paulo/SP, Brazil.
Copyright 2012 ACM 978-1-4503-1706-1/12/10...$15.00.

XBRL Dimensions allows one to restrict the dimensional information used in the instances, *XBRL Formula* allows the definition of business rules, *XBRL Rendering* provides a mechanism for transforming XBRL instances information, for a better understanding, in human language, *XBRL Versioning* communicates changes performed in XBRL taxonomy and *Generic Linkbase* allows the creation of new types of resources for the taxonomy or for relation networks (HOFFMAN, 2010).

XBRL Formula: The goals of *XBRL Formula* are related to a specific set of validations that are not available in the specification, 2.1 version, of XBRL language.

According to Hamscher, Shuetrim e Kannon (2005), since the initial development of XBRL was recognized the need for expressing, not only specific numeric facts, but also relations among these facts and other relations. In this way, according to Fischer et al. (2008), to solve these issues, a *XBRL Formula* module was developed, which defines a syntax that can be used to document business rules, through information obtained from XBRL instances (ENGEL ET. AL., 2009). These rules documentation takes place through a grouping of *links*, denominated *linkbase Formula*, which provides the taxonomy creators with a collection of XPATH functions (CLARK E DEROSE, 1999), which allow one to accomplish more complex operations in relation to the addition ones, originally foreseen in XBRL specification. An institution business policy can be expressed in *XBRL Formula* through business rules, restricting or defining some of its aspects and providing an information source for decision making.

In the processing made from *XBRL Formula*, data input happens through a XBRL instance that specifies data contexts, units and financial facts. A *XBRL Formula* processor performs the definitions of formulae processing and produces results such as output declarations and facts in XBRL.

Service: In software systems domain, Erl (2009) defines a service as a repository of related capacities created from the decomposition of a business process. Services encapsulate the logic for a task or entity in a specific context, which in a standardized and governed collection represent, according to the same author, a service inventory. Once the knowledge of the components of a basic architecture is assimilated, the extraction of pieces necessary to the construction of an automatized solution oriented toward services is made with technology use, such as *web service*. (ERL, 2011)

Web Service: A *web service* is conceptualized by Kalin (2010) as a distributed application, in which its components can be applied and executed in distinct devices through the use of *Simple Object Access Protocol*, or simply SOAP, a communication protocol that congregates a set of rules necessary to message exchanges in a decentralized way, based on XML format (KALIN, 2010). SOAP protocol has its definitions established in a WSDL document (KALIN, 2010), which, according to Gomes (2010), represents the service contract elaborated in a XML file that describes the operations that compose *web service*.

WS-BPEL: Business processes based on *web services* can have their behavior specified by BPEL language (JORDAN, EVDEMON & TC, 2007). Their implementation is similar to programming language ones and can be used in business processes for an interaction focused on messages exchange, preformed thorough orchestration or choreography. According to Rabelo (2010), in orchestration, a central process controls the services and coordinates the execution of different operations. In choreography, the dependence of a central coordinator does not exist, instead of that, each service involved identifies when to execute its operations and with whom they should interact. All of the choreography participants need to identify the business process, the operations that will be executes and the messages that will be exchanged.

These technologies usage is based on the proposal of services usage as a basis for the framework construction. Web services and BPEL technologies represent the most used technologies for these services releasing and composition, by independence platform.

3. CORRELATE WORKS

A proposal denominated EFPIF (*e-Financial Process Integration Framework*) (HUANG, HUANG E TSAI, 2006) uses *web services* as a mean to integrate financial processes of different institutions with investments analysis. From this integration it is possible to provide information for improving investment environment evaluation, reducing risks and the investment loss. These goals are pointed towards the benefit of investors, companies of investment consultancy, dealers of real estate values, banks and financial companies. This proposal goal is to provide financial services through *web services*. Financial information would be made available in XBRL and the services would be constructed and made available through the usage of UDDI repository and register (https://www.oasis-open.org/committees/tc_home.php?wg_abbrev=uddi-spec), in a way that participant systems could easily access and find the information of their interest. The services are made available through the systems connected and integrated to the *framework* through *web services* and BPEL. Some ideas in this proposal are reused in this work: financial information integration, financial flow integration and reuse.

SBR (*Standard Business Reporting*) is an initiative from the Australian government oriented to the reduction of financial reports amount, through XBRL language, based on a taxonomy, in which XBRL definitions are established for the Australian financial environment. In this way, Australian companies prepare, store and send data straight from their account systems to government agencies (A.G., 2009). This project works with five main components: (i) a national taxonomy; (ii) a services nucleus; (iii) a regime of governmental authentication (*Single Sign-on*); (iv) reports standardization; and (v) marketing implementation, as well as of a new culture for Australian financial institutions. The most important advantage in this project is the rationalization of Australian financial environment information usage, with the reduction of unnecessary data and duplication of financial demonstratives forwarded by Australian institutions.

Some other projects were researched: XBRL *Implementation Framework* (XIF), a *framework* for developing XBRL report platforms. Its goals are based on: shared knowledge, risk reduction, organized processes integralization and implementation (http://www.br-ag.eu/xbrlimplementationframework). Besides this project, there is *Integrated Framework for eChain Bank Accounting Systems*, a *framework* for integrating bank accounting systems known as eChain, which goal is to integrate various financial/accounting softwares with web service, in order to facilitate standardized business electronic files exchange among banks and other institutions. (http://www.emeraldinsight.com/journals.htm?articleid=1463426 &show=abstract&).

In the evaluation of the projects researched, it was not possible to find, in none of them, an approach for business rule processing with *XBRL Formula*, but only a performance in the general context of XBRL 2.1 specification. Besides that, it was not observed an architecture oriented to services paradigm that could provide the flexibility and scalability necessary to the incorporation of new resources, without impacting the processes already defined.

4. *Web Service – Processing Business Rules Framework*

Combining services of the business rule domain, defined in *XBRL Formula*, for the financial context, released in the form of *web services*, provides the conception of the proposed do *framework*, denominated WS–PBRF (*Web Service – Processing Business Rules Framework*). This *framework* has as its goal the processing of business rules expressed through *XBRL Formula*, based on services released in the form of *web services*. This *framework* use proposes to make business rules execution flexible, in a way that the services that represent the rules will be able to be reused and the users will have the option of using only the service necessary to their needs.

In this *framework*, each service acts independently, however they are able to compose other services together, favoring software applications interoperability, reusing information and reducing the need for accounting systems adaptation for any new requirement incorporated in the processing. The components are distributed in the three layers of this architecture, illustrated in Figure 2: presentation, application and data.

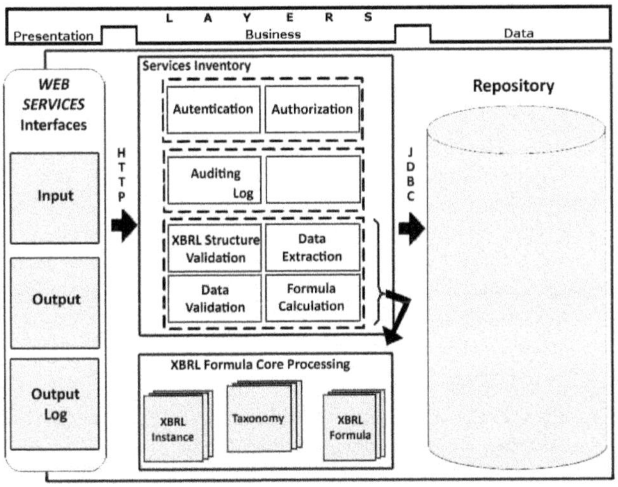

Figure 2 - Service *Framework* for *business rules*.

The first layer represents the interface for the consumers of the services provided by the *framework*: sending/receiving information (Input/Output) and the register of each consumer's action when using the *framework* services (Output Log), this one controlled by Audit Log service. The communication between this first layer and the second is performed in Web, through HTTP protocol.

In the second layer are the services released by the *framework* through an application service. These services are focused on a services inventory, which propose is illustrated in Figure 3, in which it is possible to observe the higher layer containing some proposed services identified through the numeration 1, 2 and 3 and the service candidates identified through the numeration 4, 5, 6 and 7 that, although planned, are not finalized yet. In the lower layer, one can observe a service, identified by the number 8, created from the composition of services that already exist in the higher layer. Although to the final user this is a unique service, in practice, it is an interface to execute services 1, 2 and 3 orchestrated by the composition language, WS-BPEL.

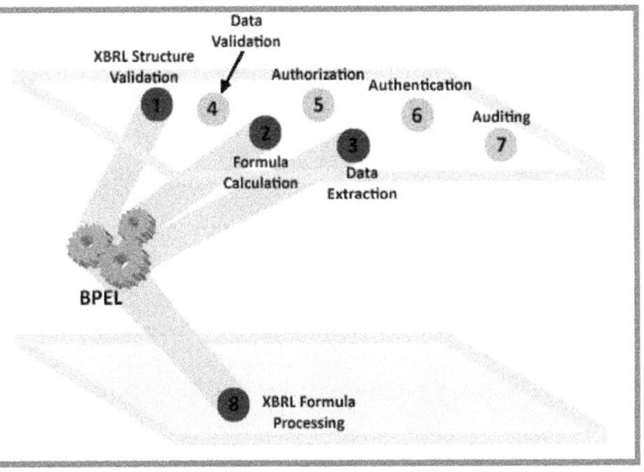

Figure 3 – Model of the proposed *framework* Services Inventory. Source: based on the model proposed by Erl (2009)

This inventory logically congregates all services incorporated to the *framework* (it means that the services do not need to be physically at the same place – server –, the consumer only needs to know where and how to localize the service registers). In this layer are the services of: (i) Audit Log, responsible for registering the consumer's actions, such as input to risk management (analysis of performance, safety, usability); (ii) Authentication, responsible for providing permission to the user in order to have access to the *framework* services; (iii) Authorization, which defines what services the authenticated user will be able to use; (iv) Structural Validation, which will analyze if the files (XBRL instance, taxonomy and linkbase formula) have their structures correctly defined, based on XBRL; (v) Data Extraction, responsible for capturing financial information contained both in the XBRL instance file and in the *linkbase Formula*, which specifies the processing rules of instance data; (vi) Formulae Calculation, responsible for processing formulae from the business rules (expressed in the *linkbase Formula*) and the forwarded data; and (vii) Data Validation, will validate the values from the formulae calculation obtained in *linkbase Formula* against the instance, the calculation service is encapsulated in this service as a subprocess. The last four listed services (iv, v, vi and vii) represent the main processing services, in this project, identified as XBRL Formula processing nucleus. *XBRL Formula* processing service is made available through the composition of three of the processing nucleus services (iv, v e vi) managed by WS-BPEL language.

The Data Extraction service uses a repository to storage the data extracted from XBRL instances and the formulae captured in the *linkbase Formula*. This repository is represented in the third layer of the model proposed for the *framework*.

In this process implementation, illustrated in Figure 2, the inventory was constructed and released through the application server, web TomCat – 7.0.4 version, in which services were inserted for the files structural validation (instance and *linkbase Formula*), data extraction of these files and formulae calculation. Client softwares consume each of these services through the forwarding of XBRL instance files and *linkbase Formula*. In the *framework* execution it is possible to identify the non-localized *links* both in the instance file and in the *linkbase*, besides the elements of the instance file absent in the taxonomy linked to the instance, performing the structural validation of the files in processing. The calculation processing takes place in the calculation service and the result released to the consumer through the output *web service* (*output*). To perform the *framework* tests, the files of taxonomy, instance and *linkbase Formula* based on US *Financial Reporting Taxonomy Framework* (USFRTF) (http://xbrl.us/taxonomies/Pages/default.aspx) were used.

5. CONCLUSION

This paper presents a solution for flexibilization and reuse of business rules processing, through the usage of services and *XBRL Formula*. This focus enables the reuse of functionalities for other situations that are not restricted to the *XBRL Formula*, but for diverse XBRL technology modules. Besides that, the incorporation of a mechanism of services register facilitates the access to the service consumer (account-financial system of an institution or physical person) and can establish the possibility of distributing business rules processing, differently from how it was implemented the example of test, because such services would be registered in only one place and remotely executed. This register represents an indicator for the service released. Thus, both the development and the implementation of the services could be made and released in any other place. It favors the elaboration of an environment that provides the incorporation of new services without the need of changing the applications that use them.

This proposal, still in the elaboration phase, has as an activity to be developed for validation the incorporation of tests and the practical application in a real environment. Besides that, it is planned the incorporation of specific services for the business safety, including safe authentication with, at least, two phases, associated to audit and cryptography.

It is also a future pretension proposing a Service Oriented Architecture (SOA) with all the components that permeates this approach in the application of *XBRL Formula* with module. For starting, it is being researched the creation of a SOA repository and register, in which the employment of the service inventory already proposed in this paper is included.

6. REFERENCES

[1] A. G. (2009). An Australian Government Initiative. Retrieved Fev 2012, from Standard Business Reporting (SBR): https://www.sbr.gov.au/content/public/au.gov.sbr.home

[2] DeRose, S., Maler, E., & Orchard, D. (2001). XML Linking Language (XLink) Version 1.0. Retrieved 2011, from W3C: http://www.w3.org/TR/xlink/

[3] Engel, P., Fischer, H., Morilla, V., Richards, J., Shuetrim, G., Kannon, D. v., et al. (2009). Formula 1.0. Acesso em 13 de setembro de 2011, disponível em XBRL International Inc: http://www.xbrl.org/Specification/formula/REC-2009-06-22/formula-REC-2009-06-22.html

[4] Erl, T. (2011). Service-Oriented Architecture Concepts, Technology and Design (11ª Edição ed.). Boston, United States of America: Prentice Hall

[5] Erl, T. (2009). SOA - Princípios do Desing de Serviços (1a ed.). (C. E. Furmankiewicz, Trad.) São Paulo, SP, Brasil: Pearson Prentice Hall.

[6] Ezell, D., Sperberg, M., & Quin, L. (2001). http://www.w3.org/XML/Schema. Retrieved 2011, from W3C.

[7] Fischer, H., Engel, P., Morilla, V., Richards, J., Shuetrim, G., Kannon, D. v., et al. (2008). Formula 1.0. Acesso em 28 de 03 de 2012, disponível em XBRL Internacional: http://www.xbrl.org/Specification/formula/CR-2008-12-31/formula-CR-2008-12-31.html

[8] Gomes, D. A. (2010). Web Services SOAP em Java. São Paulo, SP, Brasil: Novatec

[9] Hamscher, W., Shuetrim, G., & Kannon, D. v. (2005). XBRL Formula Requirements. Acesso em 14 de Setembro de 2011, disponível em XBRL International: http://www.xbrl.org/technical/requirements/Formula-Req-CR-2005-06-21.htm

[10] Hoffman, C. (2010). XBRL for Dummies. Indianapolis, Indiana, USA: Wiley Publishing.

[11] Huang, D.-Y., Huang, W.-T., & Tsai, R.-L. (2006). The Investiment Integration Framework based on XBRL and Web Services. International Journal of Electronic Business Management , p. 8.

[12] Jordan, D., Evdemon, J., & TC, O. W. (2007). Web Services Business Process Execution Language Version 2.0. (A. Alves, A. Arkin, S. Askary, C. Barreto, B. Bloch, F. Curbera, et al., Editores) Acesso em 03 de outubro de 2011, disponível em OASIS: http://docs.oasis-open.org/wsbpel/2.0/wsbpel-v2.0.html

[13] Kalin, M. (2010). Java Web Services: Implementando (1 ed.). (R. Marques, Trad.) Rio de Janeiro, RJ, Brasil: Alta Books.

[14] Rabelo, R. J. (2010). Integração de Sistemas Corporativos. Acesso em 11 de 2011, disponível em Universidade Federal de São Carlos - WS-BPEL - Web Service Business Process Execution Language: http://www.das.ufsc.br/~rabelo/Ensino/DAS5316/MaterialDAS5316/BPM/BPEL.pdf

[15] Silva, P. C. (2010). Análise Multidimensional de dados XML baseados em links: Modelos e Linguagens. Recife, PE, Brasil: Universidade Federal de Pernambuco - UFPE.

[16] Silva, P. C., Silva, L. G., & Aquino Júnior, I. J. (2006). XBRL - Conceitos e Aplicações. Rio de Janeiro, RJ, Brasil: Ciência Moderna.

[17] Clark, J., & DeRose, S. (1999). XML Path Language (XPath) Version 1.0. Acesso em 2011, disponível em W3C: http://www.w3.org/TR/xpath/

Detection of Photos from the Same Event Captured by Distinct Cameras

Hugo Feitosa de Figueirêdo[1,2], João Paulo Ribeiro da Silva[1], Daniel Farias Batista Leite[1], Cláudio de Souza Baptista[1]

[1] Universidade Federal de Campina Grande
Departamento de Sistemas e Computação
Rua Aprígio Veloso, 882 - Bairro Universitário, Campina Grande, Paraíba, Brasil

[2]Instituto Federal de Educação, Ciência e Tecnologia da Paraíba
Campus Monteiro
Ac. Rodovia PB-264 - Bairro Vila Santa Maria - CEP 58500-000, Monteiro, Paraíba, Brasil

hugo.figueiredo@ifpb.edu.br, joao.silva@ccc.ufcg.edu.br, daniel.leite@ccc.ufcg.edu.br, baptista@dsc.ufcg.edu.br

ABSTRACT

Currently one of the main features of events such as birthday party, wedding, conferences, and trips is the amount of photos taken from different digital cameras. The plethora of photo devices such as smartphones and tablets have contributed for this avalanche of photos. Social networks such as Facebook, Orkut, Flickr, and Picasa store a large volume of photos. As a consequence, the retrieval of such photos demands new systems. The automatic annotation of photo context metadata such as timestamp, and geographic coordinates, represents a challenge. In this paper, we propose a method for automatic event detection based on photos taken from different cameras in a same event. The proposed method aims to improve the retrieval of photos in a same event, to make cross tagging and to detect errors in the annotations.

Categories and Subject Descriptors

H.3.1 [**Information Storage and Retrieval**]: Content Analysis and Indexing; H.5.1 [**Information Interfaces and Presentation**]: Multimedia Information Systems.

General Terms

Algorithms, Experimentation.

Keywords

Personal Photo Collections, Photo Annotation, Event Photo Annotation, Event Detection.

1. INTRODUÇÃO

Com o advento da fotografia digital, os custos de captura e armazenamento de fotografias diminuíram e tornaram possível a integração das câmeras digitais com os telefones celulares. A captura de fotografias é uma das funções mais comuns nos dispositivos móveis atuais. Com a ubiquidade das câmeras, os usuários de dispositivos móveis têm capturado uma quantidade cada vez maior de fotografias digitais. O crescimento acentuado do número de fotografias geradas ocasiona uma onerosa tarefa para o usuário no gerenciamento das coleções de fotografias digitais pessoais, além de uma grande dificuldade no momento de busca das mesmas.

Por outro lado, o cenário atual da adição das fotografias em redes sociais demonstra a grande quantidade de fotografias geradas e a tendência dessas redes tornarem-se gerenciadores de fotografias. Como exemplo, podem ser destacados alguns números: em agosto de 2011, o Flickr obteve a marca de 6 bilhões de fotografias[1]; enquanto que o Facebook possui aproximadamente 100 bilhões de fotografias; já o Picasa possui aproximadamente 5 bilhões; e o Photobucket 8 bilhões[2]. Aproximadamente 250 milhões de fotografias são adicionadas no Facebook por dia, sendo que, em grandes eventos, esse número aumenta consideravelmente, como por exemplo, no final de semana de 1 de janeiro de 2011, mais de 750 milhões de fotografias foram adicionadas[3] por dia.

Um **evento** é caracterizado por um acontecimento que reúne pessoas com um objetivo em comum, em um determinado lugar e durante um determinado período de tempo. Exemplos de eventos incluem festas de aniversário, concertos, casamentos e natal. Dessa forma, um evento pode ser caracterizado por um conjunto de informações contextuais de um determinado acontecimento acerca de **quem**, **onde** e **quando**. Por outro lado, essas informações são consideradas as mais importantes para um usuário recordar de suas fotografias [15], tornando a detecção do evento no qual uma fotografia foi capturada, uma informação muito importante para o gerenciamento de fotografias.

A detecção automática de eventos pode ser realizada através da utilização de informações contextuais das fotografias e fontes externas, como, por exemplo, as redes sociais. As principais

Permission to make digital or hard copies of all or part of this work for personal or classroom use is granted without fee provided that copies are not made or distributed for profit or commercial advantage and that copies bear this notice and the full citation on the first page. To copy otherwise, or republish, to post on servers or to redistribute to lists, requires prior specific permission and/or a fee.
WebMedia'12, October 15–18, 2012, São Paulo/SP, Brazil.
Copyright 2012 ACM 978-1-4503-1706-1/12/10...$15.00.

[1] http://blog.flickr.net/en/2011/08/04/6000000000/, acessado em 01 de outubro de 2011.

[2] http://blog.pixable.com/2011/02/14/facebook-photo-trends-infographic/, acessado em 01 de outubro de 2011.

[3] https://www.facebook.com/press/info.php?statistics, acessado em 01 de outubro de 2011.

informações contextuais das fotografias utilizadas para a detecção automática de eventos são: a espacial e a temporal.

Alguns métodos existentes para a detecção de eventos utilizam a ideia de que o evento possui características hierárquicas, de forma que podem existir sub-eventos contidos em um evento maior. Por exemplo, "uma ida à praia" e "um churrasco na piscina" podem ser considerados sub-eventos de um evento maior chamado "Férias de Janeiro de 2011". Destarte, usuários diferentes podem possuir diferentes preferências no momento de selecionar em qual evento uma determinada fotografia foi capturada.

Por outro lado, um fator importante, denominado de evento compartilhado, tem sido comumente desconsiderado no momento de detectar os eventos. Esse fator ocorre devido à corriqueira existência de várias câmeras de pessoas distintas em um mesmo evento. A captura de várias fotografias por câmeras distintas, em um mesmo evento, é uma situação comum. Entretanto, tradicionalmente, cada pessoa possuidora de uma câmera fotográfica possui sua organização particular de fotografias. Como consequência do fato de câmeras distintas possuírem funções distintas, é possível que fotografias capturadas num mesmo evento possuam tipos de informações nos metadados diferentes. Por exemplo, as fotografias capturadas a partir da câmera de um smartphone, equipada com GPS, possuem a informação de localização geográfica nos seus metadados, enquanto que em outra câmera, equipada com bússola, as fotografias capturadas possuem apenas as informações de orientação.

Neste artigo, propõe-se a detecção de eventos compartilhados. Este termo irá ser utilizado para definir grupos de usuários que capturam fotografias de um mesmo evento para fins de registro e compartilhamento. Para esta detecção, são utilizadas redes sociais de compartilhamento de fotografias para a descoberta de eventos compartilhados na lista de contatos de um usuário. Torna-se possível, pois, a interligação entre fotografias de usuários distintos, indicando que fazem parte de um evento compartilhado.

O restante deste artigo está organizado como segue. Na seção 2, são apresentados alguns trabalhos relacionados à anotação de eventos em fotografias. Na seção 3, apresenta-se uma formalização do problema de detecção de eventos pessoais e detecção de eventos compartilhados e os algoritmos utilizados para detectar os eventos em fotografias pessoais. Na seção 4, apresenta-se o protótipo para prova de conceito que implementa os métodos apresentados neste artigo. Na seção 5, descreve-se a metodologia de avaliação utilizada e são apresentados os resultados obtidos na avaliação do método de detecção de eventos compartilhados proposto. Por fim, na seção 6, são apresentadas as conclusões e os trabalhos futuros a serem realizados.

2. TRABALHOS RELACIONADOS

Um dos problemas atuais abordados na literatura com relação à anotação de fotografias é a detecção automática de eventos. A maioria das abordagens propostas utiliza informações visuais, temporais e espaciais.

As abordagens visuais são baseadas no conteúdo da fotografia, i.e., as características visuais extraídas utilizando técnicas de recuperação de informação baseada no conteúdo (*content-based image retrieval*). Fotografias capturadas no mesmo evento, geralmente, contêm características visuais similares, tais como as cores, textura, formato e estrutura [14]. Por exemplo, fotografias capturadas durante uma caminhada na praia em um dia ensolarado possuem similaridades visuais significantes.

As abordagens baseadas em metadados temporais utilizam a data e a hora extraídas dos metadados das fotografias. A utilização da informação temporal é baseada na teoria da explosão de fotografias, na qual fotografias são capturadas em curtos intervalos de tempo durante um evento [9]. Cooper et al. [2] utilizam essa abordagem. Existem também trabalhos que combinam técnicas visuais e temporais, como O'Hare et al. [11].

As abordagens que utilizam os metadados espaciais e temporais baseiam-se no fato de que eventos ocorrem em algum lugar, em determinado momento. Dessa forma, um evento contém fotografias de lugares próximos.

O PhotoCompas [9] detecta eventos utilizando as informações espaço-temporais das fotografias. Além disso, nomeia os eventos automaticamente a partir dos nomes dos lugares e informações temporais. Porém, o PhotoCompas não realiza a detecção de eventos compartilhados.

Lacerda *et al.* [8] propuseram um algoritmo para detecção de eventos em coleções pessoais de fotografias. O algoritmo utiliza DBScan ou K-Means para realizar uma agrupamento espacial das fotografias e, em seguida, realiza uma segmentação temporal através da média e desvio padrão entre os intervalos de tempo entre fotografias consecutivas. Apesar deste algoritmo ter obtido bons resultados para eventos de coleções pessoais, não são tratados eventos compartilhados. Também, a localização geográfica nas fotografias é uma informação obrigatória.

Nenhum dos trabalhos supracitados consideram as pessoas presentes nas fotografias para a identificação dos eventos, pois trabalham com coleções pessoais de fotografias. Shimizu et al. [13] utilizaram a co-ocorrência de pessoas para buscar um grupo de fotografias em que uma pessoa tem alta probabilidade de estar presente. Entretanto, não considera a detecção de eventos nas fotografias.

Os trabalhos que consideram os metadados espaço- temporais para a separação de fotografias pessoais, obtiveram bons resultados. Entretanto, para a detecção de eventos compartilhados, estas técnicas esbarram no problema de não considerarem que podem haver diversos eventos em uma área que ocorreram em um curto período de tempo. Assim, as pessoas presentes nas fotografias podem auxiliar na separação desses eventos distintos e na detecção de eventos compartilhados.

Jang, Yoon e Cho [5] propuseram o agrupamento (*clustering)* de fotografias que foram capturadas por um grupo de pessoas durante viagens utilizando informações espaciais e temporais, sendo o agrupamento realizado de acordo com as preferências do dono de cada câmera. O algoritmo TSA proposto por Cooper et al. [2] é utilizado para separação pelo *timestamp* das fotografias em grupos. Em outro trabalho [6], os autores avaliaram a utilização de outros métodos de classificação não supervisionada. Entretanto, esse trabalho não realiza a detecção de eventos compartilhados. Além disso, os métodos propostos não utilizam as pessoas presentes nas fotografias. Outro problema dos métodos propostos é a necessidade das fotografias estarem georreferenciadas, o que diminui bastante a quantidade de fotografias que podem ser agrupadas em uma rede social.

Becker, Naaman e Gravano [1] utilizaram anotações providas por usuários e metadados das fotografias para agrupar documentos em *sites* com mídias sociais, para tanto, utilizaram uma abordagem de aprendizado de métricas de similaridade para identificação de eventos em mídias sociais. Contudo, a técnica proposta não detecta eventos compartilhados e é aplicada somente ao domínio de mídias sociais.

Nenhum dos trabalhos relacionados encontrados na área propõe métodos para a detecção de eventos compartilhados, sendo o trabalho que mais se aproxima da proposta deste artigo, o de Jang, Yoon e Cho [6]. Além disso, não foi encontrado nenhum trabalho relacionado que utilize as informações temporais, espaciais e de pessoas presentes nas fotografias para a detecção de eventos.

3. DETECÇÃO DE EVENTOS

Nesta seção, apresenta-se a solução proposta para a detecção de eventos. No escopo deste artigo, serão considerados dois tipos de detecção de eventos:

- **Detecção de eventos pessoais:** separação em eventos de coleções de fotografias pessoais, sem a existência de interseção de tempo entre eventos distintos, ou seja, dois eventos não podem ocorrer em uma mesma faixa de tempo; e
- **Detecção de eventos compartilhados:** descoberta da existência de fotografias de um mesmo evento em coleções de fotografias de donos distintos, ou seja, mais de uma pessoa capturou fotografias do evento e armazenou em sua coleção pessoal de fotografias.

No restante desta seção, serão descritos os métodos utilizados para a detecção de eventos pessoais e compartilhados.

3.1 Detecção de Eventos Pessoais

Considerando E o conjunto de todos os eventos, $Y_{ev} \subseteq F$ a coleção contendo as fotografias que foram capturadas no evento $ev \in E$ e C_f as informações contextuais relativas à fotografia $f \in F$, a detecção de eventos pessoais consiste no processo de geração de subconjuntos de fotografias $Y_{ev} \subseteq Y$, dado um conjunto de fotografias $Y \subseteq F$, de acordo com uma função de $\omega: Co \rightarrow P$, que indica se duas fotografias f_i e f_{i+1} consecutivas temporalmente fazem parte de um mesmo evento, onde $Co = \{(f_i, f_{i+1}) \mid f_i \in F \text{ e } f_{i+1} \in F\}$ e $P = \{x \mid x = 0 \text{ ou } x = 1\}$. Para a detecção de todos os eventos, para cada fotografia $f_i \in Y$, é executada a função ω. Se $\omega(f_i, f_{i+1}) = 1$, então f_i e $f_{i+1} \in Y_e$, caso contrário, se $\omega(f_i, f_{i+1}) = 0$, então $f_i \in Y_e$, $f_{i+1} \notin Y_e$ e $f_{i+1} \in Y_{e+1}$.

A detecção de eventos pessoais nas fotografias é realizada assumindo que não existem eventos paralelos na coleção de um mesmo usuário. As fotografias devem conter nos seus metadados as informações de data e hora do momento da captura, sendo a informação da localização geográfica utilizada caso já exista ou tenha sido anotada no próprio sistema anteriormente.

O algoritmo para detecção de eventos pessoais em coleções de fotografias proposto é baseado em quatro etapas e estende o proposto por Lacerda *et al.* [8], sendo os dois baseados em quatro etapas. O parâmetro de entrada do algoritmo de detecção de eventos é uma coleção de fotografias.

Na primeira etapa, caso exista a informação de localização geográfica, realiza-se uma classificação espacial das fotografias utilizando-se o algoritmo de agrupamento baseado em densidade DBSCAN [12].

Na segunda etapa, realiza-se uma classificação temporal. Nesta etapa, cada grupo detectado na etapa anterior é separado em subgrupos quando o intervalo de tempo entre duas fotografias consecutivas é superior a média mais desvio padrão de todos os intervalos de tempo entre fotografias consecutivas do grupo.

Na terceira etapa, são realizadas algumas correções de inconsistências ocorridas após as duas primeiras etapas, como eventos que ocorrerão em grandes intervalos de tempo ou em grandes áreas geográficas.

Por fim, na quarta etapa, realiza-se a nomeação dos eventos detectados. Esta etapa foi desconsiderada no escopo deste artigo.

Entretanto, no algoritmo de Lacerda *et al.* [8], todas as etapas são obrigatórias, enquanto que, a extensão realizada pelo algoritmo utilizado neste trabalho, permite que a primeira e a terceira etapas não sejam realizadas, caso a informação de localização geográfica não exista nas fotografias ou se o usuário não possuir agenda Web. Ou seja, no algoritmo ora proposto, a informação de localização geográfica não é mandatória.

Outro ponto importante, é a possibilidade de alterar o nível de granularidade do evento gerado, permitindo que, com a mesma coleção de fotografias, sejam gerados diferentes eventos.

A detecção de eventos pessoais pode ser o primeiro passo a ser realizado para a detecção de eventos compartilhados em uma rede social, pois a detecção de eventos compartilhados ocorre a partir da comparação entre eventos pessoais.

Apesar do método obter bons resultados para coleções de fotografias pessoais, para eventos compartilhados, o mesmo mostra-se ineficaz. O principal motivo dos resultados ruins é a existência de eventos que ocorrem ao mesmo tempo.

Assim, propõe-se neste artigo um método para detectar eventos compartilhados, com o intuito de realizar processamentos *a posteriori*, como de anotação cruzada automática, detecção de erros nas anotações e novas experiências na navegação e busca de fotografias. Esse método é apresentado na subseção seguinte.

3.2 Detecção de Eventos Compartilhados

O cálculo da similaridade entre eventos será realizado através da função $\varphi: V \rightarrow P$, que medirá o grau de similaridade entre dois eventos ev_1 e ev_2, sendo $V = \{(ev_1, ev_2) | ev_1 \in E_1 \text{ e } ev_2 \in E_2\}$, $P = \{x \mid x \in \mathcal{R} \text{ e } 0 < x < 1\}$ e E_u o conjunto de eventos do usuário u. A função φ é utilizada pelo módulo de anotação de eventos para a detecção de eventos compartilhados e utiliza as informações de contexto C_{E_u} do conjunto de fotografias $Y_{E_u} \subseteq F$ capturadas no evento E_u. A função φ é definida na Equação (1).

$$\varphi(ev_1, ev_2) = SE * PSE + ST * PST + SP * PSP \quad (1)$$

Onde, as funções SE, ST e SP medem o grau de similaridade espacial, temporal e de pessoas, respectivamente, entre os eventos ev_1 e ev_2. As variáveis PSE, PST e PSP são os pesos dos estimadores de similaridade espacial, temporal e de pessoas, respectivamente.

Pretende-se, com a detecção de eventos compartilhados que outras anotações possam ocorrer de forma automática ou auxiliar os algoritmos de anotação semi-automática. Por exemplo, supondo a existência de um evento compartilhado nas coleções de fotografias de dois usuários, na coleção de um dos usuários, o contato José foi anotado em uma das fotografias, já na coleção do segundo usuário, José não foi anotado nas fotografias, porém, através da detecção do evento compartilhado, José é anotado como participante do evento na coleção do segundo usuário. Outra contribuição dos eventos compartilhados é para a anotação semi-automática de pessoas presentes nas fotografias [3], pois existem estimadores, como o de recorrência no evento, que possuem melhor precisão e cobertura com um número maior de fotografias.

3.2.1 Similaridade Espacial

Na função de similaridade espacial de eventos, calcula-se a percentagem da área de intersecção das áreas dos dois eventos, com relação à soma das áreas dos dois eventos. Para isso são realizados os seguintes passos:

1. Realiza-se uma agregação das geometrias das fotografias de um mesmo evento (função *extent* do PostGIS), gerando-se uma geometria que representa o raio de abrangência dos eventos a serem comparados;
2. Gera-se um *buffer* de d metros a partir da geometria gerada pela agregação das fotografias dos eventos (função *expand* do PostGIS);
3. Verifica-se a existência de alguma interseção entre as geometrias dos dois eventos;
4. Caso não exista interseção, retorna-se uma similaridade nula;
5. Caso exista uma interseção, calcula-se a área desta interseção;
6. Em seguida, calcula-se a área da geometria de cada evento;
7. Por fim, retorna-se o resultado da aplicação da Equação 2 para o cálculo da similaridade espacial.

$$SE = \frac{2 \times Área(Interseção(ev_1, ev_2))}{Área(ev_1) + Área(ev_2)} \quad (2)$$

3.2.2 Similaridade Temporal

Na função de similaridade temporal de eventos, calcula-se a percentagem do intervalo em comum dos dois eventos sobre o tempo total dos dois, considerando um intervalo adicional t no início e fim de cada um dos eventos. Para tanto, os seguintes passos são realizados:

1. Identifica-se o início ti_{ev_1} do evento ev_1, a partir das informações temporais da primeira foto capturada entre os dois eventos. A coleção que contiver a fotografia mais antiga será considerado o ev_1;
2. Identifica-se o final tf_{ev_1} de ev_1, verificando qual a fotografia mais recente da coleção Y_{ev_1};
3. Identifica-se o início ti_{ev_2} de ev_2, verificando qual a fotografia mais antiga da coleção Y_{ev_2};
4. Identifica-se o final tf_{ev_2} de ev_2, verificando qual a fotografia mais recente da coleção Y_{ev_2};
5. Considera-se que a primeira fotografia capturada em um evento pode não ter ocorrido no início e que a última pode não ter ocorrido no final, então adiciona-se um intervalo t em tf_{ev_1}, tf_{ev_2} e diminui-se em ti_{ev_1} e ti_{ev_2};
6. Verifica-se o tempo inicial ti_{ev_C} e final tf_{ev_C} do intervalo em comum entre ev_1 e ev_2;
7. Calcula-se a ST através da Equação (3).

$$ST = \frac{2 \times Intervalo(ti_{ev_C}, tf_{ev_C})}{Intervalo(ti_{ev_1}, tf_{ev_1}) + Intervalo(ti_{ev_2}, tf_{ev_2})} \quad (3)$$

3.2.3 Similaridade de Pessoas

Na função de similaridade de pessoas em eventos, calcula-se a percentagem de pessoas em comum entre dois eventos sobre o total de pessoas. Para isso, os seguintes passos são realizados:

1. Calcula-se a quantidade de pessoas distintas anotadas $|P_{ev_1}|$ nas fotografias do evento ev_1;
2. Calcula-se a quantidade de pessoas distintas anotadas $|P_{ev_2}|$ nas fotografias do evento ev_2;
3. Calcula-se a quantidade de pessoas distintas anotadas $|P_{ev_1} \cap P_{ev_2}|$ nas fotografias do evento ev_1 que também foram anotadas nas fotografias do evento ev_2;
4. Calcula-se a SP através da Equação (4).

$$SP = \frac{2 \times |P_{ev_1} \cap P_{ev_2}|}{|P_{ev_1}| + |P_{ev_2}|} \quad (4)$$

3.2.4 Observações

As funções de similaridade de pessoas, espacial e temporal, indicam o quanto dois eventos são similares. Isoladamente, o resultado da similaridade retornada por essas funções podem ocasionar erros que não ocorreriam na detecção de eventos pessoais, e.g., dois eventos que ocorreram no mesmo horário, mas em localizações diferentes. Como em uma coleção pessoal de fotografias não pode haver dois eventos no mesmo instante de tempo, torna-se mais fácil a detecção de eventos. No entanto, tratando-se de fotografias armazenadas em uma rede social, podem existir diversos eventos que ocorreram num mesmo período de tempo. Com isso, as informações de pessoas presentes e a localização geográfica tornam-se essenciais para aumentar a eficácia da função de similaridade. Contudo, mesmo que a função SE ou a SP não possa ser calculada (devido a não existência da localização geográfica ou das pessoas presentes nas fotografias), a função φ pode ser calculada utilizando-se as outras duas funções de similaridade.

A agregação das geometrias que representam a localização geográfica das fotografias de um evento realizada na função de similaridade espacial é feita pelo método espacial *extent* de PostGIS, que retorna o MBR (*Minimum Bounding Rectangle*), que é uma geometria de menor complexidade computacional (retângulo). A desvantagem na utilização desse método de agregação é que, em alguns casos, grandes áreas que não fazem parte do evento podem ser retornadas. Ameniza-se este problema no método de detecção de eventos compartilhados através das funções de similaridade temporal e de pessoas.

Já para o cálculo da interseção das geometrias geradas pela agregação supracitada na função de similaridade espacial, foi utilizada a operação topológica *intersection* do OpenGIS [10] implementada no PostGIS, que retorna a geometria representando a área de interseção entre duas ou mais geometrias.

A função de similaridade temporal foi proposta baseada no cálculo da proporção de tempo que os dois eventos possuem em comum sobre o todo, considerando-se um intervalo adicional no início e no fim de cada evento representando o momento do início e do final do evento que não são capturadas fotografias.

4. PROTÓTIPO PARA PROVA DE CONCEITO

Para a validação dos métodos propostos, foi criado um protótipo que implementa os métodos de detecção de eventos pessoais e compartilhados.

Na Figura 1, mostra-se a arquitetura do protótipo que é dividida em camadas. A camada de dados é composta por duas bases de dados: um banco de dados objeto relacional com suporte espacial (PostgreSQL + PostGIS) e uma coleção de fotografias.

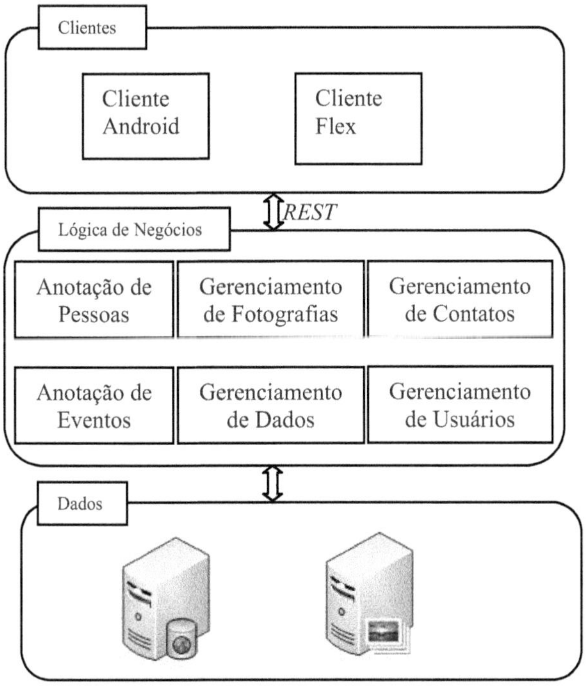

Figura 1. Arquitetura do Protótipo.

A camada de lógica de negócios é composta por seis módulos principais: módulo de gerenciamento de dados, módulo de gerenciamento de usuários, módulo de gerenciamento de contatos, módulo de gerenciamento de fotografias, módulo de anotação de pessoas e módulo de anotação de eventos.

O módulo de gerenciamento de dados é responsável pelo acesso e mapeamentos do dados em objetos. Neste módulo, utiliza-se JPA (*Java Persistence API*) para a realização de persistência dos dados.

O módulo de gerenciamento de usuários e o módulo de gerenciamento de contatos são responsáveis pelo gerenciamento dos usuários e dos contatos dos usuários no sistema. Um usuário é uma pessoa que possui permissões de acesso ao sistema, dono de uma coleção de fotografias e possui vários contatos. Os contatos são pessoas que estão presentes nas fotografias dos usuários. Todos os usuários possuem pelo menos um contato, o qual representa ele mesmo nas fotografias anotadas com as pessoas presentes. Um pessoa física só pode ter um objeto do tipo pessoa no sistema, mas podem existir diversos contatos para uma pessoa. Se uma pessoa é contato de mais de um usuário, para cada usuário, existe um contato diferente associado, mas somente uma pessoa. Ao ser adicionado um contato novo no sistema, verifica-se a existência de uma pessoa com o mesmo e-mail no sistema, caso positivo, o contato criado é associado a esta pessoa, caso negativo, é criada uma nova pessoa e o contato é associado a ela.

O módulo de gerenciamento de fotografias é responsável pela adição, remoção, extração de metadados e recuperação de fotografias. Além disso, neste módulo é verificado quem tem permissão de acessar as fotografias. As geometrias das fotografias são adicionadas ao banco de dados de duas formas: extração dos metadados (lat/long) das fotografias (EXIF) ou anotadas pelo usuário na interface gráfica, que utiliza a API do Google Maps para o georreferenciamento com o auxílio de mapa.

O módulo de anotação de pessoas é responsável por adicionar e remover as pessoas presentes nas fotografias, além de listar as pessoas mais prováveis de estarem presentes nas fotografias, para auxiliar o usuário na anotação das fotografias [7].

O módulo de anotação de eventos é responsável por organizar as fotografias em eventos. Neste módulo, foi implementado o algoritmo de detecção de eventos. Além disso, também é responsável por indicar, na visualização de eventos, os eventos similares existentes, detectados pelo algoritmo de detecção de eventos compartilhados. A detecção de eventos compartilhados foi implementado diretamente no banco de dados, utilizando-se a linguagem procedural PL/pgSQL. Periodicamente, um gatilho dispara uma ação que procura por eventos compartilhados nas listas de contatos dos usuários no banco de dados. Na implementação atual, o gatilho é disparado uma vez ao dia, entretanto, não foi realizado nenhum experimento até o momento para verificar qual o momento ideal de ser disparado este gatilho.

Na Figura 2, apresenta-se a interface do protótipo relativa à visualização de fotografias capturadas em um evento, na qual está destacado em um retângulo, a parte que apresenta para o usuário os eventos similares detectados nas coleções de fotografias de seus contatos, que representa o evento compartilhado.

A camada de cliente da arquitetura possui o cliente Flex e o cliente Android. O Cliente Flex possui a interface com o usuário disponível para acessar pela Web e o cliente Android possui funções diferenciadas para adição de fotografias diretamente do dispositivo móvel, como o auxílio na anotação das pessoas presentes nas fotografias no momento de captura da fotografia [4].

A comunicação entre a camada de cliente e a camada de lógica de negócios é realizada utilizando REST (*Representational State Transfer*). Esta comunicação facilita a utilização dos métodos propostos em outras redes sociais, como o Facebook.

5. AVALIAÇÃO

Nesta seção, apresenta-se a metodologia utilizada para avaliar o método proposto para detecção de eventos compartilhados, como também, os resultados obtidos na avaliação.

5.1 Metodologia de Avaliação

Para avaliar o método proposto para a detecção de eventos compartilhados, foi utilizada uma coleção de 4.251 fotografias, com as seguintes anotações: informações de hora e data da captura da fotografia, localização geográfica e pessoas presentes nas fotografias, sendo essas informações anotadas pelos proprietários das fotografias utilizando o protótipo supracitado. Na avaliação, foi considerada uma situação ideal, onde todas as fotografias estão anotadas de maneira correta e completa, essa situação foi utilizada para que informações incorretas não afetem na avaliação do método proposto.

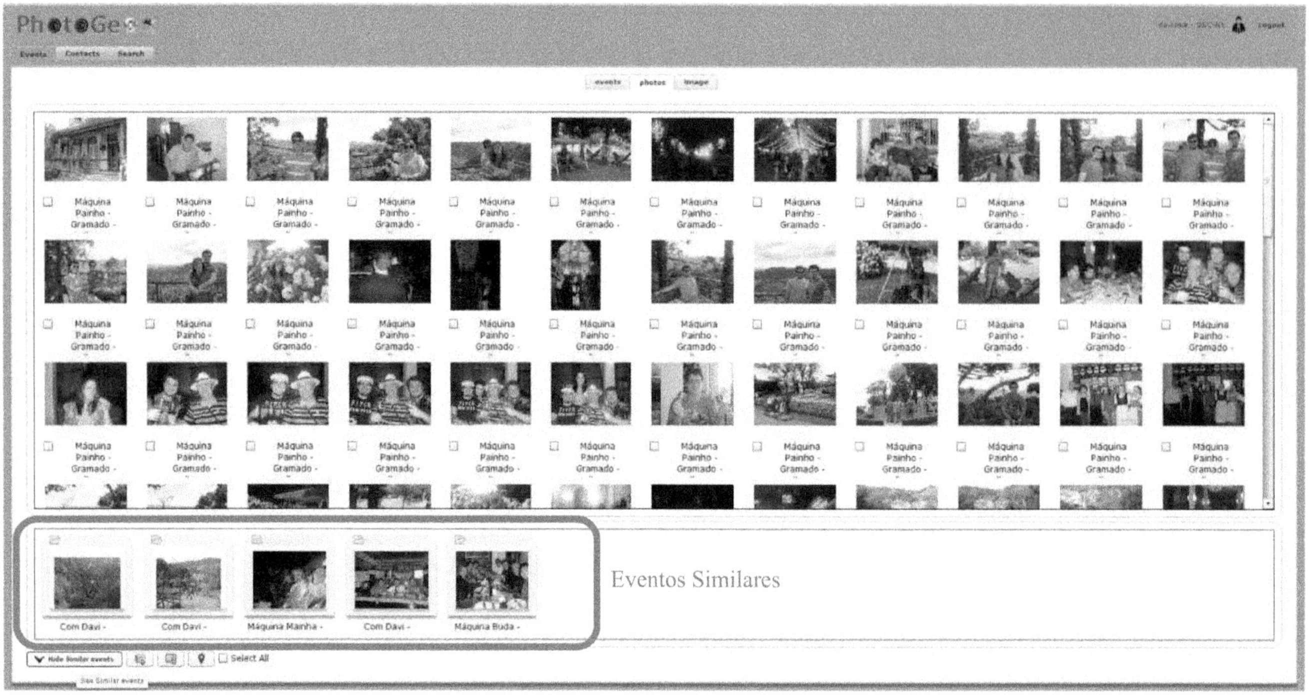

Figura 2. Protótipo de visualização de fotografias em um evento com indicação de eventos similares detectados.

As fotografias foram separadas a partir da informação do modelo da câmera fotográfica. Fotografias capturadas por câmeras distintas foram consideradas de diferentes coleções para efeito de avaliação.

Após separar as fotografias de acordo com o modelo da câmera, foi executado o algoritmo de detecção de eventos pessoais para cada coleção de fotografias gerada a partir dos modelos de câmeras. Em seguida, foi executado o algoritmo de detecção de eventos compartilhados para cada par de eventos detectados de usuários distintos, variando-se os diversos parâmetros de entrada para várias combinações. Os parâmetros de entrada do algoritmo alterados foram: os pesos das funções de similaridade espacial, de pessoas e temporal; e o limiar que separa os eventos considerados similares.

O objetivo do experimento foi detectar os melhores pesos para a função de similaridade de eventos, detectar o melhor limiar e comprovar a hipótese de que as informações de pessoas presentes, localização geográfica, horário e data das fotografias podem auxiliar na detecção de eventos similares em uma rede social.

As métricas utilizadas para avaliar os resultados foram: precisão, sensibilidade, acurácia e coeficiente de correlação de Mathews (Phi). As três primeiras métricas foram utilizadas para avaliar o quanto o método proposto é preciso e abrangente. Já o coeficiente de correlação de Mathews, foi utilizado devido à eficácia no tratamento de quantidades bem distintas de classes. A quantidade de combinações entre eventos que o classificador deve retornar como positivas é 456 e como negativas 18.265.

5.2 Avaliação dos Resultados

Na Figura 3, apresentam-se os resultados da métrica acurácia. Esta métrica obteve resultados elevados (o menor foi 79%) devido ao alto número de verdadeiros negativos. Entretanto, foi possível identificar que o detector de eventos similares possui uma melhor acurácia quando utilizadas ponderações para as três funções de similaridade maiores que 0.

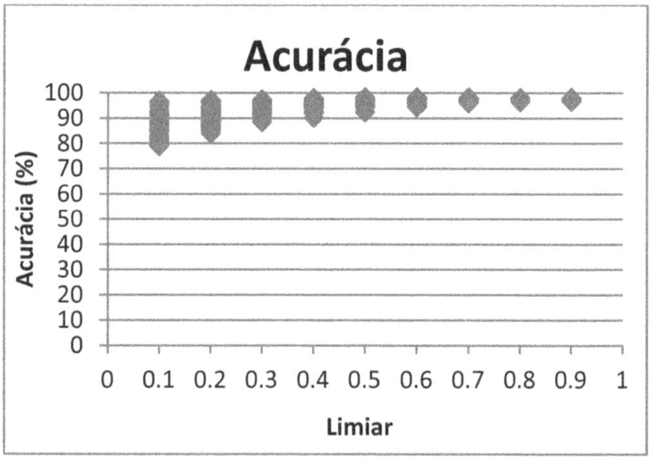

Figura 3. Acurácia da função de similaridade versus limiar.

Na Figura 4, são apresentados os resultados do experimento de variação dos parâmetros utilizando a métrica precisão. A partir desses resultados, foi identificado que o valor do limiar deve ser superior a 0,7 para que seja obtida uma precisão superior a 70%.

Na Figura 5, são apresentados os resultados para a métrica sensibilidade, que verifica a quantidade de classificações corretas em relação ao total de eventos similares. Considerando os resultados para os limiares superiores a 0,5, os resultados acima de 0,7 possuem resultados com sensibilidade não satisfatórios. Dessa forma, foram considerados valores para limiar entre 0,5 e 0,7 para a obtenção de bons resultados para a equação proposta.

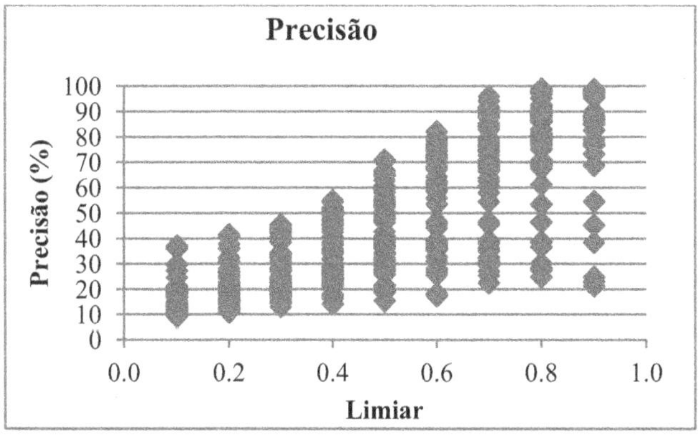

Figura 4. Precisão da função de similaridade versus o limiar.

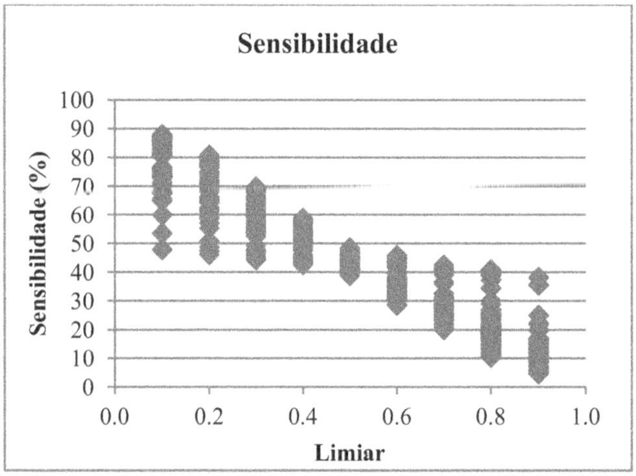

Figura 5. Sensibilidade da função de similaridade versus o limiar.

Na Tabela 1, são apresentados os melhores resultados obtidos para cada uma das métricas utilizadas na avaliação do método de detecção de eventos compartilhados. Como pode ser observado, todas as métricas obtiveram seus melhores resultados utilizando pelo menos uma ponderação de 0,2 para as funções de similaridade espacial, temporal e de pessoas. Para o protótipo implementado, foram selecionados os parâmetros com melhores resultados na métrica Phi, que são: 0,6 para o limiar; 0,2 para a ponderação da função de similaridade de pessoas; 0,3 para a função de similaridade espacial; e 0,5 para a função de similaridade temporal.

Tabela 1. Melhores resultados obtidos para cada métrica destacada.

Limiar	*PP*	*PE*	*PT*	*Prec*	*Sens*	*Acur*	*Phi*
0,6	0,2	0,2	0,6	79,3	34,4	**98,2**	0,51
0,5	0,2	0,3	0,5	70,4	41,7	98,2	**0,53**
0,1	0,4	0,4	0,2	10,6	**87,9**	81,7	0,27
0,8	0,2	0,4	0,4	**98,9**	19,5	98,0	0,43

6. CONCLUSÕES

Neste artigo, foi proposto a detecção de eventos compartilhados em coleções de fotografias de usuários de uma mesma rede social, utilizando-se as anotações de pessoas presentes, localização geográfica e hora e data da captura da fotografia.

O algoritmo proposto obteve resultados satisfatórios em termos de precisão e acurácia, para uma cobertura aceitável. Para a coleção utilizada nos experimentos, foi considerado como melhor resultado a execução do algoritmo para eventos com similaridade superior a 60%, com peso de 20% para as pessoas, de 20% para a localização geográfica e 60% para a parte temporal. Nessa execução, o algoritmo obteve uma acurácia de 98%, precisão de 79% e cobertura de 34%.

Como trabalho futuro, o algoritmo proposto será adaptado para funcionar com falta de informações. Em seguida, será avaliada a eficácia de algoritmos de anotação cruzada para os eventos detectados como similares. Além disso, será implementado o algoritmo em alguma rede social de grande escala na Internet para avaliar os aspectos relacionados a nova experiência de navegação em fotografias, através de eventos e eventos similares. Outro ponto que será explorado em trabalhos futuros é a utilização de técnicas de crowdsourcing aliado ao algoritmo de similaridade de eventos para a anotação de fotografias. Outro trabalho futuro, será o estudo do impacto da granularidade dos eventos na função de similaridade.

7. AGRADECIMENTOS

Os autores agradecem ao CNPq por financiar esta pesquisa e às pessoas que contribuíram com suas fotografias e anotaram-nas com as localizações geográfica e as pessoas presentes.

8. REFERÊNCIAS

[1] Becker, H., Naaman, M. and Gravano, L. 2010. Learning similarity metrics for event identification in social media. *Proceedings of the third ACM international conference on Web search and data mining - WSDM '10* (New York, New York, USA, 2010), 291.

[2] Cooper, M., Foote, J., Girgensohn, A. and Wilcox, L. 2005. Temporal event clustering for digital photo collections. *ACM Transactions on Multimedia Computing, Communications, and Applications*. 1, 3 (Aug. 2005), 269–288.

[3] Figueirêdo, H.F., Lacerda, Y.A., Paiva, A.C., Casanova, M.A. and Souza Baptista, C. 2011. PhotoGeo: a photo digital library with spatial-temporal support and self-annotation. *Multimedia Tools and Applications*. (Feb. 2011).

[4] de Figueirêdo, H.F., Fernandes, R.M., de Menezes, L.C., de Souza Baptista, C., Lacerda, Y.A. and de Paiva, A.C. 2009. A context-aware solution to annotate people in mobile devices. *Proceedings of the 7th International Conference on Advances in Mobile Computing and Multimedia - MoMM '09* (New York, New York, USA, 2009), 113–120.

[5] Jang, C., Yoon, T. and Cho, H.-G. 2009. A smart clustering algorithm for photo set obtained from multiple digital cameras. *Proceedings of the 2009 ACM symposium on Applied Computing - SAC '09* (New York, New York, USA, 2009), 1784.

[6] Jang, C., Yoon, T. and Cho, H.-G. 2010. Digital photo classification methodology for groups of photographers. *Multimedia Tools and Applications*. 50, 3 (Feb. 2010), 441–463.

[7] Lacerda, Y.A., de Figueirêdo, H.F., de Souza Baptista, C. and de Paiva, A.C. 2008. Expandindo e utilizando informações de contexto para a sugestao de anotações de fotografias digitais. *Proceedings of the 14th Brazilian Symposium on Multimedia and the Web - WebMedia '08* (New York, New York, USA, 2008), 162–169.

[8] Lacerda, Y.A., Figueirêdo, H.F.D., Baptista, C.D.S. and Sampaio, M.C. 2008. PhotoGeo: A Self-Organizing System for Personal Photo Collections. *2008 Tenth IEEE International Symposium on Multimedia* (Dec. 2008), 258–265.

[9] Naaman, M., Song, Y.J., Paepcke, A. and Garcia-Molina, H. 2004. Automatic organization for digital photographs with geographic coordinates. *Proceedings of the 2004 joint ACM/IEEE conference on Digital libraries - JCDL '04* (New York, New York, USA, 2004), 53.

[10] OGC 1999. *OpenGIS Simple Features Specification For SQL - Revision 1.1.*

[11] O'Hare, N. and Smeaton, A.F. 2009. Context-Aware Person Identification in Personal Photo Collections. *IEEE Transactions on Multimedia.* 11, 2 (Feb. 2009), 220–228.

[12] Sander, J., Ester, M., Kriegel, H.-P. and Xu, X. 1998. Density-Based Clustering in Spatial Databases□: The Algorithm GDBSCAN and Its Applications. *Data Mining and Knowledge Discovery.* 2, 2 (1998), 169–194.

[13] Shimizu, K., Nitta, N. and Babaguchi, N. 2011. Learning people co-occurrence relations by using relevance feedback for retrieving group photos. *Proceedings of the 1st ACM International Conference on Multimedia Retrieval - ICMR '11* (New York, New York, USA, 2011), 1–8.

[14] Vailaya, A., Figueiredo, M.A.T., Jain, A.K. and Zhang, H.-J. 2001. Image classification for content-based indexing. *IEEE transactions on image processing□: a publication of the IEEE Signal Processing Society.* 10, 1 (Jan. 2001), 117–30.

[15] Wagenaar, W.A. 1986. My memory: A study of autobiographical memory over six years. *Cognitive Psychology.* 18, 2 (Apr. 1986), 225–252.

OpenedEyes: Developing an Information Visualization Framework using Web Standards and Open Web Technologies

Caio Sacramento de Britto Almeida
Universidade Federal da Bahia
Instituto de Matemática
Departamento de Ciência da Computação
Salvador, Bahia, Brazil
caiosba@dcc.ufba.br

Antônio L. Apolinário Jr.
Universidade Federal da Bahia
Instituto de Matemática
Departamento de Ciência da Computação
Salvador, Bahia, Brazil
apolinario@dcc.ufba.br

ABSTRACT

Extract knowledge from a dataset is not trivial. Information visualization shows up to help on this task by trying to optimize the user information gathering by using suitable graphical representations. There are some tools for this, but they are often focused on desktop, require advanced knowledge or use proprietary technologies. The proposal of this work is to present OPENEDEYES, a JavaScript framework that uses web standards to implement interactive information visualization modules to be run in a web browser. From the framework core, a case study was built based on a real dataset for an empiric framework evaluation. Traditional and new techniques were implemented confirming the flexibility and extensibility of the framework.

Categories and Subject Descriptors

H.5.4 [**Information Interfaces and Presentation**]: Hypertext/Hypermedia—*Navigation*

General Terms

Information visualization

Keywords

information visualization, framework, web standards

1. INTRODUCTION

Advances in technology allow computers nowadays to store a large amount of data. Researchers from the Berkeley University estimates that every year 1 exabyte of data is produced, most of them available in digital format [19]. Being a valuable source of information is a promise that such datasets carry, while extracting these informations is often a hard task.

Permission to make digital or hard copies of all or part of this work for personal or classroom use is granted without fee provided that copies are not made or distributed for profit or commercial advantage and that copies bear this notice and the full citation on the first page. To copy otherwise, to republish, to post on servers or to redistribute to lists, requires prior specific permission and/or a fee.
WebMedia'12, October 15–18, 2012, São Paulo/SP, Brazil.
Copyright 2012 ACM 978-1-4503-1706-1/12/10 ...$15.00.

There are tools developed to help on data analysis. Visual exploration involves directly the user and has an advantage over other methods that is to be intuitive and able to handle easily heterogeneous data. As a consequence, they often lead to faster analysis and better results [19]. Visual representations and interaction techniques take advantage of the human eye broad bandwidth pathway into the mind to allow users to see, explore, and understand large amounts of information at once [28].

Regarding interactive visualizers, the proprietary technology Adobe Flash [1] is used by some tools. But Flash goes against the grain of the open standards since it requires a plug-in to be installed by the user, which is considered a usability and accessibility problem, among other implications [23]. On the other hand, the web standards were born as recommendations proposed by the World Wide Web Consortium (W3C) as an attempt to promote the Internet's evolution and to guarantee that all web technologies work well when joined. For years, W3C referred to these specifications as recommendations, and this may have contributed to a weak adoption by the companies that developed web browsers. When the Web Standards Project [25] was launched, in 1998, those recommendations were renamed to web standards, and then the support to those standards became a vital ingredient to any browser or Internet device. The web browsers modernization allows web standards-based rich internet applications to be built, even visualization tools [20].

The need to extract knowledge from large datasets motivated the development of a web-based information visualization framework using only web standards and open web technologies. This framework is composed of many interactive visualization modules, each one suitable for a certain kind of dataset, and also offers the basic infrastructure that allows it to be extended with the development of new visualization modules. As a result, it was possible to develop a fully functional framework with four visualizers developed upon it. Those visualizers are completely different since they implement different techniques suitable for different numbers of dimensions. The bubble chart module supports up to four dimensions, the great circles map represents relationships between geographic-related data, the choropleth map allows a variable to be compared across regions on a map, and finally, the parallel bars chart, an implementation of a new technique purposed by this work, allows n dimensions to be represented in a bidimensional space. The following sections will present related works, the reference model, the framework and a case study.

2. RELATED WORKS

Perhaps the first framework for information visualization was the Information Visualizer [5]. Microsoft Excel also generates charts based on a dataset, but beyond running on desktop, it's a proprietary software. Regarding end user visualization applications, Tableau [27] and Spotfire [29] are desktop applications which offer advanced information visualization tools to analyze large amount of data.

Many visualization tools were developed in the recent years to allow developers build their own visualizations. Among the Java-written ones, Processing [10] is a visual programming language and environment for people who want to create images, animations and interactions but works in a lower-level since it requires some programming skills. Besides this, there are many possibilities to build complex visualizations, but its target is the desktop environment. The target of Prefuse [14] is the web environment, and it defines itself as a toolkit for interactive visualizations creation. The Prefuse framework provides both Java and Flash tools, is freely licensed, but its strength is tree and graph structures besides also requiring coding. ManyEyes [30], written in Java, is a website which offers a service that allow users to upload datasets, create visualizations, publish and comment, but can not be downloaded and used as a product, just as a service.

Fusion Charts [11] is also another Flash tool for interactive visualization, which is largely used worldwide. Includes lots of visualization techniques, most of them traditional and simple techniques such as pie, bar and line charts. Besides not including complex visualizations, it's a paid product. Part of its code is written in JavaScript and HTML 5.

Among the JavaScript solutions, most of the existing solutions work in a lower-level. Raphael [2] makes it easy to create cross-browser SVG [34]. ProcessingJS [26] is a JavaScript port of Java Processing, so it works in a similar way as the Java tool. The solutions for charts creation are many, but include only simple charts and most of them can't be extended.

From an evolution optics, it can be noticed that many of the visualization tools were focused on the desktop environment and then started to migrate to the web environment. Finally, on the recent years, a large amount of data became available to the public on the Internet, some of them accessible through webservices. OPENEDEYES architecture is already prepared to handle with this new scenario, since the data server is independent from the application server. So, data can come from any place (regardless they are on the Internet or stored in a local file), once it is formatted according to what OPENEDEYES expects.

As exposed above, the existing tools can be divided into two main groups. In one group, web applications that implement simple techniques or require advanced knowledge. In the other group, desktop applications that implement more advanced techniques. Both groups could also be divided into free software and non free software. So, OPENEDEYES would be placed in an intersection between those two groups since it is web based, free and implements advanced techniques without requiring advanced knowledge. This way, lots of features are joined in only one product. It's written in JavaScript and based on web standards, avoiding proprietary technologies such as Adobe Flash. It runs on web browsers, making it available for all platforms. Works on both lower level and high level, so users who have programming skills can extend it by developing new visualizers, while novice users can just generate a visualization for some dataset by using one of the available visualizers. It's full available for download and licensed as free software, so anyone can download it, modify and use. Advanced techniques are available, such as a new technique introduced by this work called *parallel bars*. Conceptually, OPENEDEYES was based on the reference model to be presented in the following section.

3. REFERENCE MODEL

Some components in the information visualization process are common to many visualization techniques, regardless the data domain. These components are present in reference models [4, 6, 13], which serve as a conceptual framework for structuring infovis applications [14]. This work is based on the reference model shown in Figure 1 [22], modified to show how each component is mapped to a web technology.

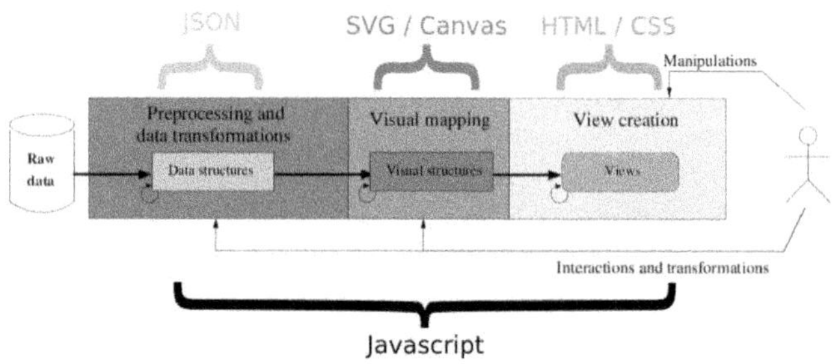

Figure 1: Adapted reference model for this work based on [22]

The process begins with the raw data. Pre-processing turns data into a JSON [8] structure. These JSON data tables can be static (stored in a file system) or dynamically returned by a data server. An advantage of this approach is that the same structured data can be used by different web applications. Data will be graphically represented as visual structures, by a process called visual mapping. Visual structures in OPENEDEYES are SVG elements (vectors), or a Canvas bitmap (HTML 5 element) [33]. Finally the views are created, which are HTML documents [33] formatted using CSS [31]. The transitions between each stage of this sequence is done by JavaScript, as the user interactions after the view creation. These interactions may not perform new requests to the server.

4. THE FRAMEWORK

Regarding its extensibility, OPENEDEYES can behave as white box or as black box. White box frameworks, or architecture driven, are those where instantiation is achieved through adding new classes. These classes should be included in the framework source code, so it requires some level of knowledge about the framework internals. On the other hand, black box frameworks, or data driven, are those that do not require much knowledge about the framework internals as instantiation is achieved through defining configuration parameters [21]. OPENEDEYES behaves as a white box framework when a developer creates a new visualizer for it and as a black box framework when a user creates a new view for some dataset using one of its visualizers. The OPENEDEYES execution flow is presented in Figure 2.

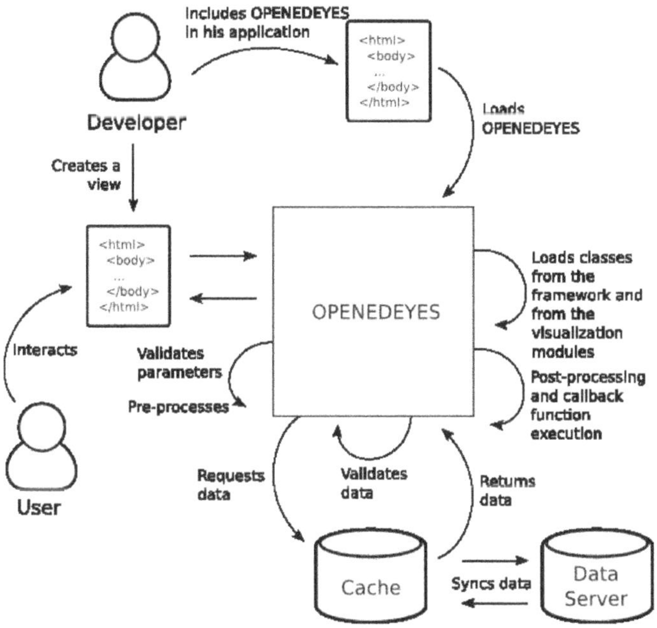

Figure 2: Global execution flow of OPENEDEYES

The developer - responsible for creating the visualization - includes OPENEDEYES in his application and defines the configuration parameters and interface controls. The user - responsible for understanding some dataset from the visualization - uses those controls to interact with the view generated by OPENEDEYES. The framework is responsible for handling the current state of visualization, current values of configuration parameters, data request and data preprocessing. Interface controls added by the developer communicate with this visualizer by message passing, calling public methods provided by OPENEDEYES. These methods allow changing configuration parameters, setting which variable is represented on each dimension, enabling and disabling dimensions, filtering the dataset, zooming in and out, and so forth.

A simplified OPENEDEYES class diagram is represented in Figure 3, hiding the methods. Five classes (wrapped in the rectangle in Figure 3) form the framework core. The other classes form the visualization modules set. This set is not limited since it includes only the visualization modules already implemented in this work as an attempt to show the expansion capabilities of the framework. A new visualization module could be implemented by creating a new class that inherits from the OpenedEyes class. The core classes are:

- Data: Manages input data. As mentioned previously, the data table for OPENEDEYES is a JSON structure, that can be returned by AJAX [12] or by JSONP [18]. The choice for JSON instead of another popular format, such as XML [32], is that JSON is lightweight (faster and cheaper to be transfered through network), easy to be read or written (can be manipulated in lots of programming languages, making it easy

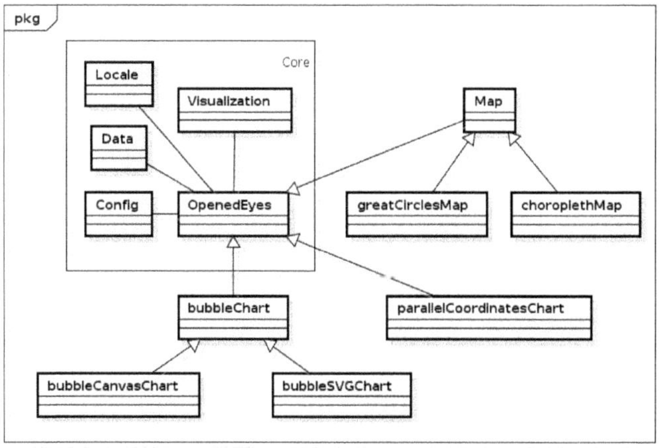

Figure 3: Simplified OPENEDEYES class diagram

to be sent by a data server), subset of JavaScript (language on which OPENEDEYES is written), among other reasons [7]. Tests also suggest that JSON requires less resources and is faster than XML [24]. XML has the advantage of being a format for universal representation of data, simple, human-readable and self-explained [24], advantages not so important as the JSON advantages, in this work.

- Visualization: Defines helper methods for visualization. Visual structures can be elements from an SVG document or part of a bitmap drawn on a Canvas element. The main differences between those two approaches is that SVG, while being actually XML, represents each scene element independently as an XML element, which allows this element to be controlled, what usually results in more smooth transactions between two states of the visualization. On the other hand, when many visual structures are present, the SVG approach can lead to performance failures, and so in this case Canvas might be a better choice. Since it's a single bitmap, it can represent complex visualizations, although it does not allow each scene element to be controlled independently, what means that any change on the visualization requires a full redrawing of the scene.

- Config: Manages configuration parameters.

- Locale: Handles translations.

- OpenedEyes: It's the main class of the framework.

The visualization modules are interactive and implement non-trivial techniques. Multiple inheritance and abstract classes are used to allow extension of the framework. For example, classes OpenedEyes, bubbleChart and Map are abstract classes, but Map and bubbleChart inherit from OpenedEyes. The Map class defines tasks that are common to many geographic visualizations, while bubbleChart calculates values for visual structures allowing its child classes to represent them in different ways. Another visualization module implemented is a variation of the parallel coordinates chart [17], proposed by this work, that consists in replacing each line for a polygon which height is proportional to the represented value. Each polygon represents a subset of the input dataset instead of a single element. The following section will show a case study that was made using these visualizers with real data.

5. CASE STUDY

As a case study for this work, it was chosen data from the database of SaferNet Brazil [3], which stores data about reports of crimes against the human rights on the Internet. The choice considered mainly the fact that this database had different data types, such as multidimensional, geographic and temporal, that are related in non-trivial ways. Then, a lot of hidden information could be revealed by using information visualization tools.

Figure 4 represents a simplified diagram of the used database (not all database). Only the used entities, relationships and attributes are represented.

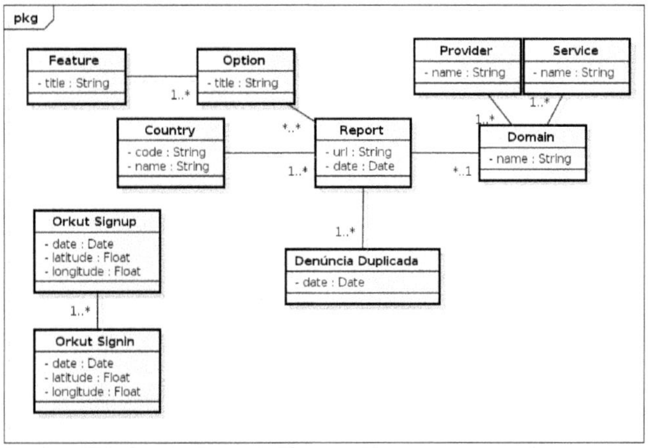

Figure 4: Database used in the case study

The report is the most important entity in the data model and represents each reported URL. Each report is associated to an Internet domain, which can be related to a provider and a service. A report has many qualifications, defined through feature options. The country where the reported website is hosted is stored. If some URL is reported twice, a new report record won't be created, instead, a duplicate report is created associated to the first one. Besides these, it was used also some geo-referenced data about an operation of Federal Police of Brazil that fought child pornography in the Orkut social network.

This dataset carried some questions. What providers were responsible for hosting the most reported content? And the ones that most removed criminal content when notified? To analyze many aspects of a report, some multidimensional visualization would be necessary. For the geo-referenced data, a geographic visualization would be probably the most intuitive way, both by region and exact location. Clarifying these questions, and following the behaviour through time (since most of this data is temporal), would help to understand the evolution of the reports and possibly predict some trends in cyber crime.

Four visualization modules were developed and each of them got as input a datafile from the above dataset. The respective results are presented in the following section.

6. RESULTS

The following subsections explain each developed visualizer and how it was used to gather information from the input dataset.

6.1 Bubble Chart: Up to four dimensions

The Bubble Chart module implements a variation of the scatter plot, where data points are replaced by bubbles that define a new dimension. In a bubble chart, each element is represented by a bubble which area is proportional to some variable from the dataset. In this implementation, each bubble has four visual properties (color, size, horizontal position and vertical position), so this chart may have from one to four dimensions (since any dimension can be disabled at any time). There are two classes,the first one uses SVG and so offers a richer experience as any modification in the chart is reflected in an animated way. The other one uses Canvas and so might be a better choice when the input dataset has lots of elements.

Each OPENEDEYES visualization module includes a default interaction interface (black box behavior), although new controls can be added (white box behavior). This default interface has four select menus where each of them defines which variable will be represented in each dimension. It's also possible to filter the dataset by clicking on some bubble, that will be removed and all the chart will be redrawn (Figure 5).

On the example on Figure 5, it's possible to verify what are the providers responsible for hosting reported content through time. Each element is an Internet service provider, like Google or Yahoo, for example. There are four attributes, that are the number of reports (plotted in y-axis), the number of distinct URLs (plotted in x-axis), the number of URLs that are still online (represented by the bubble size), and the provider name (which defines the bubble color). There is also a timeline divided by years. Figure 5 shows that in 2011, excluding reports related to Google services, Twitter (the light blue bubble) and Facebook (the dark blue bubble) were two services related to many reports.

6.2 Parallel Bars Chart: Representing n dimensions in a two-dimensional space

Parallel coordinates chart can represent, in a bi-dimensional space, n distinct dimensions of dependent attributes. Each attribute is represented by a bar, which are equally spaced and positioned parallel [17]. Parallel coordinates chart represents each element from the dataset as a line that crosses each attribute bar. The problem is that this visualization can lead to poor performance when many elements are present.

A variation of this technique, called *parallel bars* (Figure 6), is proposed in this work. Instead of representing each element as a line, each subset of elements is represented by a polygon, which height is proportional to the value at that bar, so the subset is filtered as the polygon crosses the bars. This way less lines are represented without information loss. Global analysis is possible since each line groups elements with the same characteristics.

The main difference between this visualizer and the other ones developed in this work is that this one requires the definition of not only the variables that will be plotted in each dimension, but also which are these dimensions. Each dimension is represented by a bar that is related to some attribute from the dataset. The default interface allows bars

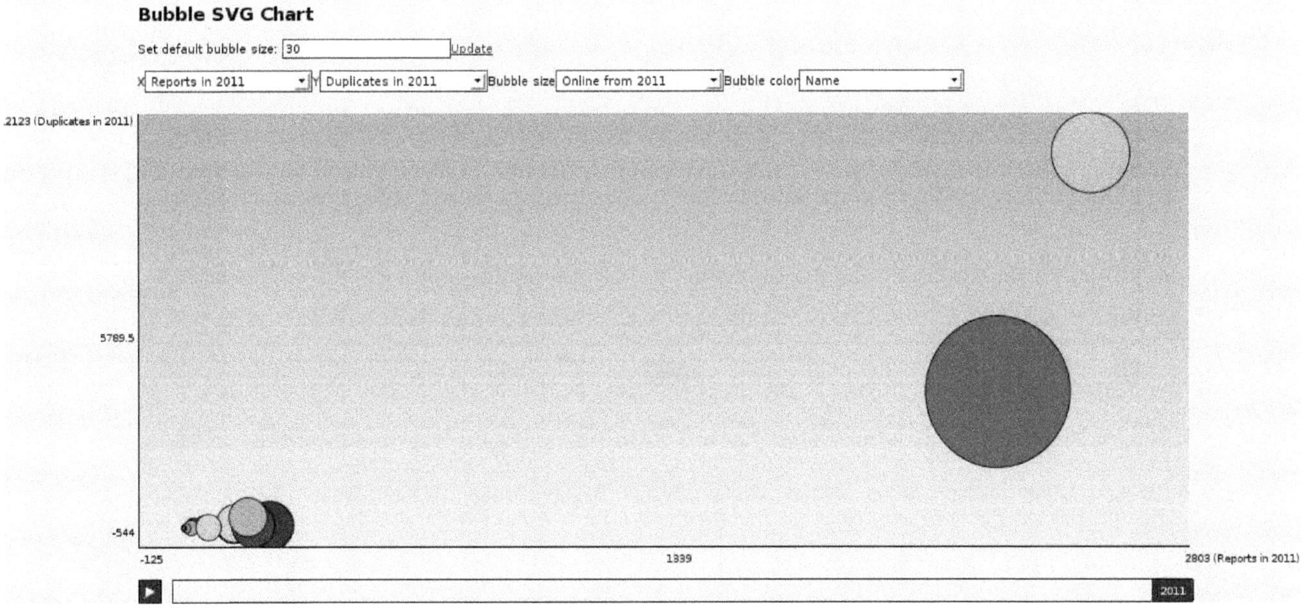

Figure 5: Reports by provider in 2011, ignoring Google

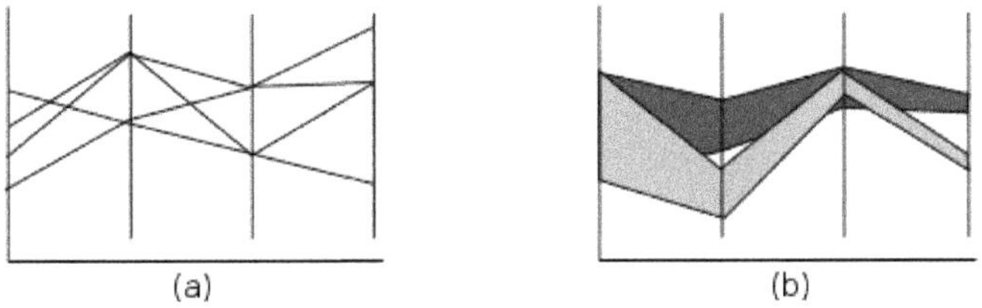

Figure 6: Main difference between the way that data is represented in (a) parallel coordinates and (b) parallel bars

to be added, removed and reordered. It also allows new polygons to be added, removed or manipulated, by just clicking on the value for some attribute. Another big difference is that Parallel Bars usually will demand new data requests. A local cache, implemented using local storage [15], is available to avoid unnecessary requests. The cache can be available even after the browser session is over, making it useful for datasets that won't change much over time.

The dataset picked to be visualized using parallel bars is formed by reports and their attributes. Figure 7 shows a parallel bars view that has seven attributes, from which three are active (the first three checked ones in the left control box). The order of the attributes in the control box is reflected in the bars order in the chart. The data shown in the chart is related to 2008, as marked in the timeline. There are four profiles of data, each one represented by a colored polygon, from which the blue one is active, what means that any interaction made directed in the chart will reflect only in this line, while interactions done through the control box will reflect in all lines.

A big dataset can be filtered as the bars are being crossed. For example, from Figure 7 it's possible to see that UOL was the Brazilian Internet service provider with most reports of cyber crimes, from which almost half of them was related to child pornography content. This view also shows the number of child pornography reports on the Internet related to other three Brazilian providers in 2008.

6.3 Choropleth Map: Shading areas in a thematic map in proportion to the measurement of a variable

Choropleth map is a conventional way to plot geographic density data [9]. This technique uses a sequence of color tones or shadows to apply over the regions. Areas with higher values get darker colors, while areas with lower values get lighter colors. In this OPENEDEYES implementation, the map regions are colored according to value of the represented numeric variable. The colored regions define a dimension of this visualization. The other dimension available is defined by bubbles over regions, which areas are proportional to the represented variable. This alternative is present because in some cases colored maps are not the best way to visualize data, since bigger regions get more attention than the smaller ones, and that can lead to misinterpretation [16].

The example on Figure 8 shows the number of reported websites hosted by countries. The United States host most of them, so it was removed from the dataset to allow other countries to be analyzed. As shown in Figure 8, in 2007 Brazil was responsible for hosting a lot of reported pages, followed by Australia. The Netherlands and the Cayman Islands are two countries that deserve attention, but using only colors is not possible to notice that, since their regions are small. This is a case where using bubbles instead of colors is a better approach, like is shown in Figure 9.

6.4 Great Circles Map: Connecting points on the surface of Earth

A great circle is a section of a sphere that contains the diameter of the sphere. The shortest path between two points in a sphere is a segment of a great circle [35]. As the Earth

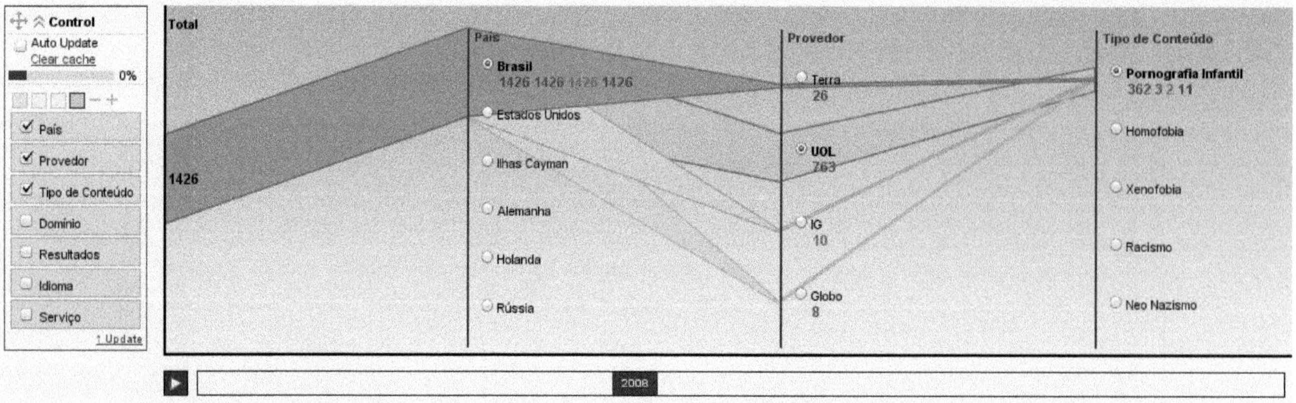

Figure 7: Brazilian providers that hosted child pornography reported content in 2008

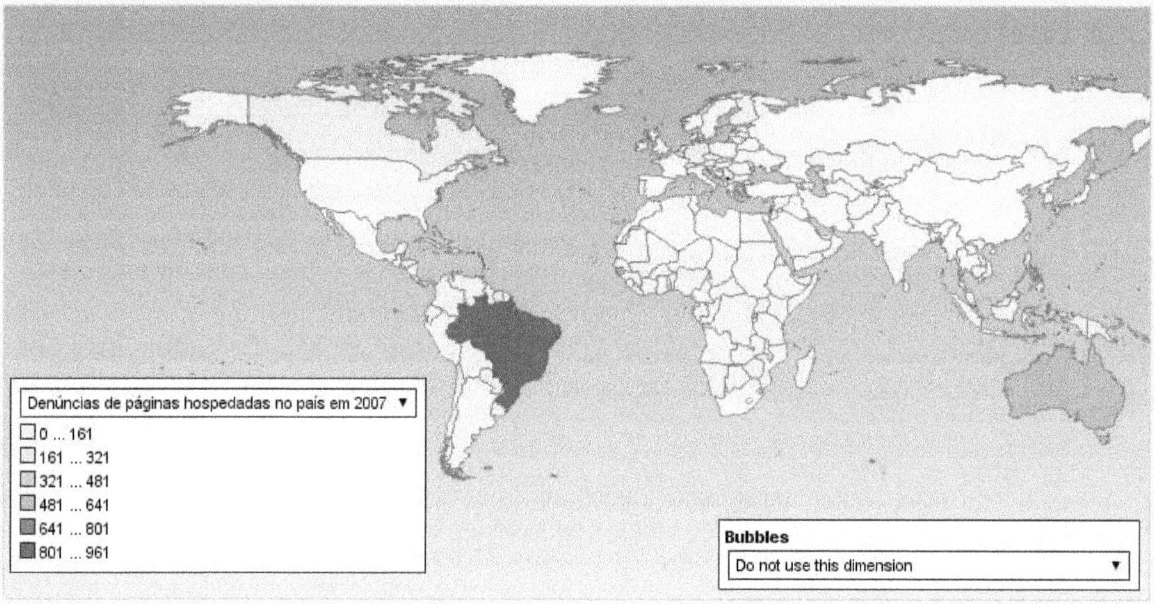

Figure 8: Countries that host most of reported content in 2007, excluding the United States

is not a perfect sphere, the shortest distance between two points is not exactly a great circle, but in this work an approximation is made and so the Earth is considered a perfect sphere, as the goal is not to measure distances, but notice relationships between points.

The example on Figure 10 shows how the Orkut child pornography offenders act. A Brazilian Federal Police operation called Turko was launched in May 2009 to search and seize computers in 103 different locations in Brazil. Data related to this operation was used to generate the map on Figure 10. The red points show the IP addresses used by the offender to create an Orkut profile to spread child sexual abuse material, and the yellow ones show the IP addresses used by the offender to access his illegal profile in Orkut. There are lines connecting the location where the profile was created to the location from where the offender accessed his account. This view shows that offenders and the victims are both located in Brazil (and also in India), despite the fact that the content was hosted in Google servers in the United States.

The empiric results obtained in this section indicates that the framework is flexible and usable, being capable of building information visualizations with different relationships, as well as implementing various visualization techniques.

7. CONCLUSION

This work presented OPENEDEYES, a web standards-based framework for information visualization on the web written in JavaScript. Its architecture is modular, defined by five core modules, responsible for common actions and basic structure, and four visualization modules, which implement advanced visualization techniques to fit distinct datasets. As a framework, its hybrid behaviour, acting sometimes as a black box framework or as a white box framework, makes it usable for developers and for users, from novice to advanced. Interaction is such an important ingredient in visualization, and so all developed visualization modules include

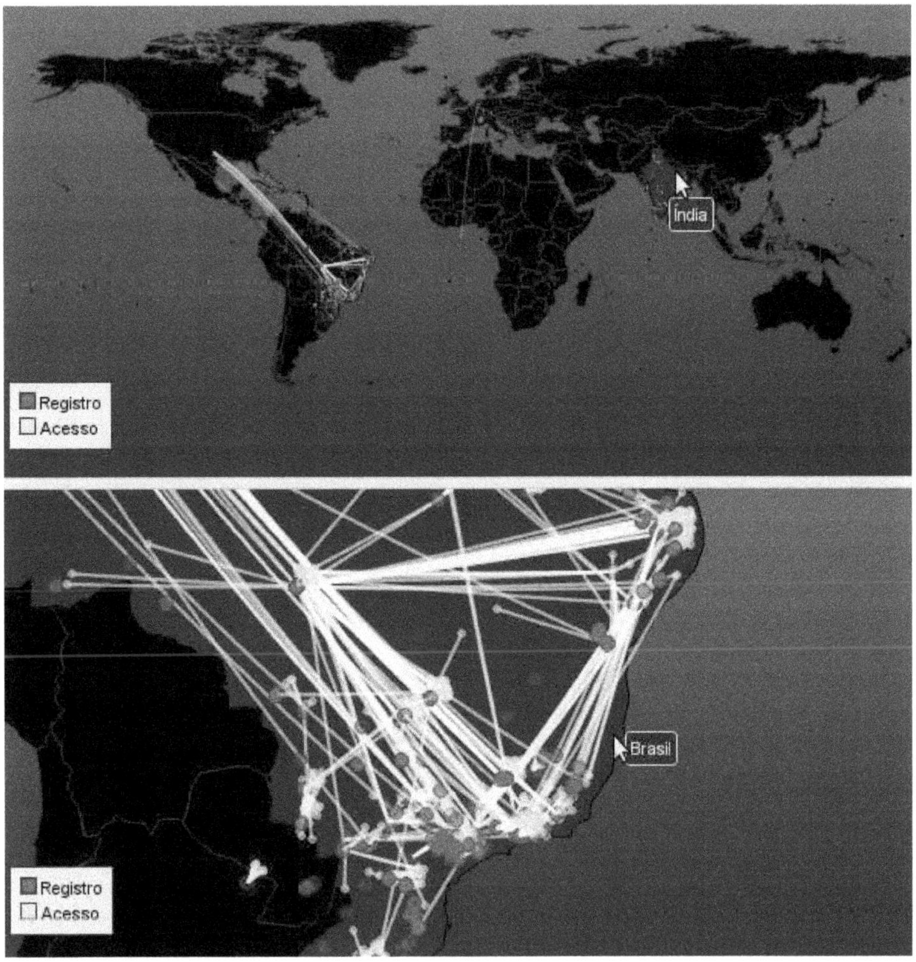

Figure 10: Great circles used to represent data about Turko operation

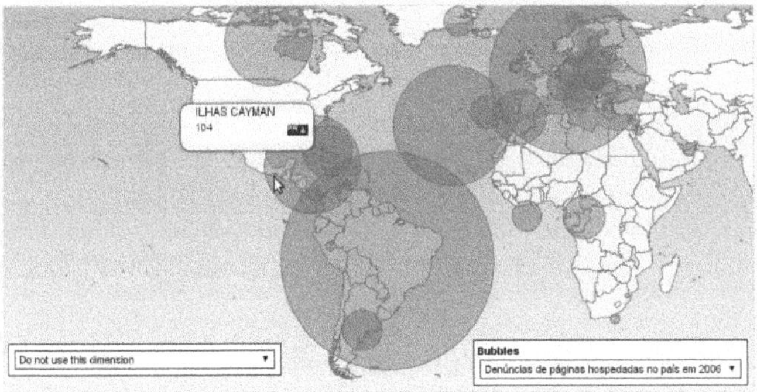

Figure 9: Cayman Islands were responsible for hosting many websites of child pornography content in 2006

a default interaction interface but also allow new controls to be added. OPENEDEYES comes to fill a gap in the visualization tools world by offering tools which are, at the same time, web based, interactive, simple but robust, and even innovative, besides providing a structure that allows new visualizers to be added. Future works include studying how this implementation scales for larger datasets, whether there are performance failures, how they can be mitigated, and evaluate the usability of the visualizers for users and developers. Future works could also try to extend OPENEDEYES by generating visualizations of real-time released data.

8. REFERENCES

[1] Adobe. Flash, 2011. URL: <http://www.adobe.com/br/products/flash.html> (last accessed December 11, 2011).

[2] D. Baranovskiy. Raphael, 2011. URL: <http://raphaeljs.com/> (last accessed December 11, 2011).

[3] S. Brasil. Quem somos, 2008. URL: <http://www.safernet.org.br/site/institucional> (last accessed December 11, 2011).

[4] S. Card, J. Mackinlay, and B. Shneiderman. *Readings in information visualization: using vision to think*. The Morgan Kaufmann series in interactive technologies. Morgan Kaufmann Publishers, 1999.

[5] S. K. Card, G. G. Robertson, and J. D. Mackinlay. The information visualizer, an information workspace. In *Proceedings of the SIGCHI conference on Human factors in computing systems: Reaching through technology*, CHI '91, pages 181–186, New York, NY, USA, 1991. ACM.

[6] E. H. Chi. A taxonomy of visualization techniques using the data state reference model. 2000.

[7] D. Crockford. JSON: The fat-free alternative to XML, 2006. URL: <http://www.json.org/fatfree.html> (last accessed December 11, 2011).

[8] D. Crockford. RFC 4627 - the application/json media type for javascript object notation (JSON), 2006. URL: <https://tools.ietf.org/html/rfc4627> (last accessed December 11, 2011).

[9] D. Cuff and M. Mattson. *Thematic maps: their design and production*. University paperbacks. Methuen, 1982.

[10] B. Fry and C. Reas. Processing: A programming handbook for visual designers and artists, 2007.

[11] FusionCharts. FusionCharts, 2011. URL: <http://www.fusioncharts.com/> (last accessed December 11, 2011).

[12] J. J. Garret. AJAX: A new approach to web applications, 2005. URL: <http://www.adaptivepath.com/publications/essays/archives/000385.php> (last accessed December 11, 2011).

[13] R. B. Haber and D. A. Mcnabb. Visualization idioms: a conceptual model for scientific visualization systems. *Visualization in Scientific Computing*, 1990.

[14] J. Heer, S. K. Card, and J. A. Landay. Prefuse: a toolkit for interactive information visualization. In *Proceedings of the SIGCHI conference on Human factors in computing systems*, CHI '05, pages 421–430, New York, NY, USA, 2005. ACM.

[15] I. Hickson. Web storage, 2011. URL: <http://dev.w3.org/html5/webstorage/> (last accessed December 11, 2011).

[16] IBM. Many Eyes: Maps, 2007. URL: <http://www-958.ibm.com/software/data/cognos/manyeyes/page/Maps.html> (last accessed December 11, 2011).

[17] A. Inselberg and B. Dimsdale. Parallel coordinates: a tool for visualizing multi-dimensional geometry. In *Proceedings of the 1st conference on Visualization '90*, VIS '90, pages 361–378, Los Alamitos, CA, USA, 1990. IEEE Computer Society Press.

[18] B. Ippolito. Remote JSON - JSONP, 2005. URL: <http://bob.pythonmac.org/archives/2005/12/05/remote-json-jsonp/> (last accessed December 11, 2011).

[19] D. A. Keim. Information visualization and visual data mining. *IEEE transactions on visualization and computer graphics*, 7(1), 2002.

[20] R. Kosara. The state of information visualization, 2011, 2011. URL: <http://eagereyes.org/blog/2011/state-of-infovis-2011> (last accessed December 11, 2011).

[21] M. E. Markiewicz and C. J. P. de Lucena. Object oriented framework development. *Crossroads*, 7:3–9, July 2001.

[22] R. Mazza. *Introduction to information visualization*. Springer, 2009.

[23] J. Nielsen. Flash: 99% bad, 2000. URL: <http://www.useit.com/alertbox/20001029.html> (last accessed December 11, 2011).

[24] N. Nurseitov, M. Paulson, R. Reynolds, and C. Izurieta. Comparison of JSON and XML data interchange formats: A case study. *Scenario*, 59715:157–162, 2009.

[25] T. W. S. Project. About the web standards project, 1998. URL: <http://www.webstandards.org/about/> (last accessed December 11, 2011).

[26] J. Resig. ProcessingJS, 2011. URL: <http://processingjs.org/> (last accessed December 11, 2011).

[27] Tableau. Tableau, 2012. URL: <http://www.tableausoftware.com> (last accessed December 11, 2011).

[28] J. J. Thomas and K. A. Cook. *Illuminating the Path: The Research and Development Agenda for Visual Analytics*. National Visualization and Analytics Ctr, 2005.

[29] TIBCO. Spotfire, 2012. URL: <http://spotfire.tibco.com/> (last accessed December 11, 2011).

[30] F. B. Viegas, M. Wattenberg, F. van Ham, J. Kriss, and M. McKeon. Many Eyes: a Site for Visualization at Internet Scale. *IEEE Transactions on Visualization and Computer Graphics*, 13:1121–1128, 2007.

[31] W3C. Cascading Style Sheets, 2011. URL: <http://www.w3.org/Style/CSS/> (last accessed December 11, 2011).

[32] W3C. Extensible Markup Language, 2011. URL: <http://www.w3.org/standards/xml/> (last accessed December 11, 2011).

[33] W3C. HTML 5, 2011. URL: <http://www.w3.org/TR/html5/> (last accessed December 11, 2011).

[34] W3C. Scalable Vector Graphics, 2011. URL: <http://www.w3.org/Graphics/SVG/> (last accessed December 11, 2011).

[35] E. Weisstein. Great circle, 2011. URL: <http://mathworld.wolfram.com/GreatCircle.html> (last accessed December 11, 2011).

Use of Information Visualization and Adaptive Hypermedia Techniques on Content Portals

Rafael Vaisset Mazariolli
Instituto de Ciência e Tecnologia - ICT, Unifesp
Rua Talim, 330 - Vila Nair
São José dos Campos/SP
rvmazariolli@unifesp.br

Ezequiel Roberto Zorzal
Instituto de Ciência e Tecnologia - ICT, Unifesp
Rua Talim, 330 - Vila Nair
São José dos Campos/SP
ezorzal@unifesp.br

ABSTRACT

This paper applies Information Visualization and Adaptive Hypermedia techniques to the development of a computational tool to adjust elements of hypermedia, based on the user profile.

Categories and Subject Descriptors

H.5.2 [**User Interfaces**]: [Ergonomics]; H.5.4 [**Hypertext/ Hypermedia**]: [Navigation]

General Terms

Human Factors

Keywords

Visualização de Informação, Hipermídia Adaptativa, portais de conteúdo

1. INTRODUÇÃO

Vários trabalhos [2, 4, 9, 3, 10, 12] podem ser encontrados com o objetivo de melhorar a usabilidade nos sítios eletrônicos por meio de adaptações de acordo com a expectativa, necessidade, preferência ou desejo do usuário. Porém, é difícil adaptar um sítio que não esteja preparado para isso. Em outras palavras, os usuários tornam-se dependentes da arquitetura do sítio e são tratados de maneira uniforme.

Visando aprimorar a experiência dos usuários com um número maior de sítios hospedados na Internet e aumentar a abrangência dos conteúdos neles contidos, propõe-se neste trabalho uma ferramenta de adaptação dos elementos de hipermídia utilizando técnicas de Hipermídia Adaptativa e Visualização da Informação.

Esta ferramenta propõe analisar o comportamento dos usuários nos sítios e extrair informações de navegação, que serão utilizadas para elaborar um modelo de preferências deste usuário. Este modelo será posteriormente aplicado aos sítios que o usuário visitar, tornando mais fácil a visualização das informações consideradas mais relevantes, além de possibilitar a inclusão de novas informações relacionadas, ampliando o conhecimento oferecido.

Este trabalho está organizado em quatro seções, a partir da introdução. A Seção 2 descreve uma breve análise dos portais de conteúdo. A Seção 3 define algumas estratégias para implementação da ferramenta, bem como a descrição da mesma. A Seção 4 descreve os testes realizados na ferramenta desenvolvida e apresenta as suas limitações. Por fim, a Seção 5 descreve as conclusões e trabalhos futuros.

Permission to make digital or hard copies of all or part of this work for personal or classroom use is granted without fee provided that copies are not made or distributed for profit or commercial advantage and that copies bear this notice and the full citation on the first page. To copy otherwise, to republish, to post on servers or to redistribute to lists, requires prior specific permission and/or a fee.
WebMedia'12, October 15–18, 2012, São Paulo/SP, Brazil.
Copyright 2012 ACM 978-1-4503-1706-1/12/10 ...$15.00.

2. PORTAIS DE CONTEÚDO

No Brasil, existem diversos portais de conteúdo disponíveis aos usuários e, segundo o serviço de análise de tráfego Alexa [1], os três portais mais acessados no país nos meses de outubro e novembro de 2011, em ordem, foram: Universo Online (UOL); Globo.com (inclusive G1) e Terra.

Baseando-se nesta pesquisa, optou-se por analisar estes três portais, devido à grande quantidade de acessos. Neste grupo também foi incluído o portal G1, já que este faz parte das estatísticas apresentadas para o portal Globo.com.

Observou-se que cada portal de conteúdo é construído de uma maneira, com seções, diagramação e conteúdo distintos, e alguns deles buscam atingir públicos mais específicos enquanto outros procuram atentar a todos. No entanto, após estudos e observação, podem-se definir algumas características comuns à maioria dos portais de conteúdo mais acessados na Internet brasileira, divididas entre àquelas referentes aos *links* presentes nos portais de conteúdo (organização em seções, título do conteúdo e data da notícia anexada ao *link*) e as que se referem à organização destes dentro do ambiente do portal (divisão de áreas e destaques na formatação do conteúdo).

3. DETALHES DE IMPLEMENTAÇÃO

3.1 Acompanhamento da navegação

Durante a navegação do usuário pelas páginas do portal de conteúdo, algumas informações serão coletadas, analisadas e armazenadas a fim de construir e atualizar um modelo para aquele usuário. Este modelo conterá as informações referentes às suas preferências e servirá de base na adaptação do conteúdo oferecido.

A captura destes dados de navegação ocorrerá de duas formas, em dois momentos distintos, e as informações coletadas serão utilizadas na adaptação do conteúdo obtido diretamente no portal de conteúdo, como descrito nas etapas a seguir:

1. O usuário acessa o portal de conteúdo desejado por meio do sistema de adaptação de navegação, que atuará como um servidor *proxy*, fazendo o intermédio entre o cliente e o servidor no qual o portal está armazenado. A cada clique dado, informações serão enviadas para o servidor do sistema de adaptação;

2. As informações recebidas pelo servidor do sistema de adaptação servem para atualizar o modelo do usuário, durante o processo de pré-captura;

3. O conteúdo solicitado pelo usuário é obtido no servidor do portal de conteúdo navegado;

4. Os dados recebidos do portal de conteúdo são analisados e, com base no modelo do usuário, adaptados;

5. As novas informações obtidas após a requisição do conteúdo ao portal servem para atualizar o modelo do usuário, durante o processo de pós-captura;

6. O conteúdo adaptado é devolvido ao usuário, que continua normalmente a navegação.

3.2 Atualização do modelo do usuário

Para a ferramenta desenvolvida, no primeiro acesso do usuário, optou-se a utilização de valores padronizados para enquadrar o usuário em um determinado grupo genérico, o que conservava as características originais dos portais de conteúdo. Após o primeiro acesso, a aplicação realiza técnicas passivas [18], onde o modelo do usuário é atualizado baseando-se na conclusão de observações do comportamento, como as páginas visitadas ou na análise do histórico do usuário.

A atualização do modelo do usuário pode ocorrer de forma automática, sempre que o usuário encerrar a aplicação, ou de forma manual, a partir da solicitação do usuário, por meio do sistema. Optou-se por utilizar as técnicas implícitas, as quais se baseiam na observação do comportamento do usuário independente de seu consentimento. Fez uso de técnicas plausíveis que requerem a representação explicita da incerteza e necessita de mecanismos para manter a consistência no modelo do usuário. A manipulação dessas incertezas foi gerenciada utilizando um classificador estatístico bayesiano [7].

3.3 Técnicas e métodos de adaptação

Neste trabalho foram aplicados alguns dos métodos e técnicas de Hipermídia Adaptativa descritos nos trabalhos de Brusilovsky [6] e Koch [15], a saber: (i) Conteúdo ou explicação adicional: este método de adaptação de conteúdo é utilizado para ocultar conteúdos que não são classificados como interessantes para o usuário, de acordo com seu modelo; (ii) Ocultação Adaptativa de *Links*: esta é uma técnica de adaptação de navegação que visa facilitar as escolhas do usuário durante o uso do portal. Ela é utilizada para ocultar os *links* que não levam a conteúdos classificados como interessantes, de acordo com o modelo do usuário; (iii) Anotação Adaptativa de *Links*: esta também é uma técnica de adaptação de navegação, que é utilizada para inserir textos e indicadores visuais aos *links*, com o intuito de ilustrar para o usuário o conteúdo que ele pode chegar se seguir aquele caminho; (iv) Variações de *Layout*: este método de adaptação da apresentação é utilizado para destacar conteúdos relevantes ao usuário, alterando sua cor, tamanho ou forma.

3.4 Técnicas de visualização

A partir das técnicas de Visualização da Informação definidas por Keim [14], com o intuito de facilitar a extração de conhecimento pelo usuário, foram utilizadas técnicas 2D/3D padrão, técnicas baseadas em ícone e técnicas baseadas em hierarquia.

As ténicas 2D/3D padrão foram apresentadas a partir de gráficos de barras e pizza para indicar a quantidade de acessos por categoria, preferências e tendências dos usuários, entre outros.

Utilizou-se representações baseadas em Faces de Chernoff [8] (ténica baseada em ícones) para determinar a categoria e a correspondência do conteúdo ao modelo do usuário, através de indicadores visuais com cores e tamanhos específicos.

Implementou-se um TreeMap [13](técnica baseada em hierarquia) para mostrar as categorias de conteúdo mais visitadas pelo usuário, agrupando os *links* pertencentes à elas dentro do seu devido espaço reservado. No caso do TreeMap, é utilizada ainda a técnica de interação de *zoom* Interativo, que detalha os *links* pertencentes a uma categoria, se for o caso. Assim, o usuário poderá visualizar de forma mais específica quais conteúdos daquela categoria estão presentes na página visitada.

3.5 Descrição do sistema

O acesso ao sistema desenvolvido neste trabalho se dá por meio do uso das credenciais de acesso do serviço de *microblog* Twitter [17], onde o usuário deverá possuir uma conta previamente criada.

A comunicação com o serviço autenticador ocorre por meio do protocolo de autenticação OAuth (*Open Authorization*), que permite que o usuário delegue acesso ao sistema sem a necessidade de criar uma nova conta ou redigitar a sua senha.

Esta forma de acesso foi utilizada para simplificar o processo de registro do usuário a fim de diminuir a dificuldade de uso do sistema, e uma vez que o número de pessoas que possuem conta no serviço supracitado é bastante alto, fazer o *login* no sistema desenvolvido neste trabalho se torna uma tarefa simples.

Uma vez conectado ao sistema, o usuário tem acesso à sua interface, que foi planejada para ser simples e fácil de ser utilizada. Dado que o objetivo deste trabalho é melhorar a usabilidade nos portais de conteúdo selecionados, o maior espaço na tela foi reservado para disponibilizar este conteúdo adaptado. Os botões e menus de ação relativos exclusivamente ao sistema ficam alocados em uma barra de ferramentas localizada na parte superior da tela, conforme apresentado na Figura 1.

Figura 1: Portal G1 (g1.globo.com) adaptado pela ferramenta desenvolvida.

A partir da barra de ferramentas, o usuário pode ativar o

uso das Faces de Chernoff como técnica de visualização aplicada aos *links* do portal visitado. As faces indicam a correspondência do conteúdo apontado por aquele *link* em relação ao perfil do usuário. Durante a navegação, o usuário poderá passar o mouse sobre qualquer *link* presente no portal de conteúdo visitado e uma pequena janela será aberta contendo *links* relacionados, obtidos através do serviço Google Notícias [11]. Nesta mesma janela, para cada *link*, é apresentada uma imagem (Face de Chernoff) que simboliza à sua correspondência ao perfil do usuário.

Outra possibilidade, a partir das opções da barra de ferramentas, é utilizar o Treemap representando as categorias de conteúdo definidas pelo usuário, onde os *links* presentes na página visitada aparecem classificados em suas respectivas categorias, quando aplicável. Cada categoria recebe uma cor aleatoriamente, e o tamanho ocupado por cada uma delas corresponde o quanto a categoria é significativa em relação ao perfil do usuário.

Dentre as opções da barra de ferramentas, o usuário ainda pode administrar as categorias e palavras-chave utilizadas para classificação do conteúdo navegado. Esta seção também permite que o usuário: redefina as suas configurações, revertendo-as para as configurações fornecidas inicialmente; atualize o seu perfil de acordo com as informações de navegação, e; verifique, através de um gráfico, a quantidade de *links* visitados de cada categoria.

Além da barra de ferramentas, outro componente da interface é a lista de *links* (nuvem de *links*), presente no lado direito da tela. Nela são mostrados, em ordem decrescente de relevância, os *links* presentes na página visitada, a fim de simplificar a exibição do conteúdo ao usuário. O tamanho de cada *link* também é alterado (aumentado ou diminuído), de acordo com o peso atribuído a ele durante as etapas de adaptação realizadas pelo sistema.

A Figura 2 apresenta um exemplo o portal Globo.com antes e depois de sofrer adaptação utilizando a ferramenta desenvolvida. Nesta simulação executada, o usuário possuía um perfil indicando forte preferência à categoria esportiva. A segunda categoria de conteúdo de preferência do usuário era referente às notícias do Brasil e a terceira às notícias relacionadas sobre economia, o que justifica o destaque dos outros *links* não relacionados a esportes.

(a) (b)

Figura 2: Portal Globo.com antes (a) e depois (b) de sofrer adaptação.

4. TESTES E RESULTADOS

Para se verificar o desempenho da ferramenta, foram executados testes de carregamento dos portais de conteúdo com e sem a sua utilização. Estes testes foram realizados sob as mesmas condições de rede e recursos de máquina.

Com base nas informações obtidas, foi possível observar que o tempo de carregamento das páginas utilizando a ferramenta de adaptação foi de cerca de 3,5 a 5,5 vezes o tempo de carregamento normal da página. Este aumento ocorreu proporcionalmente ao tempo de carregamento normal da página e principalmente à quantidade de *links* presente nela, já que todos os *links* da página passam por uma análise antes de sua exibição, e este processo consome um tempo significativo.

Além disso, devido às técnicas de programação aplicadas para a realização das etapas de adaptação, a análise da página só começa a ocorrer depois do carregamento completo do seu conteúdo, o que faz com que o tempo entre o clique do usuário no *link* e o início da renderização da página aumente, já que ela é carregada primeiramente no servidor da aplicação, analisada, adaptada e posteriormente devolvida ao navegador do usuário.

Para verificar se a ferramenta desenvolvida cumpriu o objetivo de melhorar a usabilidade dos portais de conteúdo, foi escolhido o teste de usabilidade SUS (*System Usability Scale*) [5]. Este teste apresenta bons resultados de fidelidade mesmo em amostras de pequena dimensão [16].

Antes da realização dos experimentos, os usuários foram orientados a se conectarem ao servidor da aplicação e a navegarem nos portais de conteúdo livremente, preferencialmente em mais de um dos portais. Somente após este contato com o sistema que os usuários foram instruídos a realizar os testes de usabilidade.

Neste estudo, participaram quatro usuários com idades entre 21 e 52 anos, sendo que todos consideravam-se experientes na utilização de um navegador para acessar informações de portais de conteúdo.

Todos os usuários que interagiram com a aplicação responderam o questionário sobre escala do SUS, e a média obtida nas pesquisas realizadas com os usuários para esta escala foi de 85%. Este resultado pode ser considerado satisfatório, uma vez que a pontuação da escala do SUS considera o valor 0 (zero) como o valor mais baixo para o nível de usabilidade e 100 (cem) como o valor mais alto.

A principal limitação da ferramenta desenvolvida neste trabalho foi o seu desempenho, que tornou a navegação entre as páginas dos portais de conteúdo significativamente lenta. Isso ocorreu devido ao novo processo de obtenção do conteúdo dos *links* visitados, devido ao aumento da quantidade de requisições, processamentos e respostas.

5. CONCLUSÕES E TRABALHOS FUTUROS

Neste trabalho foi possível desenvolver uma ferramenta que, aplicando os métodos e técnicas das áreas de Visualização de Informações e Hipermídia Adaptativa, conseguiu atingir o objetivo de melhorar a usabilidade em portais de conteúdo disponíveis na Internet. Os *links* mais compatíveis com o perfil do usuário ficaram mais fáceis de ser encontrados dentre todos os oferecidos, e o próximo passo a ser seguido na navegação tornou-se mais relevante.

Além disso, foi possível visualizar de forma concisa informações que demonstravam as preferências do usuário dentre as diversas categorias de conteúdo cadastradas, o que facilitou a análise do seu perfil.

Para isso, no entanto, um poder computacional maior foi necessário, tornando a troca de páginas mais lenta do que normalmente, sendo este o principal fator de influência negativa nos resultados dos testes executados. Espera-se, no futuro, pesquisar e desenvolver formas de reduzir esta dificuldade, de maneira que a navegação com o uso da ferramenta de adaptação se torne tão rápida quanto à navegação comum, porém com uma usabilidade maior.

Mesmo assim, os resultados obtidos em testes executados com usuários reais foram positivos, e mostraram uma melhora na utilização e navegação entre os conteúdos dos portais selecionados neste trabalho.

Como trabalhos futuros, pretende-se realizar a classificação automática de palavras-chave em categorias por meio de técnicas de Inteligência Artificial, melhorar o desempenho da ferramenta, aplicar outras técnicas de Visualização de Informação, criar outras formas de acesso à ferramenta e executar testes mais abrangentes, com o intuito de verificar novas possibilidades de aplicação de técnicas de adaptação visando facilitar a navegação do usuário pelos portais de conteúdo.

6. REFERÊNCIAS

[1] Alexa. top sites in brazil, 2011.disponível em http://www.alexa.com/topsites/countries/br (acessado em 23/11/2011).

[2] Aquino, m.s. et al. 2005. vepersonal: an infrastructure of virtual reality components to generate web adaptive environments. in proceedings of the 11th brazilian symposium on multimedia and the web (webmedia '05), renata pontin m. fortes (ed.). acm, new york, ny, usa, 1-8.

[3] Arora, k. and kant, k. 2012. techniques for adaptive websites and web personalization without any user effort. conference on electrical, electronics and computer science (sceecs), 2012 ieee students'. bhopal, in, 1- 4.

[4] Azevedo, r.g.a, et al. 2009. an approach for textual authoring of hypermedia documents based on the use of programmatic visualization and hypertextual navigation. in proceedings of the xv brazilian symposium on multimedia and the web (webmedia '09). acm, new york, ny, usa, , article 18 , 8 pages.

[5] Brooke, j., 1996. sus: A quick and dirty usability scale. in jordan, p.w. weerdmeester,b. thomas,a. and mclelland,i.l. editors, usability evaluation in industry. taylor and francis, london.

[6] Brusilovksy, p. 1996. methods and techniques of adaptive hypermedia. user modeling and user- adapted interaction. special issue on adaptive hypertext and hypermedia, dordrecht, v. 6.

[7] Cheeseman, p. et al, 1988. bayesian classication. in seventh national conference on articial intelligence, pages 607-611, saint paul, minnesota.

[8] Chernoff, h. 1973. the use of faces to represent points in k-dimensional space graphically. journal of the american statistica association 68(342): 361 - 368. conklin, j. 1987. hypertext: A survey and introduction. ieee computer 20, (9). 17-42.

[9] dos santos, j.a.f and saade, d.c.m. 2010. xtemplate 3.0: adding semantics to hypermedia compositions and providing document structure reuse. in proceedings of the 2010 acm symposium on applied computing (sac '10). acm, new york, ny, usa, 1892-1897.

[10] Fitchett, s. and cockburn, a. 2012. accessrank: predicting what users will do next. in proceedings of the 2012 acm annual conference on human factors in computing systems (chi '12). acm, new york, ny, usa, 2239-2242.

[11] Google, google notícias. 2011. disponível em http://news.google.com.br/ (acessado em 08/10/2011).

[12] Hu, c. et al., 2012. an adaptive recommendation system in social media. conference on system science (hicss), 45th hawaii international, maui, hi, 1759-1767.

[13] Johnson, b.; shneiderman, b. 1991. treemaps: A space-filling approach to the visualization of hierarchical information structures. ieee information visualization 91.

[14] Keim, d. a. 2002. information visualization and visual data mining. ieee transactions on visualization and computer graphics 8(1):1-8.

[15] Koch, n. 2000, software engineering for adaptive hypermedia systems: Reference model, modeling techniques and development process. phd thesis, ludwig-maximilians-university of munich, germany.

[16] Tullis, t. s.; stetson, j. n. 2004. a comparison of questionnaires for assessing website usability. usability professionals' association.

[17] Twitter. serviço de microblog twitter. 2011. disponível em http://www.twitter.com/ (acessado em 20/11/2011).

[18] Wu, h., et al, 2000. supporting user adaptation in adaptive hypermedia applications, proceedings infwet2000. rotterdam, the netherlands.

Performance of the Objective Video Quality Metrics with Perceptual Weighting Considering First and Second Order Differential Operators

Carlos D. M. Regis
Federal Institute of Education, Science and Technology of Paraíba – Campus Campina Grande
Institute for Advanced Studies in Communications – Iecom
Campina Grande, Brazil

José V. M. Cardoso
Federal University of Campina Grande – UFCG
Institute for Advanced Studies in Communications – Iecom
Campina Grande, Brazil

Ítalo P. Oliveira
Federal Institute of Education, Science and Technology of Paraíba – Campus Campina Grande
Campina Grande, Brazil

Marcelo S. Alencar
Federal University of Campina Grande – UFCG
Institute for Advanced Studies in Communications – Iecom
Campina Grande, Brazil

ABSTRACT

Objective video quality assessment is important to validate the performance of applications in video communications systems. The research on visual attention and gradient-inspired metrics improves the performance of the video quality evaluation. This paper investigates the use of first and second order differential operators as visual attention estimators. The edge information, computed by differential operators, is an important factor of visual attention. The performance of the proposed models are compared with the objective metrics, PSNR, SSIM and GSSIM, by means of the Pearson correlation coefficient, considering the blurring, blocking, salt and pepper and Gaussian noise distortions. The results suggest that for blurring, blocking and salt and pepper, the combination of objective metrics with first order operators provides a significant improvement, especially for the Sobel operator.

Categories and Subject Descriptors

D.2.8 [**Software Engineering**]: Metric

General Terms

Algorithms, Measurement.

Permission to make digital or hard copies of all or part of this work for personal or classroom use is granted without fee provided that copies are not made or distributed for profit or commercial advantage and that copies bear this notice and the full citation on the first page. To copy otherwise, to republish, to post on servers or to redistribute to lists, requires prior specific permission and/or a fee.
WebMedia'12, October 15–18, 2012, São Paulo/SP, Brazil.
Copyright 2012 ACM 978-1-4503-1706-1/12/10 ...$15.00.

Keywords

Video Quality Assessment, Differential Operators, Structural Similarity, Human Visual System

1. INTRODUCTION

Video quality assessment (VQA) is an important process to validate communications systems which provide video services, including video on demand, video streaming, IPTV and Web TV. Subjective and objective methodologies are used to evaluate the video quality. The subjective methods use psycho-visual experiments with end-users, which evaluate the video quality according to personal criteria. Although this is the correct approach to assess the video quality [9], it is resource intensive, expensive and time-consuming, and it is impractical for real-time video quality assessment.

The objective metrics, on the other hand, evaluate the video quality by means of algorithms, which permits to obtain the results rapidly, and it is ideal for real time applications. Classical objective metrics such as MSE (Mean Squared Error) and PSNR (Peak Signal-to-Noise Ratio) present an unsatisfactory correlation with the subjective perception of quality, undermining the confidence on the results, because they do not incorporate features of the human visual system (HVS).

In 2004, Wang *et al* [9] proposed the Structural SIMilarity (SSIM) to image quality assessment, based on the assumption that the HVS is highly adapted to recognize structural information in the visual environment and, therefore, the change in this structural information would provide a good improvement in the approximation of the quality perceived by the HVS.

A great deal of effort has been put on the design and improvement of image and video quality metrics. Gu *et al* [3]

proposed a novel structural similarity index using adaptive weights with gradient vectors (first order derivative) to measure the image quality considering the following characteristics: edge, smooth and texture. Chen *et al* [2] present a gradient-based structural similarity (GSSIM) based on the assumption that the edge and contour information are the most sensitive features for the human visual system (HVS).

Regis *et al* [8] proposes a technique called Perceptual Weighting (PW), which introduces the local Spatial Perceptual Information (SI) as a visual attention estimator using the SSIM, since experiments indicate that the quality perceived by HVS is more sensitive in areas of intense visual attention [6]. The SI is basically computed by the Sobel differential operator, which estimates the magnitude of the gradient vectors of the video.

This paper presents a comparative study between first and second order differential operators, used to estimate the visual attention, applied into objective video quality metrics SSIM and GSSIM, with the PW technique. The remainder of this paper is organized as follows. Section 2 presents the SSIM. Section 3 describes the proposed methods. Section 4 describes the performed subjective experiment. Section 5 presents the simulation results and their impact and Section 6 presents the conclusions.

2. STRUCTURAL SIMILARITY INDEX REVIEW

Let $f = \{f_i \mid i = 1, 2, 3, \ldots, P\}$ be the original video and $h = \{h_i \mid i = 1, 2, 3, \ldots, P\}$ be the processed video. The SSIM is computed as the set of three measures over the luminance plane: luminance comparison $l(f, h)$, the contrast comparison $c(f, h)$ and the structural comparison $s(f, h)$,

$$l = \frac{2\mu_f\mu_h + C_1}{\mu_f^2 + \mu_h^2 + C_1},\ c = \frac{2\sigma_f\sigma_h + C_2}{\sigma_f^2 + \sigma_h^2 + C_2},\ s = \frac{\sigma_{fh} + C_3}{\sigma_f\sigma_h + C_3}, \quad (1)$$

in which μ is the average, σ is the standard deviation, σ_{fh} is the covariance, $C_1 = (0.01 \cdot 255)^2$, $C_2 = 2 \cdot C_3$ and $C_3 = (0.03 \cdot 255)^2$.

The structural similarity index is described as

$$\text{SSIM}(f, h) = [l(f, h)]^\alpha \cdot [c(f, h)]^\beta \cdot [s(f, h)]^\gamma, \quad (2)$$

in which almost always $\alpha = \beta = \gamma = 1$.

In practice the SSIM is computed for an 8×8 sliding squared window or for an 11×11 Gaussian-circular window. The first approach is used in this paper. Then, for two videos which are subdivided into D blocks, the SSIM is computed as

$$\text{SSIM}(f, h) = \frac{1}{D}\sum_{j=1}^{D} \text{SSIM}(f_j, h_j). \quad (3)$$

3. DIFFERENTIAL OPERATORS APPLIED INTO VQA ALGORITHMS

Let $\mathcal{T} = \{\tau_i \mid \tau_i \in \mathbb{Z}\ [0, 255]$ and $i = 0, 1, 2, \ldots, P\}$ be a video signal with 2^8 luminance levels. The gradient vector of $\mathcal{T}$ ($\nabla\mathcal{T}$) estimate the rate of change of luminance of the pixels along the horizontal and vertical directions. Its magnitude is computed as

$$|\nabla\mathcal{T}| = \left[\left(\frac{\partial\mathcal{T}}{\partial x}\right)^2 + \left(\frac{\partial\mathcal{T}}{\partial y}\right)^2\right]^{1/2}, \quad (4)$$

in which x and y represent the horizontal and vertical directions, respectively.

Digitally, the magnitude of the gradient is computed as

$$|\nabla\mathcal{T}| = [(\mathbf{O}_1 * \mathcal{T})^2 + (\mathbf{O}_2 * \mathcal{T})^2]^{1/2}, \quad (5)$$

in which $*$ denotes the linear filtering operation and the pair of matrices ($\mathbf{O}_1$,$\mathbf{O}_2$) is called differential operator. The first order differential operators considered in this work are: Sobel (6), Prewitt (7) and Robert-cross (8). Their matrices are respectively:

$$\begin{bmatrix} -1 & 0 & +1 \\ -2 & 0 & +2 \\ -1 & 0 & +1 \end{bmatrix}, \begin{bmatrix} -1 & -2 & -1 \\ 0 & 0 & 0 \\ +1 & +2 & +1 \end{bmatrix}; \quad (6)$$

$$\begin{bmatrix} -1 & 0 & +1 \\ -1 & 0 & +1 \\ -1 & 0 & +1 \end{bmatrix}, \begin{bmatrix} -1 & -1 & -1 \\ 0 & 0 & 0 \\ +1 & +1 & +1 \end{bmatrix}; \quad (7)$$

$$\begin{bmatrix} +1 & 0 \\ 0 & -1 \end{bmatrix}, \begin{bmatrix} 0 & +1 \\ -1 & 0 \end{bmatrix}. \quad (8)$$

For the Sobel and Prewitt operators the rate of change of luminance is calculated in a coordinate system with 0 and $\frac{\pi}{2}$ rad as orthogonal directions. For the Robert-cross operator, the angle of the coordinate system is rotated in $\frac{\pi}{4}$ rad [5].

The magnitude of the second order differential operator (Laplacian) is defined as [5]

$$|\nabla^2\mathcal{T}| = \left[\left(\frac{\partial^2\mathcal{T}}{\partial x}\right)^2 + \left(\frac{\partial^2\mathcal{T}}{\partial y}\right)^2\right]^{1/2}. \quad (9)$$

In image processing, the Laplacian is an isotropic operator, i.e., its value is independent of the direction of the edge. Its matrix of convolution is

$$\begin{bmatrix} 0 & +1 & 0 \\ +1 & -4 & +1 \\ 0 & +1 & 0 \end{bmatrix}. \quad (10)$$

The gradient and the Laplacian are applied to highlight the edges of the objects, i.e., zones of transition of pixel luminance. While the high magnitude of the gradients means the presence of edges, the Laplacian creates zero-crossing to indicate the existence of edges [7], i.e., when the first derivative is at a maximum, the second derivative is zero [5], as shown in Figure 1.

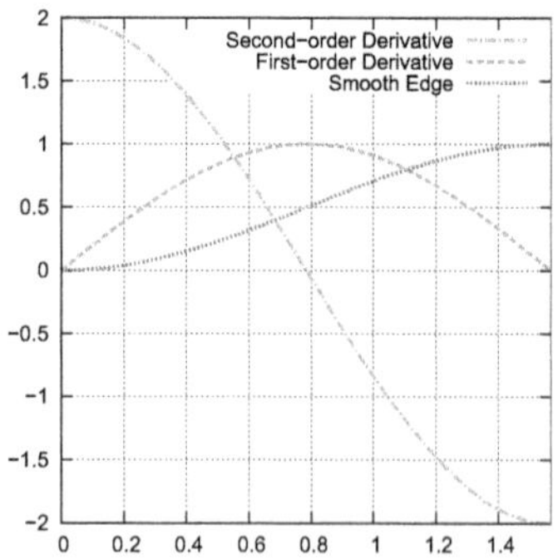

Figure 1: First and second order derivative to identify edge information.

Results of researches in perceptual vision indicated that the HVS has a different weight to sense the regions as edges, texture and smooth, i.e., these regions are structurally more important in vision environment [3], [2].

In many gradient-based image and video quality metrics, the Sobel operators are used to estimate the edge information and to identify higher visual interest regions. In the algorithm proposed by [3], the Sobel operators are used to classify the pixels in four regions: strong edge, weak edge, texture and smooth. From this division, adaptive weights are assigned to each region, intending thereby to obtain a weighted structural similarity index.

Similarly, the algorithm present in [2], called Gradient-based Structural Similarity Index (GSSIM), used the Sobel operator, and it computed as

$$\text{GSSIM}(f_j, h_j) = [l(f_j, h_j)]^{\alpha} \cdot [c_g(f_j, h_j)]^{\beta} \cdot [s_g(f_j, h_j)]^{\gamma}, \quad (11)$$

$$\text{GSSIM}(f, h) = \frac{1}{D}\sum_{j=1}^{D} \text{GSSIM}(f_j, h_j), \quad (12)$$

in which $c_g(f_j, h_j)$ and $s_g(f_j, h_j)$ are the contrast and structure comparisons calculated over the gradient vectors map from the Equation 1.

The weight (w_j) is defined to to evaluate the PW technique, with first and second order differential operators, for each squared region in the frame,

$$w_j = \left(\frac{1}{n-1}\sum_{i=1}^{n}(\nabla f_i - \mu_{f'})^2\right)^{\frac{1}{2}}, \quad (13)$$

in which $\mu_{f'}$ represent the average magnitude of the gradient vectors and n is a total of gradient vectors in j-th block. For the case that the frames are partitioned uniformly in squares 8×8, $n = 64$. For the case of the Laplacian, w_j is computed with ∇^2.

To merge the weight w_j with the considered metrics a similar approach to that used in the works of Akamine and Farias [1], Liu and Heynderickx [6] was used. It is necessary to compute a weighted average for the VQA algorithms, in which the weighting coefficients are the w_j, i.e.

$$\text{M-PW-VQA} = \frac{\sum_{j=1}^{D} \text{VQA}(f_j, h_j) \cdot w_j}{\sum_{j=1}^{D} w_j}, \quad (14)$$

in which the M = {S, R, P, L} is denoted according the used differential operator, to compute w_j, as: S (Sobel), R (Roberts), P (Prewitt) and L (Laplace); and likewise for VQA = {SSIM, GSSIM}.

4. VALIDATION PROCESS

To validate and compare the presented approach, a subjective evaluation was performed, in which real-users watched video sequences and assigned a score, according with their judgment, which corresponds to the perceived quality. The average of those scores, for each video sequence, is called Mean Opinion Score (MOS).

There are two important points which should be considered to implement a subjective experiment: the selection of the video sequences and the method. For the first, the ITU-T Recommendation P.910 suggests to observe a variety of the Spatial Perceptual Information (SI) and the Temporal Perceptual Information (TI) for the chosen video sequences, to avoid that the subjective experiment becomes boring. Accordingly, the chosen video sequences were: "Foreman", "Mobile", "Glasgow" and "Mother and Daughter", in QCIF format (ideal for mobile receivers). Their SI and TI are presented in Figure 3.

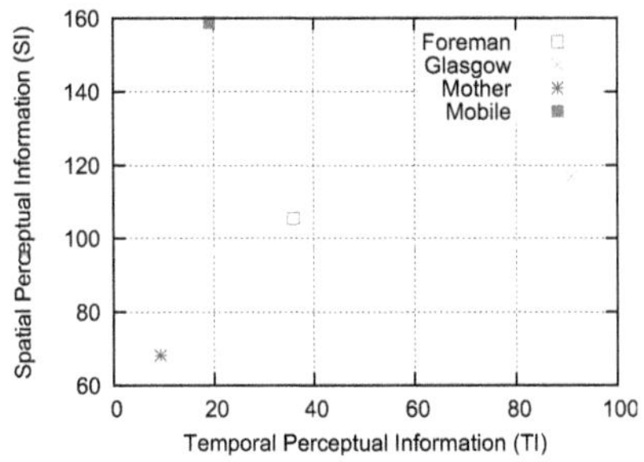

Figure 3: Spatio-temporal information of the selected video sequences.

For the second, the literature provides several methods [4], including the Absolute Category Rate (ACR), used in this work, categorized as a Single Stimulus Method (SSM), i.e., a category in which the processed video sequences are evaluated independently according a discrete scale of judgement. The main advantages of using a SSM method are the easy implementation and fast acquisition of the results [4].

The selected videos were submitted to four types of distortion: Gaussian noise, blocking, blurring and salt & pepper noise, with two levels of intensity, which resulted in a total of 32 synthetic videos, evaluated by 40 people for salt & pepper, blocking and blurring, and by 24 people for Gaussian noise. That type of distortion often occurs in video processing systems [10], therefore, it is important that they are simulated in controlled environments. The parameters used to simulate the distortions are show in Table 1.

Table 1: Distortion parameters used in the distortions simulator.

Distortion	Intensity	Parameters
Salt & Pepper Noise (**SP**)	1	Probability 1%
	2	Probability 3%
Blurring (**BR**)	1	Mean Filter with 3 × 3 mask (two applications)
	2	Mean Filter with 3 × 3 mask (four applications)
Blocking (**BK**)	1	Probability 1%
	2	Probability 3%
Gaussian Noise (**GN**)	1	$\sigma = 0.0002$
	2	$\sigma = 0.003$

5. SIMULATION RESULTS

To compare the performance of the VQA algorithms described in previous section the Pearson Linear Correlations Coefficients (PCC) was take into account, between objective measures and the MOS. The PCC quantifies the performance about to accuracy of the objective metric, when it is the closer to one the the objective metric is better.

Table 2 presents the PCC, between MOS and the predicted measure, considering the distortions in the Table 1. In general, a significant improvement for the metrics which embed the Sobel first order differential operator is noted.

(a) Original (b) Sobel (c) Prewitt (d) Roberts (e) Laplace

Figure 2: Differential Operators

Specifically, the S-PW-SSIM in scenario of videos submitted to salt and pepper noise and S-PW-GSSIM for videos which presented blurring and blocking degradations, also presented high correlation.

The Laplacian second order operator presents the highest value for the blocking scenario. It is also important to observe that none of the proposed models showed improvement in the correlation for the Gaussian noise, which can be justified by the low correlation between the Gaussian noise and SI [8].

Table 2: Pearson Linear Correlation Coefficients.

Model	SP	BR	BK	GN
PSNR	0.828	0.607	0.697	0.858
SSIM	0.902	0.776	0.792	**0.931**
S-PW-SSIM	**0.920**	0.866	0.834	0.918
R-PW-SSIM	0.883	0.870	0.831	0.903
P-PW-SSIM	0.914	0.874	0.833	0.912
L-PW-SSIM	0.907	0.882	0.840	0.915
G-SSIM	0.864	0.972	0.867	0.822
S-PW-GSSIM	0.914	**0.984**	**0.876**	0.913
R-PW-GSSIM	0.865	0.983	0.872	0.905
P-PW-GSSIM	0.911	0.984	0.875	0.911
L-PW-GSSIM	0.894	0.977	**0.876**	0.917

With respect to the computational cost, the Sobel and Prewitt first order operators present practically the same increment in time of execution, for the merge with SSIM (S-PW-SSIM and P-PW-SSIM) the period was $450ms$ and for G-SSIM (S-PW-GSSIM and P-PW-GSSIM) it was $500ms$. The Roberts and Laplacian operators present short processing times, in relation to SSIM (R-PW-SSIM and L-PW-SSIM), the time difference was of $331ms$ and $210ms$, respectively, and for the GSSIM (R-PW-GSSIM and L-PW-GSSIM) $370ms$ and $286ms$, respectively.

6. CONCLUSIONS

This paper presented an investigation on how to improve some objective metrics, with the introduction of first and second order differential operators, to identify the visual attention in a scene. The proposed technique involves the combination of the local magnitude of the first and second order differential operators, which provide an estimation of the visual attention, with objective metrics.

The experiments considered blurring, blocking, salt & pepper and Gaussian noise distortions. The performance of the proposed metrics was compared with the PSNR, GSSIM and SSIM metrics. The results suggest which the Sobel first order differential operator is the best one to estimate the visual attention, when combined with objective video quality metrics. The Laplacian second order differential operator provided a small improvement regarding the correlation coefficient, but it is fast to compute. The simulations were performed using the C programming language for a notebook with Intel(R) Core(TM) i5-2410M CPU 2.30GHz with GNU/Linux Ubuntu 10.10 operation system.

7. ACKNOWLEDGMENTS

The authors would like to thank IFPB, CNPq/PIBITI, Iecom and COPELE/UFCG for providing research support.

8. REFERENCES

[1] W. Y. L. Akamine and M. C. Q. Farias. Incorporating visual attention models into image quality metrics. In *Proceedings of the Sixth International Workshop on Video Processing and Quality Metrics for Consumer Electronics (VPQM)*, 2012.

[2] G.-H. Chen, C.-L. Yang, and S.-L. Xie. Gradient-based structural similarity for image quality assessment. In *IEEE International Conference on Image Processing*, pages 2929 –2932, oct. 2006.

[3] S. Gu, F. Shao, G. Jiang, and M. Yu. A new four-component gradient-based structural similarity metric using adaptive weights. In *Eighth International Conference onFuzzy Systems and Knowledge Discovery (FSKD)*, volume 2, pages 970 –973, july 2011.

[4] ITU-T. ITU-T Recommendation P.910: Subjective video quality assessment methods for multimedia applications. Technical report, ITU-T, April 2008.

[5] M. Juneja and P. S. Sandhu. Performance evaluation of edge detection techniques for images in spatial domain. *International Journal of Computer Theory and Engineering*, (5), Dec. 2009.

[6] H. Liu and I. Heynderickx. Studying the added value of visual attention in objective image quality metrics based on eye movement data. In *16th IEEE International Conference on Image Processing*, pages 3097 –3100, nov. 2009.

[7] E. Nadernejad, S. Sharifzadeh, and H. Hassanpour. Edge detection techniques: Evaluations and comparisons. *Applied Mathematical Sciences*, (31):1507–1520, 2008.

[8] C. D. M. Regis, J. V. M. Cardoso, and M. S. Alencar. Video quality assessment based on the effect of the estimation of the spatial perceptual information. In *Anais do XXX Simpósio Brasileiro de Telecomunicações (SBrT'12) – Accepted Paper*, 2012.

[9] Z. Wang, A. Bovik, H. Sheikh, and E. Simoncelli. Image quality assessment: from error visibility to structural similarity. *IEEE Transactions on Image Processing*, 13(4):600 –612, april 2004.

[10] S. Winkler. *Digital Video Quality: Vision Models and Metrics*. Wiley, 2005.

Effect of Visual Attention Areas on the Objective Video Quality Assessment

Carlos D. M. Regis
Federal Institute of Education, Science and Technology of Paraíba – IFPB – Campus Campina Grande
Institute for Advanced Studies in Communications – Iecom
Campina Grande, Brazil
danilo@iecom.org.br

José V. M. Cardoso
Federal University of Campina Grande – UFCG
Institute for Advanced Studies in Communications – Iecom
Campina Grande, Brazil
josevinicius@iecom.org.br

Marcelo S. Alencar
Federal University of Campina Grande – UFCG
Institute for Advanced Studies in Communications – Iecom
Campina Grande, Brazil
malencar@iecom.org.br

ABSTRACT

The objective assessment of video quality is an important area of research for the validation of video systems, and new algorithms are always in demand. Experiments indicate that the inclusion of characteristics of the human visual system into the objective metric, such as visual attention, improves the evaluation. This paper presents a new approach to evaluate the video quality based on an estimate of the local visual attention, using the structural similarity index. This approach is compared with three classical objective metrics: PSNR, SSIM and MS-SSIM, by means of the Pearson linear and Spearman rank-order correlation coefficients. The videos are submitted to several types of distortions, such as blocking, blurring and salt & pepper noise. The results indicate that the proposed approach presents good correlation with the subjective scores, for videos that contain blurring and blocking degradations.

Categories and Subject Descriptors

D.2.8 [**Software Engineering**]: Metric

General Terms

Algorithms, Measurement.

Keywords

Video Quality Assessment, Structural Similarity, Human Visual System, Visual Attention

1. INTRODUCTION

Applications involving the transmission, reproduction, storage or video processing in communication networks are present in several new technological devices. These processes often cause loss of information, introducing various artifacts in the video, such as blurring, blocking, Gaussian and salt & pepper noise, which cause loss of visual quality.

Estimate the quality of digital videos quickly and accurately has been a major challenge for communication systems and video services. Currently there are two general methodologies to evaluate the video quality, which are called objective and subjective. The first method consists of using mathematical models to measure the video quality. The second evaluates the quality of video via psychophysical experiments with human observers, and is the most precise method [9]. But, the subjective evaluation is expensive, time consuming and demands resources to achieve results, making it impractical for real time applications. The objective evaluation is fast to produce results and permits to monitor systems in real time.

Objective metrics can be classified according to the availability of the original video signal: *full reference*, when the original video signal is compared with the processed signal; *reduced reference*, when only information of the original signal are available; and *no-reference*, when only the processed video is used.

The objective metrics based on error-sensitivity, such as the Mean Squared Error (MSE) and the Peak Signal-to-Noise Ratio (PSNR), are simple to compute, but show poor correlation with subjective measures, since they do not add any features of the human visual system (HVS) [8][1].

Recently, several studies were performed to develop objective metrics, considering the fact that the efficiency of a metric is highly dependent on the attributes of the HVS that it implements. In this sense, one of the features that is intensively investigated is the visual attention. You *et al.* [12] implement the visual attention, modeled by salience regions, into objective image quality metrics. Oprea *et al.* [6] incorporates the concepts of the visual attention including elements such as color contrast, size, orientation and eccentricity in the definition of objective metrics. Gu *et al.* [3] proposed a novel image quality metric based on the gradient approach and on adaptive weights, to detect the effects of the edges, texture and smooth areas in the perceptual quality.

In this paper a new objective metric to video quality assessment is proposed based on the Structural Similarity and

Permission to make digital or hard copies of all or part of this work for personal or classroom use is granted without fee provided that copies are not made or distributed for profit or commercial advantage and that copies bear this notice and the full citation on the first page. To copy otherwise, to republish, to post on servers or to redistribute to lists, requires prior specific permission and/or a fee.
WebMedia'12, October 15–18, 2012, São Paulo/SP, Brazil.
Copyright 2012 ACM 978-1-4503-1706-1/12/10 ...$15.00.

segmentation of the visual attention areas identified by edge information, using the gradient vector approach.

The remainder of the paper is organized as follows. Section 2 describes the Structural Similarity approach. The proposed technique is described in Section 3. Section 4 presents the subjective experiments. Results, validation and discussion are presented in Section 5, and Section 6 presents the conclusions.

2. STRUCTURAL SIMILARITY INDEX

The Structural SIMilarity (SSIM) is a full-reference approach to image and video quality assessment based on the assumption that the HVS is highly adapted to recognize structural information in the visual environment and, therefore, the changes in the structural information would provide a good approximation to the quality perceived by the human visual system [9].

Let $f = \{f_i \mid i = 1, 2, 3, \ldots, P\}$ be the original video and $h = \{h_i \mid i = 1, 2, 3, \ldots, P\}$ be the processed video. The SSIM is computed as a set of three measures over the luminance plane: luminance comparison $l(f, h)$, the contrast comparison $c(f, h)$ and the structural comparison $s(f, h)$,

$$l = \frac{2\mu_f\mu_h + C_1}{\mu_f^2 + \mu_h^2 + C_1},\ c = \frac{2\sigma_f\sigma_h + C_2}{\sigma_f^2 + \sigma_h^2 + C_2},\ s = \frac{\sigma_{fh} + C_3}{\sigma_f\sigma_h + C_3}, \quad (1)$$

in which μ is the average, σ is the standard deviation, σ_{fh} is the covariance, $C_1 = (0.01 \cdot 255)^2$, $C_2 = 2 \cdot C_3$ and $C_3 = (0.03 \cdot 255)^2$.

The structural similarity index is described as

$$\text{SSIM}(f, h) = [l(f, h)]^\alpha \cdot [c(f, h)]^\beta \cdot [s(f, h)]^\gamma, \quad (2)$$

in which usually $\alpha = \beta = \gamma = 1$.

In practice the SSIM is computed for an 8×8 sliding squared window or for an 11×11 Gaussian-circular window. The first approach is used in this paper. Then, for two videos which are subdivided into D blocks, the SSIM is computed as

$$\text{SSIM}(f, h) = \frac{1}{D}\sum_{j=1}^{D} \text{SSIM}(f_j, h_j). \quad (3)$$

Since the proposal of the SSIM, several other metrics have been proposed based on the same philosophy, including the Multi-Scale Structural Similarity (MS-SSIM) [10], assuming that the multi-scale method is a convenient way to incorporate image details for different resolutions. The MS-SSIM metric is described as follows.

From the video reference and for the distorted video, the system applies a low pass filter and reduces the spatial resolution by a factor of two in each iteration. The contrast $c_k(f, h)$ and the structural $s_k(f, h)$ comparisons are computed at the k-th iteration, while the luminance comparison $l_M(f, h)$ is computed only at the M-th iteration.

This procedure is defined as

$$\text{MS-SSIM}(f, h) = [l_M(f, h)] \cdot \prod_{k=1}^{M} [c_k(f, h)][s_k(f, h)]. \quad (4)$$

3. PROPOSED MODEL

Experiments indicated that the human visual attention is not equally distributed throughout the image space, but concentrates on a few regions of interest [4], and the visual attention is an important feature of the HVS to indicate the quality of that region [12].

Based on the assumption that the edge information is closely related to the visual attention, and taking into account that the HVS is more sensitive to asses the quality for areas of higher visual attention, a new approach to objective assessment of video quality is proposed in the following.

Let $\mathcal{T} = \{\tau_i \mid \tau_i \in \mathbb{Z}\ [0, 255]$ and $i = 0, 1, 2, \ldots, P\}$ be a video signal with 2^8 luminance levels. The magnitude of the gradient vector of $\mathcal{T}$ is defined as [2]

$$\mid \nabla\mathcal{T} \mid \ = \left[\left(\frac{\partial\mathcal{T}}{\partial x}\right)^2 + \left(\frac{\partial\mathcal{T}}{\partial y}\right)^2\right]^{\frac{1}{2}} \quad (5)$$

in which x and y denotes horizontal and vertical direction, respectively.

Digitally, the magnitude of the gradient is approximated by

$$\mid \nabla\mathcal{T} \mid \ = [(\mathbf{O}_1 * \mathcal{T})^2 + (\mathbf{O}_2 * \mathcal{T})^2]^{1/2}, \quad (6)$$

in which $*$ denotes the liner filtering operation and

$$\mathbf{O}_1 = \begin{bmatrix} -1 & 0 & +1 \\ -2 & 0 & +2 \\ -1 & 0 & +1 \end{bmatrix}, \qquad \mathbf{O}_2 = \begin{bmatrix} -1 & -2 & -1 \\ 0 & 0 & 0 \\ +1 & +2 & +1 \end{bmatrix},$$

are the Sobel operators.

The gradient vectors are computed over the original video and the resulting video is subdivided into D blocks, 8×8 pixels. The average amplitude of the gradient vectors are computed for each block and the highest average among all the blocks is found. The blocks classified as of higher visual attention are those that present an average amplitude of the gradient vectors obeying the condition

$$\begin{aligned} \textbf{if } \mu_{j,n} &\geq \phi_n \Rightarrow (j, n) \in \mathcal{U}, \\ \phi_n &= \frac{\mu_{max,n}}{\mathcal{R}}, \end{aligned} \quad (7)$$

in which $\mathcal{R}$ is a constant, n is the frame number, j is the index of the block and $\mathcal{U}$ is a set that contains the blocks with higher visual attention. In the experiments $\mathcal{R} = 2.1$ was the optimal value that maximize the correlation.

(a) Original frame (b) Gradient frame (c) Relevant blocks

Figure 1: Result of the proposed algorithm.

Only blocks that are below the threshold of Inequality 7 are considered in the calculation of the metric, i.e., the blocks for which the average magnitude of the gradient vectors do not obey the criteria are ignored. Figure 1 shows an example of this method for the video Glasgow, in which the white squares in Figure 1c represent the blocks for which the SSIM metric is computed. The structural similarity with the proposed segmentation algorithm is called VAA-SSIM (Visual Attention Areas into Structural Similarity Index).

Mathematically, the local statistics μ, σ and σ_{fh} are computed using the previously selected blocks, resulting in

$$\text{VAA-SSIM} = \frac{1}{J}\sum_{j \in \mathcal{U}}^{J} \text{SSIM}(f_j, h_j). \tag{8}$$

The following algorithm summarizes the described technique.

Data: Original $\mathbf{f}(x, y, n)$ and processed $\mathbf{h}(x, y, n)$ videos.
Result: VAA-SSIM.
begin
  $k \longleftarrow 0$;
  $n \longleftarrow 0$;
  while f != EOF **do**
    $\mathbf{g}(x, y, n) = \nabla(\mathbf{f}(x, y, n))$;
    Divide $\mathbf{g}(x, y, n)$ into D blocks 8×8;
    Compute the averages $\mu_{j,n}$ for the j-th block;
    Find the highest average $\mu_{max,n}$ among the blocks;
    Compute the threshold $\phi_n = \frac{\mu_{max,n}}{\mathcal{R}}$;
    if $\mu_{j,n} > \phi_n$ **then**
      $(j, n) \in \mathcal{U}$;
      $k \longleftarrow k + 1$;
    Compute SSIM between $\mathbf{f}(x, y, n)$ and $\mathbf{h}(x, y, n)$ in $\mathcal{U}$ set;
    $n \longleftarrow n + 1$;
  VAA-SSIM $\longleftarrow \frac{\text{SSIM}}{k}$;

---

4. SUBJECTIVE EXPERIMENT

In the subjective evaluation, the observers watch selected video sequences and choose a score that corresponds to the level of video quality. The mean of the subjective scores, for each video sequence, is the Mean Opinion Score (MOS).

There are two important points that should be considered in the subjective evaluation: the method adopted and the choice of the test material. The literature provides several methods to execute a subjective evaluation of video quality [5]. The experiment used the Absolute Category Rating (ACR), that is classified as a Single Stimulus Method, i.e., a category of judgement in which the processed video sequences are presented one at a time, and are evaluated independently according to a scale of the five discrete values. The ACR was chosen because it is easy and fast to implement [5].

The ITU-T Recommendation P.910 suggests that to form a set of videos sequences for a subjective evaluation some video parameters must be taken into account, in particular the Spatial Perceptual Information (SI) and the Temporal Perceptual Information (TI), to prevent that the subjective evaluation be tiring and boring for the observers. It is important that the chosen videos present a variety of values of SI and TI. Therefore, the selected videos were: "Foreman", "Glasgow", "Mobile & Calendar" and "Mother-Daughter", in QCIF format (176 × 144 pixels). Figure 2 shows varying space-temporal information and Figure 3 shows a frame of each selected videos.

The selected videos were submitted to three types of distortions: salt and pepper, blurring and blocking, producing a total of 24 processed videos that were evaluated by 40 people. Such types of degradation often occur in video processing systems and, therefore, it is important that they be simulated in controlled environments [11]. Figure 4 shows samples of the distortions for the "Foreman" video and Table 1 shows the parameters used in the simulations.

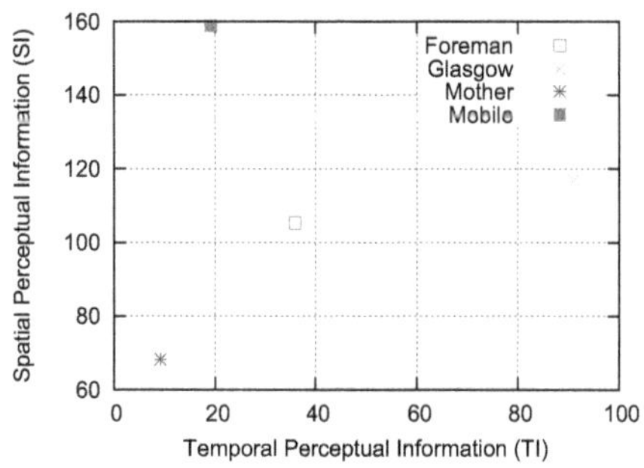

Figure 2: SI and TI values from the chosen video sequences.

(a) Glasgow (b) Foreman

(c) Mobile (d) Mother

Figure 3: Frame of the selected sequences.

Table 1: Distortions used in Experiments

Distortion	Level	Parameters
Salt & Pepper Noise	1	Probability 1%
	2	Probability 3%
Blurring	1	Average Filter with 3 × 3 mask (two applications)
	2	Average Filter with 3 × 3 mask (four applications)
Blocking	1	Probability 1%
	2	Probability 3%

5. SIMULATION RESULTS

The performance of an objective video quality assessment metric is validated by means of the correlation between the predicted measure and the MOS. The Pearson Linear Correlation Coefficient (PCC) and the Spearman Rank-order

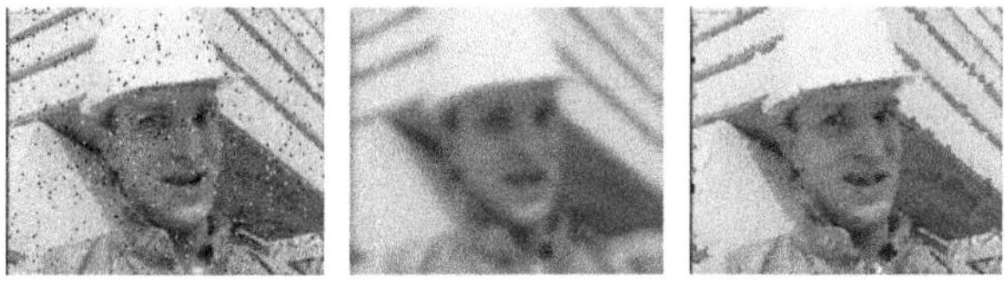

(a) Salt and Pepper (b) Blurring (c) Blocking

Figure 4: Samples of the simulated distortions.

Correlation Coefficient (SROCC) were used to validate the proposed metric. They assess the accuracy and the monotonicity of the relationship between the sets of measures.

Tables 2 and 3 present the PCC and the SROCC obtained by the quality metrics described in the previous sections, evaluated for videos with blurring, blocking and salt and pepper degradations. The boldface values correspond to the metric that presented the best performance.

Table 2: Pearson correlation coefficients.

Model	Salt and Pepper	Blurring	Blocking
PSNR	0.828	0.607	0.697
SSIM	**0.902**	0.776	0.792
MS-SSIM	0.884	0.794	0.764
VAA-SSIM	0.862	**0.911**	**0.839**

Table 3: Spearman rank-order correlation coefficients.

Model	Salt and Pepper	Blurring	Blocking
PSNR	0.595	0.738	0.667
SSIM	**0.929**	0.738	**0.881**
MS-SSIM	**0.929**	0.810	**0.881**
VA-SSIM	0.905	**0.881**	**0.881**

It is noted that the VAA-SSIM presents a significant improvement for the experiments with blocking and blurring distortions, which is due to the fact that these distortions affect, more intensively, the edges of the objects in the scene, i.e. the gradient vectors, than the salt and pepper noise [1], indicating that the regions of greatest variation of gradient vectors, that presents more visual attention, can be used to predict the quality perceived by HVS.

Due to the nonlinear relation between objective and subjective measures, the Spearman coefficients expresses, most suitably, the performance of the objective metric than Pearson coefficients, since the first compares the differences between the ranking of the measures.

6. CONCLUSIONS AND FUTURE WORKS

A *full-reference* objective video quality metric based on the visual attention of the HVS, identified by means of the gradient vectors approach, has been proposed, called VAA-SSIM. The validation process of this model was performed using the correlation coefficients between the measurements and the results from subjective experiments. The results indicate that the gradient vectors approach has significantly improved the quality predicted for the blurring and blocking degradations. On the other hand, it is not adequate for the salt and pepper noise. As future work, the model VAA-SSIM will be submitted to evaluate other distortions such as the ones present in LIVE [7] and EPFL Video Quality Databases.

7. ACKNOWLEDGMENTS

The authors would like to thank IFPB, CNPq/PIBITI, Iecom and COPELE/UFCG for providing research support.

8. REFERENCES

[1] J. V. M. Cardoso, A. C. S. Mariano, C. D. M. Regis, and M. S. Alencar. Comparação das métricas objetivas baseadas na similaridade estrutural e na sensibilidade ao erro. *Revista de Tecnologia da Informação e Comunicação (RTIC)*, (2):33–40, 2012.

[2] R. C. Gonzalez and R. E. Woods. *Digital Image Processing*. Addison-Wesley Publishing Company, 2000.

[3] S. Gu, F. Shao, G. Jiang, and M. Yu. A new four-component gradient-based structural similarity metric using adaptive weights. In *Fuzzy Systems and Knowledge Discovery (FSKD), 2011 Eighth International Conference on*, volume 2, pages 970 –973, july 2011.

[4] L. Itti and C. Koch. Computational modeling of visual attention. *Nature Reviews Neuroscience*, 2(3):194–203, 2001.

[5] ITU-T. ITU-T Recommendation P.910: Subjective video quality assessment methods for multimedia applications. Technical report, ITU-T, April 2008.

[6] C. Oprea, I. Pirnog, C. Paleologu, and M. Udrea. Perceptual video quality assessment based on salient region detection. In *Fifth Advanced International Conference on Telecommunications. AICT '09.*, pages 232 –236, may 2009.

[7] K. Seshadrinathan, R. Soundararajan, A. Bovik, and L. Cormack. Study of subjective and objective quality assessment of video. *IEEE Transactions on Image Processing*, 19(6):1427 –1441, june 2010.

[8] Z. Wang and A. Bovik. Mean squared error: Love it or leave it? a new look at signal fidelity measures. *IEEE Signal Processing Magazine*, 26(1):98 –117, jan. 2009.

[9] Z. Wang, A. Bovik, H. Sheikh, and E. Simoncelli. Image quality assessment: from error visibility to structural similarity. *IEEE Transactions on Image Processing*, 13(4):600 –612, april 2004.

[10] Z. Wang, E. Simoncelli, and B. A.C. Multi-scale structural similarity for image quality assessment. In *IEEE Asilomar Conference on Signals, Systems, and Computers*, pages 1398 –1402, 2003.

[11] S. Winkler. *Digital Video Quality: Vision Models and Metrics*. Wiley, 2005.

[12] J. You, A. Perkis, and M. Gabbouj. Improving image quality assessment with modeling visual attention. In *2nd European Workshop on Visual Information Processing (EUVIP)*, pages 177 –182, july 2010.

Assessing the Impact of the Social Network on Marking Photos as Favorites in Flickr

Luiz Alves, Matheus Maciel, Lesandro Ponciano, Andrey Brito
Departamento de Sistemas e Computação
Universidade Federal de Campinta Grande
Campina Grande, PB, Brazil
{luiz.filho,matheus.maciel}@ccc.ufcg.edu.br {lesandrop, andrey}@lsd.ufcg.edu.br

ABSTRACT

Understanding user behavior in user generated-contend systems (UGCs) is a fundamental building block for maximizing usefulness of these systems. For example, the importance of users' connections and the degree of iteration is needed in order to build meaningful recommendation systems. In this paper, we evaluate the impact of users' network on marking photos as favorites in Flickr considering various levels of distance between users in the network topology. We have observed that users' first-degree contacts are clearly the biggest contributors to the evaluation of hers/his photos (i.e., marking them as favorites). This result indicates that, in contrast to other UGCs such as Twitter and Digg, contact relations are a good indication of content interests in Flickr.

Categories and Subject Descriptors

J.4 [**Social and Behavioral Sciences**]: Miscellaneous—*Information Systems Applications*

Keywords

Social Network Analysis, User Influence, Flickr

1. INTRODUCTION

In recent years there has been great expansion of user-generated content systems (UGCs) such as Twitter, YouTube, Flickr and Digg. These systems are used daily by millions of users with the goal of sharing and/or consume content from various subjects such as art, politics and economics [6,7,9].

Several studies have investigated how content shared in a UGC is valued by users and disseminated through their contacts in the social network [3,4,8,13]. These studies have focused, for example, on characterizing how content is propagated within the network and on identifying the most popular and the most influential users [3]. Some studies have shown that users maintain large networks of contacts, but these networks have little effect on the content they consume [8]. This challenges the belief that relationship between two users indicates common interests in the types of published content.

The present work analyzes the impact of users' network on marking contents as favorites in the social network, considering various levels of distance between users in the network topology. We examine the impact of the users' network on marking photos as favorites in Flickr[1]. Flickr is a popular photo-sharing site with millions of users, more than 6 billion[2] photos posted, and thousands of new photos being posted every day. In Flickr, users can perform various activities such as: creating contacts between one another, posting photos, and marking photos as favorites. Our analysis takes into account the contact network formed by contact links among Flickr users. We analyze different distance levels between users in order to identify the relationships between the users' preference for the content posted and the users' proximity in the social network topology.

Our results show that 70% of the photos marked as favorites by users are posted by their contacts. This indicates that users show interests for contents posted by other users with whom they are connected in the social network. Moreover, unlike the behavior observed in the systems Digg.com [8] and Twitter [3], in Flickr, contacts' network has potential as a way of disseminating content. Our results show that approximately 10% of the photos marked as favorite by users have not been posted by their contacts, but disseminated by them via favorites marks. In general, the behaviors characterized in this work open several perspectives as content recommendation [11], formation of teams of specialists, and the finding of influential users [2].

In the rest of this paper, we first review related work on users activities in UGCs (Section 2). We then present our methodology of data collection, modelling and processing (Section 3). Finally, we present our results on assessing the impact of the social network on marking photos as favorites in Flickr (Section 4), and present the conclusions and future work (Section 5).

2. RELATED WORK

Several studies focus on analyzing users activities in UGCs [3–5,8]. In general, these studies concentrate on *(i)* analyzing different users' profiles in terms of production and consumption of content [4], *(ii)* modeling the content spread over the social network [5] and *(iii)* analyzing the importance of the network in content dissemination [8].

[1] `www.flickr.com`

[2] `http://blog.flickr.net/en/2011/08/04/6000000000/`

Permission to make digital or hard copies of all or part of this work for personal or classroom use is granted without fee provided that copies are not made or distributed for profit or commercial advantage and that copies bear this notice and the full citation on the first page. To copy otherwise, to republish, to post on servers or to redistribute to lists, requires prior specific permission and/or a fee.
WebMedia'12, October 15–28, 2012, São Paulo/SP, Brazil.
Copyright 2012 ACM 978-1-4503-1706-1/12/10 ...$15.00.

Burke et al. [4] investigated users' activities on Facebook by outlining different users' profiles and how they interact with their network. The study shows that users utilize the system in different ways as regards social activities and the use of the media available. Some users have a more active behavior, i.e., they are more likely to produce than to consume content, while other users exhibit a more passive behavior. In this work we analyze the contacts' network under the user's perspective. We focus on analyzing whether users show a preference for content posted by other users who are closer or distant in the network topology.

Cha et al. [5] analyze how a new content is disseminated within Flickr. The study focuses on the characterization of different patterns in which contents are propagated and on the delineation of a set of characteristics that can be used to classify them. In this study, we focus on analyzing whether users express preferences for contents posted in their network, and, conversely, whether their network is the main consumer of the contents posted by them. We do not analyze content characteristics, we take into account only the nunber of times the content has been marked as favorite.

Doerr et al. [8] analyze users influence in the news aggregator Digg.com. The study shows that some users create networks that have little influence on the content they consume or prefer. Similar behavior has been observed in Twitter [3, 12]. In these UGCs, other behaviors, such as users indirect iterations, are more representative of their influence than the social network that they maintain [3].

In this paper we focus on analyzing the impact of the users' social network on marking photos as favorites in Flickr. This system differs from Digg and Twitter in several ways. In Digg, users aggregate news that have been previously produced and transmitted by other channels, for example, news sites. In Twitter, users often post several small messages without much concern for the quality of the content posted. On the contrary, Flickr users themselves produce the photos posted in the system. Furthermore, users are usually concerned with the quality of the content posted. In many cases the content posted results from a professional or artistic activity.

3. MATERIALS AND METHODS

Our study is based on data collected in Flickr. Regarding users' interface in Flickr, it is important to note that users have access to photos posted by their contacts and those posted by users who are not in their social network. Users' home page exhibits information about photos uploaded or marked as favorites by their contacts. In the same way, users' home exhibits information about photos that are posted and marked as favorites by users who are not their direct contacts, e.g., photos most recently uploaded and photos most marked as favorite in the system.

Data collection.

The data used in this study were collected through the public Flickr's API[3]. The time window considered for data collection was four months. A summary of the data collected is presented in Table 1.

We use *Snowball Sampling* [10] as a crawling method. This method leads to an almost complete collection of data for a particular neighborhood of the social network graph, which is relevant to our analysis. The data collected contain user-user links, and user-item links. User-user links indicate the establishment of contact between a user and another user. User-item links indicate that a user has posted a photo or marked a photo as favorite.

[3]http://www.flickr.com/services/api/

Table 1: Overview of the Flickr Dataset

Period	from Nov 11, 2011 to Feb 29, 2012
#Users	2.241.714
#Photos posted	10.304.604
#favorites marks	29.249.205
#user-user links	20.684.373

Addressed questions.

Our analysis focuses on putting into perspective *(i)* how users are affected by their network, and *(ii)* how they affect the network in which they are included. When we investigate how users are affected by their network, we measure the proportion in which a reference user marks as favorite photos posted by users in their social network. When we investigate how users affect their network, we measure the proportion in which users in a social network mark as favorite the photos posted by a reference user. Thus, taking into account users at different distances in the network topology, we aim at identifying how favorites made and favorites received by each user are distributed along users' network. A scatter plot of the amount of favorites made and favorites received by each user in our dataset is shown in Figure 1.

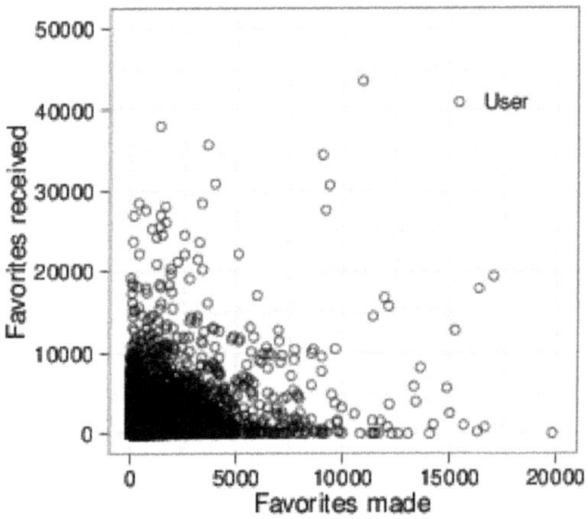

Figure 1: Scatter plot of the number of times that each user has marked as favorite photos posted by other users (favorites made) by the number of times that this user had their photos marked as favorites (favorites received).

Distance between users.

An essential factor in this work is to measure the distance between two users in Flickr. Flickr users' social network can be modeled as a directed graph $G = (U, E)$, where U is the set of users and E the set of directed edges that represent contact between users (user-user links). An example of this type of graph is shown in Figure 2. In this graph, an edge $(u_1, u_2) \in E$ indicates that the user u_1 has the user u_2 as a contact, and that there is a distance of 0 user from u_1 to u_2. In other words, the distance between a user u_a and a user u_b is the smallest number of users that are between them in the network.

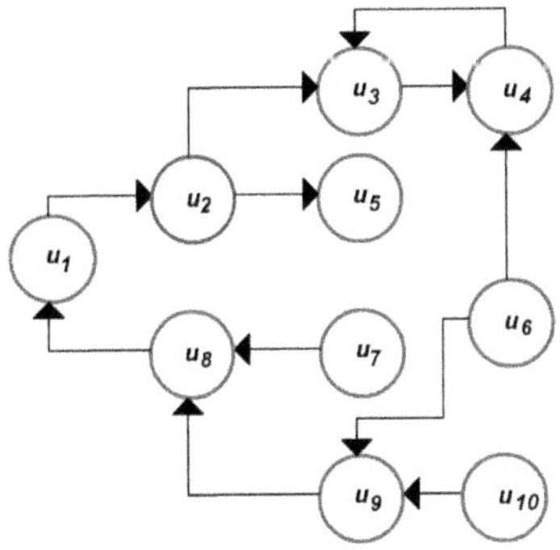

Figure 2: Example of a subgraph of the social network.

In the graph shown in Figure 2, the user u_2 is a contact of the user u_1. The user u_3, in turn, is a contact of the user u_2. In this study, we say that u_3 is at a distance of 1 user from the user u_1. Note that, the user u_7 is not in the network of the user u_1 and he/she cannot be achieved by this user by covering the social network graph. On the other hand, the user u_1 is in the network of the user u_7 and he/she can be achieved by covering the graph. The distance between users can be calculated in a breadth-first search in the graph starting from a reference user up to users on the level n.

We compute users' influence by the favorites their photos receive. For example, when a photo posted by the user u_1 is marked as favorite by the user u_8, we say that the user u_1 has influenced a contact that is at a distance 0 from him/her in the network topology. Otherwise, if the user u_1 marks as favorite a photo posted by the user u_3, we consider that the user u_1 has been influenced by a user who is distant from him/her at 1 user in the social network topology.

Method.

Given the favorites received in photos posted by a user of reference, our method aims at measuring the percentage of favorites made by users from a distance 0 up to a distance n. Similarly, given the favorites made by a reference user, we measure the percentage of such favorites that were made in photos posted by users from distance 0 up to a distance n. To define the reference users, we randomly selected a set of 50 users in our dataset. This number of users proved to be sufficient to obtain results with a satisfactory statistical error for the 95% confidence interval.

Our graph has more than 2 billion vertices (Table 1), and it is necessary to cover it by checking at the same time the photos posted and the photos marked as favorite by each user in different distances starting from the reference users. High computing power is required in this processing. To speed up our experiments, we used the MapReduce programming model to execute our method in parallel using the Hadoop platform. We have made available for download[4] all data used in this work, the scripts used to collect data through the Flickr API, and the MapReduce implementations used to identify the favorites made and favorites received at several distances between users.

4. RESULTS

The results are shown in Figures 3 and 4. In Figure 3 the vertical axis shows the percentages of all photos marked as favorites, and the horizontal axis shows at which distance in the network these photos percentages were uploaded. Each point in the graphic represents the average of the favorites made by 50 reference users. This result shows that 70% of the photos marked as favorite by users were posted by users who are at a distance 0, i.e., those who are their contacts. This indicates that Flickr users consume content shared by users with whom they maintain contact.

Furthermore, the results show that about 20% photos marked as favorite by users were posted by users at a distance of 1 and 2. These photos were disseminated via favorites made by users at the distance 0 like a cascade behavior [5]. Overall, these results show that in Flickr users' network are important in the production of relevant content to their contacts and also in the dissemination of such content.

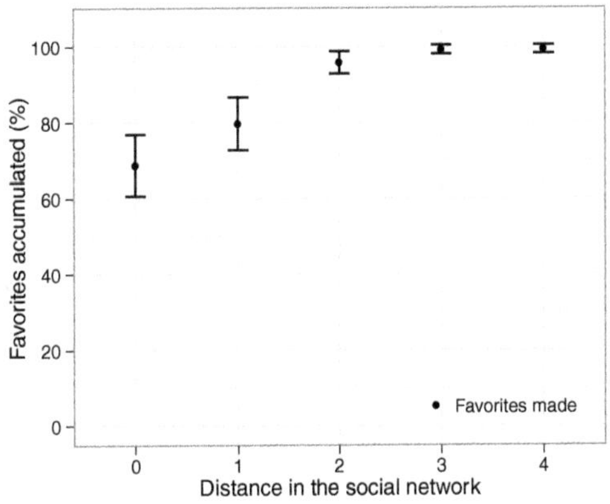

Figure 3: Distance in the social network in which were posted the photos marked as favorites by users.

Figure 4 shows the distances in the social network in which the photos posted by users were marked as favorites. In this figure the vertical axis show the percentage of favorites received in photos posted by reference users, and the horizontal axis shows at the distance in the network other users marked these photos as favorite. Each point in the graphic represents the average of the favorites received in photos posted by 50 users. The result shows that a large part (approximately 60%) of the favorites marks received in photos come from users in the network where they are included.

Implications and Limitations.

Our results indicate that in UGCs like Flickr, users show preference for content posted by their contacts and by contacts of the other users with whom they are connected. The

[4]The data are available at `http://redmine.lsd.ufcg.edu.br/projects/itemsrecommendation/wiki`. More details about implementations are described in the tech report [1].

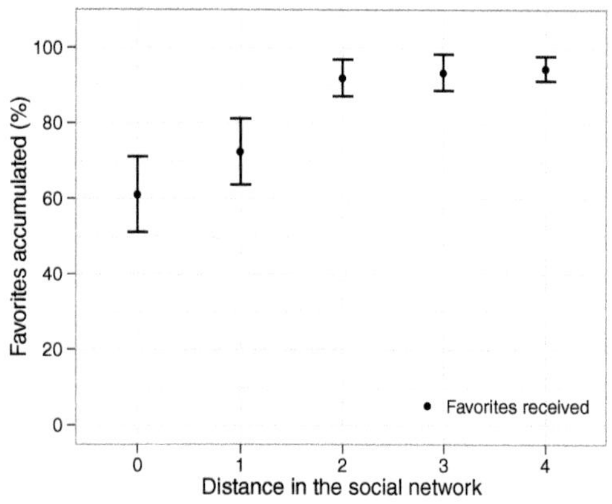

Figure 4: Distance in the social network in which the photos posted by users were marked as favorites.

greater proportion of favorites made by users is in photos posted by users who are their contacts. This result has several implications. For example, regarding content recommendation, this observation indicates that may not be a good approach to recommend photos uploaded closer in users' network, because they usually mark them as favorites even without the help of a recommendation system. However, some users may show more interest by the content posted by their contacts than others. Thus, a limitation of this study is that we have not grouped users in different profiles considering the degree of common interest with their network.

5. CONCLUSION

In this work, we analyze the impact of the users' social network on marking photos as favorites in Flickr. We analyze different distance levels between users in order to identify relationships between the users' preference for the content posted and the users' proximity in the social network topology. Our results indicate that users show preference for content posted by their contacts and by contacts of the other users with whom they are connected. Together, they represent an average of 80% of the favorites made. Moreover, more than 60% of the favorites received in users' photo comes from the network in which they are included.

As future work we intend to group users into different types of social network profiles, considering, for example, the number of contacts they have, the frequency in which they use the system, and the proportion between the amount of photos posted and the amount of favorites received. With this analysis, we intend to identify whether the observed results are more or less significante depending on the user group. Furthermore, given that our results show that users exhibit preference for content posted within their network, we intend to explore this information in a photo recommendation algorithm that find relevant content outside users' network.

Acknowledgments.

Authors are indebted to Nazareno Andrade and Leandro Marinho for their comments and suggestions on earlier versions of this paper. Authors would also like to thank the anonymous referees for their insightful comments. This paper was achieved in cooperation with Hewlett-Packard Brasil Ltda. in the context of the UFCG/HP Analytics Training Program, which uses incentives of the Brazilian Informatics Law (Law no. 8.2.48 of 1991).

6. REFERENCES

[1] L. Alves, M. Maciel, L. Ponciano, and A. Brito. Análise do impacto da rede social na marcação de fotos como favoritas no Flickr. Technical Report UFCG-LSD-2012-01, Distributed System Lab, Universidade Federal de Campina Grande, 2012. Available at `http://www.lsd.ufcg.edu.br/relatorios_tecnicos/TR-2012-01.pdf`.

[2] A. Anagnostopoulos, L. Becchetti, C. Castillo, A. Gionis, and S. Leonardi. Online team formation in social networks. In *Proceedings of the 21st international conference on World Wide Web*, pages 839–848. ACM, 2012.

[3] C. Bigonha, T. N. C. Cardoso, M. M. Moro, V. A. F. Almeida, and M. A. Gonçalves. Detecting Evangelists and Detractors on Twitter. In *18th Brazilian Symposium on Multimedia and the Web*, pages 107–114, 2010.

[4] M. Burke, R. Kraut, and C. Marlow. Social capital on facebook: differentiating uses and users. In *Proceedings of the 2011 annual conference on Human factors in computing systems*, pages 571–580. ACM, 2011.

[5] M. Cha, A. Mislove, B. Adams, and K. P. Gummadi. Characterizing social cascades in flickr. In *Proceedings of the first workshop on Online social networks*, pages 13–18. ACM, 2008.

[6] L. Chiarandini. Exploration and discovery of user-generated content in large information spaces. In *Proceedings of the fifth ACM international conference on Web search and data mining*, pages 755–756. ACM, 2012.

[7] E. David and K. Jon. *Networks, Crowds, and Markets: Reasoning About a Highly Connected World.* Cambridge University Press, New York, NY, USA, 2010.

[8] C. Doerr, N. Blenn, S. Tang, and P. Van Mieghem. Are friends overrated? a study for the social news aggregator digg.com. *Comput. Commun.*, 35(7):796–809, Apr. 2012.

[9] S. Fortunato. Community detection in graphs. *Physics Reports*, 486(35):75 – 174, 2010.

[10] L. A. Goodman. Snowball sampling. *The Annals of Mathematical Statistics*, 32(1):148–170, 1961.

[11] A. Krohn-Grimberghe, L. Drumond, C. Freudenthaler, and L. Schmidt-Thieme. Multi-relational matrix factorization using bayesian personalized ranking for social network data. In *Proceedings of the fifth ACM international conference on Web search and data mining*, pages 173–182. ACM, 2012.

[12] A. Silva, H. Valiati, S. Guimarães, and W. M. Jr. From Individual Behavior to Influence Networks: A Case Study on Twitter. In *19th Brazilian Symposium on Multimedia and the Web*, page 8, 2011.

[13] R. van Zwol. Flickr: Who is looking? In *Proceedings of the IEEE/WIC/ACM International Conference on Web Intelligence*, pages 184–190. IEEE Computer Society, 2007.

ConnecTV: An Environment to Develop and Run Component-based Customized iDTV Applications

Amirton Bezerra Chagas and Carlos André Guimarães Ferraz
Universidade Federal de Pernambuco – Centro de Informática
Av. Jornalista Anibal Fernandes, s/n – Cidade Universitária
Recife – PE / Brazil
+55 81 2126.8430
{abc, cagf}@cin.ufpe.br

ABSTRACT

Designing Interactive Digital TV (iDTV) applications is a challenging activity, due to the restrictions of having the remote control as the main and in most cases the only input device for those applications. Users of iDTV applications are used to an environment where constant concentration and intervention is not needed, so applications requiring much interaction are unfamiliar to them. Personalized applications, which behave accordingly to the context of their execution, including user's habits and preferences, tends to require less interaction. Developing such applications is however burdensome, due to the lack of tools for designing and developing the personalized behavior using contextual information. ConnecTV fills this void by combining a component-based approach to develop such applications and a runtime environment to run and give additional support to their execution.

Categories and Subject Descriptors

D.2.11 [**Software Architecture**]: Domain-specific architectures

D.3.4 [**Processors**]: Compilers, Run-time environments

General Terms

Measurement, Performance, Design, Human Factors, Languages.

Keywords

Interactive Digital TV Applications, Ginga-J, Context-awareness, Component-based software engineering, Composition.

1. INTRODUCTION

Designing and developing interactive digital TV applications is not just creating a conventional application and port it to the TV environment. Lots of extra effort must be taken to adapt the usability of this application to run on a device where users are commonly called "viewers" or "watchers", by themselves words denoting a passive behavior. Concerns about the input devices available, the device's position relative to the users, the amount of users watching TV at the same time and those users' behavior must be taken into account when developing new applications or devices to the DTV environment. Failure to do so and adapt to this setting tends to lead to a failure of the project in question.

GoogleTV's first commercially released version exposed some of the problems of turning interactive TV into a reality without considering the aforementioned concerns. Customers' overall response to the first generation of GoogleTV devices were negative, reaching the staggering point where one of the manufacturers announced that more than 50% of the devices sold were returned due to buyer's dissatisfaction[1]. User interaction on those devices is done through a QWERTY keyboard, and some models also offers a track pad, leading users to face the device as a full-fledged computer instead of a TV able to run some interactive apps specific to the television environment.

Interactive Digital TV applications require much more effort than simply attach common PC's input devices such as keyboards or pointers to a TV [1]. Freeman et al. [2] state that "The potential benefits that digital TV can bring ... are unlikely to be realized if digital TV equipment and services are not easy to use, and perceived as such", and hardly an application requiring dozens of button pressures on the remote control will be accepted as an easy-to-use application by a watcher used to just turn on the TV and tune it on the desired channel. Applications for this environment need to be designed from their inception considering this situation and the previously mentioned concerns.

Reducing the number of user intervention in the application is essential. Delivering an application personalized to the viewer's profile usually reduces the number of interactions required for the application to work properly. The knowledge of user's preferences and habits, and also other information regarding the precise environment where the TV will be running, has the potential to adapt the software to display the most interesting options for that particular user on that situation.

Knowledge from Computational Context is useful to define which available information can be used to maximize the potential success of an application running in the DTV environment. Dey and Abowd [3] define context as "any information that can be used to characterize the situation of entities (i.e., whether a person, place, or object) that are considered relevant to the interaction between a user and an application, including the user and the application themselves. Context is typically the location, identity, and state of people, groups, and computational and physical objects." This definition clearly points that context-awareness is the way-to-go to improve the application's output, adapting it to the user's scenario.

Some researches involving context-awareness and iDTV applications have already been conducted, most notably Thawani, Gopalan and Sridhar [4], who have identified which contextual information can be useful on the iDTV domain.

(c) 2012 Association for Computing Machinery. ACM acknowledges that this contribution was authored or co-authored by an employee, contractor or affiliate of the national government of Brazil. As such, the government of Brazil retains a nonexclusive, royalty-free right to publish or reproduce this article, or to allow others to do so, for Government purposes only.
Webmedia '12, October 15 - 18 2012, São Paulo, Brazil
Copyright 2012 ACM 978-1-4503-1706-1/12/10...$15.00

[1] http://online.wsj.com/article/SB10001424053111904800304564 74581913302222.html

Developing useful iDTV applications using contextual information is still a hard process. Defining the behavior changes that the application is supposed to perform, which data will trigger such changes and dealing with all the code related to the personalization of the application tends to create bad code, which on the other hand, makes software less maintainable and reusable. Setting up a good architectural model to develop those applications helps to improve this scenario.

After having analyzed the environment and the difficulties of applying personalization to an application while keeping its code maintainable, we decided for an approach using component-based software engineering. We focus on allowing the creation of different components, each responsible to deal with one module of the application and adapt this part of the application to a user's characteristic. In the following sections, we will discuss the reasons why using components to develop personalized iDTV applications makes their code cleaner when following our approach.

Our work in this research is basically developing two pieces of software: the first is a composing infrastructure, exposed as a webserver, which expects for a components repository and a configuration file that dictates how those components will be composed according to the contextual information collected from the user, delivering as its output the most appropriate application to that user according to the configuration. The second is a runtime environment that will collect the required contextual information of the user's device, send it to the composing server, receive the personalized application and run it on the DTV device. This runtime also provides extra functionality for the developers to ease the process of developing personalized applications for the DTV environment. This extra functionality is exposed to programmers through an API to be used while developing the application.

2. RELATED WORKS

GingaSC [5] project proposes a context-aware layer to the Ginga Middleware, the standardized middleware and runtime environment to the SBTVD (*Sistema Brasileiro de TV Digital /* Brazilian Digital Television System), and by using this layer, developers could easily identify and use contextual information on their Ginga iDTV applications. GingaSC is an interesting proposal, and while it does not provide the high-level abstractions that we offer on our approach, such as automatically changing the behavior of the developed application according to some information, it can be used as the low-level engine for collecting contextual information.

Some approaches for personalization and context-awareness in the DTV scenario have already been researched. Contextual Ginga [6] consists of an authoring tool to create context-aware Ginga-NCL applications. It is a visual tool where developers create profiles and associate to which screens that profile will be related to. While it is a good and easy approach to work with, it limits the possibilities of the developers to some specific information, and also the reusability of code is compromised due to the model of development proposed on the work, where all the screens and functionalities of the final application should be part of a single project, and each of those parts are not reusable in other projects.

Moreno, Soares and Cerqueira [7] discuss how component-based software development principles can be used on the DTV environment. It is mentioned that the reference implementations of Ginga-NCL, a declarative module of Ginga, and Ginga-CC, the common core that ties Ginga together, are designed in a component-based way, and already provide common components of this scenario to be used by NCL applications. This work also describes the advantages of using components in the DTV environment, due to the limited resources of such systems, where it is important to have the smaller number of functionalities loaded at a given time. It is a very motivating work that points not only the viability of the component-based approach to iDTV applications, but also shows that it already plays an important role on the development of NCL iDTV applications. However, no mention to the use of components on Ginga-J is made, neither is explored the possibility of using the component-based approach to personalize applications on this environment.

Outside the DTV environment, Sora, Verbaeten and Berbers [8] have already studied the use of component composition for customizing systems, meaning that unpredictable compositions could happen. While this is a great feature in the scenario of their study, in our environment, we prefer to restrict the options of composition, giving full control to the developer to choose under which situations, that in our case will usually be the values of contextual information about the user, each component will or will not be shipped.

Borelli, Lopes and Elias [9] also use component-based software engineering for iDTV applications. The work focuses on the definition of a XML format to define the relationship between components. It is an interesting approach, given XML's flexibility and great familiarity to most developers with the language. Together with [7], which also takes advantage of XML, this work inspired part of our own definition of the configuration file required to link the components to the personalization of the applications.

3. CONNECTV

ConnecTV is a solution to allow developers to design and create personalized iDTV applications using a component-based approach and an API to offer contextual information at runtime in a seamless way.

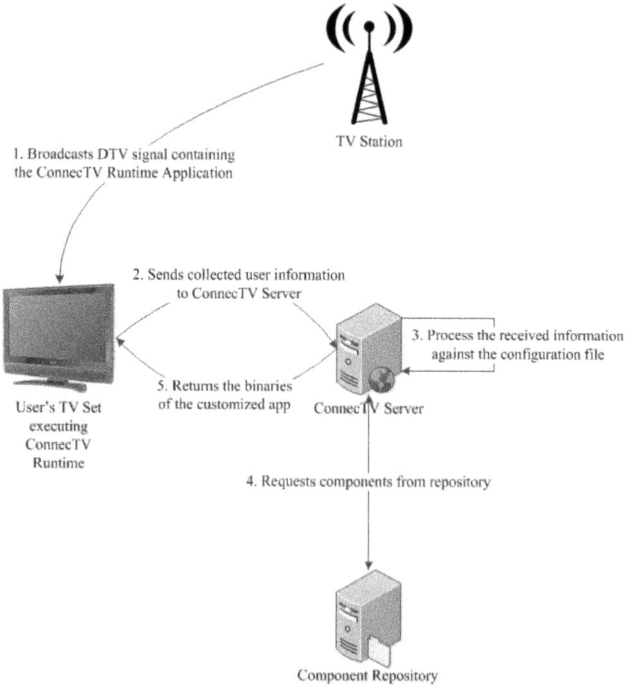

Figure 1 – ConnecTV Architecture Overview

Its architecture, depicted on Figure 1, is defined to overcome the limitations imposed by the application distribution model used by the Ginga Middleware. In this model, the iDTV application is broadcasted together in the same stream as the audio and video signal, thus, the same data will be received by all the devices tuned on a specific frequency.

SBTVD, however, defined that a device can have a return channel, a bidirectional link that makes unicast possible, so particular data can be sent to a specific device. This link generally is a connection to the Internet, so, our architecture exploits this characteristic to allow the user to receive the personalized application (Figure 1, step 5).

The solution is composed by two modules, which will be described in the next subsections.

3.1 ConnecTV Runtime

Since our component-based approach is not readily supported by the Ginga Middleware, we developed a simple runtime environment to run on top of Ginga-J, with the responsibility of setting up the environment, collecting data and executing the personalized application.

ConnecTV Runtime is actually the Ginga-J application that will be broadcasted by the TV station. However, in order to allow a better understanding of this module, we will avoid referring to it as an application, since we consider that this runtime module can be broken into three different modules which run during the lifecycle of the application:

ConnecTV Gatherer

This module is responsible for collecting the information desired by the iDTV application and making it available to it. Several different sources can be used to fetch this information from, as the default Ginga APIs available on the device, other APIs specific for collecting contextual information, as the aforementioned GingaSC project [5], external sources of profile information, as in ProfileTV [10], and in the worst case requesting the user to input some information.

It is important to point also that this module, when accessed via the ConnecTV API, can be used to register the iDTV application to be updated about the status of some particular kind of information in a timely fashion, so changes in the environment can be reflected on the iDTV application.

ConnecTV Loader

This module is responsible for requesting the personalized application to the ConnecTV Server, using data obtained through ConnecTV Gatherer. It will request to the Gatherer program the data it needs to send to the server, assemble an http request with this data and send it to the address where a ConnecTV Server application is waiting for requests.

After receiving the application data sent from the Server, ConnecTV Loader finds the main class of this application, instantiate and sends it to the ConnecTV Environment.

ConnecTV Environment

The ConnecTV Environment is responsible for starting and controlling the runtime lifecycle of the personalized iDTV application received. To understand this, the lifecycle of a generic iDTV Ginga Application, also known as an Xlet, (not necessarily a ConnecTV-enabled application) is described in Figure 2.

To support this lifecycle, regular iDTV applications implement the javax.tv.xlet.Xlet interface, which enforces the creation of 4 methods, each one to allow the developer to implement the behavior the application has to follow immediately before making the transition to one of those states.

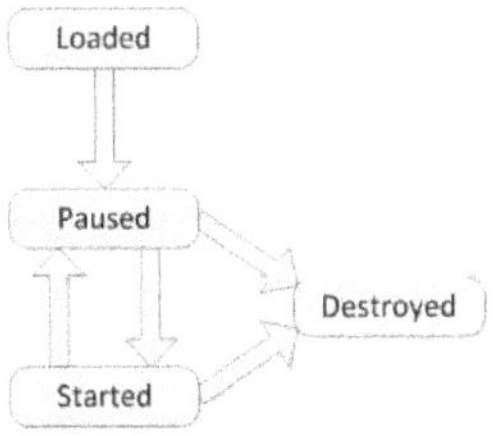

Figure 2 – Xlet lifecycle

ConnecTV-enabled applications however run inside our runtime, which already implements the Xlet interface. We provide to developers the ITVApp interface Figure 3, which also imposes the implementation of methods to deal with the event of entering in a different state, and also other methods useful for our scenario. Exactly one class in the composed application must implement this interface, and this one will be considered the main Class.

```
public interface ITVApp {
    public void initApp();
    public void startApp();
    public void pauseApp();
    public void destroyApp();
}
```

Figure 3 – ITVApp interface

ConnecTV Environment starts to run during the load phase of a Ginga-J application, being invoked immediately after Ginga Loader receives the application from the server. It calls the initApp() method as soon as possible, and after the initialization of the personalized application is done, it is responsible for calling the application's event methods whenever it receives a call from the middleware that the event is about to be changed.

ConnecTV Environment also serves to execute some scheduling functionalities present on ConnecTV. A developer has the choice of defining that the application should be started only after a predetermined time (he could also choose that the application only run in a certain timeframe). The call of startApp() will be responsible for allowing the application only to run following this choice.

3.2 ConnecTV Server

ConnecTV Server is the module responsible for composing the personalized application. It expects calls originated by a DTV device running ConnecTV Runtime, with the user's data necessary to compose and deliver the personalized application tailored to that particular user.

ConnecTV Server works as an HTTP server, expecting an HTTP POST request containing data with the user's profile. Upon the arrival of the request, the server processes the profile information against a profile configuration file provided by the developer of the application, which dictates the expected values for each of the profile information, and with this processed data it chooses which components should be included in the final application in that case.

Notice that while scale is an important requirement, it is out of the scope of this research. Our objective here is to demonstrate the viability, advantages and limitations of our approach, so, we cannot guarantee that our current implementation of the server is practical to use in a real environment with millions of requests in a short period of time. However, we consider that, given enough resources, a scalable version based on the code of our current server can be developed.

4. CONNECTV IN USE

After understanding the overall architecture of ConnecTV, developers already experienced in the development of iDTV applications shall have no difficulties in developing an application to be executed on ConnecTV.

Figure 4 describes the steps required for designing and developing a ConnecTV-enabled application. It is important to follow this flow in order to create an iDTV app that can be personalized by our engine.

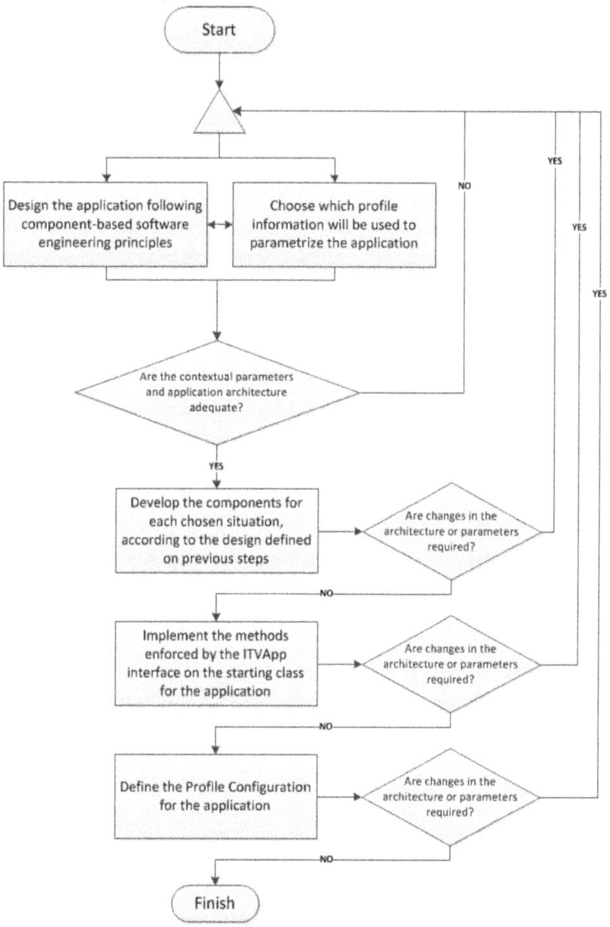

Figure 4 – Step-by-step for developing a ConnecTV-enabled application

The two first steps can occur concurrently, and are likely to benefit by doing so. Since our proposal sits on defining a type of component for each functionality that can be personalized, and this personalization arises from the value of some profile information sent by the user, choosing which information will be used to customize the application has great impact on defining the component architecture of the system. Meanwhile, the design of the application's architecture can reveal the need for more (or less) granularity on the information, or even new information that was not initially thought to be necessary.

We base the information useful to customize applications on this study basically on two previous researches already done on the iDTV area: the identification of contextual information done by Thawani, Gopalan and Sridhar [5], where they analyze the use of a context-aware software to make personalized ad insertion, and on the ProfileTV work by Coêlho and Ferraz [10], a system for profile management in interactive digital television.

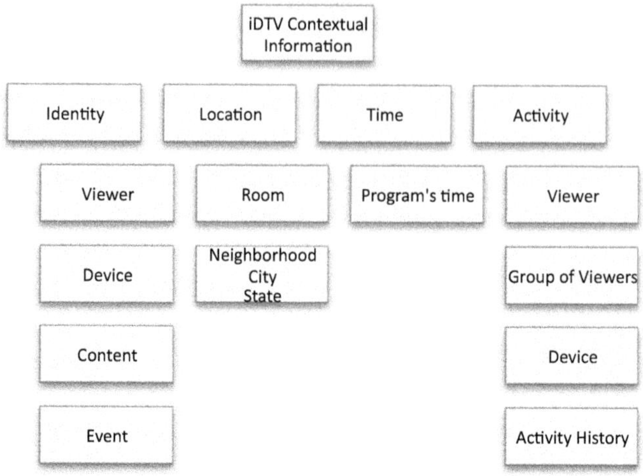

Figure 5 – Useful contextual information for iDTV applications

Figure 5 illustrates types of contextual information considered useful by the Thawani et al. research. We categorized some of the examples given in [4], since we consider that for our use it is more informative and practical to give a parameterizable broad category of information, as "Location\Room" instead of boolean information as "Location\Presence in Living Room" or "Location\Presence in Kitchen" as this kind of information is described in the former research.

While geolocational data as the neighborhood, city or state in which the viewer is going to use the application are not mentioned in [4], they are included in our classification of useful contextual information to iDTV applications.

ProfileTV [10] on the other hand does not define exact categories, and theoretically, given the required data are any retrievable information about the user, user's habits, devices and pretty much any data available, not necessarily in the TV environment only, they can be added to the system's configuration. Such approach opens several possibilities, as using the watcher's preferences on other media to personalize his iDTV applications.

Given that the architecture is well defined, and the types of information and their possible useful values are known, the next two steps are straightforward to a developer, since they are the actual implementation of the application, though both the development of the variations of the components deemed as necessary for the app to be personalized, and the development of the class implementing the ITVApp interface to control the lifecycle of the iDTV application.

The last step requires more explanation, since it is a particularity of our framework. After developing the components for each personalization condition defined on the initial steps, the developer has to write a configuration file that maps each component to the desired parameter values where this component should (or should not) be included on the application that will be sent to the requesting device.

The configuration file consists of an XML file, following the XSD schema defined on Figure 6, which specifies the structure and possible values for some of the attributes that control how ConnecTV Server will compose the personalized application.

```
<?xml version="1.0" encoding="utf-8"?>
<xs:schema id="ProfileConfiguration" xmlns=""
xmlns:xs="http://www.w3.org/2001/XMLSchema">
  <xs:element name="Property">
    <xs:complexType>
      <xs:sequence>
        <xs:element name="Component" minOccurs="1" maxOccurs="unbounded">
          <xs:complexType>
            <xs:attribute name="name" type="xs:string" use="required"/>
            <xs:attribute name="action" type="xs:string" use="required">
              <xs:simpleType>
                <xs:restriction base="xs:string">
                  <xs:enumeration value="Include"/>
                  <xs:enumeration value="AlwaysInclude"/>
                  <xs:enumeration value="Exclude"/>
                  <xs:enumeration value="AlwaysExclude"/>
                </xs:restriction>
              </xs:simpleType>
            </xs:attribute>
          </xs:complexType>
        </xs:element>
        <xs:element ref="Property" minOccurs="0" maxOccurs="unbounded" />
      </xs:sequence>
      <xs:attribute name="name" type="xs:string" use="required"/>
      <xs:attribute name="type" type="xs:string" use="required">
        <xs:simpleType>
          <xs:restriction base="xs:string">
            <xs:enumeration value="java.lang.String"/>
            <xs:enumeration value="java.lang.Integer"/>
            <xs:enumeration value="java.lang.Float"/>
            <xs:enumeration value="java.lang.Double"/>
            <xs:enumeration value="java.lang.Boolean"/>
            <xs:enumeration value="java.lang.Date"/>
          </xs:restriction>
        </xs:simpleType>
      </xs:attribute>
      <xs:attribute name="value" type="xs:string" />
      <xs:attribute name="beginValue" type="xs:string" />
      <xs:attribute name="endValue" type="xs:string" />
      <xs:attribute name="comparerType" type="xs:string" use="required">
        <xs:simpleType>
          <xs:restriction base="xs:string">
            <xs:enumeration value="EQ"/><!-- Equal -->
            <xs:enumeration value="BT"/><!-- Between -->
            <xs:enumeration value="CP"/><!-- Contains Pattern -->
            <xs:enumeration value="GT"/><!-- Greater Than -->
            <xs:enumeration value="LT"/><!-- Less Than -->
            <xs:enumeration value="IN"/><!-- In this list -->
            <xs:enumeration value="CI"/><!-- Contained in user's list -->
            <xs:enumeration value="NEQ"/><!-- Not Equal -->
            <xs:enumeration value="NBT"/><!-- Not Between -->
            <xs:enumeration value="NCP"/><!-- Doesn't contains pattern-->
            <xs:enumeration value="NGT"/><!-- Not Greater Than -->
            <xs:enumeration value="NLT"/><!-- Not Less Than -->
            <xs:enumeration value="NIN"/><!-- Not in this list -->
            <xs:enumeration value="NCI"/><!-- Not in the user's list -->
          </xs:restriction>
        </xs:simpleType>
      </xs:attribute>
    </xs:complexType>
  </xs:element>
  <xs:element name="ProfileConfiguration">
    <xs:complexType>
      <xs:choice minOccurs="1" maxOccurs="unbounded">
        <xs:element ref="Property" />
      </xs:choice>
    </xs:complexType>
  </xs:element>
</xs:schema>
```

Figure 6 – Profile Configuration XSD schema

While the XSD schema is mostly self-explanatory, some points need to be made clear about the configuration file and how ConnecTV Server processes it:

- The attributes beginValue and endValue of the Property element should only be used when the comparerType chosen is BT or NBT;
- When using the IN or NIN comparerType, the list should be written in the following notation: "{element1,element2,...,elementN}", and the type attribute for the Property must be the type of the elements.
- Lastly processed rules (meaning the rules on the last lines of the configuration file) have precedence over the first ones. So, if the first accepted rule states that component "A" action is "Exclude", but the next accepted rule states that "A" is "Include", the component will be included. Obviously, this rule would not apply if the first rule was "AlwaysExclude". If both rules have the "Always" prefix, the same precedence rule applies.
- As allowed by the XSD, the developer can chain a Property element inside other. In this case, the expected behavior is an "AND", similar to the "&&" operator, for the Component elements of the children Properties. The Component elements of the parent Property are not affected by their sibling "Property" elements.
- ConnecTV Server expects for a Property element with the name attribute set as "Default", which will have as children the default Component elements to be shipped if no rule is accepted. This Property should have at least the component with the main class which implements ITVApp.

Besides the recommendations mentioned above, developers can also use the APIs provided by ConnecTV to enhance their applications. An iDTV application created following this guidelines will be ready to be composed and served by ConnecTV Server, and consequently, will be ready to run on ConnecTV Runtime environment.

4.1 A ConnecTV-enabled iDTV application

To provide a better understanding of ConnecTV, we present here a sample iDTV application designed and developed based on ConnecTV.

The application should be available during a national-wide newscast program, and its goal is to enhance the experience of watching a news program. In short, the requirements for this application are:

- Allowing the watcher to get more information regarding the topics which are being addressed on the program;
- Displaying a dynamic ticker in the bottom of the screen, allowing the watcher to switch between news or stock market prices;
- Making available a poll during only the first block of the newscast.

This application uses the two available approaches for personalization provided by ConnecTV: It sends some profile data about the user and the device to ConnecTV Server, which composes an application tailored to the user's needs, only with those components initially evaluated as ideal to that particular user. However, some of those components can be changed, requested and loaded during runtime at the user's will.

Following the guidelines aforementioned, we define both the components for this application as well as choose which contextual information is useful to personalize it.

Figure 7 shows the component diagram for this application. Since our analysis determined that each requirement is independent from the others and can be personalized according to user data, we defined that our model will be composed by one component for each requirement.

While defining which components the application will be made of, we found the necessity of knowing upon which information each component will be personalized. We found that the following information is useful for this application.

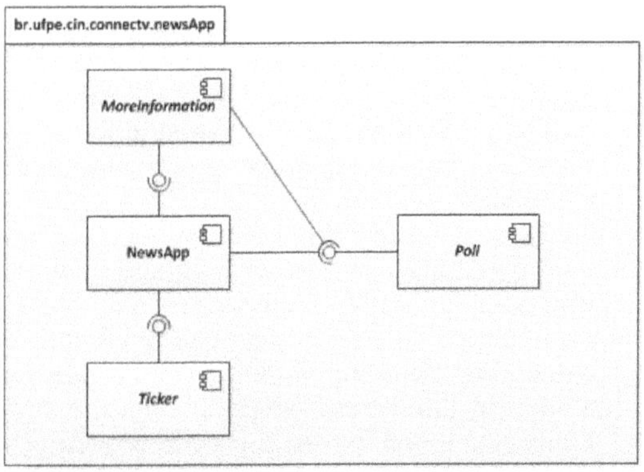

Figure 7 – Application's component diagram

A. Identity\Device\Type

If the device being used to watch the program is a mobile phone, the application will use its browser to load an Internet article about the issue of the current news report. Otherwise, it will decide which component will be included based on the information of the next item. This information also decides whether the poll component to be used is one designed for mobile phones, or a simpler poll, to be shipped on the other devices.

B. Identity\Device\ScreenSize

If the screen is larger than 30 inches, the video will be displayed on 25% of the screen, and extra text about the issue will be displayed on the 75% remaining. Otherwise, text will fill the whole screen, leaving the watcher only with the audio from the broadcast.

C. Identity\Viewer\PreferredTopics

If the user follows the stock market and this information is available, the ticker will be firstly shown as a stock prices ticker; otherwise, the application will be composed with news ticker, unless the next information changes this behavior.

D. Location\City

If the viewer is watching the program in São Paulo or Rio de Janeiro, the ticker will always come by default as a stock prices ticker.

E. Time\ProgramPart

The poll component should be included only if the program is still on the first part, since the requirement explicitly limits the polls to the first block of the newscast.

After choosing the information, we can see that our model is not complete yet, since while we define the macro architecture of our application, a developer would still not know which concrete components should be developed. Table 1 outlines which are the actual components that need to be developed for each category described in Figure 7.

Table 1. Components to be created for the news application

Category	Components
NewsApp	NewsApp (Main component)
MoreInformation	MobileInformation FullScreenInformation PartialScreenInformation
Ticker	NewsTicker StockPricesTicker
Poll	SimplePoll RichPoll

With the previous information regarding what should be done, a developer can program the application. The two development steps (developing the personalized components and the starting class which implements the ITVApp interface) is straightforward.

During the development of the Poll components, ConnecTV Runtime should be informed through a call to an API method that if the Time\ProgramPart information changes to a value different from 1, the Poll component currently loaded in the application should be unloaded.

Other use of the ConnecTV Runtime API in this application is the dynamic loading of another Ticker component, if the user chooses to change it. For instance: ConnecTV Server received information that the user follows the Stock Market, so, it should only include the StockPricesTicker component. If the viewer chooses to change the ticker to see the news instead of stock prices, ConnecTV Runtime should contact ConnecTV Server requesting this extra component, instantiate the received component and show it to the viewer. This behavior is implemented on the Ticker component itself, again, eased by using ConnecTV API.

Finally, after having developed all components, the developer will create the profile configuration to instruct ConnecTV Server to compose the application correctly according to the user's information. Figure 8 shows the XML file required by this application to be composed according to the rules previously defined in this section.

```
<ProfileConfiguration>
  <!-- Default components definition -->
  <Property name="Default" type="java.lang.Boolean" value="true"
comparerType="EQ">
    <Component name="br.ufpe.cin.connectv.newsApp.NewsApp"
action="AlwaysInclude" />
    <Component
name="br.ufpe.cin.connectv.newsApp.moreInformation.PartialScreenInformati
on" action="Include" />
    <Component name="br.ufpe.cin.connectv.newsApp.ticker.NewsTicker"
action="Include" />
    <Component name="br.ufpe.cin.connectv.newsApp.poll.SimplePoll"
action="Include" />
  </Property>

  <!-- TeamInformation components to be included -->
  <Property name="Identity.Device.Type" type="java.lang.String"
value="Mobile" comparerType="EQ">
    <Component
name="br.ufpe.cin.connectv.newsApp.moreInformation.PartialScreenInformati
on" action="Exclude" />
    <Component
name="br.ufpe.cin.connectv.newsApp.moreInformation.MobileInformation"
action="Include" />

    <Component name="br.ufpe.cin.connectv.newsApp.poll.SimplePoll"
action="Exclude" />
    <Component name="br.ufpe.cin.connectv.newsApp.poll.RichPoll"
action="Include" />
  </Property>

  <Property name="Identity.Device.Type" type="java.lang.String"
value="Mobile" comparerType="NEQ">
    <Property name="Identity.Device.ScreenSize" type="java.lang.int"
value="30" comparerType="NGT">
      <Component
name="br.ufpe.cin.connectv.newsApp.moreInformation.FullScreenInformation"
action="Include" />
    </Property>
  </Property>

  <Property name="Identity.Viewer.PreferredTopics"
type="java.lang.String" value="StockMarket" comparerType="CI">
    <Component name="br.ufpe.cin.connectv.newsApp.ticker.NewsTicker"
action="Exclude" />
```

```
    <Component
name="br.ufpe.cin.connectv.newsApp.ticker.StockPricesTicker"
action="Include" />
  </Property>

  <Property name="Location.City" type="java.lang.String" value="{Sao
Paulo,Rio de Janeiro}" comparerType="IN">
    <Component name="br.ufpe.cin.connectv.newsApp.ticker.NewsTicker"
action="Exclude" />
    <Component
name="br.ufpe.cin.connectv.newsApp.ticker.StockPricesTicker"
action="Include" />
  </Property>

  <Property name="Time.ProgramPart" type="java.lang.int" value="1"
comparerType="GT">
    <Component name="br.ufpe.cin.connectv.newsApp.poll.*"
action="AlwaysExclude" />
  </Property>

  <!-- Interfaces that should always be included -->
  <Property name="Default" type="java.lang.Boolean" value="true"
comparerType="EQ">
    <Component name="br.ufpe.cin.connectv.newsApp.miniGame.IMiniGame"
action="AlwaysInclude" />
    <Component
name="br.ufpe.cin.connectv.newsApp.teamInformation.ITeamInformation"
action="AlwaysInclude" />
    <Component
name="br.ufpe.cin.connectv.newsApp.playerInformation.IPlayerInformation"
action="AlwaysInclude" />
    <Component name="br.ufpe.cin.connectv.newsApp.statistics.IStatistics"
action="AlwaysInclude" />
    <Component name="br.ufpe.cin.connectv.newsApp.poll.IPoll"
action="AlwaysInclude" />
  </Property>
</ProfileConfiguration>
```

Figure 8 – Profile Configuration XML for this application

This simple application is an example of how using ConnecTV to create personalized iDTV applications according to contextual and profile information provided by the user. We used the component-based architecture to design the application, ConnecTV Server to provide the initial personalization of the application and ConnecTV APIs to dynamically adapt the application to changes during the execution of the app on ConnecTV Runtime. A similar iDTV application developed without the help a component-based approach and ConnecTV Runtime, API and Server would be much less reusable and maintainable, since code regarding the personalization would be spread along several classes. The next section discusses this and other advantages of ConnecTV.

5. DISCUSSION

This section states the advantages and limitations we have found by using the development approach proposed by ConnecTV's model of designing and developing personalized iDTV applications.

5.1 Consequences of enforcing the use of a component-based approach

Developing applications tailored to a specific type of user, or able to adapt to a user's behavior is a complex activity. Code produced to achieve the personalization, adaption and awareness of the environment tends to scatter across the whole codebase, and this code is also likely to become tangled with the code relative to what the application is really supposed to do and offer to its users.

Enforcing a component-based approach as ConnecTV proposes, where each component will be responsible for the behavior of a specific situation, helps reducing the scattering of code related to personalization. The fact that most of the personalization is done by the xml configuration file also helps to reduce tangling. ConnecTV already provides context awareness and large part of the code needed to adapt the application. These factors combined result in code easier to read, maintain and extend.

Designing the components correctly also leads to the creation of reusable parts of software, which can be applied to several different iDTV applications with small extra efforts. Considering the example application described in Section 4.1, we can easily foresee several applications which could use exactly the same Ticker and Poll components.

5.2 Straightforward means to develop personalized applications

As a consequence of all the amenities provided to the developer, creating a personalized application with ConnecTV is just a matter of correctly designing which parts of the application can be personalized and how each of these parts should behave for a type of user. Developers do not need to worry about how to perform the personalization, they just need to develop the components and define which of them will be shipped given some user information of their choice.

This tends to reduce the resources necessary to develop such applications, and we expect that ConnecTV also helps to raise the amount of developers creating personalized and context-aware applications on the iDTV environment, since this kind of app is generally more user friendly, a decisive quality to the success of iDTV application.

5.3 Smaller application on the data carousel

A ConnecTV-enabled application only requires that a ConnecTV Runtime application is being served on the broadcast. ConnecTV Runtime is considerably small comparing to the average size of a complete application, so it can hold very few space on the data carousel, giving freedom to the broadcaster to fit other applications, more data, repeat the sending of the Runtime more frequently or any other strategy it chooses to follow by having less data to send.

It is important to remark that by sending the Runtime more often, the average delay a user will notice between tuning his TV set on the broadcaster's channel and start using the application should decrease substantially.

5.4 Limitations

Currently, our complete proposal of just sending ConnecTV Runtime through the broadcast, relying on the return channel to download the rest of the application, is still not commercially viable, due to the low rate of TV sets connected to the Internet. Nevertheless, with the growth of Internet connectivity, we hope that soon ConnecTV is a viable option to developers planning to create iDTV applications to run on the real world. In the meantime, a modified version of ConnecTV Runtime can be added to an application sent using the data carousel, and this application can make use of the dynamic features provided by ConnecTV API to enhance viewer's experience of using interactive DTV applications.

As already mentioned, scalability of ConnecTV Server is out of the scope of this research, so we did not stress the server to test the limit of possible concurrent connections with the existing code. Some enhancements as caching the composed applications so similar requests can skip the steps 3 and 4 (the most computing intensive phases) described on Figure 1 can be used to improve the server.

6. CONCLUSIONS

This research investigated a new approach to develop personalized iDTV applications, which are beneficial compared to non-personalized apps given the limitations of the environment and habits of their potential users. We studied a way to simplify the design and development of such applications, bringing already consolidated practices for developing systems to this scenario, without removing power from developers' hands, and even expanding their possibilities through new functionalities not yet available on current frameworks.

The component-based approach, while not trivial to developer not used to it, is not complex to understand and with some practice professionals are able to develop and design component-based systems straightforwardly. As already mentioned, this approach tends to create cleaner code for this kind of application, and the positive impact of enforcing a design that results in more organized and readable code is undeniable.

The architecture and technical details of ConnecTV also have positive impact on the overall performance of a DTV system serving and running the application, due to simplicity of the application required to be broadcasted and run.

6.1 Further Work

Some of the features described in this work are still requiring more development work to be stable enough to be publicly released. Among those features are the dynamic loading of components and the event listener for changes in contextual information.

Other features considered important to provide a full-fledged framework that developers can rely on to develop their iDTV applications are still a work in progress and were not mentioned in detail in this work, as a scheduler to determine when should the application start or stop to run.

We are also considering developing a visual tool to create the parameter configuration file, since for applications with more than a dozen different components, the XML configuration can become quite large and hard to maintain, contradicting our main objective of keeping the development simple and the resulting code maintainable.

7. REFERENCES

[1] Piccolo, Lara Schibelsky Godoy and Baranauskas, Maria Cecília C. Desafios de Design para a TV Digital Interativa. In *Anais do IHC 2006* (Natal - Brazil 2006).

[2] Freeman, Jonathan, Lessiter, Jane, Williams, Allan, and Harrison, David. *Easy TV Research Report*. Independent Television Comission and Consumers' Association, 2002.

[3] Dey, Anind, Abowd, Gregory, and Salber, Daniel. A Conceptual Framework and a Toolkit for Supporting the Rapid Prototyping of Context-Aware Applications. *Human-Computer Interaction*, 16, 2-4 (2001), 97-166.

[4] Thawani, Amit, Gopalan, Srividya, and Sridhar, V. *Context Aware Personalized Ad Insertion in an Interactive TV Environment*. Applied Research Group, Bangalore, 2004.

[5] Brackmann, Christian P, Venecian, Luthiano R, Luzzardi, Paulo R G, and Yamin, Adenauer C. GingaSC: Uma Proposta de Sensibilidade ao Contexto para TV Digital Brasileira. In *Anais do VIII Seminário de Informática - RS* (Torres 2009), Ulbra.

[6] Alves, Ana Paula and Ferraz, Carlos. Development of Context-Aware Digital TV Applications using Contextual Ginga Authoring Tool. In *Anais do IX Workshop de Ferramentas e Aplicações (WFA) – WebMedia* (Belo Horizonte, Brazil 2010).

[7] Moreno, Marcio Ferreira, Soares, Luiz Fernando Gomes, and Cerqueira, Renato. Uma Arquitetura Orientada a Componentes para o Ginga. In *XXIX Simpósio Brasileiro de Redes de Computadores e Sistemas Distribuídos* (2011), 265-278.

[8] Şora, Ioana, Verbaeten, Pierre, and Berbers, Yolande. Using Component Composition for Self-customizable Systems. In *Workshop on Component-based Software Engineering* (Lund, Sweden 2002).

[9] Borelli, Frederico, Lopes, Adilson, and Elias, Glêdson. An XML-based Component Specification Model for an Adaptive Middleware of Interactive Digital Television Systems. In *Proceedings of the 18th International Conference on Advanced Information Networking and Application* (Fukuoka, Japan 2004), 457-462.

[10] Coêlho, Andrino S S and Ferraz, Carlos A G. ProfileTV: Um sistema de gerenciamento de perfís em TVDi. In *Anais do 27º Simpósio Brasileiro de Redes de Computadores e Sistemas Distribuídos* (Recife 2009), 627-640.

Towards a Generative Software Development Approach for Rapid Prototyping iDTV Applications

Raoni Kulesza,[1,2]
Silvio R. L. Meira
[1]CIN/UFPE
Cidade Universitária – Campus I
CEP 50740-560 – Recife – PE- Brasil –
[rk,srlm]@cin.ufpe.br

Thales P. Ferreira, Eduardo F. S. Alexadre,
Vicente R. S. Neto, Guido L. S. Filho
[2]LAVID/UFPB
Cidade Universitária – Campus I
CEP 58059-900 – João Pessoa – PB – Brasil
[thales,vicente,eduardo,guido]@lavid.ufpb.br

ABSTRACT
This paper presents an approach for development Interactive Digital TV applications. Methodology seeks to explore concepts and techniques already established in the area of generative software development for rapid prototyping application source code from models. The main goal is to define a systematic method using notations of high level and platform-independent to allow integration of media objects and complex application logic in applications, for example the use of Web Services. In addition, the proposed solution takes care of generating a source compatible with existing authoring tools to allow a subsequent spatial and temporal design of applications. The work also describes a case study for iTV domain for illustration purpose and an experimental pilot study to evaluate the impact of the approach usage.

Categories and Subject Descriptors
D.2.2 [**Software Engineering**]: Design Tools and Techniques - Object-oriented design methods; H.5.4 [**Information Interfaces and Presentation**]: Hypertext/Hypermedia - Multimedia Information Systems

General Terms
Design, Languages, Experimentation

Keywords
Model-driven Development, Generative Software Developmet, Authoring tool, Multimedia Application Development, Digital TV.

1. INTRODUÇÃO
O processo de convergência digital pode ser encarado sobre dois diferentes pontos de vista. No primeiro, a convergência é vista como um casamento de tecnologias ou indústrias, por exemplo, por meio da integração das redes de Internet, telefonia móvel e televisão digital. No segundo, a convergência pode ser vista como uma união de diferentes tipos de mídia por meio de uma tecnologia única. Tal cenário tem favorecido o oferecimento de novos serviços, conhecidos como aplicações multimídia [1].

Uma aplicação multimídia é definida como um software que possui interface com o usuário com pelo menos um objeto de mídia (áudio, vídeo, imagens, animações, gráficos 2D ou 3D) e que estão intimamente vinculados à lógica da aplicação. Isso implica que a relação entre os objetos de mídia pode incluir: (i) criação, exclusão, alteração de objetos de mídia a partir da lógica de aplicação em tempo de execução; e (ii) geração de eventos de objetos de mídia propagados para a lógica da aplicação. Adicionalmente, a concepção dessas aplicações também deve envolver um processo de produção de mídias [4].

O desenvolvimento de aplicações multimídia ainda é um desafio. Além da lógica de negócio, essas aplicações tipicamente oferecem uma interface gráfica sofisticada e integrada com objetos de mídia (imagens, gráficos 3D, áudio e vídeo). Consequentemente, o processo de desenvolvimento deste tipo de aplicação deve considerar o envolvimento de especialistas das áreas de projeto de software, projeto de interface gráfica e produção de mídias. Atualmente, é possível identificar uma lacuna na definição de processos, métodos e ferramentas que auxiliem o desenvolvimento sistemático e que integrem esses três aspectos do projeto das aplicações de TV Digital Interativa (TVDi) [6]. Alguns trabalhos recentes [4, 6, 8] tratam a questão do desenvolvimento de aplicações multimídia e apontam que a rota mais curta para resolver esse desafio é adaptar algumas das abordagens usadas na engenharia de software às restrições e peculiaridades da multimídia.

Uma das metodologias que procura diminuir a complexidade do desenvolvimento de aplicações de domínio específico é o Desenvolvimento Generativo de Software (*GSD – Generative Software Development*) [7], que propõe um processo para criar programas de software a partir de geradores automáticos de código-fonte de forma a aumentar a produtividade de desenvolvimento. Considerado uma metodologia do Desenvolvimento Dirigido por Modelos (MDD – *Model-driven Development*), a diferença entre o *GSD* e outras abordagens é a massiva utilização de tecnologias para automatização do desenvolvimento de software, por exemplo meta-programação, reflexão, transformação de modelos e etc. O objetivo é modelar e implementar "família de sistemas" e que a partir de uma determinada categoria de aplicação possa ser automaticamente gerada a partir de especificações descritas em uma ou mais linguagens de domínio específico (DSL- *Domain Specific Language*) textuais ou visuais. Dentre as vantagens, pode se citar: estão: custos, *time-to-market* e produtividade [20].

No entanto, para definir uma abordagem de desenvolvimento generativo é necessário considerar as várias técnicas empregadas e propriedades específicas de um determinado domínio. Assim, as

Permission to make digital or hard copies of all or part of this work for personal or classroom use is granted without fee provided that copies are not made or distributed for profit or commercial advantage and that copies bear this notice and the full citation on the first page. To copy otherwise, or republish, to post on servers or to redistribute to lists, requires prior specific permission and/or a fee.
WebMedia'12, October 15–18, 2012, São Paulo/SP, Brazil.
Copyright 2012 ACM 978-1-4503-1706-1/12/10...$15.00.

seguintes questões devem ser consideradas: (1) "*Como o GSD pode ser aplicado para o domínio das aplicações de TVDi?*"; (2) "*Como representar as características comuns e variáveis no desenvolvimento dessas aplicações?*"; (3) "*Como garantir que o código gerado seja editado posteriormente em ferramentas de autoria já existentes*"; e (4) "*Qual é o impacto do uso de uma abordagem generativa na produtividade do desenvolvimento de aplicações para TVDi*".

Nesse sentido, este trabalho apresenta uma abordagem de desenvolvimento generativo de software para a prototipação rápida de aplicações para TV Digital Interativa. A metodologia procura explorar conceitos e técnicas já bem estabelecidas na área de desenvolvimento generativo de software para permitir a geração automática do código de protótipos das aplicações a partir de modelos. O objetivo é definir um método sistemático que utilize notações de alto nível e independente de plataforma para estruturar requisitos e integrar melhor objetos de mídia e lógica de negócio complexa, por exemplo o uso de Serviços Web. Adicionalmente, a solução proposta tem a preocupação de gerar um código-fonte compatível com as ferramentas de autoria já existentes de forma a permitir uma posterior edição temporal e espacial das aplicações.

Para avaliar a proposta deste artigo, foi realizado uma prova de conceito mediante a adoção da abordagem para a especificação, projeto e implementação de aplicação de TVDi. Adicionalmente, realizou-se um experimento piloto que vai em direção da definição de um projeto de experimento que facilite a avaliação do impacto do uso de metodologias e ferramentas no desenvolvimento de aplicações multimídia interativas.

O artigo está organizado da seguinte forma: a próxima seção detalha a abordagem proposta A terceira seção descreve uma prova de conceito de utilização da proposta; A quarta discorre sobre os trabalhos relacionados. A quinta apresenta uma avaliação inicial da abordagem servindo-se de um estudo experimental piloto. A sexta e última discute as considerações finais e trabalhos futuros

2. A ABORDAGEM PROPOSTA

Nesta seção é descrita uma abordagem de desenvolvimento generativo de software, que permite a estruturação e geração de código de protótipos de aplicações de TVDi. O objetivo é aplicar metodologias de desenvolvimento para um domínio específico valendo-se de: (i) estruturação dos requisitos de família de aplicações; (ii) configuração das partes comuns e variáveis de cada categoria das aplicações por meio de um modelo de características; (iii) emprego de uma linguagem específica de domínio para modelagem das aplicações; (iv) e utilização de técnicas de meta-programação para geração automática do código das aplicações.

2.1 Visão geral

A Figura 1 exibe a visão geral da proposta dividida em 5 etapas principais. O propósito é partir de requisitos de software e definir como deve ser realizada a construção de um conjunto de modelos abstratos (representados por *templates*) e, posteriormente, a transformação desses elementos em código-fonte. No caso do domínio multimídia alguns artefatos vão possuir características específicas. Por exemplo, na especificação de requisitos é comum utilizar a técnica de *StoryBoard*, que detalham a interação dos usuários, assim como a integração e as propriedades espaciais e temporais dos objetos de mídia. Outro exemplo, e consequência do primeiro exemplo, é que os modelos gerados devem representar não apenas elementos de projeto de software (componentes, classes, interfaces e etc.), mas também objetos de mídia e interação com os usuários. É importante ressaltar também que as etapas estão em sequência, porém é possível retornar para a etapa anterior em qualquer parte do processo para refinar um modelo ou transformação definida. A seguir cada etapa da abordagem é descrita.

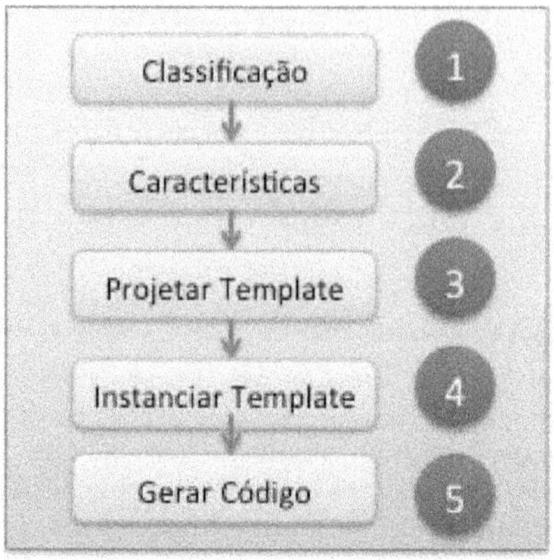

Figura 1 - Visão geral da abordagem proposta

A primeira etapa (*Classificação*) tem como objetivo estruturar os requisitos das aplicações, por intermédio das descrições de cenários de uso, histórias do usuário ou narrativas (por exemplo no formato de um *Storyboard*), que normalmente são definidos pela equipe de produção de mídia (por exemplo, projetista gráfico de jogos, roteirista de TV ou filme e etc.). A partir daí, é possível definir um escopo que representa um conjunto de elementos de uma aplicação, em outras palavras, uma família de sistemas.

A segunda etapa (*Características*) consiste na identificação das características comuns e variáveis de cada categoria de aplicação identificada na etapa anterior. Recomenda-se o uso de um *Modelo de Características* (*feature model*), o qual representa as características dos sistemas de software em um domínio [9]. Estas levam à criação de um conjunto de aplicações que facilita o projeto de cada aplicação. Tanto a primeira, como esta etapa são independentes de representação computacional

Na terceira etapa (*Projetar Template*) uma modelagem de um *Modelo de Template Abstrato* (MTA) é criada com intuito de estruturar a aplicação em termos dos aspectos comuns e variáveis presentes no modelo de características definido anteriormente. Tal elemento pode ser visto, como uma arquitetura de referência para uma determinada categoria de uma família de aplicações, sendo capaz de derivar diversos modelos diferentes decorrentes das configurações realizadas a partir do modelo de características. O MTA é independente de plataforma possuindo uma notação não ambígua e padronizada a fim de permitir a sua transformação em códigos para plataformas diferentes. Para tanto devem ser utilizada alguma linguagem de modelagem com nível de abstração que seja independente de tecnologia e até mesmo de linguagem de programação. Além disso, devido a necessidade de tratar mais do que o projeto de software das aplicações multimídia, é interessante utilizar uma linguagem ou conjunto delas que suportem mais de uma visão sistêmica das aplicações a fim de tornar o desenvolvimento mais rápido, fácil e eficiente. No domínio de aplicações multimídia sugerimos a adoção da linguagem MML (*Multimedia Modeling Language*)[8], que possui as seguintes visões: estrutural, cenas, objetos de mídia, interação do usuário, interface com o usuário.

A quarta etapa consiste em transformar um *Modelo de Template Abstrato* em *Modelos de Templates Concretos* (MTC*)*. Estes representam os modelos que estão associados a algum paradigma e linguagem de programação e são especializações dos modelos anteriores. Nesta etapa também são preenchidas as informações de instâncias, uma vez que um mesmo MTC pode gerar inúmeras aplicações diferentes.

A última etapa transforma o MTC, com informações de instância, para o código-fonte da aplicação específica para uma determinada plataforma alvo. O gerador contém um conjunto de regras de transformação, baseadas no conhecimento de origem (MTC), e da estrutura dos elementos de destino (código para uma plataforma específica). Assim, um único conjunto de MTCs pode ser transformado em código para plataformas diferentes por meio de de módulos de transformação específicos para cada plataforma.

Dentre as vantagens de um processo de desenvolvimento que utilize essas etapas é possível citar: (i) consistência entre as aplicações (*branding*), onde é possível definir e seguir um mesmo padrão para a estrutura, comportamento, identidade visual e etc.; (ii) a definição de um conjunto de aplicações permite facilmente a indexação e agrupamento das mesmas; (iii) como consequência de (i) e (ii), existe também a possibilidade de aumentar o reuso; (iv) apesar de demandar um esforço inicial para o estabelecimento de um conjunto comum de aplicações, uma vez realizado este trabalho, o desenvolvimento de aplicações a partir dos *Templates* se torna mais rápido.

2.2 Visão detalhada

Um detalhamento da abordagem é apresentada na Figura 2. No passo 1, um ator (especialista de domínio ou engenharia de requisitos) define o *Modelo de Características*. Ele representa de um modo geral o universo de possibilidades que um MTA pode tratar. São definidos dois tipos de características: (i) estruturais (especificam elementos estáticos da aplicação) e (ii) dados de instancias (especificam os valores das propriedades dos elementos da aplicação). O objetivo desta separação é possibilitar a construção automática de um formulário de configuração da aplicação. (*Wizard*). Com base no *Modelo de Características* produzido no passo anterior, um ator (Engenheiro ou Arquiteto de Software) cria no passo 2 o MTA em linguagem MML. O objetivo é conter a união dos elementos pertencentes a todas as soluções válidas que são originadas a partir das configurações do Modelo de Características. Para expressar as variabilidades da aplicação, no passo 3 são anotados os elementos do MTA utilizando dois tipos de anotações: (i) condição de presença (CP) e multiplicidade de elementos (M). Estas anotações são definidas em termos das características, e podem ser avaliadas de acordo com uma determinada configuração. Por exemplo, de acordo com uma opção num *Wizard,* um CP permite definir se uma característica deverá estar presente ou ausente num MTC. No passo 4 um ator (desenvolvedor ou engenheiro de aplicação) começa a definir a geração da aplicação com a elaboração de uma configuração manual representado mediante as opções de um *Wizard*. Baseado na definição das escolhas do *Wizard* e no MTA são especificados todos MTCs. No final, os MTCs são instanciados automaticamente e o código da aplicação é gerado (passo 5). Este processo de instanciação envolve primeiramente um mapeamento de modelo para modelo que permite uma transformação de abstrato para concreto e, em seguida, a geração de código final da aplicação.

De acordo com [7], num primeiro momento o *Modelo de Características* e o *Wizard* representam o espaço da problema e o MTA o espaço da solução. Num segundo momento os MTCs representam o espaço do problema e o código-fonte da aplicação do espaço da solução. Configurando um caso de encadeamento de mapeamentos (do inglês, *"Chaining of mappings"*). Ainda segundo [7], na Visão de Configuração, o *Modelo de Características*, o *Wizard* e o MTA representam a configuração de conhecimento e na Visão de Transformação existem dois mapeamentos: (1) MTA para MTC e (2) MTC para código-fonte da aplicação.

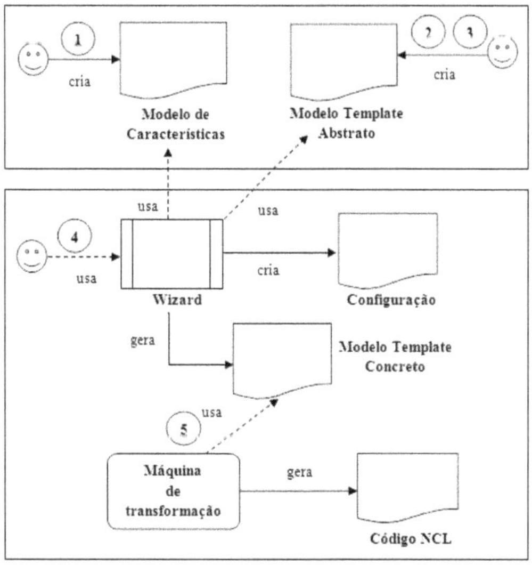

Figura 2 - Visão detalhada da abordagem

3. PROVA DE CONCEITO: TV VOTING

Além da melhoria significa da qualidade de som e imagem, um sistema de TVDi permite também a evolução na forma de acessar o conteúdo servindo-se da possibilidade de integrar softwares e dados aos fluxos audiovisuais transmitidos pelas emissoras. Esta inovação cria oportunidades para a produção e desenvolvimento de aplicações multimídia interativas dos mais diversos tipos, como por exemplo: guias eletrônicos de programas, aplicações de entretenimento (jogos) e educacionais, vídeo sob demanda (VoD), aplicações de comércio eletrônico e governamentais, entre outros. Tais serviços impõem os mesmos desafios de desenvolvimento de software citados anteriormente, pois demandam a definição de novos processos produtivos que agreguem as características de produção de TV (objetos de mídia) e de software [2, 3].

Esta seção busca avaliar a abordagem proposta, mais especificamente, tratando um caso específico de aplicação multimídia: aquelas enviadas aos receptores por uma emissora de TVDi juntamente com o conteúdo audiovisual, utilizando o canal de difusão que está sob seu controle e numa plataforma com ou sem canal de comunicação com a emissora ou a Web.

3.1 Estruturando os requisitos com uma classificação

Um fator crucial para melhorar o desenvolvimento das aplicações de TVDi é a redução do escopo da diversidade de possibilidades, até pouco tempo desconhecidas, já que surgem novos formatos e modos de interação a cada dia. Uma vez que é inviável gerar todos os MTAs de TVDi, a abordagem proposta organiza as características de cada aplicação de acordo com uma estrutura que contemple os principais cenários de uso daquele serviço.

Baseado em [5], as aplicações foram divididas em 3 categorias: *pull delivery*, *feedback channel* e *distributed.* Esta taxonomia considera que qualquer aplicação multimídia é uma estória que tem o intuito de imergir o usuário no fluxo da sua narrativa, por meio da interação com um mundo virtual comunicação entre os participantes deste mundo e acessando objetos de mídia num modo natural e guiado. Nesse contexto, abaixo o resumo das três categorias, mais detalhes em [16]:

Pull delivery: aplicações que possuem narrativas lineares e aquelas com possibilidade limitadas de opções, pois o conteúdo e os dados da aplicação se limitam ao que foi predefinido pela TV e que foi transmitido por intermédio de um canal unidirecional (difusão) controlado pela emissora, ou seja, o conteúdo é coletivo e todos os usuários recebem a mesmas possibilidades de interação.

Feedback channel: aplicações que possuem comunicação bidirecional com o gerador do conteúdo inicial, de forma a permitir a entrega de conteúdo e possibilidades de interação individual e permitir ramificações nas alternativas não-lineares e bem mais elaboradas.

Distributed: aplicações que permitem agregar conteúdo, funcionalidades ou plataformas completas já disponíveis na Web (por exemplo, um serviço Web), tornando suas narrativas evolucionárias, uma vez que o estado final da execução deste tipo de aplicação é não determinístico, já que em nenhum momento do tempo é possível determiná-lo.

Para melhor ilustrar o emprego da abordagem proposta escolhemos uma aplicação que possa ser configurada para se encaixar nas três categorias e assim representar melhor o domínio das aplicações de TVDi. A aplicação escolhida é conhecida como *TV Voting*, que permite ao usuário participar de uma enquete pela TV. A partir dessa opção foram definidas três versões da mesma: (1) enquete com envio da resposta por meio de canal indireto com a emissora (telefone, SMS, email, site Web e etc.) e recebimento do resultado apenas ao final da votação; (2) enquete com envio da resposta e recebimento de resultado "ao vivo" pelo intermédio de um canal direto com a emissora mediante um protocolo específico (por exemplo, sockets ou HTTP); e (3) enquete com envio da resposta e recebimento de resultado "ao vivo" valendo-se de canal direto com um serviço Web (SOAP ou REST) que representa um "Servidor de enquetes". A aplicação é composta por 3 cenas obrigatórias: (1) cena com ícone de interatividade (inicia interação); (2) cena de votação (com exibição da pergunta e opções de respostas) (3) cena com confirmação do envio da resposta e, se existir comunicação, resultado parcial ou final da enquete. Uma cena opcional de detalhamento da opção escolhida e confirmação do voto também é permitida.

3.2 Especificação do modelo de características

A Figura 3 apresenta algumas das características definidas para descrever as possíveis soluções de modelos para a aplicação *TV Voting*. O conjunto de características relacionadas aos aspectos estruturais e aos valores das instâncias dos *templates* são exibidos na visão *Structural* e *DataInstantiation*, respectivamente. O modelo *Structural* define, além de outras opções variáveis, a característica alternativa *QuestionFormat*, que indica as possibilidades da enquete com múltipla escolha ou da enquete com resposta aberta. A opção de exibir informações para as respostas é tratada pela característica opcional *ChoiceInformation*. A característica *InteractionMode* representa o modo de interação do usuário com a enquete e possui as opções para indicar uma interação sem comunicação (*Indirect*) ou com comunicação (*ReturnChannel*) , este último possuindo um conjunto de característica alternativas (*WebService*, *Http* e *Socket)*. Já o modelo *DataInstantiation* do *TV Voting* possui as opções para preencher os valores relativos a questão (*Question)*, as respostas (*Answers*), informações do modo de comunicação (*Interaction*) e, opções para especificar as imagens dos *backgrounds* das cenas, inclusive a cena opcional de confirmação.

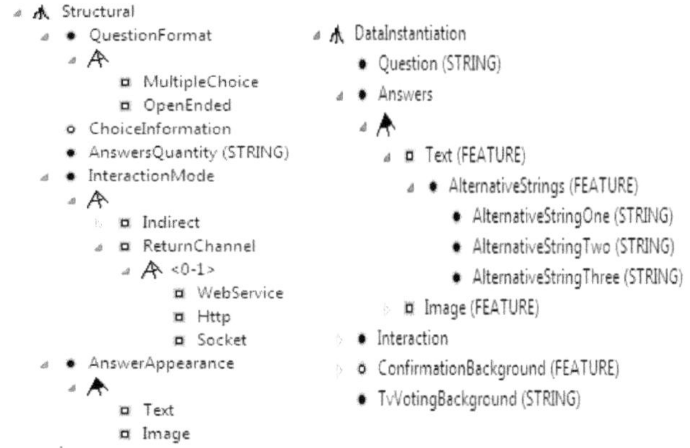

Figura 3 - Modelo de características de *TV Voting*

3.3 Modelo de Template Abstrato e variabilidades associadas

O *MTA* de *TV Voting* é descrito pelos modelos relacionado às visões estruturais e comportamentais da linguagem MML. Dessa forma, o *template* é composto pelos seguintes modelos: (i) estrutural, (i) de cena, (iii) de apresentação e; (iv) de interação. Além disso, as variabilidades de cada modelo são especificados como estereótipos UML que são anotados junto aos elementos do modelo. Cada estereótipo é mapeado para uma determinada característica. Como descrito na seção III, cada *MTA* não se limita a especificar apenas uma solução da família de modelos, mas sim conter a união de todas as possíveis soluções de *MTCs* . Por conta da limitação do espaço ilustramos apenas alguns diagramas UML a seguir.

De acordo com o MML, a primeira modelagem a ser realizada é a estrutural, nela se evidencia os elementos do domínio, bem como o seu relacionamento com as respectivas mídias. Na Figura 4 é ilustrado modelo estrutural de *TV Voting.* Ele é composto pelos elementos do modelo (classes, associações e etc.) e das anotações dos mesmos, realizadas pelos estereótipos. Estes mapeiam os elementos do modelo para as características. O modelo contém uma classe para a enquete (*Poll*), que possui uma pergunta e duas ou mais respostas (A*nswer*), e por fim o resultado parcial da votação (*Result*). Ainda nesse modelo, fica explícito os elementos do domínio associados aos elementos de mídia *AnswerIcon*, *AnswerText*, *PollBackground*, respectivamente, um objeto de mídia imagem e um objeto de mídia texto para perguntas e um objeto de mídia imagem para compor o fundo da cena de votação. Outro aspecto importante é a representação do modo de interação sem canal de retorno (*ReplyData)* e com canal de retorno (*ReturnChannel*) que permite configurar o protocolo de acesso e associá-lo a aplicação de forma modular.

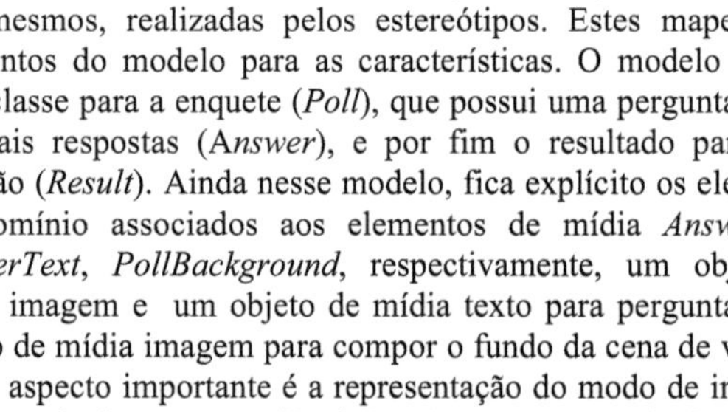

Figura 4 - Modelo *estrutural* de *TV Voting*

Já o modelo de cenas deve especificar o comportamento geral da aplicação por um conjunto de estados de transições entre eles. A Figura 5 apresenta o template com 5(cinco) estados para representar as seguintes cenas: de interatividade (*Start*), de votação (*TvVoting*), de resultado da votação (*Result*) e a cena opcional para exibir a confirmação e as informações da resposta selecionada (*InfoAnswer*). Tal modelo foi baseado nas possibilidades de cenas e sequência entre elas e de acordo com as seguintes variações: (i) permitir ou não a exibição das informações adicionais para a resposta escolhida e (ii) adição de cenas de informações adicionais de acordo com a quantidade de respostas existentes. Para a primeira variação, representado pela característica *ChoiceInformation* (Figura 3), o modelo exibe a cena *InfoAnswer* da resposta escolhida e, após o voto ter sido confirmado, a cena com o resultado da votação é exibido. Caso contrário, na ausência de *ChoiceInformation*, é exibido apenas a cena de votação (*TvVoting*) e em seguida a cena com a confirmação e resultado (*Result*). Para a segunda opção, associada a característica *AnswersQuantity*, a cena é anotada para criar cópias da cena *InfoAnswer* específicas para cada resposta. Na modelagem, cada cena representa uma tela da aplicação e esta tem a sua interface com o usuário especificada por um modelo de apresentação de cena, explicado a seguir.

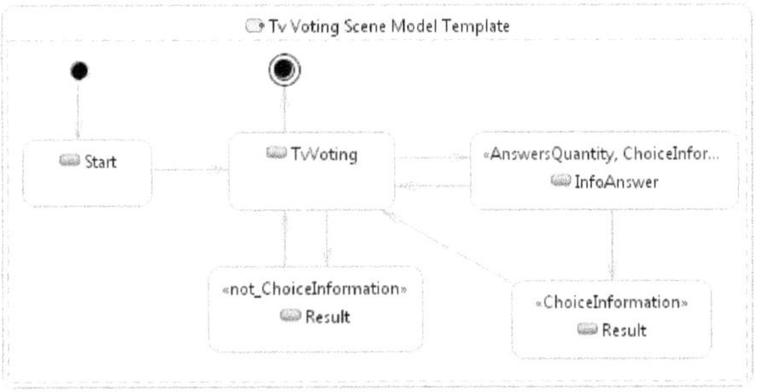

Figura 5 - Modelo de *cena* de *TV Voting*

O modelo de apresentação da cena (Figura 6) de votação descreve os elementos da interface gráfica pelas classes *AnswerText*, *QuestionText* e *Background*, que representam, respectivamente, os textos das respostas, da questão e uma imagem para compor o fundo da cena. Elas são anotadas com o estereótipo *OuputComponent* de modo a representar um componente abstrato para exibição de dados. Os valores a serem exibidos são obtidos tomando como base uma dependência para um elemento responsável por armazenar os dados. Por exemplo, o texto da resposta é obtido utilizando a dependência '*src*' cujo valor é a propriedade *aternativeString* especificada no elemento *answer*. O estereótipo *AnswersQuantity* define a variabilidade quanto a presença da quantidade de respostas especificada para a aplicação.

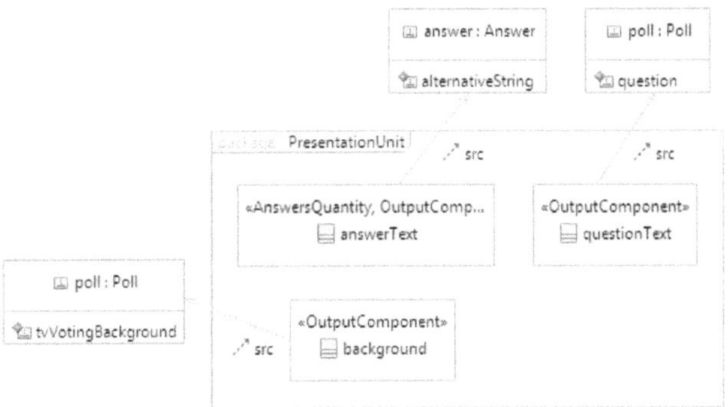

Figura 6 - Modelo de apresentação do *TV Voting*

A Figura 7 apresenta o modelo de interação para a cena *InfoAnswer*. É utilizado um diagrama de atividades para especificar o relacionamento temporal entre os objetos de mídia. Tal semântica foi baseada no modelo NCM [15] e foi definida como uma extensão do MML, pois não era considerada no projeto inicial da linguagem MML. No caso, cada partição é utilizada para especificar um elo, que indica uma relação causal entre as mídias. Os nomes das partições indicam o nome do conector utilizado pelo elo. Internamente tem-se basicamente o elemento do tipo *AcceptEventAction* para representar a condição e outros elementos do tipo *CallBehaviourAction* para representar as ações a serem disparadas. O diagrama da Figura 7 especifica a inicialização dos componentes de interface gráfica (partição *onBeginStart*) e o fluxo de voto de uma determinada opção escolhida (partição *onKeySelectionSet*). Ainda nesse modelo, mas não apresentado no diagrama, outro fluxo é responsável por encaminhar o resultado parcial da votação, retornado pelo canal de retorno, para ser exibido na cena de resultado (*Result*). O elemento *{Integer [1..*]}* especifica a variabilidade da aplicação quanto ao número da resposta escolhida. O valor para a resposta é definido de acordo com a cena atual da resposta escolhida.

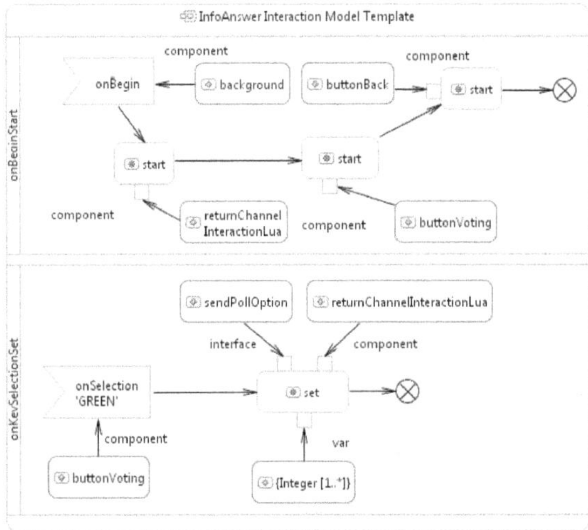

Figura 7 - Modelo de interação de *TV Voting*

3.4 Modelos de Templates Abstratos

Um MTC representa o processamento das variabilidades do MTA de acordo com as opções definidas. Estas escolhas são satisfeitas por uma configuração do *Modelo de Características* que é criada pelo *Wizard*. A seguir são ilustradas duas instâncias (MTC) do MTA: estrutural e de cenas. Assumiremos que a configuração escolhida foi uma enquete com perguntas e respostas do tipo textual, com 3 (três) opções respostas, com tela de informação das respostas e canal de retorno utilizando *Web Service*.

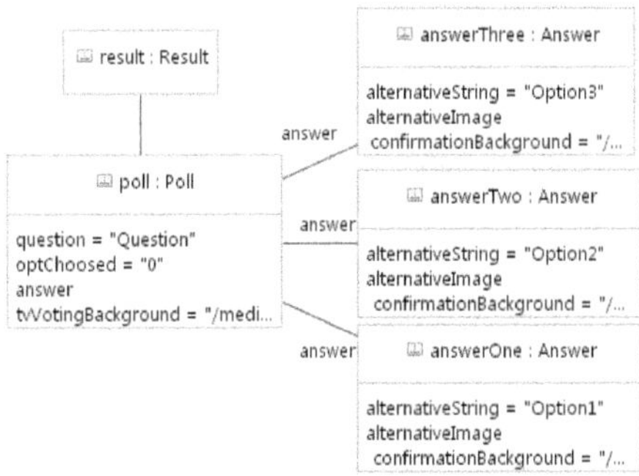

Figura 8 - Modelo estrutural instanciado de *TV Voting*

Por se tratar de um diagrama de classes, a instância do modelo estrutural da Figura 8 é obtida pela transformação para um diagrama de objetos. Cada classe é mapeada para um objeto, o qual tem seus *"slots"* criados de acordo com as propriedades das classes e seus valores preenchidos pelo *Wizard*. Adicionalmente (**Figura 9**), são criados os estados referentes a cada cena com informações adicionais das respostas e uma cena de confirmação/resultado que é apresentada logo após o voto ocorrer na cena de informações adicionais.

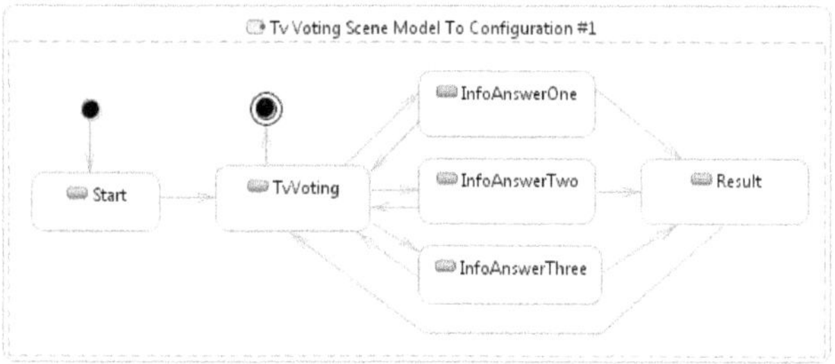

Figura 9 - Modelo de cena instanciado de *TV Voting*

3.5 Geração da Aplicação

Para auxiliar na geração de código a aplicação é disponibilizado um conjunto de formulários de aplicações (*Wizard*) que guia o usuário por intermédio de uma série de passos, para que o preenchimento das informações pendentes dos *templates* (variabilidades) aconteça e a aplicação seja gerada. O objetivo é prover uma interface de alto nível para o desenvolvedor que deseje criar e personalizar protótipos aplicações definidas utilizando a abordagem. A seguir um descrição dos principais passos realizados para geração de uma versão da aplicação *TV Voting*.

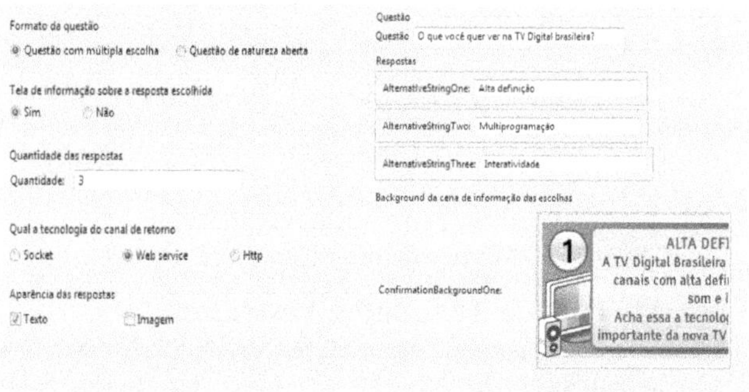

(a) (b)

Figura 10 –Wizards para configuração das característivas estruturais (a) e de valores(b) de *TV Voting*

No primeiro passo é possível escolher um tipo de protótipo disponível. No caso, também já está disponível uma aplicação de *SlideShow*, não detalhada neste artigo por questões de espaço. No segundo passo definem-se as variações das características estruturais. Por exemplo, é informado a quantidade de respostas e a se tem ou não tela de informação (Figura 10a). O terceiro passo define os dados das características de valores dos MTCs, por exemplo, informar os valores textuais da pergunta e das respostas e as imagens correspondentes a cada tela (Figura 10b). O último passo é acionar a geração, que vai utilizar a configuração e MTA para gerar os vários MTCs que instanciam uma aplicação.

Para transformar os MTCs no código da aplicação consideramos a geração para plataforma Ginga-NCL, padrão utilizado para desenvolver aplicações para TVDI no Brasil e na América Latina. O mapeamento foi realizado utilizado a ferramenta *MOFScript*. Além de outras funcionalidades, basicamente o *MOFScript*[1] define uma linguagem tipo script para realizar transformações de texto a partir de modelos MOF que representam os modelos em MML.

4. AVALIAÇÃO INICIAL

Para avaliar a abordagem proposta foi realizado um experimento piloto com estudantes com o objetivo de observar a relação causa-efeito entre uma metodologia e a produtividade no desenvolvimento de aplicações de TVDi Para tanto, foi utilizado o processo definido por [10] para definir o estudo (Tabela 1).

Tabela - Definição do estudo

Analisar o uso de uma abordagem generativa apoiada por uma ferramenta para a desenvolvimento de aplicações de TVDi
Com o objetivo de avaliar o impacto do uso da abordagem na produtividade.
Com respeito a velocidade do desenvolvimento de software por meio do emprego da abordagem.
Do ponto de vista do desenvolvedor de software.
No contexto de estudantes de graduação da área de computação com conhecimento em alguma linguagem de programação e especificação de requisitos com *storyboard* e casos de uso.

Em relação a seleção de contexto o estudo foi realizado com estudantes, com o objetivo de atuar como sujeitos do experimento. Para tanto, foram escolhidos 14 estudantes de graduação da área de Computação durante o segundo semestre de 2012. Tais sujeitos foram preparados mediante treinamento na área de desenvolvimento de aplicações multimídia, especificamente TVDI e Ginga NCL-Lua, com carga-horária de 24 horas realizado dias antes da execução do estudo. No que diz respeito a seleção das variáveis, as independentes (aplicação de TV Digital típica, especificação dos requisitos utilizando *Storyboard* e casos de uso e utilização da tecnologia Ginga NCL-Lua para implementação) foram escolhidas para configurar o uso e não uso da abordagem. Já as variáveis dependentes foram definidas por 2 (duas) métricas de desenvolvimento de softwares, descritas a seguir.

O experimento apresentou um único fator, que se trata da metodologia a ser utilizada. Diante deste fato, são definidos dois níveis desse fator:

- ***M1***: emprego do ambiente de desenvolvimento NCL-Eclipse[14], representando o uso de uma abordagem não dirigida por modelos
- ***M2***: emprego de uma ferramenta de geração de código que implementa as técnicas definidas para a abordagem generativa proposta e posterior uso da mesma ferramenta utilizada em M1 para finalização da aplicação.

A hipótese geral que se desejou investigar no experimento foi: *"O uso de uma abordagem generativa traz medidas diferentes de velocidade para o desenvolvimento de aplicações para TVDi?"*. Para tanto, o seguinte dados foi coletado :

- *TI (tempo de implementação)*: tempo para implementar um conjunto de requisitos definidos por casos de uso;

Considerando *Mx,x= 1, 2* os dois tratamentos aplicados no experimento, a métrica *TI (Mx)* (tempo de implementação dos requisitos) foi utilizada para definir as seguintes hipóteses nulas e as respectivas hipóteses alternativas:

1 Disponível em: http://www.eclipse.org/gmt/mofscript/

- ***Hipóteses Nulas (H_0 1..2):*** As metodologias de desenvolvimento são semelhantes com relação à propriedade velocidade (TI):

$$H0_1: TI(M1) \cong TI(M2)$$

- ***Hipóteses Alternativas (H_1 1..2):*** A metodologia de desenvolvimento utilizando a abordagem generativa (M2) possui valores menores do que a metodologia sem uso da abordagem (M1) em relação a velocidade (TI):

$$H1_1: TI(M1) > TI(M2)$$

O suporte instrumental foi representado por três elementos: (1) a especificação da aplicação de TVDi a ser desenvolvida (objeto); (2) documentação com interações e versões da aplicação exigidas modificações solicitadas (disponível apenas no momento da solicitação da mudança de requisitos) e instruções gerais com roteiro com todos os passos a seguir na execução do estudo (diretrizes); (3) laboratório com ambiente de desenvolvimento Ginga NCL-Lua instalado, juntamente com software para coleta de métricas de forma precisa (ferramentas de suporte).

O estudo foi caracterizado como um projeto de experimento totalmente aleatorizado e balanceado com a análise das amostras de forma independente. A ideia foi assegurar que os tratamentos tivessem igual número de participantes e para possibilitar a comparação dos efeitos das variáveis independentes. Os participantes foram divididos em dois grupos, cada um com 7 pessoas. E para cada grupo foi aplicado um tratamento diferente (M1 e M2). No caso, o objetivo da atividade foi desenvolver uma aplicação do *TV Voting* utilizando o NCL-Eclipse e uma ferramenta desenvolvida para uso da abordagem proposta. A aplicação foi especificada contendo uma tela com informação adicional sobre cada opção de resposta escolhida e o voto deveria ser enviado através de um serviço Web REST. Todos os objetos de mídia (ícone de interatividade da tela de início, figuras e background da tela de votação e figuras e background das telas de confirmação e informações adicionais) foram previamente disponibilizados para os desenvolvedores.

Após a execução do experimento e coleta de dados, uma análise calculou que a média de tempo de implementação (TI) das aplicações utilizando a abordagem generativa foi de *15494 segundos*, o que representa *4,30 horas*. Já a utilização da metodologia tradicional, gastou-se em média *18965* segundos ou *5,26 horas*. Com esses dados é possível obter que o valor da diferença média foi de *3472 segundos* ou *0,96 horas*. Porém, devido a diferença alta entre as medidas individuais de cada participante, ainda não foi possível obter nenhuma conclusão sobre as hipóteses. Acredita-se que a principal causa foi na instrumentação do experimento, como por exemplo, o uso de um mecanismo manual de coleta de tempo. Novos estudos precisam ser planejados e realizados.

5. TRABALHOS RELACIONADOS

Nesta seção é descrita uma análise de estudos divida em 2 tópicos: (i) ambientes de desenvolvimento e (ii) metodologias de desenvolvimento. O primeiro está relacionado a ambientes, normalmente representados por ferramentas de autoria, que integram várias tecnologias de implementação e visões do projeto de uma aplicação de TVDi. O segundo aborda pesquisas que tratam o desenvolvimento de aplicativos por meio de elementos do GSD para domínios específicos. É importante também lembrar que este trabalho é uma extensão e evolução dos trabalhos apresentados em [6][16] através da adoção de técnicas de GSD e realização de avaliações mais detalhadas.

No tocante a ambientes de desenvolvimento, podemos destacar: *NCL Eclipse* [14], *Composer*[13] e *MoonDo-Eclipse* [17]. Em relação ao *NCL Eclipse* e o *Composer*, este trabalho procura complementar as funcionalidades desses dois ambientes através de: (i) estruturação de requisitos através de uma classificação das aplicações e oferta de um conjunto de protótipos; (ii) reutilização de projetos de software de uma família de aplicações de TVDi de forma a garantir maior eficiência e rapidez na geração de protótipos; e (iii) configuração de pontos de extensão ou informação de instancias dos protótipos sem necessidade de conhecimento de código-fonte. Dessa forma, a partir da geração do protótipo com a abordagem proposta é possível utilizar posteriormente o *NCL-Eclipse* para uma programação mais detalhada do código-fonte da aplicação ou o *Composer* para uma edição visual que permite alterar o comportamento de layout e apresentações especial e temporal da aplicação. Porém, a estrutura da arquitetura da aplicação é tratada inicialmente na geração do protótipo. Em relação *MonDoo-Eclipse*, é possível afirmar que o mesmo contém as mesmos benefícios da metodologia proposta, entretanto, por priorizar uma geração de código da aplicação que é estruturada através do paradigma orientado a objetos e linguagens imperativas, o protótipo gerado pelo *MonDoo-Eclipse* não é compatível com as edições visuais disponíveis no *Composer*, inviabilizando uma posterior edição criativa do código.

Em relação às metodologias de desenvolvimento é possível destacar o trabalho apresentado em [8] que enfoca o desenvolvimento de aplicações multimídia interativas através da especificação da MML. O principal objetivo é permitir que o processo envolva diferentes especialistas pertencentes aos três tipos de projeto existente: projeto de software; interface gráfica com o usuário e produção de mídias. O trabalho proposto adota a MML como DSL. Porém, foi incluída uma etapa para estruturar os requisitos através de técnicas de análise de domínio (taxonomia e modelo de características) e, consequentemente, facilitar o projeto do domínio através da definição e configuração dos *templates* modelados com MML. Além disso, também foi avaliado o uso de MML num subdomínio específico de aplicações multimídia, através de: (i) extensão dos meta-modelos para tratar questões específicas de TVDi e Serviços Web; e (ii) emprego de técnicas de programação generativa para transformação de modelos para modelos e de modelos para código de aplicações.

O trabalho [18] descreve uma abordagem de prototipagem rápida adotando GSD para permitir a geração automática de um protótipo totalmente funcional de uma aplicação Web. Um ponto interessante e comum a esta proposta é que o processo e as tecnologias utilizadas para implementar essa abordagem podem ser reutilizados para a abordagem de prototipagem rápida para modelos de design diferente e/ou plataformas diferentes. Uma deficiência do trabalho é não tratar o conceito de *templates* de software para a modelagem da aplicação, tornando inviável a estruturação de requisitos para domínios específicos. Em [19] é descrita uma pesquisa que propõe uma abordagem GSD para o desenvolvimento de aplicações RIA (*Rich Internet Application*) utilizando metodologias e notações pré-existentes. Para tanto, é proposto um conjunto de metodologias GSD, que devem ser integradas em ambientes de desenvolvimento, para oferecer edição de modelos e funções de geração de código. Os principais benefícios alcançados estão relacionados da produtividade de desenvolvimento através da melhoria da expressividade da arquitetura da aplicação e maior facilidade de desenvolvimento utilizando modelos de uma DSL para geração de código de padrões arquiteturais em um ciclo de prototipagem rápida. Tal trabalho tem objetivos e questões de pesquisa bem próximas deste trabalho, mas, além de tratar domínio diferente de aplicações (Web), não realiza nenhum experimento para avaliar quantitativamente o uso da abordagem.

6. CONSIDERAÇÕES FINAIS

Este trabalho propõe uma abordagem para prototipagem rápida de aplicações de TVDI através de: (i) estruturação dos requisitos de família de aplicações; (ii) configuração das partes comuns e variáveis de cada categoria das aplicações através de um modelo de características; (iii) emprego de uma linguagem de domínio específico para estruturar os protótipos das aplicações; e (iv) utilização de técnicas de meta-programação para geração automática do código-fonte.

Através da prova de conceito foi possível analisar que o GSD pode ser aplicado no domínio de aplicações de TVDi através da estruturação de requisitos das aplicações utilizando *Wizards* e *Modelo de Características*. É possível obter a integração de visões relacionadas a lógica de aplicação (por exemplo, acesso a um serviço Web) e também a apresentação da interface gráfica e interação com o usuário através de MML, que tem como principal característica a definição de modelos para múltiplas visões de um software, permitindo atacar a natureza multidisciplinar das aplicações multimídia. A geração de código foi facilitada através de encadeamento de mapeamentos entre a estruturação de requisitos, modelagem de *templates* (abstratos e concretos) e motores de transformação (*MOFScript*) para plataformas específicas. Nesse caso, um dos principais benefícios do uso da abordagem foi a melhor estruturação dos requisitos. Por exemplo, a inclusão e configuração de serviços Web integrado com outros elementos da aplicação (elementos de interface gráfica e objetos de mídia). A principal dificuldade encontrada foi o esforço realizado para a modelagem dos *templates*.

Para avaliar o impacto do uso abordagem foi planejado e executado um experimento controlado piloto, método científico ainda pouco explorado na área de desenvolvimento de aplicações para TVDi. A ideia é procurar avaliar o desenvolvimento de uma aplicação utilizando diferentes abordagem e/ou ferramentas. Porém, apesar de representar algum ganho em relação a velocidade de implementação das aplicações, o experimento apresentou uma diferença de valores individuais muito grande entre os participantes. No prosseguimento desse trabalho, os seguintes pontos deverão ser atacados: (i) realização de novos estudos empíricos para melhorar o projeto experimental e obter mais amostras que tragam evidências que novas abordagens trazem ou não algum benefício (ii) outras provas de conceito no desenvolvimento de outras aplicações de TVDi; e (iii) implementação de um editor visual de *templates* para facilitar e acelerar a elaboração de novos modelos de templates.

REFERÊNCIAS

[1] Alfonsi, B. I Want My IPTV: Internet Protocol Television Predicted a Winner. *IEEE Distributed Systems Online*, 2005.

[2] Bachmayer S.; Lugmayr A.; Kotsis, G. Convergence of Collaborative Web Approaches And Interactive TV Program Formats. Int. *Journal of Web Information Systems*, 2010.

[3] Coppens, T.; Handekyn, K.; And Vanparijs, F. *AmigoTV: A Social TV Experience Through Triple-Play Convergence.* Alcatel Technology white paper. 4p, 2005.

[4] Engels G.; Sauer, S. Object-oriented Modeling of Multimedia Applications, *Handbook of Software Engineering and Knowledge Engineering*, S. K. Chang, Ed. Singapore: World Scientific, v. 2, p. 21–53, 2002.

[5] Kaskalis, T. H.; Tzidamis, T. D.; Margaratis, K. Multimedia Authoring Tools: The Quest for an Educational Package. *Educational Technology & Society*, p.135-162, 2007.

[6] Neto, M. C. M. e Santos, C. A. S. StoryToCode: A new model for specification of convergent interactive digital TV applications. *Journal of the Brazilian Computer Society*. p3-21, Oct.2010.

[7] K. Czarnecki, *Overview of generative software development. In* UPP 2004, vol. 3566 of LNCS, pp. 326-341, Springer, 2004.

[8] Pleuss, A. e Hussmann, H. Model-Driven Development of Interactive Multimedia Applications with MML. *Studies in Computation Intelligence.* Springer: v. 340, 199-218, 2011.

[9] Kang K. C. et a.l *Feature-Oriented Domain Analysis (FODA) – Feasibility Study*, CMU/SEI-90-TR-21, SEI/CMU, 1990.

[10] C. Wohlin, P. Runeson, M. Host, B. Regnell, and A. Wessl en. *Experimentation in Software Engineering: An Introduction.* Kluwer Academic Publishers, 2000.

[11] Raj Jain. *The art of computer systems performance analysis: techiniques for experimental design, measurement, simulation and modeling.* Wiley, 1991.

[12] Shari Pfleeger. Design and Analysis in Software Engineering, Part 1: The Language of Case Studies and Formal Experiments. *Software Engineering Notes*, 19(4):16–20, 1994.

[13] Lima, B. S. et al. Composer 3: Ambiente de autoria extensível, adaptável e multiplataforma. In: *XVI Simpósio Brasileito de Sistemas Multimídia e Web (WebMedia 2010) - Workshop de TV Digital Interativa.* 2010. Belo Horizonte.

[14] Azevedo, R. G. A. et al. Textual Authoring of Interactive Digital TV Applications. *In: Proceedings of the IX European Conference on Interactive Television.* 2011. p.235-243. ACM. Lisboa..

[15] ITU-T Recommendation H.761. *Nested Context Language (NCL) and Ginga-NCL for IPTV Services.* Geneva, April 2009.

[16] Kulesza et al. A Model-driven Approach for Integration of Interactive Applications and Web Services: A Case Study in Interactive Digital TV Platform. In: *Proceedings of the 2012 IEEE International Conference on Multimedia and Expo Workshops (ICME 2012).* p.266-271. Austrália, 2012.

[17] Prota, T. M. *MoonDo-Eclipse: Um Ambiente para Desenvolvimento de Aplicações Declarativas para o SBTVD.* 167f. Dissertação (Mestrado), Universidade Federal de Pernambuco, Recife, 2012.

[18] Bernadi, M. L.; Di Lucca G. A.; Distante D. A Model-Driven Approach for the Fast Proto-typing of Web Applications. In: *XXIII IEEE International Symposium on Web Systems Evolution* (WSE 2011). p.65-74. Benevento, 2011.

[19] Fraternali, P; Comai. S.; Bozzon, A. Engineering Rich Internet Applications with a Model-Driven Approach. *ACM Transactions on the Web.* v.4,(2). ACM. Nova Iorque, 2010.

[20] Baas, L. Clements, P.; Kazman, R. *Software Architecture in Practice.* Second Edition. SEI Series in Software Engineering. Addison-Wesley, 2003.

Reuse in Implementations of Middleware for Digital TV

César A. C. Teixeira
Universidade Federal de São Carlos
São Carlos-SP, Brazil
cesar@dc.ufscar.br

Eduardo D. Sardinha
Fundação Centro de Análise, Pesquisa e
Inovação Tecnológica (FUCAPI)
Manaus-AM, Brazil
eduardo.sardinha@fucapi.br

ABSTRACT

This paper presents an approach to develop new instances of interactive digital TV – DTV middleware based on reuse and port of existing implementations of these middlewares for other hardware platforms. Design characteristics of DTV middleware and software portability concepts are used to propose a reuse model. A proof of concept using an implementation of the Brazilian DTV middleware (Ginga) showed that the approach can be useful within specific portability contexts.

Categories and Subject Descriptors

D.2.13 [**Reusable Software**]: Reuse models; I.7.2 [**Document Preparation**]: Standards

General Terms

Design, Experimentation

Keywords

Digital TV, Middleware, Reusability, Portability

1. INTRODUCTION

The development of an implementation of DTV middleware from scratch is a complex and costly task. In such large projects, software reuse became an important tool for saving cost and time [1][2].

In past decades, reuse[1] has been used to increase quality and productivity, saving coding efforts, testing, etc [3]. Nevertheless, reusability isn't always a design requirement, because development for reuse may increase the cost of a project.

Software may be adapted or customized in order to be reused — even those weren't designed for it. Porting software to other environments (another hardware platform, for instance) is one such example; as affirmed Mooney, portability is a clear form of reusability [4].

In this paper, we present an approach to develop new instances of DTV middleware based on reuse and port of existing implementations of these middlewares for other hardware platforms.

Software portability concepts and design characteristics of DTV middleware (Sections 3 and 4) — which encompasses both middleware architecture and implementation issues — are used to propose a reuse model.

Our reuse model is mainly intended to be used with middlewares that weren't designed for full reuse of its implementation.

The remainder of this paper is organized as follows. Sections 2 and 3 review, respectively, some concepts of software portability and DTV middleware. Section 4 presents the reuse model and its application in a case study using an implementation of Ginga, the middleware for Brazilian DTV System. In Section 5 we discuss some related work, and Section 6 presents our final remarks and future work.

2. DEGREE OF PORTABILITY

The effort required to port a software depends always on the *context of portability* [5], which encompasses the differences between the original and target environments for the software to be ported. Issues on hardware, operating system – OS, and external dependencies from other softwares are aspects that may limit portability.

Thereby, portability is a context-dependent attribute and can be measured through *degree of portability* [4], a metric which relates software portability to the ratio between the cost of porting and the cost of redevelopment.

Before the porting process, all thir-party dependencies (libraries, components, etc.) must be mapped, since their use in the target environment may not be appropriate (absent source code or executable, difficult to port, etc.). The smaller the number of dependencies, greater is the degree of portability [6][5][4].

3. ITU-T J.200

DTV middleware is generally compatible with the ITU-T J.200 Recommendation [7], which specifies the middleware architecture as being composed of three major entities or subsystems: Presentation Engine (declarative environment), Execution Engine (imperative environment) and Common Subsystem, through which both engines can access resources and functions of the DTV receptor (graphics, audio and video decoders, remote control, etc.).

[1]The term reuse is also used in this paper as synonym for software reuse.

Permission to make digital or hard copies of all or part of this work for personal or classroom use is granted without fee provided that copies are not made or distributed for profit or commercial advantage and that copies bear this notice and the full citation on the first page. To copy otherwise, to republish, to post on servers or to redistribute to lists, requires prior specific permission and/or a fee.
WebMedia'12, October 15–28, 2012, São Paulo/SP, Brazil.
Copyright 2012 ACM 978-1-4503-1706-1/12/10 ...$15.00.

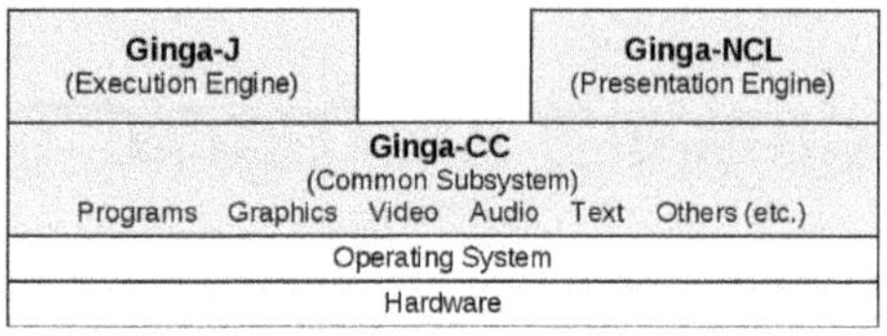

Figure 1: Ginga middleware

Figure 1 shows the architecture of Ginga [8], which is adherent to ITU-T J.200. Ginga-J and Ginga-NCL subsystems are responsible for supporting applications written in Java language and NCL, respectively; the common subsystem is known as Ginga-CC or Common Core.

4. REUSE OF DTV MIDDLEWARE

4.1 Reuse Model

Implementations of DTV middleware make use of custom hardware resources, such as video decoding and graphic rendering. Such features are typically available through custom low-level APIs whose source code often, or isn't available, or is hard to port to other platforms. Therefore, reuse and port of full implementations of middleware to different hardware platforms can be very difficult (or even impossible).

On the other hand, DTV middleware is very complex software, whose development tends to be costly and time consuming. In such large projects, software reuse became an important tool for saving cost and time.

Use of layered architectures (Figure 1), frameworks, subsystems, components, and languages that aim to portability, like C, C++ and Java — widely used to develop middleware — enhances both reusability and portability [1][2][9].

Architecture layering is a design solution widely used in the development of DTV middleware, as can be seen in [1][10][11][12], and other works. In this implementation model, levels of abstraction are used to encapsulate a set of functionality, isolating and limiting the use of custom/non-portable software to the inner layers — those closer to the OS/hardware.

Therefore, it is reasonable to assume that software at outer layers (like Presentation or Execution Engine, as shown in Figure 1) has a higher degree of portability and potential of reuse than those at the inner layers (like the Common Subsystem).

Considering this scenario and analysis, we propose a reuse model that comprises the development of DTV middleware (for a given hardware platform) based on reuse and port of software assets from existing implementations of these middlewares for other hardware platforms. Our approach consist of a two-step process (Figure 2):

1. Selection and customization of software assets from the middleware implementation, in order to create one or more reusable software components.

2. Porting the generated components to a new hardware platform, in order to integrate them into a new implementation of the middleware for this platform.

It is important to emphasize that, as seen above, the software assets to be customized (step 1) must be selected from

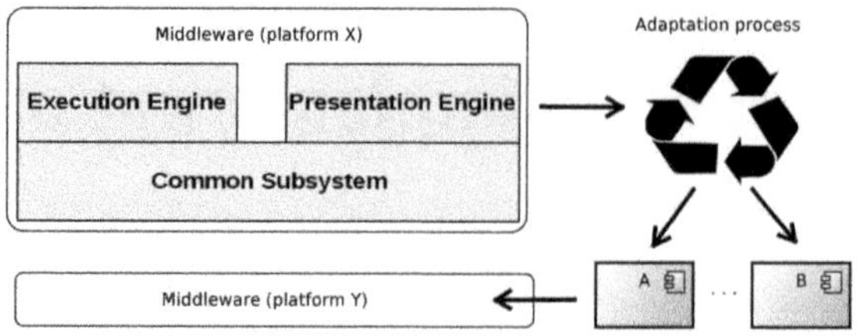

Figure 2: Reuse model for DTV middleware

those subsystems most suitable for porting and reuse activities, like Presentation and Execution Engines.

Another important issue for the model is the context of portability (step 2). In order to limit the scope of solution and to facilitate its application, a constraint for the target environment is the use of the same original operating system. It simplifies the porting process for a software asset, because, apart other external dependencies, source code can be reused in a whole — since all system calls can be maintained as at original implementation.

4.2 Case Study: Ginga

4.2.1 Ginga for Linux/PC(x86)

The reuse model proposed in previous section was applied to an existing implementation of Ginga, composed of Ginga-NCL and Ginga-CC subsystems. This used implementation was developed in C++ for Linux/PC platform and its original source code is available at `http://www.softwarepublico.gov.br/ver-comunidade?community_id=1101545` (version used was 0.11.2).

Table 1 summarizes third-party software (libraries, packages, etc.) used by this implementation of Ginga.

Table 1: Third-party dependencies for Ginga

Dependencies	List
Libraries, packages	DirectFB, Pthread, FFmpeg, video4linux, lua, Xerces-C++, ...
Total	> 30

4.2.2 Creation of Ginga-NCL Component

Our proof of concept was concerned to reuse Ginga-NCL in a whole. The main goal was to build a self-contained component to be ported and reused in different hardware platforms.

The major issue in the development of the component was the customization of Ginga-NCL to dissociate it from the Ginga-CC subsystem. The class diagram depicted in Figure 3 shows how the subsystems are coupled.

The main class of Ginga-NCL is `FormatterMediator`, which coordinates all other major classes of the subsystem, like `PlayerAdapterManager` and `FormatterScheduler`. In order to decouple Ginga-NCL from Ginga-CC, we had to identify all boundaries between the subsystems.

Ginga-NCL depends on many features and resources provided by the Ginga-CC classes. Due to page limitations, we will describe only the interfaces for media players, user input and management of graphic layouts.

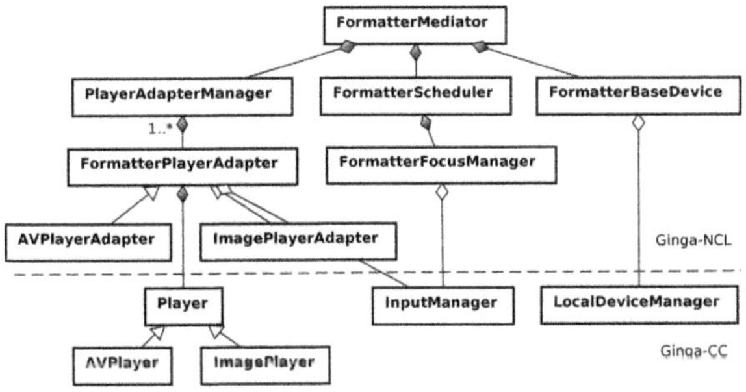

Figure 3: Associations between classes of Ginga-NCL and Ginga-CC

Media players are implemented by `Player` class and its subclasses, like `AVPlayer` (for audio and video) and `ImagePlayer` (for images). User interaction is captured through the mechanism of data input (from keyboard, remote control, etc.) implemented by `InputManager` class. The management of graphic regions depends on information on exhibition device (like its screen resolution), that are provided by `LocalDeviceManager` class.

After mapping all associations between the subsystems, we begun the customization process for the Ginga-NCL. Source code transformation was performed trough a refactoring process. Refactoring means applying some transformations to software in order to improve its internal organization and quality (modularity, reusability, etc.) [13].

A common technique used in refactoring is the introduction of design patterns [14][13]. In order to create the external interfaces for Ginga-NCL component, we have introduced some design patterns, like the Proxy pattern, shown in Figure 4.

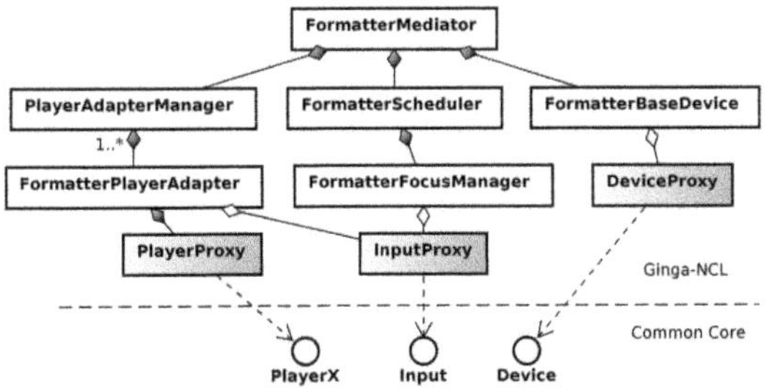

Figure 4: Integration of Ginga-NCL component with a new Common Core implementation

The Proxy pattern added a wrapper whose intent was to protect and control access to Common Core resources, while creating a flexible interface. `PlayerProxy`, `InputProxy` and `DeviceProxy` classes constitute integration points for external resources provided by an implementation of Ginga-CC.

As consequence of the refactoring process and decoupling of Ginga-NCL from Ginga-CC, the built component has just a few external dependencies. Comparing Tables 2 and 1, we can see strong reduction on number of third-party dependencies, which reflects a better degree of portability.

The effects of the decoupling process can also be perceived on some OO (object-oriented) metrics, like CBO (Coupling Between Object) [15]. Table 3 shows CBO values for several classes of Ginga-NCL before and after the refactoring process. The reduced values in the column CBO(c) suggest an improvement on reusability of Ginga-NCL.

Table 2: Third-party dependencies for Ginga-NCL component

Dependencies	List
Libraries, packages	Pthread, Xerces-C++
Total	2

Table 3: CBO values for the original and component(c) versions of Ginga-NCL

Class	CBO	CBO(c)
`FormatterMediator`	31	16
`PlayerAdapterManager`	17	11
`FormatterScheduler`	27	21
`FormatterPlayerAdapter`	32	13
`FormatterFocusManager`	15	9

4.2.3 Reuse of Ginga-NCL Component

Before to be ported, the component was compiled again to PC. As expected — due to reduced number of dependencies (only Pthread and Xerces-C++) — the build process was much simpler than that for the original middleware.

The Ginga-NCL component was ported and integrated into two new implementations of Ginga middleware, one for each platform shown in Table 4 (similar DTV platforms can be found on the websites of ST[2] and Broadcom[3]).

Table 4: DTV platforms used in the development of new implementations of Ginga

Hardware	Description
S	ST® SH4 32-bits@266MHz; dedicated audio/video/graphic processors; 1080i; 256MB RAM; Linux.
M	Broadcom® MIPS 32-bits@300MHz; dedicated audio/video/graphic processors; 1080i; 512MB RAM; Linux.

To port the component to the platforms we had to obtain only the specific versions (for each platform) of Pthread[4] and Xerces (XML parser) libraries — the first is usually distributed with the C/C++ compilers for platforms, while the second has source code freely available, which is easily compiled for any UNIX-based environment.

Table 5 shows the implementations of Ginga developed with the reuse of the Ginga-NCL. The component was integrated with two specific versions of Common Core (one

[2]http://www.st.com

[3]http://www.broadcom.com/

[4]POSIX Threads: IEEE 1003.1c Standard

for each platform). CC1 was made available in source code, whereas CC2 was provided only in its executable form.

Table 5: Implementations of Ginga developed with reuse of the Ginga-NCL component

Ginga	Ginga-CC	Hardware
A	CC1	S
B	CC2	M

5. RELATED WORK

Previous work on DTV middleware discusses the development of implementations with different approaches: from scratch [10], using frameworks [12], based on software product lines [16], using solutions for specific environments [11] and others. Most of them show a common concern: reuse [10], [12] and [16].

Our work differs from the previous in the way it proposes the reuse of existing implementations of DTV middleware, focused on implementations which weren't designed for full reuse.

6. CONCLUSIONS AND FUTURE WORK

In this paper we presented an approach to reuse existing implementations of DTV middleware in the development of new instances of these middlewares to different hardware platforms.

The proof of concept developed showed that, despite its restricted context of applicability, the approach can help to accelerate the development of new implementations of DTV middleware. As a future work, the context of portability could be expanded to include different operating systems.

Acknowledgements

We thank RNP, FINEP, FUCAPI, CAPES, and CNPq for the financial support given to research projects related to this paper, and FUCAPI and FAPESP for supporting its presentation at the conference.

7. REFERENCES

[1] S. Morris and A.S. Chaigneau. *Interactive TV Standards.* Focal Press, Elsevier, Oxford, 2005.

[2] Douglas C. Schmidt and Frank Buschmann. Patterns, frameworks, and middleware: their synergistic relationships. In *ICSE '03: Proceedings of the 25th International Conference on Software Engineering*, pages 694–704, Washington, DC, USA, 2003. IEEE Computer Society.

[3] William B. Frakes and Kyo Kang. Software reuse research: Status and future. *IEEE Trans. Softw. Eng.*, 31:529–536, July 2005.

[4] James D. Mooney. Portability and reusability: common issues and differences. In *Proceedings of the 1995 ACM 23rd annual conference on Computer science*, CSC '95, pages 150–156, New York, NY, USA, 1995. ACM.

[5] James Mooney. Developing portable software. In Ricardo Reis, editor, *Information Technology*, volume 157 of *IFIP International Federation for Information Processing*, pages 55–84. Springer Boston, 2004.

[6] Mitsuari Hakuta and Masato Ohminami. A study of software portability evaluation. *Journal of Systems and Software*, 38(2):145 – 154, 1997.

[7] ITU-T. *J.200. Series J: Cable Networks and Transmission of Television, Sound Programme and Other Multimedia Signals - Application for Interactive Digital Television - Worldwide common core – Application environment for digital interactive television services*, 2001.

[8] Luiz Fernando Gomes Soares, Rogério Ferreira Rodrigues, and Márcio Ferreira Moreno. Ginga-ncl: the declarative environment of the brazilian digital tv system. *JBCS: Journal of the Brazilian Computer Society*, 13(1):37–46, March 2007.

[9] Len Bass, Paul Clements, and Rick Kazman. *Software Architecture in Practice.* Addison-Wesley Longman Publishing Co., Inc., Boston, MA, USA, 2 edition, 2003.

[10] Chao Gao, Lei Wang, and Hong Ni. Software design methodology for set-top box. In *ICIE '09: Proceedings of the 2009 WASE International Conference on Information Engineering*, pages 302–305, Washington, DC, USA, 2009. IEEE Computer Society.

[11] Vítor Medina Cruz, Marcio Ferreira Moreno, and Luiz Fernando Gomes Soares. Ginga-ncl: implementaçao de referência para dispositivos portáteis. In *WebMedia '08: Proceedings of the 14th Brazilian Symposium on Multimedia and the Web*, pages 67–74, New York, NY, USA, 2008. ACM.

[12] Glêdson Elias, Adilson B. Lopes, Frederico Borelli, and Maurício F. Magalhães. Exploring an open, distributed multimedia framework to design and develop an adaptive middleware for interactive digital television systems. In *SAC '04: Proceedings of the 2004 ACM symposium on Applied computing*, pages 1258–1264, New York, NY, USA, 2004. ACM.

[13] Tom Mens and Tom Tourwé. A survey of software refactoring. *IEEE Trans. Softw. Eng.*, 30:126–139, February 2004.

[14] E. Gamma, R. Helm, R. Johnson, and J. Vlissides. *Design patterns: elements of reusable object-oriented software.* Addison-Wesley professional computing series. Addison-Wesley, 1995.

[15] S. R. Chidamber and C. F. Kemerer. A metrics suite for object oriented design. *IEEE Trans. Softw. Eng.*, 20:476–493, June 1994.

[16] Diego Saraiva, Lucas Pereira, Thais Batista, Flávia C. Delicato, and Paulo F. Pires. Architecting a model-driven aspect-oriented product line for a digital tv middleware: a refactoring experience. In *Proceedings of the 4th European conference on Software architecture*, ECSA'10, pages 166–181, Berlin, Heidelberg, 2010. Springer-Verlag.

MDM-KTV: A Conceptual Framework for Multi-Data-Models for Operational, Analytic, Semantic and *Linked Data* based Data Organization

Marcelle Batista Martins
Universidade Federal da Paraíba
João Pessoa – PB – Brasil
marcellebm@lavid.ufpb.br

Natasha Correia Queiroz Lino
Universidade Federal da Paraíba
João Pessoa – PB – Brasil
natasha@ci.ufpb.br

ABSTRACT

For developing applications and services in the Knowledge TV platform there is a need in structuring, organising and standardising data according to consolidating academic and industry models, however inserted in the context of interactive Digital TV (iDTV). This work presents research carried on the implementation of the Conceptual Framework MDM-KTV, which means Multi Data Models KTV, considering operational, analytical, semantic and Linked Data based data, in the context of the Knowledge TV project.

Categories and Subject Descriptors

E.1 [Data structures]: Distributed data structures; E.2 [Data Storage representations]: Composite structures, Linked representations, Object representation

General Terms

Design, Standardization, Verification

Keywords
Conceptual Framework, Linked Data, Multi-Models, TVDI

1. INTRODUÇÃO

O Sistema Brasileiro de Televisão Digital (SBTVD) [9], desde novembro de 2003, determinou normas e diretrizes para a transição do sistema de transmissão analógica para o sistema de transmissão digital. A Agência Nacional de Telecomunicações (Anatel), em abril de 2011, divulgou que 45,98% dos lares brasileiros possuem Televisão Digital e que 102 emissoras trabalham com a tecnologia digital em 480 municípios. Ela estipula que o fim da transmissão analógica em todo território nacional ocorrerá no ano de 2016 [6].

Desta forma, observamos que a Televisão Digital vem crescendo e sendo amplamente difundida, e com ela surgem novas tecnologias, dentre as quais, destacam-se os sistemas e aplicativos para promover a interatividade e a interoperabilidade com outras plataformas.

O *middleware* Ginga [11], adotado pelo SBTVD, é uma camada intermediária que faz a mediação entre o hardware e software na TV Digital Brasileira (TVD). Ele está sendo utilizado no projeto *Knowledge TV* que tem como objetivo incorporar ao Ginga uma camada semântica na plataforma de TV Digital, ou seja, a finalidade é prover serviços e aplicações multimídias baseados nos conceitos da Web Semântica [4].

O objetivo da Web Semântica é permitir que as máquinas entendam o significado da informação, não importando em que formato esteja essa informação. A Web Semântica organiza e padroniza a informação, facilitando a busca e seu o acesso na Internet por meio de Ontologias [14]. Estas, por sua vez, podem estar organizadas e interligadas dentro de um grande repositório chamado *Linked Data* [1], que também é alvo de investigação neste trabalho.

Com isso, para desenvolver as aplicações e serviços na plataforma *Knowledge TV* (KTV) surge à necessidade da estruturação, organização e padronização dos dados de acordo com modelos já consolidados no meio acadêmico, contudo inseridos no contexto da Televisão Digital Interativa (TVDI). Assim, neste trabalho, será apresentado o andamento das pesquisas relacionadas a implementação do Framework Conceitual MDM-KTV, que significa *Multi Data Models KTV,* levando em consideração os dados operacionais, analíticos, semânticos e baseados no *Linked Data* no contexto do projeto *Knowledge TV.*

2. ARQUITETURA KNOWLEDGE TV

O projeto *Knowledge TV* (KTV) [7] propõe uma camada semântica para prover serviços na plataforma da TV Digital, estendendo a visão da Web Semântica para o domínio da TV Digital, adaptando-se as suas restrições e apresentando novos desafios na busca de um ambiente de convergência digital. Essa extensão permite outras possibilidades: (i) o compartilhamento e reutilização de dados em aplicações; (ii) processamento automatizado de informações compartilhadas; (iii) conexões semânticas entre dados e objetos do mundo real, etc. Dessa forma, serão obtidos avanços ao estado da arte nas áreas de TV Digital, Inteligência Artificial e Web Semântica. A Figura 1 mostra a arquitetura conceitual do projeto *Knowledge TV*, com os principais módulos da Camada Semântica. Na referência [7] são encontradas informações detalhadas sobre a arquitetura e projeto KTV.

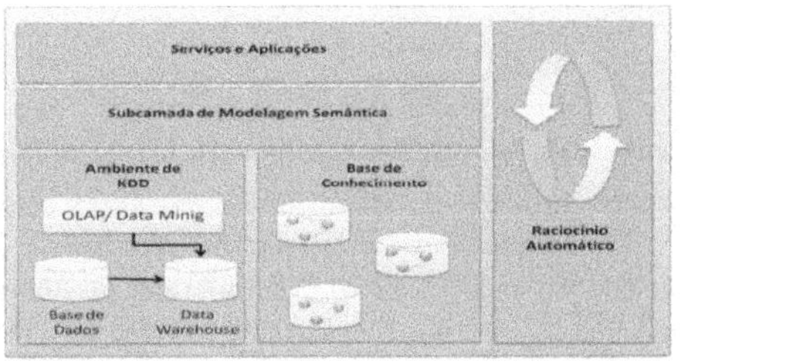

Figura 1. Arquitetura Conceitual KTV.

Permission to make digital or hard copies of all or part of this work for personal or classroom use is granted without fee provided that copies are not made or distributed for profit or commercial advantage and that copies bear this notice and the full citation on the first page. To copy otherwise, or republish, to post on servers or to redistribute to lists, requires prior specific permission and/or a fee.
WebMedia'12, October 15–18, 2012, São Paulo/SP, Brazil.
Copyright 2012 ACM 978-1-4503-1706-1/12/10...$15.00.

Inicialmente, o foco do projeto KTV é desenvolver aplicações nos cenários de *Consulta Semântica* e *Recomendação de Conteúdos* baseados no perfil do usuário.

Na *Consulta Semântica* um dos objetivos é que o usuário através do controle remoto de sua TV navegue, por meio de *tags* ou *links* sobre variados assuntos de seu interesse. As aplicações possuem modelos para consultas semânticas baseadas em um domínio específico (ex.: filmes, telejornal, novela, esporte...), que são instanciadas de acordo com um determinado contexto ou serviço.

Já o cenário de *Recomendação de Conteúdo* ao usuário, tem como finalidade ajudar o usuário na busca de conteúdo baseado na sua preferência pessoal, promovendo assim uma TV personalizada de acordo com seus interesses, comportamento e histórico de uso.

Através do MDM-KTV é possível analisar estes e demais cenários, propondo, através das vertentes operacional, analítica e semântica, meios para se alcançar resultados cada vez mais refinados e relevantes. O enriquecimento das bases de dados é permitido a partir do levantamento dos metadados emergentes da TVDI juntamente com o uso dos conceitos e padrões da Web Semântica em ambientes de convergência de Web e TV.

3. FRAMEWORK CONCEITUAL MDM-KVT

Segundo Johnson (1991) [10] um framework é um conjunto de objetos que colaboram com o objetivo de atender a um conjunto de responsabilidades para uma aplicação específica ou um domínio de aplicação. Desta forma, foram definidos para o MDM-KTV três módulos (operacional, analítico e semântico), nos quais estão especificados os modelos de dados, armazenamento e as operações realizadas em cada um destes módulos. Ao final, um modelo unificado é determinado contendo todo o conjunto de objetos, componentes, modelos núcleos de dados e seus relacionamentos.

É importante ressaltar que os dados da plataforma ou das aplicações de serviços KTV estão dispostos nas mais diferentes fontes de dados na TVDI e ambientes de convergência, requerendo acesso integrado entre eles para que a informação seja compartilhada entre os vários meios.

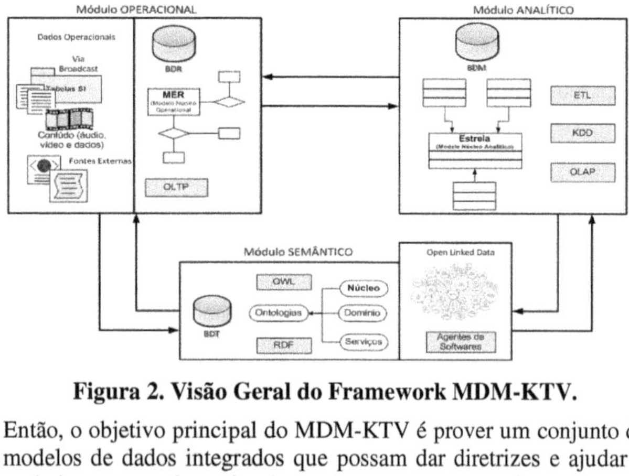

Figura 2. Visão Geral do Framework MDM-KTV.

Então, o objetivo principal do MDM-KTV é prover um conjunto de modelos de dados integrados que possam dar diretrizes e ajudar o projetista a entender o funcionamento e fluxo das informações em aplicações TVDI e, assim, auxiliá-lo na construção de novos serviços e aplicações avançadas segundo a plataforma KTV e padrões pré-definidos.

Nesta seção é demonstrada uma visão geral do Framework Conceitual MDM-KTV e uma explanação de cada módulo e seus componentes. Assim, podemos ver na Figura 2 os três módulos co-relacionados. Isto significa que os componentes dos módulos podem interagir entre si, dependendo o tipo de aplicação e resultados que se deseja obter.

3.1 Módulo Operacional

No módulo operacional, os *dados operacionais* representam as informações que descrevem o conteúdo audiovisual transmitido, via *broadcast,* através dos metadados encapsulados nas tabelas dos padrões definidos pelo SBTVD, além das informações sobre o comportamento, as preferências e o histórico dos usuários da TV.

A Figura 3 abaixo demonstra uma visão sobre o fluxo dos dados operacionais desde sua difusão através da rede broadcast até seu armazenamento em um *Banco de Dados Relacional* (BDR). Os dados são encaminhados via *broadcast* no formato de arquivo de texto (dados rígidos e flexíveis) e convertidos para o formato XML para facilitar o armazenamento no BDR, provendo maior interoperabilidade. O XML facilita declarações mais precisas do conteúdo e resultados mais significativos de busca através de múltiplas plataformas.

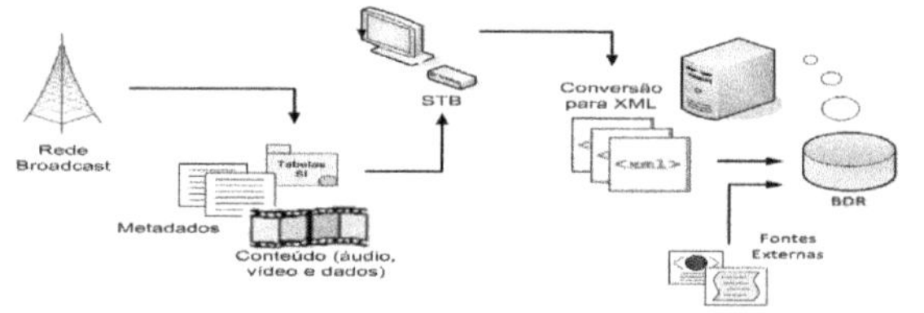

Figura 3. Fluxo dos dados operacionais – Módulo Operacional.

Assim, foi realizado um mapeamento dos padrões de metadados que atendem aos requisitos do SBTVD com o objetivo de fazer um levantamento dos *dados operacionais* importantes para ao KTV. Constatou-se, então, que as tabelas PSI/SI do padrão MPEG-2 provê conteúdo audiovisual significativos ao KTV.

Foi gerado o Modelo Entidade-Relacionamento (MER), Modelo Núcleo, conforme Figura 4 que contempla o armazenamento dos dados do ambiente operacional, coletados das *Emissoras*, *Programas* e *Usuários*, contudo passível de extensão.

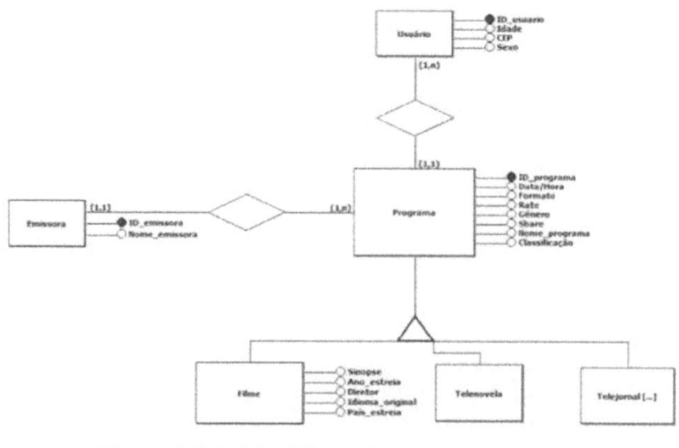

Figura 4. Modelo Núcleo Operacional (MER)

3.2 Módulo Analítico

O *Módulo Analítico* fornece subsídio para realização da análise dos dados operacionais. Através da aplicação dos processos ETL (*Extract Transform Load*), KDD (*Knowledge Discovery in. Databases*) e OLAP (*On-line Analytical Processing*) [15] são gerados os dados analíticos, os quais são armazenados em um *Data Warehouse* (DW) ou *Banco de Dados Multidimensional*, provendo, assim, novos conhecimentos, não triviais de serem descobertos, possibilitando respostas confiáveis, integradas e imediatas. Isto se faz necessário porque o *Módulo Operacional*, focado em OLTP (*Online Transaction Processing*), não fornece informações necessárias para operações de análises e acompanhamentos comportamentais, pois é destinado apenas ao controle e armazenamento. A principal finalidade do *Módulo Analítico* do MDM-KTV é dar suporte às diversas aplicações no contexto TVDI provendo novos e relevantes conhecimentos.

Ao final do processo KDD as informações serão interpretadas retornando os seguintes resultados:

- Retornará padrões descobertos em forma de novos serviços. Por exemplo, pode retornar recomendação para o usuário, como programas ou filmes semelhantes ao que ele costuma assistir, etc.;
- Encapsulará o resultado do KDD de forma semântica, em ontologias, para que estes resultados possam ser usados por qualquer serviço KTV.

As ferramentas OLAP também auxiliam na realização das pesquisas, comparações e extrações de novos conhecimentos, provendo uma melhor compreensão dos dados armazenados. Através das ferramentas OLAP é possível apresentar a multidimensionalidade em telas através de uma configuração tridimensional de linhas, colunas e páginas.

Para atender os cenários da plataforma KTV, foi gerado o Modelo Núcleo Analítico, conforme Figura 5, tendo como base o modelo Estrela, bastante difundido e utilizado na análise de informações em bases multidimensionais. Desta forma, tem-se a tabela central Fato chamada *FatoUsoTV* e as dimensões *DimensaoTempo, DimensaoHora, DimensaoUsuario, DimensaoPrograma* e *DimensaoEmissora*.

Assim, com a aplicação dos modelos e operações do *Módulo Analítico* apresentados, serão descobertas novas informações extremamente relevantes às aplicações e serviços na plataforma KTV e TVDI.

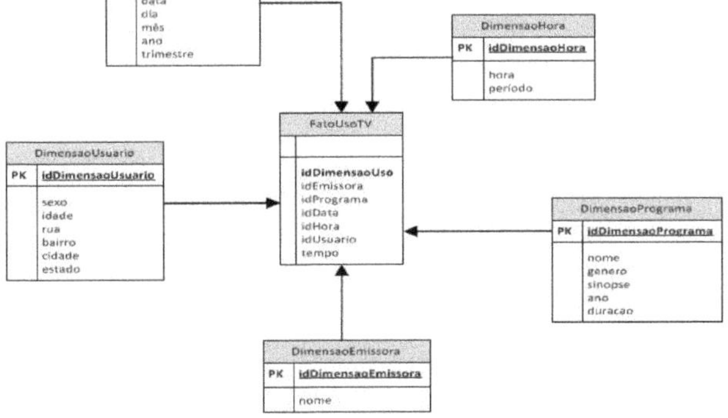

Figura 5. Modelo Núcleo Analítico (Estrela)[12]

3.3 Módulo Semântico

Um dos fundamentos do *Módulo Semântico* é especificar as representações semânticas de dados de acordo com os princípios da Web Semântica [2]. A tecnologia resultante segue os conceitos da Web Semântica e do *Open and Linked Data Movement* [8], que tem a finalidade de permitir que todos possam compartilhar dados estruturados na Web. Desta forma, por meio desta abordagem declarativa, permite-se a construção de uma ambiente de convergência digital entre a Web e TV Digital através do compartilhamento e reutilização de dados em aplicações e serviços em um formato passível de processamento automático em computadores e com conexões semânticas entre os dados.

Os componentes presentes no *Módulo Semântico* basicamente são: um BDT (Banco de Dados de Triplas), Modelos Ontológicos e operações OWL (*Web Ontology Language*) e RDF (*Resource Description Framework*). A nuvem *Linked Data* também faz parte do *Módulo Semântico* quando se introduz o termo *Linkado*. Através da nuvem do *Linked Data* é possível *linkar* (conectar) os dados, restaurando ontologias e informações para o enriquecimento das bases de dados dos cenários da TVDI. Os *Agentes de Software* são considerados um meio operacional, pois são porções de softwares que trabalham de forma autônoma e proativa, coordenando tarefas de comparação e busca por padrões de dados na nuvem do *Linked Data* [3].

O objetivo principal do *Módulo Semântico* é fornecer suporte às aplicações e serviços baseados em conhecimento na TVDI, provendo conceitos, relacionamentos e propriedades através das ontologias propostas no contexto da plataforma KTV: núcleo - CoreKTV [5], de domínios específicos ou de serviços.

Assim, acerca dos Modelos Semânticos usados no projeto *Knowledge TV* podemos ressaltar os seguintes:

- A Ontologia Núcleo (CoreKTV) [5] desenvolvida no projeto para representação semântica de conteúdo multimídia baseada em padrões de metadados tais como MPEG2 e TV Anytime. A CoreKTV é uma infraestrutura baseada em conhecimento, onde é possível extrair, classificar e estruturar o conteúdo (vídeo, áudio e dados) a partir do mapeamento para esta ontologia.
- As Ontologias de Domínio, que servirão para dar suporte, inicialmente, aos serviços de consultas semânticas e de recomendação de conteúdo e posteriormente para outros serviços a serem desenvolvidos. Para tal, técnicas como alinhamento de ontologias são usadas. Ex.: Ontologias do *Linked Data*: *DBpedia, Linked MDB, Movie Ontology*, dentre outras.
- As Ontologias de Serviços, como por exemplo, a OntoMKTV [12], onde o conhecimento descoberto é tratado de forma semântica por meio de um encapsulamento através da ontologia de Mineração de Dados. No caso do KTV foram utilizados algoritmos de regras de associação, contudo poderá ser estendido para outras tarefas como de clusterização e classificação.

O *Módulo Semântico* permitirá a realização de expansões semânticas em diferentes bases de dados semânticas (interligadas utilizando RDF). A expansão semântica consiste em trazer, através da abordagem do *Linked Data*, mais informações relacionadas ao programa assistido ou a programas que irão ser transmitidos. O *Módulo Semântico* tem como propósito principal ajudar projetistas no desenvolvimento de outras aplicações como, por exemplo, tarefas de recomendação de programas ao usuário. O módulo semântico consultará os perfis de usuário da TV com o objetivo de retornar informações mais próximas e precisas para cada Set-Top-Box.

4. METODOLOGIA ADOTADA

O *Framework Conceitual* MDM-KTV proposto neste trabalho é baseado nas regras e formalismo do desenvolvimento orientado a objeto proposto por Bosch et al. (1997) [13], seguindo os seis passos definidos para a construção de um framework, contudo de forma adaptada, sem intenção de implementação de software executável. Seguem os passos adaptados: Análise do domínio; Projeto arquitetural (definição de módulos e componentes); Projeto do Framework Conceitual MDM-KTV; Mapeamento para a Plataforma KTV; Estudos de casos nos cenários TVDI; Documentação.

A intenção é fornecer através do MDM-KTV padrões que possam ser usados como base para a modelagem conceitual de dados no domínio da TVDI.

5. CONCLUSÕES E TRABALHOS FUTUROS

Como previamente descrito, o Framework Conceitual MDM-KTV, demonstra análises dos componentes e modelos de dados na TVDI, com o objetivo de prover diretrizes aos desenvolvedores na criação de novos serviços e aplicações. Seguem algumas contribuições alcançadas até o momento:

- A análise do domínio, levantamento de requisitos, criação de casos de uso (através da UML), especificação e definição de um modelo unificado que contempla o módulo operacional, analítico, semântico e baseado no *Linked Data.*
- Análise de cada módulo levando em consideração os aspectos da obtenção dos dados/metadados, meio de armazenamento, definição dos modelos núcleos de dados e operações realizadas.
- Inserção da abordagem *Linked Data,* em um contexto novo, que é a utilização da Web Semântica e Ontologias na TVDI.

Atualmente, o MDM-KTV é um projeto em fase intermediária de desenvolvimento. Como próximas atividades do projeto são incluídas: pesquisa e especificação dos relacionamentos entre os módulos (mapeamento e conversão entre modelos); validação através de estudos de caso e mapeamento do MDM-KTV nos cenários da plataforma KTV (recomendação de conteúdo e consulta semântica) e demais cenários existentes na TVDI.

Em uma pesquisa paralela, está sendo construído um modelo de perfis de usuários para o projeto *Knowledge TV.* Este modelo se integrará ao *Módulo Semântico* do MDM-KTV. Serão usados algoritmos de recomendação baseados no conteúdo, no qual serão considerados como fator preponderante o tempo e o horário de consumo da TV. Também serão usados algoritmos de filtragem colaborativa, no qual serão consideradas informações vindas da Web. Com o uso desses algoritmos, em conjunto, espera-se oferecer serviços com resultados mais precisos aos telespectadores, como por exemplo, recomendações refinadas de conteúdos, programas ou vídeos de acordo com o seu perfil.

6. REFERENCES

[1] Berners-Lee, T. 2006. Linked Data, Design Issues. Disponível em: http://www.w3.org/DesignIssues/LinkedData.html.

[2] Shadbolt, N., Berners-Lee, T., and Hall, W. 2006. The Semantic Web Revisited. *IEEE In-telligent Systems*, 21 (3). pp. 96-101.

[3] Breitman, K. K.. Web Semântica: O Futuro da Internet. 1. ed. Rio de Janeiro: LTC - Livros Técnicos e Científicos Editora S.A., 2005. v. 1. 190 p.

[4] W3C – World Wide Web Consortium. 2009. Disponível em: http://www.w3c.br/palestras/wc3-websemantica-2009/WebSemantica.pdf

[5] Araújo, J. P.C. 2011. CoreKTV - Uma infraestrutura baseada em conhecimento para TV Digital Interativa: um estudo de caso para o middleware Ginga. UFPB-PPGI. Dissertação de Mestrado.

[6] Anatel – Agência Nacional de Telecomunicações – http://www.anatel.gov.br/Portal/exibirPortalPaginaEspecialPesquisa.do?acao=&tipoConteudoHtml=1&codNoticia=22469.

[7] Lino, N., Araújo., Anakubi, D., Júnior, J., Martins, M., Nóbrega, R., Amaro, M., Siebra, C., Lemos G. Knowledge TV. EuroITV 2011(Lisboa).

[8] Li Ding and Deborah L. McGuinness and Jim Hendler. (2010). Mash-up of Linked Government Data. Disponível em: http://data.gov. Proceedings of SemTech 2010, 2010.

[9] SBTVD (2007) – Sistema Brasileiro de TV Digital. Ministério das Comunicações. Disponível em: http://sbtvd.cpqd.com.br.

[10] Johnson, R. E. (1991): Reusing Object-Oriented Design, University of Illinois, Technical Report UIUCDCS 91-1696, 1991.

[11] Middleware Ginga. Disponível em: http://www.ginga.org.br/

[12] Patrício Júnior., J. C. A. 2012. Mining Knowledge TV: Uma Abordagem de Ambiente de KDD com Ênfase em Mineração de Dados no Ambiente da Knowledge TV. UFPB-PPGI. Dissertação de mestrado.

[13] Bosch, J; Molin, P.; Mattsson M.; Bengtsson, P. 1997. Object-Oriented Frameworks - Problems & Experiences.

[14] Gruber, T. 1993. A translation approach to portable ontology specifications. *Knowledge Acquisition*, vol 5, pp: 199-220.

[15] Han, J., and Kamber, M. 2006. *Data Mining: Concepts and Techniques*, 2nd edition. The Morgan Kaufmann Series in Data Management Systems, Jim Gray, Series Editor Morgan Kaufmann Publishers.

The Knowledge as a Service Metaphor and its Use for Building Convergence Environments

Manoel Amaro, Natasha Queiroz Lino, Clauirton Siebra and Alan Guedes
Laboratory of Digital Video Applications
Informatics Department - Federal University of Paraiba
Joao Pessoa – Paraiba - Brazil
+55 83 3216-7093
{natasha,clauirton}@di.ufpb.br; {manoel.amaro,alan}@lavid.ufpb.br

ABSTRACT

The Interactive TV (ITV) advances are enabling the development of modern applications in this platform. However, several of such applications could take advantages from a convergence environment, where they could access information and services from other platforms. The Web servers, in particular the knowledge servers, present interesting properties to the configuration of a convergence environment. This work explores such properties as a way to support convergence between the Web and ITV platforms.

Categories and Subject Descriptors

H.3.5 [**Information Storage and Retrieval**]: On-line Information Services – *data sharing, web-based services.*

Keywords

Semantic Descriptions, Convergence, ITV Services.

1. INTRODUCTION

The *Software as a Service* approach (SaaS) [1] is a consolidated Internet model to provide applications. In this model, an application is hosted in a server, becoming available to users via web. One of the main advantages of this model is to avoid that users need their own infrastructure to execute programs, once such programs are executed on the server infrastructure. According to a research from the Gartner Institution, 9 from 10 companies have planned to increase the use of SaaS in 2009. In addition, more than 30% of companies have changed their Internet applications to a SaaS approach [2]. More modern concepts related to SaaS can be seen in works associated with *Cloud Computing* [3].

Recently, and using attributes from the software as a service metaphor, several efforts have being focused on developing the concept of *Data as a Service* (DaaS) [4]. The principal property of a DaaS application is to provide commands based on common databases, which are known as CRUD (Create, Read, Update, Delete), rather than computational processes on data. This is the main difference between a SaaS and a DaaS.

Permission to make digital or hard copies of all or part of this work for personal or classroom use is granted without fee provided that copies are not made or distributed for profit or commercial advantage and that copies bear this notice and the full citation on the first page. To copy otherwise, or republish, to post on servers or to redistribute to lists, requires prior specific permission and/or a fee.
WebMedia'12, October 15–18, 2012, São Paulo/SP, Brazil.
Copyright 2012 ACM 978-1-4503-1706-1/12/10...$15.00.

The current DasS development is supported by techniques from the services oriented architectures area, which can be used to model and design access interfaces and management of data that is manipulated inside a DaaS. Models of quality for web services are already mature and several techniques, methods and tools also support the work of developers during the quality of service modeling to DaaS. However, such models focus on operational aspects of services, such as efficiency, reliability, availability and security. In this way, aspects of information related to its description and representation in a DaaS are almost ignored.

The *Knowledge as a Service* (KaaS) paradigm [5] was proposed in 2005 as a form to extend the potential of computational systems that are developed as a DaaS. Two main advantages of this paradigm can be stressed. First, its models are based on formal semantic representations, so that we do not have the same problems that are found in DaaS. Second, the knowledge servers have the capacity of accessing data of different sources, instantiating their representations and generating knowledge to be delivered via intelligent process such as Data Mining algorithms.

This work discusses representational ways to KaaS, which enable an appropriate semantic description for data that comes from different platforms. Our main aim is to use the KaaS metaphor as a form to enable convergence among different computational platforms, such as the ITV and Web. We argue that the integration of data from different platforms can be very useful to extend the services that are running on a specific platform. Practical examples are semantic query and recommendation services, which can use information from Web via a KaaS that is semantically described in accordance with the Semantic Web fundaments [6].

The remainder of this paper is organized as follows. Section 2 presents the main ideas related to the KaaS approach and its conceptual architecture. Section 3 discusses the convergence scenario, which integrates the ITV and Web platforms, showing how we intend to instantiate the components of the KaaS architecture. Finally, Section 4 brings our final considerations and research directions.

2. THE KAAS APPROACH

Knowledge as a Service (KaaS) is a service oriented computational paradigm where a knowledge based service provider, or knowledge service, answers requests sent by information consumers. These services are based on knowledge models that are in general expensive or impossible to be maintained by the own consumers.

The motivation for the development of KaaS was mainly originated from the knowledge discovery in databases and data mining techniques. Thus, in general, this service-oriented computational paradigm offers functionalities based on knowledge extracted from large volume databases and maintained by different sources. Such sources might only have dispersed information available. In this way, knowledge servers account for instantiating their models and their associated information, transforming them in knowledge. Figure 1 shows a conceptual view of the KaaS approach.

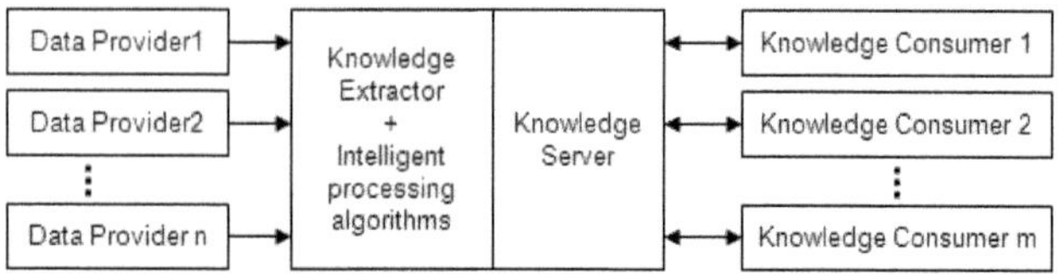

Figure 1. KaaS conceptual view [10]

According to this figure, the framework defined for KaaS has three logic components: (1) data providers, (2) knowledge server (knowledge extractor and processing algorithms) and (3) knowledge consumers. Next section presents how such components were instantiated, according to our approach. It is important to highlight three essential features of KaaS, which makes this computational paradigm appropriated for the configuration of convergence environments:

- KaaSs are based on formal semantic models, such as ontologies, which enable standardization of format and meaning. Thus, knowledge can be shared among participants that adopt a specific model;
- KaaSs act like consolidation components, since they can seek information to instantiate their models, transforming such information in knowledge;
- Intelligent processes used in KaaSs' servers, such as Data Mining algorithms, can emphasize knowledge originally implicit, or impossible to be derived from primary data sources due to the weakness and informality of their representations.

Such KaaS features have been explored end evolved as a research topic with its own discussion forum, such as the *Workshop on Knowledge as a Service,* part of *IEEE International Conference on Computer Science and Service System* - CSSS 2012.

3. ITV AND WEB CONVERGENCE

3.1 Architecture

Our architecture aims to configure a convergence environment between the ITV and Web platforms. In this architecture, the KaaS is represented by the Knowledge TV (KTV) Web Server [7]. The Digital TV network transmission, from TV content providers, accounts for sending, via broadcast, data (audio, video, applications and services) to set-top-boxes (STB) connected to TVs. Part of this broadcast information is sent to the KTV server (implemented as a KaaS), where it is transformed from the original rigid metadata format to instances of the KTV core semantic model - CoreKTV [8]. Similar and simultaneously, when users interact with applications running on Ginga (Brazilian ITV middleware), this middleware will send information to the KTV server via the return channel, implemented via sockets. This information can be associated, for example, with user profile data or interaction history. The most demanding operational, analytical and semantic operations over data are carried out in the server side. When the data manipulation is finished, requested results are sent back, also via return channel, to ITV applications. Next figure (Figure 2) shows the computational modules that account for the configuration of the convergence environment.

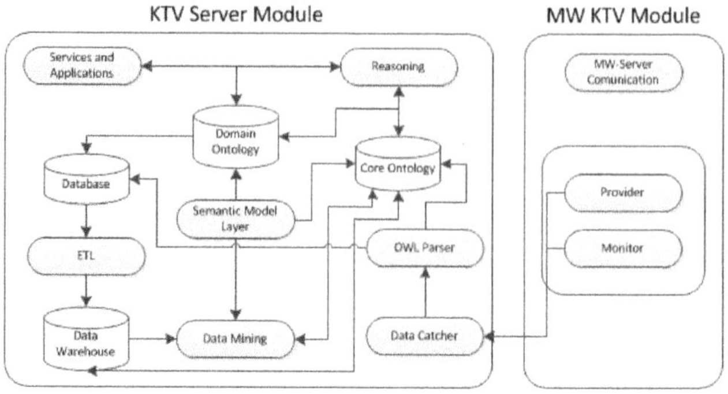

Figure 2. Modules of the convergence environment

These modules are divided between the ITV (middleware - MW) and Web platform (KaaS server). However, most of them are located in the knowledge server. This is part of the KTV strategy to implement as less as possible resources in the ITV middleware. Thus, future middleware updates will not highly impact the system. In the middleware side, there are two components or agents: *Monitor*, whose task is to obtain TV human users behavior by means of their TV interactions with programs and applications, and; *Provider* that accounts for obtaining the metadata related to ITV stream.

In the server module, the following components are highlighted: *Data Catcher* that accounts for getting information obtained from the middleware and promoting a verification phase and cleaning checking before sending the information to the *OWL Parser*. The aim of this parser is to re-organize data under a single semantic format, OWL, permitting sharing, re-use and grouping of concepts in the construction of the *Domain Ontologies* and *Core Ontology*, whose formal specification is on the *Semantic Model Layer*. This layer accounts for maintaining a knowledge base of concepts and properties regarding multimedia content in ITV that can be used, shared and extended to any specific domain or service implemented on the KTV platform.

Information in the knowledge server is maintained according to Domain Ontology models. For instance, a movie recommendation service should use a movies' domain ontology. On this data is applied a knowledge discovery in database process, including an *ETL* (Extraction, Transaction and Loading) pre-process so that the system is able to build a *Data Warehouse*. *Data Mining* algorithms are applied on the Data Warehouse to extract important patterns and knowledge, in accordance with the desired knowledge that a specific service or application needs. For example, for the movies recommendation service, one data mining task is to derive association rules and/or user clusters that have similar preferences in movies.

3.2 Information Representation and Models

In this architecture, we emphasize that data are represented via *operational*, *multidimensional* and *semantic* models. Regarding operational data (relational, textual, logs, etc.) we can list rigid broadcast metadata – for instance, MPEG-2 according to the SBTVD standard. Multidimensional models refer to the Data Warehouse and its analytical dimensional data cubes. Finally, semantic models are mainly represented in the KTV system by the core ontology and domain ontologies. The general conceptual data view is represented in Figure 3.

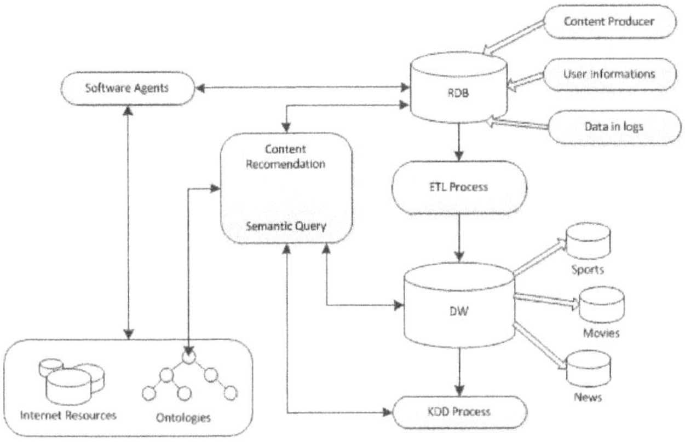

Figure 3. General conceptual data view.

One of the basis of the KTV project is to specify semantic representation of data, based on the Semantic Web principles [6]. In this way, OWL (Ontology Web Language) was used to define the core and domain ontologies. The advantage of using OWL is that it is based on real standards, such as RDF/RDFS and XML, but designed to attend the requirements of Semantic Web applications and semantic expressiveness in a domain conceptualization. Thus, OWL was suggested by the W3C consortium as a standard to specify ontologies in Web.

From the Semantic Web perspective, a broadly accepted definition for ontologies is the one proposed by Gruber [9], where ontology is defined as an explicit formal specification of a shared conceptualization of concepts and relationships, which belong to agents or agents societies. It is possible to interpret this definition as: *conceptualization* represents an abstract model of an event that identifies its relevant concepts; *explicit* means that elements and its restrictions are well defined; *formal* that the ontology is possible to be automatically processed and; *shared* reflects the consensual knowledge capturing, accepted by a group of people and programs.

One of the main goals of our project is to enable, by means of semantic aspects available via KaaS services, the creation of digital convergence environments (ITV and Web). For that end, the KTV project defines a semantic layer and a platform to provide services in convergence environments. The resulting technology follows the Semantic Web, Linked Data and Open Data Movement [10]. Therefore, this declarative approach enables the construction of a convergence environment between ITV and Web, which supports sharing and re-use of data, by applications and services, in a format able to automatically be processed in computers and with semantic connections between data.

3.3 Semantic Model and the Core Ontology

The semantic modelling of the KTV core ontology was carried on in several phases, from investigation and classification of operational data, to domains semantic modelling and mapping of operational data to ontology entities. At the end of this process, the CoreKTV was ready to be used. This means, the knowledge base, its concepts, properties and instances could be used or extended for any specific domain service, which was developed in accordance with the specifications of the KTV platform.

The semantic modelling approach of the CoreKTV initially considered the operational data classification and, after that, several concepts and concepts groups were created. The central concept of this ontology is *Multimedia Content* or *MMContent*, which represents a generic multimedia content entity. In the context of this work, this class represents the digital content transmitted via broadcast to ITV *set-top-boxes*. This content can be an audio visual service or event, together with data information associated with it. Additionally, the main modelled classes and class groups are: *ContentDescription* (description of transmitted content), *Credits* (information related to people and organisations of content authoring), *Review* (content evaluation), *EmergencyAlert* (signal transmitted by content providers to inform about an eminent emergency situation), *Language* (used language), *Genre* (genre of transmitted content), *IntendedAudience* (group of intended audience), *Classification* (content classification), *Keyword* (keyword representing content description), *Person* (person entity), *Organization* (organization entity), *Award* (prize earned or promoted by the content), *MediaFormat* (possible distributed media formats), *Group* (generic concept identified by entity grouping – same type or similar), *Origination* (primary content distribution format), User (user entity), *UserAction* (set of actions available in the remote control), *GeographicArea* (geographic position) and *Time* (date, time and time interval).

After the class definition phase, the second phase was to group concepts in hierarchies. Specialisations of concept classes were also defined to promote a more precise representation. Hierarchical modelling in the CoreKTV ontology were developed based on descriptors and descriptors schemes available in the ABNT NBR norms and the TV-Anytime specification. Protegé was used as modelling tool. The generated models are not discussed here, due to space restrictions, but they can be seen in details in [8]. Figure 4 illustrates the modeling phase with an extract of the global model related to the class hierarchy of the *ContentDescription* element, with focus on the subdivision of the *Language* element.

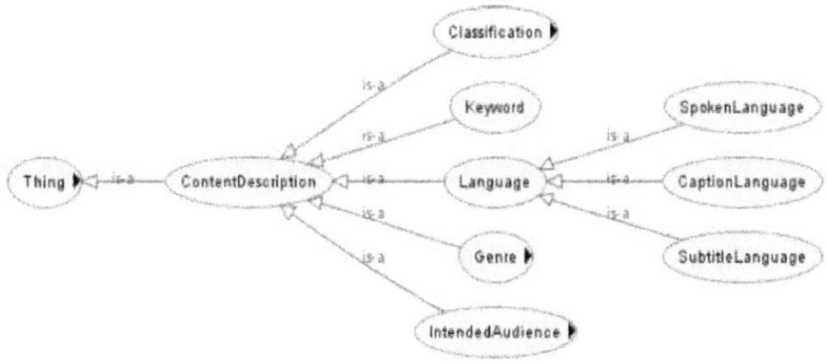

Figure 4. Hierarchy of the *ContentDescription* element

The construction of the "Content Description" hierarchy, from the *ContentDescription* class specialization, represents different ways in which a multimedia content can be described to the TV environment. In the following modelling phase, the process has established connections of classes' concepts that reflect entities links in the real world. For that end, 49 properties were defined. Such properties are extensively described in [8]. The next items are examples of these properties:

- *hasActor*: it has the *MMContent* and *Cast* classes as domain and *Actor* as contra-domain. It has functional equivalence with *hasActress* property;

- *isGroupPartOf*: it has the *MMContent* class as domain and the *MMContent* and *Series* classes as contra-domain. This property must be used when the multimedia content represents a segment or episode of a content group or a complete content.

The ontology deployment methodology recommends ontology reuse of consolidated ontologies to one or more concepts belonging to the domain in study. In our work, this guideline was used regarding the "time" element, where we have used the *OWL Time ontology* developed by the *Semantic Web Deployment Working Group*.

3.4 KTV Mining

The Data Mining component is one of the most important modules of the KTV architecture. This module accounts for supporting, for example, the semantic recommendation service. The aim of this module is to implement a KDD environment, which focuses on a data mining process performed with information from different sources. Consequently, important knowledge, which is not directly visualised in normal database models, is available to ITV applications. Such applications can be related to, for example, information loading, customization [11] and user directed advertising [12].

Traditional information for data mining comes from ITV metadata tables, which bring information about channel, time/duration of programs, classification and others. A different kind of information is related to the users' behaviour. This means, channels that they use to watch, duration that they spend in each channel and favourite TV times. In this way, the useful knowledge, which is obtained from gross data, is provided as a service to NCL or Java applications running on the middleware.

The *Mining Knowledge TV* (MKTV) is the architectural component that accounts particularly for maintaining the data and searching the useful knowledge from this data. It is important to stress that such data is related to a convergence environment, so that they may come from different sources and platforms. When this data is stored in the Data Warehouse module, it is transformed to a unique format. In fact, the Data Warehouse technique is generally used together with Data Mining, once Data Warehouse techniques present features that enable the integration of data. At the end of the KDD process, information will be interpreted and the next two types of outcomes are returned: (1) patterns of findings, which can be used, for example, for semantic recommendations to users, and; (2) instances of patterns codified according to an ontology, so that such result can be used for any KTV service.

4. CONCLUSIONS AND FUTURE WORKS

This paper discussed a computing paradigm, called Knowledge as a Service, as an appropriate way to provide convergence among different computational platforms. In particular, we focused on convergence between the ITV and Web platforms. We explored the high-level framework of this paradigm, instantiating its modules with components of the KTV architecture. The main aim was to provide semantic processes and representations, based on ontologies, to represent ITV information and also to expand this representation via knowledge from a KaaS server (KTV server).

Our future works are mainly target at implementing the remainder modules of our architecture. The *Monitor* module, for example, is an important component in ongoing implementation. It will enable the capture of the historical behavior of users, so that we can provide real recommendations based on users profiles. Initial prototypes, regarding the Semantic query and recommendations, are also in ongoing development and they will be used as form to validate our approach.

5. ACKNOWLEDGMENTS

Our thanks to RNP (Research National Network) for having provided valuable support to this project through the CTIC 2010 Research Funding Program.

6. REFERENCES

[1] Turner, M. *et al.* 2003. Turning software into a service. *Computer*, 36(10):38-44.

[2] Mertz, S., Eschinger, C., Dharmasthira, Y., and Pang, C. 2010. User Survey Analysis: Software as a Service, Enterprise Application Markets, Worldwide, 2010. *In: Gartner Group at http://www.gartner.com/resId=1337828.*

[3] Buyya, R., Yeo, C., and Venugopal, S. 2008. Market-oriented cloud computing: Vision, hype, and reality for delivering it services as computing utilities. *Proceedings of the 10th IEEE International Conference on High Performance Computing and Communications*, pp. 5–13.

[4] Truong, H., and Dustdar, S. 2009. On analyzing and specifying concerns for data as a service. *Proceedings of the IEEE Asia-Pacific Services Computing Conference*, Singapore, pp. 87-94.

[5] Xu, S., and Zhang, W. 2005. Knowledge as a Service and Knowledge Breaching. *Proceedings of 2005 IEEE International Conference on Services Computing*, vol. 1, pp: 87-94, Orlando, Florida, USA.

[6] Shadbolt, N., Berners-Lee, T., and Hall, W. 2006. The Semantic Web Revisited. *IEEE Intelligent Systems*, 21(3): 96-101.

[7] Lino, N., Araújo, J., Anabuki, D., Patrício Junior, J., Batista, M., Nóbrega, R., Amaro, M., Siebra, C., and Souza Filho, G. 2011. Knowledge TV. *Proceedings of the 9th EuroITV Conference* (EuroITV 2011), Lisbon, Portugal.

[8] Araujo, J. 2011. CoreKTV - Uma infraestrutura baseada em conhecimento para TV Digital Interativa: um estudo de caso para o middleware Ginga. *Dissertação de Mestrado*, PPGI-UFPB.

[9] Gruber, T. 1993. A translation approach to portable ontology specifications. *Knowledge Acquisition*, vol 5, pp: 199-220

[10] Ding, L., Michaelis, J., McCusker, J., and McGuinness, D. 2010. Linked Provenance Data: A Semantic Web-based Approach to Interoperable Workflow Traces, *Future Generation Computer Systems,* 27(6): 797–805.

[11] Avila, P. M., Zorzo, S. D. 2009. A personalized TV Guide System Compliant with Ginga. In: *XV Simpósio Brasileiro de Sistemas Multimídia e Web*, Fortaleza-CE. v. I. p. 35-42.

[12] Cristo, M., *et al.* 2010. Web-like Personalized Advertising System for Interactive Digital TV. In: *WTVDI/WEBMEDIA* 2010, Belo Horizonte-MG.

Shared-TV: A *Framework* to Develop Converged TV-Centric Applications

Jorge Fonseca, Carlos Ferraz
Centro de Informática – Universidade Federal de Pernambuco
Recife – Pernambuco - Brasil
{jcbf, cagf}@cin.ufpe.br

RESUMO

As plataformas de TVs Conectadas vem abrindo novos caminhos e oportunidades no desenvolvimento de aplicações interativas. Entretanto, os aplicativos hoje disponíveis não exploram todo potencial da interatividade na TV. Esses são projetados visando o uso do controle remoto convencional, permitindo apenas a participação de um usuário por vez. Este trabalho apresenta um *framework* que facilita o desenvolvimento de aplicativos interativos convergentes centrados na TV, onde os usuários podem interagir através dos seus dispositivos remotos. O *framework* proposto, chamado de *Shared-TV*, possibilita a criação de aplicativos distribuídos nas plataformas GoogleTV e Ginga-J, abstraindo a complexidade inerente à camada de comunicação e gerenciamento dos dispositivos. O desenvolvedor especifica o comportamento de *smartphones* e *tablets* a partir da aplicação de TV, não sendo necessário desenvolver as aplicações móveis. Ao final, algumas aplicações são apresentadas e um comparativo do desenvolvimento com e sem o uso do *Shared-TV* é realizado.

Categories and Subject Descriptors

D.2.11 [**Software Engineering**]: Software Architecture: *Domain-specific architecture*

General Terms

Design, Experimentation

Keywords

Architecture, connected TV, GoogleTV, Ginga-J, multiple devices

1. INTRODUÇÃO

Os recentes avanços tecnológicos e o surgimento de dispositivos como *smartphones* e *tablets* permitiram o acesso a um conteúdo digital diversificado - a qualquer hora, em qualquer lugar e nos mais variados formatos. No entanto, à medida que esse consumo aumenta, as pessoas se isolam e interagem individualmente através de dispositivos remotos [1]. Apesar disso, assistir televisão ainda é a principal atividade de entretenimento em um ambiente residencial, não apenas porque a TV é quase sempre a maior tela de uma casa, mas principalmente por seu aspecto cultural e a possibilidade de convergência de mídias [2] – cenário em destaque com o lançamento das TVs conectadas [3].

Permission to make digital or hard copies of all or part of this work for personal or classroom use is granted without fee provided that copies are not made or distributed for profit or commercial advantage and that copies bear this notice and the full citation on the first page. To copy otherwise, or republish, to post on servers or to redistribute to lists, requires prior specific permission and/or a fee.
WebMedia'12, October 15–18, 2012, São Paulo/SP, Brazil.
Copyright 2012 ACM 978-1-4503-1706-1/12/10...$15.00.

Porém, ao levar a interatividade para as TVs alguns cuidados precisam ser considerados. Para Roibás [4], toda aplicação que tenha uma interface de navegação que dependa de um controle remoto convencional está distante de aproveitar o potencial da TV interativa.

Este trabalho apresenta como proposta o *Shared-TV*: um *framework* para criação de aplicações interativas convergentes centradas na TV. O *framework* proposto considera o uso de *smartphones* e *tablets* na interação com aplicativos de TV. Para o desenvolvedor, a programação distribuída ocorre como um desenvolvimento local, não sendo necessária a criação de um aplicativo específico para cada plataforma remota. Ele fica livre para criar qualquer aplicação de TV distribuída, seja atrelada ao conteúdo da grade de programação, acessando serviços da Internet ou explorando as funcionalidades dos dispositivos remotos.

A primeira versão do *framework* foi desenvolvido na linguagem de programação Java, habilitando-o a executar tanto no sistema operacional *Android* [5], como no *middleware* Ginga-J [6]. Logo, é possível executá-lo nas TVs com plataforma *GoogleTV* [7] e aquelas compatíveis com a interatividade do Sistema Brasileiro de TV Digital, e em *smartphones* e *tablets* que possuem o sistema operacional *Android*. Este artigo está organizado da seguinte forma: a Seção 2 menciona alguns trabalhos relacionados, enquanto que *framework* proposto e sua arquitetura são apresentados na Seção 3. A Seção 4 trata da implementação Java e a Seção 5 apresenta os resultados e aplicações desenvolvidas com e sem o *Shared-TV*. Finalmente, a Seção 6 é reservada às conclusões e trabalhos futuros.

2. TRABALHOS RELACIONADOS

A ideia de integrar a TV a outros dispositivos vem sendo explorada, com diferentes objetivos, em diversos trabalhos de pesquisa. Modelos relacionados à automação residencial [8,9,10], assim como o uso de *smartphones* e *tablets* envolvendo conteúdo adicional [11,12,13] e *middlewares* capazes de se comunicar com dispositivos remotos [14,15,16] são propostos utilizando as mais diversas tecnlogias. O *Shared-TV* difere dos demais trabalhos referenciados por não depender de *APIs* existentes nos *middlewares* e não precisar de recursos externos à rede local, permitindo a configuração dos recursos remotos a partir da própria TV.

3. SHARED-TV

A Figura 1 mostra a configuração inicial dos dispositivos remotos. Quando um usuário deseja interagir com um aplicativo desenvolvido com o Shared-TV, ele precisa fazer o download de uma aplicação genérica, provida pelo próprio framework, habilitando seu dispositivo a interagir com a TV.

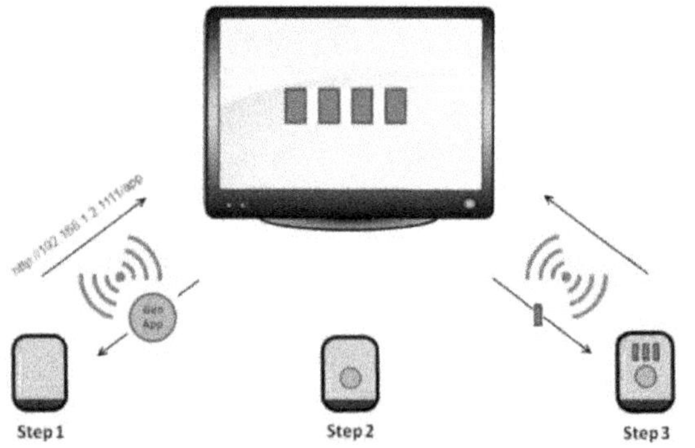

Figura 1. *Download* da aplicação móvel genérica

Neste momento os seguintes passos (Figura 1) são executados:

1. A partir de um navegador existente no dispositivo móvel, o usuário digita o IP da televisão e o *download* da aplicação genérica (círculo laranja) é realizado;
2. O dispositivo cliente instala e executa a aplicação genérica;
3. A aplicação genérica se comunica com a aplicação de TV, registrando-se e recebendo objetos compartilhados (quadrados vermelhos). À medida que os objetos são recebidos, o dispositivo mostra-os na tela permitindo interação sobre eles.

Uma vez a aplicação genérica instalada, o dispositivo remoto pode se comunicar com qualquer aplicação de TV desenvolvida com o *framework* Shared-TV. Logo, se o usuários interagirem com outros aplicativos, os passos 1 e 2 descritos acima serão ignorados.

Vale ressaltar que essa aplicação genérica não funciona apenas como um visualizador de objetos ou como um terminal sem processamento – uma vez a aplicação iniciada e moldada dinamicamente, ela apresenta o comportamento de uma aplicação móvel distribuída qualquer, gerando ações e eventos que respondem às interações do usuário.

3.1 Arquitetura Proposta

O *Shared-TV* possui seis módulos cuja principal função é gerenciar os dispositivos remotos e prover uma infraestrutura de comunicação para as aplicações. A Figura 2 apresenta a arquitetura do *framework*.

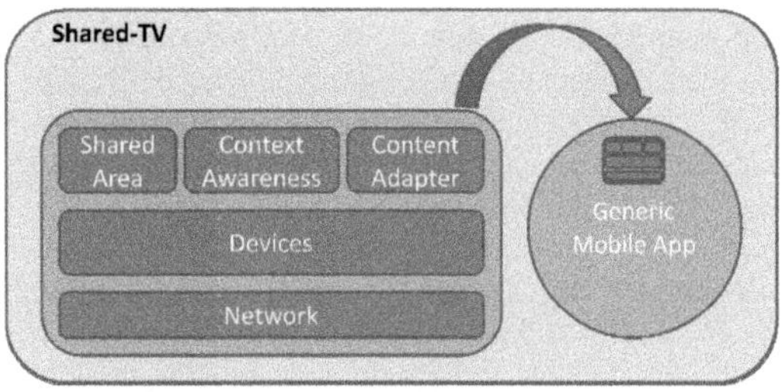

Figura 2 – Arquitetura *Shared-TV*

Cada módulo tem uma responsabilidade específica, conforme descrito a seguir.

- **Network:** Gerencia as conexões dos dispositivos, valida as requisições de acordo com o protocolo HTTP e encaminha os dados para o módulo *Devices*.
- **Devices:** Gerencia os dispositivos remotos abstraindo detalhes de comunicação para a camada de aplicação, além de identificar os dispositivos com um ID único (esses IDs simplifica a utilização por parte dos aplicativos).
- **Shared Area:** Gerencia os objetos compartilhados entre os dispositivos conectados. Cada dispositivo tem uma instância de *SharedArea*. À medida que um objeto é adicionado/removido/atualizado nessa área, ele é sincronizado com o dispositivo associado.
- **Context Awareness:** Identifica as características do dispositivo remoto relacionadas com o *hardware*, sistema operacional e configuração do usuário. Essas informações são coletadas com intuito de gerar uma resposta apropriada para cada dispositivo.
- **Content Adapter:** Apresenta os objetos compartilhados nos dispositivos conectados independente do tamanho de suas telas. Este deve garantir a identificação visual dos objetos evitando possíveis distorções/cortes dos mesmos.
- **Aplicação móvel genérica:** Usa as funcionalidades dos outros cinco módulos. É provida para *download* pelo *Shared-TV* a partir da aplicação de TV. Com a aplicação genérica os dispositivos remotos podem receber os objetos compartilhados, organizá-los e mostrá-los na tela. O *Shared-TV* deve conter uma aplicação móvel para cada sistema operacional suportado (ex.uma para *Android*, uma para *iOS* [17] e outros).

3.2 API do *Framework*

A API do *framework Shared-TV* foi especificada para prover um pequeno conjunto de classes e funcionalidades, facilitando seu entendimento e uso por parte da comunidade de desenvolvedores. A Figura 3 apresenta as classes da API, representado pelo pacote *Shared-TV Library* (omitindo apenas a classe *SharedTVEvent*).

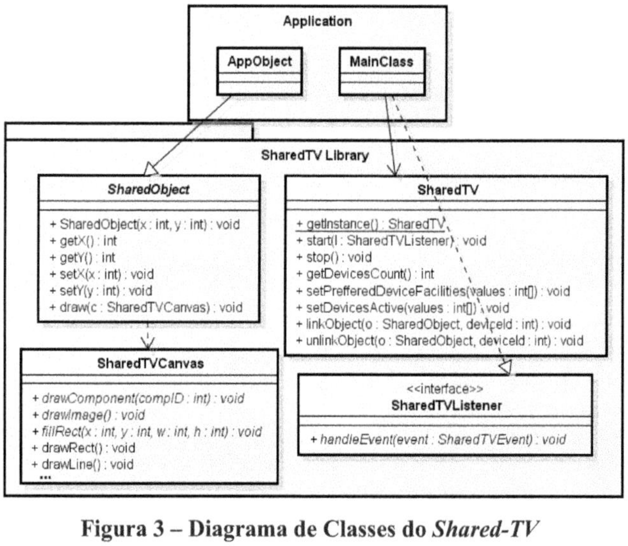

Figura 3 – Diagrama de Classes do *Shared-TV*

A classe *SharedTV* funciona como porta de entrada para o *framework*. Quando uma aplicação chama o método *start()* registrando um *SharedTVListener*, ela passa a receber notificações a respeito das ações originadas pelos dispositivos remotos. Os métodos *linkObject* e *unlinkObject* enviam e removem objetos dos dispositivos, respectivamente. Para que um objeto seja reconhecido como um objeto compartilhado, é preciso que sua classe estenda *SharedObject* e implemente o método *draw()*. Através desse método é possível especificar o comportamento gráfico dos objetos, associando componentes nativos dos dispositivos remotos (*drawComponent()*), ou desenhando através das primitivas gráficas (conjunto reduzido no diagrama de classes). A classe *SharedTVCanvas* é provida pelo *framework* dependendo da plataforma de execução.

4. IMPLEMENTAÇÃO

Um *framework* implementado na linguagem Java, atendendo a um mínimo denominador comum entre a plataforma *Android* e o middleware Ginga-J, poderá ser executado tanto nas TVs conectadas que possuam a plataforma GoogleTV integrada, como nas TVs digitais compatíveis com o padrão brasileiro.

4.1 Módulos

As classes do módulo de rede são *WebServer* e *HTTPClient*, e implementam o servidor e o cliente, respectivamente. Sempre que o servidor recebe uma requisição, os parâmetros são identificados e posteriormente analisados pelo módulo *Devices*, que detecta o tipo da solicitação, processa internamente e dispara para a aplicação de TV um evento do *framework*. Quando a aplicação precisa enviar dados ou objetos, a classe *HTTPClient* é usada. Sempre que uma nova requisição é recebida, seus dados são tratados pelo módulo *ContextAwareness*, gerando uma resposta mais adequada para cada requisição/dispositivo. Substituindo um diagrama de sequência, a Figura 4 mostra o fluxo de execução do *framework* quando uma requisição disparada pelo dispositivo conectado alcança a TV.

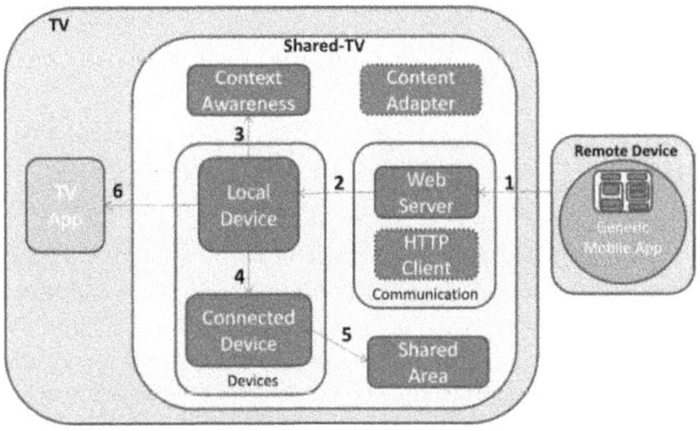

Figura 4 –Dispositivo → TV: sequência interna

A classe *LocalDevice* funciona como o *core* do *Shared-TV* e representa o dispositivo que está executando o *framework*, seja a TV ou o disposito remoto. Essa classe é responsável por receber os dados do módulo de rede (passo 2), interpretá-los e encaminhá-los aos demais módulos e aplicações. Quando o usuário interage com um objeto no *smartphone*, por exemplo, o *framework* identifica qual o dispositivo que originou a ação (passo 4), o objeto interagido (passo 5) e repassa as informações necessárias, filtradas e simplificadas, para a aplicação (passo 6). Em paralelo, a cada nova requisição, o *framework* tenta coletar informações atualizadas sobre o dispositivo e suas configurações (passo 3).

Já no sentindo inverso, quando a TV envia dados e objetos para os dispositivos remotos, a classe *ConnectedDevice*, que contém informações sobre o dispositivo remoto (IP, porta etc.) e os objetos a ele destinado (instância da *SharedArea*), fica responsável por controlar o cliente HTTP.

Nos dispositivos remotos o funcionamento é similar ao fluxo da TV, diferenciando principalmente na atuação do módulo *ContentAdapter*, que é executado posicionando os objetos de acordo com o tamanho da tela do dispositivo. A comunicação entre a TV e os dispositivos são baseadas em ações/eventos, pré-definidos pelo *framework* ou especificados pelo desenvolvedor.

As operações relacionadas à pintura dos objetos são encapsuladas no próprio objeto, através do método *SharedObject.draw()*. Como os objetos são enviados aos dispositivos, as operações gráficas são delegadas para a plataforma *Android*, encarregada por desenhar os objetos. Quando o método *drawComponent()* é executado, componentes nativos são criados, garantindo o *look and feel* padrão da plataforma. É possível também a criação de objetos inteligentes, viabilizando sua mutação visual sem necessidade de se comunicar com a TV.

5. DISCUSSÕES E RESULTADOS

Com objetivo de validar o *framework Shared-TV*, os seguintes aplicativos foram implementados (Figura 5): (a) *Shot-TV*, (b) *Pong-TV*, (c) *Domino-TV* and (d) *Question-TV*. Todos os aplicativos foram escolhidos por apresentar funcionalidades necessárias para validar os requisitos e características do *framework*. Foram implementados o uso dos sensores de aceleração e orientação, gerenciamento da interação dos usuários, uso de componentes nativos (ex. *textfield*), bem como diferentes formas de apresentação do conteúdo ao usuário. As aplicações foram desenvolvidas com e sem o suporte do *Shared-TV* e analisadas no laboratório de TV C.E.S.A.R [18]. As aplicações *Shot-TV* e *Pong-TV* foram testadas em um set-top box com a plataforma Google-TV, enquando que *Domino-TV* e *Question-TV* no middleware Ginga-J. Para o lado dos dispositivos remotos, foram utilizados *smartphones* e *tablets* configurados com o sistema operacional *Android* nas versões 2.2 and 3.1. Os testes foram realizados com as duas versões de cada aplicativo. O objetivo foi comparar a execução das funcionalidades e possíveis impactos na usabilidade dos objetos e componentes visuais.

Todas as aplicações apresentaram as mesmas funcionalidades nas duas versões desenvolvidas, e exatamente o mesmo aspecto visual, seja usando componentes nativos ou primitivas gráficas.

Em relação à usabilidade, nenhum problema foi detectado. Apesar disso, os testes mostraram a necessidade de uma análise detalhada em relação ao tempo de resposta e dados transferidos, com intuito de identificar possíveis pontos de gargalos na comunicação.

Uma vez as aplicações criadas, o número total de linhas de código (*LoC*) foi calculado, e uma comparação entre as duas versões de cada aplicativo foi realizada. A Tabela 1 mostra os valores de *LoC* coletados e seus respectivos percentuais de variação (Δ% *LoC*). Na Tabela, a coluna *Shared-TV* mostra apenas o númeto total de linhas de código, uma vez que as aplicações possuem apenas o desenvolvimento da aplicação de TV.

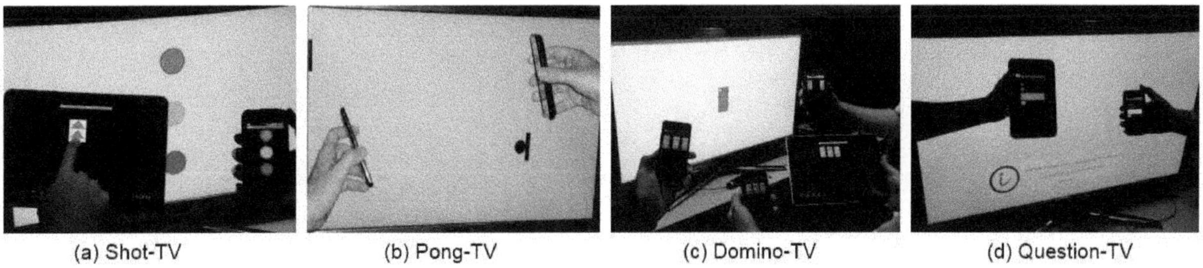

(a) Shot-TV (b) Pong-TV (c) Domino-TV (d) Question-TV

Figura 5. Aplicações desenvolvidas com e sem o Shared-TV

Tabela 1. ***LoC*** **das aplicações**

	Sem Shared-TV			Shared-TV	
	TV	*Mobile*	*Total*	*Total (TV)*	*Δ% LoC*
Shot-TV	272	314	586	304	-48.12
Pong-TV	314	93	407	286	-29.73
Domino-TV	426	370	796	476	-40.20
Question-TV	114	118	232	73	-68.53

Note que, quando o *Shared-TV* foi utilizado, o número de linhas de todas as aplicações apresentou considerável redução. Isso aconteceu principalmente pela remoção do aplicativo móvel existente na versão sem o *Shared-TV*, que no *framework* foi substituído pela aplicação móvel genérica. Apesar da aplicação de TV ter recebido novas instruções de código, com o objetivo de receber e responder aos eventos do *framework*, além de criar os objetos compartilhados, toda a camada de comunicação e gerenciamento dos dispositivos remotos é agora responsabilidade do *Shared-TV*.

Em uma aplicação sem objetos compartilhados, como *Pong-TV*, a variação do *LoC* foi menor. Porém, quando o número de objetos é alto (ex. *Domino-TV*), a variação apresentada foi mais significativa. De fato, se uma aplicação tiver um grande número de classes e objetos, provavelmente esses serão duplicados entre as plataformas quando o *Shared-TV* não é utilizado. Quando uma aplicação apresenta um conjunto de regras de negócio simples, como *Question-TV*, a variação de *LoC* é maior. Nessa aplicação a camada de comunicação representa boa parte do código desenvolvido, e que foi eliminado com o uso do *framework*.

Apesar dos resultados não serem conclusivos, devido a pequena amostragem de aplicativos analisados, pode-se inferir que o percentual da variação de LoC de uma aplicação é diretamente proporcional ao número de objetos compartilhados, e inversamente proporcional ao conjunto de regras de négocios.

6. CONCLUSÕES

Este artigo propõe um *framework* que permite o desenvolvimento de aplicativos interativos convergentes centrados na TV, chamado de *Shared-TV*. A ideia principal é facilitar a criação desse tipo de aplicativo, onde o programador desenvolve apenas a aplicação de TV, controlando e gerenciando a exibição de objetos e componentes nos dispositivos remotos, estimulando a participação dos usuários em um ambiente colaborativo. O *Shared-TV* gerencia toda a comunicação dos dispositivos, abstraindo a complexidade inerente das aplicações distribuídas. Além disso, o *framework* elimina a necessidade de uma versão do aplicativo para cada plataforma móvel, disponibilizando um aplicativo genérico capaz de se comunicar com os aplicativos de TV.

A análise do número de linhas de código das aplicações desenvolvidas mostra como o uso do *framework* pode reduzir o esforço aplicado no desenvolvimento de aplicativos convergentes para TV. Como resultado desse ganho, o desenvolvedor mantém o foco na lógica da aplicação deixando toda a parte de comunicação e gerenciamento dos dispositivos para o *Shared-TV*.

Como evolução do presente trabalho, considera-se uma análise de desempenho da camada de comunicação do *Shared-TV*, com intuito de detectar possíveis pontos de gargalo. Além dessa melhoria, planeja-se uma análise qualitativa com desenvolvedores que atuam em empresas do mercado com objetivo de validar a análise aqui realizada.

7. REFERÊNCIAS

[1] Hess, J., Lev, B., Ogonowski C., Wan, L., Wulf, V.: Jumping between devices and services: towards an integrated concept for social tv. In: EuroiTV, pp. 11-20 (2011)

[2] Viel, C.C., Melo, E.L., Teixeira, C.A.C., Trevelin, L.C.: RV-MTV: Framework para Interação Multimodal com Aplicações de Realidade Virtual em TV Digital e Dispositivos Móveis. In EuroiTV (2011)

[3] Yinghui, C.: Comprehensive analysis of the great interests of Internet TV development. In IEEE 3rd International Conference on Communication Software and Networks (ICCSN), pp. 249-351 (2011)

[4] Roibás, A. C., Sala, R., Ahmad, S. N. A. S., e Radman, M. (2005) "Beyond the remote control: Going the extramile to enhance iTV access via mobile devices & humanizing navigation experience for those with special needs", In EuroiTV 2005.

[5] Android Open Platform. Disponível em http://www.android.com/. Acessado em 15 de Maio de 2012.

[6] Ginga-J – The environment for the execution of procedural applications. Norma ABNT NBR 15606-4.

[7] GoogleTV Plataform.

[8] Cabrer, M.R., Rodondo, R.P.D, Vilas, A.F., Arias, J.J.P, Duque, J.G.: Controlling the smart home from TV. In IEEE Transactions on Consumer Electronics, pp. 421-429 (2006)

[9] Viana, N. S.; Maia, O. B.; De Lucena, V. F.: Convergence model between the IDTV Brazilian middleware and home networking software platforms. In Proceedings of the XV Brazilian Symposium on Multimedia and the Web, (2009)

[10] Freitas, G.B.; Teixeira, C.A.C.: Uma arquitetura de serviços para aplicações ubíquas em redes domésticas centrada em TV digital. In Proceedings of the 16th Brazilian Symposium on Multimedia and the Web (2010).

[11] Cesar, P., Bulterman, D.C.A., Jansen, A.J.: Usages of the Secondary Screen in an Interactive Television Environment: Control, Enrich, Share, and Transfer Television Content. In: Proceedings of the 6th European conference on Changing Television Environments, pp. 168-177 (2008)

[12] Pedrosa, D., Martins, J.A.C.Jr, Melo, E.L., Teixeira, C.A.C.: A multimodal interaction component for digital television. In Proceedings of the 2011 ACM Symposium on Applied Computing, pp. 1253-1258 (2011)

[13] IntoNow. Disponível em http://www.intonow.com. Acessado em 15 de Maio de 2012.

[14] Costa, R.M.S.; Moreno, M.F.; Soares, L.F.G.: Ginga-NCL: supporting multiple devices. In Proceedings of the 15th Brazilian Symposium on Multimedia and the Web, (2009)

[15] Silva, L.D.N.; Tavares, T.A., Souza, G.L.F.: Desenvolvimento de programas de TVDI explorando as funções inovadoras do Ginga-J. In Proceedings of the 14th Brazilian Symposium on Multimedia and the Web, (2008)

[16] MOVL company. Disponível em http://movl.com/. Acessado em 15 de Maio de 2012.

[17] Apple iOS. Disponível em http://www.apple.com/ios/. Acessado em 15 de Maio de 2012.

[18] C.E.S.A.R. Disponível em http://www.cesar.org.br. Acessado em 15 de Maio de 2012.

Multimedia Presentation Integrating Interactive Media Produced in Real Time with High Performance Processing

Caio César Viel
UFSCar, Brazil
caio_viel@dc.ufscar.br

Erick Lazaro Melo
UFSCar, Brazil
erick_melo@dc.ufscar.br

Arthur Pedro de Godoy
UFSCar, Brazil
arthur.godoy@dc.ufscar.br

Diego R. C. Dias
UFSCar, Brazil
diego.dias@dc.ufscar.br

Luis Carlos Trevelin
UFSCar, Brazil
trevelin@dc.ufscar.br

Cesar A. C. Teixeira
UFSCar, Brazil
cesar@dc.ufscar.br

ABSTRACT

Sophisticated interactive animation may be an interesting element to compose a multimedia document. However, potential demand for high performance computing can make this option impractical in digital interactive TV and mobile device environments, due to computing power restrictions of these platforms. In previous work we proposed a solution to overcome such restrictions based on video streaming. Moving forward the solution, it is described in this paper how to take advantage of media-agnostic characteristic, when present in the multimedia presentation machine, to manage this new type of media in multimedia documents. As a proof of concept we extended and tested an NCL presentation engine to add suport to this new type of media.

Categories and Subject Descriptors

C.2.4 [**Distributed Systemsl**]: Distributed applications; I.7.2 [**Document Preparation**]: Hypertext/hypermedia, Languages and systems, Multi/mixed media

General Terms

Design, Languages, Performance, Human Factors.

Keywords

High Performance Media, Declarative Languages, Multimedia, NCL, Video Streaming

1. INTRODUCTION

Multimedia presentations composed by different types of media can enrich the user experience when watching, listening and interacting with them. An interesting type of media to be considered is interactive animations with a high degree of realism and complexity, having visual and audio information following user's interactions. In this paper this type of media, wich usually requires real time and high performance processing to be produced, is called *High Performance Media (HPM)*.

One can imagine interesting applications of HPM objects in the TV environment. For example, consider a TV show based on an interactive expedition of a tourist spot, such as *Machu Picchu*. The application could be composed of a main video presenting an overview of the site and an HPM object representing a realistic 3D model of *Machu Picchu*. With the HPM object the user could explore areas and objects that were not explored or highlighted by the overview. The HPM object would be synchronized with the video of the overview. When the reporter move to another scenario, the application would move too. It would be even possible for the user to meet the news crew while navigating through the virtual environment. In addition, another media in the application, as high-resolution images or environment sound, could be added and synchronized with the user experience on HPM object. When the user enter a particular room, a specific song could start playing, for example.

Another interesting application could be a virtual contest between residents of different cities competing in a variety show. In addition to the audio and video of the program with a television presenter, participants and audience attendance, the application could also include an HPM object offering a virtual environment with competitions and events to viewers. Some viewers of the competing cities could be awarded with the opportunity to participate in the contest, competing from their homes, while all the others could follow the contest by choosing different visions of the virtual environment.

The framework RV-MTV was presented in previous work [14]. It uses a strategy based on streaming video to allow devices with low computing power - smartphones, tablets or Set-Top Boxes (STB) [1] of DTV and Internet Protocol TV (IPTV) - to interact with applications running remotely. The applications run on high-performance rendering servers. Visual and audio outputs produced by the application are captured and encoded using compression techniques. They are sent on the fly to client devices via streaming through IP or air or cable broadcast.

Using the RV-MTV one can build applications that allow viewers from environments with restricted processing power, as DTV, mobile and IPTV environments, to interact with HPM objects executed remotely. Controlling the HPM ob-

[1]The STB term is used in the text to refer to both the set-top box for IDTV and to TVs which have embbeded the features of these set-top box

Permission to make digital or hard copies of all or part of this work for personal or classroom use is granted without fee provided that copies are not made or distributed for profit or commercial advantage and that copies bear this notice and the full citation on the first page. To copy otherwise, to republish, to post on servers or to redistribute to lists, requires prior specific permission and/or a fee.
WebMedia'12, October 15–18, 2012, São Paulo/SP, Brazil.
Copyright 2012 ACM 978-1-4503-1706-1/12/10 ...$10.00.

ject requires writing an application to send messages according to some specific protocol to the HPM object. Despite the possibility of interacting with an HPM object, it would not be possible with this model to integrate HPM objects into a multimedia presentation. An HPM object would be represented by a independent video, not related to other media and subject only to the mechanisms implemented specifically for its control.

This paper presents a transparent solution to incorporate HPM objects into multimedia presentations. A dedicated player for HPM objects is proposed. The player performs the interface between the multimedia presentation machine and the HPM object, translating the instructions received from the presentation machine to messages for the HPM object. It is also proposed a way for mapping semantic concepts, common to declarative synchronization languages (anchors, links) in HPM objects. As a proof of concept, we extended the WebNCL [6], a presentation machine for Nested Context Language (NCL) [10], to add support to HPM objects. A multimedia presentation, integrating an HPM object generated by a graphic cluster, was used for testing purposes.

The remainder of this paper is organized as follows: section 2 presents some related works; section 3 defines the HPM object and discusses different strategies to enable them to run on devices with low computing power; section 4 presents the proposed mechanisms to aggregate HPM object to multimedia presentations; section 5 describes a proof of concept developed and finally section 6 presents conclusions and future works.

2. RELATED WORK

Cesar, Jansen and Bulterman proposed in [2] a way to enrich the multimedia content broadcasted in the context of IDTV. The proposal is to allow viewers to add their comments to the content transmitted by the broadcaster. The paper also discusses conceptually the incorporation of this facility in a declarative language, however it does not presents or make any reference to a proof of concept of the ideas.

Another approach to integrate HPM objects to multimedia presentations in the context of DTV, adopted in some works as in Dias et al [13], is to rely on local high performance computation. This approach may be a solution when the hardware, usually quite limited, of STB evolve to larger processing power, memory and graphics capability. This fact could lead to an increase in the cost of these devices and the need to rewrite applications for the languages supported by the embedded execution engines, which may not always be possible because of third-party resource dependencies, such as libraries and frameworks. A solution based only in local resources do not allow collaborative applications with HPM objects and remote users.

The strategy of remote execution of applications based on HPM objects is also treated in the work of Jurgelionis et al [5]. In that paper the authors propose strategies for implementation, capture, transmission and remote control of video games, allowing computers with low computational power to interact with applications. In another related work [14], the authors extend this concept to IDTV and mobile devices and present a framework that enables one to interact with remote applications through a strategy of streaming video. In both articles, applications are not integrated into the context of multimedia presentations. They are only remotely controlled by commands built with imperative languages.

In the paper of Schmitz [8], the objective is also to enhance multimedia presentations defined by a declarative language. The approach proposes an extension of the language using a model that is able to manage hybrid objects, between animation and video. Thus, it combines the control of a video sequence with the flexibility of an animation, highlighting the importance of synchronization of user interactions in a multimedia environment. The solution is restricted to the web and, as the generation of the hybrid media, respecting user interaction, is performed locally, collaborative interventions between remote users over a shared media are not supported.

Rahman, Hossain and Lornav [7] propose the inclusion of a 3D media in multimedia objects using a declarative language. However, the 3D media is treated standalone. The authors do not address its integration with other media on the composition of a multimedia object.

3. HPM AND IDTV

The class of HPM objects defined in the context of multimedia systems refers to interactive applications that produce results perceived to the human senses, usually sight and/or hearing, of very high quality and realism. The results arise from the reaction to unpredictable external stimuli caused by human interaction, by natural events or generated by other applications. The results are consumed by humans and must be created with time constraints (short delay between stimulus and response) in order to keep the quality of experience (soft real time).

Due to its characteristics, HPM objects require high performance computers or clusters to run. Thus, environments with restricted processing and/or memory, such as smartphones, STB and tablets are not suitable to run HPM objects.

To make feasible the presentation of HPM objects in IDTV environment, two approaches may be adopted. The first one is the inclusion of high-performance graphics chipsets in STB, aiming the local processing of HPM objects. The second approach is to run HPM objects remotely on high performance clusters, and transmit the visual and audible results to the STB.

The approach of local processing may prevent the reuse of legacy HPM objects, developed for running on clusters or high performance computers - environments very flexible as development platforms - due to constraints like differences on the programming languages supported. It would not be possible, for example, the reuse of HPM objects written in C / C + + in an environment that only understand IDTV applications written in Java. Moreover, this approach would not be scalable as new types of HPM objects could be designed requiring more processing power than would be available, making chipsets obsolete.

With the approach of remote processing using clusters, the restriction to reuse legacy HPM objects no longer exist. In addition, it becomes easier to build collaborative applications, since the execution of HPM objects of different users can be held in the same cluster. However, this approach requires that visual and / or audible results from an HPM object execution be transmitted via data network to the STB, which can increase the delay in consumption of the results.

Considering the remote processing approach for HPM objects that return high quality visual experience to the users, one can use different ways to transmit the output produced to the STB: (1) transmitting uncompressed frames, (2) transmission of pre-rendered frames and (3) streamming of compressed digital video .

In (1) latency time would be reduced as there would be no delay due to the compression and decompression processes. However, transmitting high quality uncompressed frames would require a large bandwidth not compatible with the found nowadays on the Internet or terrestrial broadcasting systems.

When using pre-rendered frames (2), there would be a negligible increase in latency and a significant reduction in bandwidth needed to transmit the high quality visual information back to the viewer. However, this approach assumes that local machines have sufficient processing capabilities to complete the renderization process, which can not be true with many STB and mobile devices.

Streaming compressed digital video (3) allows the transmission of high quality video over a reasonable bandwidth network. STB and mobile devices usually already have hardware support to perform video decompression. However, the problem with this approach is the increased latency due to the time spent in processes of compressing and decompressing video.

There are studies in the literature that seek ways to reduce the latency of video encoding processes. In the Holub et. al. [4] high-definition videos, which are more costly to be encoded, are considered. It is also important to consider the increased response time introduced by running applications remotely, which may be critical for some classes of HPM objects. Barker and Shenoy [1] explore this issue through empirical analysis of the performance of collaborative applications running on cloud computing.

In this work it was adopted the approach of implementing HPM objects remotely in clusters and transmitting results via streaming compressed digital video. The framework RV-MTV, which is able to perform the transmission of objects with latencies as low as one second [14], was used for capturing the HPM object video output, encoding and transmitting the video. While applications like action video game, that require instant feedback, fit the definition of HPM, the proof of concept implemented in this work obtain better results with HPM classes of objects more tolerant to response time, like virtual tours in museums and those presented as example in Section 1. Strategies to minimize inconsistencies in HPM object that could prejudice the quality of experience, when the deadline for response is difficult to be fulfilled, are addressed in this paper in Section 4.

4. HPM AS A MULTIMEDIA PRESENTATION COMPONENT

Multimedia Objects, which define the behavior of multimedia presentations and interactions, can be produced using imperative languages such as Java or Lua, declarative languages, such as SMIL and NCL, or combinations of both, in which imperative scripting languages provide support to the declarative one, as NCL and Lua in the Ginga middleware [10] or HTML and JavaScript.

The combination, declarative language supported by imperative scripting language, is a good compromise since, at the same time it eases the specification of synchronism between media it also provides facilities to define specific situations that may not be adequately supported by the declarative language, but may be implemented with the scripting language.

For the integration of HPM objects to multimedia presentations, this paper explores the possibilities of a declarative environment with support of imperative language. Two alternatives may be considered. The first, referenced here as Imperative, is based on an API in the imperative language that offers facilities for HPM objects manipulation, such as synchronization, and communication and delay control. The second approach, referenced as Declarative, as the declarative language resources are extensively exploited, defines direct interactions between the object and the HPM presentation machine. In this case, the HPM objects are in sync with the rest of the media presentation. The advantages and disadvantages of each alternative are presented below.

4.1 Declarative vs. Imperative Approach

One advantage of the Imperative approach is the flexibility for future changes and specifications due to the ease of modifying the developed API to add new features. Another advantage of this approach is a better decoupling of the API implementation and the presentation machine, which do not need to be modified. Furthermore, an imperative language always gives greater freedom for software development.

However, the Imperative approach creates a distance between the presentation machine and the HPM objects. This gap hinders the integration and interaction of HPM objects with other supported media, because the management of the HPM object is no longer under control of the presentation machine. Furthermore, the development of multimedia presentations using the Imperative approach is more complex, as it requires greater skill in programming.

In contrast with the imperative approach, declarative implementation uses the concept of presentation integrated to media management, leading to a more cohesive and natural manipulation of the multimedia document. In this approach the HPM can be used as a conventional media (such as video or audio), with support to specific demands of HPM objects, such as the address of the remote machine and the communication channel configuration. Synchronization between HPM objects and other media from multimedia object with this approach is straightforward.

The integration of HPM objects to multimedia presentations is more coupled to the presentation machine in the declarative than in the imperative approach. Specifications of the HPM objects behavior can be carried out using the same semantics of the declarative language applied to other media, making use, for example, of interaction concepts common to multimedia declarative languages, such as anchors, regions, etc. In the imperative approach, delegating the handling of HPM objects to an external controller would require re-implementation of these concepts in a language which was not designed for this.

Considering a declarative language such as NCL, for example, which allow transparent addition of new types of media , one can add support for HPM objects without the need to change the grammar of the language [11] . As a result of the delegation of responsibility for interpretation of the new elements to the presentation machine, this approach strengthens the link between multimedia presentations (with

HPM objects) and the presentation machine, since the the presentation machine must be extended to support HPM objects.

4.2 Integration Proposal

Due to the advantages of the Declarative approach presented before, that was the way we adopted for the integration of HPM objects to multimedia presentations, promoting a development model more suitable for multimedia contexts. It is necessary that the declarative language be media-agnostic, which means be able of handling and synchronizing transparently different media, without knowing the media. Examples of languages that presents such characteristic are NCL and SMIL [9] .

This class of languages uses transitions in the state machine of each media to manage synchronization. For example, synchronization points may be the beginning, end or pause of a specific media. Another intrinsic characteristic of these languages are the concepts of media properties and media anchors. The anchors refer to portions of media, such as a time interval in a video. The properties are features that can be accessed and changed during the presentation, for example, the volume of a music.

To promote the incorporation of HPM objects in multimedia presentations, some changes must be done in the presentation machine to support this new class of objects. It is necessary to map the concepts of properties, anchors and transitions of the state machine into HPM objects. The interactions between the presentation machine and the HPM object mus be encapsulated in control messages exchanged through the communication channel.

The event manipulation and transposition of an anchor type interface are illustrated in Figure 1. A syntax similar to NCL is use to exemplify the integration.

The anchor Paint1 is declared in item 1; item 2 defines its relationship with the HPM object via a link triggered in the anchor by the event onSelectionStart. The HPM object, defined in item 3 is then interpreted by the presentation machine that performs the necessary steps for synchronization, in this case pausing the return video, running the waiting resource and blocking the treatment of any other event until finishing the wait period. Then (item 4) passes to the remote application the event generated, along with control information (current timestamp) and triggers the response timeout. The remote application will apply the result of the event in the virtual environment (in this case modifying the current position of the user to the location of the anchor Paint1), thereby updating the return streaming video. The remote applicaltion also send an acknowledgment to the presentation machine, which resume the video removing it from the pause state.

Synchronization

Due to the delay inherent to the process of video encoding, decoding and transmission, the video presented to the viewer does not reflect the current state of the application running on the remote server. Although the synchronization between the states is not critical as HPM objects require only a sufficient synchronization to human perception, the latency in response time can affect the quality of experience. The upgrade of the presentation machine to integrate HPM objects must provide mechanisms to circumvent this problem.

To reduce the problem of states inconsistency, a synchro-

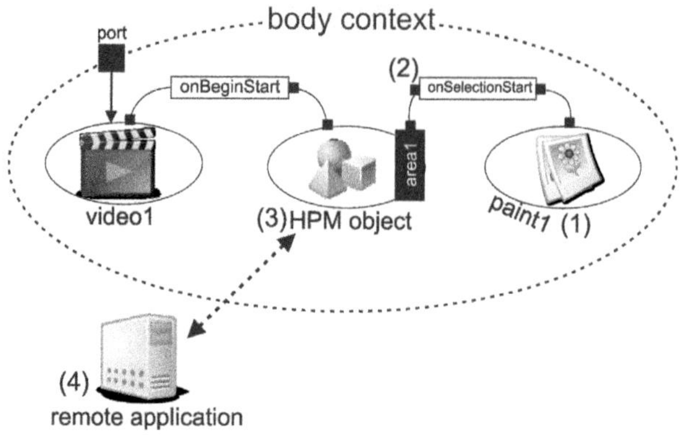

Figure 1: HPM Object in a multimedia presentation

nization mechanism between the state of the presentation and the state of the HPM object, using the clock of the involved machines (timestamp), is proposed. An initial calibration is required to synchronize the clock of local and remote machines. The calibration is repeated periodically to guarantee the sync. This synchronization does not need to be exact, tolerating differences not relevant to humans senses.

The application keeps, for each rendering iteration, the current state of its objects (eg user three-dimensional position and point of view). The presentation machine contributes with the sync process adding a timestamp in the messages when mapping events to messages and stop accepting new event requests until get confirmation message from the remote HPM object.

Further, to counterbalance the video coding/decoding delay, it is necessary that the remote application be able to evaluate the time spent in the process. Adding this time with the difference between the timestamps of control messages, the application can return back to the state the presentation was when sent the event.

There is also the need to address possible remote application freezes, discovered by the lack of response message. To do that, the extended machine triggers a timer waiting for a confirmation. In the event of a timeout, the presentation machine takes steps to alert the user, to reestablish communication or to exchange the remote server.

Application Manifest

To make simple the integration of HPM objects into multimedia presentations, we use an XML file to specify the characteristic of the HPM object. This file can hold information about the video stream address generated from the HPM object and the ways by which messages can be sent to the remote application that is generating the HPM object. It also lists the proprieties and anchors of the HPM object by which the multimedia presentation can interact with the HPM object. This Manifest File should be provide by the authors of the HPM object.

The Listing 1 contains a manifest file sample. In the lines 1 and 2 is defined the address of the video stream produced by the remote application. Between lines 3 and 8 the HPM object anchors and propriery are listed. Between lines 9 and 13 is specified how the communication with the remote application will be performed - in this case, via a message broker. Between lines 14 and 17 is specified the alternative content that will be displayed by the latency dissimulating mechanism.

```
<manifest class="HPM">
  <media type="video"
    mrl="rtmp://mediaserver/streaming" />
  <anchors>
    <area name="PAINT_001" />
    <area name="PAINT_002" />
    <area name="PAINT_003" />
    <property name="speed" />
  </anchors>
  <communication protocol="stomp">
    <address brokerURI=
    "failover:(tcp://broker:61616)" />
    <topic dest="HPM_APP" />
  </communication>
  <holdOn>
    <waitingTrick type="image"
      mrl="loading.gif" />
  </holdOn>
</manifest>
```

Listing 1: NCL Link

5. PROOF OF CONCEPT

Our proof of concept for the proposed integration of HPM objects into multimedia objects is composed of two parts. The first part is the extension of an NCL presentation machine to suport HPM objects as a new media type which was done by adding a new media player for HPM objects. The second part is building a distributed application, consisting of an application running on high-performance clusters that procudes HPM object and a NCL document which embedded this HPM object.

5.1 Adding an HPM Player to the presentation machine

The presentation machine we choose to extend was the WebNCL [6], an NCL presentation machine developed on top of web stack technologies (HTML/CSS /JavaScript) that allows the execution of NCL documents into HTML5 compatible browsers.

The WebNCL's Event Manager is responsible for controlling the processing of NCL links. It is media-agnostic-media, which means it does not need to know if the media is an image or a video - or even non-standard type such as HPM objects - to perform the processing of events. The responsibility to inform the event manager about the transitions occurred in the media presentation that can represent conditions in NCL links - as beginning of an anchor - is delegated to players of each media. Also, the media players are responsible for receiving and processing the actions triggered by links - as modify a media property.

Because of this decoupling between the event manager and the media players in WebNCL, to add support for HPM objects in WebNCL we need to implement a new media player. This new media is responsible for playing and controlling HPM objects. This approach also does not require modifications in the presentation machine core.

Figure 2 depicts the WebNCL's architecture and details the HPM object player that was added to the presentation machine. The HPM player was inserted in the presentation layer, the same layer where the other media players are situated. It is composed of components responsible for to parse the manifest file (Manifest Parser), to handle and to present the video streamed by the remote application (Video Stream Player), to exchange messages with the remote application (Communication Module) and to synchronize and to perform dissimulation delay mechanisms (Synchronization Module).

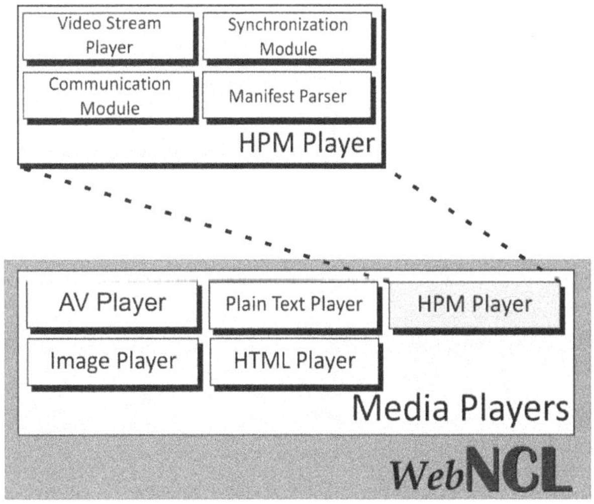

Figure 2: NCLweb and HPM Player Architecture

The HPM object player receives video stream using RTMP (Real Time Messaging Protocol)[2] and display the video frames on the screen in the position defined by the presentation machine. Whenever an action event is triggered over an HPM object media node - as to start a certain anchor - the HPM player encodes that event in a JSON (JavaScript Object Notation) [3] message and sends it to the remote application.

In a similar way, when the remote application notices any transition that can be used as a condition to NCL links - such as HPM object's anchors starts - it sends a message to the HPM player. The HPM player decodes the message received and triggers the corresponding events to the presentation machine.

The HPM player also implements synchronization mechanisms to works around possible delay resulting from the video encoding strategy. When a user's stimulus can generate some inconsistencies in the presentation due to the difference between what he sees and the HPM object state in the cluster, the HPM player sends a message to the remote application with the video packets timestamp. The remote application uses the timestamp to retrieve the HPM object state for the moment that user's stimulus has been happened. In this state, the remote application processes the stimulus, producing the right visual output. While the cluster processes the user's stimulus and adjust the HPM object state, the HPM player can display some alternative content to dissimulate the latency.

[2]RTMP - http://www.adobe.com/devnet/rtmp.html

[3]JSON - http://www.json.org

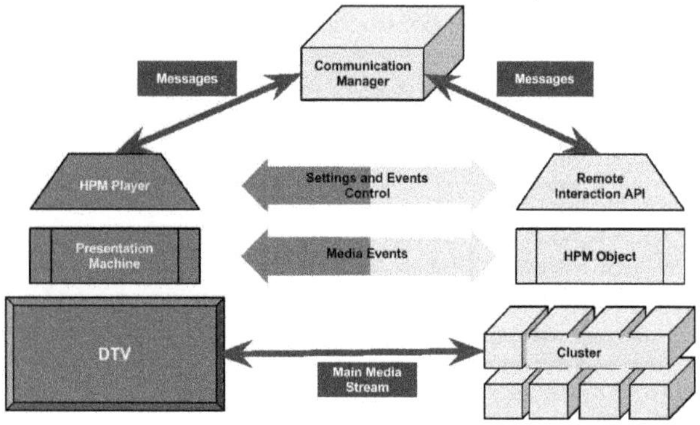

Figure 3: HPM Architecture

5.2 HPM object embedded in a NCL presentation

Figure 3 dipcts the infrastructure used for the integration of HPM objects with an NCL presentation.

The graphic cluster is an instantiation of a Cave Automatic Virtual Environment (CAVE) [12] called Mini CAVE [3]. The graphics rendering applications is done in a distributed way. Thus complex environments can be presented in a high frame rate.

The running application was developed in C++ using the OGRE 3D [4], a graphic engine. It runs on a cluster of six nodes, equipped with Intel i7 processors and NVIDIA GPU.

The application responsible for generating the HPM object is an 3D modeling of a painting of Sonia Menna Barreto, a Brazilian artist, called *Torre de Papel*. The environment has some predefined animations and other paintings spread by the environment, such as an art exhibition of her works. Users can navigate in the virtual environment, using traditional devices (mouse, keyboard) and unconventional (mobile devices, Kinect and Wii Remote).

The application has been modified to incorporate the framework RV-MTV [14] . Using the framework, the generated frames are captured and encoded, generating a video stream that is sent to the HPM player.

The anchors of the HPM object were defined as certain positions within the 3D environment (the coordinates x, y, z and the camera angle by which the image is seen). Each anchor points to an environment location that faces one of the exhibited paintings. When the application receives a message from the HPM player informing an *play event* in a certain anchor, the application adjusts its display to show the painting associated with the anchor. One can also set the speed of predefined animations by modifying the property value speed through events sent by HPM player.

Also, it was implemented a new interaction mechnism, allowing navigation through NCL application. If the user navigating in the environment, approaches to a painting associated to an anchor, the application will send an event to the HPM player, informing the start of that anchor. When the user leaves the area, an event indicating the end of an anchor will also be sent in an analogous manner. Figure 4 shows the application running on the cluster graph.

[4]OGRE 3D - http://www.ogre3d.org/

Figure 4: HPM object running.

A module for controlling the messages exchanged between the HPM Player and the HPM object running on the cluster is important. We chose to use the ActiveMQ broker [5] to accomplish the management of these messages.

The advantages of a using a broker for message exchange are its reliability and security. Furthermore, as libraries for integration with ActiveMQ are present in many different languages, the construction of distributed applications on different platforms and languages, as occurs in this proof of concept, is facilitated.

We used the STOMP protocol (Simple Text Message Oriented Protocol) [6] to realize the communication between applications, encoding messages in JSON format. Streaming video produced by the application is sent to a remote media server. The media server then retransmits the video for the presentation machine using a multimedia streaming protocol (RTMP).

The NCL document which embed the HPM object allows users to navigate among the anchors through a menu. When the user is viewing any HPM anchor, a high-resolution image of the artwork is displayed. The user can also change the speed of the animations in HPM object using the colored buttons in the remote control.

```
<media id="interactivePaint"
     src="HPM_manifest.xml"
     descriptor="dInteractivePaint">
  <area id="paint1" text="PAINT_001" />
  <area id="paint2" text="PAINT_002" />
  <area id="paint3" text="PAINT_003" />
  <property name="speed" value="1.0" />
</media>

<link id="lGoPaint1"
     xconnector="onSelectionStopStart">
  <bind component="menuItem1"
     role="onSelection" />
  <bind component="interactivePaint"
     role="stop" />
  <bind component="interactivePaint"
     interface="paint1" role="start" />
</link>

<link id="lRedKey"
     xconnector="onKeySelecionSet">
  <bind component="interactivePaint"
     role="onSelection">
```

[5]ActiveMQ - http://activemq.apache.org
[6]STOMP - http://stomp.github.com

```
24          <bindParam name="keyCode"
25       value="RED"/>
26     </bind>
27     <bind component="interactivePaint"
28       interface="speed" role="set">
29          <bindParam name="setValue"
30       value="1.5"/>
31     </bind>
32 </link>
33
34 <link id="lShowPaint2"
35       xconnector="onBeginStart">
36     <bind component="interactivePaint"
37       interface="paint2" role="onBegin" />
38     <bind component="plainPaint2"
39       role="start" />
40 </link>
41
42 <link id="lHidePaint2"
43       xconnector="onEndStop">
44     <bind component="interactivePaint"
45       interface="paint2" role="onEnd" />
46     <bind component="plainPaint2"
47       role="stop" />
48 </link>
```

Listing 2: NCL Link

Listing 2 presents some excerpts from the NCL document. Between lines 1 and 8 an HPM media node is defined. The media's source is the HPM manifest (HPM_manifest.xml). It describes the possible properties, anchors and how to communicate with the HPM object (the address of streaming and other information that defines the object). Inside the media node are defined three anchors and a property.

The link lGoPaint1 (lines 10-18) defines an action that causes the HPM object to be moved to the anchor Paint1 when a particular menu icon is selected. The link lRedKey modify the value of HPM oject speed property to 1.5 when the red button is pressed, in other words, increasing the speed of the animations in 50 %.

The links lShowPaint2 (lines 34-40) and lHidePaint2 (lines 42-48) make the image plainPaint2, a high-resolution image of an artwork, be presented when the user is near to the equivalent painting in the HPM object.

Figure 5 shows the NCL document being presented. The user can interact with the application using the arrow keys to navigate between artworks from a side menu. When the user selects a menu item, the HPM object is moved to its anchor and a high resolution image of the artwork is displayed (Figure 6).

6. FINAL REMARKS

The work presented in this paper confirms the feasibility of the proposed approach for embedding HPM objects in multimedia presentations. From a multimedia presentation platform with declarative language, complemented by imperative scripting language, interpretation capabilities, the approach adopted was to promote changes in the presentation machine so that the new media could be fully managed by the declarative part of the environment only. Thus, HPM objects can be better integrated with the multimedia presentation, as all its management is kept under the control of the presentation machine. It was also shown the feasibility of incorporating HPM objects on TVDi and mobile devices environments, using a strategy of video streaming.

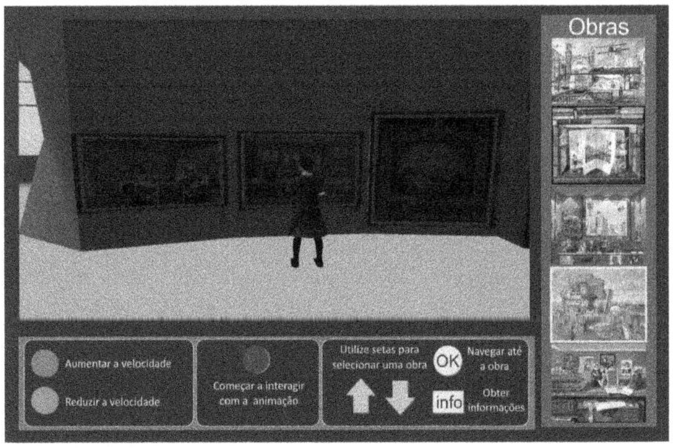

Figure 5: Navigation in the virtual environment

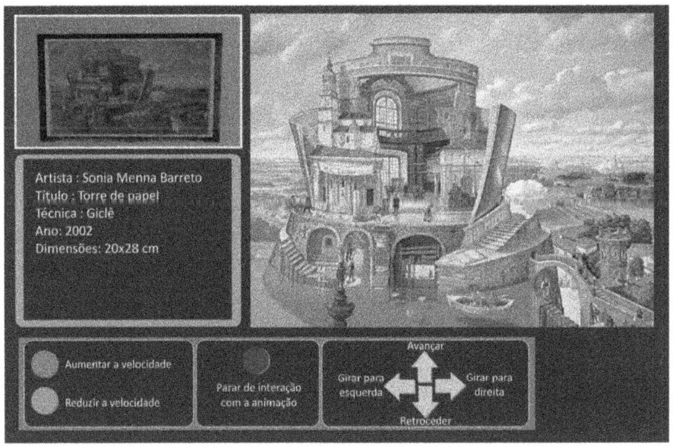

Figure 6: HPM synchronization with other media

It was presented as proof of concept the upgrade of a NCL presentation machine needed to enable it to run multimedia presentations that have HPM objects as one of their media. The new media is managed by the presentation machine generically, as it was an image or a video. Upgrading the presentation machine demanded no modification in the grammar of NCL as it is a media-agnostic language. A NCL multimedia application, including an HPM object generated remotely by a graphics cluster, was also developed and tested. This experience showed that creating a multimedia presentation with HPM objects is natural for developers who already have experience in authoring NCL documents.

The main issues that may be addressed in future works, in order to improve the proposed approach of embedding HPM objects in multimedia applications for IDTV and mobile devices environments, are related to the delay of encoding and streaming video. One can explore an approach based on the generation of pre-rendered frames at the cluster, leaving the final rendering to the local application. This process can be improved with embedded GPUs as OpenGL-ES [7] or even a web version like WebGL.

Acknowledgments

We thank CAPES, CNPq, RNP, FINEP and MinC for the financial support given to research projects related to this

[7]OpenGL-ES - http://www.khronos.org/registry/gles/

paper and FAPESP for supporting its presentation at the conference.

7. REFERENCES

[1] S. K. Barker and P. Shenoy. Empirical evaluation of latency-sensitive application performance in the cloud. In *Proceedings of the first annual ACM SIGMM conference on Multimedia systems*, MMSys '10, pages 35–46, New York, NY, USA, 2010. ACM.

[2] P. Cesar, D. Bulterman, and A. Jansen. An architecture for end-user tv content enrichment. *Journal of Virtual Reality and Broadcasting*, 3(9):14, 2006.

[3] D. R. C. Dias, J. R. F. Brega, M. Paiva Guimarães, F. Modesto, B. B. Gnecco, and J. R. P. Lauris. 3d semantic models for dental education. In M. M. Cruz-Cunha, J. a. Varajão, P. Powell, and R. Martinho, editors, *ENTERprise Information Systems*, volume 221 of *Communications in Computer and Information Science*, pages 89–96. Springer Berlin Heidelberg, 2011.

[4] P. Holub, L. Matyska, M. Liška, L. Hejtmánek, J. Denemark, T. Rebok, A. Hutanu, R. Paruchuri, J. Radil, and E. Hladká. High-definition multimedia for multiparty low-latency interactive communication. *Future Generation Computer Systems*, 22(8):856 – 861, 2006.

[5] A. Jurgelionis, P. Fechteler, P. Eisert, F. Bellotti, H. David, J. P. Laulajainen, R. Carmichael, V. Poulopoulos, A. Laikari, P. Perälä, A. De Gloria, and C. Bouras. Platform for distributed 3d gaming. *Int. J. Comput. Games Technol.*, 2009:1:1–1:15, Jan. 2009.

[6] E. L. Melo, C. C. Viel, and C. A. C. Teixeira. Webncl: A web-based presentation machine for multimedia documents. In *WebMedia 2012*, 2012.

[7] M. Rahman, M. Hossain, and A. Saddik. Lornav: A demo of a virtual reality tool for navigation and authoring of learning object repositories. In *Distributed Simulation and Real-Time Applications, 2004. DS-RT 2004. Eighth IEEE International Symposium on*, pages 240 – 243, oct. 2004.

[8] P. Schmitz. Multimedia meets computer graphics in smil2.0: a time model for the web. In *Proceedings of the 11th international conference on World Wide Web*, WWW '02, pages 45–53, New York, NY, USA, 2002. ACM.

[9] SMIL3. Synchronized multimedia integration language (smil 3.0). http://www.w3.org/TR/SMIL3/, Maio 2012.

[10] L. Soares, R. Rodrigues, and M. Moreno. Ginga-ncl: the declarative environment of the brazilian digital tv system. *Journal of the Brazilian Computer Society*, 12(4):37–46, 2007.

[11] L. F. G. Soares, M. F. Moreno, and F. Sant'Anna. Relating declarative hypermedia objects and imperative objects through the ncl glue language. In *Proceedings of the 9th ACM symposium on Document engineering*, DocEng '09, pages 222–230, New York, NY, USA, 2009. ACM.

[12] L. P. Soares. *Um Ambiente de multiprojeção totalmente imersivo baseado em aglomerados de computadores*. PhD thesis, USP, São Paulo, 2005.

[13] D. F. Souza, T. A. Tavares, L. S. Machado, and G. L. Souza Filho. Incorporating 3d technologies to the brazilian dtv standard: a study of integration strategies based on middleware ginga. In *Proceedings of the 8th international interactive conference on Interactive TV&Video*, EuroITV '10, pages 251–258, New York, NY, USA, 2010. ACM.

[14] C. C. Viel, E. L. Melo, L. Trevelin, and C. A. C. Teixeira. Rv-mtv: Framework para interação multimodal com aplicações de realidade virtual em tv digital e dispositivos móveis. In *WebMedia 2011*, 2011.

Exploration of Motion Estimation Algorithm in Graphics Processing Environment

Ronaldo Husemann
DELET – UFRGS
Av. Osvaldo Aranha, 103
Porto Alegre – RS – Brasil
rhusemann@inf.ufrgs.br

Augusto L. Lenz, Marco Gobbi
UNIVATES
Av. Alberto Tallini, 171
Lajeado – RS – Brasil
augustollenz@gmail.com
marcogobbi@universo.univates.br

Valter Roesler, José Valdeni Lima
II – UFRGS
Av. Bento Gonçalves, 9500 B. IV
Porto Alegre – RS – Brasil
roesler@inf.ufrgs.br
valdeni@inf.ufrgs.br

ABSTRACT

Currently, even considering the recent advances in the microprocessor power computing, high definition multimedia applications still require very complex demands to allow real-time video encoding. Particularly, modern video encoders (MPEG/ITU H.26x series) depend of complex and computationally exhaustive motion estimation algorithms to identify and remove temporal redundancy among consecutive (or not) frames inside a video sequence, as strategy to reduce the final compressed bit rate. In fact, the mechanism of block matching can be considered the most critical encoder algorithm, in terms of computational demands, like it is responsible for searching, in distinct reference frames, for similar pixel blocks related with each one of the input image blocks. The number of required block comparisons for high definition videos represents a clear and important restriction for real-time implementations. This paper introduces an improved strategy of block matching method, which was optimized for multiprocessing execution, mainly focusing in implementation over general purpose graphical processing unit technologies, as the NVidia CUDA® GPUs. The improved motion estimation solution was implemented in the JSVM reference code (scalable version of H.264 video encoder), when it was registered a speed up gain of more than 350% in average for 4CIF videos.

Categories and Subject Descriptors

D.1.3 [**Concurrent Programming**]: Parallel programming

General Terms

Algorithms, Performance, Design.

Keywords

SAD method, H.264 encoding, CUDA.

1. INTRODUÇÃO

Impulsionado pela indústria do entretenimento, a demanda pelo emprego de complexos codificadores de vídeo tem crescido muito nos últimos anos. Estes codificadores, que são responsáveis por comprimir as informações de vídeo, reduzindo suas demandas por espaço, requerem entretanto computação intensa, tornando necessárias técnicas computacionais sofisticadas, muitas vezes implementadas em hardware (usando, por exemplo, componentes do tipo ASIC - *Application Specific Integrated Circuit*), para tornar possível sua execução com características de tempo real [1]

A implementação de modernos padrões de codificação, para processar vídeos de alta definição, através de soluções somente por software é ainda um grande desafio. Para se ter uma idéia desta complexidade, pode-se considerar os resultados de [2] que apontam que um codificador de vídeo H.264, padrão ITU-T de 2002, para operar sobre vídeos de alta definição, chega a exigir demandas de até 3,6 TIPS (*Tera Instructions Per Second*).

Basicamente, dentro de um codificador de vídeo, se destacam por sua complexidade os algoritmos de estimativa de movimento. Estes algoritmos realizam processos extensivos de pesquisa e comparação, sobre sequências de imagens, responsáveis por analisar, para cada bloco de pixels da imagem de entrada, pela posição mais provável para onde este possa ter se movido dentro uma determinada janela de busca. Quando esta movimentação é detectada o codificador pode apenas guardar esta informação, dispensando a necessidade de retransmitir dados já recebidos pelo decodificador.

Uma estratégia possível para atender a altas demandas computacionais como dos algoritmos de estimativa de movimento, se baseia no uso de processadores gráficos de alto desempenho como motores de co-processamento, auxiliando o computador na realização de algoritmos de alta complexidade computacional.

Os modernos processadores gráficos (*Graphical Processing Units* – GPUs) possuem uma arquitetura altamente paralela, compostas por centenas de núcleos operacionais, que permitem executar, em um mesmo ciclo de instrução, um grande número de procedimentos simultâneos. Esta forma de organização é particularmente apropriada para processamento de gráficos em duas ou três dimensões (3D), mas também pode ser empregada na implementação de uma grande diversidade de algoritmos em diversos outros campos [3]. Este conceito é genericamente chamado de *General Purpose Graphics Processing* Unit (GPGPU), uma vez que visa explorar o poder de processamento das placas aceleradoras de vídeo em aplicações não necessariamente gráficas [4].

Considerando este cenário, o presente artigo apresenta uma análise investigativa do uso da tecnologia de GPGPU NVIDIA

Permission to make digital or hard copies of all or part of this work for personal or classroom use is granted without fee provided that copies are not made or distributed for profit or commercial advantage and that copies bear this notice and the full citation on the first page. To copy otherwise, or republish, to post on servers or to redistribute to lists, requires prior specific permission and/or a fee.
WebMedia'12, October 15–18, 2012, São Paulo/SP, Brazil.
Copyright 2012 ACM 978-1-4503-1706-1/12/10...$15.00.

CUDA® como plataforma de desenvolvimento para aumento de velocidade de um algoritmo de estimativa de movimento, visando uma solução aplicável para qualquer codificador de vídeo H.264 compatível.

Dentro deste enfoque, foi produzida uma versão de estimador de movimento otimizada para suportar elevado grau de paralelismo, tornando-se assim mais adequada para implementação em arquiteturas de processamento paralelo, como é o caso destas modernas GPUs.

Como estratégia de validação da solução proposta, esta foi implementada sobre o software de referência JSVM, que é disponibilizado pela entidade JVT (*Joint Video Team*), para desenvolvedores de soluções de codificação baseadas no H.264 SVC (*Scalable Video Coding*), versão mais recente do codificador ITU-T H.264 [4].

Os resultados obtidos comparando-se a nova arquitetura de estimativa de movimento em ambiente de computação convencional (monoprocessador) com uma solução que de fato utiliza uma placa de processamento gráfico apontam para ganhos de desempenho bastante relevantes.

O artigo é organizado da seguinte maneira: a seção 2 traz uma visão geral de mecanismos de estimativa de movimento, a seção 3 apresenta detalhes da arquitetura GPGPU NVIDIA CUDA; a seção 4 apresenta alguns trabalhos relacionados; a seção 5 descreve a arquitetura da solução de estimativa de movimento proposta; a seção 6 mostra os dados reais obtidos comparando o método proposto com uma arquitetura tradicional e finalmente a seção 7 apresenta as considerações finais do artigo.

2. ESTIMATIVA DE MOVIMENTO

O módulo de estimativa de movimento procura explorar a redundância temporal existente entre imagens de um mesmo vídeo. A pesquisa por movimentação ocorre no nível de blocos de pixels e é feita normalmente em uma janela de busca de tamanho fixo em imagens de referência (já previamente recebidas), utilizando-se um determinado critério de similaridade. Dentre os diferentes mecanismos de cálculo de similaridade, o mais comum é o SAD (*Sum of Absolute Differences*), que apresenta o erro residual entre dois blocos pelo cálculo das diferenças absolutas entre pixels. Este algoritmo é bastante utilizado, pois utiliza apenas operações triviais como somas e subtrações, enquanto que outros cálculos alternativos de similaridade como o MSE (*Mean Square Error*) ou SSE (*Sum of Square Errors*), demandam por operações de multiplicação ou outras funções ainda mais complexas [1].

Abaixo se apresenta a expressão usada para o cálculo de SAD entre dois blocos de pixels.

$$SAD = \sum \sum abs\,(PS_{ij} - PR_{ij})$$

Onde:

PS_{ij} = Valor do pixel do bloco de origem localizado na posição (i,j);

PR_{ij} = Valor do pixel do bloco de referência localizado na posição (i,j).

Durante um processo de estimativa de movimento, o bloco de pixels da imagem de referência que apresentar o menor valor de SAD terá o menor erro residual e por este motivo deverá ser selecionado como a melhor estimativa de movimento encontrada. Sua distância em relação ao bloco atual é chamada de vetor de movimento e identificado como resultado do algoritmo de busca.

O algoritmo de estimativa de movimento que gera o vetor de movimento mais preciso é conhecido como algoritmo de pesquisa completa (*full search*), uma vez que pesquisa na totalidade da janela de busca da(s) imagem(s) de referência pelo bloco de pixels mais próximo possível do bloco da imagem atual.

Este procedimento é efetuado para todos os possíveis blocos imagem, buscando verificar se o bloco alvo foi movimentado para qualquer outro ponto da imagem, não importando o quão longe esteja do ponto original dentro da janela de busca. Pelo fato do algoritmo de busca completa analisar todas as opções possíveis de deslocamento, ele consegue determinar com precisão o melhor vetor de movimento para aquela região pesquisada.

Apesar, entretanto, de obter o melhor resultado, na prática este procedimento de busca completa não costuma ser muito utilizado, devido ao fato de demandar um custo computacional muito elevado.

Além disso, dificilmente num vídeo ocorrem grandes movimentações de uma imagem em relação à anterior, o que indica que a maior parte dos procedimentos de busca completa seria desnecessária [5].

Visando substituir o método *full-search*, surgiram os algoritmos de busca esparsa. A principal característica destes algoritmos é de que eles não analisam todos os blocos da janela de busca, mas sim buscam por um padrão que infere o melhor caminho para encontrar o bloco mais parecido.

Alguns dos algoritmos mais conhecidos são o Three-*Step Search* (TSS), um dos primeiros desta linha [5], e também suas evoluções, o *New Three-Step Search* (NTSS) [6] e o *Four Step Search* (4SS) [7].

Um mecanismo alternativo de busca esparsa foi proposto por Chung [8], onde são utilizados cálculos estatísticos visando otimizar a área de busca.

Outra proposta menos intensiva computacionalmente e que leva a menores erros foi apresentada por Zhu, e ficou conhecida como *Diamond Search* (DS), empregando dois padrões de busca: diamante grande e diamante pequeno [9].

Na implementação do presente trabalho, utilizou-se apenas a topologia de diamante pequeno para estimativa de movimento, pois este padrão além de mais simples, se ajusta bem a aplicações que apresentam nível pequeno e médio de movimentação [10].

Uma ilustração do padrão de busca em diamante pequeno está representada na Figura 1. Neste padrão, sempre que uma busca for iniciada, deve-se conferir o bloco inicial em relação ao bloco na posição imediatamente superior, imediatamente inferior e aos seus vizinhos laterais (direita e esquerda).

Na Figura 1, a posição inicial é identificada pelo círculo claro, no centro do diamante, enquanto que os blocos vizinhos representam os círculos escuros.

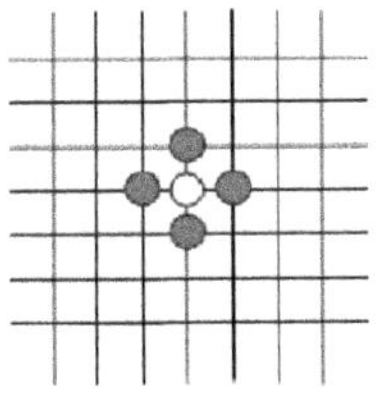

Figura 1. Visão geral da topologia de diamante pequeno.

No primeiro estágio da busca, o bloco original é comparado com todos os quatro blocos vizinhos utilizando a métrica SAD, partindo-se do bloco superior e seguindo-se o sentido horário para comparar os demais. O bloco que obtiver o menor resultado de erro absoluto indica o caminho para o próximo estágio. Se dois valores de SAD forem iguais deve-se escolher o primeiro bloco na sequencia definida (partindo-se do bloco superior no sentido horário). O algoritmo encerra a busca quando encontra o menor erro no centro do diamante.

3. TECNOLOGIA GPU NVIDIA

Nos últimos anos, as demandas crescentes por processamento tridimensional de placas aceleradoras gráficas, impulsionaram avanços das arquiteturas de processadores gráficos dedicados. Apesar do crescimento deste mercado, porém, as ferramentas e linguagens disponíveis para desenvolvimento de aplicações de processamento gráfico (ex. OpenGL) não se mostravam adequadas para outros propósitos mais gerais tais como aplicações científicas. Este cenário se modificou com a decisão das empresas fabricantes de processadores gráficos em disseminar o uso destas plataformas para fins não gráficos. Um fato marcante foi o lançamento, em 2006, da plataforma de software e hardware CUDA, que visava estimular exatamente este mercado.

CUDA é uma arquitetura de computação paralela de propósito geral que faz uso da capacidade de processamento presente nas GPUs da empresa NVIDIA. A arquitetura CUDA definiu duas alterações principais na organização das GPUs: a unificação dos *shaders* (*vertex* e *pixel shaders*) e a criação de uma memória compartilhada de alto desempenho. O componente resultante da união dos *shaders* é chamado *Stream Processor* (SP). Essas alterações transformaram as GPUs em dispositivos mais adequados ao processamento de propósito geral [11].

Grupos de *threads* (tarefas independentes previstas pelo algoritmo) podem ser escalonados para execução em um dos núcleos, sequencialmente ou simultaneamente, sem que seja necessário explicitar em qual núcleo o bloco será alocado, o que torna a solução mais flexível.

As placas de vídeo compatíveis com a tecnologia CUDA possuem um conjunto escalável de multiprocessadores, que são chamados *Streaming Multiprocessors* (SMs). Os SMs são compostos por uma série de processadores escalares (*scalar processors* – SP), uma unidade de instrução *multi thread* e memória compartilhada. Os blocos de *threads* criados pelo algoritmo são escalonados automaticamente para execução em SMs com capacidade ociosa. As *threads* dentro de um mesmo bloco são executadas concorrentemente, pois cada *thread* é mapeada em um SP distinto, com seus próprios registradores (Figura 2) [12].

O escalonador de *threads* separa-as em grupos, chamados de *warps*. A cada ciclo de operação um *warp* é selecionado para execução, então a mesma instrução pode ser executada em todas as *threads* ativas neste *warp* [11].

Apesar de todas *threads* começarem a execução no mesmo ponto do código, há a possibilidade de que haja ramificação na execução (ex. devido a conflito no acesso a memórias). Neste caso, nem todas as *threads* estarão ativas no mesmo momento, resultando na serialização da execução. Portanto, para que seja alcançada eficiência máxima na execução paralela das *threads* é necessário que não hajam ramificações no fluxo de execução dentro de um mesmo *warp* [13].

A organização das *threads* se dá na forma de blocos com uma, duas ou três dimensões. Esse arranjo particular torna simples a execução de cálculos em elementos de vetores, matrizes ou volumes. A identificação da *thread* que está sendo executada é implementada através de índices que identificam a posição da *thread* dentro do bloco (Figura 2). Os índices são disponibilizados ao programador através da variável tridimensional threadIdx que contém três campos de inteiros sem sinal: x, y, z. As *threads* que residem no mesmo bloco são executadas no mesmo SM podendo cooperar entre si através do compartilhamento de dados (pela memória compartilhada) e da sincronização da execução com funções intrínsecas que servem como barreiras na execução, de forma que a execução prossiga apenas quando todas as *threads* tiverem finalizado a execução de uma determinada sequência de instruções.

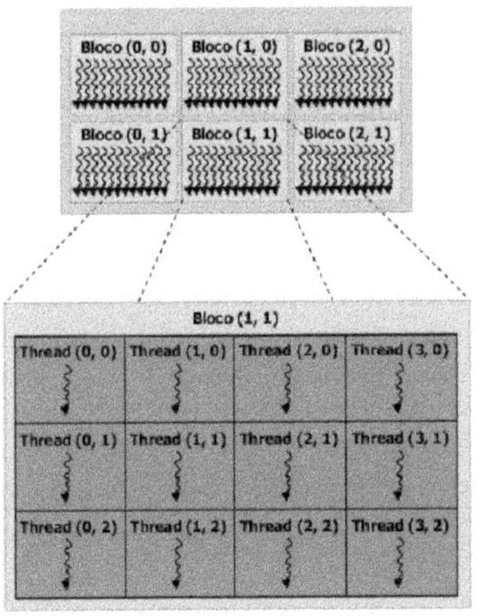

Figura 2 Organização das *threads* em uma arquitetura CUDA

Além do alinhamento de *threads* internas é interessante observar as características dos diferentes tipos de memória presentes nesta arquitetura, uma vez que sua adequada utilização pode influenciar diretamente o desempenho do algoritmo desenvolvido. Na prática, são cinco tipos de memórias previstos:

- Memória local e registradores;
- Memória compartilhada;
- Memória global;
- Memória de textura;
- Memória de constantes;

Os registradores são utilizados para armazenar as variáveis automáticas (variáveis locais). Se não houver espaço suficiente, o compilador alocará as variáveis na memória local. Como a memória local está localizada fora do chip esta apresenta tempo acesso elevado [14]. A memória local é apenas uma abstração sobre a memória global, com escopo limitado a cada *thread* [15].

A memória compartilhada está localizada dentro de cada multiprocessador e por isso possui latência cerca de cem vezes menor do que a memória global ou local, porém o tamanho total desta memória é reduzido [14]. A memória compartilhada pode ser utilizada como uma memória cache explicitamente gerenciada. A memória compartilhada é organizada em bancos, ou seja, módulos que podem ser acessados simultaneamente, a fim de obter uma alta largura de banda. Essa arquitetura permite que diversas requisições simultâneas, que acessem endereços localizados em diferentes bancos, possam ser atendidas ao mesmo tempo. Por outro lado, se uma requisição de acesso à memória contiver acessos em endereços localizados no mesmo banco poderá haver um conflito de acesso. A ocorrência de conflitos se dá quando mais de uma *thread* pertencente ao mesmo *half-warp*[1] solicitam acesso a posições de memória que localizam-se em um mesmo banco. Há uma exceção no caso de todas *threads* de um *half-warp* executarem leituras no mesmo endereço. Neste caso o conteúdo lido é disponibilizado para todas as *threads* através de uma operação de transferência global (*broadcast*).

A memória global está localizada na placa de vídeo, no entanto, não sendo integrada ao chip da GPU, possui alta latência no acesso. Esta memória pode ser acessada através de transações alinhadas de 32, 64 ou 128 bytes. Na prática, o endereço do primeiro elemento manipulado precisa ser um múltiplo do tamanho do segmento. As requisições de acesso à memória global efetuadas por um *half-warp* ou por um *warp* são combinadas resultando na menor quantidade de transações possível, que obedeça as regras de alinhamento impostas pela arquitetura de hardware. A Figura 3 ilustra padrões de acesso que permitem o acesso coalescido, ou seja, o acesso a várias posições de memória em apenas uma transação. Desta forma, os efeitos da latência de acesso são diluídos. A figura (a) exemplifica o acesso coalescido a variáveis *float* de quatro bytes. A figura (b) ilustra o acesso coalescido por um *warp* divergente, quando nem todas as *threads* acessam as respectivas variáveis.

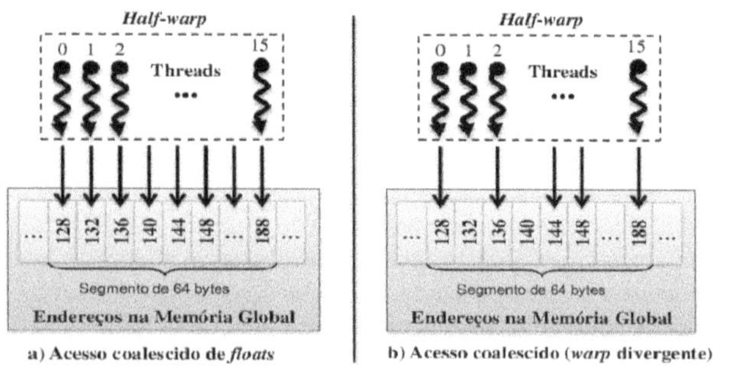

Figura 3 Padrões de acesso coalescido

---

1 *Half-warp* é um grupo de *threads*, com metade do tamanho de um *warp*.

A memória de textura ou superfície está localizada na memória interna da placa de vídeo e possui cache otimizado para acesso a dados que apresentem localidade espacial em duas dimensões, ou seja, dados localizados em posições próximas.

Além disso, esse espaço de memória é projetado de forma a obter fluxos de leitura com latência constante. Dessa forma, uma leitura do cache reduz a largura de banda demandada, mas a latência se mantém constante. Quando um *warp* necessita de um dado que está presente no cache há um ganho significativo no tempo de leitura. Caso o dado não esteja disponível no cache o tempo de acesso será o mesmo de uma leitura na memória global convencional. A memória de textura pode ser escrita a partir do computador externo, mas do ponto de vista da GPU é uma memória somente de leitura.

Por fim, a memória de constantes está localizada no interior do dispositivo e possui também memória cache. Possui acesso somente de leitura pela GPU. Esta memória pode ser utilizada pelo compilador através de instruções específicas [14].

4. TRABALHOS RELACIONADOS

Por se tratar de uma área bastante relevante, diversos autores da comunidade acadêmica têm buscado a utilização desta tecnologia como forma de aprimoramento do desempenho de codificadores de vídeo [15-18].

O trabalho [15], por exemplo, propõe um algoritmo rápido para cálculo de estimativa de movimento visando aplicação direta sobre um codificador H.264/AVC, a partir da exploração da plataforma CUDA. Foi escolhido, para este trabalho, um algoritmo de estimativa por busca completa (*full search*) para esta finalidade. Na solução desenvolvida, inicialmente, pixels do bloco atual e do quadro de referência são transferidos do domínio da CPU para a memória da GPU. As *threads* implementadas na GPU processam e acumulam seus resultados na memória compartilhada da placa. A operação de comparação de resultados (SADs dos diferentes blocos) assim como o algoritmo de soma de diferenças (SAD) em si basicamente exploram o mesmo algoritmo destacando-se apenas, que, para o caso das comparações, são utilizadas operações acumuladas de subtração e não de soma. Resultados de simulação mostram que o apoio da GPU chega a gerar uma implementação cerca de 40 a 60% mais rápida quando comparada com uma solução baseada unicamente em uma CPU.

Por sua vez, o trabalho [16], em comparação, implementa uma solução de estimativa de movimento baseado em um algoritmo esparso rápido de diamante pequeno (*small diamond*). Este algoritmo foi especialmente adaptado para explorar as características de processamento paralelo de modernas GPUs (assim como as larguras das diferentes memórias envolvidas). Como forma de validação os resultados obtidos com a solução otimizada para GPU foram comparados com o algoritmo UMHexagonS implementado para uma solução tradicional de CPU.

Testes práticos foram feitos sobre o software de referência JM9.0 (modelo de código aberto do codificador H.264), o qual foi estendido, na solução proposta, para, através do uso da API DirectX 9, conseguir acessar a GPU. Os resultados de melhoria de desempenho obtidos por esta solução otimizada apontaram para ganhos entre 1,5 e 3 vezes em relação a uma solução baseada em CPU somente.

5. ALGORITMO PROPOSTO

Visando-se contribuir com uma solução que pudesse aumentar o desempenho de algoritmos de estimativa de movimento compatíveis com o padrão H.264, foi desenvolvida uma proposta que alinha a localidade de dados deste tipo de algoritmo com a estrutura interna de processadores gráficos compatível com a arquitetura CUDA.

Conforme comentado, o algoritmo escolhido se baseia na topologia de busca por diamante pequeno. A ideia proposta está centrada na paralelização do mecanismo de cálculo de similaridade por SAD, que trabalha a cada vez com dois blocos de pixels.

O projeto, desenvolvido sob a forma de aplicativo CUDA, executa os cálculos de similaridade SAD, valendo-se do conceito de que cada diferença absoluta de pixel de uma dada posição pode ocorrer de forma independente e totalmente paralela em relação aos demais pixels vizinhos. Esta condição permite adequar o algoritmo para explorar um elevado nível de paralelismo.

Conforme visto na seção anterior, para a tecnologia CUDA, este paralelismo deve ser traduzido em *threads*, que, em última instância, podem ser interpretadas como unidades de execução simultâneas.

Particularmente, na implementação proposta, cada módulo de cálculo de cálculo de SAD foi estruturado para uma grade com tamanho básico de 16x8 *threads*. O tamanho desta grade de *threads* foi definido para permitir calcular dinamicamente a distribuição para acomodar quadros em diferentes resoluções.

De forma geral, o tamanho de bloco de 16x8 elementos permite uma arquitetura de 128 *threads* para esta implementação. O algoritmo de cálculo de SAD utiliza estas 128 *threads* durante os cálculos de diferença absoluta entre pixels dos dois blocos analisados, enquanto que as tomadas de decisão do algoritmo de busca são realizadas apenas pela *thread* (0,0).

Uma ilustração deste procedimento, conforme proposto, é apresentada na Figura 4, onde se observa à esquerda a imagem de referência e à direita a imagem corrente em processo de codificação.

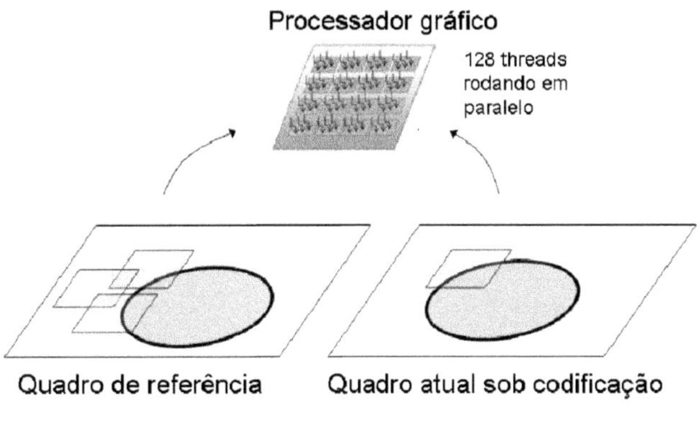

Figura 4 Alinhamento dos dados com o processador gráfico, conforme proposto.

Na prática, o cálculo completo de um SAD consiste em duas operações sequenciais:

(i) obtenção da diferença absoluta para cada pixel dos blocos analisados (bloco de pixels do quadro de referência em relação ao bloco atual da imagem que está sendo codificada);

(ii) somatório dos resultados anteriormente calculados.

A implementação dessas operações foi feita utilizando a instrução de baixo nível *usad* que recebe três argumentos e calcula a soma da diferença absoluta dos dois primeiros argumentos com o terceiro. Essa instrução de baixo nível executa as duas operações (diferença absoluta e soma) com maior velocidade quando comparada com a implementação dessas operações em código de mais alto nível (linguagem C), que seria traduzido em um maior número de instruções pelo compilador. Além disso, a capacidade desta instrução de realizar as duas operações conjuntamente permite acelerar a primeira etapa do algoritmo de redução pela junção do cálculo da diferença absoluta e a primeira etapa do somatório de resultados [19].

Para entender melhor este procedimento, pode-se considerar o caso de blocos de 16x16 (macrobloco padrão H.264). Neste caso, inicialmente calcula-se a diferença absoluta dos 128 últimos pixels (parte inferior do macrobloco). A seguir, obtém-se a diferença absoluta dos 128 primeiros pixels (parte superior) e, na mesma instrução, soma-se esse resultado com as diferenças obtidas na etapa anterior.

A partir deste resultado (vetor de 128 elementos), dá-se início ao procedimento de redução (em verdade o primeiro estágio de redução já foi implementado no sequenciamento das duas instruções *usad* a partir da soma dos dois vetores de 128 elementos em um apenas).

A seguir, o número de *threads* ativas utilizadas é reduzido para 64 (cada qual somando dois elementos) e, posteriormente, para 32. Após isso, as *threads* contidas no último *warp* (cada *warp* comporta 32 *threads*) realizam os estágios restantes do algoritmo de redução. Ao fim do processo, o vetor tem apenas um valor que é o somatório das diferenças absolutas.

A Figura 4 ilustra o procedimento da redução implementado [19]. Na figura se demonstra como um vetor de 16 elementos seria tratado para permitir o somatório de todos seus elementos em apenas cinco ciclos de operação.

É interessante observar também como, a cada etapa, o número de *threads* ativas reduz à metade, sempre lendo e escrevendo na mesma memória, chegando, no último estágio, apenas uma *thread* ativa que, por fim, determina o valor resultante desejado.

Após o cálculo do SAD para as cinco posições da busca em diamante (centro, cima, baixo, direita e esquerda), são realizados os testes para determinar qual a posição possui o menor SAD (maior similaridade) de forma a se definir, portanto, se a busca deve ser executada mais uma vez ou se a obtenção do vetor de movimento já chegou ao fim.

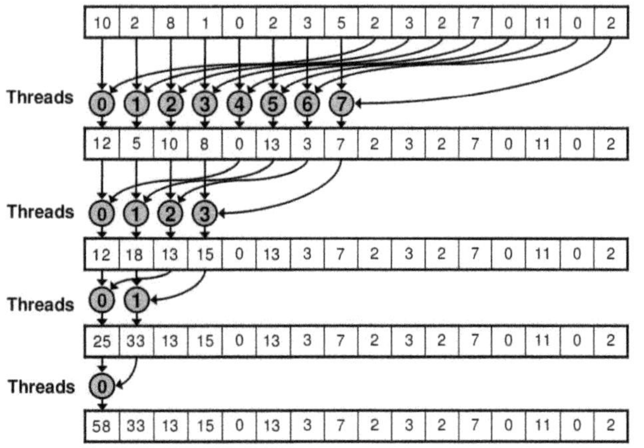

Figura 5. Procedimento de redução utilizado para o cálculo do valor de SAD.

Além do alinhamento entre *threads* e posições dos elementos internos a serem manipulados no cálculo de SAD, também foi buscado o melhor uso das memórias da plataforma. Isso é muito importante, pois as memórias disponíveis possuem diferentes velocidades de acesso, produzindo efeito direto sobre o desempenho global da solução proposta.

O quadro de referência a ser utilizado pelo algoritmo, por exemplo, foi armazenado na memória de texturas, a qual possui estrutura de cache otimizada para dados com localidade 2D [20].

Essa característica é particularmente apropriada devido à natureza do acesso aos pixels do quadro de referência, onde *threads* vizinhas acessam posições adjacentes da memória e, a cada iteração do algoritmo de busca, a posição acessada será deslocada em uma posição.

Já as variáveis de controle, índices e resultados intermediários foram armazenados na memória compartilhada,de forma que possam ser acessados por diferentes *threads* residentes em um mesmo bloco.

Esta decisão permitiu uma significativa redução na latência do algoritmo de controle em si.

Por fim, o quadro a ser codificado e os resultados a serem lidos pelo aplicativo no microprocessador da placa mãe residem na memória global.

Isso, pois a cada vez que uma transferência de dados é realizada, estes devem ser armazenados na memória global. Esta é uma memória mais lenta, o que motivou que o algoritmo proposto buscasse reduzir o número de acessos à memória global. Assim esta foi usada apenas como interface de entrada e saída de dados da placa.

As transferências de dados entre o computador e a placa ocorrem com pacotes que comportam a cada transferência múltiplos macroblocos H.264 (16x16 pixels), o que permitiu reduzir também as latências de comunicação entre o aplicativo principal e o algoritmo em GPU (latências estas fortemente dependentes do sistema operacional) [7]

6. RESULTADOS EXPERIMENTAIS

A experimentação prática da solução proposta fez uso do software de referência JSVM (*Joint Scalable Video Model*) que implementa o codificador H.264/SVC [21]. O padrão SVC (*Scalable Video Coding*) é um anexo à norma H.264, que trata da codificação de vídeo escalável. No entanto, nestes experimentos, não foi prevista a exploração dos conceitos de escalabilidade da codificação, trabalhando o aplicativo apenas como um codificador H.264 compatível.

O software JSVM precisou ser adaptado para tornar possível expor à GPU um conjunto de dados suficientemente grande para que se pudesse, com isso, fazer uso eficiente da arquitetura paralela em questão.

Na implementação original do software de referência, o módulo de estimativa de movimento recebe um macrobloco, processa-o e devolve os resultados. A alteração realizada, entretanto, fez com que o aplicativo tivesse acesso ao quadro inteiro, de forma a entregar à placa de vídeo, de uma só vez, um conjunto de diversos macroblocos a serem processados.

Nos experimentos realizados foram avaliadas duas situações: variabilidade de movimentação (diferentes sequências de vídeo) e diferença na resolução dos vídeos avaliados.

O ambiente utilizado no desenvolvimento e experimentação é composto por um computador com processador Intel Core 2 Quad de 2,66GHz com 2 GB de memória RAM e utilizando-se uma placa de vídeo NVIDIA GTX 560 Ti. Nos experimentos, foi utilizado sistema operacional GNU/Linux (distribuição Ubuntu, versão 11) e o toolkit CUDA versão 4.2, que contém o compilador e demais ferramentas necessárias ao desenvolvimento de programas que utilizem a GPU.

As tabelas a seguir resumem os resultados de ganho de velocidade registrados comparando-se a implementação da solução proposta na placa gráfica em relação ao mesmo algoritmo sendo executado no processador principal do computador (atrasos de comunicação entre computadores placa gráfica estão inclusos nestas medições).

A tabela 1 traz os resultados obtidos para a avaliação de vídeos em resolução QCIF (144x176 pixels).

Tabela 1. Ganho de desempenho para vídeos QCIF

Vídeo	médio	máximo
City	1,03	1,43
Crew	1,04	1,61
Harbour	0,79	1,06

A análise dos resultados da Tabela 1 aponta para pequenos ganhos de desempenho nesta condição (inclusive para o vídeo Harbour a solução em GPU foi, em média, mais lenta que a solução em CPU). O fato que explica este baixo desempenho é a relação entre o tamanho dos pacotes transferidos comparado com o tempo total de execução.

Para volumes pequenos de dados o tempo de transferência de dados entre computador e placa gráfica se torna significativo, o que limita bastante o desempenho da solução.

Já a Tabela 2 apresenta os resultados obtidos para a avaliação do mesmo algoritmo, porém, neste caso avaliando vídeos em resolução CIF (288x356 pixels).

Tabela 2. Ganho de desempenho para vídeos CIF

Vídeo	médio	máximo
City	1,85	2,37
Crew	2,22	3,73
Harbour	1,47	2,01

Conforme comentado o tamanho dos pacotes transferidos afeta o desempenho global do sistema. Para vídeos maiores, com é o caso da resolução CIF, o ganho se apresentou com maior evidência chegando a ser em média cerca de duas vezes mais rápido na solução em GPU.

O menor ganho de desempenho para o vídeo Harbour em relação aos demais (City e Crew) se justifica, pois este é um vídeo com movimentação horizontal muito uniforme, o que faz com que tanto as versões em CPU quanto GPU sejam muito rápidas na determinação do vetor mais adequado [22].

A Tabela 3, por fim, traz os resultados obtidos da solução proposta quando da avaliação de vídeos em resolução 4CIF (576x704 pixels).

Tabela 3. Ganho de desempenho para vídeos 4CIF

Vídeo	médio	máximo
City	3,53	4,09
Crew	4,16	5,54
Harbour	2,9	3,77

Observa-se que, para vídeos maiores, o ganho registrado se mostra ainda mais significativo, chegando-se a atingir mais de 350% na média dos três vídeos e mais de 550% no melhor caso (vídeo Crew).

A Figura 6 traz os resultados de ganho de desempenho máximos obtidos para os três vídeos. Os melhores resultados são obtidos para o vídeo CREW, que apresenta um padrão de movimentação bastante irregular (quando o maior paralelismo da tecnologia GPGPU se mostra de fato mais eficiente).

Para todos os vídeos, entretanto, os melhores resultados são obtidos quando resoluções maiores são utilizadas (efeitos da latência de comunicação são menos representativos no tempo total de transferência e execução).

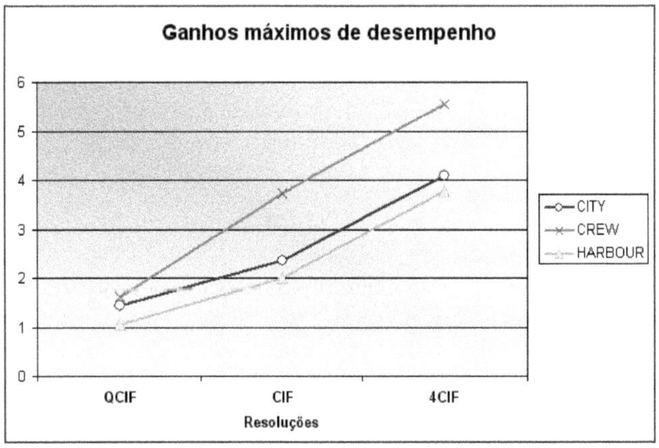

Figura 6. Ganhos máximos de desempenho obtidos para diferentes vídeos e resoluções.

Além disso, de forma resumida, o ganho ponderado da solução (considerando-se os diferentes vídeos avaliados) é apresentado na Figura 7. Mais uma vez, se percebe claramente, que os melhores resultados de ganho são obtidos para vídeos com resoluções maiores.

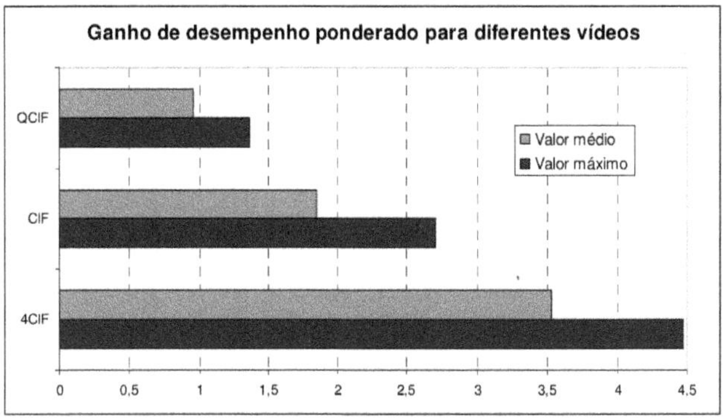

Figura 7. Ganho ponderado da solução (média para diferentes vídeos)

7. CONCLUSÕES

Considerando-se a importância dos algoritmos de estimativa de movimentos, dentro de um moderno codificador de vídeo, o presente trabalho propõe uma solução paralela para este tipo de algoritmo, que foi especialmente desenvolvida para permitir sua implementação sobre plataformas recentes de processamento gráfico.

As plataformas estudadas (GPU CUDA) foram exploradas para atingir a execução de centenas de operações simultâneas, permitindo assim um ganho real de desempenho.

Deve-se observar, entretanto, que para pequenos pacotes de dados, o tempo de transferência de dados entre computador e a placa gráfica pode limitar os ganhos globais de desempenho, como pode ser evidenciado nos experimentos práticos realizados sobre o software de referência JSVM.

No geral, a solução proposta apresentou ganhos ponderados de cerca de 350%, em média, para vídeos de resolução 4CIF, atingindo valores máximos ponderados de 550% (5,5 vezes mais rápido que a mesma solução sendo executada em um computador pessoal convencional), o que comprova a vantagem desta solução para o desenvolvimento de soluções de codificação de vídeo de alta definição.

8. AGRADECIMENTOS

Os resultados obtidos com este trabalho somente foram possíveis devido ao suporte financeiro da agência FINEP

9. REFERÊNCIAS

[1] Richardson I. E. G., H.264 and MPEG-4 Video Compression. England, Ed Wiley . Sons, v2 2003, 281p.

[2] Chen, and H.-Y Chen, "Physical Design for System-On-a Chip" in Essential Issues in SOC Design (Y.-L Lin, Editor), Springer, 2009.

[3] Do D. M. T., GPUs - Graphics Processing Units Institute of Computer Science, University of Innsbruck July 7, 2008.

[4] ITU, .H.264/AVC Reference Software Decoder (version 13.0). 2008 <http://iphome.hhi.de/suehring/tml/doc/ ldec/html.

[5] Koga T. et al. Motion-compensated interframe coding for video conferencing. In: proceedings Nat. Telecom. Conf. dez 81.

[6] Li r., Zeng B., Liou M., "A new three-step search algorithm for block motion estimation," IEEE Transaction on Circuit Systems and Video Technology, vol. 4, pp. 438–442, Aug. 1994.

[7] Po L. M. and Ma W. C., "A novel four-step search algorithm for fast block motion estimation," IEEE Transaction on Circuit Video Technology, vol. 6, pp. 313–317, June 1996.

[8] Chung K.L., Chang L.-C., A new predictive search area approach for fast block motion estimation. IEEE Transactions on Image Processing. V. 12 N. 6, pp 648-652. 2003.

[9] Zhu S. and Ma K.-K., A New Diamond Search Algorithm for Fast Block-Matching Motion Estimation. IEEE Transactions on Image Processing. V. 9, n. 2, Feb. 2000.

[10] Tourapis A. M., Au 0. C. and Liou M. L. "PredictiveMotion Vector Field Adaptive Search Technique (PMVFAST) - Enhancing Block Based Motion Estimation," in Proc. of Visual Communications and Image Processing, pp.883-892, Jan. 2001.

[11] Huang Y.-L., Shen Y.-C., Wu J.-L., Scalable computation for spatially scalable video coding using NVIDIA CUDA and multi-core CPU MM.09, October, 2009, China pp.361-370.

[12] Chen W.-N. and Hang H.-M. .H.264/AVC motion estimation implementation on Compute Unified Device Architecture (CUDA), IEEE International Conference on Multimedia and Expo 2008, pp 697-700, 2008.

[13] Han T. D. and Abdelrahman T. S., Reducing Branch Divergence in GPU programs. Proceedings of the Fourth Workshop on General Purpose Processing on Graphics Processing Units [S.l.]: 2011.

[14] NVIDIA. NVIDIA's Next Generation CUDA Compute Architecture: Fermi . 2009. 22 p.

[15] Song, T. et al. Parallel Implementation Algorithm of Motion Estimation for GPU Applications 6 p.

[16] Schwalb, M. Ewerth, R. and Freisleben, B. Fast motion estimation on graphics hardware for H.264 video encoding IEEE Transactions on Multimedia Volume 11 Issue 1, January 2009 pp. 1-10.

[17] Cheng, R. Yang, E. and Liu, T. Speeding up motion estimation algorithms on CUDA technology Asia Pacific Conference in Multimedia and Electronics 2010. pp. 93-96.

[18] Massanes F., Cadennes M. and Brankov J. G., CUDA implementation of a block-matching algorithm for Multiple GPU cards Journal of Electron Imaging. 2011 20(3) pp.1-21.

[19] Crow T. S. Evolution of the Graphical Processing Unit. 2004. 59 p.

[20] Harris M. Optimizing Parallel Reduction in CUDA 2010, 38p.

[21] ITU – International Telecommunication Unit, H.264/SVC Reference Software for H.264 advanced video coding (JSVM - Joint Scalable Video Model, software version 9.19.9), 2010.

[22] Chung K.-L. and Chang L.-C., A new predictive search area approach for fast block motion estimation. IEEE Transactions on Image Processing. V. 12 N. 6, pp 648-652. 2003.

Influence of Self-Similarity on 3D Holoscopic Video Coding Performance

Caroline Conti
Instituto de Telecomunicações
Av. Rovisco Pais, 1049-001, Portugal
caroline.conti@lx.it.pt

Luis Ducla Soares
Instituto de Telecomunicações
Av. Rovisco Pais, 1049-001, Portugal
lds@lx.it.pt

Paulo Nunes
Instituto de Telecomunicações
Av. Rovisco Pais, 1049-001, Portugal
paulo.nunes@lx.it.pt

ABSTRACT

Holoscopic imaging, also known as integral imaging, is a promising solution for glasses-free 3D technology since it allows a more natural and immersive 3D sensation with continuous full motion parallax. However, in order to provide 3D holoscopic content with convenient visual quality in terms of resolution and 3D perception, ultra-high resolution acquisition and display devices are required. Consequently, efficient video coding tools become essential to deal with this large amount of data. However, current and emerging state-of-the-art video coding technologies do not yet address the specific characteristics of 3D holoscopic content. In this context, this paper presents and studies a coding scheme based on the concept of self-similarity compensated prediction, which is used to explore the particular arrangement of 3D holoscopic content through the introduction of new prediction modes. In order to profoundly analyze these new prediction modes, two different generations of video codecs, modified to handle 3D holoscopic content, are examined and compared: the first one is derived from the H.264/AVC video coding standard while the second one is based on the recent standardization project called High Efficient Video Coding (HEVC). Experimental results clearly show the advantages of using this coding scheme in both codecs, as well as the connection between the performance of the self-similarity compensation process and the characteristics of the 3D holoscopic content.

Categories and Subject Descriptors

I.4.2 [**Image Processing and Computer Vision**]: Compression (Coding) - Approximate methods; E.4 [**Coding and Information Theory**]: Data compaction and compression.

General Terms

Algorithms, Performance, Experimentation.

Keywords

3D holoscopic content, integral imaging, image coding, video coding, H.264/AVC, HEVC.

1. INTRODUCTION

Three Dimensional (3D) video technologies created a frenzy in the recent past, which resulted in an extensive research in 3D displays and video capturing technologies. Especially with the success of the *Avatar* movie, it is shown that a new generation in visual technology has started.

Permission to make digital or hard copies of all or part of this work for personal or classroom use is granted without fee provided that copies are not made or distributed for profit or commercial advantage and that copies bear this notice and the full citation on the first page. To copy otherwise, or republish, to post on servers or to redistribute to lists, requires prior specific permission and/or a fee.
WebMedia'12, October 15–18, 2012, São Paulo/SP, Brazil.
Copyright 2012 ACM 978-1-4503-1706-1/12/10...$15.00.

Currently, the 3DTV market is in a period of less excitement, but experts still state that this is a common cycle for many new technologies and have optimistic expectations for the coming years [7]. One of the main obstacles to the wide proliferation of 3DTV is that the most used technology, referred to as 3D stereoscopic, relies on glasses to create the 3D sensation, which can induce some discomfort for the users (eyestrain and headaches) and does not allow an immersive and realistic sensation. Nevertheless, new technologies such as those based on autoestereoscopic multiview approaches have been brought out with some success in handheld devices, allowing a 3D sensation with horizontal motion parallax without requiring glasses. Moreover, with the increasing research in autostereoscopic display manufacturing, this approach may become more popular in the consumer mass-market [7] in few years.

In this context, 3D holoscopic imaging, also known as integral imaging, has been considered recently a promising approach for glasses-free 3D solutions. As a result of the optical structure, where a micro-lens array is overlaid on the camera sensor for content acquisition and on a conventional flat panel display for content display, a more natural 3D viewing experience is achieved due to the replication of the original scene light field. These 3D holoscopic systems allow continuous motion parallax throughout the viewing zone in all directions (horizontal and vertical) with accurate convergence and depth perception, reducing the eyestrain compared with current 3D stereoscopic and multiview displays.

In order to provide 3D holoscopic content with convenient resolution to fit the High Definition (HD) requirements, much higher resolution acquisition devices are required and, consequently, adequate compression tools for this particular type of content are need for efficient transmission and storage of the large amount of data involved.

Due to the micro-lens array used in acquisition and display, a 3D holoscopic image consists of an array of 2D micro-images with a slightly different perspective of the scene. To handle this type of content, several 3D holoscopic image and video coding schemes have been developed that take advantage of this inherent planar intensity distribution. In [1], a Three Dimensional Discrete Cosine Transform (3D-DCT) is applied to a stack of micro-images to exploit the existing correlation between adjacent micro-images. In [2], the 3D holoscopic image is separated into various sub-images by extracting one pixel with the same position from each micro-image and a Three-Dimensional Wavelet Transform (3D-DWT) is computed in alternative to the 3D-DCT. In this scheme, the two lower frequency bands of sub-images are assembled and compressed using a forward two-level 2D-DWT and the results are then arithmetic encoded. In [9], a scheme based in Multiview Video Coding (MVC) [11] is proposed. In this scheme, the extracted sub-images are organized as multiview video content, which is subsequently coded using MVC. A common feature of these coding schemes is the need for: i) a precise knowledge of the image structure, notably the micro-image dimensions; and ii) an integer number of pixels behind each micro-lens, which is substantially more difficult to guarantee for images that are not computer generated.

Since the 3D holoscopic content is actually a 2D image (arranged as an array of micro-images), a coding scheme based on the self-similarity compensation concept, can efficiently exploit the particular structure of this type of content to improve the coding performance. In this paper, the self-similarity compensation concept, previously proposed in [5], is incorporated in the current and emerging state-of-the-art 2D video coding technologies and an analysis of the advantages of using this new coding scheme is presented. In the first case, an H.264/AVC video codec [12] is modified to incorporate additional prediction modes to handle 3D holoscopic content. In the second case, a similar approach is followed for the new standardization project on video coding, called High Efficient Video Coding (HEVC) [10], which is coming up (by the joint efforts of MPEG and ITU-T) and promises to improve the coding efficiency of the H.264/AVC to fulfill the compression efficiency requirements, among other requirements, for high and ultra-high resolution video content. For this, the HEVC reference model 4.0 has also been modified to include new prediction modes based on the self-similarity compensation concept to efficiently handle 3D holoscopic content. These two modified codecs are then analyzed and compared with the "standard" solutions in terms of their rate-distortion performance for 3D holoscopic content with different amounts of self-similarity redundancy.

The remainder of this paper is organized as follows: Section 2 briefly describes the structure of 3D holoscopic content. Section 3 presents an overview of the self-similarity compensation concept and describes also the new prediction modes for the H.264/AVC and HEVC codecs. Section 4 discusses and compares the Rate-Distortion (RD) performance of the two modified codecs, and, finally, Section 5 concludes the paper.

2. STRUCTURE OF 3D HOLOSCOPIC CONTENT

The 3D holoscopic imaging basics were first proposed by G. M. Lippmann and referred to as integral photography in 1908 [6]. Briefly, this system is based on an array of small spherical micro-lenses, known as a "fly's eye" lens array, which is used both to record and to display 3D holoscopic images (see Figure 1a). In the acquisition side, the 3D holoscopic image is projected behind the micro-lens array creating a simple 2D array of micro-images that stores pixel intensity and direction information in the form of a 2D planar distribution. Each micro-lens can be seen as an individual small low resolution camera, recording a different perspective of the same scene at slightly different angles, as can be seen in Figure 1b. In the display side, only one pixel from each micro-image is visible by each eye of the user, which allows different views to be visible depending on the viewing angle, thus giving the user a realistic depth perception and motion parallax, because a different perspective of the scene is visible when the user moves around the display.

3. CODING SCHEME FOR 3D HOLOSCOPIC CONTENT

Due to the small angular disparity between adjacent micro-lenses, a significant cross-correlation exists between neighboring micro-images. Thus, this inherent cross-correlation of 3D holoscopic images can be seen as a type of Self-Similarity (SS) and may be exploited for improving coding efficiency.

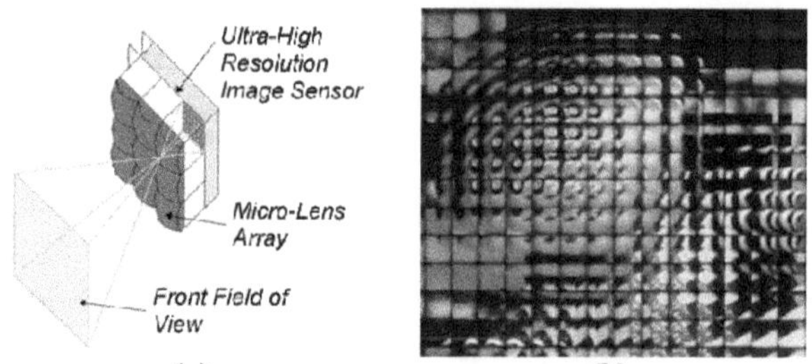

(a) (b)

Figure 1. Micro-lens array applied to an imaging sensor for capturing 3D holoscopic content; (b) Example of a 3D holoscopic image in enlargement.

Therefore, the coding scheme for 3D holoscopic presented in this paper consists of two major codec modifications: first, it introduces the self-similarity compensated prediction by defining additional prediction modes; second, as the new prediction modes are purely spatial prediction modes, they are incorporated into a modified I-slice increasing this way the degrees of freedom for improving the coding efficiency.

In the following sections, an overview of the self-similarity compensation process applied to this type of content is provided, as well as a detailed description of the coding scheme combined with the H.264/AVC standard and the HEVC, respectively.

3.1 Self-Similarity Compensated Prediction

A scheme for self-similarity estimation and compensation was first proposed by the authors in [5] in order to explore the high self-similarity between neighboring micro-images and improve the performance of the H.264/AVC. Similarly to motion estimation, the self-similarity estimation process uses block-based matching in order to find a best match – in terms of a suitable matching criterion – for prediction of a block area being encoded. However, in this case, the allowed search area is the previously coded and reconstructed area of the current picture. As a result, the chosen block becomes the candidate predictor and the relative position between the two blocks is derived as a vector (similarly to a motion vector). This vector is here referred to as the Self-Similarity Vector (SSV). This prediction process has the advantage of being able to find efficient predictions for 3D holoscopic content without the need to know the precise structure of the underlying micro-lens array, and consequently, the arrangement of the micro-images.

In the self-similarity compensation block, the inverse quantized and inversed transformed prediction residual is added to the predictor to form the reconstructed data that is stored in the prediction memory to be available for future predictions.

3.2 H.264/AVC SS Prediction Modes

This scheme introduces a set of spatial prediction modes, in addition to the existing H.264/AVC Intra prediction modes. Each additional mode (i.e., INTRA_SS 16×16, INTRA_SS 16×8, INTRA_SS 8×16, and INTRA_SS 8×8) specifies a different way to partition the macroblock (MB) to evaluate the self-similarity estimation and compensation. For the INTRA_SS 8×8 mode, each 8×8 macroblock partition can be further split into 8×4, 4×8 or 4×4 sub-partitions for self-similarity compensation, which is indicated in the bitstream with a sub-macroblock type syntax element. Furthermore, a modified skipped macroblock mode considering a 16×16 block size, called INTRA_SS SKIPPED, is also added as a candidate prediction mode, in which a predicted self-similarity vector (PSSV) is directly selected without using self-similarity compensation. The PSSV is computed as the median vector of self-similarity vectors of three neighbouring blocks, in a similar way to the rules defined in H.264/AVC [12] for the motion vector prediction.

When either the INTRA_SS 16×16, INTRA_SS 16×8, INTRA_SS 8×16 or INTRA_SS 8×8 prediction mode becomes the best mode, in a rate-distortion sense, from the set of all possible coding modes, a distinct self-similarity vector is defined for each macroblock partition or sub-partition. A self-similarity vector difference between the predicted self-similarity vector (computed with the median prediction model) and the current vector (found with the best mode) is encoded and transmitted. Up to 16 self-similarity vector differences can be encoded (i.e., for the INTRA_SS 8×8 mode, when each 8×8 macroblock partition is further partitioned into 4×4 sub-partitions). In addition to the self-similarity vector difference, the prediction residual is also encoded and transmitted. On the other hand, when the INTRA_SS SKIPPED is selected as the best mode (also in a rate-distortion sense), only a skipped macroblock indicator is transmitted.

3.3 HEVC SS Prediction Modes

In the HEVC test model version 4.0 (HM-4.0) [8], the basic unit for compression is a square 2N×2N block with up to 64×64 luma samples in size, called coding unit (CU), which can be recursively split into four smaller CUs until a pre-defined minimum size is reached (it may be as small as 8×8). A new level is defined in each split of a CU into four smaller CUs, and each level is distinguished by a depth (corresponding to the number of splits to reach this level. Each CU contains one or multiple prediction units (PU), which correspond to the basic unit that carries information related to the prediction modes. The number of PUs and their sizes are related to the associated prediction mode.

In Section 2, it was shown that there are multiple micro-lens array arrangements to produce 3D holoscopic content. Then, in a self-similarity compensation sense, it is expected that better predictions can be obtained as more flexible is the block partition scheme (in terms of block sizes and shape patterns). In this sense, two possible prediction modes are defined and referred to as Self-similarity and SS-skip prediction modes. The Self-similarity prediction mode – based on the HEVC Inter prediction mode [8] – enables the eight original PU partition patterns (i.e., 2N×2N, N×2N, 2N×N, N×N, 2N×nU, 2N×nD, nL×2N and nR×2N) to code each CU, but switch the motion estimation and compensation by the self-similarity estimation and compensation process.

In the self-similarity compensation process, for each PU partition pattern, up to four self-similarity vectors are derived. In addition, an adapted scheme from the HEVC Advanced Motion Vector Prediction (AVMP) [8] is used to select, in a Rate-Distortion Optimization (RDO) sense, a self-similarity vector prediction by checking the availability of 5 spatially neighboring PUs. On the other hand, the SS-skip prediction mode evaluates a method adapted from a merge technique to infer a self-similarity vector to the current PU. In the original merge technique [8], used in the HEVC Inter prediction, the motion vector is inferred from multiple candidates formed by motion vectors of spatially neighboring PUs, as well as temporally neighboring PUs. In the other hand, the modified merge scheme limits the self-similarity vector candidates from only spatially neighboring PUs, as well as limits the vector position to conform to the limited area defined in the self-similarity estimation process. This guarantees that the CU signaled by the chosen self-similarity vector is already available as a self-similarity reference.

4. PERFORMANCE EVALUATION

In order to evaluate the performance of the self-similarity compensated prediction scheme for 3D holoscopic video coding, four scenarios have been compared: i) the H.264/AVC reference software JMVC 8.3.1, simply referred to as H.264/AVC; ii) the proposed 3D holoscopic video codec using all the new INTRA_SS modes (referred to as H.264+SS); iii) the HEVC reference software version HM-4.0 (referred to as HEVC (HM-4.0)); and iv) the HEVC HM-4.0 plus the proposed prediction modes (referred to as HEVC+SS). The test set has been encoded according to the common test conditions defined in JCTVC-F696 [3] for "Intra, low-complexity" configuration. Four QPs values (22, 27, 32 and 37) and a full search with search range of 128 are adopted. The performance is measured in terms of luminance Peak Signal-to-Noise Ratio (PSNR Y) and by the luminance Bjontegaard (BD-PSNR/BD-BR) measurement method [4].

Four different frames from a sequence called *Plane and Toy* with resolution of 1920×1088 (Frames I, II, III and IV corresponding respectively to Figure 2a, b, c and d) have been tested to illustrate different amounts of self-similarity redundancy. These frames (Figure 2) illustrate four situations representing different distances of two scene object (plane and toy) relatively to the micro-lens array, where the redundancies between neighboring micro-images become gradually more evident from Frame I to Frame IV.

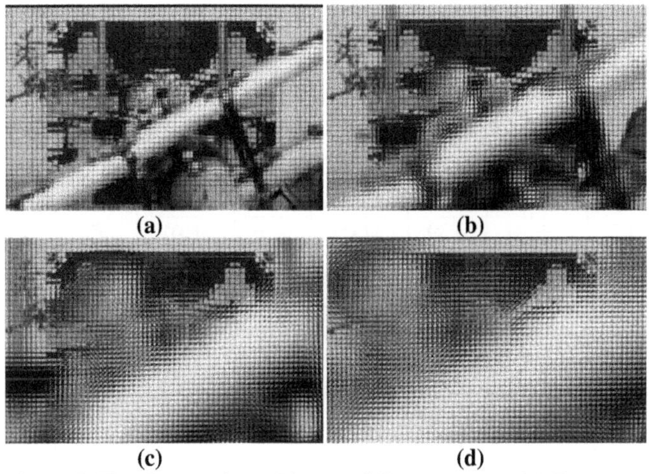

Figure 2. Test frames from *Plane and Toy* sequence. (a) Frame I (the lowest self-similarity (SS) redundancy); (b) Frame II; (c) Frame III; and (d) Frame IV (the largest SS redundancy).

As can be seen from the RD performance in Table 1 and Table 2, the proposed HEVC+SS scheme always outperforms all the other scenarios with considerable gains, even when compared with the HM-4.0 (up to 2.16 dB), the second with better performance. It can also be noticed that, as a result of the superior performance of the HEVC compared with H.264/AVC, there is also a superior performance of the HEVC+SS compared to the H.264+SS.

Comparing now the gains with the corresponding frames in Figure 2 and with the results in Table 3, it can be seen that, for the both schemes, the gains shown are directly proportional to the visual evidence of the self-similarity redundancies as well to the percentage of usage of the additional prediction modes. Therefore, it is possible to conclude that the stronger is the self-similarity redundancy the better is the performance of the self-similarity compensation process.

Moreover, since there are also substantial gains when the H.264+SS scheme is compared to the pure H.264/AVC (up to

2.12 dB), which are also proportional to the amount of self-similarity redundancy, it can be concluded that the performance of the prediction scheme is quite independent of the codec and is, in fact, more dependent on to the type of content.

Table 1. RD performance of the H.264/AVC-based scheme.

Frame	QP	H.264/AVC		H.264 + SS		BD-BR/ BD-PSNR	
		[bpp]	PSNR [dB]	[bpp]	PSNR [dB]		
I	22	1.23	43.15	1.16	42.84	-8.04 %	0.56 dB
	27	0.75	39.33	0.66	38.85		
	32	0.47	35.94	0.37	35.14		
	37	0.30	32.74	0.21	31.55		
II	22	1.56	42.19	1.44	41.86	-11.1 %	0.78 dB
	27	0.97	38.48	0.82	37.89		
	32	0.61	35.02	0.45	34.12		
	37	0.39	31.81	0.26	30.52		
III	22	1.79	43.51	1.60	42.73	-13.9 %	1.24 dB
	27	1.31	39.05	1.02	37.81		
	32	0.78	34.57	0.54	33.31		
	37	0.53	31.05	0.30	29.39		
IV	22	2.32	43.93	1.85	41.76	-22.4 %	2.12 dB
	27	1.43	37.54	1.03	36.53		
	32	0.97	33.70	0.57	32.34		
	37	0.64	30.32	0.31	28.47		

Table 2. RD performance of the HEVC-based coding scheme.

Frame	QP	HEVC (HM4.0)		HEVC + SS		BD-BR/ BD-PSNR	
		[bpp]	PSNR [dB]	[bpp]	PSNR [dB]		
I	22	1.04	43.20	0.87	42.35	-14.9 %	0.88 dB
	27	0.61	40.07	0.47	39.15		
	32	0.39	37.09	0.26	36.01		
	37	0.24	33.77	0.15	32.81		
II	22	1.32	42.34	1.13	41.63	-17.1 %	1.06 dB
	27	0.79	39.12	0.63	38.61		
	32	0.50	36.12	0.36	35.60		
	37	0.31	32.85	0.21	32.33		
III	22	1.71	42.89	1.47	42.16	-18.8 %	1.34 dB
	27	1.07	38.92	0.81	38.10		
	32	0.67	35.54	0.45	34.66		
	37	0.43	32.20	0.26	31.25		
IV	22	2.00	42.40	1.59	41.60	-28.3 %	2.16 dB
	27	1.23	38.42	0.86	37.74		
	32	0.80	34.90	0.48	34.19		
	37	0.52	31.39	0.27	30.69		

Table 3. Mode selection statistics for QP value 32.

H.264/AVC- based scheme			
Frame	**H.264/AVC Intra**	**INTRA_SS (16×16 up to 8×8)**	**INTRA_SS SKIPPED**
I	41.03 %	48.10 %	10.87 %
II	33.82 %	57.3 %	8.88 %
III	22.11 %	72.60 %	5.29 %
IV	8.27 %	88.14 %	3.59 %
HEVC- based scheme			
Frame	**HM 4.0 Intra**	**Self-similarity**	**SS-skip**
I	64.63 %	28.88 %	6.49 %
II	49.91 %	48.05 %	2.04 %
III	36.62 %	62.09 %	1.29 %
IV	21.00 %	77.95 %	1.05 %

5. CONCLUSIONS

This paper presented a self-similarity compensation scheme which was incorporated into the H.264/AVC and in the HEVC to explore the particular structure of the 3D holoscopic content and to further improve the performance for this type of 3D content. This considerably improves the rate-distortion performance of the modified codecs relatively to the original versions for Intra coding. It was also shown that the performance of the proposed self-similarity compensation process increases as the self-similarity redundancy increases. Finally, it was also shown that the gains obtained are less dependent on the underlying codec and more related to the characteristics of the 3D holoscopic content.

6. ACKNOWLEDGMENTS

The authors acknowledge the support of the European Commission under the FP7 project 3D VIVANT (Live Immerse Video-Audio Interactive Multimedia).

7. REFERENCES

1 Aggoun, A. A 3D DCT Compression Algorithm For Omnidirectional Integral Images. In *IEEE International Conference on Accoustics, Speech and Signal Processing (ICASSP 2006)* (Toulouse, France May 2006), 517-520.

2 Aggoun, A. Compression of 3D Integral Images Using 3D Wavelet Transform. *Display Technology, Journal of*, 7, 11 (Nov. 2011), 586-592.

3 Au, O. C., Zhang, X., Pang, C., and Wen, X. *Suggested Common test conditions and software reference configurations for Screen Content Coding*. JCTVC-F696 , Joint Collaborative Team on Video Coding (JCT-VC), Torino, July, 2011.

4 Bjontegaard, G. *Calculation of average PSNR differences between RD curves*. ITU-T Video Coding Experts Group (VCEG) Meeting, Austin, TX, USA, April, 2001.

5 Conti, C., Lino, J., Nunes, P., Soares, L. D., and Correia, P.L. Spatial Prediction Based on Self-Similarity for 3D Holoscopic Image and Video Coding. In *18th International Conference on Image Processing (ICIP 2011)* (Brussels, Belgium 2011), 977-980.

6 Lippmann, G. Epreuves Reversibles Donnant la Sensation du Relief. *Journal de Physique Théorique et Appliquée*, 7, 1 (November 1908), 821-825.

7 MarketsandMarkets. *Three-Dimensional (3D) Technology Market (2011 – 2016) By Products, Applications & Technology Focus, Global Forecast & Analysis – Features Introduction To 4D Technology*. 2012.

8 McCann, K., Bross, B., Sekiguchi, S., and Han, W. *HM4: High Efficiency Video Coding (HEVC) Test Model 4 Encoder Description*. JCTVC-F802, Joint Collaborative Team on Video Coding (JCT-VC), Torino, 2011.

9 Shi, S., Gioia, P., and Madec, G. Efficient Compression Method for Integral Images Using Multi-View Video Coding. In *18th International Conference on Image Processing (ICIP 2011)* (Brussels, Belgium September 2011), 141-144.

10 Ugur, K., Andersson, K., Fuldseth, A. et al. High Performance, Low Complexity Video Coding and the Emerging HEVC Standard. *IEEE Transactions on Circuits and Systems for Video Technology*, 20, 12 (December 2010), 1688-1697.

11 Vetro, A., Wiegand, T., and Sullivan, G.J. Overview of the Stereo and Multiview Video Coding Extensions of the H.264/MPEG-4 AVC Standard. *Proceedings of the IEEE*, 99, 4 (April 2011), 626-642.

12 Wiegand, T., Sullivan, G. J., Bjøntegaard, G., and Luthra, A. Overview of the H.264/AVC Video Coding Standard. *IEEE Transactions on Circuits and Systems for Video Technology*, 13, 7 (July 2003), 560-576.

Evaluation of Theora and Speex Performance in IP Videoconferencing

Douglas G. Ribeiro*, Celso S. Kurashima*§, Adilson E. Guelfi‡§, Marcelo K. Zuffo§

*Universidade Federal do ABC (UFABC)
Santo Andre, SP, 09210-580, Brasil.

‡Instituto de Pesquisas Tecnologicas de Sao Paulo (IPT)
Sao Paulo, SP, 05508-901, Brasil.

§Laboratorio de Sistemas Integraveis da Universidade de Sao Paulo (LSI-USP)
Sao Paulo, SP, 05508-900, Brasil.

douggribeiro@gmail.com, celso.kurashima@ufabc.edu.br, guelfi@lsi.usp.br, mkzuffo@lsi.usp.br

ABSTRACT

The increasing demand for applications of videoconference over IP requires not only low bandwidth but also adequate performance on networks. This paper presents the evaluation of a local network videoconferencing system based on open source codec for video and for voice signals. Specifically, these are the Theora codec and the Speex codec, which are developed under the Xiph Foundation. The satisfactory performance results we achieved indicate that both coders are potential candidates for future implementation of immersive systems.

Categories and Subject Descriptors

E.4 [**DATA**]: Coding and Information Theory – *Data Compaction and Compression.*

General Terms

Measurement, Performance, Experimentation.

Keywords

Video conferencing, video coding, speech coding, multimedia transmission.

1. INTRODUCTION

Videoconferences over the Internet are being increasingly used both in personal and in professional applications. In this latter case, the interaction between users without leaving their workplaces brings the benefit of saving time and resources. Furthermore, some videoconferencing systems offer the comfort of a natural interaction between people in the meeting by large visual displays [1]. In this sense, immersive telepresence systems have been investigated, and their implementations are reported with practical results [2] [3]. An important part in such systems is the video encoding and speech coding, since most of networks and the Internet are accessed by low bandwidth connections [4]. In applications that demand high bandwidth, such as immersive video, encoding time will impact on the overall performance of the videoconferencing [5].

Permission to make digital or hard copies of all or part of this work for personal or classroom use is granted without fee provided that copies are not made or distributed for profit or commercial advantage and that copies bear this notice and the full citation on the first page. To copy otherwise, or republish, to post on servers or to redistribute to lists, requires prior specific permission and/or a fee.
WebMedia'12, October 15–18, 2012, São Paulo/SP, Brazil.
Copyright 2012 ACM 978-1-4503-1706-1/12/10...$15.00.

The goal of this paper is to present a study on the performance of video codecs and voice in a simple experimental implementation of videoconferencing over IP, aiming future application in immersive systems. In this evaluation, we use the Theora video encoder [6] and the Speex vocoder [7], both of which are made available by the Xiph Foundation under open source license.

A related work is the Rio Internet TV [8]. This study presents videoconferencing as a way to achieve distance education, and make it a teaching resource among teachers and students. A lecture was live broadcasted so that students could attend it from their homes through the website. Another interesting application of videoconferencing is reported in [9], for building a communication and collaboration platform to be used in the Internet. They illustrate three use cases: eLearning/eUniversity, eConferencing and eCustomer Support.

In previous studies on IP videoconferencing, we used the MSU VQMT [10] for evaluation of video coders, and the PESQ metric [11] for evaluation of vocoders. The VLC Media Player [12] was used to conduct a videoconference transmission over the LAN IP [13] [14] and video signal is encoded with Theora and voice signal is encoded with Speex. Both are multiplexed in the Ogg format. Section 1 discussed the context of the present proposal of IP videoconferencing system. Section 2 presents details on the approach used in the videoconferencing implementation. Section 3 presents the obtained results. And Section 4 concludes the paper.

2. VIDEOCONFERENCE ARCHITECTURE

The implementation of video conferencing system used the Java programming language [15] and *Gstreamer* multimedia framework [16], within the Ubuntu 12.04 Linux operating system [17]. Gstreamer provides an interface to encode and to decode voice and video signals, as well as to create servers and clients for UDP data transmission over networks. Thus, our code uses Java Socket class in conjunction with the Gstreamer, for transmission and reception of multimedia signals over local area networks. The general sketch of the program is shown in Figure 1.

2.1 Speech Coding

The UDP server for the Speex encoding requires elements in the logical sequence shown in the left column of Figure 1. The process begins with the element *alsasrc*, which is responsible for capturing audio through an ALSA (Advanced Linux Sound Architecture) device. This voice stream is received by the *audioconvert* element, that converts audio buffers in *raw* format. The *audioresample* element resamples audio buffer to a different sampling rate, by using a function to increase quality. Then, the flow is sent to the *capsfilter* element which determines speech parameters as the number of channels and the new sampling rate. The signal is then directed to the Speex encoder *speexenc*, in which encoding bit-rate are set by the programmer. In the next step coded voice is multiplexed and encapsulated in Ogg format, and transmitted by UDP protocol, in the *rtpspeexpay* element. Finally, voice stream transmission to client is done in the *udpsink* element, where remote client IP and port should be defined beforehand.

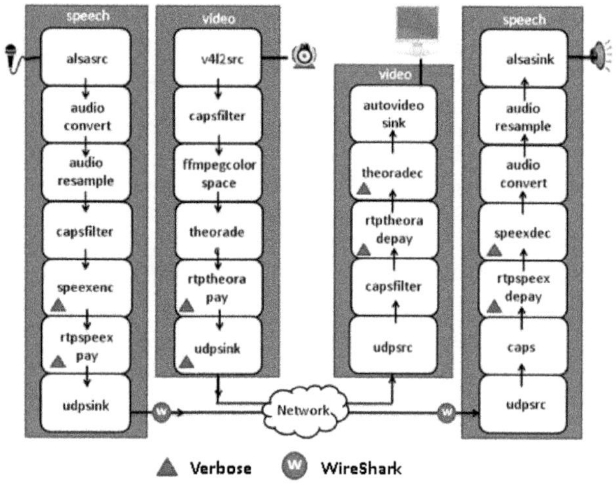

Figure 1. Connection between GStreamer elements. Speech and Video are independent process. The direction of the signal flow is indicated by the arrows.

The voice signal reception is shown in the rightmost side of Figure 1. The *udpsrc* element starts upon receiving the voice stream from the server, and indicating the port that will be used. The *caps* element verifies whether the received signal parameters match to those specified by the server, such as the sampling rate and encoder type among others. Then, the received signal is demultiplexed by the *rtpspeexdepay* element with UDP protocol. The *speexdec* element decodes the signal, and sends it to *audioconvert* and *audioresample* elements for doing the reversal process. After that, the speech stream is sent to the *alsasink* consumer element, that drives an audio output.

2.2 Video Coding

The video encoder uses the Theora elements as shown in the left side of Figure 1. The *v4l2src* element is responsible for detecting the image capture device. Once captured by a camera, video data stream is processed by the *capsfilter* element and then by the *ffmpegcolorspace* element. After being encoded by *theorade* element, multiplexing is done by *rtptheorapay* element. The encapsulated packet is sent through the network via UDP protocol. The final element is the *udpsink* sends data packets to the recipient, which should be previously defined by its IP and port number. In the video client, shown in the right side of Figure 1, video packets are received by the *udpsrc* element. The *caps* element verifies the demultiplexing and decoding parameters to be used by the *rtptheoradepay* element and the *theoradec* element, respectively. Then, video signals are handled by the *autovideosink* element, that creates a window and display the sequence of images on it.

2.3 Measurement Tools

Certain *pipeline* elements such as the encoders, decoders, and multiplexers, may be inspected by using the GStreamer *Verbose* tool in conjunction with the *debug* mode. The first one is used to obtain general settings of timestamp and clock. In debug mode, we obtain the time duration for completion of encoding, decoding, and multiplexing tasks. The elements inspected by verbose were marked with a triangle sign in Figure 1.

The WireShark software [18] was used to count the time that a data packet takes to leave the server port until reaches a specific client. This application saves in memory the following measurements: the packet size, package output time, package arrival time after being carried by the UDP protocol, the number of samples per second, and average byte rate during the period of assessment. In Figure 1, the measuring points with WireShark program is identified by a circle containing the letter 'w'. The program is triggered after data encoding and multiplexing. We captured only the packets that enter and leave the Ethernet card in each computer, regardless of previous packages.

3. RESULTS

A good videoconferencing system should offer the user an easy and effective communication. Based on this, simple and intuitive graphical interface is desirable. Also, a technical requirement is that a good system provides quality of service with the lowest data loss as possible in the communication link between two computers. The transmission time should attend real time demand for voice and video session. Therefore, from the videoconference implementation point of view, the goal is to achieve low enough processing time on the encoding, decoding, multiplexing, and demultiplexing jobs. Also, the round trip time of packets through the local network should be the lowest as possible, without data loss.

3.1 Graphical User Interface

We have developed graphical user interface for the experiments on videoconferencing shown in Figure 2. It is called "ADVENTO UFABC", and it allows user to set local and client IP numbers and to begin videoconference calls.

As seen in Figure 2, the local IP number is automatically displayed in "My IP" field (1). The remote IP must be manually inserted in the "Client IP" field (2). The "Show Video" button (3) is only available after the videoconference is already stablished. "Teleconferencing" or "videoconferencing" options in field (4) must be chosen before beginning the remote call with the "Call" button (5). Therefore, the user needs to perform only three basic steps: enter the IP of another machine, choose the form of personal communication, and click the "Call" button.

When a videoconference between two computers in a local network is running, two image windows appear on the monitor: one for the local image and the other for the remote image. In the example of Figure 3, the local video is placed on the left side (with a man standing in front of the camera) and the remote video is to the right side (with a woman showing up on the window). In this situation, voice connection is running as well, and both people can talk naturally with each other.

The system works with conventional webcam camera for video input and microphone for audio input to the computer. Headphones or speakers may be used for audio output, and computer monitor or multimedia projectors may be used for video output.

In the experiments, no other parallel process that utilizes the bandwidth of the network was running, and videoconferencing was performed satisfactorily. The system allows the view of remote images as well as to perform a natural conversation with a distant person.

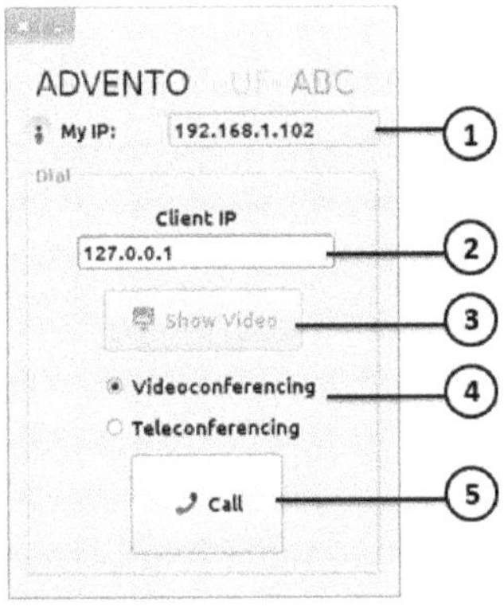

Figure 2. Graphical user interface of the IP videoconference.

Figure 3. IP Videoconference: local and remote windows.

For the video signal, the image resolution is 640 x 480 pixels at a rate of 15 frames per second. For voice signal, sampling uses 12-bit and 8 kbps rate. The Local Area Network uses 1 Gbps Ethernet connections. This configuration was used in the experiments reported throughout the rest of this is section.

3.2 Package Arrival Time

In this experiment, the goal is to measure the average bandwidth the videoconference system needs from the local network. Data flow in the network was monitored by using the WireShark tool [18]. While the videoconference is running normally, we obtained the time period between the packet data output from UDP server until the packet data input into the UDP client. The measuring tool generates a list of exit time and the arrival time at each port, as well as statistics of the transmission, such as the bit rate. We can easily compute average values after sampling a number of these data.

For the measurement of video stream performance in the network, the voice stream has been disabled in the videoconference program. And, on the other hand, for the measurement of voice stream performance in the network, the video stream was disabled in the videoconference program. Table 1 presents the results for the average packet arrival time and the average bit rate of the videoconference using either the Theora video encoder or the Speex vocoder.

The average packet arrival time are similar to both Theora and Speex configuration. This is an expected result, since the packet arrival time is related only to the network structure and does not depend on the encoder. However, the average bit rate of videoconference in the network is greater with Theora codec only than with Speex codec only. This large difference of bit rate is due to video signal contains much more information than the voice signal. By analyzing the absolute value obtained for Theora, the bit rate of about 1.25 Mbps indicates that the proposed system is practicable for use in local area networks.

Table 1. Average UDP packet arrival time from the UDP Server output until the UDP client input, and average bit rate of videoconference in the local network without interferences

CODEC	Theora	Speex
Average packet arrival time (μs)	18,60	19,10
Average bit rate (Kbits/s)	1246	50

3.3 Coding and Multiplexing Time

In this experiment, we measured encoding time, multiplexing time, and packet sending time on the UDP server side. Likewise, we measured the packet reception time, demultiplexing time, and decoding time on the UDP client side. Table 2 shows the times obtained on the server side, and Table 3 shows the times obtained on the client side. In these tables, the overall process time corresponds to the entire process of capturing, encoding, multiplexing and sending UDP; and the overall time of receipt matches the entire process of receiving, demultiplexing, decoding and display the signal. The time values shown in these two tables were obtained through the GStreamer debug tool. These measures were collected at the time of encoding or decoding the signals into existing processes of camera or microphone pipelines.

Table 2. Average times in the UDP Server side.

CODEC	Theora	Speex
Coding Time (ms)	0,51	0,02
Multiplexing Time (ms)	0,09	0,05
Overall Process Time (ms)	39,38	17,75

Table 3. Average times in the UDP Client side.

CODEC	Theora	Speex
Decoding Time (ms)	0,87	0,37
Demultiplexing Time (ms)	0,27	0,12
Overall Receiving Time (ms)	43,20	22,35

It is observed in Table 2 that the coding time and multiplexing time are smaller than the overall process time. This overall process time refers to the period the pipeline takes to perform the capture of image or speech signal, its encoding, multiplexing and sending to *udpsink* block the end of the pipeline. It is possible to conclude that this global time consists largely by capturing the media device and preparation for transmission by *udpsink* block.

It can be observed in Table 3 that the demultiplexing time and decoding time of video signals and voice are smaller than the overall receiving time. Therefore, this overall time is largely composed by the UDP data receiving process, and by the video and speech delivery process to their respective output devices.

The time spent in each process of sending and receiving has a great impact on a system that operates in real time. Delays on signal delivery may result in loss of communication quality. We have achieved fast internal processes with Speex and Theora.

3.4 Jitter Measurement

The jitter – variation of delay between successive packages – was measured by monitoring the clock times with the Verbose and debug functions of GStreamer framework. Table 4 shows the obtained jitter values and the flow rate of the signal in the packet buffer, which was named D_{R1}.

Table 4. Average Jitter and flow rate in packet buffer.

CODEC	Theora	Speex
***Jitter* (ns)**	−67676	0
Buffer Flow Rate - D_{R1}	0,999	1,000

If $0 < D_{R1}, \leq 1$, the *upstream* element is faster than real time. If $D_{R1} = 1$ the element is in perfect running speed. For $D_{R1} > 1$, then the *upstream* element buffer cannot operate in real time. Thus, D_{R1} says whether the *upstream* can reach real time speed.

For the experiment with Theora, we obtained a negative jitter, which indicates that the buffer comes at the right time to sink. The value obtained for D_{R1} is very close to 1, ie the *upstream* transmission of coded video Theora presents a perfect speed in real time, without delay.

For the experiment with Speex codec, the average jitter is zero, and there is no advance or delay in the arrival of packets. The data arrives at the sink in real time, and it is dispatched immediately, without need for synchronization due to delays or advances. With The $D_{R1} = 1$, it indicates real-time delivery of encoded speech signal.

4. CONCLUSIONS

The performance of video and speech codecs in an IP videoconference system was evaluated, through measurements of coding time and jitter. The implemented system uses the Theora video encoder and the Speex vocoder.

It was observed small coding and multiplexing time in videoconferences with Theora and Speex codecs. Additionally, UDP protocol provided appropriate bit rate for videoconferencing over a LAN. However, the overall time of transmission and reception indicates a possible limitation of the system, and it should be investigated in the future. The jitter performance and data flow results were satisfactory. This study is the basis for future research in immersive video conferencing, and the next steps are videoconferences via external networks and the Internet.

5. ACKNOWLEDGMENTS

To PDPD program of UFABC for supporting first author. To CAPES for Grant AUX-PE-RH-TVD-231/2008.

6. REFERENCES

[1] Lombard, M.; and Ditton, T. 1997. At the Heart of It All: The Concept of Presence. *Journal of Computer-Mediated Communication*. 3, 2 (September, 1997).

[2] Yang, R., Kurashima, C.S., Towles, H., Nashel, A., Zuffo, M.K. 2007. Immersive Video Teleconferencing with User-Steerable Views. *Presence*. 16, 2 (April 2007), 188–205. DOI= http://dx.doi.org/10.1162/pres.16.2.188.

[3] Gross, M., Wormlin, S., Naef, M., Lamboray, E., Spagno, C., Kunz, A. 2004. Blue-c: A spatially immersive display and 3D video portal for telepresence. *ACM Transactions on Graphics*. 22, 3 (2004), 819–827.

[4] Halsall, F. 2000. *Multimedia Communications: Applications, Networks, Protocols and Standards*. Addison Wesley.

[5] Kurashima, C.S.; Yang, R.; Lastra, A. 2002. Combining Approximate Geometry with View-Dependent Texture Mapping - A Hybrid Approach to 3D Video Teleconferencing. In: *Proceedings of XV Brazilian Symposium on Computer Graphics and Image Processing* (Fortaleza, CE, Brazil, 2002). SBC, Porto Alegre, RS, 112-119. DOI= http://dx.doi.org/10.1109/SIBGRA.2002.1167133.

[6] Xiph.org Foundation. *Theora Video Compression*. Online: <http://www.theora.com>. Accessed in June 17, 2012.

[7] Xiph.org Foundation. *Speex Speech Compression*. Online: <http://www.speex.org>. Accessed in March 17.2012.

[8] Laufer, C.; Fuks, H.; Lucena, C.J.P. 1998. Rio Internet TV - AulaNet: Videoconferência em Web-Based Learning. In *Proceedings of the IX Brazilian Symposum of Informatics on Education* (Fortaleza, CE, Brazil, 1998).

[9] Goetz, M., Igler, M., Meerkamm, S., Reithmeier, T., Jablonski, S., and Ehmann, M. 2010. Online Communication and Collaboration - A General Approach. In *Proceedings of the Fifth International Conference on Internet and Web Applications and Services (ICIW)* (Barcelona, Spain, May 9-15, 2010). 544 - 549. DOI= 10.1109/ICIW.2010.87.

[10] MSU. *Video Quality Measurement Tool*. Online: <http://compression.ru/video/quality_measure/video_measurement_tool_en.html>. Accessed in: August 4. 2011.

[11] PESQ. *Perceptual Evaluation of Speech Quality*. Online: <http://www.pesq.org>. Accessed in: August 4. 2011.

[12] VideoLan. *VLC Media Player*. Online: <http://www.videolan.org/>. Accessed in March 17.2012.

[13] Ribeiro, D.G., and Kurashima, C.S. 2010. Experimentos de Codificação de Video com o Codificador Theora. *Boletim Técnico da Faculdade de Tecnologia de São Paulo*. BT/29 (2010), 25-25.

[14] Ribeiro, D.G., and Kurashima, C.S. 2011. Experimentos de Teleconferência Usando o Codificador de Voz Speex. In: *Anais do 9º Congresso de Engenharia de Áudio da AES-Brasil*. (Sao Paulo, Brazil, 2011), AES Brasil, 124-127.

[15] Deitel, P., and Deitel, H. 2010. *Java - Como Programar*. 8.ed. Prentice Hall.

[16] *GStreamer Open Source Multimidia Framework*. Online: <http://gstreamer.freedesktop.org/>. Accessed in March 18.2012.

[17] *Ubuntu*. Online: <http://www.ubuntu.com/>. Accessed in March 17.2012.

[18] Wireshark Foundation. *Wireshark*. Online: <http://www.wireshark.org/>. Accessed in March 17.2012.

Reducing the Dimensionality of the SIFT Descriptor and Increasing its Effectiveness and Efficiency in Image Retrieval via Bag-of-Features

Glauco Vitor Pedrosa, Solange Oliveira Rezende e Agma Juci Machado Traina
Instituto de Ciências Matemáticas e de Computação - ICMC
Universidade de São Paulo - USP
{gpedrosa,solange,agma}@icmc.usp.br

ABSTRACT

The Bag-of-Features is a popular approach to describe multimedia information by using visual words. The SIFT (Scale Invariant Feature Transform) is one of the most utilized descriptor to model multimedia information in Bag-of-Features. The data is described as a set of keypoints and a feature vector is assigned for each of the keypoints. This feature vector is composed of 128 values, which represent the region around each keypoint. In general, some of the detected keypoints are not relevant and can be discarded without losing the local discriminative power. In this paper, we propose a technique to reduce the detected keypoints by SIFT, as well as a technique to reduce the feature vector dimensionality. Experiments were made in order to analyze the performance of the proposed reduction techniques using two different image databases. The results demonstrated that the proposed techniques improve the performance of the image retrieval by reducing up to 50% the feature vector dimensionality of SIFT and at the same time providing a gain of computational time of modeling an image employing Bag-of-Features.

Categories and Subject Descriptors

I.4 [**Image Processing and Computer Vision**]: Image Representation, Multidimensional

Keywords

Bag-of-features, Feature selection, Image Retrieval, SIFT

1. INTRODUÇÃO

A área de recuperação e caracterização de imagens tem avançado muito nos últimos anos, porém continua sendo um campo de pesquisa com grandes desafios a serem alcançados. O problema de analisar a dissimilaridade entre imagens requer um método que capture a essência da imagem, extraindo características perceptualmente eficientes e compactas que irão representar a imagem nos processos de mineração, análise e recuperação.

A recuperação de imagens se refere à tarefa de retornar as imagens de uma base de dados mais similares à uma dada imagem de consulta. Um sistema que realiza tal tarefa necessita de um descritor [8], cujo objetivo é agrupar imagens com características similares em uma dada região do espaço de medida, e grupos de imagens com características distintas em regiões diferentes deste espaço. Diferentes descritores podem gerar diferentes representações da imagem, levando a um agrupamento mais próximo das expectativas do usuário, sendo o descritor ideal aquele capaz de capturar informações perceptivamente similares nas imagens.

Nos últimos anos a abordagem *Bag-of-Features* (BoF) tem recebido bastante atenção da área de recuperação de imagens [6, 7, 2]. Ela é uma analogia às representações conhecidas como *Bag-of-Words* (BoW) [7], usada na representação de informações textuais. Na representação BoW, cada documento textual é descrito por um vetor formado pela freqüência das palavras que ocorrem nele e a análise da dissimilaridade entre documentos é dada pela comparação entre esses vetores. De maneira semelhante, na representação BoF as imagens são descritas por um conjunto de palavras visuais e a representação é dada pela análise da freqüência de cada palavra visual na imagem. Essa maneira de tratar o problema de recuperação de imagens torna um sistema capaz de lidar com imagens que possuem uma grande variedade de objetos presentes na cena.

O SIFT (*Scale Invariant Feature Transform*) [5] é um dos métodos mais utilizados para representar imagens em BoF. Esse método transforma as informações de uma imagem em um conjunto de pontos-de-interesse detectados via Diferença de Gaussianas (DoG). A quantidade de pontos-de-interesse pode variar entre imagens distintas e, geralmente, alguns pontos detectados não contribuem com informações relevantes para distinguir duas imagens e podem ser descartados sem afetar o poder discriminativo. Uma caracterização compacta e distintiva é útil e necessária, pois evita acrescentar informações irrelevantes ao espaço de medida, prevenindo o efeito da "maldição da dimensionalidade" [4], aumentando a eficiência e eficácia da análise da dissimilaridade entre imagens.

Além de detectar pontos-de-interesse, o SIFT descreve cada ponto utilizando a informação da magnitude e orientação do gradiente da região ao redor de cada ponto, gerando um vetor com 128 valores. A dimensão do vetor-

Permission to make digital or hard copies of all or part of this work for personal or classroom use is granted without fee provided that copies are not made or distributed for profit or commercial advantage and that copies bear this notice and the full citation on the first page. To copy otherwise, to republish, to post on servers or to redistribute to lists, requires prior specific permission and/or a fee.
WebMedia'12, October 15–28, 2012, São Paulo/SP, Brazil.
Copyright 2012 ACM 978-1-4503-1706-1/12/10 ...$15.00.

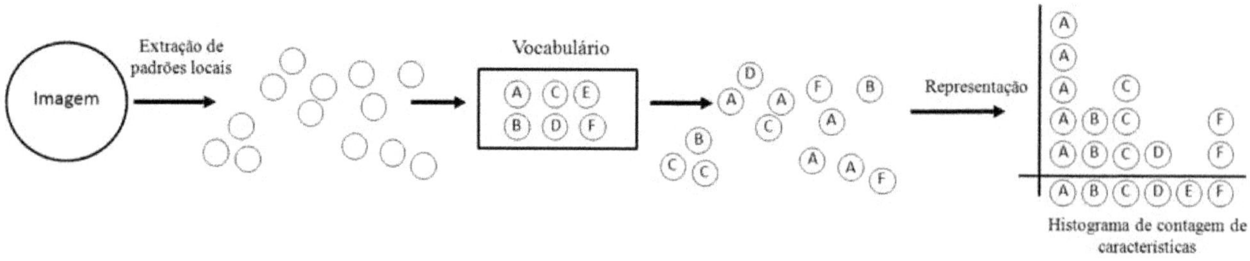

Figure 1: Abordagem *Bag-of-Features.*

de-características é um aspecto muito importante que deve ser considerado em qualquer sistema computacional, pois vetores com alta dimensionalidade influenciam diretamente no desempenho computacional do sistema, além de requerer mais espaço para armazenamento e indexação.

A proposta deste trabalho é a obtenção de uma representação robusta e compacta do descritor SIFT, visando diminuir a quantidade de pontos-de-interesse detectados e reduzir a dimensão do vetor-de-caracteristica necessário para descrever cada ponto. A idéia é eliminar pontos que possuem muitos vizinhos próximos com a mesma característica visual e utilizar o cálculo da entropia de Shannon [1] para reduzir a dimensão do vetor-de-característica de cada ponto.

Testes experimentais foram realizados com duas diferentes base de dados, analisando a performance da recuperação de imagens, via abordagem *Bag-of-Features*, utilizando as técnicas de reduções propostas neste trabalho.

2. MODELO BAG-OF-FEATURES

A abordagem *Bag-of-Features* (BoF) é uma técnica usada para modelar uma imagem através de um conjunto de padrões locais representativos. Esses padrões são descritos por um conjunto não-ordenado de pontos-de-interesse $P = \{p_1, p_2, ..., p_n\}$, em que cada ponto é representado por $p_i = (D_{p_i}, W_{p_i}, \delta_{p_i})$, tal que:

- $D_{p_i} = (d^1_{p_i}, d^2_{p_i}..., d^m_{p_i})$ representa o vetor-de-caracteristica do ponto p_i;
- W_{p_i} representa a palavra-visual correspondente ao ponto;
- $\delta_{p_i} = (x_i, y_i)$ as coordenadas do ponto na imagem.

Uma visão da abordagem BoF está sumarizada na figura 1 e pode ser definida pelas seguintes fases:

1. Extração de padrões locais: dada uma imagem, pontos-de-interesse caracterizados por terem alguma propriedade local são extraídos e descritos por um vetor-de- característica;
2. Vocabulário: as características mais representativas da imagem são codificadas em um conjunto de palavras, e cada ponto-de-interesse localizado na fase anterior são atribuídos à uma palavra-visual;
3. Representação: o vetor de características é dado pela freqüência das palavras contidas na imagem.

A fase de detecção de características corresponde a extração de padrões locais representativos de uma imagem. Esses padrões são os elementos básicos que compõem a imagem e existem diversas técnicas na literatura desenvolvidas para a detecção automática desses padrões. Para uma representação compacta, um vocabulário visual é geralmente construído por meio do agrupamento de pontos-de-interesse que possuem a mesma característica e cada grupo é tratado como uma palavra-visual no vocabulário.

O agrupamento pode ser realizado, por exemplo, utilizando o algoritmo *k-means*. Uma vez definido o vocabulário, cada ponto-de-interesse é associado à uma palavra visual. O histograma de palavras-visuais resultante compõe as características que serão usadas para representar a imagem em *Bag-of-Features*. O centróide que possui a menor distância ao ponto-de-interesse é determinado, e adiciona-se uma unidade ao seu *bin* correspondente no histograma.

3. MÉTODO PROPOSTO

Para modelar uma imagem em *Bag-of-Features*, em geral o SIFT [5] é o descritor mais utilizado e o que possui melhores resultados em diversos domínios. A ideia do SIFT é detectar pontos na imagem robustos a transformações geométricas e variações de intensidade. Para cada ponto, ele associa um vetor-de-característica que representa a magnitude e orientação da região ao redor do ponto.

A proposta deste trabalho visa a diminuir a dimensionalidade do vetor-de-característica gerado pelo SIFT, bem como reduzir a quantidade de pontos-de-interesse detectados.

3.1 Redução da dimensionalidade do vetor-de-característica

O vetor-de-característica D_{p_i} gerado pelo SIFT, para cada ponto-de-interesse p_i detectado, tem uma dimensão de $m = 128$ elementos. Para reduzir o tamanho desse vetor, a proposta é utilizar o cálculo da entropia de Shannon [1], que é definida por:

$$S = -\sum_{j=1}^{t} d^j_{p_i} ln(d^j_{p_i}) \quad (1)$$

em que t é o fator de aglutinação. Por exemplo, para $t = 128$ calcula-se o valor da entropia considerando todos os elementos do vetor e o resultado final é apenas um valor,

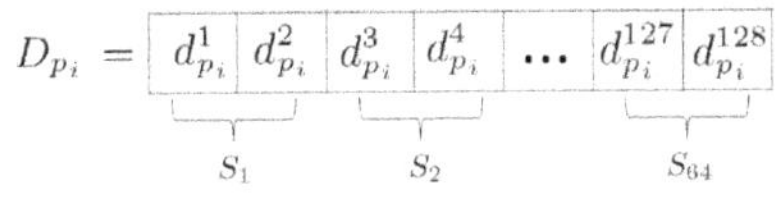

Figure 2: Redução da dimensionalidade do vetor via cálculo da entropia de Shannon em intervalo de 2 elementos.

ou seja, houve uma aglutinação do vetor de 128 elementos em apenas um único valor.

A proposta é reduzir o tamanho do vetor utilizando o cálculo da entropia em intervalos de t elementos. Por exemplo, para reduzir a dimensão do vetor pela metade, como ilustrado na figura 2, o calculo da entropia é feito em intervalos de $t = 2$ elementos, e o vetor resultante é dado por $D'_{p_i} = \{S_1, S_2, ..., S_{64}\}$.

3.2 Redução da quantidade de pontos-de-interesse detectados

O outro objetivo desse trabalho é reduzir a quantidade de pontos-de-interesse detectados, ou seja, encontrar um conjunto $P' \subseteq P$ sem redundância, eliminando pontos-de-interesse que não contribuem com informação relevante para a caracterização da imagem. A ideia proposta é descartar pontos que possuem muitos vizinhos similares, ou seja, excluir pontos muito próximos entre si que possuem a mesma palavra-visual. Formalmente, dado um raio de abrangência r, o conjunto dos pontos vizinhos similares à um dado ponto p_i é definido por:

$$\phi(p_i) = \{p_j \in P | W_{p_j} = W_{p_i}, dist(\delta_{p_i}, \delta_{p_j}) \leq r\} \quad (2)$$

em que $dist(\delta_{p_i}, \delta_{p_j})$ é a distância do ponto p_i ao ponto p_j.

A proposta é obter $P' = \{\sigma(p_1), \sigma(p_2), ..., \sigma(p_n)\}$, tal que $\sigma(p_i)$ é um critério de seleção que satisfaz a seguinte propriedade:

$$\sigma(p_i) = \begin{cases} p_i, & \text{se } \forall p_j \in \phi(p_i), |\phi(p_i)| < |\phi(p_j)|, \\ \varnothing, & \text{caso contrário.} \end{cases} \quad (3)$$

em que $|\phi(p_i)|$ denota a quantidade de vizinhos similares ao ponto p_i. A equação 3 seleciona apenas aqueles pontos que estejam em uma vizinhança que possuem poucos pontos similares com a mesma palavra-visual.

4. AVALIAÇÃO EXPERIMENTAL

Para avaliar a eficiência e a eficácia das técnicas de redução propostas, nesta seção alguns resultados experimentais são reportados. Para uma análise comparativa, foi utilizada a técnica de redução PCA (*Principal Component Analysis*) [3], que é um dos métodos mais utilizados na literatura.

Nos experimentos foram utilizadas duas bases de imagens, de diferentes domínios, para analisar os resultados:

- base Médica [1]: contendo 2400 imagens médicas de raio-x e ressonância magnética, classificadas conforme a parte do corpo e tipo de corte, sendo composta por 12 classes distintas com 200 imagens em cada classe;
- base Corel 1000 [2]: base formada por imagens de cenas naturais. Ela é composta por 1000 imagens dividas em 10 classes, 100 imagens em cada classe.

Para cada base de imagens, foi definido um dicionário com tamanho fixo de 50 palavras. Essas palavras foram geradas a partir do agrupamento dos pontos-de-interesse utilizando o algoritmo *k-means*.

Uma medida bastante utilizada para avaliação de sistemas de recuperação por conteúdo é o uso da curva de Precisão e Revocação (PR): dada uma consulta q, a precisão é definida como a fração entre o número de imagens relevantes recuperadas, $Ra(q)$, e o número de imagens recuperadas A: $Pr(q) = Ra(q)/A$. A revocação é definida como a fração entre o número de imagens relevantes recuperadas, $Ra(q)$, e o número total de imagens R relevantes na coleção: $Re(q) = Ra(q)/R$. A curva PR indica o compromisso entre essas duas medidas e, em geral, a curva mais alta no gráfico indica o descritor com a melhor eficácia.

Para uma avaliação mais robusta, também foi realizado o teste *t de Student* com nível de confiança de 95%. Esse é um teste estatístico pareado que compara a média e a variância, entre dois resultados, para definir a distribuição do ganho do desempenho. O ideal é que a melhora no desempenho seja significativo em todas as imagens, e não apenas em classes específicas.

Primeiro foi analisado o desempenho do descritor SIFT utilizando a proposta de redução da dimensão do vetor-de-características. O fator de redução utilizado, tanto na técnica proposta quanto na técnica PCA, foi de 50%, ou seja, o vetor de 128 dimensões, originalmente gerado pelo SIFT, foi reduzido para 64 elementos. Essa redução de 50% na dimensionalidade do vetor de característica reduziu o tempo computacional também em 50% para geração e indexação das palavras-visuais.

A figura 3-a-b mostra os gráficos de Precisão e Revocação para a base Corel 1000 e base Médica, respectivamente, e os resultado obtidos usando a técnica de redução proposta neste trabalho e a técnica de redução PCA. Nota-se que, a redução proposta conseguiu desempenho similar comparado com o desempenho obtido com o vetor no seu tamanho original. Inclusive, para valores altos de revocação, a técnica proposta conseguiu uma performance superior. Já a técnica de redução via PCA obteve resultados de precisão inferiores para todos os valores de revocação, comparado com o vetor de tamanho original e a técnica proposta.

O segundo experimento realizado foi a análise de desempenho utilizando a redução de pontos-de-interesse proposta neste trabalho. Empiricamente, o raio utilizado, para delimitar a área de abrangência necessária no método proposto (eq. 2), foi definido como a média das distâncias entre todos os pontos.

A figura 4-a-b mostra as curvas de Precisão e Revocação para as bases Corel e Médica, respectivamente. As curvas mostram os resultados obtidos usando a abordagem BoF sem redução dos pontos-de-interesse e o resultado obtido utilizando a redução de pontos-de-interesse proposto neste trabalho. Para todos os valores de revocação, a redução proposta contribuiu positivamente no aumento do valor da precisão. Estatisticamente, essa melhoria na recuperação foi considerado extremamente significativa com nível de 95% de confiança.

[1]Fornecida pelo Hospital das Clínicas da Faculdade de Medicina de Ribeirão Preto (HCRP) - USP

[2]Disponível em: http://wang.ist.psu.edu/docs/related/

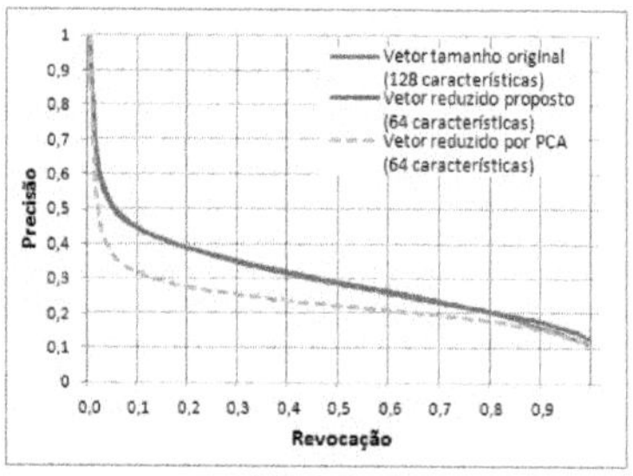

(a) base Corel

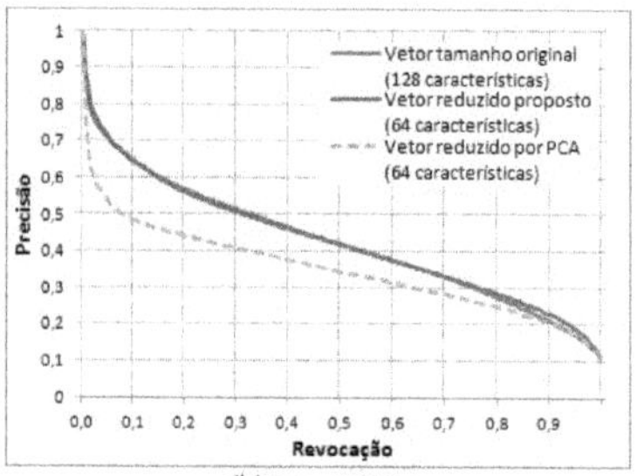

(b) base Médica

Figure 3: Resultado da redução da dimensionalidade do vetor-de-característica do SIFT.

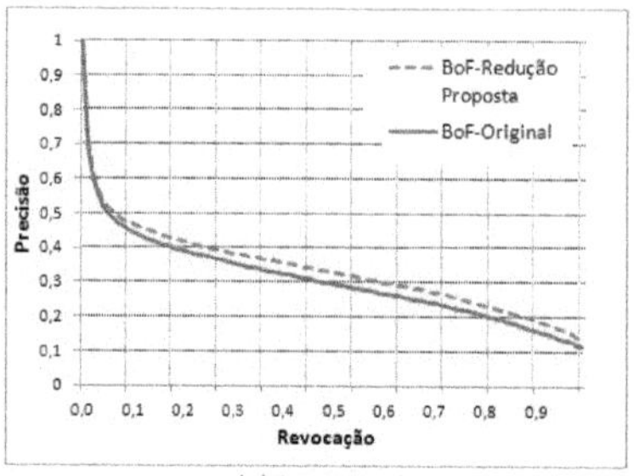

(a) base Corel

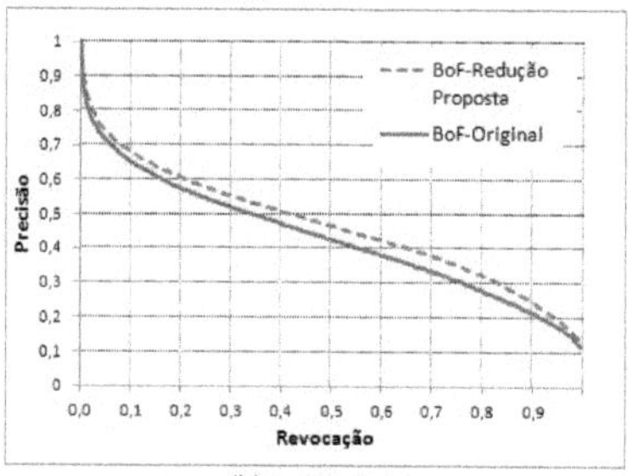

(b) base Médica

Figure 4: Resultado da redução da quantidade de pontos-de-interesse detectados pelo SIFT.

5. CONCLUSÃO

Este trabalho apresentou uma técnica, baseada no cálculo da entropia de Shannon, para a redução da dimensionalidade do vetor-de-características gerado pelo SIFT. Resultados experimentais mostraram que o desempenho na recuperação utilizando a técnica de redução proposta é similar ao desempenho do vetor-de-características sem a redução, com a vantagem da diminuição em até 50% do tempo computacional necessário para a geração e indexação das palavras-visuais.

Outra contribuição deste trabalho foi a proposta de uma técnica para a redução de pontos-de-interesse detectados pelo SIFT. A ideia é selecionar apenas pontos que estejam em uma vizinhança que possuem poucos pontos similares, com a mesma palavra-visual. Essa redução foi considerada estatisticamente significativa no aumento da precisão na recuperação de imagens via abordagem *Bag-of-Features*.

Agradecimentos

Os autores agradecem o apoio financeiro do CNPq, CAPES e FAPESP (processo n°. 2011/21460-4).

6. REFERENCES

[1] P. H. Bugatti, A. J. M. Traina, and C. Traina Jr. A new method to efficiently reducing histogram dimensionality. In *Symposium on Medical Imaging (SPIE-2008), Computer-Aided Diagnosis track*, pages 1–9, San Diego - CA, 2008.

[2] H. Jegou, M. Douze, and C. Schmid. Improving bag-of-features for large scale image search. *International Journal of Computer Vision*, 87(3):316–336, 2010.

[3] Y. Ke and R. Sukthankar. Pca-sift: A more distinctive representation for local image descriptors. In *CVPR (2)*, pages 506–513, 2004.

[4] F. Korn, B.-U. Pagel, and C. Faloutsos. On the 'dimensionality curse' and the 'self-similarity blessing'. *IEEE Transactions on Knowledge and Data Engineering*, 13:96–111, 2001.

[5] D. G. Lowe. Distinctive image features from scale-invariant keypoints. *Int. J. Comput. Vision*, 60(2):91–110, Nov. 2004.

[6] S. O'Hara and B. A. Draper. Introduction to the bag of features paradigm for image classification and retrieval. *CoRR*, http://arxiv.org/abs/1101.3354, 2011.

[7] J. Sivic and A. Zisserman. Video Google: A text retrieval approach to object matching in videos. In *Proceedings of the International Conference on Computer Vision*, volume 2, pages 1470–1477, Oct. 2003.

[8] R. D. S. Torres and A. X. Falcão. Content-based image retrieval: Theory and applications. *Revista de Informática Teórica e Aplicada*, 13:161–185.

Towards a Model to Explore Business Opportunities in Trail-aware Environments

Cládio Martins
UFSC / PPGEEL / GSE
Florianópolis – SC – Brazil
+55(48)3721-2358
cladiom@lisha.ufsc.br

João Rosa, Jorge Barbosa
Unisinos / PIPCA / Mobilab
São Leopoldo – RS – Brazil
+55(51)3591-1122
{jrosa, jbarbosa}@unisinos.br

Laerte Franco
Quality IT
São Paulo – SP – Brazil
+55(11) 3025-7082
laerte.franco@gmail.com

Eduardo Bezerra
UFSC / PPGEEL / GSE
Florianópolis – SC – Brazil
+55(48)3721-2358
bezerra.rs@gmail.com

ABSTRACT

In mobile computing environments, the tracking of users allows applications to adapt to the users' contexts (Context Awareness). Context, in this sense, is any information that can be used to characterize the users' situations and that is relevant to the interaction between the user and an application. In recent years, the use of context information and users' profiles have been considered an opportunity for ubiquitous commerce. Furthermore, the improvement and the wide adoption of location systems are stimulating the tracking of users, allowing the use of trails. A trail is the history of the contexts visited by a user during a certain period. In this article, we propose a model for trails management and its application in ubiquitous commerce. In this text, we consider that Trail Awareness is an advance of the simple use of contexts and profiles. We present a prototype and its application in a simulated commercial environment for discovery of deal opportunities using trail awareness.

Categories and Subject Descriptors

C.2.4 **[Computer-Communication Networks]**: Distributed Systems; D.2.11 **[Software Engineering]**: Software Architectures – *Domain-specific Architectures* H.0 **[Information Systems]**: General; J.7 **[Computer Applications]**: Computers in other systems.

Keywords

Context Awareness, Trail Awareness, Context History, Ubiquitous Computing, Ubiquitous Commerce.

1. INTRODUCTION

Currently, the evolution of mobile devices and high-speed wireless networks have been stimulating research related to Mobile Computing [5, 18]. In this area, the improvement and proliferation of Location Systems [8, 9] have motivated the adoption of solutions that consider the user's precise location in the providing of services (Location-Based Services [3, 22]). Mobile applications have also begun to take into account the user's current context to distribute content and services (Context Awareness [1, 10]).

Permission to make digital or hard copies of all or part of this work for personal or classroom use is granted without fee provided that copies are not made or distributed for profit or commercial advantage and that copies bear this notice and the full citation on the first page. To copy otherwise, or republish, to post on servers or to redistribute to lists, requires prior specific permission and/or a fee.

WebMedia'12, October 15–18, 2012, São Paulo/SP, Brazil.

Copyright 2012 ACM 978-1-4503-1706-1/12/10...$15.00.

State-of-the-art context-aware computing enables applications to make decisions based on users' data and their current contexts [10]. Nonetheless, we understand that would also be valuable to consider the user's past actions performed in the contexts visited during a period, such as their activities, the applications used, the contents accessed, among others. We believe this would improve the distribution of content and services in context-aware environments, because applications would use the history of the user's actions to make decisions, rather than only context and profile data.

Studies on users' monitoring in mobile computing systems have shown that is possible to record the history of the contexts visited by users and their actions performed in each context [11, 12]. Usually, this history is called Trail [6, 13, 20].

Thus, in context-aware applications, trails would enable the use of the user's past behavior to distribute content and services. Hence, we propose the application of trails to context-aware computing, considering that Trail-Aware is an advance in Context-Aware computing. In this article, we introduce a model, which is named TrailM, for trails management in mobile computing environments. TrailM is an evolution of the UbiTrail model [20], mainly, the database has been improved and the server architecture has been redesigned.

An important application area of the joint use of context and profile is commerce [23]. In this field, some applications distribute contextualized deal opportunities [7]. In the same way that occurs in context-aware applications, in the commerce domain, applications are limited to make decisions based on profile and context information. Furthermore, the use of dealers' profiles in context-aware environments is a recent research topic [7, 23].

Nevertheless, deal discovery guided by the dealers' trails is still an open research area. Hence, we propose the use of trails in the commerce scenario, aiming to improve deal opportunities. In this article, we present a case study in which TrailM was integrated with a ubiquitous commerce environment (UbiTrade [7]) and used for contextualized discovery of deal opportunities.

The article is organized as follows. Section 2 describes the TrailM architecture. The third section discusses the TrailM use in the ubiquitous commerce guided by trails. Section 4 presents the TrailM and the UbiTrade prototypes as well as the integration between them, and describes and evaluates the results obtained from a case study involving trails in discovery of deal opportunities. Section 5 discusses related works and the contribution of this work. And finally, section 6 presents the conclusions and the future works.

2. TRAILM MODEL

In Section 2.1 the adopted terminology is introduced, describing, mainly, the trails composition terms. In Section 2.2, the TrailM model architecture is described and discussed.

2.1 Entities, trails, ptrail, and trailpoint

TrailM was designed to manage entities' trails. In this context, entities represent persons, accessing computational resources (for example, a smartphone), or mobile objects (for example, a vehicle). We choose entity, instead of user, because then the model could manage trails of any mobile object. In this scenario, different applications can be developed for trails. For example, a vehicle could have a trail, recording information considered relevant, such as the occurrences of maintenances or failures.

Applications that use TrailM must temporally store data that composes a trail. For this reason, we propose that the applications have internally a structure called *ptrail* (piece of trail), which is composed of the following attributes: *entity*, *resource*, *event*, *context*, and *location*.

The values of the *entity* and *resource* attributes are stored statically in the *ptrail* after that an entity logs in the model. Nonetheless, the values of the *event*, *context*, and *location* attributes are automatically updated as the actions or movements made by the entity and monitored by the application.

The records related to the contexts visited by an entity are stored in only one trail. The trail is composed of a sequence of records of the *ptrail*. A record is composed of seven attributes organized into three categories: *identification*, *content*, and *temporality*. The first category contains only one attribute to identify the trail. The second category is used to store the *ptrail* content. The last category contains *date/time* attribute, representing the time of the record creation.

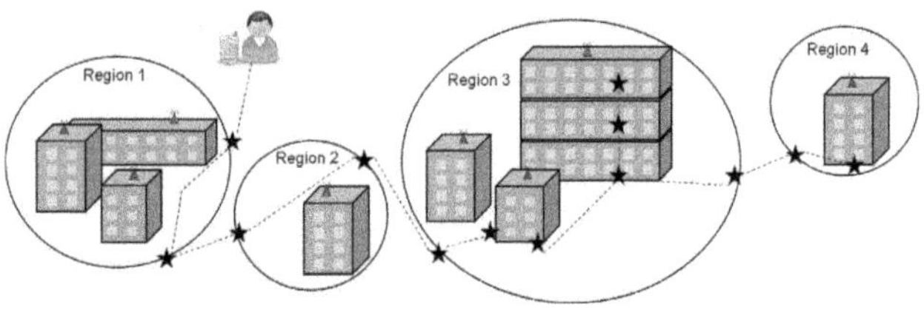

Figure 1. Example of trail composition

We named *trailpoint* the process that makes the trail composition. This process sends the values contained in the *ptrail* to be recorded in the entity's trail, which is stored in a server. The *trailpoint* occurs when the application automatically identifies that an entity performed an event, for example, entry or exit from a location, interaction with another entity, access to a file, among others. Figure 1 shows the trail creation of a mobile device user. Each star represents the occurrence of an event, which causes a *trailpoint*.

2.2 The Model Architecture

The TrailM architecture is based on the UbiTrail model [20]. The database was simplified to increase the performance. Moreover, the server architecture was remodeled, mainly, taking out the Context provider and increasing the functions of the TrailManager and TrailServices layers.

2.2.1 General Organization

Figure 2 presents a general view of the model, which is composed of a server (TrailM Server) and a client (TrailM Client). TrailM Server supports the trails management and provides services for the applications. TrailM Client runs on mobile devices and supports the communication between the applications and the server. In addition, TrailM considers the existence of an external provider that provides location information.

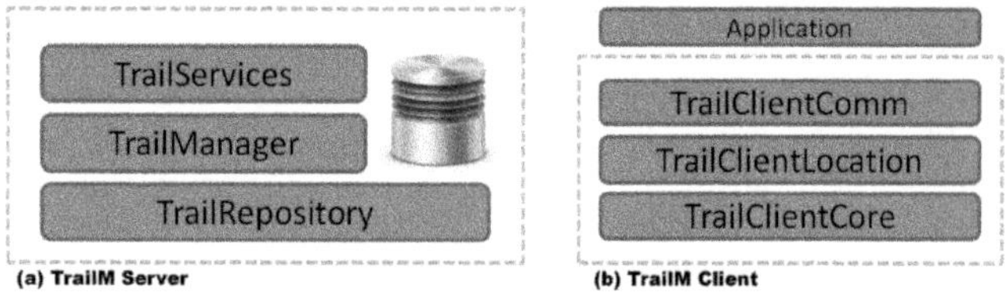

Figure 2. The TrailM architecture

2.2.2 The TrailM Server Architecture

Some of the TrailM Server basic tasks are to manage the entities' trails and to enable application to query the trails. To perform these functions, we designed the *TrailServices* module (see Figure 2a, which presents the TrailM Server architecture). The *TrailServices* provides *basic services* to manage the trails and, moreover, enables applications building their own *specialized services* according to their needs.

The *basic services* perform generic tasks which are considered strategic for the management of the server and the trails. These services are organized into three groups: *ManageTrail*, *ComposeTrail*, and *QueryTrail*. The *ManageTrail* group supports the services used for the control and management of the applications. The *ComposeTrail* group supports the services used for the trails composition. It contains the service responsable for sending the *ptrails* in the *trailpoint* process. The *QueryTrail* group contains the services that allow queries related to the trails.

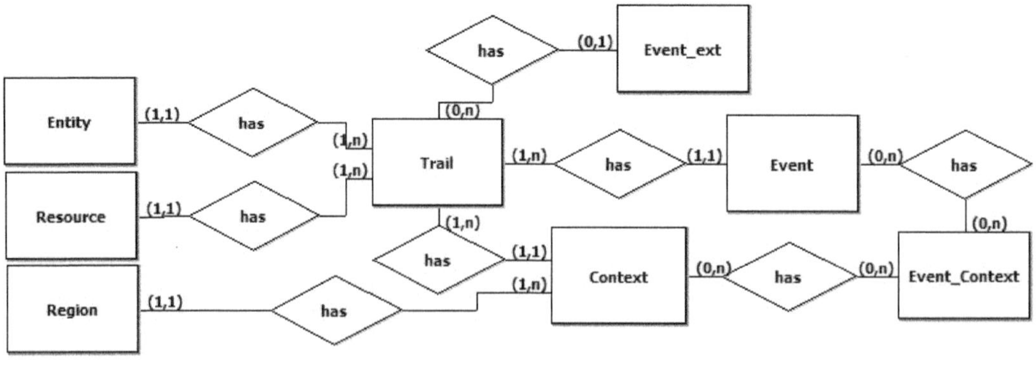

Figure 3. TrailM database

TrailM Server enables applications adding to the model their own *specialized services*, which can be composed of basic services. Section 3.2 describes four specialized services created to support the discovery of deal opportunities guided by trails. The server has a database to store entities' information, the trails, and their related content (see Figure 3). The entities table stores identification data of the entities related to the trails that are being managed. The trails table stores the *ptrails* that compose the entities' trails. The trail related content is stored in the others tables: context, region, event, extension of events and resource.

Some services can have common functions, for example, querying the database and managing the trails. For this reason, we designed the TrailManager component, which performs basic operations that can be used by the services. TrailManager has the basic functionalities for trails management, such as: (1) control of requests sent to the server; (2) registration and authentication of users; (3) access to the database; and (4) the composition of the record for the storage of a *ptrail* at the *trailpoint* solicitation moment. TrailRepository provides an interface to access the database repository, thus supporting TrailManager.

2.2.3 The TrailM Client Architecture

TrailM Client resides on the entity's mobile device and supports the applications that use TrailM to manage their trails. The client instantiates and manages the entities' *ptrails*, synchronining them with TrailM Server.

The client is organized in three layers (Figure 2b). The top layer is responsible for the communication (TrailClientComm) between the client and the server. The intermediate layer (TrailClientLocation) deals with the communication between the device and the external provider of location. The bottom layer (TrailClientCore) receives information (regarding the events performed by the entities) from the application that is using TrailM.

3. UBIQUITOUS COMMERCE

Section 3.1 describes the ubiquitous commerce environment, in which TrailM was integrated. Section 3.2 describes how the trails were used in the discovery process of Deal Opportunities (DOs).

3.1 The Ubiquitous Commerce Environment

The UbiTrade architecture [7], presented in Figure 4, is composed of eight components.

The first is the Location System, which allows the identification of the users' current context. The second is the Profile System that stores the users' data. The third is the Category Tree, which keeps a taxonomy of products and services. The fourth is the Reference System, which determines the users' reputation, according to the previous transacted businesses. The fifth is the Service Manager, which operates as a layer of messages exchange between the interface component and the others. The sixth is the Opportunity Consultant, which is the main component of the model. It operates as an analysis engine, generating business opportunities from the profiles and locations of the dealers. Finally, there are two components used as interfaces with users, the Personal Assistant and the Website.

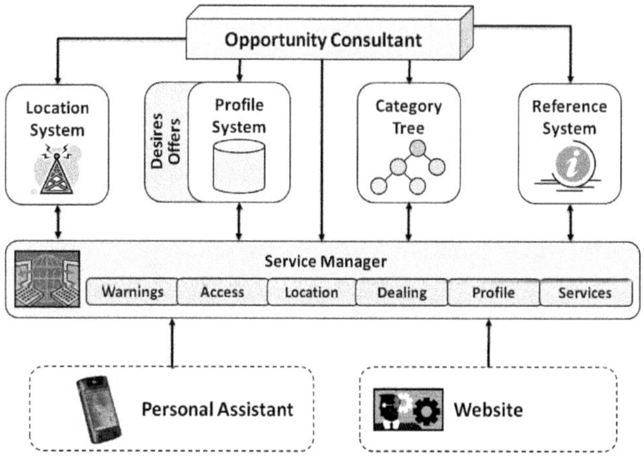

Figure 4. The UbiTrade architecture

The deal opportunity identification depends on events occurrence. The opportunities, in UbiTrade, are classified into three categories:

- The *Buy & Sell* category is generated from the desires of a dealer matched with the offers of another dealer.
- The *Knowledge Exchange* category is created based on the desires of a dealer matched with the desires of another dealer.
- The *Experience Exchange* category is produced from the matching of desires of a dealer with businesses made by another dealer.

The identification of the deal opportunities is made by Opportunity Consultant through the dealer's location and profile, and the warning to users about deal opportunities is made by Service Manager.

3.2 Deal Opportunities Using Trails

3.2.1 Specialized Services in TrailM

The deal opportunities discovery guided by trails was based on specialized services created in TrailM and accessed by Opportunity Consultant of UbiTrade. The preferences are determined considering the frequency that the user visited the contexts, and did business with other users. Table 1 summarizes the created services. The information returned by the services is obtained through the analysis of the dealers' trails.

Table 1. Specialized services created in TrailM

Name	Description
PreferredContexts	Returns a list with the dealer's preferred contexts in a trail.
DiscoveryDOs	Returns a list containing all deal opportunities of dealers that have a desire and/or offer in common based on trail.
PreferredDealingContexts	Returns a list with the dealer's preferred business conclusion contexts in a trail (for example, jewelry store, restaurant or train).
TypeOfBusinessByRegion	Returns a list with the type of business by region based on dealers' trails (for example, shopping).

3.2.2 The TrailM/UbiTrade Integration

The TrailM/UbiTrade integration was based on the following changes in UbiTrade: (1) we included the support to the TrailM services in Personal Assistant; (2) the Opportunity Consultant inferences became to consider the dealers' profiles and the services available by TrailM described in Table 1.

Figure 5 presents the dynamic of the integration. UbiTrade warns the dealers about deal opportunities. Location System informs the context in which the dealer is to Opportunity Consultant, which identifies the occurrence of one event that starts the process (step 1). Opportunity Consultant uses this information, combined with the dealer's profile and information from Reference System, to filter deal opportunities. Reference System provides data of the user's tolerated risk and of the counterpart's reputation.

The opportunity creation only continues if the user's tolerated risk is higher than the counterpart's reputation (step 2). For dealers who have the data compatible, Opportunity Consultant matches the profiles, trying to identify the type of opportunity that they are looking for (step 3). In this stage, UbiTrade uses the TrailM services to improve its inferences. When Opportunity Consultant identifies an opportunity, it sends a notification to the dealers, using the warnings service of the Service Manager component (step 4).

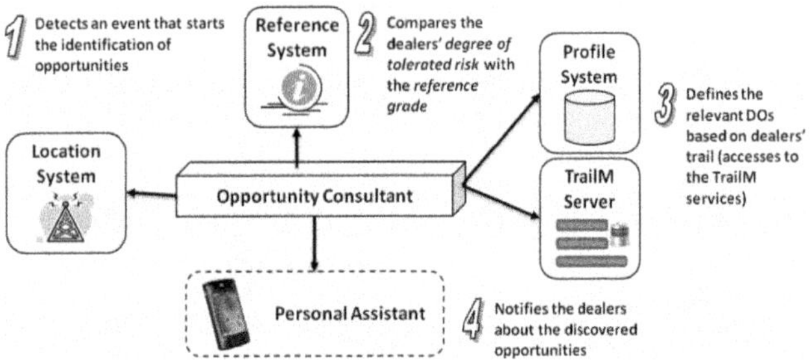

Figure 5. Discovery of DOs guided by trails

4. PROTOTYPE AND CASE STUDY

Section 4.1 describes the TrailM and the UbiTrade implementations. Furthermore, Section 4.2 discusses the case study used to validate the model.

4.1 The TrailM and the UbiTrade prototypes

The TrailM Server prototype was implemented through the Java programming language. The Hibernate framework was used to access the database information which was implemented using MySQL. The services of the *TrailServices* layer are available through the Web services technology. The choice of Web services is due to the fact that this type of architecture enabled the use of service from heterogeneous environments (such as different platforms and programming languages) using the communication based on SOAP protocol. The TrailM Client prototype was implemented using the J2ME (Java to Micro Edition).

The UbiTrade prototype was implemented through the C# programming language. The Personal Assistant was developed using .NET Compact Framework. The library of open source-code OpenNETCF was used to support wireless nets. All local storage of the profile is made in XML from the System.Xml library of the .NET.

The Personal Assistant was installed in the Smartphone HTC 4351 (Figure 6a), iPAQs 4700 (Figure 6b), and Tablet PCs tc1100 equipments, with support to Windows Mobile and Wi-Fi networks. This component captures the antennas' power, using the OpenNETCF library, and forwards this data to the Location System via the service "Localizing". UbiTrade uses this information to define the context where the mobile device is. The information of the localizing is calculated through an algorithm of neural networks, implemented using Java Neural Network Simulator (JNNS), which converts the received power into contexts. Currently, the validation environment uses four wireless antennas as will be discussed in Section 4.2.2.

The Category Tree and the Profile System were implemented using the relational database Firebird. The information of Desires, Offers, and General Configurations are registered by the user using the Personal Assistant interface installed in the mobile device or via the Web site, implemented in ASP.NET.

The Opportunity Consultant and the Reference System were implemented in C# as Windows service installed in two servers and the information is constantly monitored regarding the available environment in the database of the UbiTrade. To implement the Services Manager module, we used the established Web service technology.

(a) HTC 4351 (b) iPAQ 4700

Figure 6. Personal Assistant

4.2 Case Study

4.2.1 Obtainment of the trails

The case study was based on simulated generation of dealers' trails, which were used in the real scenario described in the validation environment. We call real scenario the physical building where we installed the infrastructure to support the experiments, we will approach this in Subsection 4.2.2.

Figure 7 presents the simulation environment used in the trails generation, which is composed of the *Houses*, *Metro*, and *Shopping* regions. We defined these regions because we wanted to monitor the dealers' activities while they were moving from their houses to the shopping. Within the regions, we mapped some locations where the users could go, for instance, the cabstand, the fast food 1, and station 2.

The *Metro* region represents the area in which the dealers move from their houses to the shopping and vice versa. This region contains a location for each one of the three stations and a location that represents the dealer's presence on the train.

Therefore, the system can record the events made by the dealer during the movement between the stations.

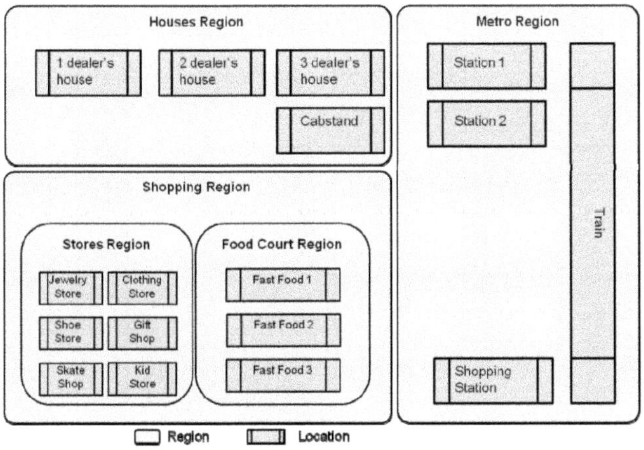

Figure 7. Map of the simulation environment

The last region corresponds to the shopping. Within the shopping region, we defined two subregions representing the stores and the food court. A region can be composed of one or more subregions, and each region contains at least one location.

In the simulation, the information of the dealers' profiles was based on two real persons, regarding their preferences and interests related to desires and offers. The trails generation was based on the possible events that the dealers could do. Furthermore, we generated the trails using an application developed specifically for this purpose.

Considering possible displacements and deals, the application generated records related to the events of entry and exit from the locations, offers and desires inclusion, creation of opportunities, and concluded businesses. Table 2 presents an example of these records.

Table 2. Example of the records

Dealer	Device	Event	Location	Extension	Date
Peter	HTC 4351	Offer inclusion	1 dealer's house	Title: Guitar Category: Sound Instrument	February. 6 08:03
Peter	HTC 4351	Exit from location	1 dealer's house	-	February. 6 08:11
Peter		Entry into location	Fast Food 1	-	February. 6 12:01
Eduard	HTC 4351	Entry into location	Shopping	-	February. 6 15:32
Eduard	HTC 4351	Entry into location	Fast Food 1	-	February. 6 16:03
Eduard	HTC 4351	Created Opportunity	Fast Food 1	DO Notification	February. 6 16:04

4.2.2 Validation environment

Figure 8 presents the map of the second floor of the Building 6B at Unisinos. The validation scenario is composed of nine rooms, in which we installed four Cisco Aironet 1100 wireless antennas. Location System of UbiTrade [7] is based on the strategy of antennas triangulation and allows the exactly determination of the rooms in which the users are. In the experiment, we used HTCs 4351. In the evaluation of the TrailM/UbiTrade prototype, the rooms presented in Figure 8 were mapped to the simulation environment presented in Figure 7. Therefore, we established a relationship between the real environment (Figure 8) and the simulated environment (Figure 7), according to the presented in Figure 9.

The rooms 206 and 215 were mapped to the representations of the locations *train* and *1 dealer's house*. The other rooms were mapped to the Shopping region. Therefore, during the prototype evaluation, the movements among the real rooms represented virtual movements.

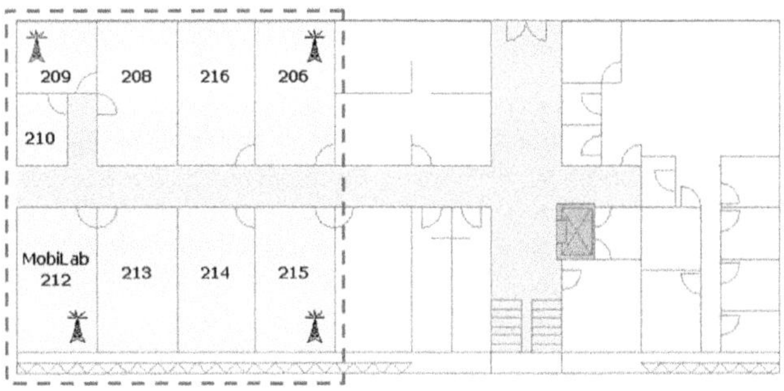

Figure 8. Map of the validation environment

For example, a movement from room 215 (house) to room 206 (train) represented the dealer's presence on the train, moving from the dealer's house to the shopping region. The presence in the virtual representation *train* makes Opportunity Consultant initiates the analysis process of deal opportunities, as the dealer actually was physically in the train location.

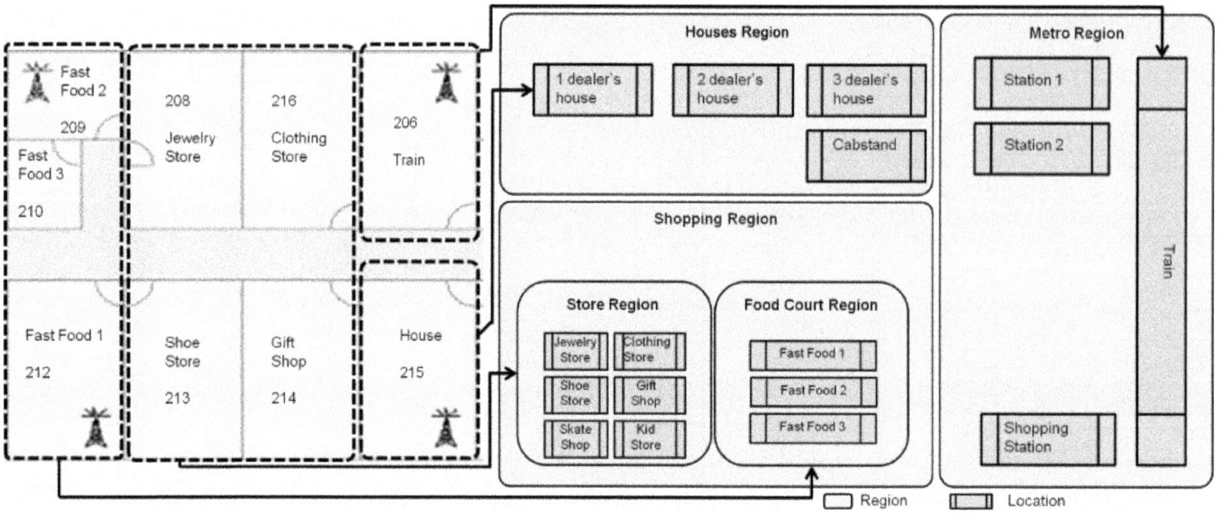

Figure 9. Validation scenario

4.2.3 Validation through a scenario

The scientific community has been using scenarios to validate context-aware environments (according to Dey's approach [4]) and ubiquitous environments (according to Satyanarayanan [17]).

Following this strategy, we created a scenario for tests and evaluations of the TrailM/UbiTrade integration, involving the daily routine of a jewelry appraiser called Peter and a music student called Eduard. This scenario focuses on the discovery of a dealing opportunity based on the dealers' trails, according to the described below:

*"Peter is a jewelry appraiser at a **jewelry store** in the shopping region. At the beginning of the day, before leaving home, he remember that he would like to sell his old guitar, which he no longer uses. So he registers an offer about his guitar in the UbiTrade's **Profile System**. After this moment, the **Opportunity Consultant** queries possible deals involving guitar every time the user enters in a new context. In this scenario the locations were mapped as the contexts.*

*To go to work, Peter goes to **station 1** and takes the **train**, usually he uses this interval to check his messages and deals through the **Personal Assistance**. Arriving at the shopping region he works until 12:00am. After, he goes to the **fast food 1** in the **food court region** to have lunch, where he remains until 12:45. After lunch, he returns to the jewelry store. Finally, at the end of the day, Peter moves to the **shopping station**, and goes home.*

*Eduard is a student of music and desires to buy a guitar, so he registers the desire in his profile in UbiTrade. Every morning, he goes to **station 2** and takes the **train** to the university. The university region is not mapped in the scenario. After the class, in the afternoon, he takes the **train** and goes to the shopping region to meet with his friends. After the meeting, he moves to the **shopping station** to go home.*

***Opportunity Consultant** uses the **PreferredContexts** service of TrailM, which takes in account the frequency in which the contexts are visited, to determine the preferred contexts of each user. In this scenario the **jewelry store** and the **fast food 1** were considered the preferred contexts of Peter.*

*In a regular day, Eduard takes the train to the university, has classes and goes to the **shopping region** to meet his friends. Sometimes, they go to the **fast food 1** in the **food court region**. At this time, Eduard and his friends go to the same place again, the **fast food 1**. **Opportunity Consultant** of UbiTrade identifies for the first time, through the **PreferredContexts** service of TrailM, the **fast food 1** as a preferred context of Eduard. Once a change in Eduard's preferences is detected, the Opportunity Consultant uses the **DiscoveryDOs** service of TrailM to infer possible deal opportunities for dealers. This service compares the users' preferences based on trails, i.e., preferred contexts, and returns the dealers which can deal between them to **Opportunity Consultant**.*

As Peter and Eduard usually pass through the fast food 1 (Preferred Context), for them would be easier to make an appointment at this place to talk about the business. So, based on similar preferred contexts and offers/desires, Eduard receives a message (see Figure 10*(a)) about the deal opportunity and has the possibility to exchange messages with the counterpart, in this case, Peter. We believe the places they visit are a factor of approchement between them, so they could meet to exchange ideas, and even deliver the product and take the money.*

Always that the dealers receive a notification of DO, they can delay the access. This action indicates that the dealers are interested in the deal, but they do not want to access it at the moment, i.e., Eduard stores the deal opportunity to see in another moment (see Figure 10*(b)) because he is in a meeting with his friends.*

*After the meeting, Eduard moves to the **shopping station**. When he enters in the **train**, UbiTrade notifies him that a postponed DO was identified (see* Figure 10*(c)). UbiTrade used the **PreferredDealingContexts** service to define the sending, once Eduard usually sends messages and performs deals at this location. So, he accesses the deal opportunity to look details (see* Figure 10*(d)) and can exchange messages to deal with Peter. So after some messages exchanged, they book a day and time in the **fast food 1** at the **Shopping Region** to perform the deal."*

The scenario was tested in the validation environment previous described in Section 4.2.2. The dealers, carrying HTC 4351, simulated the scenario moving around the environment rooms. The train and the dealer's house were simulated through the rooms 206 and 215, respectively.

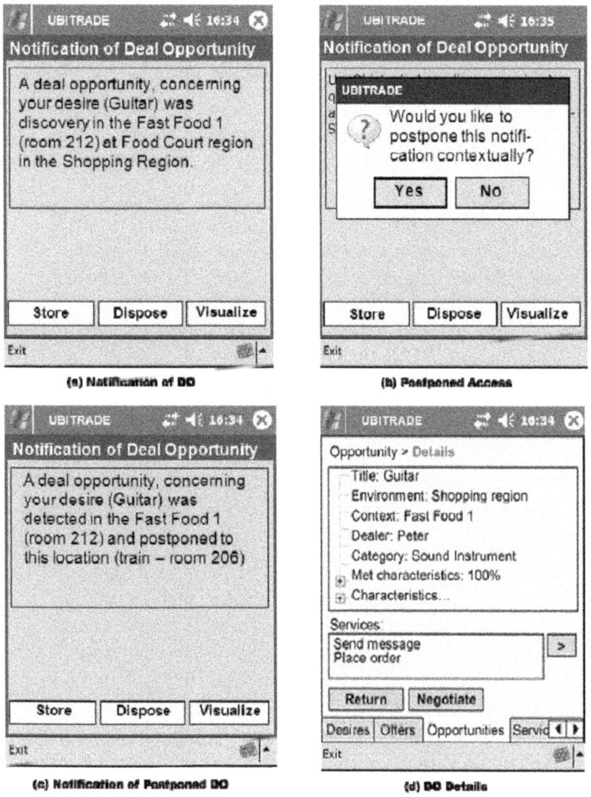

Figure 10. The scenario snapshots

5. RELATED WORKS

5.1 Ubiquitous Commerce

Some researches have proposed models for ubiquitous commerce. These models affect different areas, from the commerce of products in supermarkets to the control of parking lots. In this subsection, we discuss the main characteristics of some models for u-commerce.

For example, iGrocer, discussed by Shekar [19], was designed to be a smart assistant, aiding clients in the purchase process in supermarkets. iGrocer tracks and retains consumers' nutritional profiles, suggesting the purchase of products or even warning about items that should be avoided. This is particularly practical for elderly people or those who need help to follow a specific diet. iGrocer also identifies the desired products, through barcode scanning, and gives the user information about the nutritional facts. In order to suggest product for the consumer purchase, iGrocer also combines the client's nutritional profile with a database of nutritional facts.

Another application is MyGrocer, presented by Roussos and Mossouri [16]. It is similar to iGrocer and was designed to assist consumers in the food purchasing process. However, MyGrocer emphasizes the control of the stock of products in food-related businesses and households, using sensors on the shelves and in other locations. These sensors indicate the available quantity of a product, warning when something is missing or finishing.

Lin *et al.* [14] present a generic architecture called the Pervasive Activity Manager (PAM). Its aim is to assist clients, giving complementary information of products to help the decision on the purchase of an item. PAM uses services supplied by stores, shopping malls, or even other customers.

The u-commerce concept may also be applied to services. For example, EPARK was proposed to assist clients and employees in the process of parking payment and management [15]. Some of its functionalities are a parking map, booking a parking space, and extending the booking time for a parking space. Another example of a u-commerce application in the service market is the Ubiquitous Tourist Assistant System (UTAS) of Chiu *et al.* [2]. UTAS was designed to satisfy tourists' needs in situations where language is an obstacle. UTAS is capable of warning about delayed or canceled flights, obstructed roads, and restaurant or concert bookings, allowing the traveler's trip plans to be handled though a mobile device.

Although there are many proposals for u-commerce, UbiTrade is the only model that focuses on the generation of business opportunities for users playing the role either of clients or suppliers. UbiTrade is also generic, working with the trade of products in different areas, rather than focusing on a specific one.

5.2 Trail Management

In this subsection, we discuss the main characteristics of some works which use the trail-aware concept. In the trail management area, Hermes [6] is a framework for creating applications that involve the movement of users during the performance of actions in different locations. In Hermes, a trail consists in the route suggested to the users accomplish their tasks efficiently. The proposal does not consider the record of activities in contexts, as proposed by TrailM.

Levene and Peterson (Trail Records [13]) propose the use of a mobile device to record learning experiences using different media (for instance, text, video, and audio) while visiting different locations. The sequence of records forms a structure named trail, which can be used to recover the learner's experience in the visited path. The model is not generic, focusing specifically on the record of experiences with media.

Life Annotation [21] proposes the annotation of the places visited by users of mobile devices, thereby composing their trails. However, it does not standardize the trails information, which makes difficult to query them. TrailM standardizes the information through the use of a specific database (see section 2.2.2).

Based on the bibliographic review of this article, we can affirm that the TrailM/UbiTrade integration creates the first environment supporting deal opportunities discovery guided by trails. Furthermore, among the researched works, TrailM is the only model capable of managing trails of any kind of mobile entity (e.g., people, objects or animals).

In the several works related to ubiquitous commerce none of them use trails. To our knowledge this is the first work that focuses on the use of trails in ubiquitous commerce.

6. CONCLUSIONS AND FUTURE WORK

This paper has presented a model to manage trails and its application in the business opportunities discovery in ubiquitous commerce environments. TrailM initially has been integrated with UbiTrade, but its proposal is generic and can be used by other works.

The trails allow the use of more precise users' behavior information. The objective of the case study was to demonstrate that is viable to integrate ubiquitous commerce environments with TrailM as well as to use the trails to improve automatic decisions, in our case, business opportunities.

The main conclusions were: (1) the use of trails confirms the mobile computing potential to improve the business opportunity discovery; (2) the availability of the history of visited contexts stimulates the use of mobile devices as instruments to access contextualized contents; (3) TrailM supports content distribution guided by trails; (4) the prototype and the experiment attest the proposal feasibility.

TrailM as well as its integration with UbiTrade is an initial proposal. The following activities will allow the continuity of the study: (1) we will run additional tests with the trails obtained from simulation, for example, the *TypeOfBusinessByRegion* service was not used yet; (2) the heuristic to determine the preferred contexts (frequency of visit) can be improved through additional information, for example, time of each use; (3) the system performance involving a significant amount of records must be evaluated, because the experiment considered a few number; (4) additional simulations with different situations will be performed to proof the system effectiveness.

7. ACKNOWLEDGMENTS

The authors wish to thank CNPq (The Brazilian National Counsel of Technological and Scientific Development) for the financial support.

8. REFERENCES

[1] Baldauf, M., Dustdar, S., and Rosenberg, F. 2007. A Survey on Context-aware Systems. *International Journal of Ad Hoc and Ubiquitous Computing*, Vol. 2, No. 4, pp. 263-277. DOI= 10.1504/IJAHUC.2007.014070.

[2] Chiu, D. and Leung, H. 2005. Towards ubiquitous tourist service coordination and integration: a multi-agent and semantic web approach. *International Conference on Electronic Commerce*, Xi'an, China, August, 2005, 574–581. DOI= 10.1145/1089551.1089656

[3] Dey, A., Hightower, J., Lara, E., and Davies, N. 2010. Location-Based Services. *IEEE Pervasive Computing*, vol. 9, no. 1, pp. 11-12, Jan.-March 2010, DOI= 10.1109/MPRV.2010.10

[4] Dey, A., Salber, D., and Abowd, G. 2001. A conceptual framework and a toolkit for supporting the rapid prototyping of context-aware application. *Human-Computer Interaction*, Vol. 16, No. 2, pp. 97-166. DOI= 10.1207/S15327051HCI16234_02.

[5] Diaz, A., Merino, P., and Rivas, F.J. 2010. Mobile Application Profiling for Connected Mobile Devices. *IEEE Pervasive Computing*, Vol. 9, No. 1, pp. 54-61. DOI= 10.1109/MPRV.2009.63

[6] Driver, C. and Clarke, S. 2008. An application framework for mobile, context-aware trails. *Pervasive and Mobile Computing*, Vol. 4, No. 5, pp. 719-736. DOI= 10.1016/j.pmcj.2008.04.009

[7] Franco, L., Rosa, J. , Barbosa, J., Costa, C. and Yamin, A. 2009. Exploring Business Opportunities in Ubiquitous Environments. *VIII IADIS International Conference WWW/Internet*. Roma, Italy, pp. 469-476.

[8] Hightower, J. and Borriello, G. 2001. Location Systems for Ubiquitous Computing. *Computer*, Vol. 34, No. 8, pp. 57-66. DOI= 10.1109/2.940014

[9] Hightower, J., LaMarca, A. , and Smith, I. 2006. Practical Lessons from Place Lab. *IEEE Pervasive Computing*, Vol. 5, No. 3, pp. 32-39. DOI= 10.1109/MPRV.2006.55

[10] Hoareau, C. and Satoh, I. 2009. Modeling and Processing Information for Context-Aware Computing - A Survey. *New Generation Computing*, Vol. 27, No. 3, pp. 177-196. DOI= 10.1007/s00354-009-0060-5

[11] Hong, J., Suh, E., Kim, J. and Kim, S. 2009. Context-aware system for proactive personalized service based on context history. *Expert Systems with Applications*, Vol. 36, No. 4, pp. 7448-7457. DOI= 10.1016/j.eswa.2008.09.002

[12] Kalatzis, N., Roussaki, I., Liampotis, N., Strimpakou, M. and Pils, C. 2008. User-centric Inference Based on History of Context Data in Pervasive Environments. *Proceedings of the 3rd international workshop on Services integration in pervasive environments*, pp. 25-30. DOI= 10.1145/1387309.1387316

[13] Levene, M. and Peterson, D. 2002. *Trail Record and Ampliative Learning*. Research Report BBKCS-02-01, School of Computer Science and Information Systems. University of London.

[14] Lin, K., Yu, T., and Chith, C. 2005. The design of a personal and intelligent pervasive commerce system architecture. *Proceedings of the 2nd IEEE International Workshop on Mobile Commerce and Services*, July, 19, 2005, IEEE Computer Society Press, Los Alamitos, CA, 2005, 163–173. DOI= 10.1109/WMCS.2005.25

[15] Mazzari, D., Seraphine, P., Ahamed, S., Balasubramanian, S. 2007. Design and implementation of EPARK wireless parking payment system using pervasive computing. *Proceedings of the 2nd IEEE International Symposium on Pervasive Computing and Ad Hoc Communications*, Niagara Falls, Canada, May 21–23, 2007, IEEE Computer Society Press, Los Alamitos, CA, 2007, 219–224. DOI= 10.1109/AINAW.2007.145

[16] Roussos, G. and Moussouri, T., 2004. Consumer perceptions of privacy, security and trust in ubiquitous commerce. *Personal and Ubiquitous Computing*, Vol. 8, No. 6, pp. 416-429. DOI= 10.1007/s00779-004-0307-6

[17] Satyanarayanan, M., 2001. Pervasive computing: vision and challenges. *IEEE Personal Communications*, Vol. 8, No. 4, pp. 10-17. DOI= 10.1109/98.943998

[18] Satyanarayanan, M., Bahl, P., Caceres, P., and Davies, N. 2009. The Case for VM-Based Cloudlets in Mobile Computing. *IEEE Pervasive Computing*, Vol. 8, No. 4, pp. 14-23. DOI= 10.1109/MPRV.2009.82

[19] Shekar, S., Nair, P. , and Helal, S. 2003. iGrocer: a ubiquitous and pervasive smart grocery. *Symposium on Applied Computing*. Melbourne, USA, pp. 645-652. DOI= 10.1145/952532.952658

[20] Silva, J., Rosa, J. , Barbosa, D., Palazzo, L. and Barbosa, J. 2009. Distribuição de Conteúdo em Ambientes Cientes de Trilhas. *Proceedings of the XV Brazilian Symposium on Multimedia and the Web*, Fortaleza, Ceará, October 05–07, 2009. DOI= 10.1145/1858477.1858492

[21] Smith, A., Hall, W., Glaser, H., and Carr, L. 2006. Towards Truly Ubiquitous Life Annotation. *Memories for Life Colloquium*. The British Library, London, England.

[22] Vaughan-Nichols, S.J. 2009. Will Mobile Computing's Future Be Location? *Computer*, Vol. 42, No. 2, pp. 14-17. DOI= 10.1109/MC.2009.65.

[23] Zhang, L., Liu, Q. , and Li, a.X. 2009. Ubiquitous Commerce: Theories, Technologies, and Applications. *Journal of Networks*, Vol. 4, No. 4, pp. 271-278. DOI= 10.4304/jnw.4.4.271-278

Dynamic and Semantic Web Services Composition for Ubiquitous Computing

Frederico Lopes[1], Thais Batista[2], Everton Cavalcante[2], Thiago Pereira[2],
Flávia C. Delicato[3], Paulo F. Pires[3], Paulo Ferreira[4]

[1] School of Science and Technology, Federal University of Rio Grande do Norte – Natal, Brazil
[2] Department of Informatics and Applied Mathematics, Federal University of Rio Grande do Norte – Natal, Brazil
[3] Department of Computer Science, Federal University of Rio de Janeiro – Rio de Janeiro, Brazil
[4] INESC-ID, Technical University of Lisbon – Lisbon, Portugal

fred.lopes@gmail.com, thais@ufrnet.br, evertonranielly@gmail.com, thiago.inf@gmail.com,
fdelicato@gmail.com, paulo.f.pires@gmail.com, paulo.ferreira@inesc-id.pt

ABSTRACT
The development of complex applications is one of the major current challenges of Ubiquitous Computing. Such applications are difficult to develop because they use services provided by different context-provision middleware, thus being necessary to know the models used for communication and representation of context information for each one. This paper presents the semantic composition and Web service selection mechanisms provided by OpenCOPI, a platform designed to integrate context-provision middleware. In OpenCOPI: (i) the applications are described in a high-level of abstraction by using semantic workflows; (ii) the semantic composition is responsible for composing concrete services from abstract descriptions of the applications, and; (iii) the selection is based on service quality metadata and user preferences. This paper also presents an evaluation of the semantic composition and the Web service selection mechanisms considering a ubiquitous application.

Categories and Subject Descriptors
C.2.4 [**Computer-Communication Networks**]: Distributed Systems – *distributed applications.*

General Terms
Algorithms, Design, Experimentation.

Keywords
Ubiquitous computing, platforms integration, context provision middleware, Semantic Web services composition.

1. INTRODUCTION
Ubiquitous Computing [1] scenarios typically consist of a myriad of integrated devices, sensors, and networks in order to build a highly heterogeneous environment. Such heterogeneity requires powerful middleware infrastructures to make easier the development of ubiquitous applications thus providing mechanisms for managing sensors, interpreting and dealing with context information, etc. [2]. The current trend in Ubiquitous Computing is the emergence of complex context-aware applications in which platforms are based on heterogeneous networks, interfaces, services, and technologies are used to provide user-centric applications. In such scenarios, a *service* is an element that has functionalities provided by an entity and consumed by other software entities (*clients*). Thus, ubiquitous applications are built through the *composition of services* provided by several service providers, so that many of them can provide services with the same functionality. Thus, the composition process may consider *Quality of Service* (QoS) parameters to select services that best meet the client's needs.

In this perspective, this paper presents OpenCOPI (*Open COntext Platform Integration*), a platform that integrates context-provision services and provides an environment to support and make easier the development of context-aware applications. OpenCOPI is based on SOA (*Service-Oriented Architecture*) [3] and its implementation uses the Web services technology, thus exploring open standards and languages. Such platform enables the integration of services provided by distinct service providers, thus ranging from services provided by simple ad hoc sensor networks to more complex services, such as context-provision middleware platforms. Another important OpenCOPI's feature is the use of *semantic workflows*. SOA and workflows management are promising technologies to meet Ubiquitous Computing requirements since SOA allows the applications functionalities to be provided and consumed as a set of *services*, which can be invoked by consumers through service interfaces published by service providers. On the other hand, a *workflow* describes the order of a set of activities to be executed by several services in order to achieve a specific goal [4]. SOA and workflows were selected since they are useful in environments in which lots of services provided by several providers are available and some of these services have similar functionality. Moreover, these technologies enable selection, composition, and automatic orchestration of services.

The model of Semantic Web service composition used by OpenCOPI is based on the service functionality and service metadata. This characteristic enables a better choice among the available services with the same functionality, for example, services with the same inputs, outputs, preconditions and effects. Such compositions must be performed by choosing services that provide context data that meet the application requirements. Thus, OpenCOPI uses

Permission to make digital or hard copies of part or all of this work for personal or classroom use is granted without fee provided that copies are not made or distributed for profit or commercial advantage and that copies bear this notice and the full citation on the first page. Copyrights for components of this work owned by others than ACM must be honored. Abstracting with credit is permitted. To copy otherwise, to republish, to post on servers or to redistribute to lists, requires prior specific permission and/or a fee.
WebMedia'12, October 15–18, 2012, São Paulo, Brazil.
Copyright 2012 ACM 978-1-4503-1706-1/12/10 $15.00

Quality of Service (QoS) and *Quality of Context* (QoC)[1] attributes. The literature presents many workflow-based platforms for Ubiquitous Computing [6, 7, 8, 9], but they do not provide service composition and selection mechanisms based on quality metadata. Moreover, such platforms have limited support for heterogeneity since they are not able to access different context-provision middleware in a transparent and uniform way.

In short, OpenCOPI provides: (i) an automatic Web service composition and selection mechanisms; (ii) a standardized communication model and an ontology-based context model, so that the applications must deal only with the abstractions provided by OpenCOPI, and; (iii) a fault-tolerance mechanism [10] that is able to deal with service failures. In this paper, we present and evaluate the semantic Web services composition and selection mechanisms provided by OpenCOPI. The service integration through composion is crucial to make easier the development of applications, thus enabling the use of services from several providers in a transparent and automatic way. Therefore, the applications become independent from the underlying context-provision platforms.

This paper is structured as follows. Section 2 describes a motivational example of ubiquitous application. Section 3 presents an overview about OpenCOPI. Section 4 presents the workflow specification, service compostion, selection, and execution processes. Section 5 discusses about the evaluation of the processes presented in Section 4. Section 5 presents related works. Finally, Section 7 presents final remarks.

2. MOTIVATIONAL EXAMPLE

In order to clarify the need of a platform like OpenCOPI, we use an ubiquitous application from the gas and oil industry as our motivational example. This application monitors an oil well in production through a pumping unit machine to detect the need of changing the pumping unit configuration. These modifications may be necessary to increase the oil production and/or decrease the abrasion of the equipment. Depending on the situation, the application can trigger actions to make changes in the configuration or directly notify the human responsible for taking decisions about the pump unit reconfiguration. This application was chosen because it uses different types of context information provided by many sources. To exemplify the use of OpenCOPI in the context of this application, we monitor the *burden* of the pump unit, which denotes the charge of oil extracted from a well at each cycle of movement of the pump unit. Each pump unit has a specific maximum value (*maxBurden*) of burden for its correct operation. If this value is abruptly reached, then the pumping unit operation must be quickly stopped to prevent its damage (a reactive strategy). Furthermore, there is an intermediary value (*intermValue*), in which actions may be taken (in a proactive way) to prevent the pump unit to be stopped, consequently avoiding loss of production and risks to the equipment. Each one of these actions may be performed by more than one service and those services may be provided by different service providers.

The *OilExploration* context ontology (Figure 1) describes concepts regarding oil exploration environments. In the context ontology, these concepts are classified as *tasks* and *objects* related to the oil exploration domain. A *task–object* relationship denotes an *activity* that can be used by the applications. For instance, the *Subscribe* task is associated with the *Burden*, *BSW*, and *LimitOilFlow* objects. Thus, applications may include activities such as a subscription to receive notifications about the burden of a pump unit (*Subscribe, Burden*). Another example is the relationship between the *Send* task and the *SMS* and *Email* object.

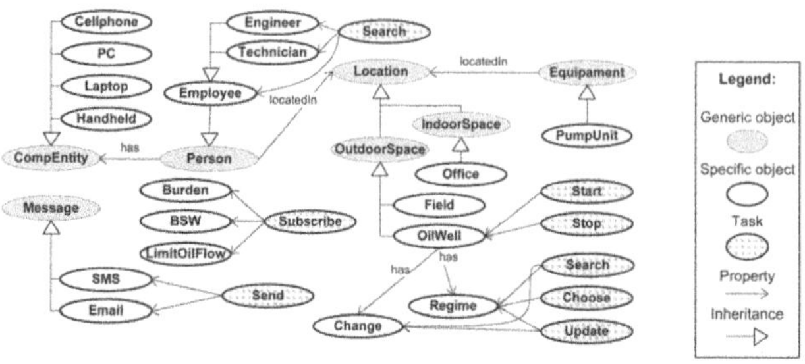

Figure 1. Description of the *OilExploration* domain ontology.

Such relationship means that it is possible to specify activities such as sending a SMS or an e-mail. Figure 2 shows the workflow that represents the motivational application in which each activity is performed at least by one service. The execution starts in the first activity, *SubscribeBurden*, which is related to a subscription to monitor the value of the pump unit burden. If the current burden value is between the pump unit's intermediary burden value and the maximum value, then the workflow follows *Flow1*. If the burden value is greater than the maximum value, then the workflow follows *Flow2*. *Flow1* encompasses activities to automatically change the *regime* (relation between the length of the pump unit's stem and its frequency in cycles per minute) of the pump unit. First, the *SearchRegimeOptions* activity looks for possible regimes of the pumping unit operation, in which each regime variable is composed of a stem length value and cycles per minute value. Then, the *searchPreviousChanges* activity finds the regimes previously used in this pumping unit. Next, the regime is changed (*ChangeRegime* activity) and this information is updated (*UpdateRegime* activity) in the registry of changes. Finally, it is performed a search for available technicians (*SearchTechnicians* activity) in the vicinity of the oil well and a message is sent to them (*SendMsgToEmployees* activity). Thus, they can check if ev-

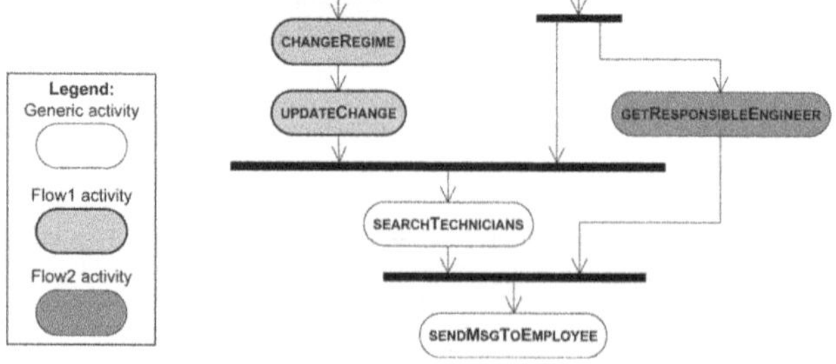

Figure 2. Workflow of the motivational example.

[1] QoC stands for any information that describes the quality of a context information, e.g. precision, probability of correctness, resolution, up-to-dateness, etc. [5].

erything is running as expected. In turn, *Flow2* describes the situation in which the burden is greater than the maximum limit of the pumping unit. To avoid damage to the pump unit, the operation of the well is stopped (*StopOilWellOperation* activity). Next, a search is performed to find the engineer that is responsible for this oil well (*GetResponsibleEngineer* activity) and the technicians near to the oil well (*SearchTechnicians* activity). Finally, warning messages are sent to them (*SendMsgToEmployees* activity).

Figure 3 presents the interaction among the application, OpenCOPI, and the underlying service providers (including context-provision middleware). *WellDatabase*[2] provides information about oil wells, being responsible for synchronously and asynchronously providing the current oil burden in each pump unit. This service performs the first workflow activity (*SubscribeBurden*). *BMDimensioner* is a platform that provides services to manage the configuration of the pump unit's operation regime. The services provided by this platform are responsible for presenting possible pump unit configurations and changing them (e.g. switching an operation regime to another one or stopping the pump unit operation). They are able to perform the *SearchRegime*, *ChangeRegime*, and *StopOilWellOperation* activities. *ChangeControlSystem* stores and retrieves configuration changes performed at the oil exploration equipment. In this case study, this system retrieves which regimes were already used in each pump unit. This system performs the *SearchPreviousChanges* and *UpdateChange* activities.

The *WifiLocalizationMiddleware*, *GPSLocalizationMiddleware*, and *CellularLocalizationMiddleware* plaforms are responsible for for providing the location of technicians spread over the oil field. Although they have the same functionality, each platform has a different quality level (QoS and QoC) and their quality will influence the selection of the service composition. Services provided by these platforms perform the *SearchTechnicians* activity. *HRDatabase* is a system that provides employees information, e.g. which employees are working at a given time. This system performs the *GetResponsibleEngineer* activity. Finally, *GSMPlatform* and *MailPlatform* provide services are used to send messages to employees. As well as location platforms, these platforms provide services with different quality level, thus performing the *SendMessageToEmployee* activity.

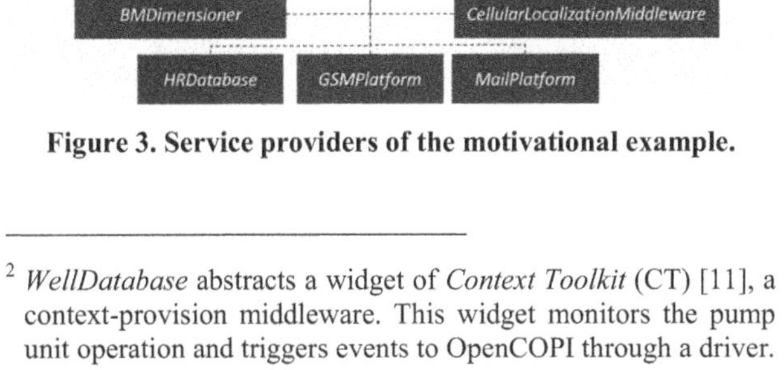

Figure 3. Service providers of the motivational example.

[2] *WellDatabase* abstracts a widget of *Context Toolkit* (CT) [11], a context-provision middleware. This widget monitors the pump unit operation and triggers events to OpenCOPI through a driver.

3. OPENCOPI: AN OVERVIEW

This Section presents OpenCOPI, a platform at the middleware level that integrates different service providers including, but not limited to, context-provision middleware platforms to make easier the task of developing context-aware adaptive ubiquitous applications. OpenCOPI enables the collaboration of different service providers to reach a high-level goal, which is to supply value-added services and contextual data to ubiquitous.

OpenCOPI provides its own communication model and an OWL [12] ontology-based context model, in which context is handled by adopting the Semantic Web services perspective [13]. Under this perspective: (i) service providers publish their services using the OWL-S language [14]; (ii) ubiquitous applications are services consumers; and (iii) OpenCOPI is a mediator that provides uniform acces to services used by ubiquitous applications. The adoption of an ontology-based context model leverages the interoperability among middleware platforms since ontologies enable knwoledgment sharing and prevent ambiguities [15]. Therefore, information received from other plaforms is translated to information that follows the ontology adopted by OpenCOPI, thus enabling applications only to know the unified context model.

OpenCOPI offers mechanisms for specifying and executing ubiquitous applications. Applications are specified through *semantic workflows*, which describe the abstract activities that represent the execution flow to reach the user goal, and each application has it own semantic workflow. A semantic workflow determines the sequence of abstract activities in terms of descriptions of semantic Web services. When specifying a semantic workflow, these activities are not linked to the services that would perform them since a semantic workflow is independent of specific concrete services, so that the link is made at the service composition phase. This approach of separating abstract activities from the concrete services able to perform them is useful mainly in cases in which there are several available similar services that are provided by different providers. In such cases, the service that best meets the user requirements can be chosen to be executed based on a given high level workflow activity.

Since a semantic workflow is an abstract representation of the execution flow, it is necessary to create at least one concrete specification for the workflow, which is called *execution plan* and contains a set of concrete, orchestrated Web services. Execution plans are built through an on-the-fly process of service discovery and composition according to the semantic enriched interface of the selected services and the semantic workflow specification. In fact, when a semantic workflow is executed, it is performed a search for Web services which are compatible with each workflow activity, i.e. services which have the same inputs, preconditions, outputs, and effects of the activity. If there is no service that performs the activity, the OpenCOPI's composition mechanism tries to compose a set of services to perform the activity. Thus, the discovered and composed services are combined in order to build one or more execution plans. The set of generated execution plans is represented as a directed acyclic graph (DAG) in which each intermediary node represents a specific service anc each directed edge represents the execution direction between two services. Each DAG starts with an *initial node* and a *final node*, which are nodes that not represent services, but are used to indicate the beginning and the end of the DAG. Thus, each complete path between the *initial node* and the *final node* represents a possible execution plans in the workflow, so that the DAG represents the workflow with all possible execution plans.

Figure 4 shows a DAG that represents eight possible execution plans regarding the workflow presented in Figure 2. It is possible to create these eight execution plans since two workflow activities are performed by more than one service. For example, the *SearchTechnicians* activity can be performed by the services provided by *GPSLocalizationMiddleware, WifiLocalizationMiddleware* and *CellularLocalizationMiddleware*, and the *SendMsgToEmployee* activity can be performed by *GSMPlatform* and *MailPlatform*. Therefore, the combination of these services can create six execution plans. In order to increase the number of execution plans to enable a better analysis of the selection process, we created a replica of the services provided by *GPSLocalizationMiddleware*. The replica and the original service have distinct quality metadada. Using this replica, there are eight different execution plans created by combining four localization services (*GPS* and *GPS2*, *Wifi* and *Cellular*, represented in Figure 4 by the *S7*, *S7'*, *S7''* and *S7'''*) and two messaging services (*SMS* and *Email*, represented in Figure 4 by *S8* and *S8'*). For example, one of the execution plans represented in Figure 4 is the execution plan that includes the services from *SubscribeBurdenAssync* (*S1*) to *UpdateChange* (*S6*), besides the GPS-based localization service (*S7* or *S7'*) and the SMS-based messaging service (*S8*). Due to space restrictions, we omit the intermediary services, i.e. the services between the *SubscribeBurdenAssync* (*S1*) and *UpdateChange* (*S6*) services.

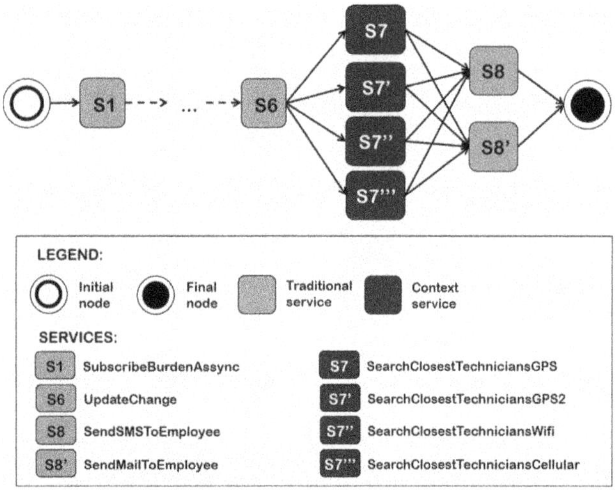

Figure 4. DAG representing the execution plans for the workflow depicted in Figure 2.

Since more than one execution plan is created, one of them must be selected. This selection is based on quality parameters regarding these services (QoS and QoC, for context services). Therefore, it is possible to select the service with the best QoS and QoC parameters among the several available services that provide the same functionality.

3.1 Architecture

OpenCOPI architecture encompasses two layers (Figure 5), namely *ServiceLayer* and *UnderlayIntegrationLayer*. *ServiceLayer* is responsible for managing abstractions of services (OWL-S descriptions) supplied by service providers. The components of *ServiceLayer* use such abstractions to support workflow creation and execution, service selection, service composition and adaptation. In addition, they support context reasoning, context storage, among other functionalities related to ubiquitous applications. These applications should implement the *IApp* interface to communicate with the OpenCOPI's *AppFacade*, which is responsible for receiving requests from the applications and forwarding them to the components of *ServiceLayer*. In turn, *UnderlayIntegrationLayer* is responsible for integrating service providers (mainly, but not only context-provision middleware), thus performing context conversion whenever it is necessary (from the middleware context model to the OpenCOPI one) and communication protocol conversion. The *IUnderlayIntegration* interface links service providers and OpenCOPI's *UnderlayIntegrationLayer*. This paper presents just the components related to the service composition and selection processes.

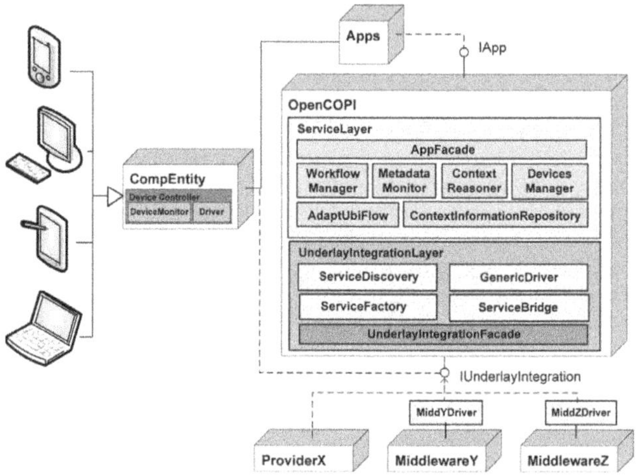

Figure 5. OpenCOPI architecture.

The *WorkflowManager* component manages workflows and is composed of the four following (sub)components, which provide support for specifying semantic workflows and generating execution plans. The *ServiceManager* component is responsing for importing OWL-S descriptions from service providers to OpenCOPI and validating such descriptions, and for proving capabilities to search for basic concepts in the knowledge base (ontology) using inputs, outputs, preconditions and effects of the available semantic Web services. *SemanticComposer* is responsible for discovering and composing Web services according to the semantc workflow specifications, i.e. it makes the mapping between abstract activities and Web services. First, it tries to discover the services (among those available at the *SemanticServicesRepository*) that can be used to compose the execution plan, given the goals in the workflow specification. Next, it tries to combine the discovered services in order to consume all inputs and preconditions and to produce all outputs and effects in the workflow specification. Then, the combined services are organized by the *SemanticComposer* according to the message flow between outputs of a service and inputs of the subsequent service. The *SemanticServicesRepository* component stores both the ontologies that describe Web services and execution plans. Finally, the *WorkflowExecutor* component supports the workflow execution. It receives the execution plan selected by the *AdaptUbiFlow* component considering QoS and QoC parameters of the services that compose each execution plan, as detailed in Section 4. At runtime, *WorkflowExecutor* executes the selected execution plan by making calls to the services provided by the underlying context-provision middleware.

MetadataMonitor is responsible for gathering metadata about the services and context provided by underlying middleware to feed the *ContextInformationRepository*. OpenCOPI adopts an SLA (*Service-Level Agreements*) [16] approach in which service providers publish the quality metadata of their services and these metadata are used to select the services to be provided to the consumers. If these metadata are not published, *MetadataMonitor* tries to assess them by invoking the services provided by underlying middleware. Details about this process are out of scope of this work.

AdaptUbiFlow component [12] is responsible for the selection and adaptation processes in OpenCOPI. After creating execution plans, *AdaptUbiFlow* selects the best execution plan (with the highest quality) to be executed. In addition, *AdaptUbiFlow* is responsible for performing an *adaptation process* in the workflow execution, thus meaning to replace the previously selected execution plan for another one, in which this new plan must meet the goals of applications specified in the workflow. This component directly works with the *MetadataMonitor* and *WorkflowManager* components to identify a fault and automatically change the execution flow in order to use another execution plan. Therefore, *WorkflowManager* and *AdaptUbiFlow* components are responsible for supporting the workflow specification and the composition, selection and execution processes.

4. FROM THE WORKFLOW SPECIFICATION TO ITS EXECUTION

This section presents the activities performed from the semantic workflow specification until its execution, also encompassing the composition, selection, and execution processes, as described in the following subsections.

4.1 Semantic workflow specification

OpenCOPI enables users to build semantic workflow even they are not familiar with the vocabulary of the process to be modelled. By using an assistant provided by OpenCOPI, the user can select the activities used for describing the application and identify the desired inputs, outputs, preconditions and effects (IOPEs) for each activity. The assistant also enables the user to specify some preferences, e.g. weights assigned to quality parameters at the selection phase.

The semantic workflow specification consists of describing the activities of a business process through the combination between a *task* and an *object* (classes in the context model). The assistant enables the user to select these activies without the need of creating each of them since they are already pre-defined according to the set of *tasks* and *objects* [17] specified in the context ontology. These activities are abstract, thus meaning that the binding to the concrete services that will perform the activity is done at runtime. The assistant shows a list of possible *tasks* and a list of possible *objects*, from which the user can select a <*task*, *object*> tuple (e.g. <*Choose*, *RegimeOption*>, <*Send*, *Message*>) to describe each activity of a semantic workflow. The assistant also shows the list of possible IOPEs related to each specified activity and that should be added to the activity definition. Thus, the user describes only the abstract activities of the workflow, so that when executing the workflow, OpenCOPI performs inferences on the ontologies to discover which services perform each workflow activity and composes the possible execution plans with these discovered services.

Figure 6 shows the process of creating workflow activities. The user requests, via OpenCOPI's GUI, the creation of a new activity. The request is received by the *WorkflowManager* component, which is responsible for creating and editing the workflow. This component asks the *ServiceManager* component for the list of possible tasks. Then, *ServiceManager* recovers the concepts described in the domain ontology stored in the *SemanticServiceRepository* component by loading all concepts in memory and returning the list of tasks and respective objects (objects related with each task) to the *WorkflowManager* component. Next, this component shows these concepts for the user, which selects the desired task and the object (e.g. the *Subscribe* task and the *Burden* object), so that this tuple is sent to *WorkflowManager*. Then, *WorkflowManager* asks the *ServiceManager* component for the list of respective IOPEs of this activity. With the concepts in memory, the *ServiceManager* returns the list of possible IOPEs for the *WorkflowManager*, which forwards this list to the user. Then, the user selects which IOPEs should be considered for this activity, thus finishing the process of including an activity. This process is repeated for each activity of the workflow.

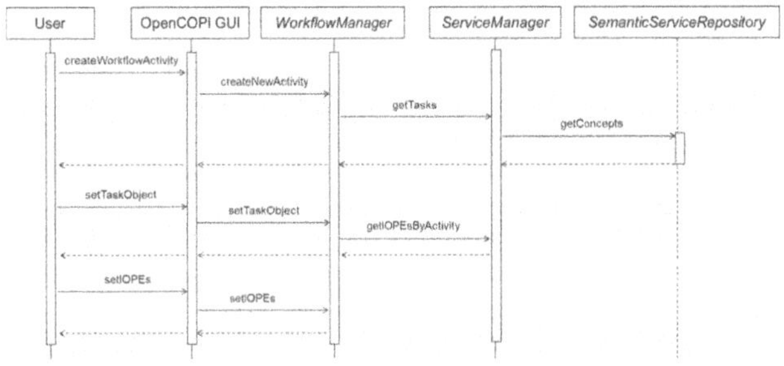

Figure 6. Process of creating a workflow activity.

OpenCOPI assistant also allows the use of flow control connectors (condition, repetition, etc.) in the semantic workflow specification. Figure 7 presents the assistant screenshot in which three activities have already been added to the workflow and the activity *Choose_RegimeOption* composed by the *Choose* task and the *RegimeOption* object is being added. Figure 7 also presents a screenshot showing that the user selected two inputs (*RegimeList* and *ChangeList*) and one output (*Regime*) for the current activity.

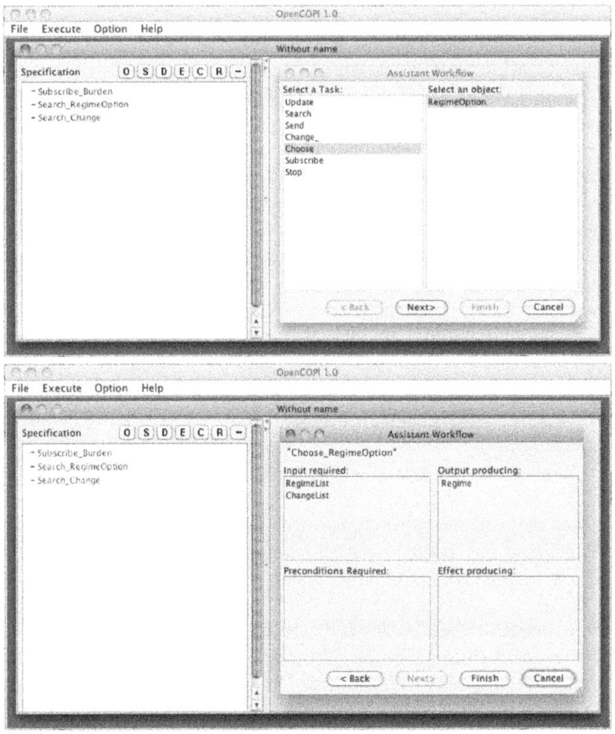

Figure 7. Assistant for creating a workflow.

4.2 Composition: Creating execution plans

Once the workflow is completed, the next step is the creation of the execution plans by the *SemanticComposer* component. First, this component discovers which registered services can be used to satisfy the activity's IOPEs. Next, it matches the selected services in order to consume inputs, produce outputs, and meets preconditions and effects of each workflow activity, so that a workflow activity may be performed by a service composed of atomic services as well as a single service may perform more than one activity. Finally, *SemanticComposer* orders the services of each created execution plan by following the sequence of activities defined in the workflow specification (service orchestration). OpenCOPI uses the matching algorithm presented by Mendes et al. [18] that composes Web services from a semantic workflow specification taking into account the required inputs and pre-conditions and the produced outputs and effects regarding each activity. With these lists, OpenCOPI generates the possible execution plans. In the presented case study, each one of these execution plans was naes as *EP1*, *EP2*, ..., *EP8* to facilitate the explanation of the evaluation. Table 1 shows the services that are different in the execution plans. The services that perform the other activities are the same for all execution plans since there is only one available service for each of these activities.

Table 1. Execution plans for the motivational example.

EPs	Distinct services in the execution plans
EP1	*SearchTechnicians**GPS**, Send**SMS**ToEmployee*
EP2	*SearchTechnicians**GPS2**, Send**SMS**ToEmployee*
EP3	*SearchTechnicians**GPS**, Send**Mail**ToEmployee*
EP4	*SearchTechnicians**GPS2**, Send**Mail**ToEmployee*
EP5	*SearchTechnicians**Wifi**, Send**SMS**ToEmployee*
EP6	*SearchTechnicians**Wifi**, Send**Mail**ToEmployee*
EP7	*SearchTechnicians**Cellular**, Send**SMS**ToEmployee*
EP8	*SearchTechnicians**Cellular**, Send**Mail**ToEmployee*

4.3 Execution plan selection

OpenCOPI selects execution plans according to quality metadata (QoS and/or QoC parameters) regarding the services that compose the execution plan. Although we have defined a built-in set of parameters, new parameters can be added to this set and others can be removed from it. OpenCOPI considers the following QoS parameters: (i) *Response time*, which represents the time between sending a service request to a service provider and receiving the response; (ii) *Availability*, which represents the probability that the service provider is up and the service is running, i.e. if the service is ready for immediate use, and; (iii) *Performance*, which describes the number of service requests fulfilled by the service provider at a given period of time. Moreover, OpenCOPI considers the following QoC parameters, as proposed by Buchholz et al. [6]: (i) *Correctness*, which denotes the probability that a piece of context information is correct (since internal problems in a temperature sensor can generate wrong temperature values, for example), and; (ii) *Freshness*, which represents the time elapsed between the generation of context data and the retrieval of this data by applications, so that a particular context data may be prioritized if is is newer than other similar data.

4.4 Aggreggation functions

The process of selecting an execution plan begins with the calculation of the quality of each plan. The quality of an execution plan is determined by quality (QoS and QoC) parameters values of all services contained in the execution plan. Before computing the execution plan quality, it is necessary to compute the *global quality* of each quality parameter. Global quality of a parameter means the quality parameter value for the whole execution plan, i.e. the value that represents the parameter of all services of this execution plan. The global quality of each parameter can be computed by aggregating the corresponding values for such parameter of all services in the respective execution plans. Different aggregation functions [19, 20] are necessary to compute the global value of each parameter. Typical quality parameter aggregation functions are addition, multiplication, minimum, and average relation. For instance, *Response time* is the QoS parameter used to measure the response time to execute each service. Thus, the value of the *Response time* parameter for an execution plan *EP* ($q_{EP(R)}$) is the sum of the *Response time* values of all servicess ($q_{R(s)}$) that compose *EP*. The *Availability* QoS parameter can be aggregated ($q_{EP(A)}$) through a multiplication function of the availability value of each services of the execution plan *EP* ($q_{A(s)}$). The *Performance* QoS parameter describes the number of service requests served by the service provider at a given period of time. Thus, the performance of an execution plan *EP* ($q_{EP(P)}$) is limited to the service with the smaller value for *Performance* attribute. *Freshness* QoC parameter describes the context information life span, i.e. how long time ago the context information was created. Thus, the value of this QoC parameter for an execution plan *EP* ($q_{F(s)}$) is the average of context life span of all services of *EP*. Similar to the *Availability* parameter, the aggregation function for the *Correctness* parameter is also a multiplication; however it refers to the correctness level of context information provided by the execution plan's services ($q_{C(s)}$).

4.5 Normalization of quality parameters

Once the value of all global (or aggregated) quality parameters were calculated, and considering that different quality parameters have different units and ranges, it is necessary to *normalize* these attributes into the same range to allow a unified and uniform measurement of the quality of the execution plans. Some quality parameters could be *positive*, i.e., a parameter in which the quality is better if the value is greater (for example, *Correctness* parameter). Other parameters are *negative*, i.e. the quality is better if the quality value is smaller (for example, the *Response time* parameter)[3]. This quality parameters normalization process is used by several authors [19, 20, 21].

Equations 1 and 2 present the formula used to normalize positive and negative parameters, respectively. In these equations, q_{Ni} is the normalized value of the parameter *i*, q_i is the global value of this parameter for the current execution plan, and q_{max} and q_{min} are respectively the minimum and the maximum global values of this parameter for all considered execution plans (if $q_{max} = q_{min}$, then $q_{Ni} = 1$). In this process, each normalized value results in a value between 0 and 1.

(1) $$q_{Ni} = \frac{q_i - q_{max}}{q_{max} - q_{min}}, q_{max} \neq q_{min}$$

(2) $$q_{Ni} = \frac{q_{max} - q_i}{q_{max} - q_{min}}, q_{max} \neq q_{min}$$

4.6 Utility of execution plans

The normalization process is followed by a weighting process to consider the user priority and preferences. Thus, users can prioritize some quality parameters and minimize the importance of

[3] We **are not** saying that the values are negative.

other quality parameters according to their needs. To do this, the user assigns a weight w_i to each quality parameter i, which must be between 0 and 1 and the sum of all of these weights must be 1. Equation 3 presents the function to calculate the execution plan quality (q_{EP}) according to a set of QoS and QoC parameters. In this formula, q_{EP} is the quality of the execution plan and it is calculated through a weighted sum between these normalized values (q_{Ni}) according each quality parameter i ($1 \leq i \leq m$) and its respective weight (w_i).

(3) $$q_{EP} = \sum_{i=1}^{m} (q_{Ni} * w_i)$$

At the selection phase, the *utility* of each execution plan is just the quality of the respective execution plan, so that the exection plan with the highest quality is selected.

4.7 Execution

After selecting an execution plan, it is started. Executing a plan means invoking each service that compose it according to the execution process defined in the workflow that have originated this selected execution plan. Thus, OpenCOPI orchestrates the invocation of each service.

5. EVALUATION

The evaluation presented in this paper is twofold. The first evaluated aspect is the execution plan *selection*, which is based on QoS and QoC parameters of each service that compose each execution plan. The second evaluated aspect is the overhead generated by OpenCOPI. This overhead is natural since OpenCOPI introduces an abstraction layer between middleware platforms and applications. This evaluation uses the motivational example presented in Section 2.

5.1 Evaluation of execution plan selection

The evaluation was performed in order to confirm the selection of the best execution plan according to different configurations in terms of prioritizing the weights regarding the quality parameters. Two or more execution plans within the same workflow may differ from each other only in a few services, so that the calculations in the selection process are really influenced by the services that differentiate an execution plan from another one. For instance, an execution plan *EP1* may differ from another execution plan *EP2* only in terms of one service, which will make a substantial difference in the final quality of these execution plans. Therefre, the quality (QoS/QoC) metadata regarding the services were populated with ficticious values (see Table 2 and Table 3) in order to verify which execution plan would be selected for each tested prioritization configuration. For this evaluation, the motivational example presented in Section 2 contains eight possible execution plans (each one named as *EP1*, *EP2*, ..., *EP8*), which differ from each other in terms of combinations of four possible localization services (*Wifi*, *Cellular*, *GPS* e *GPS2*[4]) and two messaging services (*SMS* and *Email*).

The execution plans were submitted to the selection algorithm considering the metadata of each service. After calculating the global value of each parameter for each one of the eight execution plans, these values were normalized, so that all parameters are re-

Table 2. QoS metadata for traditional and context services.

Services	*Availability*	*Performance*	*Response time*
SubscribeBurdenAssync	2	1	3
SearchRegimeOptions	2	1	3
SearchPreviousChanges	2	1	3
ChooseRegimeOptions	3	1	1
ChangeRegime	2	1	3
UpdateChange	2	1	3
SearchTechniciansGPS	9	8	4
SearchTechniciansGPS2	9	6	4
SearchTechniciansCellular	4	2	7
SearchTechniciansWifi	8	3	6
SendSMSToEmployees	7	7	9
SendMailToEmployees	9	5	7

Table 3. QoC metadata for context services.

Services	*Correctness*	*Freshness*
SubscribeBurdenAssync	5	2
SearchTechniciansGPS	10	2
SearchTechniciansGPS2	9	2
SearchTechniciansCellular	7	6
SearchTechniciansWifi	5	5

presented in an adimentional way. Table 4 shows the utility of the execution plans for different prioritization configurations for the quality parameters. For instance, the execution plan *EP1* is selected when all parameters have the same prioritization, while the execution plan *EP4* is selected when only the *Availability* parameter is prioritized. The execution plan *EP5* is selected when only the *Response time* parameter is prioritized, and the execution plan *EP7* is selected when the parameters *Availability* and *Response time* have the same prioritization (0.5). The values highlighted in Table 4 refer to the highest utility for each tested configuration. The selection process was performed as expected, *always* selecting the best execution plan.

Table 4. Utility of execution plans (EPs) for each configuration.

EPs	Same priority ($w = 0.2$)	*Availability* ($w = 1.0$)	*Responsing* ($w = 1.0$)	*Availability/ Responsing* ($w = 0.5$)
EP1	0,785	0,528	0,400	0,464
EP2	0,772	0,660	0,000	0,530
EP3	0,766	0,830	0,400	0,415
EP4	0,760	1,000	0,000	0,500
EP5	0,515	0,528	0,800	0,664
EP6	0,496	0,830	0,400	0,615
EP7	0,480	0,000	1,000	0,500
EP8	0,430	0,150	0,600	0,375

5.2 Overhead in OpenCOPI

The overhead generated by OpenCOPI was also evaluated under three aspects: (i) composition; (ii) selection, and; (iii) execution. Some overhead was expected since an additional abstraction layer was inserted between ubiquitous applications and services provided by several underlying platforms, thus increasing the response time to the users. Therefore, it is important to measure the impact of OpenCOPI in the application execution time. Furthermore, it is important to relate this overhead time with the benefits propitiated by OpenCOPI in terms of implementation and execution of ubiquitous applications.

In order to evaluate the overhead of the composition and selection processes, it was considered a single workflow and the amount of possible execution plans for this workflow was varied in eight,

[4] *GPS2* is a replica of the GPS-based location service (*GPS*). However, these services have distinct quality metadata.

six, four and two execution plans by considering all available services in the motivational example. To decrease from eight to six execution plans, the *SearchTechniciansCellular* service was removed from the OpenCOPI service repository since this service performs the *SearchTechnicians* activity in two execution plans. This process was repeated to the *SearchTechniciansWifi* and *SearchTechniciansGPS2* services in order to have four and two available execution plans. The conducted experiments were carried out on Mac OS X operating system, using a computer with processor Intel® Core^{TM} 2 Duo 2.4 GHz and 4 GB of RAM.

Figure 8 illustrates the average overhead (in miliseconds with a confidence interval of 95%) regarding the composition (Figure 8.A) and selection (Figure 8.B) processes. As the composition mechanism discovers services to perform each workflow activity and then creates the possible execution plans, this process is more computationally expensive since it requires analyzing the ontologies of each available service in the service repository. However, we can observe in the results that the time spent for the composition process is not relevant since it transforms an abstract specification (semantic workflow) in compositions of concrete services (execution plans), thus enabling a dynamic service selection and decoupling the applications form the used services. For the simplest configuration (two possible execution plans), the time spent in the semantic composition was 1008 ms on average to build both execution plans, and for the most complex configuration (eight possible execution plans) it was 1286 ms on average. The process of selecting an execution plan is cheaper. For several executions for each configuration and considering a confidence interval of 95%, the average times spent for the simplest and the more complex configurations were 2 ms and 6 ms, respectively.

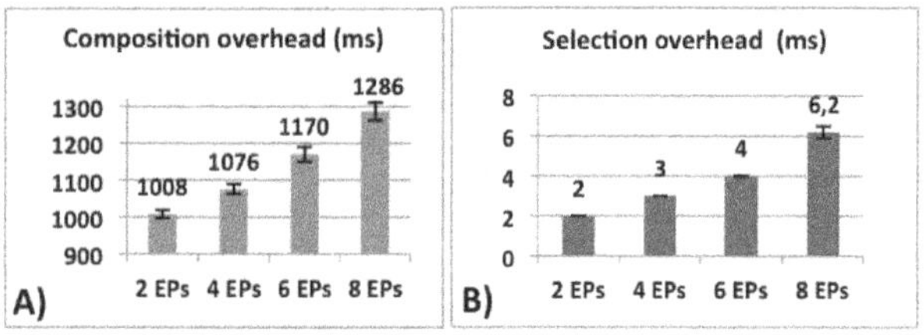

Figure 8. Overhead of the composition and selection processes.

Another aspect analyzed in the evaluation was the application execution time. Since OpenCOPI represents an additional layer between ubiquitous applications and services provided by many platforms, it is expected that the use of OpenCOPI increases the overall processing time and therefore the response time for users. Thus, it is important to measure the impact of OpenCOPI in the application execution time and if this impact is either significant or negligible from the point of view of the user's experience. For this purpose, two versions of the case study were built. The first one considered the specification and execution of a workflow using OpenCOPI, while the second one directly invokes the same services through Java source code in the same sequence followed by the workflow executed by OpenCOPI. The average execution time of the application without OpenCOPI was 1.2 s to call all services involved in the case study. In the application that uses OpenCOPI, the execution time increased to 1.9 s. According to Nah [22], the difference (about 0.7 s) between these two versions was not significant for this kind of application. Moreover, the second version does not take advantage on the benefits provided by OpenCOPI. For instance, to build the application without OpenCOPI, 139 lines of code (LOC) were necessary only to call all services specified in the workflow. However, the process to build the workflow using OpenCOPI is simpler since it was not necessary to implement source code but only to build the workflow by defining the applications activities, combining *tasks* and *objects* to satisfy the application goal. Moreover, without OpenCOPI, it is essential to know the services available in the environment and their interfaces. Consequently, the development is harder, reuse is laborious, and it is difficult to dynamically select services and also to support adaptation

6. RELATED WORKS

Several workflow-based middleware platforms have emerged over the last years to assist the development of ubiquitous applications. However, most of them do not meet the wide range of requirements demanded by highly dynamic and heterogeneous ubiquitous environments. In general, these proposals do not allow dynamic and semantic service composition based on several quality metadata parameters.

Ranganathan and McFaddin [6] present a workflow approach for modelling and managing the user interaction with the ubiquitous environment. In such approach, users can determine their overall goal and preferences and the system generates a customized workflow describing how various services should interact with one another. Montagut and Molva [7] present an architecture that supports the distributed execution of workflows in pervasive environments based on decentralized control. Both proposals lack mechanisms to allow dynamic service composition and workflow adaptation.

Tang et al. [8] present a context-adaptive workflow management algorithm, which can dynamically adjust workflow execution policies in terms of current context information and supports service selection based in bandwidth and user location. Finnaly, Mostarda et al. [9] present a workflow management approach that matches orchestration and choreography in ubiquitous environments. However, this approach does not consider metadata quality when selecting the services that will compse the workflow, thus hampering the selection of services with better quality.

Unlike all the previously mentioned proposals, this paper investigates how to automatically manage workflows by semantically composing execution plans from abstract descriptions of the application activities and then automatically selecting one of the possible execution plans, which may be composed of services provided by several context-providion middleware. In OpenCOPI, this selection process is based on several quality parameters, and each one of them has its weight defined by the user.

7. FINAL REMARKS

This paper presented the service composition and selection process performed in OpenCOPI to make easier the development of ubiquitous applications and to enable the use of services provided by several context-provision middleware in a transparent and automatic way. We presented the workflow management process by detailing the activities performed from the semantic workflow specification until its execution, also encompassing the composition, selection, and execution processes. In addition, we conducted computational experiments to evaluate OpenCOPI under two distinct aspects: (i) selection of execution plans to show that the best execution plan was selected in all tested configurations in terms of weights regarding the quality parameters, and; (ii) the overhead introduced by OpenCOPI: this overhead is natural since OpenCOPI represents an additional abstraction layer between ubiquitous computing and underlying context-provision middleware. First, the selection mechanism was performed as expected always selecting the best exectution plan. Second, the time spent in the service composition and execution plan selection processes were very low. Moreover, the difference (0.7 s) between the application executing with OpenCOPI and the application developed using the Java programming language was not significant compared with the benefits propritiated by OpenCOPI since delays in the order of 1 s are acceptable for Web applications, as stated by Nah [22]. Finally, without OpenCOPI, it is essential to know the available services and their interfaces, thus making the development more complex and the reuse impraticable.

The execution plan selection process presented in Section 4 considers all services that compose all execution plans. Therefore, the selection overhead considerably increases when there is a high number of services since it is necessary to combine the services and then calculate all aggregated values for each quality parameter for each execution plan. In this perspective, we are currently developing a strategy that aims to reduce the number of services to be considered in the selection processing, thus making the aggregations faster. Such strategy consists of desconsidering services that would be in all execution plans and thus equally contribute in the aggregation calculations. Once this new selection algorithm is implemented, we will carry out new computational experiments comparing the performance of both algorithms.

8. ACKNOWLEDGMENTS

This work is partially supported by the Brazilian National Institute for Web Science Research (Web Science Brazil), founded by the Brazilian National Council for Scientific and Technological Development (CNPq) through the grant 557128/2009-9. Thais Batista, Flavia C. Delicato, and Paulo F. Pires are partially supported by CNPq through the grants 307269/2012-8, 311363/2011-3, and 311515/2009-6 (respectively). Flavia C. Delicato is also partially supported by CNPq through the grant 470586/2011-7.

9. REFERENCES

[1] Weiser, M. 1991. The computer of the Twenty-First Century. *Scientific American* 265, 3, 94-104.

[2] Judd, G., Steenkiste, P. 2003. Providing contextual information to Pervasive Computing applications. *Proc. of the First Int. Conf. on Pervasive Computing and Communications*. PERCOM'03. IEEE Computer Society, USA, 133-142.

[3] Erl, T. 2007. *SOA principles of service design*. Prentice Hall, USA.

[4] Abbasi, A., Shaikh, Z. 2009. A conceptual framework for smart workflow management. *Proc. of the Int. Conf. on Information Management and Engineering*. IEEE Computer Society, USA, 574-578.

[5] Buchholz, T., Küpper, A., Schiffers, M. 2003. Quality of Context: What it is and why we need it. *Proc. of the 10th Workshop of the HP OpenView University Association*.

[6] Ranganathan, A., McFaddin, S. 2004. Using workflows to coordinate Web services in Pervasive Computing environments. *Proc. of the IEEE Int. Conf. on Web Services*. IEEE Computer Society, USA, 288-295.

[7] Montagut, F., Molva, R. 2005. Enabling pervasive execution workflows. *Proc. of the Int. Conf. on Collaborative Computing: Network, Applications and Worksharing*. IEEE Computer Society, USA.

[8] Tang, F. et al. 2008. Towards context-aware workflow management for Ubiquitous Computing. *Proc. of the Int. Conf. on Embedded Software and Systems*. IEEE Computer Society, USA, 221-228.

[9] Mostarda, L., Marinovic, S., Dulay, N. 2010. Distributed orchestration of pervasive services. *Proc. of the 24th IEEE Int. Conf. on Advanced Inf. Networking and Applications*. IEEE Computer Society, USA, 166-173.

[10] Lopes, F. et al. 2011. AdaptUbiFlow: Selection and adaptation in workflows for Ubiquitous Computing. *Proc. of the 9th IEEE/IFIP Int. Conf. on Embedded and Ubiquitous Computing*. EUC 2011. IEEE Computer Society, USA, 63-71.

[11] Dey, A., Abowd, G., Salber, D. 2001. A conceptual framework and a toolkit for supporting the rapid prototyping of context-aware applications. *Human Computer Interaction* 16, 2, 97-166.

[12] OWL 2 Web Ontology Language. 2009. W3C. Available at: http://www.w3.org/TR/owl-overview/

[13] Martin, D. et al. 2004. Bringing semantics to Web services: The OWL-S approach. Proc. of the First International Workshop on Semantic Web Services and Web Process Composition. SWSWPC 2004. In *Lecture Notes in Computer Science*, J. Cardoso, A. Sheth, Eds. Springer-Verlag Berlin Heidelberg, Germany, 26-42.

[14] OWL-S: Semantic Markup for Web Services. W3C. Available et: http://www.w3.org/Submission/OWL-S/

[15] Gruber, T. 1993. A translation approach to portable ontology specifications. *Journal of Knowledge Acquisition* 5, 2, 199-220.

[16] Keller, A., Ludwig, H. 2003. The WSLA Framework: Specifying and monitoring Service-Level Agreements for Web Services. *Journal of Network and Systems Management* 11, 1, 57-81.

[17] Guarino, N. 1998. Formal ontology and information systems. *Proc. of the Int. Conf. on Formal Ontology and Information Systems*. FOIS'98. 3-15.

[18] Mendes, R. et al. 2011. Using Semantic Web to build and execute ad-hoc processes. *Proc. of the 9th IEEE/ACS Int. Conf. on Computer Systems and Applications*. AICCSA 2011. IEEE Computer Society, USA, 233-240.

[19] Alrifai, M., Skoutas, D., Risse, T. 2010. Selecting skyline services for QoS-based Web service composition. *Proc. of the 19th Int. Conf. on World Wide Web*. ACM, USA, 11-20.

[20] Yanwei, Z. et al. 2010. A dynamic Web services selection based on decomposition of global QoS constraints. *Proc. of the IEEE Youth Conference on Information Computing and Telecommunications*. IEEE Computer Society, USA, 77-80.

[21] Ardagna, D., Mirandola, R. 2010. Per-flow optimal service selection for Web services based process. *Journal of Systems and Software* 83, 8, 1512-1523.

[22] Nah, F. 2004. A study on tolerable waiting time: How long are Web users willing to wait. *Behavior and Information Technology* 23, 3, 153-16.

A Model for Context Awareness in Ubicomp

João Lopes, Rodrigo Souza, Cláudio Geyer
PPGC/INF/Federal University of Rio Grande do Sul
Porto Alegre-RS, Brazil
{jlblopes,rssouza,geyer}@inf.ufrgs.br

Cristiano Costa, Jorge Barbosa
PIPCA/University of the Vale do Rio dos Sinos
São Leopoldo-RS, Brazil
{cac,jbarbosa}@unisinos.br

Márcia Gusmão, Adenauer Yamin
PPGC/CDTec/Federal University of Pelotas
Pelotas-RS, Brazil
{mzgusmao,adenauer}@ufpel.edu.br)

ABSTRACT

In this paper we present a view of EXEHDA middleware and a novel service created for dynamic adaptation. EXEHDA is service-oriented, adaptive and was conceived to support the execution of ubiquitous applications. The main concept in the proposed design for the middleware and for the application is context awareness expressed in an adaptive behavior. The middleware manages and implements the *follow-me semantics* for ubiquitous applications. This is also a key to provide functionality adapted to the constraints and unpredictability of the large-scale environment. EXEHDA provides services for distributed adaptive execution, context recognition, ubiquitous storage and access, and anonymous and asynchronous communications. To evaluate the proposed service we developed a case study, implementing an application in medical area. Analyzing the results we can see that the users found the application easy to use and usefulness for health workers at a hospital.

Categories and Subject Descriptors

C.2.4 [**Computer Systems Organization**]: Computer-Communication Networks—*Distributed Systems*

Keywords

Ubiquitous Environment, Context Awareness, Context-aware Adaptation

1. INTRODUCTION

The field of Ubiquitous Computing (Ubicomp) presupposes the provision of computing environments with information and communication technology everywhere, for everyone, all the time. In this way, human beings will be citizens of both the physical world and the augmented reality that extends this world.

In Ubiquitous Computing, systems need to sense and adapt to the environment. They have to understand the context in which they are interested. This new class of computer systems, adaptive to the context, enables the development of richer applications, more elaborated and complex, exploiting mobility of the user and the dynamic nature of modern computing infrastructures. Nevertheless, the development of applications that continuously adapt to the environment and remain running even when the user is moving or switching device, remains an open research challenge [8].

We consider that a central issue in the context-aware adaptation is the degree of expressiveness that can be achieved in the description of contextual information. In that sense, the use of technologies to support semantic processing, such as ontologies, are suitable for supporting the reasoning services in the scope of ubiquitous applications [3] [4].

Ontologies can capture the full range of concepts involved in a complex environment, increasing the expressiveness of context information and providing support for reasoning [11]. In that sense, this article proposes an architectural model and an ontology-based semantic model.

The article is structured as follows. Section 2 outlines the EXEHDA Middleware software architecture. Section 3 describes the main features of the EXEHDA middleware. Section 4 discusses the EXEHDA middleware services. Section 5 details the context-aware adaptation in the EXEHDA middleware, introducing a service for dynamic adaptation control. In Section 5 we present a case study. Finally, related work and concluding remarks are presented in sections 6 and 7, respectively.

2. EXEHDA MIDDLEWARE SOFTWARE ARCHITECTURE

The foundation of our proposal is the EXEHDA Software Architecture, in which cells form a large-scale computing environment. These cells are composed of several mobile and stationary physical resources. The computing environment components (data, code, devices, services, and resources) are ubiquitous and managed by a middleware, which provides the ever-present access to them [2].

In this computing scenario, the mobile devices are more used as interfaces. They do not store neither code nor data persistently (except for some caching strategy), but operate as portals that obtain the code to be executed and that can transfer the execution to other devices using proximity or resource availability as a selection criteria. Furthermore,

Permission to make digital or hard copies of all or part of this work for personal or classroom use is granted without fee provided that copies are not made or distributed for profit or commercial advantage and that copies bear this notice and the full citation on the first page. To copy otherwise, to republish, to post on servers or to redistribute to lists, requires prior specific permission and/or a fee.
WebMedia'12, October 15–28, 2012, São Paulo/SP, Brazil.
Copyright 2012 ACM 978-1-4503-1706-1/12/10 ...$15.00.

each user has a virtual environment that can be accessed at any location, and with the available device. Moreover, the user's location in the environment has a significant effect in the way ubiquitous applications are executed. As the user moves physically, i.e. by carrying his current device - user mobility - or changing the device being used - terminal mobility, his currently running applications, in addition to the user's virtual environment, need to be continuously available to him, following the user's movements in the ubiquitous space. Such behavior defines what we call *follow-me semantics* of ubiquitous applications [9].

The main properties of EXEHDA applications are: distributed, mobile, adaptive and reactive to the context, and capable of expressing the follow-me semantics - the application follows the user in his movement at a large-scale space. The application's code is installed on-demand on the devices used and this installation is adaptive to context of each device [1].

The EXEHDA software architecture, shown in Figure 1, aims to provide an integrated solution to build and execute large-scale ubiquitous applications [2].

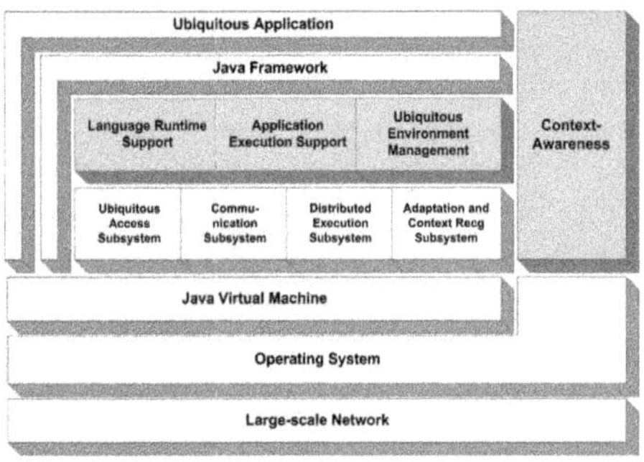

Figure 1: EXEHDA Software Architecture

3. EXEHDA MIDDLEWARE FEATURES

EXEHDA is based on services which contribute in three perspectives: (i) provide an ubiquitous environment management, through services to control the physical environment in which the processing will take place; (ii) support for execution of applications, by providing the services and abstractions needed to implement the follow-me semantics; and (iii) offers an API (Application Programming Interface) to foster ubiquitous application development.

The requirements of operation in a high heterogeneous environment, in which hardware capabilities and software availability on each device may vary, have motivated the use of pluggable services. In each node, a execution profile defines the loading policy that will be applied for each of the middleware services. This loading policy specifies one of two currently available modes: (i) bootstrap, meaning that the service should be loaded in the node startup process; or (ii) on demand, meaning that the service will be loaded in its first use.

The minimum core provides the loading policy for services and is included in each node that composes the ubiquitous environment. Using this feature, we can configure what is needed and when it should be loaded. However, there are two services that must always be present: (i) Profile Manager, in charge of interpreting the execution profiles, making these profiles available at runtime for the other middleware services; (ii) Service Manager, which activates services in anode based on the information provided by the Profile Manager. Service code is loaded on demand from a service repository, which may be local or remote depending on the device storage capacity and the nature of the service being loaded.

EXEHDA has the requirement of remaining operational during periods of planned disconnection. To support this feature, we split the services into two parts, a node instance and a cellular instance. The former is local to each device, while the latter executes in the base node. Hence, the local device will remain operational during the planned disconnection, regarding that the node instance of that service would temporary renounce the access to resources that are in the network. On the other hand, the cellular instance of the service, in execution on the base node of the cell, acts as a reference point for services that require distributed, internode or inter-cell, coordination procedures [1].

4. EXEHDA MIDDLEWARE SERVICES

EXEHDA is composed of several integrated services. An overview of these services is presented in this section. The middleware services are conceptually organized in subsystems: data and code ubiquitous access, uncoupled spatial and temporal communication, large-scale distribution, context recognition and adaptation. The subsystem integration is shown in Figure 2.

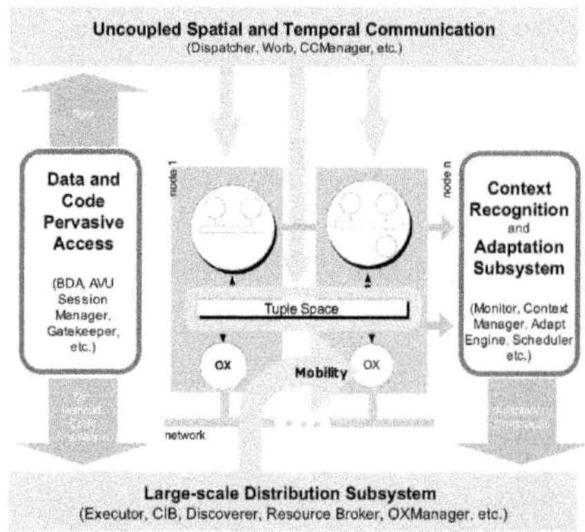

Figure 2: EXEHDA Subsystems

4.1 Multi-Level Communication Services

Regarding communications, EXEHDA currently provides, through the *Dispatcher*, *WORB*, and *CCManager* services, three types of communication primitives, each one addressing a distinct abstraction level.

The *Dispatcher Service* corresponds to the lowest abstraction level, providing message-based communications. Message delivering is done through per-application channels, which may be configured to ensure several levels of protection for the data being transmitted. Protection levels range from data integrity, using digital signatures, to privacy through encryption mechanisms. Additionally, the *Dispatcher Service* uses a checkpointing/recovery mechanism for the channels, which is activated when a planned disconnection is in course. This feature may or may not be activated by the upper communication layers depending on its particular demands.

In order to make the development of distributed services easier, EXEHDA also provides an intermediary solution for communications, based on Remote Method Invocations, through the *WORB Service*. The programming model is similar to Java RMI, but optimized to the ubiquitous environment. More specifically, WORB remote method invocations, differently from Java RMI, do not require that the device keep connected during the entire execution of the method on the remote node. Instead, WORB was built on the functionality provided by the Dispatcher Service, including a per-invocation ID. The invocation ID remains valid during the disconnection, allowing the WORB to re-sync with the remote node after reconnection and obtain the returned values from the invocation.

At a higher level, the *CCManager Service* provides tuple-space based communications. It builds on the *WORB Service*, which also handles planned disconnections, providing to applications an anonymous and asynchronous communication support. This model is provided in the *CCManager Service* and is better suited to scenarios that application components might migrate among nodes, since it does not require both sides to coexist at the same time for the communication to take place.

4.2 Management of Physical Resources

From the middleware point of view, ubiquitous environment resources fit in one of two categories: processing node or specialized resources. The former corresponds to the nodes, which effectively execute and whose access is managed by the middleware. The latter corresponds to unmanaged specialized devices, e.g. printers, scanners, etc., whose access is not done through one of the middleware services, but through the use of some specific libraries. Although unmanaged by EXEHDA, the specialized devices are also cataloged in the *CIB Service* in order to allow applications to locate and use them.

The *Discoverer Service* is in charge of finding specialized resources in the ubiquitous environment based on an abstract definition of the resource. Typically, this service interacts with the *CIB Service* from its own cell, aiming at satisfying the resource discovery request in the scope of the local cell. When the local resources fail to fulfill the request, the *Discoverer Service* interacts with the *Resource Broker service* of the neighbors cells. The strategy adopted in this extra-cell search is characteristic of the particular *Discoverer Service* instance in use. These services employ a language to describe resources and its interfaces are standardized. Since the Middleware do not manage specialized resources, the results of a *Discoverer Service* search do not imply resource allocation or even resource reservation.

4.3 Services to Build the Context Information

The *Monitor Service* implements a monitoring scheme based on sensors, which employs indexes to describe specific aspect of the environment. These sensors can be customized through parameters. The whole set of sensors installed on a node is part of the node description information registered in the *CIB Service*. The data generated by each sensor is gathered by the *Monitor Services*, which typically runs on the same node that sensors are installed. The gathered data is published by the *Monitor Service* to a *Collector Service*, which typically runs on the base-node.

Both the gathering of data by the sensors and the publication to the *Collector Service* by the Monitor occur in discrete multiples of a per-node configured *quantum*. The quantum parameter allows the resource owner to control, externally to the middleware, the degree of intrusion of the monitoring mechanism in the host. After a *quantum* of time expire, the *Monitor Service* executes a pooling operation over the active sensors in the node. Then, it applies the publishing criteria specified for the sensor data, determining, or not, the generation of a publishing event for that sensor. Thus, the events generated after a quantum expiration are grouped into a single message, reducing the amount of data that the Monitor has to transmit to the Collector.

The *Collector Service* aggregates information from several monitors in the cell and forwards them to the registered consumers. Among such consumers are other middleware services like the *Context Manager* and the *Dynamic Adaptation Service*.

5. DYNAMIC ADAPTATION CONTROL SERVICE

In order to increase the flexibility for specifying adaptations, the *DA Service* is proposed to allows an incremental development of specifications, which includes policies, rules, parameters, constraints, and adaptation actions. This feature enables reuse and customization of these specifications in the development of adaptive applications [17].

Another aspect is the utility function, which considers the parameters of adaptation and execution context, as well as user preferences. This function calculates the weighted sum of the differences between the parameters offered by the environment and required by the application, where the weights reflect the priorities of user needs. Within this model, the goal of *DA Service* can be formulated as a guarantee that at any time, the adaptation with the highest utility is performed and does not violate the resource constraints imposed by the environment.

5.1 Semantic Model

The semantic model proposed to *DA Service* includes an ontology, called OntUbi, which represents the ubiquitous environment. The OntUbi is composed by the following ontologies: (i) OntContext - Context Situation - it represents the collected contexts, notified contexts, and contexts of interest (see Figure 3); (ii) OntAdapt - Adaptation Policy - rules, parameters, operations and preferences, constraints and adaptation actions for the applications components.

In OntUbi, elements of context are entities and have three basic categories of information: (i) hardware resources: devices, peripherals and information of nodes and sensors, such as location, memory, battery, bandwidth, CPU load, among others; (ii) software resources: description of the operating system, middleware and applications, and adaptation policy; (iii) user resources: user profile and preferences.

The Adaptation Policy is in charge of registering the profiles of the application software components. This ontology consists of specifications rules that manage the adaptive behavior of application components.

In OntAdapt, we can set policies for various applications. Each application may consist of several compo-

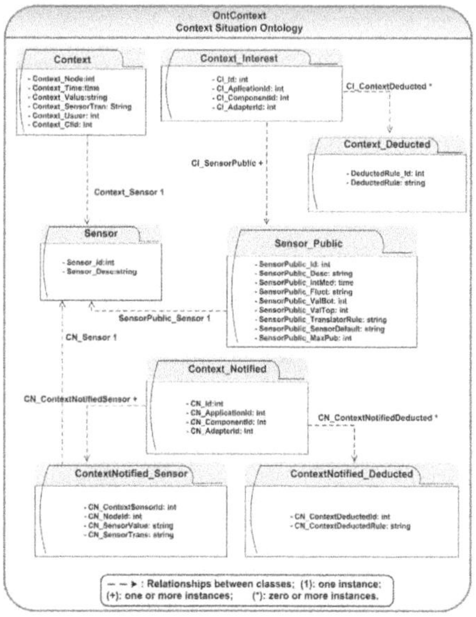

Figure 3: Context Situation Ontology

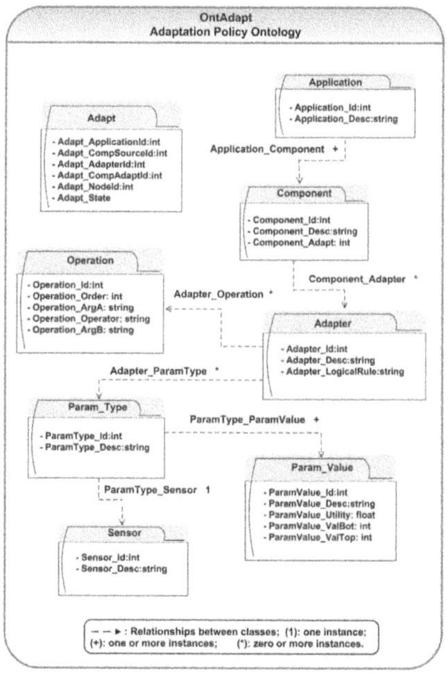

Figure 4: Adaptation Policy Ontology

nents, instances of relationship "Application_Component". Each component can have several adaptations, instances of the relationship "Component_Adapter". Each adaptation can have multiple parameters, instances of relationship "Adapter_ParamType". A parameter can have multiple instances of lower value, higher value, and utility value, which will be instances of the relationship "ParamType_ParamValue".

Figure 4 shows the attributes and relationships between classes of OntAdapt. This ontology is instantiated and maintained by the developer, using a framework, called FWADAPT. The programmer employs this framework, in development time, to instantiate the adaptation policy.

The main assumptions considered in the design of this framework were: (i) to be general, allowing different kind of applications follow the EXEHDA's programming model; (ii) to provide procedures for editing or extending definitions previously established in applications; (iii) to enable resources that foster the reuse of existing specifications to adaptations, rules, and operations.

5.2 Architectural Model

The design of the *DA Service* considers the following architectural features: (i) monitoring of context, which must be kept detached from the application, and executes through the use of reusable elements in the middleware; (ii) context processing, which executes in the middleware and must be extensible, supporting the inclusion of new elements of context and new ways of reasoning.

In the adaptation decision-making, the model considers three categories of information: (i) the context, based on monitored data, semantic information and inferences; (ii) the adaptation policy of the application; (iii) the user preferences.

The *DA Service* supports both functional (that selects the code being executed) and non-functional (related to scheduling and resource allocation) adaptations [2]. Moreover, the service includes a Multi-level Collaborative adaptation organized in two levels. At the application level, in development time, two approaches are provided: (i) creation of the following ontologies: Adaptation Policy and Context of Interest; (ii) programming of the adaptive commands in the software components. Furthermore, at the application level, at runtime, the middleware activates commands that trigger the EXEHDA adaptive services. At the same time, in the service level, the middleware makes the decision of adaptation, considering the state of the context, the adaptation policy, and of user preferences.

We present the definition of *DA Service* software architecture in Figure 5. The service is organized in the following modules:

- **Notified Contexts Handler**: this module receives the identification of notified contexts from the Context Recognition Subsystem. These contexts are accessed in order to define the possible interest of the application component, and the sensor values associated with it. This mechanism also deals with application policy, using the semantic processor, and accesses the information needed to determine the adaptation rule. In this module DA Service prepares all the needed information for deciding which adaptation to make.

- **Adapter Rules Processor**: this module produces a list with one or more actions to adapt, classified by criteria of utility. It infers the possible options for adaptive actions, using the adaptation rule and the parameters values used to evaluate it. Possible actions are classified using the utility function, from higher to lower use of adaptive action. Functional and non-functional adaptations are computed the same way, through the adaptation rule.

- **User Rules Processor**: this module accesses the user's preferences for the application in the User class on OntUbi. These preferences are sorted by utility value. This way, it selects the one with the highest utility value to the user, from the possible adaptive actions inferred in the previous module.

- **Inferred Adaptation Provider**: this module provides the information necessary for adaptation action, obtained from the previous module. The implementation of the adaptation is inserted into the code of the running component. At this moment, the *Executor Service* of the EXEHDA access the information for adaptation execution.
- **Semantic Processor**: this module accesses, instantiates, and infers the information needed to compute the adaptation rules. The product of these rules is delivered to the mechanism that makes the retention of the adaptation decisions for the applications components.

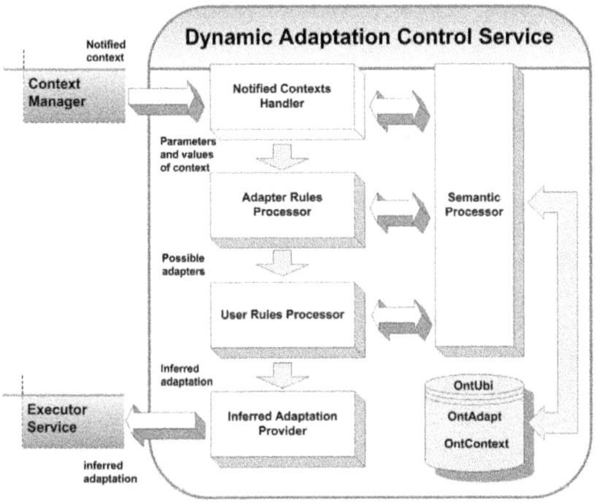

Figure 5: Software Architecture of the *DA Service*

6. CASE STUDY

The application developed uses the follow-me semantics and the context-aware adaptation, provided by the EXEHDA services, particularly the *DA Service* described in section 5. We defend a model of collaborative adaptation between application code and the execution system, as well as a semantic-oriented approach for dynamic adaptation. In that sense, the application was modeled considering these principles.

6.1 Ubiquitous Monitoring of Patients

The Ubiquitous Monitoring of Patients is an application targeted to the medical area. The functions are designed to explore the context-aware adaptation control promoted by the *DA Service*, considering the demands of ubiquitous behavior of this application.

The application uses a database created specifically for this case study. The values, alert levels, rules, and parameter adaptation are approximate averages, with no commitment to translate an accurate medical data. This is necessary to manipulate the data during the tests, avoiding the incursion at ethical aspects.

The proposition in this case study is to improve the monitoring of patients that require continuous observation, avoiding the need of admitting then in an Intensive Care Unit. The main objectives of this proposition are: (i) to show patient data, acquired dynamically using a mechanism of signals sensing; (ii) to present the different alert levels to health workers, such as physicians and nurses, in an automated way, based on the sensed data; (iii) to integrate the alerts service application in the open communication network (Google Talk); (iv) to provide access from both mobile devices and desktops; and (v) to enable health workers ubiquitous access to the history of sensed data of the patients.

The health workers can run two modules: (i) dynamic capture of patients' vital signs; and (ii) history of patients' alerts. The signals considered in this version are heart rate, blood pressure and temperature. Different alert levels to health workers are produced according to the values of the signal data. On the other hand, the history includes the date and time of the alert, its level, and the values of vital signs. This information assists the physician's decision-making regarding the patient's clinical status.

The application is designed to explore functional adaptations, managed by the *DA Service*. The adaptations are specified in the ontology OntAdapt, considering two situations: (i) the context data sensed from the patient (vital signs), determining the software component used to display the alert level; and (ii) the device (desktop, smartphone or tablet) used by the health workers, selecting the component with the most appropriate interface to the device.

To build the adaptation policy, considering the specifications provided by health workers, the application developer uses the framework FWADAPT, instantiating classes and relationships of the ontology OntAdapt, with their parameters and adaptation rules. The application is instantiated in the Application class and its software components in the Component classes of OntAdapt ontology. Furthermore, the components' adapters are instantiated in the ontology classes Adapter, Operation, Param_Type, Param_Value, and Sensor.

Figure 6 shows the values associated with the properties of the class Application and the software components instantiated in the class Component.

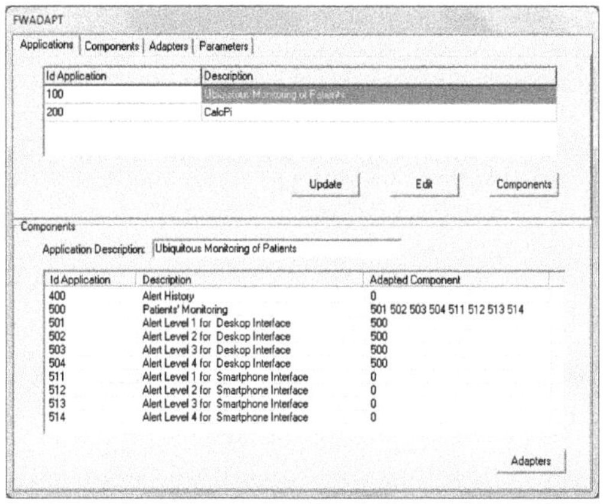

Figure 6: Application Components

The software component "Patient Monitoring (500)" can adapt to the component "501" to "514", depending on vital signs collected and the type of device used by health worker. The software component "500" is associated with adapters "Automatic Alert" and "Device Type". These adapters are related to certain types of parameters, for example, the adapter "Automatic Alert" is related to the parameters "Blood Pressure", "Temperature", and "Heart Rate".

Listing 1 shows an instance of the class "Adapter", in which the rule for determining the adapter "Automatic Alert" is specified. This rule uses information instantiated in the ontology "OntContext" by the Context Recognition Service and in the ontology "OntAdapt" by the framework FWADAPT. The module "Semantic Processor" handles this rule using SPARQL[1] and Jena API[2], and the result corresponds to the adaptive software component relative to the alert level.

Listing 1: Class "Adapter"

```
Adapter_Id = 1
Adapter_Desc = Automatic Alert
Adapter_LogicalRule = (ROUND ((CN_ContextNotifiedSensor.
     CN_SensorTrad (CN_Sensor.Sensor_Id = 100) *
     ParamType_ParamValue.ParamValue_Utility (
     ParamType_ParamValue.ParamType_Id = 001) +
     CN_ContextNotifiedSensor.CN_SensorTrad (CN_Sensor.
     Sensor_Id = 101) * ParamType_ParamValue.
     ParamValue_Utility (ParamType_ParamValue.ParamType_Id
      = 002) + CN_ContextNotifiedSensor.CN_SensorTrad (
     CN_Sensor.Sensor_Id = 102) * ParamType_ParamValue.
     ParamValue_Utility (ParamType_ParamValue.ParamType_Id
      = 003) + 0,9) + Context_Notified.CN_ComponentId
```

The devices considered in the adaptive process are smartphones and desktops. The automatic alert levels are defined by physicians for patients. The *DA Service* runs the adaptation procedures using the following levels:

- "Automatic Alert" Level 1: normal signs. Application with identification and patient vital signs: name, specialty, heart rate (HR), temperature (T), and blood pressure (BP). Interface Level 1 (green);
- "Automatic Alert" Level 2: some signs are outside normal range (HR or T). Interface Level 2 (yellow);
- "Automatic Alert" Level 3: medium problem. Just BP is outside the normal or HR and T outside the normal. Interface Level 3 (orange) and gtalk message to nurse;
- "Automatic Alert" Level 4: maximum alert. BP is outside the normal, T and/or HR are outside the normal. Interface Level 4 (red) with gtalk message to nurse and message delivery option for physicians.

The adaptations of the application are chained: the decision of the adapter "Device Type" uses the decision previously taken with the adapter "Alert Level". Figure 7 shows the Alert Level 4 for desktop and also smartphone.

6.2 Acceptance Evaluation

This section presents the experiment details and the results obtained with the application's evaluation. The evaluation regards the application acceptance, which involved São Francisco Hospital volunteer users, among physicians and nurses. These volunteers answered a questionnaire, after they used the application.

For the study we considered 10 physicians and 20 nurses, who were selected based on their activities in the hospital. Each participant used a mobile device (smartphone) and a desktop, with the application installed. We performed a basic training on the application operation beforehand.

[1]http://www.w3.org/TR/rdf-sparql-query

[2]http://jena.sourceforge.net

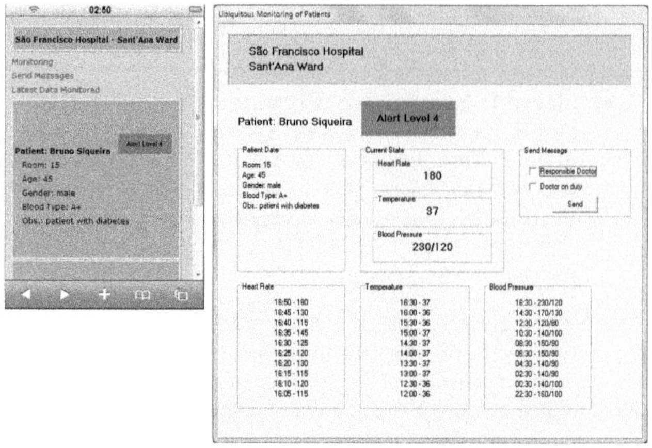

Figure 7: Automatic Alert Level 4 (smartphone and desktop versions)

Participants were asked to use the application and respond to an evaluation questionnaire regarding the experience in the use of the system.

The answers should be within a range of five points[3], ranging from 1 point (totally disagree) to 5 points (totally agree). To evaluate the model acceptability, checking the system usability, the questionnaire were defined based on the Technology Acceptance Model (TAM) proposed by [10], which was updated by [18] in their acceptance wireless networks study. The TAM model considers the following main themes for application acceptance: (i) Ease of Use: means the degree in which users evaluating the application may reduce their effort; (ii) Usefulness: means the degree in which users evaluating the application may improve their performance.

Table 1 and Table 2 contain the questionnaire applied to users, and answers obtained. The questions were designed in order to be simple, short and direct. Table 1 presents the questionnaire with answers regarding Ease of Use with the following guidance: "Regarding the ease of use of the application, tell us in which degree you agree with the following statements". The table presents the question at the first column and the percentage obtained with the number of users in brackets following from "Totally Disagree" to "Totally Agree". The last column shows the consolidation average percentage score obtained by the responses, which varied between zero and five.

Analyzing the results we can observe that approvals were higher regarding ease of use. In general most people approved the application for this requirement, since average grades were high, up to four (4.5), which means approval of more than ninety percent (90%).

Table 2 presents the questionnaire with the user's answers on the subject usefulness, with the following guidance: "Regarding the application usefulness,tell us in which degree you agree with the following statements". The last two questions were posed in order to determine the true intent of the evaluator in using the application. We could verify that the approval was also high (over eighty percent), but with values slightly lower than the previous questions. This assessment is probably not due to usability issues, since they have high

[3]http://psycnet.apa.org/psycinfo/1933-01885-001

Table 1: Ease of Use Evaluation

Question	Totally Disagree	Partially Disagree	Neutral	Partially Agree	Totally Agree	Average
1. The application is easy to understand.	0,0%(0)	0,0%(0)	0,0%(0)	30,0%(9)	70,0%(21)	4,7
2. The application is easy to use.	0,0%(0)	0,0%(0)	0,0%(0)	30,0%(9)	70,0%(21)	4,7
3. With little effort I can make the dynamic capture of patients' vital signs.	0,0%(0)	0,0%(0)	0,0%(0)	20,0%(6)	80,0%(24)	4,8
4. With little effort I can access the history of patients' alerts.	0,0%(0)	0,0%(0)	0,0%(0)	20,0%(6)	80,0%(24)	4,8
5. The application interface is properly adapted to the device (mobile or desktop).	0,0%(0)	0,0%(0)	10,0%(3)	20,0%(6)	70,0%(21)	4,6

grades, but because of other users concerns such as security and privacy, regarding the use in a hospital.

Finally, analyzing all the results we can see that in general the users found the application easy to use. Regarding the perception that these users had about the application usefulness, they also considered that application would be useful for health workers at a hospital.

7. RELATED WORK

Carisma [5] is based on a context-aware reflexive middleware for mobile applications. In Carisma the rules provide less transparency for the developer. The reasoning occurs through reconfiguration actions in a low-level, rather than an architectural design at the semantic level. In EXEHDA, reconfiguration actions of lowest level are determined automatically by the middleware and the adaptation is driven by attributes for functional and non-functional adaptations. On the other hand, Carisma's policy-based rules do not consider non-functional adaptations. In addition, Carisma only handles a fixed number of policies for a given adaptation, while in EXEHDA's approach the utility function selects the best adaptation among the alternatives inferred by the adaptation service.

Chisel [14] is a framework for dynamic context-aware adaptation of services. The system uses reflection controlled by policies. Chisel is based on the decomposition of extra-functional aspects (non-functional) in alternative behaviors. In Chisel, policies are defined with a declarative language and are essentially rule-based. EXEHDA, on the other hand relies on utility functions, besides rules, for the adaptation decisions. Another difference is that EXEHDA employs functional and non-functional adaptations.

QUO [15] is a project based on a QoS-aware middleware. One drawback of QUO architecture is that the only focus is on adapting the functional aspects of the application, depending on the state of system resources. Unlike EXEHDA, QUO does not consider non-functional adaptations and has no support for portable devices and wireless networks. As in EXEHDA, QUO is one of the few projects that address adaptation as a reusable component or service.

Rainbow [12] [7] consists of a framework, a language and an incremental process engineering of self-adaptation. The adaptation approach, proposed in Rainbow, is similar to that used in EXEHDA, regarding the separation of the adaptation from the logical application. However, Rainbow does not focus on the requirements relevant to environments with mobile devices. Moreover, the strategies for adaptation are based on situation-action rules, which specify exactly what to do in certain situations. EXEHDA, on the other hand, uses the extended objectives policy expressed as utility functions, which is a higher-level specification for adaptation strategies.

Madam [13] is a European research project with partners in industry and universities. Madam, in addition to a middleware, includes a methodology for model-driven development, based on adaptation models and the corresponding changes model-to-code. EXEHDA does not focus on software development tools, but rather in the provision of support for adaptations that can be used by components of the applications. Another consideration is that Madam does not use semantic modeling for adaptation policy application. The proposal does not explicit whether adaptation policies can be reused for further adaptations or other software components.

Proteus [16] employs a semantic model in the adaptation management of the users' access. Proteus executes adaptations in the access policies to resources, used by applications. In the management of the adaptive process, similar to EXEHDA, Proteus contemplates the use of a semantic model. However, EXEHDA provides a wider range of adaptations. Different functionalities of the applications, with different natures, are involved in the adaptive process.

SECAS [6] is a project that deals with the context adaptation, considering the preferences of the user, environment, and devices involved. SECAS covers only the functional adaptations for healthcare applications. The proposal uses logical expressions to context settings for adapters. Unlike EXEHDA, SECAS does not use semantic modeling for adaptation rules. However, SECAS employs a formalism based on Petri networks.

We consider that the employ of utility functions provide greater capability for adapt to user needs. This feature distinguishes EXEHDA from most of the related work. Moreover, EXEHDA distinguishes from most of the researched projects, because it provides a semantic model that increases the expressiveness of context representation, as well as addressing both functional and non-functional adaptations.

In addition, EXEHDA allows, at any time, that the application developer includes new instances of classes in the adaptation policy ontology, such as new adapters, new rules, and new parameters. This is due to the fact that application policy can be maintained externally, describing the configuration of the profiles of the applications, through the rules, parameters and operations of its adaptation policy.

8. CONCLUSION

In this article we presented the EXEHDA middleware, highlighting the Dynamic Adaptation Control Service (*DA Service*). This service enables the instantiation of adaptation policy, externally to the application code, using a frame-

Table 2: Usefulness Evaluation

Question	Totally Disagree	Partially Disagree	Neutral	Partially Agree	Totally Agree	Average
1. The options presented are relevant.	0,0%(0)	0,0%(0)	0,0%(0)	40,0%(12)	60,0%(18)	4,6
2. The application makes it easy to do the dynamic capture of patients' vital signs.	0,0%(0)	0,0%(0)	0,0%(0)	40,0%(12)	60,0%(18)	4,6
3. The application makes it easy to access the history of patients' alerts.	0,0%(0)	0,0%(0)	0,0%(0)	30,0%(9)	70,0%(21)	4,7
4. The application is useful for a hospital.	0,0%(0)	0,0%(0)	20,0%(6)	30,0%(9)	50,0%(15)	4,3
5. I would use this application in my work at hospital.	0,0%(0)	0,0%(0)	30,0%(9)	20,0%(6)	50,0%(15)	4,2

work. The proposal eases the development and the inclusion of new adaptations, new contexts of interest, new rules, and operating parameters.

In addition, the formalism, expressiveness, possibility of dynamic relationships, and inference between information, introduced by the semantic model, allow the definition of an adaptation policy model in high level. Furthermore, this model allows the maintenance, reuse, standardization, and sharing of information maintained in the ontological model among the various services of the middleware.

The results obtained so far are promising and they encourage the continuity of the research. In that sense, the following aspects should be explored in future work: (i) implementation of adaptation rules that modify the parameters of other rules, characterizing a context adaptation of their own middleware; and (ii) inclusion of the historical context and the history of adaptations in the adaptive decision.

9. REFERENCES

[1] I. Augustin, A. Yamin, and C. F. R. Geyer. Managing the follow-me semantics to build large-scale pervasive applications. In *Proceedings of the 3rd international workshop on Middleware for pervasive and ad-hoc computing*, MPAC '05, pages 1–8, New York, NY, USA, 2005. ACM.

[2] I. Augustin, A. C. Yamin, and L. C. d. Silva. Building a smart environment at large-scale with a pervasive grid middleware. In J. Wong, editor, *Grid Computing Research Progress*, volume 1, chapter 10, pages 323–344. Nova Science, New York, NY, USA, 2008.

[3] M. Baldauf, S. Dustdar, and F. Rosenberg. A survey on context-aware systems. *Int. J. Ad Hoc Ubiquitous Comput.*, 2(4):263–277, June 2007.

[4] C. Bettini, O. Brdiczka, K. Henricksen, J. Indulska, D. Nicklas, A. Ranganathan, and D. Riboni. A survey of context modelling and reasoning techniques. *Pervasive Mob. Comput.*, 6(2):161–180, Apr. 2010.

[5] L. Capra, W. Emmerich, and C. Mascolo. Carisma: Context-aware reflective middleware system for mobile applications. *IEEE Transactions on Software Engineering*, 29(10):929–945, 2003.

[6] T. Chaari and F. Laforest. Adaptation in context-aware pervasive information systems: the secas project. *International Journal of pervasive Computing and Communications*, 3(4):400–425, 2007.

[7] G. Chen, M. Li, and D. Kotz. Data-centric middleware for context-aware pervasive computing. *Pervasive Mob. Comput.*, 4(2):216–253, Apr. 2008.

[8] C. A. Costa, L. C. d. Silva, J. L. V. Barbosa, A. C. Yamin, and C. F. R. Geyer. A primer of ubiquitous computing challenges and trends. In F. M. M. Neto and P. F. R. Neto, editors, *Designing Solutions-Based Ubiquitous and Pervasive Computing: New Issues and Trends*, volume 1, chapter 15, pages 282–303. IGI Global Publishing, Hershey, 2010.

[9] C. A. Costa, A. C. Yamin, and C. F. R. Geyer. Toward a general software infrastructure for ubiquitous computing. *IEEE Pervasive Computing*, 7(1):64–73, 2008.

[10] F. D. Davis. Perceived usefulness, perceived ease of use, and user acceptance of information technology. *MIS Quarterly*, 13(3):319–340, 1989.

[11] K. Fujii and T. Suda. Semantics-based context-aware dynamic service composition. *ACM Trans. Auton. Adapt. Syst.*, 4:12:1–12:31, May 2009.

[12] D. Garlan, S.-W. Cheng, A.-C. Huang, B. Schmerl, and P. Steenkiste. Rainbow: Architecture-based self-adaptation with reusable infrastructure. *Computer*, 37:46–54, October 2004.

[13] K. Geihs, P. Barone, F. Eliassen, J. Floch, R. Fricke, E. Gjørven, S. Hallsteinsen, G. Horn, M. U. Khan, A. Mamelli, G. A. Papadopoulos, N. Paspallis, R. Reichle, and E. Stav. A comprehensive solution for application-level adaptation. *Software Practice & Experience*, 39(4):385–422, 2009.

[14] J. Keeney and V. Cahill. *Chisel: A Policy-Driven, Context-Aware, Dynamic Adaptation Framework.* IEEE Computer Society, 2003.

[15] P. K. Sharma, J. P. Loyall, G. T. Heineman, R. E. Schantz, R. Shapiro, and G. Duzan. *Component-Based Dynamic QoS Adaptations in Distributed Real-Time and Embedded Systems*, volume 3291 of *Lecture Notes in Computer Science.* Springer, 2004.

[16] A. Toninelli, R. Montanari, L. Kagal, and O. Lassila. Proteus: A semantic context-aware adaptive policy model. *IEEE International Workshop on Policies for Distributed Systems and Networks*, 0:129–140, 2007.

[17] N. Warken, L. Venecian, S. Rodrigues, R. Dilli, J. L. Lopes, and A. Yamin. A model of autonomous control of the adaptation to the context in ubicomp. *11th Symposium on Computing Systems-WSCAD-SSC - IEEE Computer Society*, 0:104–111, 2010.

[18] C. Yoon and S. Kim. Convenience and tam in a ubiquitous computing environment: The case of wireless lan. *Electron. Commer. Rec. Appl.*, 6(1):102–112, Jan. 2007.

DynamiCC: A Framework for Dynamic Context Composition in Ubicomp

João Lopes, Rodrigo Souza, Cláudio Geyer
PPGC/INF/Federal University of Rio Grande do Sul
Porto Alegre-RS, Brazil
{jlblopes,rssouza,geyer}@inf.ufrgs.br

Cristiano Costa, Jorge Barbosa
PIPCA/University of the Vale do Rio dos Sinos
São Leopoldo-RS, Brazil
{cac,jbarbosa}@unisinos.br

Gizele Gadotti
Federal University of Pelotas
Pelotas-RS, Brazil
gizele.gadotti@ufpel.edu.br

Márcia Gusmão, Adenauer Yamin
PPGC/CDTec/Federal University of Pelotas
Pelotas-RS, Brazil
{mzgusmao,adenauer}@inf.ufpel.edu.br

ABSTRACT

Ubiquitous computing (Ubicomp) environments are characterized by high distribution, heterogeneity and dynamism. In these environments, applications must be aware of their contexts and adapt to changes in them. A major research challenge in the area of Ubicomp is related to context awareness. Considering the characteristics of ubiquitous environments, this paper presents a framework for context awareness, called DynamiCC (Dynamic Context Composition), which includes elements to support context modeling, contextual data collection, environment actuation, composition and interpretation of contextual information. We consider that the main contributions of this work are the use of a hybrid approach for context modeling, and the proposal of an architecture that supports interpretation and composition of dynamic contexts. DynamiCC enables the construction of complex contexts at runtime. To assess the functionality of the proposed model, we developed usage scenarios.

Categories and Subject Descriptors

C.2.4 [**Computer Systems Organization**]: Computer-Communication Networks—*Distributed Systems*

Keywords

Ubiquitous Computing, Context Awareness, Dynamic Contexts

1. INTRODUCTION

The computational infrastructure for Ubicomp tends to be highly distributed, heterogeneous, and dynamic. This is because of the contextual elements, devices and software components that often change their status in the ubiquitous environment. Therefore, one of the research challenges in this area concerns the ability of software development resources to explore the context awareness for the adaptation process of applications [7].

In computational environments for ubiquitous applications, contextual information is obtained from multiple sensors. Consequently, the software components should be aware of their contexts of interest and, when appropriate, automatically adapt to their changes, characterizing by that context awareness [9].

The literature review indicates several challenges in the support of context awareness for ubiquitous applications, including: (i) representation of a context model that has features such as extensibility, standardization, expressiveness, and reasoning, (ii) context acquisition from distributed and heterogeneous sources, (iii) context processing and actuation on the environment, and (iv) context dissemination to interested consumers in a distributed and timely way [3] [4].

Considering the integration with EXEHDA middleware [2] and the fact that it does not meet these challenges, this paper presents the current state of DynamiCC framework.

The paper is organized as follows. Section 2 summarizes related works. Section 3 presents an overview of the proposal. Section 4 discusses the proposed framework, and section 5 describes the software architectural model designed for its use. In section 6 we highlight the prototypes and tests. Finally, section 7 presents the concluding remarks.

2. RELATED WORK

WComp [8] is a middleware for ubiquitous computing, based on a software infrastructure, an architecture for service composition, and a mechanism for adaptation. The proposal has some limitations in dealing with context awareness. The main constraint is not to define an expressive model for the representation of contextual information.

CARE [1] is a middleware to support context adaptation. It proposes a context modeling based on the integration of a markup model and an ontological model. This integration is achieved through the representation of context data with profiles CC/PP, which contain references to classes and relationships of the ontology. CARE has a narrower focus, including the adaptation of usual services of Internet in the context of mobile computing.

Solar [5] is a middleware to support context awareness, which collects data from heterogeneous sources and aggre-

Permission to make digital or hard copies of all or part of this work for personal or classroom use is granted without fee provided that copies are not made or distributed for profit or commercial advantage and that copies bear this notice and the full citation on the first page. To copy otherwise, to republish, to post on servers or to redistribute to lists, requires prior specific permission and/or a fee.
WebMedia'12, October 15–28, 2012, São Paulo/SP, Brazil.
Copyright 2012 ACM 978-1-4503-1706-1/12/10 ...$15.00.

gates this data to obtain high-level contexts. Solar employs an informal model for context representation, it does not record historical data context, and the data collection requires direct participation of the applications, since they need to manage sensors, operators and requests.

HiCon [6] is a framework for monitoring and composing context. It considers different levels of context, allowing the dynamic composition of different contexts and the creation of a comprehensive set of scalable applications. Hicon has a greater focus on filtering contextual data, rather than context processing.

In comparison with related works, the DynamiCC framework proposes a hybrid model for the context representation, which provides high expressiveness for context processing. This approach is not identified in the related works. DynamiCC bases its proposal on a semantic and compositional vision of the context, an approach that differs from related works discussed, and which includes the assumptions of distribution, heterogeneity, and dynamism inherent of the ubiquitous environments. Furthermore, unlike the works analyzed, the software architecture of DynamiCC enables the collection of context data and the actuation on the environment, in a distributed way.

3. PROPOSAL OVERVIEW

The applications of ubiquitous environment managed by EXEHDA are distributed, mobile, and adaptive to the context. They are available from any place, at any time. This environment is composed of cells organized in the following fashion: (i) a server in charge of all basic services of the cell (Cellular Server); (ii) computers that manage sensors and actuators (Border Servers); and (iii) user's equipment (Nodes).

In the design of the proposal we employed a hybrid approach for modeling and processing context. The integration of different models may provide greater flexibility and generality in meeting the requirements of the context aware ubiquitous applications, minimizing limitations presented individually in existing models [4]. Therefore, the proposed model integrates a semantic approach based on ontologies, to support inferences, and a logical approach, which uses a relational database to support queries on the context data.

We proposed many instances in the ontologies, representing entities and their context data and persist this context information. Moreover, storage in text files OWL (Web Ontology Language) footnote http://www.w3.org/TR/owl2-overview/ may imply in delays in the ontology's processing, not only by querying on their instances, but also in making inferences, since the entire file contents needs to be handled. In this sense, the use of databases for storing instances of the ontology has been shown an efficient way to query processing [12].

The designed model provides dynamic handling of context information, while the ubiquitous applications are been executed. Moreover, the definition, instantiation, and monitoring of the context are conceived to be external. This approach leverages aspects of modularity and reuse in building new applications.

In the proposed design we employed an event-driven approach [11], both among modules of the software architecture, as well as with the applications. In this way, we enable the possibility of associating processing rules to the contexts of interest, which can be triggered automatically whenever an event occurs. The event, in our view, relate to changes in the state of the context. The composition of dynamic contexts is a key aspect in the design of the proposal, corresponding to the ability to construct complex contexts and time of applications execution, which can be composed by the context data obtained from different sensors distributed in cells forming the ubiquitous environment. This approach enhances the expression of contextual information, which can be made available to the processes of adaptation in ubiquitous applications.

4. CONTEXT MODEL

The methodology proposed by Noy [10] is used to build the ontology that represents the context of the ubiquitous environment. This ontology, called OntUbiContext, shown in Figure 1 is integrated into the proposed architecture for context awareness and provides support for reasoning, by the use of inferences, over the contextual information.

The ontology is used to model the entities that are involved in the development and implementation of ubiquitous applications. In this sense, as a project goal, we assumed that this ontology should be general enough to model different types of applications. Another characteristic, is that the ontology should be able to model all entities used by the computational infrastructure, including resources, people, and places. Furthermore, the ontology should consider the abstractions proposed to model the real world, and represent the context information of the ubiquitous environment, which may be used for context awareness.

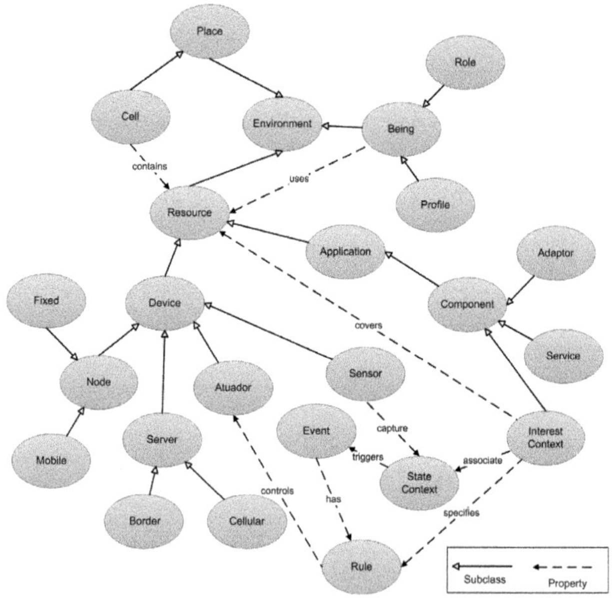

Figure 1: Proposed Ontology

The logical model of context enables the storage of contextual information, reflecting the ontology structure in a model of entities and relationships. This model, as well as the semantic model, is also integrated into the proposed architecture for context awareness. The database includes the relationships between applications, components, sensors, environments, and contexts of interest. Nevertheless, the database stores information about architecture configuration and publications from the existing sensors in ubiquitous environment.

5. ARCHITECTURAL MODEL

The software architecture for context awareness, presented in Figure 2 has the following assumptions: (i) use of a hybrid model for context (see section 4); (ii) processing information acquired by sensors in different cells of the ubiquitous environment, (iii) use notifications according to the rules for context processing employed by different applications, (iv) possibility of sensors and/or actuators to be activated, deactivated, configured and accessed at any time, through their respective handlers, in a ubiquitous way, at any cell of the environment, and (v) possibility of changing the rules for context processing, during the execution of the applications.

The software architecture consists of modules distributed between the two types of servers, Cellular and Border. These servers are located in cells of the ubiquitous environment, where each cell has one Cellular Server and can contain several Border Servers.

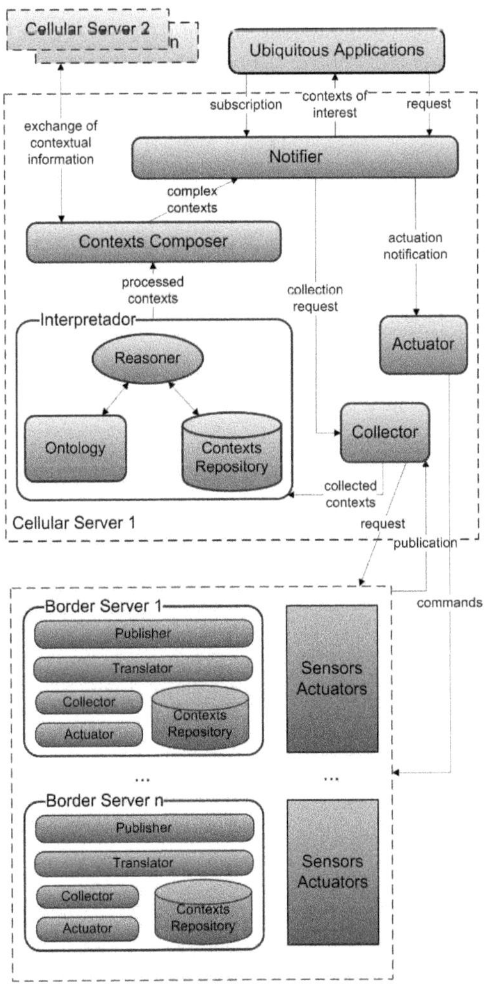

Figure 2: Overview of Software Architecture

The services of the architecture installed on the Cellular Server are in charge of: (i) request and collect the context information published by Border Servers; (ii) maintain the context model; (iii) persist the context data; (iv) interpret the context, through the processing of inference rules; (v) make the composition of dynamic contexts, received both from the Border Servers as from the other Cellular Servers in the ubiquitous environment, producing complex contexts of interest; (vi) notify the ubiquitous applications about the occurrence of the contexts of interest subscribed by them; and (vii) build action commands which are sent to Border Servers to be processed.

The architecture services in the Border Servers stores temporary records of the context data, and process translation rules related to the sensed data. The translation rules involve less complex operations, not including the reasoning and context composition made in the Cellular Server. Nonetheless, in the Border Servers we have services that activate, deactivate and configure actuators used by applications. The architecture also provides a support for communication failures in Border Servers, which stores the data acquired by sensors in a local context repository, ensuring their availability to the Cellular Server whenever communications is restored.

6. PROTOTYPING AND TESTING

The DynamiCC framework is not specific to a particular problem domain, but is designed to be comprehensive, aiming to meet different domains. In this sense, despite of the fact that the applications described in this section are related to projects in the area of agriculture (AMPLUS [1] and plenUS [2]), the DynamiCC framework enables support in other application domains.

The prototypes and tests evaluated some characteristics of the context model, the software architecture, and the technologies employed, covering aspects related to (i) data collection and actuation on the environment, (ii) composition of dynamic contexts, and (iii) context interpretation.

Current versions of servers are being developed with the Java programming language [3], to be integrated with the Jena API [4], which allows the processing of the ontological model.

A Border Server manages a network of sensors and actuators, which communicate using the 1-Wire protocol [5]. These servers are collect the data produced by sensors associated with the different contexts, as well as trigger commands on existing actuator in the environment.

For testing data collection, actuation, and composition we considered the following initial profile of the computational environment: (i) Environment: Didactic Laboratory of Seed Analysis (LDAS) [6]; (ii) Collector: LDAS Border Server; (iii) Application: Control of Physical Environment Condition of LDAS; (iv) Component: Temperature Control in the Room of Seed Germinators; (v) Context of Interest: temperature captured by digital sensors; (vi) States of Context: temperature values collected (limits for publication: $\geq$ 27ž C or $\leq$ 15ž C); (vii) Event: temperature outside the boundary; (viii) Rule: Activate Warning Light (triggers the

[1] http://amplus.ufpel.edu.br
[2] http://plenus.ucpel.tche.br
[3] http://www.java.com
[4] http://jena. apache.org
[5] http://ubiq.inf.ufpel.edu.br/1-wire/
[6] http://amplus.ufpel.edu.br/ LDAS

software component that activates an warning light in the room of the responsible for LDAS).

For the collection and actuation process we used, respectively, a digital temperature sensor and an electronic key addressable, both based on 1-Wire technology. We configured the Publisher Module of the Border Server to publish the temperatures every 30 minutes in the Cellular Server.

To test the composition of dynamic contexts, the context of interest has been modified to include the factors humidity and temperature of the external environment. This last factor is published by a Border Server, managed by the Cellular Server located at Embrapa-Lowlands cell, specialized in Agroclimatological Station and located at Capão do Leão Campus (campus of Federal University of Pelotas, where the LDAS is situated). This setting characterizes a collection of context data in a distributed way, in different cells of the ubiquitous environment.

We validate the modifying of processing rule, at runtime, using transactions. When a state of context occurred that triggers an event related to the rule "Activate Warning Light", outside the operation hours of the lab, we began to be used the rule "Send E-mail", which triggered the software component to send an email to the person responsible for the laboratory, warning the occurrence of a temperature outside the established boundary.

In this scenario, the Border Server LDAS published the context data (temperature and humidity) collected in the laboratory room and the module "Contexts Composer" of Cellular Server, added the external temperature published by the Border Server of Agroclimatological Station and made the composition, considering the states of context, events and related rules.

With respect to the context interpretation, tests were performed to evaluate the formal representation of context through ontologies and the ability to make inferences, as well as the possibility of storing the context data and make queries over them.

The tool Protégé [7] was used to model the ontology, which was represented in OWL-DL (Description Logics). To check the consistency of the ontology and taxonomy we used Pellet reasoner to classify data [8]. As a result, we found that the ontology had no conflicting events, and generated the correct class hierarchy, inferring superclasses and equivalent classes to each class modeled.

Using the data persistence module of the Jena API, the ontological model was stored in the database PostgreSQL [9], allowing queries with language SPARQL [10]. A scenario related to the project plenUS was built to test this functionality. The context of interest defined was the availability of slots (places in greenhouses free for installation of an experiment), with certain operating characteristics.

7. CONCLUDING REMARKS

The main difference of DynamiCC framework in relation to related work concerns more expressiveness in the context representation, by employing a hybrid approach for modeling contexts, as well as supporting the interpretation and composition of dynamic contexts, which enables the construction of complex situations, at runtime.

Among others, in the continuing of research, the following aspects should be explored in future works: (i) revise and expand the aspects considered in the target applications of the proposal; (ii) specify the API and protocols between the application layer and middleware, and (iii) continuing the specification of the architecture modules.

8. REFERENCES

[1] A. Agostini, C. Bettini, and D. Riboni. Hybrid reasoning in the care middleware for context awareness. *Int. J. Web Eng. Technol.*, 5(1):3–23, May 2009.

[2] I. Augustin, A. C. Yamin, and L. C. d. Silva. Building a smart environment at large-scale with a pervasive grid middleware. In J. Wong, editor, *Grid Computing Research Progress*, volume 1, chapter 10, pages 323–344. Nova Science, New York, NY, USA, 2008.

[3] M. Baldauf, S. Dustdar, and F. Rosenberg. A survey on context-aware systems. *Int. J. Ad Hoc Ubiquitous Comput.*, 2(4):263–277, June 2007.

[4] C. Bettini, O. Brdiczka, K. Henricksen, J. Indulska, D. Nicklas, A. Ranganathan, and D. Riboni. A survey of context modelling and reasoning techniques. *Pervasive Mob. Comput.*, 6(2):161–180, Apr. 2010.

[5] G. Chen, M. Li, and D. Kotz. Data-centric middleware for context-aware pervasive computing. *Pervasive Mob. Comput.*, 4(2):216–253, Apr. 2008.

[6] K. Cho, I. Hwang, S. Kang, B. Kim, J. Lee, S. Lee, S. Park, J. Song, and Y. Rhee. Hicon: a hierarchical context monitoring and composition framework for next-generation context-aware services. *Network, IEEE*, 22(4):34 –42, july-aug. 2008.

[7] C. A. Costa, A. C. Yamin, and C. F. R. Geyer. Toward a general software infrastructure for ubiquitous computing. *IEEE Pervasive Computing*, 7(1):64–73, 2008.

[8] N. Ferry, V. Hourdin, S. Lavirotte, G. Rey, M. Riveill, and J.-Y. Tigli. Wcomp, a middleware for ubiquitous computing, ubiquitous computing. In E. Babkin, editor, *Ubiquitous Computing*, volume 1, chapter 8, pages 171–176. InTech, 2011.

[9] J. Kjeldskov and M. B. Skov. Exploring context-awareness for ubiquitous computing in the healthcare domain. *Personal Ubiquitous Comput.*, 11(7):549–562, 2007.

[10] N. F. Noy and D. L. McGuinness. Ontology development 101: A guide to creating your first ontology. Technical Report KSL-01-05, Knowledge Systems, AI Laboratory, Stanford University, 2001.

[11] J.-Y. Tigli, S. Lavirotte, G. Rey, V. Hourdin, D. Cheung-Foo-Wo, E. Callegari, and M. Riveill. Wcomp middleware for ubiquitous computing: Aspects and composite event-based web services. *Annales des Télécommunications*, 64(3-4):197–214, 2009.

[12] S. N. Venturi Filho, A. M. d. C. Moura, and M. C. R. Cavalcanti. Armazenamento e manipulação de ontologias utilizando sistemas gerenciadores de banco de dados. Relatório técnico, Instituto Militar de Engenharia - IME, 2010.

[7] http://protege.stanford.edu/

[8] http://pellet.owldl.com/

[9] http://www.postgresql.org/

[10] http://www.w3.org/TR/rdf-sparql-query

Measuring Media-based Social Interactions in Online Civic Mobilization Against Corruption in Brazil

Alan Keller Gomes
Federal Institute of Goiás - IFG, Inhumas, Brazil
University of São Paulo - USP, São Carlos, Brazil
alankeller@icmc.usp.br

Maria da Graça Campos Pimentel
University of São Paulo - USP
ICMC, São Carlos-SP, Brazil
mgp@icmc.usp.br

ABSTRACT

Given the importance of new media on traditional forms of civic mobilization, it is opportune to investigate how online civic mobilization can be described in terms of the actions performed by users. In earlier work we proposed the application of established data mining procedures to evaluate rules associated with social interactions, and developed a technique for codifying, mining and evaluating social interactions. In this paper we present a method which guides the iterative application of the technique. We used the method to analyze social interactions in two online civic mobilizations against corruption occurred in Brazil. After two iterations, the results include: in terms of generic social interactions, Facebook users are more likely to perform *Likes* and *Comments* on Posts; in terms of media-based social interactions, users are more likely to choose the media *text*.

Categories and Subject Descriptors: H.5.1 [**Multimedia Information Systems**]: Evaluation/ Methodology. J.4 [Computer Applications]: Social and Behavioral Science

General Terms: Human Factors, Measurement.

Keywords: Social Networks, Civic Mobilization, Facebook, Behavioral Contingencies, Sequential Patterns, *If-then* Rules.

1. INTRODUCTION

Popular social networks may be an alternative for users to engage in civic or political activities, as it was the case in mobilizations in Egypt [25], which used Twitter, and in U.S. presidential election [18], which used Facebook.

Social interactions have been defined in Social Sciences as the acts, actions, or practices of two or more people mutually oriented towards each other's selves, that is, any behavior that tries to affect or take account of each other's subjective experiences or intentions [20]. Social network analysis [29] studies social entities (people, actors or users) and their relationships and interactions. Existing models have been investigated to allow the representation of relationships based on interactions among users — this is usually achieved applying data mining techniques such as clustering and classification [27]. Given that such models do not explain how the interactions among social media users occur, there is a demand for a descriptive model allowing the representation, mining and measuring of situations which involve users in social interactions.

Results from Experimental Social Psychology argue that social interactions may be specified as *behavioral contingencies*: *if-then* rules corresponding to observations of what people do, or not do, in a variety of situations [15]. In Data Mining, *if-then* rules are general implications in the form of $B \to H$ which can be extracted and evaluated by a variety of Rule Learning measures [7]. In our work we exploit the application of established data mining procedures [13] to evaluate *if-then* rules associated with social interactions, and have been evolving a technique for codifying and evaluating media-based social interactions [8] [9] [11].

After successfully integrating a mining stage into our technique [10], in this paper we present a method which guides the iterative application of the technique. We use our method to analyze social interactions occurring in a 45-day period in which two online civic mobilizations against corruption which mobilized thousands of protesters occurred in Brazil. We collected data from social interactions on Facebook in two different moments: September 9[1] and October 12[2] 2011.

Applying the method, the measures after two iterations indicate, among others, one expected result (in terms of *generic social interactions*, Facebook users are more likely to perform both *Likes* and *Comments* on Posts) and one less obvious result (in terms of *media-based social interactions*, users are more likely to choose the media *text* even with richer options of media types for sharing).

In this paper, Section 2 discusses related work; Section 3 summarizes our technique; Section 4 details our method and Section 5 its application; Section 6 summarizes our work.

2. RELATED WORK

Web-based social networks such as Twitter and Facebook have been exploited by users engaging in civic and political activities. Recent examples include election protests in Iran [31], political uprisings in Egypt [25], and the so-

[1] http://www1.folha.uol.com.br/poder/971643-marcha-anticorrupcao-leva-milhares-as-ruas-em-brasilia.shtml (accessed on 05/08/2012, in Portuguese).

[2] http://o-povo.jusbrasil.com.br/politica/7857285/marcha-contra-a-corrupcao-reune-20-mil-pessoas-em-brasilia (accessed on 05/08/2012, in Portuguese).

Permission to make digital or hard copies of all or part of this work for personal or classroom use is granted without fee provided that copies are not made or distributed for profit or commercial advantage and that copies bear this notice and the full citation on the first page. To copy otherwise, to republish, to post on servers or to redistribute to lists, requires prior specific permission and/or a fee.
WebMedia'12, October 15–18, 2012, São Paulo/SP, Brazil.
Copyright 2012 ACM 978-1-4503-1706-1/12/10 ...$10.00.

cial mobilization after the 2010 earthquake in Haiti [24]. In those cases, Twitter was fundamental as a platform for information diffusion and for organization of activities, and the research reported focused on the extraction of statistics associated with the propagation of information, which was achieved by observing the sharing of media and the reposting of messages. The approach does not refer to a model for representing the collective behavior associated with the social relations.

The literature also reports research efforts towards imparting meaning for social relations in the context of Twitter. Analyzing *Retweets* and *Replies*, Bigonha et al. [2] propose a technique for ranking users as evangelists and detractors. Meira Jr et al. [22] consider that a follower-followee interaction defines a potential influence relationship between users. In contrast with our work, these researches study specific interactions, and do not consider other types of shared media besides text.

Facebook was extensively used in political mobilization in USA, for example, in congressional and governor elections [30] and presidential election [18]. Facebook was also used to understand the discourse and the agenda of the political group "Join the Coffee Party Movement" [14]. Results associated with Facebook report that users are more likely to use *photos* in the maintenance of social relations among long-distance closest friends [28], and in the engagement of closest friends in private social events [17]. These results do not include an analysis of users' behavior in terms of actions performed after sharing media, as aimed by the application of our technique.

Given that research efforts outlined above focus on the extraction and on the interpretation of statistics and on measurements of social graphs, there is an opportunity for extending our previous works in the direction of proposing a method to guide the application of our technique for codifying, mining and evaluating social interactions, as discussed next.

3. REPRESENTING, MINING AND MEASURING SOCIAL INTERACTIONS

3.1 Behavioral Contingencies Representation

In behavioral science, everyday interactions among individuals can be specified as conditional relationships in the form of *if-then* statements, e.g., *behavioral contingencies* [23]. In games, for intance, behavioral contingencies determine how the game is played.

Mechner [15] was groundbreaking in proposing a notation system for codifying behavioral contingencies which combined boolean algebra with a set of diagrams. More recently, Mechner [16] presented a formal symbolic language for cod ifying any behavioral contingencies involving several participants. In the *Mechner Language*, behavioral contingencies are logic implications which can be evaluated as independent variables. Some important elements of this language are:

1. *Action (or actions)*: matching the antecedent of the contingency, i.e., $A \rightarrow$. If there is more than one action, they are represented as $A_1 \cap A_2 \cdots \rightarrow$.
2. *Agent(s) of action(s)*: represented by lowercase letters placed in front of one A. For example, the fact that agent a performed action A is representd by aA. One letter can represent a single agent or a group of agents that perform an action.
3. *Consequence*: corresponds to the consequent of the contingency, i.e., $\rightarrow C$. If there is more than one consequence, they are represented as $\rightarrow C_1 \cap C_2$.

The following statements represent contingencies codified as *if-then* rules using the Mechner Language:

- $aA_1 \cap bA_2 \rightarrow abC_1$. *If* a executes action A_1 and b executes action A_2 *then* the consequence C_1 is perceived by a and b.
- $\overline{a}A_1 \cap bA_2 \rightarrow \overline{a}bC_2$. *If* a does not execute action A_1 and b executes action A_2 *then* the consequence C is not perceived by a but is perceived by b.

It is important to observe that the action that starts the social interaction, which is the case of A_1 in the above example, is called *social stimulus* [23].

Although other notation systems have been proposed to codify behaviors(e.g. [21]), we use the Mechner Language [16] for representing behavioral contingencies as boolean expressions in disjunctive normal form, which is exploited by the data mining procedures we adopt.

We use the Mechner language to represent situations involving users of social media systems in social interactions. In other words, we have to identify *actions A*, *agents of actions* (e.g., user a, or group (of users) k and l), and *consequences C*. Behavioral contingencies codified as *if-then* statements are represented in the form $Body \rightarrow Head$ (in short, $B \rightarrow H$). For example, considering $B = aA_1 \cap bA_2$ and $H = abC_1 \cap abC_2$, an *if-then* behavioral contingency is represented as $R = aA_1 \cap bA_2 \rightarrow abC_1 \cap abC_2$.

Observing users' activities in a social media system, *if-then* statements can model causality (actions lead to consequences). However, we do not assume that all behavioral contingencies codified in Mechner language model causality. In fact, we aim to observe correlations (actions performed by users correlated with system responses perceived by users) instead of causations.

3.2 Behavioral Contingencies Mining

We observe that, in social media systems, each social situations involving users is a sequence of actions and consequences temporally-ordered. For example, *conversations* are sequences of temporally-ordered comments on the shared media object [4]. Such temporal-ordinal relation can be explored in the automatic extraction of behavioral contingencies as sequential patterns.

An approach commonly used in the extraction of sequential patterns is known as brute-force or *Apriori*-like approach [26], as it is the case of the GSP algorithm [1] which makes multiple database passes. In the first pass, all single items (1-sequences) are counted (support counting). From the frequent items, a set of candidate 2-sequences is formed, and another pass is made to identify their frequency. The frequent 2-sequences are then used to generate candidate 3-sequences, and this process is repeated until no more frequent sequences are found. Sequences which do not satisfy a user-specified minimum support[3] are eliminated in a pruning phase. It is worth observing that the GSP algorithm is not able to manipulate attributes with null/missing values.

[3]The user-specified minimum support is estimated by user before sequence extraction.

Also, the GSP is not able to start a sequence generation with length ≥ 1.

Efficient approaches for sequence mining have been proposed, mainly focusing the extraction of sequential patterns without redundant dataset scans [3] [5]. In general terms, such approaches perform a global dataset search and use minimum support threshold for the reduction of the search space. A large number of sequences is generated, from which many may be useless. Also, important sequences may be eliminated or never mined.

In order to overcome such limitations, some particular features can be useful in the task of mining behavioral contingencies as sequences patterns. Considering such particular features, we propose a modification for GSP algorithm to extract behavioral contingencies.

We preprocess the dataset in the data preparation phase: the aim is to reduce the search space. First we organize the *agent of actions* and the *actions* as attributes and, next, organize the consequences. The actions are organized in the order in which they are made available in the social media system. In Facebook, the order is of the actions is:

1. aA_1 = Post,
2. lA_2 = *Like*,
3. kA_3 = *Comment*,
4. sA_4 = *Share*.

The consequences follow the same order as the actions:

1. $alksC_1$ = notification of Post,
2. $alksC_2$ = notification of *Like*,
3. $alksC_3$ = notification of *Comment*,
4. $alksC_4$ = notification of *Share*.

The strategy employed in our algorithm for mining sequences uses to scan the intended dataset twice, as shown in algorithm 1. In *Step 1*, each different line with actions and consequences (with missing/null values) is computed as a sequence candidate. The number of behavioral contingencies observed n and the frequency of occurrence of each sequence candidate are counted. At the end the execution of this step, all sequences with maximum length are generated, for example:

- $< aA_1, lA_2, kA_3, sA_4, alksC_1, alksC_2, alksC_3, alksC_4 >$
- $< aA_1, \bar{l}A_2, \bar{k}A_3, \bar{s}A_4, alksC_1, null, null, null >$.

In *Step 2*, each sequence candidate is scanned and divided in *Body* (*agent of actions* and *actions*) and *Head* (consequences). In this pass, null values are removed from the *body* and the *head*, for example:

- $< aA_1, \bar{l}A_2, \bar{k}A_3, \bar{s}A_4, alksC_1, null, null, null >$ becomes
- $aA_1 \cap \bar{l}A_2 \cap \bar{k}A_3 \cap \bar{s}A_4 \rightarrow alksC_1$.

The final step is an adjustment of the frequencies of bh, b and h. If one *body* appears in more than one sequence, the frequency is increased; if one *Head* appears in more than one sequence, the frequency is increased. At the end of our algorithm, each sequence is represented as rules in the form $B \rightarrow H$, which have values of bh, b ($bh + b\bar{h}$) and h ($bh + \bar{b}h$) counted as the frequency of the occurrence of $B \rightarrow H$, *body* and *head*, respectively. Using these values, rule measures are computed as explained next.

3.3 Behavioral Contingencies Measurement

Using data mining procedures, the value of a rule $B \rightarrow H$ can be measured by comparison with a set of observations [13]. For example, the number n of behavioral contingencies observed during a particular social experience can be computed using classic data mining contingency values $bh, b\bar{h}, \bar{b}h, \overline{bh}$ as

$$n = bh + b\bar{h} + \bar{b}h + \overline{bh}$$

Algorithm 1 Mining Behavioral Contingencies as Sequences

```
Input:
DsOb: Dataset of Observations;
nA: number of Actions
nC: number of Consequences

Output:
Seq: list of sequences;
Bseq: list of sequences Body;
Hseq: list of sequences Head ;
Bcount: list of frequencies of sequences Body;
Hcount: list of frequencies of sequences Head ;
Count: list of frequencies of sequences;
n = number of observations;

Description:
ob = observation (line);
p, t = indexes;
Pseudo code Step 1
 t = -1; n = 0; Seq = φ; Count = φ;
 for each ob ∈ DsOb {   // scan dataset DsOb
 if ob ∉ Seq{
    t++;
    Seq_t = ob;
  } else{
    search position p of ob in Seq;
    Count_p ++;
  }
  n++
 }
 return Seq, Count, n;
 Procedure Step 1(DsOb,nA,nC)

Description:
s = sequence candidate;
Pseudo code Step 2
 s = φ; Seq = φ; Bcount = φ; Hcount = φ;
 for each s ∈ Seq {   // scan the list of Sequences
    Bseq = s position 0 to nA − 1;
    remove null ∈ Bseq;
    Hseq = s position nA − 1 to nA + nC − 1;
    remove null ∈ Hseq;
    Bcount = Hcount = Count;
  }
 return Bseq, Bcount, Hseq, Hcount;
 Procedure Step 2(Seq, Count, nA, nC)
```

As an application of the mapping of Mechner contingencies into data mining rules, contingency values can be used to calculate measures of a given rule in a set of observations. Table 1 details how the contingency values bh, $b\bar{h}$, $\bar{b}h$, and $\overline{bh}$ are used in the computation of four classic rule evaluation measures [13]:

Table 1: Rule Evaluation Measures

Support	Confidence	Cossine Correlation
$P(BH) \equiv \frac{bh}{n}$	$\frac{P(BH)}{P(B)} \equiv \frac{bh}{b}$	$\frac{P(BH)}{\sqrt{P(B)*P(H)}} \equiv \frac{bh}{n*\sqrt{\frac{b*h}{n^2}}}$

- the *Support* measure determines how the rule R is applicable to a given set of observations, determining how frequently H *and* B will appear in the set of observations. This measure reflects the usefulness of rules.
- the *Confidence* measure determines the reliability of the inference made by rule R, determining how frequently H appears in observations that contain B. This measure reflects the certainty of the rules.
- the *Cosine Correlation* measure determines the strength (or lack of strength) of association between B *and* H.

4. A METHOD FOR MEASURING SOCIAL INTERACTIONS

The application of our technique can be guided by an iterative method inspired in the process of knowledge discovery (KDD process) [6].

The method SIREMr (Social Interaction Representation Extraction Measuring rule-based) aims at detailing actions, media objects, applications types, and devices types within rules. Figure 1 presents an overview of the method as a process with inputs and outputs for each phase. The SIREMr method contains seven stages: Observe, Capture, Preparation, Representation/Extraction, Measurement, Interpretation/Validation, Specialization/Reorganization. From one stage to the other, the method has five inputs and outputs: list of attributes, datasets, rules sets, rule measures, and new specified attributes.

4.1 Observe

The first step is to obtain guidance from social psychologists in the observation of the Social Media System, aiming at identifying what is to be captured that is related to social interactions, considering the elements of the Mechner Language. This stage produces a list of attributes for the next stage.

4.2 Capture

Data capturing must be performed automatically, for example by using an API or by analyzing logs generated from the use of social media systems. The selection and the preparation of the data to be captured are typical activities of this stage. This phase produces as output the raw data for next phase.

4.3 Preparation

All collected data can be cleaned, selected and/or transformed for being used in the subsequents phases of representation and measurement of social interactions. In this stage, the identification of the elements of Mechner language (actions, users and consequences) is demanded.

4.4 Representation/Extraction

Social interactions are represented as behavioral contingencies in the form of *if-then* rules. After the identification of the elements of Mechner language, the manual identification of behavioral contingencies may be achieved by observing social situations in the social media system, with support from specialists in social interactions.

The automatic extraction of behavioral contingencies can be made by processing datasets with actions and consequences collected from social media systems. We use the algorithm presented in Section 3.2 for behavioral contingencies mining. This phase produces rules sets as output.

4.5 Measurement

Each social interaction described as an *if-then* rule is represented in the general form $B \rightarrow H$ for computing $bh, b\bar{h}, \bar{b}h, \overline{bh}$ values. After that, each rule is measured by computing rule evaluation measures such as *Support*, *Confidence*, *Utility*, *Cosine Correlation*, *Sensitivity* and *Laplace*. This phase produces rules measures as output.

4.6 Validation/Interpretation

The validation and the interpretation of the results of the representation, the extraction and the evaluation of social interactions must be performed by specialists. If the results are sufficient, the process is concluded. Otherwise, rule specialization or reorganization of data may be performed before repeating the process from the stages Representation or Preparation. If the process has not been concluded, new specified attributes can be used as output for next phase.

4.7 Specialization/Reorganization

Rule specialization may be necessary to analyze, for instance, actions involving particular media types, and is achieved by detailing elements of interest within the rules.

Reorganization of data may be demanded if the results of obtained at this stage are not valid, and the process is repeated from the Preparation stage so that new datasets are generated. On the other hand, if new elements of interest have been identified and have not been collected, the process is repeated from the phase of Capture. Moreover, if the elements of interest have not been observed, the process is repeated from the phase of Observe.

Next, we present how the process is used by means of a case study.

5. A CASE STUDY USING FACEBOOK

The objective of this case study is to show how to use the method to perform an experiment to analyze behavioral contingencies related with an online civic mobilization. We study how Facebook was used to organized two mobilizations in Brazil, one for September 7th 2011 (Brazilian Independence Day) and other for October 12th 2011 (Patron Saint of Brazil Day). Next, each stage of the process is discussed.

5.1 Observing the Social Network

Before collecting data, we were guided by one specialist in the observation of the Facebook Social Network, aiming at identifying social interactions involving elements of Mechner Language. A social interaction starts in Facebook when a user adds a post on a Wall (his Wall, or a friend's). We represent the user that provides the social stimulus as user a.

When a user a adds a post, his group of friends f is notified of this posting. From this moment on, friends of the user may *comment* or *like* that post. We call k the group of users who perform the action *comment* and l the group who perform the action *like*. In addition, $\bar{k}$ represents the group of users who do not perform the action *comment* with respect to that post, and $\bar{l}$ represents the group of users who do not perform the action *like*. The possible actions and corresponding consequences are listed in Table 2.

When mapping user actions into the Mechner language, we identify that, for instance, when user a performs the action A_1, a provides a social stimulus, and friends in groups k and l perform or not actions A_2 and A_3. Also, user a

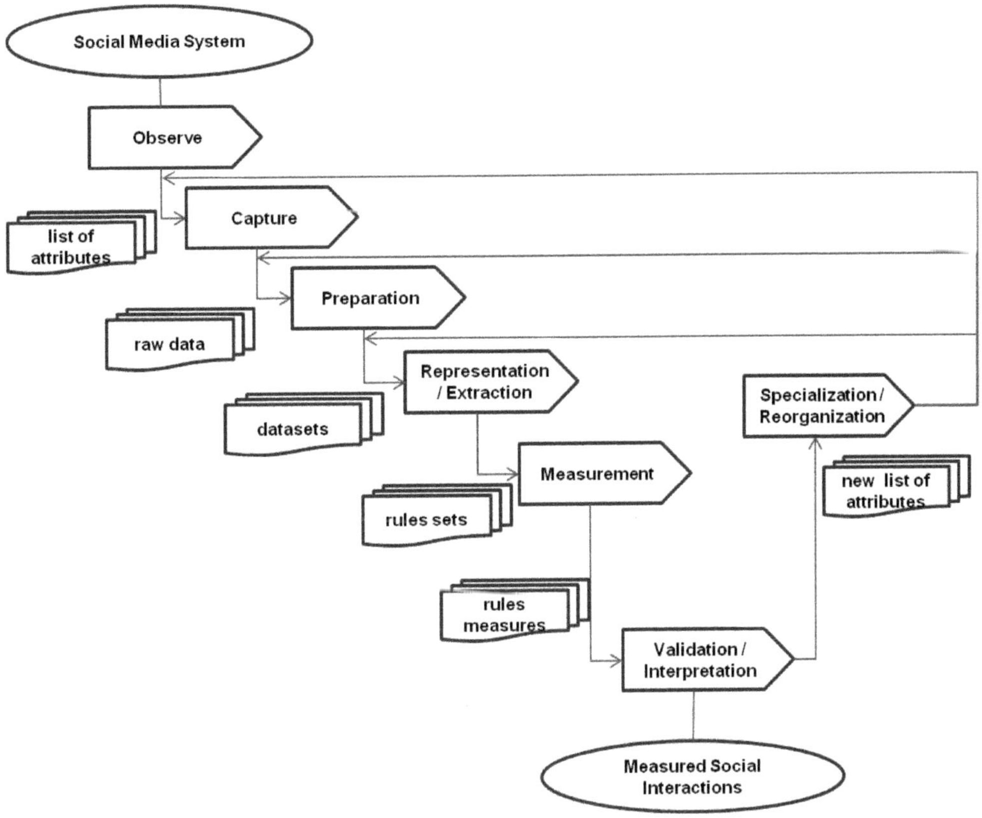

Figure 1: The SIREMr Method

Table 2: Actions and Consequences

Actions	
A_1	to make a post on the Wall
A_2	to make Like on that post
A_3	to make Comment on that post
Consequences	
C_1	to be notified of a post (social stimulus)
C_2	to be notified of a Like(s) on a post
C_3	to be notified of a Comment(s) on a post

and his friends can perceive the consequences C_1, C_2 and C_3. Such actions and consequences are used to represent, to extract and to evaluate social interactions related with the civic mobilization.

5.2 Capturing Data

We implemented a Facebook crawler using Python[4] and run the script four times between September 1st and October 14h 2011, extracting data from more than 1,400 profiles.[5]

We have collected information from 108,043 social interactions, including data about the type of the post (checkin, photo, status, video, link, swf, music, as explained after), about user's activities such as adding *comments* **or** *likes* to a post, and the number of users that add both *comments* **and** *likes* to a post. Also, we have collected the content of the *message*, the *URL*, the *source*, the *caption* and the *description* available for each post.

[4]www.python.org

[5]Most users (954) are from Brazil.

We build a bag of words[6]frequently used to identify the civic mobilization against corruption in Brazil. For each media type posted, we distinguish the posts that have or not one of the words in the bag, by searching in *message*, *URL*, *source*, *caption* and *description*.

5.3 Data Preparation

We built datasets with Social Interactions (SI) data related with the online civic mobilization: two different datasets are organized with the attributes as detailed in Table 2. The first Dataset of SI (DSI 1) registers 50,887 social interactions posted from August 30 to September 7, 2011. The second Dataset of SI (DSI 2) registers 57,156 social interactions posted from September 8 to October 12, 2011.

5.4 Generic SI: Representation

When user a makes a post which receives *Likes* and *Comments*, we represent such generic social interaction as: **if** user a makes a post (action A_1) and users l *Likes* that post (action A_2) and users k *Comment* that post (action A_3), **then** user a and his friends (users l and k) are notified of that post (consequence C_1), and they are notified of *Likes* on that post (consequence C_2), and they are notified of *Comments* on that post (consequence C_3). From now on, we refer to *Posts* as P, to *Likes* as L and to *Comments* as K in the text and in the figures.

[6]We use words in Brazilian Portuguese such as *corrupção* (corruption), *marcha* (walking) and *manisfestação* (manifestation).

5.5 Generic SI: Extraction

We compute generic social interactions presented in Listing 1 as result of mining DSI 1 and DSI 2, by using a implementation of our algorithm described in the Section 3.2, implemented as a Python script.

Listing 1: Generic Social Interactions

R1. $aA_1 \cap \bar{l}A_2 \cap \bar{k}A_3 \rightarrow aklC_1$
R2. $aA_1 \cap lA_2 \cap \bar{k}A_3 \rightarrow aklC_1 \cap aklC_2$
R3. $aA_1 \cap \bar{l}A_2 \cap kA_3 \rightarrow aklC_1 \cap aklC_3$
R4. $aA_1 \cap lA_2 \cap kA_3 \rightarrow aklC_1 \cap aklC_2 \cap aklC_3$

5.6 Generic SI: Measurement

The rules in Listing 1 were evaluated with datasets DSI 1 and DSI 2 by computing the measures presented in Table 1. The values of $ConR$ and $CosR$ for rules $R1$ to $R4$ are 100%. The measure $ConR = 100\%$ means that each rule fits with the observations related with the social interaction described in such rule. The measure $CosR = 100\%$ means that the correlation described in each rule is a strong correlation.

Figure 2 presents the value of support ($SupR$) of each social interaction in Listing 1.

The rules $R1$ to $R4$ can be ranked by value of support as $R4 = \{P, L, K\}$ $R1 = \{P\}$, $R2 = \{P, L\}$ and $R3 = \{P, K\}$. Such ranking describe the social interactions collective behavior for the users engaged in civic mobilization against corruption. To establish the rule ranking, low frequent social interactions are as important as high frequent ones.

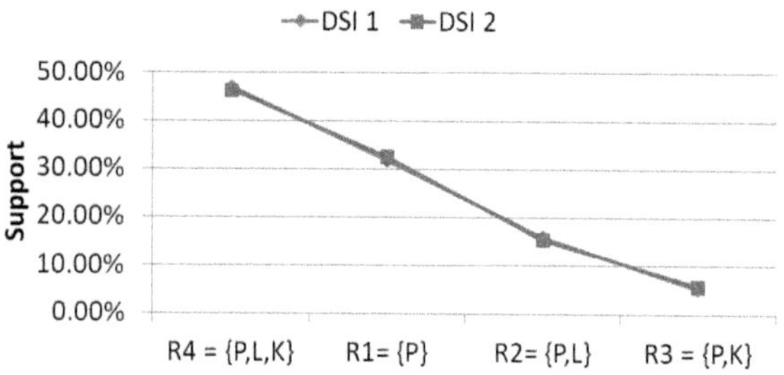

Figure 2: $SupR$ for Generic Social Interactions

5.7 Generic SI: Validation

The extracted rule sets and the results presented above are validated by specialists in social interaction analysis, as we presented in our previous work [8] [9] [11].

5.8 Generic SI: Interpretation

We have an interest result from the reported data: in terms of generic social interactions, Facebook users are more likely to perform *Likes* and *Comments* on Posts ($Sup(R4) = 46\%$). Moreover, an important percentage of posts ($Sup(R1) = 31\%$) do not engage users in social interactions, which means that users do not perform actions *Likes* and/or *Comments* on that posts. Such collective behavior is the same in the two different moments of civic mobilization.

5.9 Specialization of Action with Media Types

Aiming to observe collective behavior in terms of the actions performed by user and the sharing of media, a new iteration of our method guides the specialization of the rules $R4$ and $R1$, to observe which types of media are shared in social interactions.

Table 3: Specialization of A_1

$A_1.checkin$	to make a post type *checkin*
$A_1.link$	to make a post type *link*
$A_1.music$	to make a post type *music*
$A_1.photo$	to make a post type *photo*
$A_1.status$	to make a post type *status*
$A_1.swf$	to make a post type *swf*
$A_1.video$	to make a post type *video*

To represent and to evaluate media-based social interactions, a set of A_1 specialized with the media types categorized from Facebook was obtained as presented in Table 3.

5.10 Media-based SI: Preparation

Each type media posted on Facebook is categorized as *photo*, *status* (text), *video*, *link*, *swf*, *music* and *checkin*. The sharing of media during the two different moments of civic mobilization is presented in Table 4. It must be observed that, in the first moment, media type *checkin* (which allows users to confirm their presence in physical locations) is not shared.

Table 4: Media Types as Social Stimulus

photo	status	video	link	swf	music	checkin
35.83%	37.89%	14.90%	11.16%	0.13%	0.09%	-
34.49%	39.72%	12.27%	12.26%	0.11%	0.02%	1.13%

5.11 Media-based SI: Representation

When user a posts a *photo* which receives *Likes* and *Comments* ({photo,L,K}), we represent such media-based social interaction as: **if** user a makes a post of the type *photo* (action $A_1.photo$) and users l *Like* that post (action A_2) and users k *Comment* that post (action A_3), **then** user a and his friends (users l and k) are notified of that post (consequence C_1), and they are notified of *Like* that post (consequence C_2), and they are notified of *Comment* that post (consequence C_3).

5.12 Media-based SI: Extraction

We specialize the action A_1 with media types presented in Table 4 in datasets DSI 1 and DSI 2. From such datasets, we extract the rules presented in Listing 2 by using the implementation of the algorithm described in the Section 3.2.

Listing 2: Media-based Social Interactions

R4.1. $aA_1.status \cap lA_2 \cap kA_3 \rightarrow aklC_1 \cap aklC_2 \cap aklC_3$
R4.2. $aA_1\ photo \cap lA_2 \cap kA_3 \rightarrow aklC_1 \cap aklC_2 \cap aklC_3$
R4.3. $aA_1.video \cap lA_2 \cap kA_3 \rightarrow aklC_1 \cap aklC_2 \cap aklC_3$
R4.4. $aA_1.checkin \cap lA_2 \cap kA_3 \rightarrow aklC_1 \cap aklC_2 \cap aklC_3$
R4.5. $aA_1.link \cap lA_2 \cap kA_3 \rightarrow aklC_1 \cap aklC_2 \cap aklC_3$
R1.1. $aA_1.photo \cap \bar{l}A_2 \cap \bar{k}A_3 \rightarrow aklC_1$
R1.2. $aA_1.link \cap \bar{l}A_2 \cap \bar{k}A_3 \rightarrow aklC_1$
R1.3. $aA_1.status \cap \bar{l}A_2 \cap \bar{k}A_3 \rightarrow aklC_1$
R1.4. $aA_1.video \cap \bar{l}A_2 \cap \bar{k}A_3 \rightarrow aklC_1$
R1.5. $aA_1.checkin \cap \bar{l}A_2 \cap \bar{k}A_3 \rightarrow aklC_1$

5.13 Media-based SI: Measurement

The rule evaluation measures measures presented in Table 1 are computed for the rules sumarized in Listing 2.

Figure 3 presents the value of support ($SupR$). The values of $ConR$ for rules in Listing 2 are 100%. Figure 4 presents the value of cosine correlation ($CosR$) It must be observed that $R4.1$ and $R1.1$ are the two most frequent and the two most strong media-based social interactions.

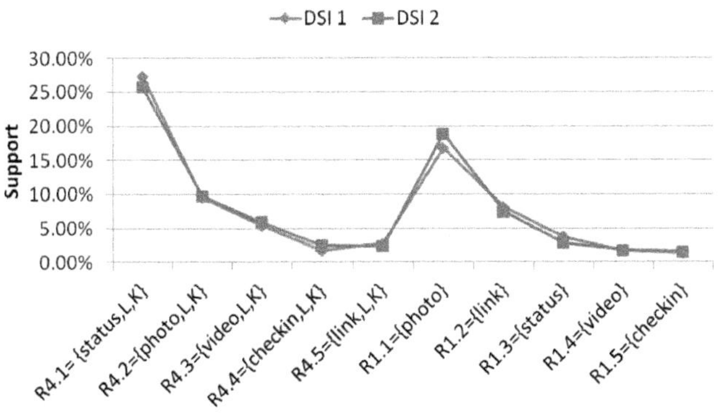

Figure 3: *SupR* for Media-based Social Interactions

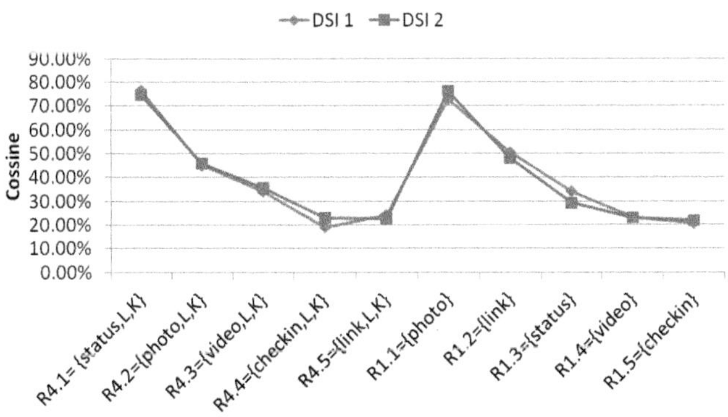

Figure 4: *CosR* for Media-based Social Interactions

5.14 Media-based SI: Validation

The media-based social interactions presented in Listing 2 are validated by specialists in social interaction analysis, as in the case of the validation of generic social interactions.

5.15 Media-based SI: Interpretation

Analyzing the media sharing, it must be observed that users perform *Likes* and *Comments* around the media type *status* (text). Also, an important percentage of posts are of the media type photo ($Sup(R1.1) \cong 18\%$), which did not instigate social interactions.

Is is interesting to observe that the collective behaviors measured by $SupR$ (Figure 3) and by $CosR$ (Figure 4) are very similar and consistent in the two different moments of online civic mobilization analysed: in terms of media-based social interactions, even being able to use rich media types for sharing, users are more likely to use the media *text* when engaged in civic mobilization.

Another interest finding is worth observing: although the media type *photo* is frequently shared, Facebook users do not perform *Likes* and/or *Comments* after such media sharing; in other words, in the scope of the datasets analyzed, users are not likely to choose the media *photo* when engaged in civic mobilization.

6. FINAL REMARKS

In earlier work we proposed the application of established data mining procedures to evaluate rules associated with social interactions, and developed a technique for codifying, mining and evaluating social interactions. In this paper we present a method which guides the iterative application of the technique. We use our method to analyze social interactions occurring in a 45-day period in which two online civic mobilizations against corruption which mobilized thousands of protesters occurred in Brazil.

After the rule mining stage, we measured social interactions and we found that the collective behavior is very similar and consistent in two different moments of the online civic mobilization.

In terms of generic social interactions, we observed that Facebook users are more likely to engage by performing *Likes* and *Comments* on Posts.

In terms of media-based social interactions, we also observed that users are more likely to perform actions *Like* and *Comment* after the sharing of media type *text* to engage in civic mobilization. On the one hand, this result is similar to that in which users are more likely to share the media *text* to engage in online civic mobilizations on Twitter [31] [25] [24]. On the other hand, this result is different from that in which users are more likely to share the media *photo* to engage closest friends to private social events (e.g., parties, dating, etc.) [17] [28].

Our technique and associated method are efforts toward an approach to analyze response behavior to understand how interactions are developed and are influenced in social media system. The approach presented supports the understanding of how people engage around specific topics of real-world life using the facilities of interaction powered by social-awared media networks. Our approach can be used in other social networks upon identification of *actions A*, *agents of actions* and *consequences C* in the context of those networks, and after permission is given by users to access the corresponding data.

One limitation of our approach is that the identification of *actions A*, *agents of actions* and *consequences C* depends on the feeling of the analyst. Also, the execution time of our algorithm during the discovery of contingencies may be improved. Moreover, we depend on previously given authorized access to social interaction data which can be collected from the social networks.

In future work we plan to design a process based on our technique, providing an implementation that potential users may deploy when developing social media applications.

Acknowledgments

The authors thank FAPESP for supporting the presentation of this paper. The authors also thank CAPES, CNPq, FAPESP, FINEP, MCT and RNP for financial support. Alan Keller also thanks the PIQS-IFG.

7. REFERENCES

[1] R. Agrawal and R. Srikant. Mining sequential patterns. In *Int. Conference on Data Engineering*, ICDE '95, pages 3–14, 1995.

[2] C. A. S. Bigonha, T. N. C. Cardoso, M. M. Moro, V. A. F. Almeida, and M. A. Gonçalves. Detecting

evangelists and detractors on twitter. In *Brazilian Symposium on Multimedia and Web (WebMedia)*, pages 107–114, 2010.

[3] C.-W. Cho, Y.-H. Wu, and A. L. Chen. Effective database transformation and efficient support computation for mining sequential patterns. *J. Intell. Inf. Syst.*, 32(1):23–51, Feb. 2009.

[4] M. De Choudhury and H. Sundaram. Why do we converse on social media?: an analysis of intrinsic and extrinsic network factors. In *Proceedings of SIGMM Int. Workshop on Social media*, WSM '11, pages 53–58, 2011.

[5] X. Dong, Z. Zheng, L. Cao, Y. Zhao, C. Zhang, J. Li, W. Wei, and Y. Ou. e-NSP: efficient negative sequential pattern mining based on identified positive patterns without database rescanning. In *Proceedings of Inter. Conf. on Information and Knowledge Management*, CIKM '11, pages 825–830, 2011.

[6] U. M. Fayyad, G. Piatetsky-Shapiro, and P. Smyth. From data mining to knowledge discovery in databases. *AI Magazine*, 17(3):37–54, 1996.

[7] J. Fürnkranz, D. Gamberger, and N. Lavrac. *Rule Learning: Essentials of Machine Learning and Relational Data Mining.* Springer, 1st edition, 2011.

[8] A. K. Gomes and M. d. G. C. Pimentel. Measuring media-based social interactions provided by smartphone applications in social networks. In *Proceedings of Workshop on Social and Behavioural Networked Media Access in ACM Multimedia*, SBNMA '11, pages 59–64, 2011.

[9] A. K. Gomes and M. d. G. C. Pimentel. A technique for human-readable representation and evaluation of media-based social interactions in social networks. In *Brazilian Symposium on Multimedia and Web (WebMedia)*, pages 119–126. ACM DL, 2011.

[10] A. K. Gomes and M. d. G. C. Pimentel. Media-based social interaction patterns: a case study in an online civic mobilization. In *Proceedings of the Inter. Workshop on Socially-Aware Multimedia in ACM Multimedia 2012 (to appear)*, IWSAM'12, pages 59–64, 2012.

[11] A. K. Gomes and M. G. C. Pimentel. A media-based social interactions analysis procedure. In *Proc. of the ACM Symposium on Applied Computing*, SAC '12, pages 1018–1024, 2012.

[12] M. Hall, E. Frank, G. Holmes, B. Pfahringer, and I. H. Witten. The Weka data mining software: an update. *SIGKDD Explor. Newsl.*, 11(1):10–18, 2009.

[13] N. Lavrac, P. A. Flach, and B. Zupan. Rule evaluation measures: A unifying view. In *Int. Work. on Ind. Logic Prog. (ILP)*, pages 174–185. Springer, 1999.

[14] C. M. Mascaro and S. P. Goggins. Brewing up citizen engagement: the coffee party on facebook. In *Proc. of the Int. Conf. on Communities and Technologies*, C&T '11, pages 11–20, 2011.

[15] F. Mechner. A notation system for the description of behavioral procedures. *Journal of Experimental Analysis of Behavioral*, 2:133–150, 1959.

[16] F. Mechner. Behavioral contingency analysis. *Behavioral Processes*, 78(2):124–144, 2008.

[17] M. Rabbath, P. Sandhaus, and S. Boll. Analysing facebook features to support event detection for photo-based facebook applications. In *Proc. of Inter. Conf. on Multimedia Retrieval*, ICMR '12, pages 11:1–11:8, 2012.

[18] S. P. Robertson, R. K. Vatrapu, and R. Medina. The social life of social networks: Facebook linkage patterns in the 2008 U.S. presidential election. In *Int. Conf. on Digital Government Research*, dg.o '09, pages 6–15. Digital Government Society of North America, 2009.

[19] R. G. Rossi and S. O. Rezende. Building a topic hierarchy using the bag-of-related-words representation. In *Proceedings of Symposium on Document Engineering*, DocEng '11, pages 195–204, 2011.

[20] R. Rummel. Social behavior and interaction – Chapter 9. In S. Publications, editor, *Understanding Conflict and War – The Conflict.* John Wiley, 1976.

[21] M. Sidman. Equivalent relations and the reinforcement contingency. *Journal of Experimental Analysis of Behavioral*, 74:127–146, 2000.

[22] A. Silva, H. Valiati, S. Guimarães, and W. M. Jr. From individual behavior to influence networks: A case study on twitter. In *Brazilian Symposium on Multimedia and Web (WebMedia)*, pages 135 –142. ACM DL, 2011.

[23] B. F. Skinner. *Science and Human Behavior.* New York Press, 1953.

[24] K. Starbird and L. Palen. "voluntweeters": self-organizing by digital volunteers in times of crisis. In *Conference on Human Factors in computing systems*, CHI '11, pages 1071–1080, 2011.

[25] K. Starbird and L. Palen. (How) will the revolution be retweeted?: information diffusion and the 2011 egyptian uprising. In *Proceedings of Conf. on Computer Supported Cooperative Work*, CSCW '12, pages 7–16, 2012.

[26] P.-N. Tan, M. Steinbach, and V. Kumar. *Introduction to Data Mining.* Addison Wesley, 2005.

[27] I. Ting, T. Hong, and L. Wang. *Social Network Mining, Analysis, and Research Trends: Techniques and Applications.* Igi Global, 2012.

[28] L. P. Tosun. Motives for facebook use and expressing "true self" on the internet. *Computers in Human Behavior*, 28(4):1510 – 1517, 2012.

[29] S. Wasserman and K. Faust. *Social Network Analysis: Methods and Applications.* Cambridge U. Press, 1994.

[30] C. B. Williams. Social networks in political campaigns: Facebook and the 2006 midterm elections. *Meeting of the American Political Science Association*, 1:49 –62, 2007.

[31] Z. Zhou, R. Bandari, J. Kong, H. Qian, and V. Roychowdhury. Information resonance on twitter: watching iran. In *ACM Workshop on Social Media Analytics*, SOMA '10, pages 123–131, 2010.

Leveraging Relationships in Social Networks for Sentiment Analysis

Juliano C. B. Rabelo, Ricardo C. B. Prudêncio, Flávia A. Barros
Centro de Informática - UFPE
Av. Prof. Moraes Rego 1235
Recife - PE - Brazil
+55 81 2126-8430 (Ext: 4304)
{jcbr, rbcp, fab}@cin.ufpe.br

ABSTRACT

The emergence of online social networks in the past few years has generated an enormous amount of valuable data containing user opinions and experiences about the most varied subjects. Aiming to identify the orientation of user postings, several sentiment analysis techniques have been proposed - mainly based on text analysis. We propose here a different perspective to treat this problem, based on a user centric approach. We adopt a graph representation in which nodes represent users and connections represent their relationships in social networks. When available, the user opinion orientation is used to tag the user node. Then, we apply link mining techniques to infer opinions of users who have not posted their opinion about the subject under analysis. Preliminary experiments on a Twitter corpus of political preferences have shown promising results.

Categories and Subject Descriptors

G.2.2 [**Discrete Mathematics**]: Graph Theory – *graph algorithms, graph labeling.*

General Terms

Theory, Algorithms.

Keywords

Sentiment analysis; node classification; link mining; collective classification; opinion mining; social networks.

1. INTRODUCTION

The World Wide Web, initially used as a mere static information repository, has turned into a huge source of different applications, containing not only information but also providing entertainment, business, relationship, etc. That diversity of applications contributed to the web popularization and, among the most accessed websites, we see e-commerce (e.g., Amazon, eBay) and, more recently, social networks such as Facebook, Twitter and Orkut [24]. Those repositories contain an enormous amount of users' opinions related to products and services. In e-commerce websites, for instance, while buying a product online, users can also provide immediate feedback (either by filling specific forms or by posting opinions on specialized websites, such as Epinions).

However, the recent explosion of social networks [4] made them the main platform for users communication on the web. In social networks, opinions are not restricted to products and services, since their users can potentially discuss any subject, ranging from politics to trips or favorite dishes. The ubiquity of online social networks, the enormous amount of available data, together with the diversity of issues about which people talk have driven researchers' focus of interest to these websites. In fact, not only researchers have great challenges to solve here, but also many interesting real applications can be developed. Clearly, all that information is highly valuable for companies which aim to improve existing products or services, evaluate competitors, estimate potential markets, etc.

This scenario requires effective techniques and algorithms to automatically mine information from those databases. This research field is commonly referred to as Sentiment Analysis [30]. Usually, sentiment analysis algorithms analyze a text snippet to classify it as positive, negative or neutral with respect to a given entity. Nevertheless, not only the text produced by social networks users make them suitable for Sentiment Analysis. Those networks also provide a new information dimension that may be leveraged: the relationships among users. By analyzing how users interact with each other within a particular social network, it may be possible to infer their opinions on specific matters, provided that we know the opinion orientation of part of the network users.

The purpose of this work is to evaluate link mining (more specifically, collective classification [12]) techniques on the context of Sentiment Analysis in a user centric approach. We adopt a graph representation in which nodes represent users and connections represent their relationships in the social network. Thus, we provide as input to the collective classification algorithm a set of users in a social network with known opinion orientation (i.e., the labeled users), and the algorithm automatically classifies the set of unlabeled users based on the known label of their connections.

In order to verify the viability of the proposed approach, we developed a case study aiming to classify political opinion of Twitter users. In this case study, we collected a dataset of around 9,000 tweets and respective users, and created a graph where which node represents a user labeled with his/her political class. In our experiments with collective classification, we evaluated the use of a Relaxation Labeling technique [7] and different strategies for choosing the users to be labeled (e.g., the most connected

Permission to make digital or hard copies of all or part of this work for personal or classroom use is granted without fee provided that copies are not made or distributed for profit or commercial advantage and that copies bear this notice and the full citation on the first page. To copy otherwise, or republish, to post on servers or to redistribute to lists, requires prior specific permission and/or a fee.
WebMedia'12, October 15–18, 2012, São Paulo/SP, Brazil.
Copyright 2012 ACM 978-1-4503-1706-1/12/10...$15.00.

users). The experiments revealed promising results, with a performance rate of more than 80% in some cases.

The rest of this paper is organized as follows: section 2 gives more background and briefly describes related work on the fields of Sentiment Analysis and Link Mining. Section 3 presents in detail the proposed approach. Section 4 explains experiments executed on Twitter, section 5 lists some of the planed extensions for this work and section 6 presents our conclusions.

2. RELATED WORK

The task of classifying opinions gathered from online data sources has received much attention from researchers recently [30]. Most of the techniques seen on the literature approach the problem by analyzing text segments containing the opinions (we will refer to those techniques as "Classical Sentiment Analysis"). In this section, we present a brief review of some classical approaches to sentiment analysis. We will also review some researches which use link information in the context of sentiment analysis (although none of those works has the same focus we gave here).

2.1 Classical Sentiment Analysis

Processing free form text to identify opinion orientation requires five basic steps:

1) Capture: collects documents to be processed.

2) Segmentation: breaks documents down to sentences. Ideally, this step should include the removal of sentences which do not contain opinionated information.

3) Attribute identification: the goal of this step is to identify relevant attributes (or features) of the object. For example, in hotel opinions, the relevant attributes would include comfort, price, food quality, location, etc. This is a refinement of the model and sometimes is not performed; in those cases, it is assumed the opinion is on the object, no matter what attribute is cited.

4) Classification: during this step, the opinion orientation on each attribute (or object) is inferred. Most of the work developed to this task is based on lexicons [9], [15]. That approach consists on the use of opinionated words and phrases to infer the sentence opinion orientation. There are works for automatic lexicon construction and semi automatic approaches for classification rule mining [33] and [26].

5) Presentation: results are presented to the users.

There were recently great advances in this area, but not rarely there are challenges which are not currently well handled by existing algorithms. Among those, we may highlight:

- Convoluted sentence constructions: automatically classifying the sentiment of a text snippet with respect to some object may get more difficult when the sentences are written in convoluted constructions. Not only the classification itself is harder, but other steps (as attribute/object identification) also become more complex [27]. Natural language processing techniques and other tools may be applied, but this is still an open issue for processing open domain documents;

- Irony/sarcasm handling: there are works devoted solely to classify opinions from ironic and sarcastic text snippets [6]. Integrating those classification algorithms in a general sentiment analysis system may also require another classifier to identify whether the text should be treated as ironic or not;

- Negation handling: the same we said for irony/sarcasm applies here. There are works which are focused on appropriately processing negation in text snippets [8], but this adds up complexity to the overall flow;

- Comparative sentences, which require specific treatment [10];

- Wrong grammar, misspellings and use of slang also increase the difficulty of this task [29] and are addressed by specific researches [25], [2].

Those issues show that a good real world classical sentiment analysis system requires special handling for some very hard problems. Another problem seen on those systems to which were found no references is the issue of external context resolution. Sometimes, the information provided in the text is not enough for classifying its opinion orientation. As an example, consider the following fictitious (but viable) text snippet: "I think the economic situation in Europe will certainly influence Brazil", which is a negative opinion on Brazilian economics, given the (external) context of Europe being in a crisis. Another, slightly different, example would be: "I think his last speech on the new Obama policy was spot on", whose opinion orientation is given by the referenced speech.

All of the above mentioned issues are frequent in opinionated documents and make the problem of assessing the expressed sentiment a lot harder.

2.2 Link Based Classification

The presence of links (or, more generally, relationships) among entities is common in information repositories. Those links usually represent information on the entities, either explicitly (e.g., the list of user friends in a social network) or implicitly (if many of my friends like a given product, chances are that I might like it as well).

Traditional data mining algorithms usually aim at finding patterns on a dataset containing instances independent from each other. If one models such instances with a graph, the problem may be seen as learning the node attributes while neglecting the links among the nodes.

However, when relationship information is available, it is important to model the instances and algorithms to leverage that information. One of the key features that made Google the most used web search engine was the use of such information via its PageRank algorithm [5]. Recommender systems had a significant improvement in precision and recall with Collaborative Filtering [23]. Like the above examples indicate, the link mining scenario usually needs to cope with heterogeneous and deeply structured data, in domains which not rarely contain many types of objects. Thus, the modeling graph may have different types of nodes and edges.

The field of Link Mining studies techniques and algorithms which appropriately model those idiosyncrasies. Among the different subfields in Link Mining, we are especially interested in Collective Classification, whose goal is to assign classes to objects based on the relationships among the objects. Our intuition is leveraging homophily, the principle that a contact between similar people occurs at a higher rate than among dissimilar people [20], which is ubiquitous in observations and theories of social networks [22], and has already been used in the context of online social networks (e.g., reference [3] monitored

Twitter users for 6 months and showed that general happiness is assortative across the Twitter social network).

We did not find references of link structure applications for sentiment analysis with the same focus we propose here. However, we did find some related works that are worth mentioning: reference [31] applies collective classification to the problem of sentiment analysis, but their focus is detecting sentence subjectivity in movie reviews. Their results suggest that discarding objective sentences make the text to be analyzed not only shorter, but also cleaner representations of the intended polarity. Reference [34] proposes a multi grain collective classification framework to exploit the information available at different granularity levels and use intra dependencies at each level and inter dependencies between the levels. Notice that both approaches make use of collective classification, but for modeling the document that must be classified as a graph, whereas our approach uses collective classification in a user centric manner, since we do not try to classify documents, but users. We assume there is a partially labeled graph of users with opinion information (which can be given or constructed with simple semi-automatic methods, like the one we used in our experiments, which is described in section 4) and use collective classification to infer opinions of the unknown nodes. In the following subsections, we describe how link information is being used in the field of Sentiment Analysis. Our approach will be explained in section 3.

2.2.1 Relationships between Document Units

A document can be seen as set of sub-document units (paragraphs or sentences) with different, possibly opposing labels, where the overall sentiment label for the document is a function of the sequence of labels at the sub-document level. Instead of seeing a document as a bag of features, there have been various attempts to model the structure of a document via analysis of sub-document units, and to explicitly utilize the relationships between those units to achieve a more accurate global labeling. Modeling the relationships between these sub-document units may also improve sub-document labeling.

An opinionated text snippet often consists of evaluative portions, which influence the overall sentiment of the document, (e.g., "this is a good restaurant") and are often called "subjective portions" and non-evaluative, or objective, portions (e.g., "the cell phone has a built-in 3.2MP camera").[1] The overlap between the vocabulary used for evaluative portions and non-evaluative portions makes it particularly important to model the context in which these text segments occur. Reference [31] proposes a two-step procedure for polarity classification in movie reviews, which first detects and removes the objective portions of a document (since they are considered uninformative) and then applies polarity classification to the remainder of the document. It is important to notice that, instead of making the subjective–objective classification for each sentence individually, they assume there might be some degree of continuity in subjectivity labels (since authors usually do not switch too frequently between subjective and objective portions), and incorporate this intuition by assigning preferences for pairs of nearby sentences to receive similar labels. All the sentences in the document are then labeled as being either subjective or objective through a collective classification process.

2.2.2 Relationships in Conversational Scenarios

An interesting scenario for opinion mining comes up when the texts to be analyzed are part of a running discussion, such as in the case of individual turns in political debates, posts to online discussion boards, or comments on blog posts. One important aspect here is the rich information source that references between those texts represent, since such information can be leveraged for better collective labeling of the documents. Using such relationships between the texts is especially useful when the texts are written in a convoluted or uncommon way (which is quite often in this scenario), what makes it difficult to classify on their own (as we mentioned in subsection 2.1). These documents can be easily categorized, despite of their complicated structure, if we find within them indications of agreement with some text that is clearly positive (or negative).[2] From manual examination of responses in newsgroups devoted to three distinct controversial topics (abortion, gun control and immigration), reference [1] observes that the relationship between two individuals in the "responded-to" network is more likely to be antagonistic (i.e., in this scenario, people tend to get into conversations more often with those with opposing opinions). Assuming that "respond-to" links imply disagreement, users are effectively classified into opposite camps via graph partitioning, outperforming methods that depend solely on the textual information within a particular document.

Similarly, reference [28] examines "quoting" behavior among users, which have been previously classified as either liberal or conservative, of the politics.com discussion site. A user can refer to another user by quoting part of some of its posts, or by addressing the other user by name or user ID. The researchers observed that a significant fraction of the posts of interest to them contained quoted material. Moreover, in accordance with findings from [1] cited above, politics.com posters tend to quote users at the opposite end of the political spectrum. To perform the final political orientation classification, users are clustered so that those who tend to quote the same entities are placed in the same cluster.

2.2.3 Relationships between Product Features

Reference [33] treats the labeling of opinion words regarding product features as a collective labeling process. That work proposes an iterative algorithm wherein the polarity assignments for individual words are collectively adjusted through a relaxation-labeling process. Starting from "global" word labels computed over a large text collection that reflect the sentiment orientation for each particular word in general settings, the label is gradually re-defined from one that is generic, to one that is specific to a review corpus, to one that is specific to some given product feature, to, finally, one that is specific to the particular context in which the word occurs. They make sure to respect sentence-level local constraints that opinions connected by conjunctions such as "but" should receive opposite polarities, whilst opinions connected by conjunctions like "and" should receive the same polarity.

[1] Notice that objective sentences may sometimes imply an opinion, e.g. "The phone battery lasted for two weeks". Correct evaluation of this type of sentence often requires external context resolution, cited in subsection 2.1 as one of the challenges faced by classical sentiment analysis techniques.

[2] This is similar to what we propose, but focused on the specific scenario of turn-based discussions.

The idea of utilizing discourse information to help with the inference of relationships between product attributes can also be found in [36], which uses agreement information in a task where one must predict ratings for multiple aspects of the same item (e.g., comfort and fuel consumption for a car). Its approach is to construct a linear classifier to predict whether all aspects of a product are given the same rating, and combine this prediction with that of individual-aspect classifiers so as to minimize a certain loss function (which they term the "grief"). Interestingly, reference [36] gives an example where a collection of independent aspect-rating predictors cannot assign a correct set of aspect ratings, but augmentation with their agreement classification allows perfect rating assignment; in their specific example, the agreement classifier is able to use the presence of the phrase "but not" to predict a contrasting rating between two aspects.

2.2.4 *Relationships between Classes*

Regression formulations (including ordinal regression) are quite well-suited to the rating reference problem of predicting the degree of positivity in opinionated documents such as product reviews, and to similar problems such as determining the strength with which an opinion is held. In a sense, regression implicitly models similarity relationships between classes that correspond to points on a scale, such as the number of "stars" given by a reviewer. In contrast, standard multi-class categorization focuses on capturing the distinct features present in each class, and ignores the fact that "5 stars" is much more like "4 stars" than "2 stars." On a movie review dataset, it is observed in [32] that a one-vs-all multi-class categorization scheme can outperform regression for a three-class classification problem (positive, neutral, and negative), perhaps due to each class exhibiting a sufficiently distinct vocabulary, but for more fine-grained classification, regression presents better results.

Furthermore, while regression-based models implicitly encode the intuition that similar items should receive similar labels, reference [32] formulates rating inference as a metric labeling problem [17], so that a natural notion of distance between classes ("2 stars" and "3 stars" are more similar to each other than "1 star" and "4 stars" are) is captured explicitly. More specifically, an optimal labeling is computed that balances the output of a classifier that considers items in isolation with the importance of assigning similar labels to similar items.

A similar version of this problem is considered in [18], with the difference that one of the classes (corresponding to "objective") does not lie on the positive-to-negative continuum. Reference [14] presents a graph-based algorithm that addresses the rating inference problem in the semi-supervised learning setting, where a closed-form solution to the underlying optimization problem is found through computation on a matrix induced by a graph representing inter-document similarity relationships, and the loss function encodes the desire for similar items to receive similar labels. In [21], the use isotonic conditional random fields is proposed to capture the ordinal labels of local (sentence-level) sentiments. Given words that are strongly associated with positive and negative sentiments, they formulate constraints on the parameters to reflect the intuition that adding a positive (negative) word should affect the local sentiment label positively (negatively).

3. PROPOSED APPROACH

Our approach to sentiment analysis in online social networks is based on collective classification. The problem may be more formally defined as follows: given a graph *G* representing (part of) a social network, composed of a set $U=\{u_1, u_2, ..., u_n\}$ of users, a set of edges $E_{UxU}=\{(u_i, u_j), ...\} \mid (u_i, u_j) \in$ E iif users u_i and u_j are connected, and a sufficiently large subset $K \subset U$ of users with known opinion orientation (i.e., the labeled users), the task is to create a model to effectively classify the set of unlabeled users $Y=\{y_1, ..., y_k\}$ where $y_i \in U$ and $y_i \notin K$ relying solely on *G*. The rationale is: by using a model which includes link information, we expect to achieve higher classification precision rates and to be able to handle cases that cannot be handled or would be very difficult to handle by Classical Sentiment Analysis techniques, such as those listed in subsection 2.1. That expectation is supported by studies which demonstrate that taking advantage of relational information can improve performance substantially [16], [37]. Moreover, this model could be used even to classify users who have not explicitly expressed their opinions, thus allowing also for a substantial improvement in coverage. Our results indicate that, when the classes of the 10% most connected nodes are known, the model is able to classify the remaining nodes with almost 80% of accuracy (see section 4).

Our algorithm receives a partially labeled graph, performs node selection (actually, a graph pruning process to generate a suitable graph for the classification task) and runs a classification algorithm which consists of a model comprised of three main components: (1) the relational classifier, which gets as input a node and its neighborhood, and produces a classification or a class-probability estimate for that node. For example, a relational classifier might combine local features and the neighbors' labels using a naive Bayes model [7]; (2) a component which addresses the problem of collective inference: what should we do when a node's classification depends on a neighbor's class and vice versa? And (3), a local classifier: such classification methods require initial ("prior") estimates of the nodes classes.

Preliminary experiments on data collected from Twitter have shown promising results. As we said before, no references on sentiment analysis were found with the same focus.

3.1 Implementation

For the implementation of the proposed model we used NetKit, a framework which contains relational and collective inference algorithms to process graph data like we explained above [19]. The three components described are configured in our implementation as follows:

- Local classifier: since we do not have local attributes on the nodes, our local classifier returns the *a priori* probabilities of each class.

- Relational classifier: we used the weighted vote relational neighbor classifier, which estimates class membership probabilities by assuming the existence of homophily. Its definition is quite simple: given $u_i \in Y$, the classifier estimates $P(u_i|N_i)$ as the weighted mean of the class-membership probabilities of the entities in N_i:

$$P(x_i = c \mid N_i) = \frac{1}{Z} \sum_{u_j \in N_i} w_{i,j} \cdot P(x_j = c \mid N_j)$$

where Z is a normalizer, N_i is the neighborhood of node u_i and c is one of the possible classes.

- Collective inferencing: a relaxation labeling algorithm based on [7] was used. It was chosen instead of other methods of collective inferencing (e.g., [11]) because, unlike those methods, relaxation labeling does not treat the graph as being in a specific labeling state at a given point; instead, it retains uncertainty, keeping track of the current probability estimations. The pseudo code for the algorithm is shown below:

Table 1: Pseudo code for the relaxation labeling algorithm.

For $u_i \in Y$, initialize the prior $\hat{c}_i^{(0)}$ using the Local Classifier (LC), where $\hat{c}_i$ is a vector of probabilities representing LC's estimates of $P(x_i\|N_i)$. $\hat{c}_i(k)$ is the k-th value in $\hat{c}_i$ and represents $P(x_i = c_k\|N_i)$.
For each $u_i \in K$, estimate class xi by applying the relational model: $\hat{c}_i^{(t+1)} \leftarrow M_R(u_i^{(t)})$, where $M_R(u_i^{(t)})$ denotes using the estimates $\hat{c}_j^{(t)}$ for $u_j \in N_i$ and t is the iteration count. This has the effect that all predictions are done pseudo-simultaneously based on the state of the graph after iteration t.

This algorithm approximately maximizes the joint probability of the labels of all nodes in the graph whose labels were initially unknown. A pre condition for its applicability is that part of the nodes on the network has already been assigned classes. In section 4 we explain how we created graphs suitable for processing by this algorithm.

4. EXPERIMENTS

The first step to execute our experiments is constructing a graph of social network users (Twitter was used in the experiments). The procedure we followed to build such a graph was as follows: we defined a subject to monitor (USA politics) and collected tweets containing mentions to well-known American politicians from both the Democrat and Republican parties, like Barack Obama, Sarah Palin, etc. Since we needed a labeled corpus for evaluating our algorithm, the first attempt to achieve that was through the application of classical text based sentiment analysis on the collected tweets. For that task, we used Twitter Sentiment [13], a web tool for sentiment analysis which takes as input the text to be processed and, optionally, the entity on which the sentiment must be calculated (our inputs were the tweet text and the respective politician name). However, we analyzed a sample of 5% of the results and observed that the precision was low at around 60%, and that would potentially have a negative effect on the experiments. Thus, we considered to manually label all the collected tweets. Although it would be feasible for our corpus of around 9,000 tweets (see Table 2), this was very labor intensive and would not scale when we need to run other experiments.

So, our approach to having a labeled corpus followed a simple, semi-automatic approach: we empirically observed that hashtags such as #obama2012, #teaparty, etc were great indicators of users' political lean. Of course, there were a few cases in which those hashtags were used in a criticizing context, but those can be seen as corpus noise and would not severally influence the results. Thus, we monitored Twitter not for the politicians' names, but for those hashtags listed on Table 2, automatically classifying posts according to them. We called as "authors" the users who posted the collected tweets. Then, we collected all users which were followers or were followed by the authors and called them "non-authors", as they had not explicitly manifested their opinion on the monitored subjects.

A directed graph is built with nodes modeling users and edges modeling the follower/follows relationship. An author is labeled with the class which has the highest count among its posts, and non-authors are assigned an unknown class. A refinement of this labeling approach would be to consider the counts proportionally, so that a user with many positive and many negative tweets gets classified as neutral, even if the tweet count for positive and negative classes are different. Another option would be to consider the user political polarity as a value in the interval [-1; 1] whose limits represent the ends of the political spectrum. Thus, users with a more radical political lean would be close to the limits of the interval, whereas users with similar numbers of posting making compliments/criticisms to both Republican and Democrat parties would lie close to the center.

Table 2: Information on the data collected from Twitter.

Period monitored	Jan, 1 2012 - Jan 9 2012
Monitored hashtags and respective postings and user counts	#dems2012 (1,260) (525) #obama2012 (3,159) (1,952) #teaparty (1,535) (742) #tcot (3,144) (1,500)
Classes of postings/users	Republican, Democrat, Unknown

We collected 9,098 posts from 4,719 users containing the monitored hashtags (approximately 50% of each class). Users (authors and non-authors) were collected as explained before. That procedure resulted in a graph with more than 97,000 nodes and almost 1 million edges (Figure 1a). Clearly, applying collective classification on such a graph is not feasible, since a very small fraction of around 5% of its nodes are labeled (i.e., the author nodes), so we developed a simple graph pruning algorithm to generate a suitable graph (see the pseudo code in Table 3). The algorithm reduced the graph to 1,244 nodes and about 78,000 edges, with around 80% of labeled nodes (Figure 1b).

Table 3: Pseudo code for the graph pruning algorithm.

$SU \leftarrow sort(U)$ is the set of users sorted in ascending degree (number of connections) order.
For each $u_i \in SU$, if removing u_i does not break connectivity in the graph G, remove u_i and its edges from G (we start with the least connected because they are less likely to break graph connectivity).
Stop when any node removal will break the graph connectivity.

To evaluate our results, we "deleted" the classes of part of the known nodes (marking those nodes as unknown) and ran the algorithm on the resulting graph, comparing the inferred classes to the expected values. We select which nodes are to be deleted in three different manners:

1) Random: randomly select *n* nodes to delete.

2) Most connected: ordering the set of nodes by degree (i.e., number of connections), remove the *n* first nodes.

3) Least connected: ordering the set of nodes by degree, remove the *n* last nodes.

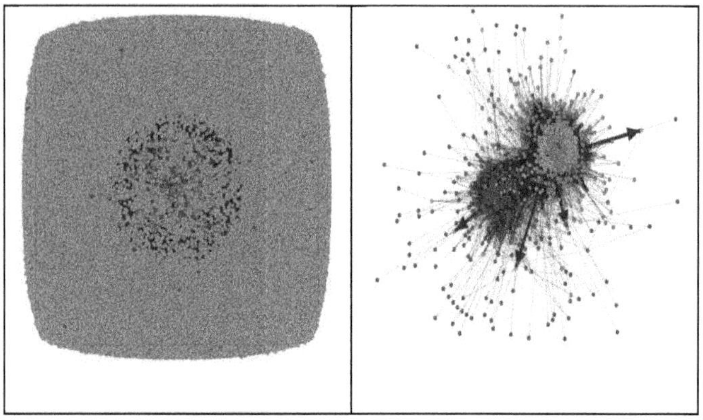

Figure 1a (left): Graph built with the method described. Blue nodes are democrats, red node are republicans and gray nodes are those who have not manifested opinion but either follow or are followed by authors ("non-authors").

Figure 1b (right): Result after pruning the graph shown in Figure 1a with the described algorithm.

The actual number *n* of nodes to delete is varied in our experiments. We start with 1% (meaning 99% of the original nodes' labels were kept), then 5%, 10%, 15%, etc. For the random node selection, we performed a 50 fold execution of the algorithm for each level, using a different random set of users to classify in each execution, and calculated the average classification precision for each level. The results are shown in Figure 2.

As expected, if we classify the least connected nodes, our precision is initially very poor since there is very little link information for the classifier to use. The precision increases as we get higher degree nodes to classify and stabilizes around 80%. It is worth noting that this performance is seen when we have as few as 10% of known nodes. That suggests we can effectively use this approach to classify 90% of a graph, once we know the classes of the 10% highest connected nodes. If this approach were to be used in real case scenarios, one could apply classical sentiment analysis techniques just to the 10% most connected users and use our method on the rest. In the lack of good text based classifiers, the classification could even be performed by a team of operators who would manually analyze the postings of the 10% most connected users, and the rest could be calculated automatically by our algorithm.

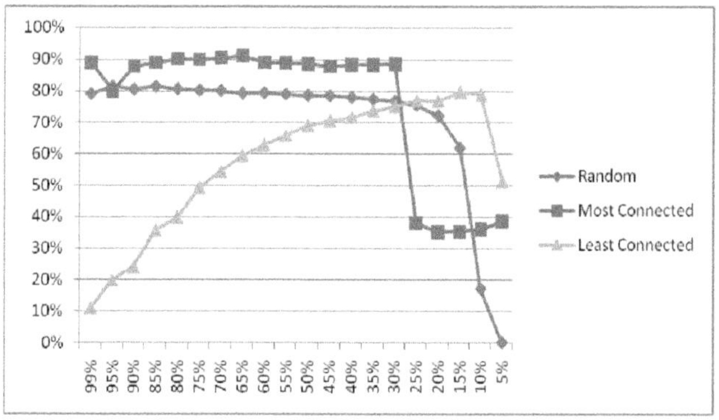

Figure 2: Precision of the algorithm for different strategies of selection for the nodes to be classified.

In the other end of the spectrum, if we know the classes of the least connected and want to classify the highest connected, our precision is initially very high at almost 90%. When we get to around 30% of known nodes (i.e., the 30% least connected), the precision drops substantially. This might be a good indicator of a threshold for the minimum amount of "degree usefulness" for this approach to be successfully applied: the 30% least connected probably do not have much utility for this algorithm, since they do not have sufficient link information to be processed. In real world applications, that would mean we would not apply the algorithm to those users (which in most cases will be of less interest for the topic being monitored anyway, given their little interaction with the rest of the community). Thus, those nodes could be neglected or handled by a text based classifier.

If we randomly select the nodes to classify, despite of their degree, we observe a consistent precision at around 80% which initially deteriorates slowly, dropping fast when there are around 20% of known nodes.

In Figure 3, we present the graph of the achieved precision considering all the nodes (including the nodes with known labels) in each step, which gives an idea of the overall precision.

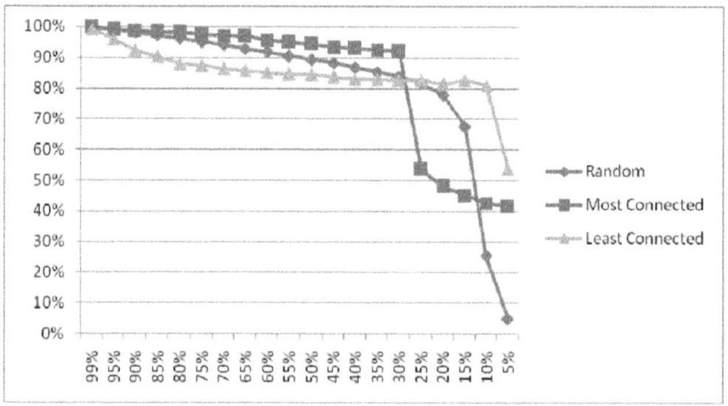

Figure 3: Overall precision considering also the known nodes.

For comparison purposes against classical text sentiment analysis techniques, we ran Twitter Sentiment on the collected postings, aggregated the postings classes for each user and labeled the users with the highest classification count (just like we had done to set up the graph in our experiment). The observed precision for users was 17.35%. Such a low precision rate for the text based sentiment classifier may be explained as follows: the tool calculates the opinion orientation of a text document with respect to some given entity. So, the expected input for this algorithm is a text segment like the following actual tweet: "Mitt Romney gave a masterful speech this weekend at Liberty University with a wonderful introduction by Mark DeMoss. Well done.", and an entity to be analyzed (in this case, "Mitt Romney"). In our experiments, the "entities" we input to the algorithm are the hashtags we use to gather Twitter postings. Since hashtags are not exactly entities in the way this text classifier expects, it cannot properly resolve the sentiment expressed about the "real" entity. For example: in the actual tweet "Anybody who says that Mitt Romney didn't create thousands of jobs has clearly never been to India or China.... #Obama2012", the algorithm would try to resolve the sentiment on "#Obama2012", which is clearly misleading (the posting is actually a criticism to the "Mitt Romney" entity; #Obama2012 is just a tag). We also ran Twitter Sentiment without specifying the entity and the results were almost the same (17.15% precision), which indicates the entity resolution in the tool is almost useless for our data, since we do not have the actual entities. Even with these limitations, the results attained by Twitter Sentiment are an indicator of how difficult it is the process of classifying opinion orientation on twitter postings considering just the text contents.

5. FUTURE WORK

We plan to further develop the research on the use of link mining techniques to the problem of sentiment analysis. We foresee several issues which would be interesting to study:

- Experiments in other domains, ideally with more than two classes, to evaluate the applicability of the technique in different scenarios;
- Evaluation of different algorithms of collective classification;
- Include in the graph information that is currently being neglected, such as retweet relationships and friendships (reciprocal followers), which might indicate a stronger correlation than the "following" relationship, and evaluate the impact of that information on the results obtained;
- Comparison of the proposed technique against other classical sentiment analysis techniques and systems, trying to better setup those tools providing plausible entities;
- Enhancement of the proposed model by using existing classical sentiment analysis techniques as the local classifier in our model. We could even study a combination model in which collective classification would not only assign classes to unlabeled nodes in graphs initially classified by classical techniques, but could also try to modify some of the nodes' classes. This would ideally combine the strengths of both techniques: classical systems would perform better on simple text structures (no sarcasm/irony handling, context resolution or deep text analysis required), and collective classification would be used for nodes with enough labeled neighbors, despite of the existence of convoluted text structures (or even the presence of any text). Studies exist which combine link and content [35], and will be evaluated.
- Study and evaluate how a user centric approach like the one proposed here can handle changes in user opinion along the time.

6. CONCLUSIONS

Sentiment analysis has recently caught a great deal of attention from the academic community. Many different algorithms have been proposed to tackle the problem of inferring the opinion orientation on a given subject by analyzing a piece of text. We propose here a different approach to that problem, which leverages the link structure available in some opinion data sources (namely online social networks, the most pervasive web application nowadays). Preliminary experiments have shown very promising results and we have a roadmap to further investigate the applicability and the improvement of the proposed technique.

7. ACKNOWLEDGEMENTS

The authors would like to thank CAPES, FACEPE and CNPq (Brazilian agencies) for their financial support.

8. REFERENCES

[1] Agrawal, R., Rajagopalan, S., Srikant, R. and Xu, Y. Mining newsgroups using networks arising from social behavior. In *12th International Conference on World Wide Web*, pp. 529–535, 2003.

[2] Amiri, H. and Chua, T. Mining slang and urban opinion words and phrases from cQA services: an optimization approach. In *5th ACM International Conference on Web Search and Data Mining*. pp. 193-202. New York, NY, USA. 2012.

[3] Bollen, J., Goncalves, B., Ruan, G., Mao, H. Happiness is assortative in online social networks. *Artificial Life* 17(3), pp. 237-251. 2011.

[4] Boyd, D. M. and Ellison, N. B. Social network sites: definition, history, and scholarship. *Journal of Computer-Mediated Communication*. pp. 210–230. 2008.

[5] Brin, S. and Page, L. The anatomy of a large-scale hypertextual Web search engine. *Computer Networks and ISDN Systems* 30: 107–117. 1998.

[6] Carvalho, P., Sarmento, L., Silva, M. J., Oliveira, E. Clues for detecting irony in user-generated contents: oh...!! it's "so easy" ;-). In *1st international ACM CIKM workshop on Topic-sentiment analysis for mass opinion*. New York, NY, USA. 2009.

[7] Chakrabarti, S., Dom, B., Indyk, P. Enhanced hypertext categorization using hyperlinks. In *ACM SIGMOD International Conference on Management of Data*, pp. 307–318, 1998.

[8] Councill, I. G., McDonald, R., Velikovich, L. What's great and what's not: learning to classify the scope of negation for improved sentiment analysis. In *ACM Workshop on Negation and Speculation in Natural Language Processing*. Stroudsburg, PA, USA. 2010.

[9] Ding, X., Liu, B. and Yu, P. A holistic lexicon-based approach to opinion mining. In *Conference on Web Search and Web Data Mining* (WSDM), 2008.

[10] Ganapathibhotla, M. and Liu, B. Mining Opinions in Comparative Sentences. In *22nd International Conference on Computational Linguistics (Coling 2008)*, pages 241–248, Manchester, August 2008.

[11] Geman, S. and Geman, D. Stochastic relaxation, Gibbs distributions and the Bayesian restoration of images. In *IEEE*

Transactions on Pattern Analysis and Machine Intelligence (PAMI), 6:721–741, 1984.

[12] Getoor, L. and Diehl, C. P. Link mining: a survey. *ACM SIGKDD Explorations*, vol. 7, issue 2. December 2005. New York, NY, USA.

[13] Go, A., Bhayani, R. and Huang, L. *Twitter sentiment classification using distant supervision*. Technical report, Stanford Digital Library Technologies Project. 2009.

[14] Goldberg, A. B. and Zhu, X. Seeing stars when there aren't many stars: Graph-based semi-supervised learning for sentiment categorization. In *TextGraphs: HLT/NAACL Workshop on Graph-based Algorithms for Natural Language Processing*, 2006.

[15] Hu, M. and Liu, B. Mining and summarizing customer reviews. In *ACM SIGKDD Conference on Knowledge Discovery and Data Mining* (KDD), pp. 168–177, 2004.

[16] Jensen, D., Neville, J. and Gallagher, B. Why collective inference improves relational classification. In *10th ACM SIGKDD International Conference on Knowledge Discovery and Data Mining* (pp. 593–598), 2004.

[17] Kleinberg, J. and Tardos, E. Approximation algorithms for classification problems with pairwise relationships: Metric labeling and Markov random fields. *Journal of the ACM*, vol. 49, pp. 616–639, ISSN 0004-5411, 2002.

[18] Koppel, M. and Schler, J. The importance of neutral examples for learning sentiment. In *Workshop on the Analysis of Informal and Formal Information Exchange During Negotiations (FINEXIN)*, 2005.

[19] Macskassy, S. A., Provost, F. NetKit-SRL: a toolkit for network learning and inference. In *Proceedings of the North American Association for Computational Social and Organizational Science (NAACSOS) Conference*, 2005.

[20] Macskassy, S. A. and Provost, F. Classification in Networked Data: A Toolkit and a Univariate Case Study. In *Journal of Machine Learning Research*. vol. 8, pp. 935-983. 2007.

[21] Mao, Y. and Lebanon, G. Isotonic conditional random fields and local sentiment flow. In *Advances in Neural Information Processing Systems*, 2007.

[22] McPherson, M., Smith-Lovin, L. and Cook, J. M. Birds of a feather: Homophily in social networks. *Annual Review of Sociology*, 27:415–444, 2001.

[23] Melville, P., Mooney, R. J. and Nagarajan, R. Content-boosted collaborative filtering for improved recommendations. In *Eighteenth National Conference on Artificial Intelligence (AAAI-2002)*, pp. 187-192, Edmonton, Canada, July 2002.

[24] Mislove , A., Marcon, M., Gummadi, K. P., Druschel P., Bhattacharjee, B. Measurement and analysis of online social networks. In *IMC'07* (San Diego, California, USA. October, 2007).

[25] Missen, M.M.S., Boughanem, M., Cabanac, G. Challenges for Sentence Level Opinion Detection in Blogs. In *8th IEEE/ACIS International Conference on Computer and Information Science*. pp. 347-351. June 2009.

[26] Morinaga, S., Yamanishi, K., Tateishi, K. and Fukushima, T. Mining product reputations on the web. In *ACM SIGKDD Conference on Knowledge Discovery and Data Mining* (KDD), pp. 341–349, 2002.

[27] Mullen, T., Malouf, R. A Preliminary Investigation into Sentiment Analysis of Informal Political Discourse. In *AAAI-2006 Spring Symposium on Computational Approaches to Analyzing Weblogs*. 2006.

[28] Mullen, T. and Malouf, R. Taking sides: User classification for informal online political discourse. *Internet Research*, vol. 18, pp. 177–190, 2008.

[29] Narayanan, R., Liu, B. and Choudhary, A. Sentiment analysis of conditional sentences. In *2009 Conference on Empirical Methods in Natural Language Processing*. Vol. 1, pp. 180-189. Stroudsburg, PA, USA.

[30] Pang, B. and Lee, L. Opinion mining and sentiment analysis. *Foundations and Trends in Information Retrieval*, vol. 2, n. 1–2, 2008.

[31] Pang, B., Lee, L. A sentimental education: sentiment analysis using subjectivity summarization based on minimum cuts. In *Proceedings of the Association for Computational Linguistics* (ACL), pp. 271–278, 2004.

[32] Pang, B. and Lee, L. Seeing stars: Exploiting class relationships for sentiment categorization with respect to rating scales. In *Proceedings of the Association for Computational Linguistics (ACL)*, pp. 115–124, 2005.

[33] Popescu, A. and Etzioni, O. Extracting product features and opinions from reviews. In *Proceedings of the Human Language Technology Conference and the Conference on Empirical Methods in Natural Language Processing* (HLT/EMNLP), 2005.

[34] Shivashankar, S. and Ravindran, B. Multi grain sentiment analysis using collective classification. In *19th European Conference on Artificial Intelligence*. 2010.

[35] Shiy, L., Zhaoy, Y. and Tang, J. Combining link and content for collective active learning. In *Proceedings of CIKM'10*, Oct, 2010. Toronto, Ontario, Canada.

[36] Snyder, B. and Barzilay, R. Multiple aspect ranking using the Good Grief algorithm. In *Proceedings of the Joint Human Language Technology/North American Chapter of the ACL Conference (HLT-NAACL)*, pp. 300–307, 2007.

[37] Taskar, B., Segal, E. and Koller, D. Probabilistic classification and clustering in relational data. In *17th International Joint Conference on Artificial Intelligence* (pp. 870–878), 2001.

Climate Quiz – A Web Application for Eliciting and Validating Knowledge from Social Networks

Arno Scharl
MODUL University Vienna
Dept. of New Media Technology
Am Kahlenberg 1, 1190 Vienna, AT
+43 1 3203555 500
arno.scharl@modul.ac.at

Marta Sabou
MODUL University Vienna
Dept. of New Media Technology
Am Kahlenberg 1, 1190 Vienna, AT
+43 1 3203555 520
marta.sabou@modul.ac.at

Michael Föls
Vienna University of Economics and Business; RICM
Augasse 2-6, 1190 Vienna, AT
+43 1 31336 5239
michael.foels@wu.ac.at

ABSTRACT
With more than 800 million monthly active users, Facebook bears significant potential for science projects. Climate Quiz is an interactive Web application in the tradition of "games with a purpose" that leverages this potential to create metadata through a crowdsourcing-based approach. It presents participants with two types of challenges: (1) selecting the correct relation to connect two environmental concepts, and (2) answering climate-related multiple choice questions. Climate Quiz aims to create shared meaning through collaborative ontology building, a process that captures emergent semantics and elicits formal knowledge in the form of a domain model. As an innovative survey instrument, the application leverages social networking platforms to capture indicators of environmental attitudes, lifestyles and behaviors.

Categories and Subject Descriptors
H.5.2 [Information Interfaces and Presentation]: User Interfaces and Interaction styles; H.5.3 [Group and Organization Interfaces]: Web-based Interaction; K.8 [Personal Computing]: Games.

General Terms
Measurement, Design, Human Factors, Verification.

Keywords
Games with a Purpose, Crowdsourcing, Climate Change, Shared Meaning, Awareness, Collaborative Ontology Building.

1. INTRODUCTION
Innovative modes of Web-based interaction enable us to validate and extend ontologies as a by-product of users playing online games, creating an entertaining yet productive setting where large-scale ontology evaluation becomes feasible. Multi-user games with a purpose (GWAPs) capture formal and informal knowledge and communication processes (in the sense of "collective mind mapping"). This reveals the "how" and "why" of the intricate knowledge relations within and across organizations. Thereby, *Climate Quiz* [18] leverages the significant potential of social networking platforms and their viral mechanisms for addressing scientific problems. Advantages include a large number of possible players, intrinsic motivation within a social context, and more effective mechanisms to detect and combat attempts of cheating and manipulating results. The use of social networking platforms also allows monitoring the propagation of the application over the network, and investigating the creation of shared meaning within a real-world setting.

Permission to make digital or hard copies of all or part of this work for personal or classroom use is granted without fee provided that copies are not made or distributed for profit or commercial advantage and that copies bear this notice and the full citation on the first page. To copy otherwise, or republish, to post on servers or to redistribute to list, requires prior specific permission and/or a fee
WebMedia'12, October 15–18, 2012, São Paulo/SP, Brazil.
Copyright 2012 ACM 978-1-4503-1706-1/12/10...$15.00.

The game with a purpose is part of the Climate Change Collaboratory [17], a research project to strengthen the relations between environmental stakeholders who recognize the need for climate change mitigation and adaptation, but differ in their specific goals and agendas. It not only develops new survey instruments such as the Climate Quiz to create shared meaning and build domain models, but also investigates the communicative strategies of various stakeholders. Thereby, the collaboratory aims to unearth hidden assumptions and misconceptions about climate change, contribute to a mutual understanding of existing problems, and suggest priorities for research and policy development.

2. RELATED WORK
Knowledge acquisition is a task that has been addressed through games from as early as 2006 when von Ahn has built Verbosity [1], a GWAP inspired from the Taboo game (where a narrator offers hints and a guesser must guess the concept), which collects a database of common-sense facts. Verbosity uses the cards metaphor to guide the types of hints that the narrator gives. For example, the "Type" card allows providing hints about the superclasses of the concept, by generating appropriate natural language templates to be filled by the Narrator. This approach ensures that the game collects a broad range of relations, such as type, purpose, is related, is opposite, spatial relations. Built an year later than Verbosity, the Common Consensus GWAP focuses on acquiring a particular type of knowledge, namely goals [6]. Inspired from the Family Feud TV show, the game asks players to answer questions such as "What are some things you would use to watch a movie?" in order to elicit commonsense knowledge about goals. The game relies on a handful of question templates which allow acquiring different types of knowledge about goals (e.g., parent and children goals or orthogonal connections between goals). As a multi-player game, players receive points in real time for all their answers that are also given by other players. Vickrey and colleagues report on three games (inspired from the Scattegories and Taboo games) that aim to collect semantically related words with their three games: Categorilla (players must

supply a phrase fitting a specific category, e.g., "Things that fly", and starting with a given letter), Categodzilla (same as Categorilla but without the letter restriction) and Free Association, where players must type words related to a given "seed" word [12].

The emergence of the Semantic Web research area has reiterated the need for formally recorded domain knowledge. Early attempts of using the GWAP paradigm in this area have primarily focused on alleviating human-input intensive tasks such as ontology learning and matching. For ontology learning, OntoPronto [11] is one of the games running on the OntoGame platform that aims to build domain ontologies from Wikipedia articles by mapping these articles to the most specific class in the Proton ontology. The Virtual Pet Game [5] aims to build a semantic network that encodes common knowledge. It runs on the popular Chinese bulletin board, PPT, and uses a pet metaphor – each player has a pet and he needs to ask and answer questions in order to earn points. The knowledge is collected and verified through this answer/question mechanism. The Raport Game [5] is a Facebook game (not accessible as of December 2011), where a semantic network of common knowledge is built through answers and questions generated by the community of its players. For ontology matching, SpotTheLink [11] is a real-time quiz running on the OntoGame platform and aiming to align concepts from DBpedia [19] and the Proton upper level ontology [21].

A current trend is building games that make use of the large body of linked open data (LOD) to build new knowledge artefacts, provide useful applications, and try to improve LOD quality:

- GuessWhat [8] creates ontologies by exploring instance data available as linked open data. Given a seed concept (e.g., banana), the game engine collects relevant instances from DBpedia, Freebase and OpenCyc and extracts the main features of the concept (e.g., fruit, yellowish) which are then verified through the collective process of game playing.
- BetterRelation [4] is a two-player game running on DFKI's website, which aims to detect which statements related to a topic make sense and are the most relevant: the players are asked to decide which of two given statements about an entity would have "come to mind first" and score points if their selections coincide. Hees et al [4] report 359 players.
- WhoKnows? [13] and RISQ [16] are developed by the same group and have a similar mechanism: they use LOD facts to generate questions and use the answers to (1) evaluate property ranking (which property of an instance is the most important/relevant); (2) detect inconsistencies; (3) find doubtful facts. The obtained property rankings reflect the "wisdom of the crowd" and are an alternative to semantic rankings generated algorithmically based on statistical and linguistic techniques. The games, however, differ in the gaming paradigm they adopt. While WhoKnows?! uses a classroom paradigm and aims towards being an educational game, RISQ is a Jeopardy-style quiz game. Although RISQ! is distributed both through Facebook and as a standalone game, Wolf et al. [16] report on only 116 distinct players.
- The recently launched UrbanGames intiative of the PlanetData project [20] will build mobile applications for the tourism domain using the GWAP paradigm where the games will reuse "clean" LOD, and, because of user interaction, they will both detect errors and acquire new facts.

3. CLIMATE QUIZ

Compared to the GWAPs described above, Climate Quiz focuses on acquiring knowledge in the domain of climate change as opposed to harvesting generic knowledge. As such, it appeals to environmental enthusiasts and leverages their interest in the domain as an additional motivational factor (besides the fun factor). Similarly to knowledge acquisition games (Virtual Pet Game, Raport Game, RISQ!) as well as games from the area of natural language processing – PhraseDetectives [2], Sentiment Quiz [9] and Climate Quiz leverage the potential of social networking systems, particularly Facebook, for attracting players. A final differentiating feature of Climate Quiz compared to other knowledge acquisition games is its pronounced educational goal, a feature resembling virtual citizen science projects [15].

3.1 Application Framework

Climate Quiz builds upon and extends the social application framework of *Sentiment Quiz*, a publicly available Facebook application and winner of the 'Online Communities, Web 2.0 and Social Networks' category of the Austrian National Award for Multimedia and e-Business [3]. Released as part of the US Election 2008 Web Monitor [10], the application asked users vote for and track their preferred candidates, and to evaluate whether quotes from election-related documents express positive or negative sentiment. Besides leveraging the wisdom of the crowds to improve algorithms for automated sentiment detection, the system helped investigate perceptions of political Web content.

3.2 Task Structure

Climate Quiz goes beyond the rather simple five-point sentence classification of Sentiment Quiz, its predecessor. It integrates multiple-choice questions, offers a separate questionnaire as a bonus challenge, and invites Facebook users and their online friends to evaluate whether two concepts presented by the system are related (e.g. "climate change", "ecosystem"), and which label is most appropriate to describe this relation (e.g. "threatens"). Similar to Verbosity and Common consensus, the system controls the types of relations between concept pairs, but our consideration set contains both generic (e.g., "is a sub-category of") and domain-specific (e.g., "opposes") relations.

Figure 1. Climate Quiz Relation Assessment

To extract the environmental concepts from Anglo-American news media coverage between January and December 2011, the project used a component for semi-automated ontology learning from unstructured text [7; 14] has been continually refined over several years as part of the webLyzard text mining framework [22]. It incorporates a range of methods from statistics, artificial intelligence and natural language processing, including co-occurrence analysis, subsumption analysis, link type detection, Hearst patterns, and spreading activation. It addresses the limited availability of expertise and qualified human resources, which is the bottleneck and cost-driver in building environmental ontologies. Automated suggestions and intuitive interfaces address this bottleneck by improving the productivity of ontology engineers. Deconstructing the complicated task of ontology building into tiny problems that can be solved by a wider community also offsets the limited availability of domain experts (the Climate Change Collaboratory does not intend to create an ontology editor; it aims at developing applications with simple and rapid user feedback mechanisms to interact with highly dynamic, evolving climate change resources).

3.3 Incentive Scheme and Dissemination

Built-in notification systems and real-time progress statistics help engage Facebook users and leverage the wisdom of the crowds for scientific purposes. Participants earn one point for each matching answers, but can also lose points if their opinion differs from the majority of players. If in doubt, the system awards a point not in order not to discourage players – if the first user selects relation A, for example, and the second user selects B, both receive a point since a majority solution has yet to be determined. If the first two players have answered A, however, the answer of a third player who does not agree with them will be considered wrong.

Participants are given immediate feedback about each in terms of the percentage of players who agreed/disagreed with their decision. This feedback constitutes a continuous training mechanism through the game, and increases transparency by explaining how the points are provided.

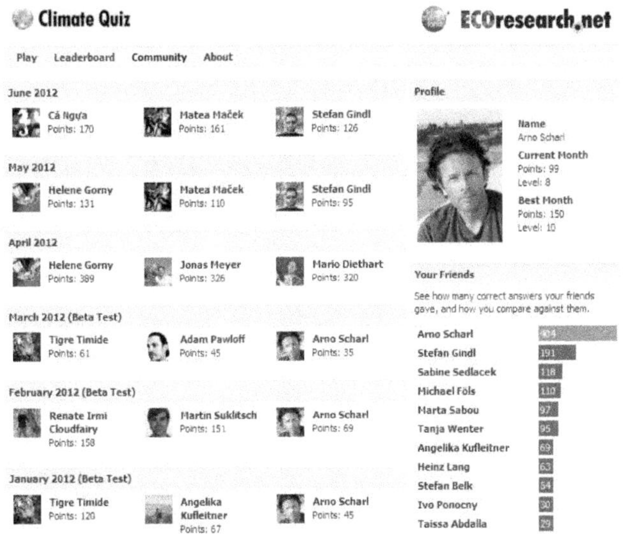

Figure 2. Climate Quiz Leaderboard

To attract a sufficient number of players, we used a combination of press releases, presentations (e.g. at an online conference organized by the World Bank's Connect4Climate initiative), paid Facebook ads, and personal networking. To maintain and grow the resulting community of players, incentives include a leveling system with the opportunity to unlock additional games features, the comparison of a player's performance vis-à-vis the network of online friends, and the leaderboard shown in Figure 2 with monthly scores and progress statistics.

3.4 Usage Statistics and Results

Climate Quiz was launched on 18 April 2012, together with a dedicated community page (see Figure 3) to assist the dissemination process.

Figure 3. Climate Quiz Community Page

Within the first week, a total number of 275 users have played the game, generating 7,836 ontology relations and 1,563 survey answers. Of these 275 players, 222 have become returning visitors and 171 (120) of them returned for at least five (ten) times. After two months, the total number of players has increased to 439, yielding 13,259 ontology relations and 2,610 survey answers. Of these 439 players, 360 have become returning visitors – 277 (208) players returning at least five (ten) times. A high level of user engagement is reflected by a typical game session lasting an average of 8.38 minutes, some for over an hour. The average speed in which players are answering is 18 seconds per ontology relation and 25 seconds per survey answer. 1,128 distinct concept pairs were assessed since the start of the game (1,076 within the first week). A final relation could be identified for 25 concept pairs; the other pairs require additional user interactions to identify the majority opinion.

3.5 Technical Implementation

Climate Quiz was implemented in PHP and JavaScript using the jQuery Framework and Facebook's Graph API. Using the Graph API enables a deep integration with the Facebook user experience and allows retrieving information about the user to use them for statistical analysis. When starting the game, Facebook provides a security token to access the information of the user (if the user grants data access to the application). The information is provided via the JavaScript Object Notation (JSON). The jQuery JavaScript framework helped avoid the need for page reloads. This not only improves the user experience, but also yields technical benefits (partial refreshes of a page reduce the total amount of SQL queries and improve the scalability of the application).

Climate Quiz uses a Model-View-Controller (MVC) design pattern to allow easy maintenance and extensibility. The data generated by playing the game and the basic information about the users are stored in a PostgreSQL database. The stored data provide rich information about the usage of the game.

4. CONCLUSION AND OUTLOOK

This paper presents Climate Quiz, a Facebook application in the tradition of "Games with a Purpose". The interactive application invites users of the social networking platform to compete with their online friends and contribute to a scientific project that aims to raise awareness and share environmental knowledge. Participants face two types of challenges: (i) select correct relations between two concepts, and (ii) answer climate change related questions. Following a literature review and overview of the task structure, the paper reports on the underlying incentive scheme and the pursued dissemination strategy, provides usage statistics and results, and summarizes the technical implementation.

Given appropriate design and authentication mechanisms, games with a purpose can also capture individual knowledge and attitudes according to the scientific criteria of objectivity, reliability, validity and representativeness. Climate Quiz provides a cost-effective tool to gain data from large worldwide samples in comparably short time intervals and in an unobtrusive setting. The application allows gaining repeated measures from the same individuals. Such data can be used to investigate emergent semantics and the temporal stability of knowledge.

5. ACKNOWLEDGMENT

The *Climate Quiz* Facebook application and the crowdsourcing methods presented in this paper were developed as part of the DIVINE (www.weblyzard.com/divine) research project, funded by FIT-IT Semantic Systems of the Austrian Research Promotion Agency (www.ffg.at) and the Federal Ministry for Transport, Innovation and Technology (www.bmvit.gv.at).

6. REFERENCES

[1] Ahn, L.v. (2006). "Games with a Purpose", *Computer,* 39(6): 92-94.

[2] Chamberlain, J., Kruschwitz, U. and Poesio, M. (2012). Motivations for Participation in Socially Networked Collective Intelligence Systems. *Collective Intelligence 2012.* T.W. Malone and L.v. Ahn. Cambridge, USA: Cornell University.

[3] Fischer, R. (2008). Election Monitor Wins Social Media Category of the Austrian National Award for Multimedia and e-Business. Vienna: MODUL University Vienna: http://www.modul.ac.at/nmt/2008-09-multimedia-award.

[4] Hees, J., Roth-Berghofer, T., et al. (2011). "BetterRelations: Using a Game to Rate Linked Data Triples", *34th Annual German Conference on Artificial Intelligence (= LNCS, Vol. 7006).* Eds. J. Bach and S. Edelkamp. Berlin: Springer. 134-138.

[5] Kuo, Y.-l., Lee, J.-C., et al. (2009). Community-Based Game Design: Experiments on Social Games for Commonsense Data Collection. *ACM SIGKDD Workshop on Human Computation (HCOMP-2009).* New York, USA: 15-22.

[6] Lieberman, H., Smith, D.A. and Teeters, A. (2007). Common Consensus: A Web-based Game for Collecting Commonsense Goals. *International Conference on Intelligent User Interfaces (IUI-2007).* Honolulu, USA.

[7] Liu, W., Weichselbraun, A., Scharl, A. and Chang, E. (2005). "Semi-Automatic Ontology Extension Using Spreading Activation", *5th International Conference on Knowledge Management (I-KNOW 2005).* Graz, Austria: Springer. 145-153.

[8] Markotschi, T. and Völker, J. (2010). "Guess What?! Human Intelligence for Mining Linked Data", *Workshop on Knowledge Injection into and Extraction from Linked Data at the International Conference on Knowledge Engineering and Knowledge Management (EKAW-2010)*Lisbon, Portugal.

[9] Rafelsberger, W. and Scharl, A. (2009). Games with a Purpose for Social Networking Platforms. *20th ACM Conference on Hypertext and Hypermedia.* C. Cattuto et al. Torino, Italy: Association for Computing Machinery: 193-197.

[10] Scharl, A. and Weichselbraun, A. (2008). "An Automated Approach to Investigating the Online Media Coverage of US Presidential Elections", *Journal of Information Technology & Politics,* 5(1): 121-132.

[11] Siorpaes, K. and Hepp, M. (2008). "Games with a Purpose for the Semantic Web", *IEEE Intelligent Systems,* 23(3): 50-60.

[12] Vickrey, D., Bronzan, A., et al. (2008). Online Word Games for Semantic Data Collection. *Conference on Empirical Methods in Natural Language Processing (EMNLP-2008).* Stroudsburg, USA: Association for Computational Linguistics: 533-542.

[13] Waitelonis, J., Ludwig, N., Knuth, M. and Sack, H. (2011). "WhoKnows? - Evaluating Linked Data Heuristics with a Quiz that Cleans up DBpedia", *International Journal of Interactive Technology and Smart Education,* 8(4): 236-248.

[14] Weichselbraun, A., Wohlgenannt, G. and Scharl, A. (2010). "Refining Non-Taxonomic Relation Labels with External Structured Data to Support Ontology Learning", *Data & Knowledge Engineering,* 69(8): 763-778.

[15] Wiggins, A. and Crowston, K. (2011). From Conservation to Crowdsourcing: A Typology of Citizen Science. *44th Hawaii International Conference on System Science (HICSS-44).* Koloa, USA: IEEE Computer Society.

[16] Wolf, L., Knuth, M., Osterhoff, J. and Sack, H. (2011). RISQ! Renowned Individuals Semantic Quiz: A Jeopardy Like Quiz Game for Ranking Facts. *7th International Conference on Semantic Systems (I-Semantics 2011).* C. Ghidini et al. Graz, Austria: ACM.

Online Resources

[17] Climate Change Collaboratory. http://www.modul.ac.at/nmt/triple-c.

[18] Climate Quiz. http://www.ecoresearch.net/tnple-c.

[19] DBpedia. http://www.dbpedia.org/.

[20] PlanetData. http://www.planet-data.eu/.

[21] Proton Ontology. http://proton.semanticweb.org/.

[22] webLyzard. http://www.webLyzard.com/.

Behavioral Analysis in Social Networks: An Approach Based on Intelligent System

Thiago Rúbio
Computing Department
Federal Center of Tech.
Education of Minas Gerais
Belo Horizonte, MG
thmunhoz@lsi.cefetmg.br

Rogério Gomes
Computing Department
Federal Center of Tech.
Education of Minas Gerais
Belo Horizonte, MG
rogerio@lsi.cefetmg.br

Adriano Pereira
Computing Department
Federal Center of Tech.
Education of Minas Gerais
Belo Horizonte, MG
adriano@decom.cefetmg.br

ABSTRACT

This paper presents a new methodology to classify Twitter users based on Artificial Neural Networks and Fuzzy Logic. Simulations are carried out using a SOM (Self Organized Maps) neural network for classifying users into four distinct groups: (0)*Unimpressive User*; (1)*Desired User: Follower*; (2)*Desired User: Follower and Publisher*; (3)*Desired User: Publisher*. The proposed methodology was validated through an autonomous agent, whose interactions with others were modeled by means of Fuzzy Inference System. The results obtained show that neural networks can be used for user classification in social networks, and we observed that the interaction of the agent with other users occurred in a transparent way, i.e., showing typical behaviors of real users.

Categories and Subject Descriptors

I.2 [**Artificial Intelligence**]: Miscellaneous; J.4 [**Social and Behavioral Sciences**]: Miscellaneous

General Terms

Algorithms, Experimentation, Human Factors

Keywords

Social Networks, Artificial Intelligence, Machine Learning, Twitter, Self Organized Maps, Fuzzy Logic

1. INTRODUCTION

Social Networks can be seen as large systems in which one can study the behavior of users by identifying individual interests, its affinity relations, as well as their common goals [8]. The analysis of the behavior of individuals is essential for assessing the relationships among them and social groups [4, 3], enabling the creation of dynamic content management systems [1].

Permission to make digital or hard copies of all or part of this work for personal or classroom use is granted without fee provided that copies are not made or distributed for profit or commercial advantage and that copies bear this notice and the full citation on the first page. To copy otherwise, to republish, to post on servers or to redistribute to lists, requires prior specific permission and/or a fee.
WebMedia'12, October 15–28, 2012, São Paulo/SP, Brazil.
Copyright 2012 ACM 978-1-4503-1706-1/12/10 ...$15.00.

There are several algorithms for classifying users in social networks in the literature, most of them related to the *PageRank* algorithm [2]. Basically, this method is based on the analysis of the complex networks, as well as the counting of the interactions between users in social networks. However, these approaches may lead to a superficial understanding of the user behavior [14].

Thus, this paper presents a new approach based on SOM (Self Organized Maps) artificial neural network [13, 12] for the classification of Twitter users [3, 7, 1]. Moreover, an autonomous agent capable of interacting with others Twitter users is modeled in order to validate the proposed classification system. This agent is modeled through a fuzzy inference system and should present the same features displayed by users of a particular group.

In a summarized manner, this paper proposes the use of artificial intelligence techniques in the analysis of user behavior in social networks. Unsupervised networks are used in the process of grouping or classifying the datasets, and are also widely used as classifiers in data mining approaches. Moreover, the autonomous agent models non-numeric linguistic concepts of user behavior, enabling to design a content-based recommendation system in social networks.

2. RELATED WORK

In the virtual environment, people want to create social relations that exist or that they would like to exist in the real world. The fundamental connection between people in a virtual social network site is performed by means of identity, the establishment of friendships, as well as by means of similarity of thoughts and goals. Thus, users with similar features can be grouped and common behaviors can be used to indicate which users with similar characteristics should be allocated in the same group [2, 5]. This group, in turn, can be accomplished through the use of neural networks, which are powerful tools for classification [12].

Another important feature regarding the classification of users is the fact that the process of validating results is not a trivial task. In dynamic networks such as social networks, it becomes a challenge due to the fact that there is not an appropriate statistical model that provides the quality of the classification [10, 8].

One approach that can be used in assessing results would be the application of autonomous agents, since we can control the types of interactions among them, as well as provide them with inherent characteristics of real users [6]. Thus, the proposed model is based on Fuzzy Logic [9] , which allows the modeling of user behavior based on their qualitative states.

3. FUNDAMENTS AND METHODOLOGY

The aim of this paper is to evaluate the result of classification of Twitter users by means of neural networks. Therefore, we implemented a version of SOM neural network algorithm (Self Organized Maps), which consists of an unsupervised neural network training [15].

The methodology used in this article may be used in any social network, since the developed techniques are independent of the adopted technology. The choice of Twitter as a case study was a matter of design decision.

3.1 SOM Neural Network

The SOM algorithm is based on unsupervised and competitive learning. It provides a topology preserving mapping from high dimensional space to map units. Map units, or neurons, usually form a two-dimensional lattice, this it provides a mapping from high dimensional space onto a plane. The property of topology preserving means that the mapping preserves the relative distance between the points. Points that are near each other in the input space are mapped to nearby map units in the SOM. Therefore the SOM can serve as a cluster analyzing tool of high dimensional data. Moreover, the SOM has the capability to generalize. Generalization capability means that the network can recognize or characterize inputs it has never encountered before. A new input is assimilated with the map unit it is mapped to [13].

The approach adopted in this work is related to analysis of individual users. Thus, the following criteria were selected: (a) Number of Tweets; (b) Number of Followers; (c) Following Number; (d) Number of Followers/Following Number; (e) Following Number/Number of Followers; (f) Number of Replies;

These criteria are used as inputs for the neural network in order to classify users into groups. The database used in the training phase of the SOM neural network was composed of 300,000 users, obtaining at the end of the calibration a configuration with four groups, namely:

- Group 0 - *Unimpressive User*: displays low number of Tweets, Following and Followers. It has no significant relevance to influence other users.
- Group 1 - *Desired User - Follower*: it has a large number of Tweets and Following, but does not have many Followers.
- Group 2 - *Desired User - Follower and Publisher*: these users have the most interesting features, since they are very active on the network and are always sharing and seeking new information. They have high rates of Tweets, Followers and Following.
- Group 3 - *Desired User - Publisher*: with a significant number of Tweets, these users have many Followers that disseminate their new content, but therefore they have a relatively low number of following.

3.2 Fuzzy based Agent

In order to validate the classification found by the SOM neural network, it was implemented an autonomous agent whose actions and decisions were modeled using a Fuzzy Inference System. In general, a Fuzzy system is a representation that defines the qualitative states and treats them quantitatively [11, 9]. Thus, it is possible to evaluate non-quantifiable linguistic concepts, such as "very happy", "somewhat solitary", etc.. This model is important because it allows the creation of a user whose typical response time of the interactions with other users ensures a constant change in states of the agent.

The Fuzzy Inference System was developed having as inspiration the mood states of a human being. The mood states modeled in the agent were: Excitation, Satisfaction and Loneliness. It is important to emphasize that this choice was arbitrary, since Fuzzy Logic works, as already described, with linguistic concepts. Therefore, this is one of the biggest advantages of Fuzzy Logic and one of the main contributions of this work.

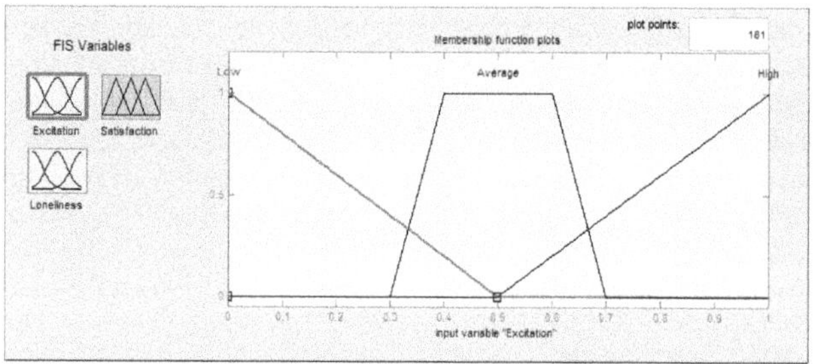

Figure 1: Fuzzy Set of the input variable Excitation

The states of Excitation and Loneliness are the linguistic variables used as input to the Fuzzy system, while Satisfaction is the linguistic variable that models the output of the system. This developed model takes into account the fact that the agent is happy when another network user interacts with him, reducing their level of Loneliness. When there are no interactions for a particular period of time, the level of Excitation decreases, followed or not by an increase in Loneliness. A critical level of Satisfaction (composed of the aggregation of the fuzzy inferences between Excitation and Loneliness) triggers an action to initiating relationships with new users (following). When the agent presents high levels of Satisfaction it generates new content, such as a comment or phrase.

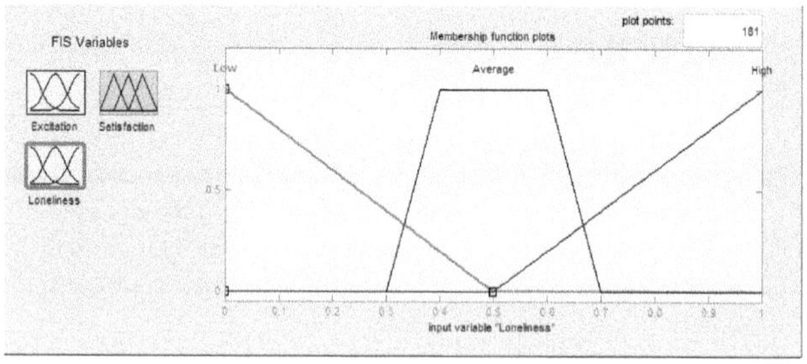

Figure 2: Fuzzy Set of the input variable Loneliness

By using the Twitter API, it was possible to integrate the agent "feelings" (implemented by the Fuzzy system) with some useful resources of the Twitter. The API works as a layer in the system, which has the responsibility to communicate with Twitter and produce the common actions of the users like posting, establishing friendship, searching etc..

The agent can call this layer as a result of the composition of the Fuzzy rules. When the output variable reaches some levels, it triggers actions in the Twitter API.

Thus, the modeled agent simulates a real user being able to perform actions, such as following users, attracting followers and posting messages (tweets). The agent implements a set of messages to post, suggest followers to other users, post comments about its mood (according to the Fuzzy state) or reference the trending topics (the most discussed terms of the network at a given time).

We identify the interest of users in the content published by the agent to the extent that users of certified accounts, such as the Official Firefox (@firefox) and others started to follow the profile of the agent. This corroborates the influence of the agent and shows that other users started to create an identifying relationship with the profile of the agent, showing interest in its content and in its friendship network.

The Fuzzy model that characterizes the agent can be seen in Figures 1, 2 and 3.

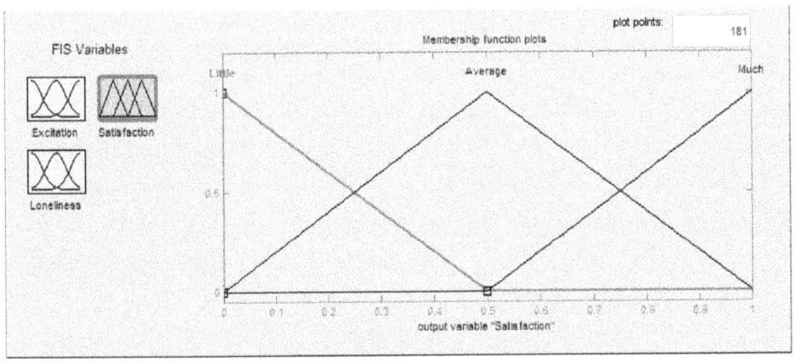

Figure 3: Fuzzy Set of the output variable Satisfaction

The fuzzy rules that implement the actions of the agent can be seen in the Code 1.

Code 1 Fuzzy model rules

```
METHOD: COG;
DEFAULT: = 0;
END_DEFUZZIFY

RULEBLOCK No1
AND: MIN / / Using 'min' for 'and'
ACT: MIN / / Using 'min' activation method
ACCU: MAX / / Using 'max' accumulation method

RULE 1: IF Excitation IS high
THEN Satisfaction IS much;

RULE 2: IF Excitation IS average
AND Loneliness IS average
THEN Satisfaction IS average;

RULE 3: IF Loneliness IS low
THEN Satisfaction IS much;

RULE 4: IF Excitation IS low
OR Loneliness IS high
THEN Satisfaction IS little;

RULE 5: IF Excitation IS high
OR Loneliness IS low
THEN happy IS very;
```

4. CASE STUDY AND EXPERIMENTS

In order to demonstrate the effectiveness of the methodology applied to Twitter, several experiments were performed to validate the system. Initially, the SOM neural network was calibrated using a database composed of 300,000 users, as described in Subsection 3.1.

After the calibration process of the SOM neural network using the training database, a system for collecting more users was developed in order to validate the classification capacity of the network. At the end, a total of 3,000 users were collected and classified. Table 1 presents a sample of 10 users classified by the neural network, highlighting the results of the classification.

It is possible to notice that the results in Table 1 are coherent with the proposed model, since users with low rates of Tweets, Followers and Following were classified in Group 0. Users with great tendency of following people content were classified, on the other hand, in Group 1. Similarly, users who are basically followed were classified in Group 3.

Table 2 shows the final result of the user classification, and it is possible to note that most users were classified as *Unimpressive User*. It is verified that this occurs because many social network users are note very participative on a global level, although they can be very influential in their circle of friendship.

Table 1: Sample data and its respective classification

Followers	Following	Tweets	Group
3	27	154	0
35	37	252	0
57	74	16	0
160	780	157	1
97	1997	602	1
1158	1641	293	1
586	268	57	1
21900	3858	5987	2
485	555	171	3
3878	1343	1057	3
1883	862	885	3

Table 2: Percentage of users rated in each group

Group	Number of Users	Percentage
0 - *Unexpressive*	1578	0.53
1 - *Follower*	846	0.28
2 - *Follower and Publisher*	109	0.04
3 - *Publisher*	467	0.16

Experiments were conducted during one week in order to promote the sort of agent to Group 2. Thus, starting from the relationship with just one user, the agent was initially classified as Group 0 by the SOM neural network (*Unimpressive User*). From that moment, the agent started the process of interaction with Twitter users, publishing content dynamically, creating following relations and seeking for followers. Every day after the interaction with other Twitter users, the agent was again classified by the SOM neural network in order to verify its performance. At this moment, we recorded the profile information of the agent, as summarized in Table 3. You can verify that in this period the agent's user passed from *Unimpressive User* (Group 0) to *Follower User*(Group 1), being finally classified as *Follower and Publisher User* (Group 2). The agent was not classified as a *Publisher User* (Group 3) due to the nature of interactions with Twitter users. The rules that trigger actions to publish massive content (tweets) were not activated and therefore the number of tweets was not very large, not allowing it to be classified as belonging to Group 3.

Figure 4 shows that there is a strong correlation between the parameters selected for the user classification, i.e., as soon as the values become more expressive it was verified that the classification performed by the SOM neural network converged to the expected results, according to the proposed model.

Table 3: Agent properties during the experiment

Followers	Following	Tweets	Date	Group
1	1	0	Day 00	0
12	27	69	Day 01	0
83	112	94	Day 02	0
192	547	448	Day 03	1
240	631	561	Day 04	1
356	712	739	Day 05	1
781	842	957	Day 06	1
1230	1035	1346	Day 07	2

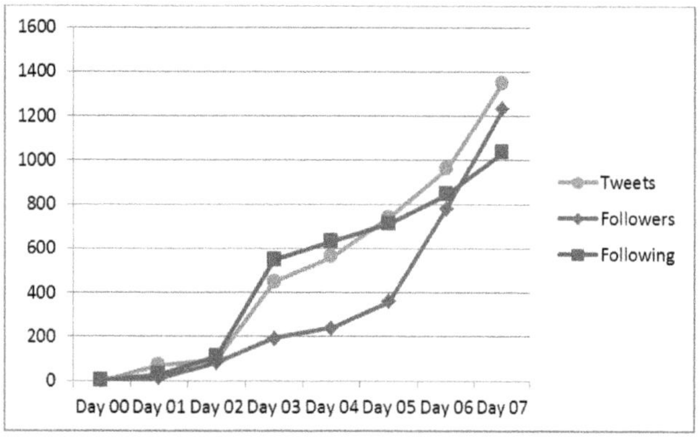

Figure 4: Growth of the agent properties

5. CONCLUSION

The analysis of Web systems is important and essential to design and implement new tools to facilitate the information retrieval by users. In order to know these users, it is necessary to characterize and evaluate their characteristics and extract information about common feelings, group formations and interactions between them.

The use of the SOM neural network to categorize Twitter users proved to be very satisfactory, being possible to characterize and identify some groups by means of user profiles.

Furthermore, it can be seen that the Fuzzy agent represented satisfactorily a human user through a Fuzzy Inference System. The agent carried out a transparent relationship with users, showing typical behaviors of common users. Although users have noticed that the agent was a computerized mechanism, it is possible to conclude that the model showed a reasonable representation of the behavior of a real user, relating to users of different ways and fulfilling its goal of being identified as a member of the group.

As future work we intend to create a refined mechanism for collecting data users to be presented to the SOM neural network, improving and refining the classification process. Moreover, studies should be made taking into account the data users filtered by subject, enabling to identify the most influential users in certain subjects, contributing to the development of new forms of advertising, as well as new content recommendation systems.

6. ACKNOWLEDGMENTS

This research is partially supported by the Brazilian National Institute of Science and Technology for the Web - INWEB (CNPq grant no. 573871/2008-6), CAPES, CNPq, Finep and Fapemig. In particular, the authors would like to thank the INWEB for the assistance in obtaining the real data mass used for the calibration of the neural network.

7. REFERENCES

[1] F. Abel, Q. Gao, G. Houben, and K. Tao. Analyzing temporal dynamics in twitter profiles for personalized recommendations in the social web. *Journal of the American Society for Information Science and Technology*, 2011.

[2] S. G. Arlei Silva, Hérico Valiati and W. M. Jr. From individual behavior to influence networks: A case study on twitter. In *WebMedia*, 2011.

[3] E. Bakshy, J. M. Hofman, W. A. Mason, and D. J. Watts. Everyone's an influencer: quantifying influence on twitter. In *Proceedings of the fourth ACM international conference on Web search and data mining*. ACM, 2011.

[4] E. Bakshy, B. Karrer, and L. A. Adamic. Social influence and the diffusion of user-created content. In *Proceedings of the 10th ACM conference on Electronic commerce*. ACM, 2009.

[5] C. Bigonha, T. N. C. Cardoso, M. M. Moro, V. A. F. Almeida, and M. A. Gonçalves. Detecting evangelists and detractors on twitter. In *WebMedia*, 2010.

[6] M. Brennan and R. Greenstadt. Coalescing twitter trends: The under-utilization of machine learning in social media. In *SocialCom*, pages 641–646. IEEE, 2011.

[7] P. Brown and J. Feng. Measuring user influence on twitter using modified k-shell decomposition. In *The Social Mobile Web*, volume WS-11-02, 2011.

[8] M. C. Fabricio Benevenuto, Tiago Rodrigues and V. Almeida. Characterizing user behavior in online social networks. *Usenix/ACM SIGCOMM Internet Measurement Conference (IMC), Chicago,USA*, 2009.

[9] Z. Liu, S. He, and W. Xiong. *A Fuzzy Logic Based Emotion Model for Virtual Human.*, pages 284–288. IEEE Computer Society, 2008.

[10] C. Meeyoung, H. Hamed, B. Fabricio, and G. Krishna. Measuring user influence in twitter: The million follower fallacy. 2010.

[11] W. Pedrycz and M. Reformat. *Evolutionary fuzzy modeling*, pages 652–665. Springer-Verlag, 2003.

[12] M. Pennacchiotti and A.-m. Popescu. A machine learning approach to twitter user classification. *Artificial Intelligence*, 46(39):281–288, 2010.

[13] B. Prieto, J. Merelo, A. Prieto, and F. Tricas. *Analyzing a Web-Based Social Network Using Kohonen's SOM*, pages 911–918. 2007.

[14] J. Weng, E.-P. Lim, J. Jiang, and Q. He. Twitterrank: finding topic-sensitive influential twitterers. In *Proceedings of the third ACM international conference on Web search and data mining*. ACM, 2010.

[15] G. P. Zhang. Neural networks for classification: a survey. *IEEE Transactions on Systems Man and Cybernetics Part C Applications and Reviews*, pages 451–462, 2000.

Generating Correct Compositions of Semantic Web Services With Respect to Temporal Constraints

Efraim Zalmoxis de Almeida Machado
FORMAS/LaSiD/DCC/IM
Federal University of Bahia (UFBA)
Av. Adhemar de Barros s/n – 40.170-110 – Salvador – BA – Brazil
efraimmachado@gmail.com

Daniela Barreiro Claro
FORMAS/LaSiD/DCC/IM
Federal University of Bahia (UFBA)
Av. Adhemar de Barros s/n – 40.170-110 – Salvador – BA – Brazil
dclaro@ufba.br

Aline Maria Santos Andrade
FORMAS/LaSiD/DCC/IM
Federal University of Bahia (UFBA)
Av. Adhemar de Barros s/n – 40.170-110 – Salvador – BA – Brazil
aline@ufba.br

ABSTRACT

Services are being widely published over the Web and many services may be composed to attend a user's need. A composition of services can demand complex requirements to get an executable composition. Temporal restrictions are one of these requirements. As compositions are dynamically composed, model checking can be applied to verify if compositions are correct in relation to the temporal restrictions required. In this work we propose an algorithm that creates semantic web service compositions and verifies the correctness of a composition checking the temporal restrictions of each iteration. Experiments were carried out and the precision of retrieved services and their execution time were analyzed.

Categories and Subject Descriptors

H.3.5 [**Information Systems**]: On-line Information Services—*Web-based services*; F.4.3 [**Theory of Computation**]: MATHEMATICAL LOGIC AND FORMAL LANGUAGES—*Formal Languages*

Keywords

semantic web services, service discovery, temporal restriction, model checking

1. INTRODUCTION

The increasing publication of services to provide data in a standardized way in emerging technologies such as Cloud Computing or Pervasive Computing is expanding and spreading the formatting of these services through WSDL (Web Service Description Language) and SOAP (Simple Object Access Protocol). In the case of large repositories of distributed web services, the task of finding a desirable service may become increasingly difficult and time consuming. Therefore the importance of automating the process of service discovery becomes a key factor in finding services that meet user needs. However, a description of the functionality of services through input and output parameters can lead to ambiguities that are not resolved automatically by machines. The incorporation of an unambiguous semantic description can facilitate this discovery and increase the chances of retrieving the service requested.

Several mechanisms can be used to describe semantic services through the use of ontologies [3]. Through the concepts, relationships and axioms of an ontology, one can analyze the inputs and outputs of a service and their preconditions and effects in particular. One possible way to describe the preconditions and effects in a semantic service is through SWRL (Semantic Web Rule Language), which uses the rule format of Horn [14].

For example: a patient is admitted to a hospital and the doctor has to carry out a procedure which has to be authorized by the patient's health insurance. This procedure must be completed within a period of three hours otherwise the patient's condition worsens. A service of *Authorization of Health Insurance procedure* has as IOPE (*Input, Output, Preconditions and Effects*) the parameters *Patient's name*, *Receipt Authorization*, *Monthly pay*, *Authorized procedure* respectively. If only IO (input and output) are considered, services not covered by the patient's insurance may be used erroneously, i.e. these services will not be available when required, delaying the process of authorizing the procedure and putting the patient's life at risk. As regards preconditions and effects, a machine can automatically analyze if a precondition has been satisfied in order to release the execution of a requested service. Preconditions and effects enable the addition of time constraints, thus preventing the services being selected outside the time interval required. Therefore, only services that satisfy this time restriction should be performed. This restriction avoids to find service authorization procedures that have a period longer than that required by the doctor.

It is important to note that a service *Authorization of Health insurance procedure*) could combine several services to meet a user's need, thus creating a composition of services. For instance, other services have to be composed so as to obtain the authorization procedure, such as *Health In-*

Permission to make digital or hard copies of all or part of this work for personal or classroom use is granted without fee provided that copies are not made or distributed for profit or commercial advantage and that copies bear this notice and the full citation on the first page. To copy otherwise, to republish, to post on servers or to redistribute to lists, requires prior specific permission and/or a fee.
WebMedia'12, October 15–28, 2012, São Paulo/SP, Brazil.
Copyright 2012 ACM 978-1-4503-1706-1/12/10 ...$15.00.

surance Number which can be obtained from the patient's medical record, *Exams authorization*, where examinations are allowed if they are necessary for the medical procedure, etc. The greater the number of services in a composition, the greater the number of attributes IOPE. This makes manual analysis difficult. Thus, the importance of a dynamic composition of service parameters which consider IOPE and time constraints is clear.

The dynamic composition of services requires an iterative analysis of each individual service which is aggregated in a composition. IOPE parameters determine the internal data flow, i.e. what data is exchanged between which services. This analysis is important because incorrect interactions between services may, for example, lead to non-execution of a service or generate problems such as *deadlocks*. Considering the example above, if a data flow between services is not analyzed, one can take the first service *Procedure authorization* to be requested after the service *Patient identification* is required. However, the *Patient identification* will not be useful if executed later in a data flow composition. The problem is further aggravated if the service required is in *deadlock*.

Going back to the example above, suppose that the doctor needs to know if the health insurance authorizes the patient's procedure. The doctor's request is sent at exactly 12:00 pm and the reply should be received in within three hours to avoid worsening the patient's condition. Considering the simple service *CheckProcedure* that informs if the procedure can be performed or otherwise. This service cannot be executed because the doctor only has the patient's name. This service requires 3 inputs: the availability of surgical resources (blood, medical supplies, etc), the hospital infrastructure resources (availability of pre-surgical, surgical and post-surgical spaces) and authorization from the health insurance. Analyzing these services in a repository, only the combination of some services can satisfy the doctor's need. This composition is shown in Figure 1 and it is explained in the course of this paper.

This paper proposes an iterative algorithm which generates correct service compositions, considering three criteria: (i) analysis of the data flow (the algorithm analyzes between data services if the functional and nonfunctional requirements are matched through the analysis of semantic similarity), (ii) the correctness of the data flow (using model checking) and (iii) temporal analysis (applying model checking and a semantic reasoner).

The remainder of this paper is structured as follows: section 2 presents a definition of correct compositions, section 3 presents the proposal of this work, section 4 describes our experiments, validations and results, section 5 presents a set of related work, and finally section 6 presents our conclusions and future work.

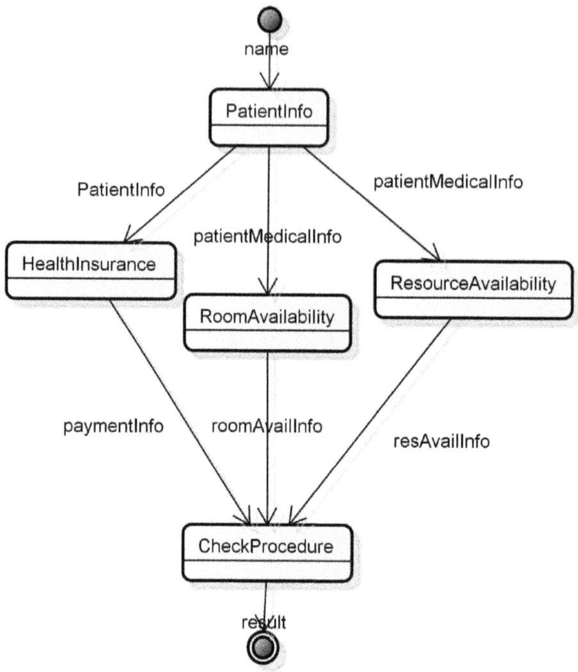

Figure 1: A doctor's request attending by a composition of services

2. CORRECT COMPOSITIONS OF SEMANTIC WEB SERVICES

This section presents some concepts and definitions to help understand the work proposed in this paper.

2.1 Services and compositions

A web service is a way of providing the functionalities of an information system in the web using standardized technologies [1]. We define a service s as a tuple $s = (I_s, O_s, P_s, E_s)$ such that I is the set of the inputs of s, O is the set of the outputs of s, P is the set of preconditions of s and E is the set of effects of s. A request r of a service is defined by the tuple (I_r, O_r, P_r, E_r), where I is the set of provided data, O is the set of required output, P are the preconditions of the provided data and E are the intended effects.

A service $s = (I_s, O_s, P_s, E_s)$ satisfies a request $r = (I_r, O_r, P_r, E_r)$ if and only if $I_s \subseteq I_r$ e $O_r \subseteq O_s$ e $P_r \rightarrow P_s$ e $E_s \rightarrow E_r$, that is, s can be executed with the inputs provided by r and it produces all the outputs and intended effects of the requirement.

Like a service, a composition c has inputs, outputs, preconditions and effects and it can be defined as $c = (I_c, O_c, P_c, E_c, R)$, where R is a relationship among the inputs and outputs of services, defining the internal flow of the composition such that $R \subseteq O_i \times I_k$, where O_i is the set of outputs of the service i and I_k is the set of input of the service k such that $\forall i, k \in S, i \neq k$. Multiple services can be composed with each other to satisfy a request, as long as certain restrictions are met. Consider the services s_1 and s_2, s_2 can be composed with s_1 if O_{s_1} can be used as input I_{s_2}, considering a sequential composition where all services are required.

2.2 Correct compositions

A service or a composition of services is correct if it returns the outputs and effects specified in the request provided that its preconditions and inputs are satisfied.

To prove that a web service composition is correct, it is necessary to prove that, respecting the preconditions, the input data are correctly transformed until the required outputs and effects are produced, i.e. the data flow of the composition is possible and the data exchanged between the services are compatible.

In order to analyze the data flow we check all possibilities of execution, i.e. the exploration of all alternative flows. We verify if the data exchanged between the services in a flow are compatible, i.e. if it refers to semantically similar data structures and if their preconditions and effects are satisfied, following [12, 15] and [8]. According to the authors [12, 15], semantic similarity can be used to analyze the compatibility between inputs and outputs of a service, increasing the precision of the analysis. In [8] the analysis of preconditions and effects of a service is also done through the semantic similarity analysis through a service or a request.

An important class of non functional requirements (preconditions and effects) which should be considered are the temporal restrictions [13], which are essential in many applications. These have not been considered in most of the works dealing with correctness of service compositions to date.

To verify the correctness of the flow and the compatibility of the exchanged data, the algorithm proposed in this paper considers that each individual service in a composition is correct. This verification comprises: if inputs, outputs, preconditions and effects of each flow are satisfied in relation to both the composition and the service by the use of semantic similarities proposed in [8]; if the flow determined by the composition is correct, using model checking; if the temporal restrictions of both the request and the services are satisfied, using model checking and a reasoner to infer temporal properties.

2.3 Temporal restrictions

Temporal restrictions presuppose a pre-established order of service execution and they are commonly presented in either individual web services systems and service compositions which must preserve the temporal dependency between the services in order to generate the intended results of the request [10, 9].

In order to analyze if the temporal preconditions of a service, which is part of a composition, are satisfied it should be checked if the service can be executed without violating the temporal restrictions of either the request or the services. This analysis can be done by a reasoner using the relations *before*, *during* and *after* to infer if the service executes without violating any temporal restrictions. Another alternative is to apply model checking.

With model checking it is possible to check all possible path of the internal flow in a composition, verifying the properties which are valid in these paths. The present work uses both alternatives: a reasoner to check time constraints and model checking to verify the properties of the composition, including the temporal properties of both the services and the requests. Model checking is an automatic technique which uses model checker tools, such as UPPAAL [6].

2.3.1 *Model checking*

Model checking consists of a model of a system, normally represented as a finite automaton which verifies if a property specified in a temporal logic is satisfied in that model.

UPPAAL is a model checker which uses a variant of a timed automaton to model a system. It uses a simplified version of the *Timed Computation Tree Logic* (TCTL) to specify and query properties [2]. A timed automaton is a finite automaton augmented with a finite set of real-valued clocks [6].

An automaton in UPPAAL contains: a finite set of localizations; an initial localization; a finite set of transitions; a set of constants; and a set of clocks (*clocks*), channels, booleans and numeric variables. An invariant condition can be associated to a location and three types of labels can be associated to the transitions: guards, synchronizations and actions. The invariants of a location must be satisfied while the automaton is in this location; if the invariant is violated, a transition to another location should be activated. A transition can only be activated if its guards are satisfied. When a transition is activated, actions can be executed, as for example, the initialization of clock variables or synchronizations through channel variables with another transition of another automaton. The variables *clocks* are used to specify temporal restrictions associated to the locations and transitions of the automaton. The Figure 2 represents an automaton of UPPAAL, with the locations Initial, Medium and Final, the guard of the transition between the location Initial and Medium specifies that the variable *input* must be greater or equal to one in order for the transition to occur.

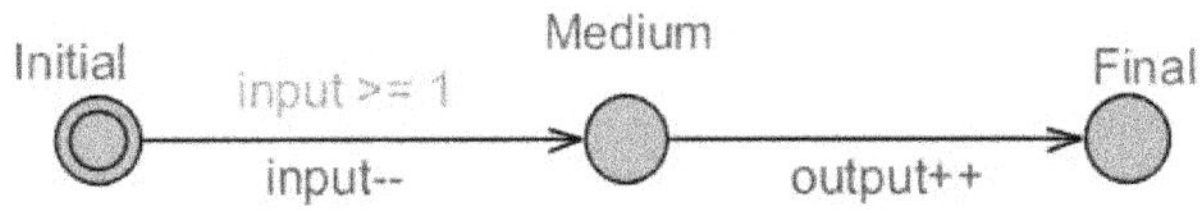

Figure 2: A service execution converted to a timed automaton

An example of invariant can be seen in Figure 3. The initial location represented by two concentric circles contains the invariant *second* ≤ 0. This invariant specifies that the initial location is active while the variable *second* is shorter or equal to 0.

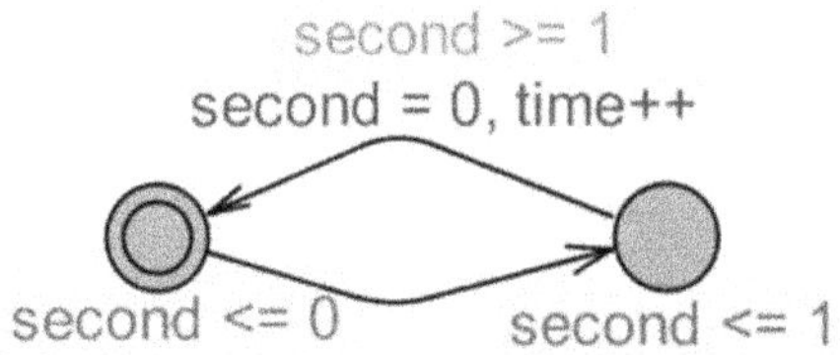

Figure 3: Timer automaton

A concurrent system is modeled in UPPAAL as a network of timed automata executing in parallel. In UPPAAL, some channels and localizations can be defined as urgent. A transition with an urgent channel will be executed as soon as possible, having priority over others. Similarly, an urgent location does not allow the evolution of the automata to other locations which are not urgent.

The temporal logic used by UPPAAL is composed of the logic operators (`and`, `or`, `imply`, `not`), the temporal operators ($\Box$ - always, $\Diamond$ - occasionally, $\rightarrow$ - leave to), and path operators (`A` - to all path, `E` - there is a path). Its syntax can be defined by: $E\Diamond p, E\Box p, A \diamond p, A\Box p, p \rightarrow q$ where p and q are p, q ::= *Automaton.location* | *Automaton.variable* | *clock* $\odot$ *value* | p or q | p and q | not p | p *imply* q | *deadlock*. Where $\odot$ is the binary relations: $\leq$, $\geq$, $<$, $>$ and $=$.

3. PROPOSED ALGORITHM

The proposed algorithm is capable of creating, iteratively, a correct composition given a request and a repository of semantically described services. Thus the algorithm performs:

- semantic similarity analysis of inputs and outputs of the services that exchange data in the composition, ensuring compatibility between the data exchanged as proposed by [12, 15];
- semantic similarity analysis of preconditions and effects of the services that exchange data in the composition, ensuring compatibility between the data exchanged as proposed by [8];
- double temporal constraints analysis: one through a semantic reasoner and the other by model checking, ensuring temporal compatibility between a request and a service;
- data flow analysis, performed by model checking.

The algorithm can be divided into three phases: (i) Discovery phase (line 11), (ii) Composition phase (lines 12 to 23) and (iii) Verification phase (line 24). These phases form a cycle that repeats until the composition is complete and correct or it is not able to be built.

Listing 1 presents the principal commands of the algorithm main loop.

Listing 1: Correct composition algorithm

```
1  correctComposition(request , repository){
2    stopCondition = true;
3    composition := nil;
4    prohibitedSolutions  := nil;
5    finalService := createFinalService(request);
6    composition.add(finalService);
7    auxiliaryService := createAuxiliaryService(
       request);
8    repository.adiciona(auxiliaryService);
9    while(stopCondition){
10     p := composition.getPendency();
11     ss := discoveryServices(repository, p);
12     if (ss != nil)
13         ss.remove(prohibitedSolutions .
             getServices(p));
14     if (ss.empty() == true){
15         if (p.service == finalService){
16                 return nil;
17         }       else{
18                 composition.remove(p.service);
19                 repository.remove(p.service);
20         }
21         continue;
22     }
23     s := selectService(ss);
24     composition.add(s, p);
25     if (formalVerification(composition) ==
           false){
26        prohibitedSolutions .add(s,p);
27        composition.remove(s,p);
28     }
29     stopCondition = analysisEnd();
30   }
31   return composition;
32 }
```

The composition is created incrementally from the outputs of a request until it can be executed, i.e., all services which constitute the composition have inputs provided by other services or/and are provided by the request. To initialize the composition, two services are created: the *auxiliaryService* (line 7) which is added to the repository and used to represent a request, this service has no input nor preconditions and takes the request inputs and preconditions as output and effects respectively; and the *finalService* (line 5) which is added to the composition. This service has no output nor effects and takes as input the outputs of the request and the preconditions of the request effects. In the first execution of the Discovery phase, a discovered service should contain an output that meets the input of *finalService*. Thus this service is added to the composition and this process is repeated for each service included in the composition until the composition can be executed. Returning to our example, the initial state of the composition contains only the *finalService*.

The process of looking for an output to match an input of a service is carried out through a pending queue (it can be seen in line 10 that the method *getPendency* returns the first pendency P in the queue) which is initialized with the inputs of the *finalService* and is updated as new services are being discovered and require other services to meet their inputs. When there is no queue, this means that the composition is complete. When a pendency cannot be resolved, i.e., there is no service in the repository whose outputs meet the required inputs, the service that generates this pendency is removed from the composition and the pending queue is rolled back to its previous status. If the service to be removed is the *finalService*, this means that this composition cannot be generated in that repository.

Returning to our example, the pendency $P = result$. The Discovery phase will return the service *CheckProcedure*, removing P from the pendency queue and adding the pendencies from *CheckProcedure*: *paymentInfo*, *roomAvalInfo* and *resAvalInfo*.

3.1 Discovery phase

The Discovery phase finds services in accordance with a composition. Given a request, this phase should match one input and all the preconditions of a service and some of its outputs and effects.

Considering the service $s = (I_s, O_s, P_s, E_s)$ of a composition that requires the input $i_i \in I_s$. A request $r = (\{\}, \{i_i\}, \{\}, P_s)$ is generated in the Composition phase and it is sent to the Discovery phase.

Services are selected according to some similarity degree which was defined in [12, 15]: *exact*, *plugin*, *subsumes*, *sibling* and *fail*. The degree of similarity corresponds to relations between the concepts within an ontology (in this case these are the output-input and effect-precondition of a request and a service).

Considering a semantic similarity function $ss(Req, Ser) = g$, which returns the degree of semantic similarity g from a request Req and a service Ser, a function $desc(Rep, Req, g) = S$, which receives a repository Rep, a request Req and a degree of semantic similarity g can be performed. This function returns a set of services S. As any request r, this set can be defined by $S = \{s \in Rep | ss(s, r) = g\}$.

After selecting the service based on the degree of similarity, each service is analyzed with regard to its temporal properties. The properties which are not temporally compatible with the composition are discarded, causing a failure in service execution or a non-compliance with temporal preconditions and effects of the request. These mechanisms are treated by the temporal compatibility analysis procedure.

3.1.1 Temporal compatibility analysis

The temporal validation is designed to find out which services can be added to the composition without violating the time constraints of the composition nor the request.

A temporal restriction of a service is a rule concerning the time that must be satisfied (temporal precondition) or it is a description of the environment after the execution of a service (temporal effect). A time restriction is not necessarily part of an input or an output, although it should be described as a precondition and an effect, specifically a post-condition. The time constraints are divided into two classes:

- Availability: Availability refers to when a service is available to run. It is defined as a range, i.e. between Monday and Friday or between 08:00am and 06:00pm;
- Duration: The duration is defined as the time from starting to finishing a service execution, i.e. from the beginning of a service execution with its inputs until the generation of its outputs.

In this paper, the time constraints are described based on OWL-Time, a temporal description ontology [11]. The semantic description allowed by OWL-*Time* makes it possible to use reasoners to verify the temporal preconditions and effects in a formal manner.

Availability is described through the properties of *hasBeginning* and *hasEnd*. The duration of the class is described by *DurationDescription*, which may be a length expressed in years, months, weeks, days, hours, minutes and seconds.

To check the temporal preconditions and effects of a composition it is necessary to position the temporal properties on the timeline and analyze through time concepts *before*, *in* and *after* if these restrictions are satisfied. The Pellet reasoner [16] is used in this work to deduce if the service that receives the outputs meets the time constraints defined and therefore can start its execution.

To better illustrate the proposed analysis, consider c a composition to be executed at time T and consists of three services s_1, s_2 and s_3 with availability intervals $disp_1(i_1, f_1)$, $disp_2(i_2, f_2)$, $disp_3(i_3, f_3)$ (i is the beginning and f is the end) and duration dur_1, dur_2 and dur_3 respectively. Consider that the services are composed in sequence so that s_2 uses output s_1 and s_3 uses the output of s_2. In this case, the services can only be compatible in time if and only if $before(t, f_1) \wedge before(t + dur_1, f_2) \wedge before(max(t + dur_1 + dur_2, i_2 + dur_2), f_3)$ and $max(x, y)$ is a function that returns the greatest value between x and y.

Returning to our example, unusual time constraints were added to some services that participate in the composition to make them (the example and consequently the composition) more complex. These restrictions are displayed in Table 1.

The following conditions must be valid (initial instant is 12:00pm):

- $before$(12:00pm, Always): the initial composition time must finish before the availability final instant of the service *PatientInfo*;
- $before$(12:00pm + 30min, 04:00pm): the *PatientInfo* must finish before the availability final instant of service *ResourceAvailability*;
- $before$(12:00pm + 30min, 03:55pm): the *PatientInfo* must finish before the availability final instant of service *RoomAvailability*;
- $before$(12:00pm + 30min, 05:00pm): the *PatientInfo* must finish before the availability final instant of service *HealthInsurance*;
- $before(max($12:00pm + 30min + 5min, 08:00 + 5min), Always): the *ResourceAvailability* must finish before the availability final instant of service *CheckProcedure*;
- $before(max($12:00pm + 30min + 45min, 11:00 + 45min), Always): the *RoomAvailability* must finish before the availability final instant of service *CheckProcedure*;
- $before(max(12:00pm{+}30min{+}1hr, 08:00{+}1hr)$, *Always*): the *HealthInsurance* must finish before the availability final instant of service *CheckProcedure*;

Service	Availability	Duration
PatientInfo	Always	30 min
ResourcesAvailability	08:00am - 04:00pm	5 min
RoomAvailability	11:00am-03:55pm	45 min
HealthInsurance	08:00am-05:00pm	1 hour
CheckProcedure	Always	5 minutes

Table 1: Composition's services time constraints

Before or *after* expressions with *Always* are always valid. To analyze the request time constraint it is necessary to know the maximum value *maxTime* between *max(12:00pm + 30min + 1hr, 08:00 + 1hr)*, *max(12:00pm + 30min + 45min, 11:00 + 45min)* and *max(12:00pm + 30min + 5min, 08:00 + 5min)* and check *before(maxTime, 12:00pm + 3hr)* (request duration is up to 3 hours).

3.2 Composition phase

The composition phase receives a set of services resulting from the Discovery phase and chooses among them the service that best suits the composition created so far, considering (in this order): (1) the reuse of services already used in the composition, minimizing the use of new services; (2) the use of services with a greater degree of similarity, facilitating compatibility between services and (3) the choice of services with fewer inputs, so that fewer services are needed to provide these inputs in the remainder of the composition.

The selected service is then added to the composition, creating a relationship between the output and the effects respectively with the inputs and the preconditions of service that generated the pendency. It is worth noting that in conjunction with the Discovery phase, this phase is responsible for ensuring the compatibility of data exchanged inside the data flow. The algorithm uses composite structures defined in OWL 1.2: *Sequence*, *joins* and *SplitJoins* to create the composition, thereby defining the data flow to be later verified by the Verification phase.

Definition. Considering $s_i = (I_i, O_i, P_i, E_i)$ a service and $i_i \in I_i$ and $req = (\{\}, \{i_i\}, \{\}, \{P_i\})$ the request created to meet the input i_i. Suppose that $s_k = (I_k, O_k, P_k, E_k)$ is the selected service to provide the input s_i. The result of the composition is given by the function $comp(c, s_i, req, s_k) = c'$, such that $c = (S_c, I_c, O_c, P_c, E_c, R_c)$ is the inputed composition and $c' = (S_c \cup s_k, (I_c \cup i_k) \backslash i_i, O_c, (P_c \cup p_k) \backslash p_i, E_c, R \cup (o_k, i_i))$ is the resultant composition.

The addition of a service in a composition results in new requests, i.e. the service added may require some inputs and these inputs (pendency) will be required by the discovery phase, as can be seen in C' by inserting the new inputs in the set of inputs $(I \cup i_k)$.

Returning to our example, Figure 4 presents a composition being assembled. The current state of the pendency queue is: *resAvalInfo, patientInfo, patientMedicalInfo.* It is important to note that although this example does not highlight the importance of *FinalService*, it becomes useful when the final result comes from more than one web service because all outputs are join in one service.

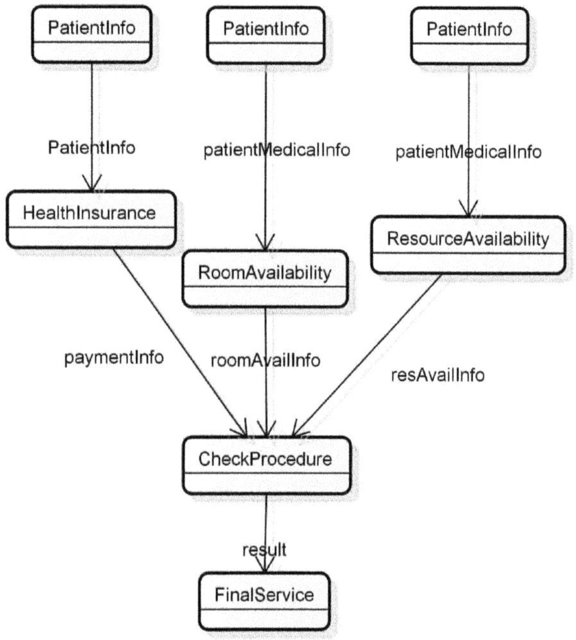

Figure 4: A composition's snapshot

Before the insertion of service *RoomAvailability* the current state of pendency queue was: *roomAvalInfo, resAvalInfo, patientInfo.* The service *RoomAvailability* solved the *roomAvalInfo* pendency but added a new pendency: *patientMedicalInfo.*

3.3 Verification phase

The verification phase converts the composition into an automaton network and verifies if the generated composition is correct in relation to the data flow (if the data flow is possible to execute) and time constraints of services, using the model checker UPPAAL. The main features of the services have been taken into account to configure the rules represented inside the model:

- Stateless services: service state is not stored, thus the same service invocation can generate the same outputs and effects if the same inputs are provided;
- Asynchronous communication: the most common protocols used to exchange data between services are asynchronous: HTTP and FTP. Thus, data are generated and cannot be consumed immediately.

The properties of the composition and their requests are represented in the automaton network as guards and invariants. As the composition is verified when a service is added, it is possible to observe which service causes a non-validation property of a composition. This ensures that in each cycle of the composition it contains no errors.

To verify the successful execution of the composition, the formula in CTL $A\Box$ *finalAutomaton.Final and* $output_0 = 1$ *and* $output_1 = 1$ *and...and* $output_n = 1$ is used, and the $output_i$, i = 0,1,...,n are the desired outputs in the request. This formula expresses that for all possible execution, the composition generates all outputs. The representation $finalAutomaton.Final$ means that the automaton $finalAutomaton$ will be in its location called $Final$. The formula above is sufficient to verify that there are no problems in the composition as *deadlocks* or non-performance of services, because it represents that for all possible execution paths the location of the automaton that represents the final execution of the composition is reached and all desired outputs from the request are generated. In our example, the formula is $A\Box$ *finalAutomaton.Final and result = 1.*

3.3.1 Conversion of composition into automata

In order to meet the stateless service model, each invocation of a service is converted into a timed automaton so that successive invocations have the same result (the *finalService* converstion creates the finalAutomaton mentionned above). This automaton has three locations: $Initial$, which represents the moment before the execution of the service; $Medium$, which represents the service running, and $Final$, which represents the moment after the execution of the service (see Figure 2). It is noteworthy that after a composition is performed, the services remain in its *Final* location. These locations are connected by two transitions: one that links the location $Initial$ to location $Medium$ and is responsible for consuming the *inputs* used in the execution of a service, and another that links the location $Medium$ to location $Final$ and is responsible for generating the *outputs* resulting from the execution of the service. Thus, for every invocation of the service $s = (I_s, O_s, P_s, E_s)$ exist a timed automaton $m = (\{(Initial, Medium, Final)\}, \{(input, output)\}, \{(Initial, Medium), (Medium, Final)\}, \{Initial\}, \{Final\})$ which represents the service and his invocation.

Figure 2 shows the conversion of service $RoomAvailability$ into a timed automaton. It is important to highlight in this example that there is a guard to check the existence of the input in that automaton. When the composition has time constraints, this guard is specified in the timer automaton. And then a channel is used to synchronize the *RoomAvailability* and Timer automaton.

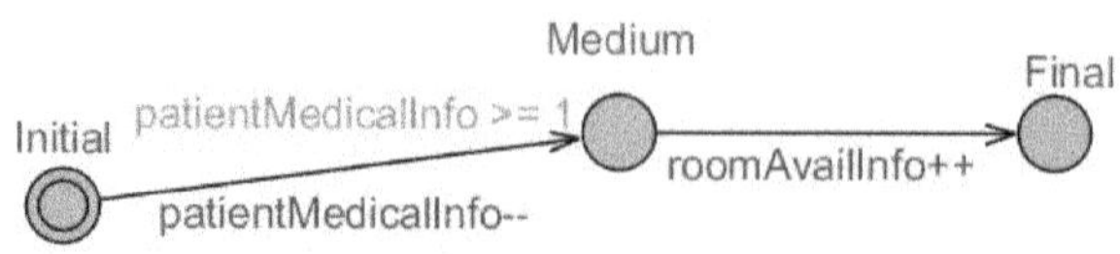

Figure 5: RoomAvailability automaton representation

3.3.2 *Inputs, outputs and data flow*

The algorithm is designed to verify asynchronous service compositions. Some inputs do not necessarily need to be consumed even if they were already generated by a request or by a service *output*. These generated inputs are stored to be consumed when possible or required. Since the channels are synchronous in UPPAAL, they were not used to represent data exchanged between the composition services.

To represent the asynchronous communication, an integer variable was used for each pair of output-input between two services. Whenever a piece of data is generated (output), it increments the variable referring to the pair and, similarly, decreases when the given data (input) is consumed. This is done because in a composition when a piece of data is generated it is sent to a specific service and other services cannot use it. Thus, for a composition $c = (S_c, I_c, O_c, P_c, E_c, R_c)$ and $(o_n, i_m) \in R$ (m and n are differents services), the timed automaton that represents the service m has the integer variable named $(s_n + o_n + i_m + s_m)$ (+ is the concatenation operation) that represents the output-input pair. It should be noted that in this way, the data flow is implicitly defined by these variables.

Returning to our example, when the service *healthInsurance* generates its output *paymentInfo*, the variable *healthInsurancepatientInfopatientInfoCheckProcedure* (the pair *paymentInfo-paymentInfo* from *healthInsurance* to *CheckProcedure*) is incremented.

3.3.3 *Temporal constraints*

In UPPAAL, as the clocks are not discrete, it is not possible to control the exact time and ensure that service execution and outputs are generated at the appropriate time.

To circumvent this problem, an automaton was modeled that acts like a timer, controlling the passage of time and firing the services that should be executed as soon as possible. To represent the passage of time, an integer variable named *time* is used instead of the variable *clock*, because of the restrictions on using *clock* expressions. For example, a constraint using *clock* expressions cannot assign a *clock* value to another variable in UPPAAL, because the *clock* variable takes real values and its values are continually changing. The automaton *timer*, shown in Figure 3, has the variable *time*, which advances only if no other action can be performed. The *clock seconds* is used to represent the passage of a second, while the integer variable *time* is used to store how many seconds have passed. The invariants ensure that only one second is spent at each turn, leaving the initial location and returning.

With each new invocation that contains temporal constraints, two new locations are added to the *timer* automaton, one to represent the availability of a service and the other to represent the end of the execution of a service, as shown in Figure 6.

The availability of a service is represented as a *urgent* location which is linked to the *timer* initial location with two transitions: one of the transition has a guard to express the condition that the necessary inputs are available. The another transition is responsible by connect the localization Availability with the localization Initial of the timer. Linked with this transition is created a synchronization action with an urgent channel that communicates with an urgent channel of the automaton that represents the service making it changes its current location to the location *Medium*. When this transition is triggered the variable that stores the duration of the execution of this service is initialized.

The ending of the execution of a service is represented by adding a new location in a similar way of the location Availability. One of the transition has a guard that specifies if the *clock* duration has reached the required value, if the service has been invoked (to prevent this transition occurs before the transition to availability) or if the service has already been executed (to avoid repetition of this transition). The other transition uses an urgent channel invocation to change the location of the automaton from *Medium* location to *Final* location (Figure 6). These urgent channels keep the assynchronism and allow the transitions to be performed as soon as possible.

All the time units of temporal properties are converted into the smallest unit of time used in the composition and are represented as a time elapsed since an initial instant until the time expressed in temporal property. Suppose there are two services: a and b. The service a can be performed after 08h:00m while the service b after 02h:35m:43s. These restrictions are expressed as the amount of seconds to a initial time (00h:00m:00s of a day). The service a can run after the time $t >$ *8*3600 segs* and the service b at time $t >$ *2*3600+35*60+43 segs*.

4. EXPERIMENTS, VALIDATIONS AND RESULTS

The proposed algorithm was implemented using the tool Verifyta (UPPAAL tool) and the Pellet reasoner in the Discovery and Composition phases. Some experiments were performed to validate our proposed approach. The test set used in [8] containing semantically web services describing OWL-S with inputs, outputs, preconditions and effects has been adapted, adding temporal semantic description (from OWL-Time and SWRL) to some services and compositions.

4.1 Accuracy and precision

Accuracy can be defined as the degree of an estimate value is closeness to its real value and precision can be expressed as the degree to which repeated values under unchanged conditions have the same results[4]. The accuracy as the proximity degree between the result and the expected result.

According to our proposal, the use of formal verification and temporal properties can create compositions that better meet user requests, i.e. improving accuracy and precision of a composition in relation to some related algorithms such as [12] and [8]).

Thus, in order to test the accuracy and the precision of our algorithm, 100 compositions were manually created. These compositions were analyzed based on three criteria (i) analysis of IOPE (*Inputs, Outputs, Preconditions and Effects*), (ii) temporal properties (using only a reasoner) and (iii) formal verification (using model checking). Tests were performed on those 100 compositions using only the criteria (i) (representing the algorithm proposed in [8], which has an accuracy greater than that proposed in [12]); criteria (i) and (ii) (Represents the algorithm proposed in this paper without formal verification) and finally all three criteria were taken into account, representing our proposed algorithm. Each test has the results for each composition: *Right Execution*, which means that using the criteria established the composition

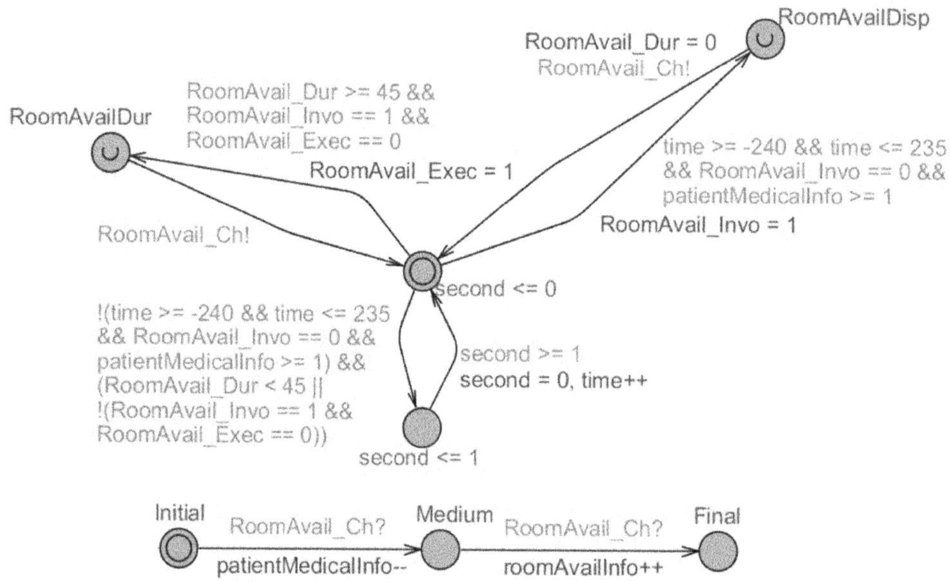

Figure 6: timer's automaton and his duration and Availability locations used to verification

can be performed and *Wrong Execution* which means the composition cannot run otherwise.

After performing these tests, all 100 compositions were manually analyzed, i.e. checked on a non-automatic way: 40 *Right Execution* compositions and 60 *Wrong Execution* compositions. The degree of similarity in this analysis was defined for *exact* and *plugin*.

The test results are shown in Table 2. The columns in Table 2 represents: : True Positive (TP) - The number of compositions that are correct and are classified as correct, True Negative (TN) - The number of compositions that are not correct and are not classified as correct; False Positive (FP) - Number of compositions which are not correct but are classified as correct; False Negative (FN) - Number of compositions that are correct but are classified as not correct.

Criteria	VP	VN	FP	FN
(i)	27	40	30	3
(i, ii)	35	49	13	3
(i, ii, iii)	36	60	1	3

Table 2: Experiment to algorithm's accuracy meansure

It can be seen in Table 2 that the use of the all criteria (i, ii, iii) is closest to the manual results obtained. However, four compositions were classified incorrectly because of the non-temporal analysis of the preconditions and effects (criteria i): a composition whose preconditions were not compatible even though it is correct, was wrongly classified as correct and three other compositions that were correct but were wrongly classified as not correct; this fault was caused because of the non-time analysis of preconditions and effects. These services were considered as incompatible in relation to its preconditions and effects, but in face they were compatible. This problem happened because the preconditions and effects were described in a different ontology so the degree of similarity between them was *fail*.

Table 3 presents the accuracy and the precision of our tests.

Critérios	Acurácia	Precisão
(i)	67%	0,473
(i, ii)	84%	0,729
(i, ii, iii)	97%	0,972

Table 3: Test's accuracy and precison result

The experimental results show that the algorithm has a greater accuracy and precision compared to other algorithms. This increase is due to the use of time constraints and a formal verification which examines the composition data flow searching for errors.

4.2 Execution time

Considering the exponential complexity of the auxiliary tools used in this project (Verifyta and Pellet), our tests on execution time were carried out to verify the feasibility of using our proposed algorithm. 20 tests were conducted with different requests.

The test results can be seen in Figure 7. Here the chart lists the number of invocations and the total time (in seconds) of our proposed algorithm, differentiating the time spent (in seconds) to analyze the *inputs*, *outputs*, preconditions and effects (including restrictions on time) and the time taken in seconds to achieve the formal verification of the composition. Despite the relatively high time for many invocations (20 seconds), this time is acceptable as it reflects the worst case scenario of our algorithm.

4.3 Analysis of our checking method of the composition

The model used in this work retains the main features

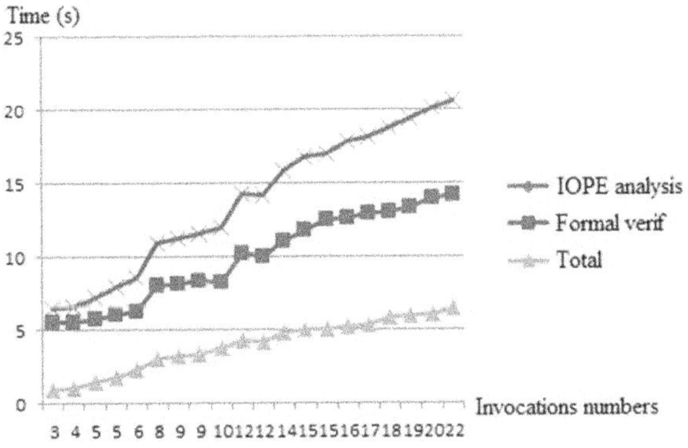

Figure 7: Numbers of invocation X time (s)

of a composition of web services in a real scenario, as the properties listed below about service composition. Therefore it is able to simulate the execution environment more closely.

- Parallelism: it is possible that services begin or finish running while other services are still running. The structure of the *timer* automaton ensures this property. Each time progress is checked to verify if a service can begin/end and to increment the duration of the services which are already running.
- Time Progress: the time progress is linear and discrete by one time unit. The structure of the automaton *timer* ensures this property. The transition that increases the *time* does this by adding one unit of time.
- Stateless: The conversion of the composition to the automaton network is through invocations. Thus each invocation of a service is exactly the same, not storing information about previous invocations of the service;
- Asynchronism: The use of the variable that represents a list allows a service only to consume the outputs generated by another service where possible, allowing the postponement of its execution;

5. RELATED WORK

The authors in [8] proposed an algorithm based on inputs, outputs, preconditions and effects specified in SWRL in order to increase precision in service discovery. The analysis of the semantic similarity is done among the predicates and the attributes of a request, and these are the main strengths in relation to other IOPE approaches. However, as mentioned, the algorithm in [8] is not able to analyze neither temporal preconditions nor effects. Unlike our work, the temporal restrictions were introduced in order to increase the accuracy of a discovery algorithm.

In [13], the authors propose an algorithm which considers the temporal restrictions represented in OWL-*Time* as inputs and outputs of a web service. More specifically, they consider the availability of a web service in the discovery phase. Unlike [13], our work uses the SWRL language with which it is also possible to analyze the semantic similarities in the predicates of the rules automatically. Moreover, we do not use preconditions or effects as inputs and outputs, our preconditions and effects are described as semantic rules.

Authors in [5] define a set of abstractions to verify the temporal restrictions through the conversion of WS-CDL. This was not the main objective of our work and, it is too restrictive in terms of choreography.

Authors in [9] and [7] define a set of abstractions in order to verify temporal restrictions in asynchronous communications of web service compositions. The work presented in [9] is based on choreography concept and uses the *timed conversational protocol* representing the internal behavior of a service in an automaton in UPPAAL. In relation to time it uses the data type *clock* to represent the data exchange and passage of time, which consequently makes the model unable to simulate parallelism between web services and to verify the principal types of temporal restrictions. Unlike our work, we define our own time structure, simulating parallelism and the verification of temporal restrictions. The model presented in [7] is also unable to simulate parallelism and some temporal restrictions.

Furthermore, this work emphasized the importance of practical analysis in the use of web services so that the restrictions inherent to this technology become more evident.

6. CONCLUSION AND FUTURE WORK

The compositions of services has been created dynamically using algorithms to combine services in order to meet a user request. Time constraints must be checked in compositions in order to ensure the time limits established. This paper proposed the development of an iterative algorithm with temporal constraints in order to capture and formally validate the composition generated.

Some analyses were carried out in order to validate the proposed algorithm, such as: (i) accuracy and precision, (ii) execution time and (iii) verification method. Our proposed algorithm had higher precision and accuracy compared to the discovery methods proposed by [12] and [8]. Although the runtime of our solution is higher than other approaches due to our formal verification, the guarantee of a correct composition for tackling temporal restrictions is one of the main strengths of this approach. As far as we know, no other approach has proposed an iterative algorithm that ensures correct compositions.

As future work, we intend to expand the use of temporal properties using OWL-Time and include some new control structures of OWL-S in the process of formal analysis of a composition, such as *repeat* and *while* thus allowing alternative flows.

Acknowledgements

The authors would like to thank PIBIC n.1759 for their funding of this research.

7. REFERENCES

[1] G. Alonso, F. Casati, H. Kuno, and V. Machiraju. *Web Services: Concepts, Architectures and Applications.* Springer, 2004.

[2] G. Behrmann, A. David, and K. G. Larsen. A tutorial on uppaal. In *SFM'04*, pages 200–236, 2004.

[3] T. Berners-Lee, J. Hendler, and O. Lassila. The semantic web. *Scientific American*, May 2001.

[4] K. H. Brodersen, C. S. Ong, K. E. Stephan, and J. M. Buhmann. The balanced accuracy and its posterior

distribution. In *Proceedings of the 2010 20th International Conference on Pattern Recognition*, ICPR '10, pages 3121–3124, Washington, DC, USA, 2010. IEEE Computer Society.

[5] M.-E. Cambronero, G. Díaz, E. Martínez, V. V. Ruiz, and M. L. Tobarra. Wst: a tool supporting timed composite web services model transformation. *Simulation*, 88(3):349–364, 2012.

[6] E. M. Clarke and F. Lerda. Model checking: Software and beyond. *J. UCS*, pages 639–649, 2007.

[7] G. Díaz, M.-E. Cambronero, M. L. Tobarra, V. Valero, and F. Cuartero. Analysis and verification of time requirements applied to the web services composition. In *Proceedings of the Third international conference on Web Services and Formal Methods*, WS-FM'06, pages 178–192, Berlin, Heidelberg, 2006. Springer-Verlag.

[8] L. Erdens, D. B. Claro, D. Lopes, and P. Albers. Discoverying cloud services by preconditions and effects for compositions. In *14th International Conference on Enterprise Information Systems (ICEIS 2012)*, 2012.

[9] N. Guermouche and C. Godart. Timed model checking based approach for web services analysis. In *ICWS'09*, pages 213–221, 2009.

[10] J. R. Hobbs and F. Pan. An ontology of time for the semantic web. *ACM Trans. Asian Lang. Inf. Process.*, pages 66–85, 2004.

[11] F. Pan and J. R. Hobbs. Temporal aggregates in owl-time. In *FLAIRS Conference'05*, pages 560–565, 2005.

[12] M. Paolucci, T. Kawamura, R. Payne, Terry, and K. Sycara. Semantic matching of web services capabilities, 2002.

[13] C. V. S. Prazeres, C. A. C. Teixeira, and M. da Graça C. Pimentel. Semantic web services discovery by matching temporal restrictions. *Applications and the Internet, IEEE/IPSJ International Symposium on*, 0:26–32, 2008.

[14] A. Rivolli, J. P. Orlando, C. H. Yamamoto, and D. Moreira. Regras swrl: Análise de similaridade e detecção de erros. In *In WebMedia'11: Proceedings of the 17th Brazilian symposium on Multimedia and the web*, 2011.

[15] J. J. Samper, F. J. Adell, L. V. D. Berg, and J. J. Martinez. Improving semantic web service discovery. *Development*, 3(1):35–42, 2008. Disponível em: http://www.academypublisher.com/ojs/index.php-/jnw/article/view/995.

[16] E. Sirin, B. Parsia, B. C. Grau, A. Kalyanpur, and Y. Katz. Pellet: A practical owl-dl reasoner. *Web Semant.*, 5:51–53, June 2007. Disponível em: http://dl.acm.org/citation.cfm?id=1265608.1265744.

An Approach to Developing Multi-Tenancy SaaS Using Metaprogramming

Josino Rodrigues
CIn-UFPE, UFRPE
jrn4@cin.ufpe.br

Andreza Leite
CIn-UFPE, UFRPE
ala4@cin.ufpe.br

Júlio César Damasceno
CIn-UFPE, UFRPE
jcd@cin.ufpe.br

Paulo Silveira
CIn-UFPE
pamsn@cin.ufpe.br

Vinícius Garcia
CIn-UFPE
vcg@cin.ufpe.br

Silvio Meira
CIn-UFPE
silvio@meira.com

ABSTRACT

In last years have seen an increase in SaaS (Software as a Service) use. The development of multi-tenancy web application (one of the main ways to provide SaaS) increased considerably after the start of call "Web 2.0 Age". This work presents an approach for implementation of a multi-tenancy SaaS application, and an architecture based on plugins and metaprogramming to achieve a high level software reuse. This approach is presented through an experience report described throughout the paper.

Categories and Subject Descriptors

D.2.8 [**Software Engineering**]: Software Architectures—*Patterns*

Keywords

Multi-Tenancy, SaaS, Metaprogramação, Software as a Service, Software como serviço, Arquitetura

1. INTRODUÇÃO

Segundo estudos da Gartner, na América Latina, a receita estimada para SaaS (Software as a Service) esta para alcançar U$ 419,7 milhões até o final de 2012, valor esse que atingiu U$ 331,1 milhões no ano anterior. Espera-se que Brasil e México conduzam a maioria das oportunidades de adoção e receita[5].

Segundo Harris e Ahmed [6] existem três tipos diferentes de aplicações SaaS:

- ***Multi-instance***: executam em ambientes onde o servidor web é compartilhado. Nessa abordagem uma cópia da aplicação é inicialmente configurada e então implantada como um contexto do servidor web.
- ***Single-instance***: as aplicações provêem serviços para um único cliente e executam em um servidor exclusivo. Essa pode ser considerada a abordagem com maior desperdício de recursos, dado que um servidor pode executar com apenas 10% de sua capacidade [6].
- ***Multi-tenancy***: provê uma única aplicação compartilhada por vários clientes. Nessa abordagem várias aplicações "virtuais" (*tenants*) são criadas na mesma instância de software.

Arquiteturas *multi-tenancy* tem sido identificadas como uma vantagem competitiva potencialmente crítica sobre as arquiteturas clássicas *single-tenant* em certos domínios[4]. Contudo desenvolvedores de software têm dificuldade em projetar e implementar arquiteturas *multi-tenancy* eficientes[9] devido à falta de documentação e formalização do entendimento dos conceitos arquiteturais.

O objetivo desse trabalho é apresentar uma experiência prática obtida durante a adoção da arquitetura *multi-tenancy*, de forma a auxiliar desenvolvedores e engenheiros de software no processo de desenvolvimento de SaaS. Esse trabalho está organizado da seguinte forma: a Seção 2 apresenta o problema solucionado durante a implementação da aplicação *multi-tenancy*, a Seção 3 apresenta a metodologia utilizada nesse trabalho, a Seção 4 descreve a escolha da arquitetura e sua implementação, por fim, a Seção 5 apresenta as conclusões e trabalhos futuros.

2. PROBLEMA

O problema a ser solucionado surgiu da necessidade de desenvolver um software para suporte ao desenvolvimento de LPS (Linha de Produtos de Software) que fosse executado no modelo de software como serviço. Esse aplicativo foi desenvolvido para atender a necessidade da empresa Rise [1], onde ocorreu uma residência em reuso de software na qual os residentes deveriam definir e documentar várias LPS para diferentes empresas.

Cavalcanti *et al.* [3] apresentam um metamodelo que tem como objetivo coordenar as atividades relacionadas ao desenvolvimento de uma LPS, pelo gerenciamento de suas diferentes fases e da manutenção da rastreabilidade e variabilidade entre os diferentes artefatos. Esse metamodelo foi representado utilizando a notação UML e divide-se em cinco sub-modelos: Gerenciamento de Projeto, Gerenciamento de Risco, Escopo, Requisitos e Testes. A descrição de cada submodelo pode ser encontrada em [3].

Além dos requisitos citados acima, ainda existiam alguns fatores que poderiam influenciar nas decisões de projeto:

- A aplicação seria inicialmente provida como SaaS para

[1] http://rise.com.br

Permission to make digital or hard copies of all or part of this work for personal or classroom use is granted without fee provided that copies are not made or distributed for profit or commercial advantage and that copies bear this notice and the full citation on the first page. To copy otherwise, to republish, to post on servers or to redistribute to lists, requires prior specific permission and/or a fee.
WebMedia'12, October 15–18, 2012, São Paulo/SP, Brazil.
Copyright 2012 ACM 978-1-4503-1706-1/12/10 ...$15.00.

um grupo de 20 clientes, que validariam os requisitos da aplicação durante o uso da versão beta;

- Os clientes deveriam ter a possibilidade de contratar e usar a aplicação sem nenhuma intervenção manual da empresa provedora do serviço;
- Cada cliente deveria poder gerenciar seus próprios usuários;
- A aplicação iria executar em um ambiente virtualizado com 613MB de memória e 30GB de armazenamento;
- Os requisitos da aplicação deveriam ser levantados e implementados de forma incremental;
- A aplicação deveria aproveitar o máximo de recursos possível.

A necessidade de prover uma aplicação web, que pudesse ser contratada pelo cliente e paga por uso, sem a intervenção do provedor de serviço fortaleceram a escolha da abordagem SaaS. Adicionalmente, os recursos limitados de hardware e a necessidade de prover a mesma aplicação para 20 clientes exige o máximo de otimização no uso do hardware. Dentre os 3 tipos de SaaS apresentados na seção anterior, *multi-tenancy* apresentou-se como a melhor escolha.

3. METODOLOGIA

Para conduzir a etapa de desenvolvimento de um aplicativo na indústria seguiremos o processo definido na Figura 1. De acordo com a figura, a primeira etapa consiste em definir uma arquitetura do aplicativo a ser desenvolvido. A segunda etapa foi escolher as tecnologias que seriam utilizadas para a implementação dos requisitos funcionais e não funcionais da aplicação, além da migração dos dados já cadastrados que anteriormente eram manipulados por uma aplicação legada, utilizada por um dos clientes iniciais da aplicação. Durante a etapa de implementação foi adotado SCRUM[1] como metodologia de desenvolvimento, o que facilitou a realização de *releases* incrementais e rápidos. Por fim, na terceira etapa é realizado a coleta de *feedback* dos usuários, de forma que seja possível melhorar a aplicação no tocante a requisitos funcionais e não-funcionais. Uma sequência de vários ciclos compostos da etapa de "implementação" e "validação da aplicação" é realizado com o objetivo de proporcionar uma evolução incremental do produto.

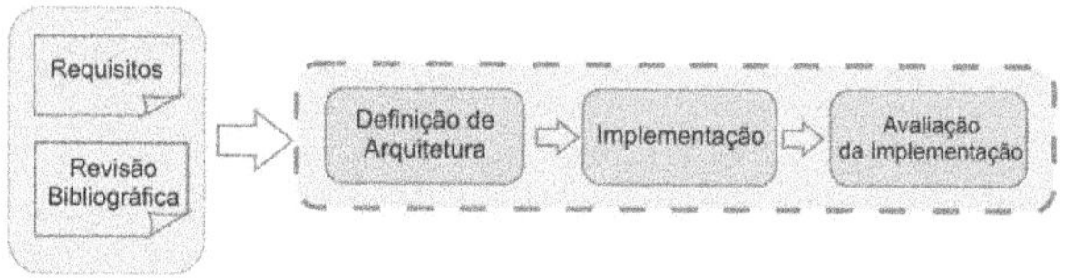

Figure 1: Metodologia Utilizada para Desenvolvimento de Aplicação na Indústria.

4. DEFINIÇÃO DE ARQUITETURA

A separação de interesses entre requisitos relacionados ao negócio principal da aplicação e requisitos inerentes a *multi-tenancy* também é um fator crítico que deve ser levado em consideração. A aplicação deveria ser implementada de forma que o código de regra de negócio sofresse o mínimo de interferência possível do código associado a implementações de *multi-tenancy*.

Estes problemas podem ser superados integrando cuidadosamente *multi-tenancy* na arquitetura. No restante desta seção, descrevemos os componentes da arquitetura abordada por Bezemer *et al.* [2] para implementação de *multi-tenancy* como um interesse transversal.

Os principais componentes da arquitetura definida por Bezemer são:

Autenticação Pelo motivo de uma aplicação multi-tenancy ter apenas uma instância da aplicação e do banco de dados, todos os *tenants* usam o mesmo ambiente físico. A fim de oferecer a customização do ambiente e ter certeza de que os *tenants* podem acessar somente os seus próprios dados, *tenants* devem ser autenticados. Como a autenticação de usuário, normalmente, já esta presente na aplicação de destino, um mecanismo específico para autenticação de *tenants* faz-se necessário por duas razões: (1) geralmente é mais fácil introduzir um mecanismo de autenticação adicional, do que mudar um já existente; e (2) a autenticação de *tenants* permite que um único usuário faça parte de uma ou mais organizações lógicas, o que estende a idéia de autenticação com grupo de usuários.

Configuração Em uma aplicação *multi-tenancy* a customização deve ser possível através de configuração. A fim de permitir que o usuário tenha uma experiência como se ele estivesse trabalhando em um ambiente dedicado, é necessário permitir pelo menos os seguintes tipos de configuração: estilo de Layout ,configurações gerais definidas pelo usuário, configurações de localização de arquivos e configurações de *workflows*.

Banco de Dados Em uma aplicação *multi-tenancy* há uma grande exigência para o isolamento dos dados. Como todos os *tenants* usam a mesma instância de um banco de dados é necessário ter certeza de que eles podem acessar somente seus próprios dados. Atualmente sistemas de gerenciamento de dados (*Data Base Management Systems* - DBMS) de prateleira não são capazes de lidar com *multi-tenancy*, isso deve ser feito em uma camada entre a camada lógica de negócios e o *pool* de banco de dados de aplicações. As principais tarefas dessa camada são as seguintes: criação de novos *tenants* no banco de dados, adaptação de consultas executadas no SGBD e balanceamento de carga.

4.1 Tecnologias

Após a escolha de uma arquitetura de referência para ser adotada por nossa aplicação, tem-se a necessidade de escolher as tecnologias que serão adotadas para a implementação. Durante a escolha dessas tecnologias avaliou-se a possibilidade do uso de tecnologias existentes na plataforma Java, como JSF[2], Struts 2[3], Spring Framework[4] e Grails[5]. A escolha da plataforma Java deve-se ao fato da mesma ser bem consolidada tanto em ambiente acadêmico quanto no mercado. A partir de reuniões com os envolvidos observou-se que Grails apresentava um conjunto de recursos que poderiam dar produtividade para a equipe de desenvolvimento que não foram encontrados nas outras tecnologias como geração de CRUD (*Create, Read, Update* e *Delete*), arquitetura baseada em *plugins* que permite a criação e reuso

[2]http://javaserverfaces.java.net
[3]http://struts.apache.org/2.3.1.2/index.html
[4]http://www.springsource.org/spring-framework
[5]http://grails.org

de componentes, e total integração com frameworks e APIs Java.

O Grails é um framework web *open-source* que utiliza a linguagem Groovy[6], e outros frameworks consagrados como Hibernate[7], Spring Framework e Sitemesh[8]. Grails propõe-se a trazer a produtividade do Ruby on Rails para a plataforma Java, porém ele possui uma grande vantagem, já que é baseado na linguagem Groovy.

A aplicação que está sendo desenvolvida, em particular se beneficiará da capacidade de definir métodos e propriedades em tempo de execução, disponibilizado pela linguagem Groovy. Essa característica da linguagem Groovy é chamada de metaprogramação. Em uma linguagem estática como java, o acesso a uma propriedade ou invocação de um método é resolvido em tempo de compilação. Em comparação, Groovy não resolve o acessos à propriedades ou invocação de métodos até que a aplicação seja executada[8]. Uma aplicação que utiliza essa linguagem pode dinamicamente definir métodos ou propriedades em tempo de execução, isso vai de encontro à necessidade de customização das aplicações, dado que com a utilização desse recurso pode-se adicionar atributos e customizar comportamentos de um *tenant* específico futuramente.

Outro ponto que influenciou bastante na escolha de Grails foi sua arquitetura baseada em *plugins*. Grails não se propões a ter todas as respostas e soluções para o desenvolvimento de aplicações web. Ao invés disso, ele provê uma arquitetura baseada em *plugins* e um repositório mantido pela comunidade de desenvolvedores onde é possível encontrar *plugins* que implementam as mais diversas funcionalidades como segurança, teste, busca, geração de relatórios, etc. Essa abordagem proporciona o reuso e permite que funcionalidades de difícil implementação possam ser adicionadas na aplicação de forma bastante simples.

Além das tecnologias relacionadas à programação, foi necessário escolher a tecnologia utilizada para armazenamento de dados. Grails Framework permite optar por qualquer SGBD relacional para armazenar dados. A opcão escolhida foi o SGBD PostgreSQL.

4.2 Prototipagem

A partir da escolha da arquitetura de referência, das tecnologias a serem adotadas e da divisão dos módulos da aplicação, chegou-se a proposta de arquitetura apresentada na Figura 2. A proposta da aplicação possui 5 módulos associados à lógica de negócio da aplicação, esses módulos foram descritos anteriormente na seção 2. Foi adotado o Framework Grails para auxílio ao desenvolvimento da aplicação web e juntamente com ele foram adotados alguns de seus *plugins*. Para validar arquitetura proposta foi desenvolvido um protótipo contendo uma parte pequena dos requisitos funcionais da aplicação. Nesse protótipo serão implementados os cadastros de Projeto, Módulo e Features. A implementação do protótipo tem o objetivo de verificar a viabilidade de implementação e o atendimento dos objetivos da arquitetura.

Com o objetivo de implementar os requisitos *multi-tenancy* de forma reutilizável, a solução foi implementar esses requisitos como um plugin do Grails, dessa forma aplicações futuras poderiam se beneficiar do código implementado. Uma vantagem do uso dessa abordagem é que dentro de um plugin

[6]http://groovy.codehaus.org
[7]http://www.hibernate.org
[8]http://www.sitemesh.org

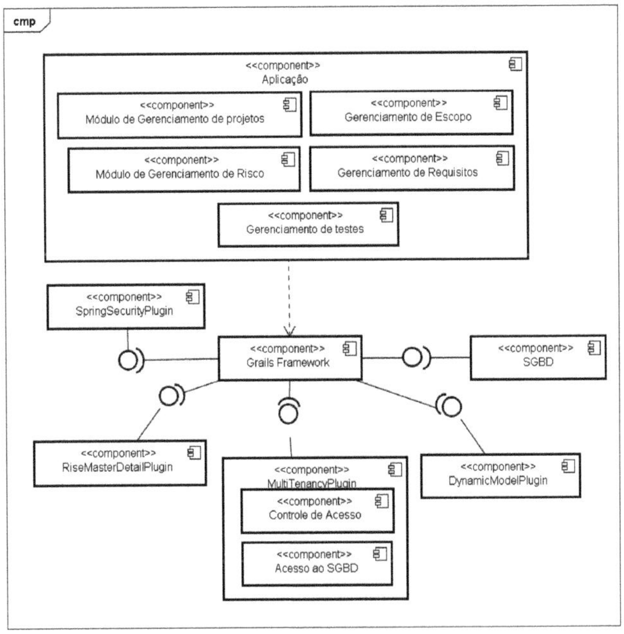

Figure 2: Arquitetura da Aplicação

grails é possível adicionar não só classes implementadas em Groovy ou Java, mas também páginas da camada de visão e outros tipos de arquivo. Antes de implementar os requisitos *multi-tenancy* como *plugin* foi realizado uma pesquisa no repositório de *plugins* do Grails para verificar se já existia algo semelhante ao que pretendia-se implementar.

Durante a pesquisa foi encontrado o *plugin Multi-Tenant Core* [9] que implementa as funcionalidades de 2 dos componentes mencionados na arquitetura de referência [2], o componente de autenticação e o componentes de acesso ao banco de dados. Esse plugin implementa a funcionalidade de associar um usuário da aplicação a um *tenant* específico e, além disso, realiza de forma dinâmica o filtro dos dados durante uma consulta ao banco de dados, de forma que um usuário da aplicação tenha acesso apenas aos dados vinculados ao seu *tenant*. A autenticação e controle de acesso pode ser realizado através da integração desse plugin com o *Spring Security*[10], um *framework* de controle de acesso bastante utilizado em aplicações Java.

O terceiro componente mencionado na arquitetura proposta, até então não implementado, é o componente de configuração. O objetivo desse componente é gerenciar as configurações relacionadas a cada *tenant* e prover funcionalidades de customização da aplicação para cada *tenant*. Essa customização pode ir desde alterações em *interface* com o usuário até alteração nas classes de negócio, tudo isso realizado de forma dinâmica. Um outro plugin encontrado Durante a pesquisa foi o *plugin Dynamic Domain Class*[11] que proporciona a criação de classes de domínio de forma dinâmica, esse plugin ajudou a validar a idéia de usar Groovy e Grails para customizar as classes de domínio em tempo de execução.

[9]http://multi-tenant.github.com/grails-multi-tenant-core
[10]http://static.springsource.org/spring-security/site/index.html
[11]http://code.google.com/p/grails-dynamic-domain-class-plugin/

ATRIBUTO	AVALIAÇÃO
Disponibilidade	Como foi adotado um SGBD PostgreSQL, é possivel agendar tarefas automáticas no servidor para executar backups periódicos.
Integridade Conceitual	Tanto as entidades de negócio quanto as classes utilitárias da aplicação foram modularizadas em plugins de forma que os interesses da aplicação foram bem definidos e separados.
Flexibilidade	A flexibilidade pode ser alcançada através do uso das característica de linguagem dinâmica existente na linguagem Groovy. Dessa forma é possivel criar Entidade de domínio e alterar entidades já existentes em tempo de execução, caso seja necessário.
Interoperabilidade	O uso de plugins Grails permite que os dados da aplicação possam ser expostos através de REST ou Web Services para os usuários.
Manutenibilidade	A arquitetura de plugins do Grails facilita a manutenção dos código já que cada plugin pode ser mantido separadamente, reduzindo as dependências entre os componentes da aplicação.
Gerenciabilidade	Não foi possivel identificar soluções para esse atributo durante a implementação do protótipo.
Performance	Não foi possivel identificar soluções para esse atributo durante a implementação do protótipo.
Reusabilidade	As partes da aplicação implementadas como plugins podem ser reutilizadas em aplicações futuras facilmente, sem a necessidade de qualquer adaptação no plugin.
Escalabilidade	Não foi possivel identificar soluções para esse atributo durante a implementação do protótipo.
Segurança	A autenticação e controle de acesso puderam ser garantidos pelo uso do Framework Spring Security, que pôde ser facilmente integrado com o plugin de multi-tenancy no atendimento do requisito de isolamento de acesso entre dados dos tenants.
Testabilidade	O Grails Framework provê uma infraestrutura para auxiliar na implementação de testes unitários que utiliza JUnit, um framework de teste para aplicações java. Durante a criação de uma classe o Grails Framework já cria uma classe de testes correspondente para otimizar o tempo de desenvolvimento.
Usabilidade	Grails trabalha com templates para geração de telas. Embora já possua um template padrão, o desenvolvedor pode implementar um template próprio que atenda à necessidades específicas de interação com o usuário. O template padrão do Grails Framework já implementa alguns padrões de usabilidade bem estabelecidos no mercado.

Table 1: Resultado da Aplicação dos Critérios de Exclusão

Durante a implementação detectou-se que o padrão de geração de telas do Grails não satisfazia aos anseios dos usuários quanto à forma de interação com o aplicativo. A partir dessa necessidade foi desenvolvido um *plugin* para implementar o padrão de tela Mestre/Detalhe [7], não implementado nativamente pelo gerador de telas padrão do Grails. Durante a implementação desse *plugin* identificou-se que poderia ser viável implementar módulos completos da aplicação como *plugins* Grails, desde classes de negócio à camada de visão.

Após a implementação do protótipo foi realizada a avaliação do protótipo para verificar quais atributos de qualidade desejáveis foram atendidos. A Tabela 1 apresenta cada atributo de qualidade e uma breve descrição de como ele foi atendido.

Após a avaliação do protótipo foi possível observar que a solução proposta atendia a 8 dos 12 atributos de qualidade desejados. Quatro atributos de qualidade (disponibilidade, gerenciabilidade, performance, escalabilidade) não puderam ser avaliados durante a implementação do protótipo inicial. A avaliação foi considerada satisfatória, considerando que os quatro atributos de qualidade da arquitetura que não foram atendidos inicialmente não geraram nenhum impedimento para a geração da primeira versão do aplicativo. Ao fim da implementação do protótipo deu-se início ao desenvolvimento da aplicação real. Ao final da implementação da primeira versão da aplicação, foi necessário criar algum mecanismo para migrar os dados já cadastrados pela aplicação legada.

5. CONCLUSÕES

Esse trabalho apresentou uma abordadgem para implementação de aplicações *multi-tenancy* que utiliza uma arquitetura de *plugins* e o recurso de metaprogramação, existente em várias linguagens dinâmicas. A arquitetura de *plugins* permitiu a modularização dos requisitos de forma que os artefatos (*plugins*) possam ser reutilizados em aplicações futuras. Já o uso de metaprogramação, permitiu a separação de interesses durante a implementação. Dessa forma os requisitos *multi-tenancy* puderam ser inseridos na aplicação de forma pouco invasiva. A separação de interesses provida pela abordagem proposta permitiu um alto grau de reuso durante o desenvolvimento da aplicação. Como trabalhos futuros serão realizados experimentos que validem essa abordagem em um ambiente com grande número de requisições e manipulação de grande massa de dados.

6. REFERENCES

[1] P. Agarwal. Continuous scrum: agile management of saas products. In *Proceedings of the 4th India Software Engineering Conference*, ISEC '11, pages 51–60, New York, NY, USA, 2011. ACM.

[2] C.-P. Bezemer, A. Zaidman, B. Platzbeecker, T. Hurkmans, and A. 't Hart. Enabling multi-tenancy: An industrial experience report. In *Software Maintenance (ICSM), 2010 IEEE International Conference on*, pages 1 –8, sept. 2010.

[3] Y. C. Cavalcanti, I. Do Carmo Machado, P. A. Da Mota, S. Neto, L. L. Lobato, E. S. De Almeida, and S. R. De Lemos Meira. Towards metamodel support for variability and traceability in software product lines. *Proceedings of the 5th Workshop on Variability Modeling of SoftwareIntensive Systems VaMoS 11*, (840):49–57, 2011.

[4] F. Chong and G. Carraro. Architecture strategies for catching the long tail. 2006.

[5] Gartner. Gartner says worldwide software-as-a-service revenue to reach 14.5 billion in 2012, 2012.

[6] I. S. Harris and Z. Ahmed. An open multi-tenant architecture to leverage smes. *European Journal of Scientific Research*, 65(4):601–610, 2011.

[7] T. Neil. 12 standard screen patterns, 2010.

[8] C. Richardson. Orm in dynamic languages. *Commun. ACM*, 52(4):48–55, Apr. 2009.

[9] Z. H. Wang, C. J. Guo, B. Gao, W. Sun, Z. Zhang, and W. H. An. A study and performance evaluation of the multi-tenant data tier design patterns for service oriented computing. In *Proceedings of the 2008 IEEE International Conference on e-Business Engineering*, pages 94–101, Washington, DC, USA, 2008. IEEE Computer Society.

Evaluation of Semantic Similarity in WSD: An Analysis to Incorporate it into the Association of Terms

Erick Nilsen Pereira de Souza
FORMAS - Semantic Formalisms and Applications
LaSiD/MMCC/IM/UFBA
Multi-Institutional Master Program on Computer Science (MMCC)
Federal University of Bahia
Av. Adhemar de Barros, s/n, Campus de Ondina, Salvador - Bahia - Brazil 40170-110
ericksouza@dcc.ufba.br

Daniela Barreiro Claro
FORMAS - Semantic Formalisms and Applications
LaSiD/MMCC/IM/UFBA
Multi-Institutional Master Program on Computer Science (MMCC)
Federal University of Bahia
Av. Adhemar de Barros, s/n, Campus de Ondina, Salvador - Bahia - Brasil 40170-110
dclaro@ufba.br

ABSTRACT

Semantic association requires an analysis on similarity in order to provide better combinations. Several semantic similarity measures have been proposed for the Word Sense Disambiguation (WSD) problem. Therefore, this work aims to evaluate the performance of five semantic similarity measures into a thesaurus by WSD approach so as to incorporate semantic similarities into association problems. Experiments were conducted using two main algorithms of WSD domain. The results showed that the application of semantic similarity improves precision and recall on disambiguation domain. In order to complement the evaluation, we proposed a hybrid approach and we evaluated it over other measures presented. According to our results, it was possible to adapt a similarity measure for the problem of finding semantic associations in texts.

Categories and Subject Descriptors

H.3.1 [**Information Storage and Retrieval**]: Content Analysis and Indexing

Keywords

semantic similarity, word sense desambiguation, semantic association, Wordnet

1. INTRODUCTION

The semantic association between two entities in texts is a inherent human task [3]. Entities such as *Lula* and *Luis Inacio* written in Brazilian texts can be inferred by a Brazilian reader that they are similar. However, when considering the large amount of unrepresentative information present in the Web, strategies for the automatic extraction of relationships between semantically meaningful entities have become a research challenge.

The degree of similarity is an important step to identify the relevance of semantic association between entities. Several measures of semantic similarity, with applications to problems in many areas such as Bioinformatics [16], GIS [7] and Information Extraction [2] have been studied and used. In the case of hierarchical ontologies, an indirect method of evaluating the quality of a similarity measure is to apply it to the problem of Word Sense Disambiguation (WSD). WSD deals with lexical ambiguity, this means, a choice of a proper sense of a word in a given context. This ambiguity is propagated in several levels of human communication: morphological, lexical, syntactic, semantic, contextual and pragmatic [5].

According to Navigli [14], WSD methods can be classified into two: those based on corpus and those based on lexical. The corpus-based methods use training corpora with machine learning algorithms. The lexical-based methods, also called knowledge-based methods, apply heuristics to computational lexicons so as to obtain the most likely meaning of a word in context. The lexicon most used in WSD domain is Wordnet [6]. Wordnet is a taxonomy where words are written in English and each word is related to a set of synonyms (*synsets*), parts of speech, meanings and usage examples.

In this paper, semantic similarity approaches in hierarchical ontologies are described and evaluated in the context of WSD methods based on a computational lexicon (Wordnet). This work has two main objectives: (i) analyze the performance of five similarity measures in DLS, through a comparative study of two algorithms and (ii) propose a hybrid approach to complement the previous evaluation in order to determine which measure is more appropriate to extracting semantic associations automatically. From the results, it could be possible to indicate which measure can be efficiently used to detect semantic similar associations, thus identifying and grouping the most representative associations in a particular context.

This paper is organized as follows: section 2 describes the main semantic similarity approaches. Section 3 presents an analysis of WSD algorithms. Our WSD hybrid method is proposed in section 4 and evaluated in section 5. Section 6 presents the analysis and partial conclusions of this work.

Permission to make digital or hard copies of all or part of this work for personal or classroom use is granted without fee provided that copies are not made or distributed for profit or commercial advantage and that copies bear this notice and the full citation on the first page. To copy otherwise, to republish, to post on servers or to redistribute to lists, requires prior specific permission and/or a fee.

WebMedia'12, October 15–28, 2012, São Paulo/SP, Brazil.

Copyright 2012 ACM 978-1-4503-1706-1/12/10 ...$15.00.

2. SEMANTIC SIMILARITY

There are basically two types of semantic similarity measures: edge-based and information content-based.

2.1 Edge-based measures

Intuitively, near concepts are more similar than far concepts in a hierarchical ontology. Therefore, the shortest path between two concepts is an important measure of similarity. This conceptual distance is defined by Mihalcea [13] as $dist(c_1, c_2) =$ *minimum number of edges separating* c_1 *and* c_2, where c_1 and c_2 represent concepts (nodes) in the ontology. With this assumption, Wu and Palmer [19] defined a similarity measure (WUP) taking into account the depth of the concepts in the hierarchy:

$$sim_{WUP}(c_1, c_2) = \frac{2 \times D(LCS(c_1, c_2))}{D(c_1) + D(c_2) + 2 \times D(LCS(c_1, c_2))}, \quad (1)$$

where $D(c_i)$ is the depth of the concept c_i and $LCS(c_i, c_j)$ is the common super concept most specific between concepts c_i and c_j (*Least Common Superconcept*).

Leacock and Chodorow [10] introduced the measure (LCH) based on the shortest distance between two concept and its depth (H) in a taxonomy:

$$sim_{LCH}(c_1, c_2) = -log\frac{dist(c_1, c_2)}{2 \times H} \quad (2)$$

One of the shortcomings of edge-based measures is that it considers that the connections between concepts have an uniform distance, which does not reflect a lack of uniformity between entities in real world [17].

2.2 Information Content-based measures

In Information Content based measures, the frequency which a term appears associated with another indicates the degree of similarity between them. According to Resnik [17], the probabilities associated to concepts in a taxonomy have the same idea of an edge-based approach without the deficiency of uniform distances.

Considering $p : C \rightarrow [0, 1]$ a probabilistic function applied to a taxonomy, for every $c \in C$, $p(c)$ is the probability of finding an instance of concept c. The probability decreases due to the specificity of the concept. According to Information Theory, $IC(c) = -log[p(c)]$, this means, the more abstract a concept is, the lower is its aggregated information.

Resnik [17] defines a similarity between two concepts as:

$$sim_{RES}(c_1, c_2) = \max_{c \in S(c_1, c_2)} IC(c), \quad (3)$$

where $S(c_1, c_2)$ is a set of all common super concepts between concepts c_1 and c_2. This measure was reformulated by Lin [12] using features of the equation 1:

$$sim_{LIN}(c_1, c_2) = \frac{2 \times IC(LCS(c_1, c_2))}{IC(c_1) + IC(c_2)}, \quad (4)$$

Then authors in [8] define a similarity measure (JCN) that combines the concepts of both edge-based and information content-based measures:

$$sim_{JCN}(c_1, c_2) = \frac{1}{IC(c_1) + IC(c_2) - 2 \times IC(LCS(c_1, c_2))} \quad (5)$$

Previous similarity measures were used into two WSD algorithms: Simplified Lesk [11] and Adapted Lesk [4]. The next section describes these algorithms and the incorporation of semantic similarity to carry out our experiments.

3. ANALYSIS OF WSD ALGORITHMS

Many WSD methods are based on the optimization of relatedness measures, which estimate the degree of correlation between two entities (words or meanings) in a text fragment. The Lesk algorithm [11] is one of the well known methods of this category. It uses a dictionary definition (gloss) to perform the word disambiguation in a given context. In its simplified version[1] (Algorithm 1), a target word w is assigned to the sense whose gloss shares the largest number of words in common[2] with the surrounding words of w.

Algorithm 1 Simplified Lesk [11]

```
Require: word, sentence.
Ensure: best-sense.
best-sense ← most frequent sense for word
max-overlap ← 0
context ← set of words in sentence
for all sense in senses of word do
    signature ← set of words in the gloss and examples of sense
    overlap ← COMPUTEOVERLAP(signature,context)
    if overlap > max-overlap then
        max-overlap ← overlap
        best-sense ← sense
    end if
end for
```

The major limitation of this algorithm is that its dictionary might not have enough words to identify their meaning due to its limitation size, i.e. they usually have few word for each meaning. This means that the intersection between the gloss and the words of the neighborhood of w often has an empty set as result. In order to solve this problem, Banerjee[4] proposes a modification in the Simplified Lesk algorithm, where the elected sense for w is the one that has greater semantic similarity degree among all senses of the words surrounding w (Algorithm 2).

Algorithm 2 Adapted Lesk[4]

```
Require: word, sentence.
Ensure: best-sense.
best-sense ← most frequent sense for word
max-similarity ← α
window ← set of words in sentence
for all sense in senses of word do
    for all window-word in window do
        for all sense-window in window-word do
            sim ← sim+SIMILARITY(sense,sense-window)
        end for
    end for
    if sim > max-similarity then
        max-similarity ← sim
        best-sense ← sense
    end if
end for
```

However, using the most voting approach to elect a sense of a word is not a good way to perform WSD experiments, since this approach can improperly increase the accuracy of

[1]A comparative study in [18] shows that the simplified Lesk algorithm is significantly better than its original version in terms of accuracy and efficiency.
[2]COMPUTOVERLAP returns the number of words in common between two sets of words.

the algorithms when applied to datasets within many frequent senses. In order to better evaluate the performance of similarity measures, the election of the most frequent sense is discarted in our evaluation. In other words, when COMPUTEOVERLAP returns the empty set in Simplified Lesk algorithm, it is unable to elect a valid sense for the target word. The same occurs when the accumulation of similarity does not exceed the threshold α of the Adapted Lesk algorithm. With this approach it could be possible to better evaluate the similarity measures on each algorithm.

It is possible observe that the recall of Algorithm 2 tends to be greater than the recall of Algorithm 1 when α is small; this occurs due to the flexibility obtained by the semantic similarity measures. In fact, unlike the simplified version, the Adapted Lesk algorithm does not require a perfect match between entities for electing a valid sense, it just needs a minimal accumulation of similarity among their possible meanings. Despite the gains in recall, results in [1] shows that a low quality of a semantic similarity measure can decrease the accuracy of disambiguation.

In face of this analysis, this paper proposes a hybrid approach that combines the simplified and adapted features of the Lesk algorithm.

4. OUR HYBRID APPROACH

The hybrid approach proposed in this paper combines the features of the simplified and adapted Lesk algorithm (described in Section 3):

Algorithm 3 Hybrid Lesk

```
Require: w, sentence.
Ensure: best-sense.
1: best-sense ← simplifiedLesk(w, sentence)
2: if best-sense = null then
3:     best-sense ← adaptedLesk(w, sentence)
4: end if
```

In Algorithm 3, the simplified component (simplifiedLesk) is first applied to identify the best sense of w. If there is no perfect matches between the word signature and the word sentence, i.e. when the algorithm returns an invalid sense (null) to a target word, the adapted component (adaptedLesk) is carried out with the same parameters. Thus, our proposal aims to join the accuracy of the Simplified Lesk algorithm with the recall of the Adapted Lesk algorithm so as to improve the quality of disambiguation.

5. EXPERIMENTS

In this work, the performance of each semantic similarity measure described in Section 2 was evaluated within WSD problem. The *SIMILARITY* function in Algorithms 2 and 3 was replaced by each aforementioned measure. Therefore, we compared our Hybrid Approach (Section 4) with both Lesk algorithms (Table 1).

The experiments were done using *Senseval-3* [9], a set of exercises to assess the quality of WSD algorithms. Each test instance is composed by a text fragment in English, containing a target word and a reference to the correct sense in Wordnet. All the similarity values were calculated using the *JWordnet::Similarity (JWS)*[3] library.

[3]http://www.sussex.ac.uk/Users/drh21/

As Wordnet's taxonomy describes relationships between nouns [1], only target words which belongs to this syntactic category were considered in our experiments, totalizing of 3593 test instances. Moreover, the Patwardhan's [15] disambiguation strategy was carried out, i.e. only words surrounding the target word that could be indexed as a noun in Wordnet were selected. Tables 1, 2 and 3 present our results.

Table 1: Performance of DLS algorithms

Algorithm	Precision	Recall	F-Measure
Hybrid Lesk	0.346	1	0.514
Adapted Lesk [4]	0.348	1	0.516
Simplified Lesk [11]	0.298	0.127	0.178

In Table 1, the values of Adapted Lesk [4] algorithm and Hybrid Lesk approach correspond to those obtained by the similarity measure JCN [8], which obtained the best precision and recall among the other evaluated measures.

Table 2: Performance of semantic similarity measures in Adapted Lesk algorithm

Measure	Precision	Recall	F-Measure
JCN [8]	0.348	1	0.516
LIN [12]	0.221	0.996	0.361
LCH [10]	0.211	1	0.349
WUP [19]	0.180	1	0.305
RES [17]	0.165	0.999	0.283

Table 3: Performance of semantic similarity measures in Hybrid Lesk approach

Measure	Precision	Recall	F-Measure
JCN [8]	0.346	1	0.514
LIN [12]	0.226	0.996	0.369
LCH [10]	0.226	1	0.369
WUP [19]	0.194	1	0.325
RES [17]	0.180	0.999	0.305

Tables 2 and 3 highlight the disambiguation results for the Adapted Lesk [4] algorithm and Hybrid Lesk approach respectively. Both tables present our results of the five similarity measures described in the Section 3. In both cases, the similarity threshold was set as $\alpha = 0$.

6. EVALUATION AND PARTIAL RESULTS

Experimental data indicates that it is possible to significantly increase the recall of WSD algorithms by using semantic similarity approaches. In terms of precision, the use of JCN [8] into adapted Lesk algorithm has gotten an increase of 5% over the simplified Lesk version. However, the other measures have presented lower results. Thus, these values suggest that the quality of a similarity measure is crucial to disambiguation.

The hybrid approach proposed in this paper obtained an improvement of 5% on precision and 87.3% on recall in comparison to the simplified Lesk algorithm, thus indicating an overall increase of 34.9% in disambiguation quality. Regarding the Adapted Lesk algorithm, our hybrid version had slightly higher precision for simpler measures: an improvement of 1.5% in comparison with Resnik measure. Considering Jiang and Conrath's proposal, which is more sophisticated, there was no improvement observed (Table 3).

In the lower measures (RES, WUP, LIN e LCH), the simplified versions helped to increase the precision of our hybrid approach, since the simplified Lesk algorithm, for such measures, has better precision than the adapted Lesk algorithm. The opposite occurs within the JCN measure, because this is the only measure that has better precision when compared over the simplified Lesk algorithm (Table 1 and Table 2). In the latter case, the simplified approach have reduced the precision of our hybrid approach.

Since simplified measures require less processing time, the improvements observed for such measures in our hybrid approach can have better cost-benefit when applied to large amounts of data.

Finally, we intend to evaluate the use of semantic similarity concepts into [3] approach to create a ranking of semantic associations as future work. Therefore, from the results obtained in this study, we expect to obtain more accurate results by using semantic similarities in order to better find semantic associations in texts.

Acknowledgements

The authors would like to thank FAPESB for their funding of this research (project number 19.573.128.2586).

7. REFERENCES

[1] E. Altintas, E. Karsligil, and V. Coskun. A new semantic similarity measure evaluated in word sense disambiguation. *In Proceedings of the 15th NODALIDA conference, S. Werner (ed.), 2006, pp. 8-11 ISBN 952-458-771-8, ISSN 1796-1114.*, 2006.

[2] H. Alves and A. Santanchè. Folksonomized ontologies - from social to formal. *In Proceedings of the XVII Brazilian Symposium on Multimedia and the Web (WebMedia)*, 2011.

[3] K. Anyanwu, A. Maduko, and A. Sheth. Semrank: Ranking complex relationship search results on the semantic web. *Proc. of the 14th International World Wide Web Conference, ACM Press, 117-127.*, 2005.

[4] S. Banerjee and T. Pedersen. An adapted lesk algorithm for word sense disambiguation using wordnet. *In Proceedings of the Third International Conference on Intelligent Text Processing and Computational Linguistics, CICLing 2002, Mexico City, February 2002.*, 2002.

[5] M. Carpuat and D. Wu. Improving statistical machine translation using word sense disambiguation. *In Proceedings of the Joint Conference on EMNLP-CoNLL, Prague, Czech Republic. pp.61-72.*, 2007.

[6] C. Fellbaum. *WordNet: An electronic lexical database. Language, Speech, and Communication.* MIT Press, Cambridge, MA., 1998.

[7] K. Janowicz, C. Keßler, M. Schwarz, M. Wilkes, I. Panov, M. Espeter, and B. Bäumer. Algorithm, implementation and application of the sim-dl similarity server. *In Second International Conference on GeoSpatial Semantics, GeoS 2007 (2007), 128-145*, 2007.

[8] J. Jiang and D. Conrath. Semantic similarity based on corpus statistics and lexical taxonomy. *In Proceedings of International Conference on Research in Computational Linguistics, 19-33, Taiwan.*, 1997.

[9] A. Kilgarriff. Senseval: An exercise in evaluating word sense disambiguation programs. *International Conference on Language Resourcesand Evaluation, LREC, Granada, May 1998. pp 581-588*, 1998.

[10] C. Leacock and M. Chodorow. Combining local context and wordnet similarity for word sense identification. *In Fellbaum 1998, pp. 265-283.*, 1998.

[11] M. Lesk. Automatic sense disambiguation using machine readable dictionaries: How to tell a pine cone from a ice cream cone. *In Proceedings of the 1986 SIGDOC Conference, pp. 24-26. Toronto.*, 1986.

[12] D. Lin. An information-theoretic definition of similarity. *In Proceedings of the 15th International Conference on Machine Learning, 296-304.*, 1998.

[13] R. Mihalcea and D. Moldovan. Word sense disambiguation based on semantic density. *Proceedings of COLING-ACL Workshop on Usage of WordNet in Natural Language Processing Systems*, 1989.

[14] R. Navigli. Word sense disambiguation: A survey. *ACM Comput. Surv. 41, 2, Article 10 (February 2009).*, 2009.

[15] S. Patwardhan, S. Banerjee, and T. Pedersen. Using measures of semantic relatedness for word sense disambiguation. *In Proceedings of the Fourth International Conference on Intelligent Text Processing and Computational Linguistics, pp. 241-257, Mexico City, Mexico, February, 2003.*, 2003.

[16] C. Pesquita, D. Faria, A. Falcão, P. Lord, and F. Couto. Semantic similarity in biomedical ontologies. *PLoS Computational Biology 5(7): e1000443. doi:10.1371/journal.pcbi.1000443*, 2009.

[17] P. Resnik. Using information content to evaluate semantic similarity. *In Proceedings of the 14th International Joint Conference on Artificial Intelligence, pages 448-453, Montreal.*, 1995.

[18] F. Vasilescu, P. Langlais, and G. Lapalme. Evaluating variants of the lesk approach for disambiguating words. *International Conference on Language Resourcesand Evaluation, LREC, Portugal, pp. 633-636.*, 2004.

[19] Z. Wu and M. Palmer. Verb semantics and lexical selection. *In Proceedings of the 32nd Annual Meeting of the Association for Computational Linguistics. Las Cruces, New Mexico.*, 1994.

Eventline: Representation of the Temporal Behavior of Multimedia Applications

José Rios Cerqueira Neto[1], Rodrigo Costa Mesquita Santos[1], Carlos de Salles Soares Neto[1,2], Mario Meireles Teixeira[1,2]
Laboratory of Advanced Web Systems – LAWS
[1]Programa de Pós-Graduação em Ciência da Computação
[2]Departamento de Informática
Universidade Federal do Maranhão
Av. dos Portugueses, Campus do Bacanga
São Luís, MA – 65085-580 – Brasil
{rios,rodrim.c,csalles,mario}@laws.deinf.ufma.br

ABSTRACT

This paper presents the concept of eventline as a visual representation proposal for the temporal behavior of multimedia applications. The main difference of this proposal when compared to the timeline paradigm is the replacement of the temporal continuous axis to a temporal discrete axis based on the occurrence of events. Media synchronization in each eventline is based on the relative time of a main media. User interaction is expressed as the navigation between multiple eventlines. The objective of this work is to provide a simplified alternative for authoring of interactive multimedia applications.

RESUMO

Este trabalho apresenta o conceito de *eventline* como proposta visual de representação do comportamento temporal de aplicações multimídia. Essa proposta é baseada na abstração *timeline,* sendo a principal diferença entre ambas a mudança da modelagem de um eixo temporal contínuo para um eixo temporal discreto baseado na ocorrência de eventos. A sincronização das mídias em cada *eventline* individualmente é pautada no tempo relativo de uma mídia principal e a interação do usuário é expressa pela navegação entre múltiplas *eventlines*. O objetivo deste trabalho é oferecer uma alternativa simplificada para a autoria de aplicações multimídia interativas.

Categories and Subject Descriptors

H.5.4 [**Information Interfaces and Presentation**]: Hypertext/hypermedia– *user issues*.

Keywords

Eventline, timeline, temporal semantics, multimedia authoring, visual abstraction, visual programming.

Permission to make digital or hard copies of all or part of this work for personal or classroom use is granted without fee provided that copies are not made or distributed for profit or commercial advantage and that copies bear this notice and the full citation on the first page. To copy otherwise, or republish, to post on servers or to redistribute to lists, requires prior specific permission and/or a fee.
WebMedia'12, October 15–18, 2012, São Paulo/SP, Brazil.
Copyright 2012 ACM 978-1-4503-1706-1/12/10...$15.00.

1. INTRODUÇÃO

Aplicações multimídia são compostas por diversas mídias sincronizadas entre si, tanto estáticas quanto contínuas, que podem oferecer ao usuário diversas formas de interação. Em [14], é discutido que essas formas de interação podem variar desde algumas bem simples, como avançar um *slide* em uma apresentação, até formas bem mais complexas, como a capacidade de mudar de perspectiva e controlar objetos de cena.

A representação do comportamento desse tipo de aplicação é um tópico bem estudado na literatura. Existem diversas soluções [8][5][13][9] que variam bastante em termos de capacidade de expressão e simplicidade, dependendo do objetivo definido. Para a autoria, por exemplo, é comum a utilização de representações gráficas que teoricamente diminuem o esforço cognitivo na leitura e construção da aplicação simplesmente por serem gráficas. Petre [17], porém, realiza um estudo que demonstra que uma abstração gráfica nem sempre é melhor, mesmo utilizando linguagem pictórica, e, principalmente, não é uma troca equivalente de uma abordagem textual. Em [17] e [4] são apontadas algumas diferenças entre as abordagens textual e gráfica.

Independente da abordagem de autoria utilizada (textual ou gráfica), ela deve ser capaz de suavizar o processo de construção de uma aplicação multimídia. Um ambiente de desenvolvimento completo deve contemplar uma série de aspectos que essas aplicações podem trabalhar. Em [6] é feita uma pesquisa desses aspectos e como diferentes ferramentas os suportam. É comum, nesses ambientes, a utilização de diversas abstrações de autoria em conjunto e sincronizadas para abrangê-los.

Dentre esses aspectos de autoria, este trabalho está interessado especialmente na capacidade de sincronização de mídias e de lidar com interações do usuário. A representação desses dois aspectos, porém, não é uma tarefa trivial que tenha uma solução universalmente aceita. Na literatura existem diversos trabalhos que abordam o tema sobre diferentes pontos de vista, como operadores lógicos entre as mídias [21], grafos compostos [8][5], *timelines* [15], etc. Esses trabalhos possuem pontos fortes e fracos que têm relevância variada de acordo com o objetivo da representação (armazenamento, autoria, representação de conhecimento, etc) e o perfil do usuário alvo.

A representação do comportamento temporal de aplicações multimídia não-interativas possui diversas soluções comerciais aceitas, como, por exemplo, [10][3][22][1], todas baseadas na abstração *timeline*. Essa abstração sincroniza as mídias precisamente em função do tempo absoluto da aplicação, permitindo, inclusive, que uma abstração espacial complementar mostre a disposição das mídias na tela e o conteúdo de cada mídia em um determinado instante de tempo da aplicação.

As limitações dessa abstração, porém, ficam evidentes ao lidar com questões imprevisíveis, como a interação do usuário. Não há como saber, em nível de autoria, o instante de tempo exato que o usuário irá interagir com a aplicação, se ele interagir. Logo, naturalmente é difícil especificar as consequências de uma interação em função do tempo absoluto da aplicação, por exemplo, o instante preciso que uma imagem aparecerá se ela advém de uma interação do usuário.

Este trabalho propõe a substituição da dimensão temporal contínua da *timeline* por outra dimensão temporal discreta, onde cada unidade de informação seja a ocorrência de um evento sobre uma mídia em um instante de tempo. Esses eventos são ancorados em função do tempo relativo de uma única mídia, denominada principal. A abstração aqui proposta, que utiliza esse eixo de eventos para representar o progresso temporal da aplicação, denomina-se *eventline*.

Em outras palavras, a *eventline* representa parte da aplicação que possui um conjunto de mídias que estão sincronizadas independentemente do resto da aplicação. A interatividade é representada através da navegação entre múltiplas *eventlines*, adaptando a solução proposta em [13]. O conjunto de *eventlines* que modela o comportamento de um segmento autocontido da aplicação é denominado, neste trabalho, de **composição narrativa**.

Este artigo está organizado da seguinte forma. Na seção 2 são apresentados alguns trabalhos relacionados. A seção 3 discorre em detalhes a abstração proposta. A seção 4 ilustra um estudo de caso. Finalmente, a seção 5 apresenta a conclusão e trabalhos futuros.

2. TRABALHOS RELACIONADOS

Allen [2] analisa o comportamento temporal de intervalos de tempo de duração fixa e define um conjunto de operadores para descrever as possíveis relações entre esses intervalos. No contexto de uma aplicação multimídia, os intervalos representam as mídias e os operadores descrevem o sincronismo da aplicação. À autoria, a principal limitação desses operadores é que eles não expressam nenhum tipo de função ou relacionamento de causalidade (e. g., ao término de *A* inicie *B*) entre os intervalos de tempo, eles apenas ilustram a disposição temporal das mídias. Consequentemente, eles acabam limitados a caracterizar aplicações já instanciadas, onde os tempos de início e fim de todos os intervalos são conhecidos [9].

Em [9] é definido um conjunto de operadores capaz de expressar relacionamentos causais entre intervalos de tempo de duração desconhecida e realizar composições lógicas entre esses intervalos. Esses operadores tomam dois intervalos como argumento e retornam um novo intervalo composto que pode ser usado como argumento por outros operadores. Isso permite aninhar e descrever operações lógicas sobre composições de intervalos. Outro fator positivo é que por esses operadores tratarem intervalos de duração desconhecida, eles são capazes de representar aplicações com elementos imprevisíveis, como interação do usuário e *feeds* em tempo real.

Existem diversos trabalhos que empregam operadores lógicos em diversas áreas da computação, como banco de dados [9], inteligência artificial [2] e até mesmo autoria [21]. Entretanto, o nível menos granular em que esses operadores atuam distancia o autor e a aplicação final, acrescentando maior dificuldade no processo de autoria.

Outra abordagem é representar os relacionamentos através de grafos direcionados. Grafos são capazes de descrever a sincronização das mídias e lidar com eventos imprevisíveis, como ativações condicionais e interação com o usuário. Tal abordagem é expressivamente comparável à codificação textual da aplicação [6]. O Firefly [5] utiliza um conjunto de grafos para representar os relacionamentos de uma apresentação multimídia. A sequência de eventos previsíveis, a partir do evento de início da mídia que começa a aplicação, forma um grafo principal. Para cada evento imprevisível, cujo tempo não pode ser calculado antes do início da apresentação, um grafo auxiliar é construído. O *Hypermedia Temporal Graph* (HTG) [8] também utiliza um conjunto de grafos para representar um documento multimídia. Nele, os nós são eventos que ocorrem sobre as mídias e as arestas são condições para se percorrer no grafo. Um evento imprevisível leva para um grafo alternativo que ilustra as consequências desse evento.

Para a autoria, a principal desvantagem dessas abordagens é que do mesmo modo que elas oferecem alto poder de expressão, é complicado para o autor representar relações complexas entre as mídias. Tanto em [6] quanto em [13] é comentado a dificuldade de acompanhar a modelagem de aplicações com diversas mídias e arestas[1].

Uma abordagem mais próxima da apresentação final, e amplamente difundida no meio acadêmico [6], é a estruturada. Nela os elementos são dispostos de uma forma organizada (geralmente em forma de árvore) de modo a expor as mídias, o instante em que elas são ativadas e os relacionamentos entre elas. Em [7] há uma abstração estrutural que organiza um documento SMIL [20] em forma de árvore, com os nós intermediários representando uma composição dos nós de mídias (folhas da árvore). Em [12] tem-se uma visão estrutural para NCL que organiza os elementos através de objetos de mídia, setas e caixas aninhadas. As caixas definem as composições hipermídia da aplicação, que no jargão NCL são chamadas de contextos, e as setas definem as relações entre os elementos de mídia.

Por fim, tem-se a abordagem através de *timelines*. Essa abordagem é simples, intuitiva e amplamente utilizada em soluções comerciais [6]. Nela as mídias são dispostas discretamente em um eixo vertical e o eixo horizontal representa o tempo da aplicação. A posição e o comprimento das mídias horizontalmente definem as características temporais dela, como quando se inicia, quanto tempo dura, quando termina. Em [1][10][3][22][15] há diversas aplicações dessa abordagem.

A abordagem de *timeline* é intuitiva e eficiente para aplicações com características temporais conhecidas ou que podem ser explicitamente especificadas [6], porém ela possui uma série de limitações. Ao deslocar uma mídia horizontalmente, é necessário rearranjar todas as outras mídias manualmente, a não ser que exista um mecanismo de agrupamento entre elas. Outro problema mais complexo, conforme mencionado anteriormente, é como lidar com eventos imprevisíveis, como interações por parte do

[1] Em [13] esse comentário é feito referindo-se especificamente ao Firefly.

usuário. O posicionamento desses eventos em função do tempo da aplicação é complexo, pois o instante em que eles talvez aconteçam só é conhecido em tempo de execução da aplicação.

Hirzalla [13] define uma maneira interessante de representar interações do usuário através de múltiplas *timelines*. Um novo objeto de mídia chamado *choice* é inserido na *timeline* e representa uma janela de oportunidade para o usuário realizar uma interação. Caso essa interação não seja concretizada, o fluxo da aplicação segue normalmente a *timeline* para os outros objetos. Caso a interação seja feita, ela leva para outra *timeline* alternativa. Elementos de duração desconhecida são representados através de alterações nos tradicionais retângulos que representam as mídias. Essas alterações "esticam" o retângulo tanto para representar o instante em que a mídia possivelmente comece, quanto aquele em que ela possivelmente termine. A ferramenta Composer [12], utiliza outra alternativa para lidar com a interatividade. O autor pode simular na visão temporal o instante em que o usuário decide fazer uma interação (por exemplo, o pressionar do botão vermelho do controle remoto em uma aplicação de TV digital), o que modifica a visualização da *timeline* daquele instante de tempo em diante.

O problema com essas alternativas é que, por tentarem representar eventos imprevisíveis e não-determinísticos (não se sabe o instante em que eles ocorrerão) em um modelo previsível e determinístico, elas abrem uma margem de possibilidade na linha temporal, distanciando o autor da aplicação final, que é o forte desse modelo. Não há como saber, por exemplo, o instante preciso que uma mídia aparecerá e terminará se ela pode ser ativada entre os instantes 10s e 20s e dure rigorosamente 10s. Para aplicações mais ricas com várias mídias e possibilidades de interação, as informações das linhas do tempo podem ficar muito imprecisas.

3. EVENTLINE

Em termos de autoria multimídia, considera-se que uma abstração deva ter um poder de expressão relevante para sincronização temporal de mídias e relacionamentos baseados em interações do usuário. Ao mesmo tempo, essa abstração deve manter um controle sobre a estrutura e a disposição dos elementos para simplificar a visualização. Este trabalho busca definir uma abstração que represente o comportamento temporal de aplicações multimídia visando estabelecer, principalmente, um equilíbrio entre expressividade e simplicidade. A *timeline* é o ponto de partida, visto que é uma abordagem bem aceita na literatura [6].

Em uma *timeline,* há essencialmente duas informações sobre as mídias: o tempo em que elas iniciam e o tempo em que elas encerram. Com base nessas duas informações é possível deduzir tanto o comportamento temporal da mídia (sua duração) como o da aplicação (a ordem das mídias). A disposição das mídias através de retângulos no eixo temporal permite uma leitura visual rápida dessas informações, porém, como dito anteriormente, a noção de tempo preciso limita a expressividade da abstração.

Este trabalho propõe uma nova abstração que utiliza uma unidade básica de representação denominada *eventline*. Uma *eventline* é uma representação de uma parte da aplicação através de eventos (uma ocorrência no tempo) que definem os relacionamentos causais entre as mídias. Nessa representação, a sincronização das mídias é pautada em eventos temporais oriundos de uma única mídia (em geral, contínua) aqui denominada principal. Para lidar com a interatividade são utilizadas múltiplas *eventlines* que compartilham a mesma instância de uma mídia principal. Essas *eventlines* são interligadas por interações do usuário (solução adaptada de [13]) e são capazes de representar as diversas possibilidades de navegação na aplicação.

Abstrações visuais são naturalmente restritivas [4]. No caso do emprego de *eventlines*, seu escopo de atuação reside em aplicações multimídia caracterizadas por um comportamento temporal que pode ser decomposto em partes isoladas, cada uma delas com sincronismo ancorado em uma mídia específica. Essas partes isoladas são representadas por *eventlines*. Em complemento, a interatividade do usuário pode ser modelada pela navegação entre *eventlines*.

Ao conjunto de *eventlines* que compartilham a mesma instância de uma mídia principal dá-se o nome de **composição narrativa**, a qual representa um segmento autocontido da aplicação. Na prática, essas composições narrativas podem ser semanticamente relacionadas para formar uma aplicação multimídia completa.

3.1 Representação Gráfica

Uma *eventline* representa uma mídia através de um conjunto de imagens, ícones, propriedades (textos) e linhas. As imagens representam os eventos previsíveis que ocorrem nas mídias, mas não especificam qual evento. Os ícones representam o tipo do evento e são baseados, em grande parte, em um estudo anterior [11]. As linhas simbolizam a progressão desses eventos no sentido da esquerda para direita. Uma imagem pode estar ligada a outra imagem à sua esquerda representando o evento que a precedeu, se houver, e à sua direita representando o próximo evento que ocorrerá, se houver. A intenção é manter a ideia de progresso temporal sem sacrificar em excesso a expressividade. Em outras palavras, a troca de uma dimensão temporal contínua por outra discreta baseada em eventos ainda torna possível simular e visualizar o tempo de ativação e término das mídias e a ordem em que elas acontecem. As linhas verticais representam os eventos que acontecem simultaneamente em mídias diferentes. Elas definem os relacionamentos de causalidade entre esses eventos. Na próxima subseção é discutido como esses relacionamentos são construídos.

A disposição individual das mídias na *timeline* possibilita a manipulação delas sem abrir mão da visão geral da aplicação, visto que é possível saber quais mídias executam em um determinado instante de tempo. Essa disposição pode também ser explorada para a visualização de relacionamentos causais, como, por exemplo, é feito em [9]. Neste trabalho optou-se também por visualizar as mídias individualmente.

As Figuras 1 (a) e (b) ilustram respectivamente uma aplicação na *timeline* convencional e a mesma aplicação na *eventline.* Na Figura 1 (a) uma mídia A é ativada no início da aplicação e aos 10s uma nova mídia B aparece. Aos 20s a mídia B encerra e aos 30s a mídia A encerra. Reescrevendo essa aplicação através de eventos, na Figura 1(b), pode-se falar que a mídia principal A passa por um evento de ativação quando a aplicação inicia; que a mídia B passa por um evento de ativação quando A passa por um evento temporal de 10s; B passa por um evento de término (brusco) quando A passa por um evento temporal de 20s; e, por último, A passa por um evento de fim (brusco) quando ela mesma passa por um evento temporal de 30s.

Por convenção, a mídia principal sempre será destacada em verde nas *eventlines*. Adicionalmente, é importante ressaltar que na

Figura 1(a) os retângulos são representados na mesma escala de tempo. Por outro lado, na Figura 1(b), a distância entre os eventos de uma mídia não requer que o tempo esteja proporcionalmente na mesma escala. Na Figura 1 (b), o terceiro evento de A (20s) poderia ser qualquer outro valor maior que 10s.

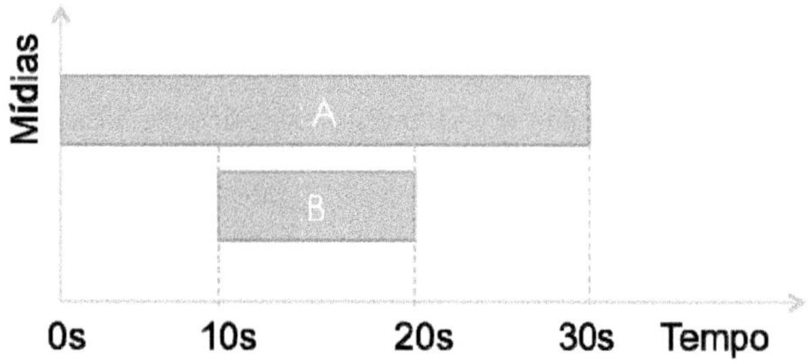

Figura 1 (a): Aplicação na *timeline* convencional

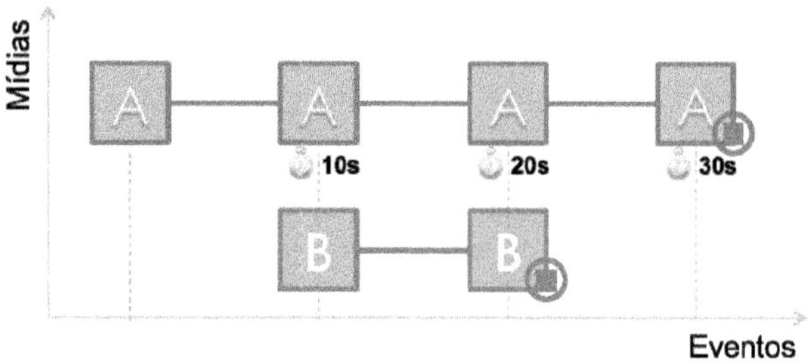

Figura 1 (b): Aplicação na *eventline*

3.2 Modelagem de Eventos

Os eventos modelados neste trabalho se baseiam nos definidos no modelo NCM (*Nested Context Model*) [18] da linguagem NCL (*Nested Context Language*) [19] para lidar com o paradigma de causalidade, onde uma determinada condição faz ser realizada uma ação resultante. NCM elabora relacionamentos causais entre as mídias através de quatro tipos de eventos: apresentação, seleção, atribuição e composição. Em um relacionamento causal, os eventos podem ser associados a um conjunto de papéis de condição e de ação pré-definidos.

Para este trabalho, são especialmente interessantes os eventos de apresentação e seleção, que são responsáveis, respectivamente, pela sincronização temporal e pela interatividade com o usuário. Eventos de atribuição consistem na manipulação de propriedades das mídias e também são representados. Eventos de composição correspondem à apresentação da estrutura de um nó de composição. Eles são representados através da sucessão de composições narrativas.

3.2.1 Eventos de Apresentação

Eventos de apresentação consistem na apresentação de um subconjunto de informações de um objeto de mídia. Uma âncora temporal, por exemplo, é um subconjunto das informações temporais de uma mídia e o seu início corresponde a um evento de apresentação. A Tabela 1 mostra a relação dos eventos de apresentação utilizados na *eventline*, os ícones que os simbolizam, e os papéis de condição e de ação pré-definidos em NCM que representam cada um desses eventos em um relacionamento causal.

Todos os ícones utilizados são posicionados na extremidade inferior direita dos eventos, com exceção do ícone de ativação de âncora temporal, que é posicionado abaixo do evento. Os eventos de ativação de mídia e fim natural são representados na *eventline*, respectivamente, pelo primeiro e último evento de uma sequência de eventos, no caso, a primeira e a última imagem de uma mídia, sem fazer uso de ícones.

Tabela 1: Relação dos eventos de apresentação utilizados na *eventline*, seus respectivos ícones, e os papéis de condição e de ação do NCM que os representam.

Evento	Ícone	Relacionamento Causal	
		Condição	Ação
Ativação de mídia	-	*onBegin*	*start*
Ativação de âncora temporal		*onBegin*	*start*
Fim de mídia (natural)	-	*onEnd*	-
Fim de mídia (brusco)		-	*stop*
Abortar mídia		-	*abort*
Pausar mídia		-	*pause*
Resumo de mídia		-	*resume*

Em um relacionamento causal, pode haver apenas uma ação de apresentação por mídia. Essa medida visa evitar incoerências, como, por exemplo, uma ação *start* e outra *stop* sobre a mesma mídia, no mesmo relacionamento. A Figura 2 ilustra um exemplo com diversos eventos de apresentação. Nela, as quatro linhas verticais representam quatro relacionamentos causais distintos e em cima de cada evento há o papel de condição ou de ação que cada evento assume no relacionamento causal.

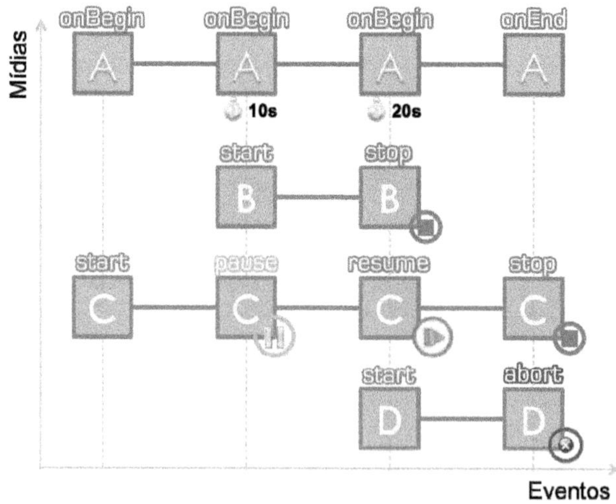

Figura 2: Ilustração de eventos de apresentação.

As condições possuem algumas restrições com o objetivo de simplificar a abstração, protegendo o autor de realizar certas inconsistências no progresso da aplicação. A principal restrição estabelecida é que os eventos de apenas uma mídia por composição narrativa podem atuar como condições de apresentação em um relacionamento causal (Figura 2). A Figura 3 ilustra o porquê dessa restrição. Suponha que nesse exemplo não exista uma mídia principal e, portanto, tanto os eventos da mídia A quanto da mídia B podem ser usados como condição em um relacionamento causal. Na mídia A, em um determinado instante, ocorre um evento temporal (10s) que é usado como condição para ativar a mídia B. Logo após ocorre em B um evento temporal (5s). No instante em que esse último evento temporal (5s) ocorre na mídia B, o tempo corrido da mídia A deve estar com 15s, visto que se passaram 5s desde o seu último evento temporal (10s). Entretanto, após o evento temporal (5s) na mídia B, ocorre em A um evento temporal de 11s. O tempo da aplicação está inconsistente nesse caso, pois na apresentação final o evento temporal (11s) que ocorre em A acontecerá antes do evento temporal (5s) que ocorre em B. Consequentemente os respectivos relacionamentos causais pautados nesses dois eventos também acontecerão na ordem errada.

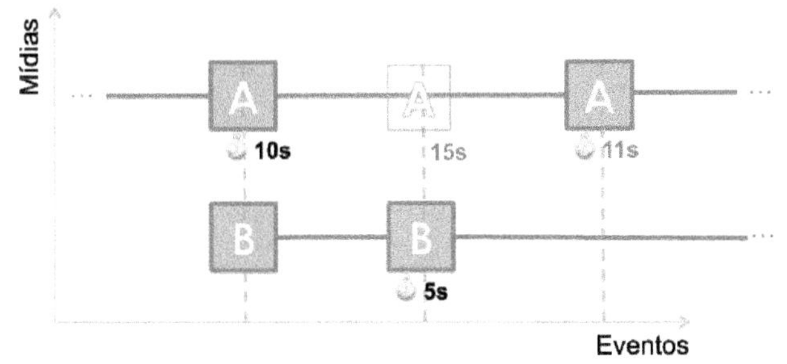

Figura 3: Inconsistência na especificação do sincronismo temporal.

Nesse exemplo, pode-se rearranjar a ordem dos eventos para deixá-lo consistente. No entanto, exigir que o autor saiba a ordem exata que as condições temporais acontecem gera um esforço adicional para utilização da abstração. Ao lidar com a imprevisibilidade da interação do usuário, a tarefa de monitorar esses tempos pode facilmente se tornar complexa e propensa a erros, mesmo no cenário de uso de uma ferramenta de autoria. Como dito anteriormente, um dos objetivos deste trabalho é que a abstração seja simples de visualizar, por isso decidiu-se que os eventos de apenas uma mídia, dita principal, podem atuar como condição de apresentação em todos os relacionamentos causais de uma composição narrativa (conjunto de *eventlines*). O sincronismo em uma *eventline*, consequentemente, é sempre feito de forma relativa ao tempo dessa mídia principal.

Os eventos de uma mídia principal podem assumir apenas dois papéis de condição de apresentação em relacionamentos causais: *onBegin* e *onEnd*, como mostra a Tabela 1. A explicação para essa limitação é que apenas esses dois papéis são suficientes para especificar cada relacionamento causal individualmente. Pode-se dividir os papéis de condição de apresentação em naturais (*onBegin* e *onEnd*) e derivados (*onPause*, *onResume* e *onAbort*). Os primeiros enquadram eventos que podem ocorrer naturalmente em uma mídia, i.e., eles não precisam que uma ação (*pause*, *resume* e *abort*) ocorra sobre a mídia para acontecerem. Os últimos enquadram eventos que são oriundos de uma ação que ocorreu sobre a mídia, o que só pode ter acontecido em virtude de uma condição natural anterior (ou de um evento imprevisível). Como cada relacionamento causal é individualmente especificado na representação, se a condição de um relacionamento for de apresentação, utiliza-se sempre um evento da mídia principal como condição para disparar todas as ações de cada relacionamento.

Uma consequência natural de limitar condições a apenas uma mídia é que a abstração não representa condições de apresentação compostas. De fato, à *eventline*, condições compostas de apresentação pouco acrescentam aos relacionamentos de causalidade, pois com o tempo de apenas uma mídia é possível definir esses relacionamentos. Como na *eventline* os eventos de um relacionamento devem ocorrer no mesmo instante de tempo, acrescentar o tempo de outra mídia como condição não enriquece o relacionamento, apenas acrescenta informações redundantes e potencialmente incoerentes. Há relacionamentos causais que utilizam condições compostas (como NCL) na qual as condições são ditas satisfeitas no momento em que todas elas passam a ser consideradas verdadeiras, independente de ocorrerem no mesmo tempo. Na abstração, porém, caso as condições temporais não ocorram ao mesmo tempo, ela não ilustrará o que de fato irá ocorrer na aplicação final, ficando, consequentemente, inconsistente.

Por a mídia principal ser a fonte de condições de apresentação dos relacionamentos causais, nela não podem ocorrer quase todas as ações de apresentação. A ação *start* pode retroceder o tempo da aplicação, tornando-a inconsistente. As ações *stop* e *abort* podem ocorrer como último evento da mídia principal, pois simbolizam o fim de uma mídia. A ação *pause* congela o tempo da mídia, impedindo-a de sair naturalmente desse estado. Nesse caso não há como definir relacionamentos de causalidade. Finalmente, a ação *resume* não alteraria o estado da mídia principal, sendo pouco útil.

Por fim, com o término da exibição de uma mídia principal, não há como elaborar relacionamentos causais disparados por condições de apresentação, já que não há condições a serem utilizadas. Com o fim de uma mídia principal, encerra-se também todas as instâncias das mídias presentes na mesma composição narrativa que ela está inserida. Se não for especificada a composição que sucede a atual, a aplicação é encerrada.

3.2.2 Eventos de Seleção

As diversas possibilidades de navegação proporcionadas pela interatividade são expressas através de múltiplas *eventlines*. Para simbolizar uma oportunidade de interação do usuário, é utilizada uma solução baseada em [13]: um objeto, semelhante aos de mídia, é inserido na *eventline* para representar uma oportunidade de interação durante um intervalo de eventos temporais da mídia principal. Esse objeto, de fato, não corresponde a nenhuma mídia que será exibida na aplicação final. Graficamente, ele é representado por um componente (e.g., o botão de um controle remoto) e exibe quais mídias são selecionáveis, e para qual *eventline* cada interação possível leva.

Uma *eventline* destino pode ser tanto uma *eventline* da mesma composição narrativa quanto a primeira *eventline* de uma composição narrativa nova. No primeiro caso, o relacionamento causal disparado pela interação pode tanto adicionar mídias novas, quanto disparar eventos sobre as instâncias das mídias correntes, isso é, alterar o estado delas. Graficamente, as mídias que são aproveitadas de uma *eventline* origem devem estar explicitamente presentes na *eventline* destino. No segundo caso, as instâncias de todas as mídia (inclusive a principal) necessariamente são encerradas e o fluxo da aplicação passa a ser guiado pela primeira *eventline* da composição narrativa destino.

As mídias contínuas da *eventline* origem podem, opcionalmente, ter uma marcação ***continue*** na *eventline* destino (apenas se for a mesma composição narrativa) para simbolizar que elas não são afetadas pelo relacionamento causal, i.e., não são afetadas pela interação. Como resultado, todas as mídias de uma *eventline* destino que não possuírem essa marcação, necessariamente são novas instâncias. A mídia principal (contínua ou estática) sempre tem essa marcação entre *eventlines* da mesma composição narrativa, pois, como dito anteriormente, nela não podem ocorrer diversos eventos de apresentação. Caso a mídia principal não possua a marcação ***continue***, significa que uma nova composição narrativa (com uma nova instância da mesma mídia principal) será iniciada e todas as instâncias dos objetos da composição narrativa corrente são encerrados. Por essa notação percebe-se que uma *eventline* (e uma composição narrativa) é encerrada ou pelo fim da mídia principal, ou por uma interação realizada.

A Figura 4 ilustra a especificação de uma oportunidade de interação por parte do usuário. Na mídia principal A ocorre um evento temporal (10s) que é utilizado como condição para os eventos de ativação de B e C. C é um objeto que não corresponde a nenhuma mídia de fato na aplicação final, ele apenas simboliza uma possibilidade de interação entre os eventos 10s e 20s da mídia principal. O quadro abaixo de C mostra quais mídias C pode selecionar (no caso apenas A) e qual a *eventline* destino daquela interação.

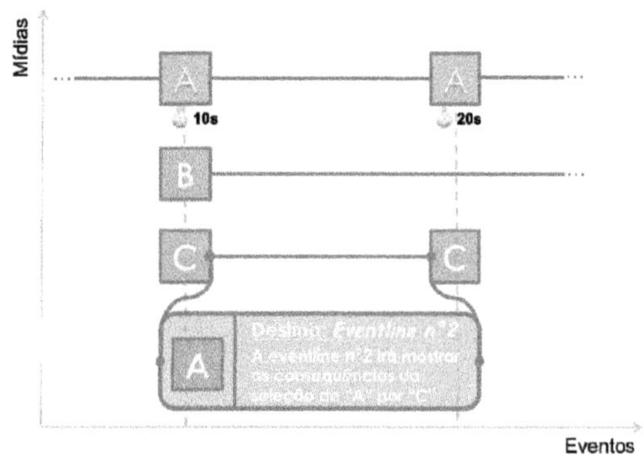

Figura 4: Evento de seleção na *eventline*.

Na Figura 5 têm-se a *eventline* destino da única interação possível na Figura 4. A *eventline* origem é encerrada com a interação, isto é, o fluxo da aplicação passa agora a ser guiado pela *eventline* destino. Essa última é independente da primeira; todas as mídias que participam dela estão explicitamente presentes. Consequentemente, percebe-se pela Figura 5 que a mídia B encerrou junto com a *enventline* origem.

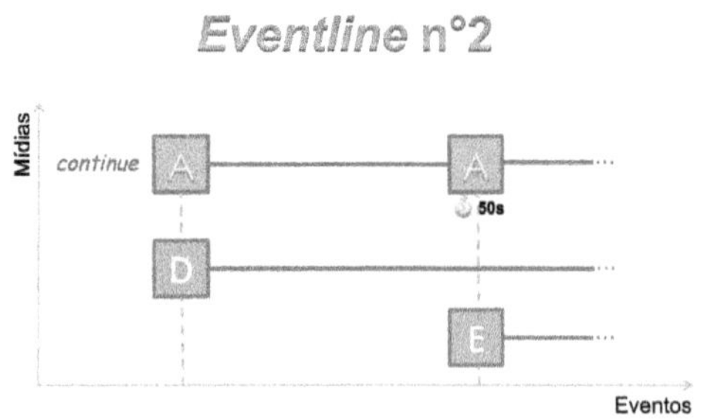

Figura 5: *Eventline* destino.

3.2.3 Eventos de Atribuição

Durante uma aplicação multimídia é comum que algumas propriedades das mídias sejam manipuladas, como a transparência, o volume, o tamanho, a posição, etc. Os eventos de atribuição são os que realizam essa manipulação. Eles são representados na abstração pelo nome da propriedade e seu novo valor embaixo da imagem que representa esse evento. A Figura 6 ilustra um exemplo. Na mídia principal A ocorre um evento temporal (50s) que atribui à propriedade *visible* da mídia D o valor *false*. A partir desse momento, D continua executando, mas não está mais visível na aplicação final até que haja outro evento de atribuição posterior que altere novamente essa propriedade em D.

Esses eventos, diferente dos de apresentação e seleção, não são utilizados como condição em nenhum relacionamento causal na abstração. A explicação é que, assim como alguns papéis de condições de apresentação (*onPause*, *onResume* e *onAbort*), os papéis de condições de atribuição (*onBeginAttribution* e *onEndAttribution* - vistos como uma só, já que os eventos são instantâneos na abstração) não precisam ser usados. Esses papéis são sempre oriundos de uma ação sobre a mídia (*pause*, *resume*, *abort* e *set*), que por sua vez deve, obrigatoriamente, ser disparada por uma condição da mídia principal ou uma interação do usuário. Cada relacionamento causal, então, utiliza essa condição natural anterior para disparar todas as suas ações.

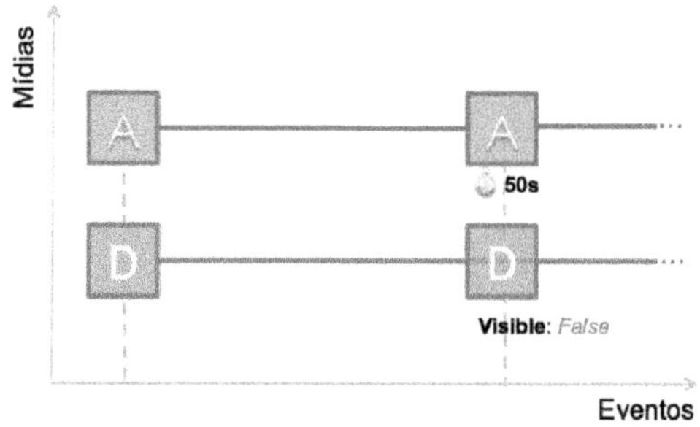

Figura 6: Manipulação da propriedade *Visível* de D.

3.2.4 Eventos de Composição

Eventos de composição correspondem aos eventos que manipulam a apresentação de composições narrativas. Como dito anteriormente, uma aplicação modelada pela abstração proposta consiste em uma composição de segmentos autocontidos. Graficamente, um evento de composição não é representado na *eventline*. Espera-se que uma ferramenta de autoria que vá instanciar a abstração forneça um mecanismo de lidar com essas composições narrativas de um modo intuitivo para o usuário.

4. ESTUDO DE CASO

Para ilustrar os conceitos apresentados, foi modelada uma aplicação interativa segundo a proposta deste trabalho. A aplicação em questão é uma versão simplificada do PrimeiroJoao[1] que pode ser encontrada no repositório Clube NCL[2]. Nessa aplicação há sempre um vídeo principal sendo exibido e, em seu decorrer, diversos relacionamentos causais ocorrem com outras mídias.

O primeiro desses relacionamentos é disparado logo no início da aplicação com a ativação de uma mídia de áudio. Aos 45s do vídeo principal, aparece uma imagem de uma chuteira que talvez dure até os 51s, dependendo de uma interação do usuário. Junto com a imagem da chuteira é ativada também uma janela de oportunidade de interação através do botão vermelho do controle remoto. Caso o usuário realize a interação, o vídeo principal é redimensionado, a imagem da chuteira é encerrada, um vídeo

[1] http://clube.ncl.org.br/node/46

[2] http://clube.ncl.org.br/

secundário é ativado e nada acontece com a mídia de áudio. Ainda no contexto da interação, aos 60s do vídeo principal o mesmo é redimensionado novamente, o vídeo secundário é encerrado e novamente nada acontece com a mídia de áudio que segue até o fim do vídeo principal (fim da aplicação). Caso o usuário não realize a interação, o vídeo principal não será redimensionado, a imagem da chuteira é encerrada aos 51s e a aplicação encerra junto com o vídeo principal (consequentemente causando o fim da mídia de áudio também).

A primeira parte da aplicação envolve apenas a sincronização de mídias. Ela é representada pela Figura 7. Nela, o vídeo principal é a primeira mídia destacada em azul, a mídia de áudio é simbolizada pelo ícone de áudio e a interatividade é representada pelo botão vermelho. Logo no início da aplicação, a ativação do vídeo principal é usada como condição em um relacionamento causal que dispara o evento de ativação da mídia de áudio. Aos 45s do vídeo principal, ocorre um evento temporal que é usado como condição para disparar a ativação da imagem da chuteira e a da janela de oportunidade de interação. Nesse instante de tempo ocorre uma ramificação da aplicação que possibilita um salto entre *eventlines*. Se o usuário não realizar a interação, ocorre um evento temporal aos 51s do vídeo principal que é usado como condição para encerrar tanto a imagem da chuteira quanto a possibilidade de interação. A partir desse momento o usuário não pode mais realizar a interação e a aplicação segue rigorosamente o fluxo da *eventline* 1.

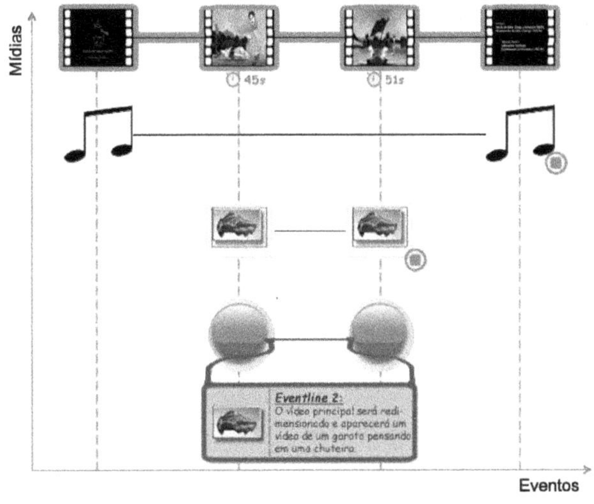

Figura 7: *Eventline* 1

Caso o usuário realize a interação, então o fluxo da aplicação salta da *eventline* 1 para a *eventline* 2 (Figura 8). Nesse ponto, todas as mídias que persistem à interação devem estar presentes na *eventline* destino. Nesse caso, o vídeo principal (obrigatoriamente) e a mídia de áudio não só persistem de uma *eventline* para outra, como também não são afetados pela interação realizada na *eventline* 1. Aos 60s do vídeo principal ocorre outro relacionamento que tanto redimensiona o próprio vídeo principal quanto encerra o vídeo secundário. Por fim, a aplicação encerra quando o vídeo principal terminar naturalmente, finalizando também a mídia de áudio.

5. CONCLUSÃO

A representação do comportamento temporal de aplicações multimídia interativas é um tema recorrente no cenário de autoria. Como visto, existem várias soluções propostas que evidenciam a complexidade do tema. Dentre essas propostas, a *timeline* destaca-se pela simplicidade e facilidade de uso.

Este trabalho realiza um levantamento de diversas propostas de representação do comportamento temporal de aplicações multimídia e propõe uma abstração denominada *eventline* que é baseada no paradigma *timeline* e representa o comportamento temporal de aplicações multimídia. Acredita-se que a proposta utilizada de substituir o eixo temporal contínuo por outro discreto baseado em eventos seja capaz de suavizar o processo de autoria dessas aplicações cuja natureza imprevisível limita a utilização da *timeline* convencional.

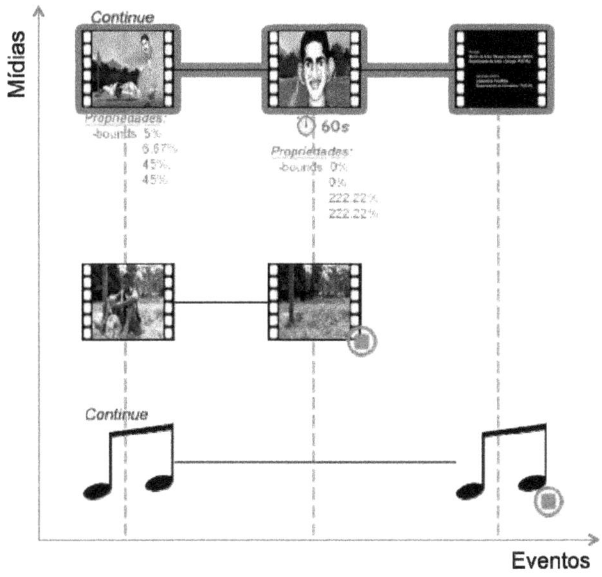

Figura 8: *Eventline* 2

A principal restrição da abordagem proposta é que o sincronismo está pautado no tempo relativo de uma única mídia, dita principal. Essa limitação visa proteger o autor de definir inconsistências temporais. Uma consequência natural dessa restrição é que os relacionamentos causais não possuem condições compostas.

A principal contribuição da abstração proposta é a capacidade de representar o progresso temporal da aplicação e a interatividade por parte do usuário sem as limitações inerentes à *timeline*. Uma ferramenta de autoria pode, inclusive, complementar a abstração proposta com uma visão espacial que mostre quais mídias estão executando e suas respectivas posições em um dado momento, aproximando o usuário e a aplicação final.

Como trabalhos futuros, destacam-se a realização de testes de usabilidade para verificar o esforço cognitivo da abstração e seus elementos, e a implementação de um *plugin* para *eventlines* na ferramenta de autoria NCL Composer [16].

6. AGRADECIMENTOS

Gostaríamos de agradecer as fundações FAPEMA e CAPES pelo apoio financeiro a esse projeto. Gostaríamos de agradecer também aos companheiros do laboratório LAWS pelos conselhos e ricos debates.

7. REFERÊNCIAS

[1] Adobe Director. 2012. http://www.adobe.com/products/director/

[2] Allen, J. F. 1983. Maintaining knowledge about temporal intervals. *Commun. ACM* 26, 11 (November 1983), 832-843. DOI=10.1145/182.358434 http://doi.acm.org/10.1145/182.358434

[3] Avid. 2012. http://www.avid.com/US/

[4] Azevedo, R. G. A., Soares Neto, C. S., Teixeira, M. M., Santos, R. C. M. and Gomes, T. A. 2011. Textual authoring of interactive digital TV applications. In *Proceddings of the 9th international interactive conference on Interactive television* (EuroITV '11). ACM, New York, NY, USA, 235-244. DOI=10.1145/2000119.2000169 http://doi.acm.org/10.1145/2000119.2000169

[5] Buchanan, M. C. and Zellweger, P. T. 2005. Automatic temporal layout mechanisms revisited. *ACM Trans. Multimedia Comput. Commun. Appl.* 1, 1 (February 2005), 60-88. DOI=10.1145/1047936.1047942 http://doi.acm.org/10.1145/1047936.1047942

[6] Bulterman, D. C. A. and Hardman, L. 2005. Structured multimedia authoring. *ACM Trans. Multimedia Comput. Commun. Appl.* 1, 1 (February 2005), 89-109. DOI=10.1145/1047936.1047943 http://doi.acm.org/10.1145/1047936.1047943

[7] Bulterman, D. C. A., Hardman, L., Jansen, J., Mullender, K. S., and Rutledge, L. 1998. GRiNS: a graphical interface for creating and playing SMIL documents. *Comput. Netw.* ISDN Syst. 30, 1-7 (April 1998), 519-529. DOI=10.1016/S0169-7552(98)00128-7 http://dx.doi.org/10.1016/S0169-7552(98)00128-7.

[8] Costa, R. M. R., Moreno, M. F. and Soares, L. F. G. 2008. Intermedia synchronization management in DTV systems. In *Proceedings of the eighth ACM symposium on Document engineering* (DocEng '08). ACM, New York, NY, USA, 289-297. DOI=10.1145/1410140.1410203 http://doi.acm.org/10.1145/1410140.1410203

[9] Duda, A. and Keramane, C. Structured temporal composition of multimedia data. *Proceedings International Workshop on MultiMedia Database Management Systems*, page 136, 1995.

[10] Final Cut Pro X. 2012. http://www.apple.com/finalcutpro/

[11] Guimarães, R. L., Soares Neto, C. S and Soares, L. F. G. 2008. A visual approach for modeling spatiotemporal relations. In *Proceedings of the eighth ACM symposium on Document engineering* (DocEng '08). ACM, New York, NY, USA, 285-288. DOI=10.1145/1410140.1410202 http://doi.acm.org/10.1145/1410140.1410202

[12] Guimarães, R.L., Costa, R.M.R., Soares, L.F.G. 2007. Composer: Ambiente de autoria de Aplicações Declarativas para TV Digital Interativa. In *Proceedings of XIII Brazilian Symposiumn Multimedia and the Web* -WebMedia'07, (RS, Brazil, October, 21-24, 2007).

[13] Hirzalla, N., Falchuk, B. and Karmouch, A. A temporal model for interactive multimedia scenarios. *IEEE MultiMedia*, 2(3):24–31, July 1995.

[14] Li, Z., and Drew, M. S. Fundamentals of Multimedia. Prentice Hall, 2004.

[15] Deltour, R., Layaida, N., Weck, D.: LimSee2: A Cross-Platform SMIL2.0 Authoring Tool. In: The European Research Consortium for Informatics and Mathematics - ERCIM News. n. 62 (2005).

[16] NCL Composer. 2012. http://composer.telemidia.puc-rio.br/doku.php

[17] Petre, M. 1995. Why looking isn't always seeing: readership skills and graphical programming. *Commun. ACM* 38, 6 (June 1995), 33-44. DOI=10.1145/203241.203251 http://doi.acm.org/10.1145/203241.203251

[18] Soares, L. F. G., Rodrigues, R. F. Nested Context Model 3.0: Part 1 - NCM Core, Technical Report, Departamento de Informática PUC-Rio, May 2005, ISSN: 0103--9741.

[19] Soares, L.F.G., Rodrigues, R.F.: Nested Context Language 3.0: Part 8 - NCL Digital TV Profiles. Technical Report - Department of Informatics - PUC-Rio. n. 35/06 (2006) ISSN 0103-9741.

[20] Synchronized Multimedia Integration Language (SMIL 3.0), 2008. http://www.w3.org/TR/REC-smil/ W3C Recommendation

[21] Vazirgiannis, M., Trafalis, M., Stamati, I. and Hatzopoulos, M. i-mu.s.e.-interactive multimedia scenario editor. In *Multi-Media Database Management Systems, 1998. Proceedings. International Workshop on*, pages 145 –152, aug 1998.

[22] Windows Movie Maker. 2007. http://www.microsoft.com/en-us/download/details.aspx?id=34

An Approach to Verify Live NCL Applications

Delcino Picinin Júnior
Federal University of Santa Catarina
picinin@das.ufsc.br

Jean-Marie Farines
Federal University of Santa Catarina
farines@das.ufsc.br

Cristian Koliver
University of Caxias do Sul
ckoliver@gmail.com

ABSTRACT

This paper describes a NCL 3.0 hypermedia application development toolchain which supports the verification of temporal and spatial consistency of NCL applications. In this toolchain, the application is translated into a TSS code and temporal logic formulas are used for checking the desired properties. It is proposed an approach for incremental verification of live NCL applications. The paper illustrates the proposed approach with a case study of a NCL-based interactive TV application.

Categories and Subject Descriptors

H.5.4 [**Hypertext/Hypermedia**]: Information and Presentation; F.4.3 [**Formal Languages**]: Verification

General Terms

Verification,Languages,Design

Keywords

NCL, interactive digital TV, incremental verification, model checking

1. INTRODUCTION

According to [15], the authoring and presentation of hypermedia applications generally are independent phases. However, sometimes these phases can be performed concurrently. This is the case, for example, of nonlinear TV programs[1] produced from live data. Still according to [15], while viewing a nonlinear live TV program, not only parts of content (such as audio and video objects[2]) but also some temporal and spatial relationships among objects are unknown *a priori*. For example, in a live broadcast show, the exact timing of the scenes of merchandising are not determined a priori. If the show is interactive, when the host promotes a product (either implicitly or explicitly), an icon can appear on the interactive screen so the viewer can get more details about the product offered. This icon is temporarily associated with the product shown at that moment. In the context of the Brazilian Terrestrial Digital TV (SBDTV-T), the integration between the authoring tool (Composer 3) and the execution platform (Ginga) provides all necessary support for the creation and execution of live NCL applications. This is done via an incremental edition in which an initial version of the application is modified during the presentation by means of commands for adding, deleting or changing objects and/or links.

The real-time authoring of a live application may result undesired behaviors. For instance, the presentation of two audio objects at the same time or the presentation of an object that never ends. The approach proposed in the present work intend to aid NCL application designers to detect and correct undesired behaviors during the live authoring phase. Such aid is achieved from techniques of formal verification.

In [14], we presented a framework for supporting the development of NCL hypermedia applications. In this framework, after the authoring phase, is carried a step whose purpose is to perform a formal verification of some application properties expressed by temporal logic formulas in LTL or CTL. Through transformation of models, a formal model more appropriate for the verification of properties is generated. Over this model, a model checker tool performs an exhaustive search in the state space (combinations of possible executions) verifying which properties are satisfied. A non satisfied property means that the application has a mismatch in the temporal relations (temporal inconsistency) or conflicts in the use of devices (spatial inconsistency). For each non satisfied property, the model checker generates a counter-example that helps the designer to identify the path of execution that led to the inconsistency or conflict. Using the authoring tool, the designer corrects errors identified in the NCL application, which is subjected to further verification. In the presentation phase (execution of the application through the Ginga platform), it is assumed that the application is free from temporal and spatial inconsistencies.

A problem related to formal verification techniques is the

[1]A TV program is nonlinear if the viewer does not have to follow linear chronology of the TV program he/she is watching but rather has the possibility to influence it and request changes [1]. Examples of such programs include video on demand and hypermedia applications designed for interactive digital TV.

[2]We adopt the term *object* to denote multimedia objects of a hypermedia application.

(c) 2012 Association for Computing Machinery. ACM acknowledges that this contribution was authored or co-authored by an employee, contractor or affiliate of the national government of Brazil. As such, the government of Brazil retains a nonexclusive, royalty-free right to publish or reproduce this article, or to allow others to do so, for Government purposes only.

WebMedia'12, October 15–18, 2012, São Paulo/SP, Brazil.
Copyright 2012 ACM 978-1-4503-1706-1/12/10 $15.00.

significant computational effort required. Even moderately sized projects require large amounts of memory and CPU cycles for property verification. This effort is enhanced upon the occurrence of a problem referred as combinatorial explosion of states - a huge number of combinations of independent state variables or processes.

The above problem does not inhibit the use of our toolchain when the phases of authoring and presentation are separated, because the model checker's runtime is not a crucial parameter in the absence of real-time constraints.

In contrast, a hypermedia application representing a live program has several versions: an initial and several subsequent versions, resulting from the edition on-the-fly. The changes of the new versions can lead to new inconsistencies of the application, requiring a new verification of properties. The full scan of a new version and the correction of errors eventually found require an amount of resources close to the initial scan, which may be impractical due to real-time constraints of live TV applications.

An alternative to the full exploration of states is the model checker to verify a partial formal model of the application, with a small number of states to be explored (using techniques such as abstraction, reduction based on equivalence, composition) or acting only on a part of the state space (based on heuristics or randomness). In the case of our toolchain for aiding the NCL application development, the complete model of each version to be evaluated is reduced to a model containing only the objects and links influenced by the live editing command.

In this article, we describe an approach for incremental verification of live-generated NCL applications. The main focus is on the description of the abstract model used to represent the NCL application and the strategy used to reduce this model as well. The reduced model, according to preliminary assessments carried out, has a number of states pretty inferior to the original model, which greatly minimizes the model checker's runtime. These initial results indicate the feasibility of using the toolchain also as a support to develop live NCL applications. The remainder of the text is divided as follows. In Section 2, we review the literature related to this proposal. In Section 3 we briefly describe the toolchain for supporting NCL application development proposed in [14]. Later, in Section 4, we detail issues concerning to the incremental evaluation of this proposal, the model used to represent NCL applications, and the rules used in the reduction of this model. In Section 5 we describe the steps of incremental verification and some principles for the translation into the formal model used for checking. In Section 6, we present a case-study to illustrate the incremental checking mechanism. Finally, in Section 7, we present conclusions and further work.

2. RELATED WORK

Many authoring tools driven to the construction of hypermedia applications have been proposed in recent years. Some of them check temporal consistency of the application in authoring time or via a post-processing. Generally, verification is based on Petri nets, automata, or axioms. Next, we describe some approaches, techniques and tools described in the literature. The list is not exhaustive, but provides a good idea of the State of the Art regarding to the temporal validation of hypermedia applications.

[16] proposes a methodology for designing interactive SMIL 2.0 hypermedia applications. For that, it maps the application code into a Real-Time LOTOS specification. Real-Time LOTOS (or simply RT-LOTOS) [7] formally describes the objects of the SMIL code by an automaton, allowing the generation of a valid schedule for processing the application. The designer must describe the components of the SMIL 2.0 application, representing objects and attributes that describe the spatial synchronization and content, among others. This description is needed to generate the data structures required for the translation. As noted in [9], this automaton assists the designer in identifying temporal inconsistencies of SMIL applications, without, however, help her/him to fix them. Moreover, the approach is not extensible: the automaton describing the behavior needs to be re-built after changes.

[4] describes the SMIL Builder tool which uses a Hierarchical SMIL Petri Net model, an extension of hierarchical Petri Nets, to incrementally (in the authoring time) check temporal consistency of SMIL applications. The tool allows to edit SMIL applications using different levels of abstraction, thus reducing the time required for verifying the application. Currently, the tool does not include the verification of non-deterministic events, such as user's interactions.

[9] describes temporal aspects of a SMIL application through a set of inference rules. The rules follow the Hoare's semantics and describe how a code fragment changes the state of computing. If any temporal conflict is identified, the system returns a message to the designer indicating the object that generated the conflict and its motivation.

[19] defines another formalism based on Petri Nets called Software Architecture Model (SAM). The SAM model of a SMIL application is translated into a set of axioms used to prove a set of logical formulas that expresses QoS requirements; semantic conflicts are not checked.

[17] describes an approach in which a NCM hypermedia application is translated into the RT-LOTOS model to be checked. Intrinsic (related to the application) and extrinsic (related to the application execution platform) time constraints are checked, as the memory load time of the video.

[8] presents the first attempt to validate NCL hypermedia applications. The NCL application is translated into a ORL (*Objects Representation Language*) model. The ORL model, in turn, is translated into a kind of timed automaton model called *Broadcaster Timed Automaton*. A set of formulas in temporal logic is then used to check the consistency of the automaton model through the UPPAAL model checker.

[18] proposes an approach to check properties related to temporal consistency of applications coded in a subset of NCL. Timed Petri Nets (TPN) are used to model the application; the properties to be checked are expressed through Visual Timed Scenarios (VTS), a graphical language to describe events. Translation is carried out using the tool VTS2-TINA [3] that generates a TPN from a VTS scenario. Next, the TINA model checker is used to verify if the TPN representation of the application satisfies the scenario.

In short, as shown in Table 1, most of the tools described in this section focuses on hypermedia applications coded in a subset of SMIL. Only one of these approaches allows incremental verification, eliminating the need for a full scan of the application. Also, despite the identification of temporal conflicts, not all proposals provide facilities for the designer to correct them. Another gap of most of the proposals is that they do not take on account non-deterministic events, such

Table 1: Comparison of related work

Proposal	Target language	Formalism	Strategy of verification	Non-deterministic events	Spatial analysis	Error detection	Aid for correcting	Incremental evaluation
[16]	SMIL	automata	RA[1]	yes	no	yes	no	no
[4]	SMIL	Petri Nets	Time computation	no	no	yes	partial	yes
[19]	SMIL	Petri Nets	MC[2] e RA	yes	no	no	no	no
[9]	SMIL	axioms	Rule validation	yes	no	yes	yes	no
[8]	NCL 1.0	automata	MC	yes	no	yes	no	no
[18]	NCL	Petri Nets	MC	yes	no	yes	no	no
Our proposal	NCL 3.0	Petri Nets	MC	yes	yes	yes	yes	yes

[1]RA: reachability analysis
[2]MC: model checking

as user's interaction, quite common in applications targeted to digital interactive TV. Finally, when using model checking, the counter-examples are presented in the language of the formal model, usually unknown by the application designer. Our approach aims to overcome these limitations by checking temporal and spatial properties in an incremental way, and mapping counter-examples to the corresponding NCL sequence of events. Moreover, it is targeted to designers lay in relation to any kind of formalism.

3. THE NCL HYPERMEDIA APPLICATION DEVELOPMENT TOOLCHAIN

In this section, we provide an overview of our NCL application development toolchain presented in [14].

3.1 The NCL Language

The Nested Context Language (NCL) [10] is a declarative language based upon the NCM conceptual model. A NCM application is compounded by nodes (representing application objects), and *link* and *connectors* establishing relationships between nodes. Composite nodes (*context* and *switch*) are nodes hierarchically organized.

The diagram of Fig. 1, adapted from [10] shows the possible states of an object of a NCL application. In the diagram, arrows represent the targeted actions (events) and the smaller circles represent logical conditions (temporal events) that occur as the action that leads to the state. NCL operates under causalities: an action can change the state of an object; the change makes a condition true. In Fig. 1, the action *Start* change the state of an object from *Sleeping* to *Occurring*. This makes the condition *onBegin* true. Table 2 present the list of possible causalities between actions and conditions. Code 1 is a NCL fragment in which a link is activated when the condition *onEnd* on object *B* trues. This generates action *Start* for objects *C* and *D*.

Due to the large semantic gap between the NCL Enhanced DTV Profile (EDTV) specification and the data structures used by the NCL machine (Ginga player), a new NCL language profile, closer to the concrete data structures for implementation, has been developed: the NCL-RAW profile [13]. On the one hand, a NCL-RAW specification is easily converted to the implementation structures. On the other hand, a NCL-RAW-coded application is difficult to be understood by designers and handled by NCL authoring tools.

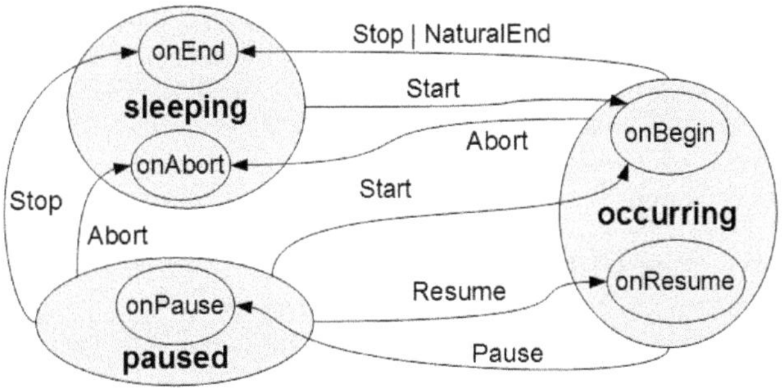

Figure 1: NCL state machine

Table 2: Causalities

	Action	Condition
1	*Stop*	*onEnd*
2	*Start + NaturalEndTime*	*onEnd*
3	*Start*	*onBegin*
4	*Resume*	*onResume*
5	*Pause*	*onPause*
6	*Abort*	*onAbort*
7	*Start + Anchor*	*DocDur = Anchor*

Hence, a NCL application will still be coded through EDTV profile. Afterwards, it is translated into the corresponding NCL-RAW profile to be executed over Ginga. We highlight that designers code the application using NCL "pure" (EDTV profile) which is then converted into the NCL-RAW profile by Composer 3 to run over Ginga player. In order to simplify, we use in the remainder of this text only *NCL* to refer to *NCL-RAW*.

3.2 The Composer Authoring Tool

According to [12], Composer is an authoring tool to help the creation of interactive TV programs for SBDTV-T. In Composer, several abstractions are defined creating different document views (structural, temporal, layout and textual). One of these views, the temporal view, preserves as much as possible the timeline paradigm, so popular in TV program editing. Using this view, authoring can be done by placing media objects on a time axis without changing the relative relationships among them. Moreover, non-deterministic

NCL Code 1 NCL connectors and links

```
...
<causalConnector id="onEndStart">
   <simpleCondition role="onEnd"/>
   <simpleAction role="start"/>
</causalConnector>
 ...
<link  id="lMusic" xconnector="onEndStart">
   <bind role="onEnd" component="B"/>
   <bind role="start" component="C"/>
   <bind role="start" component="D"/>
</link>
```

time events, like user's interactions and content adaptations, can also be represented in the temporal view. In addition, the occurrence of these unpredictable events can be simulated, and the resulting TV program played, from any starting point. Composer also supports live editing operations. On the server-side, Composer can dynamically construct live editing commands, in agreement with the SBDTV-T standard. These commands can then be transmitted in order to modify on-the-fly an interactive TV program. On the viewer-side, editing commands can be used to enhance program content.

3.3 The FIACRE Language

FIACRE has been developed within the TOPCASED project as an intermediate language to represent both temporal and behavioral aspects of systems issued for formal verification and simulation purposes [2].

The FIACRE language is a strongly typed language whose basic syntactic constructors are *process*, to describe sequential behavior, and *component*, to represent the system through the composition (possibly in a hierarchical form) of processes and other components. The behavior of a process is defined from a set of states and transitions. For each state, expressions specify transitions and how to move to the next state. These expressions are written by: (1) deterministic constructions usually available in programming languages (assignment, condition, loop, sequential composition ...), (2) non-deterministic constructions (non-deterministic selection and assignment), and (3) communication events through ports. The component *main* describes the parallel composition of components and/or processes that communicate via synchronous ports and shared variables. To make possible asynchronous communication, there is a special process called *glue* which desynchronizes sender and receiver ports.

3.4 The Toolchain Architecture

The NCL application development toolchain integrates an authoring tool (particularly, Composer 3 [12]) and the Ginga execution platform to a mechanism of formal verification of properties. It extends the toolchain presented in [14] for also including the development of live NCL applications. For that, after a formal verification of the entire application code, subsequent verifications act only on the part of the code affected by live authoring commands (hereafter, referred simply as *command*). The toolchain is targeted for designers without expertise in formal verification. The NCL application development toolchain with its elements and relationships among them is depicted in Fig. 2. Initially, designer codes the NCL application using Composer 3. During the authoring phase, she/he can also select a set of properties to be checked, some of them with arguments associated, using the Properties Visual Editor. Some properties are then converted into temporal logic formulas by using the properties library; others are a front end of FIACRE-coded observers[3]. Observers are used to check some behaviors (e.g., to check if the lower limit of presentation of an object is respected). The code of observers and NCL application input the NCL2FIACRE translator, which generates a formal model in FIACRE. Next, the FIACRE formal model is transformed into a Timed Transition System (TTS) formalism [11] by the FRAC[4] compiler. The TTS formalism and the set of properties to be checked input the TINA model checker[5] which verifies what properties are satisfied. For each non satisfied property P, TINA generates a TTS counter-example representing the execution sequence that led to the non-validation of P. As the TTS formalism is (possibly) outside of the designer's domain of knowledge, a translator attempts to map out the TTS counter-example into the NCL application code. Finally, the counter-example can be run and viewed by Ginga. The above process – NCL application authoring, NCL2FIACRE translation, FIACRE2TTS translation, model checking – may be performed several times until the designer assumes that the application is correct. Each execution of this process is a *phase*.

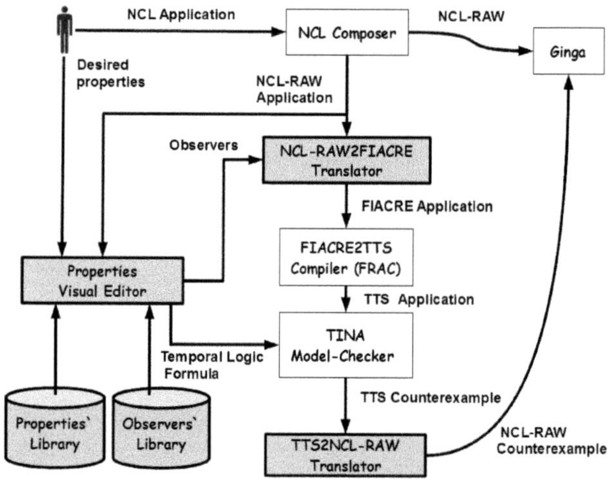

Figure 2: NCL application development toolchain

3.5 Properties

In our approach, we defined two sets of properties: *general properties* and *specific properties*.

General properties are always checked, regardless of the application semantics. They are properties that all objects

[3]A [synchronous] observer is an adjunct to a system model that monitors its state variables and raises a signal when some condition is satisfied. Observers provide an alternative to temporal logic as a means to specify safety properties but have the benefit that they are expressed in the same notation as the system model. Model checkers that do use temporal logic can nonetheless employ observers by checking for properties such as "never (signal raised)".

[4]http://projects.laas.fr/fiacre/

[5]http://projects.laas.fr/tina/

of the application must satisfy and do not establish relationships between objects. This set includes the following properties:

1. all objects are presented at least once;
2. exist objects endlessly presented;
3. all objects end after presentation; and
4. the presentation of some visual object exceeds the margins of the screen.

Specific properties involve relationships among objects. They are used to verify characteristics intrinsic to the application. Designer selects and parametrizes specific properties through the Properties Visual Editor (parameters are specific objects). Parameterized properties are then converted into temporal logic formulas or observers. This set includes the following properties:

1. mutual exclusion in the presentation of two objects;
2. the presentation of an object is inside the range of the presentation time of another object;
3. the sequence in the presentation of two objects; and
4. the presentation of an object is within its range of time.

The set of specific properties, placed in a library, comes from related work and from the BBC's specification described in the "BBC-interactive Television Style Guide"[6]. We intend to interview NCL developers in order to improve this set of properties.

4. INCREMENTAL VERIFICATION OF LIVE APPLICATIONS

Our approach here proposed is based on the *Incremental Computing* concept [5], a software feature which, whenever a piece of data changes, attempts to save time by only recomputing those outputs which "depend on" the changed data. For that, the model checking scans a reduced formal model of the NCL application achieved from the complete model. Thus, model checking uses a more modest amount of resources as compared to the verification of the entire application. In our approach, the complete model of the NCL application is internally represented as a labeled and oriented graph similar to the Hypermedia Temporal Graph (HTG) [6]. At each command, the complete graph is updated and a reduced graph is created by using properties of Graph Theory. Model checking is performed over the reduced model. Representing the NCL application through a graph makes easy: (1) the identification of dependence relationships among objects; (2) the NCL2FIACRE translation, since many algorithms used for that are based upon graph dependence; and (3) the representation as a data structure.

The abstract model G of the NCL application is a directed vertex and edge-labeled graph. The graph G is such that $G = (V, A, \lambda)$ where the set of vertices V represents the NCL objects, the set of edges A represents the NCL links and connectors, and λ is a set of edges label. Vertex labels are the names of the application objects (a specific video, audio, image ...). An edge $e = (v_1, v_2, l_{v_1 \to v_2})$ is considered to be directed from v_1 to v_2; v_2 is called the *head* of e and v_1 is called the *tail* of e; v_2 is said to be a *direct successor* of v_1, and v_1 is said to be a *direct predecessor* of v_2 (in the NCL application, this means that the object represented by v_1 activates the object v_2). In the edge $(A, B, < onBegin, start >)$ presented in Fig. 3, A and B are respectively the tail and the head. B is a direct successor of A and C is an indirect successor. For reduction purposes, we say that all direct and indirect successors of a vertex v *depends on* v.

For $e = (v_1, v_2, l_{v_1 \to v_2}) \in A$, the vertices v_1 and v_2 are said to be *incident* to the edge e, or, equivalently, e is incident to v_1 and v_2 (v_1 and v_2 are *adjacent* since they share a common edge). In Fig. 3, vertices A and B, and B and C are adjacent The *indegree* of a vertex v is the sum of edges for which v is the head endpoint. Likewise, the *outdegree* of a vertex v is the sum of edges for which v is the tail endpoint. If there are two edges $e_{v_1 \to v_2} = (v_1, v_2, l_{v_1 \to v_2})$ and $e'_{v_1 \to v_2} = (v_1, v_2, r'_{v_1 \to v_2})$, in the computation of v_1 outdegree they are counted once[7]. The *degree* of vertex v is the indegree plus the outdegree of this vertex.

The set of ingoing edges of a vertex $v \in V$ is given by $A_{in}(v)$ such as $A_{in}(v) \subset A$. Hence, $A_{in}(v)$ contains all edges $e_i = (v_i, v, l_{v_i \to v})$ $(v_i \in V,\ i = 1, 2, ..., k)$, i.e., edges where v is always the tail. It represents, in the NCL application, the actions associated to links that can change the current state of the object represented by v. Likewise, the set $A_{out}(v)$ contains all edges for which v is the head. They represent actions over the links of the object v that can change the state other objects. To the edges in $A_{in}(v)$ and $A_{out}(v)$ are also associated the conditions to occur the actions.

The existence of an edge

$e_{x \to y} = (x, y, l_{x \to y})$, $e_{x \to y} \in A_{out}(x)$, $A_{in}(y)$, $x, y \in V$, $l_{x \to y} \in \lambda$

implies a causality between x and y, as mentioned in Section 3.1.

The set of edge labels λ is a subset of the Cartesian product $Condition \times Action$ such as $Condition = \{'onBegin', 'onEnd', 'onAbort', 'onResume', 'OnPause'\}$ e $Action = \{'Start', 'Stop', 'Abort', 'Pause', 'NaturalEnd', 'Resume'\}$. These are predefined conditions related to the objects behavior. Composite conditions join behavior conditions and platform-related conditions (for example, language and resolution). For a x ingoing edge

$e_{in}(x) = (y, x, l_{y \to x})$, $l_{y \to x} = < condition_{y \to x}, action_{y \to x} >$

and a x outgoing edge

$e_{out}(x) = (x, z, l_{x \to z})$, $l_{x \to z} =< condition_{x \to z}, action_{x \to z} >$, $l_{y \to x}, l_{x \to z} \in \lambda$,

the action $action_{y \to x}$ makes true the condition $condition_{x \to z}$, according to Table 2. The Code 2 is a NCL fragment describing a causality between objects A, B e C; the graph G shown in Fig. 3 is the corresponding model. In the code, object B has the condition *explicitDur* defining its natural end (action *stop*) after 10s. The end is a relationship from B to B, represented by a loop in the graph of Fig. 3. In the code, the link identified by $l1$ defines a dependence relation between A and B, in which the presentation beginning of A triggers the presentation beginning of B; the link identified by $l2$ defines a dependence relation between B and C: the end of B triggers C presentation.

For interactive applications, the graph G always has a vertex labeled RC. This vertex represents the remote control and has only outgoing edges. An edge $e_{RC \to x} = (RC, x, l_{RC \to x})$ means that x is an interactive media (e.g., an interactive icon triggered by a remote control command). In the graphical representation used here, the edges adjacent to RC are always dashed.

[6]http://www.tvdi.inf.br/site/artigos/Guia%20de%20Estilo%20e%20Usabilidade%20-%20BBC%20Londres/iTV-DesignTrigger_v1.pdf

[7]Note that this is not the usual definition of degree in the Graph Theory.

NCL Code 2 NCL causalities

```
<media id="B" ...> explicitDur=10s ... <\media>
...
<causalConnector id="onBeginStart">
   <simpleCondition role="onBegin"/>
   <simpleAction role="start"/>
</causalConnector>
<causalConnector id="onEndStart">
   <simpleCondition role="onEnd"/>
   <simpleAction role="start"/>
</causalConnector>
 ...
<link  id="l1" xconnector="onBeginStart">
   <bind role="onBegin" component="A"/>
   <bind role="start" component="B"/>
</link>
<link  id="l2" xconnector="onEndStart">
   <bind role="onEnd" component="B"/>
   <bind role="start" component="C"/>
</link>
```

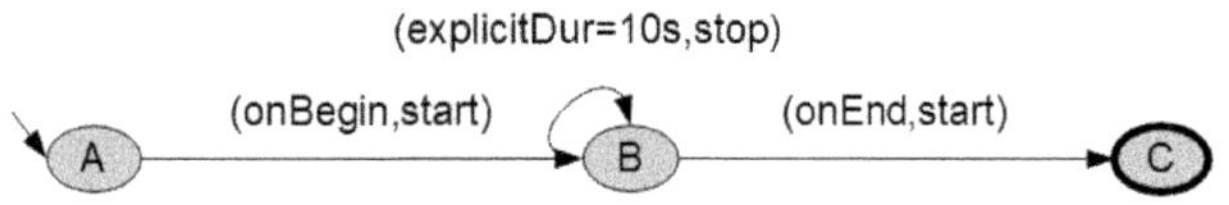

Figure 3: Graph G modeling a NCL application

4.1 Graph Reduction

As we said in Section 3.4, each new command request to perform the evaluation cycle (phase). A new phase requires to update G. At the phase k ($k = 1, 3, ..., N$), it is generated a new graph $G_k = (V_{G_k}, A_{G_k}, \lambda_{G_k})$ reflecting the new state of the NCL application. A graph $g_k = (V_{g_k}, A_{g_k}, \lambda_{g_k})$ representing only the parts of the application that were affected by the phase k is also built. Note that $g_0 = G_0$ and g_k *is not* a subgraph of G_k, but $V_{g_k} \subset V_{G_k}$.

The reduction process proposed is delimited by a set of rules defining preservation criteria and reduction strategies. Preservation criteria constraint the application of the reduction rules; the nature of the rules is related to the NCL application semantics. (In the next figures, the vertex modified in phase k has thicker lines.)

4.1.1 Preservation Criteria

Criterion C1: Preservation of vertices representing interactive objects.

The set of vertices V_{g_k} of the graph g_k contains a subset V'_{G_k} ($V'_{G_k} \subset V_{G_k}$) such as for all $v_i \in V'_{G_k}$, ($i = 1, 2, ..., n$), there is an edge $e_i = (v_i, RC, l_{v_i \to RC})$ (i.e., v and RC are adjacent).

Criterion C2: Preservation of the successors of the vertex modified in phase k.

Let $v \in V_{G_k}$ is the vertex changed in phase k. The subgraph of G_k whose root is v must remain in g_k, because the properties related to the objects contained in this part of the NCL application should be checked again.

Criterion C3: Preservation of the vertices representing objects used as arguments in specific properties.

Let $v_1, v_2 \in V_{G_k}$. If there is the specific property $P(v_1, v_2)$ and v_1 *or* v_2 were changed in phase k, then $v_1, v_2 \in V_{g_k}$.

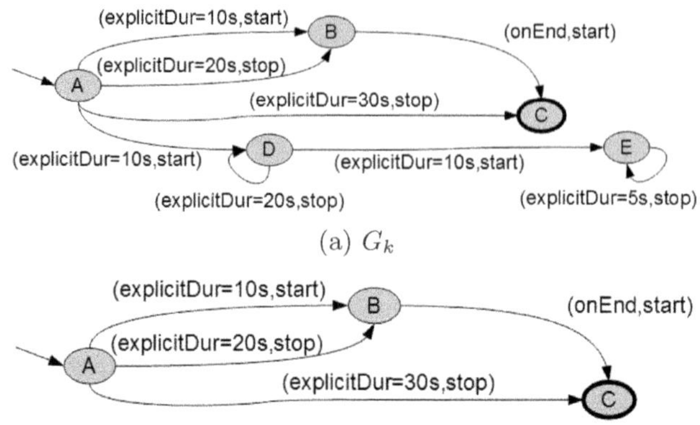

(a) G_k

(b) g_k

Figure 4: Applying R1

4.1.2 Reduction Rules

Rule R1: Elimination of the vertices unrelated to the changes.

Let $v \in V_{G_k}$ the vertex changed in phase k. If $v_1, v_2, ..., v_n \in V_{G_k}$ do not depend on v, then $v_1, v_2, ..., v_n \notin V_{g_k}$. For the graph G_k illustrated in Fig. 4(a) in which the vertex C is modified, D and E are not in A_{g_k} (Fig.4(b)) because they do not depend on C.

Rule R2: Elimination of vertices due to homeomorphism.

Let $v \in V_{G_k}$ the vertex changed in phase k and r the root of G_k. All intermediate 2-degree vertices between r and v are not in V_{g_k}. However, A_{g_k} must contain an edge $e_{r \to v}$. This new edge sums the activation times of vertices in the path between r and v, likely the approach adopted in [4]. For eliminating an intermediate vertex x,
$\forall e_i = (x, v_i, l_{x \to v_i}) \in A_{out}(x)$, $l_{x \to v_i} = < condition_{x \to v_i}, action_{x \to v_i} >$ $(i = 1, 2, ..., n)$,
we seek to verify if
$\exists e_j = (v_j, x, l_{v_j \to x}) \in A_{in}(x)$, $l_{v_j \to x} = < condition_{v_j \to x}, action_{v_j \to x} >$ $(j = 1, 2, ..., m)$
such that $action_{v_j \to x}$ makes true $condition_{x \to v_i}$. The new edge $e' \in A_{g_k}$ is
$(v_j, v_i, l_{v_j \to v_i}) \mid l_{v_j \to v_i} =< condition_{v_j \to x}, action_{x \to v_i} >$.

The intent of the example shown in Fig. 5(a) is to reduce the graph by eliminating the 2-degree intermediate vertex B. The output edge of B is $e_{B \to C} =< B, C, l_{B \to C} >$ where $l_{B \to C} =< condition_{bc}, action_{bc} >$, the input edges are $e_{A \to B} = < A, B, l_{A \to B} >$ where $l_{A \to B} =< condition_{ab1}, action_{ab1} >$ and $e'_{A \to B} = < A, B, l'_{A \to B} >$ where $l'_{A \to B} =< condition_{ab2}, action_{ab2} >$. In the reduction process, it is sought in Table 2 a row $action_{ab1}$, $condition_{bc}$ and a row $action_{ab2}$, $condition_{bc}$. For each *action* of the input edge of B that makes true *condition* of the output edge of B, a new edge is created. The new edge directly links the vertices A and C and is labeled by the *condition* of the input edge and the *action* of the output edge. Fig. 5(b) shows g_k. Note that are two new edges connecting the vertices A and C.

If there is a circuit in the intermediate vertices, V_{g_k} must at least contain two vertices of the circuit. One vertex is v; the other is any vertex of the circuit. In Fig. 6 the 2-degree vertex labeled E has to remain in V_{g_k} to keep the circuit.

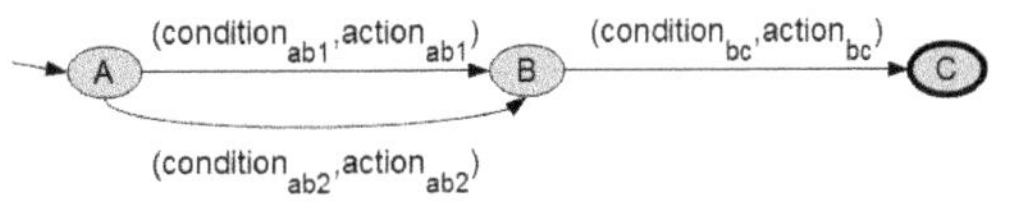

(a) G_k

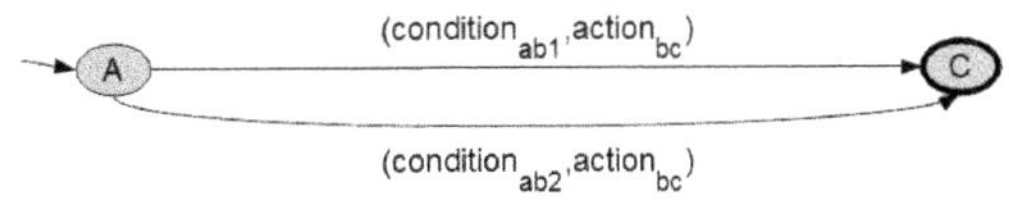

(b) g_k

Figure 5: Applying R2

Circuits must be kept because they can represent recursive causalities that cannot be reduced to a single vertex.

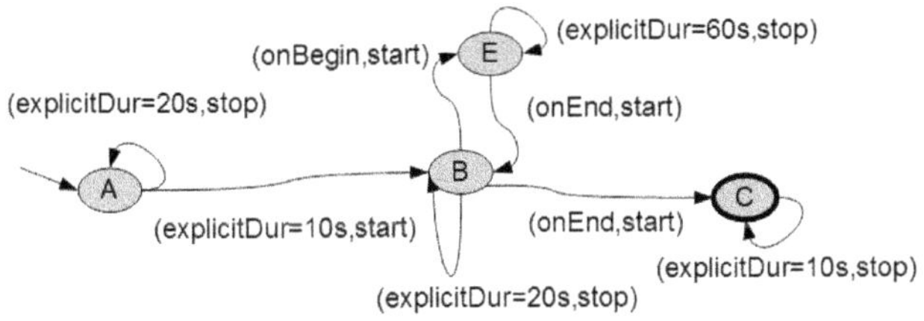

Figure 6: Graph containing a circuit

5. THE ENVIRONMENT OF INCREMENTAL VERIFICATION

The support provided by Ginga player and Composer authoring tool for live editing of NCL applications is used in our live NCL application development toolchain. In the toolchain, the NCL2FIACRE translation of Fig. 2 is performed at N-phases. The first phase (phase 0, usually performed offline) checks properties of the first version of the application. At this phase, the entire NCL code is translated into the FIACRE formal model. After the phase 0, each command results in a new phase of [incremental] verification. Fig. 7 shows the new architecture of the NCL2FIACRE translation process considering live editing. In the figure, phase 0 is distinguished from the other phases. Note that in phase 0 is generated graph G_0 presenting the entire NCL application. In the following phases, the graph G_k corresponding to the entire NCL code is generated, as the graph g_k, obtained by applying the rules presented earlier. In phase 0, the model G_0 undergoes a MDE transformation to FIACRE; in subsequent phases, the transformation is from the reduced model g_k to FIACRE.

The reduction mechanism is being coded in ANSI C. It keeps a binary-format copy of the part of the structure of G_k needed to be reduced. Consequently, the mechanism execution cost in the toolchain is also reduced. Note that the computational complexity is linear to the NCL code size.

The toolchain presented here will be integrated to the Composer as a plugin. As we said, Composer 3 provides commands for live editing and it already parses the XML syntactic structure corresponding to the NCL application during authoring. Thus, we do not need to address such issue in the toolchain.

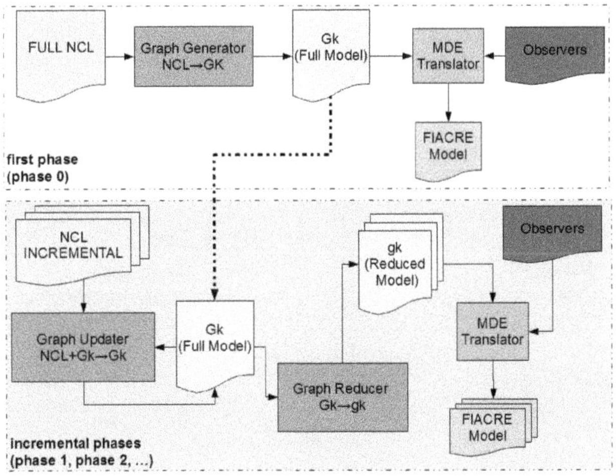

Figure 7: Phases of incremental verification

5.1 Some Translation Principles

The NCL2FIACRE translator complies with the following principles: (1) all vertices of G_k (NCL application objects) generate a FIACRE *component*. Nested NCL *contexts* generate FIACRE nested *components*; (2) for each innermost *component* (generated from the vertices of G_k) is generated two FIACRE *processes*, one representing the behavior of the object and a FIACRE glue-type process[8]; (3) FIACRE *processes* communicate through FIACRE *ports*, which are created from the edges linking the vertices of G_k (NCL *links* and *connectors*); and (4) for the remote control object (RC), is created a FIACRE *component* referred as *Control*, which has two processes: (a) *setup* responsible for assigning variables of the display platform, and (b) *Remote_Control* responsible for simulating user's interaction. The component *Control* and components generated from the first NCL hierarchical level are created by composition within the FIACRE component *main*.

6. CASE-STUDY

The graph G_k representing the NCL application *O Primeiro João* [10] used as case-study is shown in Fig. 8(a). It consists of three video-type objects, one audio-type object, three image-type objects and two form-type objects (in different languages) to be chosen by the user. In this graph, the vertex labeled *VideoV*, was incrementally added after the beginning of the application execution.

In this case-study, we want to check whether there is, at some moment, an undesired behavior. For example, the simultaneous presentation of *VideoV* and *VideoC*, since both have audio associated. The property of mutual exclusion of these two objects in the presentation is given by the LTL formula:

$$\Box\neg(VideoV\_sexec \wedge VideoC\_sexec). \qquad (1)$$

This formula, obtained automatically through the Property Visual Editor, says that these two media will never occur simultaneously. To verify this property, the graph G_k

[8]A glue process intermediates communication between process to make possible asynchronous communication, since FIACRE process communication is only synchronous.

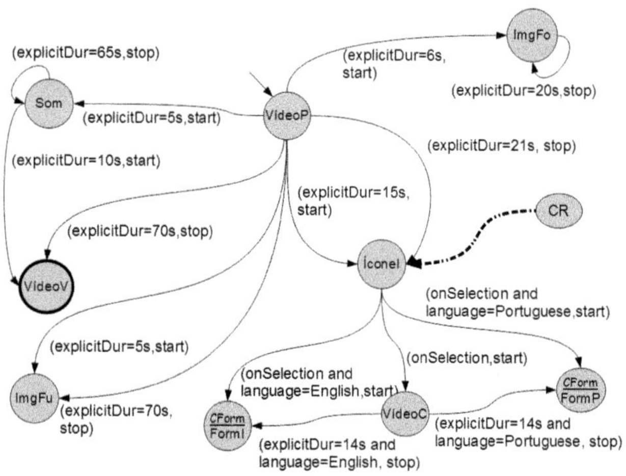

(a) Full graph G_k

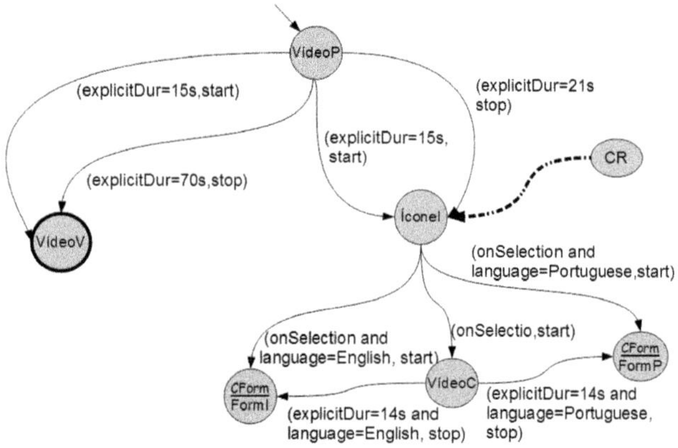

(b) Reduced Graph g_k

Figure 8: Case-study: (a) G_k, and (b) g_k

shown in Fig. 8(a) can be reduced to the graph g_k shown in Fig. 8(b), using the rules R1 and R2. We analyzed the size of G_k and g_k. On the one hand, the automaton produced by the TINA model checker (Kripke's structure) corresponding to G_k had 1,507 states and 2,880 transitions. On the other hand, the structure corresponding to g_k had only 377 states and 712 transitions. The reduction process performed in this case-study allowed to decrease the number of model states and, consequently, the computational cost of the verification process.

In the checking using the reduced model g_k, TINA returned FALSE for the formula of Equation 1, showing that there is not mutual exclusion in the presentation of objects *VideoV* and *VideoC*. TINA also presented the following counter-example: (1) after 15s, *VideoV* is presented; (2) after 15s, the interactive object *IconeI* is presented; (3) the interactive object *IconeI* is selected by the user via the remote control; and (4) selection of *IconeI* triggers *VideoC* during *VideoV* presentation. This counter-example can help the designer to modify the NCL application specification to enforce mutual exclusion between *VideoV* and *VideoC*.

7. CONCLUSION AND FURTHER WOK

In this work we described a toolchain for supporting the development of live NCL hypermedia applications driven to interactive digital TV. The toolchain performs the incremental verification of properties of the application.

In the incremental verification, the application is internally represented as a graph of the temporal dependencies among the objects. This representation, similar to that used internally by the Ginga player, allows the use of rules of graph reduction and greatly reduces the size of the model to be scanned. Hence, the computational cost for performing the model checking is also reduced.

The translations and reductions presented in this paper were also carried out manually. The automatic processes of translation and reduction are being implemented, following the rules and principles presented here.

8. ACKNOWLEDGEMENTS

The authors would like to acknowledge to CAPES - Brazilian Federal Agency for supporting this research.

9. REFERENCES

[1] F. Beer, A. Mull, and C. Forster. The odds of running a nonlinear tv program using web technologies. In *Proc. of the 2011 IEEE Int. Symp. on Broadband Multimedia Systems and Broadcasting*, pages 1 –4, june 2011.

[2] B. Berthomieu, J.-P. Bodeveix, P. Farail, M. Filali, H. Garavel, P. Gaufillet, F. Lang, and F. Vernadat. FIACRE: an intermediate language for model verification in the topcased environment. *4th European Congress on Embedded RT Software - ERTS*, 2008.

[3] B. Berthomieu, P.-O. Ribet, and F. Vernadat. The tool TINA - construction of abstract state spaces for Petri Nets and Time Petri Nets. *Int. Journal of Production Research*, 14(42), 2004.

[4] S. Bouyakoub and A. Belkhir. SMIL builder: An incremental authoring tool for SMIL documents. *ACM Trans. Multimedia Comp. Comm. Appl.*, 7:2:1–2:30, February 2011.

[5] M. Carlsson. Monads for incremental computing. *SIGPLAN Not.*, 37(9):26–35, Sept. 2002.

[6] R. M. R. Costa, M. F. Moreno, and L. F. Gomes Soares. Intermedia synchronization management in DTV systems. In *Proc. of the 8th ACM Symp. on Document engineering*, DocEng '08, pages 289–297, New York, NY, USA, 2008. ACM.

[7] J.-P. Courtiat, C. A. S. Santos, C. Lohr, and B. Outtaj. Experience with RT-LOTOS, a temporal extension of the LOTOS formal description technique. *Computer Communications*, pages 1104–1123, 2000.

[8] M. Felix, E. Haeusler, and L. Soares. *Validating Hypermedia Documents: A Timed Automata Approach.* Monografias em Ciência da Computação. PUC, 2002.

[9] O. Gaggi and A. Bossi. Analysis and verification of SMIL documents. *Multimedia Syst.*, 17(6):487–506, 2011.

[10] L. F. Gomes Soares and S. D. J. Barbosa. *Programando em NCL 3.0: desenvolvimento de aplicações para o middleware Ginga, TV Digital e Web.* Elsevier, Rio de Janeiro, Brazil, 2009.

[11] T. Henzinger, Z. Manna, and A. Pnueli. Timed transition systems. In *Proc. of the REX Workshop 1991 (REX'91)*, LNCS, pages 226–251, New York, NY, USA, 1992. Springer.

[12] R. Laiola Guimarães, R. Monteiro De Resende Costa, and L. F. Gomes Soares. Composer: Authoring tool for itv programs. In *Proc. of the 6th European conference on Changing Television Environments*, EUROITV '08, pages 61–71, Berlin, Heidelberg, 2008. Springer-Verlag.

[13] G. Lima, L. Gomes Soares, C. Soares Neto, and M. Moreno. Towards the NCL Raw Profile. *II Workshop de TV Digital Interativa - WTVDI (WebMedia)*, 2010.

[14] D. J. Picinin, J.-M. Farines, and C. A. S. Santos. Uma abordagem MDE para modelagem e verificação de documentos multimídia interativos. *WebMedia*, 2011.

[15] R. M. Resende Costa, M. F. Moreno, R. F. Rodrigues, and L. F. Gomes Soares. Live editing of hypermedia documents. In *Proc. of the 2006 ACM Symp. on Document Engineering*, DocEng '06, pages 165–172, New York, NY, USA, 2006. ACM.

[16] P. Sampaio and C. J-P. An approach for the automatic generation of RT-LOTOS specifications from SMIL 2.0 documents. *J. Braz. Comp. Soc.*, 9(3):39–51, 2004.

[17] C. A. S. Santos, L. F. Gomes Soares, G. L. de Souza, and J.-P. Courtiat. Design methodology and formal validation of hypermedia documents. *Proc. of the 6th ACM Int. Conf. on Multimedia - MULTIMEDIA '98*, pages 39–48, 1998.

[18] S. Yovine, A. Olivero, D. Monteverde, and G. Cordoba, L.and Reiter. An approach for the verification of the temporal consistency of NCL applications. *WebMedia*, 2010.

[19] H. Yu, X. He, S. Gao, and Y. Deng. Modeling and analyzing SMIL documents in SAM. In *Proc. of the 4th IEEE Int. Symp. on Multimedia Software Engineering*, MSE '02, pages 132–, Washington, DC, USA, 2002. IEEE Comp. Society.

Verification of Crossmedia Content for Interactive Digital Television

Rafaela Ponte Lisboa
Universidade Federal do Ceará
Rua Waldery Uchoa, 01
Fortaleza, Brasil
+ 558533667687
rafaela@multimeios.ufc.br

Elizabeth Furtado
Universidade de Fortaleza
Av. Washington Soares,1321
Fortaleza, Brasil
+558534773079
elizabethsfur@gmail.com

Hermínio Borges Neto
Universidade Federal do Ceará
Rua Waldery Uchoa, 01
Fortaleza, Brasil
+ 558533667687
herminio@multimeios.ufc.br

ABSTRACT

Since the standard interactive Digital Television (DTV) has been defined, there is the expectation of creation of universal network of Distance Education. But there are limitations concerning the techniques and profile of the Brazilian, however, one sees an improvement of the technology for use in educational settings and across many sectors. So this paper proposes recommendations for the production of such content, grouped into the categories of usability, communication and technology that were enriched from experiences with students of the public school system. The contribution of this research is a checklist to support in verification of production of content.

Categories and Subject Descriptors

H.5.2 **[User Interfaces]**: *Evaluation/methodology*

Keywords

Crossmedia, categories, Digital Television, learning objects.

1. INTRODUÇÃO

Em virtude das mudanças ocorridas no setor tecnológico ligado ao Sistema Brasileiro de Televisão Digital (SBTVD) nos últimos anos, a difusão e o acesso aos conteúdos televisivos vêm exigindo novos requisitos para o processo de produção dos conteúdos.

Uma transmissão pode ter agora, além do vídeo, uma aplicação interativa *fullseg* com conteúdos principais, possivelmente na forma de dados (gráficos, textos) a serem acessíveis via um aparelho de TV e/ou uma aplicação interativa *oneseg*, com conteúdos a serem acessíveis via um dispositivo móvel. O acesso a um conteúdo pelo telespectador passa a ser mais flexível, podendo acessá-lo usando várias mídias e dispositivos e em contextos de uso específicos (variando local, tempo, etc.) [1]. Um conteúdo projetado para ser acessado num dispositivo (o celular) a partir de outro dispositivo (a TVD), dá-se neste texto a noção de conteúdo crossmidiático. Um requisito que deve ser considerado em um processo de produção dos conteúdos se refere ao seu design, o qual deve levar o usuário a perceber as diversas formas de interagir e reagir frente à inovação. O usuário deve entender as possibilidades de interatividade e como realizar a convergência entre plataformas, entre o sistema televisivo e o telefônico, para ter acesso aos conteúdos disponíveis na internet via TV.

A maioria dos trabalhos que foca na produção de conteúdos para novas tecnologias não apresenta estudos sobre a definição de uma linguagem comunicativa para facilitar essa adaptação. O trabalho de Cattelen et al. [2], que apresenta de forma original princípios para o paradigma assistir e comentar um vídeo, foca na definição de protótipos para a edição colaborativa de vídeos pelos usuários.

Este artigo apresenta recomendações para a produção de conteúdos educativos crossmidiáticos, relacionadas ao design, à linguagem e aos recursos técnicos necessários para projetar formas de levar o telespectador-aluno a ter a percepção das possibilidades de interatividade e de como acessar os conteúdos via TVD. Elas foram obtidas a partir de problemas e necessidades identificados quando alunos interagiram com conteúdos educativos produzidos e transmitidos em tempo real, e estão organizadas em categorias e foram aplicadas em duas situações: no projeto de uma aplicação para TVD para apresentar conteúdos crossmidiáticos e no processo de produção de um vídeo educativo. Como contribuição relevante tem-se um *checklist* que auxilia na verificação de produtos crossmidiáticos.

Este artigo se organiza da seguinte maneira. Na seção 2, apresenta-se a conceituação sobre a produção de conteúdos educativos para TVD. Na seção 3, apresenta-se as categorias utilizadas para orientar a produção dos produtos crossmidiáticos. Na seção seguinte, as experiências de aplicação das categorias no processo de produção de conteúdos crossmidiáticos são descritas. Em seguida, apresentam-se orientações de verificação desses tipos de conteúdos e por fim a conclusão.

2. CONCEITOS E RECURSOS PARA AUTORIA DE CONTEÚDOS EDUCATIVOS

A motivação para este trabalho não foi somente fundamentada na convergência tecnológica. Ela foi inicialmente identificada a partir de experiências reais com T-VILOS, *Video Interative Learning Objects for television,* ou seja, um objeto de aprendizagem com vídeo interativo transmitido e acessado por telespectador-aluno (usuário) em um meio de comunicação - a TVD. Este conceito é oriundo do conceito de VILOS, em português: Objetos de Aprendizagem (OAs) Vídeo Interativos, que são uma evolução dos OAs tradicionais [3]. Para que um T-VILO se constitua como um OA para TVD, foi definido o uso de dois componentes: 1) o vídeo e; 2) os conteúdos multimídia. Para o desenvolvimento desse OA foi elaborado um processo de planejamento em cinco fases: produção, realização, supervisão, recepção e avaliação. Essas fases foram baseadas na proposta inicial do sistema Telensino, que visava levar a educação para cidades do estado do Ceará desprovidas de infraestrutura

Permission to make digital or hard copies of all or part of this work for personal or classroom use is granted without fee provided that copies are not made or distributed for profit or commercial advantage and that copies bear this notice and the full citation on the first page. To copy otherwise, or republish, to post on servers or to redistribute to lists, requires prior specific permission and/or a fee.

WebMedia'12, October 15–18, 2012, São Paulo/SP, Brazil.

Copyright 2012 ACM 978-1-4503-1706-1/12/10...$15.00.

tecnológica. Dentre as boas práticas desse sistema pode-se destacar: a estruturação de uma equipe multidisciplinar, o uso de diversas mídias e a produção de conteúdos complementares presentes em materiais didáticos (apostilas e manuais). Na fase de produção, há a definição do tema de interesse, seguida da estruturação do roteiro do conteúdo principal, que será abordado no vídeo televisivo, e da estruturação de conteúdos em multimídia, que serão apresentados via uma aplicação de TVD. Na fase de realização, ocorre o recrutamento de profissionais; ensaios e gravação do vídeo, no formato digital; a e elaboração dos conteúdos multimídia com questionários, textos, imagens e mais informações acerca do conteúdo apresentado no vídeo. Em situação de supervisão, sugere-se a verificação da transmissão do vídeo, dos fatores de usabilidade e de acessibilidade dos conteúdos. As duas últimas fases, de recepção e de avaliação, são destinadas, respectivamente, à organização de oficina e/ou aula, sensibilização, orientação de aprendizagem e realização de atividades; e à avaliação da aprendizagem e de usabilidade. Especificamente as duas primeiras fases são suportadas pela aplicação da metodologia pedagógica Sequência Fedathi (SF) [4], escolhida para nortear o desenvolvimento do vídeo e dos conteúdos em multimídia criados, por colocar o aluno em uma posição ativa no processo de ensino-aprendizagem e tendo a possibilidade de interagir e intervir no conteúdo apresentado.

É importante destacar que T-VILO é suportado por recursos disponíveis em três categorias: tecnológica, pedagógica e comunicacional. A categoria tecnológica de um T-VILO se refere ao seu uso na plataforma SBTVD, incluindo a aplicação que irá permitir o acesso a tal conteúdo. Neste projeto em execução [4], duas ferramentas foram desenvolvidas: o T-VILO Maker, para geração de conteúdos multimídia e o T-VILO Viewer, para exibição do conteúdo gerado. A categoria pedagógica de um T-VILO está baseada no conceito de OA, mas também na aplicação da SF. Enquanto que a categoria comunicacional se refere ao processo de comunicação a ser estabelecido entre o telespectador-aluno e o apresentador de um programa (neste caso, de um vídeo televisivo).

2.1 Perspectiva crossmidiática

As conceituações evoluíram a partir de experiências relativas ao uso dos T-VILOs no contexto educacional, especificamente em uma oficina de matemática com 10 alunos de 10 a 13 anos de uma escola de ensino fundamental e médio da rede estadual de ensino que tinha como objetivo verificar a qualidade da interação de um conteúdo educativo. Interessava observar se o conteúdo levava o usuário ao entendimento sobre as possibilidades de interatividade. Os conteúdos desenvolvidos foram transmitidos para os aparelhos de TVD situados no laboratório onde acontece esta pesquisa, que possue uma infraestrutura de transmissão própria com um canal específico de TV, para transmitir os conteúdos atingindo um raio inferior a dez metros. Como o canal se apresenta em caráter acadêmico para testes não é preciso solicitar uma concessão do Governo Federal.

A oficina de matemática iniciava como uma sensibilização, e em seguida, os alunos reunidos em grupos de 3 deveriam acessar a aplicação interativa, que possuía conteúdos em um menu, e deveriam espontaneamente realizar outras ações para fazer uso dos T-VILOs. Essas ações poderiam ser: navegar nas mídias, acessar uma mídia, ler um texto, responder um questionário, dar sua opinião, etc. Quando um grupo terminava sua experiência, havia um grupo focal para os alunos expressarem seus sentimentos.

De uma forma geral, os resultados apontaram algumas deficiências com relação à linguagem comunicativa usada na produção dos conteúdos interativos, que prejudicava a percepção dos usuários para as possibilidades de interatividade. Por exemplo, dentre os personagens do vídeo não havia um que realizasse a mediação entre os demais personagens ou que buscasse solucionar o problema posto no vídeo envolvendo o telespectador. Assim, o comportamento dos alunos era inicialmente passivo, até serem motivados a interagir pelo condutor da oficina. Alguns usuários chegaram a questionar sobre a possibilidade de obter informações mais lúdicas, animações, acerca do conteúdo, etc.

Uma solução para esta problemática e às novas necessidades reveladas não deve ser tomada por produtores sem considerar uma avaliação das especificações técnicas do SBTVD e do perfil dos usuários brasileiros. O SBTVD tem um limite de 6MB por pacote de aplicação que é transmitido por meio do sinal de TV digital (*broadcasting*). Esse problema cria uma restrição para o uso de conteúdos com animações. Essa situação poderia ser parcialmente resolvida se o usuário obtivesse o conteúdo sob demanda, com uma conexão de canal de retorno rápida. Seria então uma solução para um sistema IPTV, que transforma a TVD do usuário em algo similar a um computador com acesso à Internet. O usuário comum de TV no Brasil não tem acesso a Internet. No entanto, o acesso a Internet pelo celular cresce, chegando a 9% do total de 8,1 milhão de usuários de banda larga [5].

Para a busca de soluções percebe-se que a perspectiva crossmidiática, pode favorecer a convergência entre os dispositivos, ou seja, proporcione o acesso de conteúdos em diversas mídias de acordo com a necessidade e possibilidades.

Diante desta perspectiva foi realizada uma revisão sistemática acerca dos conceitos crossmídia na literatura científica. Chegou-se à definição de um produto crossmidiático como sendo algo que deve envolver mais de uma mídia, de modo que cada uma apoie a outra com seus pontos fortes e seja acessível por meio de computador, celular e televisão [6]. Houve então a necessidade de evoluir o conceito de OA passa a ser composto por um conjunto de mídias que se combinam com o intuito de transmitir uma mensagem comum explorando dois ou mais tipos de dispositivos. Um OA, por sua vez, precisa ter conteúdo que apresente ligações relacionando suas mídias. Esses elos devem possibilitar a navegação entre dispositivos diferentes [6], ou seja, a alternância de dispositivos. Surgem duas novas características a serem incluídas no fluxo de navegação entre mídias de um T-VILO. Trata-se do ponto de entrada, significando o início do conteúdo a ser apontado no fluxo, ou seja, é o contato inicial do usuário com o produto. A outra característica é de transição, que se refere à ação de alternar dispositivos ao longo de um produto de mídia cruzada. A alternância entre dispositivos depende de uma ação do usuário, no entanto é necessário especificar, orientar no fluxo o momento em que haverá a troca de dispositivos.

Diante da evolução desse conceito, surgiu o seguinte questionamento: como desenvolver T-VILOs que atendam a essa perspectiva, abordando elementos que levem os usuários a perceberem as possibilidades de interação e a acessarem as aplicações interativas? Resposta para esta questão é apresentada na próxima seção, onde recomendações para o desenvolvimento de conteúdos são propostas e organizadas em três categorias: usabilidade, tecnológica e de comunicação. É importante salientar que a categoria pedagógica foi substituída pela de usabilidade, visando trabalhar com estratégias que levem os usuários a terem a percepção das possibilidades de acesso às aplicações interativas.

Além disto, percebeu-se que para os usuários acessarem os conteúdos projetados nesta perspectiva, era necessário evoluir as aplicações com funcionalidades de transmídia. Desta forma, na seção seguinte, apresenta-se como as recomendações propostas servem para apoiar na evolução desse tipo de aplicações.

3. CATEGORIAS PARA A AUTORIA DE PRODUTOS CROSSMIDIÁTICOS

Nesta seção são descritas as categorias de usabilidade, tecnológica e de comunicação. Ao que se refere à usabilidade, um produto crossmidiático precisa considerar os meios de comunicação utilizados e a estrutura de navegação construída. Dois elementos foram definidos para essa categoria [6]. O primeiro é o **meio de comunicação**, que está relacionado à pertinência e à adequação do conteúdo, das mídias e dos próprios dispositivos utilizados sob o ponto de vista dos meios de comunicação selecionados. O produtor deve checar se um conteúdo principal é apresentado em um dispositivo adequado, de modo que os usuários tenham fácil acesso e familiaridade com ele; e identificar se o manuseio do dispositivo não causa restrições a usuários, principalmente, aqueles com alguma necessidade física especial. O segundo é a **navegação no conteúdo**, trata-se da percepção e do comportamento do usuário em relação às possibilidades de navegação entre diferentes dispositivos. Para um produto sequencial ou com caminhos alternativos, a navegação é um modo de envolver o usuário de modo que a sua experiência seja atraente e significativa.

Já em termos da categoria tecnológica, esta exerce influência no resultado final de um produto crossmidiático, que vai desde as estratégias adotadas para proporcionar interatividade, até a correta exploração de uma mídia em dispositivos. Foram estabelecidos dois elementos para essa categoria. Primeiramente, destaca-se a **interatividade**, que é o artifício utilizado para propiciar ao usuário liberdade sobre o conteúdo, sempre levando em consideração aspectos (como a simplicidade, adequação ao uso) ligados à tecnologia empregada na elaboração do produto crossmidiático. A interatividade deve acontecer de modo que seja natural para o usuário e não exija esforço de aprendizagem, atendendo assim a meta de usabilidade sobre a aprendizagem [6]. Em seguida, tem-se a **portabilidade do conteúdo,** ou seja, o grau de facilidade com que um conteúdo é apresentado em outra plataforma além daquela de origem. Quando necessário, o produtor deve verificar os dispositivos de interesse e para cada par deles, avaliar os níveis de portabilidade de conteúdo [6]: **Alta**, cujo conteúdo é exibido no dispositivo A e pode ser exibido sem modificações no dispositivo B; **Média**, o conteúdo é exibido no dispositivo A e precisa ser modificado para ser exibido no dispositivo B. Como exemplo, pode-se trazer um vídeo em alta definição visualizado em um computador (dispositivo A) que precisa ser convertido e reduzido para ser enviado e exibido em um celular (dispositivo B); e **Baixa**: o conteúdo exibido no dispositivo A não pode ser exibido no dispositivo B. Um vídeo pode ser visualizado no computador (dispositivo A), mas não pode ser enviado para um aparelho de TV (dispositivo B) por limitações de memória.

A categoria de comunicação está relacionada ao processo de comunicação que deve ser estabelecido entre aquele que produz o produto crossmídia e o usuário desse produto. Acredita-se também que a partir do produto, pode se estabelecer uma comunicação entre o usuário e o *designer* de aplicações e /ou o produtor do conteúdo. Um processo de comunicação ocorre quando, em um determinado contexto, um emissor emite uma mensagem a um receptor por meio de um canal. Ou seja, quando um receptor recebe a mensagem, ele gera uma ideia daquilo que o emissor quis dizer e inicia o seu processo de compreensão. Há quatro elementos essenciais da comunicação Intenção do comunicador; Objeto a comunicar; Expressão e; Linguagem interativa. **Intenção do comunicador e o objeto a comunicar:** se refere aos efeitos que o emissor deseja causar no receptor para acessar um produto crossmidiático. Desta forma, o produtor tem a intenção em disponibilizar conteúdo complementar ao vídeo televisivo passando uma mensagem (o objeto a comunicar) e usando os meios (a expressão) necessários para o usuário acessar tal conteúdo complementar. O objeto a comunicar refere-se às informações e/ou conceitos abordados nas mídias; **Expressão:** em um processo de comunicação, um emissor precisa definir a expressão a ser utilizada para o objeto que se deseja comunicar. Para tanto, faz-se necessária à utilização de um código, do qual o receptor consiga interpretar. O código é a língua, por exemplo, uma mídia áudio faz uso do ato de fala. Diante de um produto crossmidiático, o elemento expressão se refere aos códigos que serão utilizados pelo produtor da obra, o designer e o programador para juntos fazerem a produção deste tipo de produto; **Linguagem interativa:** que dependendo da intenção do comunicador (produtor da obra e/ou designer), deve levar o usuário (o receptor): (i) a se envolver com o conteúdo; (ii) a se sentir parte integrante do conteúdo; (iii) a se sentir persuadido a interagir com os *crosslinks* presentes no conteúdo; e/ou (iv) a interagir com o emissor (ver exemplos na seção 4). Ou seja, promover o diálogo entre emissor e receptor e auxiliá-los a estabelecer um diálogo orientando-os adequadamente para esta interação [6].

4. APLICAÇÃO DAS CATEGORIAS

Com o intuito de perceber a aplicabilidade dessas categorias em um processo de produção de produtos crossmidiáticos, criou-se duas situações de uso. A primeira referente a uma experiência de prototipagem da experiência em papel, onde um *designer* e um desenvolvedor da equipe do projeto em execução utilizam os elementos de usabilidade e tecnológicos para elaborar um produto crossmidiático. O objetivo era adequar as funcionalidades da aplicação às recomendações dispostas nos elementos. Para tanto, os protótipos foram verificados quanto à adequação. Ajustes foram realizados, antes de a solução ser efetivamente implementada por um desenvolvedor. A partir dessa solução prototipada analisou-se as categorias, bem como observou-se a presença de outros aspectos também pertinentes que foram explorados durante a técnica, como: de acessibilidade, de portabilidade e de transição para outros dispositivos, que são importantes para a perspectiva crossmidiática. O designer percebeu que poderia haver problemas com os elementos: Meio de comunicação e Portabilidade do conteúdo, ou seja, com o acesso a conteúdos extras no formato de vídeo pelo celular. A recomendação de verificar se o manuseio do dispositivo não causaria restrições a usuários, principalmente, aqueles com alguma necessidade física especial, não exigia nenhum tratamento em particular, mas alertou os profissionais para considerar que o vídeo no celular tivesse legenda.

Na segunda situação de uso, as categorias foram aplicadas na produção de um conteúdo, em que se visava sanar problemas referentes a percepção acerca das possibilidades de interação. Assim, verificou-se em que momentos de um roteiro as recomendações comunicacionais deveriam ser consideradas. O objetivo era definir como a linguagem/ narrativa deveria ser construída para a formação de um indivíduo participativo para o uso da tecnologia. Para tanto, a técnica usada foi *storyboard* do vídeo, com foco na linguagem interativa, antes de sua gravação. No discurso, houve a preocupação de apresentar a partir da linguagem as ***alternativas para a modalidade de interação***. Sabe-se que a partir da TVD, os telespectadores poderão interagir de forma auditiva (falando ao telefone) ou textual (entrando com informações na própria TV utilizando o controle remoto). Assim, o apresentador orienta os telespectadores para a interatividade disponível: ele apresenta o controle remoto como o meio para viabilizar a interatividade textual. Utiliza também o elemento ***inclusão do usuário no diálogo*** visando envolver o telespectador no diálogo dando-lhe a informação para fazer uso dos recursos disponibilizados, incluindo-os e alfabetizando-os para esta nova tecnologia [7]. Essas experiências de aplicações das categorias em diversas situações levaram os autores a apresentar uma proposta de verificação dos produtos gerados.

5. ORIENTAÇÕES PARA VERIFICAÇÃO DOS PRODUTOS CROSSMIDIÁTICOS

Visando a apoiar profissionais tanto no projeto de aplicações como no projeto de conteúdos crossmidiáticos, propõe-se um *checklist*, o instrumento resultante deste trabalho, intitulado *Check-Cross*. Ele é sugerido para verificar o atendimento às orientações dadas, ou seja, as explicações descritas em cada categoria, na seção 3, apresentaram os objetivos e as orientações necessárias. O *checklist* se divide em cinco segmentos, são eles: conteúdo, transições e *calls-to-action* (elementos no conteúdo que estimulam o usuário a realizar a troca de dispositivos), dispositivos escolhidos, padronização e pontos de entrada. Em cada segmento, há um conjunto de perguntas objetivas que visam a auxiliar na verificação do referido produto. As perguntas que compõem o *checklist* são:

- **Conteúdo:** Quando se faz uso de portabilidade, as mídias portadas fazem sentido? Quando se faz uso de portabilidade, a linguagem e a exibição foram realmente adaptadas de modo satisfatório para o novo meio de comunicação? Cada mídia é relevante, enriquecendo de algum modo o conteúdo do qual faz parte? A falta de acesso a um conteúdo extra pode causar algum prejuízo para o usuário?
- **Transições e *CTA*:**As *CTAs* têm o destaque necessário e são fáceis de compreender? As transições são acompanhadas facilmente? Existe motivação para que o usuário de fato siga adiante utilizando as transições?
- **Dispositivos escolhidos:** O público alvo tem fácil acesso aos dispositivos necessários para acessar as mídias? O público alvo tem familiaridade com os dispositivos?
- **Padronização:** As diferentes mídias respeitam uma identidade visual e de linguagem?
- **Sobre pontos de entrada:** Os pontos de entrada do produto são de fácil conhecimento? Os pontos de entrada são atraentes para o usuário? É fácil para o usuário obter acesso inicial ao conteúdo? Há redundância quanto às mídias de entrada?

Para exemplificar as informações apresentadas em cada categoria, considere o exemplo do seguinte item do *checklist* "**Quando se faz uso de portabilidade, a linguagem e a exibição foram realmente adaptadas de modo satisfatório para o novo meio de comunicação (dispositivo)?**", cujas informações podem ser encontradas na categoria **Portabilidade do conteúdo**. Como **objetivo** foi dito que se deve garantir certo grau de facilidade para um conteúdo ser apresentado em outra plataforma além daquela de origem. Como **orientação**, foi dito que o produtor deve verificar os dispositivos de interesse e para cada par deles, ele deve avaliar os níveis de portabilidade de conteúdo. Existem, além disto, **uma especificação dessa orientação e um exemplo**, dados como segue: na portabilidade Média, o conteúdo exibido no dispositivo A precisa ser modificado para ser exibido no dispositivo B. Como exemplo, pode-se trazer um vídeo em alta definição visualizado em um computador (dispositivo A) que precisa ser convertido e reduzido para ser enviado e exibido em um celular (dispositivo B).

6. CONCLUSÃO

Neste artigo as categorias de usabilidade, tecnológica e de comunicação foram apresentadas, como mostrado, elas abrangem desde a produção de conteúdo até a visualização do mesmo na TVD e em outros dispositivos e são aplicáveis em processos de produção de conteúdo e em projetos de ferramentas de geração e de acesso ao conteúdo produzido. Uma vez a autoria realizada e as ferramentas projetadas, é importante verificar o atendimento às características da perspectiva crossmidiática. Ainda neste artigo, um *checklist* de verificação dos produtos criados na perspectiva crossmidiática foi proposto. Como trabalhos futuros, pretende-se traçar uma metodologia que condense a perspectiva de convergência de mídias anunciadas com a TVD, que também vai ao encontro com a crossmídia, sendo esta estendida para o processo de produção de conteúdos, mas também de profissionais. O intuito é inserir a interatividade nessas produções, visando à inserção de telespectadores, usuários e alunos como coautores desses conteúdos.

7. REFERÊNCIAS

[1] Chakaveh, S.; Borgen, M. (2007). Media Convergence, An Introduction. Human-Computer Interaction. HCI Intelligent Multimodal Interaction Environments, Berlin.

[2] Cattelan, R; Teixeira C., Gularte R., Pimentel. (2008) Watch-and-Comment as a Paradigm toward Ubiquitous Interactive Video Editing. ACM transaction on Multimedia Computing, vol. 4.

[3] Wolyne, E. (2011) Objetos de aprendizagem vídeo interativos. Disponível em: http://www.techne.com.br/artigos/VILOS.pdf. Acessado em: 20 jun. 2011.

[4] Matos, I; Furtado, E. (2010) TvILOTool: Uma Ferramenta Orientada a Serviços para Produção de Conteúdos para Televisão Digital Brasileira baseada em Objetos de Aprendizagem. In: WebMedia, Belo Horizonte.

[5] Lemos, A. Arte e Mídia Locativa no Brasil. (2009). In: Lemos, A.; Josgrilberg, F. (org.) Comunicação e mobilidade: aspectos socioculturais das tecnologias móveis de comunicação no Brasil Salvador : EDUFBA.

[6] Furtado, E; Lisboa, R. P.; Palácio, R (2012). Avaliação de produtos crossmidiáticos a partir de critérios de usabilidade, tecnológicos e comunicação. In: Furtado, M.E.S.(Org.). Qualidade da Interação de Sistemas e Novas abordagens para a avaliação. 1 ed. Curitiba: EDITORA CRV.

Automatic Annotation of Tagged Content Using Predefined Semantic Concepts

Marcelo G. Manzato, Rudinei Goularte
Mathematics and Computing Institute
University of São Paulo
Av. Trabalhador Sancarlense, 400
PO Box 668 – 13560-970
São Carlos, SP – Brazil
{mmanzato, rudinei}@icmc.usp.br

ABSTRACT

User tags are an important source of information that can be used to gather semantic data about the content, reducing the semantic gap and the restrictive domain of automatic indexing approaches. In this paper, we propose an automatic technique for semantic annotation of multimedia content based on collaborative user tags. Our technique faces some of the challenges of using user-generated terms, such as noise and incompleteness. Based on the actual context of a multimedia item and the co-occurrence of concepts and tags from the training set, we are able to predict semantic concepts for new items without the need of complex multimedia indexing techniques. We describe the results of our approach with an evaluation of our algorithm using a large scale dataset composed of images and user tags.

Categories and Subject Descriptors

H.3.1 [**Information Storage and Retrieval**]: Content Analysis and Indexing—*Indexing methods*

General Terms

Design, Algorithms

Keywords

Automatic annotation, concept classification, user tags, folksonomy, enrichment.

1. INTRODUCTION

The overload of multimedia content available on the Web has introduced new challenges for search engines to retrieve, organize and classify the data according to the user's needs. Usually, Web search algorithms rely only on the text surrounding an image or video, not considering the semantics which are associated to each multimedia item.

Permission to make digital or hard copies of all or part of this work for personal or classroom use is granted without fee provided that copies are not made or distributed for profit or commercial advantage and that copies bear this notice and the full citation on the first page. To copy otherwise, to republish, to post on servers or to redistribute to lists, requires prior specific permission and/or a fee.
WebMedia'12, October 15–18, 2012, São Paulo/SP, Brazil.
Copyright 2012 ACM 978-1-4503-1706-1/12/10 ...$15.00.

The extraction of meaningful information describing the content is an important step to enable multimedia search tools. Typically, the provision of such metadata is accomplished by content authors or providers, who create well-structured information about specific media items, helping search and analysis tasks. Automatic approaches may also be adopted, which create multimedia descriptions without human intervention, analyzing low level visual features in order to infer semantic information.

It is known that automatic and manual indexing techniques have limitations that may affect the process of gathering semantic information. Indeed, the lack of methods to provide meaningful descriptions has been named semantic gap [24], and over ten years researchers have been working on the development of strategies to overcome related problems. For instance, in case of automatic approaches, usually they are highly dependent on the content domain, once they infer semantic information based on previous knowledge about the content domain [2]. In manual approaches, in turn, the description is considered a time-consuming and error prone task [18].

On the other hand, recent advances in the social media field have allowed the exploration of user-generated annotations to obtain metadata about the content. In this direction, services such as Youtube[1] and Flickr[2] encourage users to act as producers, being able to author new videos, photos, audio and documents, and make them available on the Web. Moreover, it is possible to annotate, augment and/or enrich existent data, by inserting tags, comments and links to other related media.

Tagging systems, in particular, have been well accepted by users because they provide simple mechanisms to tag their resources with the objective to facilitate further search by themselves. Considering other benefits, some authors [11, 35, 8, 28] have explored collaborative tagging to create folksonomies and semantic relationships based on co-occurrence of tags. With such structures, it is possible to gather semantic information from the content in a collaborative way, reducing the main problems related to traditional indexing approaches.

In spite of the possibility to face the semantic gap by means of user tags, researchers have reported a number of challenges which are currently being investigated [35]. First, user tags can be subjective and personalized; in Figure 1 (a),

[1] http://www.youtube.com/
[2] http://www.flickr.com/

Figure 1: Example of user tags.

for instance, the image was tagged with the terms "holiday" and "vacation", which refer to a personalized meaning to the user. Second, the terms used for tagging can have different meanings; in Figure 1 (b), the term "lion" is referring to an animal, but its meaning can also be related to celebrity or astrology. Third, the list of associated tags can be incomplete; in Figure 1 (c), the image description would be more complete with additional terms, such as "plant", "garden", "animal" and "wildlife". Finally, the descriptions may be prone to noise; still in Figure 1 (c), the tags "cautiverio", "explore" and "leef" are considered noise because the first is in a different language than the remaining tags (English), the second does not bring meaningful information about the content, and the third is a misspelled word for "leaf".

One important step of multimedia indexing is the automatic annotation (or simply classification) of the content into a number of semantic concepts or categories. Such annotation task helps applications to organize the media, supporting the retrieval of data according to meaningful queries created by users. Considering this task, and the challenges of using user tags in multimedia descriptions, in this paper we propose an algorithm that automatically annotates multimedia items into a number of semantic concepts. The process relies on the available tags, and uses different strategies based on co-occurrence of terms and concepts to reduce the aforementioned problems of noise and incompleteness. The first one is supported by a multi-phase filtering procedure that amends misspelled tags and considers only those semantically related to the actual context of the item. The second one, in turn, is reduced with a tag enrichment activity which aggregates related terms to the actual list of tags in order to make annotation more effective. The remaining challenges of subjective and ambiguous tags, in spite of their significance, are left as future work.

This paper is structured in the following way. Section 2 presents the related work which depict the actual state of art in semantic classification and multimedia content annotation. Section 3 provides the prior steps in our algorithm which consist of a preparation procedure to gather semantic information from the training set. Section 4 describes the concept annotator algorithm proposed in this paper. Section 5 presents an evaluation of our system with the goal to highlight its strengths and limitations. Finally, Sections 6 and 7 presents the final remarks, future work and acknowledgments.

2. RELATED WORK

The related work about content annotation and concept classification can be divided in three categories: i) approaches that analyze low level visual features to infer semantic information; ii) techniques that explore textual metadata, such as EXIF data from images, tags assigned previously by users and keywords; and iii) methods that combine both approaches to improve the classification results.

In the case of systems that deal only with low level visual features, most approaches use certain descriptors to gather visual information from the content. These descriptors can be obtained using different techniques, such as scale-invariant feature transform (SIFT) [21, 13, 6, 34, 30, 1], space envelope [6] features, colour histograms [5, 19], local binary patters [17], textures, global colours [26] and Gaussian mixture models [5]. All this sort of information is used to create bags of visual words, which are analyzed by concept classifiers. This step is usually accomplished using known techniques, such as support vector machine (SVM) [30, 1, 17], k-means [1], linear discriminant analysis (LDA) [19] and Naïve-Bayes classifiers [34].

One negative aspect of visual features-based approaches is that they usually have to know beforehand the characteristics of the application scenario in order to infer semantic information. Thus, after training, the classifiers will only be effective in a restrictive domain.

On the other hand, another direction of concept classifiers is those systems that deal only with textual metadata, using statistic methods based on co-occurrence in order to overcome most problems aforementioned about user tags. Indeed, Zhu et al. [35] investigate the issue of how the quality of tagged images used for training affects concept detection performance. They also propose a probabilistic model based on co-occurrence of tags and concepts in external sources, such as Wikipedia[3], WordNet[4] and folksonomies.

Li et al. [11] use textual features (user tags and EXIF information) to perform automatic annotation. It starts with a document expansion procedure which assigns additional content to concepts and image tags by consulting external information resources, such as DBpedia[5]. After that, expanded textual metadata is compared to expanded concepts in order to make concept assumptions. They also provide a method to assign concepts to images by analyzing EXIF data, such as the time a photo was shot. Finally, additional concepts are considered by infering affiliations and opposite relations among them.

The combination of EXIF data and external sources is also explored by approaches [16, 10, 32] that deal with contextual information (location, time, etc.) in order to suggest annotations to images.

Hare et al. [8] propose a linear algebric method for learning the semantic structure between terms in an annotated training set of images. Unannotated images are then projected into that structure in order to rank images based on keywords.

Tang et al. [29] propose a sparse graph-based semi-supervised learning approach for harnessing the labeled and unlabeled data. They describe an effective training label refinement strategy within this graph-based learning framework to handle the noise in the tags. An extension was proposed in [28] which uses a kNN-sparse graph-based semi-supervised learning algorithm to remove most of the semantically unrelated links among the data, resulting in a more robust and

[3]http://www.wikipedia.com
[4]http://wordnet.princeton.edu
[5]http://dbpedia.org

discriminative technique than the conventional graphs-based approaches.

The aforementioned text-based approaches differ from ours because we provide a co-occurrence-based tag enrichment phase in order to overcome the incompleteness of terms in resources that do not have enough associated tags. In addition, based on the enriched tags list, we also calculate the co-occurrence of concepts and tags during training to highlight the most frequent concepts by given tags.

Most of these textual-based techniques have to deal with the fact that lots of content may not have enough textual information in order to support the correct annotation and classification. If an image or video does not have any tag assigned or contextual information, those systems will not be able to predict the related concepts. Consequently, some authors have developed novel techniques that combine low level visual features with text when available. Motohashi et al. [15], for instance, propose a multi-modal system that combines conceptual fuzzy sets with visual words and user tags to annotate images. User tags are also used to improve the results of an approach proposed by Fakeri-Tabrizi et al. [7] that uses a fusion of different classifiers with supervised and semi-supervised methods. Similarly, Mensink et al. [14] propose a combination of the Fisher vector image representation with the TagProp method for image auto-annotation. They use a multi-modal approach combining tags with visual features in order to improve the results of a visual classifier. The TagProp [31], in particular, is a model that predicts the term relevance of images by taking a weighted sum of the annotations of the visually most similar images in an annotated training set.

Other approaches that combine visual features with textual information are the works of Srikanth et al. [25] and Shi et al. [23], which explore concept ontologies to map a visual vocabulary into a semantic hierarchy.

Although we find interesting the approach of using visual and textual information to improve the classification results, the exploration of visual features needs complex techniques which usually are computationally expensive. In addition, as argued before, the use of visual features may restrict the application domain, as the system will have to know beforehand the characteristics of the content in order to infer semantic information.

Therefore, in this paper, we propose a technique that uses only user tags, their statistic information and a lexicon database to provide automatic annotation of multimedia items into a number of semantic concepts. Based on the actual state of art, we summarize the following gaps which are covered in this paper:

- The lack of tags in certain resources which may lower the performance of classification. In our approach, this problem is reduced with a tag enrichment phase based on folksonomies.
- The fact that visual-based approaches may be computationally expensive. The expensiveness of our technique is only at the creation of statistic information during training; after that, our classification algorithm relies only on textual metadata, and thus, does not require complex processing as needed by visual features approaches.
- The restrictive characteristic of visual-based techniques according to the application domain. Our approach is generic because it relies only on folksonomies and a generic lexicon, and thus, can be automatically adapted according to the actual domain.

3. TRAINING

Our automatic annotator starts with a training procedure whose main objective is to gather semantic information from the available corpus already annotated. In addition, all user tags must be filtered and analyzed in order to remove incomplete and/or incorrect tags. Figure 2 illustrates the overall schema. Although in this paper we are considering only images, our approach may be used with any other multimedia modality, such as video and audio, unless the content does not have any associated tags.

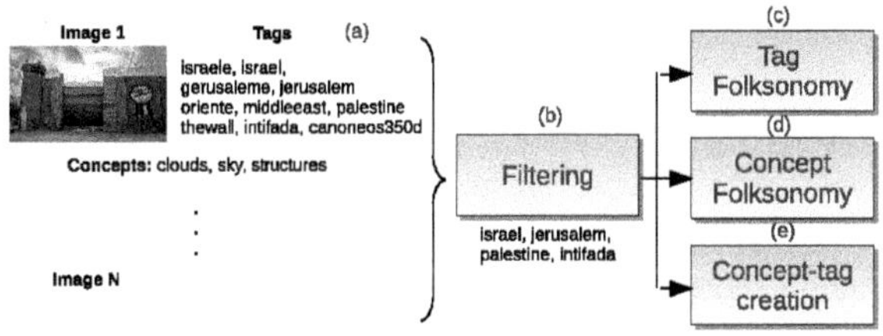

Figure 2: Training procedure.

All available tags about an item (Figure 2 (a)) are submitted into a module which will filter incorrect and/or incomplete terms. This procedure has the objective to eliminate noise which can affect later the quality of concept classification. After that, all terms are used to create a folksonomy of tags (Figure 2 (c)), so that semantically related terms can be obtained during the annotation of items with few associated tags. A folksonomy of concepts is also constructed based on their co-occurrence, as indicated in Figure 2 (d). The idea behind this process is to identify semantically related concepts, and then, assign more generic concepts based on specific ones already found. For instance, if an item was annotated with the concept "flower", so it will also be annotated with "plant_life". Finally, we use both concepts and terms of each item to create a table containing the most frequent concept for each tag (Figure 2 (e)). This table will be used during classification to predict possible concepts according to tags assigned by the user. Next subsections describe the training steps in details.

3.1 Filtering Tags

The process of filtering noisy tags is divided into two phases. The first one is conducted to amend or discard misspelled, incorrect and/or incomplete terms, being most of the process supported by lexicon resources and syntactic analysis of the terms. The second phase consists of checking the meaning of the tags in order to decide if such terms are semantically related to the most frequent concepts in the training set. Given Figure 1 (c), for instance, tags such as "yaguarete" and "cautiverio" would be discarded in the first phase of the filtering process; the tag "leef" would be replaced to the correct term "leaf" in this same phase; and the tag "explore" would be discarded during the second phase of the process.

This subsection describes the first phase of the filtering procedure; the second one, because it is executed as a further step of the annotation algorithm, is depicted in details in Subsection 4.3.

The synctatic analysis of the given tags is similar to the one proposed by Cantador et al. [3]. Figure 3 illustrates the main steps. It starts with a lexical checking (Figure 3 (a)) which will discard all stop-words and terms that contain digits and/or their length is less than 2 or bigger than 25 characters.

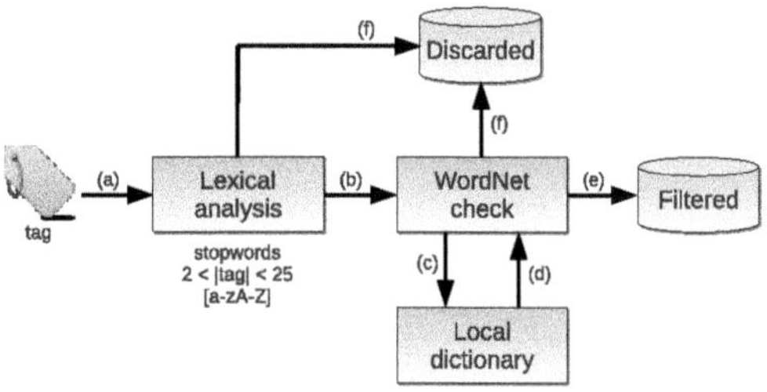

Figure 3: Filtering procedure.

After that, the tags are checked against the WordNet (Figure 3 (b)) in order to find existent words. If it was not found, the tag may be misspelled. Consequently, we check it against a local dictionary (Figure 3 (c)) to find possible correct lexical variations of that term. As opposite to the algorithm proposed by Cantador et al., which uses a Google connector to check lexical variations, we use the Levenshtein distance [12] among the tag and possible candidates, working similarly to *Google Did You Mean*, though the latter also considers proper names. The reason for not having used the Google version is that it restricts the number of queries per day. In our case, tags consisting of proper names will be investigated in future work through the use of Wikipedia ontologies, such as Yago2[6] or DBpedia.

After the local dictionary module has indicated possible lexical variations of the term, they are checked again on WordNet in order to make sure it is a valid English term existent in such database (Figure 3 (d)). If it was found, the term will be considered in the system (Figure 3 (e)); otherwise, it will be discarded (Figure 3 (f)).

3.2 Statistics Calculation

After syntactic analysis, the training items and their associated tags are used to create three statistic tables, as illustrated in Figure 2 (c), (d) and (e). The first two are the tag and concept folksonomies, and the last is the one which relates concepts and tags. As will be described in next section, they are used to infer related tags and concepts from the corpus, supporting the semantic classification.

The folksonomies are based on the relatedness measure described by Cattuto et al. [4], who create a folksonomy based on co-occurrence of tags. They define it as a weighted undirected graph whose set of vertex is the set T of all tags from all items. Two tags t_1 and t_2 are connected by an edge if and only if $t_1, t_2 \in T_s$, where T_s is the set of tags assigned to item $s \in S$. The weight of this edge is given by the number of times t_1 and t_2 co-occurred, i.e., $w(t_1, t_2) = |\{s \in S \mid t_1, t_2 \in T_s\}|$.

For the concept folksonomy, the same process is adopted, but instead of considering co-occurrence of tags, we check the co-occurrence of concepts assigned to each item from the training set. This folksonomy is used to highlight concepts which have a semantic relation. For instance, if used the 24 different concepts defined in the MIRFLICKR-25k dataset [9], the most related concepts to "people" are "female", "male" and "portrait". These relationships are used to create manually an ontology of concepts in order to collect more general concepts if a specific one was used to annotate an item. Consequently, if "female" was used, so the generic concept "people" is also considered.

Another statistic table created from the training set is the one which relates concepts and tags. We calculate the number of times a concept and a tag co-occurred in an item. Given a pair (c, t), where $c \in C$ is a concept and C is the set of all considered concepts, we assume they are related if and only if $c \in C_s$ and $t \in T_s$, where C_s is the set of concepts assigned to item s during training. A weight between them is also defined, i.e., $w(c, t) = |\{s \in S \mid c \in C_s \;\&\; t \in T_s\}|$.

4. AUTOMATIC ANNOTATION

This section describes the automatic annotation algorithm proposed in this paper. It consists of analyzing the available tags of each multimedia item in order to infer possible related concepts according to the folksonomies and statistical data constructed during training.

Figure 4 illustrates the overall schema. User tags associated to a multimedia item (e.g. an image) (Figure 4 (a)) are first filtered using the same procedure described in Subsection 3.1 (Figure 4 (b)). After that, some items may have not enough terms to support correct concept classification. Thus, we add a tag enrichment phase (Figure 4 (c)) which will expand the set of available tags with related ones obtained from the tag folksonomy created previously during training.

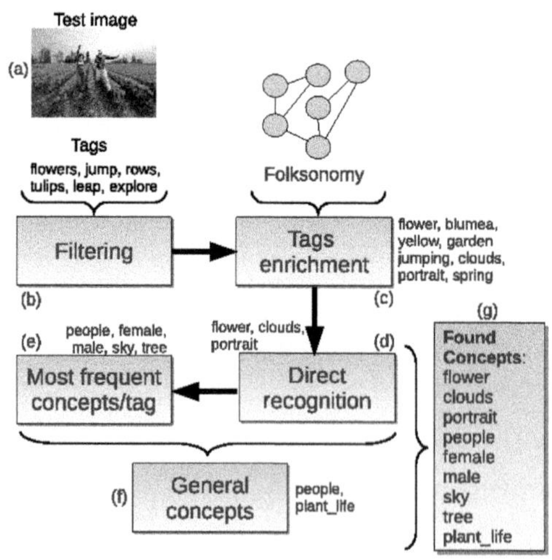

Figure 4: Annotation procedure.

When an item has enough terms, it can be annotated. This task is accomplished by means of three strategies, illustrated in Figure 4: direct recognition (d), most frequent concepts by tag (e) and definition of general concepts (f). As a result of all three classification steps, the multimedia content is annotated with all obtained concepts (Figure 4 (g)). Next subsections describe in details all involved steps.

[6]http://www.mpi-inf.mpg.de/yago-naga/yago

4.1 Tag Enrichment

Although concepts are inferred based on the content of each tag, it is possible to improve the classification results by enriching the set of tags with related terms that users usually use together to tag a resource. When more tags are available, the classifier will be able to better predict concepts because more information will be analyzed about the content.

The tag enrichment procedure is implemented in our system by considering a number of related terms t' to a given tag t. This relatedness between tags is defined proportionally to the edge weights of the tag folksonomy; consequently, given a tag $t \in T$, the tags that are most related to it are all the tags $t' \in T$ with $t \neq t'$ such that $w(t, t')$ is maximal.

As a result of gathering the related terms from all tags $t \in T_s$, we obtain a list R_s composed of related terms and associated weights. A weight value is calculated according to the corresponding term's frequency of retrieval by using all tags t. Then, these weights are used to sort the list in descending order.

We empirically define a minimal number of tags $\bar{T}$ to allow each item to be classified. We run the experiments with a development dataset ranging such parameter, and then, the best minimal number of tags was chosen to be used during evaluation on the testset.

The value of $|\bar{T}|$ includes the terms already associated by the user, plus the related terms obtained from the tag folksonomy. Thus, we consider the n_s first terms from list R_s, whose value is given by:

$$n_s = \begin{cases} |\bar{T}| - |T_s| & \text{if } |T_s| < |\bar{T}| \text{ , or} \\ 0 & \text{otherwise.} \end{cases} \quad (1)$$

4.2 Direct Recognition

The annotation task effectively starts with direct recognition (Figure 4 (d)), which will check whether a user has tagged an item with a term that explicitly refers to a concept. For instance, if one has tagged an image with "flowers", so one of the image's concepts will be "flower".

With the objective to improve the results of direct recognition, we also consider the fact that many tags may be in the plural or singular forms, and users may use a synonym word to refer to the same concept. Thus, we first use an inflector object to transform all tags and concepts to their singular form, in addition to a synonym vocabulary that contains different synonyms for each concept. Consequently, if user has tagged an item with "architecture", so the system will check it is a synonym of "structure", and finally, as all concepts and tags will be in the singular, it will classify the item with the predefined concept "structures".

4.3 Most Frequent Concepts

The next step of concept annotation is to obtain the most frequent concepts by tag using the concept-tag relation described in Subsection 3.2. Given a tag $t \in T_s$, we collect the C_t most frequent concepts related to it, i.e., C_t will have a subset of concepts $c \in C$ such that $w(c, t)$ is maximal.

Once we have some concepts candidates given by C_t, it is still necessary to check if they are semantically related to the tag t. This is because the concept-tag relation only provides concepts relying on statistic information, it does not ensure that the most frequent concepts have a semantic relation to the given tag. For instance, the tag "explore" is frequently used by users to tag resources in many contexts, though it is not semantically related to the item's actual concepts. Consequently, if this tag is used to retrieve the most frequent concepts, the list will be prone to noise. To solve this problem, we use two semantic similarity measures to decide whether $c' \in C_t$ will be adopted in final annotation or not. The first measure, sim_{wp}, is the Wu & Palmer approach [33], which is based on the topology of the WordNet ontology. The second one, sim_{res}, is the Resnik semantic similarity measure [27], which is based on information content.

Therefore, our algorithm will combine both similarity measures in order to find a concept $c' \in C_t$ that is semantically related to tag t, that is:

$$c_s = \begin{cases} c' & \text{if } sim_{wp}(\max_{c' \in C_t}[sim_{res}(c', t)], t) \geq \Gamma \\ \oslash & \text{otherwise} \end{cases} , \quad (2)$$

where Γ is a threshold.

This process is executed for all tags associated to item s. Thus, the system will find a set of concepts C_s such that each element $c_s \in C_s$ is a concept that is most semantically similar to a tag $t \in T_s$.

4.4 Generic Concepts Recognition

As the final step of the annotation task, the generic concepts recognition module uses the concepts ontology which was created during training. It is worth to mention that we use co-occurrence of concepts to highlight possible relations among them, but the real association between generic terms and specialized ones is defined manually.

Table 1: Concepts ontology.

Generic	Specialized
animals	bird, dog
people	baby, female, male
people	portrait
indoor	food
transport	car
sky	cloud
plant_life	tree, flower
water	river, lake, sea

In this paper, we consider the set of 24 different concepts which were defined in the MIRFLICKR-25k dataset [9]. This dataset was chosen because it provides a fair amount of manually annotated images with semantic concepts, in addition to textual descriptions provided by users.

Considering the set of concepts and their co-occurrence, Table 1 lists the semantic relations used in this paper. Therefore, if the classifiers direct recognition or most frequent concepts assigned one of the specialized terms illustrated in Table 1 (for instance, "car"), then in this classification phase the generic concept (in the example, "transport") will also be annotated on the multimedia item.

5. EVALUATION

This section describes the experimental results and evaluation executed in the system. It consists of comparing the performance of the proposed algorithm with other approaches available in the literature. We chose as baseline the Naïve Bayes classifier with Laplace (add-1) smoothing [12], because it also performs concept classification based on statistics information and probabilities of terms and classes. Both approaches were executed with the same datasets, and a variety of known metrics related to classification and information retrieval fields were used, harvesting different aspects of the proposed technique's performance.

5.1 Preparation

The experiments were executed over a large scale dataset composed of training and test images with associated tags. The MIRFLICKR-25k dataset [9] were adopted; it was divided into 15,000 images for training and 10,000 images for test. The training set corresponds to 133,662 raw tags, which were filtered, remaining 72,590 tags. This subset of images, tags and concepts were used to create the tag and concept folksonomies, in addition to the concept-tag relation table.

From the test subset, we selected for evaluation only those with at least one remaining tag after filtering, corresponding to 8,368 images. The associated concepts, in turn, were used as ground truth to evaluate our algorithm. The concept predictions were compared against the ground truth in order to support the evaluation metrics which will be described in the following subsections. It is worth mentioning that the MIRFLICKR dataset provides 24 different concepts which are manually associated to all 25,000 images. Some of these concepts are also divided into potential and relevant concepts; but in our experiments, we did not considered such difference, assuming that all associations are relevant for the classification. More details about the dataset used in this evaluation can be found in the dataset website[7] and corresponding paper [9].

In order to run the experiments, we empirically defined the parameters of the classifier. The value of $|\bar{T}|$ was set to 20; the value of $|C_t|$ was set to 5; and the threshold Γ was set to 0.7.

5.2 Overall Results

Table 2 presents the overall results of both classifiers. The symbols P_{micro}, R_{micro}, P_{macro}, R_{macro} and MAP correspond, respectively, to the metrics: micro average precision, micro average recall, macro average precision, macro average recall and mean average precision. The macro averaging metric computes precision and recall performance for each class, and then, average the results. The micro averaging, on the other hand, collects decisions for all classes, computes the contingency table, and then, calculates precision and recall. While the first gives the same weight for all concepts regardless of dominant and common ones, the second is dominated by score on common classes [12]. The MAP is computed according to the 11-point average precision metric, which will be described in next subsection.

Table 2: Overall Results.

Classifier	P_{micro}	R_{micro}	P_{macro}	R_{macro}	MAP
Bayes	0.3869	0.3654	0.2828	0.2970	0.4737
Proposed	0.4915	0.4174	0.4954	0.4385	0.5240

From Table 2 it is possible to visualize an overall improvement of the proposed approach performance over the baseline algorithm, whose MAP increased from 0.4737 to 0.5240. In addition, comparing the micro and macro averaging scores for a single classifier, one can note that Naïve Bayes achieved considerably different values, whose precision/recall scored 0.3869/0.3654 for the micro averaging, and 0.2828/0.2970 for the macro averaging. This high difference between micro and macro averaging scores did not occur with the proposed algorithm, whose precision/recall were 0.4915/0.4174 for the micro, and 0.4954/0.4385 for the macro averaging. Such difference in the Naïve Bayes classifier suggests that the prediction of some concepts had a significant poor performance, which decreased the component scores of the macro averaging. As the proposed algorithm achieved similar scores in micro and macro averaging, it suggests that most concepts were able to be predicted equally.

Such feature of having similar performance in all available concepts is an important factor in the context of content annotation and classification. For instance, if the annotated multimedia items are going to be used in information retrieval applications, it should be better to have as many descriptions about semantic concepts as possible, once the user may be willing to search content about a particular subject of interest.

[7]http://press.liacs.nl/mirflickr/

5.3 11-Point Average Precision

The mean average precision (MAP) provides a single-figure measure of quality across recall levels. Its calculation is based on the average precision of a single information need. As analogy, for the MAP values presented in Table 2, we consider an information need as the classification of a single image, being the set of predicted concepts the rank of retrieved documents. In addition, in order to better represent the results of this single information need, we use the 11-point average precision metric [22] to define precision scores for each standard recall value.

Figure 5 presents the averaged 11-point recall versus precision graph containing the performance of both classifiers. For each percent of concepts predicted (recall values), the average precision of all tested images was computed, being represented in Figure 5 by a single value on the y axis. It is possible to note a clear improvement of the proposed approach over the baseline algorithm for all levels of recall. In particular, when recall achieves 80% or more of all concepts predicted, one can visualize that precision has decayed significantly, suggesting that some of the concepts are being predicted wrongly.

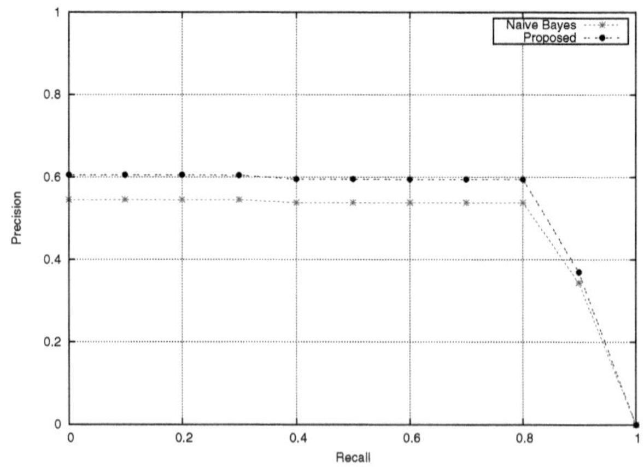

Figure 5: 11-point average precision.

5.4 Concept Results

In this subsection, we present the results for each concept using the F1 metric [20]. This metric was chosen because it captures the trade-off between precision and recall in a single value, which can be used for characterizing the system's performance.

Figure 6 shows the F1 results by concept for both considered classifiers. Comparing both approaches, it can be noted that the proposed algorithm was more effective for most considered concepts. Only in case of some generic ones, such as "female", "indoor" and "people", the Naïve Bayes predictor was able to outperform our approach. In particular, the poor performance of our algorithm can be explained by the fact that as these concepts are generic, lots of distinct tags will be used to describe the content. Consequently, if used the concept-tag relation table to infer most relevant concepts for a given tag, the results will be rather broad. For instance, according to the dataset's computed folksonomy, the most relevant tags for the concept "indoor" are: "portrait", "ikon", "food" and "dog", which are semantically broad among themselves; on the other hand, the most relevant tags for the concept "bird" are: "birds", "nature", "animal" and "wildlife", which are more semantically related to the specific concept "bird". In this way, predicting more specialized concepts using the proposed algorithm may result in better performance when compared to the prediction of more generic ones, and research about how to solve this problem is left as future work.

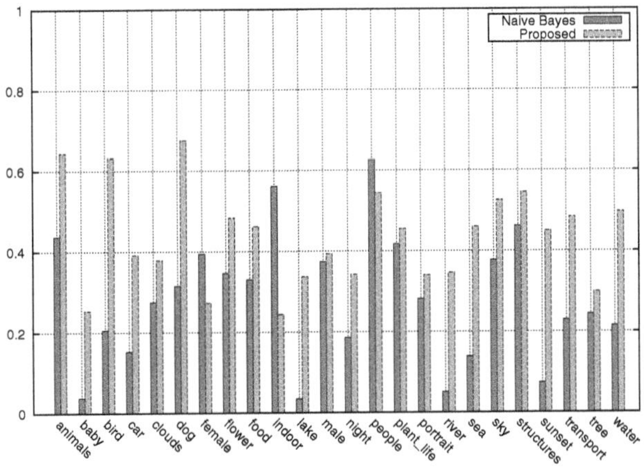

Figure 6: F1 measure histogram.

5.5 Number of Tags

In this subsection, we present the results for each classifier by clustering the images which have the same number of associated tags. For each set of images with same amount of tags, we calculated the MAP for the considered classifiers, resulting in the graph illustrated in Figure 7.

Once the value of $|\bar{T}|$ was set to 20 in our experiments, one can note that for $|T_s| \leq 20$ the proposed algorithm had better performance than the baseline. This shows the effectiveness of the tag enrichment phase, which provided related terms to those images containing only a few tags prior to classification. In addition, when $20 < |T_s| < 38$, the proposed approach outperformed Naïve Bayes in most cases, demonstrating that other modules of the algorithm were also able to improve the quality of the results.

When considering higher values for $|\bar{T}|$, our experience demonstrated that too much noise would be aggregated into the list of tags, affecting the overall results. Thus, the tag enrichment module is useful to relate more terms to items whose number of associated tags is low. This is particularly important because our technique relies only on available tags, and if this information is not present or enough, then it cannot successfully predict concepts.

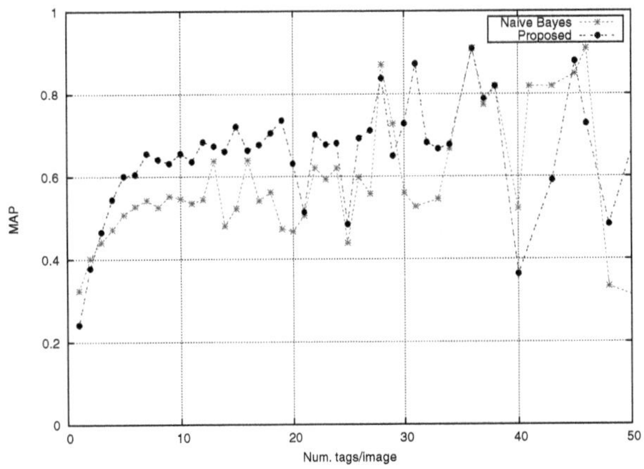

Figure 7: Results by number of tags.

6. FINAL REMARKS

This paper presented an automatic annotation algorithm which uses different strategies based on co-occurrence of tags and concepts in order to reduce two problems related to the use of tags in classification: noise and incompleteness. The first one is supported by a multi-phase filtering procedure that amends misspelled tags and considers only those semantically related to the actual context of the item. The second one, in turn, is reduced with a tag enrichment activity which aggregates related terms to the actual list of tags in order to make annotation more effective.

Our main contribution is the provision of an automatic annotation tool which can be adapted according to the application scenario, as opposite to approaches based on visual features that usually have to know beforehand the characteristics of the actual domain. Our approach is generic because it is based on folksonomies, which are a dynamic structure that reflects the actual activities of users.

As future work, we plan to investigate how to improve the results of concept annotation, in particular the generic ones which do not have significant related and meaningful tags to support statistic-based predictions. In addition, the problem of ambiguous and subjective tags will be investigated in order to define the real meaning of each tag according to the item's actual context.

7. ACKNOWLEDGMENTS

The authors would like to thank the financial support from FAPESP, process number 2011/17366-2.

8. REFERENCES

[1] R. A. Batal and P. Mulhem. MRIM-LIG at ImageCLEF 2010 Visual Concept Detection and Annotation task. In *Working Notes of CLEF 2010*, Padua, Italy, 2010.

[2] D. Brezeale and D. J. Cook. Automatic Video Classification: A Survey of the Literature. *IEEE*

Transactions on Systems, Man, and Cybernetics, 38(3):416–430, 2007.

[3] I. Cantador, M. Szomszor, H. Alani, M. Fernández, and P. Castells. Enriching Ontological User Profiles with Tagging History for Multi-Domain Recommendations. In *1st International Workshop on Collective Semantics: Collective Intelligence & the Semantic Web (CISWeb 2008)*, Tenerife, Spain, 2008.

[4] C. Cattuto, D. Benz, A. Hotho, and G. Stumme. Semantic Grounding of Tag Relatedness in Social Bookmarking Systems. In A. P. Sheth, S. Staab, M. Dean, M. Paolucci, D. Maynard, T. W. Finin, and K. Thirunarayan, editors, *The Semantic Web - ISWC 2008*, volume 5318 of *Lecture Notes in Computer Science*, pages 615–631, Berlin/Heidelberg, 2008. Springer.

[5] B. Daroczy, I. Petras, A. A. Benczur, D. Nemeskey, and R. Pethes. SZTAKI @ ImageCLEF 2010. In *Working Notes of CLEF 2010*, Padua, Italy, 2010.

[6] I. Dimitrovski, D. Kocev, S. Loskovska, and S. Dzeroski. Detection of Visual COncepts and Annotation of Images using Predictive Clustering Trees. In *Working Notes of CLEF 2010*, Padua, Italy, 2010.

[7] A. Fakeri-Tabrizi, S. Tollari, N. Usunier, M. R. Amini, and P. Gallinari. UPMC/LIP6 at ImageCLEF annotation 2010. In *Working Notes of CLEF 2010*, Padua, Italy, 2010.

[8] J. S. Hare, P. H. Lewis, P. G. B. Enser, and C. J. S. A linear-algebraic technique with an application in semantic image retrieval. In *Proceedings of the International Conference on Image and Video Retrieval*, pages 31–40. Springer, 2006.

[9] M. J. Huiskes and M. S. Lew. The mir flickr retrieval evaluation. In *MIR '08: Proceedings of the 2008 ACM International Conference on Multimedia Information Retrieval*, New York, NY, USA, 2008. ACM.

[10] Y. A. Lacerda, H. F. de Figueiredo, C. de Souza Baptista, and A. C. de Paiva. Expandindo e utilizando informacoes de contexto para a sugestao de anotacoes de fotografias digitais. In *Proceedings of the 14th Brazilian Symposium on Multimedia and the Web*, WebMedia '08, pages 162–169, New York, NY, USA, 2008. ACM.

[11] W. Li, J. Min, and G. J. F. Jones. A Text-Based Approach to the ImageCLEF 2010 Photo Annotation Task. In *Working Notes of CLEF 2010*, Padua, Italy, 2010.

[12] C. D. Manning, P. Raghavan, and H. Schtze. *Introduction to Information Retrieval.* Cambridge University Press, New York, NY, USA, 2008.

[13] E. Mbanya, C. Hentschel, S. Gerke, M. Liu, A. Nurnberger, and P. Ndjiki-Nya. Augmenting Bag-of-Words - Category Specific Features and Concept Reasoning. In *Working Notes of CLEF 2010*, Padua, Italy, 2010.

[14] T. Mensink, G. Csurka, F. Perronnin, J. Sánchez, and J. Verbeek. LEAR and XRCE's participation to Visual Concept Detection Task – ImageCLEF 2010. In *Working Notes of CLEF 2010*, Padua, Italy, 2010.

[15] N. Motohashi, R. Izawa, and T. Takagi. Meiji University at ImageCLEF2010 Visual Concept Detection and Annotation Task. In *Working Notes of CLEF 2010*, Padua, Italy, 2010.

[16] M. Naaman, S. Harada, Q. Wang, H. Garcia-Molina, and A. Paepcke. Context data in geo-referenced digital photo collections. In *Proceedings of the 12th annual ACM international conference on Multimedia*, MULTIMEDIA '04, pages 196–203, New York, NY, USA, 2004. ACM.

[17] S. Paris and H. Glotin. Linear SVM for LSIS Pyramidal Multi-Level Visual only Concept Detection in CLEF 2010 Challenge. In *Working Notes of CLEF 2010*, Padua, Italy, 2010.

[18] S. N. Patel and G. D. Abowd. The ContextCam: Automated Point of Capture Video Annotation. In F. Khendek and R. Dssouli, editors, *UbiComp 2004: Ubiquitous Computing*, volume 3205 of *Lecture Notes in Computer Science*, pages 301–318. Springer, 2004.

[19] C. Rasche and C. Vertan. A Novel Structural-Description Approach for Image Retrieval. In *Working Notes of CLEF 2010*, Padua, Italy, 2010.

[20] C. J. V. Rijsbergen. *Information Retrieval.* Butterworth-Heinemann, 2nd edition, 1979.

[21] H. Sahbi and X. Li. TELECOM ParisTech at ImageCLEF 2010 Photo Annotation Task: COmbining Tags and Visual Features for Learning-Based Image Annotation. In *Working Notes of CLEF 2010*, Padua, Italy, 2010.

[22] F. Sebastiani. Machine learning in automated text categorization. *ACM Comput. Surv.*, 34, 2002.

[23] R. Shi, C.-H. Lee, and T.-S. Chua. Enhancing image annotation by integrating concept ontology and text-based bayesian learning model. In *Proceedings of the 15th international conference on Multimedia*, MULTIMEDIA '07, pages 341–344, New York, NY, USA, 2007. ACM.

[24] A. W. M. Smeulders, M. Worring, S. Santini, A. Gupta, and R. Jain. Content-Based Image Retrieval at the End of the Early Years. *IEEE Transactions on Pattern Analysis and Machine Intelligence*, 22(12):1349–1380, 2000.

[25] M. Srikanth, J. Varner, M. Bowden, and D. Moldovan. Exploiting ontologies for automatic image annotation. In *Proceedings of the 28th annual international ACM SIGIR conference on Research and development in information retrieval*, SIGIR '05, pages 552–558, New York, NY, USA, 2005. ACM.

[26] M. Stanek and O. Maier. The Wroclaw University of Technology Participation at ImageCLEF 2010 Photo Annotation Track. In *Working Notes of CLEF 2010*, Padua, Italy, 2010.

[27] P. R. Sun. Using information content to evaluate semantic similarity in a taxonomy. In *In Proceedings of the 14th International Joint Conference on Artificial Intelligence*, pages 448–453, 1995.

[28] J. Tang, R. Hong, S. Yan, T.-S. Chua, G.-J. Qi, and R. Jain. Image annotation by kNN-sparse graph-based label propagation over noisily tagged web images. *ACM Transactions on Intelligent Systems and Technology*, 2:14:1–14:15, 2011.

[29] J. Tang, S. Yan, R. Hong, G.-J. Qi, and T.-S. Chua. Inferring semantic concepts from community-contributed images and noisy tags. In W. Gao, Y. Rui, A. Hanjalic, C. Xu, E. G. Steinbach, A. El-Saddik, and M. X. Zhou, editors, *ACM Multimedia*, pages 223–232. ACM, 2009.

[30] K. E. A. van de Sande and T. Gevers. The University of Amsterdam's Concept Detection System at ImageClEF 2010. In *Working Notes of CLEF 2010*, Padua, Italy, 2010.

[31] J. Verbeek, M. Guillaumin, T. Mensink, and C. Schmid. Image Annotation with TagProp on the MIRFLICKR set. In *11th ACM International Conference on Multimedia Information Retrieval (MIR '10)*, pages 537–546, Philadephia, USA, 2010. ACM Press.

[32] W. Viana, A. Miron, B. Moisuc, J. Gensel, M. Villanova-Oliver, and H. Martin. Towards the semantic and context-aware management of mobile multimedia. *Multimedia Tools and Applications*, 53:391–429, 2011.

[33] Z. Wu and M. Palmer. Verbs semantics and lexical selection. In *Proceedings of the 32nd annual meeting on Association for Computational Linguistics*, pages 133–138, Stroudsburg, PA, USA, 1994. Association for Computational Linguistics.

[34] D. Zhang, B. Liu, C. Sun, and X. Wang. Random Sampling Image to Class DIstance for Photo Annotation. In *Working Notes of CLEF 2010*, Padua, Italy, 2010.

[35] S. Zhu, G. Wang, C.-W. Ngo, and Y.-G. Jiang. On the sampling of web images for learning visual concept classifiers. In *Proceedings of the ACM International Conference on Image and Video Retrieval*, CIVR '10, pages 50–57, New York, USA, 2010.

Browsing Interaction Events in Recordings of Small Group Activities via Multimedia Operators

Diogo S. Martins, Maria da Graça C. Pimentel
Instituto de Ciências Matemáticas e de Computação
Universidade de São Paulo
São Carlos, SP, Brazil
{diogosm, mgp}@icmc.usp.br

ABSTRACT

The recording of multimedia sessions of small group activities, such as meetings, lectures and webconferences, is becoming increasingly popular following the improvements in recording technologies, the popularity of web-based media repositories, and the opportunity of reviewing or sharing the activity in a later moment. When reviewing a (potentially long) multimedia session, a user may not be interested in watching it linearly as a whole, but only on browsing or skimming specific fragments of interest. For tackling this requirement, the literature reports the opportunity of indexing interaction events that typically occur in these activities, such as slide transitions, speech turns and gestures. In this paper we investigate the issue of combining different types of interaction events as an aid to navigate in multimedia sessions. First, we define temporal interval-based composition operators so that the semantics of groups of annotations can be orchestrated in queries. Second, we demonstrate the operators in a web-based multimedia player that enable users to browse a multimedia session with the aid of visualizations and filters over interaction-focused annotations. In order to experiment with the model, we report a case study with multimedia information recorded by a capture environment in use.

Categories and Subject Descriptors

H.5.1 [**Information Interfaces and Presentation**]: Multimedia Information systems—*Audio, Video*; H.5.4 [**Information Interfaces and Presentation**]: Hypertext/Hypermedia—*Navigation*

Keywords

multimedia browsing, capture and access, multimedia events, document engineering

Permission to make digital or hard copies of all or part of this work for personal or classroom use is granted without fee provided that copies are not made or distributed for profit or commercial advantage and that copies bear this notice and the full citation on the first page. To copy otherwise, to republish, to post on servers or to redistribute to lists, requires prior specific permission and/or a fee.
WebMedia'12, October 15–18, 2012, São Paulo/SP, Brazil.
Copyright 2012 ACM 978-1-4503-1706-1/12/10 ...$15.00.

1. INTRODUCTION

Small group activities such as meetings, lectures and webconferences are commonly recorded so that the activity can be revisited later by the participants or shared with someone who was not present in the live experience. In the case of multimedia recordings of these activities, it is recurrent the capture of a session composed of temporally synchronized media streams (e.g. audio, video, slides, screen sharing, etc.), aggregated in a linear video or in a declarative multimedia document. In some situations, a user reviewing a session is not interested in watching all the content linearly, but he is interested in reviewing or skimming only specific fragments of interest [12]. This requirement on focused intra-session navigation raises the need for the generation of indexes to specific events that are reported in fragments of the session.

The general problem of indexing humans and their actions in visual multimedia streams has been largely studied in the multimedia literature [2]. Particularly in the case of small group activities, a recurrent alternative for tackling this problem has been the indexing of interaction events that are typical in these scenarios, gathered via sensor-based sources (e.g. via mobile devices or instrumented rooms) [24] or content-based sources (e.g. analysis of audio utterances or computer vision methods on videos) [13, 14]. The level of abstraction of the indexed interactions can vary from low-level physical actions (e.g. change of slides, live annotations, speech turn taking, primitive gestures, addressing, nodding, etc.) [15, 18] to high-level behaviors (such as decisions, disagreement, dominance, extroversion, social roles, competition, personality states, etc.) [17, 8]. The utility of interaction events as cues for reviewing a session has been positively assessed by several user studies in different small group configurations, such as meetings [17, 16] and webcasts [7].

In order to improve the level of abstraction of the events, the literature suggests the opportunity of combining low level interaction events to generate higher level interaction events by means of composition relationships. For instance, hypotheses regarding the occurrence of these patterns have been investigated in the analysis of voice utterances to derive dialogue acts [25] and the discrimination among brainstorming and decision-making discussions [11]. The analysis of composite interaction patterns have also been investigated in the context of recordings from doctor-patient interviews [15]. These research results suggest the feasibility of combining low-level interaction cues in order to make sense of specific events in small group activities, opening up possibilities for better session browsing mechanisms.

Aiming at these problems and opportunities, in this paper we tackle the issue of combining the semantics of various interaction events for reviewing a session, for instance when a user desires to express a complex information request about fragments of the recording. For this purpose, the primary contribution of this paper is the definition of a group of temporal composition operators in order to combine time-indexed multimedia annotations of interaction events. These operators, founded on interval logics and set-theoretic interval algebra, extend a model of interaction events that was developed for indexing small group activities. We demonstrate the applicability of the operators in the context of a web-based session browser that enable users to synchronously visualize and filter the recordings based on the visual formulation of queries.

The remaining of this paper is organized as follows. Section 2 compares the contribution of this research to related approaches in the field of meeting and lecture browsing. Section 3 review the conceptual background on which the composition operators are built upon, namely the Interactors conceptual model and annotation operators. Section 4 presents the definitions of the composition operators and related concepts. Section 5 discuss the most important issues on the design of multimedia player for reviewing sessions using the composition operators. Section 6 demonstrate the use of the composition operators in experimental information obtained from a capture environment. Finally, Section 7 concludes the paper and indicates directions for future research efforts.

2. RELATED WORK

Much research on multimedia applied to the domain of meetings and lectures has been concentrated on design and evaluation of specific purpose mechanisms for browsing captured sessions. These contributions include the design of meeting and lecture browsers, which are tools that provide users with access interfaces to navigate multimedia recordings using different types of annotation indexes. In the context of meetings, Whittaker et al. [23] categorize browsers according to the available types of indexes. Audio-based browsers [19] generally focus on events such as speaker turns, pause detection and emphasis; video browsers explore keyframes and observable participant behavior; artifact browsers [1, 16] enable navigation by means of user-media interaction such as slide changes, ink-based notes and document sharing; and discourse-based browsers concentrate on navigation of speech transcripts, named entities and perceivable emotions [12]. Focusing on a single modality, these browsers have limited applicability to environments that can exploit multimodal media sources, such as webconferencing systems and smart meeting rooms.

Multimodal browsers tackle this problem by providing synchronized access to multiple media streams as they use indexes obtained from several sources. Popescu-Belis et al. [17] report a meeting browser that enables the synchronized navigation of points of interest that occur in a recording based on speaker turns, speech transcripts, slide turns, etc. The browser developed by Behera et al [4] provides random access to points of interest in a meeting session considering video, whiteboard, speech transcripts and documents. Geyer et al. [9] discuss a browser for synchronized navigation of slides and video based on speaker turns, action items and agenda items.

An outstanding characteristic of multimodal browsers is that they provide synchronized access to the multimedia session using a collection of indexes which entail different perspectives of the real-world experience. On the other hand, while these browsers generally enable users to access random points in a session timeline, they do not provide means for users to establish composition relationships between the various indexes to express an information request. In order to tackle this limitation, in the remaining of this paper we define and demonstrate a family of operators that enable the composition of the various indexes available in a multimedia session, thus providing more flexible navigation and exploration of recorded information.

3. BACKGROUND: CONCEPTUAL MODEL AND ANNOTATION OPERATORS

In this section we review the conceptual model and the annotation operators that serve as an extension basis for the composition operators reported in Section 4. The Interactors model was conceived to abstract important issues in indexing and browsing of interaction events generated along a multimedia production process. The model includes three components: *i)* a conceptual model that acts as a reference for structuring interaction events; *ii)* a collection of annotation operators abstracted from selections and restrictions over the conceptual model; and *iii)* a collection of composition operators to orchestrate the annotation operators and select fragments of an indexed session. In the remaining of the section we provide an overview of the conceptual model and the annotation operators.

3.1 Interactors conceptual model

The Interactors conceptual model depicted in Figure 1 acts as a reference for modeling the interaction events that occur in a experience. To that extent, the model represents an interaction event as a central concept and structures the information that characterizes an event as associated dimensions, each one represented by the association of one or more concept hierarchies (omitted in the figure due to space restrictions). Dimensions referring to the following upper entities are defined: interaction, media, space and time. The *interaction dimension* aggregates the types of agents that participate in a interaction event and the types of interactions in which these agents engage. The *media dimension* encompasses the several media aggregated in a session and the temporal relationships between them. The *spatial dimension* is composed of valid space and session space: valid space refers to the spatial framing of an interaction event in the real world whereas session space refers to the spatial representation or rendering of the interaction event in the visual media elements comprised in a session. Finally, the *time dimension* models the concepts related to the temporal scopes of a session. The concepts in the time dimension have instrumental importance in the construction of the composition operators. Due to this fact, in the following we concentrate on the main definitions of the time dimension, starting with some temporal primitives.

Definition 1. **Temporal primitives**. A temporal domain $\{t_1, t_2, t_3, ...\}$ is an infinite connected set of totally ordered discrete points where $t_k \in \mathbb{N}$. A time interval

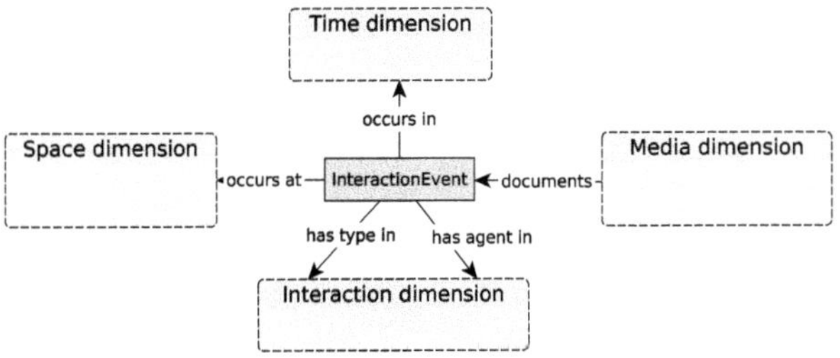

Figure 1: Overview of Interactors conceptual model

$I = [t_a, t_b]$ is a set of consecutive points in the temporal domain, so that $I = \{t_a, t_{a+1}, t_{a+2}, ..., t_b\}$. The duration Δ of a time interval $I = [t_a, t_b]$ is $\Delta_I = t_b - t_a$. An absolute timeline is an interval in the temporal domain. Let $S = \{I_1, I_2, ..., I_n\}$ be an ordered set of disjoint time intervals. The contiguous alignment E_S of S is the ordering of all time points in the interval S. If b and e denote the beginning and end of an interval in the set S respectively, the contiguous alignment of S is represented as $E_S = \{t_{1b}, ...t_{1e}, t_{2b}, ..., t_{2e}, ..., t_{nb}, ..., t_{ne}\}$. A connected transformation over a continuous alignment is obtained by sequentially indexing the positions of each element in the contiguous alignment, namely $\{0, 1, 2, 3, ..., k-1\}$, provided that $|E_S| = k$. A relative timeline of S is the result of a connected transformation over E_S.

Definition 2. The *time dimension* comprises two distinct entities: the valid time and the session time. Valid time is an interval $V = [t_v, t_x]$ that specifies the time interval of the session in the absolute timeline of the session. Session time is an interval $S = [t_0, t_{k-1}]$ that specifies a time interval in the relative timeline of the session. The absolute timeline represents the valid timeline. The relative timeline represents the session timeline.

The time dimension is also used to define the temporal scope of a session.

Definition 3. A *session* is a a tuple (E, T) where E is a set of discrete and continuous media elements and T is a set of temporal constraints specifying the synchronization of the media elements in reference to the session timeline.

3.2 The annotation operators

An annotation operator abstracts two issues: *i)* a class of interaction events; and *ii)* a mechanism for associating instances of a class to fragments of the session. An interaction event is an action that occurs when two or more agents have an effect upon each other. Interaction events physically occur in the valid space and valid time scopes and are documented in the session time and session space scopes. Moreover, events are documented by one or more media elements aggregated in a session.

Definition 4. The *event space* is a 5-ary relation $E = (A, I, T_v, S_v, M)$ that represents all interaction events captured in a session, where:

- A is a set of agents;
- I is a set of interaction instances;
- T_v is a set of valid time intervals;
- S_v is a set of valid space regions;
- M is a set of media elements in a session;

An *interaction event* is a tuple $(P, i, t, s, N) \in E$ where:

- $P \subseteq A$ is a set of participants in the event;
- $i \in I$ is an interaction instance;
- $t \in T_v$ is the valid time interval when the event occurred;
- $s \in S_v$ is the valid space region where the event occurred;
- $N \subseteq M$ is a set of media elements that report the event.

Provided that the event space aggregates heterogeneous interaction events in an experience, we need some means to associate the interaction events to corresponding fragments in a session. For this purpose we define an *Interactor* as an annotation operator that associates session fragments and interaction events.

Definition 5. An *interactor* is an annotation operator $O = (\alpha, X)$ where α is a filtering operation and X is a labeling function, both defined as follows:

- $\alpha(E, \gamma) = \{e : e \in E, e \models \gamma\}$ is a filtering operation over the event space E, where γ is a composite restriction over the domains of the event space. The composite restriction γ is a propositional formula over the domains of the dimensions involved in an event space. For instance, the composite restriction $\gamma_1 : (a = professor) \wedge (a = pen) \wedge (i = haptics) \wedge (m = ink)$ restricts the event space to the events on which the following restrictions apply: an agent in the professor role interacted with a pen; the interaction is classified as an haptic interaction; this interaction was documented in a media element of type ink stroke.
- $X : \alpha(E, \gamma) \to (l, t_s)$ is a function that associates each element in the filtered event space to a session time interval t_s via an annotation label l.

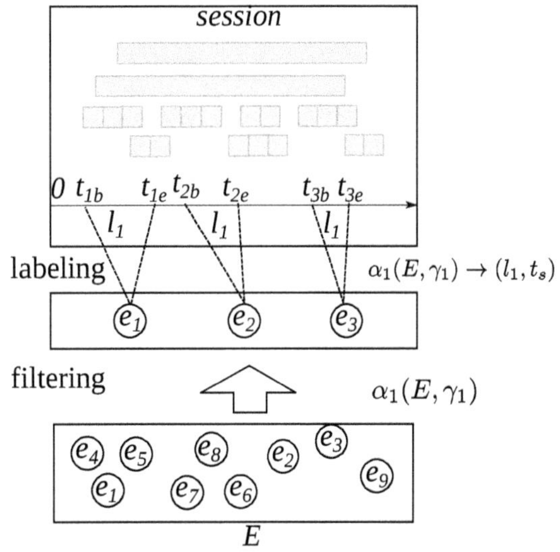

Figure 2: Example of a generic annotation operator

Figure 2 illustrates the behavior of an annotation operator. Suppose that a session defines an event space

$E = \{e_1, e_2, e_3, ..., e_9\}$ and Interactor $O_1 = (\alpha_1, l_1, X_1)$ has been defined. If O_1 applies to the session, then at least one fragment of the session has been associated to a label of type l_1. The operator at first filters the interaction events which satisfy the composite restriction γ_1, so that $\alpha(E, \gamma_1) = \{e_1, e_2, e_3\}$. Then for each filtered event the labeling function assigns a label l_1 to an interval of the session so that $X(\{e1, e2, e3\}) \rightarrow \{(l_1, [t_{1b}, t_{1e}]), (l_1, [t_{2b}, t_{2e}]), (l_1, [t_{3b}, t_{3e}])\}$.

In previous work a family of Interactors have been defined and experimented with [20], including automatic annotations obtained from digital ink annotations (Inkteractors), audio utterance patterns (AudioInteractors), board-based interaction (BoardInteractors), interaction via text messages (TextInteractors) and detection of events from videos (VideoInteractors). All of these types of annotations focus on interactions that occur in small group activities and can be modeled and labeled using the Interactors conceptual model and annotation operators. Building upon this foundation, the next section details the composition operators which enable the combination of these different classes of annotations.

4. TEMPORAL COMPOSITION OPERATORS

The composition operators enable the expression of information needs by orchestrating the semantics of the various annotation operators. Examples of situations on which such operators can be used include dynamic visualizations of the annotations, fact-finding tasks over the session, and summarization of the session based on interaction events. The basic idea of a composition operator is to perform set-theoretic joinings of annotation timelines, provided that each timeline is a sequence of non-overlapping time intervals. Bearing on these principles, we first review preliminary concepts on interval logics and set-theoretic interval arithmetic before defining the composition operators.

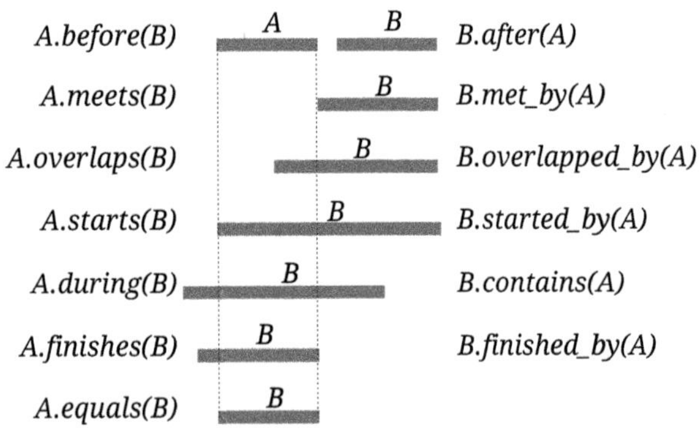

Figure 3: Allen's 13 interval relations [3].

As preliminary concepts for the composition operators, we take as reference the 13 temporal relationships from Allen's interval logic [3] (see Figure 3, where A and B are temporal intervals). Additionally to the relationships in Figure 3, we define three composite relationships as a shorthand notation to common operations.

Definition 6. The composite relationships *left overlaps*, *right overlaps* and *intersects*, among two intervals $A = [a_1, a_2]$ and $B = [b_1, b_2]$, are defined respectively as:

- $A.l\_overlaps(B)$ if $a_1 < b_1 \land a_2 \geq b_1 \land a_2 \leq b2$
- $A.r\_overlaps(B)$ if $a_1 \geq b_1 \land a_1 \leq b_2 \land a_2 > b_2$
- $A.intersects(B)$ if $a_2 \geq b_1 \land a_1 \leq b_2$

The three relationships are interpreted as composite relationships provided that they can be represented by means of atomic relationships, namely:

- $A.l\_overlaps(B) = \begin{array}{l} A.overlaps(B) \lor A.meets(B) \lor \\ A.finished\_by(B) \end{array}$
- $A.r\_overlaps(B) = \begin{array}{l} A.started\_by(B) \lor A.met\_by(B) \lor \\ A.overlapped\_by(B) \end{array}$
- $A.intersects(B)$ if $\neg(A.before(B) \lor A.after(B))$

The extended set of temporal relationships are used to define set-theoretic operations over intervals.

Definition 7. The *union*, *intersection* and *difference* of two intervals $A = [a_1, a_2]$ and $B = [b_1, b_2]$ are defined respectively as:

- $A \cup B = \begin{cases} \begin{array}{l}[min(a_1, b_1), \\ max(a_2, b_2)]\end{array} & \text{if } A.intersects(B) \\ \{[a_1, a_2], [b_1, b_2]\} & \text{otherwise} \end{cases}$
- $A \cap B = \begin{cases} \begin{array}{l}\{[max(a_1, b_1), \\ min(a_2, b_2)]\}\end{array} & \text{if } A.intersects(B) \\ \varnothing & \text{otherwise} \end{cases}$
- $A - B = \begin{cases} A & \text{if } \neg(A.intersects(B)) \\ [a_1, b_1 - 1] & \text{if } A.l\_overlaps(B) \\ [b_2 + 1, a_2] & \text{if } A.r\_overlaps(B) \\ \begin{array}{l}\{[a_1, b_1 - 1], \\ [b_2 + 1, a_2]\}\end{array} & \text{if } A.contains(b) \\ \varnothing & otherwise \end{cases}$

The next definition concerns the temporal representation of an annotation operator.

Definition 8. A sequence of intervals $S = (I_1, I_2, I_3, ..., I_n)$ is a non-overlapping interval sequence if $I_i.before(I_{i+1})$ for every $I_i \in S$. An annotation operator O_i defines its own *annotation timeline* as a finite non-overlapping interval sequence $T_i = (t_{i1}, t_{i2}, ..., t_{ik})$ where $t_{i1}, t_{i2}, ..., t_{ik}$ are intervals of the session timeline in which a label l_i is applied by O_i.

Building upon the definition of an Interactor timeline, we define set-theoretic joinings of the interval sequences. Figure 4 overviews the results of the operators applied to two timelines T_A and T_B.

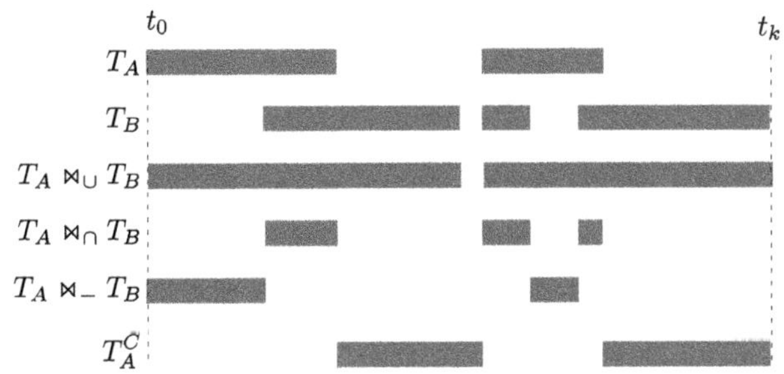

Figure 4: Overview of sample results for the composition operators

Definition 9. A *timeline join operation* is defined as $T_A \bowtie_\varphi T_B = (I_{c1}, I_{c2}, ..., I_{cn})$ where:

1. T_A and T_B are annotation timelines;
2. $T_C = (I_{c1}, ..., I_{cn})$ is a non-overlapping interval sequence;
3. $\varphi \in \{\cap, \cup, -\}$.

According to the variation of φ, different join operations are defined:

- *Intersection join* ($T_A \bowtie_\cap T_B$): $\varphi = \cap$, $I_{ci} = I_{aj} \cap I_{bk}$ where $I_{ci} \in T_C$, $I_{aj} \in T_A$ and $I_{bk} \in T_B$;
- *Union join* ($T_A \bowtie_\cup T_B$): $\varphi = \cup$, $I_{ci} = I_{aj} \cup ... \cup I_{bk}$ where $I_{ci} \in T_C$, $I_{aj} \in T_A$ and $I_{bk} \in T_B$;
- *Difference join* ($T_A \bowtie_- T_B$): $\varphi = -$, $I_{ci} = I_{aj} - I_{bk}$ where $I_{ci} \in T_C$, $I_{aj} \in T_A$ and $I_{bk} \in T_B$.

```
# sa, sb, res are non-overlapping
#   sequences of intervals
def intersection_join(sa, sb):
    ai = 0
    bi = 0
    res = []
    while ai < len(sa) and bi < len(sb):
        a = sa[ai]
        b = sb[bi]
        if a.before(b):
            ai += 1
        elif b.before(a):
            bi += 1
        elif a.intersects(b):
            c = intersect_interval(a,b)
            if a.end > b.end:
                bi += 1
            elif a.end < b.end:
                ai += 1
            else:
                ai += 1
                bi += 1
            res.append(c)
    return res
```

Figure 5: Intersection join algorithm

Provided the restrictions that T_A and T_B are ordered sets of non-overlapping intervals, the intersection join operation can be performed by a linear time algorithm (Figure 5) that in one pass traverses the sequences in parallel and performs the intersections whenever it is possible. An algorithm for the union join operation, suppressed for space limitations, can be designed via an analogous strategy, with the additional restriction that an union accumulator should be maintained so that only the maximal union intervals are included in the resulting sequence. The strategy also applies to the difference join algorithm (Figure 6), but in this case a stack (or, alternatively, an ordered linked list) can be used to help keep preliminary outcomes depending on the number of intervals resulting from interval-interval difference operations.

```
# sa, sb, rs: non-overlapping interval sequences
def difference_join(sa, sb):
    bi = 0
    res = []
    stack_a = sa[:]
    stack_a.reverse()
    while len(stack_a) > 0 and bi < len(sb):
        a = stack_a.pop()
        b = sb[bi]
        # case 1: a before b
        if a.before(b):
            res.append(a)
        # case 2: a after b
        elif a.after(b):
            stack_a.append(a)
            bi += 1
        # case 3: intersection
        elif a.intersects(b):
            c = difference_interval(a, b)
            # case 3.1: one interval
            if len(c) == 1:
                stack_a.append(c[0])
            # case 3.2: two intervals
            elif len(c) == 2:
                res.append(c[0])
                stack_a.append(c[1])
    # flush
    while len(stack_a) > 0:
        res.append(stack_a.pop())
    return res
```

Figure 6: Difference join algorithm

Based on the timeline difference join we define the unary timeline complement as follows.

Definition 10. A *complement operation* of the timeline T_A is the non-overlapping interval sequence $T_A^C = S \bowtie_- T_A$ where $S = [t_0, t_n]$ is the session timeline.

In the next sections we discuss the most important issues related to the integration of the composition operators in a multimedia player that allows users to review recorded sessions using synchronized playback, timeline visualizations and interval-based filters.

5. IMPLEMENTATION

In order to experiment with the operators in a web environment, we developed an HTML5-based multimedia player — Interactors player — that enables users to review a session using automatically generated annotations. In this section we provide an overview of the most important issues regarding the design of the player, whose architecture is depicted in Figure 7.

The majority of the annotation operators of the Interactors taxonomy take action in the capture and post-production phases of the lifecycle of a multimedia session. In the capture phase, low-level interaction events are captured by sensors in instrumented rooms or by event loggers provided by web-based synchronous communication tools; in the post-production phase, the captured signals and low level events are analyzed in order to derive additional events (e.g. speech features such as speaker diarization), and most

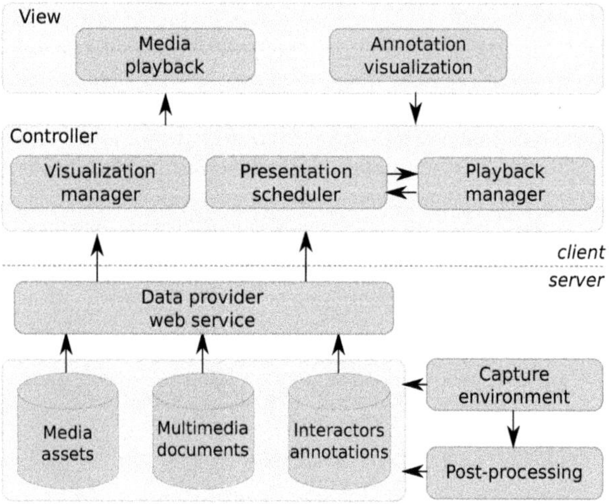

Figure 7: Architecture of the Interactors player

importantly, to apply the annotation operators based on the captured events. All the annotations are stored in a server alongside the captured media assets and their synchronization relationships, the latter used to generate multimedia documents. A web service provides access to the data sources and answers requests for results involving the composition operators.

In the web-based client application, developed in HTML5 [10] and Javascript, a controller component fetches the multimedia documents, the media assets and the annotations. In this component also occurs the construction of structures for visualizing the annotation timelines and the general control of the presentation elements, which are rendered in the view layer. For rendering timelines containing Interactor annotations, user interface widgets are built as scripted SVG (Scallable Vector Graphics) documents.

The execution of multimedia presentations within an HTML5-compliant user agent demands a proper mechanism to manage the complex synchronization relationships between the media elements. Even though the inclusion of continuous media elements is straightforward in HTML5 documents, the specification of inter-element temporal synchronization relationships is not directly supported. In this direction, proposals such as the WHATWG Media Controller [22], based on offsets over parallel media streams, are still in early stages of adoption and not yet implemented in web browsers. Alternative solutions, such as the SMIL timesheets [21] port proposed by Cazenave et al. [6], as well as scripting solutions such as Popcorn.js[1], whereas capable of providing support for many types of synchronization relationships, present limitations when working with multiple videos.

Aiming at these problems, the solution adopted in the Interactors player consists on specifying the timing relationships in structured multimedia documents whereas the presentation is controlled by a scheduling component. The multimedia documents are automatically authored at server-side in HTML5 and contain data attributes (`data-*`) for inline markup of timing relationships based on the SMIL [5] timing model. Figure 8 presents an excerpt of a sample multime-

[1]Popcorn.js media framework: `http://popcornjs.org/`

```
<!-- global container -->
<div id="presentation" data-timecontainer="par">
    <!-- slides container -->
     <div id="slides" data-timecontainer="seq">
        <img id="s0" data-begin="3" data-dur="40"
            src="data/slides/1.png"/>
        <img id="s1" data-dur="40" src="data/slides/2.png"/>
        <img id="s2" data-dur="61" src="data/slides/3.png"/>
        ...
        <img id="s80" data-dur="1" src="data/slides/81.png"/>
    </div>
    <!-- videos container -->
     <div id="videos" data-timecontainer="par">
        <video src="data/videos/lecture.webm" id="v1"
            data-begin="24"></video>
        <video src="data/videos/room.webm" id="v2"
            data-begin="22"></video>
    </div>
    ...
</div>
```

Figure 8: Excerpt of the HTML5-based multimedia document

dia document with the timing attributes highlighted. The global container `presentation` is a `par` time container that will execute the inner containers `slides` and `videos` in parallel. The sequential (`seq`) `slides` container will sequentially execute a playlist of images according to the timing specified by the timing attributes `data-begin` and `data-dur`. Analogously, the parallel (`par`) time container `videos` will execute the two inner video elements in parallel according to the offsets specified by the attribute `data-begin` and finish each video stream according to their intrinsic duration.

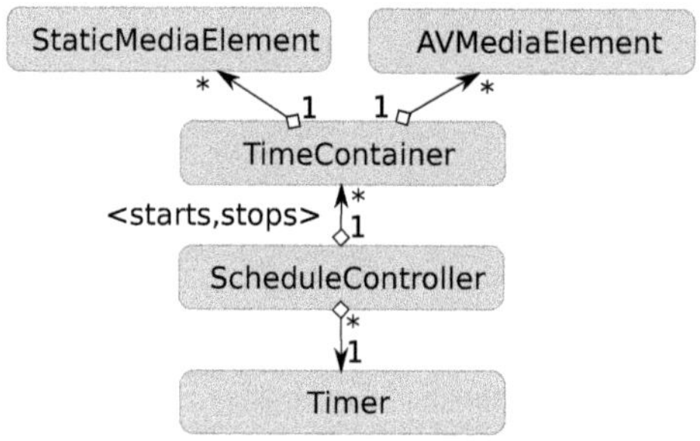

Figure 9: Presentation scheduler architecture

The presentation scheduling component (Figure 9), implemented in Javascript, parses the multimedia document and controls the timing relationships during playback. For this purpose, the class `ScheduleController` builds a schedule tree containing time containers, references to inner media elements and both their explicit and derived timing relationships. The schedule tree, which follows a timeline model, is designed to be efficiently queried for the time intervals that should be activated at any moment. Such approach also enables to seek the presentation to any moment in the session timeline, thus providing proper support for random access in the session according to time-indexed annotations. At presentation time, a global `Timer` is asynchronously and periodically updated to track the presentation timing. The timer also acts as an update trigger for the presentation and as reference to reactivelly keep the multiple videos in sync.

6. CASE STUDY

As a case study we experimented with the Interactors player using a session generated by a working capture environment for collaborative activities. We employed the cap-

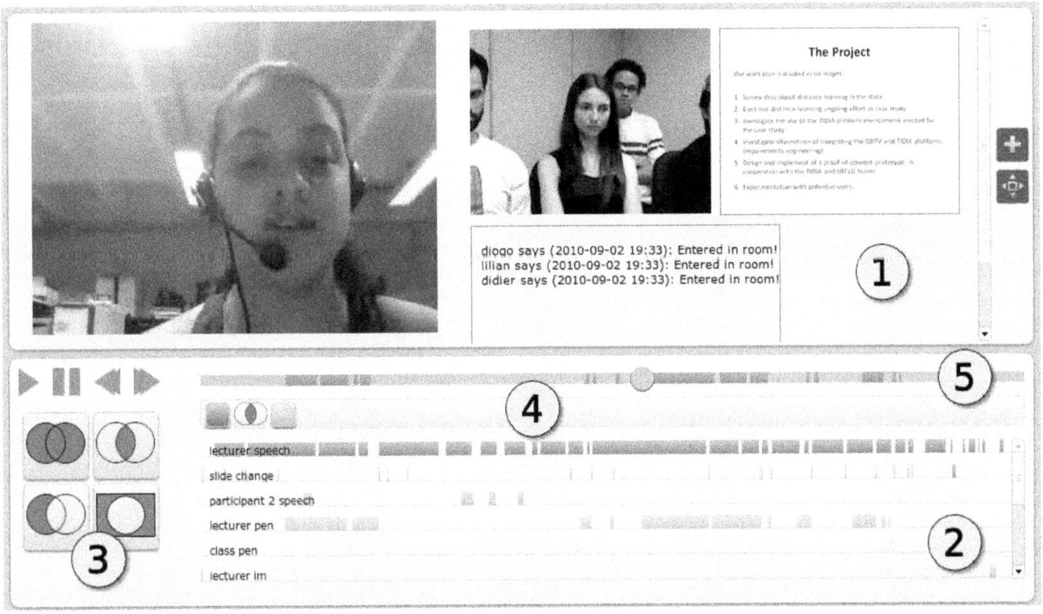

Figure 10: Overview of Interactors player interface

ture environment in a webconference with discussions between a remote lecturer and a group of attendants, which took turns with respect to talking, asking, drawing and typing text. The group of attendants shared an instrumented meeting room whereas the lecturer joined the webconference from a remote location. The lecturer used whiteboard software to load a set of slides and to make ink-based annotations, and shared a chat session and AV conferencing with the remote participants. The capture environment automatically recorded the media assets and captured both the synchronization relationships and the interaction events.

Figure 10 illustrates the Interactors player rendering the multimedia document generated from the session and the associated interaction events. The player has a media presentation region (1) with a main video occupying a large region and secondary media elements occupying a scrollable library to the right. Additional items can be added to the secondary media library (in case of sessions with many media elements) whereas the presentation has a full screen mode for the case of watching the session without the annotations. In the annotations region (2) the annotation timelines are rendered in a list that can be reordered via drag-and-drop or extended with new items from an annotation library (also in the case of sessions with too many timelines).

The playback buttons and composition operators are layed out in the toolbar region (3). Each composition operator, with an icon resembling its equivalent operation via a Venn diagram, can be used by dragging and dropping it to the query construction pane (4). To this region timelines can also be dropped and as a consequence a rectangle surrogate with the same color as the timeline is included in the query pane. The intervals resulting from the query evaluation are presented in the annotated playback timeline (5) which is also the global time slider for the presentation. Figure 10 illustrates a simple query involving a single operator (intersection join) between two timelines, namely lecturer speech (blue) and lecturer pen (yellow). As a result, the annotated playback timeline is updated with the intervals in which the lecturer was annotating a slide while speaking, possibly denoting that an important information in the slides was being subject to attention.

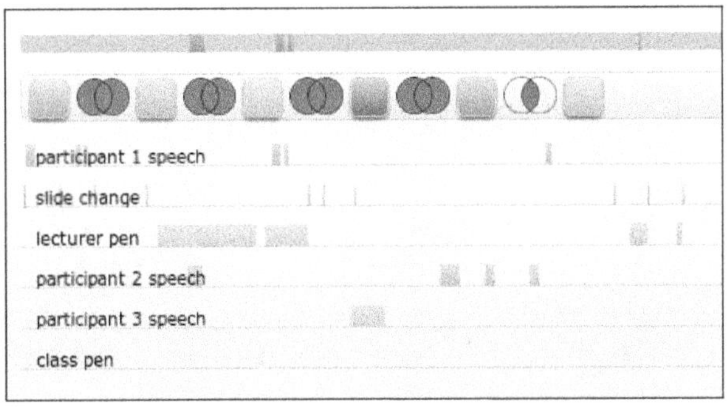

Figure 11: Query pane with a sample query involving several timelines

By combining the composition operators, users can express increasingly complex information needs involving many timelines. Figure 11 illustrates a sample query whose results include the intervals when any of the participants was speaking while the lecturer was annotating slides. This query was obtained by performing the union join of the speech timelines for all the 5 participants and performing the intersection join of the results with the timeline of the lecturer pen annotations.

7. FINAL REMARKS

In this paper we reported the definition of temporal composition operators for combining annotations of interaction events indexed from recordings of small group activities. The applicability of the operators has been verified in a session browser implemented as a web-based multimedia player. With the aid of the operators, the player enables users to visualize the annotations and to orchestrate them in more complex information requests. The most important issues on the design of the player have been stressed out, including the annotation visualization approach and the design of a presentation scheduling component for proper presentation of a session. A case study has been reported on the use of the player with information obtained from a real capture environment.

Currently, the annotation and composition operators in our model consider only intra-session navigation, provided that all Interactors are indexed in reference to the relative timeline of a session. For the situations where a user wishes to search for interaction events spawning through several sessions, for instance in a repository of online lectures, the model should be extended in future work to tackle these issues.

Another direction of future research is the investigation of methods to automatically derive higher level events from low level events. In many situations there is a gap between a high level user information need and the low level events that are indexed in the session. Even though the user-in-the-loop approach adopted in the Interactors player via the composition operators have potential of helping users to bridge this gap, we believe that not all users are willing to engage in formulating query-like information requests. In this direction, we plan to build upon the formalization of the annotation and composition operators in order to develop methods for pattern mining of higher level events and further develop simpler navigation mechanisms for multimedia sessions. This effort will be greatly helped by the execution of user studies to properly evaluate the interaction issues with the multimedia player.

Acknowledgments

We thank CNPq for directly funding this research; and also the volunteers, for participating in the case study.

References

[1] J. Adcock, M. Cooper, L. Denoue, H. Pirsiavash, and L. A. Rowe. Talkminer: a lecture webcast search engine. In *ACM MM '10*, pages 241–250, 2010.

[2] J. Aggarwal and M. Ryoo. Human activity analysis: A review. *ACM Computing Surveys*, 43(3):16,43, 2011.

[3] J. F. Allen. Maintaining knowledge about temporal intervals. *Commun. ACM*, 26(11):832–843, 1983.

[4] A. Behera, D. Lalanne, and R. Ingold. DocMIR: An automatic document-based indexing system for meeting retrieval. *Multimedia Tools and Applications*, 37(2):135–167, 2007.

[5] D. Bulterman and L. Rutledge. *SMIL 3.0: Flexible Multimedia for Web, Mobile Devices and Daisy Talking Books*. Springer Publishing, 2008.

[6] F. Cazenave, V. Quint, and C. Roisin. Timesheets.js: when SMIL meets HTML5 and CSS3. In *Proceedings of the 11th ACM Symposium on Document Engineering*, pages 43–52, 2011.

[7] C. Dufour, J. C. Bartlett, and E. G. Toms. Understanding how webcasts are used as sources of information. *J. Amer. Soc. Inf. Sci. Tech.*, 62(2), 2011.

[8] D. Gatica-Perez. Automatic nonverbal analysis of social interaction in small groups: A review. *Image and Vision Computing*, 27(12):1775–1787, 2009.

[9] W. Geyer, H. Richter, and G. D. Abowd. Towards a Smarter Meeting Record-Capture and Access of Meetings Revisited. *Multimedia Tools and Applications*, 27(3):393–410, 2005.

[10] I. Hickson and D. Hyatt. HTML5: A vocabulary and associated APIs for HTML and XHTML. *W3C Working Draft*, 19, 2010.

[11] D. Jayagopi, T. Kim, A. Pentland, and D. Gatica-Perez. Privacy-sensitive recognition of group conversational context with sociometers. *Multimedia Systems*, 18(1):3–14, 2012.

[12] V. Kalnikaitė, P. Ehlen, and S. Whittaker. Markup as you talk: establishing effective memory cues while still contributing to a meeting. In *Proceedings of the ACM 2012 conference on Computer Supported Cooperative Work*, pages 349–358, 2012.

[13] R. Kaptein and M. Marx. Focused retrieval and result aggregation with political data. *Information retrieval*, 13(5): 412–433, 2010.

[14] D. Korchagin, S. Duffner, P. Motlicek, and C. Scheffler. Multimodal Cue Detection Engine for Orchestrated Entertainment. In *Proceedings of the 18th International Conference on Multimedia Modeling (MMM'12) - LNCS 7131*, pages 662–670, 2012.

[15] Y. Koyama, Y. Sawamoto, Y. Hirano, S. Kajita, K. Mase, T. Suzuki, K. Katsuyama, and K. Yamauchi. A multi-modal dialogue analysis method for medical interviews based on design of interaction corpus. *Personal and Ubiquitous Computing*, 14(8):767–778, 2010.

[16] M. Nathan, M. Topkara, J. Lai, S. Pan, S. Wood, J. Boston, and L. Terveen. In case you missed it: benefits of attendee-shared annotations for non-attendees of remote meetings. In *Proceedings of the ACM 2012 conference on Computer Supported Cooperative Work*, pages 339–348, 2012.

[17] A. Popescu-Belis, D. Lalanne, and H. Bourlard. Finding information in multimedia meeting records. *IEEE Multimedia*, 19(2):48–57, 2012.

[18] J. Terken and J. Sturm. Multimodal support for social dynamics in co-located meetings. *Personal Ubiquitous Comput.*, 14:703–714, December 2010.

[19] G. Tur, A. Stolcke, L. Voss, S. Peters, D. Hakkani-Tur, J. Dowding, B. Favre, R. Fernández, M. Frampton, M. Frandsen, and Others. The CALO meeting assistant system. *Audio, Speech, and Language Processing, IEEE Transactions on*, 18(6):1601–1611, 2010.

[20] D. A. Vega-Oliveros, D. S. Martins, and M. G. C. Pimentel. Media-oriented operators for authoring interactive multimedia documents generated from capture sessions. In *ACM SAC '11*, volume 2, pages 1267–1272, 2011.

[21] P. Vuorimaa, D. Bulterman, and P. Cesar. SMIL Timesheets 1.0. *W3C Working Group Note*, 2008.

[22] WHATWG. The HTML5 video element. URL "http://www.whatwg.org/specs/web-apps/current-work/multipage/the-video-element.html. Accessed in May, 2012.

[23] S. Whittaker, S. Tucker, K. Swampillai, and R. Laban. Design and evaluation of systems to support interaction capture and retrieval. *Personal and Ubiquitous Computing*, 12(3):197–221, 2007.

[24] Z. Yu and Y. Nakamura. Smart meeting systems: A survey of state-of-the-art and open issues. *ACM Computing Surveys*, 42 (2):1–20, 2010.

[25] Z. Yu, Z. Yu, X. Zhou, C. Becker, and Y. Nakamura. Tree-Based mining for discovering patterns of human interaction in meetings. *IEEE Transactions on Knowledge and Data Engineering*, 24(4):759–768, 2012.

"Let Me Comment on Your Video": Supporting Personalized End-User Comments within Third-Party Online Videos

Rodrigo Laiola Guimarães[1,2], Pablo Cesar[1] and Dick C. A. Bulterman[1,2]

[1] CWI: Centrum Wiskunde & Informatica
Science Park 123
1098 XG Amsterdam, The Netherlands
+31 20 592 93 33

[2] VU: Vrije Universiteit Amsterdam
De Boelelaan 1081
1081 HV Amsterdam, The Netherlands
+31 20 598 2988

{rlaiola, p.s.cesar, dick.bulterman}@cwi.nl

ABSTRACT

Long before the first transmission in color of a World Cup in 1970, people used to gather around the few existing radio and TV sets to watch together and talk about their favorite programs. Decades later, not only the technology has significantly changed but also people's consumption and commenting habits. Nowadays, one can easily watch an online video on demand and share comments with others asynchronously. However, current video commenting facilities do not take into account the temporal nature of videos. Viewers can only add comments that will then appear statically underneath the video. Motivated by a survey research on current media watching and commenting practices, we report on our findings from the evaluation of an online video commenting system that allows users to add synchronized comments to third-party videos. Our results indicate that users appreciate the functionalities of our system and find it better to comment when compared to existing tools. Ultimately, we hope that our work can bring insights to be considered in the design of next generation online video commenting tools.

Categories and Subject Descriptors

H.1.2 [**Models and Principles**]: User/Machine Systems – *Human factors*. H.5.1 [**Information Interfaces and Presentations**]: Multimedia Information Systems - *Audio, Video*. I.7.2 [**Document and Text Processing**]: Document Preparation - *Format and notation, hypertext/hypermedia, Languages and Systems, Multi/mixed media.*

General Terms

Design, Experimentation, Human Factors.

Keywords

End-user comments, Synchronization, Timed comments, Video commenting system, YouTube.

Permission to make digital or hard copies of all or part of this work for personal or classroom use is granted without fee provided that copies are not made or distributed for profit or commercial advantage and that copies bear this notice and the full citation on the first page. To copy otherwise, or republish, to post on servers or to redistribute to lists, requires prior specific permission and/or a fee.
WebMedia'12, October 15–18, 2012, São Paulo/SP, Brazil.
Copyright 2012 ACM 978-1-4503-1706-1/12/10...$15.00.

1. INTRODUCTION

Uploading and sharing video online has become a global phenomenon as shown by the popularity of video viewing sites like YouTube[1]. Even social networks like Facebook, originally conceived for status updating, have become important distribution points for both consumer and professionally generated video [15]. At last, video has become a first class citizen of the Web. Nevertheless, there are some requirements that have yet to be met for providing rich multimedia Web experiences.

Capturing and sharing videos online reflect the human need for communicating stories (by using implicit or explicit narrative structures). After all, sharing is intended to be a catalyst for communication among viewers of that content [10]. Recent developments on online video (and other media) sharing services

Figure 1. Typical end-user comment in YouTube. It appears statically underneath the third-party video.

[1] The services and technologies mentioned in this paper, if unknown, could easily be identified via a simple Web search, therefore they will not be Web-referenced.

and social networks have created new communication channels that were not present with conventional broadcast TV or personal media. Viewers can now associate to third-party media implicit forms of comments (e.g. anonymous ratings and tags), and explicit text comments (as shown in Figure 1).

End-user generated comments have the potential to enrich and transform the video viewing experience by allowing users to express themselves and interact with others. They can also provide valuable information for better understanding users and media. For instance, the analysis of user-generated comments around media has resulted in innovative work on the semantic and temporal structure of media events [3], user commenting patterns in video on demand [5] and in live video streaming platforms [9].

In the case of online video on demand, text comments usually appear statically underneath the media player. If desired, users need to make explicit any reference to a particular event that happens within the video object (e.g. "Look at Pelé's goal at 0:40" in Figure 1). In YouTube, by typing a particular time, it automatically becomes a 'temporal link', that when clicked takes the interested viewer to that part of the video. However, such comments do not reproduce the "*commenting while watching*" activity people perform when consuming media together. In general, users cannot add comments that are synchronized with the video, unless the owner (who uploaded it) has given editing rights to the source video content.

This paper considers the scenario in which any viewer – not necessarily the owner of the video – watches online video on demand, and adds personalized comments that are synchronized to specific events within the video. By *personalized* we mean comments created to highlight a particular event that is interesting within the end-user social circle. By *synchronized* we mean that the comments will be rendered during video playback at the time the event happens, differently from the static comments available in YouTube or Facebook. Supporting this functionality we expect to 'reproduce' asynchronously the commenting experience people have when watching media together.

We have approached this scenario by considering the following research questions:

1. Do people want to have their comments synchronized to specific events within an online video?
2. If so, does this functionality provide an identifiable improvement over current video commenting tools?

In previous work we reported on a multimedia document model for structuring such synchronized comments within media [14]. In particular, we described a set of temporal transformations for multimedia documents that allow end-users to create and share personalized timed text comments within third-party online videos. The benefit over current approaches lays in the usage of a rich commenting format that is not embedded into a specific video encoding format. We also reported on a predictive timing model for helping users to incidentally synchronize text comments with specific events within a video.

Motivated by a survey research on current media watching and commenting practices, in this paper we report our findings from a user-centric evaluation of a prototype system that uses this new video commenting paradigm. Our results indicate that users appreciate the functionalities of our system and find it better to comment when compared to current video commenting tools. Ultimately, we hope that the contributions of this paper will impact on the design of next-generation video commenting tools.

This paper is structured as follows. First, we provide an overview of related work in Section 2. Then, Section 3 motivates our work, while Section 4 describes the design and implementation of our Web-based video commenting tool, which allows end-users to add timed comments to third-party YouTube videos. Next, in Section 5 we present the results and discuss the findings from the evaluation of our commenting paradigm. Finally, Section 6 dedicates to concluding remarks and future work.

2. RELATED WORK

This paper investigates the use of timed comments when watching video on demand (or asynchronously). In the rest of this section we review some representative works.

2.1 Commenting on Web Media

Previous research efforts have been dedicated to the analysis of end-user generated annotations and comments on online video. For example, [6] investigated the quality of textual information inserted by users in popular Web applications, while Benevenuto et al. [5] characterized behavioral patterns on video-based interactions in YouTube. Complementarily, Gomes and Pimentel [1] proposed a technique for representing and evaluating media-based social interactions among a group of Facebook users. Our work differs not only in focus, but also by the fact that we are interested in text comments that are synchronized with particular events within videos.

From the technical perspective, YouTube allows the video owner to add time-synchronized notes and links (enrichments) on top of the uploaded video. If enabled by the video owner, any user also can do the same, though the owner will retain final control over what appears (he may remove third-party comments and enrichments). In our work, we consider that any online user can potentially add comments to be rendered with specific events within any YouTube video (or from any other provider).

SoundCloud is an online audio distribution platform that is becoming increasingly popular on the Web. It allows for collaboration, promotion and distribution of audio recordings among amateur musicians and enthusiasts. Regular comments, similar to YouTube or Facebook posts, can be posted underneath the track's player on its individual page. These comments will not show up on the player but will appear statically underneath. Besides that, a key feature provided by this service is that when a user is listening to a third-party song, s/he can add a timed comment to specific parts of the music waveform. In spite of supporting a similar concept in the video domain, we go a step further and report on the evaluation of our commenting tool.

2.2 Commenting on Live Media

A large body of research has addressed end-user enrichments on multimedia [12][13]. Most closely related to our work, Nathan et al. [11] presented a system that allows viewers to create text comments while watching a TV show. In an asynchronous scenario, previously generated comments (temporally-linked to the media stream) are shown to later viewers as they watch that program. Our work is related, but we focus on timed text comments within online videos.

Shamma et al. [3] investigated micro-blogging around live media events. Results showed that the Twitter activity is temporally aligned to the topics of discussion during a video event. While twittering reactions to live broadcast media can yield significant insights into the semantic and temporal structure of media, the same methodology cannot easily be applied for obtaining temporal cues within a video hosted in a rich media social site such as YouTube or Facebook. Finally, Arantes et al. [7] proposed a set of operators to manipulate session information related to workspaces and tools scheduling in collaborative synchronous environments. As the result of a session, interactive multimedia documents are generated. Our work differs not only in the underlying technology, but also in the application context. While they concentrate on documenting synchronous sessions for later review, we focus on incidental commenting on third-party videos.

3. MOTIVATION

As mentioned before, we have previously reported on a set of temporal transformations for multimedia documents that allow end-users to create and share personalized timed text comments on third-party videos [14]. In this work though, we follow a user-centric approach to motivate and validate our contributions. In the remaining of this section we present the results gathered in a survey about current media watching and commenting practices around media. This discussion is followed by results that show the utility and usefulness of synchronized comments.

3.1 Survey Research

A sample group of 21 people participated in the evaluation process. All participants were regular Internet users. Eighteen (18) people declared to be in the 21-40-age range, while the other 3 were over 40 years old. Participants were from different nationalities including Brazilian, Chinese, Dutch, German, Hungarian and Irish.

We used semi-structured electronic questionnaires to collect users' feedback. While multiple-choice questions allowed us to explore patters and find trends (quantitative methods), open-ended questions aimed at capturing further insights into participants' opinions and perceptions. The user study was divided in 3 parts. The first part, which is the focus of this section, consisted of a questionnaire to gather background information about respondents' commenting practices when watching video content. Feedback answers were anonymous.

3.1.1 Media consumption and commenting practices

Figure 2 summarizes the results obtained in our survey research regarding media consumption and commenting habits. As users' practices were different, for each question we present the weighted average (colored column) and the respective standard deviation (bar). In Figure 2 the questions also have been clustered in two groups according to the consumption experience: synchronous (blue) and asynchronous watching (red). For each scenario we also asked about participants' conversational and commenting practices around media.

A wide range of TV watching habits has been reported by our participants. In average, our users watch TV *every week* (Q1.1). This was the second highest frequency score among our questions. Participants also reported having the habit (between *occasionally* and *every week*) of talking with family and friends about a TV show they have watched (Q1.2). When asked about the frequency they would converse about a TV program with collocated people while watching, the average answer was *occasionally* (Q1.3). The lowest score though was obtained in the question about how often they would send tweets related to a TV show they were watching (Q1.4). As reported elsewhere [3], this activity is becoming popular over the years and, in some cases, it is used as an

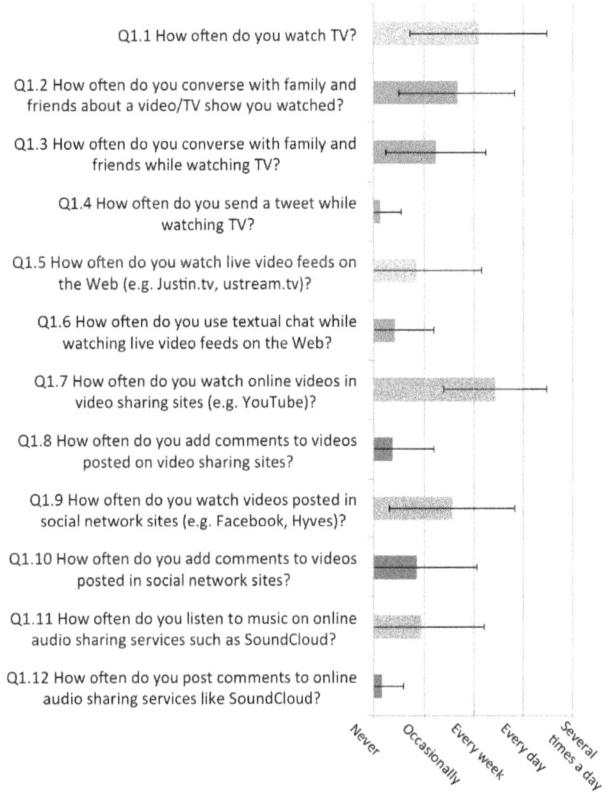

Figure 2. Survey research about media consumption and commenting practices. Blue columns indicate synchronous watching and related conversational habits. In red, on demand (asynchronous) consumption and commenting.

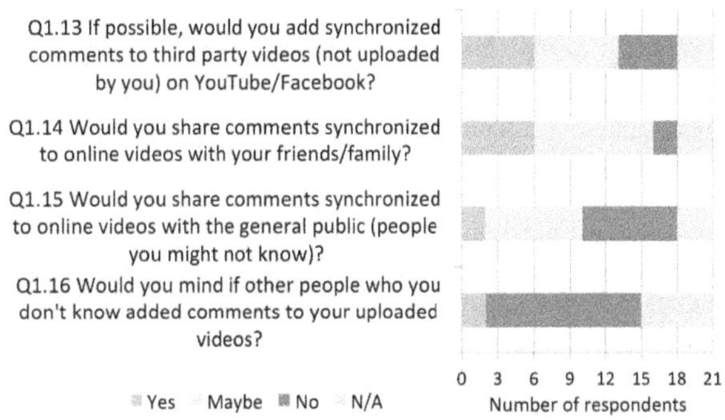

Figure 3. Requirements gathering: utility and usefulness of timed comments within media.

interactive return channel in which the audience can influence on live TV programs.

In the second media consumption scenario, we asked our participants about the habit of watching live video feeds on the Web (using e.g. Justin.tv, Ustream.tv). The average of their feedback was around *occasionally* (Q1.5). Regarding the activity of commenting on the video event while watching, we asked how often they make use of the built-in open textual chat rooms generally available on those services. Again, rather small the frequency stayed between *never* and *occasionally*, which was slightly higher than the one reported for tweet messages (Q1.6).

Regarding on demand (asynchronous) watching, we asked our participants about the usage of YouTube, Facebook and

SoundCloud. Validating previous research [15], YouTube was often (between *every week* and *every day*) used by our participants to watch online videos (Q1.7). However, posting comments to the video page did not seem to be a common practice among them (Q1.8). In conjunction with the use of YouTube, we also witnessed a fair high frequency of video viewing on social networking sites (Q1.9). In this case though, participants use to comment more on videos when compared to the comments added in YouTube (Q1.10). One possible explanation for this behavior could be that participants are more likely to post comments within their social circle than to the open public. Finally, we asked our users to report on their practices using online audio streaming services such as SoundCloud. In average, respondents *occasionally* listen to music on these platforms (Q1.11) and they do not have the habit of adding timed comments to songs (Q1.12).

3.1.2 Requirements Gathering

In the second part of the survey we asked our participants about the possibility of adding timed text comments to particular events within a third-party online video (see Figure 3). Thirteen (13) out of 21 participants said they would possibly (*yes* or *maybe*) add timed comments to YouTube or Facebook videos if they could (Q1.13). One of the participants expressed that such feature would be a *"nice way to highlight sections/points of the video"*. When asked whether they would share these synchronized comments within their social circle the number raised to 16 (Q1.14), higher than the number reported for sharing comments with the general public (Q1.15). In one case, a user justified by writing *"I'm never interested in sharing my comments with the public... but to have a link that I just could send to friends"*.

At last, we asked a question related to digital rights and ownership. In this case, only 2 participants expressed they would mind if other people could add timed comments to their videos (Q1.16). In these lines, one participant highlighted the necessity of having control over the commenting activity: *"If everybody could add comments to any video it would become a real mess. Some people would use it to damage the image of others"*.

In this study we looked at the media consumption and commenting practices of a group of Internet users in different applications. Rather small, this sample group provides strong indications that people consume media and doing so, they comment and share those moments with friends, family, and sometimes with the general public. Regarding the asynchronous media consumption scenario, our respondents provided evidences that they would comment on particular events within the media, if possible. This discussion led to the specification of the following three requirements:

- *Allow personalized timed comments:* when watching an online video, viewers should be able to add comments that are time-synchronized. This feature would reproduce (asynchronously) the watching and commenting activity people are used to have when watching collocated;
- *Allow selective viewing:* viewers might decide whether to watch synchronized comments or not. This is important because some comments might be targeted to individual users while others are intended to the general public; and
- *Retain base video integrity:* viewers should not be able to alter the base video content, either in terms of adding embedded comments or providing visual overlays on the base content — this right is reserved for the video owner.

We used these requirements as the basis for validating the online video commenting system introduced in the next section.

4. A NEW VIDEO COMMENTING PARADIGM

In this work we look at social interaction and commenting practices around online video content. This process involved the design and deployment of a video commenting system as a flexible testbed. Unlike current commenting approaches, our solution, which is called *Ambulant Captioner* (http://www.ambulantplayer.org/smilTextWebApp/), allows end-users to add timed text comments to particular events within third-party online videos. We focus on text, but a similar approach could have been followed to add other types of user-generated comments (or enrichments) to videos [12][13]. In the remaining of this section we discuss the design and implementation of our video commenting system.

4.1 Infrastructure

The high-level workflow of our video commenting system is illustrated in Figure 4. The interaction starts when a user requests a video. For that we make use of the YouTube Data API (*Application Programming Interface*), which provides programmatic access to videos stored in YouTube. It allows us to retrieve a set of videos matching a user-specified search term or retrieve standard feeds (e.g. most viewed today). The data is requested using AJAX (*Asynchronous JavaScript and XML*) and returned in the XML (*eXtensible Markup Language*) format, then parsed and presented to the end-user.

For video playback we use the YouTube Player API, which is exposed via JavaScript. It allows us to control not only the 'Look and Feel' of the player but also the playback behavior of the videos in our Web application. With the current YouTube

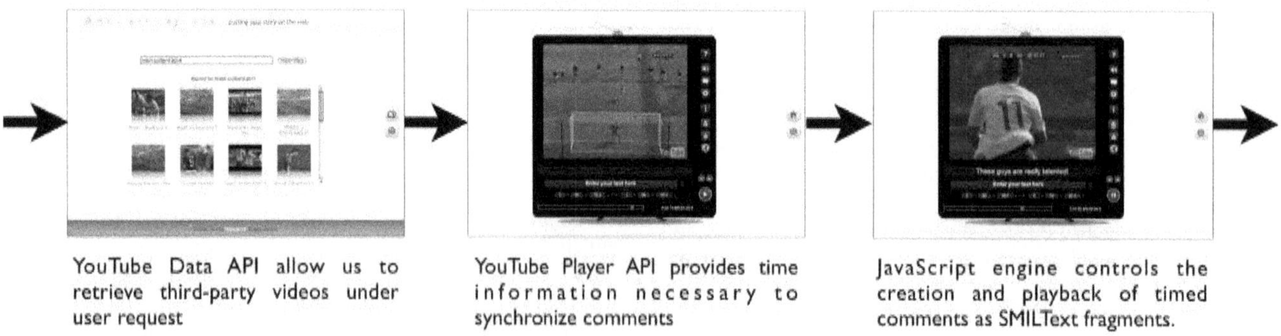

Figure 4. Workflow of our online video commenting system.

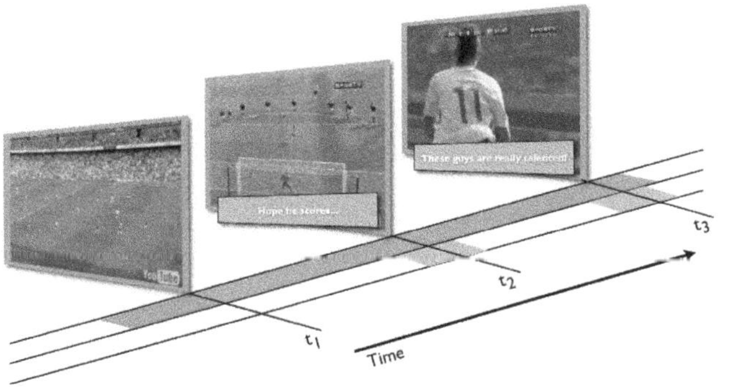


```
<smil ...>
 <head ...> ... </head>
 <body>
  <par>
   <video region="r1" id="v1" src="YouTube video"/>
   <smilText region="c1"...>
    ...
    <clear begin="t2-5s"/>
    Hope he scores...
    <clear begin="t2+2s"/>

    <clear begin="t3-5s"/>
    These guys are really talented!
    <clear begin="t3+3s"/>
    ...
   </smilText>
  </par>
 </body>
</smil>
```

Figure 5. Document model for supporting synchronized comments within a YouTube video.

infrastructure, the client Web browser must have Flash Player 10.1 or higher installed to work correctly. Most importantly, the Player API provides the time information necessary to synchronize the text comments within a video. This feature is obtained by listening to specific events, which are fired accordingly (e.g. time update event). A similar infrastructure would be necessary for making the commenting tool available for videos hosted in different providers. In this case, the YouTube Data and Player APIs should be replaced and the interfaces of the new provider adapted accordingly.

Since the viewer has no rights to add comments to the base video, the timed comments are stored separately at our Web server. The actual format used to encapsulate the multimedia presentation (base video plus a layered collection of timed comments) is W3C's SMIL 3.0 [4]. In fact, timed comments are specified in SMILText, the embedded text format for use within SMIL 3.0. This decision has been motivated by our extensive work in the development and standardization of the SMIL language. SMIL allows us to respect the video owner's rights and keep a provider-agnostic multimedia presentation. As such, comments can be shared, modified and analyzed independently (see Figure 5). It is important to notice that the same functionality could have been obtained using NCL [8], the standard XML-based application language for defining interactive multimedia presentations in the Brazilian Terrestrial Digital TV System (SBTVD-T).

For the synchronized playback of end-user comments we implemented a SMILText JavaScript engine that runs on the client's Web browser. Its API allows us to embed SMILText functionalities in Web pages and have the presentation controlled by an external source, in this case the YouTube video. The SMILText engine has reasonably complete coverage of the features defined in the SMIL 3.0 SMILText External Profile. The API also provides a number of other utilities for adding and manipulating timed text content, making possible the creation of applications such as the commenting tool presented in this paper.

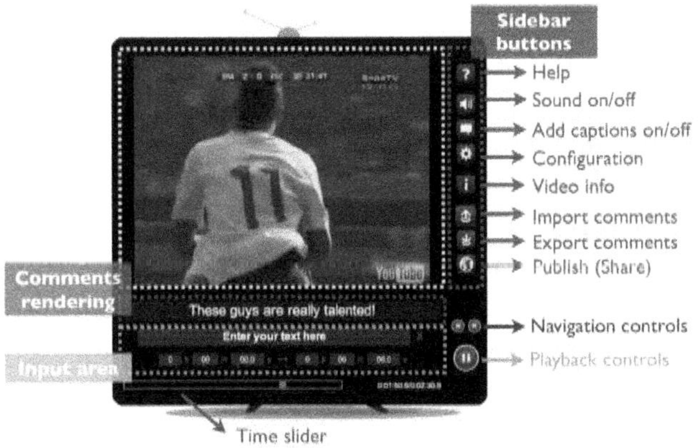

Figure 6. Video commenting interface.

4.2 User Interface

The commenting interface of our system is shown in Figure 6. It is composed by a video rendering area, a comments rendering space, an input area and sidebar controls. In most cases, relative passive end-users will simply watch a piece of video content forwarded to them. If the content itself has embedded comments, these can be selectively turned on or off via the sidebar controls interface. During playback users may also choose to insert new personalized comments in the input area.

One key feature of our video commenting system is its ability to (semi-) automatically compute the alignment of user-generated comments. To explain how this functionality works, consider the scenario illustrated in Figure 5. In an operation mode, we assume users will react only after the actual interesting moment has passed (e.g. t_3). Based on this premise, when the end-user indicates s/he wants to add a comment, the video playback is paused and the input area gains focus. Given this action was performed right after listening to or watching the event of interest, the current time moment (in this case t_3+3s) describes the end of the comment entry. As a preliminary guess, we consider the start time of the comment will be equals the current time (t_3+3s) minus a minimal duration that a short comment should stay in the screen for being effectively read. However, based on a prediction model and some parameters — e.g. the number of words in a comment — the start time can change. In our example the final start time computed for "These guys are really talented!" was t_3-5s. After the user saves the new comment entry, the video playback is resumed. The use of this feature often provides only coarse temporal support; users may fine-tune the timing if desired. In our experience, such fine-tuning is not necessary unless tightly coupled subtitles are being created. A detailed description of this temporal model can be found elsewhere [14]. In our current implementation, the system generates a link to the commented video. This link can then be sent by email or posted on the Facebook wall of a friend.

5. EVALUATION

As mentioned before, the survey discussed in Section 3 was followed by 2 other experiments. In the first one, users were instructed to interact with the prototype system presented in Section 4 and then, fill in a questionnaire to report on their experiences. In the second part, users were asked to further explore the commenting activity by close captioning a sample video (approx. 7 minutes duration) and fill in another questionnaire. Table 1 summarizes the participants involved in each part of the evaluation process presented in this paper. In the next sections we present the results and discuss the findings from the evaluation of our online video commenting tool.

5.1 Commenting on videos

In general, participants' feedback regarding our video commenting tool was very positive (see Figure 7). When asked how much they liked the service (Q2.1), 13 out of 18 answered *some* or *a lot*. This number jumps to 17 when we consider the people that said *a little bit*. All users reported that our video commenting tool is helpful for adding synchronized comments to YouTube videos (Q2.2). Some participants also expressed their appreciation by saying that *"synchronization is much better"* and *"I can easily add comments to specific moments in the video. In Facebook I think I can't. In YouTube I can but I have to type the time moment in the comment"*.

When compared to regular comment threads in YouTube or Facebook, 9 users said our tool is *better* or *much better*. In this direction, a user justified by saying that *"the possibility to comment on a specific moment in the video adds a lot of functionality. Instead of saying, 'after 16 seconds he does this', you can just comment at that moment. This also works quite well on SoundCloud as far as I have seen"*. On the other side, 5 participants said they were unable to judge. One of them explained by writing: *"I have never added comments to Facebook nor YouTube. However, the way to add comments in this (video commenting) tool is intuitive"*.

5.2 Close captioning videos

The last experiment was the most time consuming one, and for this reason, only 12 participants committed to complete it. Users were kindly requested to close caption a 7 minutes speech video. This task was first performed using our video commenting tool, and later using a standard video player and a text editor. This experiment allowed us to evaluate the effectiveness and usefulness of the time prediction algorithm provided in our commenting tool (see Figure 8).

Using our tool, participants spent in average 61 minutes (SD = 48 minutes), and other 101 minutes (SD = 33 minutes) without it. The utility of our commenting system has also been reflected in the questionnaire answers. When asked how much easier it was to add close captions with our system compared to the other method, all respondents said it was *much easier* or *easier* (Q3.1). A similar feedback has been obtained in the question regarding participants' appreciation for the predictive synchronization of captions/comments (Q3.2). In this case, 10 users reported to have

Table 1. Composition of participants in evaluation process.

Survey Questionnaire	*Number of Respondents*	*% of Respondents*
1. Current video watching and commenting practices	21	100.0%
2. Commenting on videos with our prototype system	18	85.7%
3. Captioning videos using our prototype system	12	57.1%

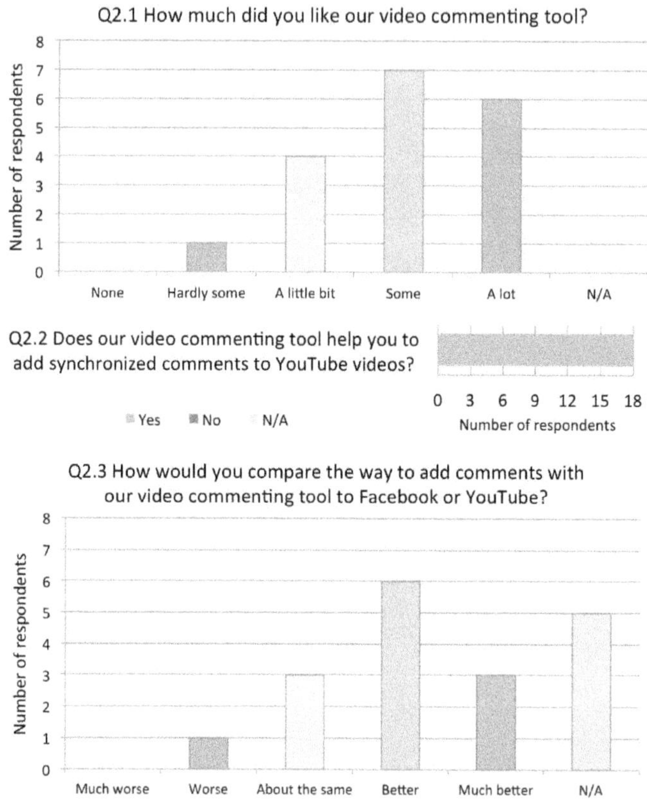

Figure 7. Results from the evaluation of our commenting tool.

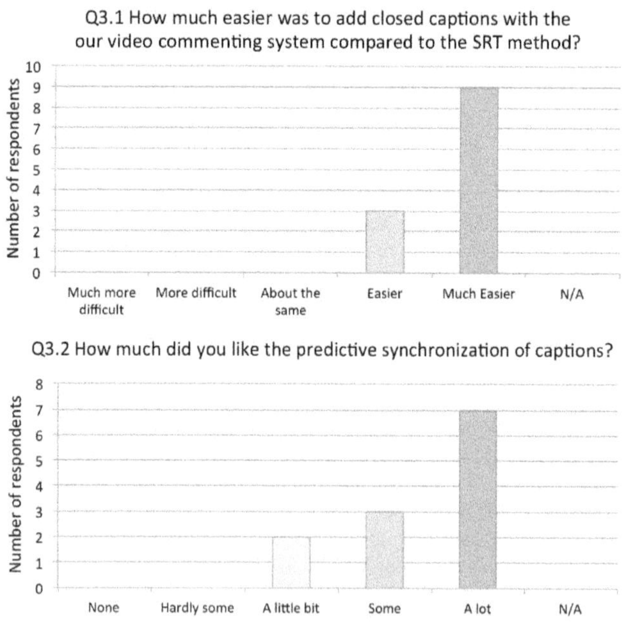

Figure 8. Results from the close captioning activity using our prototype system.

liked *some* or *a lot*. In one case, one participant mentioned that *"most captions were synchronized nice to the video, and the prediction algorithm does work. It saves a lot of time having not to fine tune the start and end point, as you have to with the SRT format"*. And another user added: *"the prediction works really good, the captions are usually where they are supposed to be!"*.

Although our primary objective was not to provide a close caption authoring tool, the point we want to make here is that video commenting systems like ours should not only allow users to add timed comments, but also help them by offering automatic processes that will make the commenting task simpler and more enjoyable. In future work we intend to further explore the effectiveness of our system in the captioning context by comparing it with other subtitling tools[2,3].

5.3 Discussion

The survey research about media watching and commenting practices characterizes the first major contribution of this paper. While in terms of contextualization, this study is very relevant; even more it is from the viewpoint of motivation. Do people actually want to add timed comments within videos? Our results provide evidences that people would add synchronized comments while consuming video on demand if they had the appropriate tools for doing that. This directly responds our first research question (see Section 1).

The video commenting tool reported in this paper also fulfills the requirements identified in Section 3. By using a rich multimedia format – in our case SMIL – we allow users to add synchronized comments to third-party videos (requirement #1). As these comments can be targeted to different audiences, they can be selectively rendered (requirement #2) while respecting the owners' rights by retaining the video integrity (requirement #3). The evaluation of our video commenting system represents the second major contribution of our work. It shows that this paradigm brings a measurable increment over existing commenting systems. This feedback answers our second research question.

It is important to make clear that we do not claim synchronized comments should replace traditional ones, but rather be complementary. Regular comments are targeted to a fundamentally different use case than the ones offered by our system. In Facebook or YouTube, people can comment about a video, but also give feedback to the author or start a conversation about something unrelated. Our video commenting system, on the other hand, could be used to highlight interesting things for other viewers, maybe to make a point about a particular event within the video. It is also important to consider that the textual comment one can read while watching a video should be rather simple, because anything more complex would be difficult to follow.

The contributions of this paper are not restricted to a specific multimedia language or service. In the context of the Brazilian Terrestrial Digital TV System, the same functionality could be obtained using NCL [8]. On the viewer-side, when integrated to the TV middleware for instance, an application could extend the traditional television-watching experience by allowing end-users to enrich the broadcast content. Such enriched content can be shared with other viewers within a distributed peer group, using for example a return channel. In this direction, Teixeira et al. [2] presented a framework that allows users to personalize a live program (e.g. a football match) with previously created media stickers — pieces of content that may be temporarily attached to the base video. With the potential of the Brazilian Digital TV, we expect our contributions can foster discussions on the design of new media experiences.

We also expect that many of the insights raised in this paper can impact the HTML5 standard. The current proposal for supporting video and WebSRT (*Web Subtitle Resource Tracks*) is far too restrictive to support the type of service we propose in this paper.

6. CONCLUSION

In this paper we presented our efforts for supporting personalized end-user comments within third-party online videos. Motivated by a survey on media watching and commenting practices, we introduced and evaluated a new video commenting paradigm. Results from this evaluation process indicate that users appreciate the functionalities of our system and would potentially use it. During this process we did not focus on drawing final conclusions about the topic, but rather on starting a discussion on whether users would comment within third-party online videos. We hope that our insights can stimulate future research in this topic not only on the Web domain.

In future work we intend to explore alternatives to represent timed comments within a video. The lack of visual representation of timed comments in the timeline of a video was a recurrent complaint during the evaluation process.

7. ACKNOWLEDGMENTS

The research leading to these results has received funding from the European Community's Seventh Framework Programme (FP7/2007-2013) under grant agreement no. ICT-2007-214793. Special thanks to all the participants involved in the user evaluations and to FAPESP for supporting the presentation of the work in the event.

8. REFERENCES

[1] A.K. Gomes and M.G.C. Pimentel. 2011. A technique for human-readable representation and evaluation of media-based social interactions in social networks. In Proceedings of Brazilian Symposium on Multimedia and the Web (WebMedia'11), Brazil.

[2] C.A.C. Teixeira, E.L. Melo, G.B. Freitas, C.A.S. Santos, M.G.C. Pimentel. 2011. Discrimination of media moments and media intervals: sticker-based watch-and-comment annotation. Multimedia Tools and Applications (29 July 2011), pp. 1-22, DOI= 10.1007/s11042-011-0846-6

[3] D.A. Shamma, L. Kennedy, and E.F. Churchill. 2009. Tweet the debates: understanding community annotation of uncollected sources. In Proceedings of the first SIGMM workshop on Social media (WSM '09). ACM, New York, NY, USA, 3-10. DOI=10.1145/1631144.1631148 http://doi.acm.org/10.1145/1631144.1631148

[4] D.C.A Bulterman and L.W. Rutledge. SMIL3.0 - Interactive Multimedia for Web, Mobile Devices and DAISY Talking Books. Springer-Verlag, 2009. ISBN: 978-3-540-78546-0

[5] F. Benevenuto, T. Rodrigues, V. Almeida, J. Almeida and K. Ross. 2009. Video interactions in online video social networks. ACM Trans. Multimedia Comput. Commun. Appl. 5, 4, Article 30 (November 2009), 25 pages.

[2] Subtitle Horse. http://subtitle-horse.org

[3] dotSUB. http://dotsub.com

DOI=10.1145/1596990.1596994
http://doi.acm.org/10.1145/1596990.1596994

[6] F. Figueiredo, F. Belém, H. Pinto, J. Almeida, M. Gonçalves, D. Fernandes, E. Moura, V. Almeida, and M. Cristo. 2009. Characterizing use and quality of textual attributes in Web 2.0 applications. In Proceedings of the XV Brazilian Symposium on Multimedia and the Web (WebMedia '09). ACM, New York, NY, USA, Article 9, 8 pages. DOI=10.1145/1858477.1858486 http://doi.acm.org/10.1145/1858477.1858486

[7] F.L. Arantes, C.R. Moraes, S.H.P. Silva, R.P.M. Fortes and M.G.C. Pimentel. 2010. Where and with whom do you wanna meet? Session-based collaborative work. In Proceedings of Brazilian Symposium on Multimedia and the Web (WebMedia'10), v.1, p.123-130, Brazil.

[8] ITU-T Rec. H.761, Nested Context Language (NCL) and Ginga-NCL for IPTV Services, Geneva, Apr. 2009. Available at http://www.itu.int/rec/T-REC-H.761

[9] J.D. Weisz, S. Kiesler, H. Zhang, Y. Ren, R.E. Kraut, and J.A. Konstan. 2007. Watching together: integrating text chat with video. In Proceedings of the SIGCHI conference on Human factors in computing systems (CHI '07). ACM, New York, NY, USA, 877-886. DOI=10.1145/1240624.1240756 http://doi.acm.org/10.1145/1240624.1240756

[10] M.D. Choudhury, H. Sundaram, A. John, and D.D. Seligmann. 2009. What makes conversations interesting?: themes, participants and consequences of conversations in online social media. In Proceedings of the 18th international conference on World wide web (WWW '09). ACM, New York, NY, USA, 331-340. DOI=10.1145/1526709.1526754 http://doi.acm.org/10.1145/1526709.1526754

[11] M. Nathan, C. Harrison, S. Yarosh, L. Terveen, L. Stead, and B. Amento. 2008. CollaboraTV: making television viewing social again. In Proceedings of the 1st international conference on Designing interactive user experiences for TV and video (UXTV '08). ACM, New York, NY, USA, 85-94. DOI=10.1145/1453805.1453824 http://doi.acm.org/10.1145/1453805.1453824

[12] P. Cesar, D.C.A. Bulterman, D. Geerts, J. Jansen, H. Knoche, and W. Seager. 2008. Enhancing social sharing of videos: fragment, annotate, enrich, and share. In Proceedings of the 16th ACM international conference on Multimedia (MM '08). ACM, New York, NY, USA, 11-20. DOI=10.1145/1459359.1459362 http://doi.acm.org/10.1145/1459359.1459362

[13] R.G. Cattelan, C. Teixeira, R. Goularte, and M.G.C. Pimentel. 2008. Watch-and-comment as a paradigm toward ubiquitous interactive video editing. ACM Trans. Multimedia Comput. Commun. Appl. 4, 4, Article 28 (November 2008), 24 pages. DOI=10.1145/1412196.1412201 http://doi.acm.org/10.1145/1412196.1412201

[14] R.L. Guimarães, P. Cesar, and D.C.A. Bulterman. 2010. Creating and sharing personalized time-based annotations of videos on the web. In Proceedings of the 10th ACM symposium on Document engineering (DocEng '10). ACM, New York, NY, USA, 27-36. DOI=10.1145/1860559.1860567 http://doi.acm.org/10.1145/1860559.1860567

[15] The Nielsen Company. 2010. How People Watch – A Global Nielsen Consumer Report. Available at http://www.nielsen.com/us/en/insights/reports-downloads/2010/How-We-Watch-The-Global-State-of-Video-Consumption.html

Video Annotation and Navigation on Mobile Devices

Bruna C. R. Cunha, Diogo Pedrosa, Rudinei Goularte, Maria da Graça Pimentel
Instituto de Ciências Matemáticas e de Computação - ICMC - USP
Avenida Trabalhador São Carlense, 400
PO Box: 668 - 13560-970 - São Carlos, SP - Brazil
{brunaru, diogo, rudinei, mgp}@icmc.usp.br

ABSTRACT

The growing ease of capturing and playing back videos using mobile devices demands the investigation of alternatives for improving the user experience, for instance by taking advantage of the expanding culture of end-user content generation. Advances in terms of end-user media capture and media combination aim at enriching and facilitating the authoring experience. This work explores the generation of textual annotations on videos played on mobile device: the approach is to offer an application that allows associating annotations to a navigation line decorated with frames that are representative of the points of interest. The aims is to improve the user experience of video annotation by allowing users to to find interesting points intuitively. Experiments with users identified of new issues, even though the application was considered easy to use.

Categories and Subject Descriptors

H.5.1 [**Information Interfaces and Presentations**]: Multimedia Information Systems—*Video*; H.5.2 [**Information Interfaces and Presentations**]: User Interfaces—*Graphical user interfaces (GUI)*; H.5.4 [**Information Interfaces and Presentations**]: Hypertext/Hypermedia—*Navigation*

General Terms

Design, Human Factors

Keywords

Navigation, Annotation, Mobile Devices

1. INTRODUCTION

Video playback on mobile devices has become usual [7] due to the increasing accessibility, practicality of use and mobility of these devices. The mobility enables people to use their idle time while traveling or make the journey from home to work or at waiting rooms, for example. In such scenarios both video for entertainment and for display of educational content are increasingly popular [5].

Permission to make digital or hard copies of all or part of this work for personal or classroom use is granted without fee provided that copies are not made or distributed for profit or commercial advantage and that copies bear this notice and the full citation on the first page. To copy otherwise, to republish, to post on servers or to redistribute to lists, requires prior specific permission and/or a fee.
WebMedia'12, October 15–28, 2012, São Paulo/SP, Brazil.
Copyright 2012 ACM 978-1-4503-1706-1/12/10 ...$15.00.

In online video display platforms, making comments via annotations is a way of entertaining and discussion that is naturally carried. Annotations on video have been shown useful also in tasks of educational videos review. In activities such as classes and tutorials, users can enrich videos with their own observations and mark points of interest used to aid and facilitate learning. O'Hara et al. [7] report that one of the observed behaviors in a group of friends reviewing videos is the nonlinear playback. As an example, the authors report that when reviewing a movie within a group it is common to fast forward to the favorite moments, commenting about the scenes, discussing and sharing opinions among the group.

Annotations generated by viewers enrich the video content at specific reproduction times , as reported in the literature. Müller et al. [6], for example, use annotations as a navigational aid on video: in a posterior playback of the video the user may not only review your comments but also navigate directly to the point of occurrence through timeline marks. This solution is restricted to desktop computers and moreover the approach of marking the video timeline limits the navigation on mobile devices due the screens limited sizes and the fingertip precision [2]. Vega-Oliveros et al. [11] propose an automatic generation of annotations based on key frames captured from the content of different TV channels watched by the user: these annotations are used for navigation between videos through a timeline. Inspired by these results the work reported in this paper aims to investigate video navigation on mobile devices using the preview of the annotations accompanied by reference frames. For this we developed a prototype for multimedia authoring and navigation on mobile devices focusing on non-expert users. Experiments carried out with users helped to point out problems and improvements to be performed and had positive results regarding easiness of use. Among the encountered problems, the difficulty of selecting points of navigation, due to the precision of touch, and the display time of the annotations stimulate studying ways to improve the user interaction.

The remainder of the paper is organized as follows. Section 2 discusses related work, Section 3 the developed prototype, Section 4 the usability evaluation performed and Section 5 the final considerations.

2. RELATED WORK

Video playback interfaces on mobile devices, such as those presented by Hürst [9] and Huber [2], usually have their navigation based on temporal dimension.

Pimentel et al. [8] explore the production of multimodal

annotations on video transmitted over digital TV using mobile devices. The main premise of this work is the naturalness of practice and the enjoyment resulting from making comments while playing media. The work focuses on the production of annotations for the generation of interactive multimedia documents. However the navigation through points of interest is not explored.

Applications that support annotation generation enable the association of the generated text with a video instant and display them simultaneously with the reference scene [6]. These associations create marking points. Müller et al. [6] propose the use of annotations to allow a dynamic and fast navigation, and make use of multiple timelines marked with the annotations occurrence points. The paper does not discuss the use of the proposal on mobile devices.

The use of thumbnail images demands attention on the influence of the size of the image in its recognition, which is a critical task on small screens. Inspired by the work of Torralba et al. [10], that studies the performance in the recognition of miniatures, Hürst et al. [3, 4] study the influence of the size of thumbnails for the retrieve of videos on devices that have screens of limited size, obtaining good results for recognition in static images of 90 pixels. The results presented encourage the use of thumbnails on mobile devices.

Vega-Oliveros [11] make use of thumbnails of frames captured from videos presented on different TV channels to offer a timeline for navigation between videos based on recent frames. The work does not allow text annotations nor discuss the use of the proposal on mobile devices.

3. NAVIGATION ON VIDEO THROUGH ANNOTATED FRAMES

To investigate the use of video navigation on mobile devices through the preview of annotations accompanied by reference frames, we developed a prototype that enables multimedia authoring and navigation on mobile devices focusing on non-expert users. Given this approach the tool should be easy to learn and give the user the possibility of authorship of their own interactive videos. Figure 1 shows the main screen of the prototype: it displays the video, the playback controls, a box for annotations addition and a button that allows the navigation through annotations already made. During the playback of the video, annotations are displayed simultaneously with its related scene.

The main functionality of the prototype is the non-linear video navigation through points of interest: points annotated by users. Points of interest are displayed on a dynamically generated navigation screen, which is displayed by pressing the navigation button. The navigation representation is composed by the captured video frame, the text inserted by the user and the time of the video when the action was taken, as shown in Figure 2. Clicking on a picture or text makes the video skips to the time referenced by the markup.

The navigation via specific points can occur not only when reviewing videos, but also in its first playback since the navigation is updated with each new annotation addition. Annotations can be shared among users allowing the enrichment of the files by another person. In the current prototype, the sharing must be done by manually copying XML files from one device to another. In future versions the sharing should

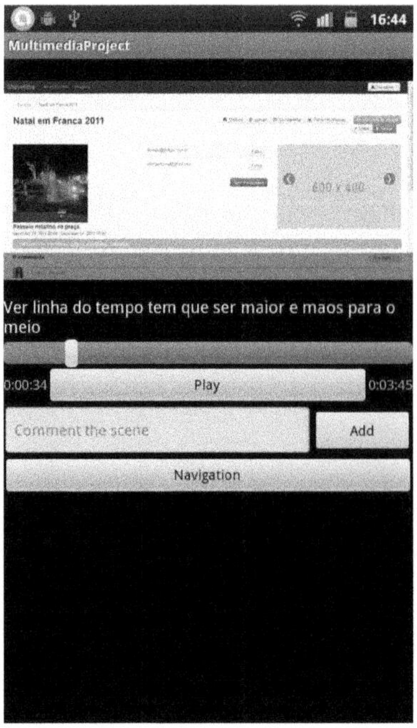

Figure 1: Main screen of the application.

be done automatically by the tool, for example, via Bluetooth[1] communication. Sharing is another distinguishing feature not attacked in reported work [8, 6]. Figure 3 shows the applicationŠs initial screen, which allows the selection of the author of the comments. In case that there is no annotation file, the system suggests the use of the username of a Google account of the device.

The prototype considers the playback on devices with different resolutions and screen sizes and the video is adjusted at the tool startup. The layout was designed in vertical position so the interaction elements could always be visible and the virtual keyboard could be displayed without modifying the video aspect ratio. The execution control and the timeline were manually controlled to enable handling the user interaction with the progress bar.

The prototype was developed using Java on Android SDK platform [2]. The annotations are stored in XML documents, which can be transmitted between users, thus allowing them to view and edit the annotations. Simple XML library[3] was used to perform the generation and manipulation of XML files. This library performs the mapping of XML schemas into classes and allows the creation of simple and elegant codes. It is not necessary to perform the XML processing explicitly. Simple XML features high performance and requires little space, which makes it very suitable for developing Android applications. The dynamic capture, i.e., the capture of images utilized for the thumbnails, is not implemented in the prototype due to the absence of the necessary infrastructure for such in Android SDK. Video thumbnails are pre-captured, at a rate of one frame per second, by a Java tool using the Xuggle[4] library, which provides solu-

[1]http://www.bluetooth.com/
[2]http://developer.android.com/sdk/
[3]http://simple.sourceforge.net/
[4]http://www.xuggle.com/

Figure 2: Navigation screen.

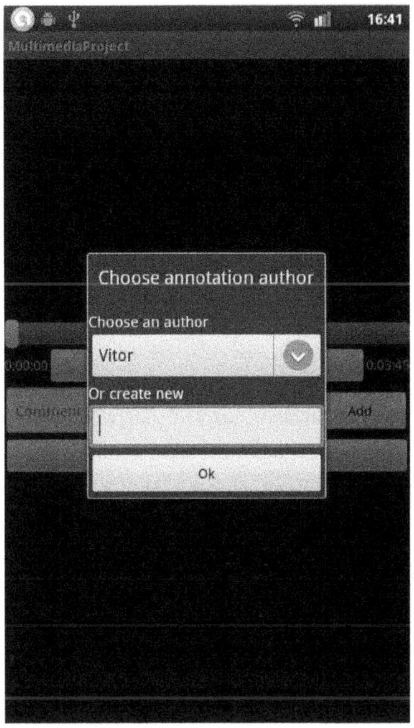

Figure 3: Author chooser.

tions to facilitate the video handling with Java language. The thumbnails must be generated previously with this tool and then added with the video to the device. Thus, instead of capturing the image directly from the video, the Android application uses the closest thumbnail of the video frame, which is already stored in memory. Because they are miniatures, the space wasted by the thumbnails in the device memory is not representative.

4. USABILITY EVALUATION

Studies were made to evaluate the developed application, identifying the easiness of use, its problems and possible improvements. Tests were done with volunteer graduate students of a Human Computer Interaction course. The videos used in the experiment were produced by the students themselves and its content is about their projects developed during the course. The videos, with approximately three minutes each, present the functionalities of three different software applications in use. Six users participated in the activity that occurred in the laboratory using a device provided by the moderators. Three of the participants were from the computer science field. The other three studied architecture, image and sound, and physics. There were male and female participants, aged 26 to 46 years, with different experiences in using touch screen devices. Most of them watch videos on their mobile devices.

The qualitative evaluation adopted a cooperative strategy in which users are encouraged to collaborate with the evaluation. In the evaluation the user first interacts with the system while observed by the moderators. When this interaction ends, user and moderators discuss the encountered problems [1]. Each evaluation session was divided into three tasks and lasted approximately 25 minutes. In the first part the user watches a video and adds annotations that he finds relevant. The users were free to choose the video and make the comments, knowing that they will have to show them to the moderators afterwards. In the second part, the user presents his/her annotations to the moderators explaining their motivation and, at the end, the user answers a questionnaire. The interactions of the participants with the tool were audio and video recorded with prior consent.

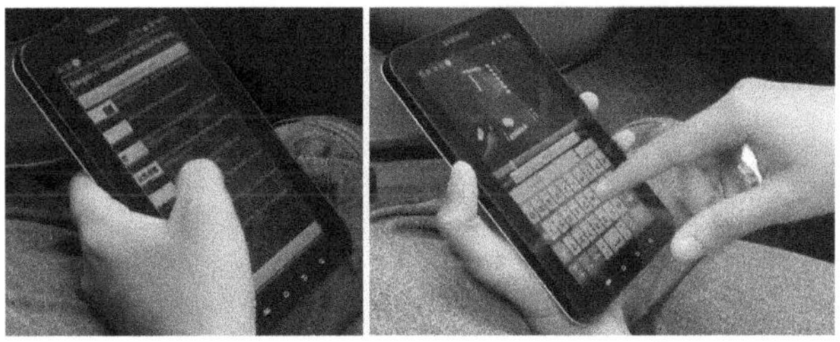

Figure 4: Experiment with users.

The main objective of the evaluations was to identify issues in the application. The analysis was performed by observing the videos recorded in each experiment and the questionnaire responses. The contributions were constructive and we were able to identify issues and improvement points to be worked on in the next prototype version.

The most critical identified points involved trouble creating new author, shows that the dialog was not intuitive, the action of pressing the button to add a new annotation without entering a text, and accuracy problems when clicking on an annotation on navigation screen. Besides these problems, some planned features that weren't available had its need reinforced: edition and removal of the annotations and a larger display of the video in horizontal layout.

The prototype met the expectations on functioning and was well received by the users. In their majority, they considered the features very easy or easy to use and were able to perform the assigned tasks successfully without assistance. The ease of reading the annotations was considered regu-

Table 1: **Results of the questionnaire for the evaluation of functionalities.**

Participant	Choose Video	Choose Author	Add Annotation	Navigation by Annotation	Annotation Reading
1	Very Easy	Easy	Easy	Very Easy	Very Easy
2	Very Easy	Very Easy	Easy	Easy	Easy
3	Very Easy	Easy	Very Easy	Very Easy	Very Easy
4	Very Easy	Easy	Regular	Regular	Regular
5	Very Easy	Very Easy	Easy	Easy	Regular
6	Easy	Easy	Very Easy	Very Easy	Regular

lar by half of the users, which, combined with discussion and analysis of the recorded interactions, showed a lacked of accuracy in the estimation of the display time of the text. Table 1 presents the questionnaire results for each functionality, rated at five levels: very easy, easy, regular, difficult and very difficult.

5. CONCLUSIONS

This work showed an authoring and navigation tool on video for mobile devices with touchscreen. The developed prototype allows adding textual annotations and it dynamically generates a navigation screen based on thumbnails of the captured frame at the annotation time and its text. The navigation through annotation proposed by Müller [6] is extended with focus on mobile devices. The usability evaluation performed contributed to the identification of problems and possibilities of interface improvements.

It is expected that this work contributes to the production of multimedia content through mobile devices, exploring authoring, navigation and facilitate collaboration, without the need of expertise in video authoring tools.

Acknowledgements

We thank FAPESP (Fundação de Amparo à Pesquisa do Estado de São Paulo) and CNPq (Conselho Nacional de Desenvolvimento Científico e Tecnológico) for financial support.

6. REFERENCES

[1] E. Frokjaer and K. Hornb. Cooperative usability testing: complementing usability tests with user-supported interpretation sessions. In *CHI '05 extended abstracts on Human factors in computing systems*, CHI EA '05, pages 1383–1386. ACM, 2005.

[2] J. Huber, J. Steimle, and M. Mühlhäuser. Toward more efficient user interfaces for mobile video browsing: an in-depth exploration of the design space. In *Proceedings of the international conference on Multimedia*, MM '10, pages 341–350. ACM, 2010.

[3] W. Hürst, C. G. Snoek, W.-J. Spoel, and M. Tomin. Keep moving!: revisiting thumbnails for mobile video retrieval. In *Proceedings of the international conference on Multimedia*, MM '10, pages 963–966. ACM, 2010.

[4] W. Hürst, C. G. M. Snoek, W.-J. Spoel, and M. Tomin. Size matters! how thumbnail number, size, and motion influence mobile video retrieval. In *Proceedings of the 17th international conference on Advances in multimedia modeling - Volume Part II*, MMM'11, pages 230–240. Springer-Verlag, 2011.

[5] W. Hürst, M. Welte, and S. Jung. An evaluation of the mobile usage of e-lecture podcasts. In *Proceedings of the 4th international conference on mobile technology, applications, and systems and the 1st international symposium on Computer human interaction in mobile technology*, Mobility '07, pages 16–23. ACM, 2007.

[6] S. Müller, G. Miller, and S. Fels. Using temporal video annotation as a navigational aid for video browsing. In *Adjunct proceedings of the 23nd annual ACM symposium on User interface software and technology*, UIST '10, pages 445–446. ACM, 2010.

[7] K. O'Hara, A. S. Mitchell, and A. Vorbau. Consuming video on mobile devices. In *CHI '07*, pages 857–866. ACM, 2007.

[8] M. d. G. C. Pimentel, R. G. Cattelan, E. L. Melo, G. B. Freitas, and C. A. Teixeira. Watch-and-comment as an approach to collaboratively annotate points of interest in video and interactive-tv programs. In A. Marcus, R. Sala, and A. C. Roibás, editors, *Mobile TV: Customizing Content and Experience*, Human-Computer Interaction Series, pages 349–368. Springer London, 2010.

[9] Q. Sun and W. Hürst. Video browsing on handheld devices-Interface designs for the next generation of mobile video players. *IEEE MultiMedia*, 15(3):76–83, July 2008.

[10] A. Torralba, R. Fergus, and W. T. Freeman. 80 million tiny images: A large data set for nonparametric object and scene recognition. *IEEE Trans. Pattern Anal. Mach. Intell.*, 30(11):1958–1970, Nov. 2008.

[11] D. A. Vega-Oliveros, D. de C. Pedrosa, M. d. G. Pimentel, and R. Goularte. Video navigation based on recent frames. In *Proc. XV Brazilian Symposium on Multimedia and the Web*, WebMedia '09, pages 36:1–36:4. ACM, 2009.

FIND: Facilitating the Identification of Intervals and Moments for Incorporation of Additional Content in Continuous Media

Kamila R. H. Rodrigues
Federal University of São Carlos - Brazil
kamila_rodrigues@dc.ufscar.br

Maria da Graça Pimentel
University of São Paulo - Brazil
mgp@icmc.usp.br

Suetônio S. Pereira
Federal University of São Carlos - Brazil
suetonio_pereira@comp.ufscar.br

Cesar A. C. Teixeira
Federal University of São Carlos - Brazil
cesar@dc.ufscar.br

ABSTRACT

As a result of many real world demands, the literature abounds with results in the form of annotation-based systems, as it is the case of systems which allow the annotation of audio or video objects as well as digital ink, paper and web pages, to name a few. Among the many types of annotations which may be of interest, annotations in the form of additional content associated with audio or video objects are likely to result in enriched media useful for several applications, including the promotion of accessibility. However, besides the highly demanding intellectual work of defining what additional content should be created for a particular segment of media, the author of that content faces the task of identifying the exact media intervals in which the additional content should be inserted. That task is particularly arduous when the media has a long duration. In this paper we propose FIND, a reference model guiding the construction of systems which aggregate software components for: 1) the specification and the recognition of patterns in audio or video; 2) the synchronized composition of the annotated media; 3) and the formatting of the annotated media into multimedia documents for presentation. We also illustrate how the model was instantiated in a configuration which allows the association of additional content to movies resulting in a multimedia document with better accessibility.

Categories and Subject Descriptors

H.1.2 **[Information Systems]:** Models and principles, Use/Machine Systems – *Human Factors*; H.5.1 **[Information Interfaces and Presentations]**: Multimedia Information Systems – *Audio, Video*.

Keywords

Media Enrichment, Additional Content, Multimedia Document Generation.

1. INTRODUCTION

Due to the demand for various application domains, the literature abounds with results in the form of annotation–based systems, as it is the case of systems which allow the annotation of audio objects [8], video [5], digital ink [7], web pages, to name a few. Among the many types of annotation which may be of interest, annotations in the form of additional content associated with audio or video objects are likely to result in enriched media useful for several applications. In this case, not only the original media may have its accessibility improved [6], but also the enriched documents can be used for purposes other than the original ones [5, 7].

However, besides the highly demanding intellectual work of defining what additional content should be created for a particular segment of media, the author faces the task of identifying the exact media intervals in which the additional content should be inserted. That task is particularly arduous when the media has a long duration.

Considering that several multimedia annotation platforms are rich in alternatives that support authors finding specific portions of the original media where to include additional content, there is an opportunity for the definition of a reference model associated with such systems.

In this paper we propose FIND, a reference model guiding the construction of systems which aggregates (1) software components for the specification and the recognition of patterns in audio or video which, are used to recommend time intervals in which authors associate additional content to the original media; (2) software components for the synchronized composition of annotated media; and (3) software components for the formatting of annotated media into multimedia documents for presentation to the viewer or listener.

As proof of concept, the model was instantiated in a restricted setting that allows the association of additional content to movies. This instantiation allowed a comparative analysis with respect to time and effort spent by the author of the additional content to carry out the enrichment media from manual steps and steps semi automated.

This paper is organized as follows: Section 2 discusses related work, Section 3 describes the proposed model, Section 4 presents the instantiation carried out from the model, and Section 5 summarizes the contributions and gives indicative of future works.

2. RELATED WORKS

Reference models for multimedia synchronization [3] and generation of multimedia applications [4] contribute significantly to building applications and environments.

The Advene model [1] and the ELAN tool [2] are more inclusive than the current instantiation (restricted) of FIND model. The Advene model (Annotate Digital Video, Exchange on the NEt) allows the realization of annotations into digital documents such as

Permission to make digital or hard copies of all or part of this work for personal or classroom use is granted without fee provided that copies are not made or distributed for profit or commercial advantage and that copies bear this notice and the full citation on the first page. To copy otherwise, or republish, to post on servers or to redistribute to lists, requires prior specific permission and/or a fee.
WebMedia'12, October 15–18, 2012, São Paulo/SP, Brazil.
Copyright 2012 ACM 978-1-4503-1706-1/12/10...$15.00.

movies, lectures and classes. The Advene allows users to share their analysis and annotations produced from the generation of documents in the hypervideo format. The model provides an interface for authoring and publishing that allows users create and edit annotations, and specify how they should be presented. Thus, users can also customize their own visualizations, in order to accommodate their specific needs. As the final multimedia document Advene generates SMIL files, CSV subtitles and SRT [1].

The ELAN is a professional tool for video and audio annotations. The tool adds components to the image recognition and signals to be processed to provide various patterns identified in a given media. Besides allowing annotations in the video and audio, the tool facilitates the visualization of information inserted and analysis of data obtained. The tool supports several audio and video formats as input and the final multimedia document is stored in XML file, allowing the export to text, HTML, SMIL and subtitles (SRT) [2].

The FIND model aims to serve as a reference for building of generic and extensible systems. Systems such as the Advene model and the ELAN tool, although more inclusive than the current instantiation of the FIND model in terms of pattern recognizers, does not report documentation regarding the possibility of extension, as proposed in the FIND model. It is interesting noting that the FIND model supports aggregation of components that, among others things, allows the annotations authoring with different levels of description, annotations that can make use of ontologies and, annotations that can be implemented using web services.

3. FIND MODEL

Figure 1 illustrates the general scenario in which an author of additional content faces the generic situation of adding additional content to an object of continuous media (such as video or audio), hereinafter referred to as original media, with some specific purpose to meet demands of different viewers or listeners.

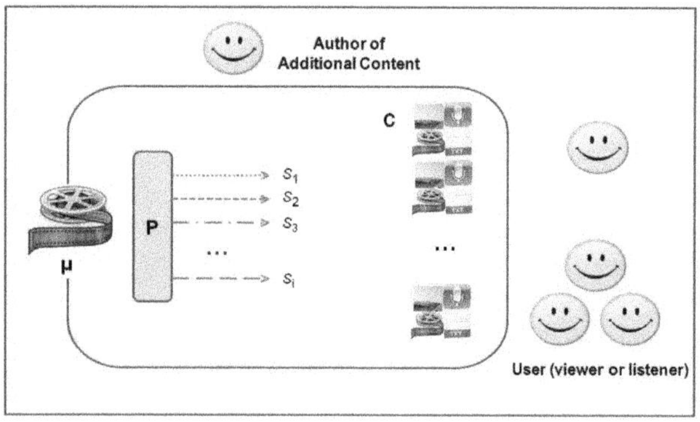

Figure 1. General scenario for media enrichment.

It is natural that additional content may require the time dimension when represented as continuous media, requiring the definition of the time or interval.

In Figure 1, μ represents the original media to be complemented. The block labeled P represents an entity to identify moments or intervals on the original media in accordance with patterns or properties p_i defined depending on the goals of the complementation of the media. The dotted arrows, obtained from functions $s_i = p_i(\mu)$, representing sequences of moments and intervals on the timeline that presents the media μ. A sequence s_i is useful for guiding authors of complements in the task of associating additional content, related to p_i, with the original media μ, mainly when the duration of the additional content and the duration of the intervals associated are relevant (duration of associated interval greater or equal than the duration of the additional content, for example). The blocks identified with the label C represent the additional content duly associated with an instance of μ, producing the appropriate multimedia object to the viewer or listener. It may be also relevant to generate a sequence *s*, in function of the different properties *p,* for guiding in the task of association of the additional content with μ. Generate one or more sequences *s* resulting from operations of union, intersection or complement on one or more properties *p* could also be relevant.

Figure 2 illustrates FIND, a versatile model of system for identification of intervals and moments, the incorporation of additional content and generation of the final multimedia object, which helps achieve the objectives of the media complementation.

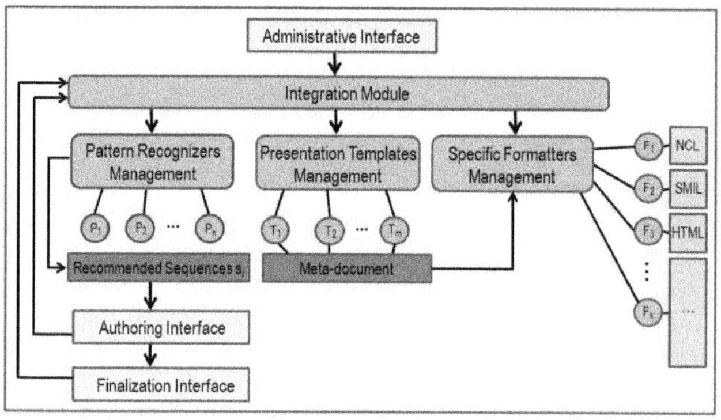

Figure 2. FIND model components.

The model is based on the aggregation of components that may be included or removed from the system by a user with administrator role using the Administrative Interface. There are three categories of components: Pattern Recognizers, Presentation Templates and Specific Formatters. For each category of component the model provides a management module that, under the control of a central Integration Module, provides interfaces for users with roles of administrator and author of additional content to provide them the relevant services. The modules for management also perform functions of allocating the appropriate component for the processing required.

The components of Pattern Recognizers are projected for specific functionality. It is reasonable to seek the reuse of existing components to save effort and development cost. Depending on the use that it aims for the multimedia document resulting from the complementation of the original media, different components or combinations of components for recognition should be used.

Through the Authoring Interface, the author specifies the set $p = \{p_a, p_b, \ldots p_k\}$ of property in the media that he wants to be recognized and the function $f(p_a, p_b, \ldots p_k)$ of union, intersection and complement to generate sequences of recommendation according to the desired goals. The Pattern Recognizers Management undertakes to trigger specific recognizers $P_a, P_b, \ldots P_k$ for the recognition of respective properties in moments and intervals in the media and to apply the function *f* to generate sequences of recommendation s_i.

With the recommended sequence and the first study on the media, the author observes the media more focused, choosing the most appropriate moments and segments for the insertion of additional content, which depends on its location in the media and also of its duration, in the case of intervals. The model also intends to provide an appropriate interface to the author and to facilitate navigation on the media using references to the sequence or recommended sequences. The interface should also make annotations easier. At this phase the author details the additional content to be produced, specifies the precise location / moment to insert the content and defines rules of interaction with the content.

In the next phase, the final art of the additional content is done with activities of locution of the audio to be added, inserting images and videos, among others. This work, done by the Finalization Interface, is guided by the annotations made by the author in the previous phase.

Concluded the human phase of the authoring, the information produced are forwarded to the generation of a meta-document. The author chooses the presentation template T_m to be used in function of the type of additional content and the interaction rules defined. The meta-document establishes the proper synchronization of the additional content with the original media, respecting also the rules of interaction established.

Finally, the F_k formatter chosen by the author, that must have compatibility with the template T_m, generates the final version of the document with additional content, in the specification language desired. This is the document that will be presented to the viewer or listener.

4. IMPLEMENTATION AND CASE STUDY

The study case carried out consists of the provision of additional multimedia content such as support for the accessibility of television programs, collaborating with viewers who have difficulties in the comprehension of the content of televise programs such as entertainment movies, providing a better enjoyment of the weft and encouraging the increased satisfaction of television viewers during the televise session [9].

Additional contents can be offered in different formats, including: audio, video, image and text. The proof of concept described in this paper uses the media in audio format, due to the preference detected in a previous study [9].

The insertion of additional content in audio format requires that the author analyzes the media several times to find intervals without the characters' speeches. It is important to identify the size of the intervals and which are best suited for the insertion.

The process of mapping the intervals without characters' speech demands a thorough manual effort of the additional content's author, which is often repetitive and requires attention and patience. The effort is grater if the author does not have a tool to identify the appropriate intervals for the content insertion.

By using a component recognition, a template for presentation and a formatter suitable to automate some steps of the production process of the additional content, it is possible to minimize the effort.

The Section 4.1 presents a scenario in which the additional content is inserted in a media by a non-automated method and a semi-automated method using an implementation of the FIND model that aggregates the basic components for the case studied.

4.1 Enriching entertainment movies with additional multimedia content

The insertion of additional content in movies is usually carried out in two stages: planning and production. At the planning stage, the author of additional content watches all the media to identify intervals without speeches of the characters or scenes that allow the insertion of text and image contents. After identifying these segments, the author makes a thorough analysis of the movie to identify the moments in which he/she concludes that the presence of a content to support the weft is necessary. Then, the author defines the additional content to be inserted, how long it will remain available and what media (audio, text and image) is more appropriate to represent this content. Also in the planning stage, related requirements to the interface (layout) of the additional content must be specified. In the production stage, the additional content requirements established in the planning are in fact associated with the media by the author. After the insertion of additional content, the author must create a final multimedia object to the assessment of the viewer and / or listener.

The planning stage is composed of five steps: 1) contact and familiarity with the media, 2) identification of intervals where additional content can be inserted, and 3) identification of moments when it is necessary to insert an additional content; 4) definition of what additional content to offer and 5) defining the layout of that content.

For a process carried out with most of the stages performed manually, first the author watches the movie without interruptions to get to know the plot and to become familiar with the media (step 1). In step 2, the author watches the media again, pausing it and delineating the intervals without characters' speeches, hereinafter referred to as silent intervals. To assist in the step of mapping the segments, the author uses a millimeter sheet (used in this project to provide a panoramic view of the media) and marks the beginning and end of each interval. At the end of this task the author has an overview of the total time of the media and snippets with intervals of silence present in the media. It is common, that in this step, the author watches the media several times to collect the appropriate intervals.

In step 3, the author analyzes the media again identifying narrative structures that may arouse doubts in viewers / listeners. After identifying the focus of possible doubts, the author takes notes about the type of content that should be inserted to help the viewer and takes notes on the next intervals for the content insertion. Then, the author draws up a script containing the content that best clarifies the snippet in analysis (step 4) and, then the narrator makes the locution of the prepared script. Finally, in step 5, the author defines the structure of the multimedia document, respecting standards and guidelines available in the literature and industry for the production of television content.

The final multimedia document's production, i.e., the synchronization between additional content, original media and rules of interaction with it, is a task usually aided by authoring tools of the language that the author wishes to express the document.

With the FIND model it is possible to automate some steps in the process of movies enrichment like the step of identifying the intervals of silence and also the step of generating the final multimedia object. The tool can also support the step of intervals of silence association to preliminary annotations made in the planning stage.

The instantiation described below follows a restricted configuration with a specific recognizer for identifying intervals without characters' speeches, a presentation template and a specific formatter to generate as final multimedia object, an NCL (Nested Context Language) document.

In the semi-automated process the author of additional content also makes movies enrichment in two stages: planning and production. However, these stages tend to be less costly to the author, because there is a tool support. The planning phase is also performed using the five steps outlined in the manual process.

The effort and the time spent by the author in steps 1 (familiarization with the media) and 4 (definition of additional content) are similar in both the manual process as in the semi-automated. In step 2 (intervals identification), however, the time and effort spent tend to decrease, because a component of recognizers, added to the system from FIND model, is responsible for returning to the author of content the recommended sequences with the intervals of silence offered in the media as input. The aggregate component to recognize the intervals in this proof of concept uses the legend provided with the movie to trace the characters' speeches and to identify the snippet where there are no speeches.

The step 3 (time identification) is also supported by the tool to facilitate the edition of additional content and its association with appropriate intervals. The step 3 is carried out through use of the component named Authoring Interface. To support step 5, in which by means of a meta-document is defined the structure of the multimedia document to be generated, it is used the aggregate component for managing the Presentation Templates. A template was aggregated and used to attend specifications this specific context.

The aggregation of a component for Finalization Interface supports the production stage allowing the narration of the audio content defined on a script in the planning stage and also allows the realization of the final art of the multimedia document.

After all content recording finalization, in the planning stage defined places, a component of Specific Formatters is aggregated for the final multimedia object generation. For this specific context, the added component generates an NCL document that will allow the viewers to interact, if they wish, with the additional content associated to the original media.

5. CONCLUSION AND FUTURE WORKS

Tests carried out with the movies enrichment using the tool componentized, following specifications of FIND model, indicate a significant reduction of effort and time spent by the author of the additional content in the analysis and media enrichment.

In a media of 40 minutes the author demands approximately 2 hours and 20 minutes to identify the intervals and to do annotations in the millimeters sheet, plus the time spent on the sheet's preparation. By aggregating a recognizer component, the same intervals are identified in approximately 1 minute.

The step 3 was carried out by the author in 3 hours and 15 minutes using the manual process in a media of 40 minutes, while the other media with similar time had the same step carried out in 2 hours and 5 minutes with the support of the tool. In this step it is necessary consider that the complexity of the media interferes in the identification time of moments of doubt and also in the additional content to be offered. However, the advantages that the author has to view the media as a whole, with its intervals of silence, and also the use of the component Authoring Interface for the additional content insertion, contribute to reducing the time and effort counted in this step.

Similarly, the step 5 has the time significantly reduced in the semi-automated process, because the meta-document is automatically generated. The aggregate component of Specific Formatters generates, from meta-document, a final multimedia document in NCL to be presented to viewers and / or listeners.

If the author needs to identify in the same media others intervals or moments with different characteristics from the absence of dialogue, one must add to the system another recognizer that identifies the specific property desired. Others components for Presentation Templates and Specific Formatters may also be required.

The case study carried out showed the versatility of the FIND model. In addition to providing a solution to a specific domain problem of associating additional content in an original media, and to contribute with research on accessibility area, the implementing generates the basis of a system to be expanded. The addition of new components to attend new demands of multimedia documents production, based on the association of additional content to media of video or audio, should promote this expansion.

6. ACKNOWLEDGEMENTS

We thank to CAPES, FAPESP and CNPq for financial support, FINEP and RNP that, through various projects of innovation and technological development, provided the physical resources to this research.

7. REFERENCES

[1] Aubert, O.; and Prié, Y. 2005. Advene: active reading through hypervideo. In *ACM Hypertext'05,* 2005.

[2] Auer, E.; Russel, A.; Sloetjes, H.; Wittenburg, P.; Schreer, O.; Masnieri, S.; Schneider, D.; and Tschöpel, S. 2010. ELAN as flexible annotation framework for sound and image processing detectors. In *Proc. of the 7th conference on International Language Resources and Evaluation (LREC'10)*, 17-23 May 2010, Valletta, Malta, pp. 890–893.

[3] Blakowski, G.; and Steinmetz, R. 1996. A Media Synchronization Survey: Reference Model, Specification, and Case Studies. In *IEEE Journal on Selected Areas in Communications* 14(1): 5-35, 1996.

[4] Bordegoni, M.; Faconti, G.; Feiner S.; Maybury, M.T.; Rist, T.; Ruggieri, S.; Trahanias, P.; and Wilson, M. 1997. A Standard Reference Model for Intelligent Multimedia Presentation Systems, Computer Standards and Interfaces .18(6, 7), North Holland, pp. 477-496, 1997.

[5] Cattelan, R. G.; Teixeira, C. A.; Goularte, R.; and Pimentel, M. G. P. 2008. Watch-and-comment as a paradigm toward ubiquitous interactive video editing. In *ACM Trans. Multimedia Comput. Commun.* Appl. 4, 4, Article 28 (November 2008), 24 pages, 2008. DOI=10.1145/1412196.1412201

[6] Hong, R.; Wang. M.; Yuan, X.; Xu, M.; Jiang, J.; Yan, S.; and Chua, T. 2011. Video accessibility enhancement for hearing-impaired users. In *ACM Trans. Multimedia Comput. Commun.* Appl. 7S, 1, Article 24 (November 2011), 19 pages. DOI=10.1145/2037676.203768

[7] Ispas, A. ;Signer, B.; and Norrie, M. C. 2011. An extensible digital ink segmentation and classification framework for natural notetaking. In *Proceedings of the 3rd ACM SIGCHI symposium on Engineering interactive computing systems - EICS '11.* ACM, New York, NY, USA, 231-240. DOI=10.1145/1996461.1996528.

[8] Junqua, J.C.; Mak, B.; and Reaves, B. 2004. A Robust Algorithm for Word Boundary Detection in the Presence of Noise. In *IEEE Trans. Speech and Audio Process,* Vol. 2, No., 3, pp. 406-412, Apr. 2004.

[9] Rodrigues, K. R. H., Pereira, S. S., Quinelato, L. G. G., Melo, E. L., Neris, V. P. A., Teixeira, C. A. C., 2011. Interação com conteúdo complementar por meio de múltiplos dispositivos para apoio à apreciação de programas televisivos. In *Anais do Simpósio Brasileiro de Sistemas Multimídia e Web – WebMedia 2011.*

Video Quality Subjective Assessment considering Cognitive Criteria and User Preferences on Video Content

Demóstenes Zegarra Rodríguez
Escola Politécnica of University of São Paulo
Brazil
demostenes@larc.usp.br

Júlia Abrahão
Escola Politécnica of University of São Paulo
Brazil
abrahao@unb.br

Dante Coaquira Begazo
Escola Politécnica of University of São Paulo
Brazil
dante@lps.usp.br

Renata Lopes Rosa
Escola Politécnica of University of São Paulo
Brazil
rrosa@usp.br

Graça Bressan
Escola Politécnica of University of São Paulo
Brazil
gbressan@larc.usp.br

ABSTRACT

There are several subjective test methodologies for assessing video quality, being that each of these methods was developed by considering specific degradation factors in video quality. Therefore, for video streaming services that use TCP as transport protocol different evaluation criteria should be considered as compared to current methods, because the impairment are only pauses. In this paper, the concepts of the mechanisms that integrate perceptual and cognitive processes are studied, relating them to a test environment for subjective evaluation of video, which is limited to streaming video service transmitted via HTTP / TCP. For this reason, some recommendations to perform subjective assessment of streaming video service are proposed, taking into account perceptual and cognitive criteria. In this work, subjective tests are conducted, evaluators with different content preferences assess 3 different video content. Results show that the assessors' QoE depends strongly on video content preferences. Thus, assessors who are interested in the video content are more drastic in the ratings. In the case of sport videos, the Mean Opinion Score (MOS) value of assesors with explicit preference in sports reachs only 54% of the MOS obtained by assessors without interest in sports. Furthermore, the roll of the instructor during the test is also evaluated.

Categories and Subject Descriptors

H.1.2 [**Models and Principles**]: User/Machine SystemsHuman factors; H.4.3 [**Information System Applications**]: Communications Applications Computer conferencing, teleconferencing, and videoconferencing; D.2.8 [**Software Engineering**]: Metrics—*complexity measures, performance measures*

Keywords

subjective assessment, video quality, perceptual and cognitive processes, video streaming, user profile, user preferences, video content.

Permission to make digital or hard copies of all or part of this work for personal or classroom use is granted without fee provided that copies are not made or distributed for profit or commercial advantage and that copies bear this notice and the full citation on the first page. To copy otherwise, to republish, to post on servers or to redistribute to lists, requires prior specific permission and/or a fee.
WebMedia'12, October 15–18, 2012, São Paulo/SP, Brazil.
Copyright 2012 ACM 978-1-4503-1706-1/12/10 ...$15.00.

1. INTRODUCTION

According to [1], the traffic estimated for video on Internet, excluding shared files and games, will reach 61% of total Internet traffic in 2015. Nowadays, there are several types of video services applications over IP networks, and according to the requirements of these applications and information, to be transmitted, a specific transport protocol can be used. The User Datagram Protocol (UDP) is not a connection oriented protocol and, therefore it is not guaranteed that the data will reach the destination; it is generally used for real-time services like VoIP, some video applications or for applications of simple request/response as Domain Name System (DNS). The Transmission Control Protocol (TCP) is a connection-oriented mechanism, thereby ensuring that the data arrives correctly and the specified string.

Video services like YouTube , Dailymotion and others have gained popularity in the recent years. These video services run over HyperText Transfer Protocol (HTTP) which uses TCP as the transport protocol. This is because communication services, based on UDP, are in some cases intercepted and blocked by firewalls or Network Address Translation (NATs), and for this reason, streaming video services based on UDP are not offered frequently. In this work, TCP prtocol is used as transport protocol of video streaming service, being analyzed the Quality of Experience (QoE) of end users, who has different preferences regarding the video content.

Human perception on the quality of voice and video materials is quantified by a score on subjective tests. The perceptual and cognitive processes occur in a continuum. Characteristics such as: color, texture, size, shapes, brightness, motion, experienced by the human senses do part of external stimuli acting in our environment; this process is named low sensory process. The central nervous system realizes this information, converted into electrochemical stimulus, and it is interpreted, organized, stored and recalled. The information through different cognitive processes, such as memory, categorization, attention, problem solving and decision making processes, which provide indicators for action. Thus, it is important considers the cognitive process to determine the perceptual video quality [2,3].

On video quality assessment are used many algorithms, some of them based on statistical and mathematical parameters of image, such as Mean Squared Error (MSE) and Peak Signal-to-Noise Ratio (PSNR). Others, based on characteristics of the Human Visual System (HVS), consider visual information stimulus as proposed in SSIM [4] and VQM [5] metrics; or considering stimulus based on attention maps to determine the quality assessment [6,7]. Nevertheless, on video streaming service over TCP that present pauses, these algorithms and models are not appropriate to assess its quality. Pauses, for instance, disrupt cognitive process mechanisms when a user watches a video. As the frequency of pauses and their duration is increased, the users' attention and interest on video also decrease proportionally.

Our main objective is to determine how the concepts of the mechanisms that integrate perceptual and cognitive processes must be related to a test environment for subjective assessment of video, which will be limited to the service of video streaming transmitted over HTTP / TCP being presented some recommendations to perform this type of tests. Furthermore, the effect that the explicit preference of assessors regarding video content has over the QoE was studied.

The remainder of this paper is structured as follows. Section 2 introduces the current Subjective Test Methods. Section 3 presents the test methodology followed to conduct subjective tests, and the test materia is described. Section 4 shows the results obtained in this work. Finally, section 5 presents the conclusions and future works.

2. VIDEO QUALITY SUBJECTIVE TESTS

Currently, the most relevant methods to assess video quality are described in ITU recommendations: ITU-R BT-500 [8] and ITU-T P.910 [9], the latter more focused on multimedia services. In [10,11] are presented other methodologies which have few variants in relation to the described in the ITU recommendations.

ITU-R BT-500 described the following methods:

- Double Stimulus Impairment Scale (DSIS),
- Double Stimulus Continuous Quality Scale (DSCQS),
- Single Stimulus Continuous Quality Evaluation (SSCQE), and
- Simultaneous Double Stimulus for Continuous Evaluation (SDSCE)

And , in ITU-T P.910 the following methods are described:

- Absoluty Category Rating (ACR),
- Absolute category rating with hidden reference (ACR-H),
- Degradation Category Rating (DCR), and
- Pair comparison method (PC)

These methods consider video length around 10 seconds, where they are more oriented to assessing the effects of spatial degradation in the video frames, except the method Single Stimulus Continuous Quality Evaluation (SSCQE). Consequently, the effects of degradation caused by pauses cannot be properly evaluated using these methods. The SSCQE methodology considers a longer duration of video sequence and a continuous assessment by the user. However, applying this methodology, it would not be reasonable to give a score during the pause.

3. TEST METHODOLOGY

In this section the practical considerations to conduct subjective test of video quality are described, these considerations were followed in the tests performed in this work. Additionally, the main characterisitics of the video sequences used in the test are presented.

3.1 Practical Recommendations to conduct Video Quality Subjective Tests

In the subjective tests conducted, the variability of the cognitive processes of individuals was considered; thus assessors have different characteristics, such as attention level, speed in processing information, short-term memory and long-term memory, in addition to prior knowledge and preferences. The following lines present the practical considerations taken in the subjective tests conducted in this paper.

- Video sequences must be longer than 10 seconds for not losing the effect of temporality of pauses. Sequences of 3-minute were used in this paper, using as reference the top videos in *YouTube*, which have a 3-minute video length.
- Assessment tests should be conducted in an environment similar to the actual use of a video streaming service. In this paper was considered that assessors make the streaming of videos according to their preferences, watching each video as many times as they deem necessary.
- The variability of assessor's attention is considered, and because this must be pertinent that the instructions for performing the tests must be specific. Thus, at the beginning of the test, the instructor advises assessors that video degradation is only due to presence of pauses, so that their attention is focused only on the degradation factor.
- The tests were not conducted in groups of assessors, all test were performed individually, because the evaluations should be performed when each user find they have understood the test procedure. The evaluators have different speeds for processing information; hence, a limited time for them to give their scores was not considered. They can not feel any kind of pressure.
- Considering the variability in individual memory characteristics of the assessors, they can watch the videos as many times each of them considers necessary, being possible to change the scores as indicated in the SAMVIQ methodology [11].
- It is important to take into account the assessor's preferences for video contents, in order to form different

groups of assessors. The quantification of this variability of preferences in the video content and assessor preferences is part of this study, and some results will be presented.

- In order to analyze the result in a better way, it is relevant know the profile of the assessors. Thus, some characteristics as, age, gender, education level, knowledge in technology, expert or naive in video quality test, etc. need to be known.

3.2 Video Sequences

ITU-T P.910 Recommendation presents a classification of video content, these categories are showed in Table 1.

Table 1: Video Scene Content Categories [6]

Category	Description
A	One person, mainly head and shoulders, limited detail and motion
B	One person with graphics and/or more detail
C	More than one person
D	Graphics with pointing
E	High object and/or camera motion (examples of broadcast TV)

In this paper, as test material, three different video categories were chosen to conduct the subjective tests. For each video category, two video sequencies are considered, the first one is the original video, and the second one is a degraded video of the same sequence. As consequense, they are six test video sequences, which are presented in Table 2. The degraded video sequencies were built inserting four pauses, each pause with a duration of four seconds. These pauses were distribuided uniformly in the time domain during the whole video.

Table 2: Video sequencies for Subjetive Video Quality Assessment

Video Sequence	Number of of pauses	Pause length (s)
E (Foorball)	0	0
E (Foorball)	4	4
B (Documentary)	0	0
B (Documentary)	4	4
A (New)	0	0
A (New)	4	4

The characteristics for all videos are: 640x360 of resolution and 29.97 fps, and the H.264/AVC video codec was used. Video length of all videos was 180 seconds

Evaluators watched each video sequence continuously from the beginning to the end without inserting interim periods for evaluation, to avoid losing the temporal efect of pauses. 41 subjects participated in the evaluation, they had no vision problems, no knowledge in the image or video evaluation and who had used the video streaming service before evaluate the test video sequencies. Each video was scored for at least 15 assessors.

4. RESULTS

Figure 1 shows the results obtained. The rating scale used was five-grade numerical quality scale described in Annex B of ITU-T recommendation P.910. It can be observed that in all videos sequences, assessors with explicit preference gave the lowest scores as compared to assessors with no preference.

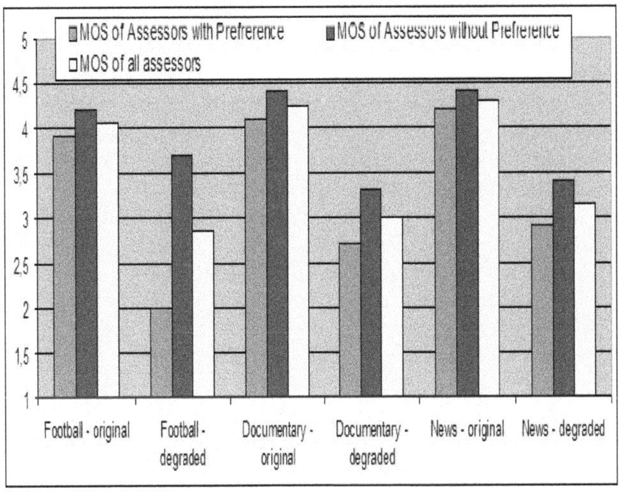

Figure 1: MOS index values considering or not the assessor's preference

In Table 3 can be observed two different ratios, the first one (Ratio 1) is obtained from MOS value of user with an explicit preference and MOS value of all users, and Ratio 2 is obtained between MOS value of user with an explicit preference and MOS value of user without preference. It can be concluded, that the video content category also plays an important roll. Thus, in football videos were obtained the lowest ratios, which mean the greatest difference, where ratio 1 and ratio 2 reach 70% and 54% respectively.

Table 3: Effects of assessors preferences

Video Sequence	Ratio 1 (%)	Ratio 2 (%)
Foorball-orig.	96.3	92.86
Foorball-degr.	70.18	54.05
Documentary-orig.	96.47	93.18
Documentary-degr.	90.00	81.82
New-orig.	97.67	95.45
New-degr.	92.06	85.29

As stated before, the instructor plays an important role in video quality subjective assessment. Table 4 shows the MOS index values obtained in two different test scenarios. In the first scenario, the instructor warns that pauses are the sole degradation factor. In the second scenario, this warning is not given. The 50% of assessors have preference for each video content and the other 50% do not have. MOS index values obtained for the first scenario are greater in relation to the second one. The video sequences used in these test were only the 3 impairment videos. It can be observed that video content category is also an important factor in the users' QoE.

Table 4: Effect of Assessor knows that pauses are the sole degradation factor

Video Sequence	MOS of Assessors warned	MOS of Assessors do not warned
Football	2.8	2.5
Documentary	3.0	2.9
News	3.1	3.0

5. CONCLUSIONS AND FUTURE WORKS

Based on the variability of the cognitive processes of assessors some practical recommendations to be considered in subjective assessment were made. These recommendations are limited a video streaming service over HTTP/TCP where the impairments are only the pauses. As a result of the tests, we highlight the importance of the relationship between the video content with the assessor's preference. Assessors who are interested in the video content are more drastic in the ratings.

Another important conclusion is that video content category can determine the level of user satisfaction. The results show that impairments in videos about sport are more sensible regarding the QoE of end users, and this was validated for both cases, users with and without preference. The impairments (pauses) in the others video content categories affect the QoE in a minor scale.

Also, we observed that if the instructor warns that pauses are the sole degradation, the subjective test results change. When the assessors are aware that the sole impairment is the pause, the MOS index values increase. This increment also depends on the video category.

As a future work, the number of both assessors and video tests of the same content category will be increased. Also, different types of video degradation will be considered. Based in the subjective test results that will be obtained, a new metric to assess video quality in video streaming service over TCP will be proposed. This metric will take into account the video content preferences of end users.

6. ACKNOWLEDGMENTS

This work was supported by FAPESP (The São Paulo Research Foundation -Brazil). FAPESP project number: 2011/12724-8.

7. REFERENCES

[1] Cisco System, *Visual Networking Index*, White Paper. Jun. 2011.

[2] G. Nyman, J. Radun, T. Leisti, J. Oja, H. Ojanen, J. Olives, T. Vuori and J. Hikkinen, *What do users really perceive - probing the subjective image quality experience.* Proceedings of the IS-T/SPIE's: Imaging Quality and System Performance III, Vol. 6059, 2006

[3] G. Nyman, J. Radun, T. Leisti, and T. Vouri, *From image fidelity to subjective quality: a hybrid qualitative/quantitative methodology for measuring subjective image quality for different image contents,* in Proc. of the International Display Workshops, Vol. 12, 1817-1820, 2007

[4] Z. Wang, A. C. Bovik, H. Sheikh, *Image Quality Assessment: From Error Visibility to Structural Similarity,* IEEE Transactions on Image Processing, vol. 13, No. 4, Apr 2004.

[5] M. Pinson and S. Wolf, *A new standardized method for objectively measuring video quality,* IEEE Trans. Broadcast., vol. 50, no. 3, pp. 312-322, Sep. 2004.

[6] J. You, A. Perkis, M. Gabbouj, and M. M. Hannuksela, *Perceptual quality assessment based on visual attention analysis*, in Proc. ACM Int. Conf. Multimedia, pp. 561-564, Mar. 2009

[7] A. K. Noorthy and A. C. Bovik, *Visual importance pooling for image quality assessment,* IEEE J. Select. Topics Signal Process., Vol. 3, no. 2, pp. 193-201, Apr. 2009.

[8] ITU, *Methodology for the Subjective Assessment of the Quality of Television Pictures,* ITU-R Recommendation BT.500-11, 2002.

[9] ITU, *Subjective Video Quality Assessment Methods for Multimedia Applications,* ITU-T Recommendation-P.910, Geneva, Abr. 2008.

[10] J. Redi, H. Liu, H. Alers, R. Zunino and I. Heynderickx. *Comparing Subjective Image Quality Measurement Methods for the Creation of Public Databases*, Electronic Imaging, SPIE Vol. 7529, pp 1-11, Apr. 2010.

[11] J. L. Blin, *New quality evaluation method suited to multimedia context: Samviq,* in Proceedings of the Second International Workshop on Video Processing and Quality Metrics, VPQM'06, Scottsdale, January 2006.

Detecção de fraudes em transações na Web (Fraud Detection in Web Transactions)

Rafael Alexandre França de Lima
DECOM - Departamento de Computação
Centro Federal de Educação Tecnológia de Minas Gerais -CEFET-MG
rafaelfrancalima@gmail.com

Adriano César Machado Pereira
DECOM - Departamento de Computação
Centro Federal de Educação Tecnológia de Minas Gerais -CEFET-MG
adriano@decom.cefetmg.br

ABSTRACT

The volume of electronic transactions has raised a lot in last years, mainly due to the popularization of e-commerce. We also observe a significant increase in the number of fraud cases, resulting in billions of dollars losses each year worldwide. Therefore it is important and necessary to develop and apply techniques that can assist in fraud detection, which motivates our research. This work aims to apply and evaluate computational intelligence techniques to identify fraud in electronic transactions, more specifically in credit card operations, using Bayesian Networks and Logistic Regression. In order to evaluate the techniques, we define a concept of economic efficiency and apply them in an actual dataset of the most popular Brazilian electronic payment service. Our results show good performance in fraud detection, presenting gains up to 35.61% compared to the actual scenario of the company.

Categories and Subject Descriptors

K.4.4 [**Computers and Society**]: Electronic Commerce; H.3.5 [**Online Information Services**]: Web based services

General Terms

Experimentation, Security

Keywords

Fraud Detection, e-Commerce, Logistic Regression, Bayesian network, e-Payment Systems, Web Applications

1. INTRODUÇÃO

A popularização e o sucesso dos serviços Web trouxeram inúmeros desafios que precisam ser endereçados. Os usuários ao utilizarem um desses serviços Web ainda encontram enormes dificuldades para alcançar seus objetivos com sucesso [2, 16]. Isso se deve não apenas à quantidade imensa de informação presente na Web e que vem aumentando consideravelmente, mas principalmente à questão da credibilidade em sistemas computacionais [27], no que diz respeito à informação, aos serviços, às fontes e à própria infraestrutura computacional.

Após o desenvolvimento de tecnologias que trazem maior facilidade de comunicação e disseminação de conteúdo na Web, houve um aumento significativo do número de fraudes em transações eletrônicas, se tornando um dos principais desafios encontrados atualmente na Web. Criminosos se aproveitam dessa facilidade de utilização e popularização dos serviços Web para obter por meio de ações fraudulentas, vantagens financeiras, informações privilegiadas, dentre outros. Na área tecnológica, pode-se citar vários tipos de fraudes como, por exemplo, fraudes em telecomunicações e no comércio eletrônico, sendo que cada uma delas possui suas características e necessitam de metodologias diferentes para serem combatidas. Devido a essas caraterísticas, o profissional encarregado de detectar fraude deve possuir um bom conhecimento da área na qual deseja-se combater o problema ou recorrer a algum especialista para auxiliá-lo na criação de modelos mais eficazes no combate à fraude.

Devido à importância do problema de detecção de fraude, vários são os trabalhos associados a essa linha de pesquisa [1, 10, 11, 17]. Em geral, esses trabalhos buscam criar metodologias que permitam o combate ou um melhor entendimento e caracterização da fraude. Normalmente esse tipo de trabalho utiliza de técnicas de Inteligência Computacional baseando-se em reconhecimento de padrões para detectar fraudes, entre as técnicas utilizadas podemos citar: Redes Neurais, Sistemas Imunológicos, Árvores de Decisão e Redes Bayesianas [12, 25].

Motivados pela crescente demanda de técnicas que sejam capazes de detectar fraudes, neste projeto aplicamos e avaliamos técnicas baseadas em inteligência computacional para identificar fraudes em transações eletrônicas, mais especificamente em operações envolvendo cartão de crédito. A fim de testar e validar a nossa metodologia, utilizamos um cenário real de um sistema para pagamento eletrônico. Além disso, adotamos um conceito (métrica) de Eficiência Econômica para avaliar o desempenho das técnicas utilizadas nesse projeto. Os resultados que serão aqui apresentados foram bastante satisfatórios, alcançando ganhos de até 36% quando comparado ao cenário real da empresa na atualidade. Isso resume as principais contribuições deste trabalho.

O restante deste artigo está organizado da seguinte forma. A Seção 2 descreve alguns trabalhos relacionados ao tema de pesquisa deste projeto. A Seção 3 apresenta uma breve descrição sobre as técnicas de redes bayesianas e de regressão logística, que foram a base dos modelos usados neste trabalho. A Seção 4 descreve a metodologia utilizada no nosso trabalho, a qual será aplicada na Seção 5 em nosso estudo de caso com dados reais providos pela

Permission to make digital or hard copies of all or part of this work for personal or classroom use is granted without fee provided that copies are not made or distributed for profit or commercial advantage and that copies bear this notice and the full citation on the first page. To copy otherwise, to republish, to post on servers or to redistribute to lists, requires prior specific permission and/or a fee.
WebMedia'12, October 15–18, 2012, São Paulo/SP, Brazil.
Copyright 2012 ACM 978-1-4503-1706-1/12/10 ...$15.00.

empresa Universo Online (UOL). Finalmente, a Seção 6 apresenta as conclusões e trabalhos futuros.

2. TRABALHOS RELACIONADOS

Métodos para detecção de fraude são bastante discutidos na literatura, com diversas pesquisas nesta área [13, 21, 3, 18], onde dependendo do tipo de fraude que deseja-se prevenir se torna necessário a utilização de um método diferente com suas características. Entretanto podemos perceber que técnicas baseadas em mineração de dados estão sendo muito utilizadas e desempenham um importante papel na detecção de fraude. Isso acontece devido a mineração de dados permitir reconhecer padrões necessários para resolução do problema a partir de um vasto conjunto de dados.

Inúmeras técnicas são utilizadas em mineração de dados para detectar fraudes. Bhattacharyya et al [4] utilizam as técnicas de *support vector machines*, *random forests* e regressão logística para detectar fraudes em cartões de crédito em um cenário real. Apesar dos autores utilizarem a técnica de regressão logística comum ao nosso trabalho, não é possível uma comparação de resultados entre os dois trabalhos, pois a técnica foi utilizada com um foco diferente. Chaochang Chiu et al [8] utilizam metódos de descoberta em redes e mineração de dados para detectar fraudes em um serviço de contas de usuários na Web, identificando possíveis usuários fraudulentos, mostrando assim que detecção de fraude é um assunto amplo e pode ser importante em diversos serviços Web.

Perols [23] faz uma comparação de seis diferentes técnicas estatísticas e de aprendizagem de máquina para prever fraudes em declarações financeiras feitas por diferentes empresas. Os resultados apresentados pelo autor mostram que as técinas de SVM *(Support Vector Machines)* e regressão logística se destacaram frente as outras técnicas utilizadas, como redes neurais e árvore de decisão.

Clifton Phua et al [24] realizaram amplo estudo e escreveram diversos artigos relacionados com detecção de fraude, usando mineração de dados e suas técnicas derivadas para solucionar o problema. O autor discute diferentes estratégias para solucionar o problema, baseando em algoritmos de treinamento não supervisionado ou supervisionado, aplicando esses em dados desbalanceados.

No treinamento supervisionado o algoritmo analisa cada transação para que matematicamente determine o padrão de uma transação de fraude e possa estimar seu risco. Redes Neurais, *Support Vector Machine* (SVM), Árvore de Decisão e Redes Bayesianas são algumas das técnicas que adotam essa estratégia. Maes et al [20] usa o algoritmo denominado *STAGE* para redes bayesianas e o algoritmo *backpropagation* para detectar fraude em transações com cartões de crédito através de Redes Neurais. Os resultados obtidos por Maes mostram que Redes Bayesianas se mostram mais precisas e simples de serem aplicadas, entretanto são mais lentas quando se precisa inserir novos registros. Técnicas como SVM são destaque como estado-da-arte, mas o SVM não apresentou eficiência, em termos de escalabilidade, em nosso caso, demandando semanas para completar uma execução do modelo.

No treinamento não supervisionado não se tem conhecimento prévio de quais transações resultaram em fraude ou não fraude. Alguns exemplos de técnicas que utilizam treinamento não supervisionado são *Clustering* e Detecção Anômala. Netmap [22] descreve o funcionamento do algoritmo de *Clustering* para previsão de fraude. Bolton and Hand [5] propõem um método de detecção de fraude em transações de cartão de crédito utilizando a Detecção Anômala.

Os trabalhos aqui brevemente descritos sugerem a crescente necessidade de prover mecanismo que sejam capazes de detectar fraudes, para que assim usuários possam utilizar com segurança os serviços online.

3. FUNDAMENTAÇÃO TEÓRICA

3.1 Redes Bayesianas

Redes Bayesianas são grafos acíclicos dirigidos que representam dependência entre as variáveis de um modelo probabilístico, onde os nós são os atributos e os arcos representam os relacionamentos de influência entre as variáveis.[19] As Redes Bayesianas podem ser representadas graficamente por um conjunto de variáveis e um conjunto de arcos que ligam essas variáveis, como mostrado na Figura 1, onde o evento A depende diretamente do evento D, que por sua vez depende diretamente de B e H e assim consecutivamente, já o evento e é um evento independente. [9].

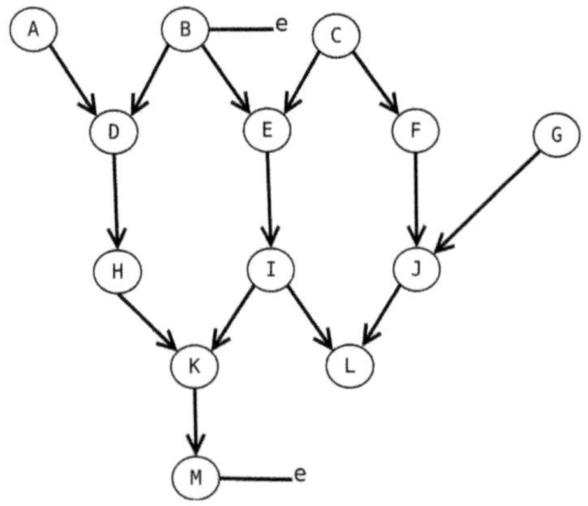

Figure 1: Exemplo de Redes Bayesianas dado um evento A.

Já do ponto de vista matemático Redes Bayesianas são derivadas do teorema de Bayes, o qual mostra que a probabilidade condicional de um evento A_i dado um evento B, pode ser calculado pela Equação 1.

$$P(A_i|B) = \frac{P(B|A_i)P(A_i)}{P(B)} \tag{1}$$

, onde $P(A_i|B)$ é a probabilidade de A dado que B ocorreu.

Logo, para aplicar a técnica de redes bayesianas em um problema de detecção de fraudes calcula-se, a partir do teorema de Bayes, a probabilidade de encontrar uma fraude, dado que outros eventos ocorreram, montando assim uma tabela de probabilidades condicionadas. De posse dessas probabilidades podemos calcular uma probabilidade final utilizando a Equação 2.

$$P(x_i, ..., x_n) = \prod_{i=0}^{n} P(x_i|Pais(X_i)) \tag{2}$$

, onde os pais de X(i) são determinados por um grafo, como da Figura 1.

No reconhecimento de padrões as dependências desse grafo são calculadas por verossimilhança, os nós pais e consequentemente a tabela de probabilidade condicionada são determinadas a partir de um treinamento sobre o conjunto de dados [29].

3.2 Regressão Logística

Regressão logística é uma técnica estatística que produz, a partir de uma série de variáveis explicativas, um modelo que permita a predição de valores tomados por uma variável dependente categórica.

Assim através de um modelo de regressão, é possível calcular a probabilidade de ocorrência de um evento, através da função de ligação, conforme descrita na Equação 3:

$$\pi(x) = \frac{e^{(\beta_0+\beta_1 x_1+\beta_2 x_2+...\beta_i x_i)}}{1+e^{(\beta_0+\beta_1 x_1+\beta_2 x_2+...\beta_i x_i)}}, \tag{3}$$

onde $\pi_i(x)$ é a probabilidade de sucesso quando o valor da variável preditiva é x, β_0 é uma constante usada para ajuste e β_i são os coeficientes das variáveis preditivas [15]. Para encontrar a estimativa dos coeficientes β na Equação 3, é usada a técnica de máxima verossimilhança que maximiza a probabilidade de obter o grupo observado de dados, através do modelo estimado. Na regressão logística essa técnica pode ser resolvida pelo método de *Newton-Raphson*, o qual gera uma sequência de soluções que convergem para o ponto máximo da função de verossimilhança [6].

O modelo de regressão logística binária é um caso especial de modelo linear generalizado, que usa a função de ligação logit para obter as estimativas dos coeficientes da Equação 3 [28]. Após encontrar os coeficientes, é possível encontrar a probabilidade de sucesso, que em nossa pesquisa é a probabilidade de fraude, aplicando na Equação 3 os valores das estimativas dos coeficientes encontrados.

4. METODOLOGIA

A metodologia adotada neste projeto iniciou-se com o entendimento e modelagem do problema de detecção de fraude, com uma completa caracterização do cenário que será descrito na Seção 5. Antes da execução das técnicas foram feitas análises sobre o conjunto de dados a fim de retirar atributos que continham grande quantidade de valores nulos ou valores inconsistentes com a natureza dos dados. Após essa análise foi feita a categorização de variáveis numéricas para melhor adequação das técnicas utilizadas, para isso transformamos cada atributo contínuo em um atributo discreto com diversas classes com amplitude (tamanho dessas faixas) fixa, onde essa amplitude (h) foi calculada pela equação 4, onde K é o número de classes e A_T é a amplitude amostral (maior valor - menor valor).

$$h = \frac{A_T}{K}, \tag{4}$$

Após esses ajustes na base de dados fizemos uma seleção dos atributos mais significativos para detectar fraude, para isso foram utilizadas as técnicas de *forward stepwise regression*, a qual baseia-se no conceito de verossimilhança e está implementada no software estatístico R [26, 29] e *Infogain*, que mostra o ganho relativo com a inclusão de cada variável. Para a realização da técnica de *Infogain* utilizamos o software Weka *(Waikato Environment for Knowledge Analysis)*, um software livre para mineração de dados, que possui sua licença baseada na GPL *(General Public Licence)* [30].

A decisão de quais atributos escolher foi tomada não somente pela eleção dos atributos através das técnicas (*Stepwise* e *Infogain*), mas também por diversos testes de caracterização que permitiram encontrar os atributos que melhor se adaptam a cada técnica. Esses atributos serão descritos na Seção 5.2.

Após selecionar os atributos, definimos os conjuntos de treinamento e testes para validar os modelos. Como nossa base de dados foi selecionada sobre transações em meses distintos,utilizamos as três primeiras semanas do mês como treinamento e as duas últimas semanas como teste. Dessa forma ficou clara a aplicação em um cenário real e preservamos a generalidade dos modelos. Além dessa abordagem, utilizamos a técnica de *K-fold-Cross-Validation*, definindo o número de subamostras como 5.

Para implementar as técnicas e criarmos os modelos de detecção de fraude utilizamos dois ambientes. O software R foi usado para regressão logística, a escolha por esse software ocorreu devido a este ser um software livre e possuir diversos pacotes estatísticos que poderiam ser utilizados. Já para Redes Bayesianas utilizamos o software Weka. Os dois softwares foram instalados em um servidor Xeon com 16 nucleos e 32 GB de RAM, sobre um sistema operacional Linux. Cada ambiente possui diferentes parâmetros para o funcionamento das técnicas, a escolha dos melhores parâmetros para cada técnica foi feita através de diversos testes de precisão. Para a realização desses testes pesquisamos na literatura os parâmetros mais utilizados para detecção de fraudes nas técnicas de regressão logística e redes bayesianas e realizamos testes com a combinação de todos parâmetros possíveis, escolhendo os que melhores se adaptaram aos modelos [14, 28, 26].

Abaixo mostramos a escolha dos parâmetros para cada técnica.

- Para construir o modelo baseado na técnica de regressão logística usamos o pacote *GLM*(modelos lineares generalizados) proveniente do software R. Nesse configuramos os parâmetros: *FORMULA* onde o atributo *ChargeBack* foi definido como variável resposta e os demais atributos como variável independente. O campo *FAMILY* foi definido como binomial e o *LINK* como logit, para caracterizar uma regressão logística binária. Após esses ajustes foi possível obter as estimativas dos coecfientes para os atributos independentes. Em seguida foi calculado a probabilidade de uma transação ser fraudulenta, usando a equação 3.

- Para a realização da técnica de redes bayesianas utilizamos o software Weka, nesse através do parâmetro **D** escolhemos usar uma estrutura de arvore chamada de ADTree para economizar tempo de execução. No parametro **Q** escolhemos o algoritmo *hill climbing* para buscar a topológia da rede, como subcategoria desse algoritmo temos os parâmetros P que define o número máximo de nós país, como a nossa base tem apenas uma variável resposta utilizamos apenas 1 pai e S onde definimos que seria utilizado o score de Bayes para montar a tabela de probabilidades. Além desses parâmetros existe o parametro **E** que define o estimador, valor que será usado como base para determinar se uma transação é fraudulenta ou não, esse valor foi irrelevante, porque nesse artigo adotamos a metodologia de criar um ranking para classificação, que será descrita abaixo.

Com os resultados obtidos pela aplicação dos modelos foi feito um *ranking* pelo grau de probabilidade de fraude para cada transação, onde no topo do *ranking* encontram-se os registros com maior probabilidade de fraude. Após a construção do *ranking* foi feita uma análise em suas diversas faixas, verificando a precisão, revocação e uma função objetivo denominada Eficiência Econômica (EE) dos modelos.

O conceito de Eficiência Econômica foi utilizado porque em transações que envolvem valores financeiros o custo de um falso positivo e um falso negativo não é o mesmo, estima-se que esse custo na grande parte das companhias é de ordem de 1:100. Ou seja, se perde bem mais prevendo que uma operação fraudulenta é legal, do que o contrário. Outro fator predominante para adotarmos a eficiência econômica foi o desbanlaceamento da nossa base de dados, tendo um volume muito maior de transações válidas, portanto não poderíamos medir somente a precisão e revocação dos modelos. Já que se classificássemos todas as transações como válidas (não fraude) e medíssemos a precisão, encontraríamos uma precisão muita alta independentemente do modelo utilizado, o que parecia ser uma boa precisão, mas na verdade estaria acarretando um prejuízo de milhares de reais, ao afirmar que 100% das fraudes eram legais.

Sendo assim, toda a análise foi feita em escalas do *ranking*, considerando a função de Eficiência Econômica que será descrita na Equação 5.

$$EE = \sum_{i=1}^{Num.Transacoes} G*k - P*(1-k) \quad (5)$$

, onde: **K** é uma constante que simboliza o percentual que o mercado eletrônico fatura em cada transação; **G** é o valor que o mercado eletrônico arrecadou após a aplicação do modelo, ou seja valores das transações que o modelo previu como confiável e realmente eram confiáveis; **P** é valor que o mercado eletrônico perdeu após a utilização do modelo, ou seja valores das transações que o nosso modelo previu que eram válidas e na verdade eram fraudes (falso positivo).

Para comparação dos modelos é preciso descrever o conceito de Eficiência Econômica Máxima (EE_{Max}), que determina o maior valor que poderia ser arrecadado pelo mercado eletrônico, sendo que esse ocorreria em um cenário fictício, onde um modelo ideal teria 100% de precisão e 100% de revocação. Ou seja, o modelo iria prever com sucesso todas as situações de fraudes, e não identificaria nenhuma situação de não fraude como sendo de fraude. Também definimos o conceito de Eficiência Econômica Real (EE_{Real}) que é a eficiência obtida pelo mercado eletrônico na atualidade com seus métodos para detecção de fraude.

Essa metodologia está ilustrada na Figura 2. Na próxima seção será apresentada a instanciação dessa metodologia aplicada a um estudo de caso utilizando dados reais.

5. ESTUDO DE CASO

Esta seção apresenta nosso estudo de caso, onde aplicamos nossa metodologia para detectar fraudes em transações eletrônicas, mais especificamente em operações com cartão de crédito, evidenciadas através das transações que ocorreram *chargeback* (estorno no cartão de crédito quando a transação não é reconhecida como válida). Devido a um acordo de confidencialidade com a empresa, não podemos divulgar informações quantitativas sobre os dados, logo serão apresentadas apenas informações gerais sobre esses, mas que são capazes de descrever o cenário utilizado nessa pesquisa.

5.1 Visão geral da base de dados

Para validar a nossa metodologia utilizamos uma base de dados real proveniente do sistema para pagamentos online PagSeguro [1] do grupo Universo Online Inc. (UOL)[2] . O PagSeguro hoje é o sistema de pagamento mais utilizado no Brasil, ficando clara a necessidade de previsão de fraudes nesse sistema, pretendendo assim trazer mais segurança para usuários que o utilizam e reduzir o déficit econômico ocasionados por esse tipo de transações.

No PagSeguro cada transação é composta por dezenas de atributos de mais diferentes tipos, sendo que um desses atributos refere-se ao status da transações, podendo acarretar em transações seguras e transações que ocorreram *chargeback*.

A Tabela 1 mostra um pequeno resumo referente aos valores médios de transações no PagSeguro, a partir dessa tabela podemos notar que as transações que ocorreram *chargeback* tem, na média, maiores valores do que as transações válidas. A cobertura desta tabela quanto dos demais resultados apresentados nesse artigo é de outubro de 2010 a março de 2011.

Cobertura (tempo)	Out/10 a Mar/11
Valor Médio de transação (R$)	75,11
Valor Médio de transação *chargeback* (R$)	167,99
Valor Médio de transação válidas (R$)	74,77

Table 1: Dataset do UOL PagSeguro - Informações Gerais

A Figura 3 apresenta o gráfico sobre a quantidade relativa de *chargeback* para cada mês. Esse gráfico mostra um fator impactante para essa pesquisa, já que em meses onde temos maior quantidade de *chargeback* as técnicas de mineração de dados tendem a ser mais eficazes. Neste gráfico também conseguimos perceber que existe uma proporção muito maior de transações legais, já que a maior porcentagem de *chargeback* em um mês é de 0.5%. Essa diferença deixa os dados desbalanceados, com a classe de transações válidas muito maior, o que foi um dos maiores desafios da nossa pesquisa. Cabe ressaltar que, apesar desse volume pequeno de chargeback,o prejuízo é muito significativo.

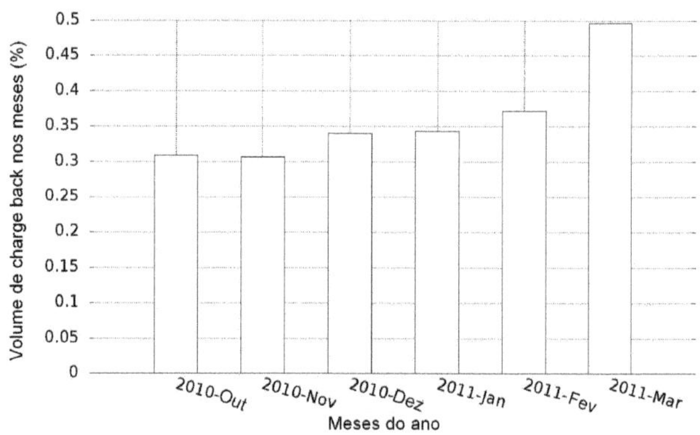

Figure 3: Quantidade relativa de *chargeback* ao longo dos meses.

Através de técnicas para seleção de atributos e análise visual de distribuições e valores semânticos explicadas na Seção 4, selecionamos um conjunto de 11 atributos que têm maior potencial para caracterizar a variável resposta como fraude. Esses são:

- **Valor:** valor em reais da transação.
- **Pontos da Transação:** pontos gerados por uma transação, os envolvidos na transação atribuem pontos para transações bem sucedidas, mal sucedidas e bem sucedidas sem pontuação (1,-1,0), respectivamente.
- **Hora da transação**: horas em formato inteiro na qual a transação foi realizada.
- **TipoConta**: define o tipo de conta do usuário, (empresarial, vendedor, comprador).

[1]http://pagseguro.uol.com.br
[2]http://www.uol.com.br

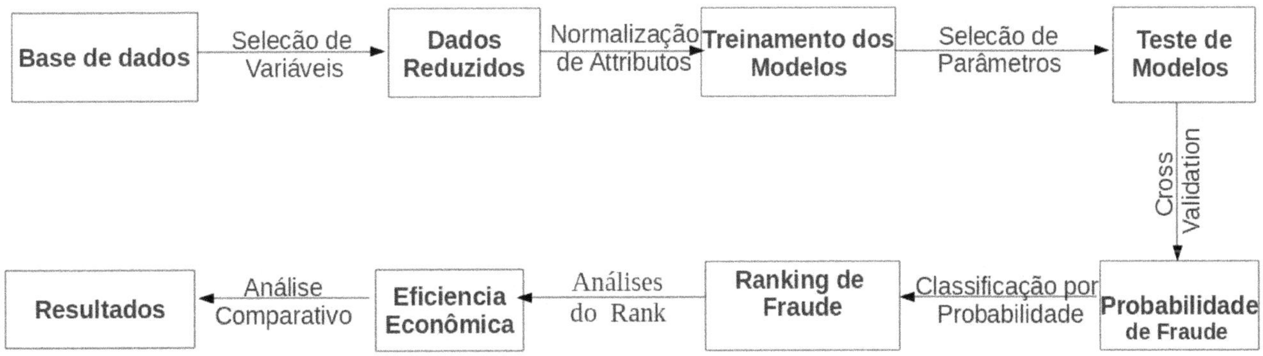

Figure 2: Metodologia para construção dos modelos de detecção de fraude

- **Tempo Cadastro Comprador**: tempo em que o comprador está registrado em dias.
- **Tempo Cadastro Vendedor**: tempo em que o vendedor está registrado em dias.
- **Categoria Principal**: categoria em que o produto comercializado pertence.
- **Bandeira do Cartão**: bandeira do cartão de crédito, que foi realizada a operação.
- **Idade**: idade do comprador da transação.
- **Flag DDD**: compara se o código DDD do usuário do PagSeguro é similar ao portador do cartão de crédito.
- **Estado de Cadastro**: campo referente à unidade federal do usuário.

5.2 Resultados

Após a aplicação das técnicas utilizando a metodologia descrita na Seção 4, obtivemos dois modelos para gerar os testes, o *Modelo de Regressão*, que utiliza a técnica de Regressão Logística para detectar fraudes, e o *Modelo Bayesiano*, que utiliza a técnica de Redes Bayesianas. Nesta seção faremos uma comparação entre esses dois modelos, comparando-os quanto ao grau de precisão, revocação e Eficiência Econômica, descrita pela Equação 5.

A Tabela 2 apresenta uma comparação entre o Modelo Regressão e o Modelo Bayesiano referente à precisão, revocação e Eficiência Econômica em um conjunto de dados de outubro/2010 a março de 2011, usando um treinamento nas três primeiras semanas de um mês e testando na quarta e quinta semana deste. Analisando essa tabela podemos notar que no geral o Modelo Bayesiano foi mais eficaz que o Modelo de Regressão Logística, ambos destacaram-se no mês de março com uma Eficiência Econômica de 35,53% e 35,61%, respectivamente, comparados ao cenário real do UOL PagSeguro.

Foram construídos gráficos de precisão, revocação e Eficiência Econômica para os diferentes períodos, possibilitando assim diversas analises sobre o comportamento dos modelos em diferentes faixas do *ranking* . Para exemplificar os resultados, daremos destaque ao mês de março/2011, uma vez que foi o que apresentou os melhores resultados.

A Figura 4(a) apresenta um gráfico comparativo das duas técnicas, analisando a precisão. Pode-se notar que o Modelo Bayesiano foi mais eficaz que o Modelo Regressão, obtendo precisão de 100% para as 10 transações que esse classificou como maior probabilidade de fraude e aproximadamente 60% de precisão até os 0,11% registros mais bem classificados para detectar fraude. Já a técnica de Regressão Logística atingiu 70% nos 0,08% primeiros registros, e 50% nos 0,10% registros a partir do topo do *ranking*.

		Bayes	**Logist**
Out.	**Prec.**	7,05	4,10
	Rev.	18,93	27,52
	Posição do Rank.	0,79	1,98
	Eficiência Econômica	**14,33**	12,03
Nov.	**Prec.**	14,70	8,33
	Rev.	32,38	36,67
	Posição do Rank.	0,73	1,47
	Eficiência Econômica	**29,70**	28,73
Dez.	**Prec.**	7,40	3,53
	Rev.	21,08	30,20
	Rank.	1,16	3,49
	Eficiência Econômica	**16,61**	10,64
Jan.	**Prec.**	8,78	9,70
	Rev.	25,56	21,19
	Posição do Rank.	1,30	0,98
	Eficiência Econômica	**16,57**	15,54
Fev.	**Prec.**	7,78	6,06
	Rev.	42,96	44,62
	Posição do Rank.	3,10	4,13
	Eficiência Econômica	**27,40**	25,75
Mar.	**Prec.**	9,93	5,38
	Rev.	43,01	49,94
	Posição do Rank.	2,22	4,76
	Eficiência Econômica	35,53	**35,61**

Table 2: Resultados - outubro/2010 a março/2011

A Figura 4(b) apresenta um gráfico comparativo do desempenho das técnicas relativo à revocação. Pode-se observar que o Modelo Bayesiano obteve as maiores coberturas classificando menos registros como fraude, quando comparado com o Modelo de Regressão Logística. A Figura 4(c) mostra um gráfico comparativo do desempenho das técnicas quanto a seu ganho sobre o modelo atual. Esse ganho é calculado pela Equação 6.

$$EE_{Relativa} = (EE - EE_{Real})/(EE_{Max} - EE_{Real}) \qquad (6)$$

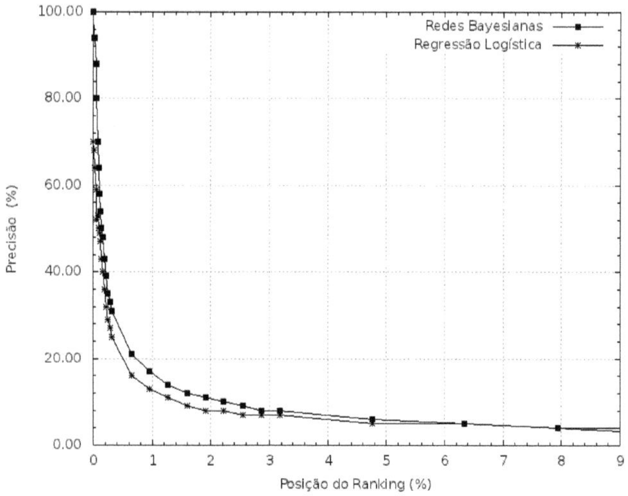

(a) Precisão

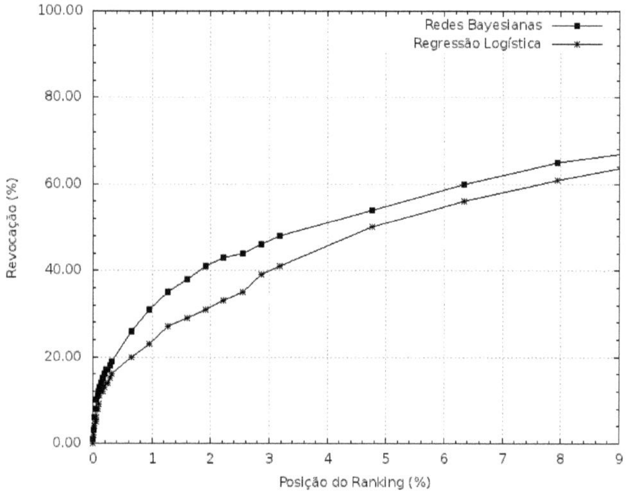

(b) Revocação

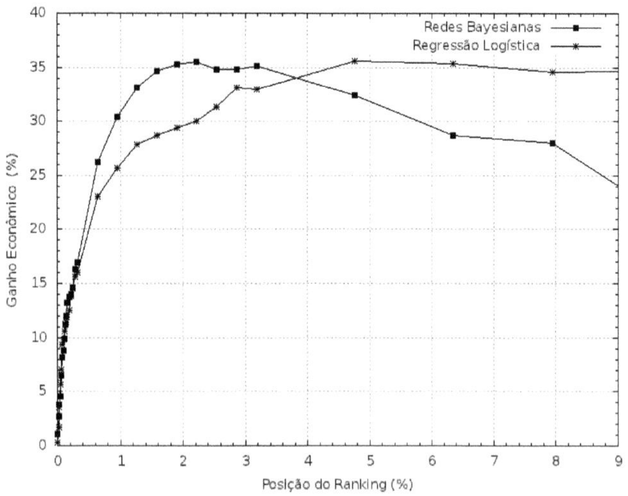

(c) Eficiência Econômica Relativa

Figure 4: Resultados Comparativos Março 2011

É possível verificar na Figura 4(c) que na maioria das faixas o Modelo Bayesiano obteve melhores resultados (Eficiência Econômica) do que o Modelo Regressão. O máximo de desempenho obtido pelo Modelo Bayesiano foi classificando 2,22% dos registros como fraude, onde o modelo obteve um ganho de 35,53% de ganho sobre o modelo real atual do PagSeguro. Já no Modelo de Regressão Logística a maior Eficiência Econômica foi alcançada ao classificar 4,76% dos registros como fraude, onde o modelo obteve ganho de 35,61%, superando levemente o Modelo Bayesiano. Os resultados aqui apresentados indicam um ganho bastante considerável quando comparados com o cenário atual utilizado pelo PagSeguro, com o potencial de reduzir em até 36% o prejuízo causado pelas fraudes eletrônicas neste serviço da empresa.

6. CONCLUSÃO

Neste artigo, aplicamos técnicas de inteligência computacional para modelar e detectar preventivamente fraudes em transações Web, mais especificamente em transações de comércio eletrônico que utilizam cartão de crédito. Utilizamos diferentes técnicas de inteligência computacional para construir modelos capazes de detectar fraude, dando destaque neste trabalho a um comparativo entre as técnicas de Regressão Logística e Redes Bayesianas.

Aplicamos os modelos para detectar fraude a um conjunto de dados providos pelo serviço de pagamento eletrônico UOL PagSeguro, contendo milhões de transações entre os meses de outubro de 2010 e março de 2011. Notamos nessa pesquisa que o desbalanceamento das classes de fraude e não fraude foi um fator determinante para a previsão de fraudes. Devido a termos uma proporção muito maior de transações válidas, as técnicas em geral encontram dificuldades para reconhecer o padrão de não fraude, assim os piores resultados foram encontrados em meses com menor volume de transações fraudulentas. Mesmo notando que o desbalanceamento dos dados dificulta bastante a eficácia das técnicas, é necessário e importante preservar as mesmas características do cenário real. Apesar dessa limitação, os resultados apresentam ganhos bastante satisfatórios quando comparado ao cenário real do serviço do UOL PagSeguro na atualidade.

Para tornar a comparação entre os modelos mais fidedigna, utilizamos o conceito de Eficiência Econômica (EE), que descreve a melhoria financeira obtida pelo modelo, sendo que a melhor Eficiência Econômica obtida foi de 35,61%. Percebemos que o Modelo Bayesiano foi mais eficaz na maioria dos experimentos, obtendo em março/2011 sua melhor Eficiência Econômica, com um ganho de 35,53% sobre o cenário real. Já o Modelo de Regressão também apresentou em março/2011 o seu melhor ganho, chegando a superar o Modelo Bayesiano, com Eficiência Econômica de 35,61%.

Um dos maiores desafios que encontramos neste trabalho foi a natureza dos dados, já que não utilizamos nenhuma técnica de balanceamento simples, pois optamos por preservar as características do cenário, e assim consequentemente tivemos que trabalhar com um volume de fraude com menos de 1% do volume total. Assim, como trabalhos futuros surge a necessidade de utilizar técnicas para lidar com dados desbalanceados sem perder a generalidade dos dados. Uma possível solução seria atribuir maiores pesos para as classe com menor volume e menor pesos para as classes com maior volume [7]. Outra solução que pretendemos estudar é a utilização de modelos híbridos que compreendem a união de mais de uma técnica de inteligência computacional, testando estas técnicas em distintos serviços web, onde possam ocorrer fraudes.

Agradecimentos

Este trabalho foi parcialmente patrocinado pelo Universo OnLine S. A. - UOL (www.uol.com.br), através do programa UOL Bolsa Pesquisa (processo número 20110212153600) e parcialmente patrocinado pelo Instituto Nacional de Ciência e Tecnologia para a Web (CNPq no. 573871/2008-6), CAPES, CNPq, Finep, e Fapemig.

7. REFERENCES

[1] D. A. Ahmed Metwally and A. E. Abbadi. Using association rules for fraud detection in web advertising networks. *31st international conference on Very large data bases*, 05:169:180, 2005.

[2] S. Amiratti. Google's udi manber- search is a hard problem. In *ReadWriteWeb Blog*. 2007.

[3] E. L. Barse, H. Kvarnström, and E. Jonsson. Synthesizing test data for fraud detection systems. In *Proceedings of the 19th Annual Computer Security Applications Conference*, ACSAC '03, pages 384–, Washington, DC, USA, 2003. IEEE Computer Society.

[4] S. Bhattacharyya, S. Jha, K. Tharakunnel, and J. C. Westland. Data mining for creditcard fraud: A comparative study. *Journal Decision Support Systems.*, 50(3):602–613, Fevereiro 2011.

[5] R. J. Bolton and D. J. Hand. Unsupervised Profiling Methods for Fraud Detection. *Statistical Science*, 17(3):235–255, 2002.

[6] G. Casella and R. Berger. *Statistical Inference*. Pacific Grove, 2nd edition, 2002.

[7] C. Chen, A. Liaw, and L. Breiman. Using random forest to learn imbalanced data. *Discovery*, (1999):1–12, 2004.

[8] C. Chiu, Y. Ku, T. Lie, and Y. Chen. Internet auction fraud detection using social network analysis and classification tree approaches. *International Journal of Electronic Commerce.*, 15(3):123–147, Março 2011.

[9] G. Cooper and E. Herskovits. A bayesian method for the induction of probabilistic networks from data. *Machine Learning*, 9(4):309–347, 1992.

[10] J. F. E. Dean W. Abbott, I. Philip Matkovsky. An evaluation of high-end data mining tools for fraud detection. *IEEE International Conference on Systems, Man, and Cybernetics*, 2:12–14, 1998.

[11] S. P. Duen Horng Chau and C. Faloutsos. Detecting fraudulent personalities in networks of online auctioneers. *Proc. ECML/PKDD*, 5:103–114, 2006.

[12] H. K. Emilie Lundin and E. Jonsson. A synthetic fraud data generation methodology. *4th International Conference on Information and Communications Security*, 02:265–277, 2002.

[13] T. Fawcett and F. Provost. Adaptive fraud detection. data mining and knowledge discovery, 1997.

[14] M. Hall, E. Frank, G. Holmes, B. Pfahringer, P. Reutemann, and I. H. Witten. The weka data mining software: an update. *SIGKDD Explor. Newsl.*, 11(1):10–18, 2009.

[15] D. W. Hosmer. *Applied Logistic Regression*. Wiley, New York, 2nd edition, 2000.

[16] W. H. T. B.-L. J. Hendler, N. Shadbolt and D. Weitzner. Web science: an interdisciplinary approach to understanding the web. *Communications of the ACM*, 51:60–69, 2008.

[17] A. Kumar and V. Nagadevara. Development of hybrid classification methodology for mining skewed data sets - a case study of indian customs data. *Computer Systems and Applications, ACS/IEEE International Conference.*, 0(2006):584–591, 2006.

[18] E. Lundin, H. Kvarnström, and E. Jonsson. A synthetic fraud data generation methodology. In *Proceedings of the 4th International Conference on Information and Communications Security*, ICICS '02, pages 265–277, London, UK, 2002. Springer-Verlag.

[19] S. Maes, karl Tuyls, B. Vanschoenwinkel, and B. Manderick. Credit card fraud detection using bayesian and neural networks. *Vrije Universiteir Brussel*, 2001.

[20] S. Maes, K. Tuyls, B. Vanschoenwinkel, and B. Manderick. Credit card fraud detection using bayesian and neural networks. In *Maciunas RJ, editor. Interactive image-guided neurosurgery. American Assoc. Neurological Surgeons*, pages 261–270, 1993.

[21] R. Maranzato, A. Pereira, M. Neubert, and A. P. do Lago. Fraud detection in reputation systems in e-markets using logistic regression and stepwise optimization. *SIGAPP Appl. Comput. Rev.*, 11:14–26, June 2010.

[22] Netmap. Fraud and crime example brochure. 2004.

[23] J. Perols. Financial statement fraude detection: An analysis of statistical and machine learning algorithms. *Journal of Practice and theory.*, 30(2):19–50, Maio 2011.

[24] C. Phua, V. Lee, K. Smith-Miles, and R. Gayler. A comprehensive survey of data mining-based fraud detection research. 2005.

[25] M. N. Rafael Maranzato, Adriano Pereira and A. P. do Lago. Fraud detection in reputation systems in e-markets using logistic regression and stepwise optimization. *SIGAPP Appl*, 11:14–26, 2010.

[26] R. Team. R: A language and environment for statistical computing. `http://www.r-project.org`, 2009. The R Development Core Team.

[27] S. Tseng and B. J. Fogg. Credibility and computing technology. *ACM*, 429:39–44, 1999.

[28] W. N. Venables, D. M. Smith, and the R Development Core Team. An introduction to r. `http://www.cran.r-project.org`, 2009.

[29] T. R. D. C. T. Version. The r project for statistical computing. `http://www.r-project.org`, 2006.

[30] I. H. Witten and E. Franku. *Data Mining: Practical Machine Learning Tools and Techniques*. Elsevier, 2005.

Compass Clustering: A New Clustering Method for Detection of Points of Interest Using Personal Collections of Georeferenced and Oriented Photographs

Yuri Almeida Lacerda[1,2], Robson Gonçalves Fechine Feitosa[2], Guilherme Álvaro Esmeraldo[2], Cláudio de Souza Baptista[1], Leandro Balby Marinho[1]

[1] Laboratory of Information Systems
Federal University of Campina Grande
Av. Aprígio Veloso, 882, Bodocongó - Campina Grande – PB, Brazil
+55 (83) 2101.1122

[2] Federal Institute of Education, Science and Technology of Ceará – Campus Crato
Rodovia CE 292, KM 15, Gisélia Pinheiro – Crato – CE, Brazil
+55 (88) 3586.8100

{yurilacerda, robsonfeitosa, guilhermealvaro}@ifce.edu.br, {baptista, lbmarinho}@dsc.ufcg.edu.br

ABSTRACT

Knowledge discovery in large online photographic repositories has been an active area of research in recent years. This is due to the great popularization of devices equipped with image capture, such as digital cameras, smartphones and tablets. Moreover, the image files generated by those devices are easily spread out on the Web through social networking sites. Typically, the photos stored in these repositories bear valuable metadata, such as, geographic coordinates, timestamp, and camera orientation. This information can be used for many interesting data mining tasks, such as detection of points-of-interest (POIs) and trip planning. This paper introduces Compass Clustering, a new clustering algorithm for detecting POIs in georeferenced and oriented photo repositories. Most of the state-of-the-art approaches for POI detection cluster photos based solely on their geographic proximity. However, in many cases, the POIs are within a certain distance from the point where the photo was taken, that is, not in the exact camera location but in the direction it is pointing to, and thus many photos would be erroneously classified by existing methods. Therefore, we propose to exploit the camera orientation in order to identify more reliable POIs that reflect the real intention of people when taking photos. We evaluated our approach on a collection of more than 8,000 georeferenced and oriented photos collected from Flickr.

Categories and Subject Descriptors

H.3.3 [**Information Search and Retrieval**]: Clustering;
H.2.8 [**Database Applications**]: Data Mining, Image Databases, Spatial Databases and GIS

General Terms

Algorithms, Management, Measurement, Experimentation.

Permission to make digital or hard copies of all or part of this work for personal or classroom use is granted without fee provided that copies are not made or distributed for profit or commercial advantage and that copies bear this notice and the full citation on the first page. To copy otherwise, or republish, to post on servers or to redistribute to lists, requires prior specific permission and/or a fee.
WebMedia'12, October 15–18, 2012, São Paulo/SP, Brazil.
Copyright 2012 ACM 978-1-4503-1706-1/12/10...$15.00.

Keywords

Clustering with Constraints; Georeferenced Photos; Point of Interest; Metadata.

1. INTRODUCTION

In the last years, we have seen a spreading of georeferenced multimedia data, especially digital photos. This volume of information is mainly due to the evolution and popularization of several electronic devices equipped with GPS (Global Positioning Systems) receivers and compass to obtain orientation, such as smartphones, tablets and digital cameras.

One kind of application which is widely used in such mobile devices is Location-Based Social Networking Services (LBSN)[1]. LBSNs allow users to share trajectories and points of interests with their social networks. Examples of LBSNs include Foursquare[1], Facebook Places[2], Bikely[3], Yelp[4], and MapMyRide[5]. With those services, users may share, for example, trajectories and routes during the practice of some sport through MapMyRide or Bikely; or, still, share a restaurant (point of interest) using Foursquare and Facebook Places.

The detection of points of interest (POIs) constitutes one of the problems, concerning LBSN services, which have been deeply investigated by the scientific community [1, 2, 3, 4]. LBSNs are capable of storing a large amount of data about the history of POIs of their users. From this history, it is possible to infer information related to the preferences of each one of those users. For example, the kind of POIs that they usually go to; time of visitation of some POI categories; what they usually visit during a touristic or business travel, among other types of information.

However, this history can be obtained from other data sources as well, such as georeferenced digital photographs. These kind of

---

[1] http://www.foursquare.com

[2] http://www.facebook.com/facebookplaces

[3] http://www.bikely.com

[4] http://www.yelp.com

[5] http://www.mapmyride.com

photos come out as an excellent data source [3] because, from them, it is possible to register, besides the geographic location at the moment of capture of the image, the date and time, camera orientation with respect to the geographic direction, descriptions about the photograph, as well as other metadata. There are standards for storing those metadata. The Exchangeable image file format - Exif [5] standard has been widely adopted by the electronic device industries. Other standards as XMP and IPTC have also been used.

Most of state-of-the-art approaches perform clustering with basis on geographic location, through the latitude and longitude coordinates obtained during the capture of the image. However, sometimes points of interest are a little distant from the place from where the picture was taken, and not in exact point, as some studies consider. This means that the point of interest is located at least some meters away from the capture location, and in the direction pointed by the camera at the moment of image registration.

We could not find, in the reviewed literature, any related work that considers, besides the geographic and temporal location, the orientation of the photograph for detection of points of interest. So, in this work we investigate the use of orientation information to infer, with more precision, the users' POIs related to their collection of georeferenced photographs.

The objective of this work is, therefore, to describe a new clustering methodology, which takes into consideration, besides geographic location, the orientation of the photograph, in order to get a more precise detection of users' POIs, using personal collections of georeferenced and oriented photographs. The rest of this work is organized as follows. In Section 2, we present some work related to the use of computational techniques related to the extraction of POIs using georeferenced images. In Section 3, we present the proposed approach. In Section 4, we illustrate a case study which uses the proposed approach. Finally, in Section 5, we present the conclusions and future work.

2. RELATED WORK

In this section, we present some work related to the identification of points of interest in georeferenced photographs. Most of the investigated studies use spatial clustering algorithms, as can be seen in [6, 7, 8]. Moreover, there are some studies which deal with the deduction of other relevant information concerning travels, from photograph collections, such as [9, 10, 11].

Among the analyzed studies, we noticed the use of the following algorithms: *k-means*, *mean shift* [12], *Density-Based Spatial Clustering of Application with Noise* (DBScan) [13], as well as spectral clustering [14]. The three first are spatial clustering algorithms which will be explained next. The last one, on the other hand, is a technique of the graph theory.

The work [6] deals with the application of the classic clustering algorithm k-means to create groups of photographs for detection of POIs in a city. With this algorithm, the author managed to detect well known places. In [7], on the other hand, the POIs are detected with basis on large volumes of data. The technique applied by the researchers used the mean shift algorithm. The authors applied, subjectively, a 100-meters parameter for the density radius, required by the algorithm. This radius is very difficult to estimate, because the area occupied by the POIs may vary much. So, if radiuses larger than the POIs are estimated, then groups larger than certain POIs will be formed. Otherwise, a same POI can be formed by several small groups.

Some studies use DBScan to cluster georeferenced photographs. However, this algorithm does not allow clusters with density variations [15]. In [8], it is proposed a new approach that uses the DBScan algorithm, taking into consideration just a local density, that is, allowing the creation of clusters with different sizes and densities.

In [3], the authors proposed an adaptive clustering algorithm based on spectral clustering, where the objects are represented as non-directional and weighted graphs. Besides, it features a reinforcement stage which takes into consideration the temporal aspects of the photograph too. In that approach, the use of parameters is abolished. Such solution was applied to collections of photographs extracted from Flickr, containing 216,092 georeferenced pictures of Paris, Hong Kong and New York. In most analyses, this technique presented better results, compared to the other studies in the literature.

Hence, we notice that no work in the reviewed literature considers the orientation of the photograph to identify the POIs. So, the main contribution of this paper is to evaluate the use of direction in the process of classifying POIs.

Furthermore, in the studies available in the literature, there is a certain difficulty in the application of clustering algorithms because, due to the high probability of variation in the size of the points of interest and of the dataset to be analyzed, it is difficult to estimate the parameters in order to optimize the clustering algorithm. However, since this work focuses on showing the influence of using orientation, we are not concerned with the estimation of those parameters.

3. COMPASS CLUSTERING

As discussed in Section 2, the studies found in the literature do not use geographic orientation information as a criterion to cluster the photographs. The use of information concerning just geographic locations (latitude and longitude) of the places where users took pictures is not always reliable for detection and extraction of POIs because, normally, these points from where the pictures were taken are some meters away from the POI, and in some geographic direction, so being able to cause inexact inferences that a picture is related to a certain POI. This is justified, since most studies use clustering algorithms that consider just the spatial aspect, such as: DBScan, k-means, spectral clustering, among others, to perform the classification of the photographs, in order to infer the clusters.

The use of orientation enables to obtain more precise information in certain scenarios. For example, in Figure 1 we present two scenarios for detection of the point of interest: (a) using just the geographic location and (b) using geographic location and orientation. Figure 1(a) presents two points of interest, *p1* and *p2*, as well as a photograph *f1*, captured near *p2*. Nevertheless, *f1* is related to the point of interest *p1*. Using the clustering algorithms of the literature, *f1* will be considered part of a group of photographs related to the POI *p2*, thus reducing the precision of the results.

The solution presented herein clusters the photographs by using data about the geographic location. Since the oriented photographs tend to be directed to the center of a certain point of interest. For example, Figure 2 presents a set of photographs captured close to a POI. So, when straight lines are drawn in the direction the pictures were taken, these lines end up crossing each other, and the result of these crossings is the creation of new points closer to the POIs than the exact location from where the pictures were taken.

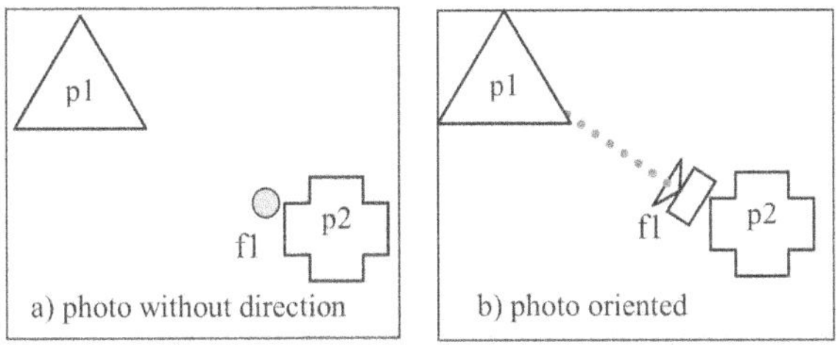

Figure 1. Importance of using orientation information of the photograph.

Nevertheless, there can be some photographs that are not directed to the center of the POI. Furthermore, the segment determined by the orientation may generate no crossing. In such cases, the geographic positions of these photographic are taken into consideration for the purpose of executing the algorithm. These photographs can be thought of as being points which do not belong to the POI (for example, the red points in Figure 2).

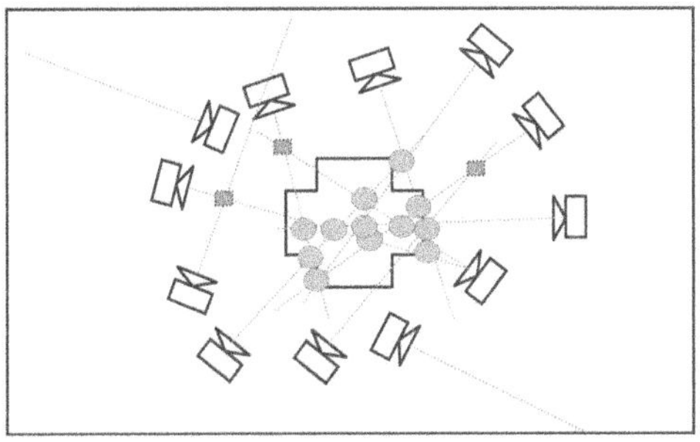

Figure 2. Example of intersection points.

Figure 3 presents a pseudocode for the clustering scheme described herein.

The algorithm comprises three steps. Firstly, it is necessary to draw a line segment sizing *d* meters according to the orientation of the respective photograph. Next, all intersections of the segments previously drawn must be detected; the second step consists in using a clustering algorithm (e.g., DBScan, k-means, etc) considering the geographic location of the intersection points of the orientation lines of the photographs. Finally, in the third step, we compute the number of intersection points for each photograph, in each cluster. When the execution of the algorithm stops, the photographs will be related to the cluster with more intersection points. In the case of equal values, the photographs will be classified for the group with higher number of intersection points.

Besides the mentioned steps, the algorithm performs a series of specific treatments to work correctly. One of them is the incorporation of geographic location data of photographs whose line segment did not result in any intersection point. Furthermore, another treatment carried out consisted in considering the photographs in the same geographic location and with the same orientation in the same manner as the photographs which did not generate intersection, that is, using just their geographic position, since the result of intersection of segments with the same position and orientation generates infinite intersection points.

```
algorithm CompassClustering(Collection<OrientedPhoto>
collection, ClusteringMethod clusteringMethod, int d):
PhotoCluster<OrientedPhoto>;

begin
   // 1st Step
   traceLines(collection, d);
   Collection<IntersectionPoints> intersectionPoints =
getPointsOfIntersection(collection);
   // 2nd Step
   PhotoCluster<IntersectionPoints> clustersOfIntersections =
clusteringMethod.clustering(intersectionPoints);
   // 3th Step
   calculatePhotoPointsPerCluster(collection,
clustersOfIntersections)
   PhotoCluster<OrientedPhoto> clusters =
createClustersToPhotos(clustersOfIntersections);
   return clusters;
end.
```

Figure 3. Pseudocode illustrating how Compass Clustering works.

4. CASE STUDY

In this section, we illustrate some results achieved with the use of the approach proposed in this work. For such, we chose a case study consisting in the detection of POIs in Paris.

So, we have implemented and incorporated the Compass Clustering algorithm to a system responsible for: collecting, treating and visualizing the clusters. This system is called MyPOIs, which is a solution for detection of POIs from a database containing oriented and georeferenced photographs. The architecture of this system is presented in Figure 4.

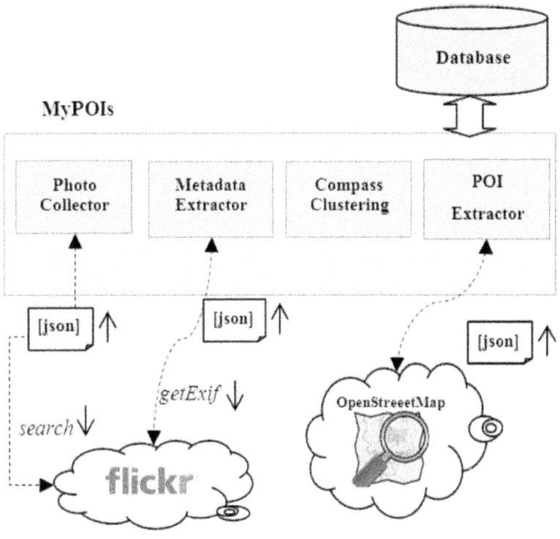

Figure 4. MyPOIs Architecture.

4.1 Data preparation

The retrieval of a personal collection of georeferenced photographs is an activity which demands a series of tasks. So, the Photo Collector is responsible for collecting a set of photographs from a large repository available online. In this work, we used Flickr[6] photographs repository, one of the most known digital photograph management system.

Besides featuring a large database with personal georeferenced photographs, Flickr also features an API (Application Programming Interface) so that developers of other platforms can

[6] http://www.flickr.com

use its functionalities. One of these functionalities is the query of data about the photographs, implemented under the method *flickr.photos.search*. This method allows the query of photographs in the whole public database. So, there are parameters that can be used, like: query keyword, the bounding box of an area from where one wishes to retrieve photographs; the return data; return format of the method (JSON, XML, etc); and many others. Figure 5 presents an excerpt of this query in JSON (JavaScript Object Notation) format.

Still in Figure 5, we illustrate some relevant information for the retrieval of the photographic file. As can be noticed, some attributes that describe the photographs are returned in *key-value* pairs, such as: the *latitude* and *longitude* information, as well as the *id*, *secret*, *server* and *farm* attributes, which will be used to compose the query to retrieve the file properly said.

{"id":"6204695215","owner":"38937706@N07", "secret":"4ae975089d", "server":"6176", "farm":7, "title":"les 10 ans du Cube", "ispublic":1, "isfriend":0, "isfamily":0, "latitude":48.819983, "longitude":2.25335, "accuracy":"16", "context":0, "place_id":"8xjQVDRUV7LYSw_eVQ", "woeid":"55843833", "geo_is_family":0, "geo_is_friend":0, "geo_is_contact":0, "geo_is_public":1}

Figure 5. Excerpt of a query result in JSON format.

So, in order to retrieve the files with the photographs, it is necessary to build an address (URL) from the data presented in Figure 5. One way to build this address is changing the text in the brackets, illustrated in the following URL, by its corresponding value, available in Figure 5. One of the formats in which the image can be extracted is the base on the following URL: http://farm[farm-id].staticflickr.com/[server-id]/[id]_[secret].jpg. So, for example, the address formed by the data presented in Figure 5 is: http://farm7.staticflickr.com/6176/6204695215_4ae975089d.jpg.

There are also other URL formats that can be built to retrieve the photograph, as described in the documentation for developers [7].

The method *flickr.photos.search* has a limitation, returning just the 4,000 first photographs in the queries. If a query were to return, for example, 100,000 results, only the first 4,000 would be retrieved. So, very specific queries must be formulated in order to get only the desired return. However, in order to get over this limitation, the module **Photo Collector** has a scheme to determine when a certain area has more than four thousand photographs and separates it recursively until it finds areas with a maximum of 4,000 photographs. This approach is similar to the presented in [16], which divides the space into smaller spaces to collect information.

For a better utilization of computational resources, this module uses multi-thread programming to make the collecting process faster. So, we developed a software component responsible for making the *k threads* control, for k>1, which will be executed in parallel to speed up the data processing.

As seen in Figure 5, the result provided by the *flickr.photos.search* does not have all the data about the georeferencing information (metadata) of the photographs, such as: orientation, capture date and time, among others. However, the metadata about the orientation of the photograph are essential for the technique proposed in this work. So, the module **Metadata Extractor** is responsible for extracting metadata from the photographs collected by **Photo Collector**.

We noticed that some of the photographs do not have metadata information (Exif), although they present geographic data in the result of the query by *flickr.photos.search*, which means that they were georeferenced by the system itself. So, a filtering process was needed, in order to discard the photographs without orientation information. The filtering process uses the following parameters: the photograph must have precise geographic data (accuracy parameters equal 16, as seen in Figure 5) and data about geographic orientation (compass).

Thus, Metadata Extractor makes a request through the method *flickr.photos.getExif*, featured by Flickr, to retrieve the metadata of a certain photograph, including: capture date, photograph orientation, local size, exposure, aperture and focus. So, this module requests data of all photographs gathered, using the *photo_id* of each of them and, next, converting the data returned by the server (in JSON format) for posterior storage the database of MyPOIs.

Using the Photo Collector module, we extracted photographs using the keyword "Paris". Besides, we retrieved the bounding box related to the areas of Paris: minimum latitude: 48.8129965, minimum longitude: 2.2498778 ; maximum latitude: 48.8925151 and maximum longitude of 2.4392203. Consequently, 516,975 photographs meeting these criteria were returned, where just 1.62% of them have metadata about orientation. These metadata were extracted using the Metadata Extractor module.

Figure 6 illustrates the the result of the process of collecting the photographs, where the blue points represent the photographs in their geographic coordinates.

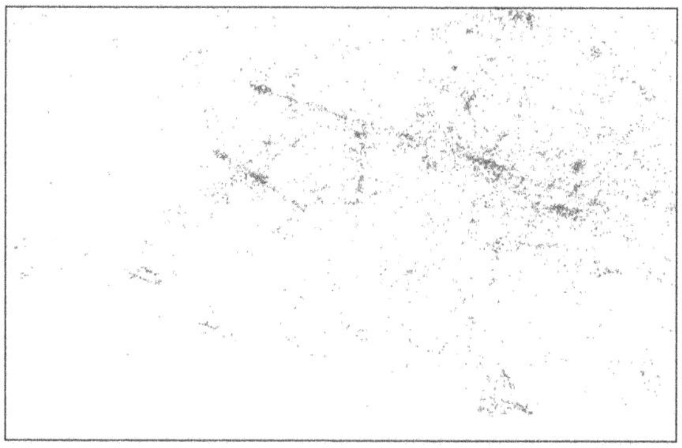

Figure 6. Geographic location of the oriented and non-classified photographs, collected by Photo Collector.

After being collected and having the metadata extracted, the photographs are classified by the **Compass Clustering** module. Figure 7 illustrates the result of the execution of 3 steps of the classification algorithm. In Figure 7(a) it is presented the result of the photographs after drawing the line segments resulting from the geographic orientation, with a **d** parameter equal 50 m. In Figure 7(b) we present the intersection points (in red) and the photographs (in blue) which did not have intersections of their line segments. Finally, in Figure 7(c), the result of set of intersection points, plus the photographs which did not generate intersections is plotted in the respective colors of each cluster inferred by the **Compass Clustering**.

[7] http://www.flickr.com/services/api/misc.urls.html

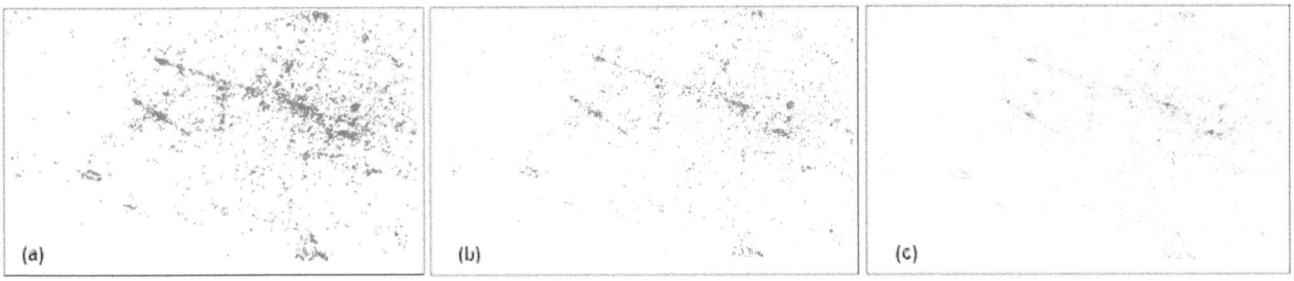

Figure 7. Photographs plotted with the line segment resulting from the geographic orientation and parameter "d" = 50 m (a). Intersection points with geographic position of the photographs that did not have intersection for d = 50 m (b). Classification result (c).

In order to validate the proposed algorithm, we need to extract the areas of the points of interest. So, the POI Extractor module extracts the points of interest of places that are geographically near to the photographs extracted by the Photo Collector. There are several POI sources available on the Web, like: Wikimapia, POI Factory, GeoNames, Java Open Street Map (JOSM), among others. So, we opted for using JOSM, since it supplies information of POIs through query procedures in a tool called Nominatim[8].

Each point of interest is classified according to its class and type. There are the classes: amenities, buildings, tourism, roads, historical, amusement, among others. Each class is divided into types. For example, the elements in the class "tourism" can be classified as one of the types: attractions, museums, theme park, among others.

So, for this work, we selected only points associated to the classes: historical, tourism and amusement. Besides, we also added to POIs type: square, park, garden and stadium. In Figure 8 we represent, through the black polygons, the POIs that were detected in the central area of Paris. Still in Figure 8, we can see the area associated to some touristic POIs in Paris, such as: (a) Eiffel Tower; (b) Arch of Triumph and (c) the Louvre Museum.

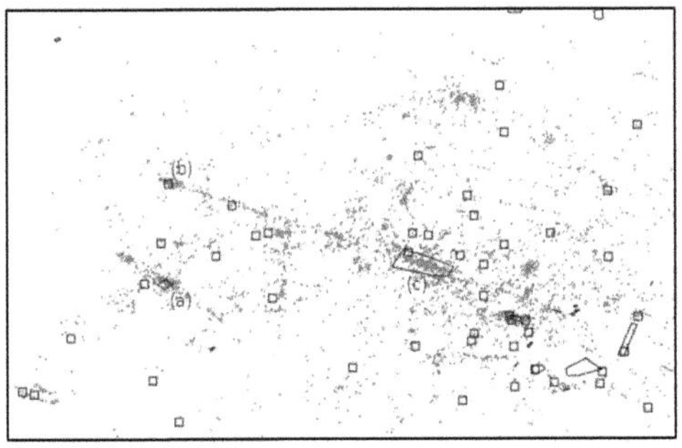

Figure 8. POIs extracted and photograph collection used.

4.2 Experimental Results

In order to validate the proposed approach, the experiments consisted of comparisons between the clustering of the photographs and the variation of the length of the line segments.

To validate the experiments, we used the precision and recall metrics [15], which are widely used in the data mining field. Precision relates the number of photographs included into the respective clusters to the photographs belonging to the POI under analysis. Recall, on the other hand, relates the number of photographs belonging to the POI to the photographs of the respective clusters.

So, for each cluster, precision was defined as the ratio between the total of elements in the cluster that are inside the Minimum Bounding Rectangle (MBR) relative to the POI and the total of elements of the cluster itself. Recall is computed as the ratio between the number of elements of the cluster that are inside the MBR of the point of interest and the total number of elements inside the MBR of the POI.

These metrics can be formally given by the following definitions:

Let C_{ij} be the set of photographs of the *i*th cluster (assuming that these photographs are in the MBR) relative to the *j*th POI, and P_j the set of photographs related to the same POI. Considering this definition, the precision of a cluster related to the respective POI can be given by the following equation:

$$p_{ij} = \frac{|P_j \cap C_{ij}|}{C_{ij}} \quad (1)$$

where p_{ij} is the precision of the *i*th cluster relative to the *j*th POI. Recall, on the other hand, can be obtained by:

$$r_{ij} = \frac{|P_j \cap C_{ij}|}{P_j} \quad (2)$$

where r_{ij} is the recall of the *i*th cluster relative to the *j*th POI.

Considering the cluster precisions relative to a certain POI, given by equation (1), the mean precision is computed through the following equation:

$$\overline{P_j} = \frac{\sum_{i=1}^{n_j}(p_{ij})}{n_j} \quad (3)$$

where $\overline{P_j}$ is the mean precision of the *j*th POI and n_j is the total number of clusters for the same POI. The total coverage of a POI is obtained from the mean of the recall of its respective clusters, given by equation (2). So, formally, we have:

$$R_j = \frac{\sum_{i=1}^{n_j}(r_{ij})}{n_j} \quad (4)$$

where R_j is the total coverage of the *j*th POI and n_j is the total number of clusters related to the POI.

Let X and Y be the sets of the mean precisions and the set of the total recall for all the POIs, respectively, and given by $X = \{\overline{P_1}, \overline{P_2}, \ldots, \overline{P_j}\}$ e $Y = \{R_1, R_2, \ldots, R_j\}$, where $j = 1, 2, \ldots, m$ and m is the total number of POIs, the minimum, maximum and mean values for both metrics can be computed by the following equations:

$$P_{min} = min\,(X) \quad (5)$$

[8] http://nominatim.openstreetmap.org

$$P_{max} = max\ (X) \tag{6}$$

$$P_{mean} = \frac{\sum_{j=1}^{m}(\overline{P_j})}{m} \tag{7}$$

Where P_{min}, P_{max} and P_{mean} indicate the lowest, the highest and the mean precision among the mean precision given to all the POIs, and m is the total number of POIs; and

$$R_{min} = min\ (Y) \tag{8}$$

$$R_{max} = max\ (Y) \tag{9}$$

$$R_{mean} = \frac{\sum_{j=1}^{m}(R_j)}{m} \tag{10}$$

where R_{min}, R_{max} and R_{mean} indicate the smallest, the largest and the mean of all the total recall values given to the POIs, and m is the total number of POIs.

4.2.1 Analysis of the influence of the intersection points on the density of clusters

In this subsection we analyze the influence of the intersection points on the identification capability of a POI. This approach is analyzed by varying the size of the orientation line segment of the photographs, evaluating the increase in the density of the points in the area inside the POIs, generated by the intersection points.

Since these points are the points of intersection of the orientation lines of photographs close to a POI, we may conclude that there will be an increase in the density of points close to and inside the POIs. Such scenario can be confirmed by analyzing Figure 9.

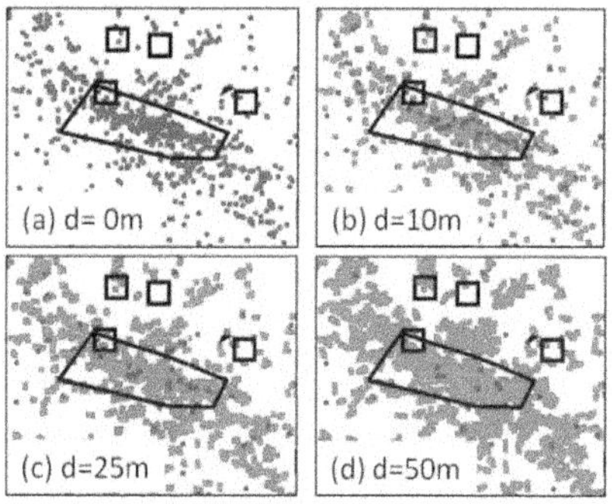

Figure 9. Cluster density as a function of d.

Figure 9 presents an area related to the case study proposed in this work. The largest polygon found in the center of the figure represents the MBR of the Louvre Museum. We present four situations in these graphs. In 9(a) we plot the capture locations of the photographs of the database researched (blue points). In Figures 9(b), 9(c) and 9(d), we present the intersection points (red points) of the line segments indicating the direction in which the pictures were taken, varying the parameter **d** in 10, 25 and 50 meters, respectively.

One may also notice that, in the area inside the POI, there is an increase in the density of points when the parameter d increases. So, the use of a higher number of points, representing the capture locations and line intersections, favors the application of clustering algorithms, since we want the exact detection of the POIs. Besides, we also consider the geographic locations of the photographs with no intersection (blue points), as seen in the blue points of Figures 9(b), 9(c) and 9(d).

*4.2.2 Analysis of the influence of the parameter **d** on the precision and recall metrics*

Still analyzing the values considered for the parameter **d**, we observed that precision and recall varied. The graph of Figure 10 shows the minimum and mean precision of all POIs, considering the respective clusters, according to equations (5) and (7). The maximum values, on the other hand, were 1 for all the variations of **d**.

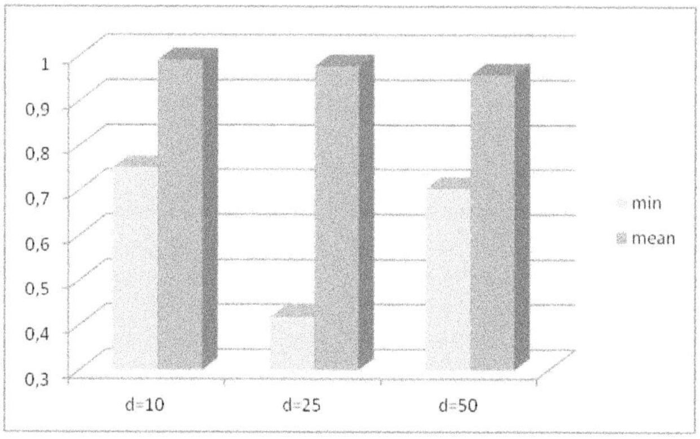

Figure 10. Comparative graph of precision for variations of the parameter d.

Observing the graph of Figure 10, we notice that, on average, the best value of the parameter d is 10. This indicates that as d increases, the clusters tend to contain more elements, even misclassifying elements that are outside the POI as if they were inside it. Figure 11, on the other hand, illustrates the minimum and the mean of recall when d is equals to 10, 25 and 50, according to equations (8) and (10). All the maximum recall values were 1.

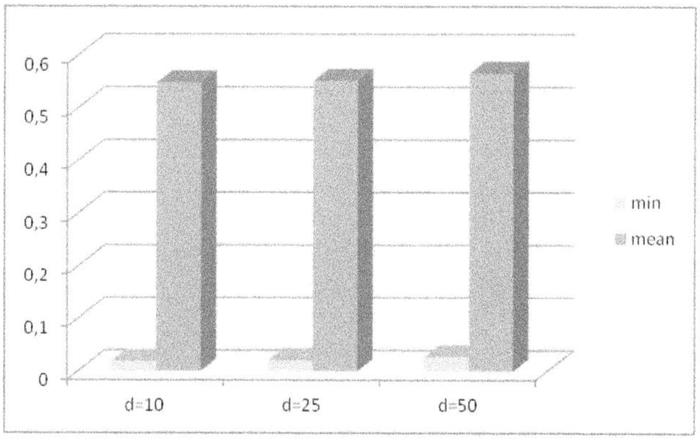

Figure 11. Comparative graph of coverage for variations of the parameter d.

Still analyzing the graph of Figure 11, we noticed that the recall value increased in function of d, with the best value of the mean for d as 50, since increasing d generates more intersection points, consequently forming clusters with more elements belonging to the POI. This can be explained by the fact that density is considered in the second step of the Compass Clustering algorithm.

The mean results presented in Figure 10 and 11 constitute an increase in precision when the values of d decrease. On the other hand, recall decreases. With those results, we can establish an engagement between the precision and recall metrics for $d = 25$.

5. CONCLUSIONS AND FUTURE WORK

This work described a new method for detection of users' points of interest using personal collections of georeferenced and oriented photographs. For such, this method, differently from other state-of-the-art approaches, takes the orientation into consideration to perform the clustering of photographs and later to detect the users' points of interest.

In order to evaluate the approach, we used two well known metrics used in data mining, namely precision and recall of the clusters with respect to the points of interest. The results showed that increasing the length of the straight line which characterizes orientation, the precision tends to fall, but recall tends to raise.

As a future work, we expect to use this technique in a Context-Aware Recommendation System [17], intending to infer information about users' preferences in systems with georeferenced information. Besides, we will carry out comparative experiments, in order to verify the performance of the methodology proposed in this work, with other clustering algorithms of the literature, such as: P-DBScan, k-means and spectral clustering.

Another proposal for a future work is the analysis of the influence of the focal distance on the estimation of the straight line length. As a form of improving the results of the experiment, we must investigate the use of statistical techniques, such as sampling, to analyze the algorithms based on photographic subsets only. Another relevant study concerns an analysis ignoring the photographs which do not generate intersections.

6. ACKNOWLEDGMENTS

The authors are grateful to the CNPq for funding this research project.

7. REFERENCES

[1] M. Ye, P. Yin, W.-C. Lee, and D-L. Lee. Exploiting geographical influence for collaborative point-of-interest recommendation. In Proceedings of the 34th International ACM SIGIR Conference on Research and Development in Information Retrieval (SIGIR '11). ACM, New York, NY, USA, 325-334, 2011.

[2] Y. Zheng, X. Xie, and W.-Y. Ma. GeoLife2.0: A location-based social networking service. In: Tenth International Conference on Mobile Data Management: Systems, Services and Middleware, n. 49, pages 4-5, 2009.

[3] Y. Yang, Z. Gong, and L. Hou. Identifying Points of Interest by Self-Tuning Clustering. SIGIR'11. Pequim, China. 2011

[4] B. Berjani, and T. Strufe. A Recommendation System for Spots in Location-Based Online Social Networks. Social Network Systems (SNS'11). Salzburg, 2011.

[5] JEITA. Design rule for Camera File system. Technical report, JEITA-49-2, 1998. http://www.exif.org/dcf.PDF.

[6] L. S. Kennedy, and M. Naaman. Generating diverse and representative image search results for landmarks. WWW, pages 297–306, 2008.

[7] D. J., L.Crandall, D. P. Backstrom, Huttenlocher, and J.M. Kleinberg. Mapping the world's photos. In WWW, pages 761-770, 2009.

[8] S. Kisilevich, F. Mansmman, F., and D. A. Keim. P-dbscan: a density based clustering algorithm for exploration and analysis of attractive areas using collections of geo-tagged photos. COM. Geo, 2010.

[9] M. Clements, P., Serdyukov, A. P. Vries, A. P. de, and M. J. T. Reinders. Using flickr geotags to predict user travel behaviour. In SIGIR, pages 851–852, 2010.

[10] S. Jain, S. Seufert, and S. J. Bedathur. Antourage: mining distance-constrained trips from flickr. In WWW, pages 1121–1122, 2010.

[11] A. Popescu, and G. Grefenstette. Deducing trip related information from flickr. In WWW, pages 1183–1184, 2009.

[12] D. Comaniciu, and P. Meer. Mean shift: A robust approach toward feature space analysis. IEEE Transactions on Pattern Analysis and Machine Intelligence, 24(5):603–619, 2002.

[13] M. H.-P. Ester, J. S. Kriegel, and X. Xu. A density-based algorithm for discovering clusters in large spatial database with noise. In KDD, pages 226-231, 1996.

[14] T. Bühler, and M. Hein. Spectral clustering based on the graph p-Laplacian. In ACM Proceedings of the 26th Annual International Conference on Machine Learning, pages 81-88, 2009.

[15] J. Han, M. Kamber, and J. Pei. Data Mining: Concepts and Techniques. 3th edition. Elsevier, 2011.

[16] F. Buccafurri, F. Furfaro, G. M. Mazzao,and D. Saccà. A quad-tree based multiresolution approach for two-dimensional summary data. "Information systems", Elsevier, Vol. 36 Issue 7, pages 1082-1103. ISSN: 0306-4379. November, 2011.

[17] G. Adomavicius, and A. Tuzhilin. Context-Aware Recommender Systems. Recommender Systems Handbook. Springer US. ISBN 978-0-387-85820-3, 2011.

Methodology for Fraud Detection in Electronic Transactions

José Felipe Júnior, Wagner Meira Júnior, Adriano Veloso
Federal University of Minas Gerais (UFMG)
Department of Computer Science
Belo Horizonte, MG, Brazil
{felipe.junior, meira, adrianov}@dcc.ufmg.br

Adriano Pereira
Federal Center of Technological Education of Minas Gerais (CEFET-MG)
Department of Computer Engineering
Belo Horizonte, MG, Brazil
adriano@decom.cefetmg.br

ABSTRACT

Due to the growing popularity of the Web, there is an increasing number of people who performs e-business transactions. On the other hand, this popularity has also attracted the attention of criminals, raising the number of fraud cases in Web and financial losses that reach billions of dollars per year. This paper proposes a methodology, based on the knowledge discovery process, to detect fraud in online payment systems. In order to evaluate this methodology we define the concept of economical efficiency and applied it to an actual dataset of one of the largest Latin American electronic payment systems. The results show a very good performance for our proposal, providing gains of up to 46.5% in comparison with the strategy currently employed.

Categories and Subject Descriptors

K.4.4 [**Computers and Society**]: Electronic Commerce

General Terms

Experimentation, Security

Keywords

Data Mining, Fraud Detection, Electronic Markets, Web Applications, KDD Applications.

1. INTRODUCTION

During the last decades we have witnessed the e-commerce popularization, and this has attracted the criminals attention because of the financial amount associated. According to Bhatla et al. (2003) [1], the rate at which fraud occurs on the Internet is 12-15 times higher than in the "physical world", so that the sales on the Web represent a significant threat to merchants. According to the Mindware Research Group (2011) [9], the total North America on-line sales revenue loss associated with frauds in 2011 was approximately US$ 3.4 billion, an increase of US$ 700 million compared to 2010.

The prevention and detection of fraud is becoming key to the success of the e-markets. Accordingly, several data mining techniques have been used for fraud detection, but, prior to its use, it is necessary that the data are prepared for the techniques in terms of format and nature. Therefore, methodologies are needed to assist in the selection, cleaning and preparing the data so that we can employ data mining techniques.

The main objective of this research is to develop a methodology that can effectively assist the fraud detection process. Our methodology is an instance of the *KDD* process with add-ons that aim to help users evaluating scenarios of fraud on the Web or other that present similar characteristics. In data selection step, when a method to support the data extraction from the database is proposed, making easier this task and also providing a auditing method to guarantee the integrity and consistency of data. In the preprocessing, when some data manipulation and test are employed to help identifying fraud and non fraud trends. In data transformation, the methodology helps finding some data evidences that can identify the best attributes for data mining. In data mining step, when fraud detection characteristics help finding the best techniques to apply for fraud detection. Finally, the last step provides a method for evaluating fraud and its impact in electronic transactions.

The remainder of this paper is organized as follows: Section 2 presents related work and Section 3 performs a description of the methodology created. Section 4 presents a case study and the results are evaluated. Finally, Section 5 presents the conclusions.

2. RELATED WORK

Due to the importance of the fraud detection problem, we may distinguish several works that discuss the subject. There are studies that seek to identify fraud classes and create methodologies that allow their classification. The objective of this research is to better understand the fraud phenomenon and identify those that share some similarity [13, 3, 5]. As a consequence of frauds specificities, these methodologies may differ significantly as a function of the particularities of each fraud type. However, we can notice that the data mining techniques have been widely used in fraud detection regardless of the methodology adopted. This is because these techniques support the extraction of useful information in databases with large volumes of data.

Phua et al. (2005) [11] perform a comprehensive study of numerous works related to fraud detection using data mining

Permission to make digital or hard copies of all or part of this work for personal or classroom use is granted without fee provided that copies are not made or distributed for profit or commercial advantage and that copies bear this notice and the full citation on the first page. To copy otherwise, to republish, to post on servers or to redistribute to lists, requires prior specific permission and/or a fee.
WebMedia'12, October 15–18, 2012, São Paulo/SP, Brazil.
Copyright 2012 ACM 978-1-4503-1706-1/12/10 ...$15.00.

and present those methods and techniques as well as their limitations. According to the authors, there are three approaches on which these algorithms are based: *(1) supervised strategy* [8], learning algorithms examine all transactions, previously labeled, to mathematically determine the profile of a fraudulent transaction and to estimate their risk; *(2) unsupervised strategy* [2], the methods do not require prior knowledge of the fraudulent and non fraudulent transactions and detect changes in behavior or unusual transactions; *(3) hybrid strategy* [15], unsupervised strategies have been used to split the data into groups for supervised approaches.

3. METHODOLOGY

The methodology for fraud detection aims to create classification models that can assist in the identification of fraud in electronic transactions. This methodology differ from others because of its scope, since it cover a lot of approaches, from data extraction and selection to the assessment of most promising techniques for fraud identification, considering the financial gain obtained by techniques. The methodology is based on the *KDD* process that has five steps that will be used to guide the fraud detection task. However, changes and directions associated with fraud context are required in order to make it more adherent to the problem domain, as will be explained.

The **Data Selection** involves identifying what information should be effectively considered. Due to the complexity and the associated risks to the data extraction, we propose a extraction method in 4 steps. *Step 1:* Database analysis and tables selection that may contain relevant information for fraud detection, performed in conjunction with experts in the area. *Step 2:* Grouping (considering the *base tables* of the groups) and joins the tables selected considering the existing information. As the audit process, we should count the number of existing records in the *base table* and in each junction of a table we have to evaluate the occurrence of change in number of records. We should also do a check of some sample records to examine whether the relationship between data remain correct. The errors must be corrected. *Step 3:* Union of groups formed to create a unique dataset, we should use the audit process proposed. *Step 4:* Extraction the generated dataset for the text file format.

In the **Preprocessing** we applied strategies for data treatment to eliminate inconsistencies. As differential we propose the use of graphs and histograms to identify fraud patterns. If a pattern is found this can provide evidence that the selected attributes are significant for the fraud detection. Thus, it allows to check in advance if the selected attributes are relevant for the fraud detection, preventing the execution of all the methodology for the occurrence of this validation.

In the **Transformation** new information or information in appropriate formats are generated from the original features. To assist in this step, a few examples of variables for fraud detection are: establishment category, list of establishment most used by the customer, average value of purchases, CPF status, registration time, number of fraud cases and time since the last transaction [7].

In the **Data Mining** refers to the act of extracting patterns or models in large volumes of data. In the fraud context, techniques that are predictive and descriptive are more interesting, since it makes clear the standards used for its prediction, is an important tool for understanding patterns associated with fraud. The selected techniques that have these characteristics are: *Decision Tree* [12], *RIPPER*[4] and *Lazy Associative Classification (LAC)*[14]. The *Naive Bayes* technique was chosen because of the good results obtained in researches [10]. *Boosting*[6], *Oversampling* and *Stacking*[10] techniques were chosen in order to improve the quality of the prediction of the classifiers defined above.

In the **Evaluation and Interpretation of the Results** the patterns obtained in data mining are analyzed and evaluated. Some common measures, such as precision and recall, despite relevant, do not represent the business rules that have to be considered to model the actual application scenario. Therefore we have proposed a new measure that indicates the relative gains achieved by considering the business rules. We denote this new measure as economical efficiency *(EE)*, Equation 1. Where n is the number of existing transactions, G is the financial value of transactions true positive, gr is the percentage gain of the company in a successful transaction, L is the financial value of transactions false negative and lr is the percentage of loss in a fraud transaction classified as non-fraud. We defined three reference limits: (1) Maximum Economic Efficiency (EE_{Max}), which represents the maximum gain possible, where the term $(L * lr)$ of the Equation 1 is 0; (2) Real Economic Efficiency (EE_{Real}), that consists in calculating the (EE) without the use of any of the proposed techniques, the results should be above this limit for them to bring some economic benefit; (3) Minimum Economic Efficiency (EE_{Min}) which represent 100% of loss, where the term $(G * gr)$ of the Equation 1 is 0.

$$EE = \sum_{j=1}^{n} G * gr - L * lr \tag{1}$$

The Equation 1 was adapted to consider a penalty in the cases where legitimate transactions are misclassified as illegitimate. The Equation 2 defines Economic Efficiency with Penalty (EE_{CP}). Where NG represents the value of the legitimate records classified as fraud and p represents the percentage of value that will be considered as a loss. To evaluate the percentage of gain obtained in relation to the maximum gain possible, we should use the Equation 3. The equation provide the relative gain where 100% represents the maximum gain possible (EE_{Max}) and 0% represents the real scenario (EE_{Real}). The Equation 3 represents the gain achieved by considering the Economic Efficiency without Penalty (EE) and to obtain the gain considering the penalty we should replace in the Equation 3 the term (EE) by the term (EE_{CP}).

$$EE_{CP} = \sum_{j=1}^{n} G * gr - L * lr + NG * p \tag{2}$$

$$Gain_{SP} = \frac{EE - EE_{Real}}{EE_{Max} - EE_{Real}} \tag{3}$$

The selected classifiers provide, as a result, the probability of a record be fraudulent or not. Therefore, in order to maximize the results obtained with the classifier, we propose the creation of a *ranking* considering the probability of a record being fraudulent. Thus, the *EE* will be analyzed along the *ranking* in order to find a point where the results quality are maximized.

4. CASE STUDY

In order to evaluate the efficiency of the proposed methodology, this case study employs actual data from *UOL PagSeguro*, which is the largest Brazilian on line safety payment system. Following the methodology will be instantiated by following their steps.

For **Data Selection** the *UOL PagSeguro* provided a database comprising a period from August 2010 to June 2011. After understanding the data, we use the extraction methodology defined in section 3. The groups created by following step 2 were: *Transaction*, *Sellers*, *Buyers* and *Credit*. he final step, *step 4*, consisted of extracting the created dataset to a text file in the *CSV* format.

In the **Preprocessing** among the inconsistencies found and eliminated, some we can cite are: Negative values for age, fields that had many null and abbreviations of states do not exist. We removed also ID fields. Some patterns that we found were: most of the cases of fraud occurs with recently registered users; fraud focus on sales made with a small number of installments; fraud is greatest in ages above 40 years. The existence of patterns provides good evidence of relevant results in data mining.

In the **Transformation** the attributes derived that were created are: *Registration period from buyer*, *Registration period from seller*, *CPF Flag* indicates difference between the user social security number and the card holder and *Area Code Flag* indicates the difference between the user Area Code and the card holder. The date attributes were divided, generating four attributes: day of week, week, month and hour. The field *card holder birth date* was transformed into age, calculated based on the field *creation date of the transaction*. Metrics such as *Entropy* and *Chi-squared* were used for evaluation of the attributes, we removed those with the lowest values.

In the **Data Mining** the algorithms chosen are those defined in section 3. For *Decision Tree* the algorithm used was *C4.5* that can also handle continuous attributes. For *boosting* the algorithm used was *AdaBoost*. The *oversampling* consisted of performing a oversampling of the minority class by creating datasets with class distribution of 10% to 50% ranging from 10 to 10. The combination of algorithms for the *Stacking* was *C4.5*, *RIPPER* and *Naive Bayes* having as *meta-learner* the *Naive Bayes* classifier.

In the **Evaluation and Interpretation of the Results** cross-validation was used and each month has been divided into five partitions, in which 4 used for training and 1 for test. The metrics are calculated assuming an average of the results of each test partition. The tables below represent the point at the *ranking* where the results are maximized. In each table we show the following measures: Precision *(Prec.)*, Recall *(Rec.)*, (EE_{SP}), (EE_{CP}), $(Gain_{SP})$, $(Gain_{CP})$ and Percentage of *ranking* where the results are maximized *(Perc. rank.)*. The best experimental result is highlighted in **bold** and marked with a (†).

Table 1: Result (%) - November.

Measure	C4.5	RIP.	LAC	NB
Prec.	15,93	**77,00**†	23,00	57,50
Rec.	**19,88**†	15,00	6,27	4,45
EE_{SP}	5,00	5,00	2,00	**6,00**†
EE_{CP}	5,00	5,00	2,00	**6,00**†
$Gain_{SP}$	15,83	14,85	7,26	**18,06**†
$Gain_{CP}$	14,98	14,78	6,65	**17,90**†
Perc. Rank.	0,40	0,06	0,09	**0,03**†

Table 2: Meta Learning Result (%) - December.

Measure	B. C4.5	B. RIP.	B. NB	Stack.
Prec.	58,64	11,71	7,60	**97,71**†
Rec.	**30,48**†	30,44	11,25	25,39
EE_{SP}	13,00	12,00	6,00	**20,00**†
EE_{CP}	13,00	11,00	5,00	**20,00**†
$Gain_{SP}$	30,78	28,48	12,84	**46,46**†
$Gain_{CP}$	30,56	26,08	12,14	**46,44**†
Perc. Rank.	0,19	0,94	0,54	**0,09**†

The Table 1 shows the result in percentage of the techniques *C4.5*, *RIPPER (RIP.)*, *LAC*, *Naive Bayes (NB)* for the month of November. The *RIP* obtained a high precision, 77%, and a good coverage of fraud, 15%. The *NB*, had a better *EE*, because the frauds detected by this classifier had higher values than those frauds obtained by *RIP.*. The *C4.5* showed a greater coverage of fraud however the low precision made their *EE* does not overcome the *NB*. The bad result with the *LAC* is associated with the need for discretization of some variables for use of this algorithm, which represents a information loss. The *NB* showed the lowest percentage of use of the *ranking* to maximize results. The Table 2 shows the results of the meta-learning techniques, the aim of this experiment is verify if the approaches defined by these techniques can improve the results quality of the classifiers defined in the first experiment. The *boosting* technique allowed a significant improvement in the *C4.5* algorithm, with an excellent Prec. and Rec. and a good *EE*. For the *RIP* this represented a deterioration in the Prec., however we obtained a considerable improvement in the Rec. and *EE*. This may be due to the strengthening of the records in the fraud classes promoted by *boosting*. However, this technique has worsened considerably the result of the *NB* algorithm, since the deterioration in Prec. does not provides a improvement in the Rev., because the samples created by this technique did not show a substantial increase in the fraud classes. The *Stacking* show the best result and the most importantly is the obtain of a gain in efficiency of 46.46% without considering the penalty and 46.44% considering the error penalty, i.e., practically the same result due to the excellent accuracy of 97.71% in a small number of occurrences near the top of the *rank*. The Table 3 shows the results of the techniques with *oversampling*. The aim of this experiment is to assess whether an improvement in the distribution fraud classes will improve the classifier's results. It was not possible to test with the *RIP.* due to problems with memory allocation. Overall, both the algorithm *C4.5* and the *NB*, improved the fraud coverage, showing that this change in the distribution contributes to an improvement in the identification of the minority class. However, both the *C4.5* and *LAC* show a degradation in Prec. and this is due to an increase in the amount of legitimate records being classified as fraud. In the case of *C4.5* this Prec. decrease did not negatively affect the *EE*, since in most cases *C4.5+Oversampling* performed best than the result of the technique where there was no change in distribution. For *LAC* changes the distribution represented by deterioration in *EE*, since there was a significant drop in Prec., because many legitimate records that were not classified as fraud came to be classified as such. The *NB* showed the best results showing significant improvements in

Table 3: *Oversampling* Result (%) - December.

Measure	10%	20%	30%	40%	50%
		C4.5			
Prec.	**9,06**†	8,11	8,07	7,80	5,89
Rec.	21,86	**27,09**†	22,75	20,23	25,13
EE_{SP}	9,00	**10,00**†	9,00	9,00	8,00
EE_{CP}	8,00	**9,00**†	8,00	8,00	7,00
$Gain_{SP}$	21,20	**22,68**†	20,58	19,58	18,89
$Gain_{CP}$	19,21	**20,09**†	18,28	17,45	15,41
Perc. Rank.	**0,88**†	1,20	1,02	0,94	1,54
		NB			
Prec.	84,33	**100,00**†	55,70	71,40	99,00
Rec.	9,39	11,14	12,40	13,25	**14,70**†
EE_{SP}	12,00	13,00	14,00	15,00	**16,00**†
EE_{CP}	12,00	13,00	14,00	15,00	**16,00**†
$Gain_{SP}$	26,52	30,65	31,90	33,64	**36,42**†
$Gain_{CP}$	26,43	30,65	31,57	33,40	**36,41**†
Perc. Rank.	**0,04**†	**0,04**†	0,08	0,07	**0,04**†
		LAC			
Prec.	**6,18**†	5,26	5,42	4,69	4,30
Rec.	24,35	**24,61**†	21,16	22,83	22,01
EE_{SP}	**8,00**†	**8,00**†	7,00	7,00	7,00
EE_{CP}	**7,00**†	6,00	6,00	5,00	5,00
$Gain_{SP}$	**19,09**†	17,88	16,83	15,72	14,89
$Gain_{CP}$	**15,12**†	13,46	13,12	11,57	10,70
Perc. Rank.	1,42	1,68	1,47	1,75	**1,84**†

all metrics and a *EE* value of 36.42% without considering the penalty and 36.41% considering the penalty.

Some hypotheses made regarding the methodology used and its effectiveness in solving the problem are: **H1 - The selected attributes are relevant for fraud detection.** All tables of results presented show gains in economic efficiency relative to the *UOL PagSeguro*. Thus, we can consider that the selected attributes are relevant to solve the problem. However, there are several other attributes that may represent evidence of fraud, and new datasets can be generated and provide an improvement in results. **H2 - Economic efficiency allows us to assess the results quality.** Generally, the best economic efficiencies are associated with better models. However, it may tend to models that identify fraud cases with high amounts. Thus, it is interesting to use Economic Efficiency together with other model evaluating measures like precision and recall. This will ensure that the best models with the best financial gains will be selected. **Q1 - Which technique showed the best results?** As shown in Table 2 the technique *Stacking* showed the best result, reaching efficiencies gains up to 46.46%. An advantage of this technique is that it combines several classifiers extracting the best result from them. Thus, this result can be improved by combining other techniques that may be more effective in fraud detection.

5. CONCLUSION

Due to financial losses caused by frauds in on-line payments by credit card, this paper proposed a methodology, based on *KDD*, for your detection considering the electronic commerce scenario. To check the effectiveness of the methodology, we developed a case study in a real dataset from company of electronic payment service, the *UOL PagSeguro*. The methodology steps were followed and the results were good, where all techniques showed gains in economic efficiency higher than those achieved by *UOL PagSeguro*. Among the best results we can mention the gain of 46.46% obtained by the *Stacking* technique, the gain of 36.42% obtained with the *oversampling* technique for the *Naive Bayes* and the gain of 18.08% obtained with the *Naive Bayes* technique. These values represent the percentage in relation to the maximum gain that can be obtained, the maximum being represented by 100%. We can see that they are expressive values, which can represent significant savings for the *UOL PagSeguro*. An important point to highlight is the excellent precision obtained with the *Stacking* technique with a value of 97.71%, showing that this classifiers combination is a good option for the fraud detection process

6. ACKNOWLEDGMENTS

This work was partially sponsored by Universo OnLine S. A. - UOL (www.uol.com.br) and partially supported by the Brazilian National Institute of Science and Technology for the Web (CNPq grant no. 573871/2008-6), CAPES, CNPq, Finep, and Fapemig.

7. REFERENCES

[1] T. P. Bhatla, V. Prabhu, and A. Dua. *Understanding Credit Card Frauds.* USA, 2003.

[2] R. J. Bolton and D. J. Hand. Unsupervised Profiling Methods for Fraud Detection. *Statistical Science*, 17(3):235–255, 2002.

[3] D. H. Chau, S. P, and C. Faloutsos. Detecting fraudulent personalities in networks of online auctioneers. In *In Proc. ECML/PKDD*, pages 103–114, 2006.

[4] W. W. Cohen. Fast effective rule induction. In *In Proceedings of the Twelfth Intl. Conf. on Machine Learning*, pages 115–123. Morgan Kaufmann, 1995.

[5] T. Fawcett and F. Provost. Adaptive fraud detection. data mining and knowledge discovery, 1997.

[6] Y. Freund and R. E. Schapire. A decision-theoretic generalization of on-line learning and an application to boosting. In *Proc. of the Second European Conf. on Computational Learning Theory*, EuroCOLT '95, pages 23–37, London, UK, UK, 1995. Springer-Verlag.

[7] M. F. A. Gadi. *Uma Comparação de Métodos de Classificação Aplicados à Detecção de Fraude em Cartões de Crédito.* São Paulo, 2008.

[8] S. Maes, K. Tuyls, B. Vanschoenwinkel, and B. Manderick. Credit card fraud detection using bayesian and neural networks. In *In: Maciunas RJ, editor. Interactive image-guided neurosurgery. American Association Neurological Surgeons*, pages 261–270, 1993.

[9] C. Mindware Research Group. *2011 Online Fraud Report.* California, USA, 12th annual edition, 2011.

[10] C. Phua, D. Alahakoon, and V. Lee. Minority report in fraud detection: classification of skewed data. *SIGKDD Explor. Newsl.*, 6(1):50–59, June 2004.

[11] C. Phua, V. Lee, K. Smith-Miles, and R. Gayler. A comprehensive survey of data mining-based fraud detection research. 2005.

[12] J. R. Quinlan. *C4.5: programs for machine learning.* Morgan Kaufmann Publishers Inc., San Francisco, CA, USA, 1993.

[13] L. Vasiu and I. Vasiu. Dissecting computer fraud: From definitional issues to a taxonomy. In *Proceedings of the 37th Annual Hawaii International Conference on System Sciences (HICSS'04) - Track 7 - Volume 7*, HICSS '04, pages 70170.3–, Washington, DC, USA, 2004. IEEE CS.

[14] A. Veloso, W. Meira, and M. J. Zaki. Lazy associative classification. In *Int. Conf. on Data Mining*, pages 645–654. 2006.

[15] G. J. Williams and Z. Huang. Mining the knowledge mine: The hot spots methodology for mining large real world databases, 1997.

Improving Location Recommendations with Temporal Pattern Extraction

Leandro Balby Marinho
Federal University of Campina Grande
Campina Grande, PB, Brazil
lbmarinho@dsc.ufcg.edu.br

Iury Nunes
Federal University of Campina Grande
Campina Grande, PB, Brazil
iurydewar@gmail.com

Thomas Sandholm
HP Labs
Palo Alto, USA
thomas.e.sandholm@hp.com

Caio Nóbrega
Federal University of Campina Grande
Campina Grande, PB, Brazil
caionobrega0@gmail.com

Jordão Araújo
Federal University of Campina Grande
Campina Grande, PB, Brazil
jordaoesa@gmail.com

Carlos Eduardo Pires
Federal University of Campina Grande
Campina Grande, PB, Brazil
cesp@dsc.ufcg.edu.br

ABSTRACT

A key challenge in mobile social media applications is how to present personalized content that is both geographically and temporally relevant. In this paper, we propose a new and generic temporal weighting function for improving location recommendations. First, we identify areas of interest to recommend by clustering geographic activity based on a trace of geotagged photos. Next, the clusters are temporally weighted using TF-IDF, in order to capture seasonality, and a decay scoring function to capture preference drift. Finally, these weights are combined with the cluster scores based on geographic relevance. We evaluate our recommender on a large dataset collected from Panoramio consisting of the top-100 most populated cities in the world and show that incorporating the proposed temporal weighting function improves recommendation quality.

Categories and Subject Descriptors

H.2.4 [**Information Storage and Retrieval**]: Information filtering

General Terms

Algorithms, Design, Experimentation

Keywords

Recommender Systems, Location-Based Applications, Time-Aware, Geographic Clustering

1. INTRODUCTION

The ubiquity of mobile devices such as tablets and smartphones with GPS capabilities resulted in a surge in popularity of Location-Based Services (LBS). Moreover, content created on these devices such as photos, or tweets are now being automatically tagged with the current geographic position of the originating device (*geotagging*). This has lead to a growing body of geotagged on-line content. Traditional search methods based on PageRank-like rankings do a poor job of finding the most relevant content as the basic assumption of the random surfer [2] is violated because of geographic relevance playing a more prominent role in the overall relevance of the content. Thus new methods are needed that exploit geographic relevance. Given that most of the geo-aware queries originate from mobile devices with limited input capabilities and restricted screen real-estate there is also a general preference for topN [3] recommendations accommodating for contextual cues automatically as opposed to keyword searches.

In the typical setting, Recommender Systems (RS) exploit a user-item matrix representing user preferences for items, e.g., the rating history of books purchased on Amazon.com or movies watched on Netflix, with the aim of recommending the items most likely to be relevant to the user. However, in LBS, the relevance score is highly dependant on the geographic context, e.g., areas within some city. It thus becomes valuable to not only recommend items to the user but also locations that are most relevant to him/her. The identified locations may then, in a second step, be further explored using traditional techniques to find items of interest. In this paper we focus on the first step of the problem, i.e., finding relevant locations given a geographic context.

Many studies have appeared recently showing the benefits of exploiting the geographic context of users for the recommendation of locations that may be of interest. Mao et al. [12], for example, showed that Foursquare users prefer points-of-interest (POIs) that are nearby the POIs they have already visited in the past, while [9] showed that the photo location similarity across users is predictable in Panoramio[1]. Although promising, these approaches ignore the time when users showed interest for a certain region. On the other hand, the state-of-the-art related work on time-aware recommendations [8, 5] ignore the location where the user demonstrated interest for an item. The area of geo and time-aware

[1]http://www.panoramio.com

Permission to make digital or hard copies of all or part of this work for personal or classroom use is granted without fee provided that copies are not made or distributed for profit or commercial advantage and that copies bear this notice and the full citation on the first page. To copy otherwise, to republish, to post on servers or to redistribute to lists, requires prior specific permission and/or a fee.
WebMedia'12, October 15–18, 2012, São Paulo/SP, Brazil.
Copyright 2012 ACM 978-1-4503-1706-1/12/10 ...$15.00.

recommender systems is still emerging. Raymond et al. [10], for example, exploits spatio-temporal correlations between locations to recommend on-demand bus rides. We on the other hand, are more interested in extracting time-period preferences (both for users and locations) and seasonal popularity automatically based on user actions in order to discover and recommend the salient locations. Furthermore, focusing on activity-based time preferences allows us to rank venues by time, as opposed to just having a binary filter (open or closed). Hence, we can recommend the most relevant items, the most relevant locations where these items reside and the most relevant times when these locations may be visited. Again, here we rely on existing recommendation techniques for item recommendations but contribute new techniques for location and time aware relevance ranking.

In this paper we consider the collection of geo- and time-tagged photos of Panoramio. In contrast to other photo sharing sites such as Flickr[2], Panoramio focuses on photos of places and landmarks, which corresponds to the entities we are interested in recommending here. This means that we do not have to filter out other kinds of photos. This also allows us to consider a photo as an endorsement of the place where it was taken. The geographical coordinate (latitude,longitude) of photos is captured by cameras equipped with GPS, smartphones, or manually entered by users via interactive maps in Panoramio. Note that if we allow photo coordinates to define places of interest directly, the co-activity matrices would be extremely sparse. Thus we want to automatically cluster coordinates into activity-based areas of interest. Various clustering algorithms have been employed for overcoming this problem, under the assumption that nearby geotagged objects belong to the same region of interest [6, 7]. The first task we tackle in this paper is thus to extract Areas of Interest (AOIs) based on the aggregate of all users' photo histories, taking into consideration the geographic metadata of photos. To this end, we employ P-DBSCAN [7], an adaptation of the classic Density-Based Spatial Clustering Applications with Noise (DBSCAN) [4].

The next step of our approach is to capture the distribution of cluster activity over time. The assumption is that clusters having more activity in the period of interest declared by the target user are more important. We split the time of interest into two levels of granularity, month and year, and use TF-IDF and a recency decay function based on the time value of money theory to define the temporal relevance of clusters. Now the final cluster scores are obtained by combining the temporal weights with the cluster scores for geographic relevance. To summarize, our contributions comprise:

1. A new and generic temporal ranking function for location recommender systems,

2. A comparison of our algorithm to a baseline popularity algorithm on a real-world dataset.

The rest of the paper is organized as follows. Section 2 presents the problem setting. Section 3 introduces a TF-IDF scheme for capturing the temporal relevance of geographic clusters. Section 4 presents the experimental setting and evaluation. Finally, Section 5 concludes the paper and discusses future work.

[2]http://www.flickr.com

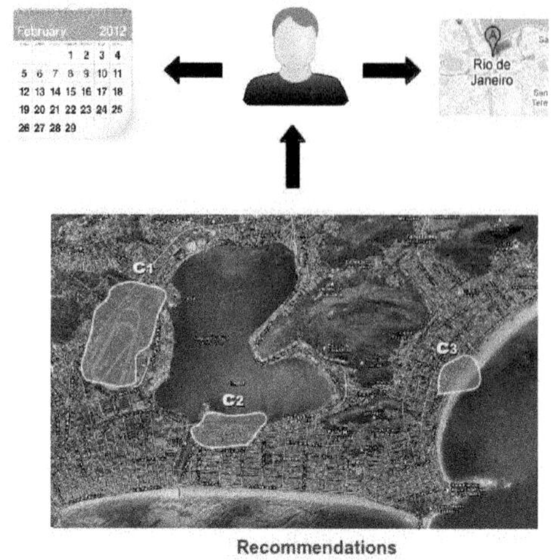

Figure 1: Example of a geo- and time-aware recommender of locations (denoted by c_1, c_2, and c_3, respectively) where a target-user is interested in popular and relevant areas in Rio de Janeiro, Brazil in February 2012.

2. PROBLEM SETTING

In this paper we tackle the problem of geo- and time-aware recommendation of locations. The recommendation scenario is as follows. A user specifies the geographic context of interest, a timestamp of interest, and the recommender engine suggests AOI (geographic clusters) within the declared geographic context and related to the declared timestamp that are likely to be relevant to the user. For example, we want to answer the following type of query: "What can I do in Rio in February, 2012?" (see Figure 1).

Let U be the set of users, G the set of geographic contexts, T the set of timestamps, and C the set of geographic clusters (AOIs). In this work geographic contexts map to city names, timestamps to (month,year) pairs, and C to geographic clusters extracted from the collection of geotagged photos. Moreover, we only consider implicit feedback data since there is no rating information in Panoramio. The data is represented by the set $S \subseteq U \times G \times T \times C$ of quaternary relations between users, geographic contexts, timestamps, and geographic clusters. The task is then to find a scoring function

$$\hat{s} : U \times G \times T \times C \to \mathbb{R} \tag{1}$$

that predicts a preference value for any given 4-tuple $(u, g, t, c) \in S$. Now, for a given user $u \in U$, a given geographic context $g \in G$, and a given time unit $t \in T$, the topN recommendations can be computed by

$$topN(u, g, t) := \operatorname*{argmax}_{c \in C_g}^{n} \hat{s}(u, g, t, c) \tag{2}$$

where n denotes the topN locations to be recommended and C_g the set of geographic clusters within city $g \in G$.

3. TEMPORAL WEIGHTING

We propose to extract the temporal relevance of all the AOI in terms of how important they are to the month and year of interest expressed by the user in a query. The assumption is that a cluster that has shown more photo activity in the month and year of interest, should be more relevant to the user.

Let t^m and t^y denote the month and year of timestamp $t \in T$ respectively and P_{c,t^m} the set of photos of cluster $c \in C$ taken on month t^m. Now, the relevance of a given cluster $c \in C$ with respect to a given month t^m is extracted based on the well-known TF-IDF scoring function as follows. The TF is defined as the ratio of photos of cluster $c \in C$ that were taken in month t^m, i.e., $|P_{c,t^m}|/|P_c|$ where P_c denotes the set of photos of cluster $c \in C$. The IDF is the number of photos taken in city $g \in G$ divided by the number of photos taken in this city in month t^m. In other words, a cluster will have a high TF-IDF with respect to a given month, if it covers many photos taken in this month but this month has a low overall popularity in terms of photos taken in the city as whole.

In order to extract the relevance of the year, we apply a decay function according to the theory of time-value of money to account for the popularity decay of clusters over the years. The assumption is that clusters having more activity in recent years should be weighted higher. This function is defined as follows:

$$v(c, t^y) = \sum_{i=x}^{t^y} \frac{P_{c,t^i}}{(1+r)^{t^y - i}} \quad (3)$$

where P_{c,t^y} is the number of photos of cluster c in year t^y, x is the year of the oldest photo in cluster c, and r is the decay rate per time step.

The final temporal score of a given cluster $c \in C$ and a timestamp $t \in T$ is a combination of the month and year weighting functions, i.e.,

$$\hat{t}(c, t) := \text{tf-idf}(c, t^m) \cdot v(c, t^y) \quad (4)$$

Now consider any geographic-aware recommender of locations that takes a user, a geographic context, and a cluster as input and returns a cluster score as output, $l : U \times G \times C \rightarrow \mathbb{R}$. We make such a recommender time-aware by just multiplying this score by our proposed temporal weighting function, i.e., the relevance of a given cluster $c \in C$ for a given user $u \in U$, a city $g \in G$, and timestamp $t \in T$ is now computed as

$$\hat{s}(u, g, t, c) := l(u, g, c) \cdot \hat{t}(c, t) \quad (5)$$

4. EVALUATION

As mentioned in Section 1, we used data from Panoramio. For the experiments, we collected users and photos from the 100 most populated cities in the world. Table 1 summarizes the characteristics of this data set. In this work we have

Table 1: Characteristics of the collected data.

#Users	#Cities	#Photos	Users per City	Photos per User
35,474	100	349,166	351	10

chosen P-DBSCAN as the clustering algorithm [7, 11]. P-DBSCAN is an adaptation of the classic DBSCAN method that has proven to be suitable to identify AOI from collections of geo-tagged photos. The following parameter values were used in P-DBSCAN: min-owners = 4[3]; $\alpha := 0.5$[4]; the radius ε was adjusted per city taking values proportional to the pairwise average distances between photos in the city of interest minus the standard deviation of these distances. Table 2 summarizes the characteristics of the generated clusters. The evaluation follows a leave-one-out protocol as follows. For each city, we select all the users having photos in at least three clusters. Next, for each of these users, we hide his/her most recent photo and use the remaining photos to predict the clusters more likely to be visited next. From the hidden photo we extract the city and timestamp of interest in order to compute the recommendation scores. The assumption is that the closer a cluster centroid is to the hidden photo the more relevant is this cluster to the user. We computed the normalized Discounted Cumulative Gain (DCG) ranking metric over top-10 recommendation lists. Since in DCG more relevant items have higher scores, we first converted distances into similarities by taking $1 - \frac{d}{d_{\max}}$ where $d_{\max}$ is the maximum pairwise distance found between the test photo and any of the cluster centroids in the city of interest and d is the actual distance. In previous work [1] we showed how to derive many neighborhood-based pure geographic-aware location recommender algorithms inspired by a simple relational classifier approach. In this paper, we investigate the impact of incorporating the temporal weights presented in Section 3 to three of these algorithms:

Table 2: Characteristics of the clusters.

#Clusters	Clusters per City	Users per Cluster	Photos per Cluster
4,615	46	> 7	75

- Most popular (MP): recommends the most popular clusters in a given city, i.e., clusters are ranked according to their number of photos;
- Collaborative Filtering: this is the geographic version of the classic user-based collaborative filtering algorithm. The profile vectors' components correspond to the clusters where the users took photos regarding the chosen city. We tested two variants of this algorithm:
  - Profile vectors filled with the number of photos took in each cluster (CF);
  - Profile vectors filled with 1, if the user took pictures in the corresponding cluster, or missing values otherwise (BCF).

The decay rate parameter of Eq. 3 was empirically set to 0.05 after a greedy search over the $[0.01, \ldots, 0.1]$ interval. Table 3 shows the results. Note that the results improve consistently over all algorithms after the temporal weights are used. Although the margin of improvement appears to be small, notice that we used the normalized version of DCG where the perfect ordering is the one where the clusters are ranked in a decreasing order of their geographic distances to the hidden photo. So even the apparently small improvements noted in Table 3 may indicate, for example, that the improved method is recommending clusters hundreds of meters closer to the hidden photo than the pure location-aware algorithms.

[3]Minimum number of photos of distinct users.

[4]Density across reachable objects should not fall below this value [7]

Table 3: Results before and after incorporating the temporal weights.

Algorithms	Location	Location-Temporal
MP	0.6842	0.6975
CF	0.6899	0.6984
BCF	0.6954	0.7004

5. CONCLUSIONS AND FUTURE WORK

In this paper we introduced a new temporal weighting function for geo and time-aware location recommender systems. The recommendation scenario we address in this paper is different from related work based on points of interest recommendation since the locations to be recommended are not given and must be inferred from data. The question that we addressed in this paper was how to leverage the temporal distribution of photos inside the inferred geographic clusters, given a timestamp of interest, in order to boost the recommendation accuracy of location recommenders. We split the time of interest into two levels of granularity, month and year, and use TF-IDF and a scoring function based on interest decay over time to define the temporal relevance of clusters. We showed that this temporal function was able to improve, consistently, the results of three neighborhood-based location recommenders presented in previous work.

Although one can adjust the density of clusters in P-DBSCAN, clusters can still assume arbitrary sizes. In practice, if the recommended areas are too large, the users may find it difficult to identify the true interesting attractions within those areas. Therefore, as future work, we plan to investigate other cluster setups as well as mechanisms to control their sizes. We note that because we measure the distance of the centroid of the recommended cluster to the exact location of the hidden photo we can effectively evaluate the viability of different clustering techniques as well. We also plan to assess the proposed temporal weights by incorporating it into more location recommendation algorithms, such as matrix-factorization methods.

6. ACKNOWLEDGEMENTS

This work was supported by Hewlett-Packard Brasil Ltda. using incentives of Brazilian Informatics Law (No. 8.2.48 of 1991). We would also like to thank Christina Aperjis, Sitaram Asur and Georgia Koutrika for insightful comments.

7. REFERENCES

[1] L. Balby Marinho, C. de Souza Baptista, T. Sandholm, I. Nunes, C. Nóbrega, and J. Araújo. Extracting Geospatial Preferences Using Relational Neighbors. *ArXiv e-prints*, Apr. 2012.

[2] S. Brin and L. Page. The anatomy of a large-scale hypertextual web search engine. In *Proceedings of the seventh international conference on World Wide Web 7*, WWW7, pages 107–117, Amsterdam, The Netherlands, The Netherlands, 1998. Elsevier Science Publishers B. V.

[3] M. Deshpande and G. Karypis. Item-based top-n recommendation algorithms. *ACM Trans. Inf. Syst.*, 22(1):143–177, 2004.

[4] M. Ester, H.-P. Kriegel, J. Sander, and X. Xu. A density-based algorithm for discovering clusters in large spatial databases with noise. In *Proc. of 2nd International Conference on Knowledge Discovery and*, pages 226–231, 1996.

[5] Z. Gantner, S. Rendle, and L. Schmidt-Thieme. Factorization models for context-/time-aware movie recommendations. In *Proceedings of the Workshop on Context-Aware Movie Recommendation*, CAMRa '10, pages 14–19, 2010.

[6] L. S. Kennedy and M. Naaman. Generating diverse and representative image search results for landmarks. In *Proceedings of the 17th international conference on World Wide Web*, WWW '08, pages 297–306, New York, NY, USA, 2008. ACM.

[7] S. Kisilevich, F. Mansmann, and D. Keim. P-dbscan: a density based clustering algorithm for exploration and analysis of attractive areas using collections of geo-tagged photos. In *Proceedings of the 1st International Conference and Exhibition on Computing for Geospatial Research & Application*, COM.Geo '10, pages 38:1–38:4, New York, NY, USA, 2010. ACM.

[8] Y. Koren. Collaborative filtering with temporal dynamics. In *Proceedings of the 15th ACM SIGKDD international conference on Knowledge discovery and data mining*, KDD '09, pages 447–456, 2009.

[9] C. Matyas and C. Schlieder. A spatial user similarity measure for geographic recommender systems. In K. Janowicz, M. Raubal, and S. Levashkin, editors, *GeoSpatial Semantics*, volume 5892 of *Lecture Notes in Computer Science*, pages 122–139. Springer Berlin / Heidelberg, 2009.

[10] R. Raymond, T. Sugiura, and K. Tsubouchi. Location recommendation based on location history and spatio-temporal correlations for an on-demand bus system. In *Proceedings of the 19th ACM SIGSPATIAL International Conference on Advances in Geographic Information Systems*, GIS '11, pages 377–380, 2011.

[11] Y. Yang, Z. Gong, and L. H. U. Identifying points of interest by self-tuning clustering. In *Proceedings of the 34th international ACM SIGIR conference on Research and development in Information Retrieval*, SIGIR '11, pages 883–892, 2011.

[12] M. Ye, P. Yin, W.-C. Lee, and D.-L. Lee. Exploiting geographical influence for collaborative point-of-interest recommendation. In *Proceedings of the 34th international ACM SIGIR conference on Research and development in Information Retrieval*, SIGIR '11, pages 325–334, 2011.

Exploiting Relevance, Novelty and Diversity in Tag Recommendation*

Fabiano Belém, Eder Martins, Jussara Almeida, Marcos Gonçalves
Departamento de Ciência da Computação
Universidade Federal de Minas Gerais, Brazil
{ederfm, fmuniz, jussara, mgoncalv}@dcc.ufmg.br

ABSTRACT

Tag recommendation methods have mostly focused on maximizing relevance, but other aspects may be as important for recommendation usefulness. We here define novelty and diversity for tag recommendation, and propose two new recommendation strategies that consider these aspects jointly with relevance. We evaluate the proposed strategies using real datasets from popular Web 2.0 applications, achieving gains over the state-of-the-art of up to 21% in relevance, 45% in novelty and 2.5% in diversity.

Categories and Subject Descriptors: H.3.5 [Information Storage and Retrieval]: Online Information Services
General Terms: Algorithms, Experimentation

Keywords: Recomendação de Tags, Novidade, Diversidade

1. INTRODUÇÃO

Tags tornaram-se bastante populares na Web. Elas tipicamente possibilitam a organização do conteúdo, provendo boas descrições e refletindo os interesses dos usuários [6]. Tags também representam uma boa fonte de dados para serviços de Recuperação de Informação, particularmente para mídias ricas (imagem, áudio, vídeo) [4]. Nesse contexto, serviços de recomendação de tags objetivam sugerir tags *relevantes* e *úteis* para o usuário, ajudando-o na tarefa de descrever o conteúdo e melhorando a qualidade das tags geradas, de forma que elas descrevam o conteúdo de forma mais precisa e completa.

A pesquisa em sistemas de recomendação tem, historicamente, dado ênfase em maximizar a *relevância* dos itens recomendados [13], isto é, o quanto eles estão de acordo com os interesses do usuário alvo. Em recomendação de tags, particularmente, relevância pode ser definida a partir de uma perspectiva centrada no objeto [2], referindo-se ao quão bem os termos recomendados descrevem o conteúdo do objeto alvo, ou a partir de uma perspectiva personalizada (isto é, um termo relevante deve não apenas descrever bem o conteúdo do objeto, como também satisfazer os interesses do usuário alvo [7]).

Entretanto, relevância apenas pode não ser suficiente para garantir a eficácia e a utilidade das recomendações [10, 13]. Por exemplo, considere uma lista de tags recomendadas a um usuário u para descrever um objeto o, em que todos os termos estão relacionados ao conteúdo de o, porém todos eles são sinônimos. Além disso, suponha que estes termos já tenham sido utilizados por u para descrever o conteúdo de o. Em ambos os casos, embora as tags recomendadas tenham relevância máxima, elas são menos interessantes e úteis do que uma lista de termos mais diversificada que traga informação nova para o dado objeto e usuário. Isso é particularmente importante porque objetos multimídia na Web 2.0 podem ser *multifacetados*, ou seja, eles podem estar relacionados a vários aspectos e temas. Assim, tags mais novas e diversas podem ajudar a capturar melhor essas várias facetas do objeto. Portanto, *novidade* e *diversidade* são também aspectos essenciais para recomendações de tags, além de sua relevância.

Vargas *et al.* [13] definem novidade como o quão diferente um item é dos itens observados em um dado contexto (por exemplo, a aplicação como um todo, um usuário, um grupo de usuários, etc). Aqui, nós analisamos a novidade de uma tag no contexto da aplicação. Uma tag é *nova* se ela não é muito frequente na aplicação, o que pode ser estimado pelo inverso da popularidade da tag. Por sua vez, a *diversidade* de uma lista de termos recomendados refere-se ao quão diferente cada item é dos demais [13]. Nós estimamos a diversidade de uma lista de tags como a média da dissimilaridade semântica [12, 5] entre cada par de tags da lista, de modo que um conjunto de palavras sinônimas ou similares tenha baixa diversidade.

Neste artigo, nós abordamos o problema de recomendar tags relevantes, novas e diversificadas. Recomendação de tags é aqui modelada como um problema de ordenar múltiplos termos candidatos por uma função da relevância, novidade e diversidade. Em outras palavras, objetivamos produzir uma função de valoração FV que associe valores a termos candidatos, baseados em várias métricas, permitindo ordená-los de tal forma que termos que representem recomendações mais relevantes, novas e diversas apareçam primeiro na lista de recomendações.

Este é o primeiro trabalho que explora diretamente novidade e diversidade no contexto de recomendação de tags.

*Esta pesquisa é parcialmente financiada pelo Instituto Nacional de Ciência e Tecnologia para a Web - INCTWeb (MCT/CNPq 573871/2008-6), CNPq, FAPEMIG e CAPES.

Permission to make digital or hard copies of all or part of this work for personal or classroom use is granted without fee provided that copies are not made or distributed for profit or commercial advantage and that copies bear this notice and the full citation on the first page. To copy otherwise, to republish, to post on servers or to redistribute to lists, requires prior specific permission and/or a fee.
WebMedia'12, October 15–18, 2012, São Paulo/SP, Brazil.
Copyright 2012 ACM 978-1-4503-1706-1/12/10 ...$10.00.

Em particular, aplicamos métricas nunca antes utilizadas em recomendação de tags e desenvolvemos duas novas estratégias de recomendação. A primeira estratégia estende um método estado-da-arte baseado em Programação Genética [3, 2], denominado PG_{rel}, para incluir as novas métricas e uma nova função objetivo que combina relevância, novidade e diversidade. A incorporação explícita dessas métricas na função objetivo que queremos otimizar muda completamente o espaço de busca por novas soluções, que resolvem simultaneamente os três aspectos do problema. Chamamos nossa nova estratégia de $PG_{rel+nov+div}$.

Nossa segunda estratégia é baseada em *relevance feedback* (RF) [1], uma técnica utilizada em Recuperação de Informação para refinar os resultados de uma consulta. Isto é, obtém-se os resultados inicialmente retornados por uma consulta e utiliza-se informação fornecida pelo usuário de quais resultados são relevantes para realizar uma nova consulta. No contexto de recomendação de tags, nossa estratégia basicamente compreende três passos: (1) uma lista contendo um conjunto inicial de tags produzida por um dado método de recomendação de tags é mostrada ao usuário alvo; (2) o usuário seleciona tags relevantes dessa lista; (3) as tags selecionadas são exploradas pelo método para recomendar novas tags. Este processo é repetido enquanto o usuário fornecer *feedback*. Nossa hipótese é que, a partir das recomendações mostradas ao usuário e das tags selecionadas por ele, é possível capturar melhor as várias facetas do objeto, que podem ser melhor percebidas por um usuário real do que por um método puramente automático, melhorando a diversidade e a novidade das recomendações, bem como aumentando a quantidade de termos relevantes retornados.

Avaliamos nossas estratégias utilizando dados coletados das aplicações YouTube, LastFM e YahooVideo, comparando-as com o método estado-da-arte PG_{rel}. Com a nossa nova estratégia baseada em Programação Genética, $PG_{rel+nov+div}$, obtivemos ganhos sobre PG_{rel} de até 14% em novidade sem causar danos à relevância. Nosso segundo método, baseado em RF, produz ganhos de até 21% em relevância e 45% em novidade. Mais ainda, verificamos que o método baseado em RF exige alguma cooperação do usuário, embora possa produzir ganhos maiores em relevância. A $PG_{rel+nov+div}$, entretanto, apresentou maiores ganhos em diversidade e novidade na maioria das coleções de dados, sendo uma estratégia promissora, flexível e que não exige esforço do usuário.

2. NOVIDADE, DIVERSIDADE: MÉTRICAS

As métricas de relevância aqui exploradas foram previamente aplicadas na tarefa de recomendação de tags [3, 12, 11, 8]. Não as apresentamos aqui por questões de espaço. A definição de cada uma delas encontra-se em [3].

Novidade está relacionada à probabilidade de que um item (no caso uma tag) não tenha sido observado anteriormente [13], e portanto quanto menor a popularidade de uma tag, mais "nova" ela será. Assim, propomos a métrica *Inverse Feature Frequency* (IFF) para estimar a novidade de uma tag. O IFF é uma adaptação do tradicional *Inverse Document Frequency* (IDF) que considera a frequência do termo em um atributo textual específico (no nosso caso, tags). Dado o número N de objetos no conjunto de treino, o IFF de um termo candidato t é definido como:

$$IFF(t) = log \frac{N+1}{f_t^{tag}+1} \tag{1}$$

onde f_t^{tag} é o número de objetos que contêm t como tag.

A ideia básica da métrica adaptada ao contexto de recomendação de tags é que termos muito frequentes tendem a ser também recomendações muito frequentes, mais óbvias e repetitivas, por exemplo a palavra "vídeo" na coleção de vídeos do YouTube.

Apesar da métrica IFF ter sido utilizada em [3], seu uso naquele artigo foi com um propósito diferente: recomendar tags que permitam discriminar melhor um objeto dos demais, uma característica relacionada com relevância. No trabalho atual, IFF é utilizada visando aumentar a novidade das recomendações, i.e., recomendar tags possivelmente relevantes mas que, por serem mais raras, dificilmente seriam recomendadas por um método de recomendação tradicional. Isso é alcançado incorporando essa métrica na função objetivo que será otimizada, o que muda o espaço de busca por boas funções de recomendação.

Outro aspecto desejável em uma lista de recomendações é a *diversidade*, i.e., cada item deve representar um conteúdo diferente dos demais itens da lista. No contexto de recomendação de tags, queremos evitar recomendações redundantes, tais como sinônimos, de forma a capturar mais facetas dos objetos. De forma similar ao que foi feito em [13], estimamos a diversidade de um termo candidato t em relação a uma lista R de outros termos candidatos à recomendação pela média das distâncias entre t e cada termo de R. Assim, definimos a *Average Distance to other Candidates* (ADC), como:

$$ADC(t, R) = \frac{1}{|R|} \sum_{i=1}^{|R|} dist(t, R_i) \tag{2}$$

onde $dist(t, R_i)$ é uma medida de de dissimilaridade entre os termos t e R_i. Há várias maneiras de se estimar essa distância. Aqui representamos cada tag pelo conjunto de objetos em que ela aparece e estimamos a distância entre duas tags t_1 e t_2 pela diferença relativa entre esses dois conjuntos:

$$dist(t_1, t_2) = \frac{|O_1 - O_2|}{|O_1 \cup O_2|} \tag{3}$$

onde O_1 e O_2 são os conjuntos de objetos que contêm as tags t_1 e t_2, respectivamente. Essa métrica corresponde ao complemento do coeficiente de Jaccard [12] entre os conjuntos O_1 e O_2. Se ambos O_1 e O_2 forem vazios, atribuímos o valor máximo de distância, ou seja, $dist(t_1, t_2) = 1$.

3. RECOMENDAÇÃO DE TAGS: MÉTODOS

Utilizamos como base de comparação o método estado-da-arte proposto em [3], denominado aqui PG_{rel}. Esse método pode ser facilmente estendido para explorar novas métricas e funções objetivo, inclusive funções que combinam múltiplos objetivos, como fizemos nesse trabalho. PG_{rel} gera como conjunto de termos candidatos: (1) termos que co-ocorrem com tags previamente associadas ao objeto alvo e (2) termos extraídos de outros atributos textuais associados ao objeto alvo, a saber *título* e *descrição*. Para cada objeto o e cada termo candidato $c \in C_o$, são computadas todas as métricas de uma lista L_m de atributos (por exemplo, o *term frequency* e o *term spread* [3]).

Cada termo candidato c é então representado por um vetor de valores de métricas $M_c \in \mathbb{R}^m$, onde m é o número de métricas consideradas. Na fase de aprendizado, um rótulo binário é associado a cada termo candidato, indicando se ele é relevante para o objeto, em objetos de um conjunto de treino. Através de um processo evolucionário que explora operações como mutação e cruzamento, PG_{rel} aprende uma função FV que maximiza uma dada função objetivo, que captura a relevância do conjunto de recomendações para cada objeto. Nós aqui utilizamos o $nDCG$ [1] nas k primeiras recomendações como função objetivo[1]. Por fim, a função aprendida FV é utilizada para ordenar por relevância e recomendar termos candidatos para novos objetos.

Nossa primeira estratégia proposta nesse artigo, chamada $PG_{rel+nov+div}$, explora os mesmos candidatos de PG_{rel}, porém introduz novas métricas na lista L_m e na função objetivo. Especificamente, nós acrescentamos a L_m a métrica *Average Distance to other Candidates* (ADC), definida na Seção 2. A PG_{rel} já inclui a métrica IFF como atributo, mas não na função objetivo. Como dito anteriormente, isso muda o espaço de busca por boas funções que maximizam ao mesmo tempo relevância, novidade e diversidade.

Em mais detalhes, para avaliar a novidade de uma lista de recomendações R, e como parte da função objetivo de $PG_{rel+nov+div}$, utilizamos a métrica *Average Inverse Popularity* nas primeiras k posições do *ranking* ($AIP@k$), adaptada de [13], definida aqui como uma média dos valores de IFF de cada um dos primeiros k termos recomendados. Essa métrica é ajustada para dar maior peso às primeiras posições do *ranking* utilizando a função $disc(i) = 1/log(1+i)$, que atribui um valor a cada posição i do *ranking*. A $AIP@k$ de uma lista de termos recomendados R é dada por:

$$AIP@k(R) = \frac{1}{K}\sum_{i=1}^{k} disc(i) \times IFF(R_i) \quad (4)$$

onde $K = \sum_{i=1}^{k} disc(i) \times IFF_{max}$ é uma constante de normalização.

Para avaliar a diversidade, utilizamos a métrica *Average Intra List Distance* nas primeiras k posições do *ranking* (AILD@k) [13], definida como:

$$AILD@k(R) = \frac{1}{K'}\sum_{i=1}^{k}\sum_{j=i+1}^{k} dist(R_i, R_j) \quad (5)$$

onde $K' = (k^2 - k)/2$ é a constante de normalização.

Por fim, definimos a nova função objetivo (*Fitness*) como uma combinação linear convexa dos três aspectos (relevância, novidade e diversidade):

$$Fit(R) = \alpha AIP@k(R) + \beta AILD@k(R) + (1-\alpha-\beta) nDCG@k(R) \quad (6)$$

onde $0 \leq \alpha \leq 1$ e $0 \leq \beta \leq 1$ são parâmetros que ponderam as métricas de avaliação.

Nossa estratégia baseada em *relevance feedback* [1] utiliza a retroalimentação fornecida pelo usuário para refinar um conjunto inicial de recomendações. O processo compreende os seguintes passos. Primeiramente, um conjunto inicial de tags I_o é gerado por um dado método-base de recomendação (aqui utilizamos o $Sum^{+}wTS$, método com melhor relação custo-benefício dentre os propostos em [3]). Em seguida, as primeiras k_{rf} tags recomendadas pelo método-base são mostradas ao usuário, que seleciona aquelas que ele considera relevantes. As tags selecionadas são então incluídas no conjunto de tags I_o, que é fornecido como entrada para o método-base que, por sua vez, gera novas recomendações explorando I_o. O processo é repetido até alcançar um número máximo de iterações M ou até o usuário parar de fornecer *feedback*. O conjunto final de recomendações consiste de todas as tags selecionadas como relevantes pelo usuário ao longo do processo seguidas das outras tags geradas pelo método-base.

[1]Resultados para Precisão nas k primeiras posições como função objetivo foram similares.

4. AVALIAÇÃO EXPERIMENTAL

Os métodos de recomendação de tags foram avaliados em três coleções de dados, cada uma contendo *título*, *tags* e *descrição* associados com objetos reais das aplicações LastFM, YouTube e YahooVideo. Os dados, obtidos de [3], compreendem os atributos textuais de 2.758.992 artistas do LastFM, 160.228 vídeos do YahooVideo e de mais de 9 milhões de vídeos do YouTube.

De forma similar à maioria dos trabalhos de recomendação de tags [3, 2, 11, 12, 9], nós adotamos uma abordagem automática de avaliação: nós utilizamos um subconjunto das tags de um objeto como *gabarito*, isto é, as tags relevantes para aquele objeto. Como tal, tais tags são desconsideradas para cálculo de métricas. O subconjunto das tags restantes é utilizado como entrada para os métodos de recomendação (I_o). Especificamente, fixamos metade das tags de cada objeto (selecionadas aleatoriamente) como gabarito e a outra metade como entrada. O gabarito também é usado para simular o processo de *relevance feedback*, isto é, dentre as primeiras k_{rf} recomendações mostradas ao usuário em uma dada iteração do método, são marcadas como relevantes aquelas que estão no gabarito. Esta metodologia foi adotada porque a avaliação manual de tags é um processo caro em termos de tempo e pessoas para avaliar, além de estar sujeito à subjetividade dos julgamentos humanos. Assim, deixamos a avaliação manual das estratégias para o futuro.

A métricas de avaliação compreendem: o $nDCG@k$, uma métrica tradicional de relevância em RI [1], o $AIP@k$ e o $AILD@k$, adaptadas de [13] e já definidas na Seção 3, utilizadas para avaliar novidade e diversidade, respectivamente.

Os experimentos foram executados utilizando validação cruzada com 5 *folds*. Isto é, os dados são divididos em 5 partes. Três são utilizadas como conjunto de treino, uma como conjunto de validação, para estimar os parâmetros e aprender a função de recomendação FV no processo evolucionário da PG. A outra parte é utilizada como teste, para comparar as estratégias. As partes são rotacionadas de modo a obter 5 configurações de conjuntos de treino, validação e teste diferentes. Os resultados reportados são médias de 5 *folds* (5 conjuntos de validação para parametrização e 5 conjuntos de teste para reportar os resultados finais da comparação dos métodos).

4.1 Resultados Representativos

Nesta seção, discutimos os principais resultados da comparação das estratégias. Mostramos médias de 25 execuções (5 *folds* × 5 sementes) para as estratégias baseadas em PG, e médias dos 5 *folds* para o método baseado em RF. Também mostramos intervalos de confiança de 95%.

Primeiramente, realizamos experimentos para determinar os melhores valores dos parâmetros dos métodos analisados, utilizando os dados do **conjunto de validação**. Omitimos tais resultados por questões de espaço.

Em seguida, utilizamos os parâmetros encontrados no conjunto de validação para executar os experimentos no con-

Tabela 1: **Resultados dos métodos de recomendação de tags no conjunto de teste e intervalos de confiança de 95%. Melhores resultados e empates estatísticos em negrito.**

Método	*nDCG@5*	*AIP@5*	*AILD@5*
	LastFM		
PG_{rel}	0.429 ± 0.002	0.293 ± 0.006	0.892 ± 0.002
$PG_{rel+nov+div}$	0.422 ± 0.004	0.334 ± 0.015	**0.910** ± 0.005
RF	**0.518** ± 0.002	**0.426** ± 0.001	0.887 ± 0.000
	YahooVideo		
PG_{rel}	0.755 ± 0.005	0.423 ± 0.005	0.892 ± 0.004
$PG_{rel+nov+div}$	0.749 ± 0.007	**0.465** ± 0.010	**0.914** ± 0.004
RF	**0.799** ± 0.002	0.430 ± 0.000	0.863 ± 0.001
	YouTube		
PG_{rel}	0.510 ± 0.004	0.613 ± 0.004	**0.973** ± 0.002
$PG_{rel+nov+div}$	0.503 ± 0.004	**0.664** ± 0.006	**0.975** ± 0.002
RF	**0.603** ± 0.003	0.621 ± 0.000	0.956 ± 0.001

junto de teste, comparando as estratégias. Os resultados são mostrados na Tabela 1.

Comparando nossa nova estratégia $PG_{rel+nov+div}$ com o método estado-da-arte PG_{rel}, obtivemos ganhos em novidade (AIP) de 14% no LastFM, 8% no YouTube e 10% no YahooVideo, perdendo no máximo 1.6% em $nDCG$. Assim, é possível obter recomendações novas mantendo o mesmo nível de relevância com a nova função objetivo proposta. Porém, é mais difícil melhorar a diversidade visto que os resultados de $AILD$ já são muito elevados na PG_{rel}: os ganhos estão abaixo de 2.5%. Isso ocorre porque os dados são esparsos, o que torna os valores de distância entre tags tipicamente altos, com pequena diferença entre eles, visto que há relativamente pouca informação sobre co-ocorrências de tags. Note também que os ganhos em novidade e diversidade são maiores no LastFM e no YahooVideo, onde as tags são criadas colaborativamente, exibindo, portanto, maior variabilidade.

Comparando nossa segunda estratégia, baseada em *relevance feedback*, com o *baseline* PG_{rel}, obtivemos ganhos em $nDCG$ de 21% no LastFM, 6% no YahooVideo e 18% no YouTube. Os ganhos em AIP variam de 45% no LastFM a menos de 2% nas outras duas aplicações. Em termos de diversidade, não houve ganhos. Isso ocorre porque o método de RF tende a recomendar termos que co-ocorrem entre si, o que tende a reduzir o valor da métrica de diversidade, maior para termos que não co-ocorrem, por eles terem maior chance de serem semanticamente diferentes. De qualquer modo, a perda em diversidade é inferior a 3% em relação ao resultado do *baseline*. Portanto, nosso método baseado em RF melhora a relevância em todas as coleções de dados, e apresenta ganhos em novidade em algumas delas. Isso ocorre porque ele é capaz de encontrar novos termos candidatos relevantes à medida que ele navega pelas co-ocorrências de termos, termos estes que não poderiam ser encontrados utilizando apenas o método-base (iteração inicial do RF, sem cooperação do usuário). O papel do usuário aqui é guiar esse processo, refinando as recomendações. Além disso, verificamos que o processo de RF converge (atinge sua máxima eficácia) rapidamente, exigindo no máximo 2 retroalimentações do usuário. O método de RF não apresenta custos adicionais em relação ao método-base, pois o treino é realizado apenas uma vez, de modo *offline*. Somente a parte *online* do método é iterativa.

Enfim, comparando nossas duas propostas, o método de RF foi o que produziu os melhores resultados em termos de relevância, porém notamos que ele exige certa cooperação do usuário, clicando nos termos que ele considerar relevantes, o que não é diferente do esperado de um usuário de um sistema de recomendação. Nossa estratégia baseada em PG, por outro lado, tem as seguintes vantagens: (1) não exige esforço do usuário, (2) tende a gerar recomendações mais novas e diversas, de acordo com nossos resultados e (3) é flexível, podendo ser facilmente modificada com uma outra função objetivo e com novas métricas de relevância, novidade e diversidade.

5. CONCLUSÕES E TRABALHOS FUTUROS

Nós definimos aqui novidade e diversidade para o problema de recomendação de tags e propomos duas novas estratégias para resolvê-lo. Uma das estratégias, baseada em Programação Genética (PG), maximiza diretamente uma função objetivo que combina relevância, novidade e diversidade. A outra estratégia baseia-se em *relevance feedback* do usuário. Nossa estratégia baseada em PG produz ganhos em novidade de até 14% sobre a alternativa estado-da-arte, sem causar perdas em relevância. Nossa estratégia baseada em RF melhora a relevância das recomendações em até 21%, e produz ganhos modestos em novidade. Trabalhos futuros incluem a exploração de novas métricas e funções objetivo (por exemplo, novidade temporal), experimentos de avaliação manual junto a usuários, avaliação do método baseado em RF sob diferentes níveis de cooperação do usuário e combinação das estratégias baseadas em PG com RF.

6. REFERÊNCIAS

[1] R. Baeza-Yates and B. Ribeiro-Neto. *Modern Information Retrieval*. Addison-Wesley, 1999.

[2] F. Belém, E. Martins, J. Almeida, M. Gonçalves, and G. Pappa. Recomendação de tags a partir de métricas de qualidade de atributos textuais em aplicações da web 2.0. In *Webmedia*, 2010.

[3] F. Belém, E. Martins, T. Pontes, J. Almeida, and M. Gonçalves. Associative tag recommendation exploiting multiple textual features. In *SIGIR*, 2011.

[4] S. Boll. MultiTube–Where Web 2.0 And Multimedia Could Meet. *IEEE MultiMedia*, 14(1), 2007.

[5] F. Figueiredo, F. Belém, H. Pinto, J. Almeida, and M. Gonçalves. Assessing the quality of textual features in social media. *Information Processing & Management*, 2012.

[6] F. Figueiredo, F. Belém, H. Pinto, J. Almeida, M. Gonçalves, D. Fernandes, E. Moura, and M. Cristo. Evidence of quality of textual features on the web 2.0. In *CIKM*, 2009.

[7] N. Garg and I. Weber. Personalized, interactive tag recommendation for flickr. In *RecSys*, 2008.

[8] P. Heymann, D. Ramage, and H. Garcia-Molina. Social tag prediction. In *SIGIR*, 2008.

[9] M. Lipczak, Y. Hu, Y. Kollet, and E. Milios. Tag sources for recommendation in collaborative tagging systems. In *ECML PKDD*, 2009.

[10] S. McNee, J. Riedl, and J. Konstan. Being accurate is not enough: how accuracy metrics have hurt recommender systems. In *CHI EA*, 2006.

[11] G. Menezes, J. Almeida, F. Belém, M. Gonçalves, A. Lacerda, E. Moura, G. Pappa, A. Veloso, and N. Ziviani. Demand-driven tag recommendation. In *ECML PKDD*, 2010.

[12] B. Sigurbjörnsson and R. van Zwol. Flickr tag recommendation based on collective knowledge. In *WWW*, 2008.

[13] S. Vargas and P. Castells. Rank and relevance in novelty and diversity metrics for recommender systems. In *RecSys*, 2011.

A Framework for Implementing Web Recommendation Agents

Danielle Medeiros[1], Uirá Kulesza[2], André Mauricio Campos[2]

[1]Instituto Federal de Educação, Ciência e Tecnologia do Rio Grande do Norte – IFRN, Natal, Brazil
[2]Departamento de Informática e Matemática Aplicada (DIMAp), UFRN, Brasil
danielle.freitas@ifrn.edu.br, {uira, andre} @dimap.ufrn.br

ABSTRACT

This paper presents the conception, design and implementation of an object-oriented framework for the development of recommendation user agents for Web-based applications. The framework agents can be plugged or unplugged in a non-invasive way from existing Web applications using aspect-oriented programming techniques. The framework was assessed through its instantiation to three different Web-based systems.

Categories and Subject Descriptors

D.3.3 [**Language Constructs and Features**]: Frameworks

Keywords

Frameworks, aspect-oriented programming, web agents.

1. INTRODUÇÃO

Aplicações Web exigem uma interação com determinadas tarefas que poderiam ser executadas de forma autônoma ou semi-autônoma. Os agentes podem inserir esses comportamentos inteligentes para facilitar e aumentar essa interação através, por exemplo, de: e-mails de resposta automática, sugestões de livros com o gosto específico do usuário, lembretes de tarefas, entre outros.

Dentro do contexto de aplicações Web, os agentes de usuário tem o objetivo de utilizar suas habilidades para enriquecer os sistemas, isto é, simplificar tarefas geralmente realizadas pelos usuários do sistema [8], desempenhando o papel de um assistente pessoal autônomo [9]. A dificuldade em implementar agentes de usuário está na definição do perfil do usuário, que deve ser elaborado de forma transparente, isto é, coletado a partir de dados pessoais (idade, gênero), assim como informações já visualizadas pelo usuário. A partir dessas informações, o perfil é definido e as recomendações são exibidas.

A engenharia de software orientada a agentes foi proposta como uma nova forma de análise, concepção e construção de sistemas complexos [1]. Várias metodologias foram propostas nos últimos anos, tais como, Gaia e Tropos [5], para auxiliar no processo de desenvolvimento de agentes. Elas motivam desde o princípio o desenvolvimento de agentes como parte integrante do sistema, não podendo ser, portanto, inseridos e removidos de acordo com a necessidade. Trabalhos de pesquisa recentes [2] [3] trazem propostas de arquiteturas para incorporação de agentes de usuário, dentro do contexto de aplicações Web, também sofrem da mesma limitação de não permitir a fácil inserção e remoção dos agentes após o desenvolvimento da aplicação. Por exemplo, em sistemas já existentes, inserir a funcionalidade de um agente de usuário requer a reengenharia de diversos componentes da arquitetura do sistema.

Nunes et al [2] [3] exploram o uso integrado das abordagens de linhas de produtos e sistemas multiagentes. Em particular, nestes trabalhos duas LPS para SMAs foram definidas: (i) o OLIS; e (ii) o ExpertCommittee [3]. Elas representam famílias de aplicações web com comportamento inteligente definidos por seus agentes de software. Ambos foram utilizados neste trabalho como estudos de caso que instanciaram o framework. Os agentes foram removidos mantendo as funcionalidades principais do sistema web. O projeto e implementação destas duas LPS são específicos e, portanto, não contemplam um framework de agentes, tal como o proposto neste trabalho e não oferecem a possibilidade dos agentes serem facilmente removidos do sistema. Além disso, estas LPSs não englobam a funcionalidade no lado cliente responsável por obter feedback do lado do cliente.

Neste contexto, este artigo propõe o desenvolvimento de um framework orientado a objetos que facilita o desenvolvimento de agentes de usuário de recomendação para aplicações Web. Um dos requisitos do framework é promover a fácil inserção e remoção de agentes de usuários em sistemas Web existentes, trazendo impacto mínimo no sistema, através do uso de técnicas de programação orientada a aspectos. O framework permite a reutilização de componentes para aplicações Web, tanto no lado servidor quanto no lado cliente. Os agentes, na interface do usuário, oferecem um painel que permite apresentar recomendações aos usuários com base em seu perfil.

2. UM FRAMEWORK DE AGENTES DE RECOMENDAÇÃO PARA WEB

Esta seção apresenta uma visão geral do framework OO para implementação de agentes de recomendação para aplicações Web de forma não invasiva. São apresentados: (i) uma visão geral do framework (Seção 2.1); (ii) sua arquitetura e principais componentes (Seção 2.2); (iii) projeto e implementação (Seção 2.3); e (iv) mecanismos de instanciação (Seção 2.4).

2.1 Visão Geral do Framework

Este trabalho se concentra no projeto e implementação de um framework que facilita a inserção de agentes de recomendação em aplicações Web de forma não invasiva, usando técnicas de programação orientada a aspectos. O framework oferece funcionalidades tanto: (i) no lado servidor – flexibilidade para definição do perfil do usuário e estratégia de recomendação; (ii) quanto no lado cliente – no qual é exibido um painel com recomendações. As recomendações baseadas no perfil definidas

Permission to make digital or hard copies of all or part of this work for personal or classroom use is granted without fee provided that copies are not made or distributed for profit or commercial advantage and that copies bear this notice and the full citation on the first page. To copy otherwise, or republish, to post on servers or to redistribute to lists, requires prior specific permission and/or a fee.
WebMedia'12, October 15–18, 2012, São Paulo/SP, Brazil.
Copyright 2012 ACM 978-1-4503-1706-1/12/10...$15.00.

no framework segue uma técnica de filtragem de informação híbrida, onde são considerados tanto históricos de navegação do usuário quanto os dos usuários com dados similares.

Os principais requisitos do framework são: (i) monitorar operações de negócio que ocorrem no sistema, com o intuito de gerar notificações; (ii) prover recomendações para usuários; (iii) atualizar perfil – a partir do seu histórico de navegação e dos usuários que tenham dados de interesse similares; (iv) avaliar itens de recomendação do framework; e (v) o framework deve ser flexível para ser integrado com sistemas Web implementados usando diferentes arquiteturas. Esse requisito é importante para garantir a reutilização do framework possibilitando sua instanciação e integração com aplicações Web existentes.

Os pontos fixos oferecidos pelo framework OO são: (i) monitoramento de operações de negócio – funcionalidade de detecção de informações no ambiente (operações executadas no sistema Web) a serem propagadas para os agentes de usuário; (ii) interface de comunicação agente-usuário – uma interface padrão que mostra recomendações dos agentes para os usuários; (iii) comportamento padrão de agentes de usuários com respectivos perfis – essa funcionalidade provê um comportamento mínimo padrão para os agentes de usuário, o qual diz respeito à sua comunicação com o sistema Web monitorado, assim, como aos perfis de usuários; (iv) comunicação entre agentes – a comunicação é por base de mensagens, as quais possibilitam a coordenação e a realização de tarefas de forma conjunta. Há comunicação entre os agentes de ambiente e os agentes de usuário para informar a mudança no ambiente; e (v) gerenciamento dos agentes - os agentes são inicializados e mantidos por um agente gerenciador. A cada novo usuário cadastrado no sistema, um novo agente de usuário que irá representá-lo no sistema é criado pelo agente gerenciador.

Os pontos flexíveis do framework são: (i) a estratégia de monitoramento do sistema Web – as operações de negócio, que serão monitoradas, devem ser definidas pelo desenvolvedor do sistema. Assim, as diferentes operações de negócio do sistema podem ser monitoradas, sejam elas de cadastro, busca, navegação, entre outras. Este ponto flexível determina a forma como o framework é integrado ao sistema Web sendo, portanto, implementado usando programação orientada a aspectos. Os aspectos são usados para projetar e implementar as variabilidades das operações de negócio ocorrendo no sistema Web de interesse. O uso de aspectos permite realizar uma composição transversal entre a aplicação Web cujos processos de negócio serão investigados; (ii) geração de recomendações – cada sistema pode definir que dados serão considerados e processados para que sejam feitas as gerações das recomendações pelos agentes; (iii) filtragem por dados – o perfil é definido, tendo por critério a técnica de filtragem dos dados, os quais dependem da estratégia de recomendação e de informações relacionadas aos interesses do usuário, a partir da sua extração pela navegação do usuário no sistema; e (iv) controle de usuários – todos os sistemas devem gerenciar usuários, e os serviços relacionados com esses devem ser configurados. O framework utiliza informações disponibilizadas pelo sistema sobre seus usuários.

2.2 Arquitetura do Framework

A arquitetura do *framework* integra o sistema *Web* com os agentes de recomendação, reduzindo assim o impacto de inserção e remoção de agentes. A Figura 1 ilustra a arquitetura do *framework* integrada com a arquitetura de um sistema *Web* estruturado em camadas. A camada de agentes é subdividida em dois componentes: monitoramento de negócio e processamento de agentes de usuários. Na camada de processamento de agentes de usuário são inseridos três comportamentos nos agentes de usuários, os quais representam pontos flexíveis para definir a estratégia de recomendação dos agentes, são eles: (i) a definição de perfil do usuário; (ii) a definição de recomendação dos usuários; e (iii) o retorno das recomendações realizadas pelos agentes para os usuários do sistema.

A camada de monitoramento de negócio realiza notificações quando alguma operação de negócio de interesse ocorre no ambiente (sistema Web). Ela está relacionada com o comportamento autônomo do sistema, e contém dois agentes: (i) agente ambiente – que observa a execução de serviços e os propaga para os outros agentes; e (ii) agente gerenciador – que inicia e gerencia os agentes no sistema. O monitoramento propriamente dito das operações de negócio do sistema Web é realizado através do uso de aspectos.

2.3 Projeto e Implementação

O framework foi desenvolvido usando as linguagens Java e AspectJ, assim como o framework Jade para apoiar a implementação da funcionalidade básica de interação do agente. O projeto do framework está organizado em três funcionalidades principais, são elas: (i) monitoramento de operações de negócio; (ii) processamento de agentes de recomendação; e (iii) consulta de recomendações.

2.3.1 Monitoramento de Operações de Negócio

Em um sistema *Web*, um processo de negócio pode ser definido como um conjunto de operações que tem o objetivo de identificar serviços específicos de utilidade dos usuários do sistema. Essas operações podem ser monitoradas com o propósito de verificar a disponibilidade do servidor ou desempenho do sistema, assim como contribuir com a análise da utilização das funcionalidades existentes no sistema. Exemplos de operações de negócio são: cadastro de usuário, inserção ou remoção de item no carrinho de compras, inserção de um novo evento, entre outros.

As classes mais importantes para o monitoramento, ilustradas na Figura 1, são: (i) `PropagateBusinessOperation` – faz a notificação de uma nova operação, definindo o tipo de operação e o conteúdo; (ii) `MonitorBusinessOperation` – aspecto abstrato que deverá ser instanciado para permitir o monitoramento de operações de negócio executadas por instâncias de classes da camada de GUI do sistema *Web*. Esse monitoramento é essencial para coletar informações que serão usadas pelo *framework* para a geração de recomendações; (iii) `ObservableBusinessService` – tem como objetivo enviar para todos os observadores uma dada operação de negócio monitorada. Assume o papel de *Subject* do padrão de projeto *Observer*; (iv) `BusinessServiceObserver` – interface que declara o método `operationPerformed()` o qual informa ao operador qual a operação que foi realizada; (v) `EnvironmentAgent` – recebe notificação sobre novas operações de negócio no sistema e propaga para outros agentes, implementa a interface `BusinessServiceObserver`; (vi) `PropagateBusinessOperBehavior` comportamento do agente ambiente que propaga a operação de negócio para os outros agentes; e (vii) `BusinessOperation` – representa uma dada operação de negócio que ocorreu na camada de negócio do sistema.

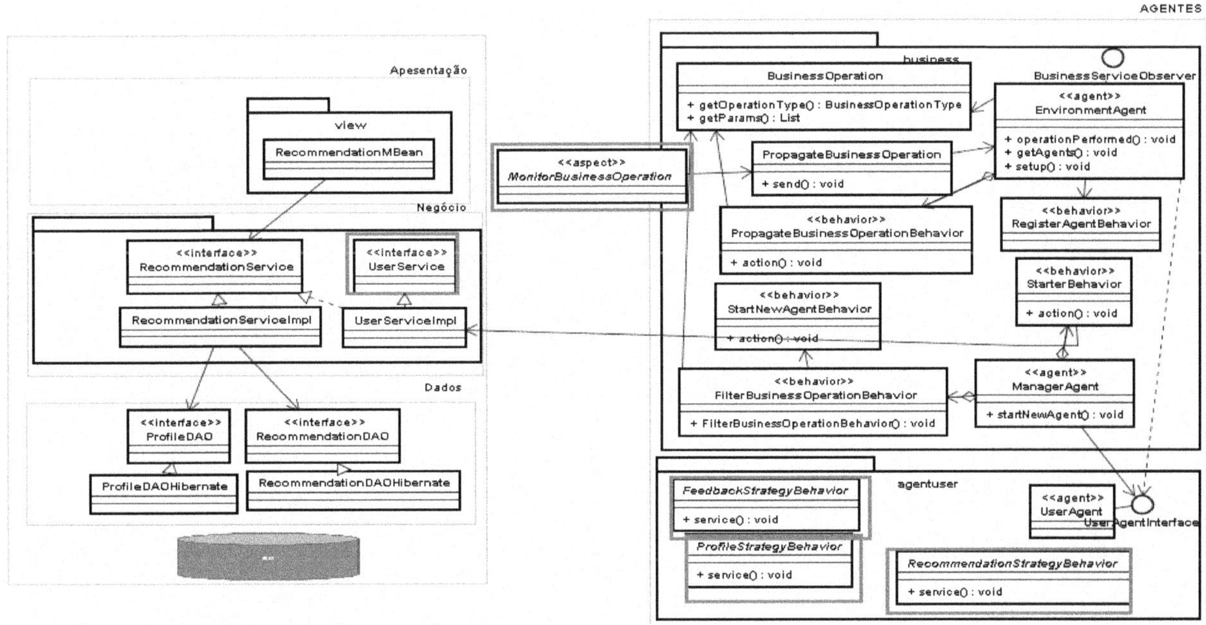

Figura 1 - Arquitetura do *Framework*

Uma das principais funcionalidades do *framework* proposto diz respeito ao monitoramento de operações de negócio de aplicações *Web*. O desenvolvedor que instancia o *framework* deve definir que operações serão monitoradas pelo *framework*, através da criação de um subaspecto do aspecto `MonitorBusinessOperation`. Uma vez capturada, a operação de negócio é propagada para os agentes do sistema, através do agente ambiente.

Quando uma operação de negócio é executada, o aspecto instanciado intercepta as classes responsáveis pela execução do equivalente e envia os dados necessários para que sejam enviados aos observadores, classes que implementam o padrão de projeto *Observer*. O agente ambiente, implementado com o suporte do *framework* JADE, recebe as notificações de operações de negócio por meio de um comportamento, classe que implementa comportamentos em JADE, este notifica, através de mensagens, a todos os agentes a operação de negócio realizada e envia os dados equivalentes a operação.

2.3.2 Processamento de Agentes de Recomendação

Os agentes do *framework* são inicializados por meio de um arquivo de configuração do sistema. Os seguintes agentes principais são criados durante a execução do *framework*: (i) agente ambiente – receberá uma mensagem com o registro do novo agente de usuário iniciado no sistema; e (ii) agente gerenciador – inicializa os agentes de usuário já inseridos no sistema e à medida que novos usuários são criados no sistema, novos agentes de usuários são criados no sistema multiagente.

As classes mais importantes, ilustradas na Figura 1, que fazem parte do módulo de inicialização são: (i) `ManagerAgent`: inicializa os agentes de usuário; (ii) `UserAgent`: inicializa um agente de usuário definindo seu *id* e comportamentos; e (iii) `UserService`: classe de serviços de usuários responsável por retornar os usuários do sistema no qual o *framework* é instanciado. A classe `UserAgent` é chamada pelo agente gerenciador a cada novo usuário inserido no sistema. Após a definição do *ID* do agente, especificado pelo JADE, são inseridos os três comportamentos que representam pontos flexíveis do *framework*. Estes comportamentos definem estratégias vinculadas para delimitar as recomendações dos usuários do sistema: (i) definição do perfil dos usuários; (ii) geração de recomendação; e (iii) o retorno das recomendações feitas pelos agentes para os usuários do sistema. Os comportamentos inseridos nos agentes tem o objetivo de delimitar as ações que devem ser executadas por eles, a partir das alterações verificadas no ambiente.

A estratégia de definição de perfil considera o histórico de uso do sistema do usuário. Essa técnica parte do princípio que os usuários tendem a terem interesses similares aos demonstrados no passado. Para isso ser controlado é salvo persistentemente a navegação do usuário. Seu objetivo no *framework* é traçar a área relacionada a cada usuário, pois todos esses 'itens' tem classificação. Ou seja, pode ser definido dentro de um esquema taxonômico, e essa faz o conteúdo do perfil. Cada usuário tem uma definição de prioridade para cada área. Por exemplo, considerando um sistema de comércio eletrônico: eletrodomésticos tem prioridade 10 e produtos de informática tem prioridade 7. Então os eletrodomésticos terão prioridade na fila de recomendação. A medida que novos itens são acessados o perfil é atualizado. Para novos usuários os itens recomendados são baseados em dados pessoais similares com outros usuários.

A estratégia de definição de recomendações faz uso da personalização dinâmica, uma vez que as preferências dos usuários podem variar com o tempo, assim o histórico gravado é atualizado continuamente, para delimitar os itens a serem exibidos para os usuários. Existem várias técnicas de filtragem de recomendação, essas têm como objetivo classificar informações relevantes e irrelevantes e assim possibilitar a diminuição das opções de escolha que os usuários têm em *Websites.*

2.3.3 Consulta de Recomendações

Para que a navegação não seja comprometida, as recomendações são exibidas em uma janela que sobrepõe à tela do sistema. Essa exibe, por exemplo, os produtos recomendados em um sistema de comércio eletrônico. Nessa os itens recomendados poderão ser acessados para mais informações que serão mostradas na tela principal e não na janela. A janela também pode ser fechada, minimizada ou maximizada. Os itens exibidos também podem ser excluídos. O painel para exibição das recomendações utiliza chamadas assíncronas ao servidor usando a tecnologia AJAX. O AJAX é atualmente utilizado em aplicações de Internet Ricas (RIA – *Rich Internet Applications*), com o objetivo de melhorar a interatividade e usabilidade da perspectiva de seus usuários.

2.4 Instanciação e Avaliação do *Framework*

A instanciação facilita a definição de agentes de recomendação em aplicações *Web*, promovendo a inserção não invasiva de agentes dentro de aplicações *Web*, e assim permitindo a reutilização de componentes.

As classes do aplicação devem implementar os comportamentos: `RecommendationStrategyBehavior`, `FeedbackStrategyBehavior` e `ProfileStrategyBehavior`. Estes são chamados pela classe `UserAgent`, na qual faz parte da camada de agentes. Esses comportamentos têm objetivo de delimitar as ações que devem ser exercidas pelos agentes de usuário, a partir das alterações verificadas no ambiente.

O comportamento `RecommendationStrategyBehavior` é acionado pela classe após o monitoramento dos itens que serão recomendados, como, por exemplo: produtos em uma loja eletrônica, eventos em um sistema de controle de eventos, apostilas em um sistema de ensino a distância, entre outros. O comportamento `ProfileStrategyBehavior` é ativado após o monitoramento da definição taxonômica dos itens, por exemplo: assunto da apostila de aula; categoria do produto da loja de *ecommerce*; área de interesse da conferência; entre outros. E o `FeedbackStrategyBehavior` é chamado ao deletar um item recomendado.

Além das classes que devem ser estendidas existem algumas configurações adicionais que devem ser feitas para permitir a instanciação do *framework* proposto para uma dada aplicação. Exemplos de tais configurações são: inclusão de bibliotecas de classes ou scripts, arquivos de configuração, arquivos que fazem parte do painel de exibição dos itens e configurações do banco de dados.

Para avaliar se o *framework* atende os requisitos previstos, ele foi instanciado para 3 diferentes aplicações [5]: (i) *Easy Commerce* - uma linha de produto para comércio eletrônico, no qual o *framework* faz recomendações de produtos aos usuários do sistema, tendo seu perfil delimitado a partir da navegação pelas categorias dos produtos; (ii) OLIS provê um serviço de agendamento de eventos, onde esses são recomendados aos usuários. No sistema, os eventos cadastrados pelos usuários são visualizados por ele, na instanciação, o OLIS pode agora realizar a recomendação de eventos a outros usuários que sejam na mesma localização ou que tenham o mesmo interesse do evento cadastrado por um diferente usuário; e (iii) *ExpertCommittee* realiza o controle e gerenciamento de conferências, essas são recomendadas para diferentes usuários de acordo com sua localização e interesse.

3. CONCLUSÃO E TRABALHOS FUTUROS

Este artigo apresentou o projeto e implementação de um *framework* que facilita a definição de agentes de recomendação em aplicações *Web*. O framework promove a inserção não invasiva de agentes dentro de aplicações *Web*, permitindo assim, a reutilização de componentes. As contribuições aos sistemas *Web*, incluem tanto o lado servidor, através das funcionalidades de recomendação do *framework*, quanto o lado cliente, no qual é exibido um painel com recomendações. As recomendações são baseadas no perfil que segue uma técnica de filtragem de informação híbrida, em que foram considerados tanto históricos de navegação do usuário quanto os de usuários com dados similares.

Pretende-se realizar como trabalhos futuros: (i) instanciação automática do *framework* com ferramentas de derivação de produto, tais como o GenArch [9], com o objetivo de automatizar (ou semi-automatizar) o processo de criação de recomendações para sistemas *Web*; (ii) instanciação de novos estudos de casos; e (iii) explorar interações diretas entre os agentes de usuário. Para a definição das recomendações que foram implementadas algumas comunicações e interações entre os agentes de usuário. Essas podem auxiliar na criação de recomendações mais ricas e precisas, a partir da criação de um *ranking* de afinidades entre agentes.

Acknowledgments. This work was partially supported by the National Institute of Science and Technology for Software Engineering (INES) – CNPq under grants 573964/2008-4 and CNPQ 560256/2010-8.

4. REFERÊNCIAS

[1] M. Wooldridge, N. R. Jennings and D. Kinny, "The Gaia Methodology for Agent-Oriented Analysis and Design," Journal of Autonomous Agents and Multi-Agent Systems, 2000.

[2] I. Nunes, C. Lucena, D. Cowan, U. Kulesza, P. Alencar and C. Nunes, "Developing multi-agent system product lines: from requirements to code," IJAOSE 4(4): 353-389, 2011.

[3] I. Nunes, U. Kulesza, C. Nunes, E. Cirilo and C. Lucena, "Extending *Web*-based applications to incorporate autonomous behavior," in Proceedings of the 14th Brazilian Symposium on Multimedia and the *Web*, Vila Velha, Brasil, 2008.

[4] A. Pokahr and L. Braubach, "The *Web*bride *Framework* for Building *Web*-Based Agent Applications," First International Workshop on LAnguages, methodologies and Development tools for multi-agent system, 2007.

[5] D. G. d. F. Medeiros, Um *framework* de agentes de recomendação para sistemas *Web*, Dissertação de Mestrado - Programa de Pós-Graduação em Sistemas e Computação, DIMAp/UFRN, Brazil, 2011.

[6] H. Yu, Y. Cai, Z. Shen, X. Tao and C. Miao, "Agents as Intelligent User Interfaces for the Net Generation," Proceedings of the 14th International Conference on Intelligent User Interfaces (IUI), 2010.

[7] J. Pena, M. Hinchey, M. Resinas, R. Sterritt and J. Rash, "Designing and managing evolving systems using a MAS product line approach," Science of Computer Programming, 2007.

[8] W. Júnior, "STAR: Um *Framework* para recomendação de artigos científicos baseado na relevância da opinião dos usuários e em filtragem colaborativa," Proceedings of ENIA 2005, pp. 22-29. São Leopoldo, Brazil.

[9] E. Cirilo, I. Nunes, U. Kulesza and C. Lucena, "Automating the product derivation process of multi-agent systems product lines," Journal of Systems and Software 85(2): 258-276, 2012.

Accelerometers Data Interoperability: Easing Interactive Applications Development

Jorge R. Carvalho, Marcelo G. Manzato, Rudinei Goularte
University of Sao Paulo
Sao Carlos-SP
Brazil
{carvalho,mmanzato,rudinei}@icmc.usp.br

ABSTRACT

Research in Natural Interfaces, sub-area of Ubiquitous Computing, investigates the use of non-traditional devices to support user interaction with applications in less intrusive ways (gestures, voice and writing based on electronic ink, for instance). With the increasing popularity of accelerometers, developers now have another tool that can be used to provide interaction between users and different applications, such as interactive TV environments. However, applications that make use of accelerometers are currently being developed for specific situations, and their implementations and handled documents are also dependent on the domain for which they were designed. This paper aims to propose a model to formalize how the accelerometer data may be handled in a generic way. In addition, the model enables the description of rules to aggregate value to these data through the addition of meanings. This is done by proposing a layered architecture to structure and share data in a flexible way. An example of use and the description of a simple application that makes use of the proposed model are also presented.

Categories and Subject Descriptors

D.2.11 [**Software Engineering**]: Software Architectures—*Data abstraction, Domain-specific architectures*

General Terms

Experimentation, Human Factors, Standardization

Keywords

Accelerometers, Document Engineering, Gesture Recognition

1. INTRODUCTION

The proliferation of interactive multimedia applications is a reality in our everyday lives. The evolution of the computing area has allowed the creation of new enabling technologies, new ways of interaction and new document formats and protocols, leading applications to produce and handle much of the digital content currently aired on the Internet, part of them pursuing interactivity innovations. The old paradigm monitor-keyboard-mouse, long used in the market, gradually gives way to natural interfaces. In a TV living room environment, the main input device is the remote control. Due to the different affordances that a TV's remote control and a PC's keyboard/mouse exhibit, suitable interaction mechanisms and widget behaviour of the two platforms are inevitably very different. Similarly to the traditional computer environments, natural interfaces could also be used during the interaction with television devices.

Research in natural interfaces investigates the use of non-traditional devices to support user interaction with applications in a less intrusive way, trying to make user-machine interaction more similar to the interactions made by people in everyday tasks [1].

The literature reports many forms of natural user interfaces, such as voice, writing and pen-based – or combinations of them, as in the case of multimodal interfaces [11]. With the lower prices and subsequent popularization of input devices equipped with sensors, e.g. accelerometers, developers now have many options of interaction with applications. Acceleration sensors have become foremost in our daily lives, and can be found in automobiles, appliances, portable devices (e.g. smartphones) and, more recently, in video games like Nintendo's current console, Wii[1]. We envisage that future remote controls will also be equipped with motion sensor and operated with few buttons in addition to motion gestures.

Essentially, accelerometers convey the absolute numerical value of the acceleration exerted on one or more axes by a certain movement over time. These values can be used in a direct (e.g. from a certain value, some action may occur) or indirect way (e.g. variation in acceleration values over time can be used to define a gesture), through the use of specific techniques, such as pattern recognition algorithms.

However, it may be noticed that applications [7, 6, 12] that make use of accelerometers are designed for specific situations and, as a result, the way they are implemented and how they manipulate document formats are also dependent on the domain for which they were designed. Moreover, a careful look at the literature [5, 8, 2, 4, 10] reveals a lack of models particularly designed to capture accelerometers data in a way to make them easily accessible for different applications, providing interoperability.

An important factor for the success of a new technology

Permission to make digital or hard copies of all or part of this work for personal or classroom use is granted without fee provided that copies are not made or distributed for profit or commercial advantage and that copies bear this notice and the full citation on the first page. To copy otherwise, to republish, to post on servers or to redistribute to lists, requires prior specific permission and/or a fee.
WebMedia'12, October 15–18, 2012, São Paulo/SP, Brazil.
Copyright 2012 ACM 978-1-4503-1706-1/12/10 ...$15.00.

[1]http://www.nintendo.com/wii

is interoperability. Eventually there might be data that needs to be transferred through different applications. It is not enough to capture and make available the accelerometer data, because it alone does not say much; it is necessary a mechanism to transform it in useful information for the applications, structuring this information along with meanings in order to aggregate value and provide interoperability. For the best of our knowledge, there is no report in the literature about an open structured method dealing with interoperability of accelerometer data associated with meaning descriptors.

Therefore, this paper aims to propose a way to treat data from accelerometers, allowing them to be manipulated by different applications and providing new ways to perform interaction in heterogeneous environments, such as iTV living rooms. This is done by proposing a layered architecture that primarily provides a loosely coupled accelerometer data acquisition model, and a structured and extensible data format with meaning descriptors, which stores data in such a way that information are made interoperable. As a result, we designed an API[2] which is responsible to implement the model and to enable the access to the stored information, as well as to provide the data to the subscribed applications.

The paper is organized as follows: Section 2 presents applications that use accelerometers in different fields of application; Section 3 describes the conceptual approach of this work; Section 4 describes the implementation of the model; Section 5 outlines the proposed model; Section 6 specifies how the model may be extended to support different applications; Section 7 shows an example of usage and implementation details of an application that makes use of this model; and finally, Section 8 presents the final remarks of this work.

2. RELATED WORK

Several studies that make use, directly or indirectly, of accelerometer data can be found in the literature. In the area of natural interfaces, Gurrin et al. [5] propose an application to naturally interact with an extensive multimedia database using gestures. They focus on the comparative analysis of interaction techniques and employ accelerometers to perform gestures recognition. However, it is not specified how the accelerometer data is treated, neither what changes would be needed to adapt the application to another environment with different devices.

The WiiNote [8] tool enables the creation of notes on images with electronic ink. Nevertheless, the device does not make use of gesture recognition, only the raw data from the sensor in a particular manner that only meets the purposes of the application. In order to perform gesture recognition, the work of Schlömer et. al. [14] proposes an API which treats the raw accelerometer data in such a way that supports different sensors, providing the results in a event-driven manner. However, it does not provide any mechanisms to add meaning to these gestures. That problem is addressed in Aoki et al. [2], where it is proposed a method of text entry using data obtained from accelerometers through gesture recognition, aiming to make it easier and more comfortable the process of inputting text in the Interactive Digital TV (IDTV) via remote controls. Nevertheless, in this case the meanings are implemented in a manner that does not provide flexibility. Also as part of the IDTV research area, Chang et al. [4] make use of the raw data obtained through accelerometers attached to remote controls, in order to propose a new and transparent method of identifying users based only on how users wield the device.

The Geolocation Working Group[3] of the World Wide Web Consortium (W3C) recently released a draft [3] describing a work in progress which aims to provide a standard way to represent movement and orientation data from devices through the definition of DOM (Document Object Model) events. Although it helps to simplify the way the data is represented, it also does not address the problem of adding meanings to the acquired data.

In medicine area, Oliveira et al. [10] implement a prototype that allows the monitoring and support of convalescence patients, or who are still being affected by diseases that require intensive medical supervision, using data obtained from various sensors, including accelerometers.

More recently, large companies such as Sony and Microsoft have implemented their products with innovative interaction capabilities, as can be seen in the new PlayStation Vita[4], which make use of the combined accceleration and multitouch data to enhance the gaming experience, and the Kinect for Xbox 360[5], with computational vision capabilitites that allow it to be used not only in a gaming environment, but in many applications as well. Although most implementation details are hidden from the public due to commercial reasons, Microsoft has released its own development API for Kinect.

In the aforementioned and studies, it is possible to observe a high degree of specificity in the way their features are defined. Different uses are made with the data obtained from various devices, either for gesture recognition or activation of pre-established routines. However, none of these studies include more specific details regarding their implementation, e.g. the models used in the creation and sharing of documents used, or how the meanings related to specific actions are defined. Such uses and routines vary from work to work, according to the problem addressed and the context and experience of the researchers involved. Moreover, the mentioned works do not provide support for application interoperability.

In this way, the main contribution of this work is the design of a model that is extensible to any applications needs, in addition to be generic enough to be used by different devices. Furthermore, as our model allows the association of meaning onto specific movements (e.g. gestures recognition), applications can benefit in the sense of not having to take care of low level implementation issues.

3. ARCHITECTURE

The architecture described in this paper (Figure 1) sets the context for the problems addressed by the proposed model, defining a conceptual separation between three layers, each one responsible for the following tasks: 1) accelerometer data acquisition; 2) categorization of the acquired data by means of gesture recognition; 3) modeling and addition of meaning to the acquired data according to a structured model.

A simple API was designed to implement the proposed

[2]Application Programming Interface

[3]http://www.w3.org/2008/geolocation/

[4]http://us.playstation.com/psvita/

[5]http://www.xbox.com/en-US/kinect

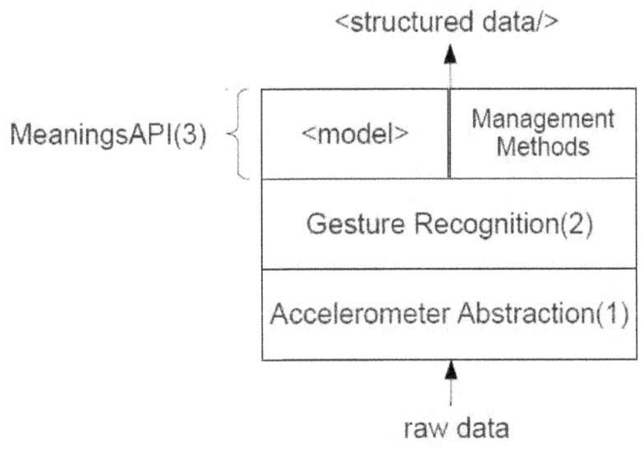

Figure 1: Proposed architecture

```
@XStreamAlias("meaning")
public class Meaning {

    @XStreamAlias("ur:id")
    private int id;
    @XStreamAlias("ur:type")
    private String type;
    @XStreamAlias("ur:value")
    private String value;
    @XStreamAlias("ur:codeSnippet")
    private String codeSnippet;
    @XStreamAlias("ur:creationDate")
    private DateTime creationDate;
    @XStreamAlias("ur:creatorName")
    private String creatorName;
    @XStreamAlias("ur:comment")
    private String comment;
```

Figure 2: Meaning class attributes

model, in particular the third layer of the architecture. This API has the main objective to provide the data from the first layer along with its corresponding meaning, according to the gestures recognized in the second layer, by generating an XML file for the requesting application. The API also provides methods to manage gestures and categories of gestures, editing and creating new ones according to the application requirements.

The second layer is needed for data categorization and identification, given that only the raw data obtained by the first layer is of little use for applications that enable natural interaction through movement provided by users. Given that most of accelerometer movements patterns remains similar (deterministic), in the related work it is possible to find many algorithms that enable gesture recognition with high accuracy and low computational cost. Among these, it can be highlighted the ones based on HMM [15] (*Hidden Markov Models*), ANN [9] (*Artificial Neural Networks*), and DTW [13] (*Dynamic Time Warping*). At the end of the recognition process, a string is returned and forwarded to the third layer, indicating which of the defined gestures was recognized.

The first layer is responsible for the acquisition of the raw data and connection with an acceleration sensor. Basically it gets the acceleration values for each axis and passes on to the layer of gesture recognition. Its implementation is closely associated with the type of device used.

The ideia behind this architecture is to get a loose coupling between its layers, allowing their implementations to be minimally dependent on each other, that is, interchangeable. Thus, the first layer's API was implemented to be agnostic to the underlying source of information, as discussed in Section 4.

4. API OVERVIEW

As illustrated in Figure 1, the API presented in this work implements the proposed model as will be described in Section 5. It receives and structures the data provided by the first and second layers, and then, creates and delivers an XML document containing the structured data to the subscribed applications, along with its categorized meanings. Along with the proposed model, it is one of the main contributions of the presented work.

The API is designed to offer its features through simple methods calls. It must contain a class whose attributes represent each of the basic accelerometer data (described later in Subsection 5.1), with methods that allow them to be set in a single object. Once the basic data is gathered, it already can be used to generate an XML document with the basic data only, in particular in the case when the application does not require further data or definition of any meanings, which in turn must be part of a category of meanings. In Figure 2 there is an example of meaning definition, based on the descriptors defined on the model. In this work the Xtream[6] library is used in order to generate the output XML file.

As for instance, if one wants to create a new category, it would be enough to call the method `createCategory` (Figure 3) and then proceed to the phase of gesture training (provided by methods in the second layer), where each new defined gesture must be assigned to a meaning and defined as part of a category.

```
MeaningsAPI mapi = new MeaningsAPI();
mapi.addCategory("GeometricForms");
```

Figure 3: Category creation example

The process of adding meanings to the raw accelerometers data is accomplished without user intervention, being the incoming data automatically associated to the identified meaning as previously trained. As an example, the API implemented for this work automatically associates the directions (`left`, `right`, `up` or `down`) to these gestures, as can be seen in Section 7.

5. PROPOSED MODEL

The model proposed in this work is defined using a set of W3C's XML Schemas[7], making use of its resources that allow the description of XML documents, vocabularies and constraints. The XML was chosen to ensure the interoperability of the accelerometers data, because of its maturity as a specification and consequent acceptance by the developers community.

The model was designed to include not only the raw data provided by accelerometers, e.g. acceleration in x, y and z axes, but also to incorporate meanings along with the data being transmitted. Depending on the application, it can be much more interesting just to get a simple command (e.g. *left*) than a long sequence of acceleration values acting on

[6]http://xstream.codehaus.org/
[7]http://www.w3.org/XML/Schema

the axes. In Figure 4 we present the basic structure of the model schema.

```
<xsd:element name="AccelerometerData">
    <xsd:complexType>
        <xsd:sequence>
            <xsd:element name="meanings" type="meaningsType" />
            <xsd:element name="data" type="sensorDataType" />
        </xsd:sequence>
        <xsd:attribute name="timeStamp" type="timeStampType"
use="required"/>
    </xsd:complexType>
</xsd:element>
```

Figure 4: AccelerometerData root element definition

The **AccelerometerData** is the root element of the XML document generated by the API described in Section 4. It must have an attribute called **timeStamp**, which specifies the date and time when the accelerometer data was captured, according to the simple type **timeStampType**, as seen in Figure 6. Also, the root element must contain, in order, the elements **meanings** and **data**, defined by the complex types **meaningsType** and **sensorDataType**, respectively.

5.1 The "data" Element

The "**data**" element is designed to store the acceleration value provided by the sensor in each axis. However, there are sensors that do not have the hardware to discount the gravity acceleration from its values. The complex type **sensorDataType** addresses this problem by defining two sets of elements to represent the acceleration on both situations, and an attribute that must specify whether the sensor is capable of discounting the gravity acceleration or not. As seen in Figure 5, the first set of elements (**valueX**, **valueY** and **valueZ**) may not appear, because they are intended to represent the acceleration values with the gravity discounted, which may not be the case. The second set of elements (**valueXwithgrav**, **valueYwithgrav** and **valueZwithgrav**) must appear in both cases, because if the sensor has the hardware to discount gravity, then it can provide both sets of data, with and without the acceleration of gravity. The acceleration values are defined by the type **accelerationValueType** and the values that the attribute **gravity** can assume are defined by the type **gravityType**, both specified in Figure 6.

```
<xsd:complexType name="sensorDataType">
    <xsd:sequence>
        <xsd:element name="valueX" type="accelerationValueType"
minOccurs="0" />
        <xsd:element name="valueY" type="accelerationValueType"
minOccurs="0" />
        <xsd:element name="valueZ" type="accelerationValueType"
minOccurs="0" />
        <xsd:element name="valueXwithgrav"
type="accelerationValueType" />
        <xsd:element name="valueYwithgrav"
type="accelerationValueType" />
        <xsd:element name="valueZwithgrav"
type="accelerationValueType" />
    </xsd:sequence>
    <xsd:attribute name="gravity" type="gravityType"
use="required"/>
</xsd:complexType>
```

Figure 5: sensorDataType complex type definition

```
<xsd:simpleType name="accelerationValueType">
    <xsd:restriction base="xsd:double"/>
</xsd:simpleType>
<xsd:simpleType name="gravityType">
    <xsd:restriction base="xsd:boolean" />
</xsd:simpleType>
<xsd:simpleType name="timeStampType">
    <xsd:restriction base="xsd:dateTime" />
</xsd:simpleType>
```

Figure 6: Schema simple types definition

5.2 The "meanings" element

In addition, the model was also designed to be extensible, i.e., depending of the application's needs, it allows the definition and subsequent incorporation of new meanings and categories of meanings. In this paper, by categories of meanings we mean the set of values which is part of a certain concept, for example, the concept of direction, which can take values such as left, right, up, down, front and back, or the concept of geometric forms, as triangle, square or circle.

The **meanings** element meets those requirements being defined by the type **meaningsType** (Figure 7), so it may contain an undefined number of **meaning** elements, each one adding a meaning to the data specified by the **data** element described in Subsection 5.1. The **meanings** element can also come with no **meaning** elements at all, i.e., it can be empty. As explained in Section 4, the user of the API may choose to generate an XML with no meanings, only with the values of acceleration measured on the axes.

```
<xsd:complexType name="meaningsType">
    <xsd:sequence>
        <xsd:element name="meaning" type="meaningType"
minOccurs="0" maxOccurs="unbounded" />
    </xsd:sequence>
</xsd:complexType>
```

Figure 7: meaningsType complex type definition

On the other hand, the **meaning** element is defined by an abstract type called **meaningType**. Because this element is abstract, it cannot be directly used. As opposite, one must first define a derived type from it, by means of a restriction or extension (see Section 6). Firstly, it should contain seven elements, as can be seen in the Figure 8. The **id** element is designed to contain a unique value representing the meaning described in the element **value**, which in turn must belong to the meaning category described in the **type** element. The **codeSnippet** element provides a place to embed a piece of code related to the meaning being defined, similarly to the comments that may be included in the **comment** element. Finally, the **creatorName** and **creationDate** elements should contain the meaning creator's name and date of creation, respectively. All elements defined here are of the type **contentType**, which basically means that they may be, for starters, of any type, as described in Figure 9.

6. USING THE MODEL

The XML Schema used to design the proposed model is intended to be used with other namespaces also defined in XML Schema, created solely to contain the concrete types derived from the abstract type **meaningType**. In other words, a new XML Schema should be defined with the meanings categories and its possible values.

```
<xsd:complexType name="meaningType" abstract="true">
    <xsd:sequence>
        <xsd:element name="id" type="contentType"/>
        <xsd:element name="type" type="contentType"/>
        <xsd:element name="value" type="contentType"/>
        <xsd:element name="codeSnippet" type="contentType"
minOccurs="0"/>
        <xsd:element name="creationDate" type="contentType"/>
        <xsd:element name="creatorName" type="contentType"/>
        <xsd:element name="comment" type="contentType"
minOccurs="0"/>
    </xsd:sequence>
</xsd:complexType>
```

Figure 8: meaningType complex type definition

```
<xsd:complexType name="contentType" abstract="true">
    <xsd:complexContent>
        <xsd:restriction base="xsd:anyType" />
    </xsd:complexContent>
</xsd:complexType>
```

Figure 9: contentType complex type definition

In this paper, we define the `directionsType` category (see Figure 10), which may take one of four values: `left`, `right`, `up` or `down`, defined as a list of possible values of the `value` element. However, more categories with other possible values may be defined, as long as it derives from the abstract type `meaningType`. The type of the other elements was also defined to be more specific, e.g. string, short or dateTime. Finally, the element `type` was defined with a fixed value, to illustrate that any `meaning` element of the type `directionsType` must contain in its element `type` the "direction" value.

```
<xsd:complexType name="directionsType">
    <xsd:complexContent>
        <xsd:restriction base="ads:meaningType">
            <xsd:sequence>
                <xsd:element name="id" type="xsd:short"/>
                <xsd:element name="type" type="xsd:string"
fixed="direction"/>
                <xsd:element name="value" type="directionsList"/>
                <xsd:element name="codeSnippet" type="xsd:string"/>
                <xsd:element name="creationDate" type="xsd:dateTime"/>
                <xsd:element name="creatorName" type="xsd:string"/>
                <xsd:element name="comment" type="xsd:string"/>
            </xsd:sequence>
        </xsd:restriction>
    </xsd:complexContent>
</xsd:complexType>
<xsd:simpleType name="directionsList">
    <xsd:restriction base="xsd:string">
        <xsd:enumeration value="left"/>
        <xsd:enumeration value="right"/>
        <xsd:enumeration value="up"/>
        <xsd:enumeration value="down"/>
    </xsd:restriction>
```

Figure 10: directionsType concrete type definition based upon the abstract type meaningType

In Figure 11 we provide another example of category defined based upon the abstract type `meaningType`. In Figure 12 we can see an instance example of the XML Schema created to define the model.

7. EXAMPLE AND IMPLEMENTATION

A usage example of the proposed model is an application that requires directions data to perform their actions or even gesture representations of shape forms associated with tasks. In this work we have implemented two prototypes that operates with XML documents derived from the

```
<xsd:complexType name="shapesType">
    <xsd:complexContent>
        <xsd:restriction base="ads:meaningType">
            <xsd:sequence>
                <xsd:element name="id" type="xsd:short"/>
                <xsd:element name="type" type="xsd:string"
fixed="shape"/>
                <xsd:element name="value" type="shapesList"/>
                <xsd:element name="codeSnippet" type="xsd:string"/>
                <xsd:element name="creationDate" type="xsd:dateTime"/>
                <xsd:element name="creatorName" type="xsd:string"/>
                <xsd:element name="comment" type="xsd:string"/>
            </xsd:sequence>
        </xsd:restriction>
    </xsd:complexContent>
</xsd:complexType>
<xsd:simpleType name="shapesList">
    <xsd:restriction base="xsd:string">
        <xsd:enumeration value="circle"/>
        <xsd:enumeration value="triangle"/>
        <xsd:enumeration value="square"/>
        <xsd:enumeration value="cross"/>
    </xsd:restriction>
</xsd:simpleType>
```

Figure 11: shapesType concrete type definition based upon the abstract type meaningType

```
<?xml version="1.0" encoding="UTF-8"?>
<AccelerometerData timestamp="2002-05-30T09:00:00"
                   xmlns="http://www.icmc.usp.br/~carvalho/AccelerometerDataSchema/"
                   xmlns:xsi="http://www.w3.org/2001/XMLSchema-instance"
                   xmlns:ur="http://www.icmc.usp.br/~carvalho/UserRepository/"
                   xsi:schemaLocation=
                       "http://www.icmc.usp.br/~carvalho/AccelerometerDataSchema/
                       AccelerometerDataSchema.xsd
                       http://www.icmc.usp.br/~carvalho/UserRepository/
                       UserRepository.xsd">
    <meanings>
        <meaning xsi:type="ur:directionsType">
            <ur:id>1</ur:id>
            <ur:type>direction</ur:type>
            <ur:value>left</ur:value>
            <ur:codeSnippet>System.out.println("Isto é um teste.")</ur:codeSnippet>
            <ur:creationDate>2002-05-30T09:00:00</ur:creationDate>
            <ur:creatorName>Aldo</ur:creatorName>
            <ur:comment>Isto é um teste.</ur:comment>
        </meaning>
        <meaning xsi:type="ur:shapesType">
            <ur:id>2</ur:id>
            <ur:type>shape</ur:type>
            <ur:value>cross</ur:value>
            <ur:codeSnippet>System.out.println("Isto é outro teste.")</ur:codeSnippet>
            <ur:creationDate>2005-05-30T09:00:00</ur:creationDate>
            <ur:creatorName>Aldo</ur:creatorName>
            <ur:comment>Isto é outro teste.</ur:comment>
        </meaning>
    </meanings>
    <data gravity="true">
        <valueX>0.0000</valueX>
        <valueY>0.0000</valueY>
        <valueZ>0.0000</valueZ>
        <valueXwithgrav>0.0000</valueXwithgrav>
        <valueYwithgrav>0.0000</valueYwithgrav>
        <valueZwithgrav>0.0000</valueZwithgrav>
    </data>
</AccelerometerData>
```

Figure 12: XML Schema instance example

proposed model. The first one identifies the corresponding gesture as one of the previously defined directions (`left`, `right`, `up` or `down`), performs a workspace change in a PC running the Ubuntu operating system, and shows the name of the movement recognized on the center of the screen.

To implement the prototype, we used the Nintendo Wii remote control, which provides a three-axis integrated acceleration sensor Analog Devices ADXL330[8].

Following the architecture outlined in Section 3, in the second layer we used the library Wiigee [14], a reusable and extensible event-driven Java implementation of the HMM algorithm. The library provides an interface for basic functions, e.g. reading raw values of acceleration, and other functions related to the recognition process, e.g. gestures training. Because the Wiigee library is implemented accor-

[8]http://www.analog.com/en/mems-sensors/inertial-sensors/adxl330/products/product.html

ding to the JABWT (*Java APIs for Bluetooth Wireless Technology*) Java standard, defined by JSR-82 community specification, in order to interface with the Wiimote we used a third-party bluetooth library called BlueCove [9]. It was choosen because it is also written in Java, it is *free* and *open source*, and it is also JSR-82 compliant. Due to the modularity of the library, there were no major problems to adapt it to be used with the prototype.

After writing the code responsible for the workspace change, we have added our API classes and libraries (WiiGee, BlueCove and XStream) to the project and created the classes representing the meanings defined in the model (as seen in Figure 2) with the appropriate attributes according to the application needs, as can be seen in Figure 10.

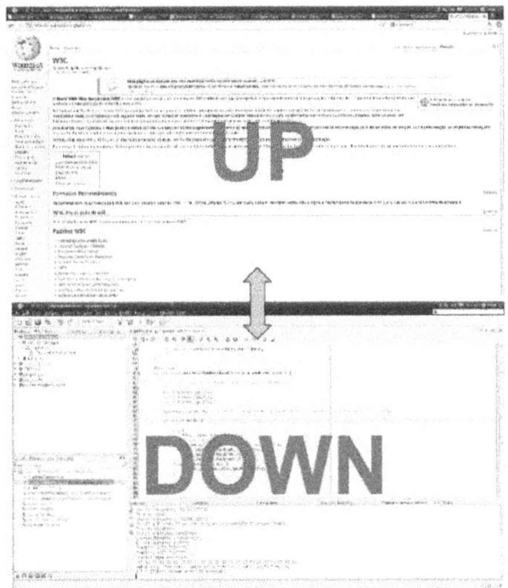

Figure 13: Result of the transition process

In Figure 13 it can be observed two screens, and the transition between them with the display of the words *up* or *down*, depending on the gesture that was recognized. In Ubuntu operating systems, users have four workspaces by default that can be easily changed through keyboard shortcuts (CTRL+ALT+ the arrow key representing where the workspace is located). After gesture training, and the assignment of each action related to changing the workspace, it is very easy to perform the same tasks, naturally handling the wiimote towards any direction. Although this is a simple application, it can be useful during a presentation or when working with multiple windows. In the Figure 16 it can be seen a user interacting with the prototype.

The second prototype is based in an old memory skill electronic game called Simon[10], whose goal was to memorize a sequence of colors and respective sounds exactly in the order they appear. It was implemented using the same hardware and programming guidelines used in the first prototype, except for the model instance that was extended to reflect a new set of meanings. We created the customized meanings `green`, `red`, `yellow` and `blue` as for the game main buttons (Figure 14) and the meanings `circle` and `cross` to represent the "restart" and "close game" functions, respectively.

[9]http://bluecove.org/

[10]http://www.hasbro.com/games/en-us/simon/

Figure 14: Original Simon

In Figure 15 we present the User Repository XML Schema definition of the custom meanings of the Simon game.

```
<xsd:complexType name="simonType">
    <xsd:complexContent>
        <xsd:restriction base="ads:meaningType">
            <xsd:sequence>
                <xsd:element name="id" type="xsd:short"/>
                <xsd:element name="type" type="xsd:string"
fixed="direction"/>
                <xsd:element name="value" type="simonList"/>
                <xsd:element name="codeSnippet" type="xsd:string"/>
                <xsd:element name="creationDate" type="xsd:dateTime"/>
                <xsd:element name="creatorName" type="xsd:string"/>
                <xsd:element name="comment" type="xsd:string"/>
            </xsd:sequence>
        </xsd:restriction>
    </xsd:complexContent>
</xsd:complexType>
<xsd:simpleType name="simonList">
    <xsd:restriction base="xsd:string">
        <xsd:enumeration value="green"/>
        <xsd:enumeration value="red"/>
        <xsd:enumeration value="yellow"/>
        <xsd:enumeration value="blue"/>
        <xsd:enumeration value="circle"/>
        <xsd:enumeration value="cross"/>
    </xsd:restriction>
</xsd:simpleType>
```

Figure 15: simonType custom meaning definition

Keeping in mind the conceptual architecture outlined in this paper and the proposed model by means of the implemented API, the identification of each part of the prototype is straightforward, as well as in which points the components interrelate. In both implemented prototypes, the Wiigee library acquires the raw accelerometer data through BlueCove library (first layer) and allows the gestures recognition by means of its HMM algorithm (second layer). Finally, the API encapsulates and validates the data according to the model, and provides an XML document through a simple method call made by the prototype.

8. FINAL REMARKS

Input devices equipped with sensors such as accelerometers play an important role in the development of new ways of interaction. Given the low cost and subsequent popularization of these devices, the number of applications found in the literature that make use of this type of sensor is relevant.

It is important to create ways to facilitate the development of applications that make use of accelerometers, specifying standards for data shared between different applications. In this work, we focus on the need of such standards, and propose a model that provides all the basic information

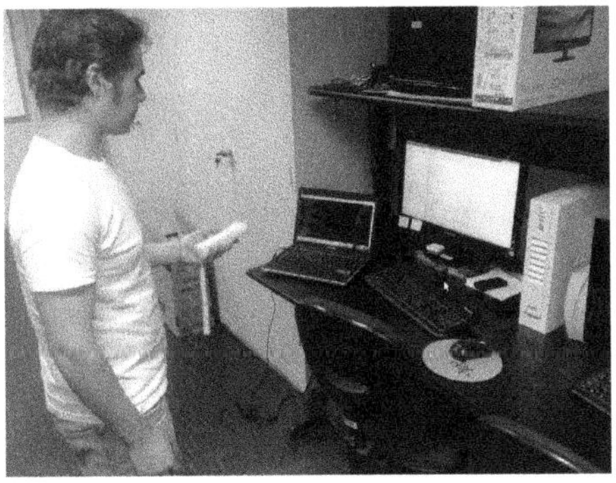

Figure 16: User performing gesture recognition

that accelerometers capture and transmit. By making use of XML documents, we turn this data readable by multiple applications and devices.

Furthermore, the proposed model provides rules to aggregate value to accelerometer data through the addition and association of meanings. The main advantage of such feature is to enable applications to be created without having to take care of particular implementation issues. In addition, the gesture recognition process may be delegated to third-part modules and tools, easing the development of new devices equipped with natural interaction characteristics.

As future work, we plan to develop more sophisticated applications that use the proposed model. Such effort will be important in the context of the digital television scenario, where users will be able to adopt different devices in order to interact with the content. In addition, we plan to analyze and incorporate other libraries and devices of gesture recognition and accelerometer acquisition onto the model. Such improvements will make the API more robust in terms of allowing users to develop new tools according to their needs.

Acknowledgements

The authors would like to thank FAPESP and CNPq for their financial support.

9. REFERENCES

[1] G. D. Abowd and E. D. Mynatt. Charting past, present, and future research in ubiquitous computing. *ACM Trans. Comput.-Hum. Interact.*, 7(1):29–58, 2000.

[2] R. Aoki, A. Maeda, T. Watanabe, M. Kobayashi, and M. Abe. *A new text input method for TV remotes using tilt sensor.* IEEE, 2010.

[3] S. Block and A. Popescu. W3C DeviceOrientation Event Specification - Editor's Draft, 2011.

[4] K. Chang, J. Hightower, and B. Kveton. Inferring identity using accelerometers in television remote controls. In *Proceedings of the 7th International Conference on Pervasive Computing*, pages 151–167. Citeseer, 2009.

[5] C. Gurrin, H. Lee, N. Caprani, Z. Zhang, N. O'Connor, and D. Carthy. Browsing Large Personal Multimedia Archives in a Lean-Back Environment. *Advances in Multimedia Modeling*, pages 98–109, 2010.

[6] J. Kela, P. Korpipää, J. Mäntyjärvi, S. Kallio, G. Savino, L. Jozzo, and S. Marca. Accelerometer-based gesture control for a design environment. *Personal and Ubiquitous Computing*, 10(5):285–299, Aug. 2006.

[7] S. Kim, J. Ok, H. Kang, M. Kim, and M. Kim. An interaction and product design of gesture based TV remote control. In *CHI'04 extended abstracts on Human factors in computing systems*, pages 1548–1548, New York, New York, USA, 2004. ACM.

[8] F. Mugellini, M. Sokhn, S. Carrino, and O. Abou Khaled. WiiNote: multimodal application facilitating multi-user photo annotation activity. In *Proceedings of the 2009 international conference on Multimodal interfaces*, pages 237–238. ACM, 2009.

[9] S. Nissen. Implementation of a fast artificial neural network library (fann). *Report, Department of Computer Science University of Copenhagen (DIKU)*, 31, 2003.

[10] M. Oliveira, P. Cunha, M. da Silva Santos, and J. Bezerra. Implementing home care application in Brazilian Digital TV. In *Information Infrastructure Symposium, 2009. GIIS'09. Global*, pages 1–7. IEEE, June 2009.

[11] S. Oviatt. *Multimodal interfaces*, chapter 21, pages 413–432. Lawrence Erlbaum Associates, Inc., Mahwah, NJ, USA, 2007.

[12] G. Pan, J. Wu, D. Zhang, Z. Wu, Y. Yang, and S. Li. GeeAir: a universal multimodal remote control device for home appliances. *Personal and Ubiquitous Computing*, 14(8):723–735, Mar. 2010.

[13] H. Sakoe and S. Chiba. *Introducing speech and language processing.* Cambridge University Press, Cambridge, U. K., 2005.

[14] T. Schlömer, B. Poppinga, N. Henze, and S. Boll. Gesture recognition with a Wii controller. In *Proceedings of the 2nd international conference on Tangible and embedded interaction*, pages 11–14, New York, New York, USA, 2008. ACM.

[15] T. Westeyn, H. Brashear, A. Atrash, and T. Starner. Georgia tech gesture toolkit: supporting experiments in gesture recognition. In *Proceedings of the 5th international conference on Multimodal interfaces*, pages 85–92. ACM, 2003.

LêbrailleTWT: Providing Visual Accessibility to *Twitter* on *Touchscreen Devices*

Agebson R. Façanha
Mestrado e Doutorado em Ciência da Computação (MDCC)
Universidade Federal do Ceará
Fortaleza-CE, Brasil
agebson@ifce.edu.br

Maria da C. C. Araújo
Projeto de Acessibilidade Virtual (RENAPI/SETEC)
Instituto Federal de Educação, Ciência e Tecnologia do Ceará
Fortaleza-CE, Brasil
marianaca@ifce.edu.br

Windson Viana
Grupo de Redes de Computadores, Engenharia de Software e Sistemas
Universidade Federal do Ceará
Fortaleza-CE, Brasil
windson@virtual.ufc.br

Mauro C. Pequeno
Grupo de Pesquisa e Produção de Ambientes Interativos e Objetos de Aprendizagem
Universidade Federal do Ceará
Fortaleza-CE, Brasil
mauro@virtual.ufc.br

ABSTRACT
The increasing use of social networks via touch screen interfaces on smartphones and tablets has brought enormous benefits to the mobile applications usability. However, access to information via these devices represents a new challenge of interaction for users with visual impairments. In this context, this paper describes a study on the issue of visual accessibility in virtual social networks, specifically on Twitter. Moreover, we have developed a mobile application to access Twitter via touch screen smartphones using the Android platform. This application provides access to blind people with audio feedback and a writing tool based on Braille. The mobile application presents itself as a solution to facilitate the interaction of the visually impaired users in this social network. In this paper, we also describe a study of use of the application with a group of blind people.

Categories and Subject Descriptors
H.5.2 [**User Interfaces**]: Input devices and strategies (e.g., mouse, touchscreen).

General Terms
Design, and Human Factors.

Keywords
Accessibility, Mobile Computing, and Social Networks.

1. INTRODUÇÃO
O uso crescente de dispositivos móveis e tecnologias de comunicação sem fio tem aumentado fortemente o acesso a Sistemas de Informação na Web, em especial sites de compartilhamento de conteúdo e redes sociais. De acordo com a pesquisa [20] realizada mundialmente em 2011, estas tecnologias estão cada vez mais inseridas nas atividades humanas diárias. Conforme a pesquisa, mais de dois terços dos participantes revelaram que usam um smartphone para fins pessoais (73%) ou de negócios (69%), e no Brasil, 89,39% responderam usar smartphones para fins pessoais e 74% para o trabalho. Dados da Anatel indicam que o Brasil terminou Agosto/11 com 224 milhões de linhas móveis e uma densidade de 114,9 cel/100 hab [9]. A maioria dessas linhas móveis também permite acesso a Internet.

Em outra recente pesquisa sobre comportamento de usuários no acesso à Web, descobriu-se que aproximadamente 4 em cada 5 usuários de internet visitam redes sociais e blogs [5]. Sendo que 40% dos usuários de redes sociais utilizam dispositivos móveis *smartphones* para acessar sua rede de relacionamentos e existe uma forte tendência de crescimento para essa modalidade de acesso.

Neste sentido, a disponibilização de conteúdos web acessíveis para estes dispositivos configura-se em uma necessidade crescente, entendendo-se que a acessibilidade deve ser provida a todos ou ao maior número possível de usuários em situações limitantes e não somente ao público deficiente [11][14]. No caso deste trabalho, o foco é a acessibilidade visual para deficientes visuais ou pessoas com baixa visão.

A problemática de acessibilidade visual nos dispositivos móveis atuais decorre de um preferencial enfoque visual dos aplicativos, principalmente, nos dispositivos com telas de toque (*touch screen)*, nas quais as interações ocorrem pela captura dos movimentos dos usuários na tela [17]. A interação com telas *touch screen* demanda ainda mais das habilidades visuais, pois até mesmo o teclado é substituído por uma versão "virtual" que não oferece retorno tátil adequado. Essas características tornam complexas as interações com esses dispositivos por parte de deficientes visuais e, muitas vezes, exigem um forte esforço cognitivo, como por exemplo, para a memorização das posições do teclado virtual [18]. Mesmo com o uso de leitores de tela, a entrada de dados por interface de toque acaba sendo um fator excludente, e por consequência, o acesso a redes sociais utilizando esses dispositivos é prejudicado para deficientes visuais.

Hoje, redes sociais não impactam apenas no entretenimento, sua influência vai desde ativismo político ao uso em ambientes educacionais [13]. Assim, é salutar o desenvolvimento de ferramentas e aplicações que permitam a inclusão dos deficientes visuais no acesso a essas redes, de preferência de forma ubíqua.

Dentro deste cenário, como forma de investigar melhores maneiras de se implantar acessibilidade em dispositivos móveis, propõe-se a concepção de um sistema acessível para dispositivos *touch screen.* O sistema, chamado de LêbrailleTWT, foi implementado para *smartphones* com a plataforma Android e provê, ao público deficiente visual, acesso ao *microblog Twitter.*

Permission to make digital or hard copies of all or part of this work for personal or classroom use is granted without fee provided that copies are not made or distributed for profit or commercial advantage and that copies bear this notice and the full citation on the first page. To copy otherwise, or republish, to post on servers or to redistribute to lists, requires prior specific permission and/or a fee.
WebMedia'12, October 15–18, 2012, São Paulo/SP, Brazil.
Copyright 2012 ACM 978-1-4503-1706-1/12/10...$15.00.

A entrada de dados nesse aplicativo faz alusão à escrita em Braille, utilizando a reglete através de um serviço chamado LêBraille, desenvolvido especialmente para tratar a entrada de dados em dispositivos *touch screen*.

Este trabalho está organizado da seguinte forma: a Seção 2 apresenta as principais motivações para a atual problematização da acessibilidade virtual em redes sociais e do uso de dispositivos com tela *touch screen*. A Seção 3 detalha o processo de desenvolvimento do LêBraille e do LêBrailleTWT. Na Seção 4, está descrita uma análise da aplicabilidade e da utilização do LêBrailleTWT e do LêBraille através de um teste piloto de utilização feito por um grupo de deficientes visuais que dominam o Braille e possuem acesso à redes sociais. Por fim, são apresentadas as conclusões na Seção 5.

2. ACESSIBILIDADE VISUAL EM REDES SOCIAIS E EM DISPOSITIVOS MÓVEIS

2.1 Acessibilidade Visual em Redes Sociais

O surgimento e difusão das redes sociais na internet é um dos mais importantes fenômenos emergentes em relação ao uso de novas tecnologias digitais [21]. Atualmente, uma das formas de criar e manter vínculos sociais é através da utilização dessas redes virtuais seja para a publicação de vídeos e de fotos (e.g., *Youtube*) ou simplesmente para compartilhar opiniões, conteúdos e status (e.g., *Facebook* e *Twitter*). Houve também um aumento do interesse da própria comunidade científica em analisar e desenvolver novas tecnologias para essas redes como se pode atestar em alguns trabalhos recentes do WebMedia [19][10].

Um dos principais problemas encontrados em redes sociais é a não garantia de acessibilidade. Resultados obtidos em estudos recentes apontam que o nível de acessibilidade nas principais plataformas de redes sociais é muito baixo [7]. Este estudo avalia resultados procedentes de análises técnicas e análises de experiências e contatos dos usuários com as plataformas.

A necessidade de acessibilidade, especialmente a visual, se baseia no acesso crítico vivenciado por deficientes visuais, visto que estes são limitados ao uso dos softwares leitores de telas. Portanto, este público necessita que as redes sociais sigam padrões mais rígidos, para que os leitores de telas possam navegar de forma satisfatória. Além disso, essa preocupação com a acessibilidade de sistemas Web deve acontecer inclusive em todas as fases do processo de desenvolvimento desses sistemas [1].

2.2 Acessibilidade Visual no *Twitter*

O *Twitter* é uma rede de informações que combina características de *blog* e rede social. Assim, seus usuários buscam, sobretudo, notícias, atualidades e compartilham relatos de situações cotidianas, tudo isso em tempo real [8]. A ferramenta ganhou bastante evidência nos últimos anos devido à expansão e uso de redes sociais, sendo uma das redes mais influentes no Brasil (terceiro país em quantidade de usuários ativos no *Twitter* mundialmente) [3]. Diferente de outras redes sociais, o *Twitter* é um *microblog* que permite a cada usuário postar frases (*tweets*) de até 140 caracteres que serão vistas por seus contatos seguidores.

Um dos primeiros passos deste trabalho foi avaliar a acessibilidade do Twitter a partir das diretrizes de acessibilidade do e-MAG 3.0 - Modelo de Acessibilidade de Governo Eletrônico Brasileiro. O teste constatou inicialmente que o site possui *links* confusos, com conteúdos em inglês e que direcionam para outra janela sem prévio aviso, algumas imagens sem descrição, contraste não adequado e níveis de cabeçalho desordenados, gerando dificuldades para que os softwares leitores de tela consigam acessar as funcionalidades do sistema.

Apesar dos problemas elencados acima e dos baixos índices de acessibilidade do Twitter obtidos nos estudos da ONCE [7], a interface padrão do mesmo ainda possui um nível aceitável de acessibilidade, pois o enfoque dessa rede é mais textual do que gráfico[22]. Ou seja, não impede, por completo, que usuários cegos a utilizem.

Existem também algumas soluções de acesso utilizando os *smartphones*, por exemplo, o TweetList (plataforma IOS da Apple) e o Tweet60 (plataforma Nokia, com teclado físico). Contudo, até este momento, não existe uma solução acessível para a plataforma *Android*.

2.3 Tecnologias Assistivas em Dispositivos Móveis

Na sua maioria, as pesquisas e produtos de tecnologia assistiva de uso geral em dispositivos móveis podem ser classificados em três grandes categorias: i) leitores de tela; ii) hardwares desenvolvidos especialmente para prover acessibilidade e iii) aplicações para entrada de dados via software;

Um leitor de tela é um software que interage com o sistema operacional do dispositivo capturando informações apresentadas textualmente na tela e as transformando em uma resposta sonora utilizando um sintetizador de voz. No caso específico de interfaces *touch screen*, a leitura deve ser baseada em gestos, ou seja, deverá permitir que pessoas com dificuldades visuais percorram e selecionem as opções através de toques na tela para ouvir uma descrição do item sob o seu dedo, podendo passar comandos para o seu dispositivo através de toques, arrastes ou deslizes. Um exemplo desses softwares está disponível nos aparelhos *iPhone*, a partir da versão 3Gs, lançado em Junho de 2009. O sistema operacional *iOS* desses *iPhones* tem integrado um leitor de telas chamado *Voice Over*, que possui funcionalidades de acessibilidade até então não disponíveis nos demais dispositivos. O leitor de tela *Voice Over*[1] é o primeiro leitor de tela baseado em movimentos/gestos, que em vez de memorizar atalhos ou pressionar pequenas teclas, com apenas o toque na tela, é possível ouvir a descrição do item, dar dois toques, arrastar ou deslizar para controlar a navegação em seu dispositivo. Outros exemplos de leitores de tela para dispositivo móvel são Nokia Braille Reader para Symbian OS e o Mobile Acessibility e Talkback para a plataforma *Android*.

Na **segunda categoria** de tecnologias assistivas para deficientes visuais, encontram-se aparelhos especificamente desenvolvidos para usuários com deficiência visual através de adaptações de hardware, visando disponibilizar as funcionalidades habitualmente encontradas em smartphones. São exemplos destas adaptações: o DrawBraille[2], o iSense[3] e o Braille E-Book[4]. Por exemplo, o Braille E-Book é uma película para ser acoplada em dispositivos e-Readers e *tablets* que permitem a leitura de texto em formato digital. Na verdade, existe um déficit de produção de livros em Braille, devido ao seu custo de produção e grande volume para

[1] http://www.apple.com/br/accessibility/ipad/vision.html

[2] http://www.yankodesign.com/2012/02/20/the-ultimate-braille-phone/

[3] http://vimeo.com/23023287

[4] http://www.yankodesign.com/2009/04/17/braille-e-book/

armazenamento. O Braille E-book se propõe a solucionar esse problema provendo uma tecnologia que permite alterar dinamicamente o padrão de superfície por meio de um sinal eletromagnético, simulando, assim, o texto em Braille. O DrawBraille, por sua vez, é um aparelho que possui área textual de 35 celas Braille, distribuídas em 5 linhas, cuja principal característica é o design inovador utilizando os pontos Braille na superfície do aparelho, sendo destinado especialmente para usuários com deficiência visual. Com o aparelho o usuário poderá utilizar vários recursos, tais como acessar menu e agenda de contatos, navegar na internet, verificar o nível da bateria, ler e-mail, mensagens e e-books. Vale ressaltar que devido ao alto nível de sofisticação dessas soluções algumas são apenas tecnologias conceituais ou possuem um custo elevado em sua comercialização, o que impede o acesso por grande parte dos deficientes visuais, sendo as soluções propostas nesse trabalho voltadas para dispositivos já existentes sem exigir mudanças estruturais nos mesmos.

Na **terceira categoria** de aplicações, encontramos soluções de entrada de texto para dispositivos com tela *touch screen*: NavTouch[17], NavTilt[18], BrailleType[2], e No-Look Notes [16] e Eyes-free [15]. A maioria dessas ferramentas são pesquisas acadêmicas recentes dos últimos quatro anos. Por exemplo, o No-Look Notes [16] é um sistema de entrada de dados usando multi-touch com retorno sonoro, implementado na plataforma iOS, que mescla o conceito do tradicional teclado SMS com toques na tela. Inicialmente, o usuário deficiente visual explora a tela de forma giratória encontrando grupos com até quatro caracteres, depois explorando tal lista de caracteres seleciona o grupo desejado.

O NavTouch[17], NavTilt[18] e BrailleType[2] foram desenvolvidos por pesquisadores portugueses da Universidade de Lisboa. NavTouch[17], é um software utilizado para entrada de texto que interage com o usuário através de movimentos direcionais (direita, esquerda, cima e baixo) e recurso sonoro. Já o NavTilt[18] se diferencia dos métodos de introdução de texto tradicionais, baseados em abordagens *multitapping*, por possuir uma interação baseada em gestos 3D e uma nova organização do alfabeto, o objetivo é permitir a entrada de textos usando somente uma das mãos. O BrailleType[2] é uma evolução das experiências anteriores e propõem um método de entrada de texto através do toque baseado na representação gráfica do alfabeto Braille. O sistema foi desenvolvido para *Android*, no qual as letras são codificadas em uma matriz de seis pontos, com retorno sonoro através do sintetizador de voz SVOX.

O serviço LêBraille, desenvolvido e utilizado no trabalho proposto neste artigo se assemelha em alguns princípios ao BrailleType e foi concebido concomitantemente ao projeto português[17].

3. LÊBRAILLETWT

A aplicação LêBrailleTWT foi desenvolvida como uma proposta de interface acessível visando facilitar o processo de inclusão de deficientes visuais no acesso ao *Twitter*.

A principal funcionalidade fornecida por esta solução é um modelo de entrada de dados que favorece a autonomia do deficiente visual na utilização do software através do toque de tela no dispositivo móvel *smartphone*. O retorno sonoro dos dados apresentados na tela é fornecido pelo sintetizador de voz instalado no celular, podem ser utilizadas diversas vozes de acordo com a preferência do usuário. O LêBrailleTWT foi implementado para a plataforma *Android* e utiliza recursos como o acesso ao acelerômetro do dispositivo para reconhecer alguns gestos e comunicação com os servidores do *Twitter* através de chamadas à Serviços Web.

O software provê acesso ao *Twitter* através de uma entrada de dados baseada em gestos e na formação de caracteres semelhantes aos do Sistema Braille, inseridos através do toque de tela. Estes caracteres formados pelos toques do usuário são dados de entrada tratados pelo software e posteriormente traduzidos para o alfabeto comum a fim de construir as mensagens enviadas ao *Twitter*. A Figura 1 apresenta uma visão geral da arquitetura e os diversos modos de comunicação entre componentes do sistema (via REST, via Intents[5] e via API).

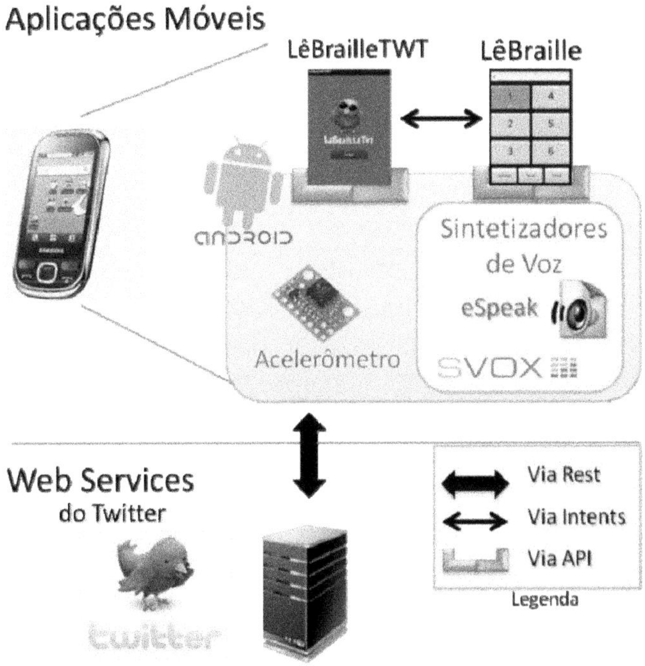

Figura 1 - Arquitetura das Aplicações Móveis Desenvolvidas.

3.1 Principais Características

A interface inicialmente planejada (ver Figura 2) segue as recomendações para acessibilidade em dispositivos móveis sugeridas em [4] a partir de testes de aceitação com deficientes visuais. O objetivo é prover um bom nível de acessibilidade às principais funcionalidades do *Twitter*.

Exemplos de recomendações adotadas foram:

a) na utilização de botões, foi incluído um modo de exploração, pois os elementos da tela devem ser identificáveis de forma tátil e/ou sonora (vibração/som);

b) opções são apresentadas em forma de lista ou em duas colunas utilizando como referência as laterais dos dispositivos; e

c) os elementos de interação possuem uma grande área de cobertura para seleção, preferencialmente com bastante espaço entre os elementos.

Após a inicialização do aplicativo em sua primeira execução, o usuário fornece informações da sua conta e senha do *Twitter*. O aplicativo móvel se comunica, então, com os servidores do

[5] A plataforma Android oferece um modelo de comunicação entre "processos" (as *Activities*) baseado na declaração e busca de intenções (Intents) .

Twitter através de chamadas a Web Services do tipo REST disponíveis na API da rede social[6] (ver Figura 1). As principais funcionalidades do *Twitter* implementadas foram:

- ***Timeline***: lista quais foram as 20 últimas postagens dos usuários.
- ***Tweet***: função para a postagem de uma mensagem de até 140 caracteres.
- ***Retweet***: função de reencaminho de um *tweet* de um contato para sua lista de contatos.
- **Configurações**: *Login* e Senha de acesso ao sistema. Esta opção é pré-configurada durante a instalação.

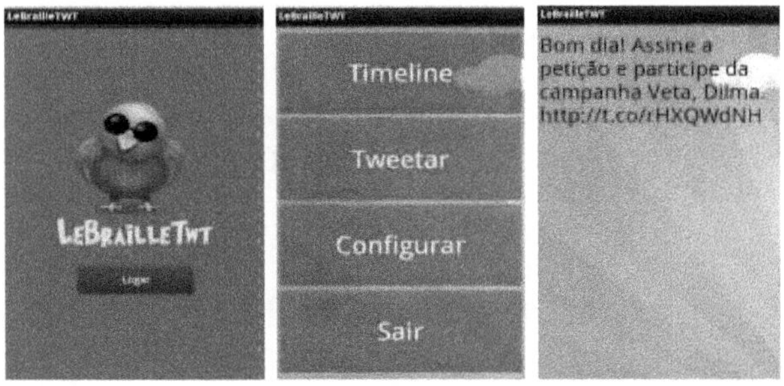

Figura 2 - Interfaces de utilização do Software LêBrailleTWT

A opção *Timeline* fornece acesso às mensagens na tela. Com o arrasto horizontal, ocorre a navegação entre as mensagens e um toque longo em qualquer ponto da tela dispara o *retweet* da mensagem. Para voltar ao menu inicial, o usuário pode utilizar a movimentação do acelerômetro (função *shake*) do aparelho. A opção *Tweetar* dispara a entrada de dados LêBraille, que traduz os caracteres da forma de escrita Braille para os caracteres do alfabeto, a fim de gerar a mensagem de texto a ser postada. A

Tabela 1 contém detalhes dos principais comandos, os gestos a serem realizados pelo deficiente visual e a ação desencadeada pelo sistema quando o gesto é detectado. Um vídeo ilustrando a utilização do aplicativo encontra-se disponível em http://www.youtube.com/watch?v=IY8cgd-jh8g&feature=plcp.

3.2 Entrada de Dados usando o LêBraille

A entrada de dados do LêBrailleTWT baseia-se no uso do serviço LêBraille, cuja versão inicial e processo de concepção são descritos em [4]. A versão final do LêBraille, também desenvolvida pelos autores deste artigo, é apresentada nessa seção.

A solução consiste na utilização de *smartphones* que utilizam recurso *touch screen*, para simular os instrumentos utilizados para escrita no Sistema Braille (i.e., reglete, punção e o papel). O papel utilizado na escrita Braille é substituído pela tela sensível ao toque, os pontos da célula Braille são elementos desta tela e a punção corresponderá à pressão exercida pelo dedo do utilizador na tela do dispositivo portátil. Ao capturar as informações puncionadas, ocorrerão manipulações no sistema para reprodução de um retorno perceptível ao usuário, seja por meio de uma saída sonora e/ou tátil. A Figura 3 ilustra os instrumentos tradicionais de uso da escrita em Braille e a tela do teclado do LêBraille.

[6] https://dev.twitter.com/docs/api

Tabela 1: *Comandos disponíveis para o LêBrailleTWT.*

Comando	Movimentação	Ação
Toque com arrasto vertical no sentido cima para baixo ou o inverso na área central da tela.		Navega entre as 4 opções do menu: *Timeline*, Tweetar, Configurar e Sair.
Após selecionar a opção do menu, o usuário deverá dar um duplo toque na tela.		Confirma acesso à opção selecionada.
Tocar com arrasto horizontalmente na tela de *timeline*, no sentido da direita para esquerda ou da esquerda para direita.		Navega entre as mensagens.
Um toque longo em uma mensagem do *Timeline*.		*(Re)Tweet* a mensagem.
Balançar (*shake*) o aparelho.		Retorna ao Menu Principal da Aplicação.

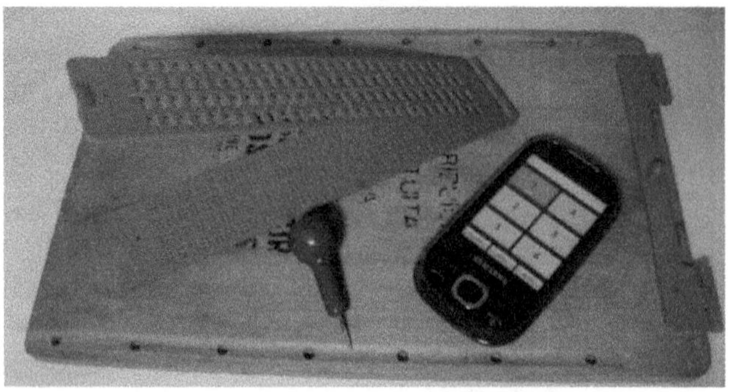

Figura 3 - Ferramentas tradicionais de escrita em Braille e uma tela do serviço LêBraille.

O aplicativo LêBraille funciona a partir na plataforma *Android 2.2.*. A Figura 3 ilustra o modo de exibição do LêBraille em um *smartphone*, exibindo uma célula Braille. Devido à diferença no tamanho das telas dos *smartphones*, o *layout* é adaptado proporcionalmente ao tamanho da tela do dispositivo.

A concepção desta interface baseou-se nos conceitos de Desenho Universal [11] que procura promover a inclusão digital dos deficientes visuais, sem realizar mudanças que contemplem somente esse público. Desta forma, o sistema pode ser utilizado por deficientes visuais, pessoas com baixa visão e videntes.

Como tela principal, Figura 4, o LêBraille dispõe de uma célula Braille virtual. Por padrão, a ordem de disposição dos pontos segue o modo de leitura em Braille. O sistema interage com o software de síntese de voz disponível para o dispositivo móvel utilizando a biblioteca padrão do Android que fará a comunicação com o sintetizador de voz configurado como padrão do dispositivo (e.g., SVOX[7], eSpeak[8]).

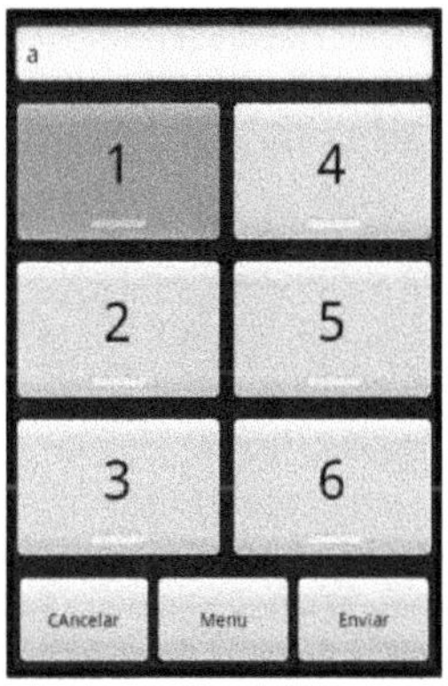

Figura 4- Interface de entrada de dados do LêBraille mostrando a escrita do caractér "a".

O aplicativo desenvolvido, além de ser acessível, implementa as principais funcionalidades de um editor de texto:

- Incluir caractere;
- Editar caractere;
- Excluir o caractere;
- Confirmar a combinação dos pontos;
- Configurar o software;
- Ler o texto gerado.

Após a instalação do software, o usuário o inicia através de um atalho instalado no dispositivo ou o mesmo é requisitado por outros aplicativos do aparelho (e.g., LêBrailleTWT) utilizando a comunicação entre processos baseadas em intenções (*Intents*) provida pela plataforma *Android.* Por oferecer interatividade sonora, cada ação do usuário no sistema é respondida com avisos de áudio, identificando qual ação foi realizada. Para utilizar o sistema, o usuário seleciona um ou mais pontos da célula Braille. Após a seleção dos pontos, os quais são sonorizados, o usuário deve deslizar o dedo horizontalmente no sentido da esquerda para a direita a fim de confirmar a combinação dos pontos. Em seguida, o sistema fará a comparação da combinação dos pontos, caso a combinação corresponda a algum caractere em Braille, então, o aplicativo retornará em áudio a identificação deste caractere e o mesmo será exibido na caixa de texto.

No caso da exclusão de um caractere, o usuário deve percorrer os caracteres digitados na caixa de texto e, ao encontrar o símbolo desejado, o usuário deve balançar o aparelho (função *shake*). A lista de comandos disponíveis para o sistema está apresentada na Tabela 2.

Tabela 2: Comandos disponíveis para o LêBraille

Comando	Movimentação	Ação
Selecionar os pontos da célula Braille e em seguida tocar e arrastar horizontalmente no sentido da esquerda para a direita.	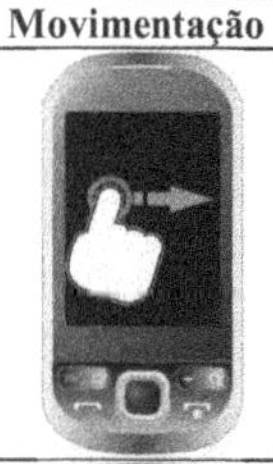	Confirma a inserção do caractere.
Um toque no botão "Menu".		Seleciona a forma de edição dos pontos entre modo de leitura ou modo de escrita.
Tocar com arrasto horizontalmente na área da tela, no sentido da direita para esquerda ou da esquerda para direita.		Navega entre os caracteres digitados. Se o comando for da direita para a esquerda a seleção do caractere move-se para a esquerda, caso contrário o cursor move-se para a direita.
Após navegar entre os caracteres, marcar/desmarcar um ou mais pontos da célula Braille.		Sobrescreve o caractere selecionado, visualmente estará com um destaque em negrito.
Após navegar entre os caracteres, toque com arrasto na diagonal principal.		Insere um espaço em branco à direita do caractere.
Balançar (shake) o aparelho.	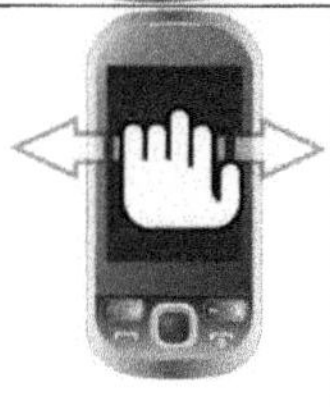	Apaga um caractere e seleciona o caractere à esquerda.
Um toque longo no campo de edição.		Sonoriza tudo que está digitado na caixa de texto.

[7] http://svoxmobilevoices.wordpress.com/

[8] http://espeak.sourceforge.net/

Um toque duplo no botão "Enviar".		Armazena na memória o conjunto de caracteres digitados.
Um toque no botão "Cancelar".		Fecha a aplicação.
Um toque duplo no botão "Menu".		Seleciona a forma de edição dos pontos entre modo de leitura / modo de escrita. Além de possuir opção para habilitar/desabilitar *feedback* através de vibração.

Esta interface de entrada de dados também pode contribuir como parte de uma solução em uma camada que provê acessibilidade, permitindo que diversas aplicações pudessem acessar o aplicativo LêBraille como uma opção de entrada de dados acessível.

4. ESTUDO PILOTO

O objetivo principal dessa avaliação é obter informações de caráter qualitativo a partir das percepções relatadas pelos participantes durante a realização ensaios com o aplicativo.

A princípio, as avaliações foram feitas em um caráter amostral com a quantidade de 10 avaliados, devido à grande dificuldade de encontrar uma quantidade maior de deficientes visuais para os testes do sistema proposto. Primeiro pelo perfil que o deficiente deveria ter para participar deste estudo (deficiente visual com experiência em Braille e com bons conhecimentos de informática, idealmente que já utilizasse sistemas *touch screen*).

Durante o experimento, foram utilizados para os testes um aparelho Galaxy 5 I5500B, tela de 2.8", com o sistema *Android* 2.2, além de instalados e configurados para síntese de voz em português os aplicativos eSpeak TTS v 1.0 e SVOX Classic Text To Speech Engine. Após o período de discussões, apenas para conhecimento da solução, foi apresentado aos participantes o *layout* da aplicação referente ao *Twitter*.

4.1 Procedimentos de Avaliação

Foi utilizada a técnica de experimentos com grupos focais, com o teste de avaliação em duas sessões com duração de 2 horas cada. O grupo foi dividido pela metade e, desse modo, em cada sessão o aplicativo foi avaliado por cinco deficientes visuais.

O teste foi realizado pelos voluntários através de uma entrevista semi-estruturada com preenchimento de questionário. Antes da interação inicial com o aplicativo LêBrailleTWT e com o LêBraille, os deficientes submeteram-se a testes práticos para comprovação de habilidades com o sistema Braille, nos quais transcreveram algumas frases para este sistema.

Durante as primeiras entrevistas com os DVs, percebeu-se a dificuldade de compreensão da localização/distribuição dos elementos na tela. Então, foi apresentado o detalhamento dos aplicativos desenvolvidos em um modelo tátil, propiciando assim uma orientação física quanto à posição dos botões virtuais do aplicativo na tela do dispositivo móvel (ver Figura 5).

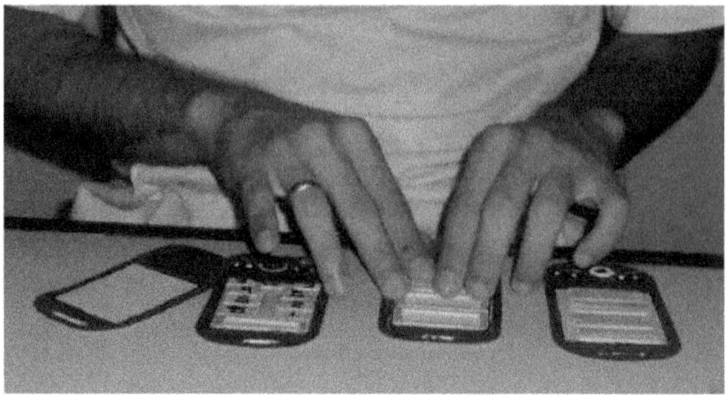

Figura 5 - Ambientação por modelo tátil.

Os deficientes visuais que participaram dessa experiência possuíam o seguinte perfil:

- 07 Homens e 03 Mulheres;
- Possuíam entre 21 e 41 anos de idade;
- 01 possuía baixa visão;
- Todos tinham conhecimentos em Braille e noção do funcionamento do *Twitter*;
- 01 utiliza o aparelho *iPhone* e outros 2 já haviam tido rápido contato com interfaces de toque usando o *iPhone*.

Em um primeiro momento, pediu-se aos usuários que navegassem no aplicativo, lessem *tweets* e reenviassem alguns tweets (*retweetar*). Em um segundo momento, um desafio prático foi proposto para cada participante no qual o tempo de execução da tarefa foi medido. O desafio era *tweetar* o alfabeto completo através da interface de entrada de dados. O objetivo do desafio era avaliar o serviço LêBraille que até o momento não havia sido avaliado com deficientes visuais letrados em Braille. Os principais resultados de interação são descritos no subtópico seguinte.

4.2 Resultados Parciais de Interação com a Tecnologia

O instrumento de avaliação, adaptado de [6], utilizado nesta investigação com usuários deficientes visuais contém 10 métricas. A seguir, apresentamos cada métrica, sua definição e o resultado relatado pelos voluntários através das entrevistas ou de observações de utilização.

I. ORGANIZAÇÃO E APRESENTAÇÃO - É uma métrica relacionada a um indicativo de aceitação do usuário, determinada pela forma de apresentar a tecnologia. Envolve, portanto, a organização geral, estrutura, estratégia de apresentação, coerência e suficiência.

Os voluntários relataram que todas as informações e materiais repassados para ambientar o acesso às tecnologias apresentadas foram necessários, os termos utilizados estavam compreensíveis e contribuíram para o aprendizado dos mesmos. E 40% dos envolvidos gostariam de mais tempo disponível para apreciação da tecnologia, não demonstrando segurança no uso do sistema, mas interessados na temática.

II. MOTIVAÇÃO - Também se constitui como outra métrica relacionada à aceitação do usuário, sendo esta relacionada à capacidade da tecnologia de causar impacto, motivação e/ou interesse.

60% dos entrevistados disseram que a tecnologia é atraente. 70% consideraram os aspectos abordados (*Twitter*, *smartphone touch screen* e Braille) importantes para a inserção dos mesmos no ambiente virtual. Apesar das necessidades de adaptações sugeridas, 90% relataram que a tecnologia tem o formato interessante para uma pessoa cega, provendo a quebra de paradigmas no uso de interfaces *touch screen*.

III. DESIGN - É determinado pelo desenho apresentado no aplicativo.

80% dos usuários deficientes visuais disseram que o aplicativo possui um *layout* que propicia a fácil localização e a operação eficiente dos elementos da interface.

IV. ESTILO DO ÁUDIO - É determinado pela compreensão e estilo do áudio apresentado.

A aplicação é portável para o sintetizador de voz que esteja definido como padrão no *smartphone*. Com isso, uma investigação foi realizada utilizando os sintetizadores de voz eSpeak e *SVOX*, verificando que 80% dos entrevistados optaram pela utilização do eSpeak devido a rapidez no tempo de resposta propiciado por esse sintetizador, gerando uma maior segurança na utilização dos aplicativos desenvolvidos. Porém, 90% não consideram o som tão atrativo para a exploração/acesso ao sistema quando comparado com a qualidade da voz sintetizada pelo SVOX.

V. NAVEGABILIDADE - Determinada pela facilidade do usuário navegar nas páginas e conteúdos correspondentes.

60% citaram que a interface está entendível e de fácil navegação, porém a mesma necessita de adaptações. 90% ratificaram que a navegação possui uma sequência lógica.

VI. CONTEÚDO - Relaciona-se ao assunto abordado na tecnologia.

Todos os entrevistados, após a manipulação do aplicativo, afirmaram que a tecnologia apresentada corresponde ao seu nível de conhecimento. O que confirma que todos os envolvidos conseguiram entender o intuito da pesquisa na qual estavam inseridos.

VII. VELOCIDADE - É determinado pela agilidade de acesso à página e aos conteúdos inseridos na mesma.

Para realização da atividade proposta, o tempo médio para escrita e postagem da mensagem foi de 05 min e 23 seg. Porém, deve-se levar em consideração que as dificuldades de navegação são decorrentes da falta de experiência do testador neste ambiente. Alguns voluntários demonstraram tempos menores, como 3min e 02 seg, o que sugere que com o tempo e familiarização com a ferramenta os mesmos diminuam significativamente.

VIII. OBJETIVOS - É determinado pelos propósitos, metas ou finalidade a que se deseja com a utilização da tecnologia.

Todos os participantes conseguiram realizar a atividade proposta, porém 70% dos mesmos afirmaram que os recursos de acessibilidade necessitam de reformulações. Estas serão detalhadas no item X. COMENTÁRIOS GERAIS E SUGESTÕES.

IX. EDUCAÇÃO ESPECIAL – Refere-se à educação de pessoas com necessidades especiais.

70 % informaram que tal recurso poderá incentivar o deficiente visual ao aprendizado Braille e estimulá-los a uma maior participação/interação nas redes sociais.

X. COMENTÁRIOS GERAIS E SUGESTÕES

a) SIMPLES: A ferramenta deve melhorar ainda o retorno sonoro ao usuário. Ou seja, melhorar a usabilidade do sistema.

b) MODERADA: Proporcionar autonomia a controladores externos à aplicação, o que é mais complexo, dado a não acessibilidade do Sistema Operacional. Portanto, deve-se estudar uma forma da própria aplicação criar tais controles, pois a proposta atual não permite a utilização de botões físicos.

c) GRAVE: Repensar a necessidade de utilização do recurso Multitouch, o qual não está sendo implementado, pois tornaria a utilização mais confusa, porém pode ajudar na resolução do conflito entre o momento de exploração da tela e o gesto que realiza uma ação.

Dentre diversas considerações, alguns avaliados destacaram que a maior contribuição deste trabalho é a inclusão do sistema Braille nas novas tecnologias.

5. CONCLUSÃO E TRABALHOS FUTUROS

Os estudos investigativos sobre a interação do deficiente com interfaces de apelo estritamente visual, como é a de toque, é uma demanda latente que requer cada vez mais estudos e pesquisas aplicadas. Nesse contexto, este artigo apresentou um aplicativo para dispositivos móveis *Android* que prover acesso ao *Twitter* para deficientes visuais, apesar da interface *touch screen* destes dispositivos. O sistema faz uso de gestos e de sintetizadores vocais para prover acessibilidade à rede social. É também apresentada a versão final do LêBraille, serviço que provê a escrita de textos digitais usando como metáfora a linguagem Braille. A avaliação realizada apresenta resultados animadores de aceitação do uso e de como a acessibilidade foi implementada tanto no aplicativo LêBrailleTWT quanto no serviço LêBraille. Como bem apontado pelos voluntários, o sistema também apresenta como benefício a inclusão do sistema Braille nas novas tecnologias.

Em curto prazo, novas avaliações continuadas ocorrerão com a realização de mais duas sessões. Deve-se propor a inserção de frases mais complexas e em dispositivos com telas maiores, visando obter melhores resultados quantitativos de aceitação da ferramenta e de sua curva de aprendizagem.

Uma modificação do aplicativo LêBrailleTWT está em andamento para prover acessibilidade a outros serviços móveis utilizados por deficientes visuais como, por exemplo, o uso de serviços de mensagens SMS (*Short Message Service*).

6. REFERÊNCIAS

[1] Maia, L. S. ; Turine, M. A.S ; Sandim, H. C ; Paiva, D.M.B. 2010. Um Modelo para o Desenvolvimento de Aplicações Web Acessíveis, In: *Webmedia*, 2010 (Belo Horizonte, Brasil).

[2] Oliveira, João; Guerreiro, Tiago; Nicolau, Hugo; Jorge, Joaquim; Gonçalves, Daniel. 2011. BrailleType: Unleashing Braille over Touch Screen Mobile Phones. In: *Human-Computer Interaction – INTERACT 2011*. Lecture Notes in Computer Science, pp 100-107. ISBN: 978-3-642-23773-7.

[3] Agência Rs. Webinar da comScore mostra dados relevantes sobre as redes sociais no Brasil – Veja gráficos. Disponível

em: http://www.agenciars.com.br/blog/webinar-da-comscore-mostra-dados-relevantes-sobre-redes-socias-brasil-veja-graficos/ (2011); Acesso em: 12 set. 2011.

[4] FAÇANHA, Agebson R.; VIANA, Windson; PEQUENO, Mauro C.. Estudo de interfaces acessíveis para usuários com deficiência visual em dispositivos móveis touch screen. XVI Congreso Internacional de Informática Educativa (TISE 2011), Santiago Chile.

[5] Nielsen. State of The Media: The Social Media Report Q3 2011. Disponível em: http://blog.nielsen.com/nielsenwire/social/ (2011). Acesso em: 12 set. 2011.

[6] Oliveira, Paula M. P. 2009. Avaliação de uma tecnologia assistiva sobre amamentação para pessoas cegas. Dissertação de Mestrado. Universidade Federal do Ceará - Departamento de Enfermagem.

[7] ONCE. 2010. Accesibilidad de Plataformas de Redes Sociales. Observatorio Accesibilidad TIC – discapnet. **Relatório Técnico**. Dec. 2010. 78 p.

[8] Rodrigues, Carla. 2009. O que você está fazendo agora? Três contribuições para o debate sobre microblogs. In: *Alceu*, v.9 – n°18, p.148-161, jan./jun. 2009.

[9] Teleco. Estatística de Celulares no Brasil. Disponível em: http://www.teleco.com.br/ncel.asp (Out. 2011). Acesso em: Nov. 2011.

[10] Fábio Khron, Jr. and Sílvio César Cazella. 2009. A framework for social networks new relationships recommendation from the use of folksonomies. In *Proceedings of the XV Brazilian Symposium on Multimedia and the Web (WebMedia '09).* ACM, New York, NY, USA, , Article 45 , 4 pages.

[11] Sanchez, Jaime; Aguayo, Fernando. 2007. Mobile Messenger for the Blind. Universal Access in Ambient Intelligence Environments. Volume 4397/2007, p.369-385. DOI = 10.1007/978-3-540-71025-7_24.

[12] Gabrilli, Mara. Desenho Universal um conceito para todos. Disponível em: http://www.vereadoramaragabrilli.com.br/files/universal_web.pdf (2009). Acesso em: 15 jan. 2011.

[13] Machado, J. R.; Tijiboy, A.V. 2005. Redes Sociais Virtuais: um espaço para efetivação da aprendizagem cooperativa. In: *Novas Tecnologias na Educação*. CINTED-UFRGS, V. 3 N° 1, Maio, 2005.

[14] Meiselwitz, G.; Lazar, Jonathan; Ozok, A. 2009. Accessibility of Registration Mechanisms in Social Networking Sites. In: Online Communities and Social Computing. Lecture Notes in Computer Science. pp 82-90. DOI: 10.1007/978-3-642-02774-1_9.

[15] Tinwala, H., and MacKenzie, I. S. 2009. Eyes-free text entry on a touchscreen phone. In: *Proceedings of the IEEE Toronto International Conference – Science and Technology for Humanity – TIC-STH 2009*, 83-89. New York: IEEE.

[16] Bonner, M.N., Brudvik, J.T., Abowd, G.D., Edwards, W.K. 2010. No-look notes: Accessible eyes-free multi-touch text entry. In: Floréen, P., Krüger, A., Spasojevic, M. (eds.) *Pervasive Computing*. LNCS, vol. 6030, pp. 409-426. Springer, Heidelberg. DOI: 10.1007/978-3-642-12654-3_24.

[17] Guerreiro, T., Lagoá, P., Nicolau, H., Gonçalves, D., Jorge, J. A. 2008. From Tapping to Touching: Making Touch Screens Accessible to Blind Users. In: IEEE MultiMedia, v.15 n.4, p.48-50. DOI: 10.1109/MMUL.2008.88

[18] Lucas, D., Nicolau, H., Guerreiro, T., Jorge, J. A. 2010. NavTilt: Interface Gestual para Cegos. In *Proceedings of the 4th National Conference on Human-Computer Interaction (Interacção 2010)*. Aveiro, Portugal.

[19] Rodrigues, T., Benevenuto, F., Almeida, V., Almeida, J., Gonçalves, M. 2009. A contextual analysis of the YouTube duplicate content. In *Proceedings of the XV Brazilian Symposium on Multimedia and the Web (WebMedia '09).* ACM, New York, NY, USA, , Article 23 , 8 pages. DOI: 10.1145/1858477.185850.

[20] CARSTENSEN, CHRISTINA. Is your marketing "Mobile Ready"?. IDG Global Solutins; 2011.

[21] SOUZA, Sérgio Augusto Freire de. As redes sociais e a liquidez na Sociedade 140 bytes: sob os olhos da Coruja de Minerva. Artigo apresentado sob a forma de palestra na XIV Semana de Letras da Universidade Federal do Amazonas - UFAM em 29 de outubro de 2009.

[22] SILVA, Fernando. R da; ZSCHORNACK, Fábio. Análise de Acessibilidade em Redes Sociais. Faculdade de Informática - UniRitter. 2009. Disponível em: <http://www.uniritter.edu.br/graduacao/informatica/sistemas/downloads/tcc2k9/TCCII_Fernando_2009_2.pdf>. Acesso em 02 abr. 2012.

Improving Photo Recommendation with Context Awareness

Fabrício D. A. Lemos
Mestrado e Doutorado em Ciência da Computação (MDCC)
Universidade Federal do Ceará
Fortaleza-CE, Brasil
fabriciolemos@great.ufc.br

Rafael A. F Carmo
Instituto UFC Virtual
Universidade Federal do Ceará
Fortaleza-CE, Brasil
carmorafael@virtual.ufc.br

Windson Viana
Grupo de Redes de Computadores, Engenharia de Software e Sistemas
Universidade Federal do Ceará
Fortaleza-CE, Brasil
windson@virtual.ufc.br

Rossana M. C. Andrade*
Grupo de Redes de Computadores, Engenharia de Software e Sistemas
Universidade Federal do Ceará
Fortaleza-CE, Brasil
rossana@great.ufc.br

ABSTRACT
One of the most important challenges in Information Systems is information overload. Recommender Systems try to cope with this problem by helping people in retrieving information (ex: videos, services, products, images, etc.) that may match their preferences and intentions. An issue of Recommender Systems is related to user's context. The use of the system in a different context than usual may cause an unsatisfactory result for the recommendation, since preferences and intentions can be influenced by user's context (location, trajectory, time of day, activity, etc.). This paper presents the MMedia2U, a mobile photo recommender system that exploits the user's context and the context when photo was created as a means to improve the recommendation. Three context dimensions area exploited: spatial, social and temporal. We describe the similarity measures used for each dimension and the results of the system evaluation with 13 users following a Gold Standard approach.

Categories and Subject Descriptors
H.3.3 [**Information Search and Retrieval**]: Information filtering.

General Terms
Algorithms, and Human Factors.

Keywords
Sistemas de Recomendação, Sensibilidade ao contexto, Computação Ubíqua.

1. INTRODUÇÃO
Um dos desafios no desenvolvimento de Sistemas de Informação Multimídia é a sobrecarga de informações. Sistemas de Recomendação tentam lidar com esse problema ajudando as pessoas na recuperação da informação (ex: vídeos, programas de TV, rotas, imagens, pessoas, etc.) que provavelmente coincidam com suas preferências e intenções. Sistemas de Recomendação tentam identificar os itens do conjunto de informação que tem uma maior chance de corresponder aos desejos de seus usuários [9][5]. No entanto, a caracterização das preferências e intenções dos usuários é uma tarefa complexa que, como regra, necessita da intervenção do usuário para ser corretamente cumprida. Outro importante ponto em Sistemas de Informação Multimídia é relacionado ao contexto do usuário. O uso do sistema em um contexto diferente do costumeiro pode causar uma recomendação com resultado insatisfatório, já que preferências e intenções podem ser influenciadas pelo contexto (localização, trajetória, período do dia, atividade, etc.) do usuário. A sensibilidade ao contexto refere-se exatamente à capacidade que um sistema possui de detectar a situação do usuário e guiar o comportamento do sistema [8]. Hoje em dia, a evolução dos dispositivos móveis e das tecnologias de sensores residenciais permite uma melhor caracterização do contexto do usuário, permitindo que esta informação seja utilizada no aperfeiçoamento das recomendações.

Neste cenário, este artigo apresenta o *Mobile Media to You* (MMedia2U), um sistema de recomendação de fotos que encaixa-se na categoria de sistemas de recomendação multimídia. O MMedia2U recomenda fotos anotadas com informações contextuais e permite que um usuário acesse os itens recomendados a partir de seu dispositivo móvel. Este domínio de aplicação é interessante devido ao grande número de fotos geradas e disponibilizadas em sites de compartilhamento como *Flickr*[1] e *Picasa Web*[2]. Muitas dessas fotos são geradas por dispositivos móveis ou câmeras eletrônicas que armazenam a localização, data, horário e possivelmente outras informações contextuais. Alguns sistemas [3], inclusive, realizam o enriquecimento das informações de contexto das fotos e as armazenam em um modelo semântico, tornando-as mais fáceis de serem exploradas por sistemas de informação, de busca e de recomendação.

O objetivo do trabalho é, portanto, mostrar que esse tipo de base de fotos anotadas com contexto pode ser usado para recomendação sem a necessidade de um treinamento prévio do sistema de forma a comportar os usuários novos sem dificuldades. Explorar fotos geolocalizadas não é novidade [15] e ferramentas como o Flickr, Picasa e Panoramio possuem essa funcionalidade como apelo central. O trabalho vai um pouco além, adotando uma abordagem de recomendação e considerando uma gama maior de atributos contextuais.

* Bolsista de Produtividade Desen. Tec. e Extensão Inovadora do CNPq - Nível 2

Permission to make digital or hard copies of all or part of this work for personal or classroom use is granted without fee provided that copies are not made or distributed for profit or commercial advantage and that copies bear this notice and the full citation on the first page. To copy otherwise, or republish, to post on servers or to redistribute to lists, requires prior specific permission and/or a fee.
WebMedia'12, October 15–18, 2012, São Paulo/SP, Brazil.
Copyright 2012 ACM 978-1-4503-1706-1/12/10...$15.00.

[1] www.flickr.com/

[2] http://picasaweb.google.com/lh/explore

O restante deste artigo é estruturado da seguinte forma: a seção 2 apresenta a fundamentação teórica dos conceitos mais importantes nas áreas de Sistemas de Recomendação e de Sensibilidade ao Contexto. A seção 3 faz a caracterização da contribuição, mostrando o cenário de incorporação de informações contextuais às técnicas tradicionais de recomendação. Na seção 4, são descritos os experimentos realizados. A quinta seção descreve a conclusão e os trabalhos futuros.

2. FUNDAMENTAÇÃO TEÓRICA E TRABALHOS RELACIONADOS

Tradicionalmente, os sistemas de recomendação lidam com dois tipos de entidade: os usuários e itens [9], onde os itens são os objetos que serão recomendados e, possivelmente, avaliados pelos usuários. A principal responsabilidade de um sistema de recomendação é prever quais os itens que melhor correspondem às preferências e necessidades do usuário. Outro conceito importante em sistemas de recomendação é a pontuação que o usuário dá a um item. Esta pontuação é basicamente uma forma de capturar a preferência de um usuário específico para um determinado item (por exemplo, atribuindo uma quantidade de estrelas, como nas primeiras versões do *Youtube*). Formalmente, um sistema de recomendação pode ser modelado com um conjunto de usuários $U = \{u_1, u_2, \ldots u_i, \ldots u_n\}$, um conjunto de itens $I = \{i_1, i_2, \ldots, i_j, \ldots, i_m\}$, e com o cálculo, para cada par (u_i, i_j), de uma pontuação r_{ij} que mede o interesse ou a utilidade esperada do item i_j para o usuário u_i usando uma base de conhecimento e um algoritmo de avaliação (ou ranking) que também deve levar em consideração padrões de preferência dos usuários. Cada elemento do conjunto U de usuários pode ser definido com um perfil que inclui várias características do usuário, tais como idade, sexo, status, e assim por diante. Similarmente, cada elemento do conjunto de itens I é definido com um conjunto de propriedades. Por exemplo, em um sistema de recomendação de conteúdo multimídia, em que o conjunto I é uma coleção de fotos, cada foto é representada pela sua descrição, data e local de geração, pessoas representadas na fotografia, etc. A pontuação r geralmente não é definida em todo o espaço $U \times I$. Ela é definida somente em um subconjunto, uma vez que a maioria dos usuários não avaliaram todas as fotos de uma coleção. Assim, o problema central de um sistema de recomendação é extrapolar r para todo o espaço $U \times I$. De acordo com Jannach et al. [5], as técnicas tradicionais de sistemas de recomendação são divididas em três paradigmas principais: *Recomendação Colaborativa*, *Baseada em Conteúdo* e *Recomendação Baseada em Conhecimento*.

A *recomendação colaborativa* parte do princípio de que usuários que demonstraram interesses similares no passado irão apresentar interesses também similares no futuro. A *recomendação baseada em conteúdo* parte do princípio de que um determinado usuário terá maior interesse em itens que tenham similaridade a itens avaliados, por ele mesmo, como positivos. Um terceiro tipo de técnica é a *recomendação baseada em conhecimento,* que realiza a recomendação a partir das preferências informadas pelo usuário. Os itens passíveis de recomendação necessitam ser anotados com características objetivas para serem avaliados quanto a sua adequação às preferências. Estas abordagens de recomendação podem ser combinadas em sistemas de recomendação híbridos, ajudando a evitar certas limitações de cada método.

Cada paradigma contem suas vantagens e desvantagens. Os sistemas colaborativos passam a ter desempenho satisfatório somente quando possuem uma extensa base histórica de recomendações e avaliações. Nos sistemas baseados em conteúdo, uma boa predição não pode ser feita até que o usuário tenha avaliado uma grande quantidade de itens. Sistemas baseados em conhecimento não possuem tais desvantagens, conhecidas como problema do início frio (*cold-start problem*), já que não dependem de uma base histórica de uso, mas sim do conhecimento das características dos itens e dos requisitos buscados pelo usuário [11]. Estes sistemas, porém, possuem como dependência um detalhado conhecimento sobre as características dos itens recomendados (e.g., formato, tamanho e qualidade dos itens) e meios de elicitar quais os valores destas características são os que mais interessam ao usuário (e.g., se o usuário está procurando conteúdo multimídia de baixa ou alta resolução).

Um conceito central das técnicas apresentadas é a necessidade de se executar cálculos de similaridade. Por exemplo, sistemas de recomendação baseados em conhecimento precisam calcular a similaridade entre as características dos itens em relação às preferências do usuário. Por outro lado, métodos baseados em conteúdo requerem o cálculo da semelhança entre itens. Existem várias medidas de similaridade: Algoritmo de Correlação de Pearson, Similaridade pelo Cosseno, Regressão, Semelhança Semântica [12]. No entanto, a descrição das propriedades dos itens e a aquisição automática de preferências do usuário continuam a ser requisitos para a execução destes cálculos.

Com a popularização da computação ubíqua, a sensibilidade ao contexto tornou-se um campo bastante relevante e tem sido utilizada para aumentar a eficiência e usabilidade de sistemas, particularmente, nas aplicações para dispositivos móveis [6]. A Sensibilidade ao Contexto em sistemas de recomendação foi motivada a partir de pesquisas que reconhecem a dependência das necessidades de longo prazo do usuário em relação ao tempo, localização, e qualquer outra informação sobre o ambiente físico em torno do usuário [4] [13]. Ela apresenta um nível adicional de personalização, considerando a influência do ambiente externo ao usuário em seu/sua apreciação dos produtos ou itens. Por depender tanto das informações dos usuários quanto dos itens recomendados, sistemas de recomendação podem se beneficiar da sensibilidade ao contexto ao considerar não somente as características intrínsecas de cada entidade, mas também as características de seu contexto.

Em Sistemas de Informação, o conceito de contexto refere-se ao estado do usuário e do ambiente adjacente no momento em que ele está usando o sistema. De acordo com Dey e Abowd [7], o contexto é construído a partir de todos os elementos de informação que podem ser utilizados para caracterizar a situação de uma entidade. Uma entidade é definida como qualquer pessoa, lugar ou coisa considerada relevante para a interação entre o usuário e o sistema, incluindo o usuário e o próprio sistema. Assim, o termo "sensível ao contexto" está associado com os sistemas que guiam o seu comportamento de acordo com seu contexto de uso. A sensibilidade ao contexto é vista como a capacidade de perceber a situação do usuário em vários aspectos, e adaptar o comportamento do sistema em conformidade [8].

No domínio de multimídia, a noção de contexto e, principalmente, a sua exploração, é ligeiramente diferente. A Sensibilidade ao Contexto é mais do que um simples mecanismo de adaptação. Esta distinção é estudada em alguns trabalhos, que estudaram o comportamento dos usuários para organizar e encontrar fotos. Na verdade, a maioria das informações referidas pelas pessoas sobre suas lembranças de imagens consistem em aspectos relacionados ao seu contexto no momento em que uma foto foi tirada (quando, onde, com quem, etc.). A popularização de dispositivos móveis equipados com sensores de localização e GIS (Sistemas de Informação Geográfica) forneceram a tecnologia e os dados necessários para desenvolver sistemas de multimídia capazes de reunir as informações de contexto desejadas. Hoje em dia, a sensibilidade ao contexto é aplicada no domínio multimídia para: anotação de multimídia, indexação de multimídia, sistemas de compartilhamento e recomendação multimídia. Uma pesquisa detalhada dessas abordagens é descrita em [3] [14].

Técnicas de recomendação sensíveis ao contexto já desenvolvidas mostram a viabilidade da implementação de sistemas de recomendação sensíveis ao contexto (por exemplo, notícias, filmes, música, serviços) [10]. Adomavicius et al. [9], por exemplo, implementaram um sistema de recomendação de filmes que leva em consideração o contexto do usuário (por exemplo, se ele vai assistir o filme em casa ou no cinema) e atestaram melhorias na precisão e no recall das recomendações. Apesar destes bons resultados iniciais, muitos problemas permanecem no uso da sensibilidade ao contexto em sistemas de recomendação, tais como: a) Como adquirir contexto de maneira precisa? b) Quais dimensões contextuais influenciam na recomendação de forma significativa? c) Como calcular similaridade de contexto? d) Como avaliar sistemas de recomendação sensíveis ao contexto?

Adomavicius et al. [9] propõem uma classificação dos sistemas sensíveis ao contexto em duas categorias. Na primeira, se encaixam os sistemas que utilizam as informações contextuais como critério de filtro dos itens. Um exemplo de sistema desta categoria é o *COMPASS* [1], que apresenta um guia turístico em que a recomendação dos pontos de interesse leva em consideração o contexto atual do usuário. *Kaialeido Photo* [2] é outro sistema desta categoria, que realiza a anotação contextual das fotos e permite que o usuário filtre os álbuns de acordo com categorias pré-estabelecidas (e.g., evento em que a foto foi gerada). Neste sistema, o usuário tem que informar explicitamente os filtros a serem utilizados, não ocorrendo uma adaptação contextual. O Columbus [15] é uma aplicação móvel mais simples que mostra fotos geolocalizadas geradas perto da localização do usuário.

Na segunda categoria, estão os sistemas que utilizam as informações contextuais no momento em que o usuário avalia algum item. Além das avaliações e características dos itens e dos usuários, os sistemas sensíveis ao contexto dessa categoria levam em consideração também as informações contextuais (e.g, localização, companhia). O trabalho descrito por Adomavicius et al. [9] é um exemplo de sistema de recomendação de filmes desta categoria que, ao registrar o momento em que o usuário assistiu algum filme, armazena tanto a nota dada pelo usuário ao filme quanto em qual contexto o filme foi assistido (e.g., em casa com a esposa). Dessa forma, por exemplo, um filme que foi bem avaliado por usuários em um determinado contexto, tem maior chance de ser recomendado a um usuário que se encontra em um contexto similar. No domínio de recomendação de conteúdo multimídia, o sistema *C2_Music* [10] incorpora informações contextuais na recomendação de músicas. De maneira geral, o comportamento deste sistema é similar ao sistema de recomendação de filmes, em que na avaliação de uma música é incorporado o contexto no qual ela foi escutada (e.g., dia da semana, condições meteriológicas).

Tais sistemas dependem, no entanto, de uma extensa base histórica em que usuários em contextos semelhantes ao usuário atual tenham utilizado e avaliado uma grande quantidade de itens. Sem essa base histórica estes sistemas não conseguem relacionar o usuário atual com nenhum contexto de utilização de itens, não sendo possível a realização de uma recomendação contextual. Um outro problema ocorre quando, mesmo na existência de uma extensa base histórica, algum item novo é adicionado à coleção. Como este item ainda não foi utilizado, não é possível recomendá-lo de acordo com técnicas de recomendação colaborativa.

Sistema	**Recomendação**	**Sensível ao contexto**	**Contexto Incorporado na Recomendação**	
			Contexto do Usuário	**Contexto dos Itens**
COMPASS	Filtragem	Sim	Localização	Localização
Kaialeido Photo	Filtragem	Não	Nenhum	Localização, Data, Contatos
Columbus	Filtragem	Sim	Localização	Localização
Adomavicius et al.	Colaborativa	Sim	Localização, Dia da Semana, Companhia	Nenhum
C2 Music	Colaborativa	Sim	Localização, Data, Condições Meteorológicas	Nenhum
MMedia2U (Nossa proposta)	Conhecimento	Sim	Localização, Data e Hora, Atividade de Interesse	Localização, Data e Hora, Atividade de Interesse

Tabela 1. Trabalhos Relacionados e MMedia2U.

O trabalho descrito neste artigo se diferencia dos trabalhos citados ao considerar não somente o contexto dos usuários, mas ao considerar, também, o contexto de geração ou contexto atual dos itens. A hipótese é que fotos tiradas em um determinado contexto *c* poderá interessar a usuários que estão em contextos similares a *c*. Consegue-se, dessa forma, um ganho em relação às técnicas de recomendação sensíveis ao contexto já conhecidas, que não se beneficiam de um repositório de itens rico em contexto e semântica. Ao utilizar uma técnica de *recomendação baseada em conhecimento*, evita-se as desvantagens das outras técnicas vistas anteriormente. Com a incorporação da sensibilidade ao contexto, além de recomendar os itens mais apropriados ao contexto do usuário, evita-se as desvantagens também da recomendação baseada em conhecimento: as características dos itens serão extraídas de seu respectivo contexto, que será comparado não com as necessidades informadas pelo usuário, mas sim com seu contexto atual de uso do sistema. As características dos sistemas citados e do MMedia2U podem ser vistas na Tabela 1.

3. MOBILE MEDIA TO YOU (MMedia2U)

No sistema proposto neste artigo, os usuários recebem recomendações de fotos geradas em um contexto similar ao seu, sendo essa similaridade função de três dimensões contextuais (espacial, social e temporal). O sistema tem como público alvo dois tipos de usuários. O primeiro tipo são aqueles que estão em um contexto não habitual (e.g., turistas visitando um local pela primeira vez) e que possam aproveitar as fotos recomendadas para ter referências de atividades ou novos locais a serem explorados.

O segundo grupo contém usuários que já tenham estado em um contexto semelhante e que podem ter nas fotos recomendadas uma nova visão e ponto de vista da situação em que se encontram. Os autores Rost et al [15], já observaram que fotos georeferenciadas podem influenciar de forma positiva e lúdica a exploração do espaço por essas duas categorias de usuários.

3.1 Modelo de Contexto

Parte fundamental na elaboração de um sistema sensível ao contexto é definição de quais informações devem compor o contexto, visto que os elementos que o descrevem dependem da tarefa do sistema e da capacidade do mesmo em observar estas informações [3]. Esta definição está associada à criação de um modelo de contexto, no qual são determinados os elementos que comporão a sua descrição e como ele deverá ser representado (e.g., usando ontologias, XML, objetos). A Figura 1 apresenta um modelo de contexto usando uma ontologia OWL-DL que possui as dimensões espacial (localização geográfica, pontos de interesse e nome do local), social (e.g., pessoa e atividade sendo desempenhada), temporal (data e hora) e computacional (dispositivo móvel). Estas dimensões são importantes na representação de elementos contextuais em diferentes domínios e em especial em aplicações multimídia [3].

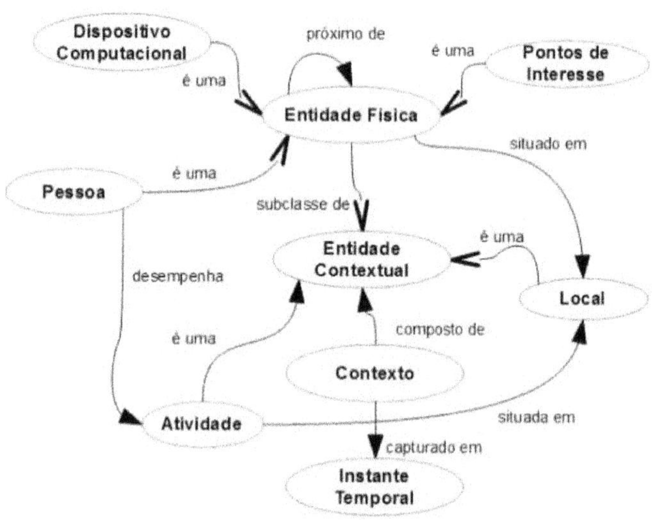

Figura 1- Modelo de Contexto

No MMedia2U, estas dimensões foram exploradas na aquisição de conhecimento dos usuários e das fotos. Tais dimensões já são exploradas em sistemas de gerenciamento contextual de conteúdo multimídia [3] e são relevantes na organização e pesquisa de fotos pessoais, sendo este um indicativo de que podem também ser exploradas em sistemas de recomendação deste tipo de documento multimídia. No MMedia2U, o atributo de localização é extraído do dispositivo móvel utilizado pelo usuário a partir de sensores de localização contidos no aparelho (e.g., GPS). Outros atributos como o local (e.g., shopping, praia,...) podem ser derivados a partir de serviços Web disponíveis gratuitamente tais como *GeoNames*[3] e *WikiMapia.*[4] A data e hora considerada é a do momento de uso do sistema. A atividade de interesse necessita ser informada pelo usuário, podendo ser escolhida entre opções apresentadas ou informadas textualmente. Exemplos de atividades de interesse são: esporte, festas, paisagens naturais, etc.

3.2 O Cálculo de Similaridade

O cálculo de similaridade é utilizado no sistema para que sejam recuperadas aquelas fotos criadas em contextos os mais similares ao contexto do usuário. O algoritmo foi desenvolvido adaptando-se a técnica de *recomendação baseada em conhecimento* [19], utilizando o contexto do usuário como indicativo de suas preferências e o contexto dos itens como representação de suas características. O cálculo de similaridade global proposto entre Usuários e Itens é uma forma bem simples de média ponderada entre os cálculos de similaridade de todos os atributos contextuais considerados relevantes. A determinação dos pesos pode ser feita manualmente (sem treinamento) ou usando uma base de treinamento (histórico de avaliações). Mais formalmente, a similaridade é calculada entre o contexto do usuário U e o contexto de um item I utilizando a seguinte fórmula:

$$\text{similaridade}(U, I) = \sum_{c \in CONT} w_c * \text{sim}_c(U, I) \quad (1)$$

Na Fórmula 1, a similaridade é calculada sem a necessidade de uma base de treinamento. Neste caso, c é um atributo pertencente a uma das dimensões do modelo de contexto utilizado (e.g., localização); w_c é o peso de influência do atributo c (e.g., localização tem peso 50%); e sim_c é a função de similaridade para o atributo c. São recomendados ao usuário U aquelas fotos que possuam o maior valor da similaridade calculada. A função sim_c é particular de cada tipo de contexto e do domínio da aplicação. Na utilização de uma base de treinamento é adicionado um limiar, de valor -1, que é ponderado de acordo com o peso calculado pelo método dos Mínimos Quadrados.

Cada dimensão do modelo de contexto deve ter um cálculo de similaridade distinto. A similaridade de localização, por exemplo, pode ser medida através da distância física entre o local em que a foto foi tirada e o local em que se encontra o usuário. Para isto, mede-se a distância entre as coordenadas de latitude e longitude das duas entidades. As fotos tiradas mais próximas ao local em que o usuário se encontra possuem uma maior similaridade de localização. Em outros casos, em que as coordenadas não são conhecidas ou em que a distância física não é a mais apropriada para o domínio da aplicação, a localização pode ainda ser mapeada em uma hierarquia (e.g., Bairro → Cidade → Unidade da Federação → País → Continente) em que a similaridade é calculada pela distância dos elementos ao nó raiz, de acordo com a fórmula [20]:

$$\text{sim}_c(U, I) = \frac{2 * N}{N_u + N_i} * PF(U, I) \quad (2)$$

Nesta fórmula, N representa a distância entre o mais próximo nó ancestral comum de U e I em relação ao nó raiz da hierarquia; e N_u e N_i representam a distância de U e I, respectivamente, ao nó raiz da hierarquia; $PF(U,I)$ é o fator de penalização para dois nós vizinhos. A similaridade para a atividade de interesse é calculada comparando-se a atividade de interesse ou ocasião em que se encontra o usuário e a atividade ou ocasião em que a foto foi gerada. Algumas das atividades mapeadas em fotos e suas respectivas similaridades encontram-se na Tabela 2.

[3] http://www.geonames.org/

[4] http://wikimapia.org/

	Compras	Festas	Lazer	Esporte
Compras	1	0	0	0
Festas	0	1	0,5	0
Lazer	0	0,5	1	0,5
Esporte	0	0	0,5	1

Tabela 2 –Similaridade entre Atividades

Em atributos numéricos, em que a similaridade é definida por quão próximos são dois valores, a Fórmula 3 é utilizada.

$$sim_c(U,I) = 1 - \frac{|V_c(U) - V_c(I)|}{max(c) - min(c)} \quad (3)$$

Na Fórmula 3, *Vc(U)* e *Vc(I)* representam os valores do contexto *c* para o usuário e o item, respectivamente; *max(c)* e *min(c)* representam, respectivamente, o valor máximo e mínimo para o atributo comparado do contexto *c*.

Comparação entre as datas da foto e do usuário	Similaridade
Mesmo dia da semana	1
Ambos finais de semana ou dia de semana	0.5
Períodos da semana distintos	0

Tabela 3 –Similaridade para o dia da semana.

A similaridade entre datas pode comparar os diversos atributos relativos ao momento em que a foto foi tirada e o instante em que se encontra o usuário. Alguns atributos comparados foram: hora do dia, dia da semana e mês do ano. Os atributos de data foram comparados individualmente para analisar a influência particular de cada um (e.g., a semelhança entre a hora do dia teria maior influência na escolha do usuário do que a semelhança do dia da semana?). A similaridade entre o mês do ano pode ser calculada pela Fórmula 3, vista acima, adaptando-a a valores cíclicos (e.g., a distância entre janeiro e dezembro é 1 ao invés de 11). A similaridade entre dias da semana pode ser calculada pela distância entre os dias da semana representados por duas datas ou pode-se, por exemplo, utilizar a Tabela 3 como critério. Da mesma forma, a similaridade entre o horário pode ser calculada pela quantidade de minutos que separam as horas ou levando em consideração se pertencem, ou não, ao mesmo turno do dia [10].

3.2.1 Reutilização da solução em outros domínios

Como exposto, existem diversas fórmulas para se calcular a similaridade entre usuários e itens. As variações podem ocorrer nos atributos a serem comparados, no cálculo de similaridade para um atributo específico ou no peso que se dá para a similaridade do atributo na Fórmula 1. Os atributos, os cálculos de similaridade e os pesos utilizados dependem do sistema de recomendação sendo desenvolvido. Um sistema de recomendação de restaurantes, por exemplo, provavelmente precisaria de cálculos de similaridade distintos do de um sistema de recomendação de fotos. A solução proposta necessita, portanto, possibilitar a inserção e remoção de cálculos de similaridade para que possa, com baixo esforço, ser reutilizada em sistemas de recomendação de diferentes domínios. Essa preocupação com a flexibilidade e a evolução dos sistemas de recomendação já foi apontada por outros pesquisadores [16].

Utilizando princípios da Orientação a Objetos e Padrões de Projeto, todo o calculo de similaridade foi abstraído do restante do sistema, tornando possível separar o algoritmo de recomendação em um componente específico e reutilizá-lo em outros sistemas que tenham cálculos de similaridade distintos. A Figura 2 mostra o diagrama de classes da modelagem utilizada.

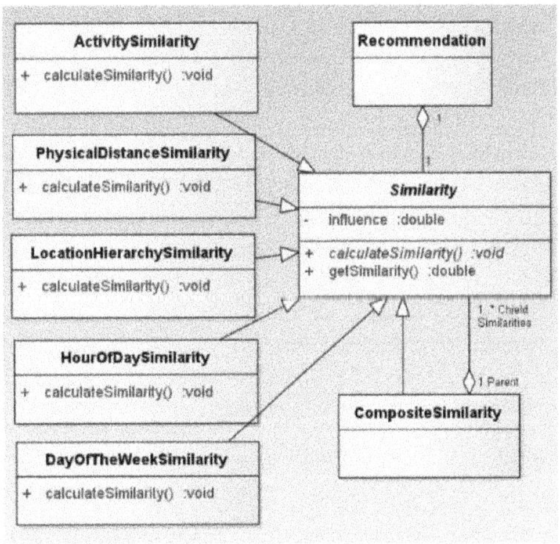

Figura 2 - Modelagem do cálculo de similaridade

A classe *Recomendation* realiza o cálculo de similaridade através de uma instância da classe *Similarity*, que abstrai toda a complexidade de composição do cálculo para todos os atributos contextuais utilizados e a atribuição de seus pesos de influência. O padrão de projeto *Composite* [18] foi utilizado, permitindo que toda uma hierarquia de objetos seja tratada uniformemente, podendo conter tanto objetos complexos (e.g., dimensões contextuais com diversas propriedades) quanto objetos simples (e.g., propriedades contextuais atômicas). O padrão permite que o cliente possa tratar a hierarquia de similaridades a partir de uma única instância da classe *Similarity*, que especifica o comportamento de todas as classes da hierarquia de objetos. A agregação de vários objetos de cálculo de similaridade pode ser feita pela classe *CompositySimilarity*. O módulo de recomendação é independente de domínio e pode ser reutilizado em outros sistemas, bastando somente que as classes de similaridades correspondentes sejam adicionadas. Além do módulo de recomendação, as próprias classes de cálculo de similaridade podem ser reaproveitadas e ainda armazenadas em componentes reutilizáveis de cálculo de similaridade.

3.3 Arquitetura do Sistema de Recomendação

A solução foi projetada seguindo uma arquitetura cliente-servidor para computação móvel baseada em *RestFul Web Services*, permitindo que dispositivos móveis de baixo processamento possam fazer uso do serviço. A Figura 3 representa uma visão geral do fluxo de execução do sistema.

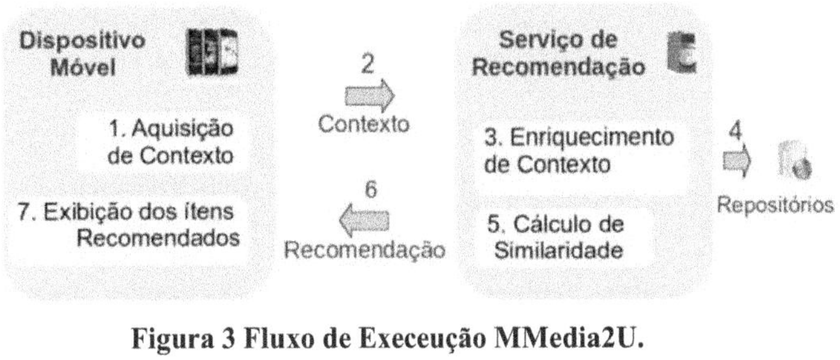

Figura 3 Fluxo de Execeução MMedia2U.

No passo 1, a aplicação de recomendação executada no dispositivo móvel é responsável por recuperar o contexto do usuário. Alguns tipos de informações (e.g., localização) podem ser adquiridos a partir de sensores (e.g., *GPS*). Outros tipos dependem de informações passadas pelo usuário (e.g., o usuário informa à aplicação qual a atividade sendo desempenhada). No segundo passo, a aplicação móvel acessa, a partir de uma chamada *HTTP*, o *Web-Service* disponibilizado pelo serviço de recomendação, informando o contexto atual do usuário. O serviço de recomendação, hospedado em um servidor *WEB*, ao receber a requisição, realiza o enriquecimento de contexto do usuário, incorporando novas informações a partir dos dados enviados. Os metadados das fotos armazenados no repositório são pesquisados e são comparados com o contexto passados. No passo 5, é elaborado um ranking de acordo com os cálculos de similaridade implementados e as fotos geradas em um contexto com maior similaridade ao do usuário são enviadas ao dispositivo móvel. O ranking retornado possui a *URL* das fotos e os seus metadados para que além do conteúdo o usuário possa também ter acesso às mesmas informações de contexto utilizadas pelo sistema.

3.4 Repositório de fotos

O sistema possui um repositório de fotos para recomendação, que precisam ter informações contextuais para que sejam comparadas com o contexto dos usuários a quem serão recomendadas. Precisa-se saber, por exemplo, a localização em que a foto foi tirada e a atividade de interesse do autor da foto no momento de sua geração. Em um primeiro momento, esperava-se utilizar diretamente bases de fotos de aplicações Web 2.0, tais como *Flickr* e *Picasa Web*. Entretanto, foi percebido que fotos destas bases não contêm todas as informações necessárias para o preenchimento do modelo de contexto e apresentavam erros em suas anotações. Assim, devido à indisponibilidade de bases corretas de fotos anotadas contextualmente, alguns atributos foram inseridos ou corrigidos nas imagens do *Picasa Web*. As fotos do repositório foram importadas do *Picasa Web* utilizando seus *web-services* para consulta de fotos georreferenciadas e disponibilizadas publicamente.

Além do conteúdo das fotos, os *web-services* do *Picasa Web* retornam os metadados no formato XML. Tais metadados contêm as informações utilizadas para alimentar o modelo de contexto das fotos com as informações de localização e data e hora. Para que estas informações possam ser lidas por visualizadores de fotos, elas precisam ser incorporadas ao arquivo da foto nos cabeçalhos *IPTC*[5] e *EXIF*[6]. A inserção, nos arquivos de cada foto, dos metadados recuperados do *Picase Web* foi feita utilizando-se a biblioteca de manipulação de metadados de imagens *Apache Sanselan*[7]. Após a incorporação dos metadados nas imagens, estes foram enriquecidos, manualmente, para que pudessem ser mais bem explorados no algoritmo de similaridade, exposto na seção 3.3. Exemplos de enriquecimento são a inferência da atividade de interesse a partir da descrição ou legendas das fotos e do dia da semana de acordo com a sua data de geração. Espera-se que com a evolução dos sistemas de gerenciamento de conteúdo multimídia, o esforço de enriquecimento e incorporação de metadados nas imagens seja bastante reduzido.

3.5 Aplicação Móvel

A Figura 4 apresenta um fluxo de execução da aplicação móvel. O usuário escolhe a "atividade/interesse", o sistema captura então as informações contextuais (localização e data/hora) e envia ao servidor. Este por sua vez, retorna uma lista de imagens recomendadas (terceira tela). Se o usuário selecionar uma foto, ele pode ver sua posição e a distância entre ele e o lugar onde a foto foi capturada e ao clicar na foto localizada no mapa seu conteúdo é exibido em tela cheia.

Figura 4 - Fluxo de execução da Aplicação Móvel

A aplicação móvel foi desenvolvida na plataforma *Android*[8], compatível com aparelhos que possuam a versão 2.2 ou superior. A comunicação com o servidor é realizada a partir de um *web-service restful* e os informações do contexto do usuário são trafegadas através de parâmetros *HTTP*. Na solicitação da recomendação ao servidor, somente um *XML* é retornado, contendo o ranking de fotos recomendadas. Para cada foto do ranking o *XML* contém a *URL* de seu conteúdo, a *URL* de sua miniatura suas informações contextuais e metadados. O retorno por *XML* poupa a banda da conexão de dados do dispositivo, já que somente o conteúdo daquelas fotos selecionadas pelo o usuário na terceira tela da Figura 4 é que será carregado.

4. EXPERIMENTOS

Avaliar um sistema de recomendação não é uma tarefa das mais simples, pois a relevância do item recomendado tem um caráter pessoal muito forte e, muitas vezes, complexo de ser medido. Esta dificuldade é potencializada em sistemas *WEB* 2.0, em que a falta de dados históricos de avaliações de referência requerem que os itens recomendados sejam avaliados manualmente, tornando estudos em larga escala muito onerosos e difíceis de serem reproduzidos [17]. Em um sistema de recomendação sensível ao contexto, a complexidade cresce ainda mais, pois é difícil variar os contextos possíveis em situações reais (i.e., diversos lugares, situações diárias, atividades, etc.). Uma validação objetiva repetível de um sistema de recomendação requer a existência de uma base histórica de avaliações dos itens pelos usuários. Os itens recomendados são então comparados com os dados históricos e se analisa quantos destes estão entre os mais bem avaliados, medindo-se a precisão [4] de acerto da recomendação.

Devido à inexistência de uma base histórica de avaliações de fotos anotadas contextualmente, foi necessária a construção de um *Gold Standard*, que consistiu em um repositório de fotos avaliadas como interessantes por usuários em determinados contextos.

O *Gold Standard* funcionou ao mesmo tempo como base para validação do sistema na versão sem treinamento (na qual os pesos do cálculo de similaridade foram atribuídos manualmente) e como base histórica na versão do sistema com treinamento (na qual os pesos do cálculo de similaridade foram atribuídos pelo método dos Mínimos Quadrados). Na construção do *Gold Standard*, foi pedido que um grupo de 13 usuários avaliassem fotos em oito diferentes contextos, cada contexto consistindo em uma etapa de avaliação. Em cada etapa, um contexto (e.g., momento de compras na orla marítima da cidade de Fortaleza no período noturno) foi apresentado ao usuário e foi pedido que ele visualizasse um conjunto de fotos e indicasse aquelas que mais despertaram o seu interesse considerando estarem inseridos no contexto sugerido. As fotos escolhidas pelos usuários passaram a compor o *Gold Standard*

5 http://www.iptc.org/IPTC4XMP/

6 http://www.cipa.jp/english/hyoujunka/kikaku/pdf/DC-008-2010_E.pdf

7 http://commons.apache.org/imaging/

8 http://developer.android.com/

e serviram de base histórica sob a qual a recomendação do MMedia2U foi comparada. O grau de sucesso da recomendação foi então avaliado pela proporção das fotos recomendadas que estão presentes no *Gold Standard* (e.g., se para um determinado contexto 10 fotos foram recomendadas e 6 destas fotos estão contidas no *Gold Standard* deste contexto, a precisão da recomendação é 0.6).

Em cada etapa de avaliação, uma média de 100 fotos foi visualizada pelos usuários, das quais 20 foram tiradas em contextos semelhantes ao passado ao usuário e 80 diferiam, em diferentes dimensões do contexto apresentado (e.g., atividade igual, localização bem distinta). Cinco dos 13 usuários não conheciam o lugar escolhido como localização do usuário (a orla turística de Fortaleza). Alguns dos usuários avaliaram as oito coleções de fotos, outros somente um subconjunto delas com um total de 66 avaliações.

4.1 RESULTADOS QUANTITATIVOS

Objetivou-se com o experimento avaliar as seguintes hipóteses:

(H-I) é possível realizar recomendações satisfatórias de fotos georeferenciadas sem conhecimento prévio do usuário, considerando apenas seu contexto atual;

(H-II) o contexto em que as fotos foram tiradas possui relevância na realização de recomendações; e

(H-III) a utilização de um modelo de contexto considerando várias dimensões contextuais pode trazer ganhos em relação a uma recomendação que utiliza somente um atributo contextual (e.g., a localização).

Para responder a estes questionamentos, o algoritmo foi executado com diferentes pesos para cada dimensão contextual sem uma base de treinamento prévio e em uma versão com treinamento prévio. Nas execuções sem treinamento, foram atribuídos pesos iguais e peso 1 para cada dimensão para validar as hipóteses. Uma combinação baseada em observações empíricas sobre a importância das dimensões contextuais para o gerenciamento de fotos pessoais também foi realizada (Comb I).

A execução baseada em histórico utilizou os pesos obtidos a partir do treinamento do algoritmo em que, para uma base de fotos, as avaliações feitas nas outras 7 bases foram utilizadas como treinamento pelo método *n-fold* [5]. A obtenção dos pesos nos dados de treinamento foi feita por regressão linear utilizando o método dos Mínimos Quadrados.

Para avaliar e comparar essas execuções foram calculadas as precisões da recomendação de acordo com a alteração da quantidade de fotos recomendadas. À medida que o tamanho da lista de fotos recomendadas aumenta, a tendência é que a proporção de recomendações corretas diminua. É salutar ressaltar que a lista de recomendação não deve ser extensa para uma visualisação em telas pequenas como a dos dispositivos móveis.

A Tabela 4 e o gráfico da Figura 5 mostram a média da precisão das execuções do algoritmo de recomendação em relação a quatro tamanhos de listas de recomendação (Top 3, Top 5, Top 10 e Top 20). Na Tabela 4, vemos que a média da precisão do algoritmo sem treinamento, atribuindo pesos iguais a todas as medidas de similaridade foi de 0.54 para o *Top 5* (5 itens recomendados). Utilizando os pesos obtidos pelos mínimos quadrados, a precisão do Top 5 foi de 0.55. Recuperando-se as fotos de maneira aleatória, sem o ranking gerado pela recomendação, a média da precisão foi de 0.28. As duas últimas linhas da tabela mostram a média da precisão ao se utilizar o cálculo de similaridade de somente uma das dimensões contextuais. A Comb I que obteve os melhores resultados foi aquela que atribuímos o dobro de importância da Atividade em relação à Localização e o quádruplo em relação aos atributos temporais.

Comparando-se os resultados obtidos sem treinamento (Comb I e Pesos Iguais) em relação ao experimento aleatório vemos que é possível recomendar com a precisão bem maior do que a escolha aleatória (corroborando com as hipóteses H-I e H-II). Além disso, o ganho não foi tão acentuado ao considerar somente uma dimensão contextual (e.g., somente localização ou somente atividade), nos levando a crer que um modelo de contexto completo é essencial para uma boa recomendação contextual (hipótese H-III).

Para dar maior validade aos resultados apresentados, a utilização de um teste estatístico foi realizada. Por exemplo, foi utilizado o teste *t-Student* nos valores de precisão para o *Top 3* obtidos pelos algoritmos comparados com o resultado obtido pela escolha aleatória de fotos. Tal utilização mostrou que a combinação dos atributos contextuais é significativamente melhor que a escolha aleatória (grau de confiança 95%, probabilidade < 0,0001) e, além disto, mostrou que a utilização de apenas um atributo (localização ou atividade, por exemplo) não é significativamente melhor que a escolha aleatória. Por fim, a comparação entre os resultados da Comb 1 e do MQ resultou em diferenças de performance sem significância estatística, o que pode indicar a não necessidade de treinamento para melhoria da precisão do sistema de recomendação.

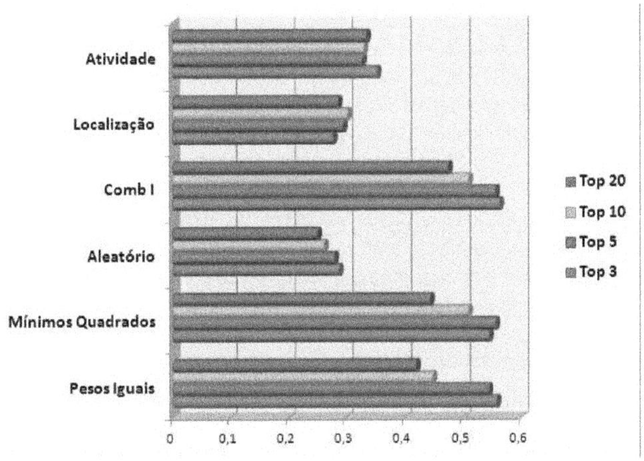

Figura 5 - Comparativo da média das precisões obtidas.

	Top 3	Top 5	Top 10	Top 20
Pesos Iguais	0.56	0.54	0.45	0.42
Mínimos Quadrados	0.54	0.56	0.51	0.44
Aleatório	0.29	0.28	0.26	0.25
Combinação 1	0.56	0.56	0.51	0.47
Somente Localização	0.28	0.30	0.30	0.29
Somente Atividade	0.35	0.33	0.33	0.34

Tabela 4. Valores médios das precisões obtidas

4.2 QUESTIONÁRIO COM OS USUÁRIOS

Em cada etapa dos experimentos, um questionário era aplicado aos usuários para que fossem investigados fatores relevantes na implementação de um sistema de recomendação contextual de fotos. Um dos fatores a ser investigado era o da própria relevância de um sistema móvel de recomendação de fotos e no caso da existência de tal sistema, se seria interessante a recomendação de fotos tiradas em um contexto parecido ao que se encontra o usuário. Nos experimentos, a cada novo contexto passado ao usuário, lhe era perguntado se, nesse contexto específico, ele gostaria de receber recomendações de fotos tiradas em um contexto parecido. O grau de interesse por um sistema de recomendação de fotos foi de 74% das ocasiões apresentadas. Os motivos variaram dentre aqueles que, em um contexto específico, não teriam interesse na recomendação. Algumas respostas foram de que a recomendação não seria interessante naquele contexto porque o usuário já conhecia bem a localização dada. Outros disseram que em uma atividade como festas, não teriam o interessem de acessar nenhum tipo de aplicativo móvel e que a recomendação seria interessante, possivelmente, em um período posterior. Quando perguntados se, de maneira geral sem considerar um contexto específico, a recomendação de fotos geradas em contextos similares seria interessante, o grau de interesse foi de 100%.

Outro ponto investigado foi a relevância relativa de cada dimensão contextual. A cada usuário foi perguntado qual a dimensão contextual, entre localização, atividade de interesse e data e hora, eles prefeririam que as fotos recomendadas mais se aproximassem das deles. Oito dos usuários responderam que acham a proximidade da localização da foto o fator mais importante para despertar seu interesse. Cinco dos usuários responderam que associação da atividade retratada pela foto com a atividade que ele está desempenhando no momento é o fator mais importante. Nenhum usuário achou a similaridade entre data e hora o fator mais importante.

5. CONCLUSÃO E TRABALHO FUTURO

Este trabalho apresentou o MMedia2U, um sistema de recomendação contextual de fotos. Na elaboração do sistema, foi construído um modelo de contexto para a representação de informações contextuais relacionadas à recomendação. Técnicas de recomendação baseadas em conhecimento foram adaptadas com a incorporação da sensibilidade ao contexto, permitindo que itens, mesmo sem nunca terem sido avaliados, possam ser recomendados somente a partir do seu contexto de geração. A extensão proposta também proporciona que um usuário, mesmo sem histórico de uso do sistema, receba recomendações de acordo com seu contexto atual. Um algoritmo de recomendação e fórmulas de cálculo de similaridade para um conjunto de dimensões contextuais foram propostos e implementados. A responsabilidade da recomendação e do cálculo de similaridade foi separada para que tanto os algoritmos de recomendação quanto as fórmulas de similaridade possam ser reutilizados em outros sistemas. A aplicação móvel de recomendação foi construída acessando remotamente o serviço de recomendação e exibindo as fotos aos usuários.

A recomendação foi validada a partir da construção de um *Gold Standard* e a média da precisão obtida pelo algoritmo nos permitiu concluir que, para os dados utilizados, a sensibilidade ao contexto pode trazer ganhos na recomendação de fotos se comparado a uma lista aleatória. Mesmo combinações de peso que não utilizaram treinamento (a Comb I e pesos iguais) obtiveram resultados satisfatórios. Assim, a utilização do sistema pode ser feita mesmo sem uma base histórica de utilização, reduzindo o inconveniente do início frio de sistemas de recomendação tradicionais. Além disso, o questionário sugere que sistemas desta natureza despertam o interesse de usuários.

É importante ressaltar que os resultados não podem ser generalizados (dependência dos usuários e da base de fotos utilizadas), entretanto funcionam como um bom indicativo de qualidade do protótipo de recomendação. A análise destes resultados foi limitada ao tamanho da base de fotos utilizada (655 fotos, com 335 de duas regiões turísticas de Fortaleza), pois o aumento da base poderia diminuir a precisão do algoritmo ou apresentar problemas de concentração de fotos em determinados lugares. Bases de fotos colaborativas, como o Flickr e o Picasa, poderão apresentar este problema. Nestes casos, novos filtros de busca e algoritmos de clusterização poderiam ser utilizados para amenizar estes desafios. Apesar disso, os resultados já são encorajadores para a construção de bases de fotos contextuais enriquecidas de pontos turísticos (e.g. pontos de interesse de cidades sede da Copa do Mundo de 2014).

Como trabalho futuro, deseja-se aumentar a base de fotos enriquecidas usando uma evolução do sistema CoMMeDiA [3], de forma a garantir a exatidão das informações anotadas contextualmente e a sua aquisição de forma automática. Em seguida, espera-se avaliar o sistema com usuários (turista ou não) em situação de mobilidade real em vários lugares de Fortaleza. Nesta nova versão do sistema, deseja-se integrar algoritmos de clusterização dos resultados e permitir aos usuários acrescentar palavras de interesse, com intuito de aumentar a precisão das recomendações.

6. REFERÊNCIAS

[1] Van Setten, M., Pokraev, S. and Koolwaaij, J. 2004. Context-aware recommendations in the mobile tourist application compass. In *Adaptive Hypermedia and Adaptative Web-Based Systems*, 235–244

[2] Xia, S., Gong, X., Wang, W., Tian, Y., Yang, X., and Ma, J. 2010. Context-Aware Image Annotation and Retrieval on Mobile Device. In *Second International Conference on Multimedia and Information Technology*, 111-114.

[3] Viana, W., Miron, A., Moisuc, B., Gensel, J., Villanova-Oliver M., and Martin, H. 2011. Towards the semantic and context-aware management of mobile multimedia. In *Multimedia Tools and Applications*, v. 53, 391-429

[4] McLaughlin , M. R. and Herlocker, J. L. 2004. A collaborative filtering algorithm and evaluation metric that accurately model the user experience. In *Proceedings of the 27th annual international ACM SIGIR conference on Research and development in information retrieval*

[5] Jannach, D., Zanker, M., Felfernig, A. and Friedrich, G. 2010. Recommender Systems, an Introduction. In *Cambridge University Press*, first edition

[6] Baldauf, M., Dustdar, S. and Rosenberg, F. 2007. A survey on context aware systems. In *International Journal of Ad Hoc and Ubiquitous Computing Volume* 2 Issue 4 , 263-277.

[7] Abowd, G. and Dey, A. 1999. Towards a Better Understanding of Context and Context-Awareness. In *Proceedings of the 1st international symposium on Handheld and Ubiquitous Computing*

[8] Marinho, F. G., Costa, A. L., Lima, F. F. P., Neto, J. B. B., Filho, J. B. F., Rocha, L., Dantas, V. L. L., Andrade, R. M. C., Teixeira, E. and Werner, C. 2010. An Architecture Proposal for Nested Software Product Lines in the Domain of Mobile and Context-Aware Applications. In *Fourth Brazilian Symposium on Software Components, Architectures and Reuse*, 51-60

[9] Adomavicius, G. and Tuzhilin, A. 2010. Context-Aware Recommender Systems. In *Recommender Systems Handbook: A Complete Guide for Research Scientists and Practitioners*, Springer Press, first edition

[10] Lee, J. S. and Lee, J. C. 2007. Context awareness by case-based reasoning in a music recommendation system. In

Proceedings of the 4th international conference on Ubiquitous computing systems

[11] Burke, R. 2000. Knowledge-Based Recommender Systems. In *Encyclopedia of Library and Information Systems,* no. 32, 180-200

[12] Albanese, M., d'Acierno, A., Moscato, V., Persia, F. and Picariello, A. 2011. A Multimedia Semantic Recommender System in Cultural Heritage Applications. In *Semantic Computing (ICSC), 2011 Fifth IEEE International Conference on* , pp.403-410, 18-21

[13] Boutemedjet , S. and Ziou , D. 2010. Using Images in Context Aware Recommender Systems, *In Proc of 1st Int'l Workshop on Adaptation, Personalization and Recommendation in the Social-semantic Web*

[14] Braga, R. B., Carvalho, W. V., Andrade, R. M. C. and Martin, H. 2011. CAPTAIN: Uma ferramenta para geração de diários de bordo digitais usando anotação contextual e conteúdo multimídia. In: *Simpósio Brasileiro de Sistemas Multimídia e Web WebMedia, 2011*

[15] Rost, M., Cramer, H., and Holmquist, L. E. 2011. Mobile exploration of geotagged photographs. In *Personal and Ubiquitous Computing*

[16] Santos, G. and Ferraz, C. 2011. Uma Arquitetura Flexível de Suporte à Execução de Algoritmos de Recomendação de Programas em TV Conectada. In *Simpósio Brasileiro de Sistemas Multimídia e Web WebMedia, 2011*

[17] Siersdorfer, S. and Sizov, S. 2009. Social recommender systems for web 2.0 folksonomies. In *Proceedings of the 20th ACM conference on Hypertext and hypermedia* (HT '09)

[18] Gamma, E., Helm, R., Johnson, R., and Vlissides , J. 1995. Design Patterns: Elements of Reusable Object-Oriented Software. Addison-Wesley Longman Publishing Co.

[19]] Mcsherry, D. 2003. Similarity and Compromise. In *Proceedings of the Fifth International Conference on Case-Based Reasoning*

[20] Slimani, T., Yaghlane, B. B. and Mellouli , K. 2006. A New Similarity Measure based on Edge Counting. In *Proceedings of* World Academy of Science, Engineering and Technology

Interacting with TV: Report of a User Experience Evaluation Considering Affective State

Ewerton M. de Menezes, Lara S. G. Piccolo, Cláudia de A. Tambascia
CPqD – Centro de Pesquisa e Desenvolvimento em Telecomunicações
Rod. Campinas Mogi-Mirim, km 118,5 – Campinas, SP
{emenezes, lpiccolo, claudiat}@cpqd.com.br

ABSTRACT

The way people relate with technology nowadays requires more from human-computer interaction methods: good usability is an essential condition, but users expect also a pleasant and funny experience, especially when entertainment is the purpose. This paper reports the usability evaluation of games and of an e-commerce application for interactive TV, which considered users' affective state, and highlights this approach benefits to analyze the interaction design.

RESUMO

A maneira como as pessoas se relacionam com a tecnologia atualmente exige mais dos métodos de interação humano-computador: boa usabilidade é uma condição essencial, mas os usuários esperam também ter uma experiência prazerosa e divertida, especialmente quando o objetivo é entretenimento. Este artigo relata a avaliação de usabilidade de jogos e de uma aplicação de comércio eletrônico na TV interativa que considerou o estado afetivo do usuário, e destaca os benefícios dessa abordagem na análise do design da interação.

Categories and Subject Descriptors

H.5.2 [**User Interface**]: Evaluation/methodology

Palavras-chave

TV interativa, usabilidade, qualidade afetiva, emoção, afeto

1. INTRODUÇÃO

Criar interfaces de usuário que sejam fáceis de aprender, eficientes e eficazes não são mais os únicos desafios do projetista de interação. Proporcionar uma boa experiência para o usuário, de forma que a utilização do artefato desperte sensações positivas, tais como prazer e conforto [5][9], é um importante desafio.

Para Ortony et al [7], as ações humanas tem componentes cognitivos e afetivos: a cognição atribui significado, e o sistema afetivo atribui valor, julgando coisas no ambiente como positivas ou negativas [6]. Há evidências de que o afeto influencia a fixação de memórias de longo-prazo, reforça processo de aprendizado, planejamento, experimentação e foco de atenção [7]. Por isso, artefatos que despertam afeto positivo são mais fáceis de aprender, mais regularmente usados, influenciam decisões de compras e produzem melhores resultados [12].

Tractinsky et al [11] comprovaram a correlação entre usabilidade, relacionada à eficiência e eficácia na interação, e a estética. Objetos considerados esteticamente atraentes funcionam melhor porque o processo de cognição envolve o sistema afetivo, que por sua vez, é influenciado pela estética [2][7]. As características da interface de usuário que levam a esse julgamento positivo podem ser atribuídas à qualidade afetiva da interface [1], conceito associado à abordagem do *Design Emocional*, proposto por Norman [6], que explica porque alguns objetos do dia-a-dia são adorados e outros não, e como o design pode influenciar o sistema afetivo de um indivíduo.

A avaliação do estado afetivo do usuário durante a interação e sua associação com o design é foco de atenção de pesquisas na área de Interação Humano-Computador. Diversas abordagens têm sido propostas, tais como coleta de medidas fisiológicas ou métodos que questionam o usuário, esse último, porém, com o desafio de lidar com a subjetividade associada inclusive para denominar emoções de maneira consensual. O *Self-Assessment Manikin* (SAM) [4], Figura 1, é exemplo de um questionário gráfico que permite mensurar o estado emocional do usuário em diferentes níveis. Em [1] e [3], o SAM foi aplicado para mensurar a qualidade afetiva de interfaces, em [1] para avaliar qualidade hedônica na TV interativa.

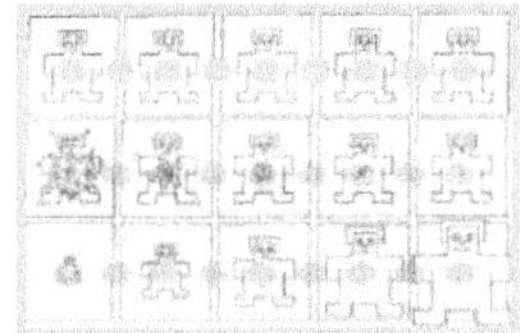

Figura 1. SAM [4], artefato de avaliação

A fim de complementar uma proposta de método avaliação de Qualidade da Experiência (QoE) na TV [8], o estado afetivo do usuário foi considerado na avaliação de dois tipos de aplicativos: comércio eletrônico e jogos. O objetivo geral da avaliação era associar parâmetros de rede de transmissão de dados e sua consequência na experiência de uso. Uma abordagem simplificada para coletar o estado afetivo do usuário a partir de imagens foi criada e aplicada experimentalmente. Essa prática permitiu obter informações importantes sobre a satisfação do usuário que dificilmente seriam obtidas por meio de avaliações tradicionais de usabilidade.

As seções subsequentes descrevem os aplicativos avaliados, o processo de avaliação desde a construção do repertório de imagens e os principais resultados. A contribuição desse trabalho é compartilhar os benefícios de considerar o estado afetivo do usuário na avaliação da experiência de uso de sistemas interativos, apontando a necessidade de aprimoramentos futuros.

2. APLICATIVOS PARA TV INTERATIVA

No escopo de um projeto de Pesquisa e Desenvolvimento de serviços multiplataforma para a TV interativa [8], foram desenvolvidos aplicativos com requisitos de rede e de interação variados. Dentre eles, um serviço de comércio eletrônico e um conjunto de jogos foram selecionados para o experimento de avaliação do estado afetivo do usuário.

Permission to make digital or hard copies of all or part of this work for personal or classroom use is granted without fee provided that copies are not made or distributed for profit or commercial advantage and that copies bear this notice and the full citation on the first page. To copy otherwise, or republish, to post on servers or to redistribute to lists, requires prior specific permission and/or a fee.
WebMedia'12, October 15–18, 2012, São Paulo/SP, Brazil.
Copyright 2012 ACM 978-1-4503-1706-1/12/10...$15.00.

2.1 Comércio eletrônico

Neste aplicativo, os produtos anunciados são organizados em categorias e subcategorias. Pelo controle-remoto, o usuário pode navegar pelos menus, fazer uma busca por palavra-chave, ou acessar produtos em destaques. Para comprar ou fazer perguntar ao vendedor, o usuário tem que ser cadastrado. Além disso, ele pode acompanhar o status da compra e avaliar o produto adquirido. O pagamento da compra pode ser feito preenchendo dados de um cartão de crédito ou por transferência de créditos de outro usuário do aplicativo.

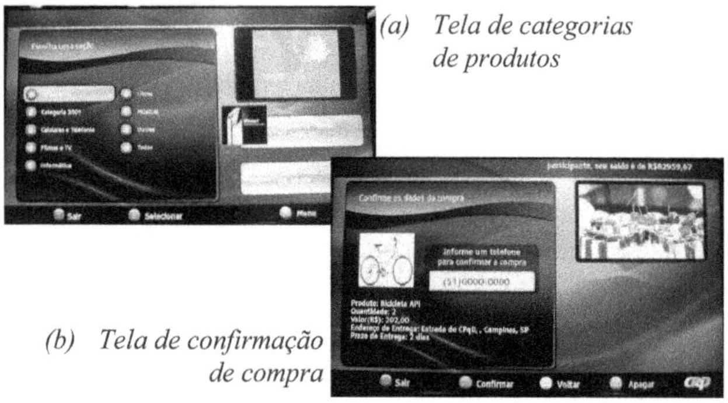

(a) Tela de categorias de produtos

(b) Tela de confirmação de compra

Figura 2. Telas do aplicativo de comércio eletrônico

Na Figura 2a, a tela inicial é ilustrada com categorias de produtos e alguns produtos em destaque. A Figura 2b se refere à tela de confirmação dos dados de compra do produto. Por ser um tipo de serviço difundido na Web, é esperada uma expectativa mais alta em relação a desempenho e efetividade de mecanismos de busca de produtos por usuários mais experientes. Além disso, é comum que provedores desse tipo de serviço invistam na boa experiência da interação visando não só ganhar novos clientes, mas também fidelizá-los. A avaliação afetiva buscou identificar os pontos em que a interação provocou respostas afetivas incompatíveis: neutras, quando era esperada certa empolgação, ou negativas.

2.2 Jogos

Cinco aplicativos de jogos foram avaliados: Campo Minado e Snake, que são adaptações de jogos populares em computadores; o Jogo da Memória, que requer a memorização de pares de cartas do baralho; o Fantasmas, um tipo de puzzle 'match 3' onde o usuário precisa completar conjuntos de 3 fantasmas de mesma cor para eliminá-los do tabuleiro; por fim, o jogo de tabuleiro Damas, projetado para dois jogadores.

Figura 3. Telas dos jogos desenvolvidos para TV Digital

Todos os jogos funcionam com interatividade local, ou seja, não requerem comunicação com a rede de dados. Na Figura 3 são apresentadas a tela inicial para seleção do jogo (a), seguida pela tela do Jogo de Damas (b), Fantasmas (c), Campo minado (d), Snake (e) e Memória (f).

A usabilidade no contexto dos jogos apresenta certas peculiaridades. Por exemplo, erros na operação indesejáveis em outros domínios são esperados em alguns jogos, uma vez que eles são projetados para desafiar usuários e forçá-los a desenvolver suas habilidades. Estratégias de engajamento, tais como níveis, geração de estímulos, etc. são também comumente aplicadas para entreter o usuário em uma meta por um período de tempo. Pinelle et al [9] definem usabilidade no contexto de jogos como a facilidade com que um jogador pode aprender, controlar e entender o jogo. Questões como entretenimento, engajamento e enredo foram avaliadas do ponto de vista de afetivo.

3. ARTEFATO PARA A AVALIAÇÃO

Como identificar, denominar e expressar o estado emocional são grandes desafios na avaliação da qualidade afetiva. A fim de criar um modelo consensual, um conjunto de imagens representando estados emocionais humanos foi proposto. O repertório foi composto por 9 imagens: 4 associadas a estados afetivos positivos, 2 associadas a estados afetivos neutros e 3 associadas a estados afetivos negativos.

O conjunto de imagens passou por um processo de validação antes de ser usado nas avaliações. Um grupo de 48 pessoas participou de uma pesquisa on-line, onde foram requisitados a atribuir uma palavra ou expressão às imagens apresentadas sem nenhum contexto ou descrição adicional. Como resultado, grande parte das imagens gerou um conjunto coerente de palavras e expressões associadas, indicando que seu significado era semelhante para a maioria dos participantes; outras apresentaram um conjunto diverso de interpretações, e por isso foram desconsideradas. Essa validação resultou nas imagens da Figura 4. Os índices dessas imagens são usados ao longo do texto para referenciá-las.

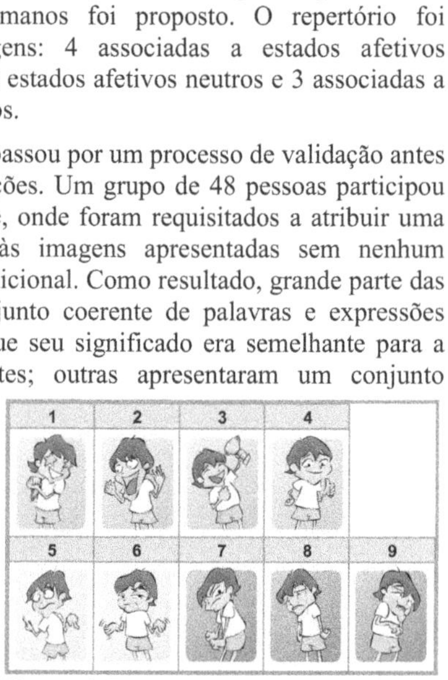

Figura 4. Imagens usadas na avaliação

4. METODOLOGIA

As interfaces interativas foram avaliadas em duas etapas: 1) inspeção de usabilidade por especialistas; 2) avaliação com usuários representativos do público-alvo, etapa que incluiu a avaliação afetiva. Nessa etapa, os usuários foram convidados a executar determinadas tarefas em um ambiente similar a uma sala de estar, interagindo por meio do controle remoto a uma distância de cerca de 2,5 metros da TV.

Um grupo de 30 participantes de perfis variados avaliou o aplicativo de comercio eletrônico. A fim de limitar o tempo da atividade, evitando assim a fadiga do participante, as tarefas descritas na Tabela 1 foram sorteadas, de forma que cada tarefa foi avaliada por no mínimo 7 usuários.

Ao final de cada tarefa o participante foi convidado a escolher a imagem da Figura 4 que melhor traduzia seu estado afetivo, e associava a imagem a uma palavra ou expressão. Dessa forma, foi possível coletar a percepção da experiência de uso de pequenos módulos que, aliados aos tempos de realização das tarefas, permitiram identificar os pontos críticos da aplicação.

Na avaliação dos jogos, os usuários eram convidados a escolher dois dos jogos apresentados na tela inicial (Damas, Fantasmas, Campo minado, Cobrinha e Memória). Não houve nenhuma restrição quanto ao tempo de execução destinado a cada jogo. Essa avaliação qualitativa contou com 5 participantes experientes no uso de jogos. O usuário era encorajado a verbalizar suas dúvidas e observações. Ao final de cada jogo o participante escolhia uma das 9 imagens da Figura 4, associando uma palavra ou expressão.

Tabela 1. Tarefas executadas no comércio eletrônico

Id	Descrição	
1	Efetuar a compra pelo nome completo do produto na busca	Mais complexas
2	Efetuar a compra utilizando ferramenta de busca de produtos	
3	Efetuar a compra buscando um produto pelo nome utilizando teclado numérico	
4	Fazer uma pergunta ao vendedor de um produto	
5	Comprar um produto escolhendo o mais barato	
6	Verificar perguntas direcionadas ao vendedor de um produto	
7	Efetuar compra de um determinado valor em créditos	
8	Verificar as qualificações do vendedor de um produto	Menos complexas
9	Comprar produto em destaque na aplicação	
10	Inserir um produto na lista de desejos	
11	Consultar produtos da lista de desejos	
12	Excluir um produto da lista de desejos	
13	Verificar informações de como comprar pela TV (help)	
14	Trocar a senha de usuário	

5. RESULTADOS

5.1 Comércio eletrônico

A Tabela 2 resume o perfil dos participantes da avaliação. A maioria tem TV interativa em suas casas, no entanto, foi identificado em entrevistas que 62% dos participantes tinham pouca familiaridade com os recursos interativos de suas TV. O recurso interativo mais conhecido foi o guia eletrônico de programação de seus provedores de TV por assinatura.

Tabela 2. Perfil dos participantes do teste

Gênero	Homens	73%
	Mulheres	27%
Faixa etária	Até 20	13%
	De 21 a 30 anos	57%
	De 31 a 40 anos	13%
	De 41 a 50 anos	17%
TV interativa	Com TV em casa	90%
	Sem TV em casa	10%

Um total de 130 imagens foram selecionadas na avaliação, sendo 63% delas associadas a estados afetivos positivos e 37% a estados afetivos negativos ou neutros. As imagens 3 e 4 foram as mais populares, selecionadas 22 e 60 vezes, respectivamente.

Considerando a frequência de utilização das imagens e as palavras associadas à seleção de cada uma delas, pode-se validar a aplicação das imagens no contexto da avaliação. A Figura 5 ilustra por meio de nuvens de palavras as mais associadas a cada imagem, por ordem de frequência geral de utilização.

A **imagem 4** foi escolhida predominantemente em situações sem grandes dificuldades, mas em que o usuário também não se surpreendeu. Já a **imagem 3** foi usada em situações de dificuldades, mas que o usuário superou gerando um sentimento de orgulho e vitória. As **imagens 5 e 6** estavam associadas a situações de confusão, dúvidas e tempo de execução maior que o tolerável; a **imagem 6** foi usada também para tarefas realizadas com pouco esforço mas confusas. A **imagem 7** já foi usada quando a aplicação de fato decepcionou o usuário provocando inclusive retrabalho. Por fim a **imagem 1** foi usada em pontos onde a aplicação surpreendeu os usuários pela sua facilidade e utilidade.

Figura 5. Palavras associadas a cada imagem

Correlacionando o tempo médio de execução das tarefas e as imagens escolhidas, podemos observar uma relação entre o tempo empreendido e o estado afetivo. As tarefas que inspiraram estados afetivos positivos foram realizadas com um tempo médio de 1 min 46 s, ao passo que as tarefas que geraram estados afetivos indiferentes ou negativos tiveram um tempo médio de 2 min 29 s. Entretanto, esse resultado precisa ser melhor investigado considerando também elementos de interface que poderiam interferir nos resultados.

Tabela 3. Imagens escolhidas por tarefa

Tarefas	Imagens 1	2	3	4	5	6	7	8	9
1	3	0	1	3	0	0	1	0	0
2	0	1	4	4	0	1	1	0	1
3	0	0	1	6	0	0	1	0	0
4	0	1	1	3	1	3	1	0	0
5	0	1	3	2	0	2	2	2	0
6	0	0	2	3	1	2	0	0	0
7	1	1	2	2	1	1	0	0	0
8	0	0	2	5	0	0	0	0	0
9	0	0	1	4	0	1	1	1	0
10	1	1	0	7	1	1	0	0	0
11	1	0	1	4	1	2	0	0	0
12	0	0	1	5	3	1	1	0	0
13	0	0	2	9	0	0	0	0	0
14	0	0	1	4	0	2	0	0	1

A Tabela 3 mostra a avaliação afetiva das 14 tarefas. Observa-se um padrão diferente entre as mais complexas e as menos complexas: enquanto as imagens atribuídas às tarefas mais complexas apresentaram uma grande variação, nas menos complexas a variação foi bem menor, se concentrando na **imagem 4**, que representam pontos onde a usabilidade não comprometeu a experiência de uso mas que também não empolgou o usuário. Essa concentração em torno da **imagem 4** é um indicativo de que as tarefas menos complexas não estimularam uma resposta afetiva significativa, nem negativa nem positiva.

A entrada de dados na TV é limitada pelas características ergonômicas do controle remoto, o que influencia negativamente a usabilidade das tarefas que envolviam inserção de textos. Na avaliação afetiva, essa influência tornou-se mais nítida nas tarefas que envolviam busca de produto e realização de perguntas ao vendedor (**Tarefas 1 a 4**), com a atribuição de várias imagens relacionadas a estados afetivos negativos. No entanto, a tarefa de compras teve uma avaliação mais positiva que a de realização de perguntas, provavelmente por estar mais alinhada com os objetivos finais da aplicação.

Os problemas de usabilidade envolvendo falta de consistência, prevenção a erros e compatibilidade com o mundo real foram os que mais influenciaram estados afetivos negativos nos participantes. A compra de produtos em destaque, por exemplo, (**Tarefa 9**) teve uma avaliação afetiva tão ruim quanto as demais compras, mesmo sendo mais rápida. Nesse caso, muitos usuários finalizavam o processo de compra sem conseguir editar todas as informações necessárias, o que causou frustração. A exclusão de itens na lista de desejo (**Tarefa 12**), por sua vez, inspirou afeto negativo em função de cores que induziam o usuário a pressionar os botões coloridos do controle remoto, quando na verdade precisavam navegar entre as opções SIM e NÃO apresentadas na tela por meio dos botões direcionais.

5.2 Jogos

Por ter como um de seus principais objetivos engajar e entreter os jogadores, espera-se que a qualidade afetiva dos jogos seja mais intensa e variada que na aplicação de comércio eletrônico.

Os 5 participantes eram todos jovem de 16 a 26 anos, tinham contato com TV digital e computadores em suas casas, com hábitos variados relacionados à jogos de computadores.

Os estados afetivos escolhidos pelos participantes ao final de cada partida indicaram que mesmo com os problemas de usabilidade, os jogos conseguiram cumprir sua função de entretenimento. Das 9 imagens selecionadas apenas duas estavam ligadas a estados afetivos neutros, e nenhuma relacionadas à estados afetivos negativos. A Tabela 4 apresenta as imagens escolhidas pelos participantes detalhando as situações e os motivos para sua escolha.

Tabela 4. Resumo das imagens escolhidas pelos participantes

	Mais escolhida pelos participantes. Relacionada a situações de dificuldades, por causa da interface ou devido as regras do jogo, mas que foram superadas. Frases dos usuários relacionadas a essa imagem: "Legal, mas difícil de jogar", "Se sentiu desafiado" e "Deu vontade de jogar mais para aprender".
	Associada ao sentimento de conquista e superação - situações nas quais os participantes desconheciam as regras ou os comandos de interação, mas conseguiram superá-los em uma segunda tentativa. Selecionada nos jogos com marcação de tempo e nas damas, que permitia dois jogadores simultaneamente.
	Imagem foi escolhida por um usuário que teve uma resposta extremamente positiva em relação ao jogo. Ela foi acompanhada da frase: "Imagina um desses (jogo) na minha TV"
	Imagem escolhida por um usuário que se sentiu extremamente confuso pela falta de consistência e coerência na interface. Foi escolhida para indicar que o jogo estava maluco.
	Escolhida para representar tédio durante o jogo. O usuário que disse ter começado o jogo animado, e no final devido à demora em terminar a partida e falta de atributos lúdicos no jogo, terminou com sono.

6. CONCLUSÕES E DIRECIONAMENTOS

Apesar de experimental e simplificada, a avaliação considerando aspectos afetivos do usuário evidenciou seu valor ao revelar incômodos na interação que passaram despercebidos como problemas de usabilidade tradicionais. Além disso, tornou o processo de avaliação mais lúdico, contribuindo para que a tensão e o estresse típicos dessas situações fossem amenizados, deixando inclusive os participantes mais propensos a oferecer feedbacks sobre o sistema.

Solicitar ao participante a associação da imagem selecionada a uma palavra ou expressão foi uma boa prática para validar o significado da escolha, clarificando a análise dos resultados. Por outro lado, também evidenciou a complexidade de lidar com os fatores subjetivos da avaliação afetiva. Apesar do repertório de imagens ter sido validado antes da execução dos testes, as ambiguidades no significado das imagens estiveram presentes, justificando um novo processo de validação das imagens para um próximo experimento.

A associação de elementos de design com o estado afetivo é um ponto que precisa ser melhor investigado nesse tipo de avaliação, provavelmente associando a escolha da imagem com perguntas específicas sobre a tela em questão. Da mesma forma, a correlação com tempo esperado e realizado de execução de uma determinada tarefa é um indicativo que pode ser mais detalhadamente explorado.

7. AGRADECIMENTOS

Agradecemos ao FUNTTEL e ao Bruno Buccolo pelo apoio.

8. REFERÊNCIAS

[1] Chorianopoulos, K., Spinellis, D. 2006. User interface evaluation of interactive TV: a media studies perspective. *Univers. Access Inf. Soc.* 5, 2 (July 2006), Springer, 209-218.

[2] Damasio, A. 1994 *Descarte's error: Emotion, Reason and the Human Brain.* G. P. Putnam.

[3] Hayashi, E. C. S.; Baranauskas, M. C. C. Meta-communication in Inclusive Scenarios: Issues and Alternatives. *Anais IHC'2010*, SBC, 111-120.

[4] Lang, P. J., Bradley, M. M., Cuthbert, B. N. 2005. International affective picture system (IAPS): Instruction manual and affective ratings. *Technical Report A-6*, University of Florida;

[5] McCarthy, J., Wright, P. 2004. *Technology as experience.* MIT. Press, NY.

[6] Norman, D. 2004. *Emotional design: why we love (or hate) everyday things*. New York: Basic Books.

[7] Ortony, A., Norman, D. A., Revelle, W. 2005. The role of affect and proto-affect in effective functioning. *Who needs emotions? The brain meets the machine.* Oxford University Press, NY.

[8] Piccolo, L. S. G., Bonadia, G. C. e Tambascia, C. A. Aplicação de Técnicas e Métodos de IHC para Avaliar a QoE de Serviços. *Anais do IHC'2010,* SBC, 225-230.

[9] Pinelle, D. Wong, N. e Stach, T. 2008. Heuristic Evaluation for Games: Usability Principles for Video Game Design. *Proc. of ACM CHI 2008*, 1453-1462

[10] Preece, J. Rogers, Y. & Sharp, H. 2011. *Interaction Design: Beyond Human-Computer Interaction.* 3rd Edition. New York, NY, John Wiley & Sons.

[11] Tractinsky, N., Katz, A. S., Ilkar, D. 2000. What is beautiful is usable. *Interacting with Computers,* 13 (2), 127-145.

[12] Zhang, P., Li, N. 2005. The Importance of Affective Quality. Communications of the ACM. Sep, Vol. 48, N 9, 105-10

Analysis of Vulnerability to Facebook Users

Cristiano Silva
Universidade Federal de São João Del Rey
Ouro Branco, Brasil
cristiano@ufsj.edu.br

Michelle Hanne
Universidade Federal de Minas Gerais
Belo Horizonte, Brasil
michelle.hanne@dcc.ufmg.br

Jussara Almeida
Universidade Federal de Minas Gerais
Belo Horizonte, Brasil
jussara@dcc.ufmg.br

Marcos Gonçalves
Universidade Federal de Minas Gerais
Belo Horizonte, Brasil
mgoncalv@dcc.ufmg.br

ABSTRACT

Facebook, the largest social network nowadays currently has 901 million active users, with 526 million of them accessing the system daily. With a very rapid growth, Facebook has become a potential site for the collection of personal information by unauthorized individuals, leaving its users vulnerable to actions of violation of privacy, spamming and phishing. This article discusses the vulnerability of Facebook users based on their exposure in the network. To this end, we propose a numerical indicator capable of estimating the degree of vulnerability of each user. This indicator is a function of both the amount of personal content published by the user and the size of her network. We demonstrate the use of the proposed indicator in real data collected from 75,000 Facebook users.

RESUMO

O Facebook, maior rede social na atualidade, possui ativos 901 milhões de usuários, sendo que cerca de 526 milhões desses acessam-no diariamente. Com um crescimento vertiginoso, o Facebook tornou-se um local privilegiado para a obtenção de informações pessoais por indivíduos não autorizados, pois seus usuários estão vulneráveis a ações de violação da privacidade, *spamming* e *phishing*. Este artigo trata da vulnerabilidade de usuários do Facebook a partir da observação do seu grau de exposição na rede. Para tal, será proposto um indicador capaz de estimar o grau de vulnerabilidade de cada usuário, indicador o qual é função tanto da quantidade de conteúdo pessoal publicado pelo usuário quanto do tamanho de suas conexões de amizades. Finalmente, foi demonstrado o uso do indicador proposto em dados reais coletados de 75 mil usuários do Facebook.

Permission to make digital or hard copies of all or part of this work for personal or classroom use is granted without fee provided that copies are not made or distributed for profit or commercial advantage and that copies bear this notice and the full citation on the first page. To copy otherwise, to republish, to post on servers or to redistribute to lists, requires prior specific permission and/or a fee.

WebMedia'12, October 15–18, 2012, São Paulo/SP, Brazil.

Copyright 2012 ACM 978-1-4503-1706-1/12/10 ...$15.00.

Categories and Subject Descriptors

C.4 [**Computer Systems Organization**]: Performance of systems—*Measurement techniques*; H.3.5 [**Information Storage and Retrieval**]: Online Information Service—*Web-based Services*; K.4.1 [**Computers and Society**]: Public Policy Issues—*Privacy*; K.6.5 [**Management of Computing and Information Systems**]: [Security and protection]

General Terms

Human Factors, Measurement, Experimentation, Security

Keywords

Vulnerability, Exposure, Social Networks, Facebook

1. INTRODUÇÃO

Sites de redes sociais tornaram-se vias populares para a comunicação entre pessoas, caracterizando como vivenciamos a Internet nos dias de hoje. A colaboração instantânea, o compartilhamento e a relação entre amigos, grupos e comunidades compõem um novo paradigma de interação na Web, o qual já supera a utilização do correio eletrônico. Tomando como exemplo a rede Facebook[1], composta por 901 milhões de usuários ativos, essa contabiliza 125 bilhões de conexões de amizades e recebe diariamente 300 milhões de novas fotos e em média 3,2 bilhões de ações de curtir e comentários [9].

As redes sociais atraem o interesse das pessoas por sua capacidade de potencializar a comunicação, o que implica em algum grau de vulnerabilidade de seus usuários. Práticas de proteção à privacidade parecem paradoxais nas redes sociais, já que o ato de compartilhar conflita com a necessidade de resguardar os dados [21], levantando questionamentos em relação à segurança da informação e ao risco de violação da privacidade de seus usuários. Ainda que essas redes permitam a customização de alguns parâmetros de privacidade, é relatado que 84% dos usuários do Facebook não alteram as configurações padrão de privacidade [3, 18].

Formalmente, a privacidade pode ser definida como a capacidade que uma pessoa tem de controlar a exposição e a disponibilidade de informações acerca de si [22]. Esse controle pode muitas vezes ser comprometido no Facebook,

[1]Facebook. http://www.facebook.com.

visto que os seus usuários possuem o hábito de publicar bastante conteúdo [2, 14] numa plataforma que é aberta à execução de aplicativos de terceiros. Desta maneira, o usuário disponibiliza, voluntariamente, um conjunto de informações sensíveis sobre si mesmo, que ficam disponíveis na rede e podem ser capturadas por coletores automáticos, tornando a rede mais suscetível às ações de *spams*[2], *phishing*[3] e outras atividades indesejadas [4].

Com o objetivo de avaliar o risco de violação da privacidade e o nível de exposição de cada usuário, este trabalho apresenta um indicador capaz de estimar o nível de vulnerabilidade de um usuário na rede Facebook. Esse indicador é gerado com base na observação das características de conexões de amizades do usuário e na quantidade de informação publicada, permitindo que o usuário seja alertado sobre o seu nível de exposição e de seus amigos. Para o desenvolvimento deste indicador foram analisados mais de 75 mil perfis públicos de usuários do Facebook e suas conexões de amizades, cujos resultados são descritos neste artigo.

O indicador proposto possui caráter qualitativo, baseado na análise de faixas geradas a partir do chamado índice de exposição, que avalia a exposição quantitativa do usuário. Após o cálculo dos índices de exposição para um grupo de usuários foi estimado o indicador de vulnerabilidade de acordo com a classificação deste usuário dentro da faixa. Este artigo também apresenta a classificação de todos os usuários da amostra em termos de seu índice de exposição e do indicador de vulnerabilidade, permitindo uma maior compreensão do nível de risco assumido pelos usuários do Facebook ao utilizar esse sistema.

Este estudo verificou que 98% dos usuários analisados não alteram a configuração padrão de privacidade do Facebook, preenchem poucos atributos e mantém em média 500 amigos em suas conexões de amizades. Informações como gênero e educação são preenchidas por mais da metade dos usuários, 59,20% e 52,67% respectivamente. Já os campos e-mail (1,12%), telefone (0,95%) e endereço (0,40%) são preenchidos pela minoria, caracterizando dessa forma, padrões de comportamento do usuário que podem ser capturado através do índice de exposição. Foi constatado que o comportamento dessa comunidade é refletido nos baixos índices de exposição, sendo que a maioria dos usuários (94,37%) possui baixo indicador de vulnerabilidade, seguida por 4,28% de vulnerabilidade média, 0,63% de alta e 0,72% de muito alta.

O restante desse trabalho encontra-se organizado da seguinte forma: A seção 2 apresenta os trabalhos relacionados. A seção 3 introduz o índice de exposição e apresenta o indicador de vulnerabilidade. A seção 4 apresenta os experimentos realizados. A seção 5 conclui o artigo e a seção 6 os agradecimentos.

2. TRABALHOS RELACIONADOS

Foram discutidos alguns trabalhos que abordam, ainda que tangencialmente, as questões relacionadas à privacidade e segurança em redes sociais (seção 2.1). Em seguida será detalhado o trabalho que mais se aproxima do que está sendo proposto (seção 2.2).

2.1 Privacidade em Redes Sociais

Na literatura é possível encontrar vários estudos de privacidade envolvendo redes sociais. Como exemplo o trabalho desenvolvido em [6], onde os autores estudam a vulnerabilidade de usuários na rede Twitter[4] através da análise dos usuários que seguem (*followers*) os *spammers*, e concluem que os *spammers* são seguidos por usuários reais. Como o Twitter usa a quantidade de seguidores como indicador de autoridade, usuários *spammers* buscam se conectar a pessoas muito populares de forma a maximizar sua importância.

Em [8] os autores propõem uma estratégia para detectar usuários maliciosos que postam vídeos na rede YouTube[5]. Para a validação da técnica, realizaram a coleta de um componente inteiro do grafo de vídeos resposta do YouTube e criaram uma coleção de testes (através de inspeção manual) com usuários classificados como legítimos, *spammers* e promotores de vídeos. O trabalho apresentou uma caracterização de aspectos que podem ser utilizados para diferenciar usuários desses grupos e aplicou estes aspectos em um algoritmo de classificação capaz de identificar corretamente 97% de promotores de vídeos, 54% de *spammers* e errando apenas 5,4% de usuários legítimos.

A análise apresentada pelos autores em [11], sobre a percepção de privacidade de usuários da rede Facebook, conclui que (i) apenas uma pequena porcentagem de usuários altera suas configurações de privacidade, (ii) uma grande quantidade de usuários expõe seu gênero publicamente, (iii) mulheres são mais preocupadas com os seus dados pessoais e (iv) muitos usuários compartilham álbuns de fotos e links publicamente para toda a rede. O estudo descrito em [16] sobre a identificação de informações pessoais analisa a combinação de atributos que podem levar a identificação de um usuário e cita que a maioria dos estadunidenses (87%) pode ser unicamente identificados a partir da data de nascimento, código postal e sexo.

O uso de *tags* em imagens e o preenchimento de atributos sensíveis é caracterizado em [15] como potencial para a invasão de privacidade e ataques pessoais. A marcação de fotos tem sido alvo de muitas críticas, principalmente considerando que o padrão de configuração de privacidade do Facebook permite a atribuição de *tags* de um determinado usuário sem a sua aprovação prévia. Os resultados apresentados demonstram que a marcação de fotos pode (inclusive) ser usada para prever alguns atributos do perfil do usuário.

Em [19] os autores propõe um *framework* colaborativo para gerenciamento da privacidade (CPM), cujo objetivo é servir como interface entre o Facebook e os aplicativos de terceiros instalados em um perfil, permitindo que o usuário seja sempre notificado sobre qualquer requisição ou ação desses aplicativos como forma de resguardar a sua privacidade.

Em [2] os autores utilizam técnicas quantitativas e qualitativas para explorar a relação entre o uso de redes sociais e o controle da privacidade. O artigo revela que a estratégia de proteção mais comumente adotada é a restrição da visibilidade do perfil para apenas o grupo de amigos e considera que esta é uma forma de proteção fraca, já que não é sufi-

[2]*Spam* é o envio de mensagens não solicitadas em massa.*Spammers* são os usuários que enviam estas mensagens

[3]*Phishing* é uma forma de fraude eletrônica caracterizada por tentativas de adquirir dados pessoais de diversos tipos. O ato consiste em um fraudador se fazer passar por uma pessoa ou empresa confiável.

[4]Twitter. http://www.twitter.com.

[5]YouTube. http://www.youtube.com.

ciente para eliminar os riscos de privacidade decorrentes da quantidade, qualidade e persistência dos dados que os usuários fornecem na rede. A conclusão do artigo é que, na visão dos usuários, os benefícios do uso do Facebook superam as ameaças à sua privacidade.

Utilizando os conhecimentos abordados nestes artigos, será proposto um indicador capaz de estimar o nível de vulnerabilidade de cada usuário na rede Facebook.

2.2 Índices de Vulnerabilidade no Facebook

Em [20] os autores propõem uma estratégia para computar a vulnerabilidade de um usuário na rede Facebook através da geração de 4 índices: (i) índice I, que avalia a quantidade de dados expostos pelo usuário através de seu perfil; (ii) índice C, que avalia a exposição de atributos comunitários; (iii) índice P, que conjuga os dois anteriores e (iv) índice V, resultante da média do índice P de todos os amigos de um usuário. O índice P representa a vulnerabilidade final de cada usuário. Cada índice é detalhado a seguir.

Índice I: O índice I varia entre 0 e 1 e indica a quantidade de dados preenchidos e tornados públicos no perfil de cada usuário, sendo calculado através da Equação 1.

$$I_u = F(A_u) = \frac{\sum_{i=1}^{n} w_i * a_{u,i}}{\sum_{i=1}^{n} w_i} \tag{1}$$

Nesta equação $a_{u,i}$ representa cada atributo passível de ser preenchido (e.g., nome, telefone, endereço e e-mail). Caso o atributo esteja preenchido, $a_{u,i}$ terá o valor 1. Caso o atributo esteja vazio, $a_{u,i}$ assumirá o valor 0. A variável w_i representa o peso do atributo calculado como o percentual de indivíduos da rede social que não preencheram este atributo. Ou seja, quanto menos disponível na rede um atributo (e.g., o número de telefone) esteja, mais sensível e valioso ele se torna.

Índice C: O índice C indica quanto o usuário pode ameaçar os seus amigos através de atributos da comunidade acessíveis a outros usuários. O estudo identifica apenas um único atributo de comunidade dado pelo percentual de usuários que utilizaram o compartilhamento de links entre seus amigos. O índice é calculado através da Equação 2.

$$C_u = \frac{\sum_{i=1}^{m} \log_{10}(b_{u,i})}{4 * m} \tag{2}$$

onde m representa a quantidade de atributos públicos da comunidade (ou seja 1), $b_{u,i}$ representa o número de amigos de u afetados pela alteração do atributo de comunidade i. Os autores argumentam que a constante 4 surge do fato de que nenhum usuário do Facebook possui mais do que 10^4 amigos.

Índice P: O índice P, construído pela combinação dos índices I e C, mostra o quão público (visível) ou privado um usuário está na rede social. O seu cálculo é mostrado na Equação (3), onde o fator α é responsável por balancear a contribuição entre I e C.

$$P_u = \alpha * \frac{\sum_{i=1}^{n} w_i * a_{u,i}}{\sum_{i=1}^{n} w_i} + (1 - \alpha) * \frac{\sum_{i=1}^{m} \log_{10}(b_{u,i})}{4 * m} \tag{3}$$

Índice V: O índice V mostra quão vulnerável é um usuário de acordo com os índices P de seus amigos, representando a soma dos índices P do próprio usuário e de seus amigos conforme apresenta a Equação (4).

$$V_u = \frac{P_u + \sum_{i \in R_u} P_i}{|R_u| + 1} \tag{4}$$

onde $|R_u|$ é a quantidade de amigos do usuário u. Os autores somam 1 para incluir o próprio usuário u no cálculo. Uma das limitações do índice V é o fato de calcular a vulnerabilidade de um usuário como a vulnerabilidade média de suas conexões de amizades. Esta solução permite, por exemplo, que um usuário abaixe seu índice de vulnerabilidade adicionando amigos de baixíssima vulnerabilidade, o que representa um comportamento contrassensual. Se um usuário está numa dada faixa de vulnerabilidade, após adicionar mais um amigo sua faixa deve se manter a mesma ou aumentar, mas nunca regredir, afinal sua exposição aumenta com o acréscimo do novo amigo. Desse modo, será proposta uma nova estratégia para estimar a vulnerabilidade com base na exposição de um usuário na rede Facebook, discutida na próxima seção.

3. INDICADOR DE VULNERABILIDADE

A partir do cálculo dos pesos dos atributos será proposto o índice de exposição de um usuário, discutido na seção 3.1. Na seção 3.2 será apresentada a proposta do indicador de vulnerabilidade.

3.1 Índice de Exposição

A exposição de cada usuário é função de quantidade de dados que ele publica multiplicado pelo tamanho do grupo de amigos, o qual está diretamente relacionado com a chance de vazamento de informações, ou seja, quanto maior a quantidade de amigos maior a chance de exposição dos dados pessoais, que podem "vazar" por meio desse grupo de amigos. A quantidade de amigos aos quais o usuário em questão encontra-se conectado (i.e, o número de arestas do nodo de um grafo que representam as conexões de amizades) pode ser expressa por um valor inteiro; já a quantidade de dados publicada por um usuário merece uma análise cuidadosa. É preciso mensurar essa quantidade, ponderando de forma diferenciada os vários atributos preenchidos pelo usuário, já que o preenchimento de atributos diferentes tem consequências distintas para a violação de sua privacidade. Logo, o desafio se encontra em como atribuir pesos para os diferentes atributos.

Uma estratégia seria arbitrar um peso para cada atributo do perfil através de um processo de análise manual do quanto cada atributo expõe o usuário. Conclui-se que a sensação de exposição varia conforme o indivíduo e que a definição de um esquema desse tipo não seria geral o suficiente para atender a todos os usuários.

Outra abordagem seria considerar a preferência de todos os usuários do Facebook para definir a sensibilidade de cada atributo, como realizado em [20]. Entretanto, não foi considerada essa abordagem adequada, por estar lidando com usuários de todas as partes do mundo, envolvendo múltiplas culturas e diferenças significativas de hábitos.

Optou-se então por considerar apenas as preferências de um grupo seleto de usuários diretamente relacionados ao usuário em análise, ou seja, sua comunidade. A formação de uma comunidade pode seguir diferentes critérios, tais como a localização geográfica, algum amigo em comum, religião, interesses e outros. A definição da comunidade serve para

Tabela 1: Obtenção de pesos relativos dos atributos.

Atributo	Freq.	Freq.%	1/Freq.%	Peso
Nome	100	100%	1	0,09
E-mail	1	1%	100	0,91
Total	-	-	101	1,00

permitir a geração do índice de exposição com menor ruído, já que costumes de usuários distantes não serão levados em consideração. Nos resultados experimentais foi considerada comunidade como sendo o conjunto de amigos de um determinado usuário.

Desta forma, para realizar o cálculo do índice de exposição será considerado o peso de cada atributo com base na sua popularidade dentro da comunidade definida. Quanto menos disponível um atributo na comunidade, maior o seu peso relativo no cálculo do indicador de exposição, pois maior o número de usuários que julgam que este atributo pode incorrer em uma exposição exagerada.

Assim, o processo de atribuição de pesos é realizado de forma inversamente proporcional à sua popularidade na comunidade. Para exemplificar, considera-se uma rede hipotética composta por 100 usuários. Suponha que todos estes usuários compõem a comunidade em análise. Através de inspeção manual verificou-se que todos os 100 usuários disponibilizam seu nome no perfil e apenas um único usuário disponibiliza, também, o seu endereço de e-mail. Suponha também que estes sejam os únicos atributos passíveis de customização no perfil do usuário desta rede social.

A Tabela 1 apresenta um exemplo de geração do peso de cada atributo (existem apenas os atributos nome e e-mail) considerando o cenário descrito acima. Nesta tabela, a coluna 1 apresenta o nome do atributo em análise. A coluna 2 apresenta a frequência com que o atributo foi preenchido pelos usuários na rede. A coluna 3 apresenta a frequência percentual de preenchimento de cada atributo. O atributo nome aparece em 100% dos usuários, enquanto que o atributo e-mail aparece em apenas 1% dos usuários.

A coluna 4 é obtida a partir do inverso das frequências percentuais apuradas e serve para definir a importância de um atributo em relação ao outro. A coluna 5 é obtida a partir da normalização da coluna 4 para que a soma de todos os pesos tenha valor 1. Esta operação é realizada a partir da divisão do peso de cada item na coluna 4 pelo somatório total desta coluna. O cálculo dos pesos W de um usuário u pode ser visto na Equação 5.

$$W_u = \sum_{i=1}^{\#atributos} w_{(i)} * a_{(i)} \qquad (5)$$

onde w representa os pesos de cada atributo e a sua ocorrência ou não (0 ou 1).

Formalizado o índice de exposição de um usuário como o produto da quantidade de dados publicados pelo tamanho de seu grupo de amigos, conforme mostrado na Equação 6. A quantidade de dados publicados é obtida a partir da soma do peso de todos os atributos públicos presentes no perfil do usuário, tendo como resultado um valor entre 0 e 1. O tamanho do grupo de amizade também é expresso como um valor entre 0 e 1, sendo obtido através da divisão da quantidade de amigos pela maior quantidade possível de amigos que ele pode ter (no Facebook cada perfil pode ter no máximo 5 mil amigos).

$$IE_u = \frac{|R_u|}{max|R|} * W_{(u)} \qquad (6)$$

Onde IE_u indica o índice de exposição do usuário u, $|R_u|$ indica a quantidade de amigos de u, $\max|R|$ indica a quantidade máxima de amigos que um usuário pode ter e $W_{(u)}$ indica o peso do atributo i para o usuário u.

Caso o índice de exposição seja próximo de 0 é possivel inferir que o usuário possui um risco muito baixo de violação de privacidade, já que disponibiliza poucos dados e possui poucos laços de amizade. Por outro lado, caso o usuário tenha um índice próximo de 1, pode ser considerada bem alta, já que possui muitos atributos públicos e possivelmente um grande número de amigos. Mas o que dizer sobre o usuário de índice 0,5, por exemplo? De fato este valor não significa muito quando avaliado isoladamente. A estratégia que este trabalho propõe é avaliar a exposição relativa entre os usuários de uma mesma comunidade para gerar o indicador de vulnerabilidade, como será discutido na próxima seção.

3.2 Indicador de Vulnerabilidade

O indicador de vulnerabilidade proposto possui caráter qualitativo gerado a partir da comparação do índice de exposição de um usuário com os índices apurados para os demais usuários da sua comunidade. Conforme já mencionado, a escolha do conjunto de usuários para formar uma comunidade pode seguir diferentes critérios. O mais intuitivo é escolher usuários que possuem um mesmo amigo em comum, embora outros critérios possam ser propostos, como localização geográfica, religião, grupo social, faixa etária, interesses e outros. Desse modo, o indicador de vulnerabilidade pode ser calculado para cada comunidade da qual o usuário faça parte.

Com base na análise da distribuição de índices de exposição dos usuários, será proposta a partição em faixas de valores de índices correspondentes a diferentes níveis de vulnerabilidade. Em particular, esta proposta abrange a divisão em quatro faixas, a saber: vulnerabilidade baixa, média, alta e muito alta.

Diferentes estratégias poderiam ser aplicadas para delimitar estas faixas. Por exemplo, poderia-se utilizar os quartis dos valores de índices observados. Assim, por definição, cada faixa conteria exatamente 25% da população de usuários analisada. Esta divisão é mais adequada quando a distribuição dos índices se aproxima de uma distribuição uniforme. Entretanto, quando a distribuição tem uma concentração maior em certos valores (que é o caso desse experimento, como será discutido na Seção 4.3), a divisão por quartis não é tão adequada, pois ela se torna mais arbitrária. Dois usuários poderiam ser classificados em faixas diferentes mesmo tendo índices de vulnerabilidade muito próximos.

Assim será proposto agrupar os usuários analisando a distribuição dos índices e buscando mudanças significativas no formato da curva (e.g., "joelhos"). Tais mudanças refletem comportamentos mais significativos nos perfis dos usuários (no que tange os valores de índices de exposição) e possivelmente delimitam regiões da distribuição com regimes diferentes. Em outras palavras, elas indicam agregação de grupos de usuários com perfis diferentes. Desse modo, foi utilizado como delimitadores das 4 faixas de perfis valores de índices que marcam mudanças maiores na distribuição.

Visando validar as faixas qualitativas geradas pelo indicador de vulnerabilidade, foi aplicado o método de aprendizado não supervisionado de agrupamento com a utilização do algoritmo K-Means. O algoritmo K-Means permite a criação de grupos a partir de instâncias de atributos semelhantes entre si, sendo um método de agrupamento não hierárquico por repartição. Utilizando a ferramenta Weka[6] para a realização dos experimentos, optou-se pelo algoritmo SimpleKMeans.

O algoritmo K-Means foi executado mais de 30 vezes, em diversos cenários, variando o número de clusters, de sementes e configuração dos parâmetros da função da distância até atingir os melhores resultados. Com os melhores parâmetros definidos, executou-se o experimento iniciando randomicamente com 10 centroides, configurando o cálculo da distância Euclidiana para calcular o quão distante um registro está do outro. Após o cálculo das distâncias o algoritmo calcula os centroides para cada um dos grupos formados e recalcula a cada nova interação, até convergir.

Os melhores resultados foram alcançados com 5 clusters, o que valida o indicador de vulnerabilidade, pois o cluster de maior percentual representa os usuários que possuem amigos igual a zero (ver seção 4.3).

Através dessa análise é possivel inferir valores típicos da comunidade, como padrões de comportamento, por exemplo. Esta abordagem é interessante, pois permite isolar diferenças culturais e de hábitos para oferecer uma indicação de vulnerabilidade considerando a comunidade em questão.

Este indicador de vulnerabilidade também pode facilmente ser integrado à interface do Facebook (ou de qualquer outra rede social), para que o usuário esteja ciente do seu nível de exposição. Além disso, a aplicação também poderia apresentar o indicador de vulnerabilidade para cada amigo do usuário, fornecendo informações para que o usuário atue ativamente na proteção de suas conexões de amizades (excluindo amigos muito vulneráveis, por exemplo). A seguir, será detalhada a análise experimental do indicador proposto em uma amostra de 75.000 usuários com perfis públicos coletados do Facebook.

4. AVALIAÇÃO EXPERIMENTAL

Nesta seção serão discutidos os resultados da avaliação do indicador de vulnerabilidade proposto em dados reais coletados do Facebook. Os dados analisados são apresentados na seção 4.1. Na seção 4.2 será apresentado como os usuários desta amostra preencheram seus atributos de perfil. Na seção 4.3 foi analisado o número de amigos por usuário da amostra. As análises 4.2 e 4.3 são importantes, pois o indicador de exposição é justamente composto da multiplicação destes dois termos. O índice de exposição é apresentado na seção 4.4. Na seção 4.5 são discutidos os resultados do indicador de vulnerabilidade e a estratégia para divisão do índice de exposição em faixas.

4.1 Conjunto de Dados

Para a realização desta pesquisa foi elaborada uma aplicação na linguagem PHP, responsável por navegar nas páginas do Facebook e realizar o armazenamento de perfis públicos. Os perfis foram escolhidos de forma aleatória, cobrindo diversas nacionalidades.

Através desta aplicação foi coletada uma amostra composta por 75.011 usuários reais e ativos do Facebook durante o 4° trimestre de 2011. Para cada usuário buscou-se

[6]Weka. http://www.cs.waikato.ac.nz/ ml/weka/.

Tabela 2: Pesos de atributos obtidos na amostra real.

Atributo	#Ocorrências	Freq.	Peso Normaliz.
Nome	75.011	100%	0,0012
Gênero	44.406	59,20%	0,0020
Educação	39.507	52,67%	0,0022
Interesses	27.190	36,25%	0,0032
Empresa	18.676	24,90%	0,0046
Sobre mim	16.946	22,59%	0,0051
E-mail	840	1,12%	0,1031
Telefone	709	0,95%	0,1222
Endereço	298	0,40%	0,2907
Sítio	186	0,25%	0,4657

11 atributos do seu perfil, sendo eles: nome, gênero, educação, interesses, empresa, sobre mim (descrição sumária do perfil do usuário), e-mail, telefone, endereço, sítio web e configuração de privacidade. Para cada um desses atributos foi armazenado um valor lógico referente ao seu preenchimento ('0' atributo vazio; '1' atributo preenchido). No caso do atributo configuração de privacidade, a coleta armazenou '0' para o perfil que não alterou nenhuma configuração dos atributos coletados e '1' para o perfil que ocultou a exibição de algum atributo.

4.2 Análise do Preenchimento do Perfi

Para gerar o índice de exposição é necessario calcular os pesos para cada atributo presente no perfil do usuário. A Tabela 2 apresenta a disponibilidade e o peso normalizado de cada atributo.

A Tabela 2 apresenta na 2ª coluna o número de usuários que preencheram cada atributo, em seguida a frequência de disponibilidade dos atributos e na 4ª coluna o cálculo do peso normalizado de cada atributo. Nota-se que o atributo menos preenchido foi o sítio web, apenas 0,25% dos perfis preencheram esta informação, já o gênero (masculino/feminino) foi preenchido por mais da metade dos usuários 59,20%. Atributos como telefone e endereço são preenchidos por menos de 1% dos usuários, mas informações sobre educação (52,67%) foram preenchidas por mais da metade dos usuários.

4.3 Número de Amigos

O índice de exposição leva em conta o número de amigos que cada usuário possui. Desta forma, apresentou-se uma breve caracterização do número de amigos por usuário presente na amostra.

É importante mencionar que a partir deste ponto em diante foram desconsiderados os usuários presentes na amostra que não continham amigos. Entende-se esta decisão adequada pois (i) a análise de um usuário sem amizades não traz contribuição para este trabalho e (ii) o usuário pode optar por não exibir os seus amigos em seu perfil ou realmente possuir 0 amigos. Foram desprezados 37.390 registros nesta condição, permanecendo 37.621 registros para as análises posteriores.

A Figura 1 apresenta o histograma do número de amigos dos usuários da amostra. Pouco mais de 6 mil usuários possuem de 1 à 250 amigos. O próximo ponto é o máximo do gráfico e indica que cerca de 8 mil usuários optaram por conexões de amizades entre 250 e 500. A partir deste ponto percebe-se uma redução do número de usuários dispostos a

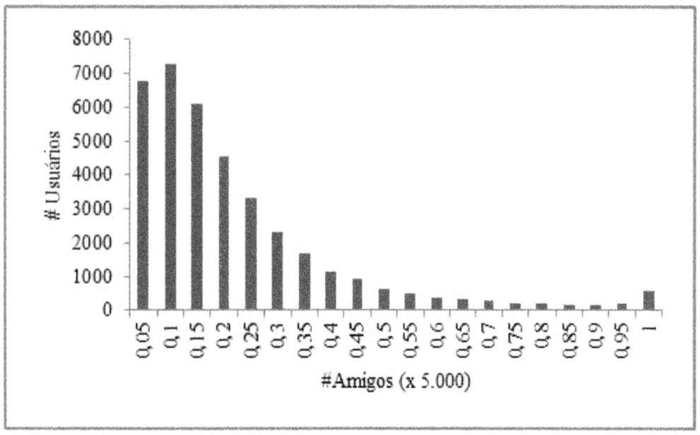

Figura 1: Distribuição do #Amigos (x 5.000).

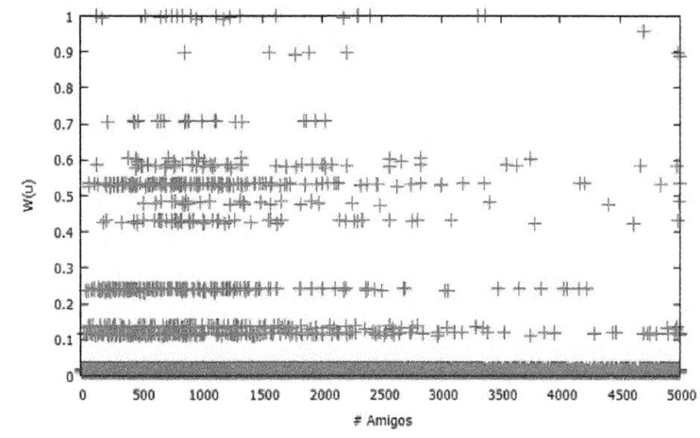

Figura 2: Gráfico do cálculo dos atributos por #amigos.

participar de grandes conexões de amizades. O gráfico apresenta uma 2ª inflexão nos usuários contendo de 4.500 até 5.000 amigos, que representa o limite de amizades na rede.

4.4 Índice de Exposição

Foi calculado o somatório dos atributos (Equação 5) para todos os usuários da base de dados e verificou-se que há formações de faixas de acordo com o preenchimento dos atributos, conforme visto na Figura 2.

Percebe-se que os usuários tendem a preencher poucos atributos no seu perfil. Um percentual de 35,67% dos usuários totalizou soma de pesos inferior à 0,001. Já 47,58% dos usuários totalizaram pesos entre 0,001 e 0,004 e 13,46% totalizaram valores acima de 0,085. Em média, os usuários preenchem 5 atributos cujos somatórios dos pesos é menor que 0,10. Apenas 1,08% dos usuários possui o somatório dos pesos igual a 0,1. É possível notar grande concentração dos usuários com peso inferior à 0,200. Um usuário que possui peso igual a 0,0137 preenche o nome, gênero, educação, interesse e a descrição sobre ele. Já o usuário que possui peso igual a 0,01 preenche o nome, gênero, educação e empresa.

Baseado na definição de pesos de cada atributo (item 4.2) e no número de amigos de cada usuário (4.3) foi calculado o índice de exposição conforme a Equação 5. A Figura 3 mostra o histograma do índice de exposição para a amostra analisada.

Analisando o gráfico nota-se que, apesar do índice variar

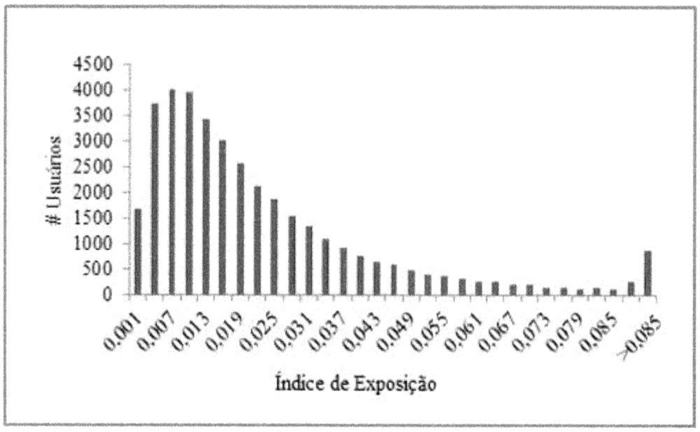

Figura 3: Histograma do índice de exposição.

Tabela 3: Faixas do indicador de vulnerabilidade.

Faixas	Análise Qualitativa
[0,000 , 0,010]	Baixa
(0,010 , 0,040]	Média
(0,040 , 0,085]	Alta
(0,085 , 1,000]	Muito Alta

entre 0 e 1, grande parte dos valores concentram-se no início da escala (até o valor 0,085). A partir do pico desse gráfico temos um movimento de queda do número de usuários dispostos a arcar com uma maior exposição. Este movimento de queda é gradativamente desacelerado conforme prosseguimos ao longo do eixo índice de exposição. O último ponto representado no gráfico demonstra um aparente crescimento no número de usuários com alto índice de exposição. É preciso levar em conta que este último ponto concentra uma faixa muito grande de índices, indo de 0,1 até 1. Ainda assim, tem-se aproximadamente 3% dos usuários da amostra neste alto patamar de exposição.

Conclui-se que os usuários tendem a preencher os atributos menos sensíveis no seu perfil e a manter conexões de amizades pequenas (entre 250 e 500 amigos). Como forma de proteger sua privacidade, os usuários optam por publicar menos dados em detrimento de terem conexões com menor número de amigos.

4.5 Indicador de Vulnerabilidade

Respeitando essas premissas, foi proposto a geração do indicador de vulnerabilidade através da classificação do usuário dentro das faixas de exposição. Para esta comunidade obteve-se a seguinte classificação apresentada na Tabela 3.

Esta tabela apresenta a análise quantitativa e qualitativa. Através da análise da derivada do gráfico de distribuição chegou-se a 4 faixas (baixa, média, alta e muito alta).

É importante ressaltar que esta divisão foi realizada desta forma apenas para fins de exposição da técnica apresentada. Na operação real da rede social, estas faixas de vulnerabilidade serão definidas dinamicamente pelo administrador da rede, de forma a sempre balancear a relação custo-benefício entre a funcionalidade da rede e a privacidade dos usuários, de forma que a discussão sobre a divisão das faixas está fora do escopo deste artigo.

A análise qualitativa da vulnerabilidade surge da comparação das faixas com a vulnerabilidade calculada para cada usuário. Como exemplo, um usuário que apresente índice de exposição no valor de 0,025 seria classificado como 'média vulnerabilidade', dado que está na segunda faixa.

A estratégia adotada aponta que o acréscimo de um amigo com vulnerabilidade superior a do usuário eleva o índice de exposição, mas esta elevação pode afetar ou não o indicador de vulnerabilidade (a depender da intensidade da vulnerabilidade do usuário adicionado e do tipo de comunidade à qual pertence). Isto porque a mudança de faixa só ocorre quando o acréscimo ou retirada de um amigo for grande o suficiente para ocasionar esse salto. Já no estudo [20], a adição deste novo amigo certamente aumenta o índice V.

5. CONCLUSÃO

Uma das principais repercussões da web 2.0 é a popularização das redes sociais, redefinindo a forma na qual usamos a internet hoje, concentrando maior demanda no usuário, o qual passa a ter um papel cada vez mais participativo e colaborativo. Com essa participação surge a exposição, muitas vezes incentivada pelas próprias redes sociais, grupos de amigos e comunidade na qual ele faz parte, o que torna as redes sociais um excelente meio de obtenção clandestina de dados pessoais.

A privacidade é a capacidade do indivíduo de controlar a exposição e a disponibilidade de informações acerca de si. Em uma rede social, esta capacidade é comprometida pela natureza colaborativa e comunicativa da própria rede. Temos certo que a participação numa rede social demanda algum nível de exposição de seus usuários, e parece justo que este nível de exposição seja apresentado ao usuário de uma forma clara e objetiva, tornando a rede social parceira do usuário na proteção dos dados da rede como um todo.

Na equalização desta situação também há que se levar em conta a multiplicidade de culturas envolvidas, com seus diversos hábitos e costumes, o que torna o tratamento da privacidade ainda mais complexo.

Diante dessa complexidade, este artigo propôs a geração de um indicador de vulnerabilidade, baseado nos costumes da comunidade na qual o usuário está inserido. Por meio desse indicador, cada usuário poderá conhecer seu nível de exposição e, de forma natural, os mesmos passarão a se conscientizar sobre a sua necessidade de preservação de privacidade.

Nos experimentos foram coletados mais de 75.000 perfis públicos da rede Facebook, constatou-se que a grande parte dos usuários (94,37%) possui baixo índice de vulnerabilidade, porém deve-se considerar que 1,35% dos usuários estão na faixa alta de vulnerabilidade. É possível perceber claramente o padrão de preenchimento de atributos, mostrado no índice de exposição, sendo que 35,67% possui o somatório dos pesos valor menor do que 0,01, seguido de 47,58% entre 0,01 e 0,04 e 13,46% entre 0,004 e 0,0085.

O trabalho futuro dessa proposta será o desenvolvimento de um aplicativo no Facebook que utilize o indicador proposto de vulnerabilidade, proporcionando ao usuário estimar a sua faixa e receber uma análise qualitativa. Esse aplicativo servirá também para analisar as conexões de amizades, podendo ser de grande valia na adição ou exclusão de amizades, servindo de alerta para o usuário e para o próprio grupo de amigos. Pretende-se realizar a avaliação do usuário para este indicador, bem como, aumentar o número de atributos a serem analisados, principalmente com foco em tags de fotos e textos publicados no mural do usuário.

Por meio da apresentação do indicador de vulnerabilidade, os usuários também poderão selecionar melhor suas conexões de amizades para autoproteção. Durante este processo, usuários com um nível de exposição muito alto poderão ser excluídos das comunidades na qual participam, e simultaneamente os administradores da rede social poderão ajustar as faixas do indicador de vulnerabilidade dinamicamente, balanceando o *tradeoff* entre a funcionalidade da rede e a privacidade dos usuários.

6. AGRADECIMENTOS

Este trabalho foi financiado por recursos da Fapemig, do Departamento de Ciência da Computação da Universidade Federal de Minas Gerais e da Pro-Reitoria de Pesquisa e Pós-Graduação da Universidade Federal de São João Del Rei.

7. REFERÊNCIAS

[1] A. Acquisti and R. Gross. Imagined communities: Wareness, information sharing, and privacy on the facebook. In *PET*.

[2] A. H. B. Debatin, J. P. Lovejoy and B. N. Hughes. Facebook and online privacy: Attitudes, behaviors and unintended consequences. In *Journal of Computer-Mediated Communication. doi: 10.1111/j.1083-6101.2009.01494.x*, page 15: 83–108.

[3] D. Boyd and E. Hargittai. Facebook privacy settings: Who cares? In *First Monday [Online], Volume 15 Number 8 (27 July 2010)*, pages 13–20.

[4] D. Boyd and A. Marwick. Social privacy in networked publics: Teens' attitudes, practices, and strategies. In *Privacy Law Scholars Conference. Berkeley, CA May.*

[5] G. Casella and R. L. Berger. *Inferência estatística.* Centage Learning, ISBN13: 9788522108947, ISBN10: 8522108943, 2010.

[6] T. R. Fabrício Benevenuto, G. Magno and V. Almeida. Detecting spammers on twitter. In *7th Annual Collaboration, Electronic messaging, Anti-Abuse and Spam Conference (CEAS).*

[7] T. R. V. A. J. A. Fabrício Benevenuto, A. Pereira and M. Gonçalves. Avaliação do perfil de acesso e navegação de usuários em ambientes web de compartilhamento de vídeos. In *Brazilian Symposium on Multimedia Systems and Web (WebMedia)*, page 149–156.

[8] V. A. J. A. Fabrício Benevenuto, T. Rodrigues and M. Gonçalves. Detectando usuários maliciosos em interações via vídeos no youtube. In *Simpósio Brasileiro de Sistemas Multimídia e Web (WebMedia).*

[9] Facebook. Facebook press room. In *Statistics, DOI= http://newsroom.fb.com/Key-Facts/Statistics-8b.aspx.*

[10] Facebook. Política de uso de dados. In *DOI= http://www.facebook.com/about/privacy/tools.*

[11] V. A. G. Rauber and P. Kumaraguru. Privacy albeit late. In *Accepted at Seventeenth edition of WebMedia, Brazilian Symposium on Multimedia and the Web (2011).*

[12] A. S. Gail-Joon, Mohamed Shehab. Security and privacy in social networks. In *IEEE Internet Computing, vol. 15, no. 3*, pages 10–12.

[13] R. Gross and A. Acquisti. Information revelation and privacy in online social networks. In *Proceedings of the*

2005 ACM workshop on Privacy in the electronic society (WPES '05). ACM, New York, NY, USA, pages 71–80.

[14] H. Jones and J. Soltren. Facebook: Threats to privacy. In *Ethics and the Law on the Electronic Frontier Course, Massachusetts Institute of Technology.*

[15] G. R. João Paulo Pesce, Diego Las Casas and V. Almeida. Privacy attacks in social media using photo tagging networks: a case study with facebook. In *Proceedings of the 1st Workshop on Privacy and Security in Online Social Media (PSOSM '12).*

[16] B. Krishnamurthy and C. E. Wills. Characterizing privacy in online social networks. In *ACM workshop on Online social networks (WOSN). ACM.*

[17] B. Krishnamurthy and C. E. Wills. On the leakage of personally identifiable information via online social networks. In *Proceedings of the 2nd ACM workshop on Online social networks (WOSN '09). ACM, New York, NY, USA*, pages 7–12.

[18] C. T. B. M. Gjoka, M. Kurant and A. Markopoulou. A walk in facebook: Uniform sampling of users in online social networks. In *Technical report, arXiv.org.*

[19] J. W. P. G. Pauline Anthonysamy, Awais Rashid and G. Larkou. Collaborative privacy management for third-party applications in online social networks. In *Proceedings of the 1st Workshop on Privacy and Security in Online Social Media (PSOSM '12).*

[20] G. B. Pritam Gundecha and H. Liu. Exploiting vulnerability to secure user privacy on a social networking site. In *Proceedings of the 17th ACM SIGKDD international conference on Knowledge discovery and data mining, KDD '11, ACM, New York, NY, USA*, pages 511–519.

[21] F. Stutzman and J. Kramer-Duffield. Friends only : Examining a privacy-enhancing behavior in facebook. In *Organization: 1553-1562. http://portal.acm.org/citation.cfm?id=175355.*

[22] T. Vianna. *Transparência pública, opacidade privada.* Revan, ISBN 978-85-7106-360-0, Rio de Janeiro, 2007.

[23] B. K. Yabing Liu, Krishna P. Gummadi and A. Mislove. Analyzing facebook privacy settings: user expectations vs. reality. In *Proceedings of the 2011 ACM SIGCOMM conference on Internet measurement conference (IMC '11).*

A Domain Engineering for Content Sharing Collaborative Features

Lucas Santos de Oliveira
Universidade Estadual do Sudoeste da Bahia
Centro de Pesquisa e Desenvolvimento de Software,
R José Moreira Sobrinho, S/N
(+55 73) 3528-9737
lsoliveira@uesb.edu.br

Marco Aurélio Gerosa
Universidade de São Paulo
Instituto de Matemática e Estatística, R do Matão 1010
(+55 11) 3091-6499
gerosa@ime.usp.br

ABSTRACT
Researchers and developers still replicate ideas with low reuse when developing Web 2.0 applications. A domain engineering identify and document commonalities and variabilities of an application family fostering reuse. In this work, we used a domain engineering approach for content sharing features of social networks. We used as a method the FODA (Feature Oriented Domain Analysis) with patterns for computer-mediated interaction to describe the collaborative features and the 3C collaboration model to classify them. To implement the commonalities, a component kit was defined and developed, based on an infrastructure named Groupware Workbench. We conducted an experiment to evaluate the artifacts generated by the domain engineering.

RESUMO
Pesquisadores e desenvolvedores continuam replicando as ideias com pouco reúso, quando desenvolvem aplicações na Web 2.0. Como alternativa, uma engenharia de domínio identifica e documenta similaridades e variações de uma família de aplicações favorecendo o reúso. Neste trabalho, é feita uma engenharia de domínio em redes sociais na Web 2.0, com o foco nas funcionalidades colaborativas relativas ao compartilhamento de conteúdo. Usamos o método FODA (Feature Oriented Domain Analysis) adaptado com padrões de interação mediados por computador para descrever e o modelo 3C de colaboração para classificar as funcionalidades de colaboração. Para implementar as similaridades, um conjunto de componentes foi definido e desenvolvido com base na infraestrutura Groupware Workbench. Conduzimos um experimento para avaliar os artefatos gerados na engenharia de domínio.

Categories and Subject Descriptors
H.5.3 [**Information Storage and Retrieval**]: Group and Organization Interfaces – *computer-supported cooperative work, web-based interaction, collaborative computing, evaluation/methodology.*

Permission to make digital or hard copies of all or part of this work for personal or classroom use is granted without fee provided that copies are not made or distributed for profit or commercial advantage and that copies bear this notice and the full citation on the first page. To copy otherwise, or republish, to post on servers or to redistribute to lists, requires prior specific permission and/or a fee.
WebMedia'12, October 15–18, 2012, São Paulo/SP, Brazil.
Copyright 2012 ACM 978-1-4503-1706-1/12/10...$15.00.

General Terms
Documentation, Design.

Keywords
Domain Engineering, 3C Collaboration Model, Interaction Patterns, Social Networks, Web 2.0, Collaborative Systems, Groupware.

1. INTRODUÇÃO
Empresas de internet que sobreviveram à crise pontocom de 2001 usavam a internet como plataforma, desenvolvendo sites colaborativos baseados em comunidades. Esse conceito foi chamado Web 2.0 [1]. Diferente do modelo anterior, em que empresas e anunciantes produzem conteúdo estático para acesso dos usuários, na Web 2.0, usuários produzem, organizam, compartilham, mesclam, criticam e atualizam conteúdos. De acordo com Prescott [2], o aumento do conteúdo na web é resultado da penetração da banda larga, *web cam*, celulares e câmeras pessoais. Esse conteúdo geralmente é compartilhado em redes sociais. No entanto, esses sites da web 2.0 contém diversas funcionalidades colaborativas recorrentes, que ficam entremeadas à lógica de negócio do sistema e normalmente são implementados sem reúso.

Greenberg [3] posiciona o desenvolvimento de sistemas colaborativos na fase de replicação no modelo BRETAM [4], que descreve como uma tecnologia evolui ao longo do tempo. Nessa fase, os pesquisadores aproveitam as ideias uns dos outros, reimplementando-as, alterando-as e inovando. O processo de construção das ferramentas ainda não está bem estabelecido e há muitas incertezas e retrabalho. Greenberg [3] argumenta que a estagnação na fase de replicação do desenvolvimento de sistemas colaborativos é decorrente da falta de um ferramental que propicie o reúso e encapsulamento das complexidades técnicas e multidisciplinares características desse tipo de sistema. Esse cenário ilustra a necessidade de uma engenharia de domínio, para construção de componentes de software reusáveis, diminuindo a necessidade de reimplementação e focando na montagem do sistema.

Este trabalho tem a seguinte estrutura: Na Seção 2 é apresentada a Engenharia de Domínio com suas etapas e seus principais métodos, detalhando o método FODA [5] utilizado neste trabalho. Na Seção 3 é mostrado os trabalhos relacionados e como esta proposta se diferencia ou os complementam. Na Seção 4 é apresentada uma engenharia de domínio, em que são levantadas as funcionalidades colaborativas relativas ao compartilhamento de conteúdo em redes sociais na Web 2.0. Foi utilizado o método FODA, estendida pelo Modelo 3C de Colaboração [6], para classificação, e padrões de interação mediados por computador [7] para descrição das funcionalidades colaborativas. Para o desenvolvimento do kit de componentes, que possibilita a criação de redes sociais de compartilhamento de conteúdo, é utilizada a infraestrutura do Groupware Workbench [8]. Na Seção 5, como forma de avaliação dos artefatos gerados, é mostrado, de maneira sucinta, um experimento e um estudo de caso. Na Seção 6 são feitas as conclusões e as considerações finais.

2. ENGENHARIA DE DOMÍNIO

Aplicações de um mesmo domínio possuem características em comum, podendo fazer uso dos mesmos processos e objetos, o que promove o reúso dos conceitos e funcionalidades. Para Ahorone e Reinhartz [9] um domínio é definido como um conjunto de aplicações que usam conceitos comuns para descrever requisitos, problemas e capacidades. O domínio é delimitado pela similaridade entre as aplicações [10].

Segundo Prieto-Diaz e Arango [11], a engenharia de domínio é o processo de identificação e organização do conhecimento sobre uma classe de problemas apoiando sua descrição e solução. Clements [12] afirma que o objetivo da engenharia de domínio é encontrar pontos comuns, identificar componentes aplicáveis e famílias de aplicações.

Alaña e Rodriguez [13] apontam as atividades do processo de engenharia de domínio, que são divididas em: Análise do Domínio, Projeto do Domínio e Implementação de Domínio, que também aparecem em outros trabalhos como em [14] [10].

A análise de domínio tem por objetivo identificar, coletar e organizar informações relevantes, utilizando o conhecimento existente do domínio e os métodos para a modelagem de informações [5]. O projeto de domínio utiliza os resultados da análise do domínio para identificar e generalizar soluções para os requisitos comuns, por meio de especificação de uma arquitetura de software [15]. Para Blois [14], é a etapa em que modelos de projeto são construídos, com base nos modelos de análise, no conhecimento obtido por estudos a respeito de projeto reusável e arquiteturas de referência. Implementação do domínio inclui o desenvolvimento de componentes reusáveis [15] [10]. Essa fase visa construir os artefatos, baseados na modelagem do domínio e nas arquiteturas de referência propostas na atividade de projeto [14].

2.1 FODA (Feature Oriented Domain Analysis)

Muitos métodos de engenharia de domínio têm sido desenvolvidos com a finalidade de prover o reúso dos artefatos gerados. Alaña e Rodriguez [13] classificam os métodos em três grupos distintos: Métodos baseados na análise do domínio, cujo objetivo é analisar e modelar, para alcançar o reúso em partes similares do domínio. Alguns de seus métodos são ODM [16], FODA [5], FORM [17], FeatureRSEB [18], DARE [19] e Odyssey-DE [20]. Métodos de Linhas de Produtos, que têm sido estendidos ou conectados a outros para cobrir todo o processo de produção. Alguns de seus métodos são: FAST [10] e PuLSE [21]. Métodos de Engenharia de domínio e OOA/D combinam engenharia de domínio com projeto e análise orientados a conteúdo. Alguns dos seus métodos são: OOram [22], JODA [23] e RiDE [24].

FODA [5], desenvolvido no SEI (Software Engineering Institute), é o método de engenharia de domínio mais conhecido e um dos precursores dos demais. Ele é baseado na identificação, análise e documentação das principais funcionalidades dos sistemas; resultando em produtos de domínio genéricos e largamente aplicáveis em um domínio. A abordagem do método FODA é relevante do ponto de vista do desenvolvimento baseado em componentes, uma vez que a captura das funcionalidades relevantes ao domínio auxilia na identificação de possíveis componentes de software [14].

Utilizamos o método FODA porque é baseado na análise do domínio e não envolve questões de implementação e arquitetura, o que o tornou propício para nosso estudo, visto que não tivemos acesso aos detalhes internos de implementação das redes sociais analisadas.

2.2 Extensão do Método FODA para Web 2.0

Neste trabalho, para dar suporte à análise de funcionalidades colaborativas na Web 2.0, o método FODA foi estendido com o Modelo 3C de colaboração e padrões para interação mediada por computador, sendo este o diferencial com relação a outros métodos. O primeiro com o objetivo de classificar as funcionalidades colaborativas e o segundo para descrevê-las. Ellis et al. [25] foram um dos primeiros a utilizar as três dimensões do modelo 3C (comunicação, coordenação e cooperação) para classificação do suporte computacional à colaboração. Esse modelo é largamente utilizado na literatura de sistemas colaborativos.

A comunicação envolve a troca de mensagens e a negociação de compromissos. Por intermédio da coordenação, as pessoas, as atividades e os recursos são gerenciados para lidar com conflitos e evitar a perda dos esforços de comunicação e cooperação. A cooperação é a produção conjunta dos membros do grupo em um espaço compartilhado, gerando e manipulando conteúdos de cooperação na realização das tarefas. Apesar da separação dessas atividades para fins de análise, a comunicação, a coordenação e a cooperação não são realizadas de maneira estanque e isolada [26]; são realizadas continuamente e iterativamente durante o trabalho em grupo [6].

Neste trabalho, adotamos o modelo 3C de colaboração para classificar e organizar as funcionalidades colaborativas. Uma vez classificadas, essas funcionalidades são mapeadas para componentes de software, que são usados para construção de sistemas colaborativos baseados nos requisitos de comunicação, coordenação e cooperação. Para classificar uma funcionalidade de compartilhamento de conteúdo em redes sociais, segundo o modelo 3C de colaboração, foram seguidos os seguintes critérios:

- Comunicação: quando a funcionalidade é utilizada pelas pessoas para trocarem mensagens e informações;
- Coordenação: quando a funcionalidade é utilizada pelas pessoas para gerenciamento do grupo, ou para estarem cientes das atividades e seus efeitos na colaboração;
- Cooperação: quando a funcionalidade é utilizada pelas pessoas para gerenciarem o espaço compartilhado ou interagirem com os conteúdos compartilhados.

Baseado na linguagem de padrões e padrões de projeto de software, Schummer e Lukosch [7] propuseram os padrões para interação mediada por computador, que descrevem o apoio recorrente a interação em grupo baseado na seguinte estrutura: nome, figura sintetizadora, intenção, contexto, problema, cenário, sintomas, solução, dinâmicas, razão, verificar, pontos de perigo, usos conhecidos e padrões relacionados. Os padrões para interação possibilitam descrever as funcionalidades colaborativas, detalhando seu comportamento e uso, suprindo parte das dificuldades de acesso aos fluxos de dados das redes sociais, que são utilizados na etapa de análise do domínio.

3. TRABALHOS RELACIONADOS

SPLSCW2.0 [27] é uma engenharia de domínio para aplicações síncronas. Segundo Gaspar et al. [27] durante o desenvolvimento de aplicações para o projeto Tidia-Ae, observou-se a existência de vários pontos de interseção na construção de aplicações de colaboração síncronas para Web. Alguns desses pontos foram de imediata identificação, ainda na atividade de requisitos, como um serviço genérico de comunicação para troca de mensagens síncronas (SCS). Porém, outros pontos, como um framework de janelas ricas (RWIF), só foram identificados após a construção de um conjunto de aplicações. Os componentes identificados foram desenvolvidos utilizando a arquitetura do Tidia-Ae e possibilitou a criação de diversos sistemas compondo alguns dos componentes.

Gadelha et al. [28] apresentam uma abordagem para solucionar alguns problemas identificados no desenvolvimento de Linha de Produtos de Groupware (LPG), que não cobre a atividade análise do domínio e das variabilidades e semelhanças do domínio. O principal objetivo dessa abordagem é desenvolver LPG incorporando os benefícios providos pelas Linhas de Produtos de Software. A análise da colaboração é realizada de acordo com o Modelo 3C de Colaboração e a análise do domínio é realizada conforme especificado no RUP 3C-Groupware [28].

Michalsky et al. [29] realizou uma análise do domínio para a Inteligência Coletiva na Web 2.0, considerando como ponto de partida o domínio do jornalismo online. Para representar o domínio, jornalismo online, foi avaliado um total de vinte sites de notícias online.

Este trabalho pode ser parte do trabalho de Gadelha et al. [28], uma vez que a engenharia de domínio é parte da linha de produto de software. Já o de Michalsky et al. [29] tem um escopo menor e um domínio diferente deste trabalho. Não foram encontrados outros trabalhos de engenharia de domínio para groupware ou redes sociais na Web 2.0, em particular.

4. ANÁLISE DO DOMÍNIO

A primeira atividade do método FODA é a análise do contexto, em que é definido o escopo do domínio, suscetível à produção de artefatos [5]. Neste trabalho, o domínio é definido como compartilhamento de conteúdo em Redes Sociais na Web 2.0.

Uma rede social é caracterizada como um grupo de pessoas conectadas entre si por meio de relacionamentos ou serviços baseados na Web, em que os usuários constroem um perfil público, possuem uma lista de usuários conectados e navegam pelas listas de outros usuários [30]. Segundo McCann [31], dois terços dos usuários da internet utilizam redes sociais. Os principais usos dessas redes estão relacionados ao compartilhamento de conteúdo, que vem crescendo desde o primeiro estudo, em 2006. Entre os anos de 2008 e 2009 foi observado que 76% dos usuários de redes sociais fazem *upload* de fotos e 33% de vídeos. O estudo também mostra que 96% dos usuários visitam as páginas de seus amigos virtuais e cerca 66% atualizam seus próprios perfis.

4.1 Funcionalidades Colaborativas em Redes Sociais

Seguindo os critérios de classificação das funcionalidades colaborativas, segundo o modelo 3C de colaboração, a Figura 1 ilustra a identificação das funcionalidades colaborativas no site Facebook (www.facebook.com). Os retângulos são elementos de comunicação, as elipses, coordenação, e as setas, cooperação. Como funcionalidade de comunicação, está identificada a possibilidade de comentário da imagem; como funcionalidade de coordenação, está identificada a denúncia de abuso na imagem e como funcionalidades de cooperação estão identificadas a marcação da foto, compartilhamento e avaliação.

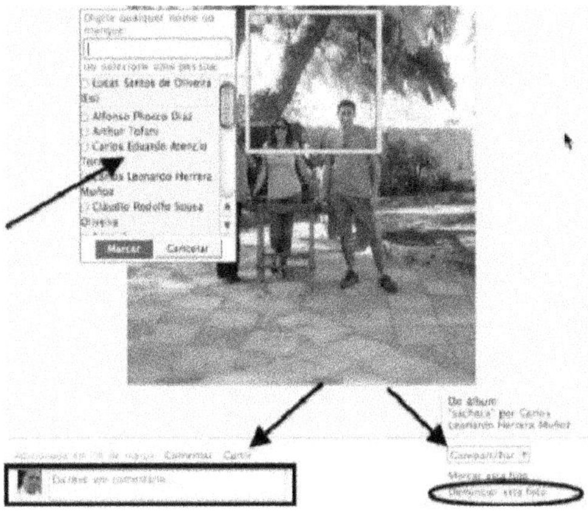

Figura 1. Funcionalidades mapeadas com base no modelo 3C

Essa análise foi replicada em diversas outras redes sociais com o objetivo de levantar as funcionalidades relativas ao compartilhamento de conteúdo mais utilizadas e outras específicas de cada rede. A Figura 2 ilustra o mapeamento das funcionalidades nas diferentes redes sociais, classificadas de acordo com o modelo 3C de colaboração. As redes sociais foram escolhidas com base no ranking de classificação do site Alexa (www.alexa.com) e Wikipédia (www.wikipedia.com), que listam as redes mais acessadas e com maior número de usuários.

Serviço	Funcionalidade	Redes Sociais														
		FACEBOOK	GROUPSITE	ORKUT	FOTOLOG	DEVIANT ART	FOTOKI	PHOTOBUCKET	PICASA	FLICKR	YOU TUBE	HI5	XANGA	NETLOG	WINDOWS LIVE	FRIENDSTER
Comunicação	Comentário	X	X	X	X	X	X	X	X	X	X	X	X	X	X	X
Coordenação	Atividades recentes	X	X	X	X	X	X	X	X	X	X	X	X	X	X	X
	Buscar pessoas	X	X	X	X		X	X	X	X		X			X	X
	Grupos		X		X	X		X	X	X	X		X	X	X	X
	Reportar abuso	X							X		X	X		X		X
Cooperação	Conteúdo compartilhado	X	X	X	X	X	X	X	X	X	X	X	X	X	X	X
	Estatísticas				X	X		X		X	X					
	Avaliação					X		X			X			X		
	Exportar									X	X		X	X	X	X
	Descrição	X	X	X	X	X	X	X	X	X	X	X	X	X	X	X
	Recomendação	X	X	X	X	X	X	X	X	X	X		X	X	X	
	Upload	X	X	X	X	X	X	X	X	X	X	X	X	X	X	X
	Marcar	X		X			X		X	X	X	X			X	X
	Categorias				X	X					X					
	Buscar conteúdo	X	X		X	X	X	X	X	X	X					
	Promover	X		X					X							
	Coleção	X	X	X	X	X	X	X	X	X	X	X	X		X	X
	Favoritos					X	X			X	X	X	X		X	X
	Anotação										X					
	Tagging							X	X	X	X		X	X		
	Permissão	X	X	X	X	X	X		X	X	X		X	X	X	

Figura 2. Funcionalidades colaborativas nas redes sociais

Foram identificadas 21 funcionalidades colaborativas relativas ao compartilhamento de conteúdo nas quinze redes sociais. Apenas uma funcionalidade foi classificada como de comunicação, quatro como coordenação, sendo que a mais recorrente foi atividades recentes, e dezesseis foram classificadas como cooperação, sendo que as mais recorrentes foram compartilhamento de objetos, descrição e upload.

A próxima atividade do método FODA é a Modelagem do Domínio, que consiste de três subatividades: Análise de Funcionalidades, Modelagem da Entidade Relacionamento e Análise Funcional. O objetivo da Análise das Funcionalidades é capturar, em um modelo, o entendimento dos usuários sobre as capacidades gerais das aplicações de um domínio [5]. Na **Error! Reference source not found.**, são representadas essas funcionalidades utilizando uma árvore proposta pelo método FODA e adaptada de [28], em que são representadas funcionalidades colaborativas obrigatórias e opcionais. Suas derivações são alternativas ou exclusivas.

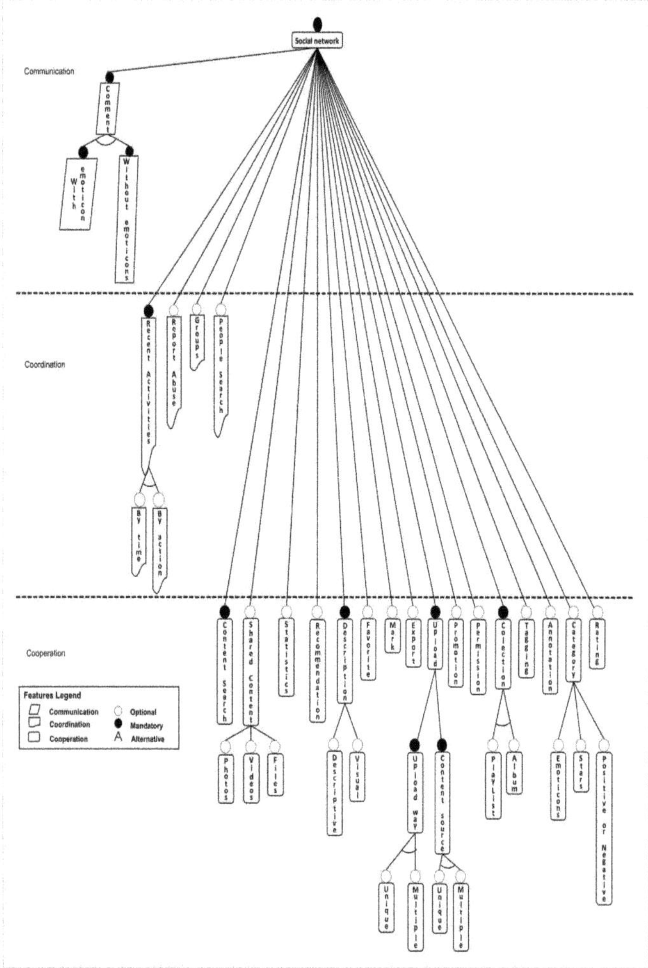

Figura 3.Árvore de funcionalidades colaborativas

A Modelagem Entidade Relacionamento captura e define o conhecimento do domínio que é essencial para implementação de aplicações [5]. Neste trabalho utilizamos o diagrama de classe em vez de entidade relacionamento, por ser mais representativo e atual. A Figura 4 exemplifica o diagrama de classe das funcionalidades colaborativas e o relacionamento entre elas.

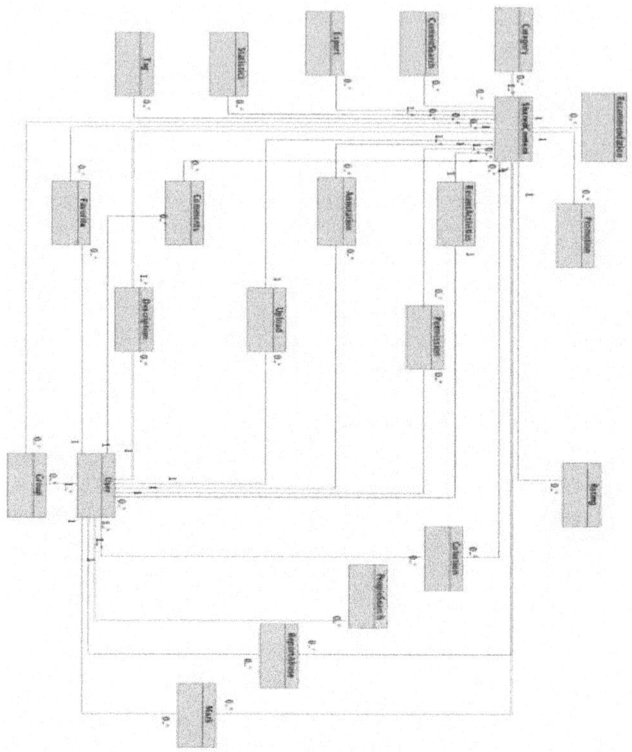

Figura 4. Diagrama de classe das funcionalidades colaborativas

Neste trabalho representamos as diferenças e semelhanças das funcionalidades de acordo com os padrões de interação propostos por Schummer e Lukosch [7]. A seguir é sumarizada a descrição do padrão "Comentário". Por razões de espaço, os outros padrões estão disponíveis no website http://www.groupwareworkbench.org.br/engenhariadedominio.

Comentário:

Figura 5. Comentário com emoticons

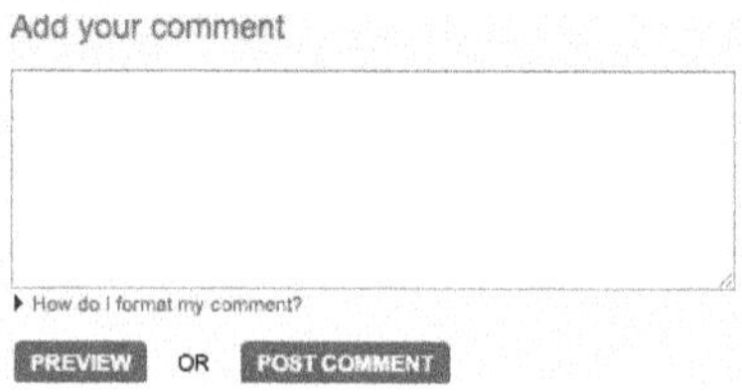

Figura 6. Comentário sem emoticons

Intenção: Possibilita ao usuário fazer uma observação sobre um determinado artefato.

Contexto: Usuário está utilizando uma ferramenta colaborativa e deseja deixar sua opinião sobre um artefato.

Problema: Usuários querem deixar sua contribuição a respeito de um conteúdo para outras pessoas, mas a ferramenta não disponibiliza um mecanismo que possibilite essa contribuição.

Cenário: João está em uma rede social e achou interessante uma imagem da igreja de sua cidade e decidiu comentar alguns fatos históricos da construção, mas não achou um lugar para deixar sua contribuição.

Sintomas: Este padrão deve ser considerado quando:

-Deseja-se que os usuários do sistema contribuam, textualmente, sobre os conteúdos compartilhados.

-Quando se deseja que haja uma discussão a respeito do conteúdo.

Solução: Integrar um mecanismo de comentários que possibilite o usuário deixar sua contribuição e iniciar uma discussão sobre do conteúdo compartilhado.

Dinâmicas: O usuário escreve o texto em campo específico para comentários, podendo adicionar recursos visuais para melhor expressar sua opinião. Após essa etapa, clica no botão de enviar mensagem, aparecendo sua contribuição na lista de discussão. Outros usuários podem acrescentar ou discordar das opiniões através de réplica.

Razões: O padrão comentário provê um fácil e rápido mecanismo de contribuição textual para os usuários.

Verificar: quando aplicar este padrão devem ser respondidas as questões:

-A aplicação permitirá réplicas dos comentários?

-Onde será alocado na interface?

-Terá apenas recursos textuais?

Pontos de perigo: Ter cuidado ao escolher o tipo de texto que será usado no seu comentário e como ele será processado. Pode ocorrer de pessoas colocarem códigos maliciosos no comentário, que podem afetar a estabilidade e segurança do sistema.

Usos conhecidos: Facebook, Orkut, Fotolog e DeviantArt.

Padrões relacionados:

-Fórum: descreve como os usuários podem discutir textualmente sobre um tópico específico.

-Thread de discussão: ajuda encontrar mensagens relacionadas quando usuários replicam um comentário existente.

-Anotação: possibilita ao usuário criar lembretes ou comentários sobre um artefato.

4.2 Implementação do Domínio

A última atividade do método FODA é a modelagem da arquitetura, que provê uma solução de software para os problemas definidos na atividade de modelagem do domínio. Um modelo de arquitetura (também conhecido como arquitetura de referência) é desenvolvido nessa atividade. Um projeto detalhado e a construção dos componentes são baseados nesse modelo [5].

Para este trabalho, tanto para arquitetura quanto para construção dos componentes, é utilizada a plataforma Groupware Workbench [8]. Ela provê um kit de componentes e uma infraestrutura de execução para sistemas colaborativos na Web 2.0. A tecnologia de componentes é vista como apropriada para o desenvolvimento de groupware e há diversos sistemas e plataformas que disponibilizam blocos modulares e relativamente independentes para a construção das aplicações colaborativas [32]. Algumas delas são [33], [34].

O Groupware Workbench estrutura as aplicações, nele desenvolvidas, utilizando componentes chamados collablets, que representam uma parte da aplicação, podendo ser acoplados e desacoplados uns dos outros em tempo de implantação ou mesmo de execução. Cada collablet é composto por algumas classes Java, a saber: entidades, uma implementação da interface de negócio (business) e controladores (controllers). Na camada de apresentação, utilizam-se páginas Java Server Pages (JSP) e alguns widgets de interface gráfica codificados como tagfiles (tagfiles são trechos de código JSP reutilizáveis armazenados em arquivos com a extensão .tag). Toda aplicação tem um collablet principal, que representa o ponto de entrada da aplicação e gerencia todos os demais componentes por meio de subordinação e dependência. Também, há uma ferramenta gráfica para montagem de aplicações, que reconhece os componentes instalados e possibilita compor essas aplicações sem a necessidade de alterar código Java. Nesta proposta, adotou-se o mapeamento um para um entre a funcionalidade levantada na análise do domínio e o componente que a implementa. Como exemplo de implementação utilizando o Groupware Workbench, é descrita a implementação da funcionalidade "comentário" instanciada como o collablet commentMgr, mostrada na Figura 7.

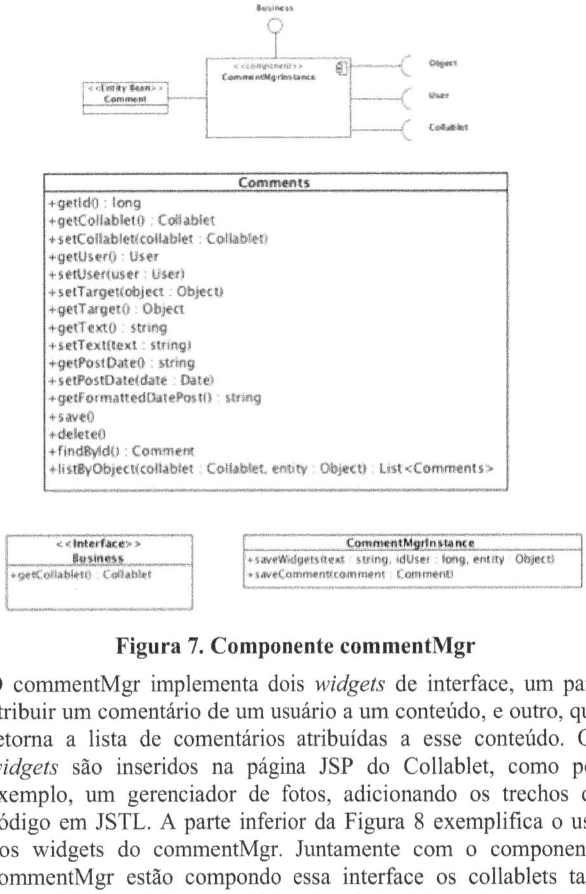

Figura 7. Componente commentMgr

O commentMgr implementa dois *widgets* de interface, um para atribuir um comentário de um usuário a um conteúdo, e outro, que retorna a lista de comentários atribuídas a esse conteúdo. Os *widgets* são inseridos na página JSP do Collablet, como por exemplo, um gerenciador de fotos, adicionando os trechos de código em JSTL. A parte inferior da Figura 8 exemplifica o uso dos widgets do commentMgr. Juntamente com o componente commentMgr estão compondo essa interface os collablets tag, counterMgr, userMgr, searchMgr, descriptionMgr e photoMgr.

Figura 8. Componente de comentário do Arquigrafia Brasil

As variabilidades das funcionalidades colaborativas identificadas na etapa de análise do domínio são tratadas nesse trabalho por meio de *widgets* de interface ou XML de configuração. Por exemplo, para a variação componente comentário com *emoticons*, será necessário implementar um *widget* de interface que provê essa característica, sem a necessidade de alterar a infraestrutura do componente.

5. AVALIAÇÃO

Para a avaliação da engenharia de domínio foi realizado um estudo experimental dividido em duas etapas, uma para avaliar a abrangência do modelo e as descrições dos padrões e outra para avaliar a facilidade de uso e utilidade dos artefatos.

Tendo como base os artefatos gerados na engenharia de domínio temos como objetivos de avaliação as seguintes perguntas:

Abrangência:

- Há funcionalidades colaborativas relativas ao compartilhamento de conteúdo nas Redes Sociais que não foram levantadas na engenharia de domínio?

Utilidade das funcionalidades levantadas:

- Os desenvolvedores entendem os artefatos disponibilizados?
- Os desenvolvedores conseguem usar os artefatos?
- Os desenvolvedores consideram os artefatos úteis?

O experimento foi dividido em duas etapas, realizadas com 9 alunos do curso de Tópicos Especiais em Desenvolvimento para Web ministrado para a graduação e pós-graduação em Ciência da Computação do IME/USP. Na primeira etapa, foi disponibilizado um questionário contendo questões sobre o grau de escolaridade e experiência no uso de redes sociais. Após o preenchimento, foi solicitado que os desenvolvedores levantassem e avaliassem funcionalidades colaborativas nas redes sociais. Ao fim dessa atividade foi passada uma lista com sete funcionalidades colaborativas, com suas respectivas descrições, para que eles lessem os padrões e tentassem identifica-los em uma rede social. Também avaliaram a facilidade de uso, detalhamento e facilidade de identificação.

Na segunda etapa do experimento, foi passado um questionário para levantar os dados sobre a experiência no desenvolvimento Web, em seguida os desenvolvedores foram separados em dois grupos e tiveram de adicionar duas funcionalidades colaborativas, comentário e tags, no sistema de FAQ desenvolvido no Groupware Workbench e outro desenvolvido utilizando o método tradicional de desenvolvimento Web. Ao termino da primeira hora e dez minutos (meia aula) ou quando terminaram a primeira atividade, os grupos inverteram e iniciaram a segunda atividade. Ao final foi passado um segundo questionário com perguntas relativas à execução do experimento, para que os desenvolvedores avaliassem os artefatos utilizados de acordo com a facilidade de uso e a utilidade.

Com relação ao *design* de experimento, o contexto supõe o processo *off-line*, porque os alunos não foram avaliados durante todo o tempo do curso, mas em determinado momento. O estudo é modelado porque as atividades executadas pelos alunos não foram realizadas durante a resolução de um problema real, mas utilizando dois experimentos controlados executados em algumas redes sociais e artefatos da engenharia de domínio previamente estabelecidos.

Para a seleção dos indivíduos, foi proposto um questionário com objetivo de caracterizar a formação dos desenvolvedores do ponto de vista acadêmico e profissional, servindo como dados para seleção dos participantes, análise e redução de viés.

Os critérios para inclusão do participante no experimento foram:

- Na primeira etapa, eles deveriam fazer parte de, pelo menos, uma rede social, utilizasse uma vez por semana e compartilhassem algum conteúdo.
- Na segunda etapa deveriam ter, pelo menos, noção em desenvolvimento Web, JSP e Java.

Com relação às variáveis, foram levados em consideração como variáveis independentes a escolaridade e experiência dos desenvolvedores, coletados por meio do questionário, e os artefatos gerados na engenharia de domínio.

Como variáveis dependentes, foram levados em consideração o grau de similaridade entre as funcionalidades colaborativas levantadas pelos desenvolvedores e as levantadas neste trabalho, o grau de entendimento dos artefatos gerados na engenharia de domínio, o grau de facilidade de uso dos artefatos gerados na engenharia de domínio, o grau de utilidade dos artefatos gerados na engenharia de domínio e o tempo gasto no desenvolvimento das aplicações.

A seguir são mostrados alguns pontos que podem ameaçar a validade do experimento.

Validade interna: é dependente do número de desenvolvedores. Para executar o experimento pressupomos utilizar entre 7 a 15 desenvolvedores para assegurar a validade interna.

Validade de conclusão: para as conclusões do experimento, foi utilizada estatística descritiva, que procura descrever e avaliar certo grupo, sem tirar quaisquer inferências ou conclusões sobre um grupo maior.

Validade de construção: escolhemos um domínio de aplicação amplamente conhecido, sistemas Web, que neutraliza o efeito da experiência dos participantes no domínio. Essa escolha evita que experiências anteriores gerem uma interpretação incorreta do impacto das técnicas propostas.

Validação externa: alguns indivíduos podem realizar o experimento de forma desleixada, sem um interesse verdadeiro na realização das atividades assim como pode acontecer em uma escala industrial. A validade externa do estudo é considerada suficiente, visto que o objetivo foi avaliar a engenharia de domínio realizada do ponto de vista da abrangência, utilidade e facilidade de uso.

Utilizando o formato GQM [35], o objetivo do experimento foi:

Analisar a engenharia de domínio realizada

Com o propósito de avaliar

Com respeito à abrangência, facilidade de uso e utilidade

Do ponto de vista dos desenvolvedores de software colaborativo

No contexto de alunos da disciplina de Tópicos Especiais em Desenvolvimento para Web.

Questões

Q1: Há funcionalidades colaborativas relativas ao compartilhamento de conteúdo em redes sociais que não foram levantadas na engenharia de domínio?

Q2: Os desenvolvedores entendem os artefatos gerados na engenharia de domínio?

Q3: Os desenvolvedores conseguem utilizar os artefatos gerados na engenharia de domínio para construírem um novo sistema?

Q4: Os desenvolvedores consideram os artefatos úteis?

Métricas

Métrica M1-(Q1): A lista de funcionalidades levantadas pelos desenvolvedores que não foram identificadas na engenharia de domínio realizada.

Métrica M2-(Q2): Porcentagem de padrões de interação que os desenvolvedores avaliam como fáceis de entender.

Métrica M3-(Q2): Porcentagem de padrões de interação que os desenvolvedores avaliam como fáceis de identificar em outras redes sociais.

Métrica M4-(Q3): Quantidade de desenvolvedores que conseguem realizar a atividade proposta dentro do tempo de duas horas e vinte minutos com dois componentes.

Métrica M5-(Q3): Porcentagem dos desenvolvedores que avaliam positivamente os artefatos quanto à facilidade de utilização.

Métrica M6-(Q4): Porcentagem dos desenvolvedores que avaliam positivamente os artefatos quanto à utilidade.

Analisando os dados coletados, obtemos:

Para a Questão 1, as funcionalidades colaborativas são equivalentes às encontradas neste trabalho e não houve registro de uma nova funcionalidade colaborativa. Para a Questão 2, 92% dos padrões de colaboração são considerados fáceis de entender e 87% dos padrões são fáceis de identificar. No entanto, alguns desenvolvedores apontaram dificuldade de entendimento dos seguintes padrões: descrição, estatísticas, *upload*, marcar e categoria.

Para Questão 3, todos os desenvolvedores realizaram o experimento, no entanto, menos de 80% avaliaram os artefatos como fáceis de usar, rejeitando a hipótese. Para a Questão 4, quase todos avaliaram como usável, apenas um desenvolvedor avaliou como neutro.

Baseado no experimento, concluímos que os desenvolvedores identificaram as mesmas funcionalidades colaborativas deste trabalho, entendem as descrições das funcionalidades e as classificam como usáveis, mas a usabilidade dos artefatos precisa ser melhorada.

Outra forma de avaliação, no entanto, menos formal, foi o estudo de caso Arquigrafia Brasil [36], que é uma rede social para estudo colaborativo da arquitetura brasileira, que tem por objetivo oferecer um amplo acervo público digital de imagens originais da arquitetura brasileira, ainda inexistente, cedidas e catalogadas pelos próprios usuários. Nesse estudo de caso, é avaliado se os artefatos produzidos na engenharia de domínio são suficientes para a construção de uma rede social.

Depois de várias reuniões de *brainstorm* e outras de levantamento e comparação de funcionalidades identificadas nos grupos foco, realizados com profissionais, especialistas fotógrafos e estudantes de arquitetura, concluímos que as funcionalidades identificadas nesta engenharia de domínio cobre grande parte dos requisitos funcionais utilizados na construção da rede social Arquigrafia Brasil.

6. CONCLUSÃO

A Web 2.0 aumentou a possibilidade de expressão e socialização por meio das ferramentas de comunicação mediada pelo computador. Os usuários não apenas modificam o conteúdo das páginas, como também o organizam, compartilham, criticam e atualizam. Neste trabalho foi proposta uma engenharia de domínio para construção de componentes de software, diminuindo a necessidade de reimplementação e focando na montagem de sistema colaborativos. Para este trabalho, o domínio foi as redes sociais na Web 2.0, com o foco nas funcionalidades colaborativas em torno do compartilhamento de conteúdo dessas redes.

Para realizar essa engenharia de domínio, foi utilizada uma adaptação do método FODA. Na atividade de análise do domínio foi utilizado o modelo 3C de colaboração [25], que classifica as funcionalidades de acordo com sua função (comunicação, coordenação ou cooperação). Ainda nessa atividade foi feita a descrição das funcionalidades com o uso dos padrões propostos por Schummer e Lukosch [7]. Essa adaptação facilitou a organização e a descrição dos artefatos gerados na engenharia de domínio. O Groupware Workbench foi usado nas atividades de projeto e implementação do domínio para desenvolver os componentes de software colaborativos.

Como avaliação dos artefatos gerados na engenharia de domínio, foram realizados um experimento e um estudo de caso. O primeiro avaliou a facilidade de uso, utilidade e entendimento dos artefatos gerados; o segundo, a aplicação desses artefatos em um contexto real, a rede social Arquigrafia Brasil. Desenvolvedores avaliaram os artefatos como usáveis e fáceis de entender. Para o caso de uso, concluímos que a engenharia de domínio realizada cobriu as funcionalidades, previamente identificas independentemente nos grupos foco e nas reuniões de exploração de ideias. Também, essas funcionalidades colaborativas mostraram um grande potencial de reúso em outros domínios, como, por exemplo, jornalismo online [29].

REFERÊNCIAS

[1] O'Reilly, T. 2005.What is Web 2.0: Design patterns and business models for the next generation of software.

[2] Prescott, L. 2007. *Hiwise US consumer generated media report*. Hitwise, fev.

[3] Greenberg, S. 2007. *Toolkits and interface creativity*. Springer Science + Business Media.

[4] Gaines, B. 1999.Modeling and forecasting the information sciences. *Information Sciences 57/58*, p. 13-22.

[5] Kang, K. C.; Cohen, S. G.; Hess, J. A.; Novak, W. E.; Peterson, A. S. 1990. *Feature-Oriented Domain Analysis (FODA) Feasibility Study*. CMU/SEI.

[6] Fuks, H.; Raposo, A. B.; Gerosa, M. A.; Lucena, C. J. P. 2005.Applying the 3C Model to Groupware Development. *International Journal of Cooperative Information Systems (IJCIS)*, v. 14, n. 2-3, p. 238-299.

[7] Schummer, T.; Lukosch, S. 2007. *Patterns for Computer-Mediated Interaction*. John Wiley & Sons Ltd.

[8] Groupware Workbench 2012. Groupware Workbench, Disponivel em: <www.groupwareworkbench.org.br>.

[9] Aharoni, A.; Reinhartz-Berger, I. 2008. *A Domain Engineering Approach for Situational Method Engineering*. University of Haifa.

[10] Harsu, M. 2005. *A survey on domain engineering*. Institute of Software Systems Tampere University of Technology.

[11] Prieto-Diaz, R.; Arango, G. 1991. *Domain Analysis Concepts and Research Directions*". In: Prieto-Diaz, R., Arango, G. (eds), Domain Analysis and Software Systems Modeling. IEEE Computer Society Press.

[12] Clements, P. C. 1997. *Successful Product Line Engineering Requires More Than Reuse*. Software Engineering Institute Carnegie Mellon University.

[13] Alaña, E.; Rodriguez, A. I. 2007. *Domain Engineering Methodologies Survey*. GMV Inovvating Solutions.

[14] Terra, A. P. 2006. *Uma Abordagem de projeto arquitetural baseado em componentes no contexto de Engenharia de Domínio*. COPPE/UFRJ, 207 p.

[15] Lima, C. M.; Marciel, R. M. 2005. A Engenharia de Domínio e o Desenvolvimento Baseado em Componentes. In: *Desenvolvimento Baseado em Componentes, Conceitos e Técnicas*. Editora Ciência Moderna.

[16] Simos, M. 1997.*Organization domain modeling and oo analysis and design: Distinctions, integration, new directions*. STJA'97 Conf. Proc, 126–132.

[17] Kang, K. C.; Kima, S.; Lee, J.; Kim, K.; Shin, E.; Huh, M. 1998.FORM: A feature-oriented reuse method with domain-specific reference architectures. *Annals of Software Engineering 5*.

[18] Griss, M. L.; Favaro, J.; D'alessandro, M. 1998.*Integrating Feature Modeling with the RSEB*.

[19] Frakes, W.; Prieto-Diaz, R.; Fox, C.Dare: Domain analysis and reuse environment. *Ann. Softw. Eng.*, p. 125–141, ISSN 1022-7091.

[20] Braga, R. M. M. 2000. *Busca e recuperac□ão de componentes em ambientes de reutilizac□ão de software*. Rio de Janeiro.

[21] Bayer, J. et al. 1999.Pulse: a methodology to develop software product lines. *Proceedings of the 1999 symposium on Software reusability*, New York, 122–131.

[22] Hoeydalsvik, G. M. 1994. *OORAM: Object-Oriented Role Analysis and Modeling*. Somerset: Wiley-QED Publishing, 141–146 p.

[23] Holibaugh, R. 1993. *Joint Integrated Avionics Working Group (JIAWG) Object-Oriented Domain Analysis Method (JODA)*. Carnegie Mellon University.

[24] DE, E. S. 2007. *RiDE: The RiSE Process for Domain Engineering*. Ph.D. Thesis in Computer Science, UFPE.

[25] Ellis, C. A.; Gibbs, S. J.; Rein, G. L. 1991. *Groupware - Some Issues and Experiences*. Communications of the ACM, v. 34. 38-58 p.

[26] Gerosa, M. A.; Pimentel, M.; Fuks, H.; Lucena, C. J. P. 2006.*Development of Groupware based on the 3C Collaboration Model and Component Technology*. 12th International Workshop on Groupware CRIWG 2006. Valladolid: Lecture Notes on Computer Science LNCS.. p. 302-309.

[27] Gaspar, T. C.; Yaguinuma, C. A.; Do, A. F. 2009.Software product lines for Web 2.0 synchronous collaboration. *WebMedia '09 Proceedings of the XV Brazilian Symposium on Multimedia and the Web*.

[28] Gadelha, B.; Cirilo, E.; Fuks, H.; P., C. J.; Castro, A.; Gerosa, M. A. 2010.Uma *Abordagem para o Desenvolvimento de Linhas de Produto de Groupware Baseados em Componentes Utilizando o Groupware Workbench*. SBSC.

[29] Michalsky, S.; Sonco, E. Z.; Gerosa, M. A. 2010.A Inteligência Coletiva na Web: Uma Análise de Domínio para o Jornalismo Online. *Simpósio Brasileiro de Sistemas Multimídia e Web - WebMedia*, v. II, p. 45-48.

[30] Kazienko, P.; Musial, K. 2006.Social Capital in Online Social Networks, v. 4252, p. 417-424.

[31] Universal Mcann. 2009. *Power to the people - social media tracker wave 4*. Universal McAnn.

[32] Gerosa, M. A. 2006. *Desenvolvimento de groupware componentizado com base no modelo 3C de colaboração*. PUC- Rio.

[33] Hill, J.; Gutwin, C. 2004.he maui toolkit: Groupware widgets for group awareness. *Computer Supported Cooperative Work (CSCW)*, 539–571.

[34] Roseman, M.; Yitbarek, S.; Greenberg., S. 1993. *Groupkit tutorial. Included in the public domain Groupkit distribution*, cpsc. ucalgary.

[35] Solingen, R. V.; Berghout, E. 1999. *The Goal/Question/Metric Method A Practical Guide for Quality Improvement of Software Development*. McGraw Hill, 198 p.

[36] Rozestraten, A. S. et al. 2010. Rede Social Arquigrafia-Brasil: Design de um ambiente online baseado em transdisciplinaridade e colaboração. *VII Simpósio Brasileiro de Sistemas Colaborativos, Anais do SBSC 2010*, v. II.

Developing a Social Network of Support to Health Care: The Experience of GenNet

Magalhães, Cleyton V.C.
UFRPE – UAST
Fazenda Saco, s/n
Serra Talhada – PE - Brazil
55-87-96033791
cleyton.vanut@gmail.com

Santos, Ronnie E.S.
UFRPE – UAST
Fazenda Saco, s/n
Serra Talhada – PE - Brazil
55-87-99027418
ronnie.gd@gmail.com

Correia Neto, Jorge S.
UFRPE – EAD
Rua D. Manoel de Medeiros, s/n, Recife – PE - Brazil
55-81-33206103
jorgecorreianeto@gmail.com

Vilar, Guilherme.
UFRPE - DEINFO
Rua D. Manoel de Medeiros, s/n, Recife – PE - Brazil
55-81- 33206103
guilherme_vilar@yahoo.com.br

ABSTRACT

Based on the context in which social networks and collaborative systems are involved, this paper presents the process of conception, projection and implementation of a collaborative social network with the goal to promote actions related to social inclusion of people with genetic disorders with physical disabilities. Using an experimental and descriptive approach the creation and development of GenNet is described and reflections are made over the particularities of this process in the healthcare environment.

General Terms

Experimentation, Human Factors, Management.

Keywords

Social network sites, collaborative environments, healthcare.

1. INTRODUCTION

In today's society there is a growing need to perform tasks and solve problems collaboratively, whether actors are in the same place at the same time or not [1, 2, 3]. Collaborative environments involve the joint development of processes and technology. The processes are, among others, developments in telemedicine, Open Distance Learning (OLD), and Geographic Information Systems (GIS) [4, 5, 6].

The tools of collaborative work create virtual environments, which allow that tasks usually carried out jointly, by two or more people, can continue to be performed even if individuals are physically distant [6, 7, 8, 9]. This kind of network configuration is peculiar to human beings. They participate in groups and establish relationships based on interests, which may develop and vary during their trajectory, including work relationships [10]. Therefore, network organizations, especially the virtual ones, produce significant transformations in the relation between the subject and the world [11].

Permission to make digital or hard copies of all or part of this work for personal or classroom use is granted without fee provided that copies are not made or distributed for profit or commercial advantage and that copies bear this notice and the full citation on the first page. To copy otherwise, or republish, to post on servers or to redistribute to lists, requires prior specific permission and/or a fee.
WebMedia'12, October 15--18, 2012, São Paulo/SP, Brazil.
Copyright 2012 ACM 978-1-4503-1706-1/12/10...$15.00.

In addition, "When a computer network connects to a network of individuals and organizations, it is a social network" [12]. This is a general definition, although complete, of the concept of virtual social networks. Just as a computer network is formed by a number of machines connected to each other, a social network is composed by a group of people (or organizations) connected via relationships based on interests, such as friendship, work, or exchange of information, for example.

Virtual social network is a kind of specific application in a specific moment which was observed on the Internet and named as *Web 2.0*. Using the expression "anyone can participate", Benioff [13] defines the *Web 2.0* as the generation of Internet applications which started to have user-generated content through collaborative participation in communities. Thus, in this environment of interaction and participation, the *Web* is treated as a platform, capable of generating communities and services in which anyone can participate in content creation [14].

Based on the context that involves social networks and collaborative environment, the purpose of this study is to report how the requirements assessment happened as well as the construction of a virtual social network project which was focused on the promotion of social inclusion actions of disabled individuals, the GenNet network. Next, the methodological procedures that guided the data collection and analysis, the results, and the final considerations will be presented.

2. METHODOLOGICAL PATH

This research is characterized as descriptive and experimental. According to Correia Neto *et al.* [15], this kind of research aims to describe how the facts and phenomena of a certain reality are and how they manifest, selecting a number of issues that will be measured independently.

In this study the following steps of GenNet development were described: a) analysis of functionalities of four major social networks, through which was possible to select the most relevant functionalities for GenNet context; b) interviews with key user profiles expected in the network; c) definition of GenNet network's functionalities, based on collected material, as well as the creation of a graphic interface design project, and; e) system implementation.

2.1 Analysis of Social Networks

In this phase, the data were collected through analysis of the functionalities of four major social networks (*Twitter, Facebook, Orkut* e *Livemocha*), chosen by using the degree of popularity on the *Web,* the nature of its services, and the participation of Brazilians. *Twitter* was one of the analyzed networks given the great popularity that this network was able to quickly achieve on the internet, becoming one of the most appreciated networks both in Brazil and worldwide. *Facebook's* functionalities were also analyzed due to the fact that it is the social network with the greatest number of users in the world, and *Orkut* because it has been the favorite among Brazilians since its creation (according data of Ibope) [17]. In the case of *Livemocha*, its feature of Practical Community (group of people gathered for a common interest) was the reason by which this network was chosen for the analysis process.

2.2 Interviews with Users

In this stage, it was decided to perform unstructured interviews, in which the interviewer follows the respondent, constituting an asymmetrical dialogue since one of the parts pursues to collect information. The researcher usually has a guide with topics that must be covered during the interview, but does not have a specific sequence to ask about them [16].

Thus, the interviews were performed with groups of potential network users who had different profiles (patients, doctors, and representatives of associations) in order to constitute a list of resources, functionalities and priorities of this network.

2.3 Project and Interface

At first, it was sought the degree of familiarity of users that will participate of the network. At this point, it was concluded that a great portion of potential participants won't have a great knowledge about the use of social networks. Thus, the graphical interface design was defined as a way to maintain a balance between what is new in the interface design of *Web* systems (especially in social networks) and the simplicity of commands commonly used in cellular phones.

2.4 Implementation

The set of tools for development, decision regarding programming language, database server, and security criteria were selected through a process of literature review of *Web* System designs. The functionalities defined for GenNet social network were grouped by affinity in five modules, which were located and developed in four iterations, with average time of two weeks for the conclusion of each module, including programming and testing.

3. GENNET SOCIAL NETWORK

The analysis of functionality of the four previously mentioned social networks suggests that the bonds among registered users on the network are well explored elements in this context. Three of the analyzed networks (Facebook, Orkut e Livemocha) have a symmetric kind of relationship, in which both users need to agree with the link between their profiles on the network. In the case of *Twitter*, users have a kind of asymmetric relationship in which a profile can be followed without necessarily having to do the same.

All the analyzed networks consider ways of sending and sharing content among users (texts, photos, videos, and web pages). The networks offer methods with which users can interact with content posted by profiles when there is a relationship. Therefore, information can circulate in the social environment through passing of users, allowing that more profiles become interrelated. To provide means for the discussion of topics of common interests among users is an important way through which social networks become environments keepers of a large amount of stored information and to stimulate relationships among members.

On the other hand, the search tools are fundamental for networks since they allow users to search for information, posts, threads, and profiles registered on the network. This is a manner of keeping the user on the network, enabling people to be found, topics of interests to be monitored, and discussions to be initiated. Finally, the social network can identify patterns between profiles and users' interests in order to suggest possible relationships among users.

The set of functionalities common to the analyzed networks that are considered important for the GenNet network are presented on Chart 1.

Chart 1. Functionalities Extracted.

Functionality	Description
Relationship	Connection between users. It is the essence of social networks.
Sharing	Tools to work on available resources simultaneously or not.
Interaction	Reciprocal action or influence favored by technology.
Threats and Discussion	Elements that users propose for debate and that remain registered for future discussions.
Search	Research for users and contents in the network.
Suggestions of Relationships	Recommendation through which the participants may find other users with common interests.

Interviews with key user profiles and discussion about the use of social networking resulted on a list of requirements that should be addressed on GenNet's construction: a) general information about diseases; b) information about associations of patients and processes; c) content management aiming to ensure the seriousness of the information exchanged; d) recognition of other users in the same condition so that relationships can be established; e) encouraging the participation of users in the topics of discussion and also on the relationship with other members of the network; f) space for the (daily) readers so that users can share experience; g) tracking the route of users in order to conduct audits, and; h) space for the inclusion of external publications, topics about nutrition, and support of judicial processes.

Using all material collected on the analysis of virtual social networks and interviews, it can be clearly defined the set of features of the network:

1. Open session for general public (virtual encyclopedia) with several information;
2. Topics for orientation about actions, aids, and activities;
3. Tools for training (not available on the current version yet);
4. Social profile of users on the network, in which they indicate their kind of representation: doctor, association or other kind of user (patient, family, lawyers, social workers);
5. Sending and receiving messages from other patients;
6. Permission to add people who are interested in establishing relationships and create groups of users to share materials;

7. Participation on discussion forums in order to exchange information with other users;
8. Space for publishing ideas and experiences as a web journal (blog) which may be accompanied by other network users;
9. Tools with which groups of users may create structures of communities to interact;
10. Methods of recommendation with which users can find participants who have the common interests when they join the network.

Through Web conference function it will be possible to obtain resources for synchronous communication with remote points using voice and video, aiming at establishing a collaborative diagnosis, monitoring treatments, training and continued education of health professionals, which demonstrated its importance, especially because patients with motor disorders are treated initially in the State capital and later on their cities of origin.

On the other hand, the elaboration of the graphical interface design of GenNet sought to establish a balance between project's needs, functional requirements defined, and attributes of a proper interface with user.

The initial screen contains the latest news of the network, which are available for user after login. There is a set menu on the left side of all screens of the network, allowing easy navigation across several options available. There will also be available the edition of profile's information, suggestions of friends, and highlighted topics on the network (Figure 1).

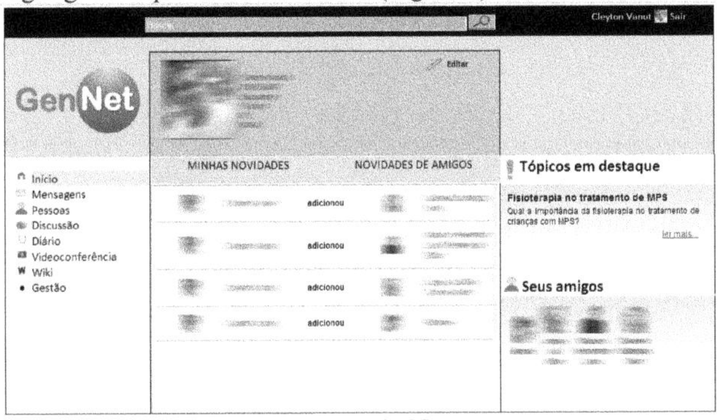

Figure 1. GenNet's Homepage.

The Messages menu has the necessary tools so that users can send various types of content to other network members with whom they established relationships. Public messages can be sent to all contacts, a specific contact, or a group of contacts. Users will be able to see messages received from other contacts, and also the ones sent by them. The messages received can be deleted and/or forwarded for other members (Figure 2).

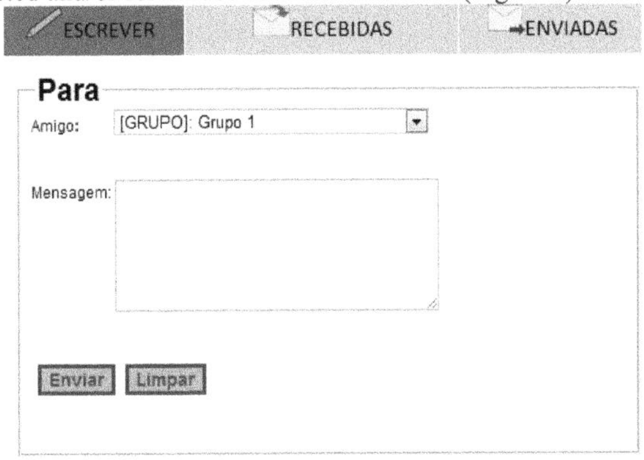

Figure 2. Management of Messages.

The People menu contains all information about relationships formed by participants. Users will be able to see and manage their list of friends, and create groups (Figure 3).

Figure 3. People Management.

By accessing the Discussion, the user is led to the categories of topics debated on the network. Within a topic, users can see, participate by commenting, and evaluate the content of information available. The Discussion menu still has a session of Recent Topics, which has a filter that allows one to see only the discussion recently updated (Figure 4).

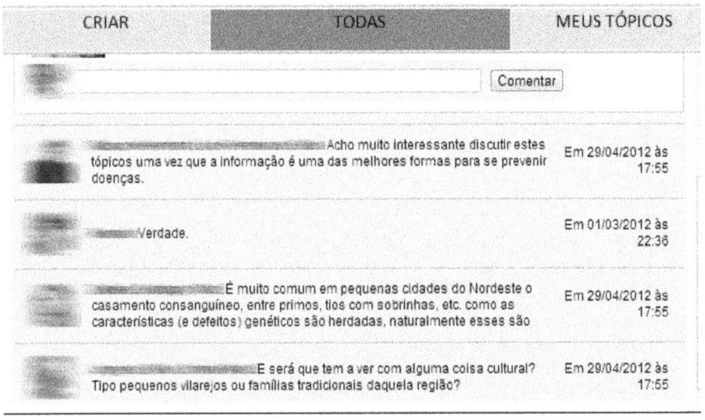

Figure 4. Management of Threads.

The Wiki is the network's area that has features of an encyclopedia (Figure 5). It was conceived with the intention of bringing together the greater number of papers, explanatory texts, and publications about issues surrounding the subject, both in medical and legal contexts. This resource will be open; therefore, it can be viewed by anyone on the *Web* not requiring login.

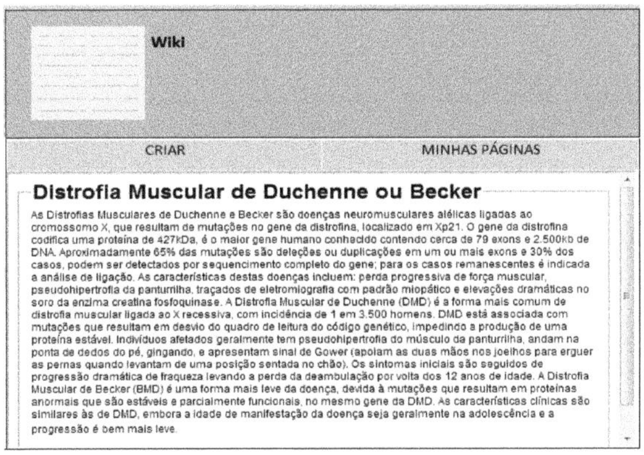

Figure 5. Wiki.

During the implementation of GenNet's first version, programming activities and tests were performed in parallel and simultaneously, i.e., a set of tests was run for every concluded functionality. This first version does not have a specific interface for mobile devices, and it is being used by a small group of users, with the objective of identifying programming flaws and additional needs that were not identified through the phase of gathering of requirements, as well as possible problems regarding the network's interface.

4. FINAL CONSIDERATIONS

GenNet aims to promote understanding, compliance, and training in aspects related to social inclusion of patients with genetic disorders and physical disabilities. Therefore, these processes will be enabled in an easier way in this virtual environment, which involves several individuals, including families, patients, and health professionals.

In this kind of social network related to health, information management is also a great challenge to be explored. Designers should have this in mind and thus strengthen aspects of communication, cooperation, and coordination, characteristics that are essential to collaborative systems. It is also worth noting that another paper will present the perception of the ones involved with the developed prototype and other aspects of security and access of information.

For future researches, this study suggests the realization of a survey seeking to understand the perception of users regarding the graphical interface and experiences of use, and another about the most appropriated algorithms of recommendation in this medical field. The system is available on www.gennet.com.br

5. REFERENCES

[1] BRITO, R. F.; PEREIRA, A. T. C. Um Estudo para Ambientes Colaborativos e suas Ferramentas. **Anais**... Congresso Nacional de Ambientes Hipermídia para Aprendizagem. Santa Catarina, 2004.

[2] ELLIS, C.A.; GIBBS, S.J.; REIN, G.L. Groupware: some issues and experiences. **Communications of the ACM**. January, 1991, v.34, n.1.

[3] McGRATH, J.E.; KRAVITZ, D.A. Group Research. **Annual Review of Psychology**. V. 33, p. 195-230.

[4] MCT. Ministério da Ciência e Tecnologia. Ciência, Tecnologia e Inovação – Desafio para a sociedade brasileira – **Livro Verde**. Brasília, 2000.

[5] MORAN, J. M.; MASETTO, M. T.; BEHRENS, M. A. **Novas Tecnologias e Mediação Pedagógica**. São Paulo, Papirus, 2002.

[6] TEIXEIRA FILHO, J. **Comunidades Virtuais**. Rio de Janeiro, SENAC, 2002.

[7] TAJRA, S.F. **Comunidades Virtuais**. São Paulo: Erica, 2002

[8] VIANNEY, J.; TORRES, P. L.; SILVA, E. F. **A Universidade Virtual no Brasil** – O ensino superior a distância no país. Santa Catarina, Unisul, 2003

[9] PETERS, O. **Didática do Ensino a Distância**. São Leopoldo, Unisinos, 2003.

[10] HOMANS, G.C. **The Human Group**. London: Routledge & Kegan Paul Ltd. 1951.

[11] TOMAÉL, M.I.; ALCARÁ, A.R.; DI CHIARA, I.G. Das redes sociais à inovação. **Revista Ciência da Informação**. Brasília, v.34, n.2, p.93-104, 2005.

[12] GARTON, L.; HAYTHORNTHWAITE, C.; WELLMAN, B. Studying Online Social Networks. **Journal of Computer-Mediated Communication.** Volume 3, 1997. Acesso em: 28 jun. 2012. Disponível em: http://onlinelibrary.wiley.com/doi/10.1111/j.1083-6101.1997.tb00062.x/full

[13] BENIOFF, M. **Welcome to *Web* 3.0**: Now Your Other Computer is a Data Center, 2008. Acesso em: 28 jun. 2012. Disponível em: http://www.techcrunchit.com/2008/08/01/welcome-to-*web*-30-now-your-other-computer-is-a-data-center/.

[14] O'REILLY, Tim. **What Is *Web* 2.0**? - Design Patterns and Business Models for the Next Generation of Software. O'Reilly Publishing, 2005. Acesso em: 07 ago. 2012. Disponível em: http://oreilly.com/web2/archive/what-is-web-20.html

[15] CORREIA NETO, J. S; ALBUQUERQUE, C. R. S; SILVA, C. R. T.; SOUZA, E. P. R. **Metodologia da Pesquisa em Computação**, Universidade Federal Rural de Pernambuco, Recife, 2010.

[16] FARIAS, E. Elaboração de Instrumentos de pesquisa - entrevistas e questionários. Rio de Janeiro: Universidade Estácio de Sá, 2002.

[17] NASCIMENTO, R.M. *E-commerce* no Brasil: perfil do mercado e do e-consumidor brasileiro.**Masters Thesis**. FGV. 2011.

Social Networks Applied to Distance Education Courses: Analysis of Interaction in Discussion Forums

Ernani Gottardo
Instituto Federal de Educação, Ciência e Tecnologia do RS - IFRS
Erechim, Rio Grande do Sul, Brazil
ernani.gottardo@erechim.ifrs.edu.br

Robinson Vida Noronha
Universidade Tecnológica Federal do Paraná - UTFPR
Curitiba, Paraná, Brazil
vida@utfpr.edu.br

ABSTRACT
Driven by public policies, distance education courses or EAD are now a reality in the Brazilian educational system. However, a major difficulty faced by professionals and institutions involved in this type of education refers to the effective monitoring of students. One alternative used by the scientific community to deal with this problem have been investigating techniques for exploring the data stored by the technological systems used, trying to turn them into useful information. This work demonstrated some possibilities of using social network analysis techniques in order to obtain information from the interaction in discussion forums. In the experiments some potentially useful information was obtained, indicating the feasibility of this proposal.

Categories and Subject Descriptors
H.3.3 [**Information Storage and Retrieval**]: Information Search and Retrieval - *Information Filtering*.

Keywords
Social Network Analysis, Distance Education, Online Forums.

1. INTRODUCTION

Research development involving distance education courses, or simply eLearning, became important in the context of the educational system in Brazil, taking into account the wide diffusion of this learning method in the country. Several public initiatives were developed with the aim of encouraging the spread of this teaching modality. Among these initiatives it's possible to highlight the creation of the Open University of Brazil (UAB), E-tec Brazil, School TV, among others.

A major challenge encountered by teachers, institutions and professionals working with this teaching modality refers to the development and operation of effective processes for monitoring tasks developed by students in an eLearning course.

Distance education courses implementation typically involves using some software to support the educational activity. The use of such software is leading to creation of large repositories that record a large amount of data about the students' learning process [9][12].

Permission to make digital or hard copies of all or part of this work for personal or classroom use is granted without fee provided that copies are not made or distributed for profit or commercial advantage and that copies bear this notice and the full citation on the first page. To copy otherwise, or republish, to post on servers or to redistribute to lists, requires prior specific permission and/or a fee.
WebMedia'12, October 15–18, 2012, São Paulo/SP, Brazil.
Copyright 2012 ACM 978-1-4503-1706-1/12/10...$15.00.

However, it is important to emphasize that simply creating large databases becomes useless to support courses management and students' monitoring. So, supplying of appropriate tools for extraction, analysis and interpretation of information from these databases is an essential task.

Thus, some research [4] [8] [12] have been developed to exploit this large amount of data and transform them into useful information for those involved in distance education courses, such as teachers, tutors, managers and students.

Take into account aspects related to the interaction (e.g. teacher-student, student-student), collaboration and feedback in the analysis process of data available in LMS (Learning Management System) is extremely important according to [8] [10].

In this context, this paper investigates the potential generated by using social network analysis techniques in order to obtain interaction patterns from discussion forums that could have influence on learning. The discovered patterns could be useful as information to support teachers in developing strategies for monitoring and management of distance education courses.

The rest of this paper is organized as follows. Section 2 presents theoretical assumptions concerning eLearning courses and the importance of interaction in these courses. In sections 3 and 4 are presented, respectively, the contextualization of the study and conducted experiments. Section 5 is dedicated to analyze the experiments' results. Finally, section 6 presents the conclusions and future works.

2. INTERACTION IN DISTANCE LEARNING COURSES

Distance education presents some characteristics that distinguish it from traditional classroom education. Distance education, in essence, is a bidirectional communication system technology (LMS) that replace the personal interaction between teacher and student in a classroom [11].

The bidirectional and dialogical aspect of communication between teacher or tutor and students is an essential factor of success in distance education courses [11].

According to [1], the interaction, dialogue and collaboration are factors that determine the nature of learning, since the quality of distance education courses is directly related to them. These factors are closely related to the quality of participation of those involved in the process of knowledge production.

The interactions in a distance learning environment have highlighted its importance for the "Theory of Interaction in Distance Education" [10]. This theory identifies the following three types of relevant interactions considering eLearning environments: I) between the student and the material of the course, II) between the student and the expert who prepared the material or some other expert acting as teacher or instructor and III) between a student and other students, alone or in groups, with or without real-time presence of an instructor.

Additionally, [13] complete that, from an abstract point of view, a significant part of the activities in any online learning experience is based on interactions.

Thus, it is noticed that there is a general acceptance about the importance of interaction and collaboration as the basis for the practice in present-day online education and recognition of social networks importance in this environment. However, it has been given little attention to evaluating the impact of the interaction network of each student in their learning [2] [3].

A technique known as Social Network Analysis provides a method to investigate the interaction patterns and the degree of connection between a defined set of actors [3]. In this work, this technique is applied to extract records from interactive discussion forums and review a few measures which represent some aspects of relations between students.

In a distance learning course some tools (e.g. chats, forums, messaging) that allow interaction between participants are usually provided by LMS. The choice of discussion forums in this work is justified given that they represent one of the most used tools to support collaborative learning, which may replace or supplement classroom activities [4] [8]. Also according to these authors, discussion forums are important as they allow students to share information, solve problems and discuss specific issues explicitly, leaving their contributions available in written form.

3. STUDY CONTEXTUALIZATION

To implement the proposed study a MOODLE[1] database will be used. This database store information of distance courses offered by a Brazilian Federal Higher Education Institution. It was chosen the course that used the largest number of discussion forums. From the discussion forums available on the selected course it was chosen which had the highest number of posts.

Considering the discussion forum selected, a procedure was developed , using SQL Language, to extract the data to be used in the study. The data were generated in a format compatible with Gephi [7], which was the tool used in this work. Gephi is an open-source interactive visualization and exploration platform for all kinds of networks, complex systems, dynamic and hierarchical graphs [7].

To use Gephi resources it's need to import data from two files. A file must contain information about the vertices or nodes and the other about the edges. Within this study, the vertices correspond to forum participants. The edges represent the interactions between the participants represented by the "post-reply" chain of messages, as usual in an online discussion forum

The file with information about the vertices must include at least one unique identifier and a label. In this study, the code of stundent at Moodle was used as a unique identifier. For confidentiality reasons, the label was composed by the unique identifier and a character to indicate the role of each participant (P: Teacher, E:Student, D: Dropout Student).

[1] Open-Source LMS available at http://moodle.org

The file with information about the edges must contain at least three columns: source, target and type. The source and target represent the participants involved in messages exchanged in a discussion forum. The type was defined as "Directed", since it intends to differentiate the directions of communication.

From the discussion forum used in the study were obtained 54 instances in the vertices file and 81 instances in edges.

4. EXPERIMENTS

After importing the data in Gephi, it is possible to visualize the representation of the graph. Figure 1 shows the graph generated, where the numbers displayed in each vertex represents the code of the student at MOODLE and letters identify the roles of participants as defined in section 3. In this figure, the size of the vertex is proportional to the out-degree (i.e. number of edges having the vertex as a source), thus allowing visualize participants that more replied posts of others.

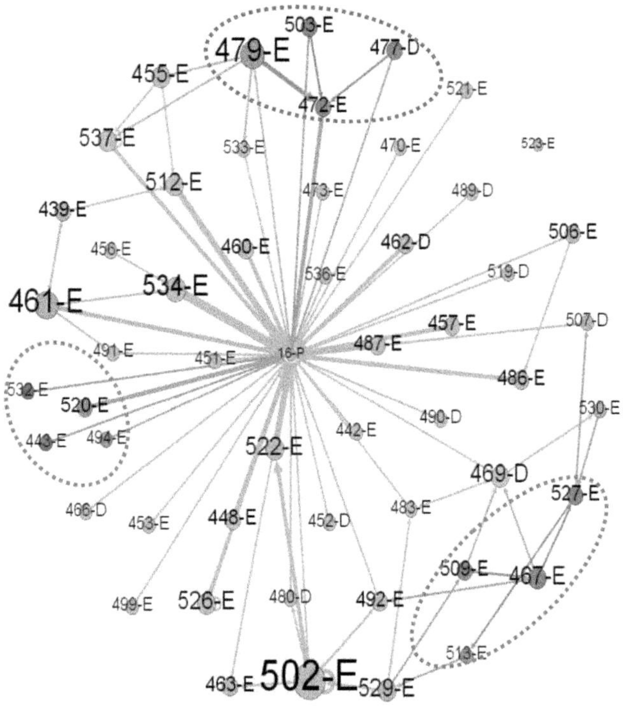

Figure 1 - Graph showing the interactions occurred in the discussion forum

In Figure 1, the edges represent the interactions occurring in the context of the forum. The thickness of the edges shows the intensity of the relationship (i.e. number of messages) occurring between the vertices. The arrows represent the direction in which the interaction occurred.

It was decided to use of directed graphs given that it is essential to consider in this scenario the direction that interaction happened. Additionally, some vertices were manually highlighted with different colors and grouped within a circle to facilitate analysis of the results in Section 5.

The layout used in Figure 1 and in all other figures presented below is known as Fruchterman-Reingold [6]. Among the layouts available in Gephi, Fruchterman-Reingold was achieved the best results in visualization of graphs used in this work.

In addition to information that can be inferred by analyzing the initial view of the graph, presented in Figure 1, it's possible to get a set of additional measures that represent several other aspects, describing the network and their relationships. Following this document, some of these measures will be presented.

4.1 Closeness Centrality

Closeness centrality is defined as the average geodesic distance (i.e. shortest path) between a vertex and all other vertices reachable from it. A vertex that is connected by several shortest paths to other vertices can be interpreted as relatively autonomous compared to other less connected. In a social network, the goal of closeness centrality is to discover if a component is close to others in the network and can interact more quickly with all other participants [5].

Figure 2 shows the graph after applying the closeness centrality to experimental data. In this figure, the size and color of each vertex are defined in terms of this measure. Vertices with larger size and darker color (e.g. 530,469) represent participants with higher values for closeness centrality.

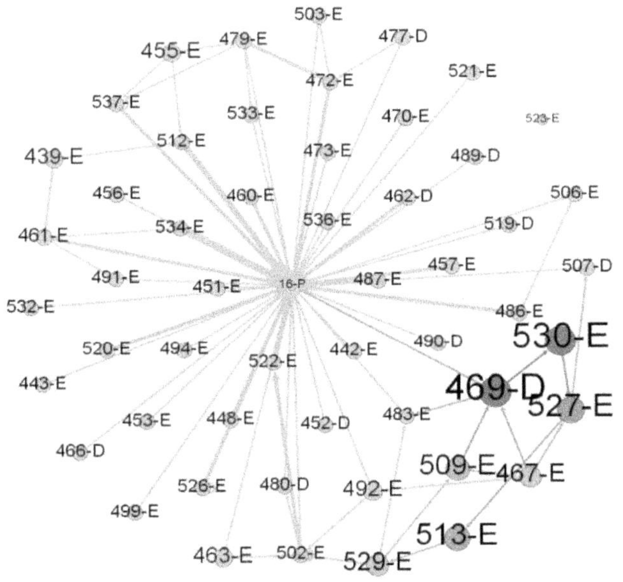

Figure 2 – Graph showing the closeness centrality of participants in the discussion forum.

4.2 Betweenness Centrality

Betweenness centrality is a measure of centrality of a vertex in a graph. Vertices that occur in many shortest paths between other vertices have higher 'betweenness'. One can understand the betweenness centrality of a vertex as the total amount of flux that it concentrates, taking into consideration the stream through all the pairs of vertices in a graph [5].

This measure was introduced to quantify the control of a vertex (e.g. humans) on the communication between other vertices in a social network (e.g. forum) [5].

The graph visualization after applying this measure on the experimental data is shown in Figure 3. Just as in the previous figure, the size and color of the vertices are directly proportional to the betweenness centrality. Thus, the participants represented by codes 529, 527, 502 and 513 are those that presented the highest values in this measure.

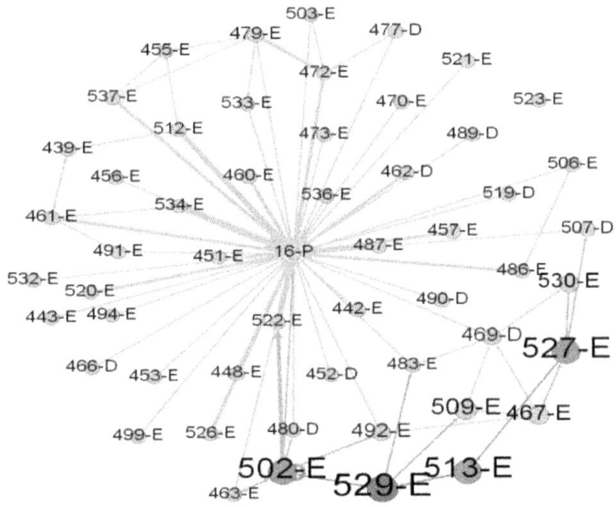

Figure 3 - Graph displaying closeness centrality measure

4.3 Clustering

Clustering is a mathematical process in which different elements of a particular set are grouped based on similarities between them [5].

In a social network, clustering algorithms try to put together individuals who make "subnetworks" or communities (e.g. population subgroups where everyone knows each other) [5].

Figure 4 shows the result of applying a clustering technique to the experimental data. In this figure, the color darkness of the vertices define the group or community of each vertex, i.e., vertices of the same color belong to the same community or group.

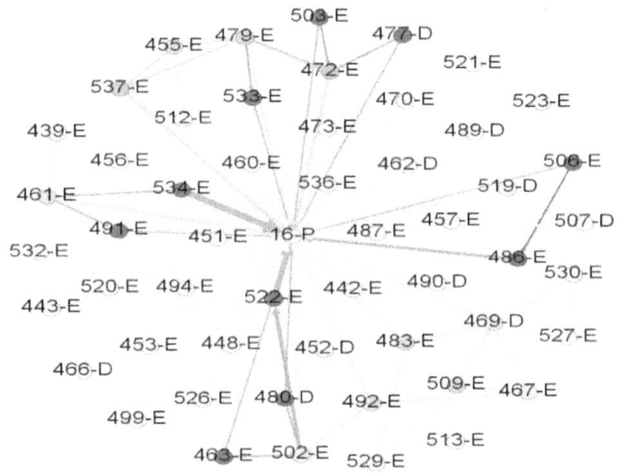

Figure 4 – Discovered clusters in forum data

The clustering algorithm implemented in Gephi and used to generate the graph shown in Figure 4 is konwn as "Louvain Method", proposed in [14].

The algorithm consists of two phases that are repeated iteratively. In the first phase, a different community is assigned to each node. Then, for each node *i* it consider the neighbours *j* of *i* and evaluate the gain of modularity that would take place by removing *i* from its community and by placing it in the community of *j*. The first phase is completed when a local maxima of the modularity is attained, i.e., when no individual move can improve the modularity. The second phase of the algorithm consists in building a new network whose nodes are now the communities found during the first phase [14].

Modularity is a measure of network structure or graphs. It measures the strength of the network division into modules (also called groups, clusters or communities). Networks with high modularity have dense connections between the vertices within modules, but the connections between vertices of different modules are sparse [5].

5. RESULTS ANALYSIS

In a preliminary analysis, considering only the visual representation of the graph shown in Figure 1, it's clear that the vertex 16, which represents the teacher (role equal to "P"), has a concentration of incident edges (i.e., edges which has the vertex as a target).

However, observing Figure 1 it is clear that the size of vertex 16 is small, indicating that it is not highlighted by the out-degree, i.e., have responded to postings of other participants. This could indicate that the teacher just started the discussion topics, and has not interacted with the class during the course of the forum.

Moreover, analyzing Figure 1 it's possible to observe some differences in behavior presented by students. Some students, highlighted with red, (e.g. 532,520,443,494) interacted only with the teacher (16). Others (e.g. 527,509,467,513), green colored, interacted only with colleagues. Finally, some students, marked in blue, (e.g. 479,503,472,477) interacted with peers and teachers.

Analyzing closeness and betweenness centrality measures, presented, respectively, in Figures 2 and 3, reveals some students which stand out. Based on this information, further analysis could be developed for the development of specific teaching strategies to be used in the course.

By analyzing the clustering graph in Figure 4, it's possible to visualize, at least, three distinct groups of students based on their interaction profile in the discussion forum. This information could be useful, for example, as a guide in definition of group members for development of jointly activities.

6. CONCLUSIONS AND FUTURE WORKS

The experiment results presented here demonstrate the feasibility of obtaining some potentially useful information to help monitoring students enrolled in distance learning courses. Information was obtained from the application of Social Network Analysis techniques on interaction data taken from discussion forums.

This information could be used as support to managers or courses' coordinators to analyze behavior aspects of teachers and tutors regarding the involvement and interaction with students in the development of courses.

Furthermore, teachers or tutors would have access to information about the profile of each student participation in discussion forums, and may establish actions aimed at improving involvement, that could result in a better performance of students. An action could involve sending a message to low engaged students and encourage their participation.

Future works could be developed in order to verify the relationship between the measures likely to be obtained by Social Network Analysis techniques (e.g. closeness centrality, betweenness centrality, clustering, etc.) and performance presented by students. This application could be useful in models that use Educational Data Mining techniques in order to make inferences about the performance of students in a distance education course.

7. REFERENCES

[1] Borba, M.C.D., Malheiros, A.P.S.D., Zulatto, R.B.A. *Educação a Distância Online*. 2.ed. Belo. Horizonte:Autêntica, 2008.

[2] Brown, J. S., & Adler, A. P. Minds on fire: Open education, the long tail, and learning 2.0. *EDUCAUSE Review*, 43(1), 16-32, 2008.

[3] Dawson, S., Mcwillian, E. *Investigating the application of IT generated data as an indicator of learning and teaching performance*. Queensland University of Technology and the University of British Columbia, 2008.

[4] Dringus, L.P., Ellis, T. Using Data Mining as a Strategy for Assessing Asynchronous Discussion Forums. *Computers & Education*, n. 45, p.141-160, 2005.

[5] Easley, D., Kleinberg, J. *Networks, Crowds, and Markets: Reasoning about a Highly Connected World*. New York, Cambridge University Press, 2010.

[6] Fruchterman, T. M. J., Reingold, E. M. Graph Drawing by Force-Directed Placement. *Software: Practice & Experience*, Vol. 21, Issue 11, p.1129-1164, 1991.

[7] Gephi, Available at http://gephi.org/, accessed on 07/2012.

[8] Li, Y. Huang, R. Analyzing Peer Interaction in Computer-Supported Collaborative Learning: Model, Method and Tool. *Lecture Notes in Computer Science (LNCS)*. n. 5169, p.125-136, 2008.

[9] Merceron, A., Yacef, K. Tada-ed for educational data mining. In *Interactive Multimedia Electronic Journal of Computer-Enhanced Learning*, 7, 2005.

[10] Moore, M. G., Kearsley, G. *Educação a distância: uma visão integrada*. São Paulo, Thomson Learning, 2007.

[11] Pereira, J.M. Educação Superior a Distância, Tecnologias de Informação e Comunicação e Inclusão Social no Brasil. *Revista de Economia Política de las Tecnologías de la Información y Comunicación*, vol. XII, n.2, Mayo-Agosto, 2010.

[12] Romero, C. Ventura, S. Educational Data Mining: A Review of the State of Art. *IEEE Transactions on Systems , Man, and Cybernetics – Part C: Application and Reviews*. VOL. 40, NO.6., p. 601-618, 2010.

[13] Romero-Zaldivar, V.A., Pardo, A., Burgos, D., Kloss, C.D. Monitoring Student Progress Using Virtual Appliances: A Case Study. *Computers & Education*, n. 58, p.1058-1067, 2012.

[14] Vincent D. Blondel, J. G, Renaud, L. Etienne, L. Fast unfolding of communities in large networks. *Journal of Statistical Mechanics: Theory and Experiment.*, p.12-20, 2008.

Interaction and Audience Analysis in Interactive Digital TV Systems

Samuel da C. A. Basílio, Marcelo F. Moreno e Eduardo Barrére
Departamento de Ciência da Computação
Universidade Federal de Juiz de Fora
Rua José Kelmer, S/n - Juiz de Fora - MG - Brasil
alvesbasilio@gmail.com, moreno@ice.ufjf.br, eduardo.barrere@ice.ufjf.br

RESUMO

Este artigo propõe e compara duas abordagens para captura de dados destinados à análise de interação de usuários e medição de audiência em sistemas de TV Digital Interativa (TVDI). A primeira abordagem é dependente do desenvolvimento de extensões aos padrões existentes e a segunda faz uso apenas de recursos comumente disponíveis em sistemas de TVDI. Ferramentas para análise de interação e audiência também são apresentadas, as quais, independente da abordagem escolhida, permitem o tratamento dos dados oriundos da interação entre usuários e seus receptores digitais.

ABSTRACT

This paper proposes and compares two approaches for data capture to support the analysis of user interaction and audience measurement in Interactive digital TV (IDTV) systems. The first approach relies on the development of extensions to existent standards and the second one depends only on resources commonly available in IDTV systems. Tools for audience and interaction analysis are also presented, which, independently from the approach chosen, allow for the handling of data originated from the interaction between users and their digital receivers.

Categories and Subject Descriptors

H.5.4 [**Hypertext**]: Hypermedia

General Terms

Algorithms, Management, Standardization.

Keywords

Ginga, TV Digital, Interação, Audiência, Medição.

Permission to make digital or hard copies of all or part of this work for personal or classroom use is granted without fee provided that copies are not made or distributed for profit or commercial advantage and that copies bear this notice and the full citation on the first page. To copy otherwise, to republish, to post on servers or to redistribute to lists, requires prior specific permission and/or a fee.
WebMedia'12, October 15–18, 2012, São Paulo/SP, Brazil.
Copyright 2012 ACM 978-1-4503-1706-1/12/10 ...$15.00.

1. INTRODUÇÃO

No Brasil, as maiores redes de televisão são de capital privado e, por isso, visam o lucro de seus proprietários. Nesse ambiente, o principal produto comercializado é o espaço publicitário e sua audiência. Mesmo provedores de conteúdo por assinatura baseiam parte de sua receita na venda de espaços para publicidade. O anunciante deseja que sua propaganda seja vista pelo maior número de pessoas possível, e mais ainda, também deseja saber se o público-alvo está sendo atingido. Afinal, não existe razão para mostrar um produto para um público que por ele não se interessaria. Por isso, é do interesse das emissoras e, mais ainda, dos anunciantes que exista uma eficiente análise de audiência.

Um dos principais institutos que realizam pesquisas em audiência na TV aberta e por assinatura no país é o IBOPE, que segue duas metodologias de trabalho [10]. A mais antiga e abrangente é chamada de caderno, na qual o telespectador recebe um formulário onde durante duas semanas ele escreve qual programação assistiu em intervalos de 15 minutos. A segunda forma, mais atual e elegante, é através de um aparelho chamado *peoplemeter*, que é instalado na casa de cada telespectador que terá a audiência mensurada. Porém, esse aparelho tem um custo alto, fato que obriga o IBOPE a restringir o número de aparelhos em funcionamento.

No sistema de medição através do *peoplemeter*, sempre que o telespectador começa a assistir TV, deve indicar quem irá utilizar o aparelho. Para isso, o aparelho tem um número previamente configurado para identificação de cada morador da casa. Essa necessidade gera alguma incerteza na análise dos dados, pois os dados recebidos são provenientes de telespectadores que sempre são lembrados que estão tendo a audiência mensurada.

O Brasil possui mais de 5000 municípios, entre os quais apenas 15 são praças regulares[1] estudadas pelo IBOPE, segundo números de 2012. Em oito dessas praças a medição é feita em tempo real. Observa-se, portanto, que há uma concentração da medição de audiência em algumas poucas cidades.

Outra característica do atual sistema de medição de audiência diz respeito aos dados que são capturados para análise. Basicamente, os dados capturados se restringem à identifi-

[1]Praças regulares são os locais onde o IBOPE realiza a medição da audiência constantemente através de *peoplemeters*. As praças regulares são Manaus, Belém, Fortaleza, Recife, Salvador, Distrito Federal, Goiânia, Belo Horizonte, Campinas, Grande São Paulo, Grande Rio de Janeiro, Vitória, Curitiba, Florianópolis e Porto Alegre.

cação dos canais, horários e perfil do usuário (idade, sexo, etc.). No entanto, em sistemas de TV digital pode-se imaginar que apenas esses dados não serão suficientes para uma medição completa, pois pode ser do interesse do anunciante ou da emissora, junto com fluxo de áudio e vídeo enviar também aplicações interativas. Se o sistema de medição for incapaz de verificar se essas aplicações estão sendo ou não utilizadas pelos telespectadores, uma importante fonte de dados pode estar sendo descartada.

Além disso, a forma com que o *peoplemeter* reconhece os canais que estão sendo assistidos impossibilita a identificação de qual programação está sendo realmente vista pelo telespectador, no caso da emissora trabalhar com a multiprogramação, como mostra o trabalho [4]. Quanto ao suporte à medição de uso de aplicações interativas, o *peoplemeter* encontra-se igualmente despreparado.

Em sistemas de TV Digital Interativa (TVDI), os receptores digitais (sejam eles *Set-Top Boxes*, TVs ou dispositivos portáteis) devem possuir instalada uma implementação de *middleware*, software responsável por gerenciar a execução de aplicações interativas. Nos casos do Sistema Brasileiro de TV Digital (SBTVD), de Sistemas a Cabo baseados na Recomendação ITU-T J.201 [2] e de Sistemas IPTV baseados na Recomendação ITU-T H.761 [1], o padrão de *middleware* comum é o Ginga-NCL[3]. Neste contexto, no projeto GingaAiyê [12], que visa a criação de aplicações não convencionais para a TV Digital, foi estabelecida a necessidade de criação de uma ferramenta de análise de interação.

O presente trabalho propõe duas abordagens para a questão da captura das interações dos usuários com a finalidade de realizar a análise de interação e medição de audiência, utilizando para isso os recursos dos próprios receptores de TVDI. Um benefício imediato destas soluções é o fato de que qualquer telespectador, possuidor de um receptor de TVDI com canal de retorno habilitado, é um potencial participante da análise, minimizando assim os problemas relacionados à pequena amostragem utilizada atualmente e à limitação de cidades participantes da medição de audiência. Com isso, a análise se tornará mais abrangente e precisa, beneficiando, principalmente, anunciantes e emissoras que terão um retorno mais preciso de quantos, quando e por quem seus anúncios e programação estão sendo assistidos.

O uso de recursos do receptor digital e sua presença intrínseca na casa do telespectador, seja qual for o sistema de TVDI, tornará latente o fato de que sua audiência está sendo medida. Evidentemente, o telespectador sempre deve, por questão de privacidade, concordar previamente com o envio dos dados. De qualquer forma, as soluções apresentadas neste trabalho possuem como benefício imediato o fato de que o telespectador não terá à vista um aparelho adicional que o lembre estar participando da medição e nem a necessidade de qualquer outro equipamento complementar.

A forma de captura de dados proposta neste artigo segue duas abordagens diferentes. A primeira abordagem é baseada em algumas das funcionalidades propostas no projeto GingaAyê, que estendem a arquitetura padrão para televisão digital. Já a segunda abordagem se baseia somente em recursos e funcionalidades normalmente disponíveis em sistemas de televisão digital interativa. Independente da abordagem para a captura de dados, é apresentada uma ferramenta que permite a análise desses dados para mensurar audiência e padrões de comportamento dos telespectadores. Uma comparação da inserção da ferramenta em cenários seguindo as duas abordagens para captura de dados é também apresentada, no intuito de subsidiar decisões de projeto para a implantação de serviços de medição de audiência.

Este artigo está estruturado da seguinte forma. A Seção 2 discute os trabalhos relacionados. Na Seção 3 dois modelos alternativos para captura dos dados nos receptores digitais são propostos. As Seções 4 e 5 são dedicadas à descrição das Ferramentas para Análise de Interação e Audiência e suas implementações. Na Seção 6 os dois modelos de captura propostos são comparados e a Seção 7 fica reservada para conclusões e discussão de trabalhos futuros.

2. TRABALHOS RELACIONADOS

Além da tradicional forma de medição de audiência, outras soluções vêm sendo propostas para a medição de audiência no Brasil. A solução proposta em [9] é baseada no reconhecimento automático, via hardware, dos logos exibidos pelas emissoras de TV durante sua programação. A medição pode ser feita de forma offline ou online, conforme recursos computacionais disponíveis. Além de necessitar um hardware específico, o trabalho não faz uso de *software* e/ou *middleware* encontrados em sistemas de TVDI.

Becker em [4] propõe uma solução em software no contexto do SBTVD. A solução permite que a identificação de canais e perfis de usuário sejam informados em tempo real a uma central. O software é um programa residente no receptor digital, que se comunica por meio de uma porta serial com um computador pessoal para realizar o registro como ponto de medição. Não fica claro na proposta se o computador pessoal continua sendo necessário ao longo da coleta e envio de dados, agindo como um intermediador. De qualquer forma, a necessidade de configuração inicial por meio de porta serial demanda a visita de técnicos do instituto de pesquisa para realizar o registro do ponto de medição. Além disso, o uso de software residente para a coleta e envio de dados traz o problema de não portabilidade entre receptores digitais disponíveis no mercado, por serem baseados nas mais variadas plataformas de hardware e software. Por fim, a medição do uso de aplicações interativas é deixada como possibilidade futura para extensão da ferramenta.

Diferentemente da proposta de Becker, este trabalho faz uso somente dos recursos do receptor digital, em ambas as abordagens apresentadas na Seção 3 para a captura de dados. Especificamente para a primeira abordagem, que depende de extensões às funcionalidades padronizadas de sistemas de TVDI, algumas das soluções resultantes do projeto GingaAyê são utilizadas. A captura de interações ocorridas no receptor digital [8] e a identificação automática dos telespectadores [5], são utilizadas para permitir, além da captura do canal e programação sintonizados, a captura de todas as interações do telespectador com as aplicações, que podem estar ou não relacionadas como o programa/propaganda. Já para a segunda abordagem, somente as habilidades usualmente encontradas em *middleware* para TVDI são exploradas para a captura de dados.

3. MODELOS DE CAPTURA DOS DADOS

Antes de qualquer tipo de análise das interações e da audiência dos usuários é necessário que os dados relevantes para a medição sejam capturados no receptor digital. Para realizar tal captura, este trabalho propõe dois modelos alternativos.

3.1 Captura por meio de extensão do middleware

Com o desenvolvimento de extensões ao padrão original de *middleware* de TVDI, muitas novas funcionalidades podem ser acrescentadas. O objetivo destas extensões é justamente agregar ao padrão possibilidades que não foram vislumbradas no momento de sua criação. Uma dessas extensões é o Componente de Captura de Interação do Usuário (CCIU) [8].

O componente de captura de interação do usuário foi desenvolvido como um módulo de um sistema de recomendação de programação. O CCIU atua monitorando constantemente o controle remoto do usuário. Qualquer interação usando o controle remoto é armazenada em uma base de dados do receptor digital.

O fato do componente de captura de interação do usuário ser um módulo de extensão a uma implementação de *middleware* garante que todos os dados necessários para a análise de interação do usuário sejam devidamente capturados. Sem dúvida, qualquer evento gerado pelo telespectador pode ser capturado, da mudança de canal ao controle de volume, da navegação por setas ao uso de botões coloridos. Também fica estabelecido um formato padrão para o armazenamento e transmissão dos dados, definido pelo CCIU [8]. Sobre a privacidade do usuário, o uso de um módulo de *middleware* pode ser benéfico, pois sempre que o módulo for ativado para início de captura dos dados o telespectador pode ser notificado e questionado sobre sua concordância.

Porém, uma importante limitação dessa abordagem é a necessidade da instalação de software nativo no receptor digital do usuário que terá sua interação analisada. Se não for possível a adição desse módulo em um determinado receptor digital, por motivos de compatibilidade, por exemplo, seu usuário não poderá participar da análise de interação.

De fato, a necessidade do componente de captura de interação do usuário ser instalado no receptor digital do cliente é um grande empecilho para o uso desta arquitetura em um ambiente real, especialmente se considerarmos os modelos de receptor digital disponíveis hoje no mercado. No entanto, esta arquitetura pode ser útil para certos planos de negócios dos institutos de pesquisa, ou mesmo em futuro próximo, com a evolução dos modelos de receptores digitais e de suas funcionalidades.

3.2 Captura por meio de aplicações interativas

Considerando a possibilidade de realização da captura de dados por meio de uma aplicação interativa, as linguagens NCL e Lua podem ser consideradas boas opções para implementação, uma vez que estão padronizadas para sistemas de TV digital terrestre, cabo e IPTV.

O maior benefício dessa abordagem é a dispensa de qualquer módulo externo não previsto no padrão. Por outro lado, trata-se de uma mudança no paradigma de medição de audiência, uma vez que os institutos de pesquisa necessitarão estabelecer parcerias com as emissoras de TV interessadas em ter sua audiência mensurada, para que estas coloquem em seu fluxo de dados (e.g. carrossel de objetos) a aplicação-base [2] de captura implementada em NCLua. Ela é sinalizada no fluxo de dados como uma aplicação de início automático.

A Figura 1 ilustra um fluxograma simplificado para a aplicação-base. Quando ela é executada, verifica se há canal de retorno habilitado no receptor digital, necessário para o envio dos dados em tempo real. Nota-se que, por interesse do instituto de pesquisa, o canal de retorno pode ser por eles subsidiado durante o período de amostragem, incentivando a participação de telespectadores. Se não houver canal de retorno habilitado, a aplicação-base é encerrada. Caso contrário, a aplicação-base verifica se já existe um arquivo de configuração no receptor. Se este arquivo não existir, o usuário é questionado se deseja participar da captura dos dados. Caso o usuário não concorde em participar da captura dos dados, o arquivo de configuração é criado informando à aplicação-base que este usuário não deseja participar. Sendo do desejo do usuário participar da captura dos dados, é solicitado que ele realize o cadastro. Após o usuário ter realizado o cadastro, o arquivo de configuração é criado, informando à aplicação que o usuário deseja participar. Dessa forma, se no arquivo de configuração já existia uma aprovação para a captura dos dados, a aplicação então começa a capturar e enviar os dados das interações e audiência para o serviço Web responsável por agregar tais dados (vide Seção 4).

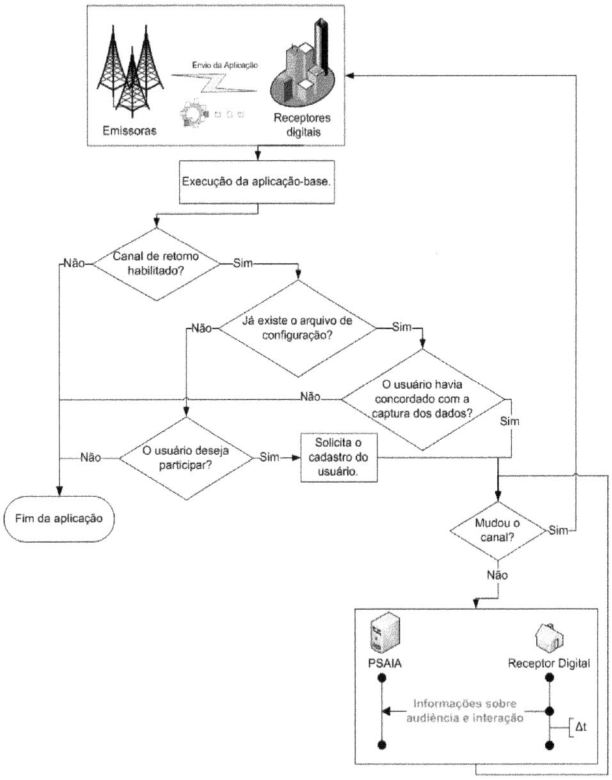

Figure 1: Modelo de captura dos dados por meio de aplicações interativas.

Após esse *handshake*, a aplicação continuará enviando os dados de audiência do usuário a cada período de tempo Δt(vide Figura 1) enquanto o usuário permanecer no mesmo canal. Quando o usuário muda de canal, o carrossel con-

[2]Chamamos de aplicação-base uma pequena aplicação, adicionada ao carrossel de objetos da emissora, responsável por iniciar e controlar a sessão entre o receptor digital e o serviço Web que recebe os dados de interação e audiência.

tido no fluxo do canal sintonizado é removido e todas as aplicações enviadas pela emissora são perdidas, inclusive a aplicação-base. Sendo assim, a aplicação-base deve ser recebida novamente, agora pelo fluxo de uma outra emissora. Reiterando o mencionado anteriormente, é necessário que todas as emissoras que desejam ter sua audiência mensurada adicionem no seu carrossel de objetos a aplicação-base a medição de audiência.

O procedimento até aqui descrito captura apenas os dados de audiência, como canal sintonizado, sub-canal selecionado, perfil de usuário, entre outros. A captura de dados originados pela navegação nas aplicações interativas, por sua vez, é implementada com ajuda de um pré-processamento feito em todas as aplicações que serão alvo da medição de interação. Um software pré-processador presente na emissora analisa o código da aplicação a ser transmitida, em busca de pontos em que a ação do usuário é permitida.

Para aplicações NCL, essa análise é extremamente facilitada devido à estruturação da linguagem. O código declarativo baseado em XML e a especificação de relacionamentos (*links*) baseados em conectores causais (*causalConnectors*) simplificam a implementação do pré-processador. O pré-processador básico busca por links cujos conectores possuem *onSelection* como tipo de papel de condição. Quando um link desse tipo é encontrado, um novo link é adicionado à aplicação, com o mesmo tipo de condição e com o mesmo componente (*media/area...*) no papel de condição. No entanto, o novo link possui no papel de ação uma interface de uma mídia Lua que, quando iniciada, envia todos os dados referentes ao link original para o serviço Web, sob a mesma sessão controlada pela aplicação-base descrita anteriormente. Dessa forma, as interações são enviadas em um formato padrão ao serviço Web (veja Seção 4) tão logo elas acontecem no receptor digital. Novamente, esta abordagem exige que todas as emissoras que desejem participar da análise de interação manipulem previamente suas aplicações, para habilitar a captura de dados de interação.

4. FERRAMENTAS DE ANÁLISE DE INTERAÇÃO E AUDIÊNCIA

O ambiente de TVDI ilustrado pela Figura 2 introduz a entidade do Provedor de Serviços de Análise de Interação e Audiência (PSAIA), [7], responsável por agregar as informações capturadas a partir de cada receptor digital. Além disso, o PSAIA atua como intermediário entre os telespectadores e as emissoras de televisão ou outro cliente interessado nas informações sobre as interações, como empresas de medição de audiência, produtores de equipamentos, companhias de publicidade, entre outros.

Portanto, com os objetivos principais de receber e armazenar os dados enviados pelos receptores digitais e disponibilizar as informações para os clientes, o Provedor de Serviços de Análise de Interação e Audiência é constituído de alguns módulos com as seguintes finalidades:

- Receber e armazenar as interações dos usuários;
- Realizar o processo de ETL (*Extract, Transform and Load*) para geração de *Datawarehouses* [3] (DW) [11];

[3] Data warehouse é um sistema de armazenamento de informações em bases de dados, de forma consolidada. A modelagem da base favorece os relatórios, a análise de grandes volumes de dados e a obtenção de informações estratégicas.

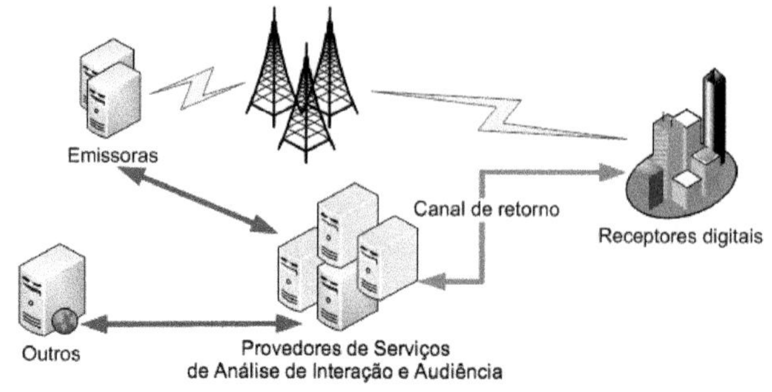

Figure 2: PSAIA no ambiente de TV Digital.

- Fornecer acesso aos dados dos DW para os clientes;
- Fornecer aplicações Web para o acesso à informação.

4.1 Ferramenta de Análise de Interação

A Ferramenta de Análise de Interação é o módulo do PSAIA dedicado a receber, armazenar e disponibilizar os dados de interação dos telespectadores. Sua lógica de funcionamento é independente do método de captura adotado no lado do receptor digital.

Utilizando o modelo de captura de dados por meio de extensões do *middleware*,conforme descrito na Seção 3.1, sempre que um usuário realiza algum tipo de interação, o componente de captura de interação do usuário armazena essa interação. A cada período de tempo $\Delta t1$(vide Figura 4), que pode variar conforme for configurado no receptor digital, um arquivo XML é enviado ao PSAIA contendo todas as interações armazenadas desde o último envio. Um exemplo simplificado de um arquivo enviado para a ferramenta de análise de interação pode ser visto na Figura 3.

```
<?xml version="1.0" encoding="UTF-8"?>
<watchTV country="Brazil"
         startDate="2012-05-18T08:30:00.0"
         endDate="2012-05-18T17:25:00.0">
  <head>
    <location zip="36035330" lat="-21.455100"
              long="-43.210100"/>
    <user birth="01-02-1972" genre="male"> ... </user>
  </head>
  <interaction type="channelChange"
               time="2012-05-18T08:30:00.0">
    <key code="CH_UP"/>
    <channel code="05" name="Globo">
      <program code="160"
               name="Campeonato Carioca"
               category="Esportes" age="10"/>
    </channel>
  </interaction>
  <interaction> ... </interaction>
</watchTV>
```

Figure 3: Exemplo de arquivo XML para a Ferramenta de Análise de Interação.

Por outro lado, utilizando o modelo de captura de dados por meio de aplicações interativas,sempre que o usuário realiza uma interação a aplicação modificada envia essa interação para o PSAIA. No entanto, o formato dos dados continua o mesmo, baseado em arquivos XML, sendo a diferença entre as duas abordagens apenas a quantidade de dados trafegados a cada comunicação entre receptor digital e PSAIA.

Após o recebimento, a ferramenta armazena os dados recebidos em uma base de dados relacional. [6]. O objetivo deste armazenamento prévio, sem nenhuma alteração dos dados é, principalmente, acelerar o processo de envio e recebimento dos arquivos XML e maximizar o número de atendimentos concorrentes suportados pelo serviço. Em um sistema como o PSAIA que possui um potencial de milhões de acessos simultâneos, a escalabilidade é fator preponderante e que guiou esta decisão de projeto. Além de uma maior velocidade e escalabilidade na comunicação entre receptor digital e PSAIA, o armazenamento prévio propicia outros benefícios, como a possibilidade da restauração de cada arquivo enviado ao PSAIA e a preservação dos dados iniciais.

A efetivação do armazenamento de dados para disponibilização é dada a cada período $\Delta t2$ (vide Figura 4), quando a ferramenta realiza um processo de ETL, a fim de fazer a carga dos últimos dados recebidos no DW. Além disso, é nesse processo que dados externos são inseridos no sistema, como datas, feriados, localidades, etc. Deste momento em diante, os dados que sofreram o processo de ETL são armazenados em um datawarehouse, por meio do qual as pesquisas podem ser realizadas pelos clientes do serviço de análise. A Figura 4 ilustra esse processo de transferência dos dados entre um receptor digital e o PSAIA.

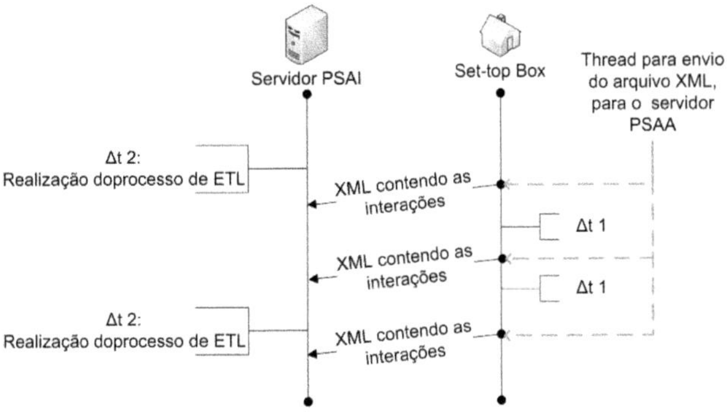

Figure 4: Comunicação PSAIA x receptor digital para a Ferramenta de Análise de Interação.

De fato, esse esquema de armazenamento prévio para posterior ETL é muito eficiente para a comunicação entre receptor digital e PSAIA, proporcionando, ainda, que pesquisas posteriores possam ser realizadas com êxito. No entanto, a disponibilização tardia dos dados pelo procedimento ETL impossibilita a realização de pesquisas em dados recentes, por exemplo para uma análise em tempo real ou quase tempo real. Para que a implantação comercial do Ferramenta de Análise de Interação do PSAIA seja viável, um estudo de escalabilidade deve ser feito. De qualquer forma, a arquitetura apresentada é válida considerando um único servidor ou mesmo um cluster capaz de suportar um número muito maior de clientes simultâneos.

O Processo de ETL

Como mostrado na Figura 4, a cada período $\Delta t2$ acontece o processo de ETL, possibilitando que os dados recentemente recebidos pelo PSAIA possam ser incluídos no DW. Este processo é computacionalmente caro, o que o torna lento e faz com que o período $\Delta t2$ deva ser escolhido com cuidado. O estudo sobre o dimensionamento deste tempo foi iniciado pelos autores. Alguns fatores que influenciam na decisão deste tempo são:

- O volume de dados recebidos;
- A capacidade de processamento do servidor/cluster;
- Quantidade de diferentes DW, e consequentemente, quantidade de processos de ETL a serem realizados;
- Necessidades dos clientes que acessam dados dos DW.

A possibilidade de realizar o processo de ETL sob demanda, mediante a necessidade do cliente, é de grande valia. Com o passar do tempo e com o crescimento das bases de dados relacionais, e, ainda, com o aumento do número de DW, o processo de ETL tende a ficar cada vez mais lento, e com isso pode ser necessário aumentar o tempo $\Delta t2$ entre cada realização do processo de ETL. Nesse contexto, caso um cliente deseje realizar pesquisas sobre dados mais recentes que a realização do último processo e se a opção de realizar o processo sob demanda não for oferecida, o cliente deverá obrigatoriamente esperar por $\Delta t2$ maior, até o próximo processo ser realizado e concluído.

4.2 Ferramenta de Análise de Audiência

A Ferramenta de Análise de Audiência é o módulo do PSAIA responsável por receber, armazenar e disponibizar os dados de audiência dos telespectadores. Da mesma forma como discutido para a Ferramenta de Análise de Interação, a Ferramenta de Análise de Audiência é independente do modelo de captura de dados adotada no receptor digital. De fato, para o caso específico dos dados capturados sobre audiência, ambas abordagens não apresentam diferenças na quantidade de dados enviada, nem na periodicidade entre envios.

No contexto de medição de audiência, a possibilidade de análise dos dados assim que recebidos pelo PSAIA é interessante e pode ser viabilizado, se algumas medidas restritivas forem adotadas. Idealmente, os dados já devem ser enviados pelos receptores no formato que a análise final será feita. Com isso, o processo de ETL, que insere o ponto de atraso nas pesquisas, pode ser removido. Como conjunto de dados relevantes para a medição de audiência é bem menor do que o conjunto de dados relevantes para a análise de interação, o tempo de processamento de cada comunicação entre receptor tende a ser reduzida. Na implementação corrente do PSAIA os pontos mais importantes para análise de audiência em tempo real foram restringidos aos dados do usuário e o programa e o canal que estão sendo assistidos. Um exemplo de um arquivo XML enviado para a ferramenta de análise de audiência pode ser visto na Figura 5.

Enquanto que para a ferramenta de análise de interação o PSAIA recebe um arquivo XML (Figura 3) que pode ter tamanho variável (e talvez exagerado seguindo a primeira abordagem de coleta de dados), para a ferramenta de análise de audiência este arquivo tem um tamanho fixo.

Assim como a ferramenta de análise de interação, a ferramenta de análise de audiência consiste em um serviço Web que receberá os dados dos receptores digitais e realizará a persistência desses dados em uma base relacional.

A cada período $\Delta t3$, o receptor digital envia os dados do usuário, do programa e do canal sendo assistidos para o PSAIA. Como dados do usuário, são enviados apenas alguns itens-chave, como número de série do receptor digital e nome do usuário, apenas o suficiente para que esse usuário

```
<?xml version="1.0" encoding="UTF-8" ?>
  <online>
    <user>
        <name>
            Samuel
        </name>
        <serial>
            200635036
        </serial>
        <birth>
            11-10-1988
        </birth>
        <zip>
            36015130
        </zip>
    </user>
    <program_cod>
        programa
    </program_cod>
    <channel_cod>
        12
    </channel_cod>
    <data>
        08-05-2012T08:30:00.0
    </data>
  </online>
```


Figure 5: Exemplo de arquivo XML para a Ferramenta de Análise de Audiência.

possa ser identificado. A partir deste ponto as pesquisas já podem ser realizadas na ferramenta de análise de audiência. A Figura 6 apresenta esse processo. Certamente, diferente do tempo $\Delta t1$ da ferramenta de análise de interação, o tempo $\Delta t3$ entre os envios dos arquivos para a ferramenta de análise de audiência não pode ser muito grande. Estudos estão sendo realizados sobre o dimensionamento deste tempo, mas nos testes realizados até o momento, o intervalo recomendado é de 1 a 3 minutos.

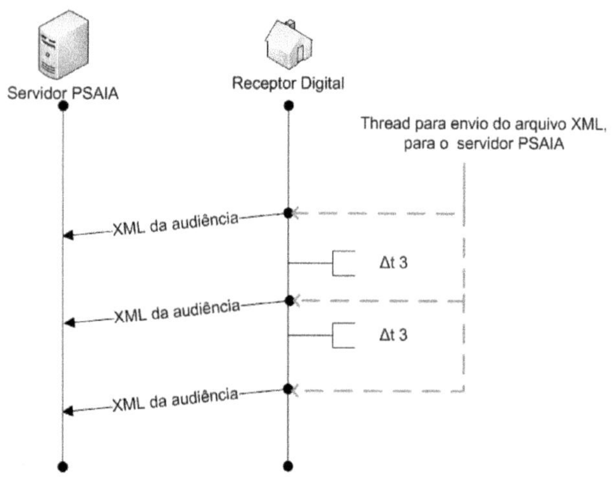

Figure 6: Comunicação PSAIA x receptor digital para a Ferramenta de Análise de Audiência.

5. IMPLEMENTAÇÃO

O PSAIA foi implantado em um servidor Tomcat e desenvolvido utilizando as tecnologias Java e MySQL. Para dar suporte a serviços Web foi utilizada a biblioteca Axis. Um DW foi desenvolvido para validar o processo e exemplificar algumas aplicações que podem ficar disponíveis na ferramenta de análise de interação. Este DW tem como atividade central a agragação de dados de interação realizada em um receptor digital. A Figura 7 apresenta um esquema simplificado do modelo dimensional desse DW.

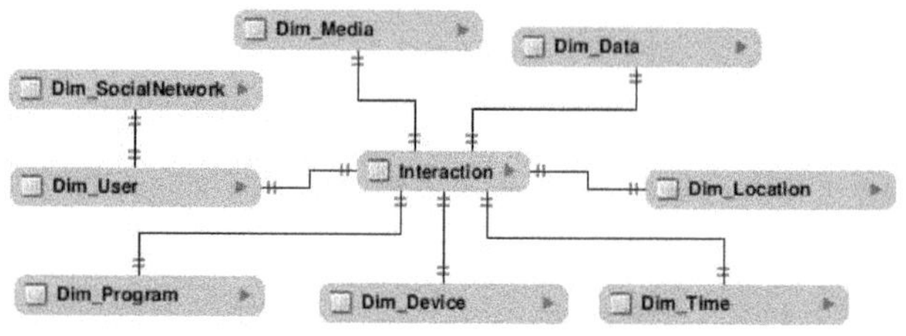

Figure 7: Modelo dimensional simplificado do DW.

No processo de ETL deste DW a maior parte dos dados vem da base de dados relacional do PSAIA, sendo apenas as dimensões Data (Dim_Data) e Location (Dim_Location) preenchidas com dados vindos de fontes externas. A dimensão Data contém informações como: feriados, finais de semanas e demais dados que trazem peculiaridade para cada dia do ano. Já a dimensão Location permite que sejam especificados: rua, bairro, região da cidade, nome da cidade, estado e país; a partir das informações contidas na tag Location (cabeçalho do arquivo XML enviado pelo receptor digital).

Após a execução do processo de ETL, os dados são atualizados no DW e então estarão disponíveis para serem consultados pelos clientes do PSAIA. Na atual versão implementada as seguintes consultas estão disponíveis:

- Quantidade de aparelhos online em certo período e em determinado canal/programa (Figura 8);
- Quantidade de aparelhos online em certo período, determinado canal/programa, durante o fim de semana dentro de um determinado período;
- Quantidade de aparelhos online em certo período, determinado canal/programa, em feriado específico;
- Aplicações executadas em certo período (Figura 9);
- Quantidade de aparelhos online em certa faixa horária;
- Quantidade de aparelhos online em certa faixa horária, em determinado canal;
- Aplicações executadas em certa faixa horária;

Além destas consultas é possível exportar os dados de um DW específico através de um arquivo XML que a ferramenta disponibiliza para download.

Para a ferramenta de análise de audiência uma nova base de dados foi criada, contendo apenas as tabelas usadas para armazenar os dados usados na análise de audiência. Através das assinaturas dos métodos disponíveis no serviço Web, o PSAIA pode identificar se um arquivo está sendo enviado para a ferramenta de análise de interação ou para a ferramenta de análise de audiência.

Todos os testes das duas ferramentas foram realizados através do uso de máquinas virtuais instaladas em computadores de uma rede local, que simulam os receptores digitais e implementam tanto o PSAIA quanto seus clientes.

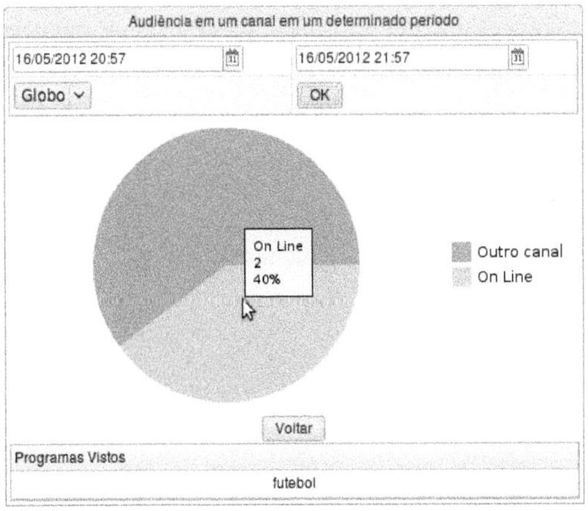

Figure 8: Audiência de uma emissora em um determinado periodo.

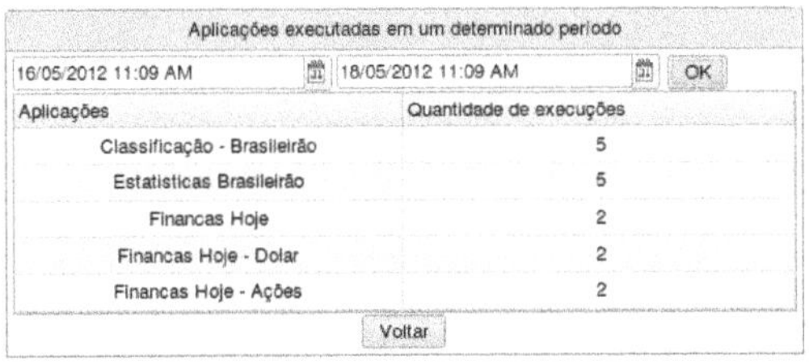

Figure 9: Aplicações executadas em um período.

6. COMPARAÇÃO DOS MODELOS DE CAPTURA PROPOSTOS

Neste artigo apresentamos dois possíveis modelos de captura de dados que podem ser adotados para análise de interação e audiência em receptores digitais. Certamente estes não são os únicos modelos possíveis, porém estes se apresentam como soluções eficientes para o aprimoramento da medição de audiência atualmente feita pelos institutos de pesquisas.

Um fator importante é a questão do custo para implantação do modelo escolhido.O modelo de extensão do *middleware* se apresenta como uma melhor solução ao modelo que utiliza *peoplemeters*, pois o custo de um *Set Top Box*, por exemplo, é menor que o do *peoplemeter*. O modelo de aplicações interativas nesse ponto é ainda melhor pois não possui custo para a sua implantação. O único requisito é que o receptor digital do telespectador seja capaz de executar aplicações interativas, escritas em NCL e Lua.

A princípio, o uso de extensões ao padrão gera maiores possibilidades. Além disso, esse modelo é bem mais semelhante ao usado atualmente através dos aparelhos *peoplemeter*. Em relação ao atual modelo de captura de dados utilizado pelo IBOPE a diferença está justamente no aparelho utilizado. Enquanto na atual captura é necessário um aparelho *peoplemeter*, no modelo proposto este aparelho poderá ser dispensado o que reduz os custos para medição de audiência.

Em relação ao modelo de captura de dados via aplicações interativas, a diferença se torna maior. Tal modelo impõe a participação ativa da emissora na análise, o que representa uma mudança substancial no paradigma de medição. Porém, seus benefícios são notáveis, como o aumento do número de usuários analisados, que pode aumentar tanto a abrangência da análise quanto sua precisão. Além disso, com a utilização de aplicações interativas, qualquer receptor digital que utilizar o Ginga-NCL como *middleware*, poderá também realizar a captura dos dados e por fim participar da análise de interação e audiência. Isto gera uma portabilidade única no sistema, que assim pode ser utilizado na Tv terrestre, Tv móvel e IPTV. A Tabela 1 evidencia estas e outras diferenças, apresentadas de forma comparativa.

Table 1: Comparação entre os modelos de captura ExM: Extensão do *middleware* ApI:Aplicações interativas

	ExM	ApI	*Peoplemeter*
Custo de implantação HW/SW	Médio	Baixo	Alto
Dependência da emisssora	Nenhuma	Total	Nenhuma
Tamanho do espaço amostral	Pequeno	Grande	Muito pequeno
Portabilidade	Não	Sim	Não
Tipo do canal de retorno	Internet	Internet	Internet ou canal dedicado
Característica do tráfego gerado	- transfers. > tamanho	+ transfers. < tamanho	+ transfers. < tamanho
Tipos de eventos capturáveis	Zapping, interação, volume, EPG...	Zapping, interação	Zapping

Algumas características do modelo de captura de dados por meio de aplicações interativas merecem ser discutidas neste momento, uma vez que tal implementação esbarra em um conjunto de limitações impostas por padrões de *middleware*.

Conforme descrito na Seção 3.2, para controlar a sessão entre receptor digital e PSAIA, a aplicação-base verifica a existência e o conteúdo de um arquivo de configuração salvo no receptor. Porém, sendo a aplicação-base enviada no carrossel de um canal, quando o telespectador mudar para outro canal, seu receptor receberá um outro carrossel, ainda que provavelmente contendo a mesma aplicação-base. Porém, é de se imaginar que aplicações oriundas de diferentes emissoras não poderiam escrever ou mesmo ler arquivos locais uns dos outros, por questão de segurança. No entanto, especificamente para a manipulação de arquivos oferecida pela API Lua I/O assíncrona [10], não há restrições no padrão que garantam a proteção dos dados entre as diferentes aplicações. Atualmente, a implementação da aplicação-base descrita na Seção 3.2 tira proveito dessa falta para permitir que o arquivo de configuração seja manipulado por ela nas suas diferentes execuções sinalizadas por diferentes canais. Os autores defendem a restrição desse tipo de funcionalidade. Ao mesmo tempo, pensam que seria perfeitamente viável o uso da API Lua I/O por aplicações assinadas digitalmente enviadas pelas emissoras. A aplicação-base seria então assinada e deveria ser identificada pelo receptor como autorizada a manipular o arquivo de configuração.

O leitor preocupado com privacidade notará também que as informações de identificação do usuário mostradas na Figura 3 incluem dados como nome do telespectador. Por enquanto, esta é a forma como o telespectador é identificado junto ao PSAIA. Isto representa um problema de privacidade na área de medição de audiência, mesmo que o sistema cuidadosamente solicite ao telespectador todos os consentimentos necessários. O problema é que o nome do telespectador não é um dado relevante para medições de audiência ou análise de interações. Os dados importantes são idade, sexo, localização, por exemplo. Em uma revisão em andamento da implementação dos programas de captura e do PSAIA, o nome será substituído por um identificador gerado automaticamente pelo serviço, sem que para isso o telespectador tenha que revelar totalmente sua identidade.

7. CONCLUSÃO E TRABALHOS FUTUROS

A especificação e implementação do PSAIA levou em conta aspectos funcionais de software. No projeto atual, buscou-se garantir que os requisitos identificados para o PSAIA fossem preenchidos de forma suficientemente robusta para servir como prova de conceito. Neste aspecto, o PSAIA se apresenta viável e como uma solução que permite além da análise de audiência tradicional, a análise das interações dos telespectadores com as aplicações interativas.

Foram apresentados, ainda, dois modelos de captura de dados, um estendendo o padrão a partir de módulos de software instaláveis e outro seguindo rigorosamente o padrão utilizando aplicações interativas. Com a implantação do modelo de captura por meio de extensão do *middleware*, os custos poderiam ser baixados e uma rica análise de interação poderia ser facilmente feita, tudo isso sem grandes alterações no atual modelo de negócio utilizado. Por sua vez, com a implantação do modelo de captura via aplicações interativas será possível multiplicar o espaço amostral usado para a análise de audiência. Não seria mais necessário o uso dos custosos aparelhos *peoplemeter*.

Como trabalhos futuros, há vários aperfeiçamentos às ferramentas, conforme discutido ao longo do texto. Medidas de desempenho e o estudo de requisitos não-funcionais, como escalabilidade, para as várias combinações de abordagens de captura e de análise dos dados encontram-se em andamento. A adaptação da proposta para melhor se adequar a serviços IPTV também está planejada para futuro próximo. Atualmente, algumas recomendações do ITU-T estão sendo finalizadas para a normalização de dados e da operação de serviços de medição de audiência em IPTV, porém nada ainda foi definido no contexto de análise de interação. Como as ferramentas mostradas estão em conformidade com os padrões ITU-T[1], pretende-se a contribuir também com as especificações normativas do ITU-T.

8. AGRADECIMENTOS

Agradecemos ao CTIC (Centro de Pesquisa e Desenvolvimento em Tecnologias Digitais para Informação e Comunicação) pelo financiamento deste projeto e ao Lapic da UFJF por prover a infraestrutura para a realização do trabalho.

9. REFERENCES

[1] Recommendation itu-t h.761 (2011), nested context language (ncl) and ginga-ncl for iptv.

[2] Recommendation itu-t j.201 (2004), harmonization of declarative content formats for interactive television applications.

[3] ABNT. Abnt nbr 15606-2 - digital terrestrial tv – data coding and transmission specification for digital broadcasting – part 2: Ginga-ncl for fixed and mobile receivers: Xml application language for application coding. 2008.

[4] V. Becker and M. K. Zuffo. Medição de audiência em ambientes de tv digital. 2010.

[5] M. Cristo, Ângelo Bitar, B. F. Guimarães, G. Penalber, R. T. S. Hanada, C. Teixeira, and E. Melo. A web-like personalized advertising system for interactive digital tv. *WTVDI/WebMedia*, 2010.

[6] S. da Costa Alves Basílio and E. Barrére. Mecanismo para armazenamento das interações dos usuários de set-top box em uma ferramenta para análise de interação. *Simpósio Internacional de Televisão Digital/SIMTVD*, 2009.

[7] S. da Costa Alves Basílio and E. Barrére. Provedor de serviços para análise de interação. *WTVDI/WebMedia*, 2010.

[8] P. M. de Ávila and S. D. Zorzo. Recommender system: A personalized tv guidesystem. *SIGMAP*, 2009.

[9] A. R. dos Santos. Medição de audiência de televisão em tempo real pelo reconhecimento de logos. Master's thesis, 2007. Disponível em: http://www.lps.usp.br/ hae/dissert-alex_ed-revisada.pdf.

[10] IBOPE. Conceitos e critérios da pesquisa de mídia para a imprensa. Disponível em: http://www.ibope.com.br/midia/downloads/conceitos_e_criteri

[11] R. Kimball and J. Caserta. *The Data Warehouse ETL Toolkit*. Wiley, 1 edition, 2004.

[12] L. F. G. Soares. Gingafrevo & gingarap evolução do middleware ginga para múltiplas plataformas (componentização) & ferramentas para desenvolvimento e distribuição de aplicações declarativas. Technical report, Rio de Janeiro, RJ, Brasil, 2008.

Advertisement Selection for Online Videos

Karla Okada
Instituto Nokia de Tecnologia
Manaus, AM, Brasil
karla.gomes@indt.org.br

Edleno S. de Moura
Univ. Fed. do Amazonas
Instituto de Computação
Manaus, AM, Brasil
edleno@icomp.ufam.edu.br

Marco Cristo
Univ. Fed. do Amazonas
Instituto de Computação
Manaus, AM, Brasil
marco.cristo@icomp.ufam.edu.br

David Fernandes
Univ. Fed. do Amazonas
Instituto de Computação
Manaus, AM, Brasil
david@icomp.ufam.edu.br

Marcos Andre Goncalves
Univ. Fed. de Minas Gerais
Dep. de Ciência da Comput.
Belo Horizonte, MG, Brasil
mgoncalv@dcc.ufmg.br

Klessius Berlt
Univ. Fed. do Amazonas
Instituto de Computação
Manaus, AM, Brasil
klessius@icomp.ufam.edu.br

ABSTRACT

The significant increase of the audience of video-sharing websites has attracted large investments on contextual advertising. In this paper we investigate alternative techniques for selecting ads to be placed in videos during their exhibitions. In order to improve the effectiveness of these ads avoiding the high cost of image processing, we explore textual metadata created by the users and stored in the page that hosts the video. Our proposal consists in assigning weights to the metadata attributes, according to their relative importance. To estimate such an importance, we apply a block importance model. Our experimental results show that the metadata attributes which perform better in the task of selecting ads are the ones that provide the best descriptions of the video content. We also observed that the application of weights according to the studied block importance model obtained gains of about 7% over the selection method without weights. Such a gain is relevant due to the possibility of increasing the profitability of ad selection systems and avoiding the negative impact on advertiser brand and credibility of placing non-relevant ads.

Categories and Subject Descriptors

H.3.7 [**Information Storage and Retrieval**]: Digital Libraries, User Issues

Keywords

Contextual Advertising, Block Importance Model, Sources of Textual Evidences, Metadata, Videos

1. INTRODUCTION

Web has become one of the major media outlets for advertising markets by exposing its products and services to large audiences at relatively low cost. Indeed, according to [14], the immediate recall of an online ad (such as a static banner) by the audience is around 40%, only 1% less effective than a 30-second television commercial. Considering the significant cost difference between the two types of ads, online advertising has become much more profitable, which has contributed for its fast and increasing adoption. Consequently, among several different media types, such as newspapers, radio, and television, Web was the one which presented the fastest growth in investments throughout its existence.

Such performance as an advertising platform is associated with the fact that online ads have unique and very interesting features for advertisers and consumers, such as (a) the possibility of measuring precisely the performance of advertising campaigns; (b) the placement of ads based on context information; and (c) the possibility of tracking consumer behavior for further analysis of interests and necessities.

Nowadays, the main approach of Web advertising is the *search advertising*. In this approach, ads are selected based on the keywords extracted from queries submitted by users to search engines and then they are matched against keywords associated with ads provided by advertisers. The success of this advertising format has motivated information gatekeepers to offer their ad services in different contexts, extending it to web pages, services and videos, which is known as *contextual advertising*.

The impact of advertising on the Web is even greater if we consider the significant increase of its audience, resulting from the proliferation of material generated by users in the so-called Web 2.0, specially with the spread of blogs, social networking sites and wikis. Many websites have been highlighted in this context, achieving great popularity and becoming promising sources for advertising. Among them, we cite YouTube[1], a video sharing website, where users can share digital media. According to statistics available on Youtube[2], videos had more than 1 trillion views in 2011, what is equivalent to around 140 views for each person in the earth.

This work aims at studying the contextual advertising applied to digital video services, exploring features of Web 2.0. Specifically, we intend to determine how metadata related

Permission to make digital or hard copies of all or part of this work for personal or classroom use is granted without fee provided that copies are not made or distributed for profit or commercial advantage and that copies bear this notice and the full citation on the first page. To copy otherwise, to republish, to post on servers or to redistribute to lists, requires prior specific permission and/or a fee.
WebMedia'12, October 15–18, 2012, São Paulo/SP, Brazil.
Copyright 2012 ACM 978-1-4503-1706-1/12/10 ...$15.00.

[1]`http://www.youtube.com`
[2]`http://www.youtube.com/t/press\_statistics`

Figure 1: Example of a video embedded into a web page where two types of metadata are highlighted: title and description.

to a video, as informed by its users, can be explored to augment the precision of algorithms to select ads. Examples of metadata contained in a typical video web page are title, description, user comments, and category. Each of them is an evidence about the video to be displayed on the page (vide Figure 1). For achieving a better quality of the selected ads, we adapt and apply the technique proposed by [8] to find the importance of metadata fields present on the pages. We then apply such importance metrics on ad selection functions.

The main contributions of this work are (1) the study of the impact of the importance block model proposed in [8] on video contextual advertising in the Web and (2) the study of the application of video metadata to retrieve relevant ads without the necessity of expensive image processing. As a result of our work, we found that the application of weights according to the importance block model has provided gains of about 7% over the traditional vector space model.

This paper is structured as follow. In Section 2, we present work related to ours. In Section 3, we provide the necessary concepts for the comprehension of our proposal. In Section 4, we present our proposal. In Section 5, we evaluate our methods, including the presentation of our experimental methodology, collections, results and discussion of results. In Section 6, we present our conclusions.

2. RELATED WORK

Online advertising growth has motivated studies on many engineering and modeling challenges of contextual and search advertising. Large scale online advertising systems deal with massive databases and transactions involving billions of pages, ads and queries.

In [2], the authors propose a project to implement contextual advertising systems in large scale, based on an information filtering model. In [19], the authors address diverse engineering restrictions since efficiency and computational costs are essential requirements for the selection of algorithms which match ads and web pages. Other aspects of search advertising were also investigated in various studies, such as the ads revenue and scoring model in the ad ranking process [10], the suggestion of ad keywords [15], the detection of fraud by means of traffic identification [9], and ranking strategies [4].

Many studies on search and contextual advertising emphasize that the most important feature for the success of these advertising formats is the relevance of the selected ads to be displayed. Particularly, the authors in [21] were the first ones to investigate this issue with the suggestion of ten strategies for ad ranking. They evaluated the efficiency of the proposed methods for contextual advertising. In a following work [16], they proposed the use of a machine learning approach to find good ranking functions for contextual ads. More specifically, they proposed a genetic programming algorithm to select the ranking function that maximizes the average precision of the selected ad. Yih et al [24] address the matching problem, not as a strategy of ad ranking but as a term selection issue. In this way, they evaluated several term extraction strategies using machine learning. To represent a keyword, they used many kinds of features such as linguistic classification and statistic metrics for measuring importance. They also considered a kind of feature close related to the page structure: the relative position of the candidate to keyword in the page.

Unlike our work, neither of these former studies have focused on video advertising. The first one to address this area was presented in [17], which proposed the VideoSense system. VideoSense is an advertising system for online video services which automatically associates relevant ads with videos. In this study, besides finding relevant ads, the authors investigate the less intrusive insertion point for the ad, in order to minimize the negative impact of an ad placement on the video watching experience. They also investigated the appropriate context for the exhibition of a certain ad [18]. In other work [7], the authors propose an architecture for contextual video advertising in a digital TV environment. They focused on the automatic identification of the user to improve targeted advertising. The work closest to our was presented in [23], where the authors studied textual pieces of evidence extracted from movies scripts. As in [24], they also treated the problem as a keyword extraction task and proposed a solution based on machine learning. Again, no evidence about the page structure was explored, besides its relative position in the surrounding page. Their main contribution was the proposition of a new kind of feature, the scene situation, which aims at describing the scene context such as *walking on the beach*, *car chasing*, etc. They have shown that such a feature was useful for identifying interesting advertising keywords.

In [22], the authors have explored the social interactions of Web 2.0. In particular, they have used the interactive search of video advertising, suggesting a three-stage process to choose relevant ads. In this process, user searches for products visually similar, sorting them using labels of aggregation, which allows them to search again, this time a textual search, based on semantic labels described by other users. This allows to the system to recommend better advertising.

Unlike previous studies, in our approach, we do not discard the page structure in which textual information is observed. In fact, we extract from this structure their text blocks as components and evaluate their importance individually, as the authors in [11] have proposed for the page ranking problem in search engines. As result, we show that the importance of the blocks is useful for improving the selection of ads in contextual video advertising.

3. CONCEPTS

In this section, we present some concepts necessary for understanding our work.

3.1 Contextual Advertising

Google[3] has introduced contextual advertising in 2002 [20]. This form of advertising can be seen as an extension of search advertising to different contexts. In search advertising [5], terms from user queries are matched to keywords associated with ads [21]. A ranking of the ads is then computed also considering the amount that the advertiser is willing to pay by placing an ad. The top-ranked ads are displayed in the page of search results along with the answers for the user query. Similarly, contextual advertising consists of the selection of ads to be displayed based on the media content being seen, instead of the user query. Once the most relevant and profitable ads are known, they are displayed to the users grouped in paid lists placed on the page where the media is embedded.

The ad selection system identifies a list of ads relevant to the content of a media target, whether it is text or not. It is expected that the attached ads are relevant to users, appropriated and cost effective for advertisers and publishers [16]. Therefore, aspects that contribute most for the order in which ads are displayed are the media content suitability to the ads and the amount that the advertiser is willing to pay when their ads are clicked on. Specifically in the context of video services, we consider that the selection system has to determine the n most relevant ads to the content of the target video.

In this paper, we consider that an ad is composed of four structural parts: title, description, keywords, and a link to a page (landing page) where a transaction can be started. These components are typically found in commercial systems [16]. The keywords, associated with an ad may be composed of one or more words (terms), and they are used by advertisers to describe topics that they believe to be present in the target media. For assigning a keyword k to one of their ads, advertisers need to make an offer for k in an auction system. The higher is the offer which the advertisers do for k, the higher are the chances that their ads will be shown at the media, whose content refers to the topic k. Advertisers pay only for offers in which users show interest (usually by *clicking on* them).

Moreover, an advertiser can associate various ads with the same product or service. This group of ads is known as *campaign*.

3.2 Using Vector Model for Advertisements Selection

In the context of video sharing websites, the selection of an ad for a video web page is made according to the relation between the contents of the ads and the web pages. This strategy might be compared to a traditional information retrieval system, whose purpose is to select the most relevant documents for user queries [3].

Thus, a possible strategy for selecting ads to be displayed on a video web page, which from now on we will call target-page, is the use of traditional information retrieval models, such as the vector space model. In this approach, each ad a and each target-page ρ are represented as vectors in an Euclidean space of dimension T, where T is the number of distinct terms in the ads collection:

$$\begin{aligned}\vec{a_j} &= (w_{1,j}, w_{2,j}, w_{3,j}, \ldots, w_{T,j})\\ \vec{\rho} &= (w_{1,\rho}, w_{2,\rho}, w_{3,\rho}, \ldots, w_{T,\rho})\end{aligned}$$

where $w_{t,j}$ is the term weight t in the ad a_j, and $w_{t,\rho}$ is the weight of t in the target-page ρ.

The weights $w_{t,j}$ and $w_{t,\rho}$ measure how well term t describes the content of ad a_j and target-page ρ, respectively. Regarding to the ads, they are calculated based on two parameters: (i) $tf(t,j)$, which corresponds to the number of times that term t occurs in the ad a_j, and (ii) $idf(t)$, which is a function of the number of ads that contain the term t. Thus, the weight of a term in ad a_j is given by:

$$w_{t,j} = tf(t,j) \times idf(t) = tf(t,j) \times \log \frac{N}{n_t} \quad (1)$$

where N is the number of ads of the collection, and n_t is the number of ads which have the term t.

The ads ranking related to a target-page is defined as the cosine of the angle between the vectors of these two elements:

$$sim(a_j, \rho) = \frac{\vec{a_j} \bullet \vec{\rho}}{|\vec{a_j}| \times |\vec{\rho}|} = \frac{\sum_{t=1}^{t} w_{t,j} \times w_{t,\rho}}{\sqrt{\sum_{t=1}^{t} w_{t,j}^2} \times \sqrt{\sum_{t=1}^{t} w_{t,\rho}^2}} \quad (2)$$

where $|\vec{a_j}|$ and $|\vec{\rho}|$ correspond to the norms of the ad and the target-page vectors, respectively. Ranking calculation is not affected by $\vec{\rho}$, once this value is the same for all the ads.

3.3 Information Retrieval Model Using Structure Information

The ad selection on video sharing services is a problem poorly studied in the literature. As we have said in the last section, a possible approach to this problem is to use the vector space model, described in that section. Our proposal is to use a more sophisticated approach, that is, an information retrieval model able to exploit the block structure typically found on the web pages where the video is embedded.

Unlike traditional documents, it is possible to divide web pages into different segments (such as menus, footers, main content, notes of copyright, title, etc.), each of them with specific content types and purposes. In [8], the authors have proposed an information retrieval model that can use this block structure of web pages to achieve significant improvements in the quality of document *rankings*.

This model was based on the idea that a page is organized on a set of structural blocks (menus, content title, content body, etc) and the similarity calculation between a query and a web page should consider the page blocks where the terms occur. For example, the occurrence of a term in the title of a page is a more significant event for the *ranking* calculation than the occurrence of this term in the menu of the page.

A key concept exploited by [8] is the block class. A block class is defined as the set of blocks, extracted from distinct pages of a same web site, which were designed with the same functional purposes across their respective pages. For example, all pages of videos from Youtube have a block containing the title of the shared media. The set composed of all these title blocks comprise which we call the title class block.

[3]http://www.google.com

Inspired on the ideas explored in traditional weighting schemes used in the vector space model [3], the authors in [8] proposed several strategies based on the structure of the pages to improve ranking calculation. They showed that simple statistics about the occurrence of terms in classes of blocks would be useful to calculate the importance of each block in the ranking. Among these strategies, we selected two that will be used in this work: the Spread and ICF.

Besides being useful for ranking systems, the Spread and ICF were also used by [1], [12] and [13] as metrics to evaluate the quality of the information available in different segments of a page. In particular, they evaluated the descriptive and discriminative power of textual features present in some Web 2.0 applications, among them, video sharing systems. Motivated by the results presented by [1], [8], [12] and [13] we intend to study in this paper the use of the AICF and SPREAD metrics for selecting contextual ads for videos web pages.

4. APPLYING BLOCK IMPORTANCE TO CONTEXTUAL ADVERTISING

There are many sources of information related to each video shared on Web 2.0 media applications, here referred to as its metadata. In particular, textual metadata, the focus of this study, comprise self-contained textual blocks that play specific roles within the videos pages. Very common examples of such metadata are the title of the video, description, keywords, comments of users, etc. Each metadata has information about the video which it is associated with, being therefore an evidence about the subject of the video, and consequently an evidence about which ads could be placed on the page of the video.

In the context of this work, a *metadata class* is a set of metadata that belong to distinct pages of a given digital video service, and that share the same role within their respective pages. For example, given a set of video pages from Youtube, the set of all titles of all videos compose a metadata class. Notice that this notion is an adaptation of the concept of block class described in Section 3.3.

In this paper we investigate the problem of using metadata and metadata classes to improve the precision of algorithms for ad selection. For this, we propose to apply the metrics presented by [8] to quantify the relative importance of metadata fields present on the video pages, and then use such importance values on ad selection functions. In the following sections we review the metrics proposed by [8], outlining the intuition that make us believe its use can be of great value to the problem we address here.

4.0.1 Class Spread

$\mathcal{C}Spread$ is a metric to estimate the ability of a metadata field to describe the video content. $\mathcal{C}Spread$ calculation involves the use of two other metrics called *Spread* and *mSpread*. Let v be a video of a collection and t a term that occurs in at least one of the metadata m of v. The *Spread* of t in v, $Spread(t, v)$, is given by the number of metadata fields of v containing the term t:

$$Spread(t,v) = \sum_{m \in v} i, \text{ where } i = \begin{cases} 1 & \text{if } t \in m \\ 0 & \text{otherwise} \end{cases} \quad (3)$$

This metric is based on the idea that the greater is the number of metadata fields v containing the term t, the better the term t represents the content of v. The spread can be seen as the structure frequency of a term, acting as a structured version of the tf adopted in vector space model (see Section 3.2).

The concept of spread can be used to calculate the value of another metric called *mSpread*, which estimates the capacity of a metadata to concentrate the keywords of the video content. Since m is a metadata associated with a video v, the mSpread of m, $Spread(m)$, is the average Spread value of all terms of m, that is:

$$mSpread(m) = \frac{\sum_{t \in m} Spread(t, v_m)}{|m|} \quad (4)$$

where v_m is the video associated with metadata m, and $|m|$ is the number of terms of m.

Based on the same reasoning, we use the mSpread metric to calculate the value of the metric $\mathcal{C}Spread$, obtained from the spread average value of the metadata field of a metadata class $\mathcal{C}$.

$$\mathcal{C}Spread(\mathcal{C}) = \frac{\sum_{m \in \mathcal{C}} mSpread(m)}{|\mathcal{C}|} \quad (5)$$

where $|\mathcal{C}|$ is the number of metadata values of $\mathcal{C}$.

4.0.2 Average Inverse Class Frequency

Inverse Class Frequency (ICF) is a measure of the quantity of information generated by the term t occurrence in the class $\mathcal{C}$. Given a class $\mathcal{C} = \{m_1, m_2, ..., m_{n_\mathcal{C}}\}$ containing $n_\mathcal{C}$ metadata and a term t which occurs at least in one metadata of $\mathcal{C}$, ICF of a term t in $\mathcal{C}$ is defined as:

$$ICF(t, \mathcal{C}) = \log \frac{n_\mathcal{C}}{n_{t,\mathcal{C}}} \quad (6)$$

where $n_{t,\mathcal{C}}$ is the number of metadata of $\mathcal{C}$ in which t occurs.

ICF is a metric similar to IDF (Inverse Document Frequency) applied in the vector model, and it aims at estimating the quantity of information associated with the occurrence of a term in a given metadata class.

In this work, we adopt a variant of ICF called *Average Inverse Class Frequency* (AICF), which is the average value of ICF of all terms that occur in a given class, and it is calculated through the following formula:

$$AICF(\mathcal{C}) = \frac{\sum_{t \in v(\mathcal{C})} ICF(t, \mathcal{C})}{|v(\mathcal{C})|} \quad (7)$$

where $v(\mathcal{C})$ is the set of distinct terms that occur in all the metadata of the class $\mathcal{C}$, and $|v(\mathcal{C})|$ is the size of this set.

When we calculate AICF, we obtain a regularity measure of the different metadata content of a class. Classes whose metadata have very repetitive content (low AICF) are less discriminative and therefore, less important. Furthermore, classes whose metadata have more diverse content (high AICF) are more important and probably they are more relevant for the ad selection.

5. EXPERIMENTS

In this Section, we present our experimental results. To this end, we describe the used collections and the evaluation method we carried out. We then discuss the results we obtained.

5.1 Collections

For experiments, two collections were used: one of ads and another of videos. The first one is composed of 93,972 ads in Portuguese language. These ads were taken from a real ads collection and they were grouped in 2,029 different campaigns, including various segments of products and services, among them: cosmetics, sportive material, electronics, etc. The ads were provided by 1,744 advertisers. Each ad of this set has a title, keywords and a description. In average, the keywords have 1 word, the descriptions have around 60 words and the titles, 6 words.

The second collection consists of 81 videos extracted from the video sharing website YouTube. In average, these videos are around 3.5 minutes long. The selected videos were collected along a random path in the YouTube page graph. Since our ads collection is in Portuguese language, we have selected only videos in which all or most of the metadata were also in Portuguese. Information about each video includes title, description, keywords, category and user comments. When sharing a video in YouTube, the Uploader (the owner of the video) is freely able to associate with the video a title, a description and keywords to describe its content. The user also needs to associate a category, which has to be chosen from a set of categories pre-defined by the system. The comments are provided by other YouTube users and, in some cases, their contents were a mix of languages (portuguese, english, spanish, etc). Only 68% of the video collection have comments. Videos belonging to the collection are about diverse subjects, such as, sports, entertainment, health, relationships, gastronomy, tourism, travels and so on.

An evaluation process was carried out with our collections of videos and ads, in order to determine which ads could be considered relevant for placement during videos exhibition. The first step of this evaluation process was to request five volunteers to watch all videos of the collection, and for each of them, associate five *keywords* (with one or more words) with the video content. For example, with a videoclip of "Racionais MC" (a Brazilian rap band) were associated keywords more specific like "racionais mc", "hip hop" and "rap", but also more general keywords such as "music" and "videoclip". Keywords were composed of 1.1 words in average. These keywords were then submitted as queries to a search system (based on the vector space model) that indexed the ads collection. Each ad retrieved for a given query was evaluated as relevant or non-relevant to the video from which the query (*keyword*) was extracted. In other words, volunteers evaluated if products or services were related to the video content and if they could generate a transaction, such as a click. For each query, in average, were identified 112 relevant ads and 124 non-relevant ads. As result of this process, we have obtained a reference collection for evaluating our advertisement selection model.

5.2 Evaluation Metric

Since we do not have reference evaluations for all ads associated with each video of our sample collection, we have decided to use evaluation metric *bpref*, proposed by Bucley et al. [6]. This metric was proposed to measure the effectiveness of a system based only on documents that were evaluated as relevant or not. Therefore, this metric is specially robust for evaluations with incomplete relevance information.

For a topic with R relevant documents where r is a relevant document and n is a member of the R first documents evaluated as non-relevant returned by a system, *bpref* formula is given by Eq. 8:

$$bpref = \frac{1}{R}\sum_{r}(1 - \frac{|n \text{ returned before of } r|}{R}) \quad (8)$$

When the number of relevant documents is very small, Eq. 8 is not conclusive due to the fact of evaluation becomes very restricted to a few pairs of documents. For this reason, we use a variant of the *bpref* metric called *bpref-10*, which guarantees the use of at least 10 pairs of documents:

$$bpref - 10 = \frac{1}{R}\sum_{r}(1 - \frac{|n \text{ returned before of } r|}{10 + R}) \quad (9)$$

where n is a member of $10 + R$ first documents evaluated as non-relevant returned by the system.

5.3 Results

In this section we present the obtained results in two groups of experiments. In group 1, we have used the vector model to select ads for each video of our collection. In group 2, we selected the ads using the vector model combined with one or more strategies to infer the importance of metadata (cf. Section 4).

In group 2, we used metadata extracted from the video page content to generate queries to submit to the ads dataset. In particular, for each video, queries were generated considering the content of: (a) only attribute title; (b) only attribute description; (c) only attribute keywords; (d) only attribute category; (e) only attribute comments; (f) the whole page excluding HTML markup; (g) attributes title and keywords; (h) attributes title, keywords and description; and (i) attributes title, keywords, description and comments.

Besides the attributes above, we also have expanded the video descriptions with other videos posted by the same user (Uploader). This information could be useful once videos of the same uploader are usually about related topics, within a small group of interest domains.

For this expansion, we used 100 additional videos posted by the same uploader, being 50 from the same category of the original video and 50 from different categories. As result, we also performed queries combining the content of all attributes of the original video with the following attributes of the videos posted by the same uploader: (a) title; (b) keywords; (c) description; and (d) the combination of title, keywords and description.

All queries were pre-processed in order to eliminate stop words, terms with high frequency and low discriminative power, such as prepositions and pronouns.

Table 2 shows results of this first group of experiments. In this table, we can observe that attribute category has obtained the worst result. This was probably due to the fact that category content is in english whereas the video and its page is in portuguese. The whole web page content also had a bad performance, due to the large amount of information not related to the video content, such as copyright notes and promotional sentences. Among the tested combinations, we have observed that the one involving all attributes was the one which presented a better performance.

In Table 3, we note that the queries expanded with in-

Table 1: **Blocks Importance Weights.**

Attributes	SPREAD	AICF	SPREAD x AICF
Title	2.176	4.304	9.366
Keywords	1.914	4.341	8.309
Description	1.388	4.210	5.841
Category	1.049	2.920	3.062
Comments	0.764	4.166	3.183

Table 2: **Bpref-10 obtained with Vector Model.**

Query	#Videos	Bpref-10
Category	81	0.0120
Title	81	0.0930
Video Page Content	81	0.1379
Keywords	81	0.1568
Comments	55	0.1690
Description	81	0.2051
Title + Keywords	81	0.1714
Title + Keywords + Description	81	0.2583
Title + Keywords + Description + Comments	81	0.2719
Title + Keywords + Description + Comments + category	81	0.2732

Table 3: **Results of Vector Model including other videos from the same Uploader**

Query	# Videos	Bpref-10 (same category)	Bpref-10 (distinct categories)
All attributes of the original Video + Title	81	0.1434	0.1285
All attributes of the original Video + Keywords	81	0.1542	0.1568
All attributes of the original Video + Description	81	0.1460	0.1118
All attributes of the original Video + Title + Description + Keywords	81	0.1454	0.1180

Table 4: **Results of Vector Model with Block Importance. The symbol '*' indicates a statistically significant difference when we compared the weighted method with a plain method did not take into consideration block importance weights.**

Query	#Videos	Bpref-10	Gain (%)
All attributes without weights application	81	0.2732	–
All attributes with AICF weight application	81	0.2907*	6.4
All attributes with SPREAD weight application	81	0.2943*	7.7
All attributes with AICF x SPREAD weight application	81	0.2942*	7.7

formation of other videos from the same uploader did not perform better than the vector model using all attributes of the video page. This suggests that information from other videos introduces much noise. We also noted slightly better results when using videos of the same category as of the original one, which reinforces the idea that there is much noise in expanded information and this is higher for less related videos. On other hand, this result suggests that videos with more-related content yield better results.

For the second group of experiments, first we calculate the importance of every metadata attribute in the video pages. The results obtained are presented in Table 4. As can be seen, the most promising attributes for ad selection are title and keywords, followed by the video description.

With metadata weights calculated, queries were generated with all attributes weighted according to (a) SPREAD values, (b) AICF values, and (c) the combination of SPREAC and AICF values. Results of these queries were evaluated using the metric Bpref-10 as shown in Table 4. The first line corresponds to the best result without the use of the weights, used here for comparison. As we can see, all three criteria for weighting (AICF, SPREAD, and SPREAD x AICF) have outperformed the no-weighting combination of attributes. In fact, the difference between the three weighting methods and the no-weighting combination was statistically significant, with p-value< 0.05 in all cases. On the other hand, there was no statistically significant difference among the performance of the three weighting methods, when compared with each other, indicating that there is no preference between these strategies. They all present a similar performance.

6. CONCLUSIONS

In this paper, we investigated the selection of ads to be displayed in videos posted on the Web, exploring the structural blocks of the page containing the video. In particular, in the case of the YouTube service, our source of videos for experimentation, these blocks correspond to textual metadata. The results of the experiments that we have performed in our collection showed that the proposed model, which explores the importance of the page blocks, presented a gain of about 7 % in precision over a traditional vector space model.

We also noted that, among the metadata of the videos for which we selected ads, the most effective are those that offer more detailed descriptions of the video content. Examples of these metadata attributes are the description of the video and the comments posted by the users. Other attributes that describe the content with words or isolated sentences, such as, title, keywords and categories, are less effective. However, all attributes contribute to a better result, when they are properly weighted.

In the future, we plan to apply the same methodology in the structure of the ad. We also intend to explore other pieces of evidence from the page which we ignored in this study, such as, users information and related videos. Finally, we intended to use the weights of the structural blocks as aditional evidence in a machine learning approach, similar to the one proposed by the authors in [23].

7. ACKNOWLEDGMENTS

The authors would like to thank INdT (Nokia Institute of Technology), UOL (grant 2011-021.521.5200) and individual grants and scholarships from CNPq (307.861/2010-4, 309.474/2011-6, and 484.816/2011-0).

8. REFERENCES

[1] J. M. Almeida, M. A. Gonçalves, F. Figueiredo, H. Pinto, and F. M. Belém. On the quality of information for web 2.0 services. *IEEE Internet Computing*, 14(6):47–55, 2010.

[2] G. Attardi, A. Esuli, and M. Simi. Best bets: thousands of queries in search of a client. In S. I. Feldman, M. Uretsky, M. Najork, and C. E. Wills, editors, *WWW (Alternate Track Papers & Posters)*, pages 422–423. ACM, 2004.

[3] R. Baeza-Yates and B. Ribeiro-Neto. *Modern Information Retrieval*. Addison-Wesley-Longman, 2st edition, 2010.

[4] H. K. Bhargava and J. Feng. Paid placement strategies for internet search engines. In *Proceedings of the 11th international conference on World Wide Web*, WWW '02, pages 117–123, New York, NY, USA, 2002. ACM.

[5] A. Broder, M. Fontoura, V. Josifovski, and L. Riedel. A semantic approach to contextual advertising. In *Proceedings of the 30th annual international ACM SIGIR conference on Research and development in information retrieval*, SIGIR '07, pages 559–566, New York, NY, USA, 2007. ACM.

[6] C. Buckley and E. M. Voorhees. Retrieval evaluation with incomplete information. In *SIGIR '04: Proceedings of the 27th annual international ACM SIGIR conference on Research and development in information retrieval*, pages 25–32, New York, NY, USA, 2004. ACM.

[7] M. Cristo, A. Bitar, B. Guimaraes, G. Penalber, R. Hanada, C. Teixeira, and E. Melo. Web-like personalized advertising system for interactive digital TV. In *WTVDI/WEBMEDIA 2010*. SBC, 2010.

[8] E. S. de Moura, D. Fernandes, B. Ribeiro-Neto, A. S. da Silva, and M. A. Gonçalves. Using structural information to improve search in web collections. *J. Am. Soc. Inf. Sci. Technol.*, 61:2503–2513, December 2010.

[9] E. Eneva. Detecting invalid clicks in online paid search listings: a problem description for the use of unlabeled data. In T. Fawcett and N. Mishra, editors, *Workshop on the Continuum from Labeled to Unlabeled Data, 20th International Conference on Machine Learning*, Washington DC, USA, August 2003. AAAI Press.

[10] J. Feng, H. K. Bhargava, and D. M. Pennock. Implementing sponsored search in web search engines: Computational evaluation of alternative mechanisms. *INFORMS J. on Computing*, 19:137–148, January 2007.

[11] D. Fernandes, E. S. de Moura, B. Ribeiro-Neto, A. S. da Silva, and M. A. Gonçalves. Computing block importance for searching on web sites. In *Proceedings of the sixteenth ACM conference on Conference on information and knowledge management*, CIKM '07, pages 165–174, New York, NY, USA, 2007. ACM.

[12] F. Figueiredo, F. Belém, H. Pinto, J. Almeida, M. Gonçalves, D. Fernandes, E. Moura, and M. Cristo. Evidence of quality of textual features on the web 2.0. In *Proceedings of the 18th ACM conference on Information and knowledge management*, CIKM '09, pages 909–918, New York, NY, USA, 2009. ACM.

[13] F. Figueiredo, H. Pinto, F. Belém, J. Almeida, M. Gonçalves, D. Fernandes, and E. Moura. Assessing the quality of textual features in social media. *Information Processing & Management*, Apr. 2012.

[14] G. Giuffrida, V. Cantone, and G. Tribulato. An apriori based approach to improve on-line advertising performance. In *Proceedings of the 2008 conference on Applications of Data Mining in E-Business and Finance*, pages 51–61, Amsterdam, The Netherlands, The Netherlands, 2008. IOS Press.

[15] D. Gleich and L. Zhukov. SVD based term suggestion and ranking system. In *ICDM '04: Proceedings of the Fourth IEEE International Conference on Data Mining (ICDM'04)*, pages 391–394, Washington, DC, USA, 2004. IEEE Computer Society.

[16] A. Lacerda, M. Cristo, M. A. Gonçalves, W. Fan, N. Ziviani, and B. Ribeiro-Neto. Learning to advertise. In *SIGIR '06: Proceedings of the 29th annual international ACM SIGIR conference on Research and development in information retrieval*, pages 549–556, New York, NY, USA, 2006. ACM.

[17] T. Mei, X. S. Hua, L. Yang, and S. Li. VideoSense: towards effective online video advertising. In *Proceedings of the 15th international conference on Multimedia*, MULTIMEDIA '07, pages 1075–1084, New York, NY, USA, 2007. ACM.

[18] T. Mei and S. Li. Contextual in-stream video advertising. In X.-S. Hua, T. Mei, and A. Hanjalic, editors, *Online Multimedia Advertising: Techniques and Technologies*, pages 223–233. IGI Global, 2011.

[19] R. Ramakrishnan, A. Tomkins, and R. Kumar. Content, metadata, and behavioral information: Directions for yahoo! research. *IEEE Data Eng. Bull.*, 29(4):10–18, 2006.

[20] M. A. Rappa. The utility business model and the future of computing services. *IBM Syst. J.*, 43:32–42, January 2004.

[21] B. Ribeiro-Neto, M. Cristo, P. B. Golgher, and E. Silva de Moura. Impedance coupling in content-targeted advertising. In *Proceedings of the 28th annual international ACM SIGIR conference on Research and development in information retrieval*, SIGIR '05, pages 496–503, New York, NY, USA, 2005. ACM.

[22] B. Wang, J. Wang, L.-Y. Duan, Q. Tian, H. Lu, and W. Gao. Interactive web video advertising with context analysis and search. In *Proceedings of the 2010 20th International Conference on Pattern Recognition*, ICPR '10, pages 3252–3255, Washington, DC, USA, 2010. IEEE Computer Society.

[23] B.-J. Yi, J.-T. Lee, H.-W. Woo, and H.-C. Rim. Contextual video advertising system using scene information inferred from video scripts. In *Proceedings of the 33rd international ACM SIGIR conference on Research and development in information retrieval*, SIGIR '10, pages 771–772, New York, NY, USA, 2010. ACM.

[24] W.-t. Yih, J. Goodman, and V. R. Carvalho. Finding advertising keywords on web pages. In *WWW '06: Proceedings of the 15th international conference on World Wide Web*, pages 213–222, New York, NY, USA, 2006. ACM.

Selecting Keywords to Represent Web Pages Using Wikipedia Information

Maisa Vidal
Univ. Fed. do Amazonas
Instituto de Computação
Manaus, AM, Brasil
maisa@icomp.ufam.edu.br

Guilherme V. Menezes
Univ. Fed. de Minas Gerais
Dep. de Ciência da Comput.
Belo Horizonte, MG, Brasil
gmenezes@dcc.ufmg.br

Klessius Berlt
Univ. Fed. do Amazonas
Instituto de Computação
Manaus, AM, Brasil
klessius@icomp.ufam.edu.br

Edleno S. de Moura
Univ. Fed. do Amazonas
Instituto de Computação
Manaus, AM, Brasil
edleno@icomp.ufam.edu.br

Karla Okada
Instituto Nokia de Tecnologia
Manaus, AM, Brasil
karla.gomes@indt.org.br

Nivio Ziviani
Univ. Fed. de Minas Gerais
Dep. de Ciência da Comput.
Belo Horizonte, MG, Brasil
nivio@dcc.ufmg.br

David Fernandes
Univ. Fed. do Amazonas
Instituto de Computação
Manaus, AM, Brasil
david@icomp.ufam.edu.br

Marco Cristo
Univ. Fed. do Amazonas
Instituto de Computação
Manaus, AM, Brasil
marco.cristo@icomp.ufam.edu.br

ABSTRACT

In this paper we present three new methods to extract keywords from web pages using Wikipedia as an external source of information. The information used from Wikipedia includes the titles of articles, co-occurrence of keywords and categories associated with each Wikipedia definition. We compare our methods with three keyword extraction methods used as baselines: (i) all the terms of a web page, (ii) a TF-IDF implementation that extracts single weighted words of a web page and (iii) a previously proposed Wikipedia-based keyword extraction method presented in the literature. We compare our three keyword extraction methods with the baseline methods in three distinct scenarios, all related to our target application, which is the selection of ads in a context-based advertising system. In the first scenario, the target pages to place ads were extracted from Wikipedia articles, whereas the target pages in the other two scenarios were extracted from a news web site. Experimental results show that our methods are quite competitive solutions for the task of selecting good keywords to represent target web pages, albeit being simple, effective and time efficient. For instance, in the first scenario our best method used to extract keywords from Wikipedia articles achieved an improvement of 33% when compared to the second best baseline, and a gain of 26% when considering all the terms.

Permission to make digital or hard copies of all or part of this work for personal or classroom use is granted without fee provided that copies are not made or distributed for profit or commercial advantage and that copies bear this notice and the full citation on the first page. To copy otherwise, to republish, to post on servers or to redistribute to lists, requires prior specific permission and/or a fee.
WebMedia'12, October 15–18, 2012, São Paulo/SP, Brazil.
Copyright 2012 ACM 978-1-4503-1706-1/12/10 ...$15.00.

Categories and Subject Descriptors

H. Information Systems [**H.3 INFORMATION STORAGE AND RETRIEVAL**]: H.3.m Miscellaneous

Keywords

Context-based advertising, keyword extraction, Wikipedia

1. INTRODUCTION

Context-based advertising has become widespread in the web in recent years due to its success in generating revenue to a large variety of web sites, ranging from small blogs to large online newspapers. A system that implements this form of advertising works by automatically associating ads with the content of the web site a user is currently visiting. The general assumption is that users have a higher probability of finding an ad interesting if the content of the ad is similar to the content of the web page the user is currently browsing in.

Traditional context-based advertising systems usually work in two phases: (i) they represent the contextual information in the target web page, e.g., by extracting the keywords that best summarize its content; (ii) they match the representations of the target page and each ad of the ad inventory database, building a ordered list of the ads to be displayed to the users. The order of the resulting ad list is determined, among other elements, by the similarity between the contents of the page and the ad.

In this paper we focus in the first phase, i.e., extraction of keywords from target web pages. We present new alternatives for representing the contextual information present in a web page. We use information from Wikipedia articles to semantically enrich the information that best summarize web pages.

Wikipedia is a source of information with some interesting characteristics. First, it is very large and covers many knowledge domains. At the time we performed our experiments, Wikipedia had approximately 3.3 million articles in English. Second, due to its popularity and the open nature of its editing process, it is frequently updated providing fresh content about many topics. As a consequence of such broader and dynamic nature, it is likely to have detailed information on new products that draw public attention, such as laptop models, game consoles or recently published books. This is very convenient to context-based advertising systems, since the user context and their interests also have a dynamic nature, that is, they change over months, weeks, and even during the same day. Further, each Wikipedia article describes an entity, such as a place, a person or an object, and is semantically precise in the sense that each article describes a "unit of knowledge" in an unambiguous way.

To take advantage of Wikipedia as a source of knowledge useful for context-based advertising systems, we propose three methods that use information from Wikipedia to represent web pages. The first one uses the titles of Wikipedia articles as a controlled vocabulary for extraction of semantically-rich keywords from target pages, using a TF-IDF weight scheme. The other two methods use the category of Wikipedia article to expand the representation of the web pages by assigning keywords that are not present in the pages, but are related to their categories.

The three methods were engineered to be simple and present small computational costs. Thus, the proposed methods are suitable for industrial context-based advertising systems that are required to process millions of requests every day. In these systems, every page view in the web site generates a request, and any method that needs too much computational effort would not be acceptable.

We evaluate the effectiveness of our proposed methods by comparing them to three keyword extraction baselines: (i) a method considering all terms of the target page; (ii) a TF-IDF implementation to select single words; (iii) a popular Wikipedia-based keyword extraction algorithm described in [15].

Experimental results show that the proposed methods are competitive in practice. For instance, when selecting keywords from Wikipedia articles, our best method outperformed the representations based on all the terms (i) and TF-IDF weighting (iii) with gains of about 33% and 26 %, respectively. In the worst scenario we found in our experiments, our methods achieved results similar to the approach proposed by [15].

The remaining of this paper is organized as follows. Section 2 covers related work. Section 3 describes the three proposed methods for selecting keywords from Web pages. In Section 4 we present experimental results comparing our methods with three baselines. Finally, in Section 5, we present our conclusions and review our contributions.

2. RELATED WORK

Wikipedia has been used in some previous work as a measure of semantic relatedness. In [6], the authors introduce a method called Explicit Semantic Analysis (ESA), with the objective of semantically enriching texts in natural language. It represents texts in a vector of Wikipedia concepts, associating a weight to each concept quantifying the relatedness between the text and the concept. They experimented with word-level and text-level semantic relatedness, obtaining better results than other approaches in the literature. They also experimented the effectiveness of their semantic relatedness measure for generating features for classification. While their focus was to address classification problems, the positive results obtained are useful to illustrate the potential benefits of using Wikipedia information to better understand and represent the content of web pages.

Hu et al [9] employ a Wikipedia based semantic relatedness measure to improve the effectiveness of document clustering. First, the method maps the text of a document to Wikipedia concepts using an algorithm to disambiguate possible candidate concepts. Next, it calculates a similarity value based on the category hierarchy of the concepts that annotate the document. It also explores Wikipedia redirects and disambiguation pages to obtain a broader representation of each concept and improve the matching. They obtained significant improvements when compared to [6].

In [11] the authors also enrich textual documents with Wikipedia concepts to improve clustering. The method maps a text to concepts by leveraging the collection of anchor texts related to Wikipedia articles, i.e., they use the anchor text of links that point to a concept to describe this concept. Each occurrence of an anchor text in the document maps the document to a candidate concept. The set of candidate concepts is subsequently reduced by using a cluster-based feature selection algorithm. A follow-up work from the same authors is presented in [12], in which they compare their method with other related methods in the literature, including [6] and [9].

In [10] the authors devised another method of Wikipedia semantic relatedness that associate texts with Wikipedia categories. They experimented with two matching techniques: exact matching and relatedness matching. The first technique performs exact string matching, which is very efficient, while the second uses the cosine measure to select concepts. Interestingly, exact matching has performed better in most cases, showing that it represented the best alternative to match textual documents and concepts. Additional applications for Wikipedia semantic relatedness include cluster labeling [2] and search [14]. All the methods mentioned above have used information available in Wikipedia to improve classification or clustering of documents. We here are interested in use Wikipedia information as a keyword extraction method.

Among the keyword extraction methods that use Wikipedia information, we can cite [15], which uses information from Wikipedia links to extract keywords. The idea behind the method is to estimate the probability that a phrase is a keyword by calculating how many times the phrase was linked to other Wikipedia articles. Another example of method that uses Wikipedia information to extract keywords is [8], which uses Wikipedia to create a semantic graph between the terms of a Web page. They use the property that keywords related to the main topic of the document usually belong to the most interconnected communities in the term graph. The work by [15] was selected to be included in our experiments to help the reader to compare our method with the other methods proposed. It gives good results in practice and has computational costs close to our proposal.

The authors in [18] introduce WikiRank, a graph-based method that extracts key Wikipedia concepts from a text. The method explores the hyperlink connections among articles and categories from Wikipedia to obtain a ranking of related concepts. They analyze their method in two applications. The first one is a Wikipedia concept linking application, which shows Wikipedia definitions related to keywords in a news text. The second one is a visualizer of the key concepts in a news collection.

The methods presented by Mihalcea and Csomai [15], Grineva et al [8], and Zhou et al [18] are all proposals to extract keywords from web pages using Wikipedia information. The main difference to our proposal is that these three works adopt graph-based strategies to extract keywords from pages, while our methods use occurrence statistics about Wikipedia titles and information about the category these titles belong to. Experimental results show that our methods outperform the work presented in [15] in the target application, which is associate ads and product offers with web pages. We do not provide a comparison to the other two methods due to the lack of detailed information about them. We also found no comparison between the previously proposed methods, so we were not able to even compare our proposal to the other two found in the literature.

Some previously proposed methods use machine learning techniques to select keywords from a given web page. Irmak et al [13] use click-through data to train a model to rank a list of pre-determined entities of a document according to their interestingness and relevance. Goodman and Carvalho [7] and Yih et al [17] use logistic regression to learn good keywords for advertising and also study a large number of features to determine the importance of a keyword. Dave and Varma [3] explore Part-of-Speech (POS) patterns that restrict the number of potential keywords which the classifiers have to handle. Although these methods present good results on selecting keywords, the difference to our approach is that they require an extra effort to perform the training step. Also note that our method is complementary to these ones since our results can be used as additional feature by the machine learning strategies proposed by those authors.

3. WIKIPEDIA-BASED KEYWORD EXTRACTION

In this section we present three new keyword extraction methods that use Wikipedia semantic information. The main objective of the proposed methods is to improve the matching between ads and target web pages.

3.1 Wiki-TF-IDF

The first method for keyword extraction uses the titles of Wikipedia articles as a controlled vocabulary to extract keywords from target web pages. The method uses a variant of the TF-IDF weighting scheme [1], which we refer to as Wiki-TF-IDF method. The terms belonging to the titles of Wikipedia articles are used to obtain their term frequency (TF) in the target page and their inverse document frequency (IDF) in Wikipedia titles. The two weights TF-IDF are used to rank the candidate keywords. The intuition behind the method is that only semantically rich units of information are extracted, thus reducing noise and ambiguity in the extracted set of keywords.

By extracting more accurate keywords, Wiki-TF-IDF improves the matching to external datasets. For example, consider that phrase "New York" is present in a target web page. If we take words as semantic units of information, the keywords "New" and "York" are extracted. The word ("New") carries very low information value, and might be considered as a stopword which would be removed by some methods. The word ("York") is ambiguous, since it may refer to the city of York or to the New York city. Since "New York" is the title of an article in Wikipedia, our method considers the phrase "New York" as a single semantic unit, avoiding the negative effect of noisy keywords.

The Wiki-TF-IDF algorithm has two steps:

1. It extracts candidate keywords from the target web page, considering that: (i) It matches the largest possible phrase present in a text fragment. For instance, in the phrase "World Wide Web" it only considers the full phrase as a candidate, discarding the subphrases "World Wide", "Wide Web", "World", "Wide", and "Web". (ii) The keywords that occur less then 3 times in the collection of Wikipedia articles are excluded. (iii) Only fragments of, at most, eight words are considered. Thus, the largest keyword to be considered has eight words, thus limiting the time taken to extract them.

2. It ranks the candidate keywords using the following TF-IDF scheme[1]:

$$w_{ij} = (1 + \log(f_{ij})) * \log(\frac{N}{n_i}) \quad (1)$$

   where f_{ij} is the frequency of the candidate keyword c_i in document d_j, N is the number of documents in Wikipedia, and n_i is the number of Wikipedia documents in which the candidate c_i occurs at least once. Then, it ranks the candidate keywords and the top k keywords are selected.

Wiki-TF-IDF is expected to perform efficiently even in large-scale systems with a large number of users. Its efficiency is due to (i) its simplicity and (ii) its use of a hash structure to store Wikipedia titles which allows it to extract all the candidate keywords in linear time.

3.2 Wiki-Categories-1

The second method for keyword extraction considers the categories that each Wikipedia article belongs to, which we refer to as Wiki-Categories-1. The Wiki-Categories-1 algorithm has three steps:

1. It selects from a given web page P a set of initial keywords IKw_P with the top 10 keywords ranked with the Wiki-TF-IDF method. The method could in fact select an initial set of any size, but when analyzing initial results provided by method Wiki-TF-IDF, we realized that it usually achieves a good precision when selecting 10 keywords, and further, the quality of results usually does not improve much when selecting more than 10 keywords.

2. Then, it identifies the set of categories in Wikipedia related to the keywords of IKw_P, creating a new set of keywords CKw_P that contains all the categories related to the titles found in IKw_P. Remember that each keyword selected by Wiki-TF-IDF is in fact a title of a Wikipedia article. Further, each Wikipedia title belongs to one or more categories in Wikipedia. Finally, each Wikipedia article presents a list of categories it belongs to.

3. The title of the categories identified in CKw_P are all listed in a single text that is then sent as input to the Wiki-TF-IDF method, just as it is done with a web page. We then use the rank provided by Wiki-TF-IDF to select keywords from this text, associating these keywords with the page P.

3.3 Wiki-Categories-2

The Wiki-Categories-2 works like the previous method, with the following difference. In step 3, to rank these categories (using the label of the categories) we use the weight of the keyword that was used to select it. For example, in Table 1, if the keyword "munition" has weight 0.8, the categories "firearms" and "artillery" will have the same weight, 0.8. The intuition behind Wiki-Categories-2 is that categories associated with keywords with a strong relation to a page P also have a strong relation to P. Notice that if the weight assigned by Wiki-TF-IDF to a keyword in a page is high, then its relation to the page is strong.

Table 1: Example of categories related to three Wikipedia titles.

Title	Categories
munition	firearms artillery
caliber	arms artillery
soldier	military forces military ranks

4. EXPERIMENTAL EVALUATION

In this section we analyze the performance of our proposed methods as part of a content targeted advertising system. Our keyword extraction methods were responsible for extracting a set of keywords from the target web page where the ads are presented. These keywords were then submitted as a query to a search system in order to select and rank advertising stored in an ad inventory database.

4.1 Datasets

A problem we endured in the experiments is that real data collections of ads are not publicly available for experiments. We then decided to create a dataset composed of 3,016,544 product offers extracted from an online shopping company called Nhemu[1]. The Nhemu is a price comparison service that crawls product offers from a large set of brazilian e-commerce shoppings. In this paper we considered that each product offer is described through the concatenation of three distinct attributes: name, brand, and category. This collection is referred to as *Ad-Collection-1* from now on.

While we recognize that this collection is different from the ones available on ad networks, such as the ones maintained by Google and Yahoo, it has the advantage of being now public, which will allow easy comparison of our results with future work. Further, we believe it will also be useful for future research in the area of content targeted advertising. The list of products available in the dataset is quite extensive, including books, CDs, electronic products, furniture, car accessories, games, groceries, clothes, shoes, and almost every type of product sold on the Internet, thus being a quite rich sample of product offers. Further, the books included in the collection cover all themes usually found in a library, thus opening possibilities to matches with pages about almost every topic. Given these properties, we believe that it can be used as a good reference collection to compare the effectiveness of keyword selection strategies for advertising. Further, the announcement of products constitutes a quite common type of advertising usually shown on the Internet.

We also used a real advertising collection composed by 93,972 ads from 1,744 distinct advertisers, which is referred to as *Ad-Collection-2* from now on.

As target pages (i.e.: the pages where the ads should be displayed) we used the following two sets of pages:

P_{Wiki}: a set of 300 random web pages obtained from the portuguese version of Wikipedia[2].

P_{News}: a set of 300 pages extracted from a brazilian newspaper[3].

As we have no preference for particular topics, both sets of pages cover diverse subjects, such as culture, music, personalities, sports, politics, technologies among others. As we use the Wikipedia database to enhance the representation of pages, our method is particularly good to extract keywords from pages that belong to Wikipedia.

We combined the ads and target pages into three distinct scenarios where the experiments were conducted, as presented in Table 2.

	Scenario 1	Scenario 2	Scenario 3
Pages	P_{Wiki}	P_{News}	P_{News}
Ads	Ad-Collection-1	Ad-Collection-1	Ad-Collection-2

Table 2: *Three scenarios where the experiments were conducted.*

The Wikipedia database used to compute the IDF and the co-occurrence of terms was a dump downloaded on February 2010, from which we obtained 533,358 distinct titles, including full articles, stub articles, disambiguation pages, category pages, list pages, and redirections. The product offer dataset, the web pages adopted in the experiments, and the relevance judgment of the ads associated with each web page will be available for future experiments. The reader can directly contact the authors to obtain the collection.

4.2 Evaluation Methodology

We evaluated the quality of the ads retrieved using the set of keywords extracted from target pages by each method. Each set of keywords was used as a query submitted to a retrieval system which returned a ranking of ads based on each set. The relevance judgment was performed by a group of 30 volunteers, each evaluating the ads returned by the methods considering an average of 10 web target pages.

Volunteers were asked to evaluate each retrieved ad as "relevant" or "non-relevant" in relation to a source web page. They were oriented to consider an ad as relevant if they considered that a user who was reading the page would likely

[1]http://nhemu.com

[2]http://pt.wikipedia.org

[3]http://www.folha.uol.com.br/

click the ad presented. Given a web page and an ad collection, we presented to the users the union of results provided by all variants of the methods studied. The results for a page were presented in a random order to avoid a possible bias caused by the order of results.

The system adopted to process the queries and selected ads is the Lucene[4], configured to rank documents using the vector space model. The keywords composed of more than one word, such as "South Africa", were submitted as phrases to Lucene for sake of simplicity. In a practical advertising system, a better option would be to change the indexing system to detect these keywords when indexing the ad collection, thus allowing fast search for keywords composed of more than one word.

The methods "TF-IDF", "Keyphraseness", "Wiki-TF-IDF", "Wiki-Categories-1" and "Wiki-Categories-2" provide a ranking of keywords and associate a weight with each of these keywords. We used as a query the top n keywords of each method ($1 \leq n \leq 30$) and included the computed weight for each keyword as part of the query (Lucene allows the assignment of weights to the words in its query processing interface). As "All terms" returns a set of unordered terms we used as keywords all the terms from the set. Thus, their results are presented as an horizontal straight line on the graphics. The "All terms" has an average of 185 keywords per web page. For the methods "TF-IDF", "Keyphraseness", "Wiki-TF-IDF", "Wiki-Categories-1" and "Wiki-Categories-2" we submitted the keywords with their weights, instructing the query processor to take the weights into account in the ranking.

The search results were evaluated using precision at 3 (p@3), which expresses the average percentage of relevant ads in the top 3 answers provided by the search system, as follows:

$$p@3 = \frac{|rel \cap answers|}{|answers|} \quad (2)$$

where rel is the set of relevant ads associated with the web page in the pool, $answers$ is the set of the top three ads displayed to this page by the evaluated method. Note that, as we consider only the top 3 results for each page, the maximum value of $|answers|$ is 3. Indeed, in some cases, the system retrieves less then 3 ads for the set of keywords used as query. The $p@3$ of a method is the average $p@3$ considering only the pages where at least one ad was returned.

A problem found when computing P@3 is that it is common to find cases where a method does not provide answers. This problem in fact might be quite common even in real case advertising collections, since ad collections may not cover the whole set of keywords and topics found on the web. In these cases, the precision for the specific query cannot be determined and we removed these cases when computing the final average value of P@3. Other option could be set the P@3 to 1 or 0, but in both cases the result would not reflect the reality.

Thus, to provide more insight about the results, we also introduced the computation of $recall@3$, which was calculated taking the number of relevant ads found in the pool as the set of relevant answers, but limiting this number to the maximum of relevant ads that could be shown by each method. Thus, the $recall@3$ of a method given a page p is:

$$recall@3 = \frac{|rel \cap answers|}{min(|rel|, 3)} \quad (3)$$

where rel and $answers$ are defined as in the previous equation and min is a function that returns the minimum value of two arguments.

[4]http://lucene.apache.org

4.3 Baselines

We used three different methods to compare the effectiveness of our approach, as follows:

1. "All terms": We simply used all the terms (except stopwords) in the web page to retrieve items, i.e., we used no keyword extraction algorithm at all.

2. We used a plain TF-IDF method [16] that uses words as semantic units. We used Wikipedia to calculate the Inverse Document Frequencies. We adopted this strategy because TF-IDF is a method largely used to select keywords from a text. Further, using the TF-IDF extracted from Wikipedia (the same source from where we select keywords using our proposed method) we are able to evaluate the improvements of our method when compared to this previously used strategy. Note that as we use TF-IDF information extracted from Wikipedia, TF-IDF can also be considered as a variant of TF-IDF proposed by us to take advantage of Wikipedia information in order to select keywords from web pages. However, we include it as a baseline, since our contribution in this case is marginal.

3. We used the method *Keyphraseness* [15] for comparison purposes. The *Keyphraseness* is a state-of-the-art keyword extraction method that also uses Wikipedia as domain knowledge base [8]. This method uses the probability of a term t_i to be selected as a keyword in a new document. It considers as keywords the terms that are linked to other Wikipedia articles, i.e., it considers link identification and keyword extraction as the same problem. The *Keyphraseness* of a term t_i is given by:

$$Keyphraseness(t_i) = P(is\ link|t_i) \approx \frac{n_{link}}{n_i} \quad (4)$$

where n_{link} is the number of documents the term t_i occurs as a link and n_i is the number of documents where the term occurs at least once. The extracted keywords are ranked and the top k keywords are used to represent the document. Following the procedure in [15], we only considered as candidate keywords the terms that occurred in more than 5 Wikipedia articles.

4.4 Results and Discussion

In this section we present the results provided by each method considering the three scenarios presented in Table 2.

4.4.1 Scenario 1

In this scenario (Wikipedia pages as target and Nhemu product offer dataset as the ad collection), the proposed methods achieved the best results. This happens because the target pages are also from Wikipedia, and thus naturally have content associated with the categories extracted by our method. We emphasize that providing effective mechanisms to select ads for Wikipedia web pages is itself an important application that could be used in practice.

Figure 1 presents the P@3 results obtained by our method in this scenario. First, when selecting from 1 to 20 keywords, our three methods outperform the baselines TF-IDF and Keyphraseness in terms of precision. Figure 1 also shows that the keyword expansion methods Wiki-categories-1 and Wiki-categories-2 caused improvements in the quality of results, achieving a gain of up to 26% when compared to "All terms" and a gain of 33% when compared to TF-IDF, the second best baseline.

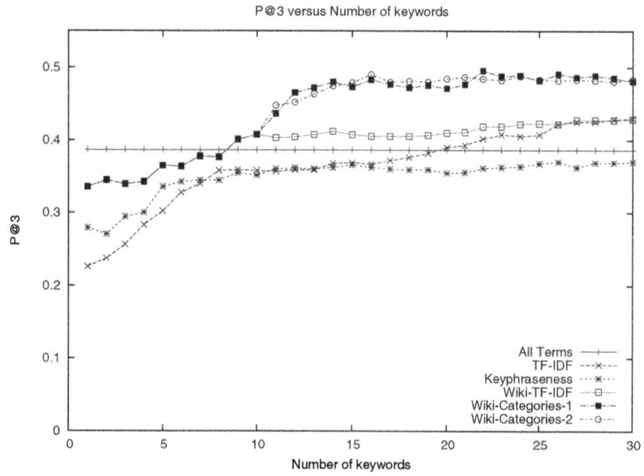

Figure 1: P@3 for each method using different number of keywords in scenario 1 (Wikipedia pages as target and Nhemu product offer dataset as the ad collection). The method "All terms" has an average of 185 keywords per web page.

The gains are statistically significant according to $t-test$ when comparing Wiki-categories-1 and Wiki-categories-2 to the baselines Keyphraseness and TF-IDF in all levels, being also significant when comparing to "All terms" and using at least 12 terms. The gains achieved by Wiki-TF-IDF are significant when compared to Keyphraseness in all points of the curve. The gains achieved by Wiki-TF-IDF are significant only for 1 to 14 keywords, being not significant when using more keywords.

An important issue in ad selection systems is the final computational costs required to select ads. While "All terms" requires an average number of 185 keywords to represent a web page, our method Wiki-TF-IDF required only about 8 keywords to achieve the same performance. This is an important property, since the computational cost to select ads is linear in the number of keywords. Thus, the expected computational cost to select ads using the keyword sets provided by our methods would be less than 1% of the cost for selecting ads when using "All terms". In this first scenario, where the target pages are extracted from Wikipedia, the improvement in time performance is obtained also with a significant improvement in the quality of the selected ads.

Figure 2 depicts the R@3 results achieved with the methods in the first scenario. As it can be seen, recall results obtained by the methods are equal to the P@3 values. This similarity in the results indicates that the ad selector has retrieved ads for virtually all the sets of keywords selected

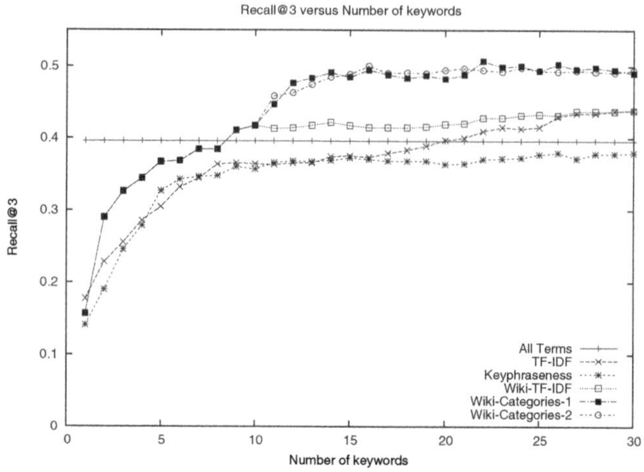

Figure 2: R@3 for each method using different number of keywords in scenario 1 (Wikipedia pages as target and Nhemu product offer dataset as the ad collection). The method "All terms" have a average of 185 keywords per web page.

by the compared methods in scenario 1. This abundance of results is related to the large variety of products found in the collection Nhemu, which includes, for instance, a large collection of books that also covers a variety of topics.

4.4.2 Scenario 2

Figure 3 presents the P@3 results obtained by our method in Scenario 2. In this second scenario, we keep Nhemu dataset as the ad collection, but changed the target pages to news pages. This change in the target pages is important to avoid the bias in favor of category methods achieved when using Wikipedia pages as targets.

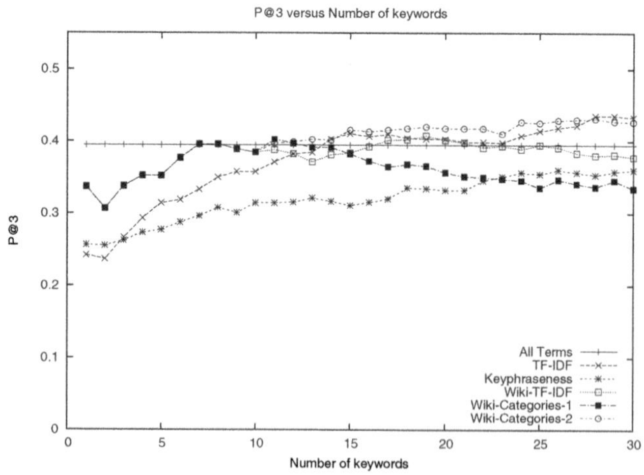

Figure 3: P@3 for each method using different number of keywords in scenario 2 (News pages as target and Nhemu product offer dataset as the ad collection). The method "All terms" have a average of 185 keywords per web page.

When selecting from 1 to 8 keywords, method Wiki-TF-IDF again outperforms the baselines TF-IDF and Keyphraseness in terms of precision, with gains statistically significant. Figure 3 also shows the keyword expansion method Wiki-Categories-2 caused just a low improvement in the quality of results, with gains achieved being not significant when compared to Wiki-TF-IDF. Method Wiki-Categories-2 in fact has caused loss of quality in this scenario.

When checking the R@3 values presented in Figure 4, conclusions are close to the ones obtained in scenario 1. The usage of Nhemu collection again allowed the values of precision and recall to be almost the same, expect for very small number of keywords (less than 3).

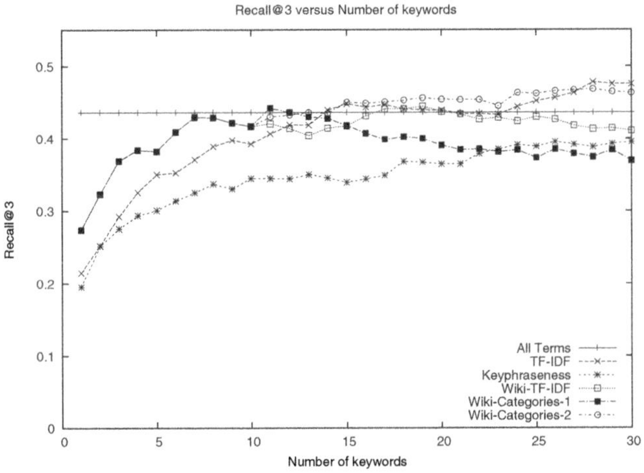

Figure 4: R@3 for each method using different number of keywords in scenario 2 (News pages as target and Nhemu product offer dataset as the ad collection). The method "All terms" have a average of 185 keywords per web page.

4.4.3 *Scenario 3*

In scenario 3, we compare the methods when the target pages contain news and the ads are extracted from a real case ad collection. Figure 5 depicts the results. Note that again method Wiki-TF-IDF achieved gains when compared to Keyphraseness. However, we notice that in this scenario the differences between our method and TF-IDF are not significant. Further, all the experimented methods are worse than an approach using all terms, with differences being statistically significant for all cases where the methods select less than 10 keywords.

Figure 5 also shows that method Wiki-Categories-2 is slightly better than Wiki-Categories-1, while again the category expansion resulted in no significant improvement in the results when compared to Wiki-TF-IDF.

Figure 6 presents the R@3 curves in this third scenario. The recall in this case is worse than precision when using just a few keywords, from 1 to 6 keywords. That means this scenario presents more cases where the ad selector was not able to find any match between the given keywords and the ad collection. This result was expected, since in this scenario the ad collection contains fewer and less diverse elements than the Nhemu database adopted in scenarios 1 and 2. Further, we can see that this scenario is less favorable to our methods. On the other hand, even in this less favor-

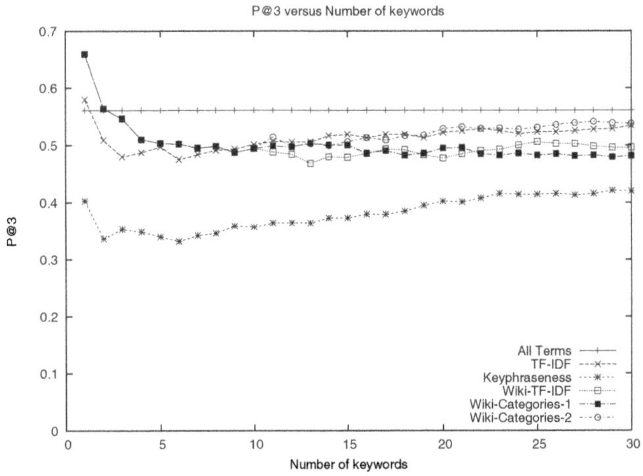

Figure 5: P@3 for each method using different number of keywords in scenario 3 (News pages as target and the ad collection dataset). The method "All terms" have a average of 185 keywords per web page.

able scenario still our methods are quite competitive when compared to the baselines.

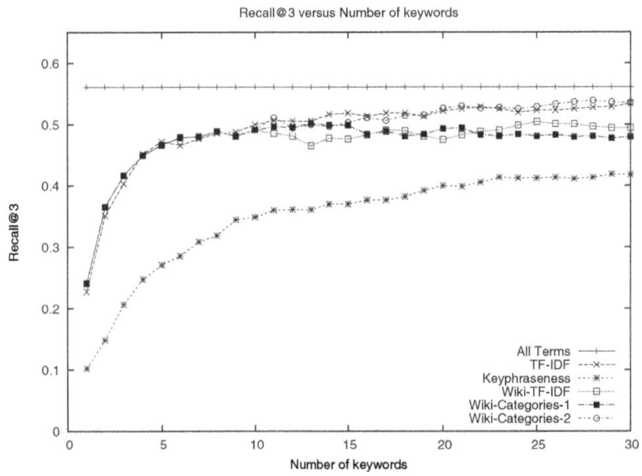

Figure 6: R@3 for each method using different number of keywords in scenario 3 (News pages as target and the ad collection dataset). The method "All terms" have a average of 185 keywords per web page.

5. CONCLUSIONS AND FUTURE WORK

In this work we proposed three novel approaches for selecting keywords on Web pages: Wiki-TF-IDF, Wiki-Categories-1 and Wiki-Categories-2. The objective was to reduce noise and improve the matching between the keywords and ads in an advertising system. To evaluate the proposed methods we used the software Lucene as the ad selector.

Experimental results have shown that the three methods are competitive in practice. For instance, when selecting keywords from Wikipedia articles, our best method outperformed the representations based on all the terms (i) and TF-IDF weighting (iii) with gains of about 33% and 26 %, respectively. In the worst scenario we found in our experiments, our methods achieved results similar to the approach proposed by [15].

We also have shown that Wiki-Categories-1 and Wiki-Categories-2 presented a good performance using small sets of keywords to represent each web page, presenting small computational costs. They achieved, in some scenarios, results with a quality even superior to the other methods experimented. For instance, on Scenario 1 they achieved results slightly superior to the ones obtained when using all terms of a page, which could be a trivial solution to the problem of representing a web page.

Although we experimented the proposed keyword selection methods only with advertising systems, the results presented indicate they may be specially useful in any application where there is a requirement of representing the content of a web page with an small set of keywords. This is the case, for instance, when this small set of keywords is used as a query to an API of web service that limits the maximum number of keywords in a query. For instance, the methods proposed could be useful to automatically select videos related to a page from online video servers, such as Youtube, or to automatically recommend books when a user is browsing a page in a Web site. We will further investigate these and other applications to our method as future work.

We are also interested in studying new strategies for selecting keywords from Web pages. For instance, we plan to improve our methods by using information about the quality of distinct textual blocks of the Web pages [4, 5]. Finally, since our methods are very cheap to compute, they could be used as complementary features for more sophisticated strategies such as the ones based in machine learning, described in Section 2.

6. ACKNOWLEDGMENTS

The authors would like to thank INdT (Nokia Institute of Technology), Brazilian National Institute of Science and Technology for the Web (grant MCT/CNPq 573.871/2008-6), National Council for Scientific and Technological Development (grants CNPq 307.861/2010-4, 309.474/2011-6 and 484.816/2011-0), UOL (grant 2011-021.521.5200) and individual scholarships from CNPq and CAPES.

7. REFERENCES

[1] R. A. Baeza-Yates and B. A. Ribeiro-Neto. *Modern Information Retrieval.* Pearson / Addison-Wesley, second edition, 2011.

[2] D. Carmel, H. Roitman, and N. Zwerdling. Enhancing cluster labeling using wikipedia. In *Proceedings of the 32nd Annual International ACM SIGIR Conference on Research and Development in Information Retrieval*, pages 139–146, 2009.

[3] K. S. Dave and V. Varma. Pattern based keyword extraction for contextual advertising. In *Proceedings of the 19th ACM international conference on Information and knowledge management*, CIKM '10, pages 1885–1888, New York, NY, USA, 2010. ACM.

[4] J. A. Fabiano M. Belém, Eder Ferreira Martins. Recomendação de tags a partir de métricas de qualidade de atributos textuais em aplicações da web 2.0. In *Proceedings of the XVI Brazilian Symposium on Multimedia and the Web*, WebMedia '10, New York, NY, USA, 2010. ACM.

[5] F. Figueiredo, F. Belém, H. Pinto, J. Almeida, M. Gonçalves, D. Fernandes, E. Moura, V. Almeida, and M. Cristo. Characterizing use and quality of textual attributes in web 2.0 applications. In *Proceedings of the XV Brazilian Symposium on Multimedia and the Web*, WebMedia '09, pages 9:1–9:8, New York, NY, USA, 2009. ACM.

[6] E. Gabrilovich and S. Markovitch. Wikipedia-based semantic interpretation for natural language processing. *J. Artif. Int. Res.*, 34:443–498, March 2009.

[7] J. Goodman and V. R. Carvalho. Implicit queries for email. In *Second Conference on Email and Anti-Spam*, `http://www.ceas.cc/papers-2005/141.pdf`, 2005.

[8] M. Grineva, M. Grinev, and D. Lizorkin. Extracting key terms from noisy and multitheme documents. In *Proceedings of the 18th International Conference on the World wide web*, pages 661–670, 2009.

[9] J. Hu, L. Fang, Y. Cao, H.-J. Zeng, H. Li, Q. Yang, and Z. Chen. Enhancing text clustering by leveraging wikipedia semantics. In *Proceedings of the 31st Annual International ACM SIGIR Conference on Research and Development in Information Retrieval*, pages 179–186, 2008.

[10] X. Hu, X. Zhang, C. Lu, E. K. Park, and X. Zhou. Exploiting wikipedia as external knowledge for document clustering. In *Proceedings of the 15th ACM SIGKDD International Conference on Knowledge Discovery and Data Mining*, pages 389–396, 2009.

[11] A. Huang, D. Milne, E. Frank, and I. H. Witten. Clustering documents with active learning using wikipedia. In *Proceedings of the 2008 Eighth IEEE International Conference on Data Mining*, pages 839–844, 2008.

[12] A. Huang, D. Milne, E. Frank, and I. H. Witten. Clustering documents using a wikipedia-based concept representation. In *Proceedings of the 13th Pacific-Asia Conference on Advances in Knowledge Discovery and Data Mining*, pages 628–636, 2009.

[13] U. Irmak, V. von Brzeski, and R. Kraft. Contextual ranking of keywords using click data. In *Proceedings of the 2009 IEEE International Conference on Data Engineering*, pages 457–468, 2009.

[14] M. Koolen, G. Kazai, and N. Craswell. Wikipedia pages as entry points for book search. In *Proceedings of the Second ACM International Conference on Web Search and Data Mining*, pages 44–53, 2009.

[15] R. Mihalcea and A. Csomai. Wikify!: linking documents to encyclopedic knowledge. In *Proceedings of the 16th ACM Conference on Information and Knowledge Management*, pages 233–242, 2007.

[16] G. Salton and C. Buckley. Term-weighting approaches in automatic text retrieval. *Inf. Process. Manage.*, 24(5):513–523, 1988.

[17] W.-t. Yih, J. Goodman, and V. R. Carvalho. Finding advertising keywords on web pages. In *Proceedings of the 15th International Conference on the World Wide Web*, pages 213–222, 2006.

[18] B. Zhou, P. Luo, Y. Xiong, and W. Liu. Wikipedia-graph based key concept extraction towards news analysis. In *Proceedings of the 2009 IEEE Conference on Commerce and Enterprise Computing*, pages 121–128, 2009.

ICT Web: Analysis of the Brazilian Governmental Web

Heitor de Souza Ganzeli
Graça Bressan
Departamento Computação e Sistemas Digitais (PCS) – EP USP
Av. Prof. Luciano Gualberto, Trav. 3 no. 158 – Cidade Universitária – 05508-900 – São Paulo, SP – Brazil
+ 55 11 30915583
heitor.ganzeli@usp.br
gbressan@larc.usp.br

Antônio Marcos Moreiras
Nic.br
Av. das Nações Unidas, 11541 – 7º A. – 04578-000 – São Paulo, SP – Brazil
+ 55 11 55093537
moreiras@nic.br

ABSTRACT
The World Wide Web is the most popular application throughout the Internet and, since its creation, it has changed people's lives in lots of ways, hence, it has become subject to several social, technological, economical and political researches. This paper presents both a project called ICT Web (Measuring Information and Communication Technologies for Development – Web) and the results it has obtained by studying the Brazilian Governmental Web. Some of the discussed topics are as follows: the importance of Open Standards, and how their conformity evaluation can be used to measure and classify the quality of Web sites. Also, more technical issues related to web crawler and web analysis tools are shown in order to reveal how all data were retrieved. Not only does this work point out some characteristics of the Brazilian governmental Web sites, which helps the creation of policies that improve this Web sites quality, but also it establishes a series of features to compare the perceived quality between Web domains.

Categories and Subject Descriptors
H.3.5 [**Information Storage and Retrival**]: On-line Information Services --- *Web-based services*; K.4.1 [**Computers and Society**]: Public policy issues --- *Regulation*;

General Terms
Measurement, Standardization, Verification.

Keywords
Web crawler, Open Standards, Accessibility, Governmental Web, Time Synchronization.

1. ICT Web
The importance of Web to the whole society is undeniable. It is the platform of most applications around the world as well as allowing the creation of new and innovative communication methods.

Therefore, the Brazilian Internet Steering Committee – CGI.br and the Brazilian Network Information Center – NIC.br, through the World Wide Web Consortium (W3C) Brazil and the Center of Study and Research in Network Technology and Operations – CEPTRO.br, have designed a project called ICT Web (Measuring Information and Communication Technologies for Development – Web) that aims to increase the knowledge and understanding of Brazilian Web. One of its main goals is to provide a novel way to characterize and analyze the Web by checking the adoption of open Internet standards.

Works on categorization of country Web domains have already been done, some examples being [3], [2] and [12]. However, the results are not directly comparable to the present ones because their analyses are mostly based on samples and their focus is mostly on Web structure, while these are to extract data from several Internet layers, trying to measure the utilization of open and recommended standards. Moreover, this study evaluates the Web periodically over time, despite analyzing it only once.

The analysis of the Brazilian Governmental Web, represented by the domain ".gov.br", was chosen as the first sub-goal of this project because, although small, it has a very substantial difference from the other domains. All its Web sites are developed by government departments or companies. Therefore, they are under government rules that require compliance with a set of interoperability standards [8], which also include an accessibility guideline named E-MAG (Electronic Government Accessibility Model) [6]. This reinforces the present project value as a way to rate Web sites and point out the ones that do not comply with the recommended guidelines and standards.

2. OPEN INTERNET STANDARDS
The Internet can be defined as a vast collection of networks that use common protocols to provide certain services [11]. Because of that, the use of standardization is essential to allow each integrated network around the world to communicate with the others. As defined by the W3C in [13], what open standards provide are transparency, relevance, openness, impartiality, consensus, availability and maintenance.

Internet uses a layer protocol model called TCP/IP. The ICT Web project aims to evaluate the usage of open and modern standards on the Internet and Application layers.

2.1 Web Standards
The application layer embraces all kinds of Internet applications. The Web is one of them and may be described as a large amount of linked documents that can only be displayed by Web browsers in such manner that humans can comprehend because they follow some standardized structures, like HTML (Hyper Text Markup Language). W3C is an international community that develops these open Web standards. Following their rules is not a straightforward process. Therefore, W3C has built an on-line

Permission to make digital or hard copies of all or part of this work for personal or classroom use is granted without fee provided that copies are not made or distributed for profit or commercial advantage and that copies bear this notice and the full citation on the first page. To copy otherwise, or republish, to post on servers or to redistribute to lists, requires prior specific permission and/or a fee.
WebMedia'12, October 15–18, 2012, São Paulo/SP, Brazil.
Copyright 2012 ACM 978-1-4503-1706-1/12/10...$15.00.

validation system called W3C Markup Validator[1], which parses Web pages to find and warn about coding mistakes.

2.2 Accessibility Standards

According to W3C definition [5], accessibility is related to the fact that people with different degrees of ability or disability might be able to understand certain contents. A working group within W3C has created a set of guidelines to assist in the development of Web content: WCAG (Web Content Accessibility Guidelines). It creates a set of requirements to classify accessible Web Sites. A Web site is considered as non-accessible if its Web pages are not consistent with any of these criteria.

Although the WCAG is one of the most referenced accessibility guidelines, Brazilian government developed E-MAG in 2007, which is based on these guidelines and tries to fulfill some local accessibility needs. However, the work [1] shows that both guidelines are very similar.

2.3 Network Time Protocol

Another relevant application layer protocol is the NTP (Network Time Protocol) [10]. NTP means a set of three things: a time synchronization algorithm, a communication protocol and an application service that can be used in devices. In practice, it is responsible to allow several devices, such as Web servers and personal computers, to synchronize their clock to the Coordinated Universal Time (UTC). Its advantages include portability, low consumption of machine resources and narrow offset.

The key factor that emphasizes the importance of time synchronization to a machine is related to computer security incidents and cybercrimes. In addition, time synchronization is fundamental to coordinate events in distributed applications. Some examples are CMSs (content management systems), messengers, e-mail clients and calendar applications.

2.4 IPv6

The Internet Protocol (IP) is the network layer protocol used on the TCP/IP stack and, currently, it is transitioning from version 4 to 6 (IPv6) [4]. This new generation started to be developed in 1990 as a solution to the problem of the IPv4 address space exhaustion.

To enlarge address space, IPv6 uses a 128-bit field instead of 32. This is one of the changes that make both protocols incompatible. Despite the existence of some communication transition methods, the non-adoption of this new version prevents the growth and evolution of the Internet. Beyond this motivation, IPv6 also brings other advantages to the network layer. Improvements in security, mobility and performance are some examples.

3. METHODOLOGY

This project methodology consists of periodically capturing the state of the part of the Web that is under study in order to build a historic series of a Web domain's states. This means that, once a year, a task of crawling and analyzing all pages hosted under some specific domains is done.

This task is performed by two pieces of software: an open source Web crawler, named WIRE (Web Information Retrieval Environment), originally developed by CWR (Center for Web Research)[2], and an analysis tool, named ConNeCTOR (Convenient Network Characteristics Testing Organized Routines), which was built by CEPTRO.br to consolidate all WIRE gathered data and to increase the variety of analyses made upon the Web sites and pages found.

3.1 Scope

The main goal of the ICT Web project is to assemble information about all Brazilian Web, which is composed by the Web sites under the ".br" domain. However, as an initial effort, a smaller domain was selected to be studied. ".gov.br" represents the Brazilian Governmental Web and is a very significant part of the main scope, since it is a domain with a restricted group of developers that can theoretically be managed by the Government. As so, public policies could be created in order to improve the quality of these Web sites.

Two data captures have already been made since 2009, when the project started. The first one was captured in the beginning of 2010 and, the second in 2011. And so, trend lines could begin to be made. Later, more details about this comparison will be presented.

3.2 Web Crawling

To seek and download Web pages, this project uses a modified version[3] of the Web crawler WIRE, an open source project developed in C++ and that has already been used to analyze other countries' Web domains [2].

To start the downloading cycle, the crawler must be fed with an initial seed of Web sites. The seed of this project were mainly compiled by DNS-based queries made to the top level DNS server of the ".gov.br" because it allows a walk through its domain records. Therefore, what this project's seed had was all domains directly under the TLD (Top Level Domain) ".gov.br", and the Web sites under those domains had to be retrieved through the crawling process.

3.3 ConNeCTOR

ConNeCTOR[4] was developed to have a modular architecture to allow an easy integration of new analyses and tests as they became necessary to the project. Currently, the performed analyses are as follows: HTML and accessibility validation; Discovery of Web server types; Time synchronization evaluation; Response delay verification; Geographic localization, and; Ipv6 utilization.

3.3.1 Web Pages Validation

According to the above-mentioned, the adoption of Web Standards provides lots of benefits to the Web Ecosystem. Despite its importance, there is very little concern about applying it, as shown in the work of Ofuonye et al. [7].

The selection of the tools to be used considered mainly the fact that they should be the official tools distributed by the organizations that are in charge of evaluating protocols and standards. Hence, the W3C Markup Validator was chosen to evaluate HTML pages and the ASES (Web Sites Accessibility Simulator and Validator)[5] was the one selected to classify the pages through the accessibilities guidelines.

Even though Web sites may use a numerous range of technologies such as PHP and Python to create dynamic pages, HTML

[1] http://validator.w3.org/
[2] http://www.cwr.cl/projects/WIRE/

[3] http://sf.net/projects/wire-nic
[4] http://sf.net/projects/connector-nic
[5] http://www.governoeletronico.gov.br/acoes-e-projetos/e-MAG/ases-avaliador-e-simulador-de-acessibilidade-sitios

validation still is relevant because these technologies do not substitute HTML content, instead they create new ways to generate it.

3.3.2 Time Synchronization Evaluation

One way to verify if a Web server is synchronized with the UTC, is to compare their times. ConNeCTOR implements two methods to obtain that information. The first one is based on the NTP specified before and it uses a Linux package called ntpdate. Because of that, this test is very accurate and the errors of its measurements are by the order of microseconds.

The second method is much simpler. By doing an HTTP HEAD request, it expects the Web server to respond with a header field that contains the timestamp of the server, which is confronted against the ConNeCTOR's time to calculate the Web server time offset.

3.3.3 Web Server Related Tests

Basic HTTP information (server type, response delay, HTTP offset, IP address) is obtained by requesting HTTP HEAD to the server. The server's geographic localization is obtained by a method called IP Geolocalization, which has been implemented by the utilization of the GeoIP API provided by MaxMind[6].

Finally, the most important and complex Web server related test is the IPv6 one. By using HTTP, DNS, and PING requests, it verifies the Web site IPv6 address, the Web site alternative hostname IPv6 address, if Web server replies to HTTP GET requests, if the Web server replies to Ping6 requests, the Web site Name Server IPv6 support and the Web site alternative hostname Name Server IPv6 support.

4. RESULTS

This section contains the evaluation of the Brazilian Governmental Web that has been done in 2010 and 2011.

4.1 Size

Table 1 shows the actual size of the Governmental Web collected. The column "Volume in Gigabytes" sums up only the size of the HTML content that was downloaded. And the number of websites only computes websites that have at least one valid Web page.

Table 1: Size of the Governmental Web

Capture	Volume in Gigabytes	Overall number of websites	Overall number of valid Web pages
2010	148	11856	6 331 256
2011	185	18229	6 874 926

It is interesting to notice that while the amount of websites and content has significantly grown, the amount of Web pages suffered a much smaller increase rate, which means that the pages are handling more content and the websites are getting smaller and, probably, more organized.

4.2 Web Page Validation

Regarding Web page validation tests, the chart presented in Figure 1 shows the percentage of pages that are in complete adherence to the HTML Standards and the pages that have at least the minimum level of accessibility defined by WCAG.

This chart indicates a steep growth in terms of accessibility adherence between these two years, which is very positive, despite the fact that the percentage of accessible Web pages is still very low. However, as the number of valid Web pages is so low, it is difficult to make a deeper analysis without data on which parts of the guidelines are failing.

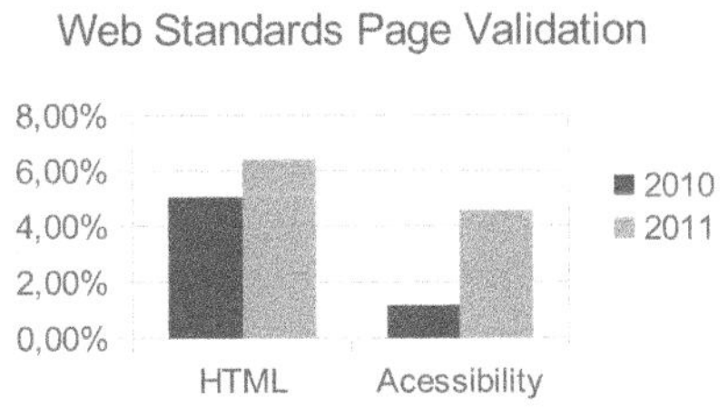

Figure 1: Percentage of page in conformity of HTML and accessibility standards in 2010 and 2011

4.3 Time Synchronization

Figure 2 shows a chart regarding the results obtained through the method of time synchronization evaluation based on HTTP requests. In this graph, the servers are divided into different levels of synchronization based on the difference between their internal clock time and the UTC. A Web server is considered synchronized when its time offset is lower or equal to 1 second. Probably, Web servers in this category have some kind of synchronization system like NTP. The other levels indicate different ranges of time offset that were observed.

In accordance to the previous indicator, the data concerning the time synchronization of the servers has also gotten a little better. The amount of servers that are considered to be synchronized with the UTC time increased by 1 percent and the number of servers that are completely unsynchronized, with more than 30 minutes of offset, has slightly dropped .

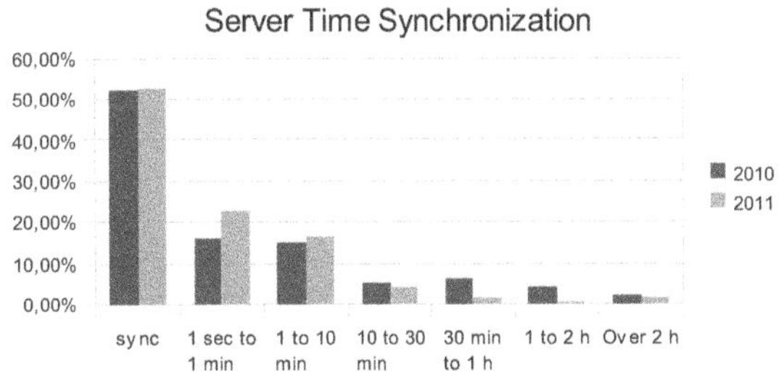

Figure 2: Percentage of Web servers in different levels of time synchronization in 2010 and 2011

4.4 IPv6

In 2010 ConNeCTOR could not find a single Web site that supported the IPv6 protocol among the governmental domain. In 2011 this scenario did not changed much: only a group of five Web sites presented some support to this protocol. Table 2 shows the distribution of these five Web sites through the 6 indicators explained in section 3.3.3.

It is important to mention that three of these Web sites use their main address instead of an alternative one to test the protocol, meaning that the systems that support IPv6 should be ready to be used in production products. Nevertheless, just three of the five responded to GET requests and so may be accessed via IPv6.

---

[6] http://www.maxmind.com/app/ip-location

Table 2: Characterization of IPv6 use in 2011

	Amount of websites
Has IPv6 address to main hostname	3
Has IPv6 address to alternative hostname	2
Replies to GET Request	3
Replies to Ping 6 Request	2
Its Name Server has IPv6 support?	3
Its alternative hostname Name Server has IPv6 support?	2

4.5 Web Server Types

As shown in the Figure 3, the scenario around the most used Web servers has not changed much between 2010 and 2011. But, surprisingly, the number of websites hosted by Nginx [9] became relevant, while the amount of Web sites that use Apache and Microsoft IIS has decreased somewhat.

A hypothesis that could be generated by analyzing the chart on Figure 4, which shows that the hosts of the Governmental Web are moving from Brazil to other countries, is that Nginx is more popular abroad than in Brazil. However, this hypothesis is denied by analyzing Figure 5, which shows that even in Brazil Nginx has become popular.

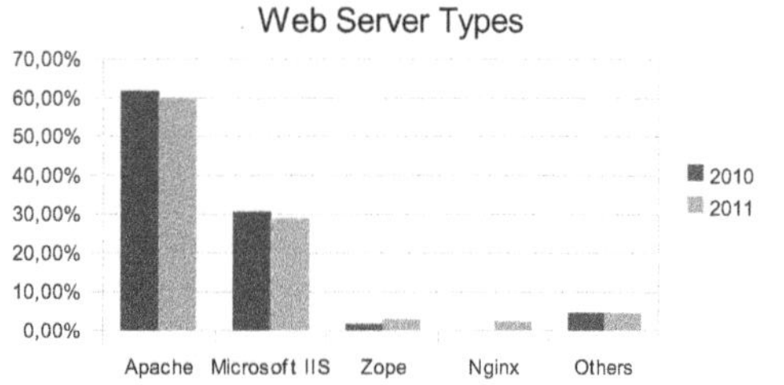

Figure 3: Distribution of Web server types in 2010 and 2011

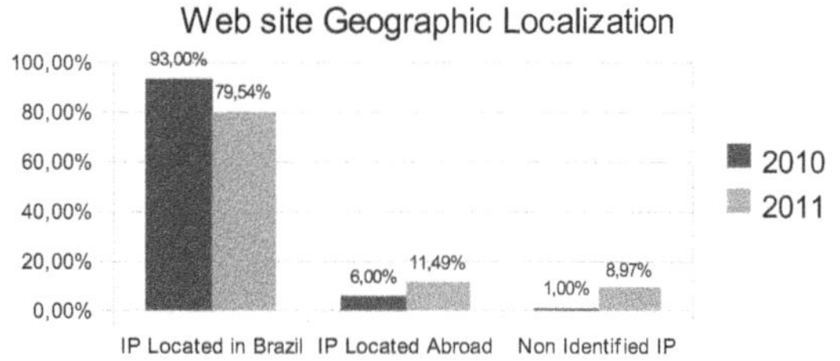

Figure 4: Percentage of Web sites that are hosted in Brazil and Abroad

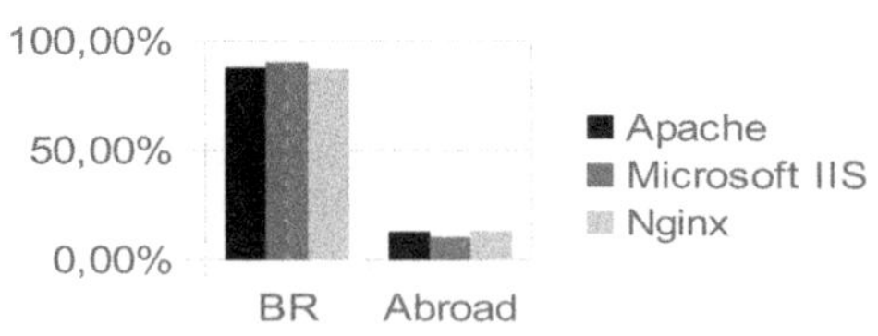

Figure 5: Percentage of Web server types that are located in Brazil and Abroad in 2011

5. Conclusion and Future Work

The ICT Web project attempts to draw a historic profile of the Brazilian Web quality regarding the utilization of open technologies. At first, data on the ".gov.br" domain was obtained. And with some data from different captures of the Governmental Web a trend line of its characteristics could begin to be defined. However, the goal is to penetrate the complete universe of Brazilian sites and, currently, sampling methods are in study to test their applicability and their capacity to gather meaningful information on larger domains like the "com.br".

Also, this paper tries to define a set of features and metrics that could be used to rate the Web sites and Web domains, which could induce the creation of policies to increase their quality.

Some future works which could follow this project include the addition of new evaluation tests, such as security validations to the servers or malware verifications of pages. Also, a better way to classify the accessibility of pages is under analysis due to the lack of information that can be acquired through WCAG classification.

6. REFERENCES

[1] Bach, C.F. et al. 2009. ACCESSIBILITY GUIDELINES: A COMPARISON BETWEEN WCAG AND E-MAG. *Revista Eletrônica de Sistemas de Informação*. 8, 1 (2009).

[2] Castillo, C. et al. 2007. Crawl.pl: Measuring Statistical and Structural Properties of the Polish Web. *Studia Informatica*. 1, 8 (2007), 43–73.

[3] Castillo, C. and Baeza-yates, R. 2005. Um novo retrato da Web brasileira. *Most*. (2005), 2005–2017.

[4] Deering, S. and Hinden, R. 1998. Internet Protocol, Version 6 (IPv6) Specification. *RFC 2460*. IETF.

[5] Henry, S.L. 2006. Introduction to Web Accessibility. *Journal of Web Engineering*.

[6] Ministério do Planejamento and Secretaria de Logística e Tecnologia da Informação 2011. *Modelo de Acessibilidade em Governo Eletrônico*. MP, SLTI, 2011.

[7] Ofuonye, E. et al. 2010. Prevalence and classification of web page defects. *Online Information Review*. 34, 1 (2010), 160–174.

[8] Padrões de Interoperabilidade de Governo Eletrônico: 2012. *http://eping.governoeletronico.gov.br/*. Accessed: 2012-05-22.

[9] Reese, W. 2008. Nginx: the high-performance web server and reverse proxy. *Linux Journal*. 2008, 173 (Sep. 2008), 2.

[10] Rybaczyk, P. 2005. *Expert Network Time Protocol*. Apress.

[11] Tanenbaum, A.S. 2002. *Computer Networks (4th Edition)*. Prentice Hall.

[12] Tolosa, G. et al. 2007. Characterization of the Argentinian Web. *Cybermetrics: International Journal of Scientometrics, Informetrics and Bibliometrics*.

[13] W3C and Open Standard: 2007. *http://www.w3.org/2005/09/dd-osd.html*. Accessed: 2011-12-09.

NEXT – Graphical Editor for Authoring NCL Documents Supporting Composite Templates

Júlia Varanda da Silva, Débora Christina Muchaluat-Saade
Laboratório MídiaCom, Departamento de Ciência da Computação
Universidade Federal Fluminense
R. Passo da Pátria, 156 – Bloco E – Sala 408 – São Domingos, Niterói, Rj, Brasil
jvaranda@ic.uff.br, debora@midiacom.uff.br

ABSTRACT

Interactive multimedia application development can be facilitated and more attractive to non-expert authors through the use of graphical editors. In a graphical environment that permits creation and edition of multimedia documents and offers different views of the document as a whole, it is possible to develop applications with less difficulty. In addition, if the editor provides templates, the development can be easier as, in that case, the author can use a pre-configured document and fulfill it with its own media content. This paper presents NEXT – NCL Editor supporting XTemplate, a graphical editor that allows development of NCL documents using hypermedia composite templates, which represent generic structures of NCL context nodes. Composite templates can be created with the XTemplate 3.0 language. Besides supporting templates, NEXT is based on a kernel and a set of plugins, which allow its extensibility and adaptability to different author skills.

Categories and Subject Descriptors

H.5.2 **[Information Interfaces and Presentation]**: User Interfaces – *graphical user interfaces (GUI), interaction styles.*

D.2.2 **[Software Engineering]**: Programming environments – *graphical environments, integrated environments.*

General Terms

Design, Languages.

Palavras-chave

NCL, TV Digital, ferramenta de autoria, plugins, XTemplate, editor gráfico, NEXT, templates de composição hipermídia.

1. INTRODUÇÃO

Aplicações para TV digital podem ser representadas como documentos multimídia, ou seja, podem conter diferentes tipos de mídia, como texto, imagem, áudio e vídeo. Além disso, essas aplicações podem permitir interatividade, oferecendo um ambiente mais rico para o telespectador uma vez que disponibilizam vários tipos de conteúdo, além do vídeo e áudio tradicionais em um sistema de televisão.

A elaboração dessas aplicações multimídia interativas requer sólidos conhecimentos de programação na linguagem de autoria utilizada, o que implica grandes gastos e considerável tempo para sua criação. Entretanto, o cenário atual de TV digital requer metodologias fáceis e rápidas para a criação dessas aplicações, de forma que autores com diferentes habilidades, inclusive aqueles que não possuem conhecimento da linguagem de autoria, possam contribuir para seu desenvolvimento.

Os sistemas de autoria multimídia visam facilitar o trabalho do autor, oferecendo um ambiente gráfico para criação e edição de documentos multimídia por pessoas com pouco ou nenhum conhecimento na linguagem de autoria utilizada. Uma forma de facilitar ainda mais o desenvolvimento desses documentos é fornecer editores gráficos com suporte a definição e uso de templates. Um template nada mais é do que um modelo de documento sem conteúdo de mídia, ou seja, ele possui apenas as partes estruturais de um documento, como por exemplo o cabeçalho e as definições de como as mídias devem se comportar durante sua execução. Desta forma, a única tarefa do autor é indicar quais mídias deverão ser utilizadas no documento a fim de completar as informações do template.

Um template de composição hipermídia é responsável por especificar a estrutura de um documento multimídia, definindo de forma genérica seus componentes (mídias ou composições) e como eles se relacionam através de elos e conectores. Um documento hipermídia que utiliza um template reúsa estruturas já especificadas, tornando sua autoria mais simples. A linguagem XTemplate 3.0 [10] permite a definição de templates de composição hipermídia utilizando o padrão XML [5]. A ferramenta de autoria EDITEC [4] permite a edição gráfica de templates, gerando o código XTemplate automaticamente. XTemplate pode ser usada em conjunto com a linguagem NCL (*Nested Context Language*) [1], adotada no Sistema Brasileiro de TV Digital (SBTVD) e na ITU H.761 [6], como padrão para criação de aplicações interativas utilizando o paradigma declarativo.

O propósito deste artigo é apresentar o NEXT - NCL Editor supporting XTemplate, uma ferramenta de autoria gráfica que foi produzida com o intuito de facilitar a criação de aplicações para TV digital, utilizando a linguagem NCL, e com suporte ao uso de templates de composição, criados com a linguagem XTemplate 3.0. NEXT exibe graficamente qualquer template de composição criado com a linguagem XTemplate 3.0, permitindo que o mesmo seja utilizado na criação de documentos NCL, o que facilita bastante o trabalho de autores com pouco ou nenhum conhecimento sobre NCL.

A arquitetura do NEXT é baseada em um núcleo capaz de se comunicar com um conjunto de plugins. Estes plugins podem ser configurados e estendidos, tornando o editor adaptável a autores com diferentes habilidades.

Permission to make digital or hard copies of all or part of this work for personal or classroom use is granted without fee provided that copies are not made or distributed for profit or commercial advantage and that copies bear this notice and the full citation on the first page. To copy otherwise, or republish, to post on servers or to redistribute to lists, requires prior specific permission and/or a fee.
WebMedia'12, October 15–18, 2012, São Paulo/SP, Brazil.
Copyright 2012 ACM 978-1-4503-1706-1/12/10...$15.00.

O restante do texto apresenta a seguinte estrutura. Na Seção 2, são apresentados alguns trabalhos relacionados. Na Seção 3, alguns requisitos básicos que um editor multimídia deve contemplar são apresentados. A Seção 4 apresenta o editor NEXT. Na Seção 5, são apresentados os plugins que foram desenvolvidos para o NEXT, com ênfase no plugin para uso de templates. Na Seção 6, uma comparação do NEXT com trabalhos relacionados e testes de usabilidade do editor com uso de templates são apresentados. As conclusões e trabalhos futuros encontram-se na Seção 7.

2. TRABALHOS RELACIONADOS

Berimbau iTV Author [2] é uma ferramenta de autoria gráfica para aplicações de TV digital, voltada para profissionais que não possuem conhecimentos de programação. A ferramenta oferece uma interface bastante simples e intuitiva, além de um repositório de mídias para uso durante a criação da aplicação. Permite gerar a aplicação final na linguagem NCL.

Apesar de facilitar a autoria de documentos NCL, Berimbau não oferece diferentes visões para edição, não contempla todas as funcionalidades da linguagem NCL, só permite a edição de documentos inicialmente criados pela própria ferramenta e somente documentos que contêm imagens. Nenhum outro tipo de mídia é suportado pelo editor. Além disso, não oferece o uso de templates para a criação do documento final.

O aplicativo Mobile Multimedia Presentation Editor [7] possibilita a criação de apresentações multimídia com diversos tipos de mídias em um dispositivo móvel. A interface do usuário é composta por diferentes visões e menus de opções, que mudam de acordo com a visão que está sendo utilizada no momento. São oferecidas visões de play (execução), de edição e de preview (simulação da execução).

As apresentações criadas utilizam a linguagem SMIL [12] e as relações temporais são baseadas em sequência das páginas. A visualização temporal é feita através de duas linhas temporais que aparecem no topo das telas. Alguns templates são oferecidos pela ferramenta, mas o autor tem a possibilidade de criar uma apresentação sem utilizá-los. O aplicativo não oferece todas as funcionalidades da linguagem SMIL e não permite a utilização de todos os tipos de mídia, como vídeo por exemplo.

EDITEC [4] é um editor gráfico para a criação de templates de composição multimídia baseado na linguagem XTemplate 3.0. O sistema oferece as visões estrutural, de leiaute e textual, permitindo ao autor ter uma melhor visualização do template durante o processo de autoria. A visão estrutural permite a criação dos elementos e definição dos relacionamentos que farão parte do template. A visão de leiaute apresenta as regiões do documento nas quais as mídias podem ser exibidas e a visão textual é dividida em duas partes, uma para exibir o código do template e, a outra, o código da base de descritores, regiões e regras do template.

Através da interface gráfica, não é possível oferecer todas as funcionalidades lógicas permitidas pela linguagem XTemplate 3.0. Sendo assim, em alguns casos especiais, é necessário usar a edição textual, o que requer mais conhecimento da linguagem por parte do autor. EDITEC permite o desenvolvimento de templates, porém não oferece a criação de documentos multimídia utilizando templates previamente criados.

O Composer 3 [8] tem como intuito oferecer um único ambiente de autoria adequado para diferentes perfis de autores. Seu padrão arquitetural é baseado em um micronúcleo, um modelo central e extensões. O micronúcleo agrupa as funcionalidades mínimas do sistema e coordena a forma como as extensões devem colaborar. As extensões são feitas por meio de plugins, que são programas capazes de interagir com o micronúcleo e que adicionam novas funcionalidades e/ou recursos à ferramenta.

Ele propõe a base para a construção de um ambiente integrado, capaz de oferecer suporte a requisitos não funcionais como, por exemplo, possibilitar a adição de novas funcionalidades à ferramenta de forma que seu desempenho não seja degradado, oferecer portabilidade e atender vários perfis de autores.

Apesar de facilitar a autoria de documentos multimídia, o Composer não possibilita o uso de templates, não realiza a simulação do documento final, assim como não verifica a consistência do comportamento de execução do mesmo. Entretanto, tais funcionalidades podem ser adicionadas à ferramenta com o desenvolvimento de novos plugins.

Em LAMP [3], o objetivo foi a geração automática de apresentações multimídia modelando esquemas de templates. A ideia é oferecer ao autor a possibilidade de definir o layout e o comportamento da apresentação, as características e atributos dos objetos, sem se preocupar com as instâncias que serão utilizadas para preencher o template. Esse trabalho teve como foco a coordenação e a sincronização de objetos de mídia contínuos. A geração automática da apresentação é dividida em duas partes: na primeira, o template é definido e, na segunda, os dados que serão utilizados na apresentação são inseridos no template. Em seguida, a apresentação é iniciada.

A ferramenta é composta por um editor visual, um simulador para testar os comportamentos, considerando as relações entre as mídias e as possíveis interações do usuário, um gerador que relaciona as mídias com o template, e o apresentador, que exibe a apresentação criada. Permite tanto a criação de layouts quanto a criação de apresentações. Embora LAMP forneça vários recursos para a autoria de documentos multimídia, ele não realiza a verificação de consistência do comportamento de execução do documento criado.

3. REQUISITOS DE UM EDITOR GRÁFICO MULTIMÍDIA

Após análise das características presentes em alguns editores multimídia que foram estudados, alguns deles apresentados na Seção 2, foi realizada a seleção de alguns requisitos considerados como essenciais para uma ferramenta de autoria gráfica. Estes requisitos são os seguintes:

- diferentes perfis de autores: a ferramenta deve alcançar o maior número de autores possíveis. Desta forma, o conhecimento da linguagem utilizada para a criação da aplicação deixa de ser impactante na elaboração da mesma;

- extensibilidade: a ferramenta deve ser capaz de suportar novas funcionalidades de forma fácil e sem comprometer seu desempenho;

- portabilidade: a ferramenta deve ser capaz de funcionar em diferentes plataformas, independentemente do sistema operacional utilizado;

- simulações: o autor deve ser capaz de visualizar/simular a aplicação que está sendo desenvolvida;

- templates: a ferramenta deve ter suporte ao uso de templates, facilitando ainda mais o desenvolvimento da aplicação. Além disso, é desejável que o conjunto de templates disponíveis possa ser facilmente estendido, permitindo a utilização de outros templates e não apenas daqueles previamente oferecidos pela ferramenta;

- diferentes visões: a ferramenta deve oferecer diversas visões do aplicativo em desenvolvimento, permitindo, assim, que o autor escolha a mais agradável de acordo com a parte do documento que o mesmo esteja editando.

- análise do documento: ao final da criação da aplicação, o documento final gerado deve ser analisado. Esta análise consiste tanto nas validações sintática e semântica como na verificação da consistência temporal da aplicação. A importância da verificação temporal reside na notificação ao autor sobre possíveis comportamentos de execução indesejados. Como exemplo, suponha uma aplicação em que o usuário deva interagir após a apresentação de 20 segundos de um vídeo, mas o vídeo nunca é apresentado. Neste caso, o usuário jamais poderá interagir com a aplicação. Outras situações mais complexas e difíceis de se detectar, como a criação de um loop infinito de apresentação de uma mídia ou a não finalização da aplicação, também devem ser encontradas através desta verificação [9].

4. NEXT

O editor NEXT – NCL Editor supporting XTemplate – proposto neste trabalho visa facilitar o desenvolvimento de aplicações para TV digital que utilizam a linguagem NCL 3.0. NEXT oferece o uso de templates de composição para criação de documentos NCL, permitindo sua utilização por autores sem conhecimento da linguagem de autoria. Templates de composição podem ser criados com a linguagem XTemplate 3.0 e com o editor gráfico EDITEC [4]. NEXT é capaz de entender e representar graficamente qualquer template criado com a linguagem XTemplate 3.0, generalizando o conjunto de templates que pode ser oferecido pelo editor.

O editor é baseado em uma arquitetura modular composta por um núcleo e um conjunto de plugins, os quais permitem que novas funcionalidades sejam facilmente adicionadas à ferramenta.

Atualmente, NEXT oferece duas opções de idiomas, português e inglês, e representa o documento NCL em forma de árvore, possibilitando sua visualização de maneira organizada. Os elementos do documento ocupam diferentes ramos na árvore de acordo com o seu tipo. A visualização do código NCL também é oferecida.

Além de permitir a criação de novos documentos NCL, também é possível editar qualquer documento NCL existente, independentemente de onde este tenha sido criado. Entretanto, qualquer comentário que o documento tenha será perdido ao ser salvo pelo NEXT.

A Figura 1, apresenta a interface gráfica que é oferecida pelo NEXT juntamente com a visão textual de um documento NCL.

O item Plugins, do Menu, apresenta uma lista com todos os plugins instalados no editor. Ao clicar neste item, a lista é exibida e o autor pode escolher qual plugin deseja utilizar. O mesmo será exibido na área central do programa, que na Figura 1 está exibindo o código NCL do documento. Além disso, este item também permite a inserção e remoção de plugins.

O item Ferramentas oferece a opção de análise do documento com uso da API aNaa – API for NCL Authoring and Analysis [9] e permite a utilização de um repositório de mídias para ser utilizado durante o desenvolvimento do documento.

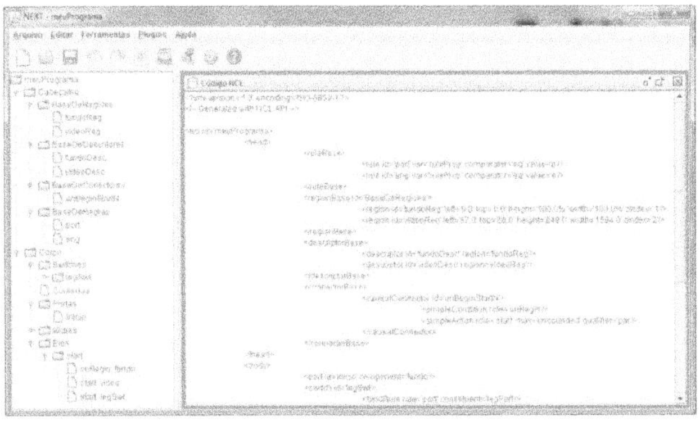

Figura 1. Interface gráfica do NEXT

4.1 Arquitetura

O trabalho realizado em [8] mostrou a importância de alguns requisitos não-funcionais relevantes para uma ferramenta de autoria, que foram considerados na arquitetura do NEXT. A fim de manter a independência das funcionalidades do editor em relação às dos plugins, foi desenvolvido um núcleo capaz de lidar com um documento NCL e, também, de se comunicar com os plugins, mantendo o sincronismo entre eles. A arquitetura do NEXT pode ser visualizada na Figura 2.

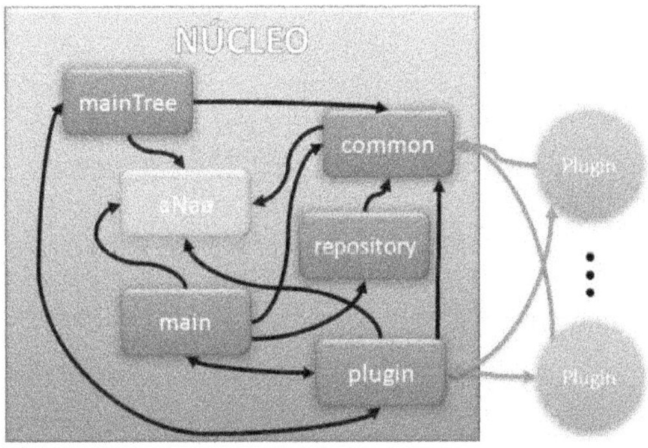

Figura 2. Núcleo do NEXT

O editor foi desenvolvido em Java a fim de oferecer portabilidade e de permitir a utilização de outras ferramentas já implementadas em Java, como a API aNaa e, futuramente, o editor EDITEC [4].

Seu núcleo é composto pelos pacotes *main*, *mainTree*, *common* e *plugin*, e pela API aNaa, que é adicionada à biblioteca. Como pode ser visto na Figura 2, o núcleo é completamente independente dos plugins.

A API aNaa cria um objeto para representação de cada elemento NCL do documento. Através de seu método *parse*, é possível a geração do código NCL do documento e, através de seu método *load*, é possível abrir um documento NCL já existente. Esta API também fornece métodos para criação e edição de elementos, que devem ser utilizados pelos plugins para que alterações no documento sejam realizadas. Além disso, ela também é responsável pela análise do documento ao final da criação. O objeto do tipo *NCLDoc* criado é analisado e, caso algum erro seja encontrado, o mesmo é informado ao autor. aNaa é capaz de encontrar erros de sintaxe, de referência e também comportamentos temporais indesejados na definição do documento [9].

Com o objeto *NCLDoc* criado pela aNaa, o pacote *mainTree* cria uma representação do documento NCL em forma de árvore, facilitando a localização dos elementos e a visualização da estrutura do documento no editor.

O pacote *main* é responsável pela interface gráfica do editor. Ele implementa botões para criação e edição de documentos NCL, além de permitir a inserção e remoção de plugins na ferramenta.

O pacote *common* permite a utilização do editor em diferentes idiomas e implementa alguns métodos auxiliares que são utilizados por outros pacotes da ferramenta.

O pacote *plugin* possui métodos que permitem a comunicação do núcleo com os plugins. Desta forma, é possível recolher informações destes, como por exemplo, a lista de elementos NCL de interesse dos plugins e mantê-los informados sobre alterações no documento. Ele também é responsável pela criação de um arquivo XML de configuração do editor, o qual possui informações dos plugins que foram instalados e, portanto, que devem ser oferecidos ao autor quando o programa for iniciado.

4.2 Plugins

Plugins são programas, geralmente leves, que adicionam funcionalidades e recursos específicos a um programa principal hospedeiro. Estes normalmente são de fácil instalação e não devem comprometer o desempenho, nem o funcionamento normal de seu hospedeiro. No NEXT, eles são responsáveis por realizar alterações no documento NCL que está sendo criado e/ou editado. Um plugin pode realizar mudanças no documento inteiro ou em apenas parte dele, esta questão ficará a cargo de seu desenvolvedor.

Para desenvolver plugins para o NEXT, o programador deverá criar um arquivo utilizando a linguagem Java (com a extensão jar), o qual será incorporado ao NEXT. Como é preciso prover comunicação entre o plugin e o núcleo, este arquivo deverá, obrigatoriamente, ter um pacote chamado *myPlugin*, o qual deverá implementar as classes *StartPlugin* e *PluginInfo*.

A classe *StartPlugin*, que obrigatoriamente deve estender uma *JInternalFrame*, é responsável por iniciar o plugin e será chamada pelo núcleo do NEXT quando o autor desejar utilizá-lo. Desta forma, é possível que o usuário utilize diferentes plugins ao mesmo tempo, onde cada um será exibido em sua *JInternalFrame*.

Já a classe *PluginInfo* é responsável por fornecer ao núcleo informações sobre o plugin. Ela é composta pelos métodos *getAlias* e *getNCLInterest*. O primeiro método, informa o *alias* do plugin, ou seja, o nome que será exibido pelo editor para representar o plugin. Já o segundo método, deve retornar uma lista com os elementos NCL de interesse do plugin. Sendo assim, sempre que um dos elementos NCL desta lista sofrer alguma alteração que não tenha sido ocasionada pelo próprio plugin, o mesmo receberá uma notificação de adição, remoção ou edição do elemento.

Para que os plugins possam ser notificados sobre as alterações no documento, é necessário que a classe *StartPlugin* também implemente o método *getUpdateAtNCLDocument*. Este método recebe três parâmetros. O primeiro é do tipo *ModType* e informa o tipo de alteração (adição, remoção ou edição). O segundo é do tipo *NCLElement* e representa o elemento NCL que foi inserido, removido ou editado. E o último é um *array* com elementos do tipo *Object*, cujo comprimento depende do tipo de modificação. Se foi uma adição ou uma remoção, o *array* terá apenas um elemento indicando qual é o elemento pai que teve o filho adicionado ou removido. Mas, se for uma edição, o *array* terá três elementos, o primeiro indica o atributo que foi editado, o segundo indica seu valor antigo e, o terceiro, o seu novo valor. De posse dessas informações e realizando as devidas providências, o plugin consegue manter a consistência com o documento que pode estar sendo editado por outro plugin do NEXT.

Para realizar alterações no documento NCL, o plugin deverá utilizar um objeto do tipo *HandleNCLDocument*, passado como parâmetro no construtor da classe *StartPlugin*. Aplicando-se o método *getNCLDocument* neste objeto, o programador receberá um objeto, do tipo *NCLDoc*, que representa o documento NCL de acordo com a API aNaa. Possuindo este objeto, as alterações no mesmo deverão ser aplicadas utilizando-se os métodos que a API disponibiliza.

Na Figura 3, apresenta-se o código Java de um plugin apenas com as importações, pacotes, classes e métodos necessários.

Para inserir um plugin no NEXT, basta utilizar a opção "Adicionar plugin", oferecida no item Plugins do menu. Uma janela será aberta e basta que o usuário informe o arquivo jar correspondente ao plugin. O NEXT se encarrega de criar uma cópia do arquivo e o insere na lista de plugins instalados, exibidos no item Ferramentas do menu.

```
package myPlugin;
import common.Constants.ModType;          // Constantes de tipo de alteração
import common.Constants.Element;          // Elementos NCL do tipo enum
import plugin.HandleNCLDocument;          // Representa o documento NCL
import common.MultiLanguage.Language;     // Idiomas oferecidos pelo NEXT

public class StartPlugin extends JInternalFrame {
    public StartPlugin (Language language, HandleNCLDocument ne){...}

    public void getUpdateAtNCLDocument (ModType type,
                    NCLElement elem, Object[ ] values) {...}
}
public class PluginInfo {
    public static String getAlias () {
        return "PluginAlias";   // Nome que será exibido no menu de plugins
    }

    public static List<Element> getInterest () {
        List elements = new ArrayList();
        elements.add (Element.REGION);
        return elements;
    }
}
```

Figura 3. Exemplo de código Java de um plugin interessado apenas no elemento region

5. PLUGINS OFERECIDOS

A fim de validar a utilização de plugins no NEXT e de permitir o uso do editor por diferentes perfis de autores, inclusive os que já conhecem NCL, verificou-se a necessidade de permitir a criação de um documento com ou sem o uso de templates. Assim sendo, quatro plugins foram desenvolvidos. O primeiro permite a criação de conectores hipermídia, o segundo, a criação de regiões e descritores e, o terceiro, a criação de contextos e seus elementos internos. Para sua utilização, estes plugins requerem que o autor possua conhecimento da linguagem NCL, mesmo que básico. Já o quarto plugin permite a utilização de templates de composição na criação do documento NCL, possibilitando seu uso por autores sem conhecimento da linguagem. Cada um destes será brevemente apresentado a seguir, com maior destaque para o plugin de utilização de templates, já que esta é a maior contribuição deste trabalho.

5.1 Visão de leiaute

O plugin da Figura 4 foi desenvolvido para permitir a criação de bases de regiões, regiões e descritores em um documento NCL. Assim sendo, sua lista de interesse engloba apenas estes três elementos NCL.

Ele oferece uma interface simples onde as regiões podem ser facilmente manipuladas utilizando-se apenas o mouse. Já para a criação de descritores, é preciso que o autor tenha um conhecimento básico do que esse elemento NCL representa no documento. Em sua criação, o autor deverá preencher alguns campos com os atributos oferecidos pelo elemento. Como nem todos são obrigatórios, o autor deve preencher apenas aqueles atributos que são desejados.

Figura 4. Plugin para criação/edição de regiões e descritores

O plugin foi desenvolvido de forma que também seja possível sua utilização independentemente do NEXT. Ou seja, ele também pode ser utilizado como uma aplicação *standalone*, onde o autor pode criar um documento NCL que contenha apenas bases de regiões e uma base de descritores. Este documento poderá ser utilizado posteriormente por outros documentos NCL, os quais poderão importar suas bases de regiões e descritores.

5.2 Editor de conectores

O plugin para a criação de conectores [11] apresenta uma interface gráfica simples baseada em *drag-and-drop* e exibe mensagens de orientação ao autor durante a criação do conector. Assim como o plugin de visão de leiaute, este plugin também pode ser utilizado como uma aplicação *standalone*, permitindo a criação de um documento NCL contendo apenas uma base de conectores. A Figura 5 mostra a interface principal do plugin.

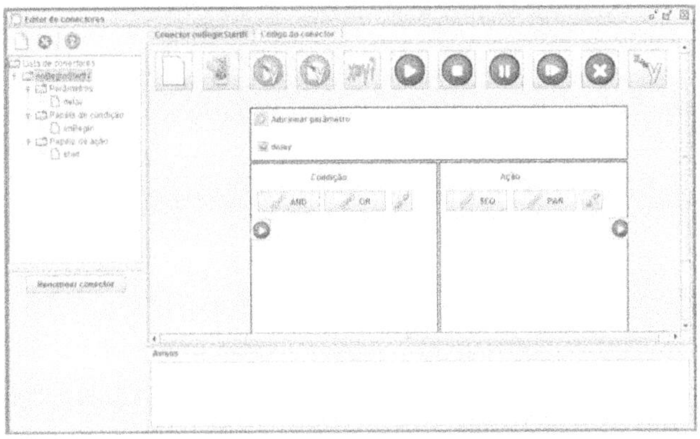

Figura 5. Plugin para criação/edição de conectores

Como este plugin manipula apenas os conectores de um documento, sua lista de interesse engloba apenas a base de conectores e os conectores nela contidos.

5.3 Visão estrutural

A Figura 6 apresenta a interface gráfica que é oferecida pelo plugin de visão estrutural, o qual permite a edição gráfica de contextos NCL. Além de oferecer a visualização dos elementos que compõem o corpo do documento ou um de seus contextos, assim como os elos entre os elementos, o plugin também permite a criação/edição dos mesmos.

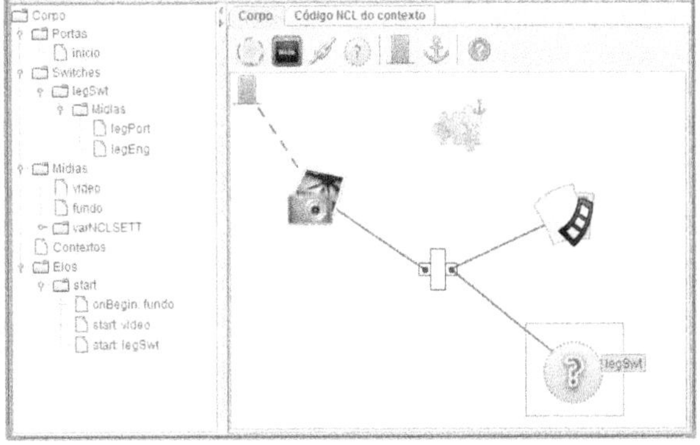

Figura 6. Plugin de visão estrutural de contextos

A interface gráfica é baseada em *drag-and-drop* com o objetivo de minimizar o trabalho durante o desenvolvimento do documento. Apesar de facilitar o desenvolvimento, este plugin requer um conhecimento básico de NCL, pois alguns elementos, como âncoras ou switches por exemplo, podem não ser tão intuitivos para o autor.

Apesar do plugin receber informações de alguns elementos do cabeçalho do documento sendo editado, o mesmo não permite sua alteração. Entretanto, quando modificações no cabeçalho implicam alterações nos elementos do corpo, essas são realizadas pelo plugin a fim de se manter a consistência do documento.

5.4 Plugin para utilização de templates de composição

Como os plugins anteriormente mencionados exigem algum conhecimento, mesmo que básico, da linguagem NCL, sua utilização por autores sem esse conhecimento é complicada. A fim de atender, também, a autores sem conhecimento de NCL, foi desenvolvido um plugin que permite a utilização de templates.

Com este plugin, é possível criar um documento NCL indicando apenas as mídias que farão parte do documento, sem a necessidade de especificar características de funcionamento da aplicação. Qualquer template de composição criado com a linguagem XTemplate 3.0 pode ser utilizado por este plugin.

Além de permitir seu uso por autores sem conhecimento de NCL, este plugin também facilita a criação de aplicações que necessitam de grande quantidade de código, muitas vezes até repetitivo, em sua especificação. Um exemplo de como a utilização de um template pode ajudar na elaboração dessas aplicações é o seguinte. Considere um vídeo com duração de 1 hora e com 50 legendas para serem exibidas durante a apresentação do mesmo. Os momentos de iniciar e de encerrar a exibição de cada uma destas legendas devem estar sincronizados com o vídeo, ou melhor, com as âncoras do vídeo. Uma âncora representa uma parte do conteúdo da mídia. Por exemplo, para este vídeo, devemos criar uma âncora para cada intervalo de tempo em que uma das legendas deve aparecer.

Esta aplicação, apesar de simples, possui muitas linhas de código NCL, que são bastante repetitivas. E, nestes casos, o autor que utiliza edição textual tende a "copiar" e "colar" os trechos repetidos, trocando-se apenas o valor dos elementos que especificam cada âncora e cada legenda. Entretanto, caso o autor se esqueça de trocar o valor de algum elemento nesta ação de "copiar" e "colar", erros podem ser facilmente gerados.

Outra questão importante é ajudar o autor a entender o que um template faz, ou seja, que tipo de aplicação pode ser criada ao se utilizar determinado template. Isso é importante pois, provavelmente, o autor utilizará uma biblioteca com diversos templates disponíveis. Cada template especificado em XTemplate possui um arquivo RDF (*Resource Description Framework*) associado cujo objetivo é explicar a funcionalidade do template [10]. Este texto explicativo é exibido pelo plugin e, além disso, uma representação gráfica do template também é apresentada, a qual apresenta ao autor como as mídias estarão dispostas para o telespectador no documento final.

O plugin realiza a leitura do documento XTemplate e cria um objeto Java do qual é possível extrair informações sobre o template. A partir destas informações, o plugin gera a visualização gráfica do template.

Na Figura 7, é ilustrada a janela de exibição dos templates encontrados em uma base de templates. Do lado esquerdo, é exibida uma lista de telas ilustrando a primeira tela de cada um dos templates. Ao selecionar uma das telas na lista, serão exibidas, do lado direito, todas as diferentes telas do template selecionado, assim como o texto explicativo do mesmo.

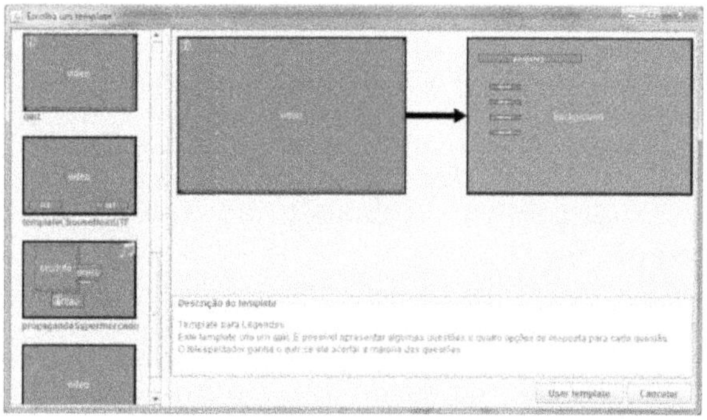

Figura 7. Janela de exibição dos templates

Uma tela é composta pelo conjunto de nós que serão exibidos ao mesmo tempo e, provavelmente, em posições diferentes na TV. Toda vez que uma nova mídia é apresentada ou termina sua exibição, de acordo com a especificação do template, uma nova tela é criada para o template. Assim sendo, um mesmo template pode ser composto por várias telas diferentes. Cada tela do template exibe as regiões criadas no mesmo, onde o autor deverá preencher com as mídias que farão parte do documento NCL. A Figura 8 exemplifica o conceito de tela para este plugin. As Telas 1 e 2 são diferentes pois o botão azul não está sendo exibido na Tela 2.

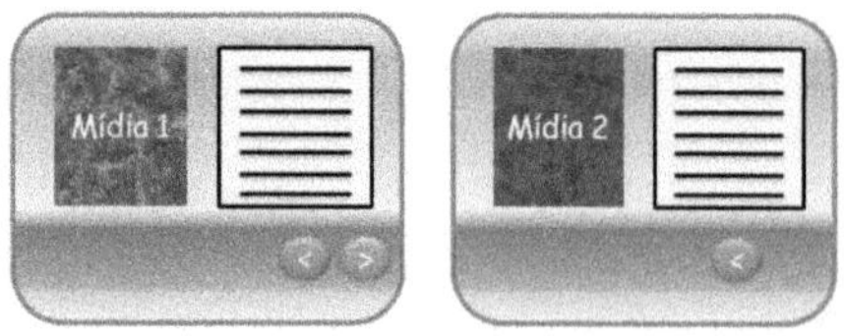

Tela 1 Tela 2

Figura 8. Diferentes telas na visão do plugin de templates

Um template de composição hipermídia especifica componentes genéricos, descrevem como estes estão relacionados e também define a posição espacial e características de apresentação dos mesmos. O plugin de templates interpreta as especificações XML do template e gera símbolos gráficos de acordo com suas definições. A Tabela 1 apresenta os símbolos gráficos utilizados pelo plugin.

Tabela 1. Símbolos usados para gerar as telas do template

Imagem	Significado
	Um retângulo azul representa um nó cujo conteúdo deverá ser escolhido pelo autor.
	Um retângulo vermelho indica um nó NCL específico que já está definido no template e cujo conteúdo não poderá ser redefinido.
	Um retângulo sombreado representa um conjunto de nós, ou seja, vários nós poderão ser exibidos na mesma região, em momentos distintos. O número máximo de nós também é definido pelo template. Neste caso, o autor pode indicar conteúdos diferentes para preencher o template.
	A nota musical indica que um componente de áudio é utilizado no template. Assim como os retângulos, a nota pode ser azul ou vermelha e pode ou não ser sombreada.
	A imagem da letra "i" sobre um componente indica que o mesmo permite interatividade, ou seja, o telespectador poderá usar o controle remoto para interagir com a aplicação.

A Figura 9 mostra como seria o template com layout das duas telas apresentadas na Figura 8.

Tela 1 **Tela 2**

Figura 9. Representação gráfica do template para o documento representado na Figura 8

Após selecionar um template, o autor deverá preenchê-lo com as mídias que irão compor o documento NCL. A Figura 10**Error! Reference source not found.** exibe a tela de preenchimento do template, especificando que nós de mídia serão incluídos no documento NCL final.

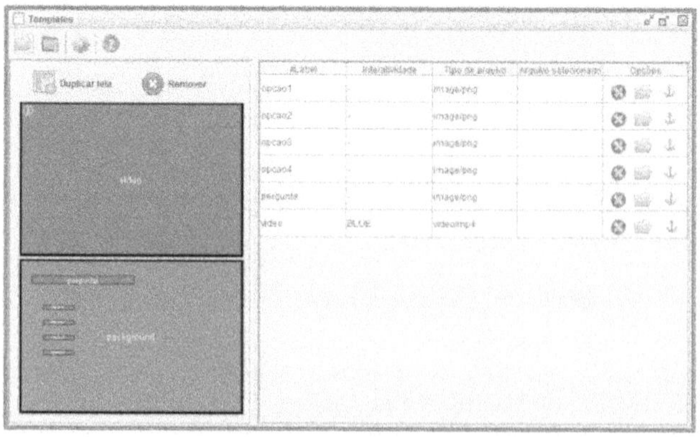

Figura 10. Tela de preenchimento do template

A Figura 10 ilustra o template de um quiz, que pode ser inicializado se o telespectador pressionar o botão azul do controle remoto, enquanto um vídeo de introdução está sendo apresentado. Para este template, o autor deverá especificar o nó de vídeo, as perguntas e quatro opções de resposta para cada pergunta do quiz. Cada pergunta e suas opções de resposta são apresentadas em telas distintas.

No lado esquerdo da Figura 10, uma lista exibe todas as telas que compõem o template escolhido. Como algumas delas podem ser duplicadas ou removidas (aquelas que apresentam retângulos ou notas sombreados), botões com estas funcionalidades são oferecidos ao autor. No exemplo, a tela de pergunta deve ser duplicada para cada pergunta diferente que irá compor o quiz. Vale ressaltar que apenas telas que foram duplicadas podem ser removidas, já que excluir uma tela do próprio template poderia causar alguma falha no documento.

Ao selecionar uma das telas do template, uma tabela é exibida no lado direito. Esta tabela apresenta informações sobre os componentes da tela, os quais devem ser preenchidos com mídias escolhidas pelo autor. Ela informa a identificação do componente (*xLabel*) e o tipo de mídia que deve ser inserida, conforme definido no template. O caminho da mídia selecionada é exibido na coluna "Arquivo selecionado". Percebe-se pela Figura 10 que os componentes predefinidos pelo template (desenhados com cor vermelha) não são exibidos na tabela.

A coluna "Opções" oferece três botões, o primeiro e o segundo estão relacionados à escolha da mídia, enquanto o terceiro permite a criação de âncoras na mídia a ser utilizada. Alguns templates requerem a especificação de âncoras e, apesar de existirem diversos tipos de âncoras, esta versão do plugin só possibilita a criação de âncoras em mídias contínuas, onde o autor pode escolher seu tempo de início e fim.

Se um componente do template permitir interatividade, a letra "i" será exibida sobre ele na tela correspondente. A coluna "Interatividade", da tabela de preenchimento do template, informa qual tecla do controle remoto deve ser utilizada neste caso. Caso esta coluna esteja preenchida com "-", significa que o componente não permite interatividade.

6. AVALIAÇÃO DO NEXT

NEXT foi desenvolvido em Java permitindo seu uso em diferentes plataformas e está disponível em dois idiomas. Além disso, adicionar novos idiomas ao mesmo não é uma tarefa difícil, uma vez que este também foi um dos seus propósitos. Ele permite a edição de qualquer documento NCL, independentemente de onde este tenha sido criado e oferece análise da consistência do documento [9], ajudando o autor a criar aplicações consistentes.

NEXT permite que autores sem nenhum conhecimento da linguagem NCL sejam capazes de criar aplicações através do uso de templates de composição. Neste caso, o autor precisa apenas preencher o documento pré-configurado. NEXT também provê uma representação gráfica do template de acordo com sua definição na linguagem XTemplate 3.0, facilitando sua compreensão por parte do autor.

O editor permite a inclusão de novas funcionalidades através de plugins, possibilitando seu uso por autores com diferentes habilidades. Plugins podem ser facilmente desenvolvidos por programadores Java, os quais apenas devem seguir algumas regras simples e bem definidas, como comentado na Seção 4.2.

A Tabela 2 lista os requisitos apresentados na Seção 3 e compara os editores apresentados na Seção 2 com o NEXT, proposto neste trabalho. NEXT satisfaz todos os requisitos exceto a simulação da apresentação do documento NCL final, o que é considerado como trabalho futuro. O Composer oferece análise estrutural de um documento NCL, porém não oferece a análise do comportamento de execução de um documento.

Tabela 2. Comparação dos editores

Requisitos/ Editores	Berimbau	MMPE	EDITEC	Composer	LAMP	NEXT
Diferentes perfis de autores	✓	✓		✓	?	✓
Extensível				✓		✓
Portável			✓	✓	✓	✓
Simulação		✓			✓	
Oferece templates		✓			✓	✓
Suporte a templates genéricos			✓		✓	✓
Diferentes visões		✓	✓	✓	✓	✓
Análise de consistência				+/-		✓

✓ contemplado pela ferramenta
? não foi possível definir
+/- atende parcialmente

Testes de usabilidade foram realizados a fim de avaliar a eficácia do NEXT e de seus plugins. O teste realizado sobre o plugin de conectores pode ser encontrado em [11]. O teste sobre o plugin para uso de templates será descrito a seguir. Já o teste sobre o uso dos demais plugins mostrou que sua utilização fica dificultada quando não se tem um bom conhecimento da linguagem NCL.

O teste do plugin para uso de templates foi realizado com 10 alunos de computação que não conheciam a linguagem NCL e dois alunos que já a conheciam.Após uma breve explicação sobre a linguagem NCL e sobre o conceito de templates, os alunos tiveram que criar uma aplicação com a utilização do plugin de templates. Nenhuma explicação sobre o funcionamento do plugin foi dada. Eles apenas foram avisados que o plugin possui um menu de ajuda, o qual poderia ser consultado durante o desenvolvimento da aplicação.

Os alunos deveriam usar um template para criar uma propaganda interativa de supermercado, onde eles deveriam sincronizar a imagem de três produtos e seus respectivos preços com âncoras de um áudio, as quais também deveriam ser criadas pelos alunos. As mídias a serem utilizadas também foram disponibilizadas.

Após a conclusão da aplicação, os alunos responderam um questionário com perguntas relacionadas especificamente ao plugin de templates. O questionário era composto por perguntas que buscavam verificar o grau de compreensão e facilidade de uso do plugin. As perguntas eram objetivas e as opções de resposta variavam numa escala de zero a cinco, onde zero era a pior opção e cinco a melhor. A Tabela 3 apresenta o resultado obtido.

Tabela 3. Perguntas e média dos resultados obtidos no questionário sobre a usabilidade do plugin de templates

Pergunta	Nota Média	Conclusão do resultado
Como você classifica o seu conhecimento em NCL?	1	Muito baixo
Qual é o seu entendimento sobre o que são templates e sua utilidade?	4	Bom
Com relação à facilidade para compreender o plugin, que nota você daria ao mesmo?	4	Fácil

Pergunta	Nota Média	Conclusão do resultado
Com que frequência você precisou utilizar a opção de ajuda do plugin para criar a aplicação?	1	Muito pouco
Você conseguiu criar a aplicação NCL final com uso do plugin?	-	Todos conseguiram
Como você classifica as imagens utilizadas para representar cada tela do template?	4	Boas
Você consegue entender a funcionalidade do template através das telas exibidas e da sua descrição?	4,5	Compreende bem
Como você classifica a tabela utilizada para definir as mídias que farão parte da aplicação?	4,5	Boa
Como você classifica a facilidade na criação de âncoras nas mídias da aplicação?	4	Fácil

Não houve nenhuma diferença no uso da ferramenta pelos dois grupos de alunos (sem e com conhecimento sobre NCL). Além de responderem o questionário, os alunos também contribuíram com sugestões para o aprimoramento do plugin. Algumas dessas sugestões foram: melhorar a indicação de quando uma âncora pode ser criada na mídia, arrastar mídias de um repositório para a tabela e exibir a imagem da mídia escolhida no lugar dos retângulos.

7. CONCLUSÃO

A principal contribuição deste artigo foi a apresentação de um editor para a criação de documentos na linguagem NCL, chamado NEXT, o qual oferece suporte ao uso de templates de composição. O trabalho visa facilitar e agilizar a criação de aplicações na linguagem NCL para televisão digital.

O editor está disponível em dois idiomas e permite a extensão de suas funcionalidades através da inclusão de plugins. Além disso, nenhum outro editor gráfico para documentos NCL oferece ao autor a possibilidade de usar um conjunto flexível de templates na criação de aplicações. NEXT permite o uso de qualquer template criado com a linguagem XTemplate 3.0 para construir documentos NCL.

Alguns plugins foram desenvolvidos, permitindo a utilização do NEXT por autores com conhecimento básico da linguagem NCL, assim como por autores sem nenhum conhecimento, como o plugin que utiliza templates.

Como trabalho futuro, mais plugins podem ser desenvolvidos para estender a ferramenta, oferecendo mais facilidade na criação de documentos. O editor EDITEC será adaptado para ser um novo plugin do NEXT. Um plugin que ofereça uma visão temporal é de grande ajuda no desenvolvimento de aplicações por auxiliar o autor a compreender o acontecimento dos eventos ao longo do tempo. Uma visão textual editável também agradaria bastante aos autores que já conhecem bem a linguagem NCL. Um plugin que permita a simulação da execução de um documento NCL também é outro importante trabalho futuro.

Outro trabalho é refinar o plugin de templates, levando em consideração as sugestões dos alunos que realizaram o teste de usabilidade.

8. AGRADECIMENTOS

Este trabalho foi parcialmente financiado pela CAPES, CNPq e FAPERJ.

REFERÊNCIAS

[1] ABNT NBR 15606-2:2007. Televisão digital terrestre - Codificação de dados e especificações de transmissão para radiodifusão digital – Parte 2: Ginga-NCL para receptores fixos e móveis – Linguagem de aplicação XML para codificação de aplicações. Setembro 2007.

[2] Berimbau iTV Author, http://www.batuque.tv/, acessado em novembro de 2011.

[3] Celentano, A. e Gaggi O. – Template-based generation of multimedia presentations. International Journal of Software Engineering and Knowledge Engineering, Vol. 13, Nº 4, 419-445, 2003.

[4] Damasceno, J. R., Santos, J. A. F., Muchaluat-Saade, D. C. EDITEC: hypermedia composite template graphical editor for interactive TV authoring. ACM Symposium on Document Engineering, pp 77-80, 2011.

[5] Extensible Markup Language (XML) 1.1 (Second Edition) - W3C Recommendation 16 August 2006, Setembro 2006, http://www.w3.org/TR/2006/REC-xml11-20060816/, acessado em abril de 2011.

[6] União Internacional de Telecomunicações (ITU), recomendação H.761, Nested Context Language (NCL) e Ginga-NCL para serviços IPTV, disponível em http://www.itu.int/itu-t/workprog/wp_item.aspx?isn=6186, 2009.

[7] Jokela T., Lehikoinen J. T., Korhonen H. Mobile multimedia presentation editor: enabling creation of audio-visual stories on mobile devices. In ACM Special Interest Group on Computer-Human Interaction, 2008.

[8] Lima, B. S., Azevedo, R. G., Moreno, M. F. e Soares, L. F. – Composer 3: Ambiente de autoria extensível, adaptável e multiplataforma. WebMedia – Workshop de TV Digital Interativa (WTVDI), 2010.

[9] dos Santos, J. A. F. Multimedia and hypermedia document validation and verification using a model driven approach. Dissertação de Mestrado. Universidade Federal Fluminense, Niterói, 2012.

[10] Santos, J. A. F., Muchaluat-Saade, D. C. XTemplate 3.0: spatio-temporal semantics and structure reuse for hypermedia compositions. ACM Multimedia Tools and Applications. Publicação online, 2011.

[11] Silva J. V. e Muchaluat-Saade D. C., Editor Gráfico de Conectores Hipermídia para Linguagem NCL 3.0. WebMedia, Florianópolis, 2011.

[12] Synchronized Multimedia Integration Language (SMIL 3.0) - W3C Recommendation, Dezembro 2008, http://www.w3.org/TR/2008/REC-SMIL3-20081201/, acessado em abril de 2011.

Luar: A Language for Agile Development of NCL Templates and Documents

Diogo Henrique D. Bezerra
LAViD/UFPB
João Pessoa, PB, Brasil
diogohenrique@lavid.ufpb.br

Dênio Mariz T. de Sousa
LAViD/UFPB
João Pessoa, PB, Brasil
denio@lavid.ufpb.br

Guido Lemos de S. Filho
LAViD/UFPB
João Pessoa, PB, Brasil
guido@lavid.ufpb.br

Aquiles Medeiros F. Burlamaqui
NatalNet/UFRN
Natal, RN, Brasil
aquiles@natalnet.br

Igor Rosberg de M. Silva
NatalNet/UFRN
Natal, RN, Brasil
igorosberg@natalnet.br

ABSTRACT
In the application's development described in NCL language, we have observed the reuse of some models and document structures, which is possible by repetition of common codes on applications. Thus, we do visualize the need to generalize this kind of development described in NCL. This need has been observed by other developers who are aiming at the possibility of the reuse of structure from some documents. This paper introduces Luar, an authoring language for NCL templates. The Luar language has been conceived through analysis of the applications' behavior for iDTV. Luar has a templates's processor developed with the Lua language and library to maintain and to aggregating template collections, sharing them among developers. The entire template system aims to facilitate the design and development of interactive applications described in NCL using the technique of reuse.

Categories and Subject Descriptors
I.7.2 [**Document and Text Processing**]: Document Preparation – *hypertext/hypermedia, languages and systems, markup languages;* D.2.3 [**Software**]: Software Engineering – *Coding Tools and Techniques;* D.2.13 [**Software**]: Software Engineering – *Reusable Software.*

General Terms
Design, Documentation, Languages, Verification

Keywords
Luar, Hypermedia Authoring, Nested Context Language, ITU-T H.761, Reuse, Template Engine.

1. INTRODUCTION
The SBTVD (Brazilian Terrestrial Digital TV System) [5] allows the televiewer to interact with TV programming from applications received along with audio/video stream from TV stations. Interactivity in SBTVD is made possible by the Ginga Middleware [20].

Permission to make digital or hard copies of all or part of this work for personal or classroom use is granted without fee provided that copies are not made or distributed for profit or commercial advantage and that copies bear this notice and the full citation on the first page. To copy otherwise, or republish, to post on servers or to redistribute to lists, requires prior specific permission and/or a fee.
WebMedia'12, October 15–18, 2012, São Paulo/SP, Brazil.
Copyright 2012 ACM 978-1-4503-1706-1/12/10...$15.00.

Ginga has two major subsystems interconnected. Ginga-J, responsible for the execution and standardization of Java applications. Ginga-NCL, with NCL (Nested Context Language) [21] as a development pattern for declarative applications. [20]

NCL has the Lua as its scripting language. Lua has a simple syntax, it is quick and easy to use and is designed to extend applications (scripting) [7].

Through the creation of interactive applications initially in NCL, it was noted the need of tools that could provide reuse and assist development of these applications. This need has been noted by authors such as Santos [18] and Neto [12], responsible for authoring languages of template XTemplate 3.0 [18] and TAL [12] respectively, which aims to promote the development of applications using the reuse afforded by templates.

There are several reasons for the development based on templates. According to Santos [19], although declarative languages like NCL become the creation of some interactive applications easier, when an application becomes more complex the hypermedia document that describes it grows. Thus, the NCL shall have many lines of code, which increases the probability of error, since the author tends to reuse settings by copying code. In this way there is a motivation to use of templates, since the use of these avoids copy code, diminishing the likelihood of errors.

Neto [12] presents several reasons for the development based on templates. The use of templates allows the TV producers follow the same style of programming. Because of the presentations of the interactivity follow the same standard interface, based on common templates, users start to use the applications more easily. A real example is the interactivity of novels Tititi [17], Passione [15] and Caminho das Índias (Passage to India) [14], all them produced by Globo TV [16]. These interactive applications follow the same model of interactivity, the change is visible only data such as images and text, making it easier to use by users. Examples like this show that templates allow indexing of document collation, also creating the concept of similar applications domain. There is also an important feature that is increasing the reuse, since the author is only concerned with filling gaps.

This paper presents the language Luar, created for the development of document templates NCL. Luar is a language inspired by languages like Lua Server Pages [3] and Java Server Pages [1] aims to blend the Lua language the NCL enabling the creation of gaps in the documents, transforming them into Luar templates. The templates are instantiated by Moonlight processor that receives the desired template and data to fill the gaps, generating the final NCL document in accordance with the restrictions of fill.

The main objective of Luar language is to promote simpler and faster development of applications described in NCL. Luar enables experienced developers create templates and others developers use it, achieving simplicity and speed in development.

The main difference of the proposed Luar language in relation to other languages is the junction of the NCL and the Lua, which dispenses with the learning of many concepts and one language to development and use of templates by NCL author.

The rest of the paper is structured as follows. Section two presents a foundation on systems for processing templates. In section three related works are discussed. Section four presents the Luar language. Finally, in section five we have the conclusion and final remarks.

2. TEMPLATES PROCESSING SYSTEMS

All templates processing system has a data model, one or more templates, a template processor and an output in document form.

The literature does not present a formal definition of the template. Henry [7] states that this is a problem in the context of template engines. So we have a simple notion of template. We define them as incomplete documents that are filled by the data model. [13] A feature that turn flexible the development based on templates. The templates can be specified with pre-existing languages, its own language for the template system or in hybrid mode, combining pre-existing languages with their own languages. [11] [6]

The data model is the mutable part in the context of a template system. Data can be varied allowing reuse of the template. The data source can be any source of data pre-formatted, such as relational database, spreadsheets, XML and others. Some template systems limit the data types used while other data allow many different data types. [11] [6]

The template processors are software or software components whose function is to match template (s) and data model to yield as output a complete document or part of a document. These documents are text files, XML, or source code. [11] [6]

Figure 1 is a schematic drawing of the templates processing system.

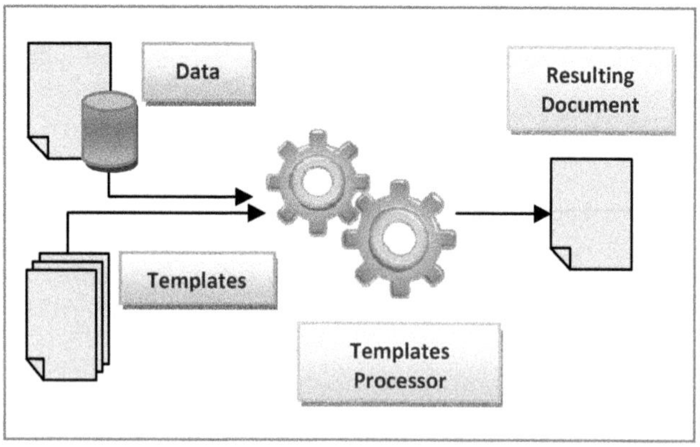

Figure 1. Basic elements and flow templates processing system.

3. RELATED WORK

This section provides a brief description of the tool iTVNews and two languages, XTemplate 3.0 and Template Authoring Language - TAL. The iTVNews is a tool used to build TV newcast applications in TVDI. The languages have been developed for authoring of templates of hypermedia documents, taking as a case study authoring of NCL document templates. Both works relate to the Luar language by providing reuse to the applications described by hypermedia documents.

3.1 XTemplate 3.0

The XTemplate language 3.0 is a solution for defining templates composition created to facilitate the programs authoring using the NCL 3.0 [21], being inspired by ADL (Architecture Description Languages) [4].

According to Santos [18] with XTemplate is possible to create templates, called templates composition, that describe in a generic way the entire contents of a context NCL. The programmer must only indicate the elements you want to use. It is as if we created an NCL document with "holes" that could be filled in later in the way we want.

The goal of the language XTemplate 3.0 is create facility to an expert author of NCL documents who have knowledge of XPath [25] and XSLT [24] as a prerequisite for use of language. The templates system XTemplate 3.0 also provides a library for creating template bases that can be shared among developers. [19]

For an NCL document using XTemplate templates can be run on a standard implementation of middleware Ginga, you need the processing of this document to be created a complete document.

3.2 TAL

The language TAL (Template Authoring Language) is an authoring language for templates of hypermedia documents [12]. According to Neto [12] TAL is a modular declarative language that works independently of the authoring language target, being an evolution of language XTemplate 3.0, having as main objective to allow expert developers specify document templates so that other developers less skilled create new documents in a simple, fast and error free form.

One goal of the language is to avoid using notations outside the context of the conceptual model and the level of abstraction of language, what happens in the XTemplate 3.0 language by using XSLT to transform documents. With that TAL may be employed in the authorship of other declarative languages.

3.3 iTVNews

iTVNews is a tool that enables the automatic creation of applications to Interactive Digital TV newscast, like polls, quizzes, chat and more. [22]

The tool in Java provides module for the creation of applications. Each module is a Java application having a graphical form for journalists fill in the data that will compose the application. The logical part of the module is fixed, as a template. And the display part is variable in order to have a visual identity for each news program, as being different templates according to the news program. After completing the form data, the module creates the document NCL of the interactive application chosen.

The iTVNews still defines repositories where developers can available the creation modules for journalists.

3.4 Luar Proposal

The Luar language aims to development of templates and their use by software engineers. Like TAL, has a proposal to facilitate the development of templates, removing the notations outside the context of the conceptual model and of the abstractions of language that occurs in language XTemplate. The Luar language tries to further facilitate the development of NCL templates, creating a notation already known by the developer NCL. The language makes it possible to use the NCL and Lua language together to create the templates, generalizing and facilitating their development.

The approach to combine languages known by the developer NCL brings advantages such as ease of learning to create and use templates, since it is not necessary to learn another type of notation. Also allows the document author understands the template developed by the author of templates, which may generate custom modifications.

In context of use by authors of documents out of the application development, the iTVNews brings a very effective approach to providing graphical forms to fill and instantiate templates. Tools like this can take advantage of the Luar language for creating templates. Requiring only the creation of graphical user interface for data completion, making it possible to instantiate Luar templates by lay people in development.

4. LUAR

The Luar language is only useful from the processing of templates that is conducted through your templates processor. The figure 2 shows the elements and flow of the processing system of Luar templates.

The basic elements and flows of the Luar system have the same elements and flows shown in Figure 1, common to all templates processing system.

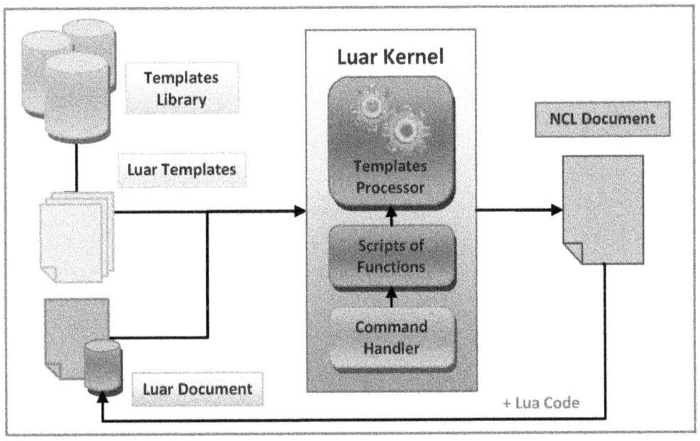

Figure 2. Basic elements and flow Luar templates processing system.

The Luar templates processing system have three well defined elements: the library, the kernel and language. The language is represented in Figure 2 by the templates and Luar document.

The system flow starts with the need for users to develop an application using templates. The templates are found in the library that holds collections of them. The templates along with the Luar document, which contains the data to form the template are sent to the kernel. The kernel interaction is given by means of commands that execute Lua scripts with specific functions of the system. The kernel's main function is to process the template through the template processor. The templates processor generates the NCL document from the template and the data passed. The NCL document can be transformed into a Luar document by adding Lua code, this is useful if the developer wants to use another template or to process code NCL. This feature will be further discussed in section 4.1.

The following is presented the Luar language in section 4.1. Section 4.2 describes kernel details of the system processing. Section 4.3 discusses the library of templates.

4.1 Language

Aiming to ease of learning and development by developers NCL, the Luar language has a simple syntax, aiming in embedding Lua in code NCL. This approach is similar to the Lua Server Pages, what the change is that instead of embedding Lua in HTML, Luar does in NCL.

The Lua language is embedded in the NCL code as scriptlets, small snippets of Lua code between the tags <% Lua code %>. So the developer does not need to learn a new syntax, just mix the two by the tag <% %>. Figure 3 shows part of the code of a slide show NCL.

```
26 <body>
27   <port id="pStart" component="slide1" />
28   <%
29     for i=1, #slides do
30       print('<media id="sld'..i..'" src="'..slides[i].. '"descriptor="dSlides" />')
31     end
32   %>
```

Figure 3. Example of Luar code

The code in Figure 3 is a simple example of Luar language. Lines 26 and 27 have code NCL, that created a port for application startup by the media "slide1." The code of a slide and its operation go and back and are common to all. In developing using NCL directly, the developer probably copy and paste the same snippet of code to each slide and swap some attributes. In lines 28 and 32 we have a Lua scriptlet. The code shows a loop to the amount of repetitions according to the number of slides wished by template user. Line 30 creates the media that will represent each slide, setting the attribute "id" with numbering according to the order passed by the user and the "src" attribute indicating the file path that represents the slide. In the same context there are still scriptlets to generate the code to go and back slides causing a great saving code.

The development based on templates has different profiles of developers. We have the authors of the templates and the authors of the documents. Below we discuss the use of language Luar by these different authors.

4.1.1 Template Authoring

The development of templates follows the example of the slide show, presented earlier, but there is a need to specify the characteristics and attributes of the template.

For a description and definition of the template, developer needs to learn to use more one tag <%! %>. Among the tags we must define the variable name followed by its description in the format attribute = "description". A general description of the template should be made in the attribute name template, as the example in Figure 4. The descriptions of the template and attributes are used for quick information on the template.

```
<?xml version="1.0" encoding="ISO-8859-1"?>
<ncl id="slideshow" xmlns="http://www.ncl.org.br/NCL3.0/EDTVProfile">
  <%!
    template="O template SlideShow cria um passador de slides."
    slides="Este atributo deve ser uma tabela Lua.
            Nas linhas da tabela deve ser indicado o caminho das..."
  %>
```

Figure 4. Descriptions of a template and its attributes.

In template authoring the authors assume the complexity for authors of documents enjoy a simple coding.

4.1.2 Authoring of NCL Document Using Luar

The authoring NCL document with Luar can be accomplished in three ways: using full templates, components templates and without the use of templates. The following sections present these three different ways of authorship.

4.1.2.1 Full Templates

The full templates generate a complete application by just filling out some data. The Slideshow template presented above is an example of a full template. This template is capable of generating an NCL document for slideshow, simply by the indication of the media files that represent the slides. The filling of the data is held in a Luar document. Figure 5 shows an example of instantiation of the Slideshow template.

```
01 <%
02     slides = { "image1.png",
03                "image2.png",
04                "image3.png",
05              }
06     includeTemplate("SlideShow")
07 %>
```

Figure 5. Instantiation of Slideshow template

The use of a full template is simple, set in a Luar scriptlet. The author of the document specifies the data template, as in lines 2 through 5 in Figure 5, and indicates which template you want to use. Line 6 shows the function used to indicate the desired template.

4.1.2.2 Components Templates

In software engineering, components are independent elements of software that can be assembled to form a complex system. [2]

From this idea was created the concept of components templates. The components templates are characterized by have independent code that can relate with others and with the NCL code directly to form an NCL application. The component template by itself generates an NCL application, but offers few features. It isn't desirable that this kind of template generate a complete application NCL, because escapes the concept of software component.

During the authorship of an NCL document, author can use the templates of components to add code that represents parts of the application, for example, a group of buttons, keyboard, form, widget, slideshow and others.

The NCL document can consist of several components templates, with the inclusion of these templates in any part of the NCL code. Figure 6 shows a snippet NCL code with inclusions of components template.

```
15 <body>
16   <port id="pStart" component="sidebar">
17   <%
18     id="sidebar"
19     leftLS={image="esquerda.png"}
20     rightLS={image="direita.png"}
21     includeComponent("LSidebar")
22   %>
23   <%
24    id="buttonGroup"
25     x=50
26     y=70
27     button={}
28     button.width=80
29     button.height=30
30     button[1]={selected="b1.png",unselected="bU1.png",start="op1"}
31     button[2]={selected="b2.png",unselected="bU2.png",start="op2"}
32     button[3]={selected="b3.png",unselected="bU3.png",start="op3"}
33     includeComponent("LButtonGroup")
34   %>
35 </body>
```

Figure 6. Code snippet using components templates.

In Figure 6 it can be observed the inclusion two templates components, LSidebar, establishing sidebars the application, and LButtonGroup, which generates a group of buttons. The way of adding a component template in the code is similar to the full templates. The difference is the function of inclusion shown in lines 21 and 33.

There is another issue in this development approach that should be taken into consideration. The templates are treated as media objects, and must have an identifier "id" handling of their states. Necessarily a component template needs to be initiated (start) and stop (stop) at some point, as well as media objects. The component template to be created should consider this detail of authorship.

In line 16 of Figure 6 we can see the "pStart" port starting "sidebar" component, example of how a component template is treated as a media object.

This model of authorship and model without use of templates, discussed in the next section, allows it to be added to the Lua language in any document NCL. This addition of Lua to the NCL through the Luar transforms him in a Luar document that can be processed and transformed in an NCL document, creating the cycle shown in Figure 2.

4.1.2.3 Authoring Without Use of Templates

In authoring of NCL documents very specific is not always possible to use templates, forcing the author to describe the document directly in NCL. Documents NCL commonly have a repeated code structures. A sample document that there is a large repetition of code is the application of the Wheel of Brazilian Television Genres [23], an application image can be seen in Figure 7.

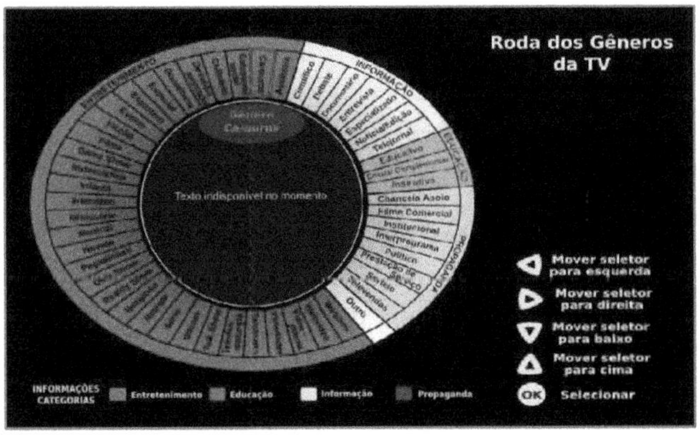

Figure 7. Application of the Wheel of Brazilian Television Genres

The Genres Wheel has the function of offering users a search engine for programming by program profiles. The user, by selecting cells in seven wheels (genre, format, transmission form, display, frequency, day of week, time and parental rating) provides a profile of program for which you want.

Once the selection mechanism of the cells is the same for the seven wheels, differing only in the number of possible choices, the code has many code snippets similar and repetitive.

The NCL code of document has approximately 23000 (twenty three thousand) lines of code. For authoring of this document, the author reported that created a C++ application to generate the description. Copy and paste code to modify some attributes lose much time.

Thus we saw that would be useful and practical to allow the processing of applications without templates. The author can use the whole structure of Lua language through Luar for automated generation of these huge repeated and similar descriptions.

The NCL document of Genres Wheel was described again with only fifteen hundred lines using Luar. Figure 8 shows the scriptlet responsible for generating the code to the move right of the first wheel. It may be seen generating fifty-one descriptions of the movement to the right of first wheel with only 18 lines, compared to approximately 459 directly using NCL.

```
<%
 for i=1, 51 do
   print('<link xconnector="onKeySelectionORStartStop">')
     print('<bind component="seltrRoda1Op'..i..'" role="onSelection">')
       print('<bindParam name="keyCode" value="CURSOR_RIGHT"/>')
     print('</bind>')
     print('<bind component="seltrRoda1Op'..i..'" role="stop"/>')
     print('<bind component="textRoda1Op'..i..'" role="stop"/>')
     if 1 < 51 then
       print('<bind component="seltrRoda1Op'..(i+1)..'" role="start"/>')
       print('<bind component="textRoda1Op'..(i+1)..'" role="start"/>')
     else
       print('<bind component="seltrRoda1Op1" role="start"/>')
       print('<bind component="textRoda1Op1" role="start"/>')
     end
   print('</link>')
 end
%>
```

Figure 8. Code to move right the first wheel.

4.2 Kernel

The Luar kernel is responsible for making entire system involving the Luar language useful. The kernel functions are to process the templates and Luar documents, allow access to new templates in the library of templates and provide information on the templates. The architecture is illustrated in Figure 10.

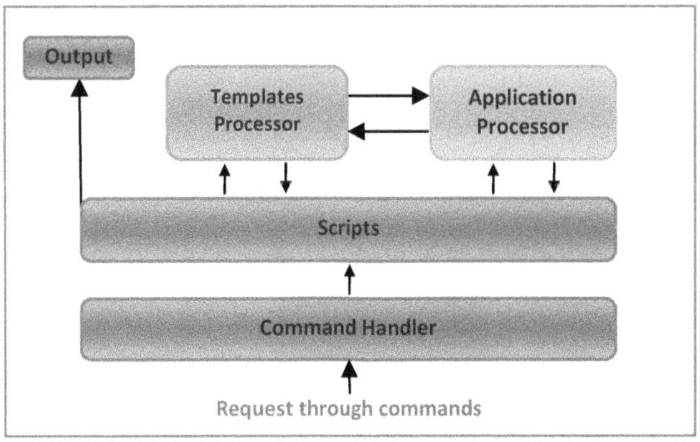

Figure 10. Basic elements and flow Luar Kernel.

The iteration is performed with the kernel through command line. The commands are processed, running the script corresponding to their function to the command. The execution of scripts produces an output according to their function. The scripts represent the functions of listing of templates, listing attributes of templates, creation project Luar, removal and addition of templates and the generation of NCL documents.

The document generation requires that the script responsible for processing the document pass the processing of Luar document for the templates processor or applications processor.

The generation of a document from a full template is requested by the script to generate documents to templates processor. The templates processor performs the processing and returns the code resulting to the script of generation. The script writes the code in a resulting NCL document.

The processing of a document without the use of templates, or with use of components templates is requested to the applications processor. The applications processor when detects the inclusion of a component template in the code, it requests to the templates processor that manage all the processing of that template. When the result code is returned, the application processor does a merge of the sintatic trees from received code with the code it already have. This is on for each template found in the document issued by the author of Luar documents. After processing, the code is returned to the generation script that writes the code in a resulting NCL document.

4.3 Templates Library

The Luar library is the element responsible for aggregate and maintaining a collection of templates that are created and shared by the authors of templates.

For sharing and search templates and components and the portal was used Ginga CDN [10], from this the authors have access to new templates, and may use them in authoring of new NCL documents.

The portal Ginga CDN is a Web service that aims to provide a means of dissemination of technologies related to the development of Ginga middleware and applications for Digital TV, more specifically to the subsystem Ginga-J [10].

Ginga CDN provides the tools and templates. In the portal you can categorize the template, describe its functionality in a textual or visual, images and videos, and save it in your repository. Other authors may view the templates and download it by portal or by using the Luar kernel, which will add the template in your local library. It is still possible that the authors qualify the templates for that author's community identifies the best. Figure 11 presents information of a template in the portal Ginga CDN.

Figure 11. Information of the Slideshow template in the GingaCDN

5. CONCLUSIONS

The Luar language makes it possible to embed Lua in NCL, an approach that seems to facilitate the authoring templates for developers experienced NCL. Making possible the instantiation of templates by authors document less specialized.

This form of development seems to cater well the creation of NCL documents, used for describing interactive applications for the Ginga middleware, already that are applications that have many similarities.

Another development approach proposed by Luar is the use of components templates, where the NCL authors can compose a NCL document with various parts of application. This form makes development based in templates more flexible.

There is still a concern to streamline the authoring of templates very specific and with large structures of repetitions. The language allows the author of document NCL embed Lua without using templates and process this document, generating an NCL document final.

Luar makes the authorship of the document agile without change with the concepts of NCL language, allowing features such as time synchronization remains in your templates or documents.

The Luar kernel, designed in Lua is available as free software. As future work, we intend to create a plugin for Composer tool [9], to make it even more readable the development with Luar language. There is still the challenge of popularizing the language for the NCL's developer community knows about it.

Another future work and of great importance is the language experimentation following techniques of experimental software engineering [26]. With this experiment we hope to have a feedback from users about learning, development speed, usability and new requirements that may arise. In this work is interesting to observe empirically the potential of the Luar approach to the authoring of NCL templates and documents.

6. REFERENCES

[1] Bergsten, Hans. *Java Server Pages*. O'Reilly Media, 2000.

[2] Brown, A.W. and Short, Keith. On Components and Objects: The Foundation of Component-Based Development. In *International Symposiumn Assessment of Software Tools and Technologies* (1997), IEEE Computer Society Press, 112-121.

[3] Burdinuk, A. Open Lua server pages (openlsp). Lua Server Pages, 2011. Disponivel em: *http://luasp.org/*. Acesso em: 20 maio 2012.

[4] Clements, P. C. A Survey of Architecture Description Languages. In *Proceedings of the 8th International Workshop on Software Specifications & Design.* (New York, NY, USA 1996), ACM.

[5] Fórum SBTVD. O que é o ISDB-TB. Fórum do Sistema Brasileiro de TV Digital, 2008. Disponivel em: *http://www.forumsbtvd.org.br/materias.asp?id=20*. Acesso em: 20 maio 2012.

[6] Fowler, Martin. *Patterns of Enterprise Application Architecture*. Addison-Wesley, 2003.

[7] Hunter, J. The Problems with JSP. Servlets.com, 2000. Disponivel em: *http://www.servlets.com/soapbox/problems-jsp.html*. Acesso em: 20 maio 2012.

[8] Ierusalimschy, Roberto, Filho, Waldemar Celes, and de Figueiredo, Luiz Henrique. Lua-an extensible extension language. *Software Practice and Experience*, 26 (Junho 1996), 635-652.

[9] Lima, Bruno Seabra, Azevedo, Roberto Gerson de Albuquerque, Moreno, Marcelo Ferreira, and Soares, Luiz Fernando Gomes. Composer: Ambiente de Autoria Extensível, Adaptável e Multiplataforma. In *XVI Simpósio Brasileiro de Sistemas Multimídia e Web - WebMedia 2010* (Belo Horizonte, MG, Brasil 2010), SBC.

[10] Lívio, A. Página Inicial. Ginga CDN - Code Development Network, 2009. Disponivel em: *http://gingacdn.lavid.ufpb.br/*. Acesso em: 20 maio 2012.

[11] Manolescu, Dragos. *Pattern Languages of Program Design 5*. Addison-Wesley Professional, 2006.

[12] Neto, Carlos de Salles Soares, Soares, Luiz Fernando Gomes, and de Souza, Clarisse Sieckenius. TAL - Linguagem para Autoria de Templates de Documentos Hipermidia. In *WebMedia - Simpósio Brasileiro de Sistemas Multimídia e Web* (Belo Horizonte, MG 2010).

[13] Parr, Terence John. Enforcing strict model-view separation in template engines. In *Proceedings of the 13th international conference on World Wide Web* (New York, NY, USA 2004), ACM, 224-223.

[14] Rede Globo de Televisão. Caminho das Índias. globo.com. Disponivel em: *http://caminhodasindias.globo.com/*. Acesso em: 6 Maio 2012.

[15] Rede Globo de Televisão. Passione. globo.com. Disponivel em: *http://tvg.globo.com/novelas/passione/index.html*. Acesso em: 6 Maio 2012.

[16] Rede Globo de Televisão. Rede Globo: Agente se liga em você. globo.com. Disponivel em: *http://redeglobo.globo.com/*. Acesso em: 6 Maio 2012.

[17] Rede Globo De Televisão. Ti ti ti. globo.com. Disponivel

em: *http://tvg.globo.com/novelas/ti-ti-ti/index.html*. Acesso em: 6 Maio 2012.

[18] Santos, Joel A. F. and Saade, Débora C. M. Linguagem XTemplate 3.0: Facilitando a Autoria de Programas NCL para TV Digital Interativa. In *WebMedia - Simpósio Brasileiro de Sistemas Multimídia e Web* (Fortaleza, CE 2009).

[19] Santos, Joel A. F. and Saade, Débora C. M. XTemplate 3.0. Adding Semantics to Hypermedia Compositions and Providing Document Structure Reuse. In *ACM Symposium on Applied Computing - ACM SAC* (2010).

[20] Soares, L. F. G. TV Interativa se faz com Ginga. *Revista da Sociedade Brasileira de Engenharia de Televisão*, 105 (Junho 2009).

[21] Soares, L.F.G., Moreno, M.F., and Neto, Carlos De Salles Soares. Ginga-NCL: Declarative Middleware for Multimedia IPTV Services. *IEEE Communications Magazine*, 48 (Junho 2010), 74-81.

[22] Sousa, Marcelo, Tavares, Tatiana, and Porto, Ed. iTVnews: Uma Ferramenta para Construção de Aplicações Telejornalísticas em TVDI.. In *Anais do XVII Simpósio Brasileiro de Sistemas Multimídia e Web – WebMedia* (Florianópolis, SC 2011), SBC.

[23] Souza, Jorge Carlos Aronchi De. Roda dos Gêneros. In *SET Broadcast \& Cable* (2010).

[24] W3C. XML Path Language (XPath). W3C, 1999. Disponivel em: *http://www.w3.org/TR/xpath/*. Acesso em: 20 maio 2012.

[25] W3C. XSL Transformation. W3C, 1999. Disponivel em: *http://www.w3.org/TR/xslt*. Acesso em: 20 maio 2012.

[26] Wohlin, C., Runeson, P., Höst, M., Ohlsson, M.C., Regnell, B., and Wesslén, A. *Experimentation in Software Engineering: An Introduction*. Kluwer Academic Publishers, Boston, Dodrecht, Londres, 2000.

WebNCL: A Web-based Presentation Machine for Multimedia Documents

Erick Lazaro Melo
UFSCar, Brazil
erick_melo@dc.ufscar.br

Caio César Viel
UFSCar, Brazil
caio_viel@dc.ufscar.br

Cesar A. C. Teixeira
UFSCar, Brazil
cesar@dc.ufscar.br

ABSTRACT

Presentation machines for multimedia declarative languages – especially the ones related with Interactive Digital TV (iDTV) and Internet Protocol TV (IPTV) – are usually embedded in devices and strongly coupled with the platforms when native code and API for the device's platform are used. Since much of the complexity to implement presentation machines lies on presenting and controlling different types of media (video, audio, image, text), and given that most of the modern browsers natively support those requirements, it becomes interesting to implement presentation machines using Web technologies to reduce their coupling with platforms. In this paper we discuss the advantages of a presentation machine for declarative multimedia languages implemented on top of Web technologies. As a proof of concept we implemented the WebNCL, a lightweight NCL presentation machine based on the web technologies stack (HTML 5/ JavaScript/ CSS). By using WebNCL, NCL documents can be presented in any device that has a HTML5 compatible browser, such as tablets, smartphones, smart TVs and PCs.

Categories and Subject Descriptors

H.5.4 [**Hypertext/Hypermedial**]: Architectures , Navigation; I.7.2 [**Document Preparation**]: Hypertext/hypermedia, Languages and systems, Multi/mixed media

General Terms

Design, Languages, Documentation, Human Factors

Keywords

Multimedia, Presentation Machine, NCL, HTML5

1. INTRODUCTION

Implementations of presentation machines for multimedia declarative languages – especially the ones related with Interactive Digital TV (iDTV) and Internet Protocol TV (IPTV) – are usually embedded in devices and strongly coupled with the platforms when the native code and API for the device's platform are used. For instance, the iDTV middleware Ginga-NCL [22, 20] contains a Nested Context Language (NCL) [21] presentation machine.

The Hypertext Markup Language (HTML) and other languages used to build Web pages, such as JavaScript and Cascading Style Sheets (CSS), are platform independent, because they are interpreted by Web browsers. Given the wide variety of browsers present in many platforms (PCs, smartphones, tablets, smartTVs, videogame consoles), it is becoming common to implement applications on top of the Web technologies to make them platform independent.

Since much of the complexity to implement presentation machines lies on presenting and controlling different types of media (video, audio, image, text), and given that most of the modern browsers natively support these requirements, it may be interesting to implement presentation machines using Web technologies to reduce their coupling with platforms.

Furthermore, there are several advantages in having a presentation machine for multimedia declarative language objects based on standard Web technologies. First it allows the reuse of declarative multimedia presentations developed for specific environment in other platforms. In addition, in a Web development perspective, a presentation machine built on top of web technologies stack (HTML5-JavaScript-CSS) is a framework which offers facilities for creating Web-applications with media synchronization requirements. The integration of multimedia declarative language objects, such as NCL documents into Webpages can enhance the capabilities of web applications and reduce the development costs.

Since a Web-based presentation machines are simpler to be used and integrated with other applications than native implementations, a more flexible and portable toolkit for development (testing and prototyping) of multimedia presentations can be provided. The presentation machine could be integrated with a text editor and provide real-time feedback or allow the presentation of multimedia objects without the necessity of sending into real or emulated devices.

Web browsers are available in many platforms. They can be found in smart TVs, smartphones, tablets and other devices. The device manufacturers can reuse the existing infrastructure provided to web browsers to integrate a multimedia presentation machine to their products. For instance, a web-based presentation machine provides a less invasive solution to add support for declarative applications in STB

Permission to make digital or hard copies of all or part of this work for personal or classroom use is granted without fee provided that copies are not made or distributed for profit or commercial advantage and that copies bear this notice and the full citation on the first page. To copy otherwise, to republish, to post on servers or to redistribute to lists, requires prior specific permission and/or a fee.
WebMedia'12, October 15–18, 2012, São Paulo/SP, Brazil.
Copyright 2012 ACM 978-1-4503-1706-1/12/10 ...$10.00.

than embedding a dedicated middleware to present declarative multimedia documents, which usually runs on system space and communicate directly with the operation system, the presentation machine can run as a Web-application in the user space.

Finally, a Web-based presentation machine allows the use of rich declarative multimedia languages, such as NCL, to create classes of presentations that are not common in embedded environments due to platform restrictions.

In this paper we discuss the advantages of a presentation machine for declarative multimedia languages implemented on top of Web technologies. As a proof of concept we have implemented the WebNCL, a NCL presentation machine based on the web technologies stack (HTML5/JavaScript/CSS). By using WebNCL, NCL documents can be presented on any device that has a HTML5 compatible browser, such as tablets, smartphones and PCs.

The remaining of this paper is organized as follows: in Section 2 we discuss related works; Section 3 describes the development process of the WebNCL and important project decisions; Section 4 presents the architecture of the WebNCL; Section 5 describes how WebNCL can be integrated into a webpage and presents the compatible platforms; in Section 6 we discuss some aspects related to embedding WebNCL; Section 7 presents the conclusions and future works.

2. RELATED WORK

The integration of web technologies with media synchronization languages has been investigated in some works. Cazenave et al. [3] propose a solution to integrate SMIL Timesheets [25] into HTML documents. Their solution allows web applications to use the SMIL temporal synchronization features through the engine *Timesheet.js*, implemented in JavaScript. A similar solution was adopted by Vouriaama [24]. The solutions proposed by these authors include only a subset of SMIL and the focus is on providing synchronization mechanisms to web pages. The creation of full portable multimedia presentation machines was not investigated by them.

Jansen and Bulterman [13, 14] present a solution for integrating SMIL documents to web pages through the use of browser plugins. A bridge between the Ambulant Annotator[4] and a *webkit*-based browser was created to perform time synchronization in web pages.

Gaggi and Danese [16] propose the *SmilingWeb*, a SMIL presentation engine that runs on any browser that supports HTML5. Our work takes this direction and uses NCL as base for discussions and proposals. The implications of this approach on DTV systems and mobile devices are also pointed in our paper.

In the context of Digital TV systems and NCL Language, Cruz et al. [7] describe a reference implementation of Ginga-NCL for mobile devices based on the Symbian platform. The focus of that study is to validate the Ginga-NCL architecture and to verify how it can be used to port the reference implementation to mobile devices. Ferreira et al. [11] present an implementation of middleware Ginga-NCL for mobile devices based on Android platform. Their paper describes the steps for porting the middleware to that platform and evaluates the transmission on applications for mobile devices using the protocol DSM-CC[6] through IP networks. Although they present the steps to port the middleware, they do not present solutions for cross platform development.

Other Digital TV middlewares have adopted web technologies for their declarative subsystems. This is the case of BML that is based on XHTML, CSS, DOM and ECMAScript [9]. The proposal described in this paper can solve some of the known problems of these systems, such as restrictions of adaptability, support for multiple devices and live presentation editing. As an example, WebNCL could be integrated to those middlewares, allowing them to display multimedia documents specified in NCL language by relying on technologies already supported (web-technologies).

3. PROJECT DECISIONS

The WebNCL was developed using agile methods. Although a specific method was not used, we used a mix of SCRUM [18] and XP [2].

We used the NCL ABNT Standards [1] as our main reference during the development. We also consulted Soares and Barbosa [19] to clarify some NCL features and concepts which were not clear in the standards. Our previous experience ([17],[8],[23]) modifying the middleware Ginga-NCL reference implementation [22] contributed to define the requirements of our presentation machine as well as its architecture.

Before starting the development itself, we conceived some proofs-of-concept to determine the viability of implementation and tested some approaches. For instance, we developed an event manager to test the NCL links condition-action mechanisms. We also performed some stressing-tests playing several videos side by side and generating events in a high rate.

After the viability tests, we have conceived an architecture for the WebNCL presentation machine. At the beginning it was similar to the Ginga-NCL reference implementation architecture [22], but it suffered many changes during the process due to the JavaScript language particularities and in order to meet project decisions.

The first goal was to develop essential and core parts of the presentation machine, such as the NCL Document parser, NCL Representation Model and the Event Manager. The remaining parts of the implementation was driven by features. We chose features, such as transition or some descriptor propriety, and added support to it. After that, a simple NCL document was written for testing purposes. That NCL document was executed into the Ginga-NCL Virtual Machine and in our presentation machine running in different browsers (Chrome, Firefox, Opera and Safari) and in different operational systems (Linux, Windows, Mac OS, Android and iOS) to verify the implementation accuracy.

3.1 Languages and Platforms

In the project conception phase, we considered implementing our NCL presentation machine based on Adobe Flash Platform[1]. Different from the HTML5 stack, Adobe Flash is already a mature platform. It also has great media support (especially video) including well-proved streaming protocols and technologies. In addition, its video formats are homogeneous – all up-to-date Adobe Flash Players support the same video formats. Another advantage is that by using the Adobe Air[2], we could easily develop a standalone desktop presentation machine.

[1]http://www.adobe.com/products/flashplayer.html
[2]http://www.adobe.com/products/air.html

However, a HTML5-based implementation can be used in more platforms since the HTML5 stack is based on open standards. For instance, iOS devices, such as iPhone, iPad and AppleTV, do not support Adobe Flash, but they have HTML5-compatible browsers.

We also believe that HTML5 is an ascending technology. Although it is only a draft and has heterogeneous support across browsers, it is already being used to build interesting and complex Web Application.

Computer power in presentation machines is required more to media presentation than to media orchestration. Since the web-browsers are responsible for media presentation and are usually implemented in native code, we believe the performance difference between WebNCL and the native-code presentation machine may be irrelevant.

3.2 Frameworks

Although HTML5 has native support for playing and controlling videos, we decided to use the Popcorn.js framework[3] for video playback. Porcorn.js is a JavaScript framework developed by the Mozilla Foundation for media synchronization and control; it also has an abstraction layer that allows developers to use HTML5 native videos via <video> tag and Adobe Flash video by a Flash Player in an agnostic way.

Popcorn.js offers a higher API for control media than pure HTML5. It is also well-tested in different browsers and platforms, which makes the presentation machine consistent across different browsers. Its abstraction layer can be used to add support for Adobe Flash based videos in our NCL presentation machine. It can be used to add features that cannot yet be used with HTML5 native videos, such as video streaming by Real Time Messaging Protocol (RTMP) [4].

A potential drawback when adopting Porcorn.js is the increased size and execution time of the JavaScript code. The size of a minified version of the framework core is 18,4KB and a version with all official plugins is 143KB. This overhead is not significant considering usual broadband Internet connection speed. We have not observed performance differences when compared a HTML5-pure and a Popcorn.js implementation. Also, the JavaScript code computing cost time is negligible when comparing to the cost of the video playback.

We also adopted the JQuery framework[5] since it makes the JavaScript development simpler and enhances presentation machine portability and reliability across different browsers and platforms.

3.3 Time-based Transition Handling

The Ginga-NCL reference implementation uses a scheduler to track the NCL presentations time-based transitions, such as the beginning of an anchor or the end of a video media. This is carried out by a thread that calculates all the presentation transitions and creates a timeline with those transitions. The thread waits the first transition and then executes the appropriated link actions. Sometimes it's necessary to recalculate the transitions timeline because the actions of the links can start or stop ', changing the order of the transitions.

Given the asynchronous and event-driven characteristics

[3]Popcorn.js - http://popcornjs.org/

[4]RMTP (Real Time Messaging Protocol) is an Adobe proprietary streaming protocol

[5]JQuery Framework - http://jquery.com

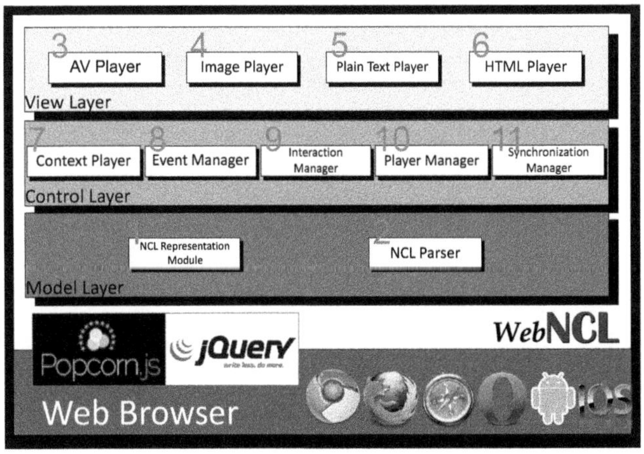

Figure 1: WebNCL Architecture

of the JavaScript language, we adopted a different strategy to process time-based transitions in our presentation machine. The responsibility to inform when transitions occur is distributed among the players. Each media player has the information about the time-based transitions associated with its media (anchors). When a transition occurs the player triggers an event to the Event Manager.

If there are links that use a transition as condition, the Event Manager creates a listener for the corresponding event triggered by the player. When an event is triggered, the listener calls the functions for each link that depends on such a condition. If all the conditions of a link have been met, the link will execute its actions, triggering events to media players. The media players listen to events performed over its medias and execute the corresponding actions.

This approach provides a decoupled architecture, since the player only needs to know the transitions related to its media and the actions that can be performed over it. The Event Manager is agnostic and does not need to know anything about the media nature.

4. ARCHITECTURE

The WebNCL was designed using the Model-View-Control (MVC) [12] design pattern. Figure 1 depicts its architecture.

The Model Layer (Figure 1 bottom) consists of two components: NCL Representation Model (Figure 1 - component 1) and NCL Parser (Figure 1 - component 2). The NCL Representation Model contains JavaScript objects to represent each entity of NCL Documents (link, media, connector and etc.) and their values. The NCL Parser is responsible for translating an NCL Document represented in Extensible Markup Language (XML) code into objects of the NCL Representation Model component.

The View Layer (Figure 1 top) contains the media players. Those players are implemented in HTML5 and JavaScript code using the Popcorn.js framework as base. There is an Audio and a Video Player (Figure 1 - component 3), an Image Player (Figure 1 - component 4), a Plain Text Player (Figure 1 component 5) and a HTML Player (Figure 1 - component 6). The media players are responsible for playing their medias and for triggering events on transitions.

In addition to the media players, there is a Context Player

(Figure 1 - component 7) that is located in the Control Layer (Figure 1 middle). The Context Player is not related to any HTML5 media - it represents an NCL context node. It contains references to the players of its nodes – Media or Context. The context player is placed on this layer because it is not directly related to "visible" elements in the presentation - it has a controller role.

The Control Layer also contains the Event Manager (Figure 1 - component 8), Interaction Manager (Figure 1 - component 9), Player Manager (Figure 1 - component 10) and Synchronization Manager (Figure 1 - component 11).

The Event Manager is the core of the presentation machine and implements the condition-action mechanism of NCL links. The Interaction Manager is responsible for handling the user's interaction via keyboard, virtual remote control, mouse and touchscreen devices. The Player Manager controls the creation and destruction of players objects and keeps track of all active media players. Finally, the Synchronization Manager is responsible for keeping the presentation synchronized when delays or errors occur due to network problems.

The remaining of this section explains how some important mechanisms work in the WebNCL implementation.

4.1 Initializing a Presentation

When an NCL document is loaded into the WebNCL, it is transformed into JavaScript objects from the *NCL Representation Model* component by the *NCL Parser*. Once the document has been translated, the *Player Manager* creates a *Context Player* for the top NCL document context node (<body>). It also creates players for all child nodes (medias and other contexts) of the NCL top context node. The media players start preloading the media, but the nested context players are not completely initialized – their internal nodes are only initialized when the context receives a play event. Each media player is associated with a HTML5 <div> element that contains a media representation tag (<img>, <audio>, <video>, etc). The initial values properties and other specific properties of the media assume the values of its associated descriptor.

After the body's nodes have been initialized, the *Event Manager* starts to create the event listeners (for transition and user interaction) for the conditions of the body's links. It also creates a function for each link and register it to a corresponding event listener.

The presentation starts only when the *Synchronization Manager* notifies that all media players are ready. When this takes place, the Event Manager triggers start events over the medias that are referred by the body's ports.

4.2 Link Processing

Listing 1 depicts an NCL link element named *sampleLink* and the connector *onBeginStart*; Figure 2 illustrates the processing of this link by the presentation machine using a simplified sequence diagram.

When the Video Player of the media named *video1* reaches the initial point of the anchor *area1*, it triggers an event (Figure 2 - step 1). Since there is a link that uses this transition as a condition (Listing 1, lines 7-8), the Event Manager creates a listener to that event beforehand. The listener executes the registered link functions, for instance, by calling the function *sampleLink* (Figure 2 - step 2).

The *sampleLink* function checks if the link's conditions

```
1  <causalConnector id="onBeginStart">
2    <simpleCondition role="onBegin"/>
3    <simpleAction role="start" max="unbounded"
4        qualifier="par"/>
5  </causalConnector>
6
7  <link id="sampleLink"
8          xconnector ="onBeginStart" />
9    <bind component="video1" interface="area1"
10         role="onBegin" />
11   <bind component="image1" role="start" />
12 </link>
```

Listing 1: NCL Link

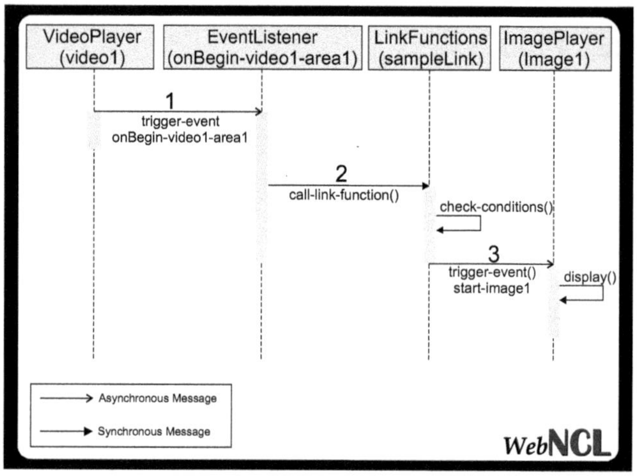

Figure 2: Link Processing Sequence

have been met. When the condition are met, the link functions trigger events to their actions. In this example, *sampleLink* has just one condition and it was met, so the *sampleLink* function will trigger events for its actions (Figure 2 - step 3). *Image1* Player receives the event and processes it, making *image1* show up.

This process is more complex when the link has a compound condition. For compound conditions that uses the AND operator the link function keeps track of the conditions met using a condition table. It registers the time when the first condition is met. When the link function is called by the event listener, it verifies the registered time - if it took place more than one second earlier, the function clears the condition table, registers the current time and checks the table for the condition entrance – in other words, conditions which are too old are discarded. If the time stored is not older than one second, the function checks the condition table for that condition. When the condition table is fully checked, the link function clears the condition table and processes the link actions.

For compound conditions that use the OR operator, the link function registers the last time when the actions were performed. When an event listener calls the link function, it verifies if the time registered took place more than one second earlier; if so, the link function processes the link actions and stores the current time. If not, the link functions just returns – in other words, the link trigger is ignored because it has just been executed.

The presentation machine also supports links that construct complex conditions by cascading different types of compound conditions.

For actions, the presentation machine supports both PAR and SEQ operators. For actions that use the PAR operator, the link function triggers the events and lets the browser scheduler handles the actions as parallel as it can. For actions that use the SEQ operator, only the first event is triggered, but this event carries a callback function. When the event is processed by Media Players, the callback function is called. This callback function triggers the next event, and this event has a callback function that will trigger the next event, and so on. Using those callback functions the presentation machine is capable of processing link actions in a sequential way.

We adopted a compound condition window of one second to trigger the actions as triggering condition events are not atomic operations. The events may be triggered in a very short window time, making us consider these events as simultaneous. Similar strategy is found in others implementations, such as the Ginga-NCL reference implementation [22].

User's interactions are implemented as they were transition events. When the user interacts with the presentation, an event is triggered. If there is a link that has user interactions as its conditions, the event will be handled by an event listener.

4.3 Synchronization Mechanisms

To keep media synchronization, even under network fluctuations, a sync mechanism was developed to pause the presentation when one or more players face some problem and resume it when all players are ready again.

The mechanism is first activated when a context starts – including the body, as this is the moment when the players start fetching the media to play. The presentation is paused and waits until all players have their media ready. The mechanism will also be activated when any player – usually continuous media players receiving their media by streaming – triggers an event notifying a problem to play its media.

The *Synchronization Manager* receives the event and forces a pause in the presentation. When the player triggers another event notifying that it is ready again, the *Synchronization Manager* resumes the presentation.

5. EMBEDDING WEBNCL IN A WEBPAGE

In order to present an NCL Document using WebNCL, it is necessary to embed it on a web page, as seen on the HTML page depicted in Listing 2.

In Lines 3-5 in Listing 2, the WebNCL source code to be imported. Between lines 6 and 14 the settings of appearance and positioning are defined as CSS style. Line 18 instantiates the presentation machine, passing the path of the NCL Document to be presented and the id of the HTML <div> where the presentation will be displayed. Finally, in line 21, the presentation is started. More than one WebNCL presentation machine can be embedded in the same HTML page.

During the experiments, an NCL Document with about 4,800 lines and 173 media nodes (videos and images) ran smoothly when submitted to WebNCL. The WebNCL was tested in several browsers and platforms. Figure 3 depicts

```
1  <html>
2    <head>
3      <script type="text/JavaScript"
4        src="js/WebNCL.js">
5      </script>
6      <style type="text/css">
7        .nclPlayer {
8          position: fixed;
9          left: 0px;
10         top: 0px;
11         width: 854px;
12         height: 480px;
13       }
14     </style>
15   </head>
16   <body>
17     <div id="ncl" class="nclPlayer"/>
18     <script type="text/JavaScript">
19       var p = new WebNclPlayer("main.ncl",
20         "ncl");
21       p.start();
22     </script>
23   </body>
24 </html>
```

Listing 2: HTML code to embed the WebNCL

the WebNCL running in different browsers in PC enviroment: Chrome in Windows (Figure 3(a)), Firefox in Linux (Figure 3(b)), Safari in Mac OSX (Figure 3(d)) and Opera in Windows (Figure 3(c)). Figure 4 depicts the WebNCL running in an Android device and Figure 5 ilustrates the execution in an iOS device. Any combination of browsers and platforms is possible.

(a) Chrome

(b) Firefox

(c) Opera

(d) Safari

Figure 3: WebNCL running on PC browsers

5.1 User Interaction

Given that many NCL applications use a TV remote control as its primary input device, we have to provide a similar way to interact with these applications. This can be done using different approaches like mapping the TV remote control on keyboard and via a virtual remote control. We implemented both solutions in the WebNCL.

Table 1 describes the mapping of TV remote control on a standard PC keyboard. When a mapped key is pressed, the Interaction Manager triggers the corresponding event.

Figure 4: WebNCL running on Android

Figure 5: WebNCL running on iPad

TV Remote Control Button	Keyboard Key
Numbers 0-9	Numbers 0-9
Arrows	Arrows
Enter | OK	Enter
RED	Q
GREEN	W
YELLOW	E
BLUE	R

Table 1: Keys mapping

The virtual remote control is built externally to the presentation machine using HTML and JavaScript. It uses the presentation machine JavaScript API to post key events. This decoupling allows creating different virtual TV remote controls without modifying the presentation machine. For instance, Figure 6(a) presents a more complete remote control while 6(b) presents a simple.

We also added support to interaction via mouse and touchscreen devices, since the WebNCL can run in environments with richer input devices. When the mouse is over a media, that media receives the focus. If the left or right button is pressed, an OK button event is triggered. In touchscreen devices, tapping in a media without the focus is equivalent to change the focus to that media. A second tap (or double tap) on that media triggers an event equivalent to pressing the OK button.

Although we used rich input devices just to mimic interactions which are already possible with TV remote controls, it is possible to extend the interaction paradigm to support new types of interaction which are more natural in PC or tablet environment (long tap, swipe, double click, drag and drop). In work in progress we are adding support to these interactions in WebNCL.

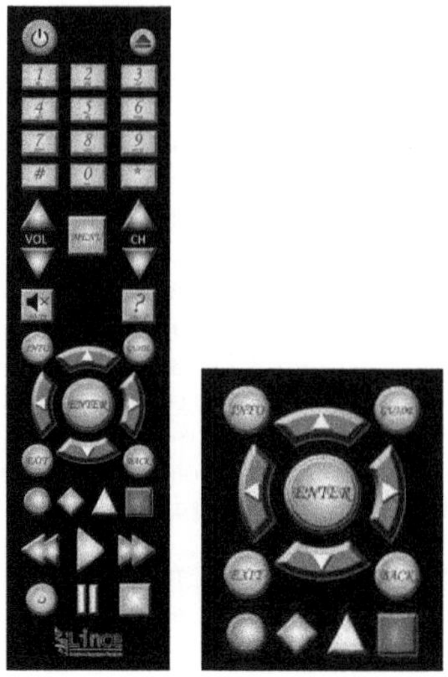

(a) Complex (b) Simple

Figure 6: Virtual remote controls

6. DISCUSSIONS

In this paper we present a solution for building a declarative presentation machine based on web-technologies. Although the WebNCL can allow the execution of NCL documents in any platform that offers a HTML5-compatible browser, it also can also be used as a component of embedded DTV middleware, since the web stacks are compatible with many embedded platforms.

However, the execution of HTML based applications is usually done in a sandbox environment. The application does not have access to the same lower-level APIs available to native codes. Efforts have been made to provide some new APIs to web-browsers, allowing the applications to access accelerometers, GPS, camera and local storage. It accomplishes many requirements of some applications but for some we still need to access native resources. This is the case of the DTV environment – there is a common core that is very platform dependent and that provides very specific services required by DTV applications (for instance: access to the EPG data).

In order to use WebNCL as a component of an iDTV middlware, we must provide low level service access to the presentation machine. Some approaches may be considered in order to extend the WebNCL to provide specific DTV services:

- The HTML5 engine may be embedded in native software, using a HTML rendering engine. This engine can be extended to provide new APIs that bridges the HTML application to the native code. This strategy has been adopted in the mobile environment with the PhoneGap framework [5], which provides some APIs to handle mobile common features, allowing the same code base to run across many platforms (iOS, Android, Symbian, WebOS, Windows Phone).
- Some web-browsers provide ways to create native extensions. The most common way is using the Pepper Plugin API[6] which is a cross platform API to build

[6]https://developers.google.com/native-client/overview

native client web browser plugins. It allows the user to execute native compiled code in the browser, which runs in a sandbox environment that tries to avoid malicious codes from damaging the system.

- Existing plugins available may be used, as Java Applets. Specifically in the DTV environment this strategy can be used to integrate declarative applications with procedural Java applications based on GEM Framework [10] or Java DTV API [15]. Java applets allow the execution of Java applications that are able to access protected resources (out of the browser sandbox).

HTML5 browser issues

WebNCL relies on the web-technologies stack. The browser imposes restrictions regarding the supported media types and its behavior. Currently, there are some limitations imposed by the browsers:

- The iOS devices are limited to playback a single audio or video stream at any time. Playback more than one video at same time is not allowed. The pre-fetching of streamings is also not supported by that platform.

- The video in HTML5 is not supported in the same way by different browsers. Only some browsers support the H.264 encoder, while others support the WebM and OGG encoders. The same goes for <audio> tag.

- The CSS3 properties are handled in different ways by the browsers. For instance, it may impact on how NCL transitions will be presented.

- Browsers eventually implement the Same Origin Policy[7], which avoid a web application to access local files. In some cases, to run local NCL applications it is necessary to access the WebNCL from a HTTP Web Server or disable that browser security mechanism.

7. FINAL REMARKS

This paper discusses the possibility of increasing the portability of declarative synchronization languages presentation machines by using web-based implementations. As a proof-of-concept we developed the WebNCL, an NCL presentation machine that presents NCL documents in HTML5 compatible browsers.

The WebNCL brings some implications and possibilities. TV stations may allow users to access the same interactive content broadcasted on TV in the web environment. The same interactive experience can be offered to web users. For instance, a soap-opera can use the same application for viewing characters profiles in both platforms. Another possibility is to offer the same interactive merchandising application in iDTV and Web.

The development of a toolkit based on WebNCL for NCL document authoring is interesting, since, according to the authors experience, the difficulties to setup an devlopment environment may be reduced to developers when compared to traditional virtual machines and emulators.

Given the possibility to embed the NCL presentation machine into webpages, many applications can be conceived. For instance, the Club NCL[8] can provide features to online previewing NCL documents. Educational tools could incorporate interactive videos in a lightweight approach using WebNCL. The traditional video lectures may be replaced by interactive multimedia lectures. This approach is being exploited by the authors.

WebNCL also helps the exploration of the multiple devices NCL support. As WebNCL runs on any HTML5 compatible browsers (which are available in most modern mobile devices) the efforts to integrate the devices - set-top-boxes and mobiles - can be smooth.

Currently, we are extending WebNCL to provide support to the Lua scripting language and implementing Lua APIs specified in ISBD-T. Through these efforts we hope that applications developed for the Ginga-NCL environment can be entirely reused in the web environment.

WebNCL is open-source and the source code and demo applications are available at http://webncl.org.

Acknowledgments

The authors thank CAPES, CNPq, FINEP and RNP for the financial support of research projects. We also thank FAPESP for supporting the paper presentation.

8. ADDITIONAL AUTHORS

Alexandre Coelho Rondon (alexcrondon@gmail.com), Daniel de Paula e Silva (danielpes@comp.ufscar.br), Danilo Gasques Rodrigues (danilod100@gmail.com) and Endril Capelli da Silva (endrilcsilva@gmail.com) from UFSCar.

9. REFERENCES

[1] N. ABNT. Associação brasileira de normas técnicas. 2007. digital terrestrial television standard 06: Data codification and transmission specifications for digital broadcasting. Technical report, Part 2–GINGA-NCL: XML Application Language for Application Coding (São Paulo, SP, Brazil, 2007.

[2] K. Beck and C. Andres. *Extreme programming explained: embrace change.* Addison-Wesley Professional, 2004.

[3] F. Cazenave, V. Quint, and C. Roisin. Timesheets. js: Tools for web multimedia. In *Proceedings of the 19th ACM international conference on Multimedia*, pages 699–702. ACM, 2011.

[4] P. Cesar, D. Bulterman, and A. Jansen. The ambulant annotator: empowering viewer-side enrichment of multimedia content. In *Proceedings of the 2006 ACM symposium on Document engineering*, pages 186–187. ACM, 2006.

[5] A. Charland and B. Leroux. Mobile application development: web vs. native. *Communications of the ACM*, 54(5):49–53, 2011.

[6] R. Crinon. The dsm-cc object carousel for broadcast data services. In *Consumer Electronics, 1997. Digest of Technical Papers. ICCE., International Conference on*, pages 246–247. IEEE, 1997.

[7] V. Cruz, M. Moreno, and L. Soares. Ginga-ncl: implementaçao de referência para dispositivos

[7] http://www.w3.org/Security/wiki/Same_Origin_Policy

[8] Club NCL is a portal to share NCL applications - http://club.ncl.org.br/

portáteis. In *Proceedings of the 14th Brazilian Symposium on Multimedia and the Web*, pages 67–74. ACM, 2008.

[8] G. De Freitas and C. Teixeira. Ubiquitous services in home networks offered through digital tv. In *Proceedings of the 2009 ACM symposium on Applied Computing*, pages 1834–1838. ACM, 2009.

[9] E. ECMAScript, E. C. M. Association, et al. Ecmascript language specification.

[10] T. ETSI. 102 819 v1. 3.1 (2005) - digital video broadcasting (dvb): Globally executable mhp (gem) specification 1.0. 2. *European Telecommunications Standards Institute, TS*, 102(819):V1.

[11] G. Ferreira, G. Nogueira, G. Comarela, F. Fabris, M. Martinello, and J. P Filho. Ginga-ncl em dispositivos portáteis: Uma implementação para a plataforma android. In *Brazilian Symposium on Multimedia and Web (WebMedia)*, 2010.

[12] E. Gamma. *Design patterns: elements of reusable object-oriented software*. Addison-Wesley Professional, 1995.

[13] J. Jansen and D. Bulterman. Enabling adaptive time-based web applications with smil state. In *Proceeding of the eighth ACM symposium on Document engineering*, pages 18–27. ACM, 2008.

[14] J. Jansen and D. Bulterman. Smil state: an architecture and implementation for adaptive time-based web applications. *Multimedia Tools and Applications*, 43(3):203–224, 2009.

[15] A. JavaDTV. Java dtv api 1.3 specification, sun microsystems (2009), 2010.

[16] L. D. O. Gaggi. A smil player for any web browser. In *Proceedings of International Conference on Distributed Multimedia Systems*, pages 114–119, Firenze, Italy, 2011.

[17] M. Pimentel, R. Cattelan, E. Melo, and A. Prado. End-user live editing of itv programmes. *International Journal of Advanced Media and Communication*, 4(1):78–103, 2010.

[18] K. Schwaber and M. Beedle. *Agile software development with Scrum*, volume 18. Prentice Hall, 2001.

[19] L. Soares. *Programando em NCL 3.0: desenvolvimento de aplicações para middleware Ginga: TV digital e Web*. Elsevier, 2009.

[20] L. Soares, M. Moreno, and C. De Salles Soares Neto. Ginga-ncl: Declarative middleware for multimedia iptv services. *Communications Magazine, IEEE*, 48(6):74–81, 2010.

[21] L. Soares and R. Rodrigues. Nested context language 3.0 part 8–ncl digital tv profiles. *Monografias em Ciência da Computação do Departamento de Informática da PUC-Rio*, 1200(35):06, 2006.

[22] L. Soares, R. Rodrigues, and M. Moreno. Ginga-ncl: the declarative environment of the brazilian digital tv system. *Journal of the Brazilian Computer Society*, 12(4):37–46, 2007.

[23] C. Teixeira, E. Melo, R. Cattelan, and M. Pimentel. Taking advantage of contextualized interactions while users watch tv. *Multimedia Tools and Applications*, 50(3):587–607, 2010.

[24] P. Vuorimaa. Timesheets javascript engine, 2007.

[25] P. Vuorimaa, D. Bulterman, and P. Cesar. Smil timesheets 1.0. *W3C Working Draft*, 2008.

Author Index

www.ingramcontent.com/pod-product-compliance
Ingram Content Group UK Ltd.
Pitfield, Milton Keynes, MK11 3LW, UK
UKHW051510290926
15471UKWH00008B/1548